Short-Term Study Abroad 2001

IIE's
Complete Guide
to Summer and
Short-Term Study

Marie O'Sullivan, Editor

INSTITUTE OF INTERNATIONAL EDUCATION
809 United Nations Plaza
New York, NY 10017-3580
www.iie.org

Contents

Programs

To Send IIE Information on New Programs

If you offer a study-abroad program not listed in this book, you may ask to be added to the mailing list. Enclose current printed information with your letter. If your program is appropriate for either ***Academic Year Abroad*** or ***Short-Term Study Abroad,*** IIE will send our New Program Questionnaire to you next summer. The books are intended to offer information on postsecondary programs up to one year in length. Mail or fax your request to:

Study Abroad Editor
IIE BOOKS
Higher Education Group
809 United Nations Plaza
New York, NY 10017-3580
USA
Fax: 212-984-5358

Credits

Senior Project Manager:	Peter Kerrigan
Editor:	Marie O'Sullivan
Assistant Editors:	Darrel Irving, Justin Kavanagh, Joy Smith, Brid Turner, MaryAnn Wrobleski
Research:	Marie Stapleton
Cover Design:	Renée Meyer
Advertising:	Mollie Melugin

Fifty-first Edition
SHORT-TERM STUDY ABROAD
was formerly published under the titles ***Summer Study Abroad*** and ***Vacation Study Abroad.***

Printed in the United States of America.
ISBN: 087206-262-7
ISSN: 1046-2104

Advertisers

Advertising Policy

Advertising in IIE's Study Abroad books is open to US and foreign higher educational institutions, private organizations, and companies that service the international educational exchange community.

The Institute of International Education does not attempt to evaluate programs listed in the books, nor can it verify statements made by advertisers in their ads. Inclusion of a program or advertisement does not imply IIE recommendation, nor does omission imply IIE disapproval. Advertisers are solely responsible for the accuracy of the information in their advertisements, and IIE may not be held responsible for any false advertising.

Program listings in ***Academic Year Abroad*** and ***Short-Term Study Abroad*** are free of charge and are provided by IIE as a public educational service. They are not contingent upon the purchase of advertising space by the sponsor. See **Index I: Sponsoring Institutions** to find the program listings for most of the advertisers listed below.

Academic Programs Abroad
AirTreks.com
American Institute for Foreign Study
American InterContinental University
American Universities International Program
American University of Paris
AustraLearn
Beaver College, Center for Education Abroad
Boston University
BUNAC
Caffe Italiano Club Centro di Lingua & Cultura Italiana
Center for Bilingual Multicultural Studies, Universidad Internacional
Center for Cross-Cultural Study
College Consortium for International Studies
College Year in Athens
Council
Cuauhnahuac
Educational Directories Unlimited
Endicott College
ENFOREX Spanish Language School
Escuela Internacional
European Heritage Institute
IES, Institute for the International Exchange of Students
IH Espana
Institute for American Universities
Institute of Spanish Studies
Instituto Cultural Oaxaca
International Council for Cultural Exchange
ISA (International Studies Abroad)
IS Aix-en-Provence
ITC-International TEFL Certificate
Ithaca College
Lingua Service Worldwide
Michigan State University
Modern Language Studies Abroad
Naropa University
New York University
Pont-Aven School of Art
Rollins College
Semester in Spain
Southern Methodist University
Studio Art Centers International
SUNY College at New Paltz
SUNY College at New Paltz, Language Immersion Institute
Syracuse University
TEFL International
Tufts University
University of Arizona
University of Joensuu
University of Kansas
University of Malta
University Studies Abroad Consortium
Villanova University

Institute of International Education

What is IIE?

- The world's most experienced global higher education and professional exchange agency;
- Administrator of the Fulbright Program, the US Government's premier public diplomacy initiative;
- Provider of training and leadership development programs for public and private sector professionals around the world;
- Organizer of democracy-building, civil society and human rights training initiatives in transitional societies;
- Initiator of projects that help students and scholars worldwide, including testing and advising, scholarships, and emergency financial assistance;
- Provider of international affairs programs and visitor and protocol services that enrich our communities and regions.

What is IIE's Mission?

An independent, nonprofit organization, the Institute is a resource for educators and institutions worldwide. Our goals are:

- to promote closer educational relations between the people of the United States and other countries;
- to increase the number of students, scholars and professionals who have the opportunity to study, teach and conduct research outside of their own country;
- to strengthen and internationalize institutions of higher learning throughout the world;
- to foster sustainable development through training programs in energy, environment, business management, and leadership development;
- to partner with corporations, foundations, and governments in finding and developing people able to think and work on a global basis.

Why is IIE Needed?

Broadening the outlook of future leaders through academic and professional exchange strengthens their ability to think and act on a cooperative basis. Academic and professional exchange is also a critical means for transferring knowledge and skills across borders and preparing a new generation of global citizens. In the century ahead, these activities will be more important than ever, since many of the world's problems can be solved only on a regional and transnational basis.

Who Participates in IIE Programs?

18,000 men and women from 175 nations participate in Institute of International Education programs each year. IIE disburses $100 million annually on programs and services. Most funds provide direct support to sponsored students and professionals. These funds also materially assist the universities and research and training institutions at which IIE grantees study and work. Individual donors, foundations and corporate grants play a critical role in enabling IIE to expand its much needed services to higher education and the community.

Statistics

IIE's *Open Doors* survey is the definitive statistical profile of 113,959 US students abroad, as well as 490,933 international students and 70,501 foreign scholars at US universities. The Institute's 400 staff members in twenty offices worldwide provide a unique resource of area expertise, skills and experience. *IIE Online*'s 12,000 digital documents form the world's largest international education information space.

Services

IIE Passport: www.iiepassport.org

IIE Passport is the Institute's brand-new US education abroad website. With additional content added by program sponsors, an option to save searches, and many other valuable new features, *IIE Passport* is now the single most complete and comprehensive web resource on study abroad for US students.

IIE Online: www.iie.org

Supported by a search engine and extensive menus designed to take advantage of the superior hypertext linking capabilities of the World Wide Web, *IIE Online* contains more than 12,000 screens of digital content and is still growing. The Fulbright section includes grant descriptions for US graduate student Fulbrights, and in-country contacts for citizens of other nations interested in securing Fulbright Fellowships.

Fulbright Program

IIE provides management services to the Fulbright Program on behalf of the US Department of State Bureau of Educational and Cultural Affairs. The US Department of State is the sponsor and funding agency.

US students enrolled in a US college or university must apply through a campus Fulbright Program Adviser. US citizens not formally enrolled in a higher educational institution may request applicant information on Fulbright Program grants from IIE's US Student Programs Office.

Foreign nationals who wish to apply for financial assistance through the Fulbright Program to study in the United States must apply through the binational Fulbright Commission or designated US diplomatic post in their home nation. IIE cannot accept applications from foreign nationals for the Fulbright Program.

Membership Services

As members of IIE, over 2,000 campus professionals worldwide receive complimentary copies of IIE's invaluable information resources, including *Academic Year Abroad* and *Short-Term Study Abroad*, now with their brand-new companion website, *IIE Passport*. Members receive IIE's electronic newsletters, *IIE.Interactive* and *Reaching Partners in International Education*; participate in IIE's seminars and university fairs; and benefit from IIE services targeted to their specific needs. Accredited US and overseas universities and US nonprofit organizations may apply for membership. Contact: Manager, Membership Services, IIE, 809 United Nations Plaza, New York NY 10017-3580 or *e-mail*: membership@iie.org.

US and Overseas Offices

The Institute's central office is located in New York City. Other US offices are located in Washington DC, Chicago, Denver, Houston and San Francisco. IIE maintains offices abroad in Brasilia, Brazil; Mexico City, Mexico; Hong Kong, China; Bangkok, Thailand; Hanoi, Vietnam; Manila, the Philippines; Budapest, Hungary; Almaty, Kazakhstan; Moscow, Russia; Kiev, Ukraine; New Delhi, India; Cairo, Egypt; and Pretoria, South Africa.
In Indonesia, IIE is represented by the Indonesian International Education Foundation in Jakarta.

IIE Study-Abroad Books

The Institute of International Education (IIE) has published guides to study abroad for over 50 years. IIE's two companion volumes, *Academic Year Abroad* and *Short-Term Study Abroad* (formerly *Vacation Study Abroad*), are the only comprehensive, annually-updated reference directories to international study for US students.

Information contained in these two books is based on a survey conducted in the summer of each year. Surveys for the 2001 edition of the IIE books were sent during the summer of 2000. The surveys were mailed to 2,000 organizational sponsors of programs listed in the 2000/2001 edition, and to all organizations that wrote to the IIE study abroad editor requesting to be listed.

US colleges and universities—over 600 of which are IIE member institutions—have traditionally been highly responsive to the Institute's surveys for *Academic Year Abroad* and *Short-Term Study Abroad*, as have many other organizations that offer international study opportunities to US nationals. Given this cooperation, the books are as comprehensive as IIE can make them.

IIE tries to make the information contained in the two books accurate and useful. Bear in mind, however, that information-gathering takes place long before these books are published—often before program arrangements are final. For this reason, it is a good idea to use the IIE books only as general resources for locating programs of interest. Final and full information on any program must be obtained directly from the program sponsor.

Criteria for Inclusion

The IIE books provide information about postsecondary study-abroad programs open to US citizens who are undergraduate, graduate or postgraduate students; adult or continuing education students; or professionals in various fields including business, education, health and law. The large majority of programs are intended for undergraduates, but IIE actively seeks information about international programs which are of interest to other categories of learners.

Most programs listed in these books are designed especially for US students. However, a substantial minority of programs are more broadly international. For example, the IIE books list the international student programs of many foreign universities. These programs are open to students from all nations who can meet the eligibility requirements, not just students from the United States.

All programs must take place outside the 50 United States. Programs sited in US territories and possessions are eligible for inclusion.

Academic Year Abroad and *Short-Term Study Abroad* describe programs that range from one week to one calendar year in length. Further information on the duration of programs listed in each of the books is provided below.

Program sponsors include US accredited colleges and universities, which sponsor the majority of programs in both books; foreign universities, language schools, educational associations, binational agencies and other organizations.

Many programs offer academic credit that may be used in partial fulfillment of requirements for an academic degree. It is not usually possible to complete all course requirements for an academic degree in the period of time covered by the programs in these books, nor is that their purpose.

Academic Year Abroad

Academic Year Abroad offers information on study-abroad programs that take place during the academic year (September through June), and that are at least one academic quarter in length (usually 8 to 10 weeks).

Of more than 2,600 programs listed in the current edition, some 75 percent are sponsored by US accredited colleges and universities. Almost 500 programs are offered by institutions without US accreditation: foreign universities and institutes, adult education centers and other US and foreign organizations.

Short-Term Study Abroad

Short-Term Study Abroad was formerly called *Vacation Study Abroad*. This new title more accurately describes the directory's focus and content. This publication lists short-term programs of varying lengths. Courses from one week to several months are listed, and include offerings for the winter and spring breaks, the summer, and other short-term overseas opportunities available throughout the year. Some 60 percent of programs are sponsored by US accredited colleges and universities.

In addition to US higher education-sponsored programs, *Short-Term Study Abroad* describes offerings of many foreign universities, language schools and other organizations. Language school programs often allow participation for lengths of time that vary from one week to several months. *Short-Term Study Abroad* also contains many programs that combine study with extensive travel over short periods of time, or that focus on topics of broad interest, and therefore are especially appealing to adults.

How to Use This Book

The information contained in this book—complemented by the guidance of an experienced study-abroad adviser if you are currently enrolled at a college or university—can help you plan what may be one of the most rewarding experiences of your life.

This section explains the overall organization of the book, how individual program entries are organized, and the terms used in the program descriptions. A list of abbreviations used in entries is also provided.

Overall Organization

Program entries are organized first by geographical region: Africa South of the Sahara, Asia and Oceania, Eastern Europe, Western Europe, the Middle East and North Africa, and the Western Hemisphere. Each world region is subdivided alphabetically by country and then by city. Within each city section, program entries are alphabetized by name of sponsoring organization.

In addition to specific country and city listings, there is a "Worldwide" section for programs that are active in more than one world region. Similarly, there are "More Than One Country" listings at the beginning of each regional section, and "More Than One City" listings at the front of each country. Remember to consult these sections in addition to listings for specific cities and countries.

The book also provides useful information in its introduction and indexes. The section you are now using provides specific information on how to use program descriptions to identify programs of interest to you. The following section, "Planning for Study Abroad," offers overall guidance on the steps students should follow in organizing a productive study-abroad experience.

Indexes are:

■ Sponsoring Institutions

This is an alphabetical index of all US and foreign colleges, universities, consortia and other organizations that sponsor study-abroad programs described in this book.

■ Consortia

A consortium in this book is a group of colleges and universities that jointly offers study-abroad programs. The index lists each consortium's member institutions.

■ Fields of Study

Programs are indexed by field of study and by country.

■ Special Options

This index is a guide to programs open to students other than undergraduates, e.g., precollege students, graduate students, adults and teachers; and to programs that offer special opportunities, e.g., internships, independent study, study tours.

■ Cost Ranges

This is an index of programs available at varying levels of cost.

■ Duration

In *Short-Term Study Abroad*, which contains entries on programs of widely varying length, there is also an index of programs by duration in weeks. *Academic Year Abroad* does not have this index, because the overwhelming number of programs of semester or academic year length would make a duration index less useful.

Sample Entry

The sample entry describes a program that does not exist. In fact, the program entry could not exist, because it offers information under virtually all headings available as options in our computer database. No study abroad program offers quite that many options, although a few come close. The advantage of this mythical program is that it allows us to provide an example of the many different kinds of useful data you may encounter in using this book, and to explain what they all mean.

Asia and Oceania

Japan

KYOTO

2001
EXEMPLARY STATE UNIVERSITY
Japanese Business and Civilization Program
Site: Japan: Kyoto *Host inst:* Kyoto Mgmt Inst
Dates: Aug-Dec or Jan-May or Jun-Jul
Subjects: Banking, Business/management, Civilization/culture, Economics, Graphic arts/design, Japanese language (int/adv), Japanese studies
Eligibility: ***Own students preferred.*** *Level:* jrs, srs, grads, adults, teachers, professionals, precoll *Requires:* 3.0 GPA, previous study in field, 2 yrs coll Japanese *Age:* min 18, max 81, avg 22
Credit: *Undergrad:* 14-15 *Grad:* 10-12 *Doc:* transcript, certificate, diploma, degree
Instruction: *In:* English, Japanese *Format:* art studio, directed field study, independent study, internship, lab, lang study, lecture, music lesson, practical training, seminar, student teaching, study tour, tutorial, volunteer/svc, workshop *Students:* mainly US
Costs: $10,000 *incl* tuition, housing, all meals, intl airfare, insurance, fees, excursions, books/materials, ISIC *Nonrefundable fee*
Housing: *Arr by pgm:* residence halls with local students, apts, homestay, pensions, hotels, hostels
Deadline: Feb 1 for fall; Oct 1 for spring
Other Info: *US accredited sponsor:* yes *Began:* 1970 *In coop with:* Kyoto Higher Educ Authority *Orient:* in US & abroad *Activities:* excursions, field trips, pgm travel, cultural events, sports *Misc:* 2 wk bus internship Kyoto Corporation. May contact former participants. *Financial aid:* scholarships, work-study *URL:* http://www.esu/intpgms.edu
Contact: Intl Pgms, Exemplary State Univ, Exemplary CA 99009 *Ph:* 800-222 1111; 714-999 8877 *Fax:* 714-999 6655 *E-mail:* ip@esu.edu
Or Contact: Exemplary State in Kyoto, Kyoto 111, Japan *Ph:* 99-222-552 222 *Fax:* 99-222-553 344

Major headings are printed in **boldface**. Subheads under the major headings are printed in *italic* type. The paragraphs below explain the terms used under each major heading in a program description, using the sample entry as an example.

Program Sponsor and Name

2001
EXEMPLARY STATE UNIVERSITY
Japanese Business and Civilization Program

Each entry begins with its program number, followed by the sponsor name and program title.

Programs are numbered in consecutive order throughout the book. All indexes are to the program number, rather than to the page number on which the program entry appears.

Name of sponsor institution is the second item of information to appear. All entries are indexed by sponsor in **Index I: Sponsoring Institutions**. Entries may list up to three cosponsors. In some cases, a consortium—group of more than three colleges and/or universities—sponsors a program. For such listings, the sponsor name used in the entry and in **Index I** is the consortium name.

Consortium-sponsored programs are also indexed by consortium name in **Index II: Consortia**, which provides lists of all member colleges and universities in each consortium. In consortia program entries, the Contact heading refers the user to the index for the consortium's membership, using the standard phrase, "See Index II for members."

Site

Site: Japan: Kyoto *Host inst:* Kyoto Mgmt Inst

The country and city in which the program takes place are provided first under the *Site:* heading.

Name of host institution is next. The host institution is the school or organization that provides the premises and facilities for classes connected with the program, typically through a contract or other agreement with the sponsor. The sponsor, not the host institution, is the organization with legal, financial and administrative responsibility for the program. The host institution may provide staff and services to the sponsor in addition to the use of its facilities.

Dates

Dates: Aug-Dec or Jan-May or Jun-Jul

Exact dates are stated if provided by the program sponsor. Remember that final program dates are often not available at the time our survey is conducted, many months before the program actually begins. For current information, contact the sponsor.

Subjects

Subjects: Banking, Business/management, Civilization/culture, Economics, Graphic arts/design, Japanese language (int/adv), Japanese studies

Up to fifteen fields of study offered by the program are listed here. Some programs provide opportunities in more than fifteen fields of study, e.g., the international student program of a foreign university. In these cases, "Full curriculum" appears as the first subject listing, to indicate the availability of a wide range of courses. Contact the sponsor for a course catalog to learn about the full range of fields of study.

Many study-abroad programs offer opportunities to learn foreign languages. When sponsors provide the information, program entries indicate the proficiency level of language courses offered: beginning, intermediate and/or advanced (beg/int/adv).

Consult **Index III: Fields of Study** for assistance in locating programs in a specific field. Contact the program sponsor for more detailed course information.

Eligibility

Eligibility: *Own students preferred.* *Level:* jrs, srs, grads, adults, teachers, professionals, precoll *Requires:* 3.0 GPA, previous study in field, 2 yrs coll Japanese *Age:* min 18, max 81, avg 22

If a program restricts eligibility, the phrase "own students only," or a similar phrase defining the restriction, e.g., "own students preferred," "state residents only," will be highlighted in bold italics. A program that does not include a highlighted restriction is open to all applicants at the appropriate academic levels from other institutions.

The IIE books include programs that colleges and universities limit to their own students, or otherwise restrict, because many students first learn of their own institution's programs from these books. Also, study-abroad advisers find it useful to know about the programs of other colleges and universities, and can occasionally arrange access to another institution's program. For these and other reasons, IIE tries to make its study-abroad reference books as complete as possible.

Level: lists the academic levels that may enroll in the program. Most programs are intended primarily for undergraduates, and the abbreviations used for the four undergraduate levels are: fresh, sophs, jrs, srs, for freshmen, sophomores, juniors and seniors. Many programs are also open to graduate students (grads), adult learners, precollege students (precoll), teachers and professionals. "Adults" usually refers to high school graduates who are at least 18 years of age, are often older than the typical undergraduate and are not currently enrolled in a degree program at a US college. "Precollege" generally means high school graduates who have not yet entered college. "Professionals" are those actively working in a field as a career who may wish to improve their skills by international study, e.g., health professionals studying the public health systems of other nations.

Adult learners often wish to study abroad as a way to productively combine travel and learning. Precollege students may want overseas experience before they begin their undergraduate education. Teachers and professionals enhance their qualifications through international study. To help graduate students, adult learners, precollege students, teachers and professionals find the programs accessible to them, use **Index IV: Special Options**.

The *Requires:* subheading lists eligibility specifications, which most typically are a minimum Grade Point Average (GPA), previous study in the field, or a minimum level of language proficiency or other course prerequisite, e.g., 2 yrs coll Japanese. Since space considerations do not allow us to describe requirements in complete detail, it is a good idea to ask the program sponsor for full information.

Some programs have minimum (min) or maximum (max) age limits. Others provide an average (avg) student age as an indication of the typical age/academic level of enrolled students.

Credit

Credit: *Undergrad:* 14-15 Grad: 10-12 *Doc:* transcript, certificate, diploma, degree

Availability of academic credit is indicated. If a unit other than semester hours is used by the program sponsor to define credit, it is specified. Undergraduate credits are listed first, then graduate credits.

Most foreign institutions do not use the US system of academic credit and, thus, do not actually grant credit for successful completion of courses. Many of them are familiar with US credit requirements, however, and have indicated the number of credits generally accepted by US colleges for the program or course listed.

Foreign schools and other organizations sometimes arrange to transfer credit through an accredited US college. When programs offer the transfer credit option, the name of the US school granting transfer credit is given.

The document awarded for successful completion of the program is listed after the subhead *Doc:*.

Remember that the award of credit by your home institution is never automatic. It must be arranged in advance. Consult your academic or study-abroad adviser about receiving academic credit before you enroll in a program.

Instruction

Instruction: *In:* English, Japanese
Format: art studio, directed field study, independent study, internship, lab, lang study, lecture, music lesson, practical training, seminar, student teaching, study tour, tutorial, volunteer/svc, workshop
Students: mainly US

Language of instruction appears first under this heading. Where more than one language is used in teaching classes, consult the program sponsor for exact information. Foreign language courses are usually taught in the language being studied. Other courses may be taught in English or the language of the host country. For courses taught exclusively in a foreign language, be sure to determine in advance whether your level of fluency is sufficient.

Entries then indicate *Format:* which may be lab, language study (lang study), lectures, seminars, tutorials—or such special options as art studio, internship, independent study, music lesson, practical training, student teaching, study tour, directed field study, volunteer/svc (voluntary service projects), or workshop. Special options such as these are indexed in **Index IV.**

The final subhead, *Students:*, provides information on class composition. Some programs are arranged especially for US students (mainly US). Others mix US students with other foreign students (international classes, abbreviated as "intl"). Still others integrate US students into classes taken mainly by local students to provide greater exposure to the host country culture (mainly host country). Many programs offer a variety of class experiences to US students. For example, US students may take some classes as a group and be integrated with host country students for other classes (an option indicated as "US & host country.") Other combinations that occur: intl & host country, US & intl.

Costs

Costs: $10,000 *incl* tuition, housing, all meals, intl airfare, insurance, fees, excursions, books/materials, ISIC
Nonrefundable fee

We have asked sponsors to provide a package amount for participation in the full program. This information is followed by a list of items the program fee includes: tuition, housing, all meals (where three meals per day are usually provided), some meals (fewer than three per day), international airfare (between the US and the program site), health/accident insurance, fees connected with participation in the program, excursions, books and materials, railpasses and other items.

If the program sponsor requires a nonrefundable application fee, the requirement is indicated by the words "Nonrefundable fee."

Since IIE conducts research for this book well in advance of actual program dates, costs that are included in this year's edition are sometimes not yet finally established at the time sponsors provide information. In such cases, sponsors typically provide information on their current fees instead. In either case, the figure given may require clarification or adjustment. Many factors can affect costs, e.g., fluctuations in exchange rates, a change in the mix of services provided for the program fee, etc. Always contact the sponsor directly for the most current information in this important area.

Index V: Cost Ranges provides guidance to programs at varying levels of cost.

Housing

Housing: *Arr by pgm:* residence halls with local students, apts, homestay, pensions, hotels, hostels

Most programs provide housing for members of the group. Entries indicate first who arranges housing—the sponsor ("Arr by pgm"=Arranged by program) or the student ("Arr by student"= Arranged by student), and second, what types of housing are available: residence halls, apartments, homestays (living with a family in a private home), pensions, hotels or other accommodations.

Deadline

Deadline: Feb 1 for fall; Oct 1 for spring

In most cases, deadlines are for the receipt of completed applications with all necessary supporting material: transcripts, recommendations, deposits, etc. Find out well in advance what application material is needed.

Some programs will admit students after the deadline is past, but usually only when a program has not filled all allotted places. It is best not to count on luck. *Apply early!*

If there is a financial aid deadline for students applying for scholarships offered by the program, it will be indicated here.

Other Info

Other Info: *US accredited sponsor:* yes *Began:* 1970 *In coop with:* Kyoto Higher Educ Authority *Orient:* in US & abroad *Activities:* excursions, field trips, pgm travel, cultural events, sports *Misc:* 2 wk bus internship Kyoto Corporation. May contact former participants. *Financial aid:* scholarships, work-study *URL:* http://www.esu/intpgms.edu

All program descriptions indicate whether an accredited US college or university sponsors the program. This information is especially important for those students who need academic credit for their study abroad.

The year in which the program began is provided next, followed by the name of any organization cooperating with the sponsor in offering the program.

Also included is the availability of orientation (*Orient:*) in the US and/or abroad. Additionally, many programs offer activities such as excursions, field trips, program-related travel (pgm travel), cultural events and sports. An excursion or field trip is usually local and does not involve extended time away from the program site. In contrast, program travel may last up to one month or more and involve extensive distances and lectures or research on distant sites.

The miscellaneous *(Misc:)* subheading is used for information that does not fit other headings, but is nonetheless significant. The phrase "May contact former participants" indicates that the sponsor, if requested, will facilitate contact with a former student—by mail, phone or in person. Some sponsors routinely invite former students to their orientation sessions. Make every effort to attend these sessions. The information you acquire from other students can be valuable in selecting the right program and preparing for a rewarding experience abroad.

If financial aid other than loans is available to program participants, the *Financial aid:* subheading will specify either "scholarships" and/or "work-study."

The *URL* (Uniform Resource Locator) subheading indicates the program sponsor's home page address on the World Wide Web.

Contact

Contact: Intl Pgms, Exemplary State Univ, Exemplary CA 99009 *Ph:* 800-222 1111; 714-999 8877 *Fax:* 714-999 6655 *E-mail:* ip@esu.edu **Or Contact:** Exemplary State in Kyoto, Kyoto 111, Japan *Ph*: 99-222-552 222 *Fax:* 99-222-553 344

The primary contact's mailing address for information and applications is listed first, with a toll-free phone number, if available, and other phone, fax and internet numbers. A second or third contact may also be listed, often in cases in which two or three colleges cosponsor a program, or in which a foreign school has both a US representative and a foreign admissions office.

Programs sponsored by consortia typically indicate the administering school as the primary contact, preceded in the program description by a reference to "See Index II for members." **Index II: Consortia** lists all member colleges and universities of a given consortium. The usual rule in this situation is that students at member schools apply to their campus study-abroad office, while students at nonmember schools should contact the main consortium office or the administering school.

Important Notice

The Institute of International Education does not attempt to review or evaluate programs listed in this book. Inclusion of a program does not imply IIE recommendation, nor does omission imply IIE disapproval. Program evaluations and additional information must be requested directly from the program sponsor, NOT from IIE.

Abbreviations

In an effort to keep this large book from becoming unwieldy, many abbreviations are used in a concise entry format. Abbreviations frequently used are:

Acad	academy, academic
Addtl	additional
Admin	administration, administrator
Adv	advanced
Amer	American
Apdo	apartado postal (Spanish for PO Box)
Apt	apartment
Arr	arranged
Assn	association
Assoc	associate
Asst	assistant
Avail	available
Ave	avenue
Avg	average
Beg	beginning
Bldg	building
Blvd	boulevard
Bus	business
CC	community college
Col	colegio
Coll	college
Comm	community; committee
Coop	cooperation
Coord	coordinator
Ctr	center, centro, centre
Cty	county
Dept	department
Dir	director
Div	division
Doc	document
Dr	title: doctor; address: drive
Econ	economics
Educ	education, educational
Equiv	equivalent
Exam	examination
Exch	exchange
Exec	executive
Fdn	foundation
FH	Fachhochschule (German university)
Fresh	freshmen
Genl	general
Govt	government
Grads	graduates
Hrs	hours
Incl	includes, including
Info	information
Inst	institute, institut, instituto
Int	intermediate
Intl	international
ISIC	International Student Identification Card
Ist	istituto (Italian for "institute")
Jrs	juniors
Lang	language
Mgmt	management
Mgr	manager
Misc	miscellaneous
Mo	month
Natl	national
Off	office
Orient	orientation
Pgm	program
Ph	phone
Pl	place
PO	post office
Precoll	precollege
Pres	president
Prof	professor
Qtr	quarter
Rd	road
Rep	representative
Rm	room
Sch	school
Sci	science
Secy	secretary
Sem	semester
Socy	society
Sophs	sophomores
Sq	square
Srs	seniors
St	street; Saint
Ste	suite; feminine "Sainte" (French)
Str	strasse (German for "street"), straat (Dutch for "street")
Svc	service
Undergrad	undergraduate
UK	United Kingdom
Univ	university, universidad, université, etc.
US	United States
VP	vice president
Wk	week
Yr	year

Planning for Study Abroad

Study abroad can be an extraordinary adventure. For the broad-minded student who seeks cultural enrichment and experience beyond the classroom, on campus and off, it really is a wonderful world of opportunity.

In contrast to the relatively sheltered life found at many US colleges, study in a foreign setting exposes the student to an exciting kaleidoscope of new cultural experiences—experiences that open up fresh perspectives on international, political and economic issues, interpersonal relationships and ultimate career choices.

Even an adventure, however, benefits from planning. How well you achieve your immediate personal and academic objectives, as well as your long-range career goals, depends largely on choosing the right country, institution and program. Because of the complexity of the choices to be made, planning should begin a full year before you expect to depart.

Researching the Options

In this age of growing globalization, the range of study-abroad programs is expanding every year. Many programs focus on specific academic disciplines, while others feature both academic and language study. A number of programs combine independent study or internships with traditional coursework.

Your choice of program should be determined by a realistic assessment of your academic preparation and objectives. If you are currently enrolled at a US college or university, be sure to consult with either a study-abroad or Fulbright Program adviser, or a faculty member knowledgeable about foreign-study programs. The adviser can help determine whether the programs you are considering will advance your educational goals—and if you will receive academic credit for them.

It remains your responsibility, however, to research the alternatives thoroughly: contact the designated persons or departments to request program literature, ask specific questions and obtain and review background information on the country you plan to visit. Get in touch with previous participants in programs that interest you. Arrange to meet with students from other countries to learn about life as a foreign student. Allow plenty of time for this research—and expect to discover exciting educational possibilities.

Language Proficiency

Foreign language proficiency is perhaps the single most important factor in choosing where to study abroad. Be completely realistic about your level of fluency. Holding a simple conversation or ordering a meal in another language is one thing; following a complicated lecture and reading scholarly books is an entirely different challenge.

US college-sponsored programs may be conducted in cooperation with a foreign institution or may be taught by foreign faculty. In such cases, the language of instruction is typically the language of the host country. The minimum requirement for most US-sponsored programs is two years of college-level language study or its equivalent.

Study abroad offers an incomparable opportunity to learn the language and immerse oneself in the culture of another country. This book provides information on language and culture/civilization programs available worldwide.

Geographic Location

Geographic setting may be as important as academic qualities in determining whether a program is appropriate for you. Large cities offer excellent cultural opportunities but are expensive and impersonal. Small towns offer more contact with local residents and a traditional way of life, but the provincial lifestyle may seem too limiting.

No foreign-study program can be a guaranteed perfect choice. Even when your needs are well matched to the program, you may suffer periods of loneliness and disorientation simply because of the unfamiliar environment. Remember that one of the most important lessons of time spent abroad is adaptability: the student who develops the ability to go on enjoying and learning, even when confronting unexpected circumstances, has truly broadened his/her horizons.

Developing Nations

Study in developing nations can be especially meaningful and rewarding for US students. We often overlook the fact that nearly three-quarters of the world's population live in such countries—a fact which will have a significant bearing on the course of world history.

The cultures of developing countries pose a sharp contrast to that of the United States. They effectively challenge our customary assumptions about our own society and values and provide a unique perspective on our place in the world.

In today's global economy, a measure of our interdependence is that US trade with developing countries now approaches 40 percent of all imports and exports. Thus, knowledge of developing nations and their cultures will prove a tremendous long-term benefit to any student.

The language of instruction is often English, Spanish or French rather than the native tongue. This after-effect of colonialism does not apply universally, however: Many countries, such as China, boast rich and historic cultures which attract large numbers to study their literature, languages and sciences.

Disabled Students

Many educational institutions provide facilities for students with disabilities. The extent to which these students can be accommodated, however, depends on the nature of the accommodation needs, the available services and the general standards of accessibility in the particular country. The student, staff and faculty are encouraged to use creativity and flexibility in addressing reasonable accommodations. Students with disabilities should discuss their accommodation needs as early as possible with the program sponsors, so arrangements can be made.

Information for exchange participants with disabilities is available from Mobility International USA/National Clearinghouse on Disability and Exchange, which produces a newsletter, videos and several publications. For full details, write to MIUSA, PO Box 10767, Eugene, OR 97440, or visit their website at: *www.miusa.org*.

Adult Learners

While most study-abroad programs are organized with the needs of college students in mind, a significant number admit adults with a personal or professional interest in study overseas. This is particularly true of summer and short-term programs, many of which are sponsored by adult or continuing education schools. The listings in IIE's study-abroad guides indicate whether a program admits adults and/or professionals. Even when the entry indicates that the program is geared to the undergraduate or graduate level, it may be worthwhile contacting the sponsor to inquire if adults can be admitted as auditors.

Adults over the age of 60 may be interested in the international programs of Elderhostel, which combine the best traditions of education and hosteling for those of retirement age. For information, write to Elderhostel, 75 Federal Street, 3rd Floor, Boston, MA 02110-1941.

The Interhostel program of the University of New Hampshire is designed for those age 50 and over. For details, write to Interhostel, Division of Continuing Education, University of New Hampshire, 6 Garrison Avenue, Durham, NH 03824-3529.

Educational Choices

Before enrolling in a study-abroad program, you must determine its effect on your degree and graduation requirements. Your advisers can help evaluate study-abroad in relation to your academic needs and may assist in arranging credit.

US college-sponsored programs generally award credit. Never assume, however, that credit will be granted automatically, or that you can wait until you complete the program to establish credit. Each school makes its own rules regarding transferable credits, and, if the program you select is not sponsored by your home institution, academic credit may not be accepted by it.

Once a proposed study program is approved by your adviser—and prior to departing from the United States—follow your school's specific procedure to ensure receipt of credit. It is strongly recommended that you secure a written document confirming that credit will be awarded. At some colleges or universities this may be done through the study-abroad office. At others, it will be handled by the admissions office or registrar. If there is no study-abroad adviser, your academic adviser can provide information.

Many US colleges and universities allow students planning to study abroad to preregister for courses to be taken upon their return. This option should also be discussed with your study-abroad adviser prior to departure.

Types of Study-Abroad Programs

Most undergraduates enroll in programs sponsored by their own or other US colleges. One advantage of US college-sponsored programs is that they allow students to study in a foreign environment while remaining within a US academic framework. Even where much of the actual coursework is completed at a foreign university, academic credit is arranged through the sponsoring US institution.

In addition, special courses in the language and culture of the foreign country may be provided, and language requirements may be relaxed. Finally, the sponsoring college usually either provides or facilitates nonacademic essentials, such as housing and round-trip transportation.

Most programs fall into one of these categories:

1. Study in a foreign institution combined with courses arranged for the group by the sponsoring US institution.

These programs usually require some knowledge of the language of the country. Nonetheless, special university courses for US or other foreign students generally have less exacting language requirements than regular university courses. Some programs offer a choice of foreign institutions, depending on the level of the student's language skills.

One benefit of this type of program is that it lets you study at a foreign institution while meeting requirements for your US degree. It also offers readily available help with any difficulties you may encounter in the foreign courses.

2. The fully integrated program at a foreign university or other college-level institution.

Students enroll in regular academic courses in the foreign institution, where fluency in the language of instruction is expected. Students must be able to follow lectures and take examinations as part of the student body. These programs can be very exciting and challenging for students who qualify.

Since students enrolled in these programs will not have the opportunity to take any US courses overseas, they must be sure to schedule required coursework at their home campuses.

3. The "island" program, in which all courses are arranged for the US group and taught by faculty members of the sponsoring US school or by foreign faculty engaged specifically for the program.

Some of these programs offer intensive language study for language majors. More often, however, these programs are conducted largely in English. In many areas of the world, they offer the only opportunity for meaningful study for students without a good command of a foreign language.

An advantage of this type of program is that the sponsoring US institution has as much control over the nature and quality of instruction as it has at home. The chief disadvantage is that US students are isolated from the foreign academic milieu and may find themselves isolated socially, as well.

A few programs offer only independent study opportunities, in which qualified students carry out preapproved research projects abroad and receive credit from their home institutions. In others, US students enroll in foreign universities and receive credit from their own schools for coursework abroad. Independent study arrangements like these are made on an individual basis by the students and their schools.

Sponsorship by Consortia

Many of the programs listed in IIE's study abroad guides are sponsored cooperatively by groups of US colleges or consortia. Some are administered through central consortium offices, others by the participating schools which rotate administrative duties among themselves.

It is unlikely to make any real difference to the student whether a program is offered by one school or by a consortium. The chief advantage of co-sponsorship is that a consortium may be able to offer specialized programs that individual schools find difficult to provide. See **Index II** for lists of consortia and their member schools.

Direct Enrollment

It is also possible to enroll directly in many foreign universities. Direct enrollment is an option more often chosen by graduate students than by undergraduates, both because graduate students are more likely to be able to profit from specialized study programs abroad, and because many foreign universities require that new US students already possess a bachelor's degree.

To enroll directly in a foreign university, look into the laws affecting higher education in the country where you plan to study. Some countries have quotas for the number of international students at their universities and restrictions on the numbers of foreign students admitted to particular fields, such as medicine, dentistry, the sciences and law. Because such restrictions may change from year to year, investigate current regulations early in the planning process.

Since admission policies vary from country to country and institution to institution, it is advisable to write directly to institutions you are interested in for specific information on their policies, requirements, costs and facilities. Addresses of foreign institutions can be found in the *World List of Universities* or the *International Handbook of Universities* (Palgrave Publishers Ltd), reference directories on higher education worldwide that can be found in many US college and university libraries. The *International Handbook of Universities* in also available on CD-ROM as part of the *World Higher Education Database*. To ensure a response, enclose an International Reply Coupon (available from any Post Office) with your enquiry.

Remember that, because educational systems vary, no foreign degree is exactly equivalent to a US degree. If you are interested in graduate studies abroad, be sure to conduct extensive research on the educational systems of the countries which interest you. Study abroad advisers can be invaluable in helping you acquire the information you need to make a decision.

Another useful source of information is the *World Education Series*, published by the American Association of Collegiate Registrars and Admissions Officers (AACRAO). Although designed for college admissions officers who need to evaluate foreign academic credentials, these publications provide an overview of each country's educational system. Write AACRAO, One DuPont Circle NW, Ste 520, Washington, DC 20038, for a complete list of titles, or visit their website at: *www.aacrao.org.*

Short-Term or Vacation Study Programs

A study program abroad is a highly productive way to spend a vacation, whether from school or work. Many colleges, language schools and other organizations offer a variety of summer and short-term programs that provide serious academic study for college students, heritage courses for adults interested in finding their roots, technical programs for professionals and a wide range of courses for those who simply want to expand their horizons.

IIE's *Short-Term Study Abroad* lists over 2,200 such programs, most of which take place during the summer. Recognizing that the desire to learn knows no age or season, however, many organizations now offer study tours and other programs throughout the year.

Internships

Many foreign study programs feature internships designed to provide hands-on experience in a particular field, with placements at museums, schools, government offices, international organizations, etc. Most are developed in close consultation with faculty advisers and are tailored to suit the special needs of the student. An internship's success depends almost entirely on the initiative and creativity of the student.

Because of the growing popularity of internship programs and the special arrangements they involve, you must apply for a position and begin making arrangements well in advance. As with other types of programs, don't forget to clarify issues of cost, credit, salary and housing. Use **Index IV: Special Options** in this book to locate internship listings.

Voluntary Service Projects

International service projects offer opportunities to young people from all over the world to live and work together with local people in community development. Usually, no special skills are required. Many projects take place during the summer for short periods, but it is also possible to participate in semester or academic year programs for which academic credit can be arranged. There is no pay, but volunteers generally receive room and board. Good sources of information on volunteer service are the Council on International Educational Exchange and the International Partnership for Service-Learning. Contact: CIEE International Workcamps, 633 Third Avenue, 20th Fl, New York, NY 10017, website: *www.ciee.org;* and, International Partnership for Service-Learning, 815 Second Avenue, Ste 315, New York, NY 10017, website: *www.ipsl.org.*

Finances

Establish a budget to help determine which programs meet both your academic needs and financial capacity. Package fees for programs sponsored by US colleges generally include transportation to and from the United States, tuition, fees, room and board and program-related travel. Other major items are books, local transportation and health and accident insurance.

Be especially careful to find out what program package fees do *not* cover. Admissions to cultural sites and events, gifts, optional travel, bank charges for exchanging money and miscellaneous personal expenses are rarely included and can add up to a considerable sum. Always set aside some money for unexpected contingencies as they invariably occur.

The program costs listed in this book should *always* be viewed as approximate: they were submitted to IIE some

12 to 18 months prior to the actual program dates. Inflation and fluctuations in exchange rates over this period of time may force significant changes in these figures. Again, it is your responsibility to confirm program costs by contacting the sponsor directly.

Large amounts of cash should not be carried abroad. Traveler's checks are available in US dollars and major foreign currencies. International charge cards and ATM cards can also be used to avoid carrying large amounts of cash. In some countries, hard currency restrictions limit the amount of foreign currency which can be changed back into US dollars, particularly if the original exchange receipts have been misplaced. Do *not* under any circumstances exchange money on the black market.

Scholarships

At present, most financial assistance available for study abroad is for graduate and postgraduate study. Undergraduates with regular university scholarships, however, are generally allowed to use them for their own school's overseas programs. Your study-abroad adviser, financial aid officer or bursar can advise you on the possibility of using federal and state aid for foreign study.

Work Abroad

The practice of working one's way through college is not common overseas, although some study programs include nonpaid work experience. Part-time work-study and trainee positions, which pay a small salary, are occasionally available, but cannot be relied upon to cover the bulk of your expenses overseas.

Summer work programs geared towards students, trainees and volunteers characteristically offer room and board rather than a salary. Archaeological excavations, for example, often fall into this category.

Foreign labor laws are often highly restrictive. Be sure to investigate them thoroughly if you plan to seek work abroad—and don't plan to rely on work in the private sector to pay your way.

The Council on International Educational Exchange has organized a work-abroad program with the cooperation of several nations. Academic credit is sometimes available through special arrangement. For information, contact CIEE Work Abroad, 633 Third Avenue, 20th Fl, New York, NY 10017, or visit their website: *www.ciee.org*.

Travel and Living

After selecting a study program, it is time to prepare for life in a foreign country. Your study-abroad experience will have greater personal value if you take an active role in learning about the language, history and culture of the country, as well as current social and political conditions.

Attend any orientation sessions offered by your program sponsor. The history and culture of the host country are usually reviewed in some detail. There may also be language exams and assigned readings. You may have the opportunity to ask questions about issues that confuse you before they present real problems.

Books, periodicals, plays, films and museum exhibits can provide additional information, as will the embassy, consulate or tourist office of the country in which you plan to study.

People abroad are frequently curious about the United States. As a consequence, you can expect to be hit with a barrage of questions about US history, economics, culture, government policies and current events. To be forewarned is to be forearmed!

Laws and Customs

Orientation sessions usually review the more important laws and customs students must comply with. These are not empty warnings. One of the biggest mistakes you can make is to assume that behavior and actions acceptable in the United States are appropriate everywhere, or that other countries will excuse inappropriate or illegal acts simply because you are a foreigner.

In many countries, for example, local cultural values dictate that certain parts of the body be covered, particularly in sacred places. Flouting such customs is perceived as a deliberate affront. In such situations, verbal protestations can escalate into threats or physical assaults. This is particularly true if the US student is thought to be indifferent to the initial objections.

It is important to realize that the issue of one's civil rights is often simply irrelevant. US notions regarding freedom of speech and expression simply do not apply in many countries. Even where the potential for violence is not an issue, students should realize that inappropriate behavior will tend to alienate them from the local populace.

Close adherence to the laws of the country in which you are living or traveling is even more important. It is unwise to rationalize that you are committing only a minor infraction when exchanging money on the black market or making purchases for foreign friends in hard currency shops that are off-limits for natives. Breaking the law—even what seems a repressive, irrational or antiquated one-is still breaking the law and can lead to severe penalties. At the very least, you can expect to be expelled from the program and deported from the country. US programs are there at the discretion of their hosts, and sponsors will not risk their programs to protect law-breaking students. Neither should you expect special intervention from US consulates.

Narcotics laws are strictly enforced overseas, particularly when the offenders are foreigners. Harsh sentences, including life imprisonment or death, are not unknown, even in countries where natives may break such laws with impunity.

Warnings aside, there are few experiences to compare with friendships formed with people who have spent their entire lives in a different milieu and who can communicate whole new perspectives on the most ordinary of life's experiences. Be sensitive rather than brash, and discover what life is like for others on this planet.

Accommodations

Student housing is difficult to find almost everywhere. Dormitory space is often so limited that many foreign universities have strict quotas for the number of rooms allotted to international students. Generally, US students live in apartments, pensions, student hostels or with families. Be sure to find out whose responsibility it is to make housing arrangements. Check with the program sponsors to see what arrangements they have made, and investigate the available alternatives. Remember to confirm all housing arrangements well ahead of departure.

Passports, Visas and Vaccinations

Valid passports are required for travel abroad. You may apply in person to a passport agent at US Department of State agencies in Boston, Chicago, Honolulu, Houston, Los Angeles, Miami, New Orleans, New York City, Philadelphia, San Francisco, Seattle, Stamford (Connecticut) or Washington, DC. Passports are also issued through selected post offices, or by clerks of any federal court or state court of records. Proof of US citizenship (birth certificate, naturalization certificate, or previous US passport), two recent photographs (2" x 2") and current identification with a personal signature and photograph or physical description (such as a driver's license) are required. Social security cards are not acceptable.

For citizens 16 years or older, a passport valid for ten years costs $60. A five-year passport for citizens under 16 is $40. You must appear in person if you are applying for the first time, are renewing a passport issued over twelve years ago or were younger than 16 when your last passport was issued. Apply early: processing an application takes *four to six weeks*—longer during the travel season.

A visa is written permission to visit a country granted by the government of that country. Visa requirements vary from country to country and are fully described in *Visa Requirements of Foreign Governments* (Publication M-264) available at any passport agency or by writing to: Office of Passport Services, Room 386, 1425 K Street NW, Washington, DC 20524.

Anyone planning to study in a country for an extended period of time may need to get a special student visa. Information relating to all visas may be obtained from the nearest embassy or consulate of the country concerned. Many visa applications require that you submit passport-type photographs to be kept on file or incorporated into the visa itself. It is always wise to obtain extra prints of your passport photographs for such purposes.

AIDS testing or vaccination certificates for inoculation against yellow fever or cholera are required by some countries. Check current regulations with your local public health department.

Medical Insurance and Other Health Concerns

The importance of having adequate insurance when visiting another country cannot be overestimated. Before leaving the United States, check your medical and accident insurance policies to be sure they are valid while traveling overseas. If coverage does not extend to travel abroad, you may want to obtain supplemental medical and accident policies. Holders of the International Student Identity Card receive basic medical/accident insurance coverage for their travel outside the continental United States.

While it is easy to stay healthy abroad, in certain countries this requires taking some elementary precautions. Some countries, particularly those in tropical regions, have bacterial, fungal and parasitical diseases which can be difficult to cure. Do not hesitate to ask about these during orientation sessions, and take the advice seriously.

If you require prescription medicines, even intermittently, be aware that foreign drugs are not necessarily closely related to those standard in the United States. Drugs may be marketed under different names and may not be available in the strengths you desire. It is wise to bring an adequate supply of any medication you need. Label all bottles clearly and carry copies of the prescriptions to avoid problems with Customs. In the case of narcotic medicines, it may not be prudent to carry additional supplies because of possible Customs difficulties. Reasonable amounts of nonprescription drugs, such as aspirin and stomach remedies, can come in handy when staying in some of the more remote regions of the world.

Finally, if you wear prescription eyeglasses or contact lenses, bring an extra pair and your prescription. This is particularly important with contact lenses, because the specific type of lens you wear may not be available abroad.

Transportation

Many US-sponsored programs include group transportation to and from the program site. In others, students make their own arrangements. Government tourist offices provide a variety of free travel literature and are good places to begin researching your travel options.

Deregulation in the airline industry has resulted in a proliferation of discounted airfares. Shop carefully if you are looking for an inexpensive flight; the cheapest flight is not necessarily the one that best suits your needs. Fares that specify a return date should be examined with particular care, as these may not allow the flexibilityyou need.

Aim to travel lightly, especially if you will be participating in a study-tour. You will have to carry whatever you bring, so restrict yourself to one or two moderate-sized bags and a small carry-on bag in which to keep valuables, passport and camera equipment. Insure your baggage and personal effects for the full period abroad. If you bring a camera, purchase a lead-lined film bag. Contrary to airport claims, some X-ray devices are ruinous to film.

Once abroad, railroads are often an economical and convenient way to travel. In Europe and Great Britain, Eurail and BritRail passes offer unlimited train travel at considerable savings to those who travel extensively. Eurailpasses are not valid in Britain but can be used on ferries between Italy and Greece, France and Ireland, and in Scandinavia. Rail passes are available from many travel agencies and must be purchased in the United States before your departure.

If you are considering renting a car, remember that in Britain, many Commonwealth countries and Japan, cars are driven on the left-hand side of the road. Your US driver's license is generally accepted abroad, but it may be necessary to supplement it with an International Driver's License, which provides a multilingual translation of the information on your US license. One may be obtained from your local AAA office.

An excellent source of information about student travel is the Council on International Educational Exchange (CIEE). CIEE publishes the *Student Travel Catalog* (available free of charge), and offers the International Student Identity Card as well as a wide range of student travel services. The International Student ID entitles the bearer to numerous discounts on transportation, accommodations, museum entrance fees and more. Contact CIEE headquarters at 633 Third Avenue, 20th Fl, New York, NY 10017, or Council Travel offices, or visit their website: *www.ciee.org.*

IIE-Administered Programs

IIE administers US student applications for the following study-abroad program:

■ **Studio Art Centers International**, Florence, Italy. 4- to 16-week courses in studio arts and culture.

Studio Art Centers International (SACI) is a complete, accredited program for serious students seeking excellence in studio art, liberal art and art conservation instruction at the United States university level in Florence, Italy. SACI offers courses in 33 different studio and academic disciplines at all levels: Semester/ Year Abroad, Summer Studies, Two Year Diploma, MFA/ MA and Post-Baccalaureate. Space is limited, so early application is suggested.

For applications and information, contact SACI at: 1-800-344-9168; *e-mail:* saci@iie.org; or visit their website: *www.saci-florence.org.*

Additional Resources for Study Abroad

The following bibliography lists publications and websites concerned with study and research abroad as well as funding opportunities. The list is current at time of publication. Contact publishers and websites for the most up-to-date information.

Websites

Academy for Educational Development
www.aed.org/
AED offers the PPIA Fellowship Program and the National Security Education Program Graduate International Fellowships. The site provides information on international exchange, fellowships and training.

The American Association of Intensive English Programs (AAIEP)
www.aaiep.org/
AAIEP provides help in choosing an English program in the United States. There are AAIEP member programs in most of the 50 states in the United States.

American Society of Civil Engineers
www.asce.org/
This site list scholarships and fellowships available only to ASCE members.

Directory of Graduate & Undergraduate Programs & Courses in Middle East Studies in the US, Canada & Abroad
Middle East Association of North America
w3fp.arizona.edu/mesassoc/directory/directory.htm
This online directory presents general information on institutions, courses and faculty members in Middle East studies, in all parts of the world, for those who are interested in or are pursuing studies or careers in this area.

E-Conflict World Encyclopedia
www.emulateme.com
This resource provides country information from around the world. It is an excellent source for business professionals, tourists, students and teachers.

Educational Directories Unlimited, Inc.
www.edudirectories.com/
An online study-abroad information resource listing study-abroad programs worldwide. Contains links to study-abroad home pages as well as related information.

FastWEB
www.fastweb.com
This site generates a personalized list of awards based on criteria selected by the user.

Federal Information Exchange
www.rams-fie.com/
Fedix, an online database of federal grant and research opportunities for the education and research communities, and Molis, an online database of 164 minority institutions, deliver e-mail announcements of grant opportunities from any of 12 federal agencies, depending upon specific interests of the recipient. Registration for this service is available on the website.

Gardinet
German American Resource Directory on the Internet
www.aicgs.org/gardinet/
This site lists information on a broad range of predominantly American-supported programs fostering German-American cooperation, primarily in the social sciences. Listings include government, university and college, association, corporate, and foundation resources. Also incorporates German resources for Germans and Americans.

IIE Online
Institute of International Education
www.iie.org
The Institute of International Education (IIE) is the largest not-for-profit international educational organization in the United States. This site provides information regarding IIE's programs, services and resources, including the Fulbright Fellowship.

IIE Passport: Living and Learning Abroad
Institute of International Education
www.iiepassport.org
A comprehensive student guide on the web to 5,000 learning opportunities worldwide.

International Research and Exchanges Board
www.irex.org
Administers academic exchanges between the United States and Russia, the Newly Independent States (NIS), Central and Eastern Europe (CEE), Mongolia and China. Lists a variety of programs as well as grant and fellowship opportunities.

National Science Foundation: Guide to Programs
www.nsf.gov
The NSF encourages exchange in science and engineering. The site has an international component, providing links with valuable information on fellowships, grants and awards, summer institutes, workshops, research and education projects, and international programs. Targeted for students as well as professionals.

Office of Higher Education Programs, US Department of Education
www.ed.gov/offices/OPE/OHEP/iegps/index.html
Administered by the Center for International Education, this site describes programs and fellowships offered by the International Education and Graduate Programs office of the US Department of Education.

Pitsco's Launch to Grants and Funding
www.pitsco.com/p/resframe.htm
This site provides links to dozens of grant and funding sources information.

Scholarship News
www.free-4u.com/newpage54.htm
This site provides links to scholarships, grants, fellowships and internships for students. Listings are organized by topic.

The Smithsonian
www.si.edu/
Contains a fellowships link to Smithsonian Opportunities for Research and Study.

StudyAbroad.com
www.studyabroad.com/
A commercial site with thousands of study-abroad programs in over 100 countries with links to study abroad program home pages. Includes the Study Abroad Forum link, which contains a multitude of financial aid resources.

TESOL: Teachers of English to Speakers of Other Languages, Inc
www.tesol.org/
TESOL's mission is to develop the expertise of its members and others involved in teaching English to speakers of other languages to help them foster effective communication in diverse settings while respecting individuals' language rights.

UCIEP: A Consortium of University and College Intensive English Programs in the US
www.uciep.org/
Founded in 1967, UCIEP's purpose is the advancement of professional standards and quality instruction in intensive English programs at universities and colleges in the United States. The member programs are committed to the consortium's effort to ensure that students receive the highest quality intensive English instruction from trained, professional teachers.

An Unofficial Guide to Youth Exchange, Foundation Scholarships, and Group Study Exchange
www.tecc.co.uk/public/PaulHarris/youthdoc.html
Although it is "unofficial," this site offers some helpful information about Rotary activities and funding opportunities.

US Department of State International Information Programs
US Department of State
www.usinfo.state.gov/
This site offers comprehensive descriptions of all IIP programs, including the Fulbright Fellowship, as well as sections on policy issues, global and regional issues and IIP publications.

World Education Services
www.wes.org/
This site for international education professionals features information on WES' foreign credentials evaluation services, world education workshops, and the journal *World and News Reviews*.

World Wide Arts Resources
www.world-arts-resources.com/
Focusing solely on the arts, this site provides links for funding sources, university programs and arts organizations all over the world.

Youth for Understanding (YFU)
www.yfu.org/index2.html
Offers opportunities for young people around the world to spend a summer, semester or year with a host family in another culture.

Publications

Advisory List of International Educational Travel and Exchange Programs 2000-2001, Council on Standards for International Educational Travel, 2000.
www.csiet.org/csiet/AdvisoryList.html
CSIET publishes this list annually as a service to schools, prospective international high school students, and host families. The *Advisory List* provides a resource from which prospective exchange students and/or their parents and school leaders can confidently glean an understanding of

the scope, background, and operations of programs that have been reviewed.

Annual Register of Grant Support, 32nd edition, 2000, RR Bowker/Reed Publishing, 1999.
www.bowker.com.catalog
This comprehensive reference is organized by subject area and offers information on both traditional (corporate, private, and public) and nontraditional (educational associations and unions) sources of funding.

Assistantships and Graduate Fellowships in the Mathematical Sciences, American Mathematical Society Publications, 1999-2000.
www.ams.org/employment/gradstudents.htm
This resource provides up-to-date information on graduate programs for prospective graduate students and their advisers. Updated annually.

Athletic Scholarships: Thousands of Grants–and Over $400 Million–for College-Bound Athletes, 4th edition, by Andy Clark and Amy Clark General, Facts on File, 2000.
www.factsonfile.com
Lists grants awarded to college-bound male and female athletes at every playing level. An introduction guides readers through the application process, with sample cover letters and resumés included. A state-by-state directory lists every four- and two-year college that offers athletic aid and scholarship money for a wide range of sports.

Awards, Honors & Prizes: US and Canada, Volume 1, 17th edition, Gale Group, 2000.
www.gale.com/
This international directory describes awards given for achievements in virtually every field. Awards are listed alphabetically by the name of the administering organization, followed by alphabetical listings and descriptions of each of the awards it offers. Organization, award and subject indexes are included.

Barron's Complete College Financing Guide, 4th edition, by Marguerite J Dennis, Barron's Educational Series, Inc, 1997.
www.barronseduc.com
This book gives parents and students the facts they need about financing an education. General advice on budgeting, managing debt, and working out a personal college financing plan is provided. Also included is advice on how to obtain information on low-interest student loans, scholarships and grant sources.

Directory of Biomedical and Healthcare Grants 2000, 14th edition, Oryx Press, 1999.
www.oryxpress.com
Lists over 3,600 government and privately-sponsored funding programs concerned with human health and biomedicine. Arranged alphabetically and indexed by subject, sponsoring organizations, program type (28 categories), and geographic area (state or regional restrictions).

Directory of Financial Aids for Women 1999-2001, Reference Service Press, 1999.
www.rspfunding.com/
Focusing on financial aid sources set aside specifically for women from secondary school to postdoctoral and professional levels, this resource provides full program descriptions for scholarships, fellowships, loans, grants, awards and internships. Indexed by program title, sponsoring organization, residency, tenability (focuses on geographical areas), subject and calendar (stresses filing dates for fundseekers facing time constraints).

Directory of Grants in the Humanities, 1999/2000, 13th edition, Oryx Press, 1999.
www.oryxpress.com
Contains 3,484 current funding programs that support research, travel, internships, fellowships, dissertations, conferences, exhibitions, performances and study in the humanities sponsored by government and private institutions. Indexed by subject, sponsoring organization, program type (26 categories) and geographic area (state or regional restrictions).

Directory of International Grants and Fellowships in the Health Sciences, US Government Fogarty International Center, 2000.
www.nih.gov/fic/
Fellowships and grants are listed separately in this guide. Each listing includes a complete program description with contact information.

Directory of Research Grants 2000, Oryx Press, 1999.
www.oryxpress.com
Taken from the GRANTS database, this resource lists a wide range of research programs in medicine, physical and social sciences, arts, humanities and education sponsored by both private and governmental sources. Programs are indexed by subject, sponsoring organization, program type (26 categories), and geographic area (state or regional focus).

Fellowships in International Affairs-A Guide to Opportunities in the US & Abroad, Lynne Rienner Publishers, 1994.
www.rienner.com
Published in conjunction with WIIS (Women in International Service), this guide lists fellowships designed to encourage women to pursue careers in international security. Fellowships are listed alphabetically and indexed by title, area and type.

Foundation Grants to Individuals, 11th edition, Foundation Center, 1999.
www.fdncenter.org
Including scholarships, student loans, fellowships, travel internships, residencies, arts and cultural projects, research and general welfare, this guide is the most comprehensive listing available of private US foundations that provide financial assistance to individuals. Indexed by geographic focus, company employee grants, specific schools, types of support, subject and foundation name.

Free Money for College, 5th edition, by Laurie Blum, Henry Holt & Co, 1999.
www.hholt.com
Provides current information on grants and scholarships available for undergraduate study. Scholarship information is organized by state and area of study, and special scholarship sections list sources of funding for women, various ethnic groups, and the disabled. A section on miscellaneous scholarships covers a broad range of eligibility requirements.

Free Money for Graduate School, 4th edition, by Laurie Blum, Henry Holt & Co, 2000.
www.hholt.com
Covers an extensive list of sources for grants and scholarships to help readers attain their advanced degrees. Each entry contains contact information, a description of the program, eligibility requirements, the maximum grant amount, and the application deadline.

German-American Scholarship Guide-Exchange Opportunities for Historians and Social Scientists, German Historical Institute, 1999-2000.
www.ghi-dc.org
This guide is divided into two sections: scholarships for study and research in the US, and scholarships for study and research in Germany. Programs in each section are listed alphabetically and indexed by category.

Grant Opportunities for US Scholars and Host Opportunities for US Universities 2000-2001, IREX.
www.irex.org
Geared toward academic faculty members and doctoral candidates, this pamphlet lists programs in advanced research, language and development, short-term travel, special projects and institutional opportunities.

Grants and Awards for Teachers: A Guide to Federal and Private Funding, 3rd edition, Aspen Publishers, Inc, 1998.
www.grantscape.com
This guide describes the how-to's of applying for funding. Entries are indexed by subject and by type of support.

Grants Register, 18th edition, St Martin's Press, 2000.
www.stmartins.com
This directory offers a comprehensive list of programs organized alphabetically with special attention to eligibility requirements. Indexed by subject.

Grants, Fellowships, and Prizes of Interest to Historians, AHA Publications, 1999-2000.
www.theaha.org
This guide offers information on awards for historians from undergraduate to postgraduate grants, fellowships, prizes, internships and awards. It also includes a section on article, book and essay prizes.

Guide to Medical and Dental Schools, 9th edition, by Dr Saul Wischnitzer, with Edith Wischnitzer, Barron's Educational Series, Inc, 2000.
www.barronseduc.com
A complete career guide manual and school directory, this book presents profiles of all accredited medical, dental, and osteopathic schools in the US and Canada, and advice on negotiating the admissions process.

Harvard College Guide to Grants, 11th edition, Harvard University Office of Career Services, 1998.
www.ocs.fas.harvard.edu
Geared toward college students and recent graduates, this guide describes national and regional grants and fellowships for study in the US, study abroad and work and practical experience. It contains appendixes and a bibliography.

Higher Education Moneybook for Women and Minorities, by Doris Marie Bruce-Young and William C Young (Contributor), Young Enterprises International, Inc, 1997.
Includes chapters on federal programs, general undergraduate programs, graduate programs by major, general postdoctoral programs, and postdoctoral programs by academic area. Program description and contact information are provided for each award.

Hispanic Yearbook-Anuario Hispano, TIYM Publishing Co, 2000.
www.tiym.com
This guide lists Hispanic organizations, publications, radio and TV stations, though not specifically for grant-giving purposes. The 1995 edition includes a diskette of 800 financial aid programs for minorities.

The International Directory of Voluntary Work, 7th edition, by David Woodworth, Vacation Work/ Peterson's Guides, 2000.
www.petersons.com
Covering much of the globe, this book sets out to explore the full range of both short- and long-term volunteer opportunities.

International Exchange Locator, Alliance for International Educational and Cultural Exchange, 1998. Available from IIE books.
www.laurasian.org/Alliance
This is a guide to US organizations, federal agencies, and congressional committees active in international educational exchange. It lists over 400 Federal agency officials in 21 agencies with complete address and fax information.

The International Foundation Directory 2000, 9th edition, Europa Publications Limited, 2000.
www.europapublications.com/ifd.htm
This directory of international foundations, trusts and other similar non-profit institutions provides a comprehensive picture of foundation activity on a world scale. Entries are arranged alphabetically by country. Includes an index of foundations and a separate index of their main activities.

Journalist's Road to Success—A Career and Scholarship Guide, The Dow Jones Newspaper Fund, 1999.
www.dowjones.com/newsfund/
Suitable for guidance offices as well as individual students who want to research the offerings at more than 400 colleges listed, this guide provides scholarship information for students pursuing journalism/mass communication degrees. Lists of internships, training programs, and continuing education opportunities for professional journalists and journalism educators are also provided.

Mathematical Sciences Professional Directory, American Mathematical Society, 1999-2000.
www.ams.org/employment/gradstudents.htm
This directory is a handy reference to: various organizations in the mathematical sciences community; academic departments in the mathematical sciences; mathematical units in nonacademic organizations; and, alphabetic listings of colleges and universities. Updated annually.

Money for Film and Video Artists, American Council for the Arts, 1993.
www.artsusa.org
The listings are organized by sponsoring organization and entries include basic application and program information. Entries are indexed by organization, geographic area, medium and format, and type of support.

Money for International Exchange in the Arts, American Council for the Arts, 1992.
www.artsusa.org
Offers a comprehensive guide to the various resources available to support artists and arts organizations in international work. Profiles 160 organizations that offer information and technical assistance, exchange programs and travel grants, exhibitions and presentations, grants, fellowships and awards, research and study opportunities, and artists' residencies and colonies.

Money for Visual Artists, ACA American Council for the Arts, 1993.
www.artsusa.org
Programs are listed alphabetically by sponsor with detailed program description. Indexed by organization, geographic area and type of support.

Music, Dance & Theater Scholarships, Conway Greene Publishing Co, 2nd edition, 1998.
www.conwaygreene.com
This resource is divided by type of scholarship and schools are listed alphabetically. It is indexed by school, and there is also a city/state locator.

Prentice Hall Guide to Scholarships & Fellowships for Math and Science Students, Prentice Hall, 1993.
This guide includes basic college and graduate school information plus admissions and financial aid expectations. The listing of scholarships and fellowships is by organization with program description and contact information.

Scholarships and Fellowships (Publication 520), IRS Tax Forms Distribution Center

Study Abroad 2000-2001, UNESCO Publishing, 1999.
www.unesco.org
With programs listed in English, French and Spanish, this directory provides comprehensive information on national and international scholarships and courses open to foreign students. National scholarships and courses are listed by

country. Indexed by international organizations, national institutions and subjects of study. Publication also available on CD-ROM.

Work Your Way Around the World, by Susan Griffith, Vacation Work/Peterson's Guides, 1999.
www.petersons.com
This unique book provides practical and realistic advice about where and how to get jobs around the world.

Working Holidays 1999: The Complete Guide to Seasonal Jobs, Central Bureau, 2000. Available from IIE Books.
www.britcoun.org/cbeve
Listed alphabetically by country/area and arranged into categories of work on offer, this annual guide provides useful information on agencies, organizations and businesses that offer paid and voluntary vacation jobs worldwide, varying in duration from 3-365 days.

World List of Universities and Other Institutions of Higher Education, 22nd edition, Palgrave Publishers, Ltd, 1999.
www.palgrave.com
An invaluable reference tool for all those concerned with higher education in its international context. This concise directory includes, in addition to universities, other institutions offering terminal degrees after three to four years of higher education. Latest edition modified and enhanced to facilitate reference.

The World of Learning 2000, 50th edition, Gale Group, 2000.
www.galegroup.com
Contains information for over 26,000 universities, colleges, schools of art and music, libraries, archives, learned societies, research institutes, museums and art galleries in more than 180 countries. Lists more than 400 major international organizations concerned with education worldwide and includes a 100-page index of institutions and organizations.

A World of Options: A Guide to International Exchange, Community Service and Travel for Persons with Disabilities, 3rd edition, Mobility International USA, 1997.
www.miusa.org
This unique directory lists an impressive array of information regarding international study, living, travel, funding and contact organizations for people with disabilities.

A Year Between: The Complete Guide to Taking a Year Out, 4th edition, Central Bureau, 2000.
Available from IIE Books.
www.britcoun.org/cbeve
This book provides detailed information on over 150 organizations offering job placements, work experience, volunteer recruitment, expeditions and study-abroad opportunities for students taking a "year out" between school and higher education, school and work, or higher education and a career.

How to Read Study-Abroad Literature

The late Lily von Klemperer trained a generation of study-abroad advisers as one of the most active members of NAFSA: Association of International Educators. Before and after her retirement from IIE, she brought a strong concern for ethics to her work. The following article, first printed in a NAFSA newsletter of the mid-1970's, has been reprinted frequently ever since.

How to Read Study-Abroad Literature

By Lily von Klemperer

This is a sample advertisement for a summer program abroad:

TWA
Spend Your Summer in Sunny Spain
Live in a Medieval Castle
Learn Spanish at a Famous University
College Credit Available
Outstanding Faculty
International Student Body
Limited Enrollment—All Ages Eligible
Inclusive Charge
Write for Fully Illustrated Brochure
Director of Admissions
PO Box 000, Grand Central Station
New York, NY 10017

This advertisement probably never existed in its entirety. Its components, however, appear in many advertisements, posters and brochures. Advertisements and posters may have to be somewhat flashy and overstated to catch the eye. Brochures, on the other hand, should be factual, realistic and totally honest.

Let us analyze the components of the sample ad, line by line, in order to remind ourselves (1) how to read, interpret and *write* descriptive literature on study-programs abroad, and (2) what questions to ask ourselves and others before enrolling in a program.

TWA. If the advertisement or brochure is "crowned" by TWA, a travel agency or a similar commercial organization, while the name of the sponsoring US college or university appears in small print elsewhere, whose program is it? And who is responsible for the program's academic standards, if any?

Spend Your Summer in Sunny Spain. A pleasant prospect! But look at the prominence of this statement and ask what the real purpose of this program is: a summer in the sun—or a summer spent studying a foreign language and culture? How many hours will be spent in class and how many on the beach? What is the curriculum? Who teaches what, where and when?

Live in a Medieval Castle. How romantic! But where is that castle? Is it near that "famous university" or will you have to commute to classes each day? Are the rooms shared or single? Are study facilities available? Are the inexpensive eating places nearby?

If family living is suggested, is it a family that has experience with US students? Will they converse with you in the language you are studying? Is the housing offered close to the center of town and cultural events? Is there public transportation after 6 pm or do students have to rely on expensive taxis?

Learn Spanish at a Famous University. Why isn't the name of the host institution given? Foreign universities generally suspend regular operations during the summer months, when their facilities may be available to anyone willing to pay the rent. The "famous university" may not actually be involved in the curriculum at all. The ad may refer to courses arranged by the sponsoring organization or to a special program for foreigners, which may or may not be organized by the host institution.

Some ads refer to "accredited" institutions or programs. To check the US accreditation of a college or university, consult *Accredited Institutions of Postsecondary Education*, published annually by the American Council on Education for the Council on Postsecondary Accreditation. Information on foreign universities is available in *The World of Learning* (Europa Publications), the *International Handbook of Universities* (de Gruyter) and the *Commonwealth Handbook of Universities Yearbook* (Association of Commonwealth Universities).

College Credit Available. The crucial questions here are (1) who makes this college credit available? and (2) does the student's home institution accept credit offered by this program?

If receiving academic credit for your studies abroad is important to you, check the brochure to see if your school is listed as a participating institution or as a school that has accepted program credits in the past. Then consult your academic or study-abroad adviser *before you enroll in the program* to see whether the credits offered can be applied to your degree program.

Outstanding Faculty. Who are they? Where do they teach? What are their credentials? And, are they accessible to the students outside of class?

International Student Body. Look closely at the roster of students in the back of the brochure. Are they swelling the ranks of "international students" by listing the children of US parents residing abroad? Or will you in fact be mixing with bona fide representatives of other cultures?

Limited Enrollment—All Ages Eligible. Does the statement "limited enrollment" presuppose selectivity when all ages are eligible? How homogeneous is a program open to everybody, unless it includes classes specifically geared to the various academic levels?

It would be more helpful to know the type of student for whom the program is designed—his academic level, educational or professional background, motivation and goals.

Inclusive Charge. There are almost as many variations to this term as there are programs. Is there an estimate of total expenses? Read the small print. Find out exactly what is covered and, more importantly, what is NOT covered. For example, are there periods of time abroad NOT covered by the inclusive fee? Will you have to pay for transportation to and from classes each day?

Ask about refund policies: Is there a nonrefundable application fee? Will tuition and program fees be refunded if circumstances force you to drop out of the program?

Write for Fully Illustrated Brochure. Even organizers of high-quality programs love to publicize them with attractive photographs of breathtaking scenery, lively cafe scenes, marble columns and Gothic spires. Unless the brochure devotes equal space to academic facilities, however, one may well question whether there is any provision at all for serious study.

Director of Admissions. Is there a name of a responsible person or just a title—or not even that? If you search the "fully illustrated brochure" and find no board of advisers, no trustees listed—no names whatsoever—what conclusions would you reach?

PO Box 000, Grand Central Station. Is there a street address or just a postal number? Is there a phone number? How can one get hold of the program director in an emergency? And does a box number or street address in Ann Arbor necessarily imply University of Michigan sponsorship?

All these remarks—negative and positive—are a bid for honesty. Descriptive literature on foreign study should reflect the serious intent of the organizers. It should reflect quality, selectivity and effective academic control. A meaningful and solid program cannot accommodate all tastes, all needs, all levels of maturity. But whatever it is meant to represent should be stated clearly and honestly.

Worldwide

0001
ALLIANCES ABROAD
Long and Short Term Language Study Abroad
Site: Africa, Australia, China, Costa Rica, Ecuador, France, Germany, Guatemala, Italy, Mexico, Spain
Dates: 2 wks or longer, yr-round
Subjects: Art, Business/management, Civilization/culture, Community service projects, Conservation, Culinary arts, Field study, Geography, History, Hotel management, Internships, Languages (beg/int/adv), Literature, Music, Political science/politics
Eligibility: *Level:* fresh, sophs, jrs, srs, grads, adults, teachers, professionals, precoll *Age:* min 16, avg 22
Credit: *Undergrad:* avail *Grad:* avail *Doc:* transcript
Instruction: *In:* host country lang *Format:* art studio, directed field study, independent study, internship, lang study, lecture, music lesson, practical training, student teaching, study tour, tutorial, volunteer/svc, workshop *Students:* intl
Costs: $1,700 per mo *incl* tuition, housing, some meals, insurance, fees, excursions, books/materials *Nonrefundable fee*
Housing: *Arr by pgm:* residence halls with local students, apartments, homestay, pensions, hotels, hostels
Deadline: 3 mos before pgm
Other info: *US accredited sponsor:* no *Began:* 1993 *Orient:* abroad (1-3 days) *Activities:* excursions, field trips, program travel, cultural events, sports *Misc:* Individually-designed svc pgms. May contact former participants. *URL:* http://www.alliancesabroad.com
Contact: Victoria Lynden, Pres, or Beatrice Tijerina, Outbound Pgm Dir, Alliances Abroad, 702 West Ave, Austin TX 78701 *Ph:* 888-622 7623; 512-457 8062 *Fax:* 512-457 8132 *E-mail:* info@alliancesabroad.com

---

0002
AMERICAN JEWISH WORLD SERVICE
International Jewish College Corps
Site: Ghana or Honduras and Israel *Host inst:* local NGOs
Dates: 7 wks, Jun 18-Aug 8
Subjects: Development studies, Homestay, Human rights, Jewish/judaic studies, Justice
Eligibility: *Level:* fresh, sophs, jrs, srs, grads *Requires:* Spanish recommended for Honduras option *Age:* min 18, max 25, avg 20
Credit: *Undergrad:* avail *Grad:* none
Instruction: *In:* English *Format:* volunteer/svc *Students:* mainly US
Costs: $3,500 *incl* tuition, housing, all meals, intl airfare, insurance, fees, excursions
Housing: *Arr by pgm:* homestay, hostels
Deadline: Mar 15
Other info: *US accredited sponsor:* no *Began:* 1994 *Orient:* avail in New York City (2 days) *Misc:* May contact former participants. *Financial aid:* scholarships *URL:* http://www.ajws.org
Contact: IJCC Pgm Coord, Amer Jewish World Svc, 989 Ave of the Americas, New York NY 10018 *Ph:* 800-889 7146; 212-736 2597 *Fax:* 212-736 3463 *E-mail:* jvcvol@jws.org

---

0003
AMERICAN JEWISH WORLD SERVICE
Jewish Volunteer Corps
Site: Africa, Asia, Central America, Middle East, Russia, Ukraine *Host inst:* local NGOs
Dates: 1 mo or longer, yr-round
Subjects: Agriculture, Business/management, Community service projects, Computer sciences, Development studies, Education/teaching, Health/health education, Homestay, Information technology
Eligibility: *Level:* adults, professionals *Requires:* must be Jewish & citizen or permanent resident of US or Canada
Credit: *Undergrad:* none *Grad:* none
Instruction: *In:* English *Format:* volunteer/svc *Students:* mainly US
Costs: Contact sponsor
Housing: *Arr by pgm:* apartments, homestay
Deadline: None
Other info: *US accredited sponsor:* no *Orient:* in US *Misc:* Volunteers work as consultants to local grassroots NGOs in healthcare, education, agriculture & fundraising. May contact former participants. *URL:* http://www.ajws.org
Contact: Jewish Volunteer Corps, Amer Jewish World Svc, 989 Ave of the Americas, 10th Fl, New York NY 10018 *Ph:* 800-889 7146; 212-736 2597 *Fax:* 212-736 3463 *E-mail:* jvcvol@jws.org

---

0004
ASSOCIATION FOR INTERNATIONAL PRACTICAL TRAINING (AIPT)
Professional Programs
Site: Various countries
Dates: 1-4 wks, yr-round
Subjects: Agriculture, Architecture, Business/management, Ecology/environmental studies, Engineering, Hospitality management, Information science/systems, Media studies, Tourism, Trade
Eligibility: *Level:* jrs, srs, grads, adults, professionals *Age:* min 18
Credit: *Undergrad:* none *Grad:* none *Doc:* certificate
Instruction: *In:* English *Format:* lecture, seminar, study tour *Students:* mainly US
Costs: Contact sponsor
Housing: *Arr by pgm:* residence halls, apartments, hotels, hostels
Deadline: Contact sponsor
Other info: *US accredited sponsor:* no *Orient:* in US & abroad (1 day) *Activities:* excursions, field trips, program travel, cultural events *URL:* http://www.aipt.org

Contact: Dan Ewert, Dir of Pgm Development, AIPT, 10400 Little Patuxent Parkway, Ste 250, Columbia MD 21044-3510 *Ph:* 410-997 2200 *Fax:* 410-997 0139 *E-mail:* aipt@aipt.org

---

0005
CENTER FOR CULTURAL INTERCHANGE
Independent Homestay
Site: Argentina, Chile, Ecuador, France, Germany, Ghana, Ireland, Italy, Japan, Mexico, New Zealand, Spain, others
Dates: 1-4 wks, yr-round
Subjects: Civilization/culture, Homestay, Independent study, Languages
Eligibility: *Level:* adults, precoll *Age:* min 16
Credit: *Undergrad:* none *Grad:* none
Instruction: *In:* host country lang *Format:* independent study *Students:* US & intl
Costs: $1,000 per mo *incl* housing, all meals, insurance, fees *Nonrefundable fee*
Housing: *Arr by pgm:* homestay
Deadline: 6 wks before pgm
Other info: *US accredited sponsor:* no *Began:* 1985 *Orient:* in US & abroad *Misc:* Focus on culture & homelife. No structured lang course. *URL:* http://www.cci-exchange.com
Contact: Karen Hindhede, Pgm Dir, Ctr for Cultural Interchange, 17 N 2nd Ave, St Charles IL 60174 *Ph:* 888-227 6231; 630-377 2272 *Fax:* 630-377 2307 *E-mail:* info@cci-exchange.com

---

0006
EASTERN MICHIGAN UNIVERSITY
European Cultural History Tour
Site: Austria, Belgium, Czech Republic, Egypt, England, France, Germany, Greece, Israel, Italy, Turkey
Dates: 40 & 78-day study tours departing May 17, May 24, Jun 14, Jun 26, Jul 3
Subjects: Art, History
Eligibility: *Level:* fresh, sophs, jrs, srs *Requires:* good acad standing, references *Age:* min 18
Credit: *Undergrad:* 6-12 *Grad:* none *Doc:* transcript
Instruction: *In:* English *Format:* lecture, seminar, study tour *Students:* mainly US
Costs: $3,995-$7,895 *incl* tuition, housing, some meals, insurance, fees, excursions
Housing: *Arr by pgm:* pensions, hotels, hostels
Deadline: Apply early
Other info: *US accredited sponsor:* yes *Began:* 1974 *Orient:* abroad & by mail *Activities:* excursions, cultural events *Misc:* May contact former participants. *URL:* http://www.emich.edu/abroad
Contact: Acad Pgms Abroad, Eastern Michigan Univ, 127 Boone Hall, Ypsilanti MI 48197 *Ph:* 800-777 3541; 734-487 2424 *Fax:* 734-487 4377 *E-mail:* programs.abroad@emich.edu

---

0007
EMI INTERNATIONAL
Summer and Year-Abroad Study Programs
Site: Canada: Quebec; France; Guadeloupe; Italy; Martinique; Spain; Switzerland *Host inst:* more than 60 schs
Dates: 1 wk or longer, yr-round
Subjects: Art, Culinary arts, Fine arts, French language (beg/int/adv), Italian language (beg/int/adv), Photography, Spanish language
Eligibility: *Level:* fresh, sophs, jrs, srs, grads, adults, teachers, professionals, precoll *Age:* min 18
Credit: *Undergrad:* avail *Grad:* avail *Doc:* certificate, diploma
Instruction: *In:* French, German, Italian, Spanish *Format:* art studio, lang study, lecture, study tour *Students:* intl
Costs: Contact sponsor
Housing: *Sponsor assists:* residence halls, apartments, homestay, pensions, hotels
Deadline: Contact sponsor
Other info: *US accredited sponsor:* no *Activities:* excursions, field trips, cultural events, sports *Misc:* May contact former participants.
Contact: Michael Giammarella, EMI Intl, PO Box 640713, Oakland Gardens NY 11364-0713 *Ph:* 718-631 0096 *Fax:* 718-631 0316 *E-mail:* mgiamma@prodigy.net

---

0008
EXPLORATIONS IN TRAVEL
International Volunteer Placements
Site: Australia, Belize, Costa Rica, Ecuador, Mexico, Nepal, New Zealand, Puerto Rico, Samoa
Dates: 1 wk or longer, yr-round
Subjects: Community service projects, Conservation, Education/teaching, Wildlife
Eligibility: *Level:* adults *Requires:* background in biology, teaching &/or Spanish lang for some placements *Age:* min 18
Credit: *Undergrad:* none *Grad:* none
Instruction: *In:* English, Spanish *Format:* directed field study, internship, lang study, student teaching, volunteer/svc *Students:* intl
Costs: $750-$1,000 placement fees *Nonrefundable fee*
Housing: *Sponsor assists:* residence halls, homestay
Deadline: Rolling admissions
Other info: *US accredited sponsor:* no *Began:* 1990 *Orient:* abroad *Misc:* May contact former participants. *URL:* http://volunteertravel.com
Contact: John Lee, Pgm Dir, or Debbie Jacobs, Pres, Explorations in Travel, 1922 River Rd, Guilford VT 05301 *Ph:* 802-257 0152 *Fax:* 802-257 2784 *E-mail:* explore@sover.net

---

0009
FOUNDATION FOR INTERNATIONAL EDUCATION
Overseas Practicum for Experienced Teachers
Site: Australia, Costa Rica, England, India, Ireland, Kenya, New Zealand, Scotland, Taiwan, others *Host inst:* various schs & colls
Dates: 3-4 wks, yr-round
Subjects: Education/teaching, Elementary education, Secondary education
Eligibility: *Level:* grads, teachers *Requires:* teaching experience *Age:* avg 50
Credit: *Undergrad:* none *Grad:* avail *Transfer credit through:* Hamline Univ
Instruction: *In:* English *Format:* independent study, internship, volunteer/svc *Students:* mainly US
Costs: About $125 per wk *incl* housing, all meals
Housing: *Sponsor assists:* homestay
Deadline: None
Other info: *US accredited sponsor:* no *Began:* 1989 *Orient:* in US *Activities:* excursions, field trips, program travel, cultural events, sports *Misc:* May contact former participants. *Financial aid:* scholarships, work study
Contact: Dr Ross Korsgaard, Fdn for Intl Educ, 121 Cascade Ct, River Falls WI 54022-2805 *Ph:* 715-425 1774 *Fax:* 715-525 5101 *E-mail:* korsgaard@worldnet.att.net

---

0010
GLOBAL EXCHANGE
Reality Tours
Site: Brazil, Costa Rica, Cuba, Guatemala, Haiti, India, Iran, Ireland, Israel, Mexico, others
Dates: 1 wk or longer, yr-round
Subjects: Agriculture, Arts, Civilization/culture, Development studies, Ecology/environmental studies, Film studies, Human rights, Internships, Languages (beg/int/adv), Peace studies, Public health, Social change, Third World studies, Women's studies
Eligibility: *Level:* fresh, sophs, jrs, srs, grads, adults, teachers, professionals, precoll
Credit: *Undergrad:* none *Grad:* none
Instruction: *In:* English, Spanish, host country lang *Format:* study tour *Students:* mainly US
Costs: About $750-$3,500 *incl* housing,

most meals, books/materials, activities, local transport
Housing: *Arr by pgm:* homestay, hotels, guest house
Deadline: Contact sponsor
Other info: *US accredited sponsor:* no *Orient:* abroad (1 day) *Activities:* program travel, cultural events *Misc:* Costs incl guides & translators. May contact former participants. *Financial aid:* scholarships *URL:* http://www.globalexchange.org
Contact: Global Exch, Reality Tours, 2017 Mission, #303, San Francisco CA 94110 *Ph:* 800-497 1994; 415-255 7296 *Fax:* 415-255 7498 *E-mail:* realitytours@globalexchange.org

---

0011
GLOBAL SERVICE CORPS
Service Learning Projects in Environment, Health and Education
Site: Costa Rica, Tanzania, Thailand
Dates: 2 wks or longer, yr-round
Subjects: Agriculture, Alternative medicine, Biodiversity, Civilization/culture, Development studies, East Asian studies, Ecology/environmental studies, Education/teaching, Health sciences, HIV/AIDS education, Internships
Eligibility: *Level:* adults *Requires:* good health, immunizations, travel insurance, applicable lang skills *Age:* min 20, avg 25
Credit: *Undergrad:* avail *Grad:* avail *Doc:* certificate
Instruction: *In:* English, Spanish *Format:* directed field study, independent study, internship, practical training, study tour, volunteer/svc *Students:* US & intl
Costs: $1,795 to $2,000, $595 for each addtl mo *incl* housing, all meals, excursions, local transport
Housing: *Arr by pgm:* residence halls, homestay, hotels
Deadline: 90 days before pgm
Other info: *US accredited sponsor:* no *Began:* 1994 *Orient:* abroad *Activities:* excursions, program travel, cultural events *Misc:* Opportunities for adult participants to volunteer on projects that serve Earth's people & her environment. May contact former participants. *URL:* http://www.globalservicecorps.org
Contact: Rick Lathrop, GSC Exec Dir, 300 Broadway, San Francisco CA 94133-3312 *Ph:* 415-788 3666 ext 128 *Fax:* 415-788 7324 *E-mail:* gsc@earthisland.org

---

0012
GLOBAL VOLUNTEERS
Global Volunteers
Site: Worldwide
Dates: Contact sponsor
Subjects: Community service projects
Eligibility: *Level:* fresh, sophs, jrs, srs, grads, adults, teachers, professionals, precoll *Requires:* good health
Credit: *Undergrad:* avail *Grad:* none *Transfer credit through:* St Thomas Aquinas Coll
Instruction: *In:* English, host country lang *Format:* volunteer/svc *Students:* mainly US
Costs: $450-$2,395 depending on pgm *incl* housing, all meals, fees, books/materials, team leader, ground transport
Housing: *Arr by pgm:* homestay, hotels, comm ctr, guest house
Deadline: Contact sponsor
Other info: *US accredited sponsor:* no

Orient: abroad & pre-trip material *Activities:* excursions, cultural events *Misc:* May contact former participants. *URL:* http://www.globalvolunteers.org
Contact: Volunteer Coords, Global Volunteers, 375 E Little Canada Rd, St Paul MN 55117 *Ph:* 800-487 1074; 651-407 6100 *Fax:* 651-482 0915 *E-mail:* email@globalvolunteers.org

---

0013
HOLBROOK EDUCATIONAL TRAVEL
Holbrook Educational Trips
Site: Latin America and Africa
Dates: Contact sponsor
Subjects: Field study
Eligibility: *Level:* fresh, sophs, jrs, srs, grads, adults, teachers, precoll
Credit: *Undergrad:* avail *Grad:* avail
Instruction: *In:* English *Format:* study tour *Students:* mainly US
Costs: $850-$2,000 *incl* housing, all meals, excursions
Housing: *Arr by pgm:* hotels
Deadline: Contact sponsor
Other info: *US accredited sponsor:* no *Began:* 1974 *Activities:* excursions, field trips, program travel *Misc:* May contact former participants. *URL:* http://www.holbrookeducationtrips.com
Contact: Sandy Doss, Holbrook Educ Travel, 3540 NW 13th St, Gainseville FL 32609 *Ph:* 888-890 0632 *E-mail:* sdoss@swbell.net

---

0014
INDIANA UNIVERSITY
Overseas Practicum for Experienced Teachers
Site: Australia, India, Ireland, Kenya, New Zealand, Taiwan, United Kingdom *Host inst:* natl schs, some private & intl schs
Dates: 3-4 wks, summer
Subjects: Education/teaching, Elementary education, Homestay, Preschool education, Secondary education
Eligibility: *Level:* teachers *Requires:* previous study in field, 1 yr teaching experience
Credit: *Undergrad:* none *Grad:* 3
Instruction: *In:* English *Format:* practical training *Students:* mainly host country
Costs: Contact sponsor
Housing: *Arr by pgm:* homestay
Deadline: May 1
Other info: *US accredited sponsor:* yes *Began:* 1996 *In coop with:* Fdn for Intl Educ *Orient:* in US *Misc:* May contact former participants. *URL:* http://www.education.indiana.edu
Contact: Dr Laura L Stachowski, Dir, Indiana Univ, Educ Bldg 1044, Bloomington IN 47405 *Ph:* 812-856 8507 *Fax:* 812-856 8518 *E-mail:* stachows@indiana.edu

---

0015
INSTITUTE FOR SHIPBOARD EDUCATION
Summer Term-Shipboard Education
Site: Belgium, Egypt, Greece, Italy, Morocco, Norway, Russia, Spain, Turkey
Dates: 8 wks, mid-Jun-mid-Aug
Subjects: Anthropology, Biology, Business administration, Communications, Economics, English, Geography, History, Music, Political science/politics, Religion/theology, Sociology, Theater arts
Eligibility: *Level:* fresh, sophs, jrs, srs *Requires:* 2.75 GPA *Age:* min 18, avg 21
Credit: *Undergrad:* 9 *Grad:* none *Doc:* transcript
Instruction: *In:* English *Format:* directed field study, independent study, lecture *Students:* mainly US
Costs: $11,325 *incl* tuition, housing, all meals, insurance, fees, books/materials *Nonrefundable fee*
Housing: *Arr by pgm:* ship
Deadline: Rolling admissions
Other info: *US accredited sponsor:* yes *Began:* 2000 *In coop with:* Univ of Pittsburgh *Misc:* Pgm focus on Europe and the Mediterranean, and is open to up to 430 undergrads. May contact former participants. *Financial aid:* scholarships, work study *URL:* http://www.semesteratsea.com
Contact: Julian Asenjo, Assoc Dir, 811 William Pitt Union, Univ of Pittsburgh, Pittsburgh PA 15260 *Ph:* 800-854 0195; 412-648 7490 *Fax:* 412-648 2298 *E-mail:* shipboard@sas.ise.pitt.edu

---

0016
INTERNATIONAL LANGUAGE HOMESTAYS
Language Homestay
Site: Argentina, Brazil, France, Germany, Italy, Japan, Mexico, Netherlands, Portugal, Russia, Spain, Sweden
Dates: 1 wk or longer, yr-round
Subjects: Homestay, Languages
Eligibility: *Level:* adults *Requires:* basic knowledge of chosen lang *Age:* avg 30
Credit: *Undergrad:* none *Grad:* none
Instruction: *In:* Dutch, French, German, Italian, Japanese, Portuguese, Russian, Spanish, Swedish, Russian, Swedish *Format:* lang study *Students:* intl
Costs: UK 470 per wk *incl* tuition, housing, all meals, books/materials
Housing: *Arr by pgm:* homestay
Deadline: 4 wks before pgm
Other info: *US accredited sponsor:* no *Began:* 1993 *Activities:* excursions, sports *URL:* http://www.student-reservations.co.uk
Contact: Mr Adam Wilton or Mr Richard Lewis, Intl Lang Homestays, Student Reservations, 38 Hawley Sq, Margate, Kent CT9 1PH, UK

0017
INTERNATIONAL PARTNERSHIP FOR SERVICE-LEARNING
Service-Learning in International/ Intercultural Settings
Site: Ecuador, France, India, Jamaica, Mexico, Philippines, US
Dates: Jan intersession (India only), summer
Subjects: Community service projects, Field study, French language (beg/int/adv), Homestay, Humanities, Independent study, Liberal arts, Social sciences, Spanish language (beg/int/adv), Student teaching
Eligibility: *Level:* fresh, sophs, jrs, srs, grads, adults, precoll *Age:* min 18, avg 21
Credit: *Undergrad:* 9-16 *Grad:* none *Doc:* transcript
Instruction: *In:* English, host country lang *Format:* directed field study, independent study, lang study, lecture, seminar, student teaching, volunteer/svc *Students:* intl
Costs: $3,000-$7,000 for summer *incl* tuition, housing, some meals, fees, excursions, svc placement
Housing: *Arr by pgm:* residence halls, homestay
Deadline: 2 mos before pgm
Other info: *US accredited sponsor:* no *Began:* 1982 *Orient:* abroad (1-3 wks) *Activities:* field trips, cultural events *Misc:* Pgm integrates acad studies with comm svc. Sem & yr pgms also avail. May contact former participants. *Financial aid:* work study *URL:* http://www.ipsc.org
Contact: Intl Partnership for Svc-Learning, 815 2nd Ave, Ste 315, New York NY 10017 *Ph:* 212-986 0989 *Fax:* 212-936 5039 *E-mail:* pslny@aol.com

---

0018
INVOLVEMENT VOLUNTEERS ASSOC INC
Networked International Volunteering
Site: Worldwide
Dates: 2-6 wks or longer, yr-round
Subjects: Agriculture, Community service projects, Conservation, Ecology/environmental studies, Education/teaching, Forestry, History, Horticulture, Medicine, Natural resource management, Social welfare/services, Special education, Veterinary science
Eligibility: *Level:* adults *Requires:* English or Spanish fluency, visa *Age:* min 19, avg 22

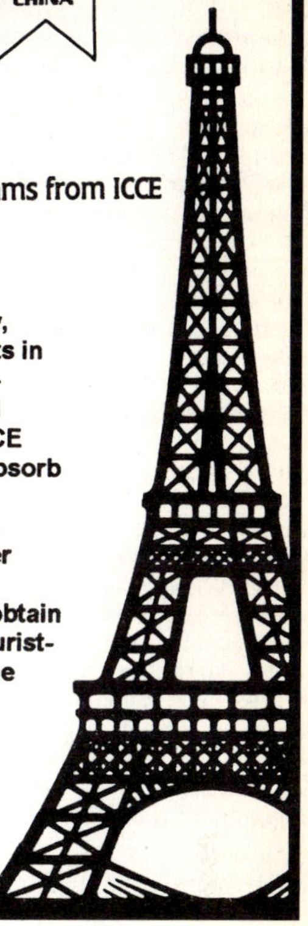

Credit: *Undergrad:* none *Grad:* none
Instruction: *In:* English, host country lang *Format:* volunteer/svc *Students:* intl
Costs: AUS $200 *incl* fees *Nonrefundable fee*
Housing: *Arr by pgm*
Deadline: None
Other info: *US accredited sponsor:* no *URL:* http://www.volunteering.org.au
Contact: Tim B Cox, Involvement Volunteers Assn Inc, PO Box 218, Port Melbourne, Victoria 3207, Australia *E-mail:* ivworldwide@volunteering.org.au

---

0019
MICHIGAN STATE UNIVERSITY
International Business Management
Site: Czech Republic, Germany, Ireland, Netherlands
Dates: 3 wks, May-Jun
Subjects: Business/management, International business
Eligibility: *Level:* jrs, srs, grads *Requires:* 2.75 GPA, good acad standing, resume *Age:* min 18
Credit: *Undergrad:* 6 *Grad:* none *Doc:* transcript
Instruction: *In:* English *Format:* lecture *Students:* mainly US
Costs: About $2,900 *incl* housing, some meals, insurance, excursions *Nonrefundable fee*
Housing: *Arr by pgm:* hotels
Deadline: Mar 2
Other info: *US accredited sponsor:* yes *Began:* 1982 *Orient:* in US & abroad *Misc:* Loans avail. May contact former participants. *Financial aid:* scholarships *URL:* http://studyabroad.msu.edu
Contact: Cheryl Benner, Study Abroad, Michigan State Univ, 109 Intl Ctr, East Lansing MI 48824-1035 *Ph:* 517-353 8920 *Fax:* 517-432 2082 *E-mail:* bennerc@msu.edu ▲

0020
MOBILITY INTERNATIONAL USA (MIUSA)
Mobility International USA (MIUSA)
Site: Worldwide
Dates: 2-4 wks, yr-round
Subjects: Community service projects, Disability studies, Homestay, Human rights, Leadership, Recreation
Eligibility: *Level:* fresh, sophs, jrs, srs, grads, adults, teachers, professionals, precoll *Age:* min 16
Credit: *Undergrad:* none *Grad:* none
Instruction: *In:* English *Format:* practical training, volunteer/svc, workshop *Students:* intl
Costs: Contact sponsor
Housing: *Arr by pgm:* homestay
Deadline: Varies depending on pgm
Other info: *US accredited sponsor:* no *Began:* 1981 *Orient:* in US & abroad *Activities:* excursions, field trips, program travel, cultural events, sports *Misc:* Equal opportunities for persons with disabilities in intl educ exch, leadership development, rights training & comm svc. May contact former participants. *Financial aid:* scholarships *URL:* http://www.miusa.org
Contact: Rhonda Neuhaus, or Melissa Mueller, Mobility Intl USA, PO Box 10767, Eugene OR 97440 *Ph:* 541-343 1284 *Fax:* 541-343 6812 *E-mail:* info@miusa.org

---

0021
NEW YORK UNIVERSITY, TISCH SCHOOL OF THE ARTS
Anthropological Origins of Performing & Visual Arts
Site: varies from year to year
Dates: 6-7 wks, May 17-Jul 1
Subjects: Art, Drama/theater, Interdisciplinary studies, Performing arts
Eligibility: *Level:* fresh, sophs, jrs, srs, grads, adults *Requires:* previous study in field *Age:* min 18
Credit: *Undergrad:* 8 per sem *Grad:* 8 per sem *Doc:* transcript
Instruction: *In:* English *Format:* lecture, music lesson, practical training, seminar, study tour, tutorial *Students:* mainly US
Costs: $8,593 *incl* tuition, housing, some

meals, intl airfare, fees, excursions, student support svcs *Nonrefundable fee*
Housing: *Arr by pgm:* hotels
Deadline: Mar 15 priority deadline; rolling admissions
Other info: *US accredited sponsor:* yes *Began:* 2000 *Orient:* in US (1 day) *Activities:* excursions, field trips, program travel, cultural events *Misc:* May contact former participants. *Financial aid:* scholarships *URL:* http://www.nyu.edu/tisch/international
Contact: Linda Kow, Assoc Dir, Tisch Sch of the Arts, Intl Pgms, 721 Broadway, 12th Fl, New York NY 10003 *Ph:* 212-998 9175 *Fax:* 212-995 4578

0022
NICHOLLS STATE UNIVERSITY
Study Programs Abroad
Site: Austria, Costa Rica, Ecuador, France, Germany, Italy, Mexico, Spain
Dates: Contact sponsor
Subjects: French language (beg/int/adv), German language (beg/int/adv), Homestay, Italian language (beg/int/adv), Spanish language (beg/int/adv)
Eligibility: *Level:* adults
Credit: *Undergrad:* avail *Grad:* avail *Doc:* transcript
Instruction: *In:* French, German, Italian, Spanish *Format:* lang study, lecture, tutorial *Students:* intl
Costs: Contact sponsor
Housing: *Sponsor assists:* residence halls, apartments, homestay, hotels
Deadline: Contact sponsor
Other info: *US accredited sponsor:* yes *Began:* 1975 *Orient:* in US & abroad (intensive lang study) *Activities:* excursions, field trips, cultural events *Misc:* May contact former participants. *URL:* http://www.nich.edu
Contact: Cynthia Webb, Dir, Study Abroad Pgm, Nicholls State Univ, PO Box 2080, Thibodaux LA 70310 *Ph:* 504-448 4400 *Fax:* 504-449 7028 *E-mail:* fl-caw@nich-nsunet.nich.edu

---

0023
NORTH CAROLINA STATE UNIVERSITY
Four Worlds
Site: Guatemala, Nepal, Egypt, Austria
Dates: 3 mos, May-Aug
Subjects: Art, International studies, Philosophy, Political science/politics, Religion/theology
Eligibility: *Level:* fresh, sophs, jrs, srs, grads
Credit: *Undergrad:* 12-15 *Grad:* 12 *Doc:* transcript
Instruction: *In:* English *Format:* directed field study, independent study, lecture, seminar, study tour *Students:* mainly US
Costs: $5,300 *incl* tuition, housing, insurance, fees, excursions *Nonrefundable fee*
Housing: *Arr by pgm:* hostels
Deadline: Feb 21
Other info: *US accredited sponsor:* yes *Began:* 1999 *In coop with:* Society for Intl Development *Orient:* in US *Activities:* excursions, field trips, program travel, cultural events, sports *Misc:* May contact former participants. *URL:* http://www.sid-vienna.org
Contact: David Greene, NC State Univ, MDS, Raleigh NC 27695-7344 *Ph:* 919-513 1903 *Fax:* 919-515 4403 *E-mail:* david-greene@ncsu.edu

Or Contact: Philipp Tavakoli, NC State Univ, Dept of Multidisciplinary Studies, Raleigh NC 27695-7344 *Ph:* 919-513 1903 *Fax:* 919-515 4403 *E-mail:* tavakoli@unity.ncsu.edu

---

0024
OPERATION CROSSROADS AFRICA
Africa Diaspora Program
Site: Brazil, Burkina Faso, Gambia, Ghana, Kenya, Malawi, Mali, Senegal, South Africa, Tanzania, Uganda
Dates: 8 wks, Jun 18-Aug 14
Subjects: Agriculture, Community service projects, Education/teaching, Forestry, Health/health education, Women's studies
Eligibility: *Level:* adults *Requires:* previous lang study for Francophone countries, pre-med or med students for med projects *Age:* min 17
Credit: *Undergrad:* none *Grad:* none *Doc:* certificate
Instruction: *In:* English, French *Format:* volunteer/svc *Students:* intl
Costs: $3,500 *incl* tuition, housing, all meals, intl airfare, insurance *Nonrefundable fee*
Housing: *Arr by pgm:* guest house
Deadline: Feb 1
Other info: *US accredited sponsor:* no *Began:* 1958 *Orient:* avail in New York City (3 days) *Activities:* program travel *Misc:* Live & work in a village for 6 wks, travel for 1 wk as a group in the host country. Educ project pgm avail in Brazil. May contact former participants. *Financial aid:* scholarships, work study *URL:* http://www.igc.org/oca
Contact: Kate Shackford, Dir, Pgm Svcs, Operation Crossroads Africa, 475 Riverside Dr, Ste 1366, New York NY 10115 *Ph:* 212-870 2106 *Fax:* 212-870 2644 *E-mail:* oca@igc.apc.org

---

0025
PEACEWORK DEVELOPMENT FUND, INC
Peacework International Volunteer Programs
Site: Belize, Bolivia, Costa Rica, Cuba, Dominican Republic, El Salvador, Honduras, Mexico, Nicaragua, Russia, Vietnam, others *Host inst:* various relief & development orgs in each country
Dates: 1-4 wks, yr-round
Subjects: Community service projects
Eligibility: *Level:* fresh, sophs, jrs, srs, grads, adults, teachers, professionals, precoll *Requires:* willingness to live & work in challenging conditions *Age:* min 16, avg 25
Credit: *Undergrad:* none *Grad:* none
Instruction: *In:* English *Format:* volunteer/svc *Students:* US & intl
Costs: $800-$2,800 depending on site *incl* housing, all meals, intl airfare, fees, excursions, orient *Nonrefundable fee*
Housing: *Arr by pgm*
Deadline: 2 mos before pgm
Other info: *US accredited sponsor:* no *Began:* 1989 *Orient:* abroad *Activities:* excursions, cultural events *Misc:* Volunteers assist renovations or construction of homes, schs, clinics or comm ctrs. May contact former participants. *URL:* http://www.peacework.org
Contact: Stephen Darr, Exec Dir, Peacework, 305 Washington St SW, Blacksburg VA 24060-4745 *Ph:* 540-953 1376 *Fax:* 540-552 0119 *E-mail:* sdarr@compuserve.com

---

0026
RAMAPO COLLEGE OF NEW JERSEY
Germany/Prague
Site: Germany: Bochum; Czech Republic: Prague
Dates: 3 wks, Jun-Jul
Subjects: Civilization/culture, History, Political science/politics
Eligibility: *Level:* fresh, sophs, jrs, srs, adults, teachers, professionals *Requires:* 2.0 GPA, good physical condition *Age:* min 18, avg 22
Credit: *Undergrad:* 3 *Grad:* none *Doc:* transcript
Instruction: *In:* English *Format:* lecture, study tour *Students:* mainly US
Costs: $2,900 for Ramapo students, $3,100 for others *incl* tuition, housing, most meals, fees, excursions *Nonrefundable fee*
Housing: *Arr by pgm:* residence halls
Deadline: May 1
Other info: *US accredited sponsor:* yes *Orient:* in US (1 day) *Activities:* excursions, field trips, program travel, cultural events *Financial aid:* scholarships, work study
Contact: Ms Robyn Perricelli, Study Abroad, Ramapo Coll of New Jersey, 505 Ramapo Valley Rd, Mahwah NJ 07430 *Ph:* 201-684 7030 *Fax:* 201-684 7561 *E-mail:* rperrice@ramapo.edu

0027
SAINT JOSEPH'S UNIVERSITY (PA)
International Study Tours
Site: Sites vary annually: Asia, Australia, Latin America, Western Europe
Dates: 2-3 wks, Jan or May-Aug
Subjects: Art, History, International business, Marketing, Political science/politics, Sociology
Eligibility: *Level:* jrs, srs, grads
Credit: *Undergrad:* avail *Grad:* avail *Doc:* transcript
Instruction: *In:* English *Format:* study tour *Students:* mainly US
Costs: $1,800-$4,000 *incl* tuition, housing, some meals, intl airfare, fees, excursions, ground transport *Nonrefundable fee*
Housing: *Arr by pgm:* pensions, hotels
Deadline: Dec
Other info: *US accredited sponsor:* yes *Began:* 1987 *Misc:* May contact former participants.
Contact: Ms Karen Lefebvre-Christou, Asst Dir, Ctr for Intl Pgms, St Joseph's Univ, 5600 City Ave, Philadelphia PA 19131 *Ph:* 610-660 1675 *Fax:* 610-660 1697 *E-mail:* klefebvr@sju.edu

0028
SUNY COLLEGE AT NEW PALTZ
Political Science Study Mission
Site: Site varies each yr
Dates: 3 wks, early Jul-mid-Jul
Subjects: Conflict studies, Government, International relations, Peace studies, Political science/politics
Eligibility: *Level:* fresh, sophs, jrs, srs, adults, precoll *Requires:* good acad standing *Age:* min 17
Credit: *Undergrad:* 6 *Grad:* none *Doc:* transcript
Instruction: *In:* English *Format:* directed field study, lecture, seminar *Students:* mainly US
Costs: $2,700 *incl* tuition, housing, some meals, insurance, fees, excursions *Nonrefundable fee*
Housing: *Arr by pgm:* hotels
Deadline: Mar 1
Other info: *US accredited sponsor:* yes *Misc:* Scholarships & loans for own students only. May contact former participants. *URL:* http://www.newpaltz.edu/oie/
Contact: Ctr for Intl Pgms, SUNY at New Paltz, 75 S Manheim Blvd, Ste 9, New Paltz NY 12561 *Ph:* 914-257 3125 *Fax:* 914-257 3129 *E-mail:* international@newpaltz.edu ▲

0029
THUNDERBIRD, THE AMERICAN GRADUATE SCHOOL OF INTERNATIONAL MANAGEMENT
Winterim in Austria: Business in Central and Eastern Europe
Site: Austria: Graz, Vienna; Croatia; Hungary
Dates: 3 wks, Jan 8-26
Subjects: Austrian studies, Civilization/culture, Field study, German language, International business
Eligibility: *Level:* grads *Requires:* 3.0 GPA, faculty permission
Credit: *Undergrad:* none *Grad:* 3
Instruction: *In:* English *Format:* directed field study, lecture, study tour *Students:* intl
Costs: $2,625 *incl* tuition, off-campus pgm fee
Housing: *Arr by pgm:* hotels
Deadline: Dec 1
Other info: *US accredited sponsor:* yes *Activities:* excursions, field trips, program travel *URL:* http://www.t-bird.edu
Contact: James Scott, AVP of Acad Operations, Thunderbird, 15249 N 59th Ave, Glendale AZ 85306 *Ph:* 602-978 7251 *Fax:* 602-547 1356 *E-mail:* scottj@t-bird.edu

---

0030
UNIVERSITY OF CALIFORNIA, EDUCATION ABROAD PROGRAM
Language and Area Studies in Various Countries
Site: Host countries worldwide
Dates: Summer, Fall, Winter, Spring
Subjects: Civilization/culture, Danish language, Danish studies, Field study, Homestay, Italian language, Italian studies, Languages, Mexican studies, Spanish language
Eligibility: Own students only. *Level:* sophs, jrs, srs, grads *Requires:* contact sponsor for previous study requirements
Credit: *Undergrad:* avail *Grad:* avail
Instruction: *In:* Host country lang *Format:* directed field study, lang study, lecture, tutorial *Students:* mainly US
Costs: Contact sponsor
Housing: *Arr by pgm:* residence halls, apartments, homestay
Deadline: 6-10 mos before pgm; contact sponsor
Other info: *US accredited sponsor:* yes *URL:* http://www.uoeap.ucsb.edu
Contact: Randy Arnold, Educ Abroad Pgm, Univ of California, Santa Barbara CA 93106 *Ph:* 805-893 4139

0031
UNIVERSITY OF CALIFORNIA, SANTA BARBARA EXTENSION
Expanding Your Classroom with Travel Study
Site: Any country
Dates: 10 days or longer, yr-round
Subjects: Art, Civilization/culture, Geography, History, Independent study, Languages, Sciences
Eligibility: *Level:* teachers
Credit: *Undergrad:* none *Grad:* avail *Doc:* transcript
Instruction: *In:* English *Format:* independent study *Students:* mainly US
Costs: $225 for 2 qtr units *incl* tuition *Nonrefundable fee*

Housing: *Arr by student*
Deadline: Rolling admissions
Other info: *US accredited sponsor:* yes *Began:* 1977 *Misc:* Independent travel. *URL:* http://www.extension.ucsb.edu
Contact: Lili Byall, Travel Study Coord, Univ of California Extension, Santa Barbara CA 93106-1110 *Ph:* 805-893 4200 *Fax:* 805-893 4943 *E-mail:* drichards@els.ucsb.edu
Or Contact: Steven Tash, Travel Study Instructor, Univ of California Extension, PO Box 16501, Irvine CA 92623-6501 *Ph:* 800-484 1081 ext 7775 *Fax:* 949-552 0740 *E-mail:* travelstudy@yahoo.com

---

0032
UNIVERSITY OF IOWA
International Perspectives in Water Resources Planning
Site: Asia, Europe, Latin America
Dates: 3 wks, Jan or May
Subjects: Water management
Eligibility: *Level:* srs, grads, professionals *Requires:* previous study in field, designed for engineers, planners, environmental, social & political scientists *Age:* avg 26
Credit: *Undergrad:* 3 *Grad:* 3 *Doc:* transcript
Instruction: *In:* English *Format:* seminar, study tour *Students:* mainly US
Costs: $2,800 *incl* tuition, housing, all meals, intl airfare, fees, excursions *Nonrefundable fee*
Housing: *Arr by pgm:* hotels
Deadline: 2 mos before pgm
Other info: *US accredited sponsor:* yes *Began:* 1997 *Orient:* in US (2 days) *Activities:* program travel *Financial aid:* scholarships *URL:* http://www.uiowa.edu/~uiabroad
Contact: Study Abroad, Univ of Iowa, 28 Intl Ctr, Iowa City IA 52245 *Ph:* 319-335 0353 *Fax:* 319-353 2021 *E-mail:* study-abroad@uiowa.edu

---

0033
UNIVERSITY OF MINNESOTA
Global Seminars
Site: 10 sites per yr
Dates: 3 wks, Dec 26-Jan 13 or May 17-Jun 9
Subjects: Full curriculum
Eligibility: Own students preferred. *Level:* fresh, sophs, jrs, srs *Requires:* 2.5 GPA, priority given to U of MN undergrads, others accepted on a space avail basis *Age:* min 18
Credit: *Undergrad:* 3 *Grad:* none
Instruction: *In:* English *Format:* directed field study, lecture, seminar, study tour *Students:* mainly US
Costs: $2,900-$4,000 for U of MN students, $3,150-$4250 others *incl* tuition, housing, some meals, intl airfare, insurance, fees, excursions, local transport *Nonrefundable fee*
Housing: *Arr by pgm:* residence halls with local students, apartments, hotels
Deadline: Oct 1 for winter; Dec 1 for spring
Other info: *US accredited sponsor:* yes *Began:* 1999 *Orient:* in US & abroad (2 days) *Activities:* excursions, field trips, program travel, cultural events *Misc:* May contact former participants. *Financial aid:* scholarships *URL:* http://www.UMabroad.umn.edu
Contact: Global Campus, Study Abroad, Univ of Minnesota, 230 Heller Hall, 271 19th Ave S, Minneapolis MN 55455 *Ph:* 612-626 9000 *Fax:* 612-626 8009 *E-mail:* UMabroad@umn.edu

---

0034
UNIVERSITY OF NEW HAMPSHIRE
Interhostel Learning Vacations
Site: Worldwide
Dates: 1- & 2-wk learning vacations, yr-round
Subjects: Art, Civilization/culture, History, Music
Eligibility: *Level:* adults *Age:* min 50, avg 67
Credit: *Undergrad:* none *Grad:* none
Instruction: *In:* English *Format:* study tour *Students:* mainly US
Costs: $2,000-$3,500 *incl* tuition, housing, all meals, intl airfare, fees, excursions, ground transport, activities
Housing: *Arr by pgm:* hotels, 3- and 4-star accommodations
Deadline: Until pgm filled; apply early
Other info: *US accredited sponsor:* yes *Began:* 1978 *Activities:* excursions, field trips, program travel, cultural events, sports *Misc:* INTERHOSTEL offers unique learning vacations for adults 50 yrs & older in the US, Canada, & abroad. *URL:* http://www.learn.unh.edu/Interhostel
Contact: Carol Bense or Robert McCaffery, Univ of New Hampshire, 6 Garrison Ave, Durham NH 03824-3529 *Ph:* 800-733 9753; 603-862 1147 *Fax:* 603-862 1113 *E-mail:* learn.dce@unh.edu

---

0035
UNIVERSITY OF SAN DIEGO, SCHOOL OF BUSINESS ADMINISTRATION
Graduate Business Study Abroad in Munich and Prague
Site: Germany: Munich; Czech Republic: Prague *Host inst:* FH Munchen; Prague Intl Bus Sch
Dates: Mid-Jul-mid-Aug (3 wks distance learning, 2 wks in Munich & Prague)
Subjects: Business/management, European studies, Finance, Human resources, International business, International marketing, Organizational behavior
Eligibility: *Level:* grads, professionals *Requires:* enrollment in or graduation from grad bus or related grad pgm, good acad standing
Credit: *Undergrad:* none *Grad:* 3 per course *Doc:* transcript
Instruction: *In:* English *Format:* lecture, seminar *Students:* US & intl
Costs: $1,450 for 1 course, $2,400 for 2 courses *incl* tuition *Nonrefundable fee*
Housing: *Sponsor assists:* residence hotel
Deadline: None
Other info: *US accredited sponsor:* yes *Began:* 1998 *Orient:* abroad (1 day) *Activities:* excursions, field trips, program travel, cultural events *Misc:* Company visits. May contact former participants. *URL:* http://business.acusd.edu/ib/germany.html
Contact: Kira Mendez, Coord, or Amanda Ryan, Admin Asst, Ahlers Ctr for Intl Bus, Univ of San Diego Sch of Bus Admin, 5998 Alcala Park, San Diego CA 92110-2492 *Ph:* 800-248 4873; 619-260 4896 *Fax:* 619-260 4891 *E-mail:* ib@acusd.edu

---

0036
VIRGINIA POLYTECHNIC INSTITUTE & STATE UNIVERSITY
Global Workplace
Site: various countries in Eastern and Western Europe
Dates: 1 mo, May 17-Jun 14
Subjects: Field study, Intercultural studies, International business
Eligibility: *Level:* jrs, srs, grads *Requires:* 2.5 GPA, good acad standing
Credit: *Undergrad:* 6 *Grad:* 6
Instruction: *In:* English *Format:* seminar, study tour *Students:* mainly US
Costs: $3,450 *incl* housing, all meals, intl airfare, excursions, books/materials, railpass *Nonrefundable fee*
Housing: *Arr by pgm:* hotels
Deadline: Mar 1
Other info: *US accredited sponsor:* yes *Began:* 1993 *Orient:* in US *Activities:* excursions, field trips, program travel, cultural events *Misc:* Normal group size is 15-20. Scholarships for own students only. May contact former participants. *URL:* http://www.cob.vt.edu/mgmt/robinson/studyabroad
Contact: Prof Jerald Robinson, Pamplin Coll of Bus, Virginia Polytechnic Inst & State Univ, Mail Code 0233-VA Tech, Blacksburg VA 24061 *Ph:* 540-231 9622, 540-231 6585 *Fax:* 540-951 1360 *E-mail:* jfr@vt.edu

---

0037
VOLUNTEERS FOR PEACE
International Workcamps
Site: 70 countries in Asia, Eastern & Western Europe, North & West Africa, the Americas, former Soviet Union
Dates: 2-3 wks, yr round
Subjects: Agriculture, Archaeology, Community service projects, Ecology/environmental studies, Historical preservation/restoration, Homestay, Social work
Eligibility: *Level:* fresh, sophs, jrs, srs, adults, precoll *Age:* min 16, avg 22
Credit: *Undergrad:* none *Grad:* none
Instruction: *In:* English *Format:* volunteer/svc *Students:* US & intl
Costs: $200 per project *incl* housing, all meals, fees
Housing: *Arr by pgm:* residence halls, homestay, hostels, churches, tents
Deadline: none
Other info: *US accredited sponsor:* no *Began:* 1980 *Misc:* Optional travel. Call or write for free newsletter. *URL:* http://www.vfp.org
Contact: Peter Coldwell, Volunteers for Peace, 1034 Tiffany Rd, Belmont VT 05730 *Ph:* 802-259 2759 *Fax:* 802-259 2922 *E-mail:* vfp@vfp.org

Africa, South of the Sahara

More Than One Country

0038
AMERICAN UNIVERSITIES INTERNATIONAL PROGRAM (AUIP) and **UNIVERSITY OF PRETORIA**
Safari Field Study in Southern Africa
Site: Botswana, Mozambique, South Africa, Swaziland, Zimbabwe *Host inst:* Univ of Pretoria
Dates: 4 wks, mid-Jun-mid-Jul
Subjects: African studies, Conservation, Ecology/environmental studies, Field study, Hotel management, Natural resources, Parks management, Recreation, Tourism, Wildlife
Eligibility: *Level:* sophs, jrs, srs, grads, adults, teachers, professionals *Requires:* 2.0 GPA, coll coursework in bio *Age:* min 18
Credit: *Undergrad:* 8 *Grad:* none *Doc:* transcript
Instruction: *In:* English *Format:* directed field study, lecture *Students:* mainly US
Costs: $3,995 *incl* tuition, housing, all meals, fees, books/materials, in-country travel, ISIC *Nonrefundable fee*
Housing: *Arr by pgm:* park housing, lodges, tent camps
Deadline: Apr 1
Other info: *US accredited sponsor:* no *Began:* 1999 *Orient:* in US & abroad *Activities:* field trips, program travel *Misc:* Travel to tribal villages, game parks, rock art sites, Victoria Falls, private protected areas & guest ranches. *URL:* http://www.auip.com
Contact: Linda Tomson or Tim Wakefield, AUIP, PMB 221, 305 W Magnolia St, Ft Collins CO 80521 *Ph:* 970-495 0869 *Fax:* 970-484 6997 *E-mail:* info@auip.com ▲

0039
GEORGIA INSTITUTE OF TECHNOLOGY
Field Work in Animal Behavior
Site: Kenya, South Africa
Dates: Jun 27-Jul 21
Subjects: Animal sciences, Behavioral sciences, Field study, Psychology
Eligibility: *Level:* jrs, srs, adults *Requires:* good acad standing
Credit: *Undergrad:* 6 *Grad:* none *Doc:* transcript
Instruction: *In:* English *Format:* directed field study, lecture *Students:* mainly US
Costs: About $6,800 *incl* tuition, housing, most meals, intl airfare, excursions
Housing: *Arr by pgm*
Deadline: Contact sponsor
Other info: *US accredited sponsor:* yes *Activities:* excursions
Contact: Tara Stoinski, Georgia Inst of Technology, Atlanta GA 30332-0284 *Ph:* 404-624 5826 *E-mail:* stoinskit@mindspring.com
Or Contact: Intl Educ, Georgia Inst of Technology, J S Coon Bldg, Ste 203, Atlanta GA 30332-0284 *Ph:* 404-894 7475 *Fax:* 404-894 9682 *E-mail:* study.abroad@gatech.edu

---

0040
INTERNATIONAL BICYCLE FUND
Eritrea/Ethiopia: Stelae, Style and Seashores
Site: Eritrea, Ethiopia
Dates: 2 wks, Sep-Oct
Subjects: African studies, Agriculture, Civilization/culture, Development studies, Ecology/environmental studies, Economics, Education/teaching, Field study, Geography, Geology, Health care/hospitals, History, Independent study, Political science/politics, Religion/theology
Eligibility: *Level:* adults
Credit: *Undergrad:* none *Grad:* none
Instruction: *In:* English *Format:* directed field study, independent study, seminar, study tour *Students:* mainly US
Costs: $1,090 *incl* tuition, housing, some meals, fees, excursions *Nonrefundable fee*
Housing: *Arr by pgm:* homestay, hotels, hostels
Deadline: Until pgm filled
Other info: *US accredited sponsor:* no *Began:* 1996 *Orient:* avail pre-departure packet *Misc:* May contact former participants. *URL:* http://www.ibike.org/bikeafrica
Contact: David Mozer, Dir, Intl Bicycle Fund, 4887 Columbia Dr S, Seattle WA 98108 *Ph:* 206-767 0848 *Fax:* 206-767 0848 *E-mail:* ibike@ibike.org

---

0041
INTERNATIONAL BICYCLE FUND
West Africa: People-to-People in Benin, Ghana, Togo
Site: Benin, Ghana, Togo
Dates: 2 wks, Nov
Subjects: African studies, Agriculture, Civilization/culture, Development studies, Ecology/environmental studies, Economics, Education/teaching, Field study, Geography, Geology, Health care/hospitals, History, Independent study, Political science/politics, Religion/theology
Eligibility: *Level:* adults
Credit: *Undergrad:* none *Grad:* none
Instruction: *In:* English *Format:* directed field study, independent study, seminar, study tour *Students:* mainly US
Costs: $1,090 *incl* tuition, housing, some meals, fees, excursions *Nonrefundable fee*
Housing: *Arr by pgm:* homestay, hotels, hostels
Deadline: Until pgm filled
Other info: *US accredited sponsor:* no *Began:* 1987 *Orient:* avail pre-departure packet *Misc:* May contact former participants. *URL:* http://www.ibike.org/bikeafrica

Contact: David Mozer, Dir, Intl Bicycle Fund, 4887 Columbia Dr S, Seattle WA 98108 *Ph:* 206-767 0848 *Fax:* 206-767 0848 *E-mail:* ibike@ibike.org

---

0042
INTERNATIONAL BICYCLE FUND
West Africa: People-to-People in Gambia, Guinea, Senegal
Site: Gambia, Guinea, Senegal
Dates: 2 wks, Nov
Subjects: African studies, Agriculture, Civilization/culture, Development studies, Ecology/environmental studies, Economics, Education/teaching, Field study, Geography, Geology, Health care/hospitals, History, Independent study, Political science/politics, Religion/theology
Eligibility: *Level:* adults
Credit: *Undergrad:* none *Grad:* none
Instruction: *In:* English *Format:* directed field study, independent study, seminar, study tour *Students:* mainly US
Costs: $1,090 *incl* tuition, housing, some meals, fees, excursions *Nonrefundable fee*
Housing: *Arr by pgm:* homestay, hotels, hostels
Deadline: Until pgm filled
Other info: *US accredited sponsor:* no *Began:* 1990 *Orient:* avail pre-departure packet *Misc:* May contact former participants. *URL:* http://www.ibike.org/bikeafrica
Contact: David Mozer, Dir, Intl Bicycle Fund, 4887 Columbia Dr S, Seattle WA 98108 *Ph:* 206-767 0848 *Fax:* 206-767 0848 *E-mail:* ibike@ibike.org

---

0043
MICHIGAN STATE UNIVERSITY
Food, Agriculture and Natural Resource Systems
Site: Lesotho, South Africa, Swaziland
Dates: 3 wks, May-Jun
Subjects: Agriculture, Natural resources
Eligibility: *Level:* jrs, srs, grads *Requires:* 2.0 GPA, good acad standing *Age:* min 18
Credit: *Undergrad:* 4-6 *Grad:* 4-6 *Doc:* transcript
Instruction: *In:* English *Format:* lecture, seminar *Students:* mainly US
Costs: About $2,300 *incl* housing, all meals, insurance, excursions, support svcs *Nonrefundable fee*
Housing: *Arr by pgm:* hotels
Deadline: Mar 2
Other info: *US accredited sponsor:* yes *Began:* 1993 *Orient:* in US *Activities:* excursions, field trips *Misc:* Loans avail. *Financial aid:* scholarships *URL:* http://studyabroad.msu.edu
Contact: Cheryl Benner, Study Abroad, Michigan State Univ, 109 Intl Ctr, East Lansing MI 48824 *Ph:* 517-353 8920 *Fax:* 517-432 2082 *E-mail:* bennerc@msu.edu ▲

0044
UNIVERSITY OF SOUTHERN MISSISSIPPI
Service Learning in Africa
Site: Africa: various sites
Dates: May 13-May 30
Subjects: African studies, Community service projects, Field study
Eligibility: *Level:* sophs, jrs, srs, grads *Requires:* 2.0 GPA, good acad standing
Credit: *Undergrad:* 4 *Grad:* none *Doc:* transcript
Instruction: *In:* English *Format:* directed field study, volunteer/svc *Students:* mainly US
Costs: Contact sponsor
Housing: *Arr by pgm*
Deadline: Early Mar
Other info: *US accredited sponsor:* yes *Misc:* May contact former participants. *URL:* http://www.usm.edu
Contact: Dr Tim Hudson, Dean, CICE, or Dir, Univ of Southern Mississippi, Box 10047, Hattiesburg MS 39406-0047 *Ph:* 601-266 4344 *Fax:* 601-266 5699 *E-mail:* melissa.ravencraft@usm.edu

Burkina Faso

OUAGADOUGOU

0045
BOWLING GREEN STATE UNIVERSITY
Summer Program in Burkina Faso, West Africa
Site: Burkina Faso: Ouagadougou
Dates: 3 wks, Jul 2-23
Subjects: Civilization/culture, Film studies, History, Homestay, Media studies, West African studies
Eligibility: *Level:* sophs, jrs, srs, grads *Requires:* 2.75 GPA, previous study in field, 2 yr coll French, 1 sem in French-speaking country, good acad standing
Credit: *Undergrad:* 6 *Grad:* 6-9 *Doc:* transcript
Instruction: *In:* French *Format:* directed field study, lecture, practical training, seminar, study tour *Students:* mainly US
Costs: $1,815 UG,$2,200-$3,000 grad OH residents, $3,400/$5,400 others *incl* tuition, housing, all meals, fees, excursions, books/materials *Nonrefundable fee*
Housing: *Arr by pgm:* homestay
Deadline: Mar 15
Other info: *US accredited sponsor:* yes *Began:* 1998 *Orient:* in US (1 day) *Activities:* excursions, field trips, program travel, cultural events *Misc:* Participants in BGSU MA pgm in French may receive full waiver of tuition, fees, housing, meals, excursions & airfare. May contact former participants. *Financial aid:* scholarships *URL:* http://www.bgsu.edu/departments/roml/homepage.htm
Contact: Dr Opportune Zongo, Romance Langs, Bowling Green State Univ, Bowling Green OH 43403 *Ph:* 419-372 7396 *Fax:* 419-372 7332 *E-mail:* ozongo@bgnet.bgsu.edu

Cameroon

MORE THAN ONE CITY

0046
DICKINSON COLLEGE
Ethnographic Field School
Site: Cameroon: Duala or Limbe
Dates: 6 wks, late May-early Jul
Subjects: Anthropology
Eligibility: *Level:* fresh, sophs, jrs *Requires:* good acad standing, 1 course in anthropology; some French helpful
Credit: *Undergrad:* avail *Grad:* none
Instruction: *In:* English *Format:* directed field study *Students:* mainly US
Costs: About $5,900 *incl* tuition, housing, all meals, intl airfare, excursions
Housing: *Arr by pgm:* homestay
Deadline: Mar 1
Other info: *US accredited sponsor:* yes *Orient:* in US & abroad *Activities:* program travel *URL:* http://www.dickinson.edu/departments/ocs/summer.html
Contact: Global Educ, Dickinson Coll, PO Box 1773, Carlisle PA 17013-2896 *Ph:* 717-245 1341 *Fax:* 717-245 1688 *E-mail:* ocs@dickinson.edu

---

YAOUNDE

0047
DICKINSON COLLEGE
Francophone Africa Summer Institute
Site: Cameroon: Yaounde *Host inst:* Univ of Yaounde I
Dates: 5 wks, late May-early Jul
Subjects: African studies, French language, Literature
Eligibility: *Level:* fresh, sophs, jrs, srs, grads *Requires:* 2.75 GPA, previous study in field, 3 yrs coll French *Age:* min 18, max 25
Credit: *Undergrad:* avail *Grad:* avail
Instruction: *In:* French *Format:* directed field study, lang study, lecture, seminar *Students:* mainly US
Costs: About $5,800 *incl* tuition, housing, all meals, intl airfare, fees, excursions
Housing: *Arr by pgm:* apartments, homestay

Deadline: Mar 1
Other info: *US accredited sponsor:* yes *Began:* 1998 *Orient:* in US & abroad *Activities:* excursions *Misc:* Offered on a 2-yr cycle. *URL:* http://www.dickinson.edu/departments/ocs/summer.html
Contact: Global Educ, Dickinson Coll, PO Box 1773, Carlisle PA 17013-2896 *Ph:* 717-245 1341 *Fax:* 717-245 1688 *E-mail:* ocs@dickinson.edu

Ethiopia

MORE THAN ONE CITY

0048
INTERNATIONAL BICYCLE FUND
Ethiopia: Abyssinian Adventure
Site: Ethiopia: various sites
Dates: 2 wks, Oct
Subjects: African studies, Agriculture, Civilization/culture, Development studies, Ecology/environmental studies, Economics, Education/teaching, Field study, Geography, Geology, Health care/hospitals, History, Independent study, Political science/politics, Religion/theology
Eligibility: *Level:* adults
Credit: *Undergrad:* none *Grad:* none
Instruction: *In:* English *Format:* directed field study, independent study, seminar, study tour *Students:* mainly US
Costs: $1,090 *incl* tuition, housing, some meals, fees, excursions *Nonrefundable fee*
Housing: *Arr by pgm:* homestay, hotels, hostels
Deadline: Until pgm filled
Other info: *US accredited sponsor:* no *Began:* 1996 *Orient:* avail pre-departure packet *Misc:* May contact former participants. *URL:* http://www.ibike.org/bikeafrica
Contact: David Mozer, Dir, Intl Bicycle Fund, 4887 Columbia Dr S, Seattle WA 98108 *Ph:* 206-767 0848 *Fax:* 206-767 0848 *E-mail:* ibike@ibike.org

Ghana

MORE THAN ONE CITY

0049
DEPAUL UNIVERSITY (IL)
Culture, Spirituality and Psychology: Studies in Ghana
Site: Ghana: Accra, Cape Coast, Kumasi
Host inst: Univ of Ghana
Dates: 3 wks, about Nov 30-Dec 20
Subjects: Psychology, Religion/theology
Eligibility: *Level:* sophs, jrs, srs, grads *Requires:* 3.0 GPA
Credit: *Undergrad:* avail *Grad:* avail *Doc:* transcript
Instruction: *In:* English *Format:* directed field study, lecture, volunteer/svc *Students:* mainly US
Costs: $6,200 *incl* tuition, housing, some meals, intl airfare, excursions, books/materials, ground transport *Nonrefundable fee*
Housing: *Arr by pgm:* hotels
Deadline: Apr 1
Other info: *US accredited sponsor:* yes *Began:* 1996 *Orient:* in US *Activities:*

excursions, field trips, program travel, cultural events *Misc:* May contact former participants. *URL:* http://www.depaul.edu/~forstudy
Contact: Christopher Swanson, Asst Dir, DePaul Univ, 2320 N Kenmore, SAC 530, Chicago IL 60614 *Ph:* 800-433 7285; 773-325 7450 *Fax:* 773-325 7452 *E-mail:* cswanson@wppost.depaul.edu

---

0050
LEHIGH UNIVERSITY
Lehigh in Ghana
Site: Ghana: Accra, Kumasi
Dates: Dec 26 - Jan 14
Subjects: African studies, Anthropology, Education/teaching, Social sciences
Eligibility: *Level:* fresh, sophs, jrs, srs, grads *Requires:* 2.0 GPA
Credit: *Undergrad:* 3 *Grad:* none
Instruction: *In:* English *Format:* directed field study, study tour *Students:* mainly US
Costs: $3,400 *incl* tuition, housing, excursions, ISIC *Nonrefundable fee*
Housing: *Arr by pgm:* hotels
Deadline: Sep 15
Other info: *US accredited sponsor:* no *Began:* 1998 *Orient:* in US & abroad *Misc:* May contact former participants. *URL:* http://www.lehigh.edu/~incis
Contact: Dr Sandi Smith, Dir, Study Abroad, Lehigh Univ, 5 E Packer Ave, Bethlehem, 354 Whitaker Lab PA 18015-3198 *Ph:* 610-758 3351 *Fax:* 610-758 5156 *E-mail:* incis@lehigh.edu

---

0051
SUNY COLLEGE AT BROCKPORT
African Studies Winter Intersession Program
Site: Ghana: Accra, Legon *Host inst:* Univ of Ghana, Inst for African Studies
Dates: 3 wks, Dec 27-Jan 19
Subjects: African studies, Civilization/culture
Eligibility: *Level:* jrs, srs *Requires:* 2.5 GPA
Credit: *Undergrad:* 3-6 *Grad:* none *Doc:* transcript
Instruction: *In:* English *Format:* lecture, study tour *Students:* intl
Costs: $3,600 *incl* tuition, housing, all meals, intl airfare, insurance, fees
Housing: *Arr by pgm:* residence halls
Deadline: Sep 15
Other info: *US accredited sponsor:* yes *Began:* 1993 *Orient:* abroad *Activities:* excursions, field trips, cultural events *Misc:* Faculty dir. *URL:* http://www.brockport.edu/study_abroad
Contact: Dr John Perry, Intl Educ, SUNY Brockport, 360 New Campus Dr, Brockport NY 14420 *Ph:* 800-298 7869 *Fax:* 716-637 3218 *E-mail:* overseas@brockport.edu

---

0052
WILLIAM JEWELL COLLEGE
Ghana Summer Study
Site: Ghana: various sites *Host inst:* SYTO: Student & Youth Travel Org
Dates: 5 wks, May 26-Jun 29
Subjects: Civilization/culture, Literature, West African studies
Eligibility: *Level:* fresh, sophs, jrs, srs, adults, teachers, professionals *Age:* min 17
Credit: *Undergrad:* 6 *Grad:* none
Instruction: *In:* English *Format:* study tour *Students:* mainly US
Costs: About $3,200 *incl* tuition, housing, some meals, intl airfare, fees, excursions
Housing: *Arr by pgm:* residence halls
Deadline: Contact sponsor
Other info: *US accredited sponsor:* yes *Orient:* in US & abroad *Activities:* cultural events *URL:* http://www.jewell.edu/academia/continues/Ghana/default.ht
Contact: Ian H. Munro, William Jewell Coll, 500 College Hill, Liberty MO 64068 *Ph:* 816-781 7700 ext 5692 *Fax:* 816-415 5027 *E-mail:* munroi@william.jewell.edu
Or Contact: Tami Jones, Marketing Coord, William Jewell Coll, 500 College Hill, Liberty MO 64068 *Ph:* 816-781 7700 ext 5396 *Fax:* 816-415 5013 *E-mail:* jonest@william.jewell.edu

---

ACCRA

0053
DUKE UNIVERSITY
Duke in Ghana
Site: Ghana: Accra *Host inst:* Univ of Ghana
Dates: Late May-early Jul
Subjects: Anthropology, Arts, Civilization/culture, West African studies
Eligibility: *Level:* fresh, sophs, jrs, srs *Requires:* good acad standing, transcript
Credit: *Undergrad:* 2 credits *Grad:* none *Doc:* transcript
Instruction: *In:* English *Format:* lecture, seminar *Students:* mainly US
Costs: $5,175 *incl* tuition, housing, all meals, fees, excursions
Housing: *Arr by pgm:* hotels
Deadline: Feb 16
Other info: *US accredited sponsor:* yes *Began:* 1999 *Orient:* in US (1 day) *Activities:* excursions, program travel, cultural events *Misc:* May contact former participants. *URL:* http://www.aas.duke.edu/study_abroad/
Contact: Study Abroad, Duke Univ, 121 Allen Bldg, Box 90057, Durham NC 27708-0057 *Ph:* 919-684 2174 *Fax:* 919-684 3083 *E-mail:* abroad@asdean.duke.edu

---

0054
NORTH CAROLINA STATE UNIVERSITY
Ghana Humanities Summer Program
Site: Ghana: Accra *Host inst:* Univ of Ghana
Dates: 6 wks, Jul-Aug
Subjects: African studies, Civilization/culture, Field study, History, Homestay, Political science/politics, Psychology, Social work
Eligibility: *Level:* fresh, sophs, jrs, srs, grads *Age:* min 18, avg 21
Credit: *Undergrad:* 6 *Grad:* 6 *Doc:* transcript
Instruction: *In:* English *Format:* directed field study, lecture *Students:* mainly US
Costs: $3,900 *incl* tuition, housing, some meals, intl airfare, insurance, fees, excursions *Nonrefundable fee*
Housing: *Arr by pgm:* homestay, hotels
Deadline: Feb 15
Other info: *US accredited sponsor:* yes *Began:* 1997 *Orient:* abroad (2 days) *Activities:* excursions, field trips, program travel, cultural events *Misc:* May contact former participants. *URL:* http://www.ncsu.edu/studyabroad
Contact: Anne Haberkern, Study Abroad, North Carolina State Univ, 2118 Pullen Hall, Box 7344, Raleigh NC 27695-7344 *Ph:* 919-515 2087 *Fax:* 919-515 6021 *E-mail:* study_abroad@ncsu.edu

---

0055
TEMPLE UNIVERSITY
Temple in West Africa
Site: Ghana: Accra *Host inst:* Univ of Ghana
Dates: 6 wks, Jul-Aug
Subjects: Aesthetics, Civilization/culture, West African studies
Eligibility: *Level:* jrs, srs, grads, teachers *Requires:* 2.5 GPA
Credit: *Undergrad:* 6 *Grad:* 6 *Doc:* transcript
Instruction: *In:* English *Format:* lecture, seminar *Students:* mainly US
Costs: $2,700-$3,300 for PA residents, $3,500-$4,000 for others *incl* tuition, housing, all meals, fees, excursions
Housing: *Arr by pgm:* residence halls
Deadline: Mar 15
Other info: *US accredited sponsor:* yes *Began:* 1993 *Orient:* in US & abroad *Activities:* field trips, cultural events *Misc:* Scholarships avail for Temple students only *URL:* http://www.temple.edu/intlprog/

Contact: Intl Pgms, Temple Univ, 200 Tuttleman Learning Ctr, 1809 N 13th St, Philadelphia PA 19122 *Ph:* 215-204 0720 *Fax:* 215-204 0729 *E-mail:* intlprog@vm.temple.edu

---

0056
UNIVERSITY OF KANSAS
Journalism in Ghana, West Africa
Site: Ghana: Accra *Host inst:* Univ of Ghana
Dates: 1 mo, Jun 23-Jul 30
Subjects: African studies, Internships, Journalism
Eligibility: *Level:* fresh, sophs, jrs, srs, grads, adults *Requires:* good acad standing *Age:* min 18
Credit: *Undergrad:* 4 *Grad:* none *Doc:* transcript
Instruction: *In:* English *Format:* independent study, internship, lecture *Students:* mainly US
Costs: $2,475 *incl* tuition, housing, some meals, excursions *Nonrefundable fee*
Housing: *Arr by pgm:* residence halls
Deadline: Rolling admissions
Other info: *US accredited sponsor:* yes *Began:* 1999 *Orient:* in US (1 day) *Misc:* May contact former participants. *URL:* http://www.ukans.edu/~osa
Contact: Susan MacNally, Asst Dir, Study Abroad, Univ of Kansas, 108 Lippincott Hall, Lawrence KS 66045 *Ph:* 785-864 3742 *Fax:* 785-864 5040 *E-mail:* osa@ukans.edu ▲

HO

0057
CROSS-CULTURAL SOLUTIONS
Ghana Progam
Site: Ghana: Ho
Dates: 3 wks-1 yr, yr-round
Subjects: Community service projects
Eligibility: *Level:* adults, precoll *Age:* min 18, avg 27
Credit: *Undergrad:* none *Grad:* none *Doc:* certificate
Instruction: *In:* English *Format:* volunteer/svc *Students:* intl
Costs: $1,950 for 3 wks *incl* housing, all meals, excursions *Nonrefundable fee*
Housing: *Arr by pgm*
Deadline: Rolling admissions
Other info: *US accredited sponsor:* no *Began:* 1999 *Orient:* abroad (3 days) *Activities:* excursions *Misc:* May contact former participants. *URL:* http://www.crossculturalsolutions.org
Contact: Volunteer Coord, Cross-Cultural Solutions, 47 Potters Ave, New Rochelle NY 10801 *Ph:* 800-380 4777; 914-632 0022 *Fax:* 914-632 8494

KUMASI

0058
NORTH CAROLINA STATE UNIVERSITY
Ghana Art and Design Summer Program
Site: Ghana: Kumasi *Host inst:* Univ of Sci & Technology, Ghana
Dates: 6 wks, Jul-Aug
Subjects: Art history, Ceramics/pottery, Graphic arts/design, Metalworking, Sculpture, Textiles
Eligibility: *Level:* fresh, sophs, jrs, srs, grads *Age:* min 18, avg 21
Credit: *Undergrad:* 6 *Grad:* 6 *Doc:* transcript
Instruction: *In:* English *Format:* art studio, lecture *Students:* mainly US
Costs: $3,900 *incl* tuition, housing, some meals, intl airfare, insurance, fees, excursions *Nonrefundable fee*
Housing: *Arr by pgm:* hotels
Deadline: Feb
Other info: *US accredited sponsor:* yes *Began:* 1997 *Orient:* in US & abroad (2 days) *Activities:* excursions, field trips, program travel, cultural events *Misc:* May contact former participants. *URL:* http://www.ncsu.edu/studyabroad
Contact: Anne Haberkern, Study Abroad, North Carolina State Univ, 2118 Pullen Hall, Box 7344, Raleigh NC 27695-7344 *Ph:* 919-515 2087 *Fax:* 919-515 6021 *E-mail:* study_abroad@ncsu.edu

---

LEGON

0059
COUNCIL ON INTERNATIONAL EDUCATIONAL EXCHANGE (COUNCIL)
International Faculty Development Seminars-Ghana
Site: Ghana: Legon *Host inst:* Univ of Ghana
Dates: 1 wk, Jul
Subjects: Economics
Eligibility: *Level:* teachers, professionals *Requires:* must be faculty at 2- or 4-yr inst
Credit: *Undergrad:* none *Grad:* none
Instruction: *In:* English *Format:* seminar *Students:* mainly US
Costs: $1,600 *incl* tuition, housing, some meals, excursions, books/materials, receptions *Nonrefundable fee*
Housing: *Arr by pgm:* hotels
Deadline: Mar 15
Other info: *US accredited sponsor:* no *Began:* 1997 *Orient:* abroad *Activities:* excursions, field trips, cultural events *Misc:* Pgm seminar title: Ghana & the Dynamics of Economic Development. *URL:* http://www.ciee.org/ifds
Contact: Jennifer Ley, Dir, Council, 633 3rd Ave, New York NY 10017 *Ph:* 800-407 8839; 212-822 2747 *Fax:* 212-822 2779 *E-mail:* ifds@ciee.org ▲

0060
GEORGE MASON UNIVERSITY
Culture, History and the Leadership Role of Ghanian Women
Site: Ghana: Legon *Host inst:* Univ of the Cape Coast
Dates: 2 wks, Jun 5-20
Subjects: Civilization/culture, Family studies, History, Rural studies, Urban studies, Women's studies
Eligibility: *Level:* fresh, sophs, jrs, srs, grads, adults, teachers, professionals *Requires:* 2.25 GPA *Age:* min 18
Credit: *Undergrad:* 3 *Grad:* 3 *Doc:* transcript
Instruction: *In:* English *Format:* lecture *Students:* mainly US
Costs: About $2,800 for VA residents, $3,300 for others *incl* tuition, housing, some meals, insurance, fees, excursions, ISIC *Nonrefundable fee*
Housing: *Arr by pgm:* hotels
Deadline: Apr 10
Other info: *US accredited sponsor:* yes *Began:* 1996 *Orient:* in US (1 day) *Misc:* May contact former participants. *Financial aid:* scholarships, work study *URL:* http://www.gmu.edu/departments/cge
Contact: Ctr for Global Educ, George Mason Univ, Johnson Ctr, Rm 235, 4400 University Dr, Fairfax VA 22030-4444 *Ph:* 703-993 2154 *Fax:* 703-993 2153 *E-mail:* cge@gmu.edu

---

0061
JAMES MADISON UNIVERSITY
JMU in West Africa: Ghana
Site: Ghana: Legon *Host inst:* Univ of Ghana
Dates: 4 wks, May 30-Jul 1
Subjects: African studies, History
Eligibility: *Level:* fresh, sophs, jrs, srs, grads, adults, teachers, professionals, precoll *Requires:* 2.5 GPA *Age:* min 18
Credit: *Undergrad:* 6 *Grad:* none *Doc:* transcript
Instruction: *In:* English *Format:* lecture, study tour *Students:* mainly US
Costs: $2,500 for VA residents, $3,700 for others *incl* tuition, housing, some meals, excursions *Nonrefundable fee*
Housing: *Arr by pgm:* hotels
Deadline: Feb 1

Other info: *US accredited sponsor:* yes *Began:* 1997 *Orient:* in US & abroad (1 wk) *Activities:* excursions, field trips, program travel, cultural events *Misc:* May contact former participants. *Financial aid:* scholarships *URL:* http://www.jmu.edu/international/
Contact: Dr David Owusu-Ansah, James Madison Univ, Harrisonburg VA 22807 *Ph:* 540-568 6743 *E-mail:* owusuadx@jmu.edu
Or Contact: Intl Pgms, James Madison Univ, Harrisonburg VA 22807 *Ph:* 540-568 6419 *Fax:* 540-568 8080 *E-mail:* international@jmu.edu

Ivory Coast

MORE THAN ONE CITY

0062
DREW UNIVERSITY
Drew in West Africa: Cote d'Ivoire
Site: Ivory Coast: Abidjian, Bouake, Korhogo
Dates: 4 wks, Jul-Aug
Subjects: African studies, Anthropology, Art, Art history
Eligibility: *Level:* fresh, sophs, jrs, srs, grads, teachers, professionals
Credit: *Undergrad:* 8 *Grad:* 6 *Doc:* transcript
Instruction: *In:* English *Format:* directed field study, independent study, lecture, seminar *Students:* mainly US
Costs: $4,250 *incl* tuition, housing, some meals, intl airfare
Housing: *Arr by pgm:* hotels
Deadline: Apr 1
Other info: *US accredited sponsor:* yes *Began:* 1984 *Orient:* abroad *Activities:* excursions, program travel, cultural events *URL:* http://www.drew.edu/cla/depts/offcampus
Contact: Drew in West Africa: Cote d'Ivoire, African-Amer/African Studies Pgm, Drew Univ, 36 Madison Ave, Madison NJ 07940 *Ph:* 973-408 3383 *Fax:* 973-408 3004 *E-mail:* ppeek@drew.edu

Kenya

MORE THAN ONE CITY

0063
GLOBAL SERVICE CORPS
Kenya Rural Self-Help Project
Site: Kenya: various sites *Host inst:* Fdn Agency for Rural Development (FARD)
Dates: 1 mo or longer, yr-round
Subjects: Agriculture, Agronomy, Civilization/culture, Health/health education
Eligibility: *Level:* fresh, sophs, jrs, srs, grads, adults, teachers, professionals *Requires:* good health, proper immunizations, travel insurance, svc/learning orient *Age:* min 20, avg 25
Credit: *Undergrad:* avail *Grad:* avail
Instruction: *In:* English *Format:* directed field study, independent study, internship, practical training, student teaching, study tour, volunteer/svc *Students:* intl
Costs: $1,795 for 27 days, $495 for each addtl mo *incl* housing, all meals, excursions, local transport
Housing: *Arr by pgm:* homestay
Deadline: 90 days before pgm
Other info: *US accredited sponsor:* no *Began:* 1994 *In coop with:* Earth Island Inst *Orient:* abroad & pre-trip material *Activities:* excursions, field trips, cultural events *Misc:* All trip costs, incl airfare, are normally tax-deductible. May contact former participants. *URL:* http://www.globalservicecorps.org
Contact: Rick Lathrop, Exec Dir, or Jamie Kemsey, Pgm Coord, Global Svc Corps, 300 Broadway, Ste 28, San Francisco CA 94133 *Ph:* 415-788 3666 ext 128 *Fax:* 415-788 7324 *E-mail:* gsc@igc.apc.org

---

0064
GLOBAL SERVICE CORPS
Sustainable Agriculture Project
Site: Kenya: Machakos, various sites
Dates: 1 mo or longer, yr-round
Subjects: Agriculture, Agronomy, Civilization/culture, Development studies, Ecology/environmental studies, Sustainable development
Eligibility: *Level:* fresh, sophs, jrs, srs, grads, adults, teachers, professionals *Requires:* Good health,proper immunizations,travel insurance *Age:* min 20, avg 25
Credit: *Undergrad:* avail *Grad:* avail *Doc:* certificate *Transfer credit through:* San Francisco State Univ
Instruction: *In:* English *Format:* directed field study, independent study, internship, practical training, student teaching, study tour, volunteer/svc *Students:* US & intl
Costs: $1,995 for 1 mo, $595 for each addtl mo *incl* housing, all meals, excursions, local transport
Housing: *Arr by pgm:* homestay
Deadline: 90 days before pgm
Other info: *US accredited sponsor:* no *Began:* 1994 *Orient:* abroad *Activities:* excursions, field trips, cultural events *Misc:* May contact former participants. *URL:* http://www.globalservicecorps.org
Contact: Rick Lathrop or Petula Dias, Global Svc Corps, 300 Broadway, Ste 28, San Francisco CA 94133 *Ph:* 415-788 3666 ext 128 *Fax:* 415-788 7324 *E-mail:* gsc@earthisland.org

---

0065
MICHIGAN STATE UNIVERSITY
Behavioral Ecology of African Mammals
Site: Kenya: Masai Mara Natl Reserve
Dates: 3 wks, May-Jun
Subjects: Field study, Zoology
Eligibility: *Level:* fresh, sophs, jrs, srs, grads *Requires:* 2.5 GPA, previous study in field, essay *Age:* min 18
Credit: *Undergrad:* avail *Grad:* avail *Doc:* transcript
Instruction: *In:* English *Format:* directed field study *Students:* mainly US
Costs: About $2,600 *incl* housing, all meals, insurance, fees, excursions *Nonrefundable fee*
Housing: *Arr by pgm:* tents
Deadline: Mar 2
Other info: *US accredited sponsor:* yes *Began:* 1999 *Orient:* in US (1 day) *Activities:* excursions, field trips *Misc:* Not handicapped accessible. *URL:* http://studyabroad.msu.edu
Contact: Cheryl Benner, Study Abroad, Michigan State Univ, 109 Intl Ctr, East Lansing MI 48824-1035 *Ph:* 517-353 8920 *Fax:* 517-432 2082 *E-mail:* bennerc@msu.edu ▲

0066
MICHIGAN STATE UNIVERSITY
Wildlife Ecology and Management
Site: Kenya: various sites
Dates: 3 wks, May-Jun
Subjects: Fishing/fisheries, Natural resources, Wildlife
Eligibility: *Level:* sophs, jrs, srs, grads *Requires:* 2.0 GPA, good acad standing, completion of zoology 355, letter of interest *Age:* min 18
Credit: *Undergrad:* 6 *Grad:* 6 *Doc:* transcript
Instruction: *In:* English *Format:* lecture, seminar, study tour *Students:* mainly US
Costs: About $2,600 *incl* housing, all meals, insurance, excursions, support svcs *Nonrefundable fee*
Housing: *Arr by pgm:* lodges in natl parks
Deadline: Mar 2
Other info: *US accredited sponsor:* yes *Began:* 1995 *Orient:* in US & abroad *Activities:* excursions, field trips, program travel *Misc:* Loans avail. *Financial aid:* scholarships *URL:* http://studyabroad.msu.edu
Contact: Cheryl Benner, Study Abroad, Michigan State Univ, 109 Intl Ctr, East Lansing MI 48824 *Ph:* 517-353 8920 *Fax:* 517-432 2082 *E-mail:* bennerc@msu.edu ▲

0067
NORTHERN ILLINOIS UNIVERSITY
Public Health and African Cultural Studies in Kenya
Site: Kenya: various sites
Dates: May 28-Jun 11
Subjects: African studies, Public health
Eligibility: *Level:* sophs, jrs, srs, grads, professionals *Requires:* 2.5 GPA *Age:* min 18, avg 22
Credit: *Undergrad:* avail *Grad:* 3 *Doc:* transcript
Instruction: *In:* English *Format:* directed field study, lecture *Students:* mainly US
Costs: $1,890 *incl* tuition, housing, some meals, insurance, excursions
Housing: *Arr by pgm:* hotels, camps
Deadline: Apr 1 or until pgm filled
Other info: *US accredited sponsor:* yes *Orient:* in US *Misc:* Pgm is in response to the growing importance of intl health to our public health curriculum. May contact former participants. *URL:* http://www.niu.edu/niuabroad/
Contact: Anne Seitzinger, Pgm Coord, Study Abroad, Williston 417, Northern Illinois Univ, DeKalb IL 60115 *Ph:* 815-753 0700 *Fax:* 815-753 0825 *E-mail:* niuabroad@niu.edu
Or Contact: Professor Gina Piane, Public & Comm Health Pgm, Northern Illinois Univ, DeKalb IL 60115 *Ph:* 815-753 6324 *E-mail:* gpiane@niu.edu
Or Contact: Prof LaVerne Gyant, Ctr for Black Studies, Northern Illinois Univ, DeKalb IL 60115 *Ph:* 815-753 1423 *E-mail:* lgyant@niu.edu

---

0068
PENNSYLVANIA STATE UNIVERSITY
Kenya Language and Cultural Studies
Site: Kenya: Lamu, Malindi, Mombasa
Dates: 6 wks, May-Jun
Subjects: African studies, Field study, Homestay, Languages
Eligibility: CIC students only *Level:* fresh, sophs, jrs, srs *Requires:* 2.5 GPA
Credit: *Undergrad:* avail *Grad:* none
Instruction: *In:* English, Kiswahili *Format:* directed field study, lang study, lecture, study tour *Students:* mainly US
Costs: Contact sponsor
Housing: *Arr by pgm:* homestay
Deadline: Rolling admissions
Other info: *US accredited sponsor:* yes *Began:* 2000 *Orient:* in US & abroad *Activities:* excursions, field trips *Misc:* May contact former participants. *Financial aid:* scholarships
Contact: Summer Abroad, Pennsylvania State Univ, 225 Penn State Conference Ctr, University Park PA 16802 *Ph:* 814-863 5170
Or Contact: Intl Pgm Adviser, Pennsylvania State Univ, 222 Boucke Bldg, University Park PA 16802 *Ph:* 814-865 7681 *Fax:* 814-865 3336

0069
UNIVERSITY OF SOUTHERN MISSISSIPPI
African Studies Program
Site: Kenya: various sites
Dates: 4 wks, Jun 8-Jul 4
Subjects: Anthropology, Geography, Sociology
Eligibility: *Level:* sophs, jrs, srs, grads, adults *Requires:* 2.0 GPA *Age:* min 18, max 40, avg 25
Credit: *Undergrad:* 4 *Grad:* 4 *Doc:* transcript
Instruction: *In:* English *Format:* seminar *Students:* mainly US
Costs: $4,899 for undergrads, $5,199 for grads *incl* tuition, housing, intl airfare, fees, excursions *Nonrefundable fee*
Housing: *Arr by pgm:* hostels
Deadline: Apr 24
Other info: *US accredited sponsor:* yes *Began:* 1997 *Orient:* avail avail *Misc:* May contact former participants. *Financial aid:* scholarships *URL:* http://www.usm.edu
Contact: Dr Tim W Hudson, Dean, or Dir, African Studies Pgm, Univ of Southern Mississippi, Box 10047, Hattiesburg MS 39406 *Ph:* 601-266 4344 *Fax:* 601-266 5699 *E-mail:* melissa.ravencraft@usm.edu

---

MACHAKOS

0070
GLOBAL SERVICE CORPS
HIV/AIDS Education Project
Site: Kenya: Machakos
Dates: 1 mo or longer, yr-round
Subjects: Civilization/culture, Health care/hospitals, Health sciences, HIV/AIDS education
Eligibility: Good health, proper immunizations, travel insurance *Level:* fresh, sophs, jrs, srs, grads, adults, teachers, professionals *Age:* min 20, avg 25
Credit: *Undergrad:* avail *Grad:* avail *Doc:* certificate *Transfer credit through:* San Francisco State Univ
Instruction: *In:* English *Format:* student teaching, study tour, volunteer/svc *Students:* US & intl
Costs: $1,995 for 1 mo, $595 for each addtl mo *incl* housing, all meals, excursions, local transport
Housing: *Arr by pgm:* homestay
Deadline: 90 days before pgm
Other info: *US accredited sponsor:* no *Began:* 1994 *In coop with:* Earth Island Institute *Orient:* abroad *Activities:* excursions, field trips, cultural events *Misc:* May contact former participants. *URL:* http://www.globalservicecorps.org
Contact: Rick Lathrop or Petula Dias, Global Svc Corps, 300 Broadway, Ste 28, San Francisco CA 94133 *Ph:* 415-788 3666 ext 128 *Fax:* 415-788 7324 *E-mail:* gsc@earthisland.org

---

NAIROBI

0071
INTERNATIONAL CAMPUS CONSORTIUM and **THUNDERBIRD, THE AMERICAN GRADUATE SCHOOL OF INTERNATIONAL MANAGEMENT**
Winterim in Kenya
Site: Kenya: Nairobi
Dates: 3 wks, Jan 3-21
Subjects: Business/management, Ecology/environmental studies, Environmental law, Environmental system analysis, International studies, Public policy
Eligibility: *Level:* grads *Requires:* 3.0 GPA
Credit: *Undergrad:* none *Grad:* 3 *Doc:* transcript
Instruction: *In:* English *Format:* lecture *Students:* intl
Costs: $2,555 *incl* tuition, insurance, fees
Housing: *Sponsor assists:* hotels
Deadline: Contact sponsor
Other info: *US accredited sponsor:* yes *Orient:* abroad *Activities:* field trips *Misc:* Study at headquarters of United Nations Environmental Pgm. Camp study at Maasai Mara game reserve. *Financial aid:* scholarships *URL:* http://www.t-bird.edu
Contact: *See Index II for Members* Dr Earl Gibbons, Assoc VP, Overseas Pgms, Thunderbird, 15249 N 59th Ave, Glendale AZ 85306 *Ph:* 602-978 7252 *Fax:* 602-978 7419 *E-mail:* gibbonse@t-bird.edu
Or Contact: Diane Hayton, Coord, Overseas Pgms, Thunderbird, 15249 N 59th Ave, Glendale AZ 85306 *Ph:* 602-978 7252 *Fax:* 602-978 7419 *E-mail:* haytond@t-bird.edu

---

0072
RUTGERS UNIVERSITY
Rutgers Summer Study in Kenya
Site: Kenya: Nairobi *Host inst:* Natl Museums of Kenya
Dates: 6 wks, mid-Jun-late Jul
Subjects: Anthropology, Archaeology, Ecology/environmental studies, Field study, Geology, Paleontology, Taphonomy
Eligibility: *Level:* jrs, srs, grads *Requires:* 2.5 GPA, recommendation letter
Credit: *Undergrad:* 8 *Grad:* none *Doc:* transcript
Instruction: *In:* English *Format:* directed field study *Students:* mainly US
Costs: $3,875 for NJ residents, $4,625 for

others *incl* tuition, housing, all meals, insurance *Nonrefundable fee*
Housing: *Arr by pgm:* hotels, campsite
Deadline: Apr 15
Other info: *US accredited sponsor:* yes *Began:* 1997 *Activities:* field trips *Misc:* Loans avail. *Financial aid:* scholarships *URL:* http://studyabroad.rutgers.edu
Contact: Dir, Study Abroad, Rutgers Univ, 102 College Ave, New Brunswick NJ 08901 *Ph:* 732-932 7787 *Fax:* 732-932 8659 *E-mail:* ru_abroad@email.rutgers.edu
Or Contact: Jack Harris or Michael Rogers, Anthropology, Rutgers Univ, Ruth Adams Bldg, Douglass Campus, New Brunswick NJ 08903 *Ph:* 732-932 9886 *Fax:* 732-932 1564 *E-mail:* jwharris@rci.rutgers.edu

---

0073
SCHOOL FOR FIELD STUDIES
SFS Kenya: Community Wildlife Management
Site: Kenya: Athi River & Kuku Maasai Group Ranch (near Nairobi)
Dates: 1 mo, mid-Jun-mid-Jul or mid-Jul-mid-Aug
Subjects: African studies, Anthropology, Biology, Conservation, Development studies, Ecology/environmental studies, Field study, Natural resources, Wildlife, Zoology
Eligibility: *Level:* fresh, sophs, jrs, srs, precoll *Age:* min 16, avg 20
Credit: *Undergrad:* avail *Grad:* none *Doc:* transcript *Transfer credit through:* Boston Univ
Instruction: *In:* English *Format:* directed field study *Students:* mainly US
Costs: $3,795 *incl* tuition, housing, all meals, excursions *Nonrefundable fee*
Housing: *Arr by pgm:* campsites, rustic cabins
Deadline: Rolling admissions
Other info: *US accredited sponsor:* no *Began:* 1980 *Orient:* abroad *Activities:* excursions, field trips, program travel, cultural events, sports *Misc:* Loans avail. May contact former participants. *Financial aid:* scholarships *URL:* http://www.fieldstudies.org
Contact: Admissions Off, Sch for Field Studies, 16 Broadway, Beverly MA 01915-4499 *Ph:* 800-989 4435; 978-927 7777 *Fax:* 978-927 5127 *E-mail:* admissions@fieldstudies.org

Mali

MORE THAN ONE CITY

0074
INTERNATIONAL BICYCLE FUND
Mali: Sahel Journey
Site: Mali: various sites
Dates: 2 wks, Oct-Nov
Subjects: African studies, Agriculture, Civilization/culture, Development studies, Ecology/environmental studies, Economics, Education/teaching, Field study, Geography, Geology, Health care/hospitals, History, Independent study, Political science/politics, Religion/theology
Eligibility: *Level:* adults
Credit: *Undergrad:* none *Grad:* none
Instruction: *In:* English *Format:* directed field study, independent study, seminar, study tour *Students:* mainly US
Costs: $1,290 *incl* tuition, housing, some meals, fees, excursions *Nonrefundable fee*
Housing: *Arr by pgm:* homestay, hotels, hostels
Deadline: Until pgm filled
Other info: *US accredited sponsor:* no *Began:* 1990 *Orient:* avail pre-departure packet *Misc:* May contact former participants. *URL:* http://www.ibike.org/bikeafrica
Contact: David Mozer, Dir, Intl Bicycle Fund, 4887 Columbia Dr S, Seattle WA 98108 *Ph:* 206-767 0848 *Fax:* 206-767 0848 *E-mail:* ibike@ibike.org

Senegal

MORE THAN ONE CITY

0075
INTERCULTURAL DIMENSIONS, INC
Crossing Cultures: Travel and Study to West Africa
Site: Senegal: various sites
Dates: 3 wks, Jun 26-Jul 17; extended stays avail
Subjects: Art, Civilization/culture, Community service projects, Dance, Education/teaching, Family services, Journalism, Languages, Law, Public health, Religion/theology, Theater arts, Traditional medicine, West African studies
Eligibility: *Level:* fresh, sophs, jrs, srs, grads, adults, teachers, professionals, precoll *Requires:* French recommended *Age:* min 17, avg 30
Credit: *Undergrad:* 3 *Grad:* none *Doc:* transcript *Transfer credit through:* North Shore CC
Instruction: *In:* French, others *Format:* independent study, lang study, practical training, seminar, study tour, volunteer/svc *Students:* mainly host country
Costs: $3,306 *incl* tuition, housing, all meals, intl airfare, excursions, railpass
Housing: *Arr by pgm:* homestay, hotels, hostels
Deadline: 45 days before pgm
Other info: *US accredited sponsor:* no *Began:* 1993 *Orient:* in US & abroad (intensive lang study) *Activities:* field trips, program travel, cultural events *Misc:* Custom-tailored to individual's interests. May contact former participants. *URL:* http://www.geocities.com/thetropics/coast/2323/idhome.html
Contact: Janet L Ghattas, Intercultural Dimensions Inc, PO Box 391437, Cambridge MA 02139 *Ph:* 617-864 8442 *Fax:* 617-868 1273 *E-mail:* janetid@aol.com

---

DAKAR

0076
NEW YORK UNIVERSITY, SCHOOL OF EDUCATION
Applied Psychology and Education
Site: Senegal: Dakar
Dates: Jul 2-20
Subjects: Child development, Family studies, Intercultural studies, International education, International studies, Psychology of education
Eligibility: *Level:* grads *Requires:* 3.0 GPA
Credit: *Undergrad:* none *Grad:* avail
Instruction: *In:* English *Format:* lecture, seminar *Students:* mainly US
Costs: $6,500 *incl* tuition, housing, some meals, books/materials
Housing: *Arr by pgm:* residence halls
Deadline: Contact sponsor
Other info: *US accredited sponsor:* yes *Orient:* abroad *Activities:* field trips *Misc:* Intl studies in child & adolescent development for psychologists & teachers. *URL:* http://www.nyu.edu/summer
Contact: Prof Suzanne Carothers, Teaching & Learning, Sch of Educ, NYU, 239 Greene St, 2nd Fl, New York NY 10003 *Ph:* 212-998 5717 *E-mail:* suzanne.carothers@nyu.edu
Or Contact: Helen J Kelly, Dir, Special Pgms, NYU, 82 Washington Sq E, Rm 62, New York NY 10003 *Ph:* 212-998 5090 *Fax:* 212-995 4923 ▲

South Africa

MORE THAN ONE CITY

0077
CONSULTANTS FOR GLOBAL PROGRAMS
Winter School: University of Natal
Site: South Africa: Durban, Pietermaritzburg *Host inst:* Univ of Natal, Intl Winter Sch
Dates: Jun 18-Aug 4
Subjects: Architecture, Art, Field study, Film studies, History, Languages, Literature, Music, Political science/politics, South African studies, Zulu language
Eligibility: *Level:* fresh, sophs, jrs, srs, grads *Requires:* 2.5 GPA
Credit: *Undergrad:* 4-8 *Grad:* avail *Doc:* certificate
Instruction: *In:* English *Format:* art studio, directed field study, lab, lang study,

lecture, music lesson, practical training, study tour, volunteer/svc, workshop *Students:* intl
Costs: $2,500 for 1 course, $3,000 for full pgm *incl* tuition, housing, all meals, insurance, fees, excursions, books/ materials *Nonrefundable fee*
Housing: *Arr by pgm:* residence halls
Deadline: Apr 2
Other info: *US accredited sponsor:* no *Orient:* abroad (2 days) *Activities:* excursions, field trips, cultural events, sports *URL:* http://www.globalprograms.com
Contact: Larry Kavich, Pres, Consultants for Global Pgms, 2019 Central Ave, McKinleyville CA 95519 *Ph:* 800-270 6870; 707-839 0478 *Fax:* 707-839 2991 *E-mail:* cgpusa@aol.com

---

0078
COUNCIL ON INTERNATIONAL EDUCATIONAL EXCHANGE (COUNCIL)
International Faculty Development Seminars-South Africa
Site: South Africa: Cape Town, Pretoria *Host inst:* Univ of Pretoria, Univ of the Western Cape
Dates: 11 days, Jun
Subjects: Contemporary issues, South African studies
Eligibility: *Level:* teachers, professionals *Requires:* must be full-time faculty at 2-yr or 4-yr inst
Credit: *Undergrad:* none *Grad:* none
Instruction: *In:* English *Format:* lecture, seminar *Students:* mainly US
Costs: $1,995 *incl* tuition, housing, most meals, fees, excursions, ITIC
Housing: *Arr by pgm:* hotels
Deadline: Mar 15
Other info: *US accredited sponsor:* no *Began:* 1995 *Orient:* abroad *Activities:* excursions, field trips, cultural events *Misc:* Seminar title: Nation Building in South Africa. May contact former participants. *URL:* http://www.ciee.org/ifds
Contact: Jennifer Ley, Council, 633 3rd Ave, New York NY 10017 *Ph:* 212-822 2747 *Fax:* 212-822 2779 *E-mail:* ifds@ciee.org ▲

0079
EASTERN MICHIGAN UNIVERSITY
African-American Studies in Transkei
Site: South Africa: Cape Town, Johannesburg, Umtata *Host inst:* Univ of Cape Town, Univ of Transkei
Dates: 4 wks, Jul 1-Aug 3
Subjects: African studies, African-American studies, Contemporary issues
Eligibility: *Level:* fresh, sophs, jrs, srs, grads *Requires:* 2.0 GPA *Age:* min 18
Credit: *Undergrad:* 6 *Grad:* none *Doc:* transcript
Instruction: *In:* English *Format:* directed field study, independent study, lecture, seminar *Students:* mainly US
Costs: $4,000 *incl* tuition, housing, some meals, intl airfare, insurance, fees, excursions
Housing: *Arr by pgm:* residence halls with local students
Deadline: Mar 1
Other info: *US accredited sponsor:* yes *Began:* 1997 *In coop with:* Univ of Transkei *Orient:* in US & abroad *Activities:* excursions, field trips, program travel, cultural events *Misc:* May contact former participants. *URL:* http://www.emich.edu/abroad
Contact: Acad Pgms Abroad, Eastern Michigan Univ, 212 Bus & Finance, Ypsilanti MI 48197 *Ph:* 800-777 3541; 734-487 2424 *Fax:* 734-487 4377 *E-mail:* programs.abroad@emich.edu

---

0080
RAMAPO COLLEGE OF NEW JERSEY
The New South Africa
Site: Africa: Alice, Capetown
Dates: 3 wks, Jun-Jul
Subjects: Field study, South African studies
Eligibility: *Level:* fresh, sophs, jrs, srs, adults, teachers, professionals *Requires:* 2.0 GPA, good physical condition *Age:* min 18, avg 22
Credit: *Undergrad:* 3 *Grad:* none *Doc:* transcript
Instruction: *In:* English *Format:* directed field study, lecture, study tour *Students:* mainly US
Costs: $3,700 for Ramapo students, $3,900 for others *incl* tuition, housing, most meals, fees, excursions *Nonrefundable fee*
Housing: *Arr by pgm:* residence halls
Deadline: May 1
Other info: *US accredited sponsor:* yes *Began:* 2000 *Orient:* in US *Activities:* excursions, field trips, program travel, cultural events *Financial aid:* scholarships, work study
Contact: Ms Robyn Perricelli, Study Abroad, Ramapo Coll of New Jersey, 505 Ramapo Valley Rd, Mahwah NJ 07430 *Ph:* 201-684 7030 *Fax:* 201-684 7561 *E-mail:* rperrice@ramapo.edu

---

0081
SCHOOL OF THE MUSEUM OF FINE ARTS, BOSTON
South Africa: Journeys in Art Making
Site: South Africa: Cape Town, Johannesburg *Host inst:* Johannesburg Art Fdn
Dates: Jun 24-Jul 14
Subjects: Studio arts (beg/int/adv)
Eligibility: *Level:* fresh, sophs, jrs, srs, grads, adults, teachers, professionals *Age:* min 18
Credit: *Undergrad:* avail *Grad:* none *Doc:* transcript
Instruction: *In:* English *Format:* art studio *Students:* mainly US
Costs: $2,760 *incl* tuition, housing, some meals, excursions, host facilities, studio space *Nonrefundable fee*
Housing: *Arr by pgm:* pensions, hotels
Deadline: Mar 23 or until pgm filled
Other info: *US accredited sponsor:* yes *Began:* 2001 *Activities:* excursions, program travel *Misc:* One hr info session at the Sch of the Museum of Fine Arts on Mar 5. *URL:* http://www.smfa.edu
Contact: Nathaniel Bradley, SMFA Continuing Educ, 230 The Fenway, Boston MA 02115 *Ph:* 617-267 1219 *Fax:* 617-369 3679 *E-mail:* coned@smfa.edu

---

0082
SUNY UNIVERSITY AT ALBANY
Language and Cultural Studies at the University of Natal
Site: South Africa: Durban, Pietermaritzburg *Host inst:* Univ of Natal
Dates: 6 wks, Jun 26-Aug 4
Subjects: African studies, Art, Community service projects, History, Political science/politics, South African studies, Zulu language
Eligibility: *Level:* jrs, srs, grads *Requires:* 3.0 GPA
Credit: *Undergrad:* 8 *Grad:* avail *Doc:* transcript
Instruction: *In:* English *Format:* lecture, seminar, volunteer/svc *Students:* intl
Costs: $3,278 for NY residents *incl* tuition, housing, all meals, insurance, fees, excursions, student support svcs *Nonrefundable fee*
Housing: *Arr by pgm:* residence halls
Deadline: Apr 1
Other info: *US accredited sponsor:* yes *Began:* 1999 *Orient:* in US & abroad (1 day) *Activities:* excursions, field trips *Misc:* May contact former participants. *URL:* http://www.albany.edu/intled
Contact: Joan N Savitt, Assoc Dir, SUNY Univ at Albany, LI 66, Albany NY 12222 *Ph:* 518-442 3525 *Fax:* 518-442 3338 *E-mail:* oipua@csc.albany.edu

---

0083
THUNDERBIRD, THE AMERICAN GRADUATE SCHOOL OF INTERNATIONAL MANAGEMENT
Winterim in the Republic of South Africa
Site: South Africa: Cape Town, Johannesburg, Pretoria
Dates: 3 wks, Jan 8-26
Subjects: Business/management,

Contemporary issues, South African studies
Eligibility: *Level:* grads *Requires:* 3.0 GPA, Faculty permission
Credit: *Undergrad:* none *Grad:* 3
Instruction: *In:* English *Format:* lecture *Students:* intl
Costs: $2,250, $375 off-campus fee *incl* tuition
Housing: *Sponsor assists:* hotels
Deadline: Contact sponsor
Other info: *US accredited sponsor:* yes *Orient:* abroad *Activities:* field trips *Misc:* Interact with bus comm & public officials. *URL:* http://www.t-bird.edu
Contact: James Scott, Overseas Pgms, Thunderbird, 15249 N 59th Ave, Glendale AZ 85306 *Ph:* 602-978 7251 *Fax:* 602-547 1356 *E-mail:* scottj@t-bird.edu

---

0084
UNIVERSITY OF DELAWARE
Winter Session in South Africa
Site: South Africa: Cape Town, Johannesburg, Pretoria
Dates: 5 wks, beg Jan
Subjects: Education/teaching, History, Women's studies
Eligibility: *Level:* fresh, sophs, jrs, srs *Requires:* 2.0 GPA
Credit: *Undergrad:* 6 *Grad:* none *Doc:* transcript
Instruction: *In:* English *Format:* lecture *Students:* mainly US
Costs: Contact sponsor
Housing: *Arr by pgm:* hotels
Deadline: Early Oct
Other info: *US accredited sponsor:* yes *Orient:* avail yes *Activities:* excursions, field trips, program travel, cultural events *Misc:* Contact sponsor to arrange honors credit. *Financial aid:* scholarships *URL:* http://www.udel.edu/studyabroad/
Contact: Intl Pgms & Special Sessions, Univ of Delaware, 4 Kent Way, Newark DE 19716-1450 *Ph:* 888-831 4685; 302-831 2852 *Fax:* 302-831 6042 *E-mail:* studyabroad@udel.edu

---

0085
UNIVERSITY OF NATAL
International Winter School
Site: South Africa: Durban, Pietermaritzburg
Dates: 6 wks, late Jun-early Aug
Subjects: Art, Civilization/culture, Drama/theater, English literature, History, Liberal arts, Music, Political science/politics, Zulu language (beg)
Eligibility: *Level:* sophs, jrs, srs, grads *Age:* min 19
Credit: *Undergrad:* 8 *Grad:* none *Doc:* transcript
Instruction: *In:* English *Format:* internship, lang study, lecture *Students:* mainly US
Costs: $3,000 *incl* tuition, housing, all meals, insurance, fees, excursions, books/materials *Nonrefundable fee*
Housing: *Arr by pgm:* residence halls
Deadline: Feb 29
Other info: *US accredited sponsor:* no *Began:* 1998 *Orient:* abroad (1 day) *Activities:* field trips, cultural events *URL:* http://www.und.ac.za/und/winter/index.html
Contact: Coord, Univ of Natal-IWS, Durban 4041, South Africa *E-mail:* iws@nu.ac.za

---

CAPE TOWN

0086
BARD COLLEGE and **UNIVERSITY OF CAPE TOWN**
International Human Rights Exchange
Site: South Africa: Cape Town
Dates: Jun 25-Jul 20
Subjects: Civilization/culture, Human rights
Eligibility: *Level:* sophs, jrs, srs *Age:* min 19, avg 21
Credit: *Undergrad:* 4 *Grad:* none *Doc:* transcript
Instruction: *In:* English *Format:* directed field study, lecture, seminar *Students:* intl
Costs: $1,500 *incl* tuition, housing, some meals, insurance, fees
Housing: *Arr by pgm:* hostels
Deadline: Mar 1; late applications considered
Other info: *US accredited sponsor:* yes *Began:* 2001 *Orient:* avail *Misc:* 4-wk course on theory & practice of human rights. *Financial aid:* scholarships *URL:* http://www.ihre.org
Contact: Carlton Rounds, Intl Pgms Asst, IILE, Bard Coll, Annandale-On-Hudson NY 12504 *Ph:* 845-758 7076 *Fax:* 845-758 7040 *E-mail:* iile@bard.edu
Or Contact: Laura Greene, Intl Projects Mgr, IILE, Bard Coll, Annandale-On-Hudson NY 12504 *Ph:* 845-758 7080 *Fax:* 845-758 7040 *E-mail:* greene@bard.edu
Or Contact: Lisa Hantout, Admin Asst, Bard Coll, Annandale-On-Hudson NY 12504 *Ph:* 845-758 7835 *Fax:* 845-758 7040 *E-mail:* hantout@bard.edu

---

0087
COOPERATIVE CENTER FOR STUDY ABROAD
South Africa
Site: South Africa: Cape Town
Dates: 3 wks, Jun 12-Jul 4
Subjects: Biology, Communications, Education/teaching, Safety management
Eligibility: *Level:* fresh, sophs, jrs, srs, grads, adults, teachers, professionals *Requires:* 2.0 GPA, recommendation letter *Age:* min 18
Credit: *Undergrad:* 3 *Grad:* 3
Instruction: *In:* English *Format:* lecture, seminar, study tour, tutorial *Students:* mainly US
Costs: $4,795 *incl* housing, some meals, intl airfare, excursions, ISIC/ITIC *Nonrefundable fee*
Housing: *Arr by pgm:* residence halls, hotels
Deadline: Mar 1
Other info: *US accredited sponsor:* yes *Began:* 1999 *Orient:* in US *Activities:* excursions, field trips, cultural events *Misc:* May contact former participants. *Financial aid:* scholarships *URL:* http://www.nku.edu/ccsa
Contact: *See Index II for Members* Dr Michael Klembara, or Robin Byerly, Coop Ctr for Study Abroad, Northern Kentucky Univ, BEP 301, Highland Heights KY 41099 *Ph:* 800-319 6015; 606-572 6512 *Fax:* 606-572 6650 *E-mail:* ccsa@nku.edu

---

0088
HOWARD UNIVERSITY SCHOOL OF LAW
Comparative and International Law Program in South Africa
Site: South Africa: Cape Town *Host inst:* Univ of Western Cape
Dates: Jun 15 - Jul 25
Subjects: Comparative law, Human rights, International business, International law, Southern African studies
Eligibility: *Level:* grads *Requires:* 2.5 GPA, previous study in field
Credit: *Undergrad:* none *Grad:* 12 *Doc:* transcript
Instruction: *In:* English *Format:* study tour *Students:* mainly US
Costs: $3,390 *incl* tuition, housing, excursions, books/materials, local transport *Nonrefundable fee*
Housing: *Arr by pgm:* apartments
Deadline: Apr 1
Other info: *US accredited sponsor:* yes *Began:* 1996 *Orient:* abroad *Activities:* excursions, field trips, cultural events *Misc:* May contact former participants. *Financial aid:* scholarships
Contact: Kim Gray, Asst Dir, HUSL Off of Admission, 2900 Van Ness Street, NW, Washington DC 20008 *Ph:* 202-806 8069 *Fax:* 202-806 8162 *E-mail:* zgray@law.howard.edu
Or Contact: Ruby Sherrod, Asst Dean, Howard Univ Sch of Law (HUSL), 2900 Van Ness Street, NW, Washington DC 20008 *Ph:* 202-806 8138 *Fax:* 202-806 8162 *E-mail:* rsherrod@law.howard.edu

---

See "How To Use This Book" for definitions of terms used above. ▲ = See program sponsor's ad(s) in this book.

0089
LEXIA INTERNATIONAL
LEXIA Summer in Cape Town
Site: South Africa: Cape Town *Host inst:* Univ of the Western Cape
Dates: 8 wks, mid-Jun-mid-Aug
Subjects: African studies, Afrikaans language (beg/int/adv), Anthropology, Arts, Civilization/culture, Community service projects, Ecology/environmental studies, Economics, Fine arts, History, Internships, Literature, Political science/politics, Sociology, Xhosa language (beg/int/adv)
Eligibility: *Level:* fresh, sophs, jrs, srs, grads, adults *Requires:* 2.5 GPA *Age:* min 18, avg 21
Credit: *Undergrad:* 8-10 *Grad:* 8-10 *Doc:* transcript *Transfer credit through:* Western Washington Univ
Instruction: *In:* English, Afrikaans *Format:* internship, lang study, lecture, seminar, volunteer/svc *Students:* mainly US
Costs: $4,650 *incl* tuition, housing, most meals, insurance, fees, excursions, ISIC, computer access *Nonrefundable fee*
Housing: *Arr by pgm:* residence halls with local students, homestay
Deadline: Apr 15; Apr 1 for scholarships
Other info: *US accredited sponsor:* no *Began:* 1995 *In coop with:* Western Washington Univ *Orient:* abroad *Activities:* excursions, field trips, program travel, cultural events, sports *Misc:* Student support svcs. May contact former participants. *Financial aid:* scholarships, work study *URL:* http://www.lexiaintl.org
Contact: LEXIA Intl, 25 S Main St, Hanover NH 03755 *Ph:* 800-775 3942; 603-643 9898 *Fax:* 603-643 9899 *E-mail:* info@lexiaintl.org
Or Contact: LEXIA Intl, West Coast, 378 Cambridge Ave, Palo Alto CA 94306-1544 *Ph:* 650-327 9191 *Fax:* 650-327 9192

0090
NEW YORK UNIVERSITY, SCHOOL OF EDUCATION
International Community Health
Site: South Africa: Cape Town *Host inst:* Univ of Cape Town
Dates: 4 wks, Jul 9-Aug 3
Subjects: Public health
Eligibility: *Level:* srs, grads *Requires:* 3.0 GPA, previous study in field
Credit: *Undergrad:* none *Grad:* avail *Doc:* transcript
Instruction: *In:* English *Format:* directed field study, lab, lecture *Students:* mainly US
Costs: $4,700 *incl* tuition, housing, some meals, books/materials *Nonrefundable fee*
Housing: *Arr by pgm:* pensions
Deadline: Apr 1
Other info: *US accredited sponsor:* yes *Began:* 1998 *Orient:* abroad (3 days) *Activities:* field trips *Misc:* Loans avail. May contact former participants. *URL:* http://www.nyu.edu/summer
Contact: Sally Guttmacher, Health Studies, Sch of Educ, New York Univ, 35 W 4th St, Rm 1221, New York NY 10003 *Ph:* 212-998 5616 *Fax:* 212-995 4260 *E-mail:* sg2@is.nyu.edu
Or Contact: Helen J Kelly, Dir of Special Pgms, New York Univ, 82 Washington Square E, Rm 62, New York NY 10003 *Ph:* 212-998 5090 *Fax:* 212-995 4923 ▲

FLORISBAD

0091
DUKE UNIVERSITY
Duke in South Africa: Paleoanthropology Field School
Site: South Africa: Florisbad *Host inst:* Natl Museum of Bloemfontein's Florisbad Quaternaly Research Ctr
Dates: 6 wks, mid-May-early Jul
Subjects: Anthropology, Paleontology, Prehistoric studies, South African studies
Eligibility: *Level:* sophs, jrs, srs *Requires:* previous study in field, good acad standing, transcript
Credit: *Undergrad:* 2 credits *Grad:* none
Instruction: *In:* English *Format:* directed field study, lab, lecture, practical training, seminar *Students:* mainly US
Costs: $4,495 *incl* tuition, housing, all meals, fees, excursions
Housing: *Arr by pgm:* residence halls
Deadline: Feb 16
Other info: *US accredited sponsor:* yes *Began:* 1999 *Orient:* in US (1 day) *Activities:* excursions, field trips, program travel, cultural events *Misc:* May contact former participants. *URL:* http://www.aas.duke.edu/study_abroad/
Contact: Study Abroad, Duke Univ, 121 Allen Bldg, Box 90057, Durham NC 27708-0057 *Ph:* 919-684 2174 *Fax:* 919-684 3083 *E-mail:* abroad@asdean.duke.edu

---

PRETORIA

0092
NEW YORK UNIVERSITY, SCHOOL OF EDUCATION
Higher Education/Educational Administration
Site: South Africa: Pretoria
Dates: Jul 2-27
Subjects: Administration, Adult education, Education/teaching, Secondary education, Technology
Eligibility: *Level:* grads *Requires:* 3.0 GPA
Credit: *Undergrad:* none *Grad:* avail
Instruction: *In:* English *Format:* lecture, seminar *Students:* mainly US
Costs: $6,500 *incl* tuition, housing, some meals, books/materials
Housing: *Arr by pgm:* residence halls
Deadline: Contact sponsor
Other info: *US accredited sponsor:* yes *Orient:* abroad *Activities:* field trips *URL:* http://www.nyu.edu/summer
Contact: Prof Teboho Moja, Admin, Leadership & Technology, Sch of Educ, NYU, 239 Greene St, Ste 300, New York NY 10003 *Ph:* 212-995 4041 *E-mail:* teboho.moja@nyu.edu
Or Contact: Helen J Kelly, Dir, Special Pgms, NYU, 82 Washington Sq E, Rm 62, New York NY 10003 *Ph:* 212-998 5090 *Fax:* 212-995 4923 ▲

STELLENBOSCH

0093
AMERICAN INSTITUTE FOR FOREIGN STUDY (AIFS)
University of Stellenbosch-South Africa
Site: South Africa: Stellenbosch *Host inst:* Univ of Stellenbosch
Dates: 4 wks, Jun 26-Jul 27
Subjects: African studies, Field study, Forestry, Homestay, Literature, Political science/politics, Wine
Eligibility: *Level:* sophs, jrs, srs, adults *Requires:* 2.00 GPA
Credit: *Undergrad:* 6 *Grad:* none *Doc:* transcript
Instruction: *In:* English *Format:* directed field study, lecture, seminar *Students:* intl
Costs: $4,999 *incl* tuition, housing, all meals, intl airfare, excursions *Nonrefundable fee*
Housing: *Arr by pgm:* residence halls, homestay
Deadline: Mar 15
Other info: *US accredited sponsor:* no *Began:* 2000 *Orient:* abroad *Activities:* excursions, field trips, cultural events *Misc:* 1-wk field trip, resident dir. May contact former participants. *Financial aid:* scholarships *URL:* http://www.aifsabroad.com
Contact: Solandy Meza, Coll Div, AIFS, River Plaza, 9 W Broad St, Stamford CT 06902 *Ph:* 800-727 2437 ext 5163 *E-mail:* college.info@aifs.com ▲

Swaziland

NGWANE

0094
OHIO UNIVERSITY
Teacher Education in Swaziland
Site: Swaziland: Ngwane *Host inst:* Ngwane Coll
Dates: 5 wks, mid-Jun-mid-Jul

Subjects: African studies, Education/teaching
Eligibility: *Level:* sophs, jrs, srs *Requires:* previous study in field
Credit: *Undergrad:* avail *Grad:* avail *Doc:* transcript
Instruction: *In:* English *Format:* practical training, student teaching *Students:* US & host country
Costs: About $2,200 for OH residents, $4,000 for others *incl* tuition, housing, all meals, intl airfare, excursions, local transport *Nonrefundable fee*
Housing: *Arr by pgm:* residence halls
Deadline: Feb 15
Other info: *US accredited sponsor:* yes *Orient:* in US *Activities:* excursions *URL:* http://www.ohiou.edu/studyabroad/
Contact: Dr Stephen Howard, Educ Studies, Ohio Univ, McCracken Hall, Athens OH 45701 *Ph:* 740-593 4467 *Fax:* 740-593 1837 *E-mail:* showard1@ohiou.edu
Or Contact: Polly Sandenburgh, Ctr for Intl Studies, Ohio Univ, 56 E Union St, Athens OH 45701 *Ph:* 740-593 1842 *Fax:* 740-593 1837 *E-mail:* sandenbu@ohiou.edu

Tanzania

MORE THAN ONE CITY

0095
INTERNATIONAL BICYCLE FUND
Tanzania: Surf to Summit
Site: Tanzania: various sites
Dates: 17 days, Feb
Subjects: African studies, Agriculture, Civilization/culture, Development studies, Ecology/environmental studies, Economics, Education/teaching, Field study, Geography, Geology, Health care/hospitals, History, Independent study, Political science/politics, Religion/theology
Eligibility: *Level:* adults
Credit: *Undergrad:* none *Grad:* none
Instruction: *In:* English *Format:* directed field study, independent study, seminar, study tour *Students:* mainly US
Costs: $1,490 *incl* tuition, housing, some meals, fees, excursions *Nonrefundable fee*
Housing: *Arr by pgm:* homestay, hotels, hostels
Deadline: Until pgm filled
Other info: *US accredited sponsor:* no *Began:* 1994 *Orient:* avail pre-departure packet *Misc:* May contact former participants. *URL:* http://www.ibike.org/
Contact: David Mozer, Dir, Intl Bicycle Fund, 4887 Columbia Dr S, Seattle WA 98108 *Ph:* 206-767 0848 *Fax:* 206-767 0848 *E-mail:* ibike@ibike.org

---

0096
UNIVERSITY OF DELAWARE
Winter Session in Tanzania
Site: Tanzania: various sites
Dates: 4 wks, Jan
Subjects: Behavioral sciences, Ecology/environmental studies, Entomology, Field study
Eligibility: *Level:* fresh, sophs, jrs, srs *Requires:* 2.0 GPA
Credit: *Undergrad:* 4-6 *Grad:* none *Doc:* transcript
Instruction: *In:* English *Format:* directed field study, lecture, seminar, study tour *Students:* mainly US
Costs: Contact Sponsor
Housing: *Arr by pgm:* safari
Deadline: mid-Oct
Other info: *US accredited sponsor:* yes *Orient:* in US *Activities:* excursions, field trips *Misc:* Contact sponsor to arrange honors credit. *Financial aid:* scholarships *URL:* http://www.udel.edu/studyabroad
Contact: Int Pgm & Special Sessions, Univ of Delaware, 4 Kent Way, Newark DE 19716 *Ph:* 888-662 4685; 302-831 2852 *Fax:* 302-831 6042 *E-mail:* studyabroad@udel.edu

---

0097
UNIVERSITY OF GEORGIA
Maymester in Tanzania
Site: Tanzania: various cities *Host inst:* Univ of Dar-es-Salaam, Marine Inst, St Augustine Univ
Dates: 4 wks, May 12-Jun 12
Subjects: African studies, Anthropology, Drama/theater, Education/teaching, Geology, Journalism, Literature, Marine sciences, Political science/politics, Swahili language, Women's studies
Eligibility: *Level:* sophs, jrs, srs, grads, adults, teachers, professionals *Requires:* 2.0 GPA, 1 sem of Swahili encouraged; ability to adapt to new cultures
Credit: *Undergrad:* 3 *Grad:* 3 *Doc:* transcript
Instruction: *In:* English *Format:* directed field study, independent study, lang study, lecture, music lesson, seminar, student teaching, study tour, volunteer/svc *Students:* intl
Costs: Contact sponsor
Housing: *Arr by pgm:* residence halls, hotels, hostels
Deadline: Nov 3; Feb 1 for scholarships
Other info: *US accredited sponsor:* yes *Began:* 2000 *Orient:* in US & abroad (4-6 days) *Activities:* excursions, field trips, program travel, cultural events *Misc:* May contact former participants. *Financial aid:* scholarships *URL:* http://www.uga.edu/~afrstu
Contact: Lioba Moshi, Dir, Univ of Georgia, 314 Candler Hall, Athens GA 30602 *Ph:* 706-542 5314, 706-583 0575 *Fax:* 706-583 0482 *E-mail:* africa@arches.uga.edu
Or Contact: Freda Scott-Giles, Univ of Georgia, 314 Candler Hall, Athens GA 30602 *Ph:* 706-542 2102 *Fax:* 706-542 2080 *E-mail:* fsgiles@arches.uga.edu

---

DAR ES SALAAM

0098
UNIVERSITY OF PENNSYLVANIA
Penn-in-Dar Es Salaam
Site: Tanzania: Dar Es Salaam *Host inst:* Univ of Dar Es Salaam
Dates: 5 wks, Jul-Aug
Subjects: Archaeology, Civilization/culture, Development studies, Drama/theater, History, Homestay, Political science/politics, Sociology, Swahili language
Eligibility: *Level:* fresh, sophs, jrs, srs, grads, professionals
Credit: *Undergrad:* 6 *Grad:* avail *Doc:* transcript
Instruction: *In:* English *Format:* lang study, lecture *Students:* mainly US
Costs: About $5,300 *incl* tuition, housing, intl airfare *Nonrefundable fee*
Housing: *Arr by pgm:* homestay
Deadline: Apr 1
Other info: *US accredited sponsor:* yes *Began:* 2000 *Orient:* in US *Activities:* excursions *Misc:* May contact former participants. *URL:* http://www.sas.upenn.edu/cgs/
Contact: Elizabeth Sachs, University of Pennsylvania, Penn Summer Abroad, 3440 Market Street, Suite 100, Philadelphia PA 19104-3335 *Ph:* 215-898 5738 *Fax:* 215-573 2053

Uganda

MORE THAN ONE CITY

0099
INTERNATIONAL BICYCLE FUND
Uganda: Pearl of Africa
Site: Uganda: various sites
Dates: 13 days, Jan-Feb
Subjects: African studies, Agriculture, Civilization/culture, Development studies, Ecology/environmental studies, Economics, Education/teaching, Field study, Geography, Geology, Health care/hospitals, History, Independent study, Political science/politics, Religion/theology
Eligibility: *Level:* adults
Credit: *Undergrad:* none *Grad:* none
Instruction: *In:* English *Format:* directed field study, independent study, seminar, study tour *Students:* mainly US
Costs: $990 *incl* tuition, housing, some meals, fees, excursions *Nonrefundable fee*
Housing: *Arr by pgm:* homestay, hotels, hostels

Deadline: Until pgm filled
Other info: *US accredited sponsor:* no *Began:* 1993 *Orient:* avail pre-departure packet *Misc:* May contact former participants. *URL:* http://www.ibike.org/bikeafrica
Contact: David Mozer, Dir, Intl Bicycle Fund, 4887 Columbia Dr S, Seattle WA 98108 *Ph:* 206-767 0848 *Fax:* 206-767 0848 *E-mail:* ibike@ibike.org

---

KIWANGALA VILLAGE

0100
UNITED CHILDREN'S FUND, INC
Uganda Country Program
Site: Uganda: Kiwangala Village *Host inst:* Karudeo
Dates: 1 wk or longer, yr-round
Subjects: African studies, Community service projects, Development studies, Homestay
Eligibility: *Level:* adults *Age:* min 18, avg 30
Credit: *Undergrad:* none *Grad:* none
Instruction: *In:* English *Format:* volunteer/svc *Students:* intl
Costs: Contact sponsor
Housing: *Arr by pgm:* homestay
Deadline: None
Other info: *US accredited sponsor:* no *Began:* 1996 *Orient:* abroad (2-3 days) *Activities:* excursions, cultural events *Misc:* May contact former participants. *URL:* http://www.unchildren.org
Contact: Norman McKinney, Dir, United Children's Fund, PO Box 20341, Boulder CO 80308-3341 *E-mail:* united@children.org

Zimbabwe

MORE THAN ONE CITY

0101
INTERNATIONAL BICYCLE FUND
Zimbabwe: Mashonaland Sojourn
Site: Zimbabwe: various sites
Dates: 2 wks, Jul
Subjects: African studies, Agriculture, Civilization/culture, Development studies, Ecology/environmental studies, Economics, Education/teaching, Field study, Geography, Geology, Health care/hospitals, History, Independent study, Political science/politics, Religion/theology
Eligibility: *Level:* adults
Credit: *Undergrad:* none *Grad:* none
Instruction: *In:* English *Format:* directed field study, independent study, seminar, study tour *Students:* mainly US
Costs: $1,090 *incl* tuition, housing, some meals, fees, excursions *Nonrefundable fee*
Housing: *Arr by pgm:* homestay, hotels, hostels
Deadline: Until pgm filled
Other info: *US accredited sponsor:* no *Began:* 1990 *Orient:* avail pre-departure packet *Misc:* May contact former participants. *URL:* http://www.ibike.org/bikeafrica
Contact: David Mozer, Dir, Intl Bicycle Fund, 4887 Columbia Dr S, Seattle WA 98108 *Ph:* 206-767 0848 *Fax:* 206-767 0848 *E-mail:* ibike@ibike.org

---

0102
INTERNATIONAL BICYCLE FUND
Zimbabwe: Matabeleland Sojourn
Site: Zimbabwe: various sites
Dates: 2 wks, Jul-Aug
Subjects: African studies, Agriculture, Civilization/culture, Development studies, Ecology/environmental studies, Economics, Education/teaching, Field study, Geography, Geology, Health care/hospitals, History, Independent study, Political science/politics, Religion/theology
Eligibility: *Level:* adults
Credit: *Undergrad:* none *Grad:* none
Instruction: *In:* English *Format:* directed field study, independent study, seminar, study tour *Students:* mainly US
Costs: $1,290 *incl* tuition, housing, some meals, fees, excursions *Nonrefundable fee*
Housing: *Arr by pgm:* homestay, hotels, hostels
Deadline: Until pgm filled
Other info: *US accredited sponsor:* no *Began:* 1990 *Orient:* avail pre-departure packet *Misc:* May contact former participants. *URL:* http://www.ibike.org/bikeafrica
Contact: David Mozer, Dir, Intl Bicycle Fund, 4887 Columbia Dr S, Seattle WA 98108 *Ph:* 206-767 0848 *Fax:* 206-767 0848 *E-mail:* ibike@ibike.org

---

BULAWAYO

0103
SCHOOL FOR INTERNATIONAL TRAINING
Zimbabwe: Grassroots Development and NGO Management
Site: Zimbabwe: Bulawayo
Dates: May-Jul
Subjects: Development administration/management, Development studies, Field study, Homestay, Independent study, Ndebele language (beg)
Eligibility: *Level:* sophs, jrs, srs *Requires:* 3.0 GPA, previous study in field, adv coursework in development studies, involvement in campus or comm svc, intercultural exper
Credit: *Undergrad:* avail *Grad:* none *Doc:* transcript, certificate
Instruction: *In:* English *Format:* directed field study, independent study, lang study, lecture, seminar *Students:* intl
Costs: $14,900 *incl* tuition, housing, all meals, intl airfare, insurance, fees, excursions
Housing: *Arr by pgm:* residence halls, homestay, hotels
Deadline: Contact sponsor
Other info: *US accredited sponsor:* yes *Began:* 1998 *In coop with:* Org of Rural Assn for Progress (ORAP) *Orient:* abroad (1 wk) *Activities:* excursions, cultural events *Financial aid:* scholarships *URL:* http://www.sit.edu
Contact: CSA Admissions, Box DA1AY, Kipling Rd, Brattleboro VT 05302-0676 *Ph:* 888-272 7881; 802-257 7751 *Fax:* 802-258 3296 *E-mail:* csa@sit.edu

---

HARARE

0104
MICHIGAN STATE UNIVERSITY
Education, Society and Learning
Site: Zimbabwe: Harare
Dates: 6 wks, May-Jun
Subjects: Education/teaching, Homestay, Independent study, Social sciences
Eligibility: *Level:* jrs, srs, grads, teachers *Requires:* 2.5 GPA, good acad standing *Age:* min 18
Credit: *Undergrad:* 9 *Grad:* 9 *Doc:* transcript
Instruction: *In:* English *Format:* independent study, lecture *Students:* mainly US
Costs: About $1,900 *incl* housing, some meals, insurance, excursions, support svcs *Nonrefundable fee*
Housing: *Arr by pgm:* homestay, hotels
Deadline: Mar 2
Other info: *US accredited sponsor:* yes *Began:* 1993 *Orient:* in US & abroad *Activities:* excursions, program travel, cultural events *Misc:* Loans avail. *Financial aid:* scholarships *URL:* http://studyabroad.msu.edu
Contact: Cheryl Benner, Study Abroad, Michigan State Univ, 109 Intl Ctr, East Lansing MI 48824-1035 *Ph:* 517-353 8920 *Fax:* 517-432 2082 *E-mail:* bennerc@msu.edu ▲

0105
MICHIGAN STATE UNIVERSITY
Expressive Culture in Zimbabwe
Site: Zimbabwe: Harare
Dates: 6 wks, May-Jun
Subjects: Civilization/culture, Field study, Literature, Music, Visual arts

Eligibility: *Level:* fresh, sophs, jrs, srs *Requires:* 2.5 GPA *Age:* min 18
Credit: *Undergrad:* 7 *Grad:* none *Doc:* transcript
Instruction: *In:* English *Format:* directed field study, lecture *Students:* mainly US
Costs: About $2,200 *incl* housing, insurance, fees, excursions *Nonrefundable fee*
Housing: *Arr by pgm:* hotels
Deadline: Mar 2
Other info: *US accredited sponsor:* yes *Began:* 2000 *Orient:* in US 1 day *Activities:* excursions, field trips, cultural events *Financial aid:* scholarships *URL:* http://studyabroad.msu.edu
Contact: Cheryl Benner, MSU Study Abroad, 109 Intl Ctr, East Lansing MI 448824-1035 *Ph:* 517-353 8920 *Fax:* 517-432 2082 *E-mail:* bennerc@msu.edu ▲

0106
SYRACUSE UNIVERSITY
Law in Zimbabwe
Site: Zimbabwe: Harare
Dates: 7 wks, Jun 12-Jul 29
Subjects: Internships, Law
Eligibility: *Level:* grads *Requires:* 2.8 GPA, 1 yr law sch
Credit: *Undergrad:* none *Grad:* 6
Instruction: *In:* English *Students:* mainly US
Costs: About $5,300 *incl* tuition, housing, some meals, fees, excursions, books/materials *Nonrefundable fee*
Housing: *Arr by pgm:* residence halls
Deadline: Mar 15
Other info: *US accredited sponsor:* yes *Began:* 1995 *In coop with:* Univ of Zimbabwe Coll of Law *Orient:* abroad *Activities:* excursions, field trips, cultural events *Misc:* May contact former participants. *Financial aid:* scholarships *URL:* http://sumweb.syr.edu/dipa/summer
Contact: Daisy Fried, Assoc Dir, or Darlene Grome, Admissions Counselor, Syracuse Univ, 119 Euclid Ave, Syracuse NY 13244 *Ph:* 800-251 9674; 315-443 9419, 315-443 9420 *Fax:* 315-443 4593 *E-mail:* dipasum@suadmin.syr.edu ▲

Asia and Oceania

More Than One Country

0107
AMERICAN INSTITUTE FOR FOREIGN STUDY (AIFS)
Southeast Asia: International Relations and Business
Site: China: Guangzhou, Hong Kong; Singapore; Vietnam: Ho Chi Minh City
Dates: 4 wks, Jun 25-Jul 18
Subjects: International business, International relations
Eligibility: *Level:* sophs, jrs, srs, grads, adults *Requires:* 2.0 GPA
Credit: *Undergrad:* 4 *Grad:* none *Doc:* transcript
Instruction: *In:* English *Format:* lecture, study tour *Students:* mainly US
Costs: $4,799 *incl* tuition, housing, some meals, most meals, intl airfare
Housing: *Arr by pgm:* residence halls, hotels
Deadline: Mar 15
Other info: *US accredited sponsor:* no *Began:* 1998 *Orient:* abroad *Misc:* 4-wk intro to development in Southeast Asia for students of intl relations & bus. May contact former participants. *Financial aid:* scholarships *URL:* http://www.aifsabroad.com
Contact: Solandy Meza, Coll Div, AIFS, River Plaza, 9 W Broad St, Stamford CT 06902 *Ph:* 800-727 2437 ext 5163 *E-mail:* college.info@aifs.com ▲

0108
COOPERATIVE CENTER FOR STUDY ABROAD
Australia/New Zealand Program
Site: Australia: Cairns, Sydney; New Zealand: Auckland, Wellington
Dates: 4 wks, Jun 21-Jul 19
Subjects: Art, Education/teaching, Mathematics
Eligibility: *Level:* fresh, sophs, jrs, srs, grads, adults, teachers, professionals *Requires:* 2.0 GPA, recommendation *Age:* min 18
Credit: *Undergrad:* 3-6 *Grad:* 3-6 *Doc:* transcript
Instruction: *In:* English *Format:* lecture, seminar, study tour, tutorial *Students:* mainly US
Costs: $5,295 *incl* housing, some meals, intl airfare, excursions, ISIC/ITIC
Housing: *Arr by pgm:* residence halls, hotels, budget accommodations
Deadline: Mar 1
Other info: *US accredited sponsor:* yes *Began:* 1999 *Orient:* in US & abroad *Activities:* excursions, field trips, cultural events *Misc:* May contact former participants. *Financial aid:* scholarships *URL:* http://www.nku.edu/ccsa
Contact: *See Index II for Members* Dr Michael A Klembara or Robin Byerly, Coop Ctr for Study Abroad, Northern Kentucky Univ, BEP 301, Highland Heights KY 41099 *Ph:* 800-319 6015; 859-572 6512 *Fax:* 859-572 6650 *E-mail:* ccsa@nku.edu

---

0109
INTERNATIONAL CAMPUS CONSORTIUM and THUNDERBIRD, THE AMERICAN GRADUATE SCHOOL OF INTERNATIONAL MANAGEMENT
Winterim in Asia
Site: Japan: Tokyo; Korea: Seoul
Dates: 3 wks, Jan 3-21
Subjects: Business language, Business/management, Communications, Finance, Industrial studies, International business, International marketing, International studies, Marketing, Retailing, Trade
Eligibility: *Level:* grads *Requires:* 3.0 GPA
Credit: *Undergrad:* none *Grad:* 3 *Doc:* transcript
Instruction: *In:* English *Format:* lecture *Students:* intl
Costs: $2,555 *incl* tuition, insurance, fees
Housing: *Sponsor assists:* hotels
Deadline: Contact sponsor
Other info: *US accredited sponsor:* yes *Orient:* abroad *Activities:* field trips *Misc:* Focus on the automobile industry. *Financial aid:* scholarships *URL:* http://www.t-bird.edu
Contact: *See Index II for Members* Dr Earl Gibbons, Assoc VP, Overseas Pgms, Thunderbird, 15249 N 59th Ave, Glendale AZ 85306 *Ph:* 602-978 7252 *Fax:* 602-978 7419 *E-mail:* gibbonse@t-bird.edu
Or Contact: Diane Hayton, Coord, Overseas Pgms, Thunderbird, 15249 N 59th Ave, Glendale AZ 85306 *Ph:* 602-978 7252 *Fax:* 602-978 7419 *E-mail:* haytond@t-bird.edu

---

0110
INTERNATIONAL COUNCIL FOR CULTURAL EXCHANGE (ICCE)
Asian, Japanese and Chinese Studies
Site: China, Japan
Dates: 2-5 wks, Jun-Sep
Subjects: Asian studies, Chinese language (beg/int/adv), Civilization/culture, Field study, Homestay, Japanese language (beg/int/adv)
Eligibility: *Level:* fresh, sophs, jrs, srs, grads, adults, teachers, professionals, precoll
Credit: *Undergrad:* avail *Grad:* avail *Doc:* transcript, certificate
Instruction: *In:* Chinese, English, Japanese *Format:* directed field study, lab, lang study, lecture, practical training, study tour *Students:* intl
Costs: Contact sponsor
Housing: *Sponsor assists:* residence halls, homestay, hotels
Deadline: 1 mo before pgm
Other info: *US accredited sponsor:* no *Began:* 1982 *Orient:* abroad *Activities:* excursions, field trips, program travel, cultural events
Contact: Dr Stanley Gochman, ICCE, 5 Bellport Ln, Bellport NY 11713 *Ph:* 631-286 5228 ▲

0111
LANGUAGE LIAISON
Chinese in Beijing or Taiwan
Site: China: Beijing; Taiwan
Dates: Varying pgm lengths, yr-round
Subjects: Chinese language (Mandarin), Chinese studies, Civilization/culture, Homestay, Taiwanese language
Eligibility: *Level:* adults *Age:* min 18
Credit: *Undergrad:* avail *Grad:* avail
Instruction: *In:* Mandarin, Taiwanese *Format:* lang study *Students:* intl
Costs: Contact sponsor
Housing: *Sponsor assists:* residence halls, homestay, hotels
Deadline: 45 days before pgm
Other info: *US accredited sponsor:* no *Orient:* avail avail *Activities:* excursions, field trips, cultural events, sports *Misc:* Scholarship research svc. *URL:* http://www.languageliaison.com
Contact: Nancy Forman, Dir, Lang Liaison, 4 Burnham Pkwy, Morristown NJ 07960 *Ph:* 800-284 4448 *Fax:* 973-898 1710 *E-mail:* learn@languageliaison.com

---

0112
MEKONG TOURS
Month in Thailand and Laos
Site: Thailand: Chiang Mai; Laos: Luang Prabang, Vientiane
Dates: 1 mo, Jun 20-Jul 20
Subjects: Civilization/culture, Ecology/environmental studies, Economics, Geography, Independent study, Internships, Languages, Women's studies
Eligibility: *Level:* sophs, jrs, srs, grads, adults, teachers, professionals *Age:* min 19
Credit: *Undergrad:* 3-6 *Grad:* 3-6
Instruction: *In:* English *Format:* independent study, internship *Students:* mainly US
Costs: Contact sponsor
Housing: *Arr by pgm:* hotels
Deadline: May 1
Other info: *US accredited sponsor:* no *Began:* 1991 *Orient:* in US *Activities:* excursions, field trips, program travel, cultural events *Misc:* May contact former participants.
Contact: Robert Phillips, Mekong Tours, 7135 Fawcett Cr Rd, Tillamook OR 97141 *Ph:* 503-842 7198 *Fax:* 503-842 4961 *E-mail:* mekongtour1@hotmail.com

---

0113
MICHIGAN STATE UNIVERSITY
Food, Environmental and Social Systems
Site: Australia, New Zealand
Dates: 3 wks, May-Jun
Subjects: Agribusiness, Agriculture, Field study, Independent study, Natural resources, Social sciences
Eligibility: *Level:* sophs, jrs, srs, grads *Requires:* 2.5 GPA, good acad standing, good physical condition *Age:* min 18
Credit: *Undergrad:* 6 *Grad:* 6 *Doc:* transcript
Instruction: *In:* English *Format:* directed field study, independent study, seminar, study tour *Students:* mainly US
Costs: About $1,900 *incl* housing, most meals, insurance, excursions, support svcs *Nonrefundable fee*
Housing: *Arr by pgm:* hotels, hostels
Deadline: Mar 2
Other info: *US accredited sponsor:* yes *Began:* 1992 *Orient:* in US & abroad *Activities:* excursions *Misc:* Loans avail. *Financial aid:* scholarships *URL:* http://studyabroad.msu.edu
Contact: Cheryl Benner, Study Abroad, Michigan State Univ, 109 Intl Ctr, East Lansing MI 48824-1035 *Ph:* 517-353 8920 *Fax:* 517-432 2082 *E-mail:* bennerc@msu.edu ▲

0114
MICHIGAN STATE UNIVERSITY
International Food Laws
Site: China, Japan, Korea
Dates: 3 wks, May
Subjects: Agriculture, Food production, Natural resources
Eligibility: *Level:* jrs, srs, grads *Requires:* 2.5 GPA, good acad standing, food science experience *Age:* min 18
Credit: *Undergrad:* 6 *Grad:* 6 *Doc:* transcript
Instruction: *In:* English *Format:* lecture, seminar *Students:* mainly US
Costs: About $1,700 *incl* housing, some meals, insurance, excursions
Housing: *Arr by pgm:* hotels
Deadline: Mar 2
Other info: *US accredited sponsor:* yes *Began:* 1996 *Orient:* in US *Activities:* excursions, field trips *Misc:* Loans avail. May contact former participants. *Financial aid:* scholarships *URL:* http://studyabroad.msu.edu
Contact: Cheryl Benner, Study Abroad, Michigan State Univ, 109 Intl Ctr, East Lansing MI 48824 *Ph:* 517-353 8920 *Fax:* 517-432 2082 *E-mail:* bennerc@msu.edu ▲

0115
NORTHERN ILLINOIS UNIVERSITY
Business and Culture in China and Korea
Site: China, Korea *Host inst:* Kyung Hee Univ, Shanghai Univ of Finance & Econ
Dates: 3 wks, May-Jun
Subjects: Business/management, Information science/systems
Eligibility: *Level:* jrs, srs, grads, professionals *Requires:* 2.5 GPA, previous study in field *Age:* avg 22
Credit: *Undergrad:* 3-6 *Grad:* 3-6 *Doc:* transcript
Instruction: *In:* English *Format:* lecture, seminar *Students:* mainly US
Costs: $4,000 per term *incl* tuition, housing, some meals, intl airfare, insurance, excursions
Housing: *Arr by pgm:* residence halls, hotels
Deadline: Mar 15
Other info: *US accredited sponsor:* yes *Began:* 1996 *Orient:* in US *Misc:* May contact former participants. *Financial aid:* scholarships *URL:* http://www.niu.edu/niuabroad/
Contact: Anne Seitzinger, Pgm Coord, Study Abroad, Williston 417, Northern Illinois Univ, DeKalb IL 60115 *Ph:* 815-753 0700 *Fax:* 815-753 0825 *E-mail:* niuabroad@niu.edu
Or Contact: Mona Salmon, Graduate Studies in Bus, Northern Illinois Univ, DeKalb IL 60115 *Ph:* 815-753 6162 *E-mail:* msalmon@niu.edu

---

0116
NORTHERN ILLINOIS UNIVERSITY
Business and Culture in Malaysia, Thailand and Vietnam
Site: Malaysia, Thailand, Vietnam *Host inst:* Chiang Mai Univ, Univ of Thailand Chamber of Commerce, Vietnam Natl Univ
Dates: 2-1/2 wks, Dec-Jan
Subjects: Business/management, Information science/systems, International business
Eligibility: *Level:* jrs, srs, grads, professionals *Requires:* 2.5 GPA, previous study in field *Age:* min 18, avg 25
Credit: *Undergrad:* 3-6 *Grad:* 3-6 *Doc:* transcript
Instruction: *In:* English *Format:* lecture, seminar *Students:* mainly US
Costs: $3,900 *incl* tuition, housing, some meals, intl airfare, insurance, fees, excursions
Housing: *Arr by pgm:* residence halls, hotels
Deadline: Nov 1
Other info: *US accredited sponsor:* yes *Began:* 1998 *Orient:* in US *Misc:* May contact former participants. *Financial aid:* scholarships *URL:* http://www.niu.edu/niuabroad/
Contact: Anne Seitzinger, Pgm Coord, Study Abroad Office, Williston 417, Northern Illinois Univ, DeKalb IL 60115 *Ph:* 815-753 0700 *Fax:* 815-753 0825 *E-mail:* niuabroad@niu.edu
Or Contact: Mona Salmon, Grad Studies in Bus, Northern Illinois Univ, DeKalb IL 60115 *Ph:* 815-753 6162 *E-mail:* msalmon@niu.edu

---

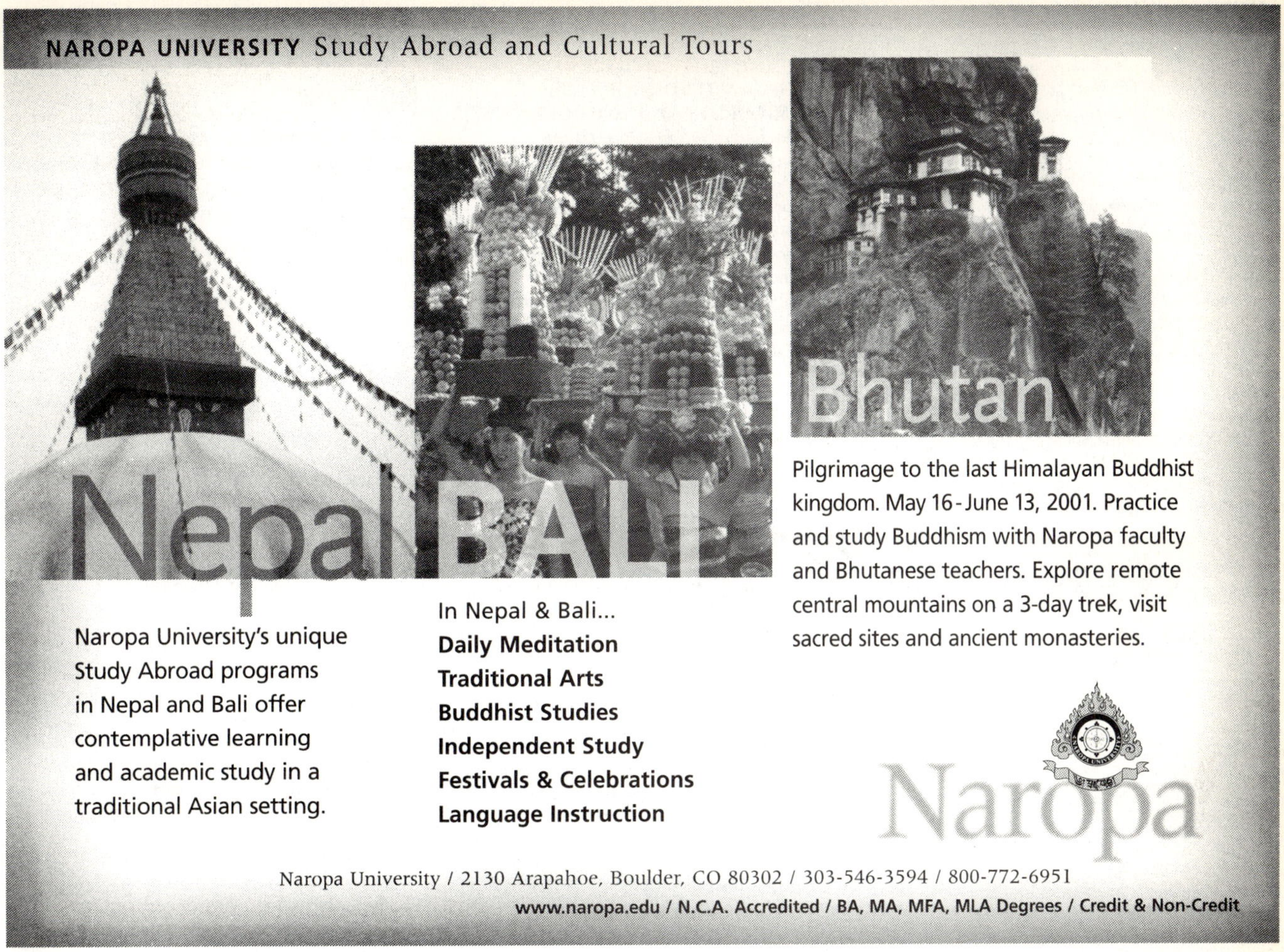

0117
THUNDERBIRD, THE AMERICAN GRADUATE SCHOOL OF INTERNATIONAL MANAGEMENT
Asia: The Automobile Industry: Japan, China and India
Site: China: Shanghai; India: Delhi, Mumbai; Japan: Tokyo
Dates: 3 wks, Jan 8-26
Subjects: Asian studies, Automotive mechanics, Field study
Eligibility: *Level:* grads *Requires:* 3.0 GPA, faculty permission
Credit: *Undergrad:* none *Grad:* 3
Instruction: *In:* English *Format:* directed field study *Students:* intl
Costs: $2,625 *incl* tuition, off-campus pgm fee
Housing: *Arr by pgm:* hotels
Deadline: Dec 1
Other info: *US accredited sponsor:* yes *Activities:* excursions, field trips, program travel *URL:* http://www.t-bird.edu
Contact: James Scott, AVP of Acad Operations, Thunderbird, 15249 N 59th Avenue, Glendale AZ 85306 *Ph:* 602-978 7251 *Fax:* 602-547 1356 *E-mail:* scottj@t-bird.edu

---

0118
UNIVERSITY OF HAWAII AT MANOA
Field Study Abroad: Industry of Asia
Site: China: Hong Kong, other sites; Japan; Korea; Thailand
Dates: 4 wks, Jul 6-Aug 3
Subjects: Business/management, Field study, Industrialization
Eligibility: *Level:* jrs, srs, grads, professionals *Requires:* 3.0 GPA *Age:* min 18
Credit: *Undergrad:* 6 *Grad:* 6
Instruction: *In:* English *Format:* directed field study, lecture *Students:* mainly US
Costs: $3,800 *incl* housing, some meals, intl airfare, excursions
Housing: *Arr by pgm:* hotels
Deadline: Early Apr
Other info: *US accredited sponsor:* yes *Began:* 1984 *Orient:* in US *Activities:* excursions *Financial aid:* scholarships *URL:* http://www2.hawaii.edu/study-abroad
Contact: Pacific Asian Mgmt Inst, Univ of Hawaii at Manoa, 2404 Maile Way C-202, Honolulu HI 96822 *Ph:* 808-956 8041 *Fax:* 808-956 3261

0119
UNIVERSITY OF SOUTHERN MISSISSIPPI
Australia/New Zealand Expedition
Site: Australia: Brisbane, Cairns, Canberra, Sydney, Townsville, other sites; New Zealand: Auckland, Hamilton, Rotorua, Taupo *Host inst:* James Cook Univ, Univ of Sydney, others
Dates: 3 wks, May 12-Jun 15
Subjects: Anthropology, Education/teaching, Field study, Geography, Health care/hospitals, Nursing, Sociology
Eligibility: *Level:* sophs, jrs, srs, grads *Requires:* 2.0 GPA, good acad standing
Credit: *Undergrad:* 4 *Grad:* 4 *Doc:* transcript
Instruction: *In:* English *Format:* directed field study, lecture *Students:* mainly US
Costs: $3,699 for undergrads, $3,999 for

grads *incl* tuition, housing, intl airfare, fees, excursions, ground transport by minivan *Nonrefundable fee*
Housing: *Arr by pgm:* hotels, hostels, motels
Deadline: Apr 1
Other info: *US accredited sponsor:* yes *Began:* 1991 *Orient:* in US & abroad *Activities:* excursions, field trips, program travel, cultural events *Misc:* Grants & loans avail. Group accompanied by USM prof & instructed by local lecturers, govt experts & parliamentarians. May contact former participants. *URL:* http://www.usm.edu
Contact: Dr Tim W Hudson, Australian Studies, Univ of Southern Mississippi, Box 10047, Hattiesburg MS 39406-0047 *Ph:* 601-266 4344 *Fax:* 601-266 5699 *E-mail:* melissa.ravencraft@usm.edu

Australia

MORE THAN ONE CITY

0120
AMERICAN UNIVERSITIES INTERNATIONAL PROGRAM (AUIP) and **UNIVERSITY OF SOUTH AUSTRALIA**
Heritage Management: Field Study Tour of Australia
Site: Australia: Adelaide, Alice Springs, Cairns, Great Barrier Reef, others
Dates: 4 wks, late Jun-mid-Jul
Subjects: Aboriginal studies, Civilization/culture, Conservation, Field study, Natural resource management, Wildlife
Eligibility: *Level:* sophs, jrs, srs, grads *Requires:* 2.0 GPA *Age:* min 18
Credit: *Undergrad:* 3 *Grad:* none *Doc:* transcript
Instruction: *In:* English *Format:* directed field study, lecture, seminar *Students:* mainly US
Costs: $1,750 per sem, $3,350 *incl* tuition, housing, all meals, excursions, local transport, ISIC *Nonrefundable fee*
Housing: *Arr by pgm:* hostels, tents, cabins
Deadline: Feb 1
Other info: *US accredited sponsor:* no *Began:* 1990 *Activities:* excursions, field trips, program travel *Misc:* May contact former participants. *URL:* http://www.auip.com
Contact: Linda Tomson or Tim Wakefield, AUIP, PMB 221, 305 W Magnolia St, Ft Collins CO 80521 *Ph:* 970-495 0869 *Fax:* 970-484 6997 *E-mail:* info@auip.com ▲

0121
AMERICAN UNIVERSITIES INTERNATIONAL PROGRAM (AUIP)
Reef to Rainforest - Northern Australian Field Study Tour
Site: Australia: various sites *Host inst:* Univ of Queensland
Dates: 3 wks, Jun 19-Jul 11
Subjects: Aboriginal studies, Conservation, Ecology/environmental studies, European studies, Field study, Historical preservation/restoration, History, Natural resource management, Wildlife
Eligibility: *Level:* jrs, srs, grads *Requires:* 2.0 GPA, previous study in field, essay, transcript, major in wildlife, natural resources, ecotourism, conservation, environmental studies, etc
Credit: *Undergrad:* avail *Grad:* none *Doc:* transcript
Instruction: *In:* English *Format:* directed field study, lecture, study tour *Students:* US & host country
Costs: $3,650 *incl* tuition, housing, all meals, insurance, fees, excursions, ISIC, materials *Nonrefundable fee*
Housing: *Arr by pgm:* campgrounds, tents
Deadline: Apr 1
Other info: *US accredited sponsor:* no *Began:* 2000 *In coop with:* Univ of Queensland *Orient:* abroad (1 day) *Activities:* excursions, field trips, program travel, cultural events *URL:* http://www.auip.com
Contact: Linda Tomson or Tim Wakefield, AUIP, PMB 221, 305 W Magnolia St, Ft Collins CO 80521 *Ph:* 888-921 2847; 970-495 0869 *Fax:* 970-484 6997 *E-mail:* info@auip.com ▲

0122
AUSTRALEARN: NORTH AMERICAN CENTER FOR AUSTRALIAN UNIVERSITIES
Australian Aboriginal Studies
Site: Australia: Brisbane, Sydney
Dates: 4 wks, about Jul 5-Aug 2
Subjects: Aboriginal studies, Civilization/culture, Field study, Homestay
Eligibility: *Level:* sophs, jrs, srs, grads, adults, professionals *Requires:* 2.5 GPA, previous study in field *Age:* min 18, avg 20
Credit: *Undergrad:* avail *Grad:* avail *Doc:* transcript *Transfer credit through:* Univ of Colorado at Denver
Instruction: *In:* English *Format:* directed field study, lecture, study tour *Students:* mainly US
Costs: About $3,750 *incl* tuition, housing, most meals, fees, excursions, books/materials, local transport *Nonrefundable fee*
Housing: *Arr by pgm:* residence halls, homestay, hotels
Deadline: Apr 1
Other info: *US accredited sponsor:* no *Began:* 1998 *Orient:* abroad *Activities:* excursions, field trips, program travel, cultural events *Misc:* 6-day field pgm in the bush learning from Aboriginal people about traditional relationships between people & the land. May contact former participants. *URL:* http://www.australearn.org
Contact: Cynthia Flannery-Banks, Dir, US Off, AustraLearn, Colorado State Univ Denver Ctr, 110 16th St, 2nd Fl, Denver CO 80202 *Ph:* 800-980 0033; 303-446 2214 *Fax:* 303-446 5955 *E-mail:* studyabroad@australearn.org ▲

0123
AUSTRALEARN: NORTH AMERICAN CENTER FOR AUSTRALIAN UNIVERSITIES
Certificate in Veterinary Studies
Site: Australia: Brisbane, Goondiwindi, Toowoomba
Dates: 3 wks, about Jul 7-27
Subjects: Field study, Homestay, Veterinary science
Eligibility: *Level:* sophs, jrs, srs, grads, adults, professionals *Requires:* 2.5 GPA
Credit: *Undergrad:* avail *Grad:* avail *Doc:* certificate
Instruction: *In:* English *Format:* directed field study, lecture, study tour *Students:* mainly US
Costs: About $2,960 *incl* housing, some meals, fees, excursions, books/materials, local transport *Nonrefundable fee*
Housing: *Arr by pgm:* residence halls, homestay, hotels
Deadline: Apr 1
Other info: *US accredited sponsor:* no *Began:* 1998 *Orient:* abroad *Activities:* excursions, field trips, program travel, cultural events *Misc:* Exposure to veterinary practices & Australian indigenous animals. May contact former participants. *URL:* http://www.australearn.org
Contact: Cynthia Flannery-Banks, Dir, US Off, AustraLearn, Colorado State Univ Denver Ctr, 110 16th St, 2nd Fl, Denver CO 80202 *Ph:* 800-980 0033; 313-446 2214 *Fax:* 303-446 5955 *E-mail:* studyabroad@australearn.org ▲

0124
AUSTRALEARN: NORTH AMERICAN CENTER FOR AUSTRALIAN UNIVERSITIES
Engineering in Environmental Management
Site: Australia: Biloela, Brisbane, Gladstone, Rockhampton
Dates: 4 wks, about Jul 4-Aug 1
Subjects: Environmental engineering, Field study, Homestay
Eligibility: *Level:* adults *Requires:* 2.5 GPA

Credit: *Undergrad:* avail *Grad:* avail *Doc:* transcript *Transfer credit through:* Univ of Colorado at Denver
Instruction: *In:* English *Format:* directed field study, lecture, study tour *Students:* mainly US
Costs: About $3,770 *incl* housing, most meals, fees, excursions, books/materials, local transport *Nonrefundable fee*
Housing: *Arr by pgm:* residence halls, homestay, hotels
Deadline: Apr 1
Other info: *US accredited sponsor:* no *Began:* 1998 *Orient:* abroad *Activities:* excursions, field trips, program travel, cultural events *Misc:* On-site case studies. May contact former participants. *URL:* http://www.australearn.org
Contact: Cynthia Flannery-Banks, Dir, US Off, AustraLearn, Colorado State Univ Denver Ctr, 110 16th St, 2nd Fl, Denver CO 80202 *Ph:* 800-980 0033; 303-446 2214 *Fax:* 303-446 5955 *E-mail:* studyabroad@australearn.org ▲

0125
AUSTRALEARN: NORTH AMERICAN CENTER FOR AUSTRALIAN UNIVERSITIES
Exploring Australian Education
Site: Australia: Brisbane, Sydney
Dates: 5 wks, about Jul 4-Aug 8
Subjects: Education/teaching, Special education
Eligibility: *Level:* sophs, jrs, srs, grads, adults, professionals *Requires:* 2.5 GPA, previous study in field
Credit: *Undergrad:* 6 *Grad:* 6 *Doc:* transcript *Transfer credit through:* Univ of Colorado at Denver
Instruction: *In:* English *Format:* directed field study, lecture, study tour *Students:* mainly US
Costs: About $3,800 *incl* housing, some meals, fees, excursions, books/materials, local transport *Nonrefundable fee*
Housing: *Arr by pgm:* residence halls, homestay, hotels
Deadline: Apr 1
Other info: *US accredited sponsor:* no *Began:* 1998 *Orient:* abroad *Activities:* excursions, field trips, program travel, cultural events *Misc:* Special educ issues for gifted, physically/intellectually disadvantaged children, immigrants & indigenous Australians. May contact former participants. *URL:* http://www.australearn.org
Contact: Cynthia Flannery-Banks, Dir, US Off, AustraLearn, N Amer Ctr for Australian Univs, Colorado State Univ Denver Ctr, 110 16th St, 2nd Fl, Denver CO 80202 *Ph:* 800-980 0033; 303-446 2214 *Fax:* 303-446 5955 *E-mail:* studyabroad@australearn.org ▲

0126
AUSTRALEARN: NORTH AMERICAN CENTER FOR AUSTRALIAN UNIVERSITIES
Internships
Site: Australia: various sites
Dates: Yr-round
Subjects: Business/management, Communications, Field study, Health sciences, Internships, Liberal arts, Political science/politics, Sciences, Sports science
Eligibility: *Level:* fresh, sophs, jrs, srs, grads, adults
Credit: *Undergrad:* none *Grad:* none

Instruction: *In:* English *Format:* directed field study, internship, lecture, study tour *Students:* mainly US
Costs: About $3,240 for 6 wks, $4,120 for 12 wks *incl* tuition, housing, fees *Nonrefundable fee*
Housing: *Arr by pgm:* apartments
Deadline: 4 mos before pgm
Other info: *US accredited sponsor:* no *Began:* 1997 *Orient:* avail avail *Activities:* excursions, program travel *Misc:* Custom-designed professional development internships. May contact former participants. *URL:* http://www.australearn.org
Contact: Cynthia Flannery-Banks, Dir, US Off, AustraLearn, Colorado State Univ Denver Ctr, 110 16th St, 2nd Fl, Denver CO 80202 *Ph:* 800-980 0033; 303-446 2214 *Fax:* 303-446 5955 *E-mail:* studyabroad@australearn.org ▲

0127
AUSTRALEARN: NORTH AMERICAN CENTER FOR AUSTRALIAN UNIVERSITIES
Politics in Australia
Site: Australia: Brisbane, Canberra
Dates: 4 wks, about Jul 2-31
Subjects: Australian studies, Field study, Homestay, International studies, Political science/politics, Public administration
Eligibility: *Level:* sophs, jrs, srs, grads, adults, professionals *Requires:* 2.5 GPA, previous study in field
Credit: *Undergrad:* avail *Grad:* avail *Doc:* transcript *Transfer credit through:* Univ of Colorado at Denver
Instruction: *In:* English *Format:* directed field study, lecture, study tour *Students:* mainly US
Costs: About $3,700 *incl* housing, some meals, fees, excursions, books/materials, local transport *Nonrefundable fee*
Housing: *Arr by pgm:* residence halls, homestay, hotels
Deadline: Apr 1
Other info: *US accredited sponsor:* no *Began:* 1998 *Orient:* abroad *Activities:* excursions, field trips, program travel, cultural events *Misc:* Trips to sessions of federal & state parliaments & local govt. May contact former participants. *URL:* http://www.australearn.org
Contact: Cynthia Flannery-Banks, Dir, US Off, AustraLearn, Colorado State Univ Denver Ctr, 110 16th St, 2nd Fl, Denver CO 80202 *Ph:* 800-980 0033; 303-446 2214 *Fax:* 303-446 5955 *E-mail:* studyabroad@australearn.org ▲

0128
AUSTRALEARN: NORTH AMERICAN CENTER FOR AUSTRALIAN UNIVERSITIES and COLORADO STATE UNIVERSITY
Rural Field Studies
Site: Australia: Canberra, Melbourne, Queensland, Sydney
Dates: 3 wks, May-Jun
Subjects: Agriculture, Animal sciences
Eligibility: *Level:* sophs, jrs, srs, grads, adults, professionals *Requires:* 2.50 GPA, previous study in field *Age:* min 18, avg 20
Credit: *Undergrad:* avail *Grad:* none *Doc:* transcript
Instruction: *In:* English *Format:* directed field study, independent study, lecture, seminar, study tour *Students:* mainly US
Costs: About $4,100 *incl* tuition, housing, all meals, intl airfare, fees, excursions, books/materials *Nonrefundable fee*
Housing: *Arr by pgm*
Deadline: Apr 1
Other info: *US accredited sponsor:* yes *Began:* 1993 *In coop with:* Agritours Australia *Orient:* in US & abroad *Activities:* excursions, field trips, program travel, cultural events, sports *Misc:* Tours of ranches, wineries, agricultural research sites, city attractions. May contact former participants. *URL:* http://www.australearn.org
Contact: Cynthia Flannery-Banks, Dir, US Off, AustraLearn, Colorado State Univ Denver Ctr, 110 16th St, 2nd Fl, Denver CO 80202 *Ph:* 800-980 0033; 303-446 2214 *Fax:* 303-446 5955 *E-mail:* studyabroad@australearn.org
Or Contact: Tom Field, Colorado State Univ, 7C Animal Scis, Ft Collins CO 80523 *Ph:* 303-491 6642 ▲

0129
AUSTRALEARN: NORTH AMERICAN CENTER FOR AUSTRALIAN UNIVERSITIES and LONG ISLAND UNIVERSITY, SOUTHAMPTON CAMPUS
Tropical Marine Ecology
Site: Australia: Great Barrier Reef research stations *Host inst:* Central Queensland Univ
Dates: 4 wks, Jun-Jul
Subjects: Ecology/environmental studies, Field study, Independent study, Marine biology
Eligibility: *Level:* sophs, jrs, srs, grads, adults, professionals *Requires:* 2.5 GPA *Age:* min 18, avg 20
Credit: *Undergrad:* 4 *Grad:* none *Doc:* transcript
Instruction: *In:* English *Format:* directed field study, independent study, lab, lecture, practical training, seminar, study tour *Students:* mainly US
Costs: About $3,710 *incl* tuition, housing, all meals, fees, excursions, books/materials
Housing: *Arr by pgm*
Deadline: Apr 1
Other info: *US accredited sponsor:* yes *Began:* 1994 *In coop with:* TraveLearn *Orient:* in US & abroad *Activities:* excursions, field trips, program travel, cultural events, sports *Misc:* Discount group airfare arranged. Hands-on marine sci experience. May contact former participants. *URL:* http://www.australearn.org
Contact: Cynthia Flannery-Banks, Dir, US Off, AustraLearn, Colorado State Univ Denver Ctr, 110 16th St, 2nd Fl, Denver CO 80202 *Ph:* 800-980 0033; 303-446 2214 *Fax:* 303-446 5955 *E-mail:* studyabroad@australearn.org
Or Contact: Dr Art Goldberg, Long Island Univ, Southampton NY 11968 *Ph:* 516-287 8404 *Fax:* 516-287 8419 ▲

0130
AUSTRALIAN TRUST FOR CONSERVATION VOLUNTEERS (ATCV)
Conservation Experience
Site: Australia: Adelaide, Brisbane, Canberra, Darwin, Hobart, Melbourne, Mildura, Perth, Sydney, Townsville
Dates: 6 wks, yr-round
Subjects: Conservation, Ecology/environmental studies, Forestry, Natural resource management, Wildlife
Eligibility: *Level:* adults *Requires:* good physical health *Age:* min 15, max 70, avg 20
Credit: *Undergrad:* none *Grad:* none *Doc:* certificate
Instruction: *In:* English *Format:* volunteer/svc *Students:* intl
Costs: AUS $920 *incl* housing, all meals, pgm travel, GST *Nonrefundable fee*
Housing: *Arr by pgm:* hostels, camping, caravans
Deadline: 1 mo before pgm
Other info: *US accredited sponsor:* no *Began:* 1982 *Activities:* field trips, program travel *URL:* http://www.atcv.com.au
Contact: Volunteer Enquiries or, Rachel Measham, ATCV, Box 423, Ballarat, Victoria 3353, Australia *E-mail:* info@atcv.com.au

---

0131
BEAVER COLLEGE, CENTER FOR EDUCATION ABROAD
Coral Reef Ecology
Site: Australia: Cairns, Townsville *Host inst:* James Cook Univ
Dates: 4 wks, Jul
Subjects: Ecology/environmental studies
Eligibility: *Level:* fresh, sophs, jrs, srs, grads *Requires:* 3.0 GPA, previous study in field
Credit: *Undergrad:* 4 *Grad:* none *Doc:* transcript

Instruction: *In:* English *Format:* directed field study, lecture *Students:* mainly US
Costs: $2,995 *incl* tuition, housing, some meals, insurance, excursions, ISIC, orient, transcript *Nonrefundable fee*
Housing: *Arr by pgm:* residence halls, hostels
Deadline: Apr 15
Other info: *US accredited sponsor:* yes *Began:* 1999 *Orient:* avail in Townsville (2 days) *Activities:* excursions, field trips *Misc:* May contact former participants. *URL:* http://www.arcadia.edu/cea/
Contact: Ctr for Educ Abroad, Beaver Coll, 450 S Easton Rd, Glenside PA 19038 *Ph:* 888-232 8379 *E-mail:* cea@beaver.edu ▲

0132
CAMP COUNSELORS USA
Australia Work-Travel Program
Site: Australia: various sites
Dates: 4 mos, yr-round
Subjects: Full curriculum
Eligibility: *Level:* fresh, sophs, jrs, srs, grads, adults *Age:* min 18, max 30
Credit: *Undergrad:* none *Grad:* none
Instruction: *In:* English *Format:* directed field study, internship *Students:* mainly host country
Costs: Contact sponsor
Housing: *Sponsor assists*
Deadline: Contact sponsor
Other info: *US accredited sponsor:* no *Began:* 1998 *Orient:* abroad *Activities:* excursions *URL:* http://www.campcounselors.com
Contact: Justin Johnston, Outbound Pgm Dir, Camp Counselors USA, 2330 Marinship Way, Ste 250, Sausalito CA 94965 *Ph:* 800-999 2267; 415-339 2728 *Fax:* 415-339 2744 *E-mail:* outbound@campcounselors.com

---

0133
CITY COLLEGE OF SAN FRANCISCO
Cultural Study Tour of Australia
Site: Australia: Cairns, Cooktown, Jowalbinna, Sydney
Dates: 17 days, Jun-Jul
Subjects: Ecology/environmental studies
Eligibility: *Level:* fresh, sophs, jrs, srs, grads, adults, teachers, professionals *Requires:* 2.0 GPA *Age:* min 17, max 80, avg 30
Credit: *Undergrad:* avail *Grad:* none *Doc:* transcript
Instruction: *In:* English *Format:* study tour *Students:* mainly US
Costs: About $2,999 *incl* tuition, housing, some meals, intl airfare, insurance, excursions, orient *Nonrefundable fee*
Housing: *Arr by pgm:* hotels, hostels
Deadline: Apr 1
Other info: *US accredited sponsor:* yes *Began:* 1999 *Orient:* in US & abroad (2 days) *Activities:* excursions, field trips, program travel, cultural events *Misc:* Loans & grants avail. *Financial aid:* scholarships *URL:* http://www.ccsf.org/studyabroad
Contact: Jill Heffron, Study Abroad Coord, City Coll of San Francisco, 50 Phelan Ave, Box C212, San Francisco CA 94112 *Ph:* 415-239 3778 *Fax:* 415-239 3804 *E-mail:* jheffron@ccsf.org

---

0134
COOPERATIVE CENTER FOR STUDY ABROAD
Australia Winter Program
Site: Australia: Cairns, Sydney
Dates: 2 wks, Dec 26-Jan 9
Subjects: Animal sciences, Arts, Biology, Communications, Education/teaching, Field study, Homestay, Women's studies
Eligibility: *Level:* fresh, sophs, jrs, srs, grads, adults, teachers, professionals *Requires:* 2.0 GPA, recommendation *Age:* min 18
Credit: *Undergrad:* 3 *Grad:* 3 *Doc:* transcript
Instruction: *In:* English *Format:* directed field study, lecture, study tour, tutorial *Students:* mainly US
Costs: $4,195 *incl* housing, some meals, intl airfare, excursions, airport transfers, ISIC/ITIC *Nonrefundable fee*
Housing: *Arr by pgm:* homestay, hotels, budget accommodations
Deadline: Oct 6
Other info: *US accredited sponsor:* yes *Began:* 1994 *Orient:* in US & abroad *Activities:* excursions, field trips, program travel, cultural events *Misc:* May contact former participants. *Financial aid:* scholarships *URL:* http://www.nku.edu/ccsa
Contact: *See Index II for Members* Dr Michael A Klembara or Robin Byerly, Coop Ctr for Study Abroad, Northern Kentucky Univ, BEP 301, Highland Heights KY 41099 *Ph:* 800-319 6015; 859-572 6512 *Fax:* 859-572 6650 *E-mail:* ccsa@nku.edu

---

0135
DUKE UNIVERSITY
Duke in Australia
Site: Australia: Lady Elliott Island, Sydney *Host inst:* Univ of New South Wales
Dates: Late Jun-early Aug
Subjects: Biology, Ecology/environmental studies, Geography, History
Eligibility: *Level:* fresh, sophs, jrs, srs *Requires:* good acad standing, transcript
Credit: *Undergrad:* 2 credits *Grad:* none *Doc:* transcript
Instruction: *In:* English *Format:* lecture *Students:* mainly US
Costs: $5,060 for 2 courses *incl* tuition, housing, all meals, excursions
Housing: *Arr by pgm:* residence halls
Deadline: Feb 16
Other info: *US accredited sponsor:* yes *Began:* 1994 *Orient:* avail in Sydney *Activities:* excursions, program travel *URL:* http://www.aas.duke.edu/study_abroad/
Contact: Study Abroad, Duke Univ, 121 Allen Bldg, Box 90057, Durham NC 27708-0057 *Ph:* 919-684 2174 *Fax:* 919-684 3083 *E-mail:* abroad@asdean.duke.edu

---

0136
EDUCATION AUSTRALIA
Internships in Australia
Site: Australia: Brisbane, Sydney, others
Dates: 6-16 wks, yr-round
Subjects: Animal sciences, Art history, Arts management, Australian studies, Biology, Ecology/environmental studies, Education/teaching, Field study, Forestry, Internships, Journalism, Political science/politics, Social work
Eligibility: *Level:* fresh, sophs, jrs, srs, grads, adults, precoll *Requires:* high sch diploma *Age:* min 17
Credit: *Undergrad:* none *Grad:* none
Instruction: *In:* English *Format:* directed field study, internship *Students:* mainly US
Costs: $2,455 for 6 wks *incl* housing, some meals, fees
Housing: *Arr by pgm:* homestay
Deadline: None
Other info: *US accredited sponsor:* no *Began:* 1988 *Orient:* abroad *Activities:* excursions, field trips *Misc:* May contact former participants. *URL:* http://www.javanet.com/~edaust
Contact: Dr Maurice A Howe, Educ Australia, PO Box 2233, Amherst MA 01004 *Ph:* 800-344 6741; 413-549 6741 *Fax:* 413-549 0741 *E-mail:* edaust@javanet.com

---

0137
FLINDERS UNIVERSITY
Marine Ecology of Temperate Australia
Site: Australia: Adelaide, Port Lincoln
Dates: 4 wks, Jan
Subjects: Biodiversity, Marine biology
Eligibility: *Level:* jrs, srs, grads *Requires:* 2.5 GPA, previous study in biology & sci *Age:* min 18
Credit: *Undergrad:* avail *Grad:* none *Doc:* certificate
Instruction: *In:* English *Format:* directed field study, lab, lecture, practical training, study tour *Students:* intl
Costs: $3,500 *incl* tuition, housing, all meals, insurance, fees, excursions, books/materials
Housing: *Arr by pgm:* Lincoln Marine Sci Ctr
Deadline: Oct 30
Other info: *US accredited sponsor:* no *Began:* 2000 *Orient:* abroad (1 day) *Activities:* excursions, field trips, program travel *URL:* http://www.flinders.edu.au
Contact: Sarah Mitchell, Study Abroad & Exch Off, Flinders Univ, GPO Box 2100, Adelaide SA 5001, Australia *Ph:* 800-686 3562 *E-mail:* intl.office@flinders.edu.au
Or Contact: Dr Jon Havenhand, Flinders Univ, GPO Box 2100, Adelaide SA 5001, Australia *E-mail:* jon.havenhand@flinders.edu.au

---

0138
GEORGETOWN UNIVERSITY
Georgetown in Australia-Australian Studies
Site: Australia: Alice Springs, Cairns, Darwin, Sydney *Host inst:* Univ of New South Wales
Dates: 6 wks, mid-Jun-Jul
Subjects: Australian studies, History, Literature
Eligibility: *Level:* adults
Credit: *Undergrad:* 6 *Grad:* 6 *Doc:* transcript
Instruction: *In:* English *Format:* lecture, study tour *Students:* mainly US
Costs: About $4,200 *incl* tuition, housing, some meals, fees, excursions, books/materials
Housing: *Arr by pgm:* apartments with local students
Deadline: Mid-Mar
Other info: *US accredited sponsor:* yes *Activities:* excursions, field trips, cultural events *Misc:* May contact former participants. *URL:* http://www.georgetown.edu/programs/oip/os
Contact: Rachel Rubin, Georgetown Univ, Intl Pgms, Box 571013, Washington DC 20057-1013 *Ph:* 202-687 5620 *E-mail:* rubinr@georgetown.edu

---

0139
MICHIGAN STATE UNIVERSITY
Fisheries and Wildlife
Site: Australia: various cities
Dates: Jun-Jul
Subjects: Field study, Fishing/fisheries, Natural resources, Wildlife
Eligibility: *Level:* jrs, srs, grads *Requires:* 2.0 GPA, previous study in field, letter of interest *Age:* min 18
Credit: *Undergrad:* 6 *Grad:* 6 *Doc:* transcript
Instruction: *In:* English *Format:* directed field study, lecture *Students:* mainly US
Costs: About $2,300 *incl* housing, some meals, insurance, excursions, books/materials *Nonrefundable fee*
Housing: *Arr by pgm:* hotels, campsites
Deadline: Mar 2
Other info: *US accredited sponsor:* yes *Began:* 1998 *Orient:* in US *Activities:* excursions, field trips, program travel *Misc:* May contact former participants. *Financial aid:* scholarships *URL:* http://studyabroad.msu.edu
Contact: Cheryl Benner, Study Abroad, Michigan State Univ, 109 Intl Ctr, East Lansing MI 48824 *Ph:* 517-353 8920 *Fax:* 517-432 2082 *E-mail:* bennerc@msu.edu ▲

0140
SUNY COLLEGE AT NEW PALTZ
Summer Study in Australia-Eco Tour
Site: Australia: various sites

Dates: 4 wks, Jun 22-Jul 23
Subjects: Aboriginal studies, Anthropology, Ecology/environmental studies, Education/teaching, Field study, Wildlife
Eligibility: *Level:* fresh, sophs, jrs, srs, precoll *Requires:* good acad standing *Age:* min 17
Credit: *Undergrad:* 6 per term *Grad:* none *Doc:* transcript
Instruction: *In:* English *Format:* directed field study, lecture, seminar *Students:* intl
Costs: $4,082 for NY residents, $5,336 for others *incl* tuition, housing, all meals, intl airfare, insurance, fees, excursions *Nonrefundable fee*
Housing: *Arr by pgm:* campgrounds, bunk houses
Deadline: Mar 1
Other info: *US accredited sponsor:* yes *Orient:* in US & abroad *Activities:* excursions, field trips, program travel *Financial aid:* scholarships *URL:* http://www.newpaltz.edu/oie/
Contact: Ctr for Intl Pgm, SUNY New Paltz, 75 S Manheim Blvd, New Paltz NY 12561 *Ph:* 845-257 3125 *Fax:* 845-257 3129 *E-mail:* international@newpaltz.edu ▲

0141
SUNY UNIVERSITY AT BUFFALO
Rainforests to Reefs: Environmental Management in Australia
Site: Australia: Brisbane, Cairns *Host inst:* Griffith Univ
Dates: 3 wks, Jun 10-Jul 4
Subjects: Ecology/environmental studies
Eligibility: *Level:* sophs, jrs, srs *Requires:* 3.0 GPA *Age:* min 18
Credit: *Undergrad:* 6 *Grad:* none *Doc:* transcript
Instruction: *In:* English *Format:* directed field study *Students:* mainly US
Costs: $2,125 *incl* tuition, housing, excursions, meal stipend
Housing: *Arr by pgm:* hotels
Deadline: May 1
Other info: *US accredited sponsor:* yes *Began:* 1997 *Orient:* in US & abroad (1 day) *Activities:* field trips *Misc:* Field trips to sites of current issues & conflicts. *Financial aid:* scholarships *URL:* http://www.buffalo.edu/studyabroad/
Contact: Dr Sandra J Flash, Dir, Study Abroad Pgms, Intl Educ, SUNY Univ at Buffalo, 210 Talbert Hall, Box 601604, Buffalo NY 14260-1604 *Ph:* 716-645 3912 *Fax:* 716-645 6197 *E-mail:* studyabroad@acsu.buffalo.edu

---

0142
UNIVERSITY OF DELAWARE
Winter Session in Australia
Site: Australia: Adelaide, Brisbane, Melbourne, Sydney, other sites
Dates: 1 mo, Jan
Subjects: Economics, Finance
Eligibility: *Level:* fresh, sophs, jrs, srs *Requires:* 2.0 GPA
Credit: *Undergrad:* 6 *Grad:* none *Doc:* transcript
Instruction: *In:* English *Format:* lecture, seminar, study tour *Students:* mainly US
Costs: Contact sponsor
Housing: *Arr by pgm:* residence halls
Deadline: Early Oct
Other info: *US accredited sponsor:* yes *Began:* 2000 *Orient:* avail yes *Activities:* excursions, field trips, cultural events *Misc:* Contact sponsor to arrange honors credit. *Financial aid:* scholarships *URL:* http://www.udel.edu/studyabroad/
Contact: Intl Pgms & Special Sessions, Univ of Delaware, 4 Kent Way, Newark DE 19716-1450 *Ph:* 888-831 4685; 302-831 2852 *Fax:* 302-831 6042 *E-mail:* studyabroad@udel.edu

---

0143
UNIVERSITY OF PITTSBURGH and **UNIVERSITY OF NEW SOUTH WALES**
Energy Today and Energy Tomorrow
Site: Australia: Cairns, Darwin, Sydney
Dates: 12 wks, May-early Aug
Subjects: Conservation, Desert studies, Ecology/environmental studies, Energy sciences, Engineering, Natural resource management, Natural resources, Water management
Eligibility: *Level:* sophs, jrs, srs *Requires:* 2.75 GPA, previous study in field *Age:* avg 21
Credit: *Undergrad:* 12 *Grad:* none *Doc:* transcript
Instruction: *In:* English *Format:* directed field study, lecture *Students:* mainly US
Costs: About $2,000 for Energy Today, $3,500 for Energy Tomorrow *incl* tuition, housing, some meals, fees, excursions *Nonrefundable fee*
Housing: *Arr by pgm:* residence halls, apartments, hotels
Deadline: Jan-Mar 30; rolling admissions;
Other info: *US accredited sponsor:* yes *Orient:* in US & abroad *Activities:* excursions, field trips *Misc:* Students who complete both pgms receive a Certificate in Energy Resource Utilization. May contact former participants. *Financial aid:* scholarships *URL:* http://www.pitt.edu/~stdyabrd/
Contact: Erin Sunday, Study Abroad Adviser, Univ of Pittsburgh, B80G Benedum Hall, Pittsburgh PA 15261 *Ph:* 412-624 5942 *Fax:* 412-624 2827 *E-mail:* abroad@engrng.pitt.edu

---

0144
WILLING WORKERS ON ORGANIC FARMS (WWOOF) AUSTRALIA
WWOOF
Site: Australia: various sites
Dates: 2 days or longer, yr-round
Subjects: Agriculture, Community service projects, Farm management, Homestay
Eligibility: *Level:* adults *Age:* min 18
Credit: *Undergrad:* none *Grad:* none
Instruction: *In:* English *Format:* volunteer/svc *Students:* intl
Costs: AUS $45 for 1, AUS $50 for 2, per yr *incl* insurance, placement list
Housing: *Arr by student:* homestay
Deadline: None
Other info: *US accredited sponsor:* no *Activities:* excursions, field trips, cultural events *Misc:* Volunteers work 3-6 hrs a day in exch for rm & board. *URL:* http://www.wwoof.com.au
Contact: Garry Ainsworth, WWOOF, Buchan, Vic 3885, Australia *E-mail:* wwoof@net-tech.com.au

---

BRISBANE

0145
SUNY COLLEGE AT OSWEGO
Adventure Australia
Site: Australia: Brisbane *Host inst:* Univ of Queensland
Dates: 6 wks, late Jun-early Aug
Subjects: Art, Earth sciences, Political science/politics, Sociology
Eligibility: *Level:* fresh, sophs, jrs, srs *Requires:* 2.5 GPA
Credit: *Undergrad:* 6 *Grad:* none *Doc:* transcript
Instruction: *In:* English *Format:* lecture, seminar, tutorial *Students:* mainly US
Costs: $4,500 *incl* tuition, housing, all meals, intl airfare, insurance, fees, excursions, books/materials *Nonrefundable fee*
Housing: *Arr by pgm:* residence halls
Deadline: Mar 15
Other info: *US accredited sponsor:* yes *Began:* 1998 *Orient:* abroad *Activities:* excursions, field trips, program travel *URL:* http://www.oswego.edu/~intled
Contact: Susan Ansara, Dir, Intl Educ, SUNY Coll at Oswego, 102 Rich Hall, Oswego NY 13126 *Ph:* 888-467 9346; 315-341 2118 *Fax:* 315-341 2477 *E-mail:* intled@oswego.edu

---

0146
SUNY COLLEGE AT OSWEGO
Winter Down Under
Site: Australia: Brisbane *Host inst:* Univ of Queensland
Dates: 3 wks, late Dec-mid-Jan

Subjects: Business/management, Sociology
Eligibility: *Level:* sophs, jrs, srs *Requires:* 2.5 GPA
Credit: *Undergrad:* 3 *Grad:* none
Instruction: *In:* English *Format:* lecture, seminar, study tour *Students:* mainly US
Costs: $3,900 *incl* tuition, housing, all meals, intl airfare, insurance, fees, excursions, books/materials *Nonrefundable fee*
Housing: *Arr by pgm:* residence halls with local students
Deadline: Oct 15
Other info: *US accredited sponsor:* yes *Began:* 1998 *Orient:* abroad *Activities:* excursions, field trips *URL:* http://www.oswego.edu/~intled
Contact: Susan Ansara, Dir, Intl Educ, SUNY Coll at Oswego, 102 Rich Hall, Oswego NY 13126 *Ph:* 888-467 9346; 315-341 2118 *Fax:* 315-341 2477 *E-mail:* intled@oswego.edu

---

CANBERRA

0147
AUSTRALIAN INTERNATIONAL HOTEL SCHOOL (AIHS)
Summer in Australia
Site: Australia: Canberra
Dates: May 28-Aug 24
Subjects: Hospitality management, Hotel management, Tourism
Eligibility: *Level:* sophs, jrs, srs *Requires:* 2.5 GPA
Credit: *Undergrad:* 12-15 *Grad:* none *Doc:* transcript
Instruction: *In:* English *Format:* internship, seminar, study tour *Students:* intl
Costs: $8,500 *incl* tuition, housing, all meals, excursions, orient *Nonrefundable fee*
Housing: *Arr by pgm:* residence halls with local students
Deadline: Mar 1
Other info: *US accredited sponsor:* no *Began:* 1996 *In coop with:* Cornell Univ Hotel Sch *Orient:* abroad *Activities:* excursions, field trips, cultural events, sports *Misc:* May contact former participants. *Financial aid:* work study *URL:* http://hotelschool.cornell.edu/AIHS/
Contact: Prof Richard Penner, AIHS, 182 Statler Hall, Ithaca NY 14853 *Ph:* 800-235 8220; 607-255 1842 *Fax:* 607-255 4179 *E-mail:* aihs@cornell.edu

---

FREMANTLE

0148
COUNCIL ON INTERNATIONAL EDUCATIONAL EXCHANGE (COUNCIL)
University of Notre Dame Australia
Site: Australia: Fremantle *Host inst:* Univ of Notre Dame Australia
Dates: Jun 17-Aug 8
Subjects: Full curriculum, Homestay
Eligibility: *Level:* jrs, srs *Requires:* 2.75 GPA *Age:* min 18
Credit: *Undergrad:* avail *Grad:* none *Doc:* transcript
Instruction: *In:* English *Format:* lecture, seminar, tutorial *Students:* mainly host country
Costs: $3,850 *incl* tuition, insurance, ISIC *Nonrefundable fee*
Housing: *Arr by pgm:* residence halls with local students, apartments, homestay
Deadline: Feb 15
Other info: *US accredited sponsor:* no *Began:* 1998 *Orient:* abroad *Misc:* May contact former participants. *Financial aid:* scholarships *URL:* http://www.ciee.org/study
Contact: Laura Gunlogson, Pgm Adviser, Australia/New Zealand, Council-ISP, 633 3rd Ave, 20th Fl, New York NY 10017-6706 *Ph:* 800-407 8839; 212-822 2669 *Fax:* 212-822 2779 *E-mail:* studyinfo@ciee.org ▲

GOLD COAST

0149
AUSTRALIAN EDUCATION CONNECTION
Study Abroad in Australia
Site: Australia: Gold Coast *Host inst:* Bond Univ
Dates: May-Aug
Subjects: Asian studies, Australian studies, Business/management, Communications, Engineering, Film studies, Finance, International relations, Television/video, Tourism
Eligibility: *Level:* sophs, jrs, srs, grads *Requires:* 3.0 GPA *Age:* min 18
Credit: *Undergrad:* 12-16 per sem *Grad:* 12-16 per sem *Doc:* transcript
Instruction: *In:* English *Format:* directed field study, independent study, internship, lecture, practical training, tutorial *Students:* mainly host country
Costs: About $4,200 per sem *incl* tuition, insurance, ISIC, phone card
Housing: *Sponsor assists:* apartments with local students, residence halls with local students, residence halls, apartments, homestay
Deadline: 3 mos before pgm
Other info: *US accredited sponsor:* no *Orient:* abroad *Activities:* excursions, field trips, cultural events *Misc:* Backpacker discount card. May contact former participants. *Financial aid:* work study *URL:* http://www.studyabroad.com/australia
Contact: Alda Nimmo, Australian Educ Connection, 5722 S Flamingo Rd, Ste 303, Ft Lauderdale FL 33330 *Ph:* 800-565 9553; 954-680 0453 *Fax:* 954-680 0597 *E-mail:* auststudy@aol.com

---

0150
CENTER FOR INTERNATIONAL STUDIES (CIS)
CIS-Bond University
Site: Australia: Gold Coast *Host inst:* Bond Univ
Dates: 3-12 wks, May-Aug
Subjects: Business/management, Communications, Computer sciences, Film studies, Hospitality management, Humanities, Information technology, International studies, Journalism, Languages (beg/int/adv), Law, Psychology, Television/video
Eligibility: *Level:* sophs, jrs, srs, grads *Requires:* 2.5 GPA *Age:* min 18
Credit: *Undergrad:* 14 per sem *Grad:* 9 per sem *Doc:* transcript
Instruction: *In:* English *Format:* lang study, lecture *Students:* intl
Costs: $8,750 per sem *incl* tuition, housing, some meals, insurance, fees, excursions
Housing: *Arr by pgm:* residence halls
Deadline: Mar 1
Other info: *US accredited sponsor:* no *Began:* 2000 *Orient:* abroad *Activities:* excursions, cultural events, sports *URL:* http://www.studyabroad-cis.com
Contact: Jeff Palm, CIS, PO Box 247, Boston MA 02133 *Ph:* 877-617 9090; 617-227 2307 *Fax:* 617-227 2398 *E-mail:* inof@studyabroad-cis.com

---

0151
COLLEGE CONSORTIUM FOR INTERNATIONAL STUDIES and **TRUMAN STATE UNIVERSITY** and **SAINT BONAVENTURE UNIVERSITY**
Summer Program in Australia
Site: Australia: Gold Coast *Host inst:* Bond Univ
Dates: May 16-Aug 22
Subjects: Accounting, Asian studies, Business/management, Communications, Computer sciences, European studies, Finance, International relations, Journalism, Languages, Law, Marketing, Pacific area studies, Philosophy, Psychology
Eligibility: *Level:* sophs, jrs, srs, adults *Requires:* 2.9 GPA *Age:* min 18, avg 20
Credit: *Undergrad:* 12-16 *Grad:* none *Doc:* transcript

See "How To Use This Book" for definitions of terms used above. ▲ = See program sponsor's ad(s) in this book.

Instruction: *In:* English *Format:* lecture, seminar, tutorial *Students:* intl & host country
Costs: $5,250 *incl* tuition, housing, some meals, fees, excursions *Nonrefundable fee*
Housing: *Arr by pgm:* residence halls with local students
Deadline: Mar 1
Other info: *US accredited sponsor:* yes *Began:* 1996 *Orient:* abroad (1 wk) *Misc:* May contact former participants. *URL:* http://www.ccisabroad.org
Contact: *See Index II for Members* CCIS, 2000 P St NW, Ste 503, Washington DC 20036 *Ph:* 800-453 6956; 202-223 0330 *Fax:* 202-223 0999 *E-mail:* info@ccisabroad.org
Or Contact: Ctr for Intl Educ Abroad, Truman State Univ, Kirk Bldg 120, Kirksville MO 63501 *Ph:* 660-785 4076 *Fax:* 660-785 7473 *E-mail:* ciea@truman.edu
Or Contact: Study Abroad Pgms, St Bonaventure Univ, St Bonaventure NY 14778 *Ph:* 716-375 2574 *Fax:* 716-375 2381 *E-mail:* asayegh@sbu.edu ▲

0152
COUNCIL ON INTERNATIONAL EDUCATIONAL EXCHANGE (COUNCIL)
Bond University
Site: Australia: Gold Coast *Host inst:* Bond Univ
Dates: May 8-Aug 21
Subjects: Full curriculum
Eligibility: *Level:* jrs, srs *Requires:* 2.5 GPA *Age:* min 18
Credit: *Undergrad:* avail *Grad:* none *Doc:* transcript
Instruction: *In:* English *Format:* lecture, seminar, tutorial *Students:* mainly host country
Costs: $5,830 *incl* tuition, insurance, ISIC
Housing: *Arr by pgm:* residence halls with local students
Deadline: Mar 1
Other info: *US accredited sponsor:* no *Began:* 1998 *Orient:* abroad *Misc:* May contact former participants. *URL:* http://www.ciee.org/study
Contact: Laura Gunlogson, Pgm Adviser, Australia/New Zealand, Council-ISP, 633 3rd Ave, 20th Fl, New York NY 10017-6706 *Ph:* 800-407 8839; 212-822 2669 *Fax:* 212-822 2779 *E-mail:* studyinfo@ciee.org ▲

QUEENSLAND

0153
LIVING ROUTES-ECOVILLAGE EDUCATION CONSORTIUM
Crystal Waters Permaculture Practicum
Site: Australia: Queensland *Host inst:* Crystal Waters Permaculture comm
Dates: 3-1/2 wks, Jan 3-27
Subjects: Anthropology, Ecology/environmental studies, Natural sciences, Sustainable development
Eligibility: *Level:* fresh, sophs, jrs, srs, grads, adults, teachers, professionals *Requires:* 2.5 GPA *Age:* min 18, max 80, avg 21
Credit: *Undergrad:* 4 *Grad:* none *Doc:* transcript *Transfer credit through:* Pacific Lutheran Univ

Instruction: *In:* English *Format:* directed field study, independent study, internship, lecture, practical training, seminar, study tour, volunteer/svc, workshop *Students:* mainly US
Costs: $3,200 per mo *incl* tuition, housing, all meals, fees, excursions *Nonrefundable fee*
Housing: *Arr by pgm:* comm guest houses
Deadline: Rolling admissions
Other info: *US accredited sponsor:* no *Began:* 1997 *Misc:* Students complete a Permaculture Certification Pgm & visit Fraser Island, the world's largest sand island. May contact former participants. *Financial aid:* scholarships *URL:* http://www.livingroutes.org
Contact: Daniel Greenberg, Exec Dir, Living Routes, 72 Baker Rd, Shutesbury MA 01072 *Ph:* 888-515 7333; 413-259 0025 *Fax:* 413-259 1299 *E-mail:* info@livingroutes.org

SCRUB HILL

0154
AMIZADE
Australia Aboriginal Volunteer Project
Site: Australia: Scrub Hill
Dates: 1-4 wks, yr-round
Subjects: Community service projects
Eligibility: *Level:* adults *Age:* min 18
Credit: *Undergrad:* none *Grad:* none
Instruction: *In:* English *Format:* volunteer/svc *Students:* intl
Costs: $3,200 for 3 wks *incl* tuition, housing, all meals, intl airfare, fees, excursions
Housing: *Arr by pgm:* residence halls
Deadline: Contact sponsor
Other info: *US accredited sponsor:* no *Began:* 1999 *Orient:* abroad (1 day) *Activities:* excursions, field trips, program travel, cultural events, sports *Misc:* May contact former participants. *URL:* http://amizade.org/Australia.htm
Contact: Mike Sandy, Ex Dir, Amizade Ltd, 367 S Graham St, Pittsburgh PA 15232 *Ph:* 888-973 4443 *Fax:* 412-648 1492 *E-mail:* volunteer@amizade.org

SYDNEY

0155
BEAVER COLLEGE, CENTER FOR EDUCATION ABROAD
Australian Environment
Site: Australia: Sydney *Host inst:* Univ of New South Wales
Dates: 6 wks, mid-Jun-early Aug
Subjects: Australian studies, Ecology/environmental studies
Eligibility: *Level:* fresh, sophs, jrs, srs, grads *Requires:* 3.0 GPA
Credit: *Undergrad:* 6 *Grad:* none *Doc:* transcript
Instruction: *In:* English *Format:* directed field study, lecture, seminar, study tour *Students:* mainly US
Costs: $4,390 *incl* tuition, housing, some meals, insurance, excursions, ISIC, transcript, orient *Nonrefundable fee*
Housing: *Arr by pgm:* residence halls, hostels
Deadline: Apr 15
Other info: *US accredited sponsor:* yes *Began:* 1995 *Orient:* avail in Darwin (2 days) *Activities:* field trips, program travel, cultural events *Misc:* May contact former

participants. *URL:* http://www.arcadia.edu/cea/
Contact: Ctr for Educ Abroad, Beaver Coll, 450 S Easton Rd, Glenside PA 19038 *Ph:* 888-232 8379 *E-mail:* cea@beaver.edu ▲

0156
BOSTON UNIVERSITY
Sydney Internship Program
Site: Australia: Sydney
Dates: 14 wks, May-Aug
Subjects: Civilization/culture, Film studies, Internships, Media studies, Political science/politics
Eligibility: *Level:* sophs, jrs, srs *Requires:* 3.0 GPA, in major, good acad standing
Credit: *Undergrad:* 16 *Grad:* none *Doc:* transcript
Instruction: *In:* English *Format:* internship, lecture, seminar *Students:* mainly US
Costs: $10,100 *incl* tuition, housing
Housing: *Arr by pgm:* residence halls
Deadline: Mar 1; Apr 1 for scholarships
Other info: *US accredited sponsor:* yes *Began:* 1992 *Orient:* in US & abroad *Activities:* field trips *Misc:* Full-time resident dir. May contact former participants. *Financial aid:* scholarships *URL:* http://www.bu.edu/abroad/
Contact: Intl Pgms, Boston Univ, 232 Bay State Rd, Boston MA 02215 *Ph:* 617-353 9888 *Fax:* 617-353 5402 *E-mail:* abroad@bu.edu ▲

0157
MICHIGAN STATE UNIVERSITY
Its Media, Environment and Culture
Site: Australia: Sydney
Dates: 6 wks, Jun-Jul
Subjects: Field study, Journalism, Natural resources
Eligibility: *Level:* jrs, srs, grads *Requires:* 2.5 GPA *Age:* min 18
Credit: *Undergrad:* avail *Grad:* avail *Doc:* transcript
Instruction: *In:* English *Format:* directed field study *Students:* mainly US
Costs: About $3,200 *incl* housing, some meals, insurance, fees, excursions *Nonrefundable fee*
Housing: *Arr by pgm:* residence halls
Deadline: Mar 2
Other info: *US accredited sponsor:* yes *Began:* 1999 *Orient:* in US (1 day) *Activities:* excursions, field trips, program travel, cultural events *URL:* http://studyabroad.msu.edu
Contact: Cheryl Benner, Study Abroad, Michigan State Univ, 109 Intl Ctr, East Lansing MI 48824-1035 *Ph:* 517-353 8920 *Fax:* 517-432 2082 *E-mail:* bennerc@msu.edu ▲

0158
SYRACUSE UNIVERSITY
Exploring Australia: The Land and the People
Site: Australia: Sydney
Dates: 4 wks, Jun 9-Jul 4
Subjects: Civilization/culture, Ecology/environmental studies
Eligibility: *Level:* sophs, jrs, srs, grads, adults, teachers, professionals *Requires:* 2.5 GPA
Credit: *Undergrad:* 6 *Grad:* 6 *Doc:* transcript
Instruction: *In:* English *Format:* seminar, study tour *Students:* mainly US
Costs: $7,000 *incl* tuition, housing, some

meals, fees, excursions, books/materials *Nonrefundable fee*
Housing: *Arr by pgm:* residence halls, hotels
Deadline: Mar 15
Other info: *US accredited sponsor:* yes *Began:* 1997 *Orient:* abroad *Activities:* excursions, field trips, program travel, cultural events *Misc:* May contact former participants. *Financial aid:* scholarships *URL:* http://sumweb.syr.edu/dipa/summer
Contact: Daisy Fried, Assoc Dir, Syracuse Univ, 119 Euclid Ave, Syracuse NY 13244 *Ph:* 800-251 9674; 315-443 9419 *Fax:* 315-443 4593 *E-mail:* dsfried@summon3.syr.edu ▲

TOWNSVILLE

0159
BEAVER COLLEGE, CENTER FOR EDUCATION ABROAD
Indigenous Identities/Indigenous Writers
Site: Australia: Townsville *Host inst:* James Cook Univ
Dates: 4 wks, Jul
Subjects: Australian studies, Literature
Eligibility: *Level:* fresh, sophs, jrs, srs, grads *Requires:* 3.0 GPA
Credit: *Undergrad:* 4 *Grad:* none *Doc:* transcript
Instruction: *In:* English *Format:* directed field study, lecture, seminar *Students:* mainly US
Costs: $2,675 *incl* tuition, housing, some meals, insurance, excursions, ISIC, orient, transcript *Nonrefundable fee*
Housing: *Arr by pgm:* residence halls, Cabins or tents during field excursions
Deadline: Apr 15
Other info: *US accredited sponsor:* yes *Began:* 1999 *Orient:* abroad (2 days) *Misc:* Incl travel to tropical rainforest in far north of Australia to meet the Jirrbal peoples of the Davidson River area. May contact former participants. *URL:* http://www.arcadia.edu/cea
Contact: Ctr for Educ Abroad, Beaver Coll, 450 S Easton Rd, Glenside PA 19038 *Ph:* 888-232 8379 *E-mail:* cea@beaver.edu ▲

0160
BEAVER COLLEGE, CENTER FOR EDUCATION ABROAD
Tropical Ecosystems
Site: Australia: Townsville *Host inst:* James Cook Univ
Dates: 4 wks, late Jun-late Jul
Subjects: Ecology/environmental studies, Marine biology
Eligibility: *Level:* sophs, jrs, srs, grads *Requires:* 3.0 GPA
Credit: *Undergrad:* 4 *Grad:* none *Doc:* transcript
Instruction: *In:* English *Format:* directed field study, lecture *Students:* mainly US
Costs: $2,995 *incl* tuition, housing, some meals, insurance, excursions, ISIC, orient, transcript *Nonrefundable fee*
Housing: *Arr by pgm:* residence halls, Cabins or tents during field excursions
Deadline: Apr 15
Other info: *US accredited sponsor:* yes *Began:* 1999 *Orient:* avail in Townsville (2 days) *Activities:* excursions, field trips *Misc:* May contact former participants. *URL:* http://www.arcadia.edu/cea
Contact: Ctr for Educ Abroad, Beaver Coll, 450 S Easton Rd, Glenside PA 19038 *Ph:* 888-232 8379 *E-mail:* cea@beaver.edu ▲

0161
JAMES COOK UNIVERSITY
Geology Field Training
Site: Australia: Townsville
Dates: 4 wks, Jun 29-Jul 26
Subjects: Field study, Geology
Eligibility: *Level:* sophs, jrs, srs *Requires:* previous study in field
Credit: *Undergrad:* avail *Grad:* avail *Doc:* transcript
Instruction: *In:* English *Format:* directed field study, independent study, practical training, seminar *Students:* mainly host country
Costs: AUS $3,600 *incl* tuition, housing, all meals, excursions *Nonrefundable fee*
Housing: *Arr by pgm:* residence halls with local students, field stations with local students
Deadline: Mid-Apr
Other info: *US accredited sponsor:* no *Began:* 1999 *Orient:* abroad *URL:* http://www.oia.jcu.edu.au
Contact: Peter Robertson, Intl Affairs, James Cook Univ, Townsville, QLD 4811, Australia *E-mail:* peter.robertson@jcu.edu.au

0162
JAMES COOK UNIVERSITY
Narratives of Australia
Site: Australia: Townsville
Dates: 4 wks, Jul 5-30
Subjects: Australian studies, Literature
Eligibility: *Level:* sophs, jrs, srs *Requires:* previous study in field
Credit: *Undergrad:* avail *Grad:* avail *Doc:* transcript
Instruction: *In:* English *Format:* independent study, seminar, workshop *Students:* intl
Costs: AUS $3,600 *incl* tuition, housing, all meals, excursions
Housing: *Arr by pgm:* residence halls with local students
Deadline: Mid-Apr
Other info: *US accredited sponsor:* no *Began:* 1999 *Orient:* abroad (1 day) *Activities:* excursions *URL:* http://www.oia.jcu.edu.au
Contact: Peter Robertson, Undergrad Pgms, Intl Affairs, James Cook Univ, Townsville, QLD 4811, Australia *E-mail:* peter.robertson@jcu.edu.au

0163
JAMES COOK UNIVERSITY
Tropical Ecosystems
Site: Australia: Townsville
Dates: 4 wks, Jul 5-30
Subjects: Ecology/environmental studies, Field study, Independent study
Eligibility: *Level:* sophs, jrs, srs
Credit: *Undergrad:* avail *Grad:* avail *Doc:* transcript
Instruction: *In:* English *Format:* directed field study, independent study, lab, practical training, seminar, tutorial *Students:* intl
Costs: AUS $3,600 *incl* tuition, housing, all meals
Housing: *Arr by pgm:* residence halls with local students, field stations
Deadline: Mid-Apr
Other info: *US accredited sponsor:* no *Began:* 1999 *Orient:* abroad (1 day) *Activities:* excursions *URL:* http://www.oia.jcu.edu.au
Contact: Peter Robertson, Intl Affairs, James Cook Univ, Townsville QLD 4811, Australia *E-mail:* peter.robertson@jcu.edu.au

YUNGABURRA

0164
SCHOOL FOR FIELD STUDIES
SFS Australia: Tropical Reforestation
Site: Australia: Yungaburra
Dates: 1 mo, mid-Jun-mid-Jul or mid-Jul-mid-Aug
Subjects: Anthropology, Australian studies, Biology, Botany, Conservation, Ecology/environmental studies, Field study, Forestry, Natural resource management, Natural resources
Eligibility: *Level:* fresh, sophs, jrs, srs, precoll *Age:* min 16, avg 20
Credit: *Undergrad:* avail *Grad:* none *Doc:* transcript *Transfer credit through:* Boston Univ
Instruction: *In:* English *Format:* directed field study, lecture, practical training *Students:* mainly US
Costs: $3,475 *incl* tuition, housing, all meals, excursions *Nonrefundable fee*
Housing: *Arr by pgm:* campsites, rustic cabins
Deadline: Rolling admissions

Other info: *US accredited sponsor:* no *Began:* 1980 *Orient:* abroad *Activities:* excursions, field trips, program travel, cultural events, sports *Misc:* Loans avail. May contact former participants. *Financial aid:* scholarships *URL:* http://www.fieldstudies.org
Contact: Admissions Off, Sch for Field Studies, 16 Broadway, Beverly MA 01915-4499 *Ph:* 800-989 4435; 978-927 7777 *Fax:* 978-927 5127 *E-mail:* admissions@fieldstudies.org

Bangladesh

DHAKA

0165
HIGHER EDUCATION CONSORTIUM FOR URBAN AFFAIRS
Development and Community in Bangladesh
Site: Bangladesh: Dhaka (Comilla District) *Host inst:* Independent Univ
Dates: 1 mo, Jan 2-28
Subjects: Anthropology, Asian studies, Development studies, Ecology/environmental studies, Economics, International organizations, International studies, Justice, Peace studies, Political science/politics, Rural development, Social policy, Social welfare/services, Sociology, Women's studies
Eligibility: *Level:* sophs, jrs, srs
Credit: *Undergrad:* 4 *Grad:* none *Doc:* transcript *Transfer credit through:* Hamline Univ
Instruction: *In:* English *Format:* directed field study, lecture, seminar *Students:* US & host country
Costs: $3,400 *incl* tuition, housing, all meals, intl airfare, excursions *Nonrefundable fee*
Housing: *Arr by pgm:* hotels, hostels
Deadline: Oct 4
Other info: *US accredited sponsor:* yes *Began:* 2000 *Orient:* in US & abroad *Activities:* excursions, field trips, program travel, cultural events *Misc:* Village field study. *URL:* http://www.hecua.org
Contact: *See Index II for Members* Rebecca Rassier, Dir, Campus Relations & Student Svcs, HECUA, Mail #36 at Hamline Univ, 1536 Hewitt Ave, St Paul MN 55104-8831 *Ph:* 800-554 1089; 651-646 8831 *E-mail:* info@hecua.org

China

MORE THAN ONE CITY

0166
BEMIDJI STATE UNIVERSITY
Sinosummer Program
Site: China: Beijing, Guangzhou, Guilin, Hong Kong, Shenyang, Xi'an *Host inst:* Liaoning Univ
Dates: Early Jun-early Jul
Subjects: Agriculture, Arts, Chinese studies, Civilization/culture, Economics, Education/teaching, Field study, Government, History, Independent study, Industry, Sociology
Eligibility: Enroll for minimum 12 undergrad credits *Level:* fresh, sophs, jrs, srs, grads *Requires:* 2.0 GPA, application, recommendation letters *Age:* min 18, avg 35
Credit: *Undergrad:* 12 *Grad:* 9 *Doc:* transcript
Instruction: *In:* Chinese, English *Format:* directed field study, independent study, lecture, study tour *Students:* mainly US
Costs: About $5,772 for MN residents, $7,438 for others *incl* tuition, housing, all meals, intl airfare, fees, excursions, books/materials *Nonrefundable fee*
Housing: *Arr by pgm:* residence halls, hotels
Deadline: Jan 1
Other info: *US accredited sponsor:* yes *Began:* 1989 *Orient:* in US & abroad *Activities:* excursions, field trips, program travel, cultural events, sports *Misc:* Visits to Chinese villages, supper with Chinese families, significant interaction with Chinese students.
Contact: Mrs Jan Weiskopf-Smith, Dir, Intl Svcs, Bemidji State Univ, 1500 Birchmont Dr NE, Bemidji MN 56601 *Ph:* 218-755 3829 *Fax:* 218-755 2074 *E-mail:* jweiskopf@vax1.bemidji.msus.edu
Or Contact: Dr Peter Smith, Acad Dir, Intl Studies Pgm, Bemidji State Univ, Hagg Sauer Hall, 1500 Birchmont Dr NE, Bemidji MN 56601 *Ph:* 218-755 2946 *Fax:* 218-755 4048 *E-mail:* petesmith@vax1.bemidji.msus.edu

---

0167
COUNCIL ON INTERNATIONAL EDUCATIONAL EXCHANGE (COUNCIL)
International Faculty Development Seminars-China
Site: China: Beijing, Shanghai, Xi'an *Host inst:* China Northwestern Univ, Peking Univ
Dates: 11 days, Jun
Subjects: Contemporary issues, History
Eligibility: *Level:* teachers, professionals *Requires:* must be faculty at 2-yr or 4-yr inst
Credit: *Undergrad:* none *Grad:* none
Instruction: *In:* English *Format:* lecture, seminar *Students:* mainly US
Costs: $1,995 *incl* tuition, housing, some meals, excursions, books/materials, receptions *Nonrefundable fee*
Housing: *Arr by pgm:* univ guest houses
Deadline: Mar 15
Other info: *US accredited sponsor:* no *Began:* 1996 *Orient:* abroad *Activities:* excursions, field trips, program travel, cultural events *Misc:* Seminar title: The Historic Cities of China. *URL:* http://www.ciee.org/ifds
Contact: Jennifer Ley, Pgm Mgr, Council, 633 3rd Ave, New York NY 10017 *Ph:* 800-407 8839; 212-822 2747 *Fax:* 212-822 2779 *E-mail:* ifds@ciee.org ▲

0168
EASTERN MICHIGAN UNIVERSITY
China Cultural History Tour
Site: China: Beijing, Luoyang, Nanjing, Shanghai, Xi'an, Zhengzhou
Dates: 1 mo, Jun 1-Jul 1
Subjects: History, Literature, Political science/politics
Eligibility: *Level:* fresh, sophs, jrs, srs *Requires:* 2.0 GPA, 2 faculty references *Age:* min 18
Credit: *Undergrad:* 6 *Grad:* none *Doc:* transcript
Instruction: *In:* English *Format:* lecture, seminar, study tour *Students:* mainly US
Costs: $2,990 *incl* tuition, housing, some meals, insurance, fees, excursions
Housing: *Arr by pgm:* residence halls, pensions, hotels, hostels
Deadline: None; apply early
Other info: *US accredited sponsor:* yes *Began:* 2000 *Orient:* abroad (2 days) *Activities:* excursions, field trips, program travel, cultural events *Misc:* May contact former participants. *URL:* http://www.emich.edu/abroad
Contact: Acad Pgms Abroad, Eastern Michigan Univ, 212 Bus & Finance, Ypsilanti MI 48197 *Ph:* 800-777 3541; 734 487 2424 *Fax:* 734-487 4377 *E-mail:* programs.abroad@emich.edu

---

0169
FUDAN MUSEUM FOUNDATION and **XI'AN JIAOTONG UNIVERSITY** and **SINO-AMERICAN FIELD SCHOOL OF ARCHAEOLOGY (SAFSA)**
Archaeological Practicum in Xi'an, China
Site: China: Beijing, Shanghai, Xi'an *Host inst:* Xi'an Jiaotong Univ, Archaeological Insts of Shaanxi Province
Dates: 4 wks, early Jul-early Aug

Subjects: Archaeology, Art, Chinese studies, Civilization/culture, History
Eligibility: *Level:* fresh, sophs, jrs, srs, grads, adults, teachers, professionals, precoll *Age:* min 17, max 65, avg 30
Credit: *Undergrad:* 3 or 6 *Grad:* 3 or 6 *Doc:* transcript, certificate
Instruction: *In:* English *Format:* directed field study, lecture, practical training, study tour
Costs: $3,795 *incl* tuition, housing, all meals, intl airfare, fees, excursions *Nonrefundable fee*
Housing: *Arr by pgm:* hotels, univ foreign guest house
Deadline: Until pgm filled
Other info: *US accredited sponsor:* no *Began:* 1991 *In coop with:* Xian Jiaotong Univ *Orient:* abroad *Activities:* excursions, field trips, program travel, cultural events *Misc:* 1st Chinese-Amer archaeological field sch in China. Excavation. SAFSA accredited by Society-Professional Archaeologists. May contact former participants. *Financial aid:* scholarships
Contact: Prof Alfonz Lengyel, Fudan Museum Fdn, 4206 73rd Terrace East, Sarasota FL 34243 *Ph:* 941-351 8208 *Fax:* 941-351 8208 *E-mail:* fmfsafsa@juno.com

---

0170
GEORGE MASON UNIVERSITY
History and Culture
Site: China: Beijing, Hong Kong, Shanghai
Dates: 2 wks, summer
Subjects: Geography, Government
Eligibility: *Level:* fresh, sophs, jrs, srs, grads, adults, teachers, professionals *Requires:* 2.25 GPA
Credit: *Undergrad:* 3 *Grad:* 3 *Doc:* transcript
Instruction: *In:* English *Format:* directed field study, lecture, seminar, study tour *Students:* mainly US
Costs: About $3,389 for VA residents, $3,989 for others *incl* tuition, housing, most meals, intl airfare, fees, excursions, ISIC, travel insurance *Nonrefundable fee*
Housing: *Arr by pgm:* hotels
Deadline: Apr 15
Other info: *US accredited sponsor:* yes *Began:* 1995 *Orient:* in US *Activities:* excursions, field trips, program travel, cultural events *Misc:* May contact former participants. *Financial aid:* scholarships, work study *URL:* http://www.gmu.edu/departments/cge
Contact: Ctr for Global Educ, George Mason Univ, Johnson Ctr, Rm 235, 4400 University Dr, Fairfax VA 22030-4444 *Ph:* 703-993 2154 *Fax:* 703-993 2153 *E-mail:* cge@gmu.edu

---

0171
GEORGE WASHINGTON UNIVERSITY
Business Environment in China
Site: China: Beijing, Shanghai, others
Dates: 4 wks, summer
Subjects: Business/management, Economics, Finance, International business
Eligibility: *Level:* grads *Age:* min 20
Credit: *Undergrad:* none *Grad:* 6 *Doc:* transcript
Instruction: *In:* English *Format:* directed field study, lecture *Students:* US & intl
Costs: $4,005 *incl* tuition, housing, excursions
Housing: *Arr by pgm:* hotels
Deadline: Contact sponsor
Other info: *US accredited sponsor:* yes *Began:* 1997 *Orient:* in US (2 days) *Activities:* excursions, field trips, program travel, cultural events *Misc:* First 2 wks in US. *URL:* http://www.gwu.edu/~specprog/
Contact: Summer, Special & Intl Pgms, George Washington Univ, 609 22nd St NW, Washington DC 20052 *Ph:* 202-994 6360 *Fax:* 202-994 9133 *E-mail:* sumprogs@gwu.edu

---

0172
IES, INSTITUTE FOR THE INTERNATIONAL EDUCATION OF STUDENTS
IES Beijing Summer Intensive Language Program
Site: China: Beijing, Chengde *Host inst:* Beijing Foreign Studies Univ (Beiwai)
Dates: 7 wks, May 26-Jul 7
Subjects: Chinese language (beg), Community service projects
Eligibility: *Level:* fresh, sophs, jrs, srs, grads, adults *Requires:* good acad standing *Age:* min 18, avg 20
Credit: *Undergrad:* 6 *Grad:* none *Doc:* transcript
Instruction: *In:* Chinese *Format:* lang study, tutorial *Students:* mainly US
Costs: $2,850 *incl* tuition, housing, health insurance *Nonrefundable fee*
Housing: *Arr by pgm:* residence halls
Deadline: Mar 15
Other info: *US accredited sponsor:* yes *Began:* 1993 *Orient:* abroad *Activities:* excursions *Misc:* $500 reduction for students continuing with IES Beijing in fall. Student support svcs. May contact former participants. *Financial aid:* scholarships *URL:* http://www.IESabroad.org
Contact: *See Index II for Members* IES, 33 N LaSalle St, 15th Fl, Chicago IL 60602-2602 *Ph:* 800-995 2300; 312-944 1750 *Fax:* 312-944 1448 *E-mail:* info@iesabroad.org ▲

0173
INTERNATIONAL CAMPUS CONSORTIUM and THUNDERBIRD, THE AMERICAN GRADUATE SCHOOL OF INTERNATIONAL MANAGEMENT
China Program
Site: China: Beijing, Hong Kong, Shanghai
Dates: 14 wks, May 22-Aug 25
Subjects: Business/management, Chinese language (beg/int/adv), Chinese studies, Finance, International business, International studies
Eligibility: *Level:* grads *Requires:* 3.0 GPA, previous lang study recommended
Credit: *Undergrad:* none *Grad:* 9-12 *Doc:* certificate
Instruction: *In:* English *Format:* lang study, lecture *Students:* intl
Costs: $11,000 *incl* tuition, insurance, fees
Housing: *Sponsor assists:* residence halls, apartments, hotels
Deadline: Contact sponsor
Other info: *US accredited sponsor:* yes *Orient:* abroad *Activities:* field trips *Misc:* May contact former participants. *Financial aid:* scholarships *URL:* http://www.t-bird.edu
Contact: *See Index II for Members* Dr Earl Gibbons, Assoc VP, Overseas Pgms, Thunderbird, 15249 N 59th Ave, Glendale AZ 85306 *Ph:* 602-978 7252 *Fax:* 602-978 7419 *E-mail:* gibbonse@t-bird.edu
Or Contact: Diane Hayton, Coord, Overseas Pgms, Thunderbird, 15249 N 59th Ave, Glendale AZ 85306 *Ph:* 602-978 7252 *Fax:* 602-978 7419 *E-mail:* haytond@t-bird.edu

---

0174
INTERNATIONAL COUNCIL FOR CULTURAL EXCHANGE (ICCE)
Chinese Culture and Language: Exploring China
Site: China: Beijing, various sites *Host inst:* Beijing Univ, others
Dates: 4-5 wks, Jul & Aug
Subjects: Asian studies, Chinese language (beg/int/adv), Chinese studies, Civilization/culture, Field study, Homestay
Eligibility: *Level:* fresh, sophs, jrs, srs, grads, adults, teachers, professionals, precoll
Credit: *Undergrad:* avail *Grad:* avail *Doc:* transcript, certificate
Instruction: *In:* Chinese, English *Format:* directed field study, lab, lang study, lecture, practical training, study tour *Students:* intl
Costs: From $2,400 *incl* tuition, housing, some meals, intl airfare, fees, excursions, transfers
Housing: *Sponsor assists:* residence halls, homestay, hotels
Deadline: 3 mos before pgm
Other info: *US accredited sponsor:* no *Began:* 1982 *Orient:* abroad *Activities:*

See "How To Use This Book" for definitions of terms used above. ▲ = See program sponsor's ad(s) in this book.

excursions, cultural events, sports *Misc:* Yr-round pgms of 2 wks or longer for pre-arr groups.
Contact: Dr Stanley Gochman, ICCE, 5 Bellport Ln, Bellport NY 11713 *Ph:* 631-286 5228 ▲

0175
LEHIGH UNIVERSITY
Lehigh in China
Site: China: Beijing, Shanghai, Xian *Host inst:* Jiaotong Univ, Beijing & Xian Shanghai Intl Studies Univ
Dates: 6 wks, late May-early Jul
Subjects: Economics, International relations
Eligibility: *Level:* sophs, jrs, srs *Requires:* 2.0 GPA, previous study in field, previous econ study
Credit: *Undergrad:* 6 *Grad:* none *Doc:* transcript
Instruction: *In:* English *Format:* study tour *Students:* mainly US
Costs: $4,600 *incl* tuition, housing, some meals, intl airfare, excursions *Nonrefundable fee*
Housing: *Arr by pgm:* residence halls, hotels
Deadline: Mar 1
Other info: *US accredited sponsor:* yes *Began:* 1996 *Orient:* in US *Activities:* excursions, field trips, program travel, cultural events *Misc:* Pgm administered in alternate yrs. May contact former participants. *URL:* http://www.Lehigh.edu/~incis/incis.html
Contact: Dr Sandi Smith, Dir, Study Abroad, Lehigh Abroad, 5 E Packer Ave, Whitaker Lab 343, Lehigh Univ, Bethlehem PA 18015 *Ph:* 610-758 3351 *Fax:* 610-758 5156 *E-mail:* incis@lehigh.edu

---

0176
LINGNAN UNIVERSITY
Lee Shiu Institute
Site: China: Guangzhou, Hong Kong
Dates: 1 mo, summer
Subjects: Business/management, Civilization/culture, Languages, Sociology
Eligibility: *Level:* sophs, jrs, srs
Credit: *Undergrad:* none *Grad:* none *Doc:* certificate
Instruction: *In:* English *Format:* directed field study, lang study, lecture, tutorial, workshop *Students:* mainly host country
Costs: $2,450 *incl* tuition, housing, some meals, insurance
Housing: *Arr by pgm:* residence halls with local students, hotels, hostels
Deadline: May
Other info: *US accredited sponsor:* no *Began:* 1998 *Orient:* abroad (2 days) *Misc:* May contact former participants. *URL:* http://www.LN.edu.hk/summerint
Contact: Jerome Hon, Pgm Officer, Lee Shiu Summer Inst, Lingnan Univ, Tuen Mun, Hong Kong *E-mail:* jhoncc@ln.edu.hk
Or Contact: Chen Hua-Ling, Dir, Lee Shiu Summer inst, Lingnan Univ, Tuen Mun, Hong Kong *E-mail:* lssi@ln.edu.hk

---

0177
NEW YORK UNIVERSITY, SCHOOL OF EDUCATION
Photography as Art
Site: China: Beijing, Shanghai
Dates: 3 wks, May 25-Jun16
Subjects: Photography
Eligibility: *Level:* srs, grads *Requires:* 3.0 GPA, previous study in field
Credit: *Undergrad:* none *Grad:* 6 *Doc:* transcript
Instruction: *In:* English *Format:* art studio, directed field study, lab, lecture *Students:* mainly US
Costs: $6,000 *incl* tuition, housing, some meals, books/materials, lab equipment *Nonrefundable fee*
Housing: *Arr by pgm:* hotels
Deadline: Apr 1
Other info: *US accredited sponsor:* yes *Began:* 1997 *In coop with:* Beijing Film Inst *Orient:* in US *Activities:* excursions, field trips, cultural events *Misc:* Loans avail. May contact former participants. *URL:* http://www.nyu.edu/summer
Contact: Prof Gerald Pryor, Art & Art Professions, New York Univ, Barney Bldg, New York NY 10003 *Ph:* 212-998 5732
Or Contact: Helen J Kelly, Dir, Special Pgms, New York Univ, 82 Washington Square E, Rm 62, New York NY 10003 *Ph:* 212-998 5090 *Fax:* 212-995 4923 ▲

0178
PENNSYLVANIA STATE UNIVERSITY
Summer Education Abroad Chinese Language and Culture
Site: China: Beijing, Nanjing *Host inst:* Beijing Univ, Nanjing Normal Univ
Dates: 7 wks, Jun-Jul
Subjects: Calligraphy, Chinese language (beg/int/adv), Chinese studies, Civilization/culture
Eligibility: *Level:* sophs, jrs, srs *Requires:* 2.5 GPA *Age:* min 18, avg 20
Credit: *Undergrad:* 9-10 *Grad:* none *Doc:* transcript
Instruction: *In:* Chinese *Format:* lang study, study tour *Students:* mainly US
Costs: About $3,930 for PA residents, $6,594 for others *incl* tuition, housing, excursions *Nonrefundable fee*
Housing: *Arr by pgm:* residence halls, hotels
Deadline: Mar 15
Other info: *US accredited sponsor:* yes *Orient:* in US (1 day) *Activities:* field trips, program travel, cultural events *Misc:* Lang class required, other courses optional & taught in English. May contact former participants. *URL:* http://www.outreach.psu.edu/PSSEA/
Contact: Summer Abroad, Pennsylvania State Univ, 225 Penn State Conference Ctr, University Park PA 16802 *Ph:* 814-863 5170 *Fax:* 814-863 5190 *E-mail:* SummerAbroad@outreach.psu.edu

---

0179
UNIVERSITY OF ARKANSAS
International Business Seminar in China
Site: China: Beijing, Shanghai *Host inst:* Northern Jiaotong Univ, Fudan Univ
Dates: May 20-Jun 18
Subjects: Economics
Eligibility: *Level:* sophs, jrs, srs *Requires:* 3.0 GPA, previous study in field, prerequisites microecon & macroecon *Age:* avg 22
Credit: *Undergrad:* 6 *Grad:* none *Doc:* transcript
Instruction: *In:* English *Format:* directed field study, study tour *Students:* mainly US
Costs: Contact sponsor
Housing: *Arr by pgm:* residence halls, hotels
Deadline: Feb 15
Other info: *US accredited sponsor:* yes *Orient:* in US & abroad *Activities:* excursions, field trips *Misc:* Opportunities to interact with Chinese students. May contact former participants. *URL:* http://www.uark.edu/~studyabr
Contact: Michelle Morris, 722 W Maple, Univ of Arkansas, Fayetteville AR 72701 *Ph:* 501-575 7582 *Fax:* 501-575 7402 *E-mail:* studyabr@cavern.uark.edu

---

0180
UNIVERSITY OF DELAWARE
Winter Session in China
Site: China: Beijing, Shanghai
Dates: 1 mo, Jan
Subjects: Civilization/culture, Education/teaching, Homestay, International studies, TEFL/TESL
Eligibility: *Level:* fresh, sophs, jrs, srs *Requires:* 2.0 GPA
Credit: *Undergrad:* 6 *Grad:* none *Doc:* transcript
Instruction: *In:* English *Format:* lang study, lecture, study tour *Students:* mainly US
Costs: Contact sponsor
Housing: *Arr by pgm*
Deadline: Early Oct
Other info: *US accredited sponsor:* yes *Orient:* avail yes *Activities:* excursions, field trips, program travel, cultural events *Misc:* Contact sponsor to arrange honors

credit. *Financial aid:* scholarships *URL:* http://www.udel.edu/studyabroad/
Contact: Intl Pgms, Univ of Delaware, 4 Kent Way, Newark DE 19716 *Ph:* 888-831 4685; 302-831 2852 *Fax:* 302-831 6042 *E-mail:* studyabroad@udel.edu

---

0181
UNIVERSITY OF SAN DIEGO, SCHOOL OF BUSINESS ADMINISTRATION
Graduate Business Study Abroad in Beijing/Shanghai
Site: China: Beijing, Shanghai *Host inst:* Beijing Univ of Sci & Technology, Shanghai Univ
Dates: 5 wks, Jun-early Jul (3 wks distance learning, 2 wks in country)
Subjects: Asian studies, Business/ management, Finance, Human resources, International business, International marketing
Eligibility: *Level:* grads, professionals *Requires:* enrollment in or graduation from grad bus or related grad pgm, good acad standing
Credit: *Undergrad:* none *Grad:* 3 per course *Doc:* transcript
Instruction: *In:* English *Format:* lecture, seminar *Students:* US & intl
Costs: $1,450 for 1 course, $2,400 for 2 courses *incl* tuition, housing, intl airfare, local transport *Nonrefundable fee*
Housing: *Sponsor assists:* hotels, assist in reserving rms
Deadline: None
Other info: *US accredited sponsor:* yes *Began:* 1994 *Orient:* abroad (1 day) *Activities:* excursions, field trips, program travel, cultural events *Misc:* Company visits. May contact former participants. *URL:* http://business.acusd.edu/ib/china.html
Contact: Kira Mendez, Coord, or Amanda Ryan, Admin Asst, Ahlers Ctr for Intl Bus, Univ of San Diego Sch of Bus Admin, 5998 Alcala Park, San Diego CA 92110-2492 *Ph:* 800-248 4873; 619-260 4896 *Fax:* 619-260 4891 *E-mail:* ib@acusd.edu

---

0182
UNIVERSITY OF WISCONSIN-STEVENS POINT
The Culture of China: Art, Architecture & Design
Site: China: Beijing, Chengdu, Guangzhou, Guilin, Hong Kong, Qufu, Xi'an
Dates: 3 wks, May-Jun
Subjects: Intercultural studies
Eligibility: *Level:* adults *Requires:* good physical condition *Age:* min 18
Credit: *Undergrad:* avail *Grad:* avail *Doc:* transcript
Instruction: *In:* English *Format:* study tour *Students:* mainly US
Costs: $3,795 for WI residents *incl* tuition, housing, some meals, intl airfare, excursions, entrance fees
Housing: *Arr by pgm:* hotels
Deadline: 10 wks before pgm (or when full)
Other info: *US accredited sponsor:* yes *Began:* 1998 *Orient:* in US (1 day) *Activities:* excursions, program travel, cultural events *URL:* http://www.uwsp.edu/acad/internat/
Contact: Intl Pgms, Univ of Wisconsin-Stevens Point, 108 CCC, Stevens Point WI 54481 *Ph:* 715-346 2717 *Fax:* 715-346 3591 *E-mail:* intlprog@uwsp.edu
Or Contact: Dr George Kung, Univ of Wisconsin-Stevens Point, 356D Sci, Stevens Point WI 54481 *Ph:* 715-346 4135 *E-mail:* gkung@uwsp.edu

---

BEIJING

0183
BOSTON UNIVERSITY
Beijing: Intensive Chinese Language
Site: China: Beijing *Host inst:* Capital Normal Univ Coll of Foreign Lang
Dates: 9 wks, Jun-Aug
Subjects: Chinese language (beg/int/adv)
Eligibility: *Level:* sophs, jrs, srs *Requires:* 3.0 GPA, in major, good acad standing
Credit: *Undergrad:* 8 *Grad:* none *Doc:* transcript
Instruction: *In:* Chinese *Format:* lang study *Students:* mainly US
Costs: $5,400 *incl* tuition, housing, all meals, insurance, fees, excursions, books/ materials, visa fees
Housing: *Arr by pgm:* residence halls
Deadline: Mar 1; Apr 1 for scholarships
Other info: *US accredited sponsor:* yes *Began:* 1993 *Orient:* in US & abroad *Activities:* excursions, field trips, cultural events *Misc:* Full-time resident dir. May contact former participants. *Financial aid:* scholarships *URL:* http://www.bu.edu/abroad/
Contact: Intl Pgms, Boston Univ, 232 Bay State Rd, Boston MA 02215 *Ph:* 617-353 9888 *Fax:* 617-353 5402 *E-mail:* abroad@bu.edu ▲

0184
CET ACADEMIC PROGRAMS
CET Chinese Language Programs in Beijing
Site: China: Beijing *Host inst:* Beijing Inst of Educ
Dates: Jun 12-Aug 13
Subjects: Calligraphy, Chinese language (Mandarin) (beg/int/adv), Chinese studies, Culinary arts, Economics, History, Literature, Martial arts, Painting, Social sciences
Eligibility: *Level:* fresh, sophs, jrs, srs, grads, adults, professionals, precoll *Age:* min 17, max 55, avg 20
Credit: *Undergrad:* avail *Grad:* avail *Doc:* transcript, certificate
Instruction: *In:* Chinese, Mandarin *Format:* lang study, lecture, seminar, study tour, tutorial *Students:* mainly US
Costs: $4,890 *incl* tuition, housing, all meals, insurance, excursions, books/ materials, visa
Housing: *Arr by pgm:* residence halls with local students
Deadline: Mar 1
Other info: *US accredited sponsor:* no *Began:* 1982 *Orient:* abroad *Activities:* excursions, field trips, program travel, cultural events, sports *Misc:* May contact former participants. *Financial aid:* scholarships *URL:* http://www.cetacademicprograms.com
Contact: Paula Miller, CET China Pgm, CET Acad Pgms, 1000 16th St NW, Ste 350, Washington DC 20036 *Ph:* 800-225 4262; 202-530 0800 *Fax:* 202-342 0317 *E-mail:* cet@academic-travel.com

---

0185
COLLEGE OF WILLIAM & MARY
China-Summer
Site: China: Beijing *Host inst:* Beijing Normal Univ
Dates: Jun 17-Aug 25
Subjects: Chinese language (int/adv), Chinese studies (adv)
Eligibility: *Level:* sophs, jrs, srs *Requires:* 2.85 GPA
Credit: *Undergrad:* avail *Grad:* none
Instruction: *In:* English *Format:* lang study, lecture *Students:* mainly US
Costs: $6,550 *incl* tuition
Housing: *Arr by pgm*
Deadline: Contact sponsor
Other info: *US accredited sponsor:* yes
Contact: Guru Ghosh, Reves Ctr for Intl Studies, Coll of William & Mary, Williamsburg VA 23187-8795 *Ph:* 757-221 3595 *E-mail:* gxghos@wm.edu

---

0186
COLUMBIA UNIVERSITY
Summer Program in Beijing
Site: China: Beijing *Host inst:* Tsinghua Univ
Dates: 9 wks, Jun 11-Aug 14
Subjects: Chinese language (beg/int/adv)
Eligibility: *Level:* fresh, sophs, jrs, srs, grads *Requires:* knowledge of Chinese only, formal study not required *Age:* min 18, avg 19
Credit: *Undergrad:* 10 *Grad:* none *Doc:* transcript

Instruction: *In:* Chinese *Format:* lang study, lecture *Students:* mainly US
Costs: $4,200 *incl* tuition, housing, intl airfare, insurance, fees, excursions, books/materials, railpass *Nonrefundable fee*
Housing: *Arr by pgm:* hotels
Deadline: Mar 8
Other info: *US accredited sponsor:* yes *Began:* 1997 *Orient:* abroad *Misc:* May contact former participants. *URL:* http://www.ce.columbia.edu/op
Contact: Student Svcs Ctr, Columbia Univ, 2970 Broadway, MC 4119, New York NY 10027-6902 *Ph:* 212-854 9666 *Fax:* 212-854 7400 *E-mail:* beijing@columbia.edu

---

0187
COUNCIL ON INTERNATIONAL EDUCATIONAL EXCHANGE CONSORTIUM
Council Study Center at Peking University
Site: China: Beijing *Host inst:* Peking Univ
Dates: 8 wks, Jun-Aug
Subjects: Chinese language (Mandarin) (int/adv)
Eligibility: *Level:* sophs, jrs, srs, grads, teachers *Requires:* 2.75 GPA, 1 yr coll Mandarin, area studies course *Age:* avg 22
Credit: *Undergrad:* 8 *Grad:* none
Instruction: *In:* Mandarin *Format:* lang study, lecture *Students:* mainly US
Costs: $4,090 *incl* tuition, housing, all meals, insurance, fees, excursions, visa, ISIC, orient
Housing: *Arr by pgm:* residence halls
Deadline: Mar 15
Other info: *US accredited sponsor:* yes *Began:* 1980 *Orient:* abroad *Activities:* excursions, cultural events *Misc:* Full-time resident dir. Grade report. Faculty from host country univs. Summer camp with Chinese middle sch students. May contact former participants. *Financial aid:* scholarships *URL:* http://www.ciee.org/study
Contact: *See Index II for Members* Council-ISP, 633 3rd Ave, 20th Fl, New York NY 10017-6706 *Ph:* 800-407 8839; 212-822 2600 *Fax:* 212-822 2779 *E-mail:* studyinfo@ciee.org

---

0188
CSA, CENTER FOR STUDY ABROAD
Beijing Language and Culture University
Site: China: Beijing *Host inst:* Beijing Lang & Culture Univ
Dates: 4-12 wks, Sep-Jul; sem/yr pgms also avail
Subjects: Chinese language (beg/int/adv), Chinese studies, History, Independent study, Literature, Political science/politics
Eligibility: *Level:* adults *Requires:* student visa *Age:* min 17, avg 23
Credit: *Undergrad:* avail *Grad:* avail *Doc:* transcript, certificate
Instruction: *In:* Mandarin *Format:* independent study, lang study, lecture *Students:* intl
Costs: $1,295 for 4 wks, $2,195 for 8 wks, $3,195 for 12 wks *incl* tuition, housing, insurance, fees *Nonrefundable fee*
Housing: *Sponsor assists:* residence halls
Deadline: May 30 or until pgm filled
Other info: *US accredited sponsor:* no *Began:* 1962 *Orient.* abroad *Activities:* excursions, field trips *URL:* http://www.studyabroad.com/csa

Contact: Alima Khan, Assoc Dir, CSA, Ctr for Study Abroad, 2802 E Madison St, MS #160, Seattle WA 98112 *Ph:* 206-726 1498 *Fax:* 206-583 8192 *E-mail:* virtuecsa@aol.com

---

0189
DICKINSON COLLEGE
China Practicum
Site: China: Beijing
Dates: 5 wks, late May-late Jun
Subjects: Chinese studies, Civilization/culture, History
Eligibility: *Level:* fresh, sophs, jrs
Credit: *Undergrad:* 4 *Grad:* none
Instruction: *In:* English *Format:* directed field study, seminar, study tour *Students:* mainly US
Costs: About $3,850 *incl* tuition, housing, all meals, intl airfare, excursions *Nonrefundable fee*
Housing: *Arr by pgm:* residence halls
Deadline: Mar 1
Other info: *US accredited sponsor:* yes *Began:* 1999 *Orient:* avail avail *Activities:* excursions, program travel, cultural events, sports *URL:* http://www.dickinson.edu/departments/ocs/abroad.html
Contact: Global Educ, Dickinson Coll, PO Box 1773, Carlisle PA 17013-2896 *Ph:* 717-245 1341 *Fax:* 717-245 1688 *E-mail:* ocs@dickinson.edu

---

0190
DUKE UNIVERSITY and **WASHINGTON UNIVERSITY (MO)**
Duke in China Summer Program
Site: China: Beijing *Host inst:* Capital Normal Univ
Dates: 9 wks, mid-Jun-mid-Aug
Subjects: Chinese language
Eligibility: *Level:* fresh, sophs, jrs, srs *Requires:* 1 yr Chinese, good acad standing, transcript
Credit: *Undergrad:* 2 credits *Grad:* none *Doc:* transcript
Instruction: *In:* Chinese *Format:* lang study, tutorial *Students:* mainly US
Costs: $4,760 *incl* tuition, housing, all meals, excursions, books/materials
Housing: *Sponsor assists:* residence halls
Deadline: Feb 16
Other info: *US accredited sponsor:* yes *Began:* 1982 *Orient:* abroad (2 days) *Activities:* excursions *Misc:* May contact former participants. *Financial aid:* scholarships *URL:* http://www.aas.duke.edu/study_abroad
Contact: Study Abroad, Duke Univ, 121 Allen Bldg, Box 90057, Durham NC 27708-0057 *Ph:* 919-684 2174 *Fax:* 919-684 3083 *E-mail:* abroad@asdean.duke.edu

---

0191
IES, INSTITUTE FOR THE INTERNATIONAL EDUCATION OF STUDENTS
IES Beijing Summer: Contemporary Issues in Urban China Program
Site: China: Beijing *Host inst:* IES, Beijing Foreign Studies Univ
Dates: 6 wks, May 26-Jul 7
Subjects: Chinese language (Mandarin) (beg), Chinese studies, Contemporary issues, Urban studies
Eligibility: *Level:* fresh, sophs, jrs, srs, grads, adults *Requires:* good acad standing, *Age:* min 18
Credit: *Undergrad:* 6 *Grad:* none *Doc:* transcript
Instruction: *In:* Chinese, English *Format:* lang study, lecture *Students:* mainly US
Costs: $2,850 *incl* tuition, housing, insurance, excursions, support svcs *Nonrefundable fee*
Housing: *Arr by pgm:* residence halls
Deadline: Mar 15
Other info: *US accredited sponsor:* yes *Began:* 2001 *Orient:* abroad *Activities:* excursions, field trips, cultural events *Misc:* $500 fee reduction for students continuing with IES in the fall. May contact former participants. *URL:* http://www.IESabroad.org
Contact: *See Index II for Members* IES, 33 N La Salle St, 15th Fl, Chicago IL 60602-2602 *Ph:* 800-995 2300; 312-944 1750 *Fax:* 312-944 1448 *E-mail:* info@IESabroad.org ▲

0192
ILLINOIS STATE UNIVERSITY
Discover China
Site: China: Beijing *Host inst:* Beijing Inst of Printing
Dates: 3 wks, May 17-Jun 10
Subjects: Chinese studies, Civilization/culture, Independent study, Printing
Eligibility: *Level:* sophs, jrs, srs, grads, adults *Requires:* 2.5 GPA
Credit: *Undergrad:* 3 *Grad:* 3
Instruction: *In:* English *Format:* independent study *Students:* intl
Costs: $4,300 *incl* housing, all meals, intl airfare, insurance, excursions *Nonrefundable fee*
Housing: *Arr by pgm:* guesthouses
Deadline: Feb 14
Other info: *US accredited sponsor:* yes *Orient:* in US (1 day) *Activities:* excursions, field trips, cultural events *Misc:* English-speaking hosts/interpreters. Loans avail. *Financial aid:* scholarships *URL:* http://www.its.ilstu.edu/intlstudies/
Contact: Adviser/chairperson, Illinois State Univ, Campus Box 5100, Normal IL 61790-5100 *Ph:* 309-438 3661 *Fax:* 309-438 3987 *E-mail:* www.oisp@ilstu.edu
Or Contact: Intl Studies & Pgms, Illinois State Univ, Campus Box 6120, Normal IL 61790-6120 *Ph:* 309-438 5365 *Fax:* 309-438 3987 *E-mail:* oisp@ilstu.edu

---

0193
INTER-UNIVERSITY PROGRAM FOR CHINESE LANGUAGE STUDIES
IUP-Tsinghua University Summer Intensive Program
Site: China: Beijing *Host inst:* Tsinghua Univ
Dates: 8 wks, Jun-Aug
Subjects: Chinese language (Mandarin)
Eligibility: *Level:* sophs, jrs, srs, grads, adults, teachers, professionals *Requires:* 2 yrs coll Chinese *Age:* avg 26
Credit: *Undergrad:* avail *Grad:* none
Instruction: *In:* Mandarin *Format:* lang study, tutorial *Students:* mainly US
Costs: $4,200 *incl* tuition, housing, insurance, fees
Housing: *Arr by pgm:* residence halls
Deadline: Mid-Jan
Other info: *US accredited sponsor:* yes *Began:* 1963 *Activities:* excursions, field trips, cultural events *Misc:* May contact former participants. *URL:* http://ieas.berkeley.edu/iup
Contact: *See Index II for Members* Brian Pierini, Pgm Admin, Inter-Univ Pgm, Inst of East Asian Studies, 2223 Fulton #2318, Berkeley CA 94720-2318 *Ph:* 510-642 3873 *Fax:* 510-643 7062 *E-mail:* iub@socrates.berkeley.edu
Or Contact: Jeff Crosland, Field Dir, Inter-Univ Pgm, Wenke Lou, Rm 502, Tsinghua Univ, Beijing, China *E-mail:* iupchina@uclink.berkeley.edu

---

0194
LANGUAGES ABROAD
Language and Cultural Immersion Programs-Beijing
Site: China: Beijing
Dates: 2 wks or longer, yr-round
Subjects: Chinese language (beg/int/adv), Civilization/culture
Eligibility: *Level:* adults *Age:* min 17, max 65, avg 25
Credit: *Undergrad:* none *Grad:* none *Doc:* certificate
Instruction: *In:* Chinese *Format:* lang study *Students:* intl
Costs: About $3,250 for 4 wks *incl* tuition, housing, some meals, excursions, books/materials
Housing: *Arr by pgm:* apartments, homestay
Deadline: None
Other info: *US accredited sponsor:* no *Misc:* May contact former participants. *URL:* http://www.languagesabroad.com

Contact: Ms Jesse Philippe, Langs Abroad, 317 Adelaide St W, Ste 900, Toronto, Ontario M5V 1P9, Canada *Ph:* 800-219 9924; 416-925 7117 *E-mail:* info@languagesabroad.com

---

0195
MICHIGAN STATE UNIVERSITY
Food, Agriculture and Environment
Site: China: Beijing *Host inst:* Chinese Acad of Agricultural Scis (CAAS)
Dates: 3 wks, May-Jun
Subjects: Agriculture, Animal sciences, Natural resources, Soil/pasture management
Eligibility: *Level:* fresh, sophs, jrs, srs *Requires:* 2.0 GPA *Age:* min 18
Credit: *Undergrad:* avail *Grad:* none *Doc:* transcript
Instruction: *In:* English *Format:* lecture *Students:* mainly US
Costs: About $1,000 *incl* housing, some meals, insurance, fees, excursions *Nonrefundable fee*
Housing: *Arr by pgm:* residence halls
Deadline: Mar 2
Other info: *US accredited sponsor:* yes *Began:* 1999 *Orient:* in US (1 day) *Activities:* excursions, field trips, cultural events *Financial aid:* scholarships *URL:* http://studyabroad.msu.edu
Contact: Cheryl Benner, Study Abroad, Michigan State Univ, 109 Intl Ctr, East Lansing MI 48824-1035 *Ph:* 517-353 8920 *Fax:* 517-432 2082 *E-mail:* bennerc@msu.edu ▲

0196
MONTCLAIR STATE UNIVERSITY
Montclair in Beijing
Site: China: Beijing *Host inst:* UIBE
Dates: 10 days, Jun 15-25
Subjects: Field study, International business
Eligibility: *Level:* grads *Requires:* 2.5 GPA, previous study in field, must be MBA student or alnmni
Credit: *Undergrad:* none *Grad:* 3 *Doc:* transcript
Instruction: *In:* English *Format:* directed field study, study tour *Students:* mainly US
Costs: About $2,000 *incl* housing, some meals, intl airfare, insurance, fees, excursions *Nonrefundable fee*
Housing: *Arr by pgm:* hotels
Deadline: May 1
Other info: *US accredited sponsor:* yes *Began:* 2000 *In coop with:* UIBE *Orient:* in US 3 days *Activities:* excursions, field trips, program travel *Misc:* May contact former participants. *URL:* http://www.montclair.edu/pages/globaled/students.html
Contact: Wendy Gilbert-Simon, Montclair State Univ, Global Educ Ctr, Upper Mountclair NJ 07043 *Ph:* 973-655 4185 *Fax:* 973-655 7654 *E-mail:* simonw@mail.montclair.edu
Or Contact: Dr Chungkue Hse, Montclair State Univ, Marketing, Upper Mountclair NJ 07043 *Ph:* 973-655 4245 *E-mail:* hsuc@mail.montclair.edu

---

0197
PRINCETON UNIVERSITY
Princeton in Beijing
Site: China: Beijing *Host inst:* Beijing Normal Univ
Dates: 8 wks, Jun 23-Aug 19
Subjects: Chinese language (Mandarin) (beg/int/adv)
Eligibility: *Level:* adults *Requires:* Chinese lang study for adv levels *Age:* avg 20
Credit: *Undergrad:* 8 *Grad:* none *Doc:* transcript
Instruction: *In:* Mandarin *Format:* lang study *Students:* mainly US
Costs: About $3,900 *incl* tuition, housing, some meals, fees, excursions, books/materials *Nonrefundable fee*
Housing: *Arr by pgm:* residence halls
Deadline: Feb 1; Jan 15 for scholarships
Other info: *US accredited sponsor:* yes *Began:* 1993 *Activities:* field trips, cultural events *Financial aid:* scholarships *URL:* http://www.princeton.edu/pib
Contact: Coord, Princeton in Beijing, Princeton Univ, 211 Jones Hall, Princeton NJ 08544 *Ph:* 609-258 4269 *Fax:* 609-258 6198 *E-mail:* pib@princeton.edu
Or Contact: Carrie Gordon, Exec Dir, Princeton-in-Asia, Princeton Univ, 12 Dillon Ct E, Princeton NJ 08544 *Ph:* 609-258 5358 *Fax:* 609-258 6198 *E-mail:* pia@princeton.edu

---

0198
SOUTHWEST TEXAS STATE UNIVERSITY
SWT in China
Site: China: Beijing *Host inst:* Peking Univ
Dates: 3 wks, May
Subjects: Independent study, Philosophy
Eligibility: *Level:* jrs, srs *Age:* min 18, avg 22
Credit: *Undergrad:* 3 *Grad:* none *Doc:* transcript
Instruction: *In:* English *Format:* independent study, lecture, study tour *Students:* mainly US
Costs: $2,320 *incl* tuition, housing, intl airfare, insurance, fees, excursions
Housing: *Arr by pgm:* residence halls
Deadline: Contact sponsor
Other info: *US accredited sponsor:* yes *Began:* 2000 *Orient:* in US (1 day) *Activities:* excursions, cultural events *Misc:* May contact former participants. *Financial aid:* scholarships *URL:* http://www.ideal.swt.edu/extension/study-abroad/
Contact: Dr Rui Zhu, Southwest Texas State Univ, 601 Universit Dr, San Marcos TX 78666 *Ph:* 512-245 8826 *Fax:* 512-245 8335 *E-mail:* rz01@swt.edu
Or Contact: Isis Gomez Extension Studies Coord, Southwest Texas State Univ, 601 University Dr, San Marcos TX 78666 *Ph:* 512-245 2322 *Fax:* 512-245 8934 *E-mail:* ig02@swt.edu

---

0199
UNIVERSITY OF PITTSBURGH
Pitt in China-Beijing
Site: China: Beijing *Host inst:* Beijing Univ
Dates: 3 wks, late Jun-Jul
Subjects: Chinese studies, Civilization/culture, Contemporary issues, East Asian studies, Economics, History, Independent study, Political science/politics
Eligibility: *Level:* sophs, jrs, srs, grads, adults *Requires:* 2.75 GPA
Credit: *Undergrad:* 6 *Grad:* none *Doc:* transcript
Instruction: *In:* English *Format:* lang study, lecture *Students:* mainly US
Costs: Contact sponsor
Housing: *Arr by pgm:* residence halls
Deadline: Feb 15
Other info: *US accredited sponsor:* yes *Began:* 1997 *Orient:* in US & abroad *Misc:* May contact former participants. *Financial aid:* scholarships *URL:* http://www.pitt.edu/~stdyabrd/
Contact: Matthew McMullen, Study Abroad, Univ of Pittsburgh, 802 William Pitt Union, Pittsburgh PA 15260 *Ph:* 412-648 7421 *Fax:* 412-383 7166 *E-mail:* stdyabrd+@pitt.edu

---

0200
US-CHINA PEOPLES FRIENDSHIP ASSOCIATION
Chinese Language Study
Site: China: Beijing *Host inst:* Beijing Lang & Culture Univ
Dates: 4, 5, 6 or 12 wks, late Feb-Dec
Subjects: Business language, Calligraphy, Chinese language (Mandarin) (beg/int/adv), Martial arts, Painting, Translating/interpreting, Written composition
Eligibility: *Level:* fresh, sophs, jrs, srs, adults, precoll *Age:* min 16, max 55
Credit: *Undergrad:* none *Grad:* none *Doc:* certificate
Instruction: *In:* Chinese *Format:* lang study, lecture *Students:* intl
Costs: About $2,300-$3,150 *incl* tuition, housing, intl airfare, fees, excursions *Nonrefundable fee*
Housing: *Arr by pgm:* residence halls

Deadline: 3 mos before pgm
Other info: *US accredited sponsor:* no *Began:* 1982 *Orient:* in US (briefing) *Activities:* program travel *Misc:* Sem pgms also avail.
Contact: Ruby M Fong, US-China Peoples Friendship Assn, 1175 Volz Dr, Sacramento CA 95822-1059 *Ph:* 916-447 3313 *Fax:* 916-444 2288 *E-mail:* info@chinatours.org

CHENGDU

0201
UNIVERSITY STUDIES ABROAD CONSORTIUM
Chinese Studies-Chengdu, China
Site: China: Chengdu *Host inst:* Sichuan Union Univ
Dates: May 31-Jun 29 and /or Jun 30-Jul 28
Subjects: Chinese language (beg/int/adv), Chinese studies, Civilization/culture, Economics, Government, History, Philosophy, Political science/politics
Eligibility: *Level:* fresh, sophs, jrs, srs, grads, adults, teachers, professionals, precoll *Requires:* 2.5 GPA
Credit: *Undergrad:* avail *Grad:* avail *Doc:* transcript
Instruction: *In:* Chinese, English *Format:* lang study, lecture *Students:* mainly US
Costs: $1,480 for 1 mo, $2,760 for 2 mos *incl* tuition, housing, insurance, fees, ISIC *Nonrefundable fee*
Housing: *Arr by pgm:* residence halls with local students
Deadline: Apr 15
Other info: *US accredited sponsor:* yes *Began:* 1998 *Orient:* abroad (2 days) *Activities:* excursions, field trips, cultural events *Misc:* May contact former participants. *Financial aid:* scholarships *URL:* http://www.usac.unr.edu
Contact: *See Index II for Members* Dr Carmelo Urza, Univ Studies Abroad Consortium, Univ of Nevada Reno/323, Reno NV 89557 *Ph:* 775-784 6569 *Fax:* 775-784 6010 *E-mail:* usac@admin.unr.edu ▲

GUANGXI

0202
CONSULTANTS FOR GLOBAL PROGRAMS
Chinese Interactive English Institute and Travel Program
Site: China: Guangxi *Host inst:* Guangxi Normal Univ
Dates: 4 wks, Jun 30-Jun 27
Subjects: Independent study
Eligibility: *Level:* srs, grads, adults, teachers, professionals *Requires:* 2.75 GPA, recommendation letter from adviser/ professional, transcript, resume, health statement & letter of intent *Age:* min 21, max 55, avg 35
Credit: *Undergrad:* none *Grad:* none *Doc:* certificate
Instruction: *In:* English *Format:* directed field study, independent study, lab, lang study, lecture, practical training, seminar, study tour, tutorial *Students:* intl
Costs: $3,150 per term *incl* tuition, housing, all meals, intl airfare, 3 days in Hong Kong with breakfasts *Nonrefundable fee*
Housing: *Arr by pgm:* residence halls, hotels
Deadline: Apr 20
Other info: *US accredited sponsor:* no *Began:* 1992 *Orient:* in US & abroad *Activities:* excursions, field trips, program travel, cultural events *Misc:* Team-taught interactive conversational English. May contact former participants. *Financial aid:* scholarships *URL:* http://www.globalprograms.com
Contact: Larry Kavich, CGP, 2019 Central Ave, McKinleyville CA 95519 *Ph:* 800-270 6870 *Fax:* 707-839 2991 *E-mail:* cgpusa@aol.com

GUANGZHOU

0203
ZHONGSHAN UNIVERSITY
Short-Term Chinese Language Program
Site: China: Guangzhou *Host inst:* Ctr for Teaching Chinese as a Foreign Lang
Dates: 4 wks, Jul 1-27
Subjects: Chinese language (beg/int)
Eligibility: *Level:* adults, precoll *Requires:* min 10 students per class *Age:* min 17, max 60
Credit: *Undergrad:* none *Grad:* none *Doc:* certificate
Instruction: *In:* Chinese, English *Format:* lang study, lecture, study tour *Students:* intl
Costs: $480 for 4 wks, $405 for 3 wks, $295 for 2 wks *incl* tuition, excursions, books/materials *Nonrefundable fee*
Housing: *Arr by pgm:* residence halls, apartments, hotels
Deadline: Jun 1
Other info: *US accredited sponsor:* no *Began:* 1983 *Activities:* excursions, cultural events *Misc:* May contact former participants. *URL:* http://www.zsu.edu.cn/English/
Contact: Ms Huang Zhao, Dir, Off Intl Cooperation & Exch, Zhongshan Univ, 135 Xingang Rd W, 510275 Guangzhou, China *E-mail:* adeao@zsulink.zsu.edu.cn
Or Contact: Tan Jinxiong Deputy Head, Intl Student's Off, Zhongshan Univ, 135 Xingang Rd W, 510275 Guangzhou, China *E-mail:* adeao01@zsulink.zsu.edu.cn

HAINAN

0204
UNIVERSITY OF HAWAII AT MANOA
Chinese Language and Culture in Hainan
Site: China: Hainan *Host inst:* Hainan Univ
Dates: 9 wks, mid-May-late Jul
Subjects: Chinese language (Mandarin) (int/adv)
Eligibility: *Level:* sophs, jrs, srs *Requires:* 3.0 GPA, 1 yr coll Mandarin
Credit: *Undergrad:* 8 *Grad:* none *Doc:* transcript
Instruction: *In:* Mandarin *Format:* lang study, lecture, seminar *Students:* mainly US
Costs: $3,930 *incl* tuition, housing, all meals, intl airfare, insurance, fees, excursions, books/materials, visa *Nonrefundable fee*
Housing: *Arr by pgm:* residence halls
Deadline: Feb 17
Other info: *US accredited sponsor:* yes *Began:* 1998 *Orient:* in US & abroad *Activities:* excursions, cultural events *Misc:* UHM financial aid avail to eligible UHM students. *URL:* http://www2.hawaii.edu/study-abroad
Contact: Dir or Study Abroad Adviser, Study Abroad Ctr, Univ of Hawaii at Manoa, Moore Hall 115, 1890 East-West Rd, Honolulu HI 96822 *Ph:* 808-956 5143, 808-956 6958 *Fax:* 808-956 9319 *E-mail:* uhmsac@hawaii.edu

HONG KONG

0205
COOPERATIVE CENTER FOR STUDY ABROAD
Hong Kong
Site: China: Hong Kong
Dates: Jun 8-23
Subjects: International business, Photography
Eligibility: *Level:* fresh, sophs, jrs, srs, grads, adults, teachers, professionals *Requires:* good acad standing, 1 reference *Age:* min 18
Credit: *Undergrad:* 3 *Grad:* avail *Doc:* transcript *Transfer credit through:* Northern Kentucky Univ
Instruction: *In:* English *Format:* directed field study, lecture, seminar, tutorial *Students:* mainly US
Costs: $3,595 *incl* housing, some meals,

intl airfare, excursions, ISIC *Nonrefundable fee*
Housing: *Arr by pgm:* hotels
Deadline: Mar 1
Other info: *US accredited sponsor:* yes *Began:* 1997 *Orient:* in US & abroad *Misc:* Scholarships for consortium students only. May contact former participants. *URL:* http://www.nku.edu/ccsa
Contact: *See Index II for Members* Dr Michael A Klembara, CCSA, Northern Kentucky Univ, BEP 301, Highland Heights KY 41099 *Ph:* 800-319 6015; 606-572 6512 *Fax:* 606-572 6650 *E-mail:* ccsa@nku.edu

---

0206
FASHION INSTITUTE OF TECHNOLOGY
Summer Internship in Asia
Site: China: Hong Kong
Dates: 1 mo, May 24-Jun 23
Subjects: Fashion design, Fashion house management, Fashion merchandising, Internships, Retailing, Textiles, Trade
Eligibility: *Level:* jrs, srs *Requires:* 2 recommendation letters *Age:* min 18
Credit: *Undergrad:* 4 *Grad:* none *Doc:* transcript
Instruction: *In:* English *Format:* internship *Students:* intl
Costs: About $3,850 for NY residents, $4,600 for others *incl* tuition, housing, intl airfare
Housing: *Arr by pgm:* hotels
Deadline: Mar 3
Other info: *US accredited sponsor:* yes *Began:* 1993 *Orient:* in US *Activities:* excursions, field trips, program travel *URL:* http://www.fitnyc.suny.edu
Contact: Georgianna Appignani, Dir, FIT, 7th Ave at 27th St, New York NY 10001-5992 *Ph:* 212-217 7633 *Fax:* 212-217 7010
Or Contact: Carole De Santis, Coord, FIT, 7th Ave at 27th St, New York NY 10001-5992 *E-mail:* desantca@sfitva.cc.fitsuny.edu

---

0207
GEORGETOWN UNIVERSITY
Comparative Business: The Asia-Pacific Perspective
Site: China: Hong Kong *Host inst:* Chinese Univ of Hong Kong
Dates: 5 wks, late Jun-early Aug
Subjects: Business/management, International business, International marketing
Eligibility: *Level:* jrs, srs *Requires:* 3.0 GPA, previous study in field
Credit: *Undergrad:* 6 *Grad:* none *Doc:* transcript
Instruction: *In:* English *Format:* directed field study, lecture, seminar, study tour *Students:* mainly US
Costs: About $4,700 *incl* tuition, housing, some meals, fees, excursions, books/materials
Housing: *Arr by pgm:* residence halls
Deadline: Early Mar
Other info: *US accredited sponsor:* yes *Activities:* excursions, field trips, cultural events *Misc:* May contact former participants. *URL:* http://www.georgetown.edu/programs/oip/os/sites/summer
Contact: Ilkka Ronkainen or Rachel Rubin, Georgetown Univ, Intl Pgms, Box 571013, Washington DC 20057-1013 *Ph:* 202-687 3788, 202-687 5620 *Fax:* 202-687 5944 *E-mail:* rubinr@georgetown.edu

---

0208
HONG KONG BAPTIST UNIVERSITY
International Summer Institute
Site: China: Hong Kong
Dates: Late Jun-mid-Jul
Subjects: Full curriculum
Eligibility: *Requires:* good acad standing for jrs
Credit: *Undergrad:* avail *Grad:* avail *Doc:* transcript
Costs: $1,500 per course
Deadline: Apr
Other info: *US accredited sponsor:* no *URL:* http://www.hkbu.edu.hk/~oice/
Contact: Ms Christina Chan, Exec Asst, Intl Coop & Exch, David C Lam Bldg 921, HKBU, 34 Renfrew Rd, Kowloon, Hong Kong *E-mail:* cchanfh@hkbu.edu.hk
Or Contact: Ms Queenie Chu, Exec Asst, Intl Coop & Exch, David C Lam Bldg 917, HKBU, 34 Renfrew Rd, Kowloon, Hong Kong *E-mail:* iibd@hkbu.edu.hk

---

0209
OHIO UNIVERSITY
Global Competitiveness Institute-Southeast Asia
Site: China: Hong Kong
Dates: 5 wks, mid Jun-mid Jul
Subjects: Business/management, International business, Southeast Asian studies
Eligibility: *Level:* sophs, jrs, srs, grads *Requires:* previous study in field *Age:* min 18, avg 22
Credit: *Undergrad:* 16 qtr hrs *Grad:* none *Doc:* transcript
Instruction: *In:* English *Format:* practical training, study tour *Students:* mainly US
Costs: $5,000 *incl* housing, some meals, intl airfare, fees, excursions
Housing: *Arr by pgm:* residence halls, hotels
Deadline: Mar 15
Other info: *US accredited sponsor:* yes *Began:* 1997 *Orient:* in US (10 days) *Activities:* excursions, field trips, program travel, cultural events *Misc:* Internship with companies within country of study. Loans avail. *Financial aid:* scholarships *URL:* http://www.ohiou.edu/studyabroad/
Contact: John Keifer, Dir, Ctr for Intl Bus, Ohio Univ, Copeland 514, Athens OH 45701 *Ph:* 740-593 2021 *Fax:* 740-593 1388 *E-mail:* keiferj@ohiou.edu

---

0210
RAMAPO COLLEGE OF NEW JERSEY
Summer Study in China
Site: China: Hong Kong
Dates: 4 wks, Jun-Jul
Subjects: Chinese language (Mandarin), Chinese studies, Civilization/culture, Economics, History, Political science/politics
Eligibility: *Level:* fresh, sophs, jrs, srs, grads, teachers, professionals *Requires:* 2.0 GPA
Credit: *Undergrad:* 7 *Grad:* none *Doc:* transcript
Instruction: *In:* Chinese, English *Format:* lang study, seminar *Students:* mainly US
Costs: $3,500-$3,700 *incl* tuition, housing, most meals, intl airfare, fees, excursions
Housing: *Arr by pgm:* residence halls
Deadline: May 1
Other info: *US accredited sponsor:* yes *Began:* 1993 *Orient:* in US (intensive lang study) *Activities:* excursions, cultural events *Misc:* May contact former participants.
Contact: Ms Robyn Perricelli, Study Abroad, Ramapo Coll of New Jersey, 505 Ramapo Valley Rd, Mahwah NJ 07430 *Ph:* 201-684 7030 *Fax:* 201-684 7561 *E-mail:* rperrice@ramapo.edu

---

KUNMING

0211
KENTUCKY INSTITUTE FOR INTERNATIONAL STUDIES (KIIS)
Summer Program in China
Site: China: Kunming *Host inst:* Yunnan Normal Univ
Dates: 6 wks, about Jun 1-Jul 10
Subjects: Chinese studies, Civilization/culture, Contemporary issues, History
Eligibility: *Level:* fresh, sophs, jrs, srs, grads, adults, teachers, professionals *Requires:* 2.0 GPA, good acad standing, transcript, faculty recommendation *Age:* min 18
Credit: *Undergrad:* 3-6 *Grad:* 3-6 *Doc:* transcript *Transfer credit through:* Murray State Univ
Instruction: *In:* English *Format:* lecture, study tour *Students:* mainly US
Costs: About $3,600 for students at member schs, $3,900 for others *incl* tuition, housing, all meals, intl airfare, fees, excursions, ISIC *Nonrefundable fee*
Housing: *Arr by pgm:* univ guest houses
Deadline: Feb 15 ($100 late fee)
Other info: *US accredited sponsor:* yes *Began:* 1998 *Orient:* in US & abroad *Activities:* excursions, program travel, cultural events *Financial aid:* scholarships *URL:* http://www.kiis.org
Contact: *See Index II for Members* Dr J Milton Grimes, Exec Dir, KIIS, Murray State Univ, PO Box 9, Murray KY 42071 *Ph:* 270-762 3091 *Fax:* 270-762 3434 *E-mail:* kiismsu@murraystate.edu
Or Contact: Nancy Martin, Coord, KIIS, Murray State Univ, PO Box 9, Murray KY 42071 *Ph:* 270-502 3091 *Fax:* 270-502 3434 *E-mail:* nancy.martin@murraystate.edu

---

NANJING

0212
CET ACADEMIC PROGRAMS and **JOHNS HOPKINS UNIVERSITY**
CET/HNC Nanjing Immersion
Site: China: Nanjing *Host inst:* Hopkins-Nanjing Ctr (Nanjing Univ)
Dates: 6 wks, mid-Jun-mid Aug
Subjects: Business language (int/adv), Chinese language (Mandarin) (int/adv)
Eligibility: *Level:* srs, grads, adults, professionals *Requires:* previous study in field, 3 sems Chinese or equiv *Age:* min 17, max 60, avg 23
Credit: *Undergrad:* avail *Grad:* avail *Doc:* transcript, certificate
Instruction: *In:* Chinese, Mandarin *Format:* lang study, lecture, seminar, tutorial *Students:* mainly US
Costs: $4,690 *incl* tuition, housing, most meals, intl airfare, insurance, fees, excursions, books/materials *Nonrefundable fee*
Housing: *Arr by pgm:* residence halls
Deadline: Mar 1; Apr 1 for scholarships
Other info: *US accredited sponsor:* yes *Began:* 1999 *Orient:* abroad (3 days) *Activities:* excursions, field trips, program travel, cultural events *Misc:* 24-hr Chinese lang pledge. *Financial aid:* scholarships *URL:* http://www.cetacademicprograms.com
Contact: Paula Miller, China Pgm, CET Acad Pgms, 1000 16th St NW, Ste 350, Washington DC 20036 *Ph:* 800-225 4262; 202-530 0800 *Fax:* 202-342 0317 *E-mail:* cet@academic-travel.com

---

0213
UNIVERSITY OF PITTSBURGH
Pitt in China - Nanjing
Site: China: Nanjing *Host inst:* Nanjing Univ of Chemical Technology
Dates: 6 wks, Jun-Jul
Subjects: Chinese language (beg/int/adv), Engineering, Sciences
Eligibility: *Level:* fresh, sophs, jrs, srs *Requires:* 2.75 GPA *Age:* avg 20
Credit: *Undergrad:* 8 *Grad:* none *Doc:* transcript
Instruction: *In:* Chinese, English *Format:* lab, lang study *Students:* mainly US
Costs: About $3,500 *incl* tuition, housing, some meals, fees, excursions, books/materials, visa *Nonrefundable fee*
Housing: *Arr by pgm:* residence halls
Deadline: Feb 15
Other info: *US accredited sponsor:* yes *Began:* 1996 *Orient:* in US *Activities:* excursions, field trips *Misc:* May contact former participants. *Financial aid:* scholarships *URL:* http://www.pitt.edu/~stdyabrd/

Contact: Erin Sunday, Study Abroad, Univ of Pittsburgh, B80G Benedum Hall, Pittsburgh PA 15261 *Ph:* 412-624 5942 *Fax:* 412-624 2827 *E-mail:* abroad@engrng.pitt.edu

SHANGHAI

0214
COUNCIL ON INTERNATIONAL EDUCATIONAL EXCHANGE CONSORTIUM
Shanghai Summer Language/Culture Program at Fudan University
Site: China: Shanghai *Host inst:* Fudan Univ
Dates: 8 wks, late Jun-early Aug
Subjects: Chinese language (Mandarin) (beg/int/adv), Chinese studies
Eligibility: *Level:* sophs, jrs, srs, grads, teachers, professionals *Requires:* 2.75 GPA
Credit: *Undergrad:* 8 *Grad:* none
Instruction: *In:* English, Mandarin *Format:* lang study, lecture, seminar *Students:* mainly US
Costs: $4,200 *incl* tuition, housing, all meals, insurance, fees, excursions, visa, ISIC, orient
Housing: *Arr by pgm:* residence halls
Deadline: Mar 15
Other info: *US accredited sponsor:* yes *Began:* 1981 *Orient:* abroad *Activities:* excursions, field trips, cultural events *Misc:* Full-time resident dir. Grade report. Wkly field trips to sites related to subject matter. One-on-one lang tutorials. May contact former participants. *Financial aid:* scholarships *URL:* http://www.ciee.org/study
Contact: *See Index II for Members* Council-ISP, 633 3rd Ave, 20th Fl, New York NY 10017-6706 *Ph:* 800-407 8839; 212-822 2600 *Fax:* 212-822 2779 *E-mail:* studyinfo@ciee.org

0215
CROSS-CULTURAL SOLUTIONS
China Program
Site: China: Shanghai
Dates: 3 wks-1 yr, yr-round
Subjects: Community service projects
Eligibility: *Level:* adults, precoll *Age:* min 18, avg 27
Credit: *Undergrad:* none *Grad:* none *Doc:* certificate
Instruction: *In:* English *Format:* volunteer/svc *Students:* intl
Costs: $2,300 for 3 wks *incl* housing, all meals, excursions *Nonrefundable fee*
Housing: *Arr by pgm:* hotels
Deadline: Rolling admissions
Other info: *US accredited sponsor:* no *Began:* 2000 *Orient:* abroad (3 days) *Activities:* excursions *Misc:* May contact former participants. *URL:* http://www.crossculturalsolutions.org
Contact: Volunteer Coord, Cross-Cultural Solutions, 47 Potters Ave, New Rochelle NY 10801 *Ph:* 800-380 4777; 914-632 0022 *Fax:* 914-632 8494

0216
CSA, CENTER FOR STUDY ABROAD
Chinese Language and Culture
Site: China: Shanghai *Host inst:* Fudan Univ
Dates: 4, 8 or 12 wks, Jan-Mar & Jun-Aug; sem/yr pgms also avail
Subjects: Art, Chinese language (Mandarin) (beg/int/adv), Chinese studies, Contemporary issues, History, Independent study, Literature, Political science/politics
Eligibility: *Level:* adults *Requires:* student visa *Age:* min 17, avg 23
Credit: *Undergrad:* avail *Grad:* avail *Doc:* transcript, certificate
Instruction: *In:* Mandarin *Format:* independent study, lang study, lecture *Students:* intl
Costs: $1,295 for 4 wks, $2,195 for 8 wks, $3,195 for 12 wks *incl* tuition, housing, insurance, fees *Nonrefundable fee*
Housing: *Sponsor assists:* residence halls
Deadline: May 30 or until pgm filled
Other info: *US accredited sponsor:* no *Began:* 1905 *Orient:* abroad *Activities:* excursions, field trips, cultural events *URL:* http://www.studyabroad.com/csa
Contact: Alima Khan, Assoc Dir, CSA, Ctr for Study Abroad, 2802 E Madison St, MS #160, Seattle WA 98112 *Ph:* 206-726 1498 *Fax:* 206-583 8192 *E-mail:* virtuecsa@aol.com

0217
GEORGIA INSTITUTE OF TECHNOLOGY
Political Economy of China
Site: China: Shanghai *Host inst:* Fudan Univ
Dates: 8 wks, summer
Subjects: Chinese studies, Economics, International studies, Political science/politics, Public policy, Social policy
Eligibility: *Level:* sophs, jrs, srs *Requires:* good acad standing
Credit: *Undergrad:* 9 *Grad:* none *Doc:* transcript
Instruction: *In:* English *Format:* lecture *Students:* mainly US
Costs: $4,200 for GA residents, $4,450 for others *incl* tuition, housing, some meals, intl airfare, fees, excursions
Housing: *Arr by pgm:* residence halls
Deadline: Mar 1
Other info: *US accredited sponsor:* yes *Began:* 1996 *Orient:* in US (1 day) *Activities:* excursions, field trips *Misc:* Next pgm offered summer 2002.
Contact: Ms B J Hewitt, Georgia Inst of Technology, Sam Nunn Sch of Intl Affairs, Atlanta GA 30332-0525 *Ph:* 404-894 4452 *Fax:* 404-894 9286 *E-mail:* brenda.hewitt@inta.gatech.edu
Or Contact: Intl Educ, Georgia Inst of Technology, J S Coon Bldg, Ste 203, Atlanta GA 30332-0284 *Ph:* 404-894 7475 *Fax:* 404-894 9682 *E-mail:* study.abroad@gatech.edu

0218
LEXIA INTERNATIONAL
LEXIA Summer in Shanghai
Site: China: Shanghai *Host inst:* Fudan Univ
Dates: 8 wks, mid-Jun-mid-Aug
Subjects: Anthropology, Arts, Asian studies, Chinese language (beg/int/adv), Civilization/culture, Community service projects, Ecology/environmental studies, Economics, Fine arts, History, Homestay, Internships, Literature, Political science/politics, Sociology
Eligibility: *Level:* fresh, sophs, jrs, srs, grads, adults *Requires:* 2.5 GPA *Age:* min 18, avg 21
Credit: *Undergrad:* 8-10 *Grad:* 8-10 *Doc:* transcript *Transfer credit through:* Western Washington Univ
Instruction: *In:* Chinese, English *Format:* internship, lang study, lecture, seminar, volunteer/svc *Students:* mainly US
Costs: $4,650 *incl* tuition, housing, all meals, insurance, fees, excursions, ISIC, computer access *Nonrefundable fee*
Housing: *Arr by pgm:* residence halls with local students, homestay
Deadline: Apr 15; Apr 1 for scholarships
Other info: *US accredited sponsor:* no *Began:* 1997 *In coop with:* Western Washington Univ *Orient:* abroad *Activities:* excursions, field trips, cultural events, sports *Misc:* Student support svcs. May contact former participants. *Financial aid:* scholarships, work study *URL:* http://www.lexiaintl.org
Contact: LEXIA Intl, 25 S Main St, Hanover NH 03755 *Ph:* 800-775 3942; 603-643 9898 *Fax:* 603-643 9899 *E-mail:* info@lexiaintl.org
Or Contact: LEXIA Intl, West Coast, 378 Cambridge Ave, Palo Alto CA 94306-1544 *Ph:* 650-327 9191 *Fax:* 650-327 9192

0219
SOUTHERN ILLINOIS UNIVERSITY AT CARBONDALE
Media Studies in China
Site: China: Shanghai *Host inst:* Shanghai Intl Studies Univ
Dates: 2 wks, May 25-Jun 8

Subjects: Communications, Journalism, Media studies
Eligibility: *Level:* fresh, sophs, jrs, srs, adults, professionals *Requires:* previous study in field *Age:* min 18
Credit: *Undergrad:* avail *Grad:* none *Doc:* transcript
Instruction: *In:* English *Format:* lecture *Students:* mainly US
Costs: Contact sponsor
Housing: *Arr by pgm:* hotels
Deadline: Feb 28
Other info: *US accredited sponsor:* yes *Began:* 2000 *Orient:* in US & abroad *Activities:* excursions, field trips *URL:* http://www.siu.edu/departments/study_abroad
Contact: Thomas Saville, Study Abroad Pgms, Southern Illinois Univ, Carbondale IL 62901-6885 *Ph:* 618-453 7670 *Fax:* 618-453 7647 *E-mail:* studyabr@siu.edu

---

0220
SYRACUSE UNIVERSITY
Global Entrepreneurship: Experiencing China's Global Market
Site: China: Shanghai
Dates: 5 wks, May 28-Jul 4
Subjects: Finance, Independent study, International business
Eligibility: *Level:* sophs, jrs, srs, grads, adults *Requires:* 2.5 GPA
Credit: *Undergrad:* 6 *Grad:* 6 *Doc:* transcript
Instruction: *In:* English *Format:* independent study, seminar *Students:* mainly US
Costs: $7,000 *incl* tuition, housing, all meals, fees, excursions *Nonrefundable fee*
Housing: *Arr by pgm:* residence halls, hotels
Deadline: Mar 15
Other info: *US accredited sponsor:* yes *Began:* 2001 *Orient:* abroad *Activities:* excursions, field trips *Misc:* May contact former participants. *Financial aid:* scholarships *URL:* http://sumweb.syr.edu/dipa/summer
Contact: Daisy Fried, Assoc Dir, Syracuse Univ, 119 Euclid Ave, Syracuse NY 13244 *Ph:* 800-251 9674; 315-443 9419 *Fax:* 315-443 4593 *E-mail:* dsfried@summon3.syr.edu
Or Contact: Linda Stevens, Admissions Counselor, Syracuse Univ, 119 Euclid Ave, Syracuse NY 13244 *Ph:* 800-251 9674; 315-443 9420 *Fax:* 315-443 4593 *E-mail:* dipasum@summon3.syr.edu ▲

0221
UNIVERSITY OF ILLINOIS URBANA-CHAMPAIGN, SCHOOL OF ARCHITECTURE
UIUC/Tongji China Study Abroad Program
Site: China: Shanghai *Host inst:* Tongji Univ
Dates: 6 wks, May 29-Jul 9
Subjects: Architectural history, Architecture, Chinese studies, Field study, Gardens/gardening, Homestay, Housing, Landscape architecture, Urban planning
Eligibility: *Level:* jrs, srs, grads *Requires:* 2.5 GPA, previous study in field *Age:* min 21, avg 23
Credit: *Undergrad:* avail *Grad:* 6-8 *Doc:* certificate
Instruction: *In:* English *Format:* directed field study, independent study, lecture, seminar, study tour *Students:* mainly US
Costs: $7,500 *incl* tuition, housing, all meals, intl airfare, fees, excursions
Housing: *Arr by pgm:* residence halls, apartments, hotels
Deadline: Dec 1
Other info: *US accredited sponsor:* yes *Began:* 1988 *In coop with:* Tongji Univ *Orient:* in US (4 days) *Activities:* excursions, field trips, program travel, cultural events *URL:* http://www.arch.uiuc.edu
Contact: Jane Cook, 611 Taft Dr, Champaign IL 61820 *Ph:* 217-333 1330 *Fax:* 217-244 2900 *E-mail:* j-cook1@uiuc.edu
Or Contact: Prof Alejandro Lapunzina, Sch of Architecture, 611 Taft Dr, Champaign IL 61820 *Ph:* 217-244 4384 *Fax:* 217-244 8866 *E-mail:* alejlapu@uiuc.edu

---

0222
UNIVERSITY OF MASSACHUSETTS AMHERST
Fudan University Summer Program
Site: China: Shanghai *Host inst:* Fudan Univ
Dates: 8 wks, Jul-Aug
Subjects: Chinese language
Eligibility: *Level:* fresh, sophs, jrs, srs, grads, adults, teachers, professionals *Requires:* 2.75 GPA, 1 sem of Mandarin
Credit: *Undergrad:* 10 *Grad:* none *Doc:* transcript
Instruction: *In:* Mandarin *Students:* intl
Costs: $2,100 *incl* tuition, housing, excursions
Housing: *Arr by pgm:* residence halls
Deadline: Mar 15
Other info: *US accredited sponsor:* yes *Began:* 2000 *Orient:* in US & abroad 1 day *Activities:* excursions *Misc:* May contact former participants. *URL:* http://www.umass.edu/ipo/exchange.html
Contact: Dir,China-Taiwan Exch Pgm, Asian Langs & Literatures, Thompson Hall, Univ of Massachusetts, Amherst MA 01003 *Ph:* 413-545 4350 *Fax:* 413-545 4975 *E-mail:* kcroke@acad.umass.edu
Or Contact: Laurel Foster-Moore, Intl Pgms, Univ of Massachusetts, Amherst MA 01003 *Ph:* 413-545 2710 *Fax:* 413-545 1201 *E-mail:* fostermo@ipo.umass.edu

---

TIANJIN

0223
UNIVERSITY OF MINNESOTA
Chinese in Tianjin
Site: China: Tianjin *Host inst:* Nankai Univ
Dates: About 9 wks, Jun-Aug
Subjects: Calligraphy, Chinese language (Mandarin) (beg/int/adv), Performing arts
Eligibility: *Level:* fresh, sophs, jrs, srs, grads *Requires:* 2.5 GPA
Credit: *Undergrad:* 10-12 *Grad:* 1-6
Instruction: *In:* English, Mandarin *Format:* lang study, lecture *Students:* US & intl
Costs: About $3,300 *incl* tuition, housing, some meals, fees
Housing: *Arr by pgm:* residence halls
Deadline: Apr 1
Other info: *US accredited sponsor:* yes *Began:* 1980 *Orient:* in US & abroad *Activities:* excursions, field trips *Misc:* 4-day Beijing tour. Scholarships for own students only. May contact former participants. *URL:* http://www.UMabroad.umn.edu
Contact: Chinese in Tianjin, Global Campus, Univ of Minnesota, Study Abroad, 230 Heller Hall, 271 19th Ave S, Minneapolis MN 55455 *Ph:* 612-626 9000 *Fax:* 612-626 8009 *E-mail:* UMabroad@umn.edu

---

ZHOUKOUDIAN

0224
GEORGE WASHINGTON UNIVERSITY
Paleoanthropological Field Program in China
Site: China: Zhoukoudian *Host inst:* IVPP
Dates: Jun 12-Jul 16
Subjects: Anthropology, Life sciences
Eligibility: *Level:* sophs, jrs, srs, grads, adults, teachers, professionals *Age:* min 21
Credit: *Undergrad:* 3 *Grad:* 3 *Doc:* transcript
Instruction: *In:* English *Format:* directed field study, lecture, seminar, study tour *Students:* mainly US
Costs: $4,384 *incl* tuition, housing, some meals, fees, excursions *Nonrefundable fee*
Housing: *Arr by pgm:* hotels, hostels

See "How To Use This Book" for definitions of terms used above. ▲ = See program sponsor's ad(s) in this book.

Deadline: Contact sponsor
Other info: *US accredited sponsor:* yes *Began:* 1995 *Orient:* abroad (1 day) *Activities:* field trips, program travel *Misc:* Summer pgms are updated in Dec. Contact sponsor for new info. *URL:* http://www.summer.gwu.edu
Contact: Summer, Special & Intl Programs, George Washington Univ, 609 22nd St NW, Washington DC 20052 *Ph:* 202-994 6360 *Fax:* 202-994 9133 *E-mail:* sumprogs@gwu.edu

Fiji

MORE THAN ONE CITY

0225
SAN FRANCISCO STATE UNIVERSITY, WILDLANDS STUDIES PROGRAM
Ecosystems and Cultures in Fiji
Site: Fiji: various sites
Dates: 6 wks, Oct 11-Nov 22
Subjects: Biology, Ecology/environmental studies, Ethnography, Field study
Eligibility: *Level:* adults *Requires:* application, essay *Age:* min 18, avg 22
Credit: *Undergrad:* 9 per term *Grad:* none *Doc:* transcript
Instruction: *In:* English *Format:* directed field study *Students:* mainly US
Costs: $1,900 *incl* tuition
Housing: *Arr by pgm:* tents in camps
Deadline: Rolling admissions
Other info: *US accredited sponsor:* yes *Began:* 1999 *Orient:* abroad *Activities:* field trips, cultural events *Misc:* May contact former participants. *URL:* http://www.wildlandsstudies.com/ws
Contact: Crandall Bay, Dir, or Marcene Bay, Asst, Wildlands Studies, San Francisco State Univ, 3 Mosswood Circle, Cazadero CA 95421 *Ph:* 707-632 5665 *Fax:* 707-632 5665 *E-mail:* wildlnds@sonic.net

India

MORE THAN ONE CITY

0226
INTERNATIONAL CAMPUS CONSORTIUM and THUNDERBIRD, THE AMERICAN GRADUATE SCHOOL OF INTERNATIONAL MANAGEMENT
Winterim in India
Site: India: Bangalore, Delhi, Mumbai
Dates: 3 wks, Jan 3-21
Subjects: Civilization/culture, Economics, Indian studies, International business, International studies, Political science/politics
Eligibility: *Level:* grads *Requires:* 3.0 GPA
Credit: *Undergrad:* none *Grad:* 3 *Doc:* transcript
Instruction: *In:* English *Format:* lecture *Students:* intl
Costs: $2,555 *incl* tuition, insurance, fees
Housing: *Sponsor assists:* hotels
Deadline: Contact sponsor
Other info: *US accredited sponsor:* yes *Orient:* abroad *Activities:* field trips *Misc:* May contact former participants. *Financial aid:* scholarships, work study *URL:* http://www.t-bird.edu
Contact: *See Index II for Members* Dr Earl Gibbons, Assoc VP, Overseas Pgms, Thunderbird, 15249 N 59th Ave, Glendale AZ 85306 *Ph:* 602-978 7252 *Fax:* 602-978 7419 *E-mail:* gibbonse@t-bird.edu
Or Contact: Diane Hayton, Coord, Overseas Pgms, Thunderbird, 15249 N 59th Ave, Glendale AZ 85306 *Ph:* 602-978 7252 *Fax:* 602-978 7419 *E-mail:* haytond@t-bird.edu

---

0227
INTERNATIONAL INSTITUTE FOR SCIENTIFIC & ACADEMIC COLLABORATION (IISAC)
Study India Program
Site: India: Kerala, Pondicherry, Trivandrum *Host inst:* Calicut Univ, Cochin Univ of Sci & Tech, MG Univ Kottayam, Pondicherry Univ, Univ of Kerala
Dates: 3 wks-3 mos, Jun-Sep
Subjects: Alternative medicine, Arts, Civilization/culture, Ecology/environmental studies, Engineering, Independent study, Indian languages, Indian studies, Internships, Life sciences, Martial arts, Medicine, Natural resources, Sociology, Traditional medicine
Eligibility: *Level:* fresh, sophs, jrs, srs, grads, adults, teachers, professionals, precoll *Age:* min 18, max 60, avg 35
Credit: *Undergrad:* avail *Grad:* avail *Doc:* transcript, certificate
Instruction: *In:* English *Format:* art studio, directed field study, independent study, internship, lab, lang study, lecture, music lesson, practical training, seminar, student teaching, study tour, tutorial, volunteer/svc, workshop *Students:* intl
Costs: $150-$200 per wk *incl* tuition, housing, all meals, insurance, fees, excursions, books/materials *Nonrefundable fee*
Housing: *Arr by pgm:* apartments, homestay, hotels
Deadline: Rolling admissions
Other info: *US accredited sponsor:* no *Began:* 1999 *Orient:* in US & abroad (1 wk) *Activities:* excursions, field trips, program travel, cultural events, sports *Misc:* May contact former participants. *Financial aid:* scholarships *URL:* http://www.iisac.com
Contact: Alex Koshy, Exec Dir, Intl Inst for Sci & Acad Collaboration, 15 Honiss Pl, Ste 1, Newark NJ 07104 *Ph:* 973-483 0888 *Fax:* 973-483 0888 *E-mail:* alexkoshy@erols.com
Or Contact: Dr Sunny Luke, Chairman, Intl Inst for Sci & Acad Collaboration, 201 Hopkins Ave, Jersey City NJ *Ph:* 201-963 1024 *Fax:* 201-963 1024 *E-mail:* sunnyluke@aol.com

---

HYDERABAD

0228
FAIRFIELD UNIVERSITY
Summer in India
Site: India: Hyderabad *Host inst:* Univ of Hyderabad
Dates: 1 mo, May 17-Jun 12
Subjects: Anthropology, Civilization/culture, Indian studies, Literature, Political science/politics
Eligibility: *Level:* sophs, jrs, srs, grads, adults, teachers, professionals *Requires:* 2.5 GPA, essay, recommendation letters *Age:* min 18, avg 20
Credit: *Undergrad:* 6 *Grad:* none *Doc:* transcript
Instruction: *In:* English *Format:* internship, lecture, tutorial *Students:* mainly US
Costs: $3,900 *incl* tuition, housing, all meals, intl airfare, excursions
Housing: *Arr by pgm:* residence halls with local students
Deadline: Feb 15 or until pgm filled
Other info: *US accredited sponsor:* yes *Began:* 1999 *In coop with:* Univ of Hyderabad *Orient:* in US *Activities:* excursions, field trips, cultural events *URL:* http://www.fairfield.edu/sce/studyabroad
Contact: Christine Bowers, Study Abroad Coord, Fairfield Univ, Dolan House, Fairfield CT 06430 *Ph:* 888-254 1566; 203-254 4220 *Fax:* 203-254 4106 *E-mail:* cbbowers@fair1.fairfield.edu

---

0229
UNIVERSITY OF PITTSBURGH
Pitt in India
Site: India: Hyderabad *Host inst:* Univ of Hyderabad
Dates: 9 wks, late Jun-late Aug
Subjects: Anthropology, Civilization/culture, Economics, Ethnography, Gender studies, Geography, History, Human rights, Independent study, Indian studies, Linguistics, Literature, Religion/theology, Urban studies
Eligibility: *Level:* sophs, jrs, srs, grads, adults *Requires:* 2.75 GPA
Credit: *Undergrad:* 9 *Grad:* none *Doc:* transcript

Instruction: *In:* English *Format:* independent study, lecture *Students:* mainly US
Costs: Contact sponsor
Housing: *Arr by pgm:* residence halls
Deadline: Feb 15
Other info: *US accredited sponsor:* yes *Began:* 1997 *Orient:* in US & abroad *Misc:* May contact former participants. *Financial aid:* scholarships *URL:* http://www.pitt.edu/~stdyabrd/
Contact: Elizabeth Royal, Study Abroad, Univ of Pittsburgh, 802 William Pitt Union, Pittsburgh PA 15260 *Ph:* 412-383 7163 *Fax:* 412-383 7166 *E-mail:* stdyabrd+@pitt.edu

---

KERALA

0230
UNIVERSITY OF WISCONSIN-MADISON
Kerala Summer Program
Site: India: Kerala *Host inst:* Univ of Kerala
Dates: Early Jun-mid-Aug
Subjects: Anthropology, Indian languages (beg), Performing arts
Eligibility: *Level:* sophs, jrs, srs, grads *Requires:* 2.5 GPA
Credit: *Undergrad:* 6-9 *Grad:* none *Doc:* transcript
Instruction: *In:* English *Format:* art studio, lang study, lecture, practical training *Students:* mainly US
Costs: $4,750 for WI residents, $5,000 for others *incl* tuition, housing, all meals, intl airfare, local transport, area travel *Nonrefundable fee*
Housing: *Arr by pgm:* pgm house
Deadline: 1st Fri in Feb
Other info: *US accredited sponsor:* yes *Began:* 1993 *Orient:* in US *Misc:* Loans for qualifying degree seeking undergrads. May contact former participants. *Financial aid:* scholarships *URL:* http://www.wisc.edu/studyabroad
Contact: Intl Studies & Pgms, Univ of Wisconsin-Madison, 261 Bascom Hall, 500 Lincoln Dr, Madison WI 53706 *Ph:* 608-265 6329 *Fax:* 608-262 6998 *E-mail:* peeradvisor@bascom.wisc.edu

---

MADRAS

0231
ILLINOIS STATE UNIVERSITY
Criminal Justice's Summer Program in Madras, India
Site: India: Madras
Dates: 2 wks, mid-Jul
Subjects: Criminal justice
Eligibility: *Level:* sophs, jrs, srs *Requires:* 2.5 GPA, previous study in field
Credit: *Undergrad:* 6 *Grad:* none *Doc:* transcript
Instruction: *In:* English *Format:* study tour *Students:* mainly US
Costs: $3,570 *incl* tuition, housing, all meals, intl airfare, insurance, fees, excursions, ISIC *Nonrefundable fee*
Housing: *Arr by pgm:* guest houses
Deadline: Mar 1
Other info: *US accredited sponsor:* yes *Orient:* avail (1 day) *Activities:* excursions, field trips, program travel, cultural events *URL:* http://www.its.ilstu.edu/intlstudies/
Contact: Dr Sesha Kethineni, ILlinois State Univ, Campus Box 5250, Normal IL 61790-6120 *Ph:* 309-438 5566
Or Contact: Intl Studies & Pgms, Illinois State Univ, Campus Box 6120, Normal IL 61790-6120 *Ph:* 309-438 5365 *Fax:* 309-438 3987 *E-mail:* oisp@ilstu.edu

---

NEW DELHI

0232
CROSS-CULTURAL SOLUTIONS
India Program
Site: India: New Delhi
Dates: 3 wks-1 yr, yr-round
Subjects: Community service projects
Eligibility: *Level:* adults, precoll *Age:* min 18
Credit: *Undergrad:* none *Grad:* none *Doc:* certificate
Instruction: *In:* English *Format:* volunteer/svc *Students:* intl
Costs: $1,950 for 3 wks *incl* housing, all meals, excursions *Nonrefundable fee*
Housing: *Arr by pgm:* apartments
Deadline: Rolling admissions
Other info: *US accredited sponsor:* no *Began:* 1999 *Orient:* abroad (3 days) *Activities:* excursions, cultural events *Misc:* May contact former participants. *URL:* http://www.crossculturalsolutions.org
Contact: Volunteer Coord, Cross-Cultural Solutions, 47 Potters Ave, New Rochelle NY 10801 *Ph:* 800-380 4777; 914-632 0022 *Fax:* 914-632 8494

0233
NORTH CAROLINA STATE UNIVERSITY
Hindi Language and Indian Culture
Site: India: New Delhi *Host inst:* Jawaharlal Nehru Univ
Dates: 5 wks, May-Jun
Subjects: Civilization/culture, Hindi language (beg/int), Indian studies, Literature
Eligibility: *Level:* fresh, sophs, jrs, srs *Requires:* 2.0 GPA *Age:* min 18
Credit: *Undergrad:* 6 *Grad:* none *Doc:* transcript
Instruction: *In:* English, Hindi *Format:* lang study, lecture, study tour *Students:* mainly US
Costs: $2,900 *incl* tuition, housing, all meals, intl airfare, insurance, excursions *Nonrefundable fee*
Housing: *Arr by pgm:* residence halls, hotels
Deadline: Feb
Other info: *US accredited sponsor:* yes *Began:* 1999 *Orient:* abroad *Activities:* excursions, field trips *Misc:* Excursions to Jaipur, Agra, Taj Mahal, Himalayan Hill Station. May contact former participants. *URL:* http://www.ncsu.edu/studyabroad
Contact: Anne Haberkern, North Carolina State Univ, 2118 Pullen Hall, Box 7344, Raleigh NC 27695-7344 *Ph:* 919-515 2087 *Fax:* 919-515 6021 *E-mail:* study_abroad@ncsu.edu

---

PUNE

0234
UNIVERSITY OF PENNSYLVANIA
Penn-in-India
Site: India: Pune (Poona) *Host inst:* Univ of Poona
Dates: 6 wks, mid Jun-early Aug
Subjects: Civilization/culture, Community service projects, Economics, Homestay, Independent study, Indian languages (beg/int/adv), Indian studies, Internships, Performing arts, Religion/theology, Traditional medicine
Eligibility: *Level:* fresh, sophs, jrs, srs, grads
Credit: *Undergrad:* 6 *Grad:* 3 *Doc:* transcript
Instruction: *In:* English *Format:* independent study, internship, lang study, lecture, tutorial, volunteer/svc *Students:* mainly US
Costs: About $5,200 *incl* tuition, housing, intl airfare, excursions *Nonrefundable fee*
Housing: *Arr by pgm:* homestay
Deadline: Mar 1
Other info: *US accredited sponsor:* yes *Began:* 1994 *Orient:* in US & abroad *Activities:* field trips, cultural events *URL:* http://www.sas.upenn.edu/CGS/
Contact: Elizabeth Sachs, Penn Summer Abroad, Univ of Pennsylvania, 3440 Market St, Ste 100, Philadelphia PA 19104-3335 *Ph:* 215-898 5738 *Fax:* 215-573 2053 *E-mail:* sdanti@mail.sas.upenn.edu

Indonesia

MORE THAN ONE CITY

0235
GEORGE MASON UNIVERSITY
Contemporary Java and Bali
Site: Indonesia: Java, Bali
Dates: 2 wks, Dec 29-Jan 13
Subjects: Anthropology, History
Eligibility: *Level:* fresh, sophs, jrs, srs, adults, teachers, professionals *Requires:* 2.25 GPA *Age:* min 18
Credit: *Undergrad:* 3 *Grad:* none *Doc:* transcript
Instruction: *In:* English *Format:* lecture *Students:* mainly US
Costs: Contact sponsor
Housing: *Arr by pgm:* hotels
Deadline: Mid-Oct
Other info: *US accredited sponsor:* yes *Orient:* in US 1 day *Activities:* excursions, program travel, cultural events *Financial aid:* scholarships, work study *URL:* http://www.gmu.edu/departments/cge
Contact: Ctr for Global Educ, George Mason Univ, Johnson Ctr, Rm 235, 4400 University Dr, Fairfax VA 22030-4444 *Ph:* 703-993 2154 *Fax:* 703-993 2153 *E-mail:* cge@gmn.edu

---

BALI

0236
ARTIS-ART RESEARCH TOURS AND INTERNATIONAL STUDIOS
Arts in Paradise
Site: Indonesia: Bali
Dates: 2-4 wks, summer
Subjects: Batik, Painting, Woodcarving
Eligibility: *Level:* fresh, sophs, jrs, srs, grads, adults, teachers, professionals *Requires:* good physical & mental health *Age:* min 18, max 78, avg 25
Credit: *Undergrad:* avail *Grad:* none *Doc:* transcript
Instruction: *In:* English *Format:* art studio, directed field study, independent study, lecture, study tour, workshop *Students:* mainly US
Costs: $3,525 *incl* housing, some meals, intl airfare, insurance, fees, excursions, art workshops, museum fees
Housing: *Arr by pgm:* hotels
Deadline: Contact sponsor
Other info: *US accredited sponsor:* no *Began:* 1980 *In coop with:* Danu Enterprises *Orient:* abroad (2 days) *Activities:* excursions, field trips, program travel, cultural events *Misc:* May contact former participants. *Financial aid:* scholarships *URL:* http://www.artis-tours.org
Contact: David Renfrow, Dir, ARTIS, 1616 Princeton Dr, Columbia MO 65203 *Ph:* 573-886 9688 *Fax:* 573-447 3495 *E-mail:* dfro@socket.net
Or Contact: Robert Renfrow, Coord, ARTIS, 1102 W Huron St, Tucson AZ 85745 *Ph:* 800-232 6893; 520-620 6613 *Fax:* 520-620 6613 *E-mail:* rfro@azstarnet.com

---

MANADO

0237
CONSORTIUM FOR THE TEACHING OF INDONESIAN AND MALAY (COTIM) and **UNIVERSITAS SAM RATULANGI**
Advanced Indonesian Abroad
Site: Indonesia: Manado (North Sulawesi) *Host inst:* UNSRAT
Dates: Jun 6-Aug 16
Subjects: Civilization/culture, Field study, Homestay, Independent study, Indonesian language (adv), Indonesian studies
Eligibility: *Level:* jrs, srs, grads, teachers, professionals *Requires:* int Indonesian or Malay
Credit: *Undergrad:* none *Grad:* none *Doc:* certificate
Instruction: *In:* Indonesian *Format:* directed field study, lang study, lecture *Students:* mainly US
Costs: $1,850 *incl* tuition, fees *Nonrefundable fee*
Housing: *Arr by pgm:* homestay
Deadline: Jan 31
Other info: *US accredited sponsor:* yes *In coop with:* US Dept of Educ *Orient:* abroad *Misc:* Intensive lang study in small groups for 9 wks, 1-wk field study on individual research project & immersion in Indonesian culture. *URL:* http://www.wisc.edu/ctrseasia/cotim.html
Contact: *See Index II for Members* Ms Marie Kruger, Pgm Asst, COTIM, Ctr for Southeast Asian Studies, 1155 Observatory Dr, Ingraham Hall, Rm 207, Univ of Wisconsin-Madison, Madison WI 53706 *Fax:* 608-263 3735 *E-mail:* mkruger@students.wisc.edu

Japan

MORE THAN ONE CITY

0238
GEORGE MASON UNIVERSITY
Pagodas and Pachinko Parlors: Tradition in Postmodern Japan
Site: Japan: Kyoto, Tokyo
Dates: 2 wks, Jun 27-Jul 12
Subjects: History
Eligibility: *Level:* fresh, sophs, jrs, srs, grads, adults, teachers, professionals *Requires:* 2.25 GPA *Age:* min 18
Credit: *Undergrad:* 3 *Grad:* 3 *Doc:* transcript
Instruction: *In:* English *Format:* lecture, seminar *Students:* mainly US
Costs: $4,500 for GMU students, $5,192 for others *incl* tuition, housing, some meals, intl airfare, insurance, fees, excursions
Housing: *Arr by pgm:* hotels
Deadline: May 15
Other info: *US accredited sponsor:* yes *Orient:* in US 1 day *Financial aid:* scholarships, work study *URL:* http://www.gmu.edu/departments/cge
Contact: Ctr for Global Educ, George Mason Univ, Johnson Ctr, Rm 235, 4400 University Drive, Fairfax VA 22030-4444 *Ph:* 703-993 2154 *Fax:* 703-993 2153 *E-mail:* cge@gmu.edu

---

0239
INTERNATIONAL COUNCIL FOR CULTURAL EXCHANGE (ICCE)
Japanese Language and Culture and Asian Studies
Site: Japan: Tokyo, various sites *Host inst:* regional univs
Dates: 5 wks or less, Jun-Aug
Subjects: Asian studies, Civilization/culture, Japanese language (beg/int), Japanese studies
Eligibility: *Level:* fresh, sophs, jrs, srs, grads, adults, teachers, professionals, precoll
Credit: *Undergrad:* avail *Grad:* avail *Doc:* transcript, certificate
Instruction: *In:* English, Japanese *Format:* lab, lang study, lecture, practical training, study tour *Students:* intl
Costs: Contact sponsor
Housing: *Sponsor assists:* residence halls, hotels
Deadline: Jun 1
Other info: *US accredited sponsor:* no *Began:* 1982 *Activities:* excursions, cultural events, sports
Contact: Dr Stanley Gochman, ICCE, 5 Bellport Ln, Bellport NY 11713 *Ph:* 631-286 5228 ▲

0240
JAPAN-AMERICA STUDENT CONFERENCE, INC (WASHINGTON DC) and **INTERNATIONAL EDUCATION CENTER (TOKYO)**
Japan-America Student Conference (JASC)
Site: Japan: various sites (2001); USA (2002)
Dates: 4 wks, Jul-Aug
Subjects: Arts, Business/management, Ecology/environmental studies, Education/teaching, Intercultural studies, Law,

Media studies, Peace studies, Philosophy, Political science/politics, Religion/theology, Sciences, Security issues, Third World studies, Trade
Eligibility: *Level:* fresh, sophs, jrs, srs, grads *Requires:* full-time student, US citizenship or permanent residency
Credit: *Undergrad:* avail *Grad:* avail *Doc:* certificate
Instruction: *In:* English *Format:* lecture, seminar *Students:* US & host country
Costs: $1,900 *incl* housing, all meals, intl airfare, books/materials, orient
Housing: *Arr by pgm:* residence halls, homestay
Deadline: Mar 1
Other info: *US accredited sponsor:* no *Began:* 1934 *Orient:* in US & abroad *Activities:* field trips, program travel *Misc:* Pgm alternates Japan (2001) & USA (2002). Meetings with govt, bus & acad leaders. Guest speakers, presentations. May contact former participants. *Financial aid:* scholarships *URL:* http://www.jasc.org
Contact: Gretchen Hobbs Donaldson, Japan-America Student Conference, 606 18th St NW, 2nd Fl, Washington DC 20006-5202 *Ph:* 202-289 4231 *Fax:* 202-709 8265 *E-mail:* jascinc@jasc.org
Or Contact: Intl Educ Ctr, 1-21 Yotsuya, Shinjuku-ku, Tokyo 160-0004, Japan

---

0241
KENTUCKY INSTITUTE FOR INTERNATIONAL STUDIES (KIIS)
Japan
Site: Japan: various sites *Host inst:* Aichi Inst of Technology
Dates: 5 wks, Jun-Jul
Subjects: Civilization/culture, Japanese language, Japanese studies
Eligibility: *Level:* fresh, sophs, jrs, srs, grads, adults *Requires:* 2.0 GPA *Age:* min 18, avg 21
Credit: *Undergrad:* 6 *Grad:* 6 *Doc:* transcript *Transfer credit through:* Murray State Univ
Instruction: *In:* English *Format:* lang study, lecture, study tour *Students:* mainly US
Costs: About $3,890 *incl* tuition, housing, some meals, intl airfare, excursions, ISIC *Nonrefundable fee*
Housing: *Arr by pgm:* hotels
Deadline: Feb 15; Mar 15 for scholarships
Other info: *US accredited sponsor:* yes *Began:* 2000 *Orient:* in US & abroad *Activities:* excursions, field trips, program travel, cultural events *Misc:* May contact former participants. *Financial aid:* scholarships *URL:* http://www.kiis.org
Contact: *See Index II for Members* Dr J Milton Grimes, Exec Dir, KIIS, Murray State Univ, PO Box 9, Murray KY 42071 *Ph:* 270-762 3091 *Fax:* 270-762 3434 *E-mail:* kiismsu@murraystate.edu

---

0242
LANGUAGE LIAISON
Japanese Language
Site: Japan: Kanazawa, Tokyo
Dates: 2 wks-1 yr, yr-round
Subjects: Calligraphy, Civilization/culture, Homestay, Japanese language (beg/int/adv)
Eligibility: *Level:* fresh, sophs, jrs, srs, grads, adults, teachers, professionals, precoll *Age:* min 14
Credit: *Undergrad:* avail *Grad:* avail *Doc:* transcript, certificate
Instruction: *In:* Japanese *Format:* lang study *Students:* intl
Costs: Contact sponsor
Housing: *Arr by pgm:* homestay, guest house
Deadline: 30 days before pgm
Other info: *US accredited sponsor:* no *Activities:* excursions, cultural events *Misc:* Scholarship research svc. *URL:* http://www.languageliaison.com
Contact: Nancy Forman, Dir, Lang Liaison, 4 Burnham Pkwy, Morristown NJ 07960 *Ph:* 800-284 4448 *Fax:* 973-898 1710 *E-mail:* learn@languageliaison.com

---

0243
LANGUAGE LIAISON
Japanese Saturation
Site: Japan: Kanazawa, Tokyo *Host inst:* Live in Learn
Dates: 1 wk or longer, yr-round
Subjects: Civilization/culture, Homestay, Japanese language (beg/int/adv)
Eligibility: *Level:* fresh, sophs, jrs, srs, grads, adults, teachers, professionals, precoll *Age:* min 10
Credit: *Undergrad:* none *Grad:* none *Doc:* transcript, certificate
Instruction: *In:* Japanese *Format:* lang study *Students:* intl
Costs: Contact sponsor
Housing: *Arr by pgm:* teacher's home
Deadline: 45 days before pgm
Other info: *US accredited sponsor:* no *Misc:* Live & learn in your teacher's home. Scholarship research svc. *URL:* http://www.languageliaison.com
Contact: Nancy Forman, Dir, Lang Liaison, 4 Burnham Pkwy, Morristown NJ 07960 *Ph:* 800-284 4448 *Fax:* 973-898 1710 *E-mail:* learn@languageliaison.com

---

0244
LINGUA SERVICE WORLDWIDE
Total Immersion/Intensive Language and Culture in Japan-Osaka, Tokyo
Site: Japan: Osaka, Tokyo *Host inst:* Home Lang Intl
Dates: 1 wk-1 yr, yr-round
Subjects: Civilization/culture, Homestay, Japanese language (beg/int/adv)
Eligibility: *Level:* adults *Age:* min 14
Credit: *Undergrad:* avail *Grad:* avail *Doc:* transcript, certificate
Instruction: *In:* Japanese *Format:* lang study *Students:* intl
Costs: Contact sponsor
Housing: *Arr by pgm:* teacher's home
Deadline: 45 days before pgm
Other info: *US accredited sponsor:* no *Began:* 1993 *Activities:* excursions, cultural events *Misc:* Participate in teacher's family & social life. May contact former participants. *URL:* http://www.linguaserviceworldwide.com
Contact: Dir, Lingua Svc Worldwide, 75 Prospect St, Ste 4, Huntington NY 11743 *Ph:* 800-394 5327; 631-424 0777 *Fax:* 631-271 3441 *E-mail:* itctravel@worldnet.att.net ▲

0245
UNIVERSITY OF ARKANSAS
International Business Seminar in Japan
Site: Japan: various sites
Dates: May 15-Jun 17
Subjects: Economics
Eligibility: Own students preferred. *Level:* sophs, jrs, srs *Requires:* 3.0 GPA, previous study in field, prerequisites in microecon & macroecon *Age:* avg 22
Credit: *Undergrad:* 6 *Grad:* none *Doc:* transcript
Instruction: *In:* English *Format:* study tour *Students:* mainly US
Costs: $3,900 *incl* tuition, housing, intl airfare, insurance, fees, excursions, railpass
Housing: *Arr by pgm:* hostels
Deadline: February 15
Other info: *US accredited sponsor:* yes *Began:* 1998 *Orient:* in US & abroad *Activities:* program travel *Misc:* Visits to several Japanese companies. *URL:* http://www.uark.edu/~studyabr
Contact: Dr Joseph Ziegler, Econ, Walton Coll 422, Univ of Arkansas, Fayetteville AR 72701 *Ph:* 501-575 3266
Or Contact: Michelle Morris, 722 W. Maple Street, University of Arkansas, Fayetteville AR 72701 *Ph:* 501-575 7582, 501-575 7582 *Fax:* 501-575 7402 *E-mail:* studyabr@cavern.uark.edu

---

0246
UNIVERSITY OF RICHMOND
Summer Study in Japan
Site: Japan: Hamamatsu, Tenryu
Dates: 6 wks, May-Jun or Jun-Jul
Subjects: Civilization/culture, Homestay, Japanese language (beg/int), Japanese studies
Eligibility: *Level:* fresh, sophs, jrs, srs, adults
Credit: *Undergrad:* 3-8 *Grad:* none *Doc:* transcript

Instruction: *In:* Japanese *Format:* independent study, lang study, lecture *Students:* mainly US
Costs: About $5,000 *incl* housing, some meals, intl airfare
Housing: *Arr by pgm:* homestay
Deadline: Rolling admissions
Other info: *US accredited sponsor:* yes *Activities:* excursions, field trips, cultural events
Contact: Prof Akira Suzuki, Univ of Richmond, Studies, Richmond VA 23173 *Ph:* 804-289 8293 *Fax:* 804-379 3761 *E-mail:* asuzuki@richmond.edu
Or Contact: Jeanne Burkett, Sch of Continuing Studies, Univ of Richmond, Richmond VA 23173 *Ph:* 804-289 8133 *Fax:* 804-289 8138 *E-mail:* jburkett@richmond.edu

---

0247
WHITWORTH COLLEGE
Sports Medicine Seminar
Site: Japan: Kanazawa, Nishinomiya, Tokyo
Dates: 1 mo, about May 20-Jun 20; offered in even-numbered yrs
Subjects: Medicine, Sports
Eligibility: *Level:* sophs, jrs, srs *Requires:* 2.5 GPA, major in sports medicine
Credit: *Undergrad:* 3 *Grad:* none *Doc:* transcript
Instruction: *In:* English *Format:* lecture, study tour *Students:* mainly US
Costs: About $4,000 *incl* housing, some meals, intl airfare, excursions, in-country transport
Housing: *Arr by pgm:* residence halls, hotels
Deadline: Oct 1
Other info: *US accredited sponsor:* yes *Began:* 1994 *Activities:* excursions, program travel, cultural events *Misc:* May contact former participants. *URL:* http://www.whitworth.edu
Contact: Sue Jackson, Coord, Off-Campus Pgms, Ctr for Intl & Multicultural Educ, Whitworth Coll, Spokane WA 99251-2702 *Ph:* 509-777 4596 *Fax:* 509-777 3723 *E-mail:* sjackson@whitworth.edu

---

ASAHIKAWA

0248
ILLINOIS STATE UNIVERSITY
Asahikawa, Japan Summer Program
Site: Japan: Asahikawa *Host inst:* Hokkaido Univ
Dates: 4 wks, Jun-Jul
Subjects: Civilization/culture, Education/teaching, Homestay, Japanese studies
Eligibility: *Level:* sophs, jrs, srs, grads *Requires:* 2.5 GPA, previous study in field, major in educ
Credit: *Undergrad:* 6 *Grad:* 6 *Doc:* transcript
Instruction: *In:* English *Format:* lecture, seminar, study tour *Students:* mainly host country
Costs: $2,700 *incl* tuition, housing, all meals, intl airfare, insurance, fees, excursions *Nonrefundable fee*
Housing: *Arr by pgm:* homestay
Deadline: Feb 14
Other info: *US accredited sponsor:* yes *Began:* 1997 *Orient:* in US & abroad (1 day) *Activities:* excursions, field trips, cultural events *Financial aid:* scholarships *URL:* http://www.its.ilstu.edu/intlstudies/
Contact: Intl Studies & Pgms, Illinois State Univ, Campus Box 6120, Normal IL 61790-6120 *Ph:* 309-438 5365 *Fax:* 309-438 3987 *E-mail:* oisp@ilstu.edu

---

CHIBA

0249
UNIVERSITY OF ALABAMA
Alabama in Japan
Site: Japan: Chiba *Host inst:* Chiba Univ
Dates: 3 wks, May 15-Jun 5
Subjects: Economics, Homestay, Japanese studies
Eligibility: *Level:* jrs, srs, grads *Requires:* 3.0 GPA, intro econ or instructor's permission
Credit: *Undergrad:* 3 *Grad:* 3
Instruction: *In:* English *Format:* lecture *Students:* mainly US
Costs: $850 *incl* tuition, housing, some meals, books/materials
Housing: *Arr by pgm:* homestay
Deadline: Mar 1
Other info: *US accredited sponsor:* yes *Orient:* in US (1 day) *Activities:* field trips, program travel *Misc:* May contact former participants. *Financial aid:* scholarships *URL:* http://www.ua.edu/international
Contact: Dr CB Hilton, Dir, Intl Bus Pgms, Coll of Commerce & Bus Admin, Univ of Alabama, Box 870225, Tuscaloosa AL 35487-0225 *Ph:* 205-348 9432 *Fax:* 205-348 6695 *E-mail:* chilton@cba.ua.edu
Or Contact: Angie Channell, Intl Pgms, Univ of Alabama, Box 870254, 135 BB Comer Hall, Tuscaloosa AL 35487-0250 *Ph:* 205-348 5256 *Fax:* 205-348 5298 *E-mail:* achannel@aalan.ua.edu

---

HIKONE

0250
JAPAN CENTER FOR MICHIGAN UNIVERSITIES
Summer Intensive Japanese Language
Site: Japan: Hikone
Dates: 9-10 wks, Jun-Aug
Subjects: Field study, Homestay, Japanese language (beg/int/adv), Japanese studies
Eligibility: *Level:* sophs, jrs, srs, grads, adults, teachers, professionals *Requires:* 2.5 GPA
Credit: *Undergrad:* 10 *Grad:* none *Doc:* transcript *Transfer credit through:* Michigan State Univ
Instruction: *In:* Japanese *Format:* directed field study, lab, lang study, lecture, practical training, seminar, tutorial *Students:* US & intl
Costs: $5,300 *incl* tuition, housing, some meals, intl airfare, fees, excursions, books/materials
Housing: *Arr by pgm:* apartments, homestay
Deadline: Mar 1
Other info: *US accredited sponsor:* yes *Began:* 1992 *Orient:* abroad (intensive lang study) *Activities:* excursions, field trips, program travel, cultural events, sports *Misc:* May contact former participants. *Financial aid:* scholarships *URL:* http://www.isp.msu.edu/JCMU/
Contact: *See Index II for Members* John Hazewinkel, JCMU, Michigan State Univ, 108 Intl Ctr, East Lansing MI 48824-1035 *Ph:* 517-355 4654 *Fax:* 517-353 8727 *E-mail:* jcmu@msu.edu

---

HIRATSUKA

0251
UNIVERSITY OF KANSAS
Exploring Contemporary Japan
Site: Japan: Hiratsuka *Host inst:* Kanagawa Univ
Dates: 5 wks, Jun 4-11
Subjects: Business/management, Civilization/culture, Japanese language (beg/int/adv), Japanese studies
Eligibility: *Level:* fresh, sophs, jrs, srs, grads *Requires:* 2 references
Credit: *Undergrad:* 6 *Grad:* none *Doc:* transcript
Instruction: *In:* English, Japanese *Format:* lang study, lecture, seminar, study tour *Students:* mainly US
Costs: $3,500 *incl* tuition, housing, some meals, fees, excursions
Housing: *Arr by pgm:* homestay, city guest house
Deadline: Mar 1
Other info: *US accredited sponsor:* yes *Began:* 1991 *In coop with:* Kanagawa Univ *Orient:* abroad *Activities:* excursions, field trips, program travel, cultural events *Misc:* 3-day excursion to Kyoto, Tanabata Festival. May contact former participants. *URL:* http://www.ukans.edu/~osa

Contact: Renee Bergene, Coord, Study Abroad, Univ of Kansas, 108 Lippincott Hall, Lawrence KS 66045 *Ph:* 785-864 3742 *Fax:* 785-864 5040 *E-mail:* osa@ukans.edu ▲

KANAZAWA

0252
NATIONAL REGISTRATION CENTER FOR STUDY ABROAD (NRCSA)
Language Study in Japan
Site: Japan: Kanazawa *Host inst:* Euroctr
Dates: 4-12 wks, yr-round
Subjects: Civilization/culture, Japanese language (beg/int/adv), Japanese studies
Eligibility: *Level:* fresh, sophs, jrs, srs, grads, adults *Age:* min 18
Credit: *Undergrad:* avail *Grad:* avail *Doc:* certificate
Instruction: *In:* Japanese *Format:* lang study, lecture *Students:* intl
Costs: About $3,220 for 4 wks, $9,500 for 12 wks *incl* tuition, housing, some meals, insurance, fees
Housing: *Arr by pgm*
Deadline: None
Other info: *US accredited sponsor:* no *Misc:* Optional excursions. *URL:* http://www.nrcsa.com
Contact: Mary Croy, NRCSA, 823 N 2nd St, #206, Milwaukee WI 53203 *Ph:* 414-278 0631 *Fax:* 414-271 8884 *E-mail:* info@nrcsa.com

KAWASAKI

0253
COLLEGE OF BUSINESS AND COMMUNICATION, KAWASAKI
Short-Period Course
Site: Japan: Kawasaki
Dates: 4 wks or longer, yr-round
Subjects: Japanese language (beg/int/adv)
Eligibility: *Level:* fresh, sophs, jrs, srs, grads, adults, teachers, professionals, precoll
Credit: *Undergrad:* none *Grad:* none *Doc:* certificate
Instruction: *In:* Japanese *Format:* lang study, lecture *Students:* intl
Costs: 57,000 yen for 4 wks *incl* tuition, fees
Housing: *Sponsor assists:* apartments
Deadline: None
Other info: *US accredited sponsor:* no *URL:* http://www.cbc.ac.jp
Contact: Japanese Dept, Coll of Bus & Communication, Kawasaki, 20-7 Ekimae-honcho, Kawasaki-k, Kawasaki-shi 210-0007, Japan *E-mail:* jpn@cbc.ac.jp

0254
COLLEGE OF BUSINESS AND COMMUNICATION, KAWASAKI
Special Summer Course for Beginners
Site: Japan: Kawasaki
Dates: 4-11 wks, beg Jun 26
Subjects: Japanese language (beg)
Eligibility: *Level:* fresh, sophs, jrs, srs, grads, adults, teachers, professionals, precoll *Requires:* knowledge of hiragana and katakana
Credit: *Undergrad:* none *Grad:* none *Doc:* certificate
Instruction: *In:* Japanese *Format:* lang study *Students:* intl
Costs: 57,000 yen for 4 wks *incl* tuition *Nonrefundable fee*
Housing: *Sponsor assists:* apartments
Deadline: Jun 15
Other info: *US accredited sponsor:* no *Began:* 1987 *URL:* http://www.cbc.ac.jp
Contact: Ms Mutsumi Harada, Japanese Dept, Coll of Bus & Communication, Kawasaki, 20-7 Ekimae-honcho, Kawasaki-ku, Kawasaki-shi 210-0007, Japan *E-mail:* jpn@cbc.ac.jp

KOBE

0255
CSA, CENTER FOR STUDY ABROAD
Japanese Language and Society-Kobe
Site: Japan: Kobe *Host inst:* YMCA
Dates: 4 wks, Jul 7-Aug 7
Subjects: Civilization/culture, Homestay, Japanese language (beg/int/adv), Japanese studies
Eligibility: *Level:* adults *Age:* min 17, avg 22
Credit: *Undergrad:* avail *Grad:* none *Doc:* certificate
Instruction: *In:* Japanese *Format:* lang study, study tour *Students:* mainly US
Costs: $2,395 *incl* tuition, housing, some meals, intl airfare, insurance, fees, excursions, books/materials, railpass *Nonrefundable fee*
Housing: *Sponsor assists:* homestay
Deadline: Jun 15
Other info: *US accredited sponsor:* no *Began:* 1997 *Orient:* in US & abroad (1 day) *Activities:* excursions, field trips, program travel, cultural events *Misc:* May contact former participants. *URL:* http://www.studyabroad.com/csa
Contact: Alima Khan, Pgm Dir, CSA, Ctr for Study Abroad, 2802 E Madison St, MS #160, Seattle WA 98112 *Ph:* 206-726 1498 *Fax:* 206-583 8192 *E-mail:* virtuecsa@aol.com

0256
SUNY UNIVERSITY AT BUFFALO
Intensive Japanese Course for Communicative Competence
Site: Japan: Kobe *Host inst:* Konan Univ
Dates: 6 wks, Jun 3-Jul 15
Subjects: Civilization/culture, Homestay, Japanese language (int), Japanese studies
Eligibility: *Level:* sophs, jrs, srs, grads, adults, teachers, professionals *Requires:* 2.67 GPA, Japanese 102 or equiv *Age:* min 18
Credit: *Undergrad:* 6 *Grad:* 6 *Doc:* transcript
Instruction: *In:* English, Japanese *Format:* lecture, seminar *Students:* mainly US
Costs: $3,300 *incl* housing, most meals, books/materials, transfers
Housing: *Arr by pgm:* homestay
Deadline: Mar 1; rolling admissions
Other info: *US accredited sponsor:* yes *Began:* 1997 *Orient:* abroad *Misc:* Noncredit option avail. *Financial aid:* scholarships *URL:* http://www.buffalo.edu/studyabroad/
Contact: Dr Sandra J Flash, Dir, Study Abroad Pgms, SUNY Univ at Buffalo, 210 Talbert Hall, Box 601604, Buffalo NY 14260-1604 *Ph:* 716-645 3912 *Fax:* 716-645 6197 *E-mail:* studyabroad@acsu.buffalo.edu

0257
UNIVERSITY OF DELAWARE
Summer Session in Japan
Site: Japan: Kobe *Host inst:* Shoin Univ
Dates: 5 wks, Jun
Subjects: Japanese language (beg/int)
Eligibility: *Level:* fresh, sophs, jrs, srs, adults *Requires:* 2.0 GPA
Credit: *Undergrad:* 6-7 *Grad:* none *Doc:* transcript
Instruction: *In:* English, Japanese *Format:* lang study, lecture, study tour *Students:* mainly US
Costs: Contact sponsor
Housing: *Arr by pgm:* residence halls
Deadline: Mid-Mar
Other info: *US accredited sponsor:* yes *Orient:* avail yes *Activities:* excursions, field trips, cultural events *Misc:* Contact sponsor to arrange honors credit. *Financial aid:* scholarships *URL:* http://www.udel.edu/studyabroad/
Contact: Lisa Chieffo, Univ of Delaware, Foreign Langs & Literatures, 326 Smith Hall, Newark DE 19716-1450 *Ph:* 302-831 6458 *Fax:* 302-831 6459 *E-mail:* lchieffo@udel.edu
Or Contact: Intl Pgms & Special Sessions, Univ of Delaware, 4 Kent Way, Newark DE 19716-1450 *Ph:* 888-831 4685; 302-831 2852 *Fax:* 302-831 6042 *E-mail:* studyabroad@udel.edu

0258
UNIVERSITY OF HAWAII AT MANOA
Japanese Language and Culture in Kobe
Site: Japan: Kobe *Host inst:* Konan Univ
Dates: 6 wks, early Jun-mid-Jul
Subjects: Civilization/culture, Homestay, Japanese language (int), Japanese studies
Eligibility: *Level:* sophs, jrs, srs *Requires:* 3.0 GPA, previous study in field, 1 yr coll Japanese
Credit: *Undergrad:* 8 *Grad:* none *Doc:* transcript
Instruction: *In:* Japanese *Format:* lang study, lecture *Students:* US & intl
Costs: $4,481 *incl* tuition, housing, some meals, intl airfare, insurance, fees, excursions, books/materials *Nonrefundable fee*
Housing: *Arr by pgm:* homestay
Deadline: Feb 17
Other info: *US accredited sponsor:* yes *Began:* 1997 *Orient:* in US & abroad (3 days) *Activities:* excursions, field trips, cultural events *Misc:* Course credit avail for 2nd yr Japanese only. Financial aid for UHM students only. *Financial aid:* scholarships *URL:* http://www2.hawaii.edu/study-abroad
Contact: Dir or Adviser, Study Abroad, Univ of Hawaii at Manoa, Moore Hall 115, 1890 East-West Rd, Honolulu HI 96822 *Ph:* 808-956 5143, 808-956 6958 *Fax:* 808-956 9319 *E-mail:* uhmsac@hawaii.edu

---

KYOTO

0259
CET ACADEMIC PROGRAMS
CET Japanese Language and Internship Program
Site: Japan: Kyoto *Host inst:* Kyoto Intl Ctr of Langs
Dates: Jun 6-Jul 24
Subjects: Civilization/culture, Homestay, Internships, Japanese language (beg/int/adv), Japanese studies
Eligibility: *Level:* fresh, sophs, jrs, srs, grads, adults, professionals *Requires:* int Japanese for internship *Age:* min 17, avg 20
Credit: *Undergrad:* avail *Grad:* avail *Doc:* transcript, certificate
Instruction: *In:* English, Japanese *Format:* internship, lang study, seminar, tutorial *Students:* mainly US
Costs: $4,990 *incl* tuition, housing, some meals, fees, excursions, books/materials
Housing: *Arr by pgm:* residence halls, homestay
Deadline: Mar 1; Apr 1 for scholarships
Other info: *US accredited sponsor:* no *Began:* 2000 *Orient:* abroad (3 days) *Activities:* excursions, field trips, cultural events, sports *Misc:* May contact former participants. *Financial aid:* scholarships *URL:* http://www.cetacademicprograms.com
Contact: Katie Smithson, Pgm Development, CET Acad Pgms, 1000 16th St NW, Ste 350, Washington DC 20036 *Ph:* 800-225 4262; 202-530 0800 *Fax:* 202-342 0317 *E-mail:* cet@academic-travel.com

---

0260
UNIVERSITY OF GEORGIA
Study Abroad Program-Japan
Site: Japan: Kyoto
Dates: May 13-Jun 13
Subjects: Civilization/culture, Japanese studies, Studio arts
Eligibility: *Level:* jrs, srs, grads, teachers, professionals *Requires:* 2.3 GPA, previous study in field *Age:* min 18
Credit: *Undergrad:* 6 *Grad:* 6 *Doc:* transcript
Instruction: *In:* English *Format:* art studio, study tour *Students:* mainly US
Costs: $5,000-$5,500 *incl* tuition, housing, some meals, intl airfare, insurance, fees, some local transport *Nonrefundable fee*
Housing: *Arr by pgm:* residence halls, traditional Japanese Inn
Deadline: Feb 15
Other info: *US accredited sponsor:* yes *Began:* 1999 *Orient:* abroad (1 day) *Activities:* excursions, field trips, cultural events *Misc:* Interact with Japanese artists & students. Studio workshops taught by Japanese artists. May contact former participants. *URL:* http://www.uga.edu/oie
Contact: Prof Glen Kaufman, Sch of Art, Univ of Georgia, Athens GA 30602 *Ph:* 706-542 1660 *Fax:* 706-542 0226 *E-mail:* japanart@uga.edu

---

NAGANO

0261
UNIVERSITY OF UTAH
Nagano, Japan
Site: Japan: Nagano *Host inst:* Shinshu Univ
Dates: 4 wks, Jun-Jul
Subjects: Homestay, Japanese language (beg/int/adv)
Eligibility: *Level:* fresh, sophs, jrs, srs, grads, adults *Requires:* 2.5 GPA, 1-2 qtrs Japanese recommended *Age:* min 18, avg 21
Credit: *Undergrad:* avail *Grad:* none *Doc:* transcript
Instruction: *In:* Japanese *Format:* lang study *Students:* intl
Costs: $2,450 *incl* tuition, housing, all meals, fees
Housing: *Arr by pgm:* homestay
Deadline: Feb 15
Other info: *US accredited sponsor:* yes *Orient:* in US *Activities:* excursions, cultural events *Misc:* Scholarships for Univ of UT students only. *Financial aid:* scholarships *URL:* http://www.saff.utah.edu/inter/
Contact: Laura Ashton, Study Abroad Adviser, Intl Ctr, Univ of Utah, 159 Olpin Union, Salt Lake City UT 84112 *Ph:* 801-581 5849 *Fax:* 801-581 5914 *E-mail:* lashton@saff.utah.edu

---

NAGOYA

0262
UNIVERSITY OF ARIZONA
Arizona Summer in Japan
Site: Japan: Nagoya *Host inst:* Trident Sch of Langs
Dates: Jun 1-Jul 10
Subjects: Civilization/culture, Homestay, Japanese language (beg/int/adv), Japanese studies
Eligibility: *Level:* sophs, jrs, srs *Requires:* 2.5 GPA
Credit: *Undergrad:* 6 *Grad:* none *Doc:* transcript
Instruction: *In:* English, Japanese *Format:* lang study, lecture *Students:* mainly US
Costs: $3,000 *incl* tuition, housing, all meals, excursions, books/materials, orient, ground transport
Housing: *Arr by pgm:* homestay
Deadline: Apr 24
Other info: *US accredited sponsor:* yes *Began:* 1992 *Activities:* excursions, field trips *Misc:* Scholarships for University of Arizona students only. *Financial aid:* scholarships *URL:* http://w3.arizona.edu/~ciss/
Contact: Caroline Patrick, Ctr for Global Student Pgms, Univ of Arizona, 939 N Tyndall Ave, Tucson AZ 85721 *Ph:* 520-626 7180 *Fax:* 520-626 9004 *E-mail:* cpatrick@u.arizona.edu ▲

OSAKA

0263
LANGUAGES ABROAD
Language and Cultural Immersion Programs-Osaka
Site: Japan: Osaka
Dates: 2 wks or longer, yr-round
Subjects: Civilization/culture, Japanese language (beg/int/adv)
Eligibility: *Level:* adults *Age:* min 17, max 65, avg 25
Credit: *Undergrad:* none *Grad:* none *Doc:* certificate
Instruction: *In:* Japanese *Format:* lang study *Students:* intl
Costs: From $3,650 for 4 wks *incl* tuition,

housing, some meals, excursions, books/materials
Housing: *Arr by pgm:* apartments, homestay
Deadline: None
Other info: *US accredited sponsor:* no *Misc:* May contact former participants. *URL:* http://www.languagesabroad.com
Contact: Ms Jesse Philippe, Langs Abroad, 317 Adelaide St W, Ste 900, Toronto, Ontario M5V 1P9, Canada *Ph:* 800-219 9924; 416-925 7117 *E-mail:* info@languagesabroad.com

---

SAPPORO

0264
UNIVERSITY OF MASSACHUSETTS AMHERST
Summer in Japan at Hokkaido University
Site: Japan: Sapporo *Host inst:* Hokkaido Univ
Dates: 4 wks, Jul
Subjects: Aboriginal studies, Civilization/culture, Economics, Education/teaching, Family studies, Homestay, Industry, Intercultural studies, Japanese language (beg/int), Japanese studies, Political science/politics
Eligibility: Five Colls & MaCIE students preferred. *Level:* fresh, sophs, jrs, srs
Credit: *Undergrad:* 6 *Grad:* none *Doc:* transcript
Instruction: *In:* English, Japanese *Format:* lang study, lecture *Students:* US & intl
Costs: About $2,900 *incl* tuition, housing, all meals, intl airfare, excursions
Housing: *Arr by pgm:* homestay
Deadline: Apr 1
Other info: *US accredited sponsor:* yes *Began:* 1974 *Orient:* in US & abroad *Misc:* Pgm offered in even-numbered yrs. May contact former participants. *URL:* http://www.umass.edu/ipo/
Contact: Laurel Foster-Moore, Intl Pgms, Univ of Massachusetts, Amherst MA 01003 *Ph:* 413-545 2710 *Fax:* 413-545 1201 *E-mail:* abroad@ipo.umass.edu

---

SHIZUOKA

0265
AMERICAN INSTITUTE FOR FOREIGN STUDY (AIFS) and RICHMOND, THE AMERICAN INTERNATIONAL UNIVERSITY IN LONDON
Richmond in Shizuoka, Japan
Site: Japan: Shizuoka *Host inst:* Prospera Lang Inst
Dates: 4 wks, Jun 21-Jul 22
Subjects: Art, Civilization/culture, Current events, Homestay, Japanese language
Eligibility: *Level:* fresh, sophs, jrs, srs, precoll *Requires:* 2.0 GPA
Credit: *Undergrad:* avail *Grad:* none *Doc:* transcript
Instruction: *In:* English *Format:* lang study, lecture *Students:* mainly US
Costs: $5,639 *incl* tuition, housing, all meals, intl airfare, excursions, books/materials, airport transfer
Housing: *Arr by pgm:* homestay
Deadline: Mar 15
Other info: *US accredited sponsor:* yes *Began:* 1994 *In coop with:* Prospera Lang Inst *Orient:* abroad *Activities:* excursions, field trips, cultural events *Misc:* Resident dir. May contact former participants. *Financial aid:* scholarships *URL:* http://www.aifsabroad.com
Contact: Solandy Meza, Coll Div, AIFS, River Plaza, 9 W Broad St, Stamford CT 06902 *Ph:* 800-727 2437 ext 5163 *E-mail:* college.info@aifs.com ▲

TOKYO

0266
IES, INSTITUTE FOR THE INTERNATIONAL EDUCATION OF STUDENTS
IES Tokyo Summer
Site: Japan: Makuhari New City (Tokyo suburb)
Dates: About 6 wks, May 31-Jul 15
Subjects: Civilization/culture, Homestay, Japanese language, Japanese studies
Eligibility: *Level:* fresh, sophs, jrs, srs, grads, adults *Requires:* good acad standing *Age:* min 18
Credit: *Undergrad:* 6 *Grad:* none *Doc:* transcript
Instruction: *In:* English, Japanese *Format:* lang study *Students:* mainly US
Costs: About $3,850 *incl* tuition, housing, some meals, insurance, excursions, field trips
Housing: *Arr by pgm:* residence halls, homestay
Deadline: Mar 15
Other info: *US accredited sponsor:* yes *Began:* 2000 *Orient:* abroad *Activities:* excursions, field trips, cultural events *Misc:* Student support svcs. May contact former participants. *URL:* http://www.IESabroad.org
Contact: *See Index II for Members* IES, 33 N LaSalle St, 15th Fl, Chicago IL 60602-2602 *Ph:* 800-995 2300; 312-944 1750 *Fax:* 312-944 1448 *E-mail:* info@iesabroad.org ▲

0267
INTERNATIONAL CAMPUS CONSORTIUM and THUNDERBIRD, THE AMERICAN GRADUATE SCHOOL OF INTERNATIONAL MANAGEMENT
Thunderbird Japan Center
Site: Japan: Tokyo
Dates: 14 wks, May 22-Aug 25
Subjects: Business/management, Finance, International business, International marketing, International studies, Japanese language (beg/int/adv), Japanese studies
Eligibility: *Level:* grads *Requires:* 3.0 GPA, previous lang study recommended
Credit: *Undergrad:* none *Grad:* 9-12 *Doc:* certificate
Instruction: *In:* English *Format:* lang study, lecture *Students:* intl
Costs: $11,000 *incl* tuition, insurance, fees
Housing: *Sponsor assists:* apartments, hotels
Deadline: Contact sponsor
Other info: *US accredited sponsor:* yes *Orient:* abroad *Activities:* field trips *Misc:* May contact former participants. *Financial aid:* scholarships *URL:* http://www.t-bird.edu
Contact: *See Index II for Members* Dr Earl Gibbons, Assoc VP, Overseas Pgms, Thunderbird, 15249 N 59th Ave, Glendale AZ 85306 *Ph:* 602-978 7252 *Fax:* 602-978 7419 *E-mail:* gibbonse@t-bird.edu
Or Contact: Diane Hayton, Coord, Overseas Pgms, Thunderbird, 15249 N 59th Ave, Glendale AZ 85306 *Ph:* 602-978 7252 *Fax:* 602-978 7419 *E-mail:* haytond@t-bird.edu

---

0268
INTERNATIONAL CHRISTIAN UNIVERSITY TOKYO
Summer Courses in Japanese
Site: Japan: Tokyo (Mitaka)
Dates: 6 wks, Jul-mid-Aug
Subjects: Japanese language (beg/int/adv)
Eligibility: *Level:* fresh, sophs, jrs, srs, grads *Age:* min 18
Credit: *Undergrad:* 6 *Grad:* none *Doc:* certificate
Instruction: *In:* Japanese *Format:* lang study, lecture *Students:* intl
Costs: 250,000-284,000 yen depending on housing *incl* tuition, housing
Housing: *Sponsor assists:* residence halls, apartments, homestay
Deadline: Apr 1
Other info: *US accredited sponsor:* no *Began:* 1973 *Orient:* abroad *Activities:* excursions, cultural events *URL:* http://www.icu.ac.jp
Contact: Summer Courses in Japanese, Research Ctr for Japanese Lang Fdn, Intl Christian Univ, 3-10-2 Osawa, Mitaka-shi, Tokyo 181-8585, Japan *E-mail:* scj@icu.ac.jp

---

0269
LANGUAGE STUDIES ABROAD, INC
Intensive Japanese
Site: Japan: Tokyo (Shibuya-ku) *Host inst:* LIC Kokusai Gakuin
Dates: 3 wks or longer, yr-round
Subjects: Calligraphy, Civilization/culture, Homestay, Japanese language (beg/int/adv), Japanese studies
Eligibility: *Level:* fresh, sophs, jrs, srs, grads, adults, teachers, professionals, precoll
Credit: *Undergrad:* avail *Grad:* avail
Instruction: *In:* Japanese *Format:* lang study *Students:* intl
Costs: $895 for 4 wks *incl* tuition *Nonrefundable fee*
Housing: *Sponsor assists:* apartments, homestay, hotels, guest housing
Deadline: 4 wks before pgm
Other info: *US accredited sponsor:* no *Began:* 1977 *Orient:* abroad *Activities:* excursions, field trips, program travel, cultural events *Misc:* May contact former participants. *URL:* http://www.languagestudiesabroad.com
Contact: Lang Studies Abroad, Inc, 103 Londonderry Ct, Reno NV 89511-2718 *Ph:* 800-424 5522; 775-849 9206 *Fax:* 775-849 9217 *E-mail:* info@languagestudiesabroad.com

---

0270
LANGUAGE STUDIES ABROAD, INC
Japanese Language
Site: Japan: Tokyo *Host inst:* LSA Tokyo
Dates: 2 wks or longer, yr-round
Subjects: Japanese language
Eligibility: *Level:* adults *Age:* min 18
Credit: *Undergrad:* avail *Grad:* avail
Instruction: *In:* Japanese *Format:* lang study *Students:* intl
Costs: $700 for 4 wks *incl* tuition, housing
Housing: *Arr by pgm:* residence halls
Deadline: 4 wks before pgm
Other info: *US accredited sponsor:* no *Began:* 1986 *Orient:* abroad 1 day *Misc:* May contact former participants. *URL:* http://www.languagestudiesabroad.com
Contact: Lang Studies Abroad, Inc, 103 Londonderry Ct, Reno NV 89511 *Ph:* 800-424 5522; 775-849 9206 *Fax:* 775-849 9217 *E-mail:* info@languagestudiesabroad.com

---

0271
LINGUA SERVICE WORLDWIDE
Total Immersion/Intensive Language and Culture in Japan-Tokyo
Site: Japan: Tokyo (Ikebukuru, Shibuya, Shijuku) *Host inst:* LIC Kokusai Kaiwa Gakuin
Dates: 1 wk-1 yr, yr-round
Subjects: Calligraphy, Civilization/culture, Homestay, Japanese language (beg/int/adv)
Eligibility: *Level:* adults *Age:* min 17
Credit: *Undergrad:* avail *Grad:* avail *Doc:* transcript, certificate
Instruction: *In:* Japanese *Format:* lang study *Students:* intl
Costs: Contact sponsor
Housing: *Arr by pgm:* apartments with local students, residence halls with local students, homestay, pensions, hotels, hostels
Deadline: 45 days before pgm
Other info: *US accredited sponsor:* no *Began:* 1993 *Activities:* excursions, cultural events *Misc:* Flower arrangement, tea ceremonies. May contact former participants. *URL:* http://www.linguaserviceworldwide.com
Contact: Dir, Lingua Svc Worldwide, 75 Prospect St, Ste 4, Huntington NY 11743 *Ph:* 800-394 5327; 631-424 0777 *Fax:* 631-271 3441 *E-mail:* itctravel@worldnet.att.net ▲

0272
MICHIGAN STATE UNIVERSITY
Packaging-Japan
Site: Japan: Tokyo
Dates: 2 wks, Jun
Subjects: Packaging
Eligibility: *Level:* fresh, sophs, jrs, srs, grads *Requires:* 2.35 GPA, previous study in field, packaging majors *Age:* min 18
Credit: *Undergrad:* 3-6 *Grad:* 1-3 *Doc:* transcript
Instruction: *In:* English *Format:* lecture *Students:* mainly US
Costs: About $1,600 *incl* housing, some meals, insurance, fees, excursions *Nonrefundable fee*
Housing: *Arr by pgm:* residence halls
Deadline: Mar 2
Other info: *US accredited sponsor:* yes *Orient:* in US (1 day) *Activities:* excursions, field trips *Misc:* May contact former participants. *Financial aid:* scholarships, work study *URL:* http://studyabroad.msu.edu
Contact: Cheryl Benner, MSU Study Abroad, 109 Intl Ctr, East Lansing MI 448824-1035 *Ph:* 517-353 8920 *Fax:* 517-432 2082 *E-mail:* bennerc@msu.edu ▲

0273
NATIONAL REGISTRATION CENTER FOR STUDY ABROAD (NRCSA)
KCP International Language Institute
Site: Japan: Tokyo *Host inst:* KCP Intl Lang Inst
Dates: 10-12 wks, beg Jan 9, Apr 4, Jul 4 or Oct 8
Subjects: Homestay, Japanese language
Eligibility: *Level:* adults
Credit: *Undergrad:* avail *Grad:* avail
Instruction: *In:* Japanese *Format:* lang study *Students:* intl
Costs: $5,600 for 12 credit semester *incl* tuition, housing, some meals, insurance *Nonrefundable fee*
Housing: *Arr by pgm:* residence halls, homestay
Deadline: Rolling admissions
Other info: *US accredited sponsor:* no *Activities:* field trips *Misc:* May contact former participants. *URL:* http://www.nrcsa.com
Contact: Reuel Zielke, NRCSA, 823 N 2nd St, #206, Milwaukee WI 53203 *Ph:* 414-278 0631 *Fax:* 414-271 8884 *E-mail:* info@nrcsa.com

---

0274
NATIONAL REGISTRATION CENTER FOR STUDY ABROAD (NRCSA)
Study Japanese in Tokyo
Site: Japan: Tokyo *Host inst:* LIC Kokusai Gakuin
Dates: 4 wks, Jan-Feb, Apr-May, Jul-Aug or Oct-Nov
Subjects: Japanese language
Eligibility: *Level:* fresh, sophs, jrs, srs, grads, adults, teachers, professionals
Credit: *Undergrad:* none *Grad:* none *Doc:* certificate
Instruction: *In:* Japanese *Format:* lang study, lecture *Students:* intl
Costs: $1,109 *incl* tuition, insurance *Nonrefundable fee*
Housing: *Arr by pgm:* hostels
Deadline: 6 wks before pgm
Other info: *US accredited sponsor:* no *Misc:* May contact former participants. *URL:* http://www.nrcsa.com
Contact: Reuel Zielke, NRCSA, 823 N 2nd St, #206, Milwaukee WI 53203 *Ph:* 414-278 0631 *Fax:* 414-871 8884 *E-mail:* info@nrcsa.com

---

0275
SOPHIA UNIVERSITY
Summer Session of Asian Studies
Site: Japan: Tokyo *Host inst:* Sophia Univ
Dates: Jul 25-Aug 20
Subjects: Asian studies, Japanese language (beg)
Eligibility: high school students with AP credits *Level:* fresh, sophs, jrs, srs, teachers
Credit: *Undergrad:* 6 *Grad:* 6 (high sch teachers)
Instruction: *In:* English *Format:* lang study, lecture, study tour *Students:* intl
Costs: About $1,400 *incl* tuition, excursions *Nonrefundable fee*
Housing: *Arr by pgm:* residence halls, hotels
Deadline: Jun 30
Other info: *US accredited sponsor:* no *Began:* 1961 *Activities:* field trips *Misc:* Tours of cultural sites; graduate credits for high school teachers. *URL:* http://133.12.40.67

Contact: Summer Session, Dir, Sophia Univ, Ichigaya Campus, 4 Yonbancho, Chiyoda-ku, Tokyo 102, Japan *E-mail:* c-takeda@hoffman.cc.sophia.ac.jp

---

0276
TEMPLE UNIVERSITY
Temple University Japan
Site: Japan: Tokyo *Host inst:* Temple Univ Japan campus
Dates: 10 wks, May-Jul
Subjects: Art history, Asian studies, Economics, English, Geography, History, Japanese language (beg/int/adv), Philosophy, Political science/politics, Religion/theology, Sociology
Eligibility: *Level:* sophs, jrs, srs *Requires:* 2.5 GPA
Credit: *Undergrad:* 10-15 *Grad:* none
Instruction: *In:* English, Japanese *Format:* lang study, lecture *Students:* mainly host country
Costs: $6,400-$8,400 *incl* tuition, housing, fees
Housing: *Arr by pgm:* Student Apts
Deadline: Mar 1
Other info: *US accredited sponsor:* yes *Began:* 1982 *Orient:* in US & abroad *Activities:* field trips *Misc:* Bachelor's & master's degree pgms avail, Internships avail. *URL:* http://www.temple.edu/intlprog/
Contact: Intl Pgms, Temple Univ, 200 Tuttleman Learning Ctr, 1809 N 13th St, Philadelphia PA 19122 *Ph:* 215-204 0720 *Fax:* 215-204 0729 *E-mail:* intlprog@vm.temple.edu

---

0277
UNIVERSITY OF IDAHO
Intensive Japanese Language and Culture Program
Site: Japan: Tokyo *Host inst:* KCP Intl Lang Inst
Dates: Jun 23-Aug 15, Jul 6-Sep 19
Subjects: Homestay, Japanese language (beg/int/adv)
Eligibility: *Level:* fresh, sophs, jrs, srs *Requires:* 2.5 GPA *Age:* min 18
Credit: *Undergrad:* avail *Grad:* none *Doc:* transcript
Instruction: *In:* English, Japanese *Format:* lang study *Students:* US & intl
Costs: $4,025 Jun 23-Aug 15, $5,225-$5,575 Jul 6-Sep 19 *incl* tuition, housing, most meals, fees, field trips *Nonrefundable fee*
Housing: *Arr by pgm:* residence halls, homestay, (Jun-Aug is residence hall only)
Deadline: Mar 27 (for Jun-Aug), Apr 7 (for Jul-Sep)
Other info: *US accredited sponsor:* yes *Began:* 1997 *Orient:* in US & abroad *Activities:* field trips, cultural events *Misc:* May contact former participants. *URL:* http://www.kcp-usa.com/
Contact: Bob Neuenschwander, Idaho Abroad, Univ of Idaho, Morrill Hall, Rm 209, Moscow ID 83844-3013 *Ph:* 208-885 4075 *Fax:* 208-885 2859 *E-mail:* bobn@uidaho.edu
Or Contact: Michael Anderson, KCP Intl USA, PO Box 28028, Bellingham WA 98228 *Ph:* 888-527 7020; 360-647 0072 *Fax:* 360-647 0736 *E-mail:* kcp@kcp-usa.com

---

0278
UNIVERSITY OF MIAMI (FL)
Asian Studies in Tokyo, Japan
Site: Japan: Tokyo *Host inst:* Sophia Univ
Dates: Mid-Jul-mid-Aug
Subjects: Art, Business/management, Civilization/culture, Japanese language (beg/int), Japanese studies, Literature, Religion/theology, Sociology
Eligibility: *Level:* fresh, sophs, jrs, srs *Requires:* 3.0 GPA, 2 faculty recommendations, transcript for Univ of Miami students only
Credit: *Undergrad:* 6 *Grad:* none *Doc:* transcript
Instruction: *In:* English *Format:* directed field study, lang study, lecture, seminar *Students:* intl
Costs: $3,450 *incl* tuition
Housing: *Arr by pgm:* residence halls with local students, hotels
Deadline: May 15
Other info: *US accredited sponsor:* yes *Began:* 1990 *Activities:* excursions, field trips *Misc:* May contact former participants. *URL:* http://www.studyabroad.miami.edu
Contact: Intl Educ & Exch Pgms, Univ of Miami, Allen Hall 212, 5050 Brunson Dr, PO Box 248005, Coral Gables FL 33124-1610 *Ph:* 800-557 5421; 305-284 3434 *Fax:* 305-284 6629 *E-mail:* ieep@miami.edu

---

0279
UNIVERSITY OF MONTANA
Group Study Abroad Summer Program in Japan
Site: Japan: Tokyo *Host inst:* Toyo Univ
Dates: 1 mo, late May-late Jun
Subjects: Civilization/culture, Field study, Homestay, Independent study, Japanese language (beg/int)
Eligibility: Own students only. *Level:* fresh, sophs, jrs, srs, grads, adults, teachers, professionals *Age:* avg 21
Credit: *Undergrad:* 2-4 *Grad:* none *Doc:* transcript
Instruction: *In:* English, Japanese *Format:* directed field study, independent study, lang study, lecture, study tour *Students:* mainly US
Costs: Contact sponsor
Housing: *Arr by pgm:* residence halls, homestay
Deadline: Feb
Other info: *US accredited sponsor:* yes *Began:* 1990 *Orient:* in US *Activities:* excursions, field trips, cultural events *Misc:* Pgm offered in even-numbered years. *Financial aid:* scholarships *URL:* http://www.umt.edu/oip
Contact: Intl Pgms, Univ of Montana, Main Hall 022, Missoula MT 59812 *Ph:* 406-243 2288 *Fax:* 406-243 6194 *E-mail:* goabroad@selway.umt.edu

---

0280
UNIVERSITY OF TEXAS AT AUSTIN
Obirin Summer Program
Site: Japan: Tokyo *Host inst:* Obirin Univ
Dates: 5 wks, mid-Jul-mid-Aug
Subjects: Civilization/culture, Homestay, Japanese language (int/adv)
Eligibility: *Level:* sophs, jrs, srs *Requires:* 3.0 GPA, 2-4 sems coll Japanese or equiv
Credit: *Undergrad:* 7 *Grad:* none *Doc:* transcript
Instruction: *In:* English, Japanese *Format:* lang study, lecture *Students:* mainly US
Costs: Contact sponsor
Housing: *Arr by pgm:* homestay
Deadline: Mar 1
Other info: *US accredited sponsor:* yes *Began:* 1992 *Orient:* abroad *Activities:* excursions, program travel, cultural events *Misc:* 20 students only. May contact former participants. *URL:* http://www.utexas.edu/student/abroad
Contact: Joy Williamson, Adviser, Study Abroad, Univ of Texas at Austin, Drawer A, Univ Station, Austin TX 78713-7206 *Ph:* 512-471 6490 *Fax:* 512-232 4363 *E-mail:* studyabroadinfo@mozart.io.utexas.edu

---

0281
WASEDA OREGON OFFICE
Waseda/Oregon Summer Japanese Program
Site: Japan: Tokyo
Dates: 6 wks, Jul 9-Aug 18
Subjects: Business language, Japanese language (beg/int/adv), Japanese studies, Multimedia
Eligibility: *Level:* adults *Requires:* 2.5 GPA, completion of 1 sem at a 2-yr or 4-yr coll *Age:* avg 23
Credit: *Undergrad:* none *Grad:* none *Doc:* transcript, certificate *Transfer credit through:* Portland State Univ
Instruction: *In:* English, Japanese *Format:* lang study *Students:* mainly US
Costs: $4,975 *incl* tuition, housing, excursions, books/materials
Housing: *Arr by pgm:* residence halls with local students

Deadline: Mar 31
Other info: *US accredited sponsor:* yes *Began:* 1999 *Orient:* abroad (2 days) *Activities:* excursions, field trips, cultural events *Misc:* May contact former participants. *URL:* http://www.opie.org
Contact: *See Index II for Members* Sally Strand, Coord Officer, Oregon Partnership for Intl Educ, 921 SW Morrison, #548, Portland OR 97205 *Ph:* 800-823 7938; 503-223 7938 *Fax:* 503-223 7946 *E-mail:* info@opie.org
Or Contact: Dean Takehiko Kawase, Ctr of Intl Educ, Waseda Univ, 1-7-14 Nishi-Waseda, Shinjuku-ku, Tokyo 169-0051, Japan

Korea, Republic of

SEOUL

0282
LANGUAGES ABROAD
Language and Cultural Immersion Programs-Seoul
Site: Korea: Seoul
Dates: 2 wks or longer, yr-round
Subjects: Civilization/culture, Korean language (beg/int/adv)
Eligibility: *Level:* adults *Age:* min 17, max 65, avg 25
Credit: *Undergrad:* none *Grad:* none *Doc:* certificate
Instruction: *In:* Korean *Format:* lang study *Students:* intl
Costs: About $2,950 for 4 wks *incl* tuition, housing, some meals, excursions, books/materials
Housing: *Arr by pgm:* apartments, homestay
Deadline: None
Other info: *US accredited sponsor:* no *Misc:* May contact former participants. *URL:* http://www.languagesabroad.com
Contact: Ms Jesse Philippe, Langs Abroad, 317 Adelaide St W, Ste 900, Toronto, Ontario M5V 1P9, Canada *Ph:* 800-219 9924; 416-925 7117 *E-mail:* info@languagesabroad.com

---

0283
SUNY UNIVERSITY AT ALBANY
Language and Cultural Studies at Yonsei University
Site: Korea: Seoul *Host inst:* Yonsei Univ
Dates: 7 wks, mid-Jun-mid-Aug
Subjects: Anthropology, Art, Business/management, Communications, Economics, History, Korean language (beg/int/adv), Law, Literature, Philosophy, Political science/politics, Religion/theology, Sociology
Eligibility: *Level:* sophs, jrs, srs *Requires:* 2.5 GPA
Credit: *Undergrad:* 6-9 *Grad:* none *Doc:* transcript
Instruction: *In:* English *Format:* lecture *Students:* intl
Costs: $3,322 for NY residents *incl* tuition, housing, all meals, fees, student support svcs *Nonrefundable fee*
Housing: *Arr by pgm:* residence halls
Deadline: Apr 1; late applications considered
Other info: *US accredited sponsor:* yes *Began:* 1994 *Orient:* in US & abroad *Activities:* field trips *Misc:* May contact former participants. *URL:* http://www.albany.edu/intled
Contact: Joan N Savitt, Intl Pgms, SUNY Univ at Albany, LI 66, Albany NY 12222 *Ph:* 518-442 3525 *Fax:* 518-442 3338 *E-mail:* intled@usmail.albany.edu

---

0284
UNIVERSITY OF PENNSYLVANIA
Penn-in-Seoul
Site: Korea: Seoul *Host inst:* Kyung Hee Univ
Dates: 7 wks, late Jun-mid-Aug
Subjects: Economics, Internships, Social sciences
Eligibility: *Level:* fresh, sophs, jrs, srs, grads, professionals
Credit: *Undergrad:* 6 *Grad:* 3-6 *Doc:* transcript
Instruction: *In:* English *Format:* internship, lecture *Students:* mainly US
Costs: About $5,000 *incl* tuition, housing *Nonrefundable fee*
Housing: *Arr by pgm:* residence halls
Deadline: Mar 7
Other info: *US accredited sponsor:* yes *Began:* 1993 *Orient:* in US & abroad *Activities:* excursions, program travel, cultural events *Misc:* Korean lang pgm offered before departure. May contact former participants. *URL:* http://www.sas.upenn.edu/CGS/
Contact: Elizabeth Sachs, Penn Summer Abroad, Univ of Pennsylvania, 3440 Market St, Ste 100, Philadelphia PA 19104-3335 *Ph:* 215-898 5738 *Fax:* 215-573 2053 *E-mail:* sdanti@mail.sas.upenn.edu

Mongolia

MORE THAN ONE CITY

0285
AMERICAN UNIVERSITIES INTERNATIONAL PROGRAM (AUIP)
Mongolia: Field Study Tour
Site: various sites *Host inst:* Ulaanbaatar Univ
Dates: 1 mo, Jun 15-Jul 17
Subjects: Anthropology, Biology, Civilization/culture, Conservation, Ecology/environmental studies, Field study, History
Eligibility: *Level:* sophs, jrs, srs, grads, adults, teachers, professionals *Requires:* 2.0 GPA *Age:* min 18
Credit: *Undergrad:* 6 *Grad:* none
Instruction: *In:* English *Format:* directed field study, lecture, study tour *Students:* mainly US
Costs: $4,495 *incl* tuition, housing, all meals, insurance, fees, excursions, books/materials, ISIC *Nonrefundable fee*
Housing: *Arr by pgm:* hotels, campgrounds
Deadline: Apr 1
Other info: *US accredited sponsor:* no *Began:* 2000 *Orient:* abroad *Activities:* excursions, field trips, program travel, cultural events, sports *URL:* http://www.auip.com
Contact: Linda Tomson or Tim Wakefield, AUIP, PMB 221, 305 W Magnolia St, Fort Collins CO 80521 ▲

Nepal

MORE THAN ONE CITY

0286
SAN FRANCISCO STATE UNIVERSITY, WILDLANDS STUDIES PROGRAM
Environments of Nepal: The Himalayan Ecosystem Program
Site: Nepal: various field sites
Dates: Jul 1-Aug 19, Sep 20-Nov 8, Apr 12-May 31
Subjects: Biology, Ecology/environmental studies, Ethnography, Field study
Eligibility: *Level:* adults *Requires:* application essay *Age:* min 18, avg 22
Credit: *Undergrad:* 9 per term *Grad:* none *Doc:* transcript
Instruction: *In:* English *Format:* directed field study *Students:* mainly US
Costs: $1,900 *incl* tuition
Housing: *Arr by pgm:* basecamp, backpacking
Deadline: Rolling admissions
Other info: *US accredited sponsor:* yes *Began:* 1988 *Orient:* abroad *Activities:* field trips *Misc:* May contact former participants. *URL:* http://www.wildlandsstudies.com/ws
Contact: Crandall Bay, Dir, or Marcene Bay, Asst, Wildlands Studies, San Francisco State Univ, 3 Mosswood Circle, Cazadero CA 95421 *Ph:* 707-632 5665 *Fax:* 707-632 5665 *E-mail:* wildlnds@sonic.net

---

0287
UNIVERSITY OF MONTANA
Nepal Intersession
Site: Nepal: various sites *Host inst:* Tribhuvan Univ, Sann Research Inst
Dates: 4 wks, Dec 26-Jan 19
Subjects: Asian studies, Ecology/

environmental studies, Homestay, Social work, Sociology
Eligibility: *Level:* sophs, jrs, srs, grads, adults, teachers, professionals *Requires:* 2.8 GPA *Age:* avg 22
Credit: *Undergrad:* 6 *Grad:* none *Doc:* transcript
Instruction: *In:* English *Format:* study tour *Students:* mainly US
Costs: $3,480 *incl* tuition, housing, some meals, intl airfare, fees, excursions *Nonrefundable fee*
Housing: *Arr by pgm:* homestay
Deadline: Oct 2
Other info: *US accredited sponsor:* yes *Began:* 2000 *In coop with:* Sann Research Inst *Orient:* in US & abroad (2 days) *Activities:* excursions, field trips, cultural events *Misc:* May contact former participants. *URL:* http://www.umt.edu/oip
Contact: Intl Pgms, Univ of Montana, Missula MT 59812 *Ph:* 406-243 2288 *Fax:* 406-243 6194 *E-mail:* goabroad@selway.umt.edu
Or Contact: Cindy Garthwait, Sch of Social Work, Univ of Montana, Missoula MT 59812 *Ph:* 406-243 2954 *Fax:* 406-243 5275 *E-mail:* cgarth@selway.umt.edu

KATHMANDU

0288
CULTURAL DESTINATION NEPAL
Volunteer Nepal
Site: Nepal: Kathmandu
Dates: 2-4 mos, beg Feb, Apr, Aug & Oct; other dates upon request
Subjects: Civilization/culture, Community service projects, Health/health education, History, Homestay, Nepali language, Nepali studies, Political science/politics, Women's studies
Eligibility: *Level:* adults *Age:* min 18, max 65, avg 25
Credit: *Undergrad:* none *Grad:* none *Doc:* certificate
Instruction: *In:* English *Format:* study tour, volunteer/svc *Students:* intl
Costs: $650 for 2-4 mos *incl* housing, some meals, fees, excursions, books/materials *Nonrefundable fee*
Housing: *Arr by pgm:* homestay, hostels
Deadline: 2-1/2 mos before pgm
Other info: *US accredited sponsor:* no *Began:* 1996 *Orient:* abroad (2 wks, intensive lang study) *Activities:* excursions, field trips, program travel, cultural events *Misc:* Rafting, jungle safari. May contact former participants.
Contact: Rajesh Shrestha, Dir, Cultural Destination Nepal, GPO Box 11535, Kathmandu, Nepal *E-mail:* cdnnepal@wlink.com.np

0289
GEORGE WASHINGTON UNIVERSITY
Women and Development in Nepal
Site: Nepal: Kathmandu
Dates: 3 wks, May 24-Jun 15
Subjects: International studies, Women's studies
Eligibility: *Level:* sophs, jrs, srs, grads *Age:* min 19
Credit: *Undergrad:* 3 *Grad:* 3 *Doc:* transcript
Instruction: *In:* English *Format:* lang study, lecture, seminar, study tour, volunteer/svc *Students:* mainly US
Costs: $2,645 *incl* tuition, housing, some meals, fees, excursions *Nonrefundable fee*
Housing: *Arr by pgm:* hostels, camp sites
Deadline: Contact sponsor
Other info: *US accredited sponsor:* yes *Began:* 2000 *Orient:* abroad (1 day) *Activities:* excursions, field trips, program travel, cultural events *Misc:* Summer pgms are updated in Dec. Contact sponsor for new info. *URL:* http://www.summer.gwu.edu
Contact: Summer, Special & Intl Programs, George Washington Univ, 609 22nd St NW, Washington DC 20052 *Ph:* 202-994 6360 *Fax:* 202-994 9133 *E-mail:* sumprogs@gwu.edu

0290
HORIZONS TO GO
Nepal: The Kathmandu Valley/A Craft and Culture Trip
Site: Nepal: Kathmandu
Dates: 2 wks, Apr 20-May 4
Subjects: Civilization/culture, Crafts, Nepali studies, Painting, Papermaking, Weaving
Eligibility: *Level:* fresh, sophs, jrs, srs, grads, adults, teachers, professionals *Age:* min 19, max 85, avg 45
Credit: *Undergrad:* none *Grad:* none
Instruction: *In:* English *Format:* workshop *Students:* mainly US
Costs: $2,950 *incl* tuition
Housing: Contact sponsor
Deadline: Contact sponsor
Other info: *US accredited sponsor:* no *Began:* 1983 *Activities:* excursions, field trips, cultural events *Misc:* Workshops with local artisans. Visits to Buddhist & Hindu temples in Kathmandu Valley. May contact former participants. *URL:* http://www.horizons-art.org
Contact: Jane Sinauer, Horizons To Go, PO Box 2206, Amherst MA 01004 *Ph:* 413-549 5995 *Fax:* 413-549 5995 *E-mail:* horizons@horizons-art.org

0291
UNIVERSITY OF IDAHO
Summer Nepal Program
Site: Nepal: Kathmandu *Host inst:* Sann Research Inst
Dates: 10 wks, May 30-Aug 15
Subjects: Ecology/environmental studies, Nepali language (beg), Philosophy, Political science/politics, Religion/theology
Eligibility: *Level:* fresh, sophs, jrs, srs *Requires:* 2.5 GPA, good physical health *Age:* min 18, avg 21
Credit: *Undergrad:* 9 *Grad:* none *Doc:* transcript
Instruction: *In:* English *Format:* lecture, seminar, study tour *Students:* mainly US
Costs: $4,200 *incl* tuition, housing, all meals, fees, excursions *Nonrefundable fee*
Housing: *Arr by pgm:* homestay
Deadline: Apr 1
Other info: *US accredited sponsor:* yes *Began:* 1998 *Orient:* in US & abroad (1 day) *Activities:* field trips, program travel *Misc:* 8-day trip to Tibet. May contact former participants. *URL:* http://www.uidaho.edu/ipo/abroad/nepal.html
Contact: Bob Neuenschwander, Study Abroad Coord, Idaho Abroad, Univ of Idaho, Morrill Hall, Rm 209, Moscow ID 83844-3013 *Ph:* 208-885 4075 *Fax:* 208-885 2859 *E-mail:* bobn@idaho.edu
Or Contact: Narayan Shrestha, Sann Research Inst, 948 Pearl St, Boulder CO 80302 *Ph:* 888-241 0710 *E-mail:* info@sannr.com

0292
UNIVERSITY OF KANSAS
Nepal 2000: Challenge and Discovery
Site: Nepal: Kathmandu
Dates: 4 wks, May 18-Jun 18
Subjects: Anthropology, Civilization/culture, Homestay
Eligibility: *Level:* fresh, sophs, jrs, srs, grads, adults
Credit: *Undergrad:* 6 *Grad:* none *Doc:* transcript
Instruction: *In:* English *Format:* lecture *Students:* mainly US
Costs: $4,100 *incl* tuition, housing, all meals, intl airfare, fees, excursions
Housing: *Arr by pgm:* homestay
Deadline: Rolling admissions
Other info: *US accredited sponsor:* yes *Began:* 2000 *Orient:* in US & abroad (1 day) *Activities:* excursions, field trips, cultural events *URL:* http://www.ukans.edu/~osa
Contact: Susan MacNally, Asst Dir, Univ of Kansas, 108 Lippincott Hall, Lawrence KS 66045-1731 *Ph:* 785-864 3742 *Fax:* 785-864 5040 *E-mail:* osa@ukans.edu ▲

KHUMBU

0293
UNIVERSITY OF IDAHO
International Expeditions
Site: Nepal: Khumbu, Everest National Park
Dates: 4 wks, May 22-Jun 17
Subjects: Anthropology, Civilization/culture, Ecology/environmental studies, Economics, Interdisciplinary studies
Eligibility: *Level:* fresh, sophs, jrs, srs, grads, teachers, professionals *Requires:* 2.5 GPA, good physical health *Age:* min 18, avg 21
Credit: *Undergrad:* 6 *Grad:* 6 *Doc:* transcript
Instruction: *In:* English *Format:* directed field study, study tour *Students:* mainly US
Costs: $2,800 *incl* tuition, housing, all meals, insurance, fees, excursions, books/materials, railpass, airfare Kathmandu to Lukla *Nonrefundable fee*
Housing: *Arr by pgm:* hotels, campsites
Deadline: Mar 21
Other info: *US accredited sponsor:* yes *Began:* 2000 *In coop with:* Mountain Inst *Orient:* in US & abroad *Activities:* excursions, field trips, program travel *Misc:* May contact former participants. *URL:* http://www.mountain.org
Contact: Amy Darter, Idaho Abroad, Rm 209, Univ of Idaho, Morrill Hall, PO Box 443013, Moscow ID 83844-3013 *Ph:* 208-885 4075 *Fax:* 208-885 2859 *E-mail:* amyd@uidaho.edu
Or Contact: Ryan Bidwell, Mountain Inst, 245 Newman Ave, Harrisburg VA 22801 *Ph:* 1-800 390 1885 *Fax:* 540-437 0494 *E-mail:* rbidwell@mountain.org

---

LADAKH

0294
SOJOURN NEPAL
Sojourn Ladakh
Site: Nepal: Ladakh
Dates: 6 wks, summer
Subjects: Apprenticeships, Hiking/trekking, Homestay, Internships
Eligibility: *Level:* fresh, sophs, jrs, srs *Age:* min 17, max 25, avg 20
Credit: *Undergrad:* none *Grad:* none
Instruction: *In:* Nepali *Format:* internship, volunteer/svc *Students:* mainly US
Costs: $3,750 *incl* tuition, housing, all meals, fees, excursions *Nonrefundable fee*
Housing: *Arr by pgm:* homestay
Deadline: 4 wks before pgm
Other info: *US accredited sponsor:* no *Began:* 1986 *Orient:* abroad *Activities:* excursions, field trips, program travel, cultural events *Misc:* Volunteer opportunities avail. May contact former participants. *URL:* http://www.sojournnepal.org
Contact: Jennifer Warren, Amer Dir, Sojourn Nepal, 2440 N 56th St, Phoenix AZ 85008 *Ph:* 602-840 9197 *Fax:* 602-840 9197 *E-mail:* snepal@aol.com
Or Contact: Sam Chapin, Sojourn Nepal, Box 2187, Kathmandu, Nepal *E-mail:* soujourn@wlink.com.np

New Zealand

MORE THAN ONE CITY

0295
CAMP COUNSELORS USA
New Zealand Work-Travel Program
Site: New Zealand: various sites
Dates: 4 mos, yr round
Subjects: Full curriculum
Eligibility: *Level:* fresh, sophs, jrs, srs, grads, adults *Age:* min 18, max 30
Credit: *Undergrad:* none *Grad:* none
Instruction: *In:* English *Format:* directed field study, internship, volunteer/svc *Students:* mainly host country
Costs: Contact sponsor
Housing: *Arr by student*
Deadline: Apr 20
Other info: *US accredited sponsor:* no *Began:* 1998 *Orient:* abroad *Activities:* cultural events *URL:* http://www.campcounselors.com
Contact: Anne Haddad, Outbound Pgm Dir, Camp Counselors USA, 2330 Marinship Way, Ste 250, Sausalito CA 94965 *Ph:* 800-999 2267; 415-339 2728 *Fax:* 415-339 2744 *E-mail:* outbound@campcounselors.com

---

0296
SAN FRANCISCO STATE UNIVERSITY, WILDLANDS STUDIES PROGRAM
Ecosystems and Cultures of the South Pacific
Site: New Zealand: various sites
Dates: Jan 4-Feb 15
Subjects: Biology, Ecology/environmental studies, Ethnography, Field study
Eligibility: *Level:* adults *Requires:* application essay *Age:* min 18, avg 22
Credit: *Undergrad:* 9 per term *Grad:* none *Doc:* transcript
Instruction: *In:* English *Format:* directed field study *Students:* mainly US
Costs: $1,900 *incl* tuition
Housing: *Arr by pgm:* basecamp, backpacking
Deadline: Rolling admissions
Other info: *US accredited sponsor:* yes *Began:* 1992 *Orient:* abroad *Activities:* field trips *Misc:* May contact former participants. *URL:* http://www.wildlandsstudies.com/ws
Contact: Crandall Bay, Dir, or Marcene Bay, Asst, Wildlands Studies, San Francisco State Univ, 3 Mosswood Circle, Cazadero CA 95421 *Ph:* 707-632 5665 *Fax:* 707-632 5665 *E-mail:* wildlnds@sonic.net

---

0297
UNIVERSITY OF DELAWARE
Winter Session in New Zealand-Animal Science
Site: New Zealand: various sites
Dates: 1 mo, Jan
Subjects: Animal sciences
Eligibility: *Level:* fresh, sophs, jrs, srs *Requires:* 2.0 GPA
Credit: *Undergrad:* 6 *Grad:* none *Doc:* transcript
Instruction: *In:* English *Format:* lecture, seminar, study tour *Students:* mainly US
Costs: Contact Sponsor
Housing: *Arr by pgm:* residence halls
Deadline: Mid-Oct
Other info: *US accredited sponsor:* yes *Orient:* in US *Activities:* excursions, field trips, cultural events *Misc:* Contact sponsor to arr honors credit. *Financial aid:* scholarships *URL:* http://www.udel.edu/studyabroad
Contact: Intl Pgms & Special Sessions, Univ of Delaware, 4 Kent Way, Newark DE 19711 *Ph:* 888-831 4685; 302-831 2852 *Fax:* 302-831 6042 *E-mail:* studyabroad@udel.edu

---

0298
UNIVERSITY OF NEW HAMPSHIRE
Ecoquest New Zealand
Site: New Zealand: Southern Hauraki Gulf (Kaiaua) *Host inst:* Ecoquest New Zealand
Dates: 5 wks, May 22-Jun 26
Subjects: Biodiversity, Ecology/environmental studies, Environmental law, Evolution, Field study, Natural resource management
Eligibility: *Level:* jrs, srs *Requires:* 2.5 GPA, good physical condition *Age:* avg 20
Credit: *Undergrad:* 8 *Grad:* none *Doc:* transcript
Instruction: *In:* English *Format:* directed field study, study tour *Students:* intl
Costs: $4,700 *incl* tuition, housing, all meals, fees, excursions *Nonrefundable fee*
Housing: *Arr by pgm:* residence halls, homestay
Deadline: Mar 15
Other info: *US accredited sponsor:* yes *Began:* 1999 *Orient:* abroad (1 wk) *Activities:* excursions, field trips, program travel, cultural events, sports *Misc:* Rural seaside campus. Applied field studies in ecology, resource mgmt & environmental policy. May contact former participants.

Financial aid: scholarships *URL:* http://www.ecoquest.unh.html
Contact: Dr Mimi Larsen Becker, Natural Resources Dept, Univ of New Hampshire, 215 James Hall, Durham NH 03824 *Ph:* 603-862 3950 *Fax:* 603-862 4976 *E-mail:* mlbecker@christa.unh.edu
Or Contact: Donna Dowal, Natural Resources, Univ of New Hampshire, 215 James Hall, Durham NH 03824 *E-mail:* ecoquest@unh.edu

CHRISTCHURCH

0299
UNIVERSITY OF DELAWARE
Winter Session in New Zealand - Art
Site: New Zealand: Christchurch
Dates: 1 mo, Jan
Subjects: Photography
Eligibility: *Level:* fresh, sophs, jrs, srs *Requires:* 2.0 GPA
Credit: *Undergrad:* 6 *Grad:* none *Doc:* transcript
Instruction: *In:* English *Format:* lecture, seminar, study tour *Students:* mainly US
Costs: Contact sponsor
Housing: *Arr by pgm*
Deadline: Early Oct
Other info: *US accredited sponsor:* yes *Orient:* avail yes *Activities:* excursions, field trips, program travel, cultural events *Misc:* Contact sponsor to arrange honors credit. *Financial aid:* scholarships *URL:* http://www.udel.edu/studyabroad/
Contact: Intl Pgms & Special Sessions, Univ of Delaware, 4 Kent Way, Newark DE 19716 *Ph:* 888-831 4685; 302-831 2852 *Fax:* 302-831 6042 *E-mail:* studyabroad@udel.edu

Philippines

MORE THAN ONE CITY

0300
FERRIS STATE UNIVERSITY
Study Abroad in the Philippines
Site: Philippines: various cities and sites
Dates: May 14-Jun 29
Subjects: Civilization/culture, Field study, Filipino studies, Geography, Urban studies
Eligibility: *Level:* fresh, sophs, jrs, srs
Credit: *Undergrad:* 3 *Grad:* none
Instruction: *In:* English *Format:* directed field study, lecture, seminar *Students:* mainly US
Costs: $3,050 *incl* housing, all meals, intl airfare, fees, airport transfer, local transport
Housing: *Arr by pgm:* hotels, jungle campsite (1 night)
Deadline: Contact sponsor
Other info: *US accredited sponsor:* yes *Began:* 2001 *Orient:* in US (2 days) *Activities:* excursions, field trips, program travel, cultural events *Misc:* Students must submit daily journal, final paper & participate in online bulletin board.
Contact: Debbie Carley, Study Abroad Coord, Intl Affairs, Ferris Univ, Bishop Hall 317, Big Rapids MI 49307 *Ph:* 231-591 3921 *Fax:* 231-591 2400 *E-mail:* carleyd@ferris.edu

MANILA

0301
UNIVERSITY OF WISCONSIN-MADISON
Manila, the Philippines
Site: Philippines: Manila *Host inst:* Ateneo de Manila Univ
Dates: 8 wks, mid-Jun-mid-Aug
Subjects: Anthropology, Filipino studies, History, Homestay, Literature, Political science/politics, Tagalog language (beg/int)
Eligibility: *Level:* sophs, jrs, srs *Requires:* 2.5 GPA
Credit: *Undergrad:* 6-9 *Grad:* none *Doc:* transcript
Instruction: *In:* English *Format:* lang study, lecture *Students:* intl
Costs: $5,100 for WI residents, $5,200 for others *incl* tuition, housing, all meals, intl airfare, books/materials, local transport
Housing: *Arr by pgm:* homestay, hotels
Deadline: 1st Fri in Feb
Other info: *US accredited sponsor:* yes *Began:* 1998 *Orient:* in US & abroad *Misc:* May contact former participants. *Financial aid:* scholarships *URL:* http://www.wisc.edu/studyabroad
Contact: Intl Studies & Pgms, Univ of Wisconsin-Madison, Bascom Hall 261, 500 Lincoln Dr, Madison WI 53706 *Ph:* 608-265 6329 *Fax:* 608-262 6998 *E-mail:* peeradvisor@bascom.wisc.edu

Singapore

SINGAPORE

0302
IMD INTERNATIONAL and **SINGAPORE INSTITUTE OF MANAGEMENT**
Job of the Chief Executive
Site: Singapore
Dates: 1 wk, Jul 30-Aug 4 or Jul 29-Aug 3
Subjects: Business administration, Business/management, Contemporary issues, International marketing, Internet, Organizational behavior
Eligibility: *Level:* professionals *Age:* min 33, max 46
Credit: *Undergrad:* none *Grad:* none *Doc:* certificate
Instruction: *In:* English *Format:* seminar *Students:* intl & host country
Costs: S $5,500 *incl* tuition, some meals, books/materials
Housing: *Arr by pgm:* hotels
Deadline: 2 mos before pgm
Other info: *US accredited sponsor:* no *Began:* 1981 *Orient:* abroad *Misc:* Pgm designed for sr mgrs from multinatl companies in Asia & the Pacific Rim. *URL:* http://www.imd.ch
Contact: David Forster, Pgm Adviser, IMD, chemin de Bellerive 23, PO Box 915, CH-1001 Lausanne, Switzerland *E-mail:* info@imd.ch
Or Contact: Lena Chia, Singapore Inst of Mgmt, Mgmt Hse, 41 Namly Ave, 267616 Singapore *E-mail:* lenachia@sim.edu.sg

0303
SYRACUSE UNIVERSITY
Management Internships in Singapore
Site: Singapore
Dates: 7 wks, Jun 25-Aug 10
Subjects: Business/management, Field study, International business, Internships
Eligibility: *Level:* jrs, srs, grads *Requires:* 2.8 GPA, previous study in field
Credit: *Undergrad:* 6 *Grad:* 6
Instruction: *In:* English *Format:* directed field study, independent study, lecture, practical training, seminar *Students:* mainly US
Costs: About $5,800 *incl* tuition, housing, some meals, fees, excursions *Nonrefundable fee*
Housing: *Arr by pgm:* hotels
Deadline: Mar 15
Other info: *US accredited sponsor:* yes *Began:* 1992 *Orient:* abroad *Activities:* excursions, field trips, cultural events *Financial aid:* scholarships *URL:* http://sumweb.syr.edu/dipa/summer
Contact: Summer Pgms, Intl Pgms Abroad, Syracuse Univ, 119 Euclid Ave, Syracuse NY 13244-4170 *Ph:* 800-251 9674; 315-443 9420 *Fax:* 315-443 4593 *E-mail:* dipasum@summon3.syr.edu ▲

Taiwan

MORE THAN ONE CITY

0304
NATIONAL REGISTRATION CENTER FOR STUDY ABROAD (NRCSA)
Taipei Language Institute
Site: Taiwan: Kaohsiung, Shihlin, Taichung, Taipei *Host inst:* Taipei Lang Inst
Dates: 4 wks or longer, yr-round
Subjects: Chinese language (Mandarin), Homestay, Taiwanese language
Eligibility: *Level:* adults
Credit: *Undergrad:* none *Grad:* none

Instruction: *In:* Mandarin, Taiwanese *Format:* lang study, tutorial *Students:* intl
Costs: $897 for 4 wks *incl* tuition, insurance
Housing: *Arr by student:* homestay, hostels
Deadline: Rolling admissions
Other info: *US accredited sponsor:* no *Misc:* May contact former participants. *URL:* http://www.nrcsa.com
Contact: Reuel Zielke, NRCSA, 823 N 2nd St, #206, Milwaukee WI 53203 *Ph:* 414-278 0631 *Fax:* 414-271 8884 *E-mail:* info@nrcsa.com

TAICHUNG

0305
UNIVERSITY OF MASSACHUSETTS AMHERST
Tunghai Summer Program, Taiwan
Site: Taiwan: Taichung *Host inst:* Tunghai Univ
Dates: 8 wks, Jul-Aug
Subjects: Chinese language (Mandarin) (beg/int), Chinese studies, Civilization/culture, Literature, Taiwanese studies
Eligibility: *Level:* fresh, sophs, jrs, srs, grads, adults *Requires:* B avg, 1 yr coll Mandarin or equiv
Credit: *Undergrad:* 10 *Grad:* none
Instruction: *In:* Mandarin *Format:* lang study, lecture *Students:* mainly US
Costs: $2,500 *incl* tuition, housing, fees, excursions
Housing: *Arr by pgm:* residence halls with local students
Deadline: Mar 15
Other info: *US accredited sponsor:* yes *Began:* 1981 *Orient:* in US & abroad *Activities:* excursions *Misc:* May contact former participants. *URL:* http://www.umass.edu/ipo/
Contact: Tunghai Summer Pgm Dir, Asian Langs & Literatures, Univ of Massachusetts, Thompson Hall, Amherst MA 01003 *Ph:* 413-545 4350 *Fax:* 413-545 4975 *E-mail:* abroad@ipo.umass.edu

TAIPEI

0306
LANGUAGE LIAISON
Chinese Language in Taipei
Site: Taiwan: Taipei
Dates: 4, 8 or 12 wks, yr-round
Subjects: Chinese language (beg/int/adv), Chinese language (Mandarin) (beg/int/adv), Chinese studies, Civilization/culture
Eligibility: *Level:* adults *Age:* min 18
Credit: *Undergrad:* avail *Grad:* avail *Doc:* transcript, certificate
Instruction: *In:* Mandarin, Taiwanese *Format:* lang study, lecture *Students:* intl
Costs: Contact sponsor
Housing: *Sponsor assists:* hotels, hostels, guest houses
Deadline: 45 days before pgm
Other info: *US accredited sponsor:* no *Activities:* excursions *Misc:* Scholarship research svc. *URL:* http://www.languageliaison.com
Contact: Nancy Forman, Dir, Lang Liaison, 4 Burnham Pkwy, Morristown NJ 07960 *Ph:* 800-284 4448 *Fax:* 973-898 1710 *E-mail:* learn@languageliaison.com

0307
LANGUAGE LIAISON
Chinese Saturation
Site: Taiwan: Taipei *Host inst:* Live in Learn
Dates: 1 wk or longer, yr-round
Subjects: Chinese language (beg/int/adv), Civilization/culture, Homestay
Eligibility: *Level:* fresh, sophs, jrs, srs, grads, adults, teachers, professionals, precoll *Age:* min 10
Credit: *Undergrad:* none *Grad:* none *Doc:* transcript, certificate
Instruction: *In:* Chinese *Format:* lang study *Students:* intl
Costs: Contact sponsor
Housing: *Arr by pgm:* teacher's home
Deadline: 45 days before pgm
Other info: *US accredited sponsor:* no *Misc:* Live & learn in your teacher's home. Scholarship research svc. *URL:* http://www.languageliaison.com
Contact: Nancy Forman, Dir, Lang Liaison, 4 Burnham Pkwy, Morristown NJ 07960 *Ph:* 800-284 4448 *Fax:* 973-898 1710 *E-mail:* learn@languageliaison.com

0308
LANGUAGES ABROAD
Language Study-Taipei
Site: Taiwan: Taipei
Dates: 2 wks or longer, yr-round
Subjects: Chinese language (Mandarin) (beg/int/adv), Homestay
Eligibility: *Level:* adults *Age:* min 17, max 65, avg 25
Credit: *Undergrad:* none *Grad:* none *Doc:* certificate
Instruction: *In:* Mandarin *Format:* lang study *Students:* intl
Costs: $1,000 per mo *incl* tuition
Housing: *Arr by pgm:* residence halls, homestay
Deadline: None
Other info: *US accredited sponsor:* no *Began:* 1995 *Activities:* excursions, field trips, program travel, cultural events, sports *Misc:* May contact former participants. *URL:* http://www.languagesabroad.com
Contact: Ms Jesse Philippe, Langs Abroad, 317 Adelaide St W, Ste 900, Toronto, Ontario M5V 1P9, Canada *Ph:* 800-219 9924; 416-925 7117 *E-mail:* info@languagesabroad.com

0309
LINGUA SERVICE WORLDWIDE
Total Immersion/Intensive Language and Culture in Taipei
Site: Taiwan: Taipei *Host inst:* Home Lang Intl
Dates: 1 wk-1 yr, yr-round
Subjects: Chinese language (beg/int/adv), Civilization/culture, Homestay
Eligibility: *Level:* adults *Age:* min 14
Credit: *Undergrad:* avail *Grad:* avail *Doc:* transcript, certificate
Instruction: *In:* Chinese *Format:* lang study *Students:* intl & host country
Costs: Contact sponsor
Housing: *Arr by pgm:* teacher's home
Deadline: 45 days before pgm
Other info: *US accredited sponsor:* no *Began:* 1993 *Activities:* excursions, cultural events *Misc:* May contact former participants. *URL:* http://www.linguaserviceworldwide.com
Contact: Dir, Lingua Svc Worldwide, 75 Prospect St, Ste 4, Huntington NY 11743 *Ph:* 800-394 5327; 631-424 0777 *Fax:* 631-271 3441 *E-mail:* itctravel@worldnet.att.net ▲

0310
NATIONAL TAIWAN NORMAL UNIVERSITY
Chinese Language and Culture Studies
Site: Taiwan: Taipei
Dates: 8 wks, Jul 1-Aug 31
Subjects: Calligraphy, Chinese language, Chinese studies, Civilization/culture, Culinary arts, Fine arts, Literature, Martial arts, Opera, Painting, Religion/theology, String instruments
Eligibility: *Level:* fresh, sophs, jrs, srs, grads, adults, teachers, professionals *Requires:* 2.0 GPA, high sch diploma *Age:* min 17, avg 22
Credit: *Undergrad:* avail *Grad:* avail
Instruction: *In:* Chinese *Format:* lang study *Students:* intl
Costs: $600 *incl* tuition *Nonrefundable fee*
Housing: *Arr by student:* residence halls, apartments, homestay, hotels, hostels
Deadline: 3 mos before pgm
Other info: *US accredited sponsor:* no *Began:* 1956 *Orient:* abroad (1 day) *Activities:* field trips, cultural events, sports *Financial aid:* scholarships *URL:* http://www.ntnu.edu.tw/mtc/index.htm
Contact: Doris YS Owyang, CCLC, NTNU, 162 Hoping E Rd, Sec 1, Taipei, Taiwan *E-mail:* mtc@mtc.ntnu.edu.tw

Thailand

MORE THAN ONE CITY

0311
NORTHWESTERN UNIVERSITY
Northwestern University in Bangkok
Site: Thailand: Bangkok, Chiang Mai *Host inst:* Chula Longkorn Univ
Dates: Jun 19-Aug 6
Subjects: Anthropology, Buddhism, Political science/politics, Religion/theology, Southeast Asian studies, Thai studies
Eligibility: *Level:* fresh, sophs, jrs, srs *Requires:* 3.0 GPA
Credit: *Undergrad:* 3 per course *Grad:* none *Doc:* transcript
Instruction: *In:* English *Format:* lecture, study tour *Students:* mainly US
Costs: $7,205 for 2 courses *incl* tuition, housing, some meals, intl airfare, fees, excursions *Nonrefundable fee*
Housing: *Arr by pgm:* hotels
Deadline: Mar 31
Other info: *US accredited sponsor:* yes *Orient:* in US (1 day) *Activities:* excursions *Misc:* Students must take 2 courses. May contact former participants. *URL:* http://www.northwestern.edu/summersa
Contact: Christina Kyres, Asst Dir, Sch of Continuing Studies, Northwestern Univ, 339 E Chicago Ave, Chicago IL 60611-3021 *Ph:* 312-503 3021 *Fax:* 312-503 3003 *E-mail:* summersa@northwestern.edu

---

0312
PRINCE OF SONGKLA UNIVERSITY
International Program in Thai Studies
Site: Thailand: Hat Yai, Phuket
Dates: 8 wks, Jun-Jul
Subjects: Arts, Civilization/culture, Communications, Economics, Field study, History, Homestay, Independent study, Political science/politics, Thai language (beg), Thai studies
Eligibility: *Level:* adults
Credit: *Undergrad:* 9 *Grad:* none *Doc:* certificate
Instruction: *In:* English *Format:* directed field study, independent study, lang study, lecture, seminar, study tour *Students:* intl
Costs: $1,125 *incl* tuition, excursions, books/materials
Housing: *Arr by student:* residence halls, apartments
Deadline: May 7
Other info: *US accredited sponsor:* no *Orient:* abroad (1 day) *Activities:* cultural events *URL:* http://www.psu.ac.th
Contact: Ms Yupin Karanyadech, Intl Officer, Prince of Songkla Univ, PO Box 102, Hat Yai, Songkhla 90110, Thailand *E-mail:* intl@ratree.psu.ac.th
Or Contact: Asst Prof Pimpaporn Suwatthiqul, Dir, Lang Inst, Prince of Songkla Univ, Phuket Campus, Kathu, Phuket 83120, Thailand *E-mail:* spimpapo@ratree.psu.ac.th

---

0313
SAN FRANCISCO STATE UNIVERSITY, WILDLANDS STUDIES PROGRAM
Thailand Ecosystem and Culture Program
Site: Thailand: various field sites
Dates: Jan 5-Mar 12
Subjects: Biology, Ecology/environmental studies, Ethnography, Field study
Eligibility: *Level:* adults *Requires:* application essay *Age:* min 18, avg 22
Credit: *Undergrad:* 9 per term *Grad:* none *Doc:* transcript
Instruction: *In:* English *Format:* directed field study *Students:* mainly US
Costs: $1,900 *incl* tuition
Housing: *Arr by pgm:* basecamp, backpacking
Deadline: Rolling admissions
Other info: *US accredited sponsor:* yes *Began:* 1992 *Orient:* abroad *Activities:* field trips *Misc:* May contact former participants. *URL:* http://www.wildlandsstudies.com/ws
Contact: Crandall Bay, Dir, or Marcene Bay, Asst, Wildlands Studies, San Francisco State Univ, 3 Mosswood Circle, Cazadero CA 95421 *Ph:* 707-632 5665 *Fax:* 707-632 5665 *E-mail:* wildlnds@sonic.net

---

BANGKOK

0314
LANGUAGES ABROAD
Language and Cultural Immersion Programs-Bangkok
Site: Thailand: Bangkok
Dates: 2 wks or longer, yr-round
Subjects: Civilization/culture, Thai language (beg/int/adv)
Eligibility: *Level:* adults *Age:* min 17, max 65, avg 25
Credit: *Undergrad:* none *Grad:* none *Doc:* certificate
Instruction: *In:* Thai *Format:* lang study *Students:* intl
Costs: From $3,350 for 4 wks *incl* tuition, housing, some meals, excursions, books/materials
Housing: *Arr by pgm:* apartments, homestay
Deadline: None
Other info: *US accredited sponsor:* no *Misc:* May contact former participants. *URL:* http://www.languagesabroad.com
Contact: Ms Jesse Philippe, Langs Abroad, 317 Adelaide St W, Ste 900, Toronto, Ontario M5V 1P9, Canada *Ph:* 800-219 9924; 416-925 7117 *E-mail:* info@languagesabroad.com

---

CHA-AM

0315
WEBSTER UNIVERSITY
Degree Program
Site: Thailand: Cha-am *Host inst:* Webster Univ Thailand campus
Dates: Yr-round
Subjects: Business/management, Computer sciences, International relations, Media studies
Eligibility: *Level:* fresh, sophs, jrs, srs, adults *Requires:* 2.5 GPA *Age:* avg 22
Credit: *Undergrad:* avail *Grad:* avail *Doc:* degree
Instruction: *In:* English *Students:* intl
Costs: About $6,440 *incl* tuition, housing, all meals, books/materials, activities
Housing: *Sponsor assists:* residence halls
Deadline: Feb 15
Other info: *US accredited sponsor:* yes *URL:* http://www.websteruniv.edu
Contact: Study Abroad Ctr, Webster Univ, 470 E Lockwood, St Louis MO 63119 *Ph:* 800-984 6857; 314-968 6988 *Fax:* 314-968 7119 *E-mail:* worldview@webster.edu

---

CHIANG MAI

0316
GLOBAL SERVICE CORPS
English Instruction, Cross Cultural Learning and Service
Site: Thailand: Lamphun Province, near Chiang Mai *Host inst:* Pasang Sch District
Dates: 25 days or longer, yr-round
Subjects: Civilization/culture, Education/teaching, English, Health/health education, HIV/AIDS education, Media studies, Special education, TEFL/TESL
Eligibility: *Level:* jrs, srs, grads, adults, teachers, professionals *Requires:* good health, proper immunizations, travel insurance *Age:* min 21, avg 35
Credit: *Undergrad:* avail *Grad:* avail
Instruction: *In:* English *Format:* directed field study, independent study, internship, practical training, student teaching, study tour, volunteer/svc *Students:* US & intl
Costs: Contact sponsor
Housing: *Arr by pgm:* homestay, hotels
Deadline: 90 days before pgm
Other info: *US accredited sponsor:* no *Began:* 1995 *In coop with:* Earth Island Inst *Orient:* abroad *Activities:* excursions, field trips, program travel, cultural events *Misc:* May contact former participants.

See "How To Use This Book" for definitions of terms used above. ▲ = See program sponsor's ad(s) in this book.

URL: http://www.globalservicecorps.org
Contact: Jamie Kemsey, Admin Asst, Global Svc Corps, 300 Broadway, Ste 28, San Francisco CA 94133 *Ph:* 415-788 3666 ext 128 *Fax:* 415-788 7324 *E-mail:* gsc@igc.apc.org
Or Contact: Bruce Houser, Thailand Project Coord, Global Svc Corps, 2740 Gunnison Dr, El Paso TX 79904 *Ph:* 915-755 0964 *E-mail:* rucbaj@aol.com

---

0317
LEXIA INTERNATIONAL
LEXIA Summer in Chiang Mai
Site: Thailand: Chiang Mai *Host inst:* Chiang Mai Univ
Dates: 8 wks, mid-Jun-mid-Aug
Subjects: Anthropology, Arts, Asian studies, Civilization/culture, Community service projects, Ecology/environmental studies, Economics, Fine arts, History, Independent study, Internships, Literature, Political science/politics, Sociology, Thai language (beg/int/adv)
Eligibility: *Level:* fresh, sophs, jrs, srs, grads *Requires:* 2.5 GPA, 1 yr postsecondary educ completed *Age:* min 18, avg 21
Credit: *Undergrad:* 8-10 *Grad:* 8-10 *Doc:* transcript
Instruction: *In:* English, Thai *Format:* independent study, internship, lang study, lecture, seminar, volunteer/svc *Students:* mainly US
Costs: $4,650 *incl* tuition, housing, insurance, fees, excursions, ISIC, computer access *Nonrefundable fee*
Housing: *Arr by pgm:* residence halls with local students, homestay
Deadline: Apr 15; Apr 1 for scholarships
Other info: *US accredited sponsor:* no *Began:* 2000 *In coop with:* Western Washington Univ *Orient:* abroad (2 days, intensive lang study) *Activities:* excursions, field trips, program travel, cultural events, sports *Misc:* Student support svcs. May contact former participants. *Financial aid:* scholarships, work study *URL:* http://www.lexiaintl.org
Contact: LEXIA Intl, 25 S Main St, Hanover NH 03755 *Ph:* 800-755 3942; 603-643 9898 *Fax:* 603-643 9899 *E-mail:* info@lexiaintl.org
Or Contact: LEXIA Intl, West Coast, 378 Cambridge Ave, Palo Alto CA 94306 *Ph:* 650-327 9191 *Fax:* 650-327 9192

0318
PAYAP UNIVERSITY
Intensive Thai
Site: Thailand: Chiang Mai
Dates: 1 wk or longer, yr-round
Subjects: Thai studies
Eligibility: *Level:* adults *Requires:* interview
Credit: *Undergrad:* none *Grad:* none
Instruction: *In:* English, Thai *Format:* lang study *Students:* intl
Costs: 6,000-12,000 baht *incl* tuition
Housing: *Arr by student*
Deadline: None
Other info: *US accredited sponsor:* no *Orient:* abroad *Activities:* field trips, cultural events *URL:* http://www.payap.ac.th/int

Contact: Dr Philip E Lyon, Dir, Intl Pgms, Payap Univ, A Muang, Chiang Mai 50000, Thailand *E-mail:* philip_l@payap.ac.th

KANCHANABRI

0319
GLOBAL SERVICE CORPS
English Instruction, Cross Cultural Learning and Service
Site: Thailand: Kanchanabri
Dates: 23 days or longer, yr-round
Subjects: Civilization/culture, Education/teaching, English, Health sciences, HIV/AIDS education, Media studies, Special education, TEFL/TESL
Eligibility: *Level:* fresh, sophs, jrs, srs, grads, adults, teachers, professionals *Requires:* good health, proper immunizations, travel insurance *Age:* min 20, avg 25
Credit: *Undergrad:* avail *Grad:* avail *Doc:* certificate *Transfer credit through:* San Francisco State Univ
Instruction: *In:* English *Format:* directed field study, independent study, internship, practical training, student teaching, study tour, volunteer/svc *Students:* US & intl
Costs: $1,895 for 23 days, $595 for each addtl mo *incl* housing, all meals, excursions, local transportation
Housing: *Arr by pgm:* homestay, hotels
Deadline: 90 days before pgm
Other info: *US accredited sponsor:* no *Began:* 1994 *In coop with:* Earth Island Inst *Orient:* abroad *Activities:* excursions, field trips, program travel, cultural events *Misc:* May contact former participants. *URL:* http://www.globalservicecorps.org
Contact: Rick Lathrop, Global Svc Corps, 300 Broadway Ste 28, San Francisco CA 94133 *Ph:* 415-788 3666 *Fax:* 415-788 7324 *E-mail:* gsc@earthisland.org
Or Contact: Bruce Houser, Global Svc Corps, 2740 Gunnisor Dr, El Paso TX 79904 *Ph:* 915-755 0969 *E-mail:* rucbaj@aol.com

KHON KAEN

0320
COUNCIL ON INTERNATIONAL EDUCATIONAL EXCHANGE CONSORTIUM
Council Study Center-Khon Kaen University
Site: Thailand: Khon Kaen *Host inst:* Khon Kaen Univ
Dates: 8 wks, Jun-Aug
Subjects: Development studies, Ecology/environmental studies, Thai language
Eligibility: *Level:* sophs, jrs, srs, grads *Requires:* 2.75 GPA
Credit: *Undergrad:* 8-9 *Grad:* none
Instruction: *In:* English, Thai *Format:* lecture *Students:* mainly US
Costs: $4,300 *incl* tuition, housing, all meals, intl airfare, excursions, orient, ISIC, activities
Housing: *Arr by pgm:* residence halls, local villages
Deadline: Apr 1
Other info: *US accredited sponsor:* yes *Began:* 1995 *Orient:* abroad *Activities:* field trips, cultural events *Misc:* Full-time resident dir. Grade report. May contact former participants. *Financial aid:* scholarships *URL:* http://www.ciee.org/study
Contact: *See Index II for Members* Council-ISP, 633 3rd Ave, 20th Fl, New York NY 10017-6706 *Ph:* 800-407 8839; 212-822 2600 *Fax:* 212-822 2779 *E-mail:* studyinfo@ciee.org

0321
NATIONAL REGISTRATION CENTER FOR STUDY ABROAD (NRCSA)
Language Study in Thailand
Site: Thailand: Khon Kaen *Host inst:* Khon Kaen Univ
Dates: Contact sponsor
Subjects: Taiwanese language (beg/int/adv)
Eligibility: *Level:* fresh, sophs, jrs, srs, grads, adults, teachers, professionals *Age:* min 18
Credit: *Undergrad:* none *Grad:* none *Doc:* certificate
Instruction: *In:* Thai *Format:* lang study, tutorial *Students:* intl
Costs: $475 for 1 wk *incl* tuition, housing, insurance *Nonrefundable fee*
Housing: *Arr by pgm:* guest house
Deadline: 6 wks before pgm
Other info: *US accredited sponsor:* no *Misc:* May contact former participants. *URL:* http://www.worldwide.edu
Contact: Reuel Zielke, NRCSA, 823 N 2nd St, #206, Milwaukee WI 53203 *Ph:* 414-278 0631 *Fax:* 414-271 8884 *E-mail:* info@nrcsa.com

PATTANI

0322
PRINCE OF SONGKLA UNIVERSITY
International Program in Thai Studies
Site: Thailand: Pattani
Dates: 8 wks, Jan-Feb
Subjects: Art, Civilization/culture, Economics, Field study, History, Homestay, Independent study, Political science/politics, Thai language (beg), Thai studies
Eligibility: *Level:* fresh, sophs, jrs, srs, grads, adults, teachers, professionals, precoll
Credit: *Undergrad:* 13 *Grad:* none *Doc:* certificate
Instruction: *In:* English, Thai *Format:* directed field study, independent study, lang study, lecture *Students:* intl
Costs: $1,000 *incl* tuition, excursions, books/materials
Housing: *Arr by student:* apartments with local students, residence halls with local students, homestay
Deadline: Nov 30; $200 late application fee
Other info: *US accredited sponsor:* no *Began:* 1995 *Orient:* abroad (1 day) *Activities:* cultural events *Misc:* May contact former participants. *URL:* http://www.psu.ac.th
Contact: Dean, Faculty of Humanities & Social Scis, Prince of Songkla Univ, Pattani 94000, Thailand *E-mail:* humansoc@bunga.pn.psu.ac.th
Or Contact: Ms Yupin Karanyadech, Intl Officer, Prince of Songkla Univ, PO Box 102, Hat Yai, Songkhla 90110, Thailand *E-mail:* intl@ratree.psu.ac.th

RANGSIT

0323
UNIVERSITY STUDIES ABROAD CONSORTIUM
Southeast Asian Studies
Site: Thailand: Rangsit *Host inst:* Rangsit Univ
Dates: May 18-Aug 28
Subjects: Anthropology, Business/management, Economics, Finance, Marketing, Philosophy, Political science/politics, Sociology, Thai language
Eligibility: *Level:* fresh, sophs, jrs, srs, grads, adults, teachers, professionals, precoll *Requires:* 2.50 GPA *Age:* min 18
Credit: *Undergrad:* 6 *Grad:* 4 *Doc:* transcript
Instruction: *In:* English *Format:* lang study, lecture *Students:* mainly host country
Costs: $2,680 *incl* tuition, insurance, fees, ISIC
Housing: *Sponsor assists:* residence halls
Deadline: Apr 15
Other info: *US accredited sponsor:* yes *Began:* 1995 *Orient:* abroad *Activities:* cultural events, sports *Misc:* May contact former participants. *Financial aid:* scholarships *URL:* http://www.usac.unr.edu
Contact: *See Index II for Members* Carmelo Urza, Univ Studies Abroad Consortium, Univ of Nevada Reno 323, Reno NV 89557-0093 *Ph:* 775-784 6569 *Fax:* 775-784 6010 *E-mail:* usac@unr.edu ▲

Vietnam

MORE THAN ONE CITY

0324
CITY COLLEGE OF SAN FRANCISCO
Re-Picturing Vietnam
Site: Vietnam: Ha Noi, Ho Chi Minh City, Mekong Delta, Nha Trang
Dates: 19 days, Dec 26-Jan 13
Subjects: Asian-American studies, Photography
Eligibility: *Level:* adults *Requires:* 2.0 GPA *Age:* min 17, max 80, avg 30
Credit: *Undergrad:* avail *Grad:* none *Doc:* transcript
Instruction: *In:* English *Format:* study tour *Students:* mainly US
Costs: $2,999 *incl* housing, some meals, intl airfare, insurance, excursions
Housing: *Arr by pgm:* hotels, hostels
Deadline: Contact sponsor
Other info: *US accredited sponsor:* yes *Began:* 2000 *Orient:* in US & abroad (2 days) *Activities:* excursions, field trips, program travel, cultural events *Financial aid:* scholarships *URL:* http://www.ccsf.org/studyabroad
Contact: Jill Heffron, Study Abroad Coord, City Coll of San Francisco, 50 Phelan Ave, Box C212, San Francisco CA 94112 *Ph:* 415-239 3778 *Fax:* 415-239 3804 *E-mail:* jheffron@ccsf.org

---

0325
COUNCIL ON INTERNATIONAL EDUCATIONAL EXCHANGE (COUNCIL)
International Faculty Development Seminars-Vietnam
Site: Vietnam: Hanoi, Ho Chi Minh City *Host inst:* The Vietnam-USA Society
Dates: 11 days, Jul
Subjects: Civilization/culture, Contemporary issues, Economics, History, Vietnamese studies
Eligibility: *Level:* teachers, professionals *Requires:* must be full-time faculty at 2-yr or 4-yr inst
Credit: *Undergrad:* none *Grad:* none
Instruction: *In:* English *Format:* lecture, seminar *Students:* mainly US
Costs: $1,850 *incl* tuition, housing, most meals, fees, excursions, airfare in Vietnam, ITIC
Housing: *Arr by pgm:* hotels
Deadline: Mar 15
Other info: *US accredited sponsor:* no *Began:* 1991 *Orient:* abroad *Activities:* excursions, field trips, cultural events *Misc:* Seminar title: Tradition & Transformation in Vietnam. May contact former participants. *URL:* http://www.ciee.org/ifds
Contact: Jennifer Ley, Council, 633 3rd Ave, New York NY 10017 *Ph:* 212-822 2746 *Fax:* 212-822 2779 *E-mail:* ifds@ciee.org ▲

0326
PEACEWORK DEVELOPMENT FUND, INC
Peacework in Vietnam
Site: Vietnam: various cities
Dates: 2-3 wks, Jan
Subjects: Community service projects, Field study, Intercultural studies, Peace studies
Eligibility: *Level:* adults *Age:* min 18
Credit: *Undergrad:* none *Grad:* none
Instruction: *In:* English *Format:* volunteer/svc *Students:* US & intl
Costs: About $2,200 *incl* housing, all meals, intl airfare, insurance, fees, excursions, books/materials *Nonrefundable fee*
Housing: *Arr by pgm:* pensions, hotels
Deadline: 2 mos before pgm
Other info: *US accredited sponsor:* no *Began:* 1997 *Orient:* in US & abroad *Activities:* excursions, cultural events *Misc:* Cultural pgms combined with svc pgms, such as bldg schs & clinics. May contact former participants. *URL:* http://www.peacework.org
Contact: Stephen Darr, Peacework, 305 Washington St, SW, Blacksburg VA 24060-1376 *Ph:* 540-953 1376 *Fax:* 540-552 0119 *E-mail:* sdarr@compuserve.com
Or Contact: Don Voth, Univ of Arkansas, Fayetteville AR 72701 *Ph:* 501-575 2409 *E-mail:* dvoth@comp.uark.edu

---

0327
UNIVERSITY OF SOUTHERN MISSISSIPPI
An Academic Excursion in Vietnam
Site: Vietnam: various sites
Dates: May 13-May 30
Subjects: History, International studies
Eligibility: *Level:* jrs, srs, grads *Requires:* 2.0 GPA, prereq of 1 History of Vietnam class; permission of instructor
Credit: *Undergrad:* 4 *Grad:* 3 *Doc:* transcript
Instruction: *In:* English *Format:* directed field study, lecture, study tour *Students:* mainly US
Costs: $3,599 for undergrads, $3,899 for grads *incl* tuition, housing, some meals, intl airfare, fees, excursions *Nonrefundable fee*
Housing: *Arr by pgm:* hotels
Deadline: Apr 3
Other info: *US accredited sponsor:* yes *Began:* 2000 *Misc:* May contact former participants. *URL:* http://www.usm.edu
Contact: Dr Tim Hudson, Dean, CICE, o Dir, Excursion in Vietnam, Univ of Southern Mississippi, Box 10046, Hattiesburg MS 39406-0047 *Ph:* 601-266 4344 *Fax:* 601-266 5699 *E-mail:* melissa.ravencraft@usm.edu

---

HANOI

0328
INSTITUTE OF LINGUISTICS OF VIETNAM
Vietnamese Language and Culture
Site: Vietnam: Hanoi *Host inst:* Ctr for the Vietnamese Lang & Applied Linguistics
Dates: Contact sponsor
Subjects: Civilization/culture, History, Vietnamese language, Vietnamese studies
Eligibility: *Level:* grads, adults, teachers, professionals, precoll *Requires:* recommendation letter *Age:* min 18, max 50
Credit: *Undergrad:* none *Grad:* none *Doc:* certificate
Instruction: *In:* English, French, Russian *Format:* directed field study, lang study, lecture, tutorial *Students:* intl
Costs: Contact sponsor
Housing: *Arr by student*
Deadline: Rolling admissions
Other info: *US accredited sponsor:* no *Activities:* excursions, cultural events
Contact: Dr Vu Thi Thanh Huong, Ctr for Vietnamese Lang, 20 Ly Thai To St, Hanoi, Vietnam *E-mail:* litha@vietnam.org.vn

---

HO CHI MINH CITY

0329
CET ACADEMIC PROGRAMS
Vietnam Immersion
Site: Vietnam: Ho Chi Minh City *Host inst:* Vietnamese Lang Sch for Foreigners
Dates: Jun 14-Aug 11
Subjects: Independent study, Vietnamese language (beg/int/adv), Vietnamese studies
Eligibility: *Level:* fresh, sophs, jrs, srs, grads, adults, professionals *Age:* min 17, avg 21
Credit: *Undergrad:* avail *Grad:* avail *Doc:* transcript, certificate
Instruction: *In:* English, Vietnamese *Format:* independent study, lang study, seminar, study tour, tutorial *Students:* mainly US
Costs: $4,690 *incl* tuition, housing, all meals, insurance, excursions, books/materials *Nonrefundable fee*
Housing: *Arr by pgm:* apartments with local students, residence halls with local students
Deadline: Mar 1
Other info: *US accredited sponsor:* no

Began: 2001 *Orient:* abroad (3 days) *Activities:* excursions, field trips, program travel, cultural events *Misc:* May contact former participants. *Financial aid:* scholarships *URL:* http://www.cetacademicprograms.com
Contact: Katie Smithson, Pgm Development, CET Acad Pgms, 1000 16th Street NW, Ste 350, Washington DC 20036 *Ph:* 800-225 4262; 202-530 0800 *Fax:* 202-342 0317 *E-mail:* cet@academic-travel.com

---

0330
FLORIDA STATE UNIVERSITY
Vietnam Summer Program
Site: Vietnam: Ho Chi Minh City
Dates: 6 wks, May 10-Jun 20
Subjects: Civilization/culture, Liberal arts, Music, Vietnamese language, Vietnamese studies
Eligibility: *Level:* fresh, sophs, jrs, srs, grads, precoll *Requires:* 2.5 GPA
Credit: *Undergrad:* 9 *Grad:* avail
Instruction: *In:* English *Format:* lang study, lecture *Students:* mainly US
Costs: $4,495 *incl* tuition, housing, some meals, intl airfare
Housing: *Arr by pgm:* hotels
Deadline: Jan 19
Other info: *US accredited sponsor:* yes *Began:* 2000 *Orient:* in US & abroad (2 days) *Activities:* excursions, field trips, program travel, cultural events *Misc:* May contact former participants. *URL:* http://www.international.fsu.edu
Contact: Elizabeth Trelenberg or Bonnie Snyder, Intl Pgms, Florida State Univ, 5500 UCA, Tallahassee FL 32306-2420 *Ph:* 800-374 8581; 850-644 3272 *Fax:* 850-644 8817 *E-mail:* intprog@www.fsu.edu

Eastern Europe

More Than One Country

0331
COUNCIL ON INTERNATIONAL EDUCATIONAL EXCHANGE (COUNCIL)
International Faculty Development Seminars-Eastern Europe
Site: Hungary: Budapest; Poland: Warsaw *Host inst:* Budapest Univ of Econ Scis (BUES), Warsaw Sch of Econ
Dates: 9 days, Jun
Subjects: Central European studies, Contemporary issues, Current events, East European studies, Social change
Eligibility: *Level:* teachers, professionals *Requires:* must be full-time faculty at 2-yr or 4-yr inst
Credit: *Undergrad:* none *Grad:* none
Instruction: *In:* English *Format:* lecture, seminar *Students:* mainly US
Costs: $1,995 *incl* tuition, housing, most meals, fees, excursions, ITIC
Housing: *Arr by pgm:* hotels
Deadline: Mar 15
Other info: *US accredited sponsor:* no *Began:* 1995 *Orient:* abroad *Activities:* excursions, field trips, cultural events *Misc:* Seminar title: Central Europe in Transition. May contact former participants. *URL:* http://www.ciee.org/ifds
Contact: Jennifer Ley, Council, 633 3rd Ave, New York NY 10017 *Ph:* 212-822 2747 *Fax:* 212-822 2779 *E-mail:* ifds@ciee.org ▲

0332
GEORGE WASHINGTON UNIVERSITY
Central and East European Politics
Site: Czech Republic: Prague; Slovakia: Bratislava *Host inst:* Charles Univ
Dates: 2 wks, summer
Subjects: Central European studies, East European studies, Field study, Independent study, Political science/politics
Eligibility: *Level:* jrs, srs, grads
Credit: *Undergrad:* none *Grad:* 3 *Doc:* transcript
Instruction: *In:* English *Format:* directed field study, independent study, lecture, study tour *Students:* US & intl
Costs: $2,590 *incl* tuition, housing, some meals
Housing: *Arr by pgm:* residence halls, hostels
Deadline: Contact sponsor
Other info: *US accredited sponsor:* yes *Began:* 1998 *Orient:* in US (1 day) *Activities:* excursions, field trips, program travel, cultural events *Misc:* New summer pgm announced in December. Contact sponsor for updated info. *URL:* http://www.summer.gwu.edu
Contact: Summer, Special & Intl Pgms, George Washington Univ, 609 22nd St NW, Washington DC 20052 *Ph:* 202-994 6360 *Fax:* 202-994 9133 *E-mail:* sumprogs@gwu.edu

---

0333
LANGUAGE LIAISON
Russian Saturation
Site: Belarus: Minsk; Russia: Moscow, St Petersburg *Host inst:* Live in Learn
Dates: 1 wk or longer, yr-round
Subjects: Civilization/culture, Homestay, Russian language (beg/int/adv)
Eligibility: *Level:* fresh, sophs, jrs, srs, grads, adults, teachers, professionals, precoll *Age:* min 10
Credit: *Undergrad:* none *Grad:* none *Doc:* transcript, certificate
Instruction: *In:* Russian *Format:* lang study *Students:* intl
Costs: Contact sponsor
Housing: *Arr by pgm:* teacher's home
Deadline: 45 days before pgm
Other info: *US accredited sponsor:* no *Misc:* Live & learn in your teacher's home. Scholarship research svc. *URL:* http://www.languageliaison.com
Contact: Nancy Forman, Dir, Lang Liaison, 4 Burnham Pkwy, Morristown NJ 07960 *Ph:* 800-284 4448 *Fax:* 973-898 1710 *E-mail:* learn@languageliaison.com

---

0334
MICHIGAN STATE UNIVERSITY
Economic and Political Transition in Eastern Europe
Site: Czech Republic: Prague; Hungary: Budapest
Dates: 4 wks, Jun-Jul
Subjects: International relations, Political science/politics
Eligibility: *Level:* sophs, jrs, srs *Requires:* 2.3 GPA *Age:* min 18
Credit: *Undergrad:* avail *Grad:* none *Doc:* transcript
Instruction: *In:* English *Format:* lecture, seminar *Students:* mainly US
Costs: About $950 *incl* housing, insurance, excursions, support svcs *Nonrefundable fee*
Housing: *Arr by pgm:* residence halls, pensions
Deadline: Mar 2
Other info: *US accredited sponsor:* yes *Began:* 1996 *Orient:* in US (1 day) *Activities:* excursions, field trips, program travel, cultural events *Financial aid:* scholarships *URL:* http://studyabroad.msu.edu
Contact: Cheryl Benner, Study Abroad, Michigan State Univ, 109 Intl Ctr, East Lansing MI 48824-1035 *Ph:* 517-353 8920 *Fax:* 517-432 2082 *E-mail:* bennerc@msu.edu ▲

0335
MICHIGAN STATE UNIVERSITY
Retail Distribution
Site: Poland: Warsaw; Russia: St Petersburg
Dates: 2 wks, May
Subjects: Business/management, Fashion

merchandising, Homestay, Independent study, Retailing
Eligibility: *Level:* fresh, sophs, jrs, srs *Requires:* 2.0 GPA *Age:* min 18
Credit: *Undergrad:* 4 *Grad:* 4 *Doc:* transcript
Instruction: *In:* English *Format:* independent study, lecture *Students:* mainly US
Costs: About $900 *incl* housing, some meals, insurance, excursions *Nonrefundable fee*
Housing: *Arr by pgm:* homestay, hotels
Deadline: Mar 2
Other info: *US accredited sponsor:* yes *Began:* 1998 *Orient:* in US *Activities:* excursions, field trips, program travel, cultural events *Misc:* May contact former participants. *Financial aid:* scholarships *URL:* http://studyabroad.msu.edu
Contact: Cheryl Benner, Study Abroad, Michigan State Univ, 109 Intl Ctr, East Lansing MI 48824 *Ph:* 517-353 8920 *Fax:* 517-432 2082 *E-mail:* bennerc@msu.edu ▲

0336
MICHIGAN STATE UNIVERSITY
Toward a New Central Europe
Site: Hungary: Budapest; Romania: Cluj
Dates: 6 wks, May-Jun
Subjects: Agriculture, Natural resources, Social sciences
Eligibility: *Level:* fresh, sophs, jrs, srs, grads *Requires:* 2.0 GPA *Age:* min 18
Credit: *Undergrad:* avail *Grad:* none *Doc:* transcript
Instruction: *In:* English *Format:* directed field study, lecture *Students:* mainly US
Costs: About $1,700 *incl* housing, insurance, fees, excursions, ground transport *Nonrefundable fee*
Housing: *Arr by pgm:* residence halls
Deadline: Mar 2
Other info: *US accredited sponsor:* yes *Began:* 1999 *Orient:* in US (1 day) *Activities:* excursions, field trips, program travel *Financial aid:* scholarships *URL:* http://studyabroad.msu.edu
Contact: Cheryl Benner, Study Abroad, Michigan State Univ, 109 Intl Ctr, East Lansing MI 48824-1035 *Ph:* 517-353 8920 *Fax:* 517-432 2082 *E-mail:* bennerc@msu.edu ▲

0337
NEW YORK UNIVERSITY, TISCH SCHOOL OF THE ARTS
Alternative Theater Festivals in Eastern Europe
Site: Bulgaria, Romania, Poland *Host inst:* Natl Acad for Theater, Natl Sch of Folk Arts, Sibiu Intl Theater Festival, Bulgarian Natl Theater
Dates: 6 wks, late May-early Jul
Subjects: Acting, Drama/theater, East European studies, Folk arts, Folk dance, Performing arts, Puppetry
Eligibility: *Level:* sophs, jrs, srs, grads, adults, teachers, professionals *Requires:* interview, previous acting training &/or experience or instructor's permission *Age:* min 18
Credit: *Undergrad:* 8 *Grad:* avail *Doc:* transcript
Instruction: *In:* English *Format:* lab, lecture, practical training, study tour, workshop *Students:* mainly US
Costs: $6,803 *incl* tuition, housing, some meals, intl airfare, fees, excursions, festival fees *Nonrefundable fee*
Housing: *Arr by pgm:* pensions, hotels
Deadline: Mar 15; rolling admissions
Other info: *US accredited sponsor:* yes *Began:* 1998 *In coop with:* Natl Acad for Theater, others *Orient:* in US (1 day) *Activities:* excursions, field trips, program travel, cultural events *Misc:* Scholarships & loans for own students only. *Financial aid:* scholarships *URL:* http://www.nyu.edu/tisch/international/
Contact: Linda Kow, Assoc Dir, Tisch Intl Pgms, New York Univ, 721 Broadway, 12th Fl, New York NY 10003 *Ph:* 212-998 9175 *Fax:* 212-995 4578 *E-mail:* tisch.international@nyu.edu

Bulgaria

PLOVDIV

0338
COLLEGE CONSORTIUM FOR INTERNATIONAL STUDIES and TRUMAN STATE UNIVERSITY
Summer Program in Bulgaria
Site: Bulgaria: Plovdiv *Host inst:* Acad of Music & Dance
Dates: 1 mo, Jul 1-31
Subjects: Balkan studies, Civilization/culture, Homestay, Music, Music history
Eligibility: *Level:* sophs, jrs, srs, adults *Requires:* 2.5 GPA, previous study in field, coll-level coursework in music *Age:* min 18
Credit: *Undergrad:* 6 *Grad:* none *Doc:* transcript
Instruction: *In:* English *Format:* lecture, music lesson *Students:* mainly US
Costs: $1,950 *incl* tuition, housing, some meals, excursions
Housing: *Arr by pgm:* residence halls, apartments, homestay
Deadline: May 1
Other info: *US accredited sponsor:* yes *Began:* 1999 *Orient:* in US & abroad (3 days) *Activities:* excursions *Misc:* May contact former participants. *URL:* http://www.ccisabroad.org
Contact: *See Index II for Members* Ctr for Intl Educ Abroad, Truman State Univ, Kirk Bldg 120, Kirksville MO 63501 *Ph:* 660-785 4076 *Fax:* 660-785 7473 *E-mail:* ciea@truman.edu ▲

SOPHIA

0339
LANGUAGES ABROAD
Language and Cultural Immersion Programs-Sophia
Site: Bulgaria: Sophia
Dates: 2 wks or longer, yr-round
Subjects: Bulgarian language (beg/int/adv), Civilization/culture
Eligibility: *Level:* adults *Age:* min 17, max 65, avg 25
Credit: *Undergrad:* none *Grad:* none *Doc:* certificate
Instruction: *In:* Bulgarian *Format:* lang study *Students:* intl
Costs: $3,995 for 4 wks *incl* tuition, housing, some meals, excursions, books/materials
Housing: *Arr by pgm:* apartments, homestay
Deadline: None
Other info: *US accredited sponsor:* no *Misc:* May contact former participants. *URL:* http://www.languagesabroad.com
Contact: Ms Jesse Philippe, Langs Abroad, 317 Adelaide St W, Ste 900, Toronto, Ontario M5V 1P9, Canada *Ph:* 800-219 9924; 416-925 7117 *E-mail:* info@languagesabroad.com

Croatia

MORE THAN ONE CITY

0340
COUNCIL ON INTERNATIONAL EDUCATIONAL EXCHANGE (COUNCIL)
International Faculty Development Seminars-Croatia
Site: Croatia: Dubrovnik, Zagreb *Host inst:* Inter-Univ Ctr
Dates: 10 days, Jun
Subjects: Balkan studies, Contemporary issues, Ethnology, History, War studies
Eligibility: *Level:* teachers *Requires:* must be faculty at 2-yr or 4-yr inst
Credit: *Undergrad:* none *Grad:* none
Instruction: *In:* English *Format:* lecture, seminar *Students:* mainly US
Costs: $1,950 *incl* tuition, housing, some meals, insurance, fees, excursions, books/materials
Housing: *Arr by pgm:* hotels
Deadline: Mar 15
Other info: *US accredited sponsor:* no *Began:* 1998 *Activities:* excursions, field

trips *Misc:* Seminar title: Present & Future Perspectives on the Balkans. *URL:* http://www.ciee.org/ifds
Contact: Jennifer Ley, Dir, Intl Faculty Development Seminars, Council, 633 3rd Ave, New York NY 10017 *Ph:* 212-822 2747 *Fax:* 212-822 2779 *E-mail:* jley@ciee.org ▲

DUBROVNIK

0341
FLORIDA INTERNATIONAL UNIVERSITY
Study Abroad in Dubrovnik
Site: Croatia: Dubrovnik
Dates: 2 wks, Mar 17-26
Subjects: Business/management, International business
Eligibility: *Level:* jrs, srs *Requires:* previous study in field
Credit: *Undergrad:* 6 *Grad:* none *Doc:* transcript
Instruction: *In:* English *Format:* study tour *Students:* mainly US
Costs: $1,400 *incl* housing, some meals, intl airfare, excursions
Housing: *Arr by pgm:* hotels
Deadline: Feb 15
Other info: *US accredited sponsor:* yes *Began:* 1998 *Orient:* in US (1 day) *Activities:* excursions, field trips, cultural events *Misc:* May contact former participants. *URL:* http://www.fiu.edu/~intered
Contact: Intl Studies, Florida Intl Univ, 11200 SW 8th St, DM 300B, Miami FL 33199 *Ph:* 305-348 1913, 305-348 1918 *Fax:* 305-348 1941 *E-mail:* intered@fiu.edu

ZAGREB

0342
UNIVERSITY OF KANSAS
Summer Language and Culture Institute in Zagreb, Croatia
Site: Croatia: Zagreb *Host inst:* Univ Zagreb, Croatian Heritage Fdn
Dates: Jun 30-Aug 6
Subjects: Croatian studies, Field study, Homestay, Literature, Slavic languages, Slavic studies
Eligibility: *Level:* fresh, sophs, jrs, srs, grads, adults *Requires:* good acad standing *Age:* min 18
Credit: *Undergrad:* 8 *Grad:* none *Doc:* transcript
Instruction: *In:* Serbo-Croatian *Format:* directed field study, lecture, tutorial *Students:* intl
Costs: $2,300 *incl* tuition, housing, medical evacuation svcs, *Nonrefundable fee*
Housing: *Arr by pgm:* residence halls, homestay
Deadline: Rolling admissions
Other info: *US accredited sponsor:* yes *Began:* 1980 *Orient:* in US (1 day) *URL:* http://www.ukans.edu/~osa
Contact: Susan MacNally, Asst Dir, Univ of Kansas, Study Abroad, 108 Lippincott Hall, Lawrence KS 66045 *Ph:* 785-864 3742 *Fax:* 785-864 5040 *E-mail:* osa@ukans.edu ▲

Czech Republic

BRNO

0343
ITHACA COLLEGE
Music with a Central European Accent
Site: Czech Republic: Brno *Host inst:* Janacek Acad of Music,Masaryk Univ
Dates: 3-1/2 wks, late May-late Jun
Subjects: Chamber music, Civilization/culture, Composition, Czech studies, Music history
Eligibility: *Level:* sophs, jrs, srs, grads, adults, teachers, professionals *Requires:* 2.5 GPA, previous study in field
Credit: *Undergrad:* 6 *Grad:* 6 *Doc:* transcript
Instruction: *In:* English *Format:* music lesson, practical training, seminar *Students:* mainly US
Costs: $2,500 no credit, $3,250 for 3 credits, $4,000 for 6 credits *incl* tuition, housing, some meals, intl airfare, fees, excursions *Nonrefundable fee*
Housing: *Arr by pgm:* residence halls
Deadline: Mar 15
Other info: *US accredited sponsor:* yes *Began:* 2000 *Orient:* abroad (2 days) *Activities:* excursions, field trips, program travel, cultural events *Misc:* May contact former participants. *Financial aid:* scholarships *URL:* http://www.ithaca.edu/oip/czech/
Contact: Rachel Gould, Asst Dir, Study Abroad, Intl Pgms, Ithaca Coll, Ithaca NY 14850 *Ph:* 607-274 3306 *Fax:* 607-274 1515 *E-mail:* intlprog@ithaca.edu ▲

OLOMOUC

0344
PALACKY UNIVERSITY
Summer School of Slavic Languages
Site: Czech Republic: Olomouc
Dates: 4 wks, Jul-Aug
Subjects: Czech language (beg/int/adv), Homestay, Russian language (beg/int), Ukrainian language (beg/int)
Eligibility: *Level:* fresh, sophs, jrs, srs, grads, adults, teachers, professionals *Age:* min 18
Credit: *Undergrad:* none *Grad:* none *Doc:* certificate
Instruction: *In:* English, German, Czech *Format:* lang study, lecture, practical training, seminar *Students:* intl
Costs: 32,400 Kc *incl* tuition, housing, all meals, excursions, books/materials *Nonrefundable fee*
Housing: *Arr by pgm:* residence halls, homestay
Deadline: Jun 30; Apr 30 for scholarships
Other info: *US accredited sponsor:* no *Began:* 1987 *Activities:* excursions, cultural events *Financial aid:* scholarships *URL:* http://lsss.upol.cz
Contact: Mgr Magdalena Vintrova, Palacky Univ, FF UP, Kri'zkovskeho 10, 771 80 Olomouc, Czech Republic *E-mail:* vintrova@tunw.upol.cz
Or Contact: Dr Milada Hirschova, CSC, Palacky Univ, FF UP, Kri'zkovskeho 10, 771 80 Olomouc, Czech Republic *E-mail:* hirsch@risc.upol.cz

PILZEN

0345
LANGUAGES ABROAD
Language and Cultural Immersion Programs-Pilzen
Site: Czech Republic: Pilzen
Dates: 2 wks or longer, yr-round
Subjects: Civilization/culture, Czech language (beg/int/adv)
Eligibility: *Level:* adults *Age:* min 17, max 65, avg 25
Credit: *Undergrad:* none *Grad:* none *Doc:* certificate
Instruction: *In:* Czech *Format:* lang study *Students:* intl
Costs: About $2,995 for 4 wks *incl* tuition, housing, some meals, excursions, books/materials
Housing: *Arr by pgm:* apartments, homestay
Deadline: None
Other info: *US accredited sponsor:* no *Misc:* May contact former participants. *URL:* http://www.languagesabroad.com
Contact: Ms Jesse Philippe, Langs Abroad, 317 Adelaide St W, Ste 900, Toronto, Ontario M5V 1P9, Canada *Ph:* 800-219 9924; 416-925 7117 *E-mail:* info@languagesabroad.com

PRAGUE

0346
AMERICAN INSTITUTE FOR FOREIGN STUDY (AIFS)
University of Economics, Prague with Charles University
Site: Czech Republic: Prague *Host inst:* Charles Univ, Univ of Econ, Prague
Dates: 5 wks, Jun 11-Jul 21

Subjects: Business/management, Czech language, Economics, Literature, Philosophy, Political science/politics, Sociology
Eligibility: *Level:* fresh, sophs, jrs, srs, adults *Requires:* 2.0 GPA
Credit: *Undergrad:* avail *Grad:* none *Doc:* transcript
Instruction: *In:* English *Format:* lang study, lecture, seminar *Students:* intl
Costs: $4,139 *incl* tuition, housing, all meals, intl airfare, excursions
Housing: *Arr by pgm:* residence halls
Deadline: Mar 15
Other info: *US accredited sponsor:* no *Began:* 1995 *Orient:* abroad *Activities:* excursions, field trips, cultural events *Misc:* Field trip to Vienna, resident dir. May contact former participants. *Financial aid:* scholarships *URL:* http://www.aifsabroad.com
Contact: Solandy Meza, Coll Div, AIFS, River Plaza, 9 W Broad St, Stamford CT 06902 *Ph:* 800-727 2437 ext 5163 *E-mail:* college.info@aifs.com ▲

0347
CET ACADEMIC PROGRAMS
Jewish Studies in Prague
Site: Czech Republic: Prague *Host inst:* Charles Univ
Dates: Jun 7-Aug 2
Subjects: Central European studies, Czech language (beg/int/adv), Czech studies, East European studies, Jewish/judaic studies
Eligibility: *Level:* fresh, sophs, jrs, srs, grads, adults, professionals *Age:* min 17, avg 21
Credit: *Undergrad:* avail *Grad:* avail *Doc:* transcript, certificate
Instruction: *In:* English, Czech *Format:* lang study, lecture, seminar, study tour, volunteer/svc *Students:* mainly US
Costs: $5,190 *incl* tuition, housing, all meals, intl airfare, insurance, excursions, books/materials
Housing: *Arr by pgm:* residence halls with local students
Deadline: Mar 1
Other info: *US accredited sponsor:* no *Began:* 2001 *Orient:* abroad (3 days) *Misc:* May contact former participants. *Financial aid:* scholarships *URL:* http://www.cetacademicprograms.com
Contact: Katie Smithson, Pgm Development, CET Acad Pgms, 1000 16th Street, NW, Ste 350, Washington DC 20036 *Ph:* 800-225 4262; 202-530 0800 *Fax:* 202-342 0317 *E-mail:* cet@academic-travel.com

---

0348
FLORIDA INTERNATIONAL UNIVERSITY
FIU in Prague
Site: Czech Republic: Prague
Dates: 5 wks, Jun 23-Jul 29
Subjects: Literature, Political science/politics, Women's studies
Eligibility: *Level:* fresh, sophs, jrs, srs, grads, adults, teachers, professionals
Credit: *Undergrad:* 9 *Grad:* 6 *Doc:* transcript
Instruction: *In:* English *Format:* lecture, study tour *Students:* mainly US
Costs: $3,800 *incl* housing, some meals, intl airfare, fees, excursions, books/materials, railpass, local transport *Nonrefundable fee*
Housing: *Arr by pgm:* homestay
Deadline: May 15
Other info: *US accredited sponsor:* yes *Began:* 1998 *Orient:* in US (1 day) *Activities:* excursions, field trips, program travel, cultural events *Misc:* May contact former participants. *URL:* http://www.fiu.edu/~intered
Contact: Intl Studies, Florida Intl Univ, 11200 SW 8th St, DM 300B, Miami FL 33199 *Ph:* 305-348 1913, 305-348 1918 *Fax:* 305-348 1941 *E-mail:* intered@fiu.edu

---

0349
FUND FOR AMERICAN STUDIES
American Institute on Political and Economic Systems
Site: Czech Republic: Prague *Host inst:* Charles Univ
Dates: 3 wks, Jul
Subjects: Business/management, Economics, International relations, Journalism, Political science/politics
Eligibility: *Level:* jrs, srs, grads *Requires:* recommendation letters, essays, transcript, resume
Credit: *Undergrad:* 3 *Grad:* 3 *Doc:* certificate *Transfer credit through:* Georgetown Univ
Instruction: *In:* English *Format:* seminar *Students:* intl
Costs: $2,500 *incl* tuition, housing, some meals, fees, books/materials
Housing: *Arr by pgm:* residence halls
Deadline: Mar 15
Other info: *US accredited sponsor:* no *Began:* 1993 *Orient:* abroad (2 days) *Activities:* excursions, cultural events *Misc:* All students receive scholarships, which vary in amount. *Financial aid:* scholarships *URL:* http://www.aipes.org
Contact: Leslie Berlin, Dir, Intl Pgms, Fund for Amer Studies, 1706 New Hampshire Ave NW, Washington DC 20009 *Ph:* 800-741 6964; 202-986 0384 *Fax:* 202-986 0390 *E-mail:* aipes@tfas.org

---

0350
GEORGE MASON UNIVERSITY
Government and Public Administration in Central Europe
Site: Czech Republic: Prague *Host inst:* Charles Univ
Dates: 6 wks, May 25-Jul 3
Subjects: Central European studies, Government, Public administration
Eligibility: *Level:* fresh, sophs, jrs, srs, grads, adults, teachers, professionals *Requires:* 2.25 GPA *Age:* min 18
Credit: *Undergrad:* 6 *Grad:* 6 *Doc:* transcript
Instruction: *In:* English *Format:* study tour *Students:* mainly US
Costs: About $3,300 for VA residents, $3,800 for others *incl* tuition, housing, insurance, fees, excursions, ISIC *Nonrefundable fee*
Housing: *Arr by pgm:* residence halls
Deadline: Apr 10
Other info: *US accredited sponsor:* yes *Began:* 1996 *Misc:* May contact former participants. *Financial aid:* scholarships, work study *URL:* http://www.gmu.edu/departments/cge
Contact: Ctr for Global Educ, George Mason Univ, Johnson Ctr, Rm 235, 4400 University Dr, Fairfax VA 22030-4444 *Ph:* 703-993 2154 *Fax:* 703-993 2153 *E-mail:* cge@gmu.edu

---

0351
LEHIGH UNIVERSITY
Lehigh in Prague
Site: Czech Republic: Prague *Host inst:* Charles Technical Univ
Dates: 5 wks, late May-late Jun
Subjects: Administration, Economics
Eligibility: *Level:* sophs, jrs, srs *Requires:* 2.0 GPA, previous study in field
Credit: *Undergrad:* 6 *Grad:* none *Doc:* transcript
Instruction: *In:* English *Format:* lecture, seminar *Students:* mainly US
Costs: $3,800 *incl* tuition, housing, some meals, excursions
Housing: *Arr by pgm:* residence halls
Deadline: Feb 20
Other info: *US accredited sponsor:* yes *Began:* 1995 *Orient:* in US *Activities:* excursions, field trips, cultural events *Misc:* May contact former participants. *URL:* http://www.Lehigh.edu/~incis/incis.html
Contact: Dr Sandi Smith, Dir, Study Abroad, Lehigh Abroad, 5 E Packer Ave, Whitaker Lab 343, Lehigh Univ, Bethlehem PA 18015 *Ph:* 610-758 3351 *Fax:* 610-758 5156 *E-mail:* incis@lehigh.edu

---

0352
LEXIA INTERNATIONAL
LEXIA Summer in Prague
Site: Czech Republic: Prague *Host inst:* Charles Univ
Dates: 8 wks, mid-Jun-mid-Aug
Subjects: Anthropology, Arts, Civilization/culture, Community service projects, Czech language (beg/int/adv), East European studies, Ecology/environmental studies, Economics, Fine arts, History, Independent study, Internships, Literature, Political science/politics, Sociology
Eligibility: *Level:* fresh, sophs, jrs, srs, grads, adults *Requires:* 2.5 GPA *Age:* min 18, avg 21
Credit: *Undergrad:* 8-10 *Grad:* 8-10 *Doc:* transcript *Transfer credit through:* Western Washington Univ
Instruction: *In:* English *Format:* independent study, internship, lang study, lecture, seminar, volunteer/svc *Students:* mainly US
Costs: $4,350 *incl* tuition, housing, insurance, fees, excursions, ISIC, computer access *Nonrefundable fee*
Housing: *Arr by pgm:* residence halls, homestay
Deadline: Apr 15; Apr 1 for scholarships
Other info: *US accredited sponsor:* no *Began:* 1991 *In coop with:* Western Washington Univ *Orient:* abroad *Activities:* excursions, field trips, program travel, cultural events, sports *Misc:* Student support svcs. Costs incl medical insurance. May contact former participants. *Financial aid:* scholarships, work study *URL:* http://www.lexiaintl.org
Contact: LEXIA Intl, 25 S Main St, Hanover NH 03755 *Ph:* 603-643 9898 *Fax:* 603-643 9899 *E-mail:* info@lexiaintl.org
Or Contact: LEXIA Intl, West Coast, 378 Cambridge Ave, Palo Alto CA 94306 *Ph:* 800-775 3942; 650-327 9191 *Fax:* 650-327 9192

0353
NEW YORK UNIVERSITY, TISCH SCHOOL OF THE ARTS
Master Class in Filmmaking and Seminar in Czech Cinema and Culture
Site: Czech Republic: Prague *Host inst:* FAMU
Dates: 5 wks, May 21-Jun 22
Subjects: Central European studies, Film studies, Media studies
Eligibility: *Level:* sophs, jrs, srs, grads, adults, teachers, professionals *Requires:* previous study in field, coll-level coursework in filmmaking or 16mm film production experience *Age:* min 18
Credit: *Undergrad:* 8 *Grad:* 8 *Doc:* transcript
Instruction: *In:* English *Format:* lang study, lecture, practical training, seminar *Students:* mainly US
Costs: $6,212 *incl* tuition, housing, some meals, fees, excursions, books/materials, basic lang training *Nonrefundable fee*
Housing: *Arr by pgm:* residence halls
Deadline: Mar 15; rolling admissions
Other info: *US accredited sponsor:* yes *Began:* 1998 *In coop with:* FAMU *Orient:*

in US & abroad (1 day, intensive lang study) *Activities:* excursions *Misc:* Draft script for students wishing to direct. 35mm film format. Scholarships & loans for own students only. *Financial aid:* scholarships *URL:* http://www.nyu.edu/tisch/international/
Contact: Linda Kow, Assoc Dir, Tisch Intl Pgms, New York Univ, 721 Broadway, 12th Fl, New York NY 10003 *Ph:* 212-998 9175 *Fax:* 212-995 4578 *E-mail:* tisch.international@nyu.edu

---

0354
NORTH CAROLINA STATE UNIVERSITY
Summer Study in Art, Landscape Architecture and Architecture
Site: Czech Republic: Prague
Dates: Jun-Jul
Subjects: Architecture, Art, Czech language (beg), Drawing, Field study, Graphic arts/design, Illustration, Independent study, Landscape architecture, Painting, Printmaking, Urban studies
Eligibility: *Level:* fresh, sophs, jrs, srs, grads, adults, teachers, professionals *Requires:* previous study in field, good standing, recommendation letter for fresh & sophs
Credit: *Undergrad:* 6 *Grad:* 6
Instruction: *In:* English *Format:* art studio, directed field study, independent study, lang study, practical training, seminar, study tour *Students:* mainly US
Costs: $2,800 *incl* tuition, housing, fees, excursions
Housing: *Arr by pgm*
Deadline: Feb
Other info: *US accredited sponsor:* yes *Orient:* abroad *Activities:* excursions, field trips, program travel, cultural events *Misc:* Students participate in 2 pgms: Architecture, Landscape architecture, Urban design or Art & Design. May contact former participants. *URL:* http://www.ncsu.edu/studyabroad
Contact: Anne Haberkern, North Carolina State Univ, 2118 Pullen Hall, Box 7344, Raleigh NC 27695-7344 *Ph:* 919-515 2087 *Fax:* 919-515 6021 *E-mail:* study_abroad@ncsu.edu

---

0355
NORTHWESTERN UNIVERSITY
Northwestern University in Prague
Site: Czech Republic: Prague *Host inst:* Coll Hieronymi Pragnensis
Dates: Jun 16-Jul 29
Subjects: Civilization/culture, Czech language (beg), Czech studies, History, Political science/politics, Slavic languages, Slavic studies
Eligibility: *Level:* fresh, sophs, jrs, srs *Requires:* 3.0 GPA
Credit: *Undergrad:* 3 per course *Grad:* none *Doc:* transcript
Instruction: *In:* English, Czech *Format:* lecture, study tour *Students:* mainly US
Costs: $5,200 for 2 courses *incl* tuition, housing, some meals, intl airfare, fees, excursions *Nonrefundable fee*
Housing: *Arr by pgm*
Deadline: Mar 31
Other info: *US accredited sponsor:* yes *Orient:* in US (1 day) *Activities:* excursions *Misc:* Students must take 2 courses. May contact former participants. *URL:* http://www.northwestern.edu/summersa
Contact: Christina Kyres, Asst Dir, Sch of Continuing Studies, Northwestern Univ, 339 E Chicago Ave IL 60611-3008 *Ph:* 312-503 3021 *Fax:* 312-503 3003 *E-mail:* summersa@northwestern.edu

---

0356
RAMAPO COLLEGE OF NEW JERSEY
Winter Session in Prague
Site: Czech Republic: Prague *Host inst:* Czech Technical Univ
Dates: 3 wks, Jan
Subjects: Field study
Eligibility: *Level:* fresh, sophs, jrs, srs, grads *Requires:* good physical condition
Credit: *Undergrad:* 3 *Grad:* none
Instruction: *In:* English *Format:* directed field study, lang study *Students:* mainly US
Costs: $2,000 for Ramapo students, $2,200 for others *incl* tuition, housing, most meals, intl airfare, fees, excursions, most meals
Housing: *Arr by pgm:* residence halls
Deadline: Nov 1
Other info: *US accredited sponsor:* yes *Began:* 1995 *Orient:* in US *Activities:* excursions, field trips, cultural events *URL:* http://www.ramapo.edu/Academics/Abroad/
Contact: Ms Robyn Perricelli, Ramapo Coll of New Jersey, 505 Ramapo Valley Rd, Mahwah NJ 07430 *Ph:* 201-684 7463 *Fax:* 201-684 7651 *E-mail:* studabrd@ramapo.edu

---

0357
SOUTHERN METHODIST UNIVERSITY
SMU-in-Prague
Site: Czech Republic: Prague
Dates: 5 wks, Jul 6-Aug 13
Subjects: Civilization/culture, Slavic studies
Eligibility: *Level:* sophs, jrs, srs *Requires:* 2.5 GPA
Credit: *Undergrad:* 6 *Grad:* none *Doc:* transcript
Instruction: *In:* English *Format:* lecture *Students:* mainly US
Costs: $4,360 per term *incl* tuition, housing, some meals, excursions *Nonrefundable fee*
Housing: *Arr by pgm:* residence halls with local students
Deadline: Mar 1
Other info: *US accredited sponsor:* yes *Began:* 2000 *Orient:* in US & abroad *Activities:* excursions, field trips *Misc:* May contact former participants. *Financial aid:* scholarships *URL:* http://www.smu.edu/studyabroad
Contact: Intl Off, Southern Methodist Univ, PO Box 0391, 3108 Fordham Dr, Dallas TX 75275-0391 *Ph:* 214-768 2338 *Fax:* 214-768 1051
Or Contact: Prof Gary Cox, Foreign Lang & Literature, Southern Methodist Univ, PO Box 0391, 3108 Fordham Dr, Dallas TX 75275-0391 *Ph:* 214-768 2294 *E-mail:* gcox@mail.smu.edu ▲

0358
UNIVERSITY OF ECONOMICS, PRAGUE
Summer School of Central and East European Studies Program
Site: Czech Republic: Prague
Dates: 5 wks, Jun 18-Jul 21
Subjects: Business/management, Central European studies, Czech language (beg), Ecology/environmental studies, Economics, European studies, Government
Eligibility: *Level:* sophs, jrs, grads *Age:* min 19, avg 21
Credit: *Undergrad:* avail *Grad:* avail *Doc:* transcript, certificate
Instruction: *In:* English *Format:* lang study, lecture, seminar, study tour *Students:* intl
Costs: $1,100 *incl* tuition, housing, excursions, books/materials *Nonrefundable fee*
Housing: *Arr by pgm:* residence halls
Deadline: May 15
Other info: *US accredited sponsor:* no *Began:* 1992 *Orient:* abroad *Activities:* excursions, cultural events *Misc:* May contact former participants. *URL:* http://www.vse.cz/
Contact: Prof Miroslav Manas, Univ of Econ, NAM W Churchilla 4, 13067 Praha 3, Czech Republic *E-mail:* manas@nb.vse.cz
Or Contact: Dr Arlyn R Rubash, Bradley Univ, 1501 W Bradley Ave, Peoria IL 61625-9989 *Ph:* 309-677 2258 *E-mail:* arr@bradley.bradley.edu

---

0359
UNIVERSITY OF MIAMI (FL)
Motion Picture Program in Prague
Site: Czech Republic: Prague *Host inst:* Film Acad of Performing Arts
Dates: Early Jul-early Aug
Subjects: Film studies
Eligibility: *Level:* sophs, jrs, srs, grads *Requires:* 3.0 GPA, some film study recommended, 2 faculty recommendation letters
Credit: *Undergrad:* 6 *Grad:* 6 *Doc:* transcript
Instruction: *In:* English *Format:* lecture, practical training, seminar, study tour, tutorial *Students:* mainly US
Costs: Contact sponsor
Housing: *Arr by pgm:* hostels
Deadline: Mar 30
Other info: *US accredited sponsor:* yes *Began:* 1991 *Orient:* abroad *Activities:* excursions, field trips, program travel, cultural events *Misc:* May contact former participants. *URL:* http://www.studyabroad.miami.edu
Contact: Intl Educ & Exch Pgms, Allen Hall 212, 5050 Brunson Dr, PO Box 248005, Univ of Miami, Coral Gables FL 33124-1610 *Ph:* 800-557 5421; 305-284 3434 *Fax:* 305-284 6629 *E-mail:* ieep@miami.edu

---

0360
UNIVERSITY OF NEW ORLEANS
Prague Summer Seminars
Site: Czech Republic: Prague *Host inst:* Charles Univ
Dates: 1 mo, Jul
Subjects: Creative writing, Film studies, Fine arts, Independent study, Jewish/judaic studies, Literature, Music, Opera, Photography, Poetry, Political science/politics, Sociology, Television/video, Written composition
Eligibility: *Requires:* 2.0 GPA
Credit: *Undergrad:* 6 *Grad:* 6 *Doc:* transcript
Instruction: *In:* English *Format:* independent study, lecture, workshop *Students:* intl
Costs: $2,295 *incl* tuition, housing, most meals, fees, books/materials
Housing: *Arr by pgm:* residence halls, apartments
Deadline: May 1
Other info: *US accredited sponsor:* yes *Began:* 1993 *Orient:* abroad *Activities:* excursions, field trips, cultural events *Misc:* May contact former participants. *URL:* http://www.uno.edu/~inst/Welcome.html
Contact: Bill Lavender, Univ of New Orleans, PO Box 1340, New Orleans LA 70148 *Ph:* 504-280 7457 *Fax:* 504-280 7317 *E-mail:* wlavende@uno.edu

---

0361
UNIVERSITY OF PENNSYLVANIA
Penn-in-Prague
Site: Czech Republic: Prague *Host inst:* Charles Univ
Dates: 6 wks, early Jul-mid-Aug
Subjects: Civilization/culture, Czech language (beg/int), Czech studies, Folklore, Jewish/judaic studies, Political science/politics
Eligibility: *Level:* fresh, sophs, jrs, srs, grads, professionals
Credit: *Undergrad:* 6 *Grad:* 3-6 *Doc:* transcript
Instruction: *In:* English *Format:* lecture *Students:* mainly US
Costs: About $3,800 *incl* tuition, housing, excursions *Nonrefundable fee*
Housing: *Arr by pgm:* residence halls
Deadline: Mar 15
Other info: *US accredited sponsor:* yes *Began:* 1993 *Orient:* in US & abroad *Activities:* excursions, program travel, cultural events *Misc:* May contact former participants. *URL:* http://www.sas.upenn.edu/CGS/
Contact: Elizabeth Sachs, Penn Summer Abroad, Univ of Pennsylvania, 3440 Market, St Ste 100, Philadelphia PA 19104-3335 *Ph:* 215-898 5738 *Fax:* 215-573 2053 *E-mail:* sdanti@mail.sas.upenn.edu

---

0362
UNIVERSITY OF SOUTH FLORIDA
USF in Prague
Site: Czech Republic: Prague *Host inst:* Anglo-Amer Coll
Dates: 6 wks, Jun-Jul
Subjects: Czech language, Economics, Humanities, International business, Social sciences
Eligibility: *Level:* fresh, sophs, jrs, srs, adults, teachers, professionals *Requires:* 2.5 GPA *Age:* min 18, avg 22
Credit: *Undergrad:* 6 *Grad:* none *Doc:* transcript, certificate
Instruction: *In:* English *Format:* lang study, lecture, seminar *Students:* intl
Costs: About $1,600 *incl* tuition, housing, fees, excursions *Nonrefundable fee*
Housing: *Arr by pgm:* apartments with local students, residence halls with local students, homestay, hostels
Deadline: Mar 31
Other info: *US accredited sponsor:* yes *Began:* 1999 *Orient:* in US & abroad (1 day) *Activities:* excursions, field trips, program travel, cultural events *URL:* http://www.usf.edu/~iac/
Contact: Julie Hale, Coord, Overseas Study Pgms, Univ of South Florida, 4202 E Fowler Ave, CPR 107, Tampa FL 33620-5550 *Ph:* 813-974 3933 *Fax:* 813-974 4613 *E-mail:* jhale@iac.usf.edu
Or Contact: Dr Warren Hampton or Brendan Calandra, Div of Lang & Linguistics, Univ of South Florida, 4202 E Fowler Ave, CPR 107, Tampa FL 33620-5550 *Ph:* 813-974 6747 *Fax:* 813-974 4613

0363
UNIVERSITY OF TEXAS AT AUSTIN
Czech Studies Summer Program
Site: Czech Republic: Prague *Host inst:* Charles Univ
Dates: 7 wks, late May-early Jul
Subjects: Architecture, Art, Civilization/culture, Czech language (beg/int), Czech studies, Drama/theater, Film studies
Eligibility: *Level:* fresh, sophs, jrs, srs, grads *Requires:* good acad standing *Age:* avg 20
Credit: *Undergrad:* 9 *Grad:* 6-9 *Doc:* transcript
Instruction: *In:* English, Czech *Format:* lang study, lecture *Students:* mainly US
Costs: Contact sponsor
Housing: *Arr by pgm:* residence halls
Deadline: Mar 1
Other info: *US accredited sponsor:* yes *Began:* 1998 *Orient:* in US & abroad *Activities:* excursions, field trips *Misc:* May contact former participants. *URL:* http://www.utexas.edu/student/abroad
Contact: Joy Williamson, Adviser, Study Abroad, Univ of Texas at Austin, Univ Station, Drawer A, Austin TX 78713-7206 *Ph:* 512-471 6490 *Fax:* 512-232 4363 *E-mail:* studyabroadinfo@mozart.io.utexas.edu

Estonia

TALLINN

0364
LANGUAGES ABROAD
Language and Cultural Immersion Programs-Tallinn
Site: Estonia: Tallinn
Dates: 2 wks or longer, yr-round
Subjects: Civilization/culture, Estonian language (beg/int/adv)
Eligibility: *Level:* adults *Age:* min 17, max 65, avg 25
Credit: *Undergrad:* none *Grad:* none *Doc:* certificate
Instruction: *In:* Estonian *Format:* lang study *Students:* intl
Costs: About $2,250 for 4 wks *incl* tuition, housing, some meals, excursions, books/materials
Housing: *Arr by pgm:* apartments, homestay
Deadline: None
Other info: *US accredited sponsor:* no *Misc:* May contact former participants. *URL:* http://www.languagesabroad.com

Contact: Ms Jesse Philippe, Langs Abroad, 317 Adelaide St W, Ste 900, Toronto, Ontario M5V 1P9, Canada *Ph:* 800-219 9924; 416-925 7117 *E-mail:* info@languagesabroad.com

Hungary

BUDAPEST

0365
BUDAPEST UNIVERSITY OF ECONOMIC SCIENCES (BUES)
Summer University
Site: Hungary: Budapest
Dates: 3 wks, mid-Jun-mid-Jul
Subjects: Business/management, East European studies, Economics, Hungarian studies, Marketing, Political science/politics
Eligibility: *Level:* jrs, srs, grads
Credit: *Undergrad:* avail *Grad:* avail *Doc:* transcript
Instruction: *In:* English *Format:* lecture, seminar *Students:* intl & host country
Costs: $450 per course *incl* tuition, fees *Nonrefundable fee*
Housing: *Arr by student*
Deadline: Apr 30
Other info: *US accredited sponsor:* no *Began:* 1992 *URL:* http://www.isc.bkc.hu
Contact: Hanna Varjas, ISC Pgm Coord, or Prof Jozsef Temesi, ISC Acad Dir, BUES-ISC, Fovam ter 8, Budapest, Hungary 1093 *Ph:* 36-1-217 1153 *Fax:* 36-1-217 0608 *E-mail:* postmaster@isc.bke.hu

---

0366
GEORGE MASON UNIVERSITY
Budapest: Intercultural Communications
Site: Hungary: Budapest
Dates: 4 wks, Jun 29-Jul 25
Subjects: Communications, Intercultural studies
Eligibility: *Level:* fresh, sophs, jrs, srs, grads, adults, teachers, professionals *Requires:* 2.25 GPA *Age:* min 18
Credit: *Undergrad:* 6 *Grad:* 6 *Doc:* transcript
Instruction: *In:* English *Format:* study tour *Students:* mainly US
Costs: About $3,000 for VA residents, $3,600 for others *incl* tuition, housing, some meals, insurance, fees, excursions, ISIC *Nonrefundable fee*
Housing: *Arr by pgm:* apartments with local students
Deadline: Apr 10
Other info: *US accredited sponsor:* yes *Began:* 1996 *Orient:* in US (1 day) *Misc:* May contact former participants. *Financial aid:* scholarships, work study *URL:* http://www.gmu.edu/departments/cge
Contact: Ctr for Global Educ, George Mason Univ, Johnson Ctr, Rm 235, 4400 University Dr, Fairfax VA 22030-4444 *Ph:* 703-993 2154 *Fax:* 703-993 2153 *E-mail:* cge@gmu.edu

---

0367
GEORGE MASON UNIVERSITY
Budapest: Political Economy of Transition in Hungary
Site: Hungary: Budapest *Host inst:* Budapest Univ Assn, Sch of Public Admin
Dates: 4 wks, Jul-Aug
Subjects: Business/management, East European studies, Economics, European Union, Political science/politics, Social change, Trade
Eligibility: *Level:* sophs, jrs, srs, grads, teachers, professionals *Requires:* 2.25 GPA, 3.0 for grads *Age:* avg 30
Credit: *Undergrad:* 6 *Grad:* 6 *Doc:* transcript
Instruction: *In:* English *Format:* lecture *Students:* mainly US
Costs: About $3,000 for VA residents, $3,600 for others *incl* tuition, housing, some meals, ISIC, travel insurance *Nonrefundable fee*
Housing: *Arr by pgm:* residence halls
Deadline: Apr 15
Other info: *US accredited sponsor:* yes *Began:* 1992 *Orient:* in US *Activities:* excursions *Misc:* Min 20 students for pgm. *URL:* http://www.gmu.edu/departments/cge
Contact: Ctr for Global Educ, George Mason Univ, Johnson Ctr, Rm 235, 4400 University Dr, Fairfax VA 22030-4444 *Ph:* 703-993 2154 *Fax:* 703-993 2153 *E-mail:* cge@gmu.edu

---

0368
LANGUAGE LIAISON
Hungarian Saturation
Site: Hungary: Budapest *Host inst:* Live in Learn
Dates: 1 wk or longer, yr-round
Subjects: Civilization/culture, Homestay, Hungarian language (beg/int/adv)
Eligibility: *Level:* fresh, sophs, jrs, srs, grads, adults, teachers, professionals, precoll *Age:* min 10
Credit: *Undergrad:* none *Grad:* none *Doc:* transcript, certificate
Instruction: *In:* Hungarian *Format:* lang study *Students:* intl
Costs: Contact sponsor
Housing: *Arr by pgm:* teacher's home
Deadline: 45 days before pgm
Other info: *US accredited sponsor:* no *Misc:* Live & learn in your teacher's home. Scholarship research svc. *URL:* http://www.languageliaison.com
Contact: Nancy Forman, Dir, Lang Liaison, 4 Burnham Pkwy, Morristown NJ 07960 *Ph:* 800-284 4448 *Fax:* 973-898 1710 *E-mail:* learn@languageliaison.com

---

0369
LEXIA INTERNATIONAL
LEXIA Summer in Budapest
Site: Hungary: Budapest *Host inst:* Eotvos Coll, Pazmany Univ
Dates: 8 wks, mid-Jun-mid-Aug
Subjects: Anthropology, Arts, Civilization/culture, East European studies, Ecology/environmental studies, Economics, Fine arts, History, Homestay, Hungarian language (beg/int/adv), Hungarian studies, Internships, Literature, Political science/politics, Sociology
Eligibility: *Level:* fresh, sophs, jrs, srs, grads, adults *Requires:* 2.5 GPA *Age:* min 18, avg 21
Credit: *Undergrad:* 8-10 *Grad:* 8-10 *Doc:* transcript *Transfer credit through:* Western Washington Univ
Instruction: *In:* English, Hungarian *Format:* internship, lang study, lecture, seminar, volunteer/svc *Students:* mainly US
Costs: $4,350 *incl* tuition, housing, insurance, fees, excursions, ISIC *Nonrefundable fee*
Housing: *Arr by pgm:* residence halls with local students, homestay
Deadline: Apr 15; Apr 1 for scholarships
Other info: *US accredited sponsor:* no *Began:* 1991 *In coop with:* Western Washington Univ *Orient:* abroad *Activities:* excursions, field trips, program travel, cultural events, sports *Misc:* Student support svcs. May contact former participants. *Financial aid:* scholarships, work study *URL:* http://www.lexiaintl.org
Contact: LEXIA Intl, 25 S Main St, Hanover NH 03755 *Ph:* 800-775 3942; 603-643 9898 *Fax:* 603-643 9899 *E-mail:* info@lexiaintl.org
Or Contact: LEXIA Intl, West Coast, 378 Cambridge Ave, Palo Alto CA 94306-1544 *Ph:* 650-327 9191 *Fax:* 650-327 9192

0370
LINGUA SERVICE WORLDWIDE
Total Immersion/Intensive Language and Culture in Hungary
Site: Hungary: Budapest *Host inst:* Home Lang Intl
Dates: 1 wk-1 yr, yr-round
Subjects: Civilization/culture, Homestay, Hungarian language (beg/int/adv)
Eligibility: *Level:* adults *Age:* min 14
Credit: *Undergrad:* avail *Grad:* avail *Doc:* transcript, certificate
Instruction: *In:* Hungarian *Format:* lang study *Students:* intl
Costs: Contact sponsor

Housing: *Arr by pgm:* apartments with local students, residence halls with local students, homestay, pensions, hotels, hostels
Deadline: 45 days before pgm
Other info: *US accredited sponsor:* no *Began:* 1993 *Activities:* excursions, cultural events *Misc:* Participate in teacher's family & social life. May contact former participants. *URL:* http://www.linguaserviceworldwide.com
Contact: Dir, Lingua Svc Worldwide, 75 Prospect St, Ste 4, Huntington NY 11743 *Ph:* 800-394 5327; 631-424 0777 *Fax:* 631-271 3441 *E-mail:* itctravel@worldnet.att.net ▲

0371
NATIONAL REGISTRATION CENTER FOR STUDY ABROAD (NRCSA)
Hungarian in Budapest
Site: Hungary: Budapest *Host inst:* Home Lang Schs Intl
Dates: 1 wk or longer, yr-round
Subjects: Homestay, Hungarian language
Eligibility: *Level:* fresh, sophs, jrs, srs, grads, adults, teachers, professionals
Credit: *Undergrad:* none *Grad:* none *Doc:* certificate
Instruction: *In:* Hungarian *Format:* lang study, tutorial *Students:* intl
Costs: $1,135 per wk *incl* tuition, housing, all meals, insurance *Nonrefundable fee*
Housing: *Arr by pgm:* homestay
Deadline: 6 wks before pgm
Other info: *US accredited sponsor:* no *Misc:* Student lives in teacher's home. *URL:* http://www.nrcsa.com
Contact: Reuel Zielke, NRCSA, 823 N 2nd St, #206, Milwaukee WI 53203 *Ph:* 414-278 0631 *Fax:* 414-271 8884 *E-mail:* info@nrcsa.com

---

0372
SAINT JOHN'S UNIVERSITY (NY)
College Europa Hungary
Site: Hungary: Budapest *Host inst:* Technical Univ of Budapest
Dates: 3 wks, May
Subjects: Economics, International business
Eligibility: *Level:* sophs, jrs, srs *Requires:* 2.75 GPA, 2 recommendation letters, interview
Credit: *Undergrad:* 3 *Grad:* none *Doc:* transcript
Instruction: *In:* English *Format:* internship, lecture, seminar *Students:* US & host country
Costs: $3,400 *incl* housing, some meals, intl airfare
Housing: *Arr by pgm:* hotels
Deadline: Mar 1
Other info: *US accredited sponsor:* yes *Began:* 1985 *Orient:* in US & abroad (1 day) *Activities:* excursions, field trips, cultural events *Misc:* May contact former participants.
Contact: Dean Joyce Lawlor, Study Abroad Pgm, St John's Univ, Bent Hall, Rm 388, 8000 Utopia Pkwy, Jamaica NY 11439 *Ph:* 718-990 6105 *Fax:* 718-990 2321 *E-mail:* intled@stjohns.edu

---

0373
TEXAS CHRISTIAN UNIVERSITY BUSINESS IN BUDAPEST CONSORTIUM and TEXAS CHRISTIAN UNIVERSITY
Business-In-Budapest
Site: Hungary: Budapest *Host inst:* Hungarian Ministry of Culture & Educ
Dates: 4 wks, Jul-Aug
Subjects: Business/management
Eligibility: *Level:* jrs, srs *Requires:* 2.75 GPA *Age:* min 18, avg 20
Credit: *Undergrad:* 6 *Grad:* none
Instruction: *In:* English *Format:* lecture, study tour *Students:* intl
Costs: $4,200 *incl* tuition, housing, some meals, fees, excursions, books/materials
Housing: *Arr by pgm:* guest house of Ministry of Culture & Educ
Deadline: Mar 1
Other info: *US accredited sponsor:* yes *Began:* 1996 *Orient:* abroad (1 day) *Activities:* excursions, field trips, cultural events *URL:* http://www.neeley.tcu.edu
Contact: *See Index II for Members* Kristi Dill, Asst Dean, Texas Christian Univ, PO Box 298530, Fort Worth TX 76129 *Ph:* 817-257 7527 *Fax:* 817-257 6049 *E-mail:* k.dill@tcu.edu

---

0374
UNIVERSITY OF DELAWARE
Winter Session in Hungary
Site: Hungary: Budapest
Dates: 1 mo, Jan
Subjects: Business/management, Field study, International business, International marketing
Eligibility: *Level:* fresh, sophs, jrs, srs *Requires:* 2.0 GPA, previous study in field
Credit: *Undergrad:* 6 *Grad:* none *Doc:* transcript
Instruction: *In:* English *Format:* directed field study, lecture, seminar, study tour *Students:* mainly US
Costs: Contact sponsor
Housing: *Arr by pgm*
Deadline: Early Oct
Other info: *US accredited sponsor:* yes *Activities:* excursions, field trips, program travel *Misc:* Contact sponser to arrange honors credit. Pgm offered in even-numbered years. *Financial aid:* scholarships *URL:* http://www.udel.edu/studyabroad/
Contact: Intl Pgms, Univ of Delaware, 4 Kent Way, Newark DE 19716 *Ph:* 888-831 4685; 302-831 2852 *Fax:* 302-831 6042 *E-mail:* studyabroad@udel.edu

---

DEBRECEN

0375
DEBRECEN SUMMER SCHOOL
Special Autumn Course
Site: Hungary: Debrecen *Host inst:* Univ of Debrecen
Dates: Oct 24-Nov 4
Subjects: Hungarian language (beg/int/adv)
Eligibility: *Level:* adults *Age:* min 17
Credit: *Undergrad:* none *Grad:* none *Doc:* certificate
Instruction: *In:* English, German *Format:* lang study *Students:* intl
Costs: EUR 1,110 *incl* tuition, housing, all meals
Housing: *Arr by pgm:* hotels
Deadline: Contact sponsor
Other info: *US accredited sponsor:* no *URL:* http://summer06.sum.klte.hu
Contact: Mr Karoly Rozsa, Debrecen Summer Sch, PO Box 35, 4010 Debrecen, Hungary *E-mail:* nyariegy@tigris.klte.hu

---

0376
DEBRECEN SUMMER SCHOOL
Summer Course
Site: Hungary: Debrecen *Host inst:* Univ of Debrecen
Dates: 4 wks, Jul 22-Aug 18
Subjects: Civilization/culture, Hungarian language (beg/int/adv), Hungarian studies
Eligibility: *Level:* adults *Age:* min 17
Credit: *Undergrad:* none *Grad:* none *Doc:* certificate
Instruction: *In:* English, French, German, Hungarian, Italian *Format:* lang study, lecture *Students:* intl
Costs: EUR 505 for 2 wks, EUR 940 for 4 wks *incl* tuition, housing, all meals, excursions, trampass, cultural events *Nonrefundable fee*
Housing: *Arr by pgm:* hotels, hostels
Deadline: Contact sponsor
Other info: *US accredited sponsor:* no *URL:* http://summer06.sum.klte.hu
Contact: Mr Karoly Rozsa, Debrecen Summer Sch, PO Box 35, 4010 Debrecen, Hungary *E-mail:* nyariegy@tigris.klte.hu

---

0377
DEBRECEN SUMMER SCHOOL
Super-Intensive Course
Site: Hungary: Debrecen *Host inst:* Univ of Debrecen

Dates: 2 wks, May 27-Jun 10
Subjects: Hungarian language (beg/int/adv)
Eligibility: *Level:* adults *Age:* min 17
Credit: *Undergrad:* none *Grad:* none *Doc:* certificate
Instruction: *In:* English, German *Format:* student teaching *Students:* intl
Costs: EUR 740 *incl* tuition, housing, all meals, trampass *Nonrefundable fee*
Housing: *Arr by pgm:* hotels
Deadline: Contact sponsor
Other info: *US accredited sponsor:* no *URL:* http://summer06.sum.klte.hu
Contact: Mr Karoly Rozsa, Debrecen Summer Sch, PO Box 35, 4010 Debrecen, Hungary *E-mail:* nyariegy@tigris.klte.hu

---

0378
DEBRECEN SUMMER SCHOOL
Winter Course
Site: Hungary: Debrecen *Host inst:* Univ of Debrecen
Dates: 2 wks, Jan 7-20
Subjects: Hungarian language (beg/int/adv), Hungarian studies
Eligibility: *Level:* adults *Age:* min 17
Credit: *Undergrad:* none *Grad:* none *Doc:* certificate
Instruction: *In:* English, German *Format:* student teaching *Students:* intl
Costs: EUR 635 *incl* tuition, housing, all meals, excursions, trampass, cultural events *Nonrefundable fee*
Housing: *Arr by pgm:* hotels, hostels
Deadline: Contact sponsor
Other info: *US accredited sponsor:* no *URL:* http://summer06.sum.klte.hu
Contact: Mr Karoly Rozsa, Debrecen Summer Sch, PO Box 35, 4010 Debrecen, Hungary *E-mail:* nyariegy@tigris.klte.hu

---

0379
LANGUAGES ABROAD
Language and Cultural Immersion Programs-Debrecen
Site: Hungary: Debrecen
Dates: 2 wks or longer, yr-round
Subjects: Civilization/culture, Hungarian language (beg/int/adv)
Eligibility: *Level:* adults *Age:* min 17, max 65, avg 25
Credit: *Undergrad:* none *Grad:* none *Doc:* certificate
Instruction: *In:* Hungarian *Format:* lang study *Students:* intl
Costs: About $2,950 for 4 wks *incl* tuition, housing, some meals, excursions, books/materials
Housing: *Arr by pgm:* apartments, homestay
Deadline: None
Other info: *US accredited sponsor:* no *Misc:* May contact former participants. *URL:* http://www.languagesabroad.com
Contact: Ms Jesse Philippe, Langs Abroad, 317 Adelaide St W, Ste 900, Toronto, Ontario M5V 1P9, Canada *Ph:* 800-219 9924; 416-925 7117 *E-mail:* info@languagesabroad.com

---

PECS

0380
OHIO UNIVERSITY
Institute for Global Competitiveness
Site: Hungary: Pecs *Host inst:* Janus Pannonius Univ
Dates: 5 wks, mid-Jun-mid-Jul
Subjects: Business administration, International business, Internships
Eligibility: *Level:* sophs, jrs, srs *Requires:* previous study in field
Credit: *Undergrad:* 16 qtr hrs *Grad:* none *Doc:* transcript
Instruction: *In:* English *Format:* internship, practical training, study tour *Students:* mainly US
Costs: $3,500-$5,000 *incl* housing, all meals, intl airfare
Housing: *Arr by pgm:* residence halls, hotels
Deadline: Mar 15
Other info: *US accredited sponsor:* yes *Began:* 1997 *Activities:* excursions, program travel *Misc:* Internship with Hungarian company. Max 30 students. Loans avail. *Financial aid:* scholarships *URL:* http://www.ohiou.edu/studyabroad/
Contact: John Keifer, Dir, Ctr for Intl Bus Educ & Development, Ohio Univ, 514 Copeland Hall, Athens OH 45701 *Ph:* 740-593 2021 *Fax:* 740-593 1388 *E-mail:* keiferj@ohiou.edu

---

0381
UNIVERSITY OF PECS
Emerging New Democracies and Economies in Central Europe
Site: Hungary: Pecs
Dates: 3 wks, Jul 16 - Aug 4
Subjects: Central European studies, Civilization/culture, Ecology/environmental studies, Economics, Folklore, History, Hungarian studies, Literature, Philosophy, Political science/politics
Eligibility: *Level:* fresh, sophs, jrs, srs, grads, adults, precoll *Age:* min 18, avg 25
Credit: *Undergrad:* 32 per 3 wks *Grad:* none *Doc:* transcript
Instruction: *In:* English *Format:* lecture, seminar, study tour *Students:* intl
Costs: $1,300 *incl* tuition, housing, some meals, excursions *Nonrefundable fee*
Housing: *Sponsor assists:* residence halls, pensions, hotels
Deadline: Jul 1
Other info: *US accredited sponsor:* no *Began:* 1999 *Activities:* excursions, field trips, cultural events *URL:* http://www.isc.pte.hu
Contact: Gabriella Kis Halas, Study Adviser, Univ of Pecs, Intl Studies Ctr, Szanto Kovacs J U 1/B, H-7633 Pecs, Hungary *E-mail:* almos@isc.pte.hu

---

0382
UNIVERSITY OF PECS
Environmental Problems and Issues in Central Europe
Site: Hungary: Pecs
Dates: 3 wks, Jul 16 - Aug 4
Subjects: Central European studies, Demography, Ecology/environmental studies, Economics, Environmental law, European Union, Geography, Hungarian studies, Urban planning
Eligibility: *Level:* fresh, sophs, jrs, srs, grads, adults, precoll *Age:* min 18, avg 27
Credit: *Undergrad:* 44 per 3 wks *Grad:* none *Doc:* transcript
Instruction: *In:* English, Italian *Format:* directed field study, lecture, seminar, study tour *Students:* intl
Costs: $1,300 *incl* tuition, housing, some meals, excursions *Nonrefundable fee*
Housing: *Sponsor assists:* residence halls, pensions, hotels
Deadline: Jul 1
Other info: *US accredited sponsor:* no *Began:* 1999 *Activities:* excursions, field trips, program travel, cultural events, sports *URL:* http://www.isc.pte.hu
Contact: Gabriella Kis Halas, Study Adviser, University of Pecs, Intl Studies Ctr, Szanto Kovacs J U 1/B, Pecs, Hungary H-7633 *E-mail:* kishalas@isc.pte.hu

---

0383
UNIVERSITY OF PECS
Hungarian for the Entire Family
Site: Hungary: Pecs
Dates: 2 wks, Jul 23-Aug 4
Subjects: Hungarian language
Eligibility: *Level:* fresh, sophs, jrs, srs, grads, adults, precoll *Age:* min 12, avg 30
Credit: *Undergrad:* none *Grad:* none *Doc:* certificate
Instruction: *In:* English *Format:* lang study, seminar, study tour *Students:* intl
Costs: $760 *incl* tuition, housing, all meals, excursions *Nonrefundable fee*
Housing: *Sponsor assists:* residence halls, pensions, hotels
Deadline: Jul 9
Other info: *US accredited sponsor:* no *Began:* 1999 *Activities:* excursions, cultural events *URL:* http://www.isc.pte.hu
Contact: Gabriella Kis Halas, Study Adviser, University of Pecs, Intl Studies Ctr, Szanto Kovacs J U 1/B, Pecs, Hungary H-7633 *E-mail:* kishalas@isc.pte.hu

---

See "How To Use This Book" for definitions of terms used above. ▲ = See program sponsor's ad(s) in this book.

0384
UNIVERSITY OF PECS
Summer School - Hungarian Language and Culture
Site: Hungary: Pecs
Dates: 1 mo, Aug 13-Sep 9
Subjects: Central European studies, Civilization/culture, Economics, Folklore, History, Hungarian language, Hungarian studies, Political science/politics
Eligibility: *Level:* fresh, sophs, jrs, srs, grads, adults, precoll *Age:* min 18, avg 29
Credit: *Undergrad:* 120 per 1 mo *Grad:* none *Doc:* transcript, certificate
Instruction: *In:* English *Format:* lang study, seminar *Students:* intl
Costs: $750 *incl* tuition, housing, some meals *Nonrefundable fee*
Housing: *Sponsor assists:* residence halls, pensions, hotels
Deadline: Aug 1
Other info: *US accredited sponsor:* no *Began:* 1999 *Activities:* excursions, field trips, cultural events *URL:* http://www.isc.pte.hu
Contact: Gabriella Kis Halas, Study Adviser, University of Pecs, Intl Studies Ctr, Szanto Kovacs J. str. 1/B, Pecs, Hungary H-7633 *E-mail:* kishalas@isc.pte.hu

Macedonia

OHRID

0385
ARIZONA STATE UNIVERSITY
Macedonia
Site: Macedonia: Ohrid
Dates: 2-1/2 wks, Jul 31-Aug 18
Subjects: Civilization/culture, Macedonian language (int)
Eligibility: *Level:* adults *Requires:* previous study in field, 8-wks intensive Macedonian in ASU pgm
Credit: *Undergrad:* 2 *Grad:* none
Instruction: *In:* English *Format:* lang study, lecture, study tour *Students:* mainly US
Costs: $1,100 *incl* tuition, housing, all meals, fees, excursions, ISIC
Housing: *Arr by pgm:* pensions
Deadline: May 1
Other info: *US accredited sponsor:* yes *Began:* 1997 *Activities:* excursions, field trips, cultural events *Misc:* Loans avail. All students pay equiv of ASU resident tuition. *Financial aid:* scholarships *URL:* http://www.asu.edu/ssc/StudyAbroad
Contact: Ara Pachmayer, Pgm Coord, Summer Sessions, Arizona State Univ, PO Box 873003, Tempe AZ 85287-3003 *Ph:* 480-965 0101 *Fax:* 480-965 3851 *E-mail:* study.programs@asu.edu
Or Contact: Carol Withers, Russian & East European Studies, Arizona State Univ, PO Box 872601, Tempe AZ 85287-2601 *Ph:* 480-965 4188 *Fax:* 480-965 0310 *E-mail:* carol.withers@asu.edu

Poland

MORE THAN ONE CITY

0386
LANGUAGES ABROAD
Language and Cultural Immersion Programs-Poland
Site: Poland: Krakow, Warsaw
Dates: 2 wks or longer, yr-round
Subjects: Civilization/culture, Polish language (beg/int/adv)
Eligibility: *Level:* adults *Age:* min 17, max 65, avg 25
Credit: *Undergrad:* none *Grad:* none *Doc:* certificate
Instruction: *In:* Polish *Format:* lang study *Students:* intl
Costs: About $3,250 for 4 wks *incl* tuition, housing, some meals, excursions, books/materials
Housing: *Arr by pgm:* apartments, homestay
Deadline: None
Other info: *US accredited sponsor:* no *Misc:* May contact former participants. *URL:* http://www.languagesabroad.com
Contact: Ms Jesse Philippe, Langs Abroad, 317 Adelaide St W, Ste 900, Toronto, Ontario M5V 1P9, Canada *Ph:* 800-219 9924; 416-925 7117 *E-mail:* info@languagesabroad.com

---

KRAKOW

0387
AMERICAN INSTITUTE FOR FOREIGN STUDY (AIFS)
Jagiellonian University-Poland
Site: Poland: Krakow *Host inst:* Jagiellonian Univ
Dates: 4 wks, Jun 30-Jul 28
Subjects: Art history, Civilization/culture, History, Literature, Music, Polish language, Polish studies, Political science/politics
Eligibility: *Level:* sophs, jrs, srs, adults, precoll *Requires:* 2.0 GPA
Credit: *Undergrad:* avail *Grad:* none *Doc:* transcript
Instruction: *In:* English *Format:* lang study, lecture *Students:* intl
Costs: $3,999 *incl* tuition, housing, all meals, intl airfare, e-mail *Nonrefundable fee*
Housing: *Arr by pgm:* residence halls
Deadline: Mar 15
Other info: *US accredited sponsor:* no *Began:* 2001 *Orient:* abroad *Activities:* cultural events *Financial aid:* scholarships *URL:* http://www.aifsabroad.com
Contact: Solandy Meza, Coll Div, AIFS, River Plaza, 9 W Broad St, Stamford CT 06902 *Ph:* 800-727 2437 ext 5163 *E-mail:* college.info@aifs.com ▲

0388
CATHOLIC UNIVERSITY OF AMERICA, COLUMBUS SCHOOL OF LAW and JAGIELLONIAN UNIVERSITY
International Business and Trade Summer Law Program
Site: Poland: Krakow *Host inst:* Jagiellonian Univ
Dates: 6 wks, about Jun 16-Jul 28
Subjects: Business/management, Central European studies, Comparative law, East European studies, Economics, European Union, International business, International law, Law, Trade
Eligibility: *Level:* grads, professionals *Requires:* previous study in field, good acad standing at accredited law sch, completion of 20 law credits
Credit: *Undergrad:* none *Grad:* 5-7 credits *Doc:* transcript, certificate
Instruction: *In:* English *Format:* lecture, seminar *Students:* intl
Costs: About $3,725-$4,575 *incl* tuition, housing, some meals, fees, excursions *Nonrefundable fee*
Housing: *Arr by pgm:* residence halls, hotels
Deadline: Mar 15
Other info: *US accredited sponsor:* yes *Began:* 1992 *Orient:* avail avail *Activities:* field trips *Misc:* Loans avail. Visits to cultural sites & courts. May contact former participants. *Financial aid:* scholarships *URL:* http://www.law.edu
Contact: Amy Miller, Pgm Coord, Columbus Sch of Law, Catholic Univ, Cardinal Station, Washington DC 20064 *Ph:* 800-787 0300; 202-319 6725 *Fax:* 202-319 4459 *E-mail:* poland@law.edu
Or Contact: Prof Rett Ludwikowski, Pgm Dir, Columbus Sch of Law, Washington DC 20064 *Ph:* 800-787-0300; 202-319-5140 *Fax:* 202-319-4459 *E-mail:* ludwikowski@law.edu

---

0389
LEXIA INTERNATIONAL
LEXIA Summer in Krakow
Site: Poland: Krakow *Host inst:* Jagiellonian Univ
Dates: 8 wks, mid-Jun-mid-Aug
Subjects: Anthropology, Arts, Civilization/culture, Community service projects, East European studies, Ecology/environmental studies, Economics, Fine arts, History, Independent study, Internships,

Literature, Polish language (beg/int/adv), Political science/politics, Sociology
Eligibility: *Level:* fresh, sophs, jrs, srs, grads, adults *Requires:* 2.5 GPA *Age:* min 18, avg 21
Credit: *Undergrad:* 8-10 *Grad:* 8-10 *Doc:* transcript *Transfer credit through:* Western Washington Univ
Instruction: *In:* English, Polish *Format:* independent study, internship, lang study, lecture, seminar, volunteer/svc *Students:* mainly US
Costs: $4,350 *incl* tuition, housing, insurance, fees, excursions, ISIC, computer access *Nonrefundable fee*
Housing: *Arr by pgm:* residence halls with local students, homestay
Deadline: Apr 15; Apr 1 for scholarships
Other info: *US accredited sponsor:* no *Began:* 1991 *In coop with:* Western Washington Univ *Orient:* abroad *Activities:* excursions, field trips, program travel, cultural events, sports *Misc:* Support svcs. May contact former participants. *Financial aid:* scholarships, work study *URL:* http://www.lexiaintl.org
Contact: LEXIA Intl, 25 S Main St, Hanover NH 03755 *Ph:* 800-775 3942; 603-643 9898 *Fax:* 603-643 9899 *E-mail:* info@lexiaintl.org
Or Contact: LEXIA Intl, West Coast, 378 Cambridge Ave, Palo Alto CA 94306-1544 *Ph:* 650-327 9191 *Fax:* 650-327 9192

WARSAW

0390
UNIVERSITY OF PENNSYLVANIA
Penn-in-Warsaw
Site: Poland: Warsaw *Host inst:* Warsaw Sch of Econ
Dates: 6 wks, mid-Jun-Jul
Subjects: Economics, Internships, Polish language (beg), Political science/politics
Eligibility: *Level:* fresh, sophs, jrs, srs, grads, adults, teachers, professionals *Requires:* basic econ
Credit: *Undergrad:* 6 *Grad:* avail *Doc:* transcript
Instruction: *In:* English *Format:* lang study, lecture, music lesson *Students:* mainly US
Costs: About $3,700 *incl* tuition, housing *Nonrefundable fee*
Housing: *Arr by pgm:* residence halls
Deadline: Mar 1
Other info: *US accredited sponsor:* yes *Began:* 1989 *Orient:* in US & abroad *Activities:* excursions, cultural events *Misc:* May contact former participants. *URL:* http://www.sas.upenn.edu/CGS/
Contact: Elizabeth Sachs, Penn Summer Abroad, Univ of Pennsylvania, 3440 Market St, Ste 100, Philadelphia PA 19104-3335 *Ph:* 215-898 5738 *Fax:* 215-573 2053 *E-mail:* sdanti@mail.sas.upenn.edu

Romania

CLUJ

0391
ARIZONA STATE UNIVERSITY
Romania
Site: Romania: Cluj *Host inst:* Babes-Bolyai Univ
Dates: 4 wks, Jul 3-31
Subjects: Civilization/culture, Romanian language (beg/int)
Eligibility: *Level:* fresh, sophs, jrs, srs, grads, adults, teachers, professionals *Requires:* 1 sem Romanian *Age:* min 18
Credit: *Undergrad:* 7 *Grad:* 6
Instruction: *In:* English *Format:* lang study, lecture, study tour *Students:* mainly US
Costs: $2,745 *incl* tuition, housing, all meals, fees, excursions, ISIC *Nonrefundable fee*
Housing: *Arr by pgm:* univ hotel
Deadline: Early Mar
Other info: *US accredited sponsor:* yes *Began:* 1999 *Activities:* excursions, program travel, cultural events *Misc:* Loans avail. All students pay equiv of ASU resident tuition. *Financial aid:* scholarships *URL:* http://www.asu.edu/ssc/StudyAbroad
Contact: Ara Pachmayer, Pgm Coord, Summer Sessions, Arizona State Univ, PO Box 873003, Tempe AZ 85287-3003 *Ph:* 480-965 0101 *Fax:* 480-965 3851 *E-mail:* study.programs@asu.edu

Russia

MORE THAN ONE CITY

0392
CAMP COUNSELORS USA
Russian Summer Camp Volunteer Program
Site: Russia: various sites *Host inst:* various summer youth camps
Dates: 1-2 mos, Jun-Aug
Subjects: Arts, Crafts, Drama/theater, East European studies, English, History, Music, Recreation, Russian language, Slavic studies, Sports
Eligibility: *Level:* fresh, sophs, jrs, srs, grads, adults, teachers, professionals *Requires:* youth work experience &/or lang study recommended *Age:* min 19, avg 22
Credit: *Undergrad:* avail *Grad:* none
Instruction: *In:* English, Russian *Format:* student teaching, study tour, volunteer/svc *Students:* mainly host country
Costs: $1,600 *incl* housing, all meals, intl airfare, fees, excursions
Housing: *Arr by pgm:* summer camp dormitories with local students
Deadline: Apr 15
Other info: *US accredited sponsor:* no *Began:* 1990 *Orient:* in US & abroad *Activities:* excursions, program travel, cultural events *Misc:* May contact former participants. *URL:* http://www.campcounselors.com
Contact: Desmond Gribben, Camp Counselors USA, 2330 Marinship Way, Ste 250, Sausalito CA 94965 *Ph:* 800-999 2267; 415-339 2728 *Fax:* 415-339 2744 *E-mail:* outbound@campcounselors.com

---

0393
COLLEGE OF SAINT SCHOLASTICA
Russian Language Camp
Site: Russia: Moscow, Petrozavodsk, St Petersburg *Host inst:* Karelian Pedagogical Univ
Dates: 5 wks, Jun-Jul
Subjects: Art, Civilization/culture, Contemporary issues, Music, Painting, Political science/politics, Russian language, Russian studies
Eligibility: *Level:* fresh, sophs, jrs, srs, grads, adults, teachers, professionals, precoll *Requires:* 2.00 GPA *Age:* min 17, max 65, avg 22
Credit: *Undergrad:* avail *Grad:* none *Doc:* transcript
Instruction: *In:* Russian *Format:* lang study, study tour *Students:* mainly US
Costs: $3,000 *incl* tuition, housing, all meals, intl airfare, excursions, books/materials, railpass *Nonrefundable fee*
Housing: *Arr by pgm:* residence halls
Deadline: Mar 30
Other info: *US accredited sponsor:* yes *Began:* 1990 *Orient:* in US (intensive lang study) *Activities:* excursions, field trips, program travel, cultural events, sports *Misc:* May contact former participants.
Contact: Prof Tom Morgan, Coll of St Scholastica, 1200 Kenwood Ave, Duluth MN 55811 *Ph:* 800-447 5444; 218-723 6442 *Fax:* 218-723 6290 *E-mail:* tmorgan@css.edu
Or Contact: Prof Tom Zelman, Coll of St Scholastica, 1200 Kenwood Ave, Duluth MN 55811 *Ph:* 218-723 6183 *Fax:* 218-723 6290 *E-mail:* tzelman@css.edu

---

0394
LANGUAGE LIAISON
Russian Saturation in Moscow and Saint Petersburg
Site: Russia: Moscow, St Petersburg
Dates: 2 wks or longer, yr-round
Subjects: Civilization/culture, Homestay, Russian language, Russian studies
Eligibility: *Level:* adults *Age:* min 18
Credit: *Undergrad:* avail *Grad:* avail
Instruction: *In:* Russian *Format:* lang study *Students:* intl
Costs: Contact sponsor

See "How To Use This Book" for definitions of terms used above. ▲ = See program sponsor's ad(s) in this book.

Housing: *Sponsor assists:* homestay, hotels
Deadline: 45 days before pgm
Other info: *US accredited sponsor:* no *Orient:* abroad *Activities:* excursions, field trips, cultural events, sports *Misc:* Scholarship research svc. *URL:* http://www.languageliaison.com
Contact: Nancy Forman, Dir, Lang Liaison, 4 Burnham Pkwy, Morristown NJ 07960 *Ph:* 800-284 4448 *Fax:* 973-898 1710 *E-mail:* learn@languageliaison.com

---

0395
LANGUAGE STUDIES ABROAD, INC
Intensive Russian and Standard Group Course
Site: Russia: Moscow, St Petersburg *Host inst:* LSA Moscow, LSA St Petersburg
Dates: 1 wk or longer Moscow/2 wks or longer St Petersburg, yr-round
Subjects: Art, Business/management, Civilization/culture, Education/teaching, History, Homestay, Hotel management, Literature, Media studies, Russian language (beg/int/adv), Russian studies, Tourism
Eligibility: *Level:* fresh, sophs, jrs, srs, grads, adults, teachers, professionals, precoll *Age:* min 16, avg 32
Credit: *Undergrad:* avail *Grad:* avail *Doc:* certificate
Instruction: *In:* English, French, German, Italian, Russian, Spanish *Format:* lang study *Students:* intl
Costs: Contact sponsor
Housing: *Sponsor assists:* apartments, homestay, hotels
Deadline: 4 wks before pgm
Other info: *US accredited sponsor:* no *Orient:* abroad *Activities:* excursions, field trips, cultural events *Misc:* May contact former participants. *URL:* http://www.languagestudiesabroad.com
Contact: Lang Studies Abroad, Inc, 103 Londonderry Ct, Reno NV 89511-2718 *Ph:* 800-424 5522; 775-849 9206 *Fax:* 775-849 9217 *E-mail:* info@languagestudiesabroad.com

---

0396
LANGUAGES ABROAD
Language and Cultural Immersion Programs-Russia
Site: Russia: Moscow, St Petersburg
Dates: 2 wks or longer, yr-round
Subjects: Civilization/culture, Russian language (beg/int/adv)
Eligibility: *Level:* adults *Age:* min 17, max 65, avg 25
Credit: *Undergrad:* none *Grad:* none *Doc:* certificate
Instruction: *In:* Russian *Format:* lang study *Students:* intl
Costs: From $2,195 for 4 wks *incl* tuition, housing, some meals, excursions, books/materials
Housing: *Arr by pgm:* apartments, homestay
Deadline: None
Other info: *US accredited sponsor:* no *Misc:* May contact former participants. *URL:* http://www.languagesabroad.com
Contact: Ms Jesse Philippe, Langs Abroad, 317 Adelaide St W, Ste 900, Toronto, Ontario M5V 1P9, Canada *Ph:* 800-219 9924; 416-925 7117 *E-mail:* info@languagesabroad.com

---

0397
LINGUA SERVICE WORLDWIDE
Total Immersion/Intensive Language and Culture in Russia
Site: Russia: Moscow, St Petersburg *Host inst:* Home Lang Intl
Dates: 1 wk-1 yr, yr-round
Subjects: Civilization/culture, Homestay, Russian language (beg/int/adv)
Eligibility: *Level:* adults *Age:* min 14
Credit: *Undergrad:* avail *Grad:* avail *Doc:* transcript, certificate
Instruction: *In:* Russian *Format:* lang study *Students:* intl
Costs: Contact sponsor
Housing: *Arr by pgm:* apartments with local students, residence halls with local students, homestay, pensions, hotels, hostels
Deadline: 45 days before pgm
Other info: *US accredited sponsor:* no *Began:* 1993 *Activities:* excursions, cultural events *Misc:* May contact former participants. *URL:* http://www.linguaserviceworldwide.com
Contact: Dir, Lingua Svc Worldwide, 75 Prospect St, Ste 4, Huntington NY 11743 *Ph:* 800-394 5327; 631-424 0777 *Fax:* 631-271 3441 *E-mail:* itctravel@worldnet.att.net ▲

0398
TULANE UNIVERSITY
Tulane University Summer Abroad in Russia
Site: Russia: Moscow, St Petersburg
Dates: 15 days, summer
Subjects: History, Russian studies
Eligibility: *Requires:* 2.0 GPA, good acad standing *Age:* min 18
Credit: *Undergrad:* 3 *Grad:* none *Doc:* transcript
Instruction: *In:* English *Format:* study tour *Students:* mainly US
Costs: About $3,350 *incl* tuition, housing, all meals, intl airfare, insurance, fees, excursions *Nonrefundable fee*
Housing: *Arr by pgm:* hotels
Deadline: Mar 13
Other info: *US accredited sponsor:* yes *Began:* 1990 *Orient:* in US (1 day) *Activities:* excursions, field trips *URL:* http://www.Tulane.EDU/~ummer/abroad/russia
Contact: Dr William Brumfield, Germanic & Slavic Langs, Tulane Univ, New Orleans LA 70118 *Ph:* 504-865 5276
Or Contact: Jenifer Thiel, Tulane Univ Summer Sch, 125 Gibson Hall, New Orleans LA 70118 *Ph:* 504-865 5555 *Fax:* 504-865 5562

0399
UNIVERSITY OF ARIZONA
Arizona in Russia-Language and Business Internship Program
Site: Russia: Moscow, St Petersburg *Host inst:* Inst of Youth (Moscow), St Petersburg State Univ
Dates: May 30-Jul 4 and/or Jul 3-Aug 1
Subjects: Business/management, Civilization/culture, Homestay, Internships, Russian language (beg/int/adv), Russian studies
Eligibility: *Level:* sophs, jrs, srs, adults, teachers *Requires:* 2.5 GPA *Age:* min 18
Credit: *Undergrad:* 6-12 *Grad:* 6-12 *Doc:* transcript
Instruction: *In:* Russian *Format:* internship, lang study, lecture *Students:* mainly US
Costs: About $3,000 per term *incl* tuition, housing, all meals, intl airfare, fees, excursions
Housing: *Arr by pgm:* residence halls, homestay
Deadline: Apr 1
Other info: *US accredited sponsor:* yes *Began:* 1985 *In coop with:* Intourist & Ministry of Higher Educ *Orient:* in US & abroad *Activities:* excursions, cultural events *Misc:* St Petersburg offers lang pgm only. May contact former participants. *Financial aid:* scholarships *URL:* http://w3.arizona.edu/~ciss/
Contact: Dr Delbert Phillips, Russian, Univ of Arizona, 340 Modern Langs, Tucson AZ 85721 *Ph:* 520-621 7341 *E-mail:* dphillip@u.arizona.edu
Or Contact: Renee Griggs, Ctr for Global Student Pgms, Univ of Arizona, 939 N Tyndall Ave, Tucson AZ 85721 *Ph:* 520-626 7180 *E-mail:* griggsr@u.arizona.edu ▲

0400
UNIVERSITY OF SAN DIEGO, SCHOOL OF LAW
Moscow Institute on International and Comparative Law
Site: Russia: Moscow, St Petersburg *Host inst:* ANO Pericles
Dates: May 29-Jul 1 for classes, Jul 3-Aug 4 for internship
Subjects: International law, Internships, Russian studies, Trade law
Eligibility: *Level:* grads, teachers,

professionals *Requires:* law or bus students
Credit: *Undergrad:* none *Grad:* 5--9 *Doc:* certificate
Instruction: *In:* English *Students:* mainly US
Costs: $2,200 for classes,$3,950 for internship, $900 housing, $500 for trip *incl* tuition, housing, books/materials *Nonrefundable fee*
Housing: *Arr by pgm:* hotels
Deadline: Mar 11
Other info: *US accredited sponsor:* yes *Began:* 1979 *Orient:* in US & abroad *Misc:* Legal & some tourist visits arr from site. Correspondence re: pgm must be in English. Loans avail for US students only. *URL:* http://www.acusd.edu/lawabroad
Contact: Cindy King, Law Pgms Abroad, Univ of San Diego, 5998 Alcala Park, San Diego CA 92110-2492 *Ph:* 619-260 7460 *Fax:* 619-260 2230 *E-mail:* cking@acusd.edu

---

EKATERINBURG

0401
UNIVERSITY OF GEORGIA
Field Biology Studies in the Ural Mountains of Russia
Site: Russia: Ekaterinburg *Host inst:* Ecology Ctr of the Urals State Univ
Dates: 6 wks, May 15-Jun 30
Subjects: Asian studies, Biochemistry, Biology, Botany, Ecology/environmental studies, Economics, Entomology, Natural history, Ornithology, Physiology
Eligibility: *Level:* fresh, sophs, jrs, srs *Requires:* good acad standing
Credit: *Undergrad:* 3 *Grad:* none
Instruction: *In:* English *Format:* directed field study, lab, lecture *Students:* mainly US
Costs: $1,200 *incl* housing, all meals, insurance, fees, excursions, visa
Housing: *Arr by pgm:* residence halls
Deadline: Apr 2
Other info: *US accredited sponsor:* yes *Began:* 2000 *Activities:* excursions, field trips, program travel, cultural events *Misc:* Guided tour to Moscow & optional tour to St Petersburg. May contact former participants. *URL:* http://www.uga.edu/biochem/bio13900/
Contact: Prof Clanton C Black, Biochem & Molecular Biology, Univ of Georgia, Life Sci Bldg, Athens GA 30602 *Ph:* 706-542 1778 *Fax:* 706-542 1786 *E-mail:* ccblack@bmb.uga.edu
Or Contact: Prof Vladimir I Pyankov, Plant Physiology/Biology, Urals State Univ, Ekaterinburg 620083, Russia *E-mail:* vladimir.pyankov@usu.ru

---

IRKUTSK

0402
MIDDLEBURY COLLEGE
Eco-Baikal
Site: Russia: Irkutsk
Dates: 1 mo, Jul
Subjects: Ecology/environmental studies, Russian language (beg/int)
Eligibility: *Level:* fresh, sophs, jrs, srs *Requires:* 2.75 GPA
Credit: *Undergrad:* 3 *Grad:* none
Instruction: *In:* English *Format:* lang study, lecture, seminar *Students:* mainly US
Costs: Contact sponsor
Housing: *Arr by pgm*
Deadline: Feb 1
Other info: *US accredited sponsor:* yes *Began:* 2001 *Orient:* abroad *Activities:* excursions, field trips, program travel *Misc:* May contact former participants. *URL:* http://www.middlebury.edu/~msa
Contact: Off-Campus Study, Sunderland Lang Ctr, Middlebury Coll, Middlebury VT 05753 *Ph:* 802-443 5745 *Fax:* 802-443 3157 *E-mail:* schoolsabroad@middlebury.edu

---

KAZAN

0403
UNIVERSITY OF VIRGINIA
UVA in Kazan
Site: Russia: Kazan *Host inst:* Kazan State Univ
Dates: 1 mo, late May-late Jun
Subjects: Homestay, Russian language
Eligibility: *Level:* fresh, sophs, jrs, srs, grads *Requires:* previous study in field, 1 yr of Russian
Credit: *Undergrad:* 6 *Grad:* none *Doc:* certificate
Instruction: *In:* Russian *Format:* lang study, lecture, study tour *Students:* intl
Costs: $2,000 *incl* tuition, housing, some meals, excursions *Nonrefundable fee*
Housing: *Arr by pgm:* homestay
Deadline: Mar 15
Other info: *US accredited sponsor:* yes *Began:* 1996 *Orient:* in US *Activities:* excursions, cultural events *URL:* http://minerva.acc.Virginia.EDU/~slavic/
Contact: Prof Karen Ryan, Slavic Dept, Univ of Virginia, 109 Cabell Hall, Charlottesville VA 22903 *Ph:* 804-924 3548 *Fax:* 804-982 2744 *E-mail:* klr8p@virginia.edu

---

MOSCOW

0404
ARIZONA STATE UNIVERSITY
Moscow
Site: Russia: Moscow *Host inst:* Moscow State Linguistic Univ
Dates: Jun 5-Jul 28
Subjects: Internships, Russian language
Eligibility: *Level:* fresh, sophs, jrs, srs, grads, adults, teachers, professionals *Requires:* 1 yr Russian *Age:* min 18
Credit: *Undergrad:* 12 *Grad:* none
Instruction: *In:* Russian *Format:* internship, lang study, lecture *Students:* mainly US
Costs: $3,590 *incl* tuition, housing, some meals, ISIC *Nonrefundable fee*
Housing: *Arr by pgm:* residence halls
Deadline: Early Mar
Other info: *US accredited sponsor:* yes *Began:* 1997 *Orient:* in US *Misc:* Loans avail. All students pay equiv of ASU resident tuition. *Financial aid:* scholarships *URL:* http://www.asu.edu/ssc/StudyAbroad
Contact: Ara Pachmayer, Pgm Coord, Arizona State Univ, PO Box 873003, Tempe AZ 85287-3003 *Ph:* 480-965 0101 *Fax:* 480-965 3851 *E-mail:* study.programs@asu.edu

---

0405
COLLEGE CONSORTIUM FOR INTERNATIONAL STUDIES and **TRUMAN STATE UNIVERSITY**
Russia Studies Summer Program
Site: Russia: Moscow *Host inst:* Inst of Youth
Dates: Early Jun-late Jul
Subjects: History, Music, Political science/politics, Russian language (beg/int/adv)
Eligibility: *Level:* sophs, jrs, srs, adults, teachers, professionals *Requires:* 2.5 GPA *Age:* min 18
Credit: *Undergrad:* 9 *Grad:* none *Doc:* transcript
Instruction: *In:* English *Format:* lang study, lecture, seminar *Students:* mainly US
Costs: $3,990 *incl* tuition, housing, all meals, fees, excursions, books/materials, visa
Housing: *Arr by pgm:* residence halls
Deadline: Apr 15
Other info: *US accredited sponsor:* yes *Began:* 1994 *Orient:* abroad (intensive lang study) *Activities:* excursions, field trips, program travel, cultural events, sports *Misc:* May contact former participants. *URL:* http://www.ccisabroad.org
Contact: *See Index II for Members* CCIS, 2000 P St NW, Ste 503, Washington DC 20036 *Ph:* 800-453 6956; 202-223 0330 *Fax:* 202-223 0999 *E-mail:* info@ccisabroad.org

Or Contact: Ctr for Intl Educ Abroad, Truman State Univ, Kirk Bldg 120, Kirksville MO 63501 *Ph:* 660-785 4076 *Fax:* 660-785 7473 *E-mail:* ciea@truman.edu ▲

0406
DICKINSON COLLEGE
Moscow Summer Immersion Program
Site: Russia: Moscow *Host inst:* Mendeleev Univ
Dates: 5 wks, late May-early Jul
Subjects: Civilization/culture, Russian language (int/adv), Social sciences
Eligibility: *Level:* fresh, sophs, jrs *Requires:* 2 yrs coll Russian
Credit: *Undergrad:* 4 *Grad:* none
Instruction: *In:* Russian *Format:* lang study, lecture *Students:* mainly US
Costs: About $4,100 *incl* tuition, housing, all meals, intl airfare, fees, excursions, railpass
Housing: *Arr by pgm:* homestay
Deadline: Mar 1
Other info: *US accredited sponsor:* yes *Began:* 1984 *Orient:* in US *Activities:* excursions *Misc:* Must pledge to speak Russian during pgm. *URL:* http://www.dickinson.edu/departments/ocs/summer.html
Contact: Global Educ, Dickinson Coll, PO Box 1773, Carlisle PA 17013-2896 *Ph:* 717-245 1341 *Fax:* 717-245 1688 *E-mail:* ocs@dickinson.edu

---

0407
EDUVACATIONS
Intensive Russian and Cultural Courses at All Levels
Site: Russia: Moscow
Dates: 1 wk-1 yr, yr-round
Subjects: Art, Business language (int/adv), Civilization/culture, Current events, History, Literature, Music, Russian language (beg/int/adv), Russian studies
Eligibility: *Level:* adults *Age:* min 14
Credit: *Undergrad:* avail *Grad:* none *Doc:* certificate
Instruction: *In:* Russian *Format:* lang study, lecture, study tour *Students:* intl
Costs: Contact sponsor
Housing: *Arr by pgm:* homestay, hotels, hostels
Deadline: Contact sponsor
Other info: *US accredited sponsor:* no *Began:* 1992 *Activities:* excursions, field trips, cultural events, sports *Misc:* May contact former participants. *URL:* http://www.eduvacations.com
Contact: Mary Ann Puglisi, eduVacations, 1431 21st St NW, Ste 302, Washington DC 20036 *Ph:* 202-857 8384 *Fax:* 202-463 8091

0408
FLORIDA STATE UNIVERSITY
Moscow Summer Program
Site: Russia: Moscow
Dates: 6 wks, May 3-Jun 13
Subjects: Civilization/culture, History, Liberal arts, Russian language, Russian studies
Eligibility: *Level:* fresh, sophs, jrs, srs, grads, precoll *Requires:* 2.5 GPA
Credit: *Undergrad:* 10 *Grad:* avail
Instruction: *In:* English *Format:* lang study, lecture *Students:* mainly US
Costs: $4,150 *incl* tuition, housing, intl airfare
Housing: *Arr by pgm:* residence halls
Deadline: Jan 19
Other info: *US accredited sponsor:* yes *Began:* 1996 *Orient:* in US & abroad (2 days) *Activities:* excursions, field trips, program travel, cultural events *Misc:* May contact former participants. *URL:* http://www.international.fsu.edu
Contact: Elizabeth Trelenberg or Bonnie Snyder, Intl Pgms, Florida State Univ, 5500 UCA, Tallahassee FL 32306-2420 *Ph:* 800-374 8581; 850-644 3272 *Fax:* 850-644 8817 *E-mail:* intprog@www.fsu.edu

---

0409
NATIONAL REGISTRATION CENTER FOR STUDY ABROAD (NRCSA)
Eurocentre
Site: Russia: Moscow
Dates: 2-4 wks, May 15-Jun or Jul 2-31
Subjects: Homestay, Russian language (beg/int/adv)
Eligibility: *Level:* fresh, sophs, jrs, srs, grads, adults *Age:* min 17
Credit: *Undergrad:* avail *Grad:* avail
Instruction: *In:* Russian *Format:* lang study *Students:* intl
Costs: $1,614 for 4 wks *incl* tuition, housing, some meals, insurance
Housing: *Arr by student:* residence halls, homestay
Deadline: Contact sponsor
Other info: *US accredited sponsor:* no *Orient:* abroad (intensive lang study) *Activities:* excursions, cultural events *URL:* http://www.nrcsa.com
Contact: Reuel Zielke, NRCSA, 823 N 2nd St, #206, Milwaukee WI 53203 *Ph:* 414-278 0631 *Fax:* 414-271 8884 *E-mail:* info@nrcsa.com

---

0410
RUSSIAN LANGUAGE STUDY CENTER
Russian Language Courses
Site: Russia: Moscow *Host inst:* Moscow M V Lomonosov State Univ
Dates: 2 wks or longer, yr-round
Subjects: Homestay, Russian language (beg/int/adv)
Eligibility: *Level:* adults *Requires:* ability to read Cyrillic alphabet *Age:* min 16
Credit: *Undergrad:* none *Grad:* none
Instruction: *In:* Russian *Format:* lang study *Students:* intl
Costs: From $210 per wk *incl* tuition, housing, fees *Nonrefundable fee*
Housing: *Arr by pgm:* residence halls, homestay, hostels
Deadline: 4 wks before pgm
Other info: *US accredited sponsor:* no *Began:* 1989 *Orient:* in US & abroad 1 day *Activities:* excursions, program travel, cultural events *Misc:* Students may enroll at Moscow State Univ. Travel & visa support. May contact former participants. *Financial aid:* work study *URL:* http://studyrussian.com
Contact: Dr Marco Ziegler, Russian Lang Study, 314 Panoramic Way, Berkeley CA 94704 *Ph:* 510-644 3745 *Fax:* 510-644 3745 *E-mail:* mziegler@uclink4.berkeley.edu
Or Contact: Prof Vladimir N Pautov, Moscow M V Lomonosov State Univ, MSU, A-161, 119899 Moscow, Russia *E-mail:* centre@garnet.ru

---

0411
SUNY UNIVERSITY AT ALBANY
Language and Cultural Studies at Moscow State University
Site: Russia: Moscow *Host inst:* Moscow State Univ
Dates: 6 wks, Jun-Aug
Subjects: Russian language
Eligibility: *Level:* fresh, sophs, jrs, srs, grads *Requires:* 2.5 GPA
Credit: *Undergrad:* 6 *Grad:* none *Doc:* transcript
Instruction: *In:* Russian *Format:* lang study *Students:* mainly US
Costs: $2,952 for NY residents *incl* tuition, housing, all meals, fees, excursions, books/materials, student support svcs
Housing: *Arr by pgm:* residence halls
Deadline: Mar 15; late applications considered
Other info: *US accredited sponsor:* yes *Orient:* in US & abroad *Activities:* excursions, field trips, cultural events *Misc:* May contact former participants. *URL:* http://www.albany.edu/intled
Contact: Joan N Savitt, Intl Pgms, SUNY Univ at Albany, LI 66, Albany NY 12222 *Ph:* 518-442 3525 *Fax:* 518-442 3338 *E-mail:* intled@uamail.albany.edu

---

0412
UNIVERSITY OF MONTANA
Group Study Abroad Summer Program in Moscow
Site: Russia: Moscow *Host inst:* Russian State Univ for the Humanities
Dates: 5 wks, May 15-Jun 23

Subjects: Civilization/culture, Independent study, Literature, Russian language (int/adv), Russian studies
Eligibility: Own students only. *Level:* sophs, jrs, srs, grads *Requires:* 1 yr Russian preferred
Credit: *Undergrad:* 6 *Grad:* none
Instruction: *In:* English, Russian *Format:* independent study, lang study, lecture *Students:* mainly US
Costs: About $3,500 for MT residents; $4,500 for non-residents *incl* tuition, housing, most meals, intl airfare, fees
Housing: *Arr by pgm:* residence halls
Deadline: Oct 10
Other info: *US accredited sponsor:* yes *Began:* 1994 *Orient:* in US (spring term) *Activities:* excursions *URL:* http://www.umt.edu/oip
Contact: Intl Pgms, Univ of Montana, Main Hall 022, Missoula MT 59812 *Ph:* 406-243 2288 *Fax:* 406-243 6194 *E-mail:* goabroad@selway.umt.edu

---

0413
VIRGINIA POLYTECHNIC INSTITUTE & STATE UNIVERSITY
Russian Language and Culture
Site: Russia: Moscow *Host inst:* Moscow State Univ
Dates: 7 wks, Jun 6-Jul 27
Subjects: Russian language (beg/int/adv)
Eligibility: *Level:* adults *Age:* min 18
Credit: *Undergrad:* 6 *Grad:* 6 *Doc:* certificate
Instruction: *In:* English, Russian *Format:* lang study *Students:* mainly US
Costs: $3,000 *incl* tuition, housing, some meals, intl airfare, fees, excursions, books/materials, public trans pass *Nonrefundable fee*
Housing: *Arr by pgm:* residence halls
Deadline: Apr 1
Other info: *US accredited sponsor:* yes *Began:* 1997 *In coop with:* Univ of Pittsburgh *Activities:* excursions, field trips, program travel, cultural events *Misc:* May contact former participants.
Contact: Irina Makoveena, PhD Student, Univ of Pittsburgh, 2552 Beechwood Blvd, Pittsburgh PA 15217 *Ph:* 412-521 5328 *Fax:* 412-624 9714
Or Contact: Prof Stephen Baehr, Virginia Tech, 351 Major Williams Hall, Blacksburg VA 24061-0225 *Ph:* 540-231 8323 *Fax:* 540-231 4812

NOVGOROD

0414
MIAMI UNIVERSITY (OH)
Russian Study-Tour at Novgorod State University
Site: Russia: Novgorod *Host inst:* Novgorod State Univ
Dates: 4 wks, early Jun-early Jul
Subjects: Homestay, Russian language (beg/int/adv)
Eligibility: *Level:* fresh, sophs, jrs, srs, grads, adults, teachers, professionals, precoll *Requires:* 2.0 GPA *Age:* min 16
Credit: *Undergrad:* 6 *Grad:* 4 *Doc:* transcript
Instruction: *In:* Russian *Format:* lang study, study tour *Students:* mainly US
Costs: About $1,900 *incl* tuition, housing, all meals, intl airfare, excursions, books/materials *Nonrefundable fee*
Housing: *Arr by pgm:* homestay, hotels
Deadline: Feb 1
Other info: *US accredited sponsor:* yes *Began:* 1999 *In coop with:* Novgorod State Univ *Activities:* excursions, program travel, cultural events *Misc:* May contact former participants. *URL:* http://www.cas.muohio.edu/~greal/forst/Novgorod.html
Contact: Dr Irina Goncharenko, German, Russian & East Asian Langs, Miami Univ, Oxford OH 45056 *Ph:* 513-529 2526 *Fax:* 513-529 1807 *E-mail:* gonchai@muohio.edu
Or Contact: Dr Margaret Ziolkowski, German, Russian & East Asian Lang, Miami Univ, Oxford OH 45056 *Ph:* 513-529 2526 *Fax:* 513-529 1807 *E-mail:* ziolkom@muohio.edu

---

0415
SUNY COLLEGE AT BROCKPORT
Russian Language and Culture Immersion Program
Site: Russia: Novgorod *Host inst:* Novgorod State Univ
Dates: 5 wks, late Jun-Aug
Subjects: Arts, Business language, Civilization/culture, History, Homestay, Independent study, Russian language, Russian studies
Eligibility: *Level:* sophs, jrs, srs, adults *Requires:* 2.5 GPA, some Russian useful *Age:* min 18
Credit: *Undergrad:* 6 *Grad:* none *Doc:* transcript
Instruction: *In:* English, Russian *Format:* independent study, lang study, lecture, seminar, study tour *Students:* mainly host country
Costs: $3,500 *incl* tuition, housing, some meals, intl airfare, insurance, fees, excursions, books/materials *Nonrefundable fee*
Housing: *Arr by pgm:* homestay
Deadline: May 1
Other info: *US accredited sponsor:* yes *Began:* 1997 *Orient:* abroad (2 days) *Activities:* excursions, program travel, cultural events *Misc:* Faculty dir. May contact former participants. *URL:* http://www.brockport.edu/study_abroad
Contact: Dr John J Perry, Dir, Intl Educ, SUNY Coll at Brockport, 350 New Campus Dr, Brockport NY 14420 *Ph:* 800-298 7869; 716-395 2119 *Fax:* 716-637 3218 *E-mail:* jperry@brockport.edu

---

SAINT PETERSBURG

0416
AMERICAN INSTITUTE FOR FOREIGN STUDY (AIFS)
Saint Petersburg State Polytechnic University
Site: Russia: St Petersburg
Dates: 5 wks, Jun 7-Jul 17
Subjects: Art history, Political science/politics, Russian language, Sociology
Eligibility: *Level:* fresh, sophs, jrs, srs, grads, adults, precoll *Requires:* 2.0 GPA
Credit: *Undergrad:* avail *Grad:* none *Doc:* transcript
Instruction: *In:* English *Format:* lang study, lecture *Students:* mainly US
Costs: $4,299 *incl* tuition, housing, all meals, intl airfare, excursions
Housing: *Sponsor assists:* residence halls
Deadline: Mar 15
Other info: *US accredited sponsor:* no *Began:* 1989 *Orient:* abroad *Activities:* excursions, cultural events *Misc:* Resident dir. May contact former participants. *Financial aid:* scholarships *URL:* http://www.aifsabroad.com
Contact: Solandy Meza, Coll Div, AIFS, River Plaza, 9 W Broad St, Stamford CT 06902 *Ph:* 800-727 2437 ext 5163 *E-mail:* college.info@aifs.com ▲

0417
BOWLING GREEN STATE UNIVERSITY
Summer Russian Language and Culture
Site: Russia: St Petersburg *Host inst:* St Petersburg State Univ
Dates: About May 17-Jun 24
Subjects: Arts, Homestay, Humanities, Russian language, Russian studies
Eligibility: *Level:* sophs, jrs, srs, grads, adults, teachers *Age:* min 18
Credit: *Undergrad:* 6-9 *Grad:* 4-6 *Doc:* certificate
Instruction: *In:* English, Russian *Format:* directed field study, lang study, lecture *Students:* mainly US
Costs: $3,050-$3,747 *incl* tuition, housing, all meals, intl airfare, fees, excursions, books/materials, railpass
Housing: *Arr by pgm:* homestay
Deadline: Apr 1

Other info: *US accredited sponsor:* yes *Began:* 1992 *Orient:* in US & abroad *Activities:* excursions, field trips, cultural events *URL:* http://www.bgsu.edu/departments/greal
Contact: Dr Irina Stakhanova, German, Russian & East Asian Langs, Bowling Green State Univ, Bowling Green OH 43403-0219 *Ph:* 419-372 7135 *Fax:* 419-372 2571 *E-mail:* irina@bgnet.bgsu.edu
Or Contact: Dr Timothy Pogacar, German, Russian & East Asian Langs, Bowling Green State Univ, Bowling Green OH 43403-0219 *Ph:* 419-372 2268 *Fax:* 419-372 2571 *E-mail:* pogacar@bgnet.bgsu.edu

---

0418
COUNCIL ON INTERNATIONAL EDUCATIONAL EXCHANGE (COUNCIL)
International Faculty Development Seminars-Russia
Site: Russia: St Petersburg *Host inst:* European Univ of St Petersburg
Dates: 8 days, Jun
Subjects: Art
Eligibility: *Level:* teachers, professionals *Requires:* must be full-time faculty at 2-yr or 4-yr inst
Credit: *Undergrad:* avail *Grad:* none
Instruction: *In:* English *Format:* lecture, seminar *Students:* mainly US
Costs: $1,995 *incl* tuition, housing, some meals, fees, excursions, books/materials, ITIC, train in Russia
Housing: *Arr by pgm:* hotels
Deadline: Mar 15
Other info: *US accredited sponsor:* no *Began:* 1992 *Orient:* abroad *Activities:* excursions, field trips, cultural events *Misc:* Seminar title: Art Treasures of the Romanovs at the Hermitage Museum. May contact former participants. *Financial aid:* scholarships *URL:* http://www.ciee.org/ifds
Contact: Jennifer Ley, Council, 633 3rd Ave, New York NY 10017 *Ph:* 212-822 2747 *Fax:* 212-822 2699 *E-mail:* ifds@ciee.org ▲

0419
DUKE UNIVERSITY
Duke in Russia
Site: Russia: St Petersburg *Host inst:* St Petersburg State Univ
Dates: Early May-mid-Jun
Subjects: Civilization/culture, Russian language (int)
Eligibility: *Level:* fresh, sophs, jrs, srs *Requires:* good acad standing, transcript, 2 sems coll Russian
Credit: *Undergrad:* 2 credits *Grad:* none *Doc:* transcript
Instruction: *In:* Russian *Format:* lang study, lecture *Students:* mainly US
Costs: $5,515 for 2 courses *incl* tuition, housing, all meals, intl airfare, excursions, visa
Housing: *Arr by pgm:* residence halls, apartments
Deadline: Feb 16
Other info: *US accredited sponsor:* yes *Began:* 1985 *Activities:* program travel *URL:* http://www.aas.duke.edu/study_abroad/
Contact: Study Abroad, Duke Univ, 121 Allen Bldg, Box 90057, Durham NC 27708-0057 *Ph:* 919-684 2174 *Fax:* 919-684 3083 *E-mail:* abroad@asdean.duke.edu
Or Contact: Prof Edna Andrews, Slavic Langs & Literatures, Duke Univ, 314 Langs Bldg, Box 90259, Durham NC 27708-0259 *Ph:* 919-660 3140 *Fax:* 919-660 3141

0420
EDUVACATIONS
Intensive Russian Language at All Levels
Site: Russia: St Petersburg
Dates: 1 wk or longer, yr-round
Subjects: Russian language (beg/int/adv)
Eligibility: *Level:* adults *Requires:* knowledge of Cyrillic alphabet *Age:* min 16
Credit: *Undergrad:* avail *Grad:* none *Doc:* certificate
Instruction: *In:* Russian *Format:* lang study, lecture *Students:* intl
Costs: Contact sponsor
Housing: *Arr by student*
Deadline: Contact sponsor
Other info: *US accredited sponsor:* no *Began:* 1992 *Activities:* excursions, field trips, program travel, cultural events *Misc:* May contact former participants. *URL:* http://www.eduvacations.com
Contact: Mary Ann Puglisi, eduVacations, 1431 21st St NW, Ste 302, Washington DC 20036 *Ph:* 202-857 8384 *Fax:* 202-463 8091

0421
LINGUA SERVICE WORLDWIDE
Intensive Language and Culture in Russia
Site: Russia: St Petersburg *Host inst:* Liden & Denz Lang Ctr, Saldi Lang Training, St Petersburg Technical Univ
Dates: 1 wk-1 yr, yr-round
Subjects: Civilization/culture, Russian language (beg/int/adv), Sociology
Eligibility: *Level:* adults
Credit: *Undergrad:* avail *Grad:* avail *Doc:* transcript, certificate
Instruction: *In:* Russian *Format:* lang study, lecture *Students:* intl
Costs: Contact sponsor
Housing: *Arr by pgm:* residence halls, hostels
Deadline: 45 days before pgm
Other info: *US accredited sponsor:* no *Orient:* abroad *Activities:* excursions, field trips *Misc:* May contact former participants. *URL:* http://www.linguaserviceworldwide.com
Contact: Dir, Lingua Svc Worldwide, 75 Prospect St, Ste 4, Huntington NY 11743 *Ph:* 800-394 5327; 631-424 0777 *Fax:* 631-271 3441 *E-mail:* itctravel@worldnet.att.net ▲

0422
NATIONAL REGISTRATION CENTER FOR STUDY ABROAD (NRCSA)
Liden and Denz Language Center
Site: Russia: St Petersburg *Host inst:* Liden & Denz Lang Ctr
Dates: 1 wk or longer, yr-round
Subjects: Homestay, Russian language
Eligibility: *Level:* adults
Credit: *Undergrad:* none *Grad:* none
Instruction: *In:* Russian *Format:* lang study *Students:* intl
Costs: $675 for 2 wks *incl* tuition, housing, some meals, insurance *Nonrefundable fee*
Housing: *Arr by pgm:* homestay
Deadline: Rolling admissions
Other info: *US accredited sponsor:* no *Activities:* field trips *Misc:* May contact former participants. *URL:* http://www.nrcsa.com
Contact: Reuel Zielke, NRCSA, 823 N 2nd St, #206, Milwaukee WI 53203 *Ph:* 414-278 0631 *Fax:* 414-271 8884 *E-mail:* info@nrcsa.com

---

0423
UNIVERSITY OF ILLINOIS AT URBANA-CHAMPAIGN
Illinois Programs Abroad: Summer in St Petersburg
Site: Russia: St Petersburg *Host inst:* St Petersburg State Univ
Dates: 8 wks, late May-late Jul
Subjects: Homestay, Literature, Russian language (int/adv), Russian studies
Eligibility: *Level:* sophs, jrs, srs, grads *Requires:* B avg, 1 yr Russian
Credit: *Undergrad:* 8 *Grad:* none *Doc:* transcript
Instruction: *In:* Russian *Format:* lang study, lecture *Students:* mainly US
Costs: Contact sponsor
Housing: *Arr by pgm:* apartments, homestay
Deadline: Mar 1
Other info: *US accredited sponsor:* yes *Began:* 1992 *Orient:* abroad *Activities:* excursions, field trips, program travel, cultural events *Misc:* Meals with homestay only. Unpaid internships. Financial aid for own students only. May contact former participants. *URL:* http://www.uiuc.edu/providers/ips/sao

Contact: Illinois Pgms Abroad, Univ of Illinois, 115 Intl Studies Bldg, 910 S Fifth St, Champaign IL 61820 *Ph:* 800-531 4404; 217-333 6168 *Fax:* 217-244 0249 *E-mail:* ipa@uiuc.edu

---

0424
UNIVERSITY OF KANSAS
Summer Language Institute: St Petersburg, Russia
Site: Russia: St Petersburg *Host inst:* Univ of St Petersburg
Dates: 5 wks, Jun 1-Jul 10
Subjects: Civilization/culture, Homestay, Russian language, Russian studies
Eligibility: *Level:* fresh, sophs, jrs, srs, grads *Requires:* 4 sems coll Russian or eqiv
Credit: *Undergrad:* 6 *Grad:* none
Instruction: *In:* Russian *Format:* lang study, lecture, study tour *Students:* mainly US
Costs: $2,600 *incl* tuition, housing, all meals, fees, excursions, visa *Nonrefundable fee*
Housing: *Arr by pgm:* homestay
Deadline: Rolling admissions
Other info: *US accredited sponsor:* yes *Began:* 1997 *Activities:* excursions, field trips, cultural events *Misc:* May contact former participants. *URL:* http://www.ukans.edu/~osa
Contact: Susan MacNally, Asst Dir, Study Abroad, Univ of Kansas, 108 Lippincott Hall, Lawrence KS 66045 *Ph:* 785-864 3742 *Fax:* 785-864 5040 *E-mail:* osa@ukans.edu ▲

0425
UNIVERSITY OF RICHMOND
Russian Language and Culture
Site: Russia: St Petersburg
Dates: 6 wks, May-Jun
Subjects: Arts, Civilization/culture, Ecology/environmental studies, Economics, Political science/politics, Russian language, Russian studies
Eligibility: *Level:* jrs, srs *Requires:* int Russian or equiv
Credit: *Undergrad:* 6 *Grad:* none *Doc:* transcript
Instruction: *In:* Russian *Format:* lang study, lecture *Students:* mainly US
Costs: About $3,850 *incl* tuition, housing, some meals, intl airfare, insurance, fees, excursions
Housing: *Sponsor assists:* homestay
Deadline: Rolling admissions
Other info: *US accredited sponsor:* yes *Began:* 1990 *Orient:* in US *Activities:* excursions, field trips, cultural events *Misc:* May contact former participants.
Contact: Prof Joe Troncale, Univ of Richmond, Richmond VA 23173 *Ph:* 804-289 8118 *Fax:* 804-379 3761 *E-mail:* jtroncal@richmond.edu
Or Contact: Jeanne Burkett, Univ of Richmond, Richmond VA 23173 *Ph:* 804-287 6835 *Fax:* 804-289 8138 *E-mail:* jburkett@richmond.edu

---

0426
UNIVERSITY OF ROCHESTER
Russian in Russia
Site: Russia: St Petersburg *Host inst:* St Petersburg Univ
Dates: 4 wks, late May-late Jun
Subjects: Russian language
Eligibility: *Level:* fresh, sophs, jrs, srs, adults
Credit: *Undergrad:* 6 *Grad:* none *Doc:* transcript
Instruction: *In:* Russian *Format:* lang study *Students:* mainly US
Costs: About $2,700 *incl* tuition, housing, all meals, fees, excursions
Housing: *Arr by pgm:* apartments
Deadline: Mar 15
Other info: *US accredited sponsor:* yes *Activities:* cultural events *URL:* http://www.rochester.edu/College/study-abroad/sa/global.html
Contact: Anne Lutkus, Modern Langs & Cultures, Univ of Rochester, Lattimore 403, Rochester NY 14627-0082 *Ph:* 716-275 2235 *E-mail:* adlt@mail.rochester.edu

---

TVER

0427
SUNY UNIVERSITY AT BUFFALO
Program on Russian Culture
Site: Russia: Tver *Host inst:* Tver State Univ
Dates: Jul 7-Aug 5
Subjects: Communications, Literature, Russian language, Russian studies
Eligibility: *Level:* fresh, sophs, jrs, srs, grads, adults, teachers, professionals *Requires:* 2.5 GPA *Age:* min 18
Credit: *Undergrad:* 6-7 *Grad:* 6-7 *Doc:* transcript
Instruction: *In:* English *Format:* lang study, lecture *Students:* mainly US
Costs: $2,500 *incl* tuition, housing, all meals, excursions
Housing: *Arr by pgm:* homestay
Deadline: May 15
Other info: *US accredited sponsor:* yes *Began:* 1993 *Orient:* in US & abroad *Activities:* field trips *Financial aid:* scholarships *URL:* http://www.buffalo.edu/studyabroad/
Contact: Dr Sandra J Flash, Dir, Study Abroad Pgms, SUNY Univ at Buffalo, 210 Talbert Hall, Buffalo NY 14260-1604 *Ph:* 716-6453912 *Fax:* 716-645 6197 *E-mail:* studyabroad@acsu.buffalo.edu

---

0428
TVER INTERCONTACT GROUP
Intensive Short/Medium Term Program
Site: Russia: Tver *Host inst:* Inst of Russian Lang & Culture
Dates: 1 wk or longer, yr-round
Subjects: Civilization/culture, History, Linguistics, Literature, Political science/politics, Russian language (beg/int/adv), Russian studies
Eligibility: *Level:* adults *Age:* min 16, max 70, avg 20
Credit: *Undergrad:* none *Grad:* none *Doc:* certificate
Instruction: *In:* Russian *Format:* internship, lang study, lecture, seminar *Students:* intl
Costs: $195 per wk *incl* tuition, housing, some meals, fees, excursions, books/materials
Housing: *Arr by pgm:* apartments, homestay
Deadline: None
Other info: *US accredited sponsor:* no *Began:* 1995 *In coop with:* Tver State Univ *Activities:* excursions, cultural events, sports *Misc:* May contact former participants. *URL:* http://www.volga.net
Contact: Dr Marina Oborina, Tver InterContact Group, Central Post Off, PO Box 0565, 170000 Tver, Russia *E-mail:* infodesk@potman.ru
Or Contact: Anne Dwyer, Tver InterContact Group, Central Post Off, PO Box 0565, 170000 Tver, Russia *E-mail:* inforuss@postman.ru

---

0429
TVER INTERCONTACT GROUP
Summer School of Russian Language and Area Studies in Tver
Site: Russia: Tver *Host inst:* Inst of Russian Lang & Culture
Dates: 2-12 wks, Jun 18 -Sep 8
Subjects: Civilization/culture, History, Linguistics, Literature, Political science/politics, Russian language (beg/int/adv), Russian studies
Eligibility: *Level:* adults *Age:* min 16, max 70, avg 20
Credit: *Undergrad:* none *Grad:* none *Doc:* certificate *Transfer credit through:* Western Maryland Coll
Instruction: *In:* Russian *Format:* internship, lang study, lecture, seminar *Students:* intl
Costs: $195 per wk *incl* tuition, housing, some meals, fees, excursions, books/materials
Housing: *Arr by pgm:* apartments, homestay
Deadline: None
Other info: *US accredited sponsor:* no *Began:* 1995 *In coop with:* Tver State Univ *Activities:* excursions, cultural events, sports *Misc:* May contact former

participants. *URL:* http://www.volga.net
Contact: Dr Marina Oborina, Tver InterContact Group, PO Box 0565, Central Post Off, Tver 170000, Russia *E-mail:* infodesk@postman.ru
Or Contact: Anne Dwyer, Tver InterContact Group, PO Box 0565, Central Post Off, Tver 170000, Russia *E-mail:* inforuss@postman.ru

---

0430
TVER INTERCONTACT GROUP
Winter School of Russian Language and Culture
Site: Russia: Tver *Host inst:* Inst of Russian Lang & Culture
Dates: 6 wks, Jan 4-Feb 22
Subjects: Civilization/culture, History, Linguistics, Literature, Political science/politics, Russian language (beg/int/adv), Russian studies
Eligibility: *Level:* adults *Age:* min 16, max 70, avg 20
Credit: *Undergrad:* avail *Grad:* avail *Doc:* certificate *Transfer credit through:* Western Maryland Coll
Instruction: *In:* Russian *Format:* lang study, lecture, seminar *Students:* intl
Costs: $195 per wk *incl* tuition, housing, some meals, fees, excursions, books/materials
Housing: *Arr by pgm:* apartments, homestay
Deadline: None
Other info: *US accredited sponsor:* no *Began:* 1995 *In coop with:* Tver State Univ *Activities:* excursions, cultural events, sports *Misc:* May contact former participants. *URL:* http://www.volga.net
Contact: Dr Marina Oborina, Tver InterContact Group, PO Box 0565, Central Post Off, Tver 170000, Russia *E-mail:* infodesk@postman.ru
Or Contact: Anne Dwyer, Tver InterContact Group, PO Box 0565, Central Post Off, Tver 170000, Russia *E-mail:* inforuss@postman.ru

---

VLADIMIR

0431
ILLINOIS STATE UNIVERSITY
Crime and Criminal Justice in Russia
Site: Russia: Vladimir
Dates: 2 wks, May 12-26
Subjects: Criminal justice
Eligibility: *Level:* sophs, jrs, srs, adults, professionals *Requires:* 2.5 GPA, previous study in field
Credit: *Undergrad:* 3 *Grad:* none *Doc:* transcript
Instruction: *In:* English *Format:* study tour *Students:* mainly US
Costs: $3,400 *incl* tuition, housing, all meals, intl airfare, insurance, fees, excursions, ISIC *Nonrefundable fee*
Housing: *Arr by pgm:* hotels
Deadline: Mar 1
Other info: *US accredited sponsor:* yes *Orient:* in US (1 day) *Activities:* excursions, field trips, cultural events *URL:* http://www.its.ilstu.edu/intlstudies/
Contact: Dr Fran Morn, Illinois State Univ, Box 5250, Normal IL 61790-5250 *Ph:* 309-438 7853
Or Contact: Intl Studies & Pgms, Illinois State Univ, Campus Box 6120, Normal IL 61790-6120 *Ph:* 309-638 5365 *Fax:* 309-438 3987 *E-mail:* oisp@ilstu.edu

---

0432
ILLINOIS STATE UNIVERSITY
Russia Educational Exchange Program
Site: Russia: Vladimir *Host inst:* Vladimir State Univ
Dates: 2 wks, May 12-26
Subjects: Civilization/culture, Homestay, Independent study, Industrial studies, Russian studies, Technology
Eligibility: *Level:* sophs, jrs, srs, grads, adults *Requires:* 2.5 GPA
Credit: *Undergrad:* 3 *Grad:* 3
Instruction: *In:* English *Format:* independent study *Students:* mainly US
Costs: $2,300 *incl* tuition, housing, all meals, intl airfare, insurance, fees, excursions, ISIC *Nonrefundable fee*
Housing: *Arr by pgm:* homestay
Deadline: Mar 1
Other info: *US accredited sponsor:* yes *Orient:* avail avail (1 day) *Activities:* excursions, field trips, cultural events *URL:* http://www.its.ilstu.edu/intlstudies/
Contact: Paul Brauchle, Illinois State Univ, Campus Box 5100, Normal IL 61790-5100 *Ph:* 309-438 2696
Or Contact: Intl Studies & Pgms, Illinois State Univ, Campus Box 6120, Normal IL 61790-6120 *Ph:* 309-438 5365 *Fax:* 309-438 3987 *E-mail:* oisp@ilstu.edu

---

0433
ILLINOIS STATE UNIVERSITY
Summer Russia Program
Site: Russia: Vladimir *Host inst:* Vladimir Pedagogical State Univ
Dates: 2 wks, May
Subjects: Field study, Geography, Geology, History, Homestay, Independent study
Eligibility: *Level:* sophs, jrs, srs, grads *Requires:* 2.5 GPA, previous study in field, history majors preferred
Credit: *Undergrad:* 3 *Grad:* 3 *Doc:* transcript
Instruction: *In:* English *Format:* directed field study, independent study, lecture *Students:* mainly US
Costs: $2,000 *incl* tuition, housing, all meals, intl airfare, insurance, fees, excursions
Housing: *Arr by pgm:* residence halls, homestay
Deadline: Mar 1
Other info: *US accredited sponsor:* yes *Orient:* in US *Activities:* excursions, field trips, program travel *URL:* http://www.its.ilstu.edu/intlstudies/
Contact: Dr Shannon O'Lear, Illinois State Univ, Campus Box 4400, Normal IL 61790-4400 *Ph:* 309-438 8120
Or Contact: Intl Studies, Illinois State Univ, Campus Box 6120, Normal IL 61790-6120 *Ph:* 309-438 5365 *Fax:* 309-438 3987 *E-mail:* oisp@ilstu.edu

---

VLADIVOSTOK

0434
UNIVERSITY OF HAWAII AT MANOA
Russian Language and Culture in Vladivostok
Site: Russia: Vladivostok *Host inst:* Far Eastern State Univ
Dates: 6 wks, mid-May-late Jun
Subjects: Russian language (int/adv)
Eligibility: *Level:* sophs, jrs, srs *Requires:* 3.0 GPA, 1 yr coll Russian
Credit: *Undergrad:* 6 *Grad:* none *Doc:* transcript
Instruction: *In:* Russian *Format:* lang study, lecture *Students:* mainly US
Costs: $3,540 *incl* tuition, housing, some meals, intl airfare, insurance, excursions, books/materials *Nonrefundable fee*
Housing: *Arr by pgm:* residence halls
Deadline: Feb 17
Other info: *US accredited sponsor:* yes *Began:* 1990 *Orient:* in US & abroad (intensive lang study) *Activities:* excursions, field trips, cultural events *Misc:* UHM financial aid avail to eligible UHM students. *URL:* http://www2.hawaii.edu/study-abroad
Contact: Dir or Study Abroad Adviser, Study Abroad Ctr, Univ of Hawaii at Manoa, Moore Hall 115, 1890 East-West Rd, Honolulu HI 96822 *Ph:* 808-956 5143, 808-956 6958 *Fax:* 808-956 9319 *E-mail:* uhmsac@hawaii.edu

---

VOLGOGRAD

0435
PENNSYLVANIA STATE UNIVERSITY
Russian Language Studies
Site: Russia: Volgograd *Host inst:* Volgograd Pedagogical Univ
Dates: 5 wks, mid-Jun-late Jul
Subjects: Homestay, Russian language (int)

Eligibility: *Level:* sophs, jrs, srs, grads *Requires:* 2.5 GPA, 1 sem Russian
Credit: *Undergrad:* 8 *Grad:* none
Instruction: *In:* Russian *Format:* lang study, lecture *Students:* mainly US
Costs: Contact sponsor
Housing: *Arr by pgm:* homestay
Deadline: Apr 1
Other info: *US accredited sponsor:* yes *Began:* 1992 *Orient:* in US *Activities:* excursions *Misc:* May contact former participants. *Financial aid:* scholarships *URL:* http://www.cde.psu.edu/PSSEA/
Contact: Lori Benson, Conferences & Insts, Penn State Univ, University Park PA 16802 *Ph:* 814-863 5170 *Fax:* 814-863 5190 *E-mail:* conferenceinfo1@cde.psu.edu
Or Contact: Kristi Wormhoudt, Asst Dir, Educ Abroad Pgms, Penn State Univ, 222 Boucke Bldg, University Park PA 16802 *Ph:* 814-865 7681 *Fax:* 814-865 3336

Slovakia

MORE THAN ONE CITY

0436
COMENIUS UNIVERSITY
Intensive Summer Course of Slovak Language
Site: Slovakia: Bratislava, Kosice
Dates: 3 wks, Jul-Aug
Subjects: Slovak language
Eligibility: *Level:* adults *Age:* min 18
Credit: *Undergrad:* none *Grad:* none
Instruction: *In:* Slovak *Format:* lang study, lecture, practical training *Students:* intl
Costs: $500 *incl* tuition, housing, books/ materials
Housing: *Arr by pgm:* residence halls
Deadline: May 30
Other info: *US accredited sponsor:* no *Began:* 1960 *Orient:* avail (intensive lang study) *Activities:* excursions, field trips, program travel, cultural events, sports *Misc:* Pgm in Bratislava in July, Kosice in August. *URL:* http://www.uniba.sk/ujop
Contact: Lubica Gallova, Mgr, Inst for Lang & Acad Preparation, Comenius Univ, Soltesovej 4,, Bratislava, Slovak Republic 81108 *E-mail:* gallova@ujop.uniba.sk

Slovenia

LJUBLJANA

0437
LEHIGH UNIVERSITY
Lehigh in Slovenia
Site: Slovenia: Ljubljana *Host inst:* Univ of Ljubljana Ctr for Experimental Mechanics
Dates: Jun 3-Jul 7
Subjects: Engineering
Eligibility: *Level:* fresh, sophs, jrs, srs *Requires:* 2.0 GPA, previous study in field, engineering major
Credit: *Undergrad:* 6 *Grad:* none
Instruction: *In:* English *Format:* directed field study, practical training *Students:* mainly US
Costs: $3,400 *incl* tuition, housing, excursions *Nonrefundable fee*
Housing: *Arr by pgm:* residence halls
Deadline: Mar 1
Other info: *US accredited sponsor:* yes *Began:* 1997 *Orient:* abroad *Misc:* Students will work on research & development projects. May contact former participants. *URL:* http://www.Lehigh.edu/incis/~incis.html
Contact: Dr Sandi Smith, Dir, Study Abroad, Lehigh Univ, 5 E Packer Ave, Whitaker Lab 343, Bethlehem PA 18015 *Ph:* 610-758 3351 *Fax:* 610-758 5156 *E-mail:* incis@lehigh.edu

---

NOVA GORICA

0438
UNIVERSITY OF IOWA
Environmental Studies in Slovenia
Site: Slovenia: Nova Gorica *Host inst:* Sch of Environmental Scis
Dates: 3 wks, early Jun-late Jun
Subjects: Ecology/environmental studies, Field study
Eligibility: *Level:* srs, grads, professionals *Requires:* previous study in field *Age:* avg 24
Credit: *Undergrad:* 3 *Grad:* 3 *Doc:* transcript
Instruction: *In:* English *Format:* directed field study, seminar *Students:* mainly host country
Costs: About $900 *incl* tuition, housing, fees *Nonrefundable fee*
Housing: *Arr by pgm:* residence halls
Deadline: Apr 1
Other info: *US accredited sponsor:* yes *Began:* 1997 *Orient:* abroad (1 day) *Misc:* May contact former participants. *URL:* http://www.uiowa.edu/~uiabroad
Contact: Study Abroad, Univ of Iowa, 120 Intl Ctr, Iowa City IA 52245 *Ph:* 319-335 0353 *Fax:* 319-353 2021 *E-mail:* study-abroad@uiowa.edu

Ukraine

MORE THAN ONE CITY

0439
MICHIGAN STATE UNIVERSITY
In Search of a New Democracy
Site: Ukraine: Kiev, L'viv, Odessa
Dates: 4 wks, May-Jun
Subjects: Criminal justice, Homestay, Independent study, Social sciences
Eligibility: *Level:* fresh, sophs, jrs, srs *Requires:* 2.0 GPA *Age:* min 18
Credit: *Undergrad:* 7 *Grad:* none *Doc:* transcript
Instruction: *In:* English *Format:* independent study, lecture *Students:* mainly US
Costs: About $1,700 *incl* housing, most meals, insurance, excursions, ground transport *Nonrefundable fee*
Housing: *Arr by pgm:* homestay, hotels
Deadline: Mar 2
Other info: *US accredited sponsor:* yes *Began:* 1998 *Orient:* in US *Activities:* excursions, field trips, program travel, cultural events *Misc:* May contact former participants. *Financial aid:* scholarships *URL:* http://studyabroad.msu.edu
Contact: Cheryl Benner, Study Abroad, Michigan State Univ, 109 Intl Ctr, East Lansing MI 48824 *Ph:* 517-353 8920 *Fax:* 517-432 2082 *E-mail:* bennerc@msu.edu ▲

0440
PENNSYLVANIA STATE UNIVERSITY
Ukrainian Language and Cultural Studies
Site: Ukraine: various sites
Dates: 6 wks, mid-May-early Jul
Subjects: Civilization/culture, Homestay, Ukrainian language (beg/int/adv), Ukrainian studies
Eligibility: *Level:* fresh, sophs, jrs, srs, grads, adults, teachers, professionals *Requires:* 2.5 GPA
Credit: *Undergrad:* 8 *Grad:* 8
Instruction: *In:* English, Ukrainian *Format:* lang study, lecture, study tour *Students:* mainly US
Costs: Contact sponsor
Housing: *Arr by pgm:* residence halls, homestay
Deadline: Apr 1
Other info: *US accredited sponsor:* yes *Began:* 1994 *Orient:* in US *Activities:* excursions, field trips *Misc:* May contact former participants. *Financial aid:* scholarships
Contact: Lori Benson, Conferences & Insts, Penn State Univ, University Park PA 16802 *Ph:* 814-863 5170 *Fax:* 814-863 5190 *E-mail:* conferenceinfo1@cde.psu.edu
Or Contact: Kristi Wormhoudt, Asst Dir, Penn State Univ, 222 Boucke Bldg, University Park PA 16802 *Ph:* 814-865 7681 *Fax:* 814-865 3336

L'VIV

0441
UNIVERSITY OF KANSAS
Ukrainian Language and Area Studies
Site: Ukraine: L'viv *Host inst:* Ivan Franko Univ
Dates: 6 wks, mid-Jun-late Jul
Subjects: Area studies, Homestay, Independent study, Ukrainian language, Ukrainian studies
Eligibility: *Level:* jrs, srs, grads, adults *Requires:* previous study in field, 3 yrs coll Russian
Credit: *Undergrad:* 6 *Grad:* none *Doc:* transcript
Instruction: *In:* Ukrainian *Format:* independent study, lang study, lecture, study tour *Students:* mainly US
Costs: $1,925 *incl* tuition, housing, all meals, fees, excursions
Housing: *Arr by pgm:* homestay
Deadline: Rolling admissions
Other info: *US accredited sponsor:* yes *Activities:* excursions, field trips *URL:* http://www.ukans.edu/~osa
Contact: Susan MacNally, Asst Dir, Study Abroad, Univ of Kansas, 108 Lippincott Hall, Lawrence KS 66045 *Ph:* 785-864 3742 *Fax:* 785-864 5040 *E-mail:* osa@ukans.edu ▲

Western Europe

More Than One Country

0442
AMERICAN INSTITUTE FOR FOREIGN STUDY (AIFS) and **RICHMOND, THE AMERICAN INTERNATIONAL UNIVERSITY IN LONDON**
European Art and Architecture
Site: Austria: Salzburg; Belgium: Bruges; England: London; France: Paris; Germany: Munich; Italy: Rome; Netherlands: Amsterdam
Dates: 4 wks, Jul 2-29
Subjects: Architecture, Art, Civilization/culture
Eligibility: *Level:* fresh, sophs, jrs, srs, grads, adults, precoll *Requires:* 2.0 GPA
Credit: *Undergrad:* avail *Grad:* none *Doc:* transcript
Instruction: *In:* English *Format:* lecture, study tour *Students:* mainly US
Costs: $4,999 *incl* tuition, housing, some meals, intl airfare, excursions
Housing: *Arr by pgm:* residence halls, hotels
Deadline: Mar 15
Other info: *US accredited sponsor:* yes *Began:* 1991 *Orient:* abroad *Activities:* excursions *Misc:* May contact former participants. *Financial aid:* scholarships *URL:* http://www.aifsabroad.com
Contact: Solandy Meza, Coll Div, AIFS, River Plaza, 9 W Broad St, Stamford CT 06902 *Ph:* 800-727 2437 ext 5163 *E-mail:* college.info@aifs.com ▲

0443
AMERICAN INSTITUTE FOR FOREIGN STUDY (AIFS) and **RICHMOND, THE AMERICAN INTERNATIONAL UNIVERSITY IN LONDON**
International Business and Finance in Europe
Site: Belgium, England, France, Germany, Luxembourg, Spain
Dates: 4 wks, Jun 21-Jul 19
Subjects: European Union, Finance, International marketing, Political science/politics
Eligibility: *Level:* sophs, jrs, srs, grads, adults *Requires:* 2.0 GPA
Credit: *Undergrad:* avail *Grad:* none *Doc:* transcript
Instruction: *In:* English *Format:* lecture *Students:* intl
Costs: $4,699 *incl* tuition, housing, some meals, intl airfare
Housing: *Arr by pgm:* residence halls, hotels
Deadline: Mar 15
Other info: *US accredited sponsor:* yes *Began:* 1984 *Activities:* program travel *Misc:* May contact former participants. *Financial aid:* scholarships *URL:* http://www.aifsabroad.com
Contact: Solandy Meza, Coll Div, AIFS, River Plaza, 9 W Broad St, Stamford CT 06902 *Ph:* 800-727 2437 ext 5163 *E-mail:* college.info@aifs.com ▲

0444
CENTER FOR CULTURAL INTERCHANGE
Language School Programs
Site: France: Antibes, Paris; Germany: Berlin, Hamburg, Munich; Italy: Florence; Spain: Barcelona, El Puerto, Madrid, others *Host inst:* Colon, Estudio Intl Sampere, Scuola Linguaviva
Dates: 2-12 wks, yr-round
Subjects: French language (beg/int/adv), German language (beg/int/adv), Homestay, Italian language (beg/int/adv), Spanish language (beg/int/adv)
Eligibility: *Level:* adults, precoll *Requires:* 3.0 GPA, beg-adv host country lang *Age:* min 15, avg 22
Credit: *Undergrad:* avail *Grad:* none *Doc:* certificate
Instruction: *In:* French, German, Italian, Spanish *Format:* lang study *Students:* intl
Costs: About $2,200 per mo *incl* tuition, housing, some meals, insurance, fees, books/materials, activities *Nonrefundable fee*
Housing: *Arr by pgm:* homestay
Deadline: 6 wks before pgm
Other info: *US accredited sponsor:* no *Began:* 1985 *Orient:* in US & abroad *Activities:* excursions, field trips, cultural events, sports *Misc:* May contact former participants. *URL:* http://www.cci-exchange.com
Contact: Karen Hindhede, Pgm Dir, Ctr for Cultural Interchange, 17 N 2nd Ave, St Charles IL 60174 *Ph:* 888-227 6231; 630-377 2272 *Fax:* 630-377 2307 *E-mail:* info@cci-exchange.com

---

0445
DICKINSON COLLEGE
Classics Immersion Programs
Site: Greece: Crete, various sites on mainland; Italy: Naples, Rome
Dates: 4 wks, late May-late Jun
Subjects: Classical studies, Latin language (adv), Literature
Eligibility: *Level:* fresh, sophs *Requires:* 2 yrs coll Latin or Greek
Credit: *Undergrad:* 4 *Grad:* none
Instruction: *In:* English *Format:* lang study, lecture *Students:* mainly US
Costs: About $4,200 *incl* tuition, housing, all meals, intl airfare, fees, excursions
Housing: *Arr by pgm:* residence halls
Deadline: Mar 1
Other info: *US accredited sponsor:* yes *Began:* 1984 *Orient:* in US *Activities:* excursions *Misc:* Two immersion pgms offered on a 2-yr cycle. *URL:* http://www.

dickinson.edu/departments/ocs/summer.html
Contact: Global Educ, Dickinson Coll, PO Box 1773, Carlisle PA 17013-2896 *Ph:* 717-245 1341 *Fax:* 717-245 1688 *E-mail:* ocs@dickinson.edu

---

0446
DUKE UNIVERSITY
Duke in Flanders and the Netherlands
Site: Belgium: Flanders; Netherlands
Dates: Late Jun-early Aug
Subjects: Art history, Civilization/culture, History
Eligibility: *Level:* fresh, sophs, jrs, srs, grads *Requires:* good acad standing, transcript
Credit: *Undergrad:* 2 credits *Grad:* 6-8 sem hrs *Doc:* transcript
Instruction: *In:* English *Format:* lecture, seminar, study tour *Students:* mainly US
Costs: $5,475 *incl* tuition, housing, some meals, excursions
Housing: *Arr by pgm:* hotels
Deadline: Feb 16
Other info: *US accredited sponsor:* yes *Orient:* in US *Activities:* excursions, cultural events *URL:* http://www.aas.duke.edu/study_abroad/
Contact: Prof Hans J Van Miegroet, Art & Art History, Duke Univ, 112 East Duke Bldg, Box 90764, Durham NC 27708-0764 *Ph:* 919-684 2499 *Fax:* 919-684 4398 *E-mail:* hvm@acpub.duke.edu
Or Contact: Study Abroad, Duke Univ, 121 Allen Bldg, Box 90057, Durham NC 27708-0057 *Ph:* 919-684 2174 *Fax:* 919-684 3083 *E-mail:* abroad@asdean.duke.edu

---

0447
EDUVACATIONS
Arts Workshops and Tours
Site: France, Greece, Italy
Dates: 1 wk or longer, yr-round
Subjects: Art restoration, Ceramics/pottery, Creative writing, Drawing, Jewelry/jewelry-making, Languages, Painting, Photography, Sculpture, Textiles
Eligibility: *Level:* adults *Age:* min 16
Credit: *Undergrad:* avail *Grad:* none *Doc:* certificate
Instruction: *In:* English, French, Italian *Format:* art studio, directed field study, independent study, lecture, practical training, study tour, workshop *Students:* intl
Costs: Contact sponsor
Housing: *Arr by pgm:* apartments, homestay, hotels, villas, restored farmhouses
Deadline: Contact sponsor
Other info: *US accredited sponsor:* no *Activities:* excursions, field trips, cultural events *Misc:* May contact former participants. *URL:* http://www.eduvacations.com
Contact: Mary Ann Puglisi, eduVacations, 1431 21st St NW, Ste 302, Washington DC 20036 *Ph:* 202-857 8384 *Fax:* 202-463 8091

0448
EDUVACATIONS
Cooking Courses in France and Italy
Site: France, Italy
Dates: 1 wk or longer, yr-round
Subjects: Culinary arts, French language (beg/int/adv), Italian language (beg/int/adv)
Eligibility: *Level:* adults *Age:* min 16
Credit: *Undergrad:* none *Grad:* none *Doc:* certificate
Instruction: *In:* English, French, Italian *Format:* lang study, practical training, workshop *Students:* intl
Costs: Contact sponsor
Housing: *Arr by pgm:* apartments, homestay, hotels, farmhouse, French chateau
Deadline: Contact sponsor
Other info: *US accredited sponsor:* no *Activities:* excursions, field trips, cultural events *Misc:* Walking & cooking tour. Non-participating partners of participants welcome. May contact former participants. *URL:* http://www.eduvacations.com
Contact: Mary Ann Puglisi, eduVacations, 1431 21st St NW, Ste 302, Washington DC 20036 *Ph:* 202-857 8384 *Fax:* 202-463 8091

0449
EN FAMILLE OVERSEAS
Language Study Holidays
Site: France, Germany, Spain
Dates: 1 wk or longer, yr-round
Subjects: French language, German language, Spanish language
Eligibility: *Level:* adults *Requires:* 1 yr lang study recommended *Age:* min 13, avg 18
Credit: *Undergrad:* none *Grad:* none
Instruction: *In:* French, German, Spanish *Format:* lang study *Students:* intl
Costs: UK 430 per wk *incl* tuition, housing, all meals *Nonrefundable fee*
Housing: *Arr by pgm:* homestay
Deadline: 4 wks before pgm
Other info: *US accredited sponsor:* no *Began:* 1945 *Orient:* abroad (7 days or longer, intensive lang study) *Activities:* excursions, cultural events
Contact: Mrs S D Baxendale or Mrs J Tourell, En Famille Overseas, 60B Maltravers St, Arundel BN18 9BG, UK

0450
FASHION INSTITUTE OF TECHNOLOGY
European Cosmetics and Fragrance Industry
Site: England: London; France: Grasse, Paris
Dates: 3 wks, end-May - Jun
Subjects: Commercial art, Industrial studies, International marketing, Marketing, Retailing
Eligibility: *Level:* fresh, sophs, jrs, srs *Requires:* interview by faculty member teaching course *Age:* min 18
Credit: *Undergrad:* 3 *Grad:* none *Doc:* transcript
Instruction: *In:* English *Format:* study tour *Students:* mainly US
Costs: About $4,300 for NY residents, $4,795 for others *incl* tuition, housing, some meals, intl airfare, fees, excursions, railpass
Housing: *Arr by pgm:* hotels
Deadline: Mar 3
Other info: *US accredited sponsor:* yes *Began:* 1992 *Orient:* in US *Activities:* excursions, field trips, program travel *Misc:* May contact former participants. *URL:* http://www.fitnyc.suny.edu
Contact: Georgianna Appignani, Dir, Intl Educ, FIT, 7th Ave at 27th St, New York NY 10001-5992 *Ph:* 212-217 7633 *Fax:* 212-217 7010
Or Contact: Carole De Santis, Coord, FIT, 7th Ave at 27th St, New York NY 10001-5992 *Ph:* 212-217 7633 *Fax:* 212-217 7010 *E-mail:* desantca@sfitva.cc.fitsuny.edu

---

0451
FASHION INSTITUTE OF TECHNOLOGY
Fashion in France and Italy
Site: France: Paris; Italy: Florence, Milan, Rome, Venice
Dates: 3 wks, late May-Jun 20
Subjects: Fashion design
Eligibility: *Level:* fresh, sophs, jrs, srs, grads, adults, professionals *Requires:* interview by faculty member teaching course *Age:* min 18
Credit: *Undergrad:* 3 *Grad:* none *Doc:* transcript
Instruction: *In:* English *Format:* study tour *Students:* mainly US
Costs: About $5,345 for NY residents, $5,750 for others *incl* tuition, housing, some meals, intl airfare, fees, excursions
Housing: *Arr by pgm:* hotels
Deadline: Mar 3
Other info: *US accredited sponsor:* yes *Began:* 1978 *Orient:* in US *Activities:* excursions, field trips, program travel *Misc:* Visits to couture & ready-to-wear establishments, accessory houses, fabric mills, design studios & museums. May contact former participants. *URL:* http://www.fitnyc.suny.edu

Contact: Georgianna Appignani, Dir, Intl Educ, FIT, 7th Ave at 27th St, New York NY 10001-5992 *Ph:* 212-217 7633 *Fax:* 212-217 7010
Or Contact: Carole De Santis, Coord, Intl Educ, FIT, 7th Ave at 27th St, New York NY 10001-5992 *Ph:* 212-217 7633 *Fax:* 212-217 7010 *E-mail:* desantca@sfitva.cc.fitsuny.edu

---

0452
FASHION INSTITUTE OF TECHNOLOGY
International Buying and Marketing
Site: England: London; France: Paris; Italy: Milan, Venice
Dates: 3 wks, Jun 1-23
Subjects: European studies, Fashion merchandising, International business, International marketing, International shipping
Eligibility: *Level:* fresh, sophs, jrs, srs *Requires:* interview by faculty member teaching course *Age:* min 18
Credit: *Undergrad:* 3 *Grad:* none *Doc:* transcript
Instruction: *In:* English *Format:* study tour *Students:* mainly US
Costs: About $4,350 for NY residents, $4,755 for others *incl* tuition, housing, some meals, intl airfare, fees, excursions
Housing: *Arr by pgm:* hotels
Deadline: Mar 3
Other info: *US accredited sponsor:* yes *Began:* 1972 *Orient:* in US *Activities:* excursions, field trips, program travel *Misc:* May contact former participants. *URL:* http://www.fitnyc.suny.edu
Contact: Georgianna Appignani, Dir, Intl Educ, FIT, 7th Ave at 27th St, New York NY 10001-5992 *Ph:* 212-217 7633 *Fax:* 212-217 7010
Or Contact: Carole De Santis, Coord, FIT, 7th Ave at 27th St, New York NY 10001-5992 *Ph:* 212-217 7633 *Fax:* 212-217 7010 *E-mail:* desantca@sfitva.cc.fitsuny.edu

---

0453
FLORIDA INTERNATIONAL UNIVERSITY
Art Education in Plein Air
Site: France: Giverny, Honfleur, Mont St Michel, Paris, Rouen, Versailles;Netherlands: Amsterdam
Dates: 16 days, Jun 17-Jul 2
Subjects: Art, Art education
Eligibility: *Level:* jrs, srs, grads, adults, teachers, professionals *Requires:* previous study in field, FIU seminar
Credit: *Undergrad:* avail *Grad:* none *Doc:* transcript
Instruction: *In:* English *Format:* art studio, directed field study *Students:* US & intl
Costs: $2,985 *incl* housing, some meals, intl airfare, fees, excursions, books/materials, art supplies *Nonrefundable fee*
Housing: *Arr by pgm:* hotels
Deadline: May 15
Other info: *US accredited sponsor:* yes *Began:* 1998 *Orient:* avail avail *Activities:* excursions, field trips, program travel, cultural events, sports *Misc:* May contact former participants. *URL:* http://www.fiu.edu/~intered
Contact: Intl Studies, Florida Intl Univ, 11200 SW 8th St, DM 300B, Miami FL 33199 *Ph:* 305-348 1913, 305-348 1918 *Fax:* 305-348 1941 *E-mail:* intered@fiu.edu

---

0454
GEORGE MASON UNIVERSITY
United States-European Relations
Site: England: London; France: Paris; Netherlands: Amsterdam
Dates: 2 wks, Dec 26-Jan 10
Subjects: Business/management, European Union, International relations, Security issues, Social sciences, Trade
Eligibility: *Level:* sophs, jrs, srs, grads, adults, teachers, professionals *Requires:* 2.25 GPA, 3.0 for grads *Age:* min 18
Credit: *Undergrad:* 3 *Grad:* 3 *Doc:* transcript
Instruction: *In:* English *Format:* directed field study, practical training, seminar, study tour *Students:* mainly US
Costs: About $3,800 for VA residents, $4,400 for others *incl* tuition, housing, intl airfare, excursions, ISIC, travel insurance *Nonrefundable fee*
Housing: *Arr by pgm:* hotels
Deadline: Oct 16
Other info: *US accredited sponsor:* yes *Began:* 1996 *Orient:* in US *Activities:* excursions, field trips, program travel, cultural events, sports *Misc:* Min 12 students for pgm. May contact former participants. *URL:* http://www.gmu.edu/departments/cge
Contact: Ctr for Global Educ, George Mason Univ, Johnson Ctr, Rm 235, 4400 University Dr, Fairfax VA 22030-4444 *Ph:* 703-993 2154 *Fax:* 703-993 2153 *E-mail:* cge@gmu.edu

---

0455
GEORGIA INSTITUTE OF TECHNOLOGY
Modern Architecture and the Modern City: 1900-1997
Site: France, Germany, Netherlands
Dates: May 15-Aug 3
Subjects: Architectural history, Architecture, Urban planning, Urban studies
Eligibility: *Level:* srs, grads *Requires:* previous study in field
Credit: *Undergrad:* avail *Grad:* 12 *Doc:* transcript
Instruction: *In:* English *Format:* lecture, seminar, study tour *Students:* mainly US
Costs: $3,750 for GA residents, $4,000 for others *incl* tuition, housing, fees, excursions *Nonrefundable fee*
Housing: *Arr by pgm:* apartments, hotels
Deadline: Apr 1
Other info: *US accredited sponsor:* yes *Orient:* in US *Activities:* field trips, program travel, cultural events
Contact: Dr Richard Dagenhart, Coll of Architecture, Georgia Inst of Technology, Atlanta GA 30332-0155 *Ph:* 404-894 2992 *Fax:* 404-894 0572 *E-mail:* richard.dagenhart@arch.gatech.edu
Or Contact: Intl Educ, Georgia Inst of Technology, J S Coon Bldg, Ste 203, Atlanta GA 30332-0284 *Ph:* 404-894 7475 *Fax:* 404-894 9682 *E-mail:* study.abroad@gatech.edu

---

0456
GEORGIA INSTITUTE OF TECHNOLOGY
Oxford Summer Program
Site: England: Oxford; various countries in Europe
Dates: Jun 5-Aug 14
Subjects: Architecture, Electrical/electronic engineering, English, History, International relations, Mechanical engineering, Music
Eligibility: *Level:* sophs, jrs, srs, grads *Requires:* good acad standing
Credit: *Undergrad:* 12 *Grad:* none *Doc:* transcript
Instruction: *In:* English *Format:* study tour *Students:* mainly US
Costs: $5,132 for GA residents, $5,382 for others *incl* tuition, housing, some meals, excursions *Nonrefundable fee*
Housing: *Arr by pgm:* residence halls, hotels
Deadline: Contact sponsor
Other info: *US accredited sponsor:* yes *Began:* 1993 *In coop with:* Worcester Coll *Activities:* excursions, field trips *Misc:* 1 wk in Atlanta, 6 wks in Oxford, 3 wks in various European cities. May contact former participants. *URL:* http://www.ece.gatech.edu/academic/oxford
Contact: Oxford Pgm Coord, Georgia Inst of Technology, Van Leer E 396, Atlanta GA 30332-0250 *Ph:* 404-894 1794 *Fax:* 404-894 4641 *E-mail:* oxford@ece.gatech.edu

---

0457
INTERNATIONAL CAMPUS CONSORTIUM and **THUNDERBIRD, THE AMERICAN GRADUATE SCHOOL OF INTERNATIONAL MANAGEMENT**
Winterim in Europe
Site: France: Archamps; Spain: Barcelona; Switzerland: Geneva

Dates: 3 wks, Jan 3-21
Subjects: Business/management, International studies
Eligibility: *Level:* grads *Requires:* 3.0 GPA
Credit: *Undergrad:* none *Grad:* 3 *Doc:* transcript
Instruction: *In:* English *Format:* lecture *Students:* intl
Costs: $2,555 *incl* tuition, insurance, fees
Housing: *Sponsor assists:* hotels
Deadline: Contact sponsor
Other info: *US accredited sponsor:* yes *Orient:* abroad *Activities:* field trips *Misc:* Special econ zones in the European econ area. *Financial aid:* scholarships *URL:* http://www.t-bird.edu
Contact: *See Index II for Members* Dr Earl Gibbons, Assoc VP, Overseas Pgms, Thunderbird, 15249 N 59th Ave, Glendale AZ 85306 *Ph:* 602-978 7252 *Fax:* 602-978 7419 *E-mail:* gibbonse@t-bird.edu
Or Contact: Diane Hayton, Coord, Overseas Pgms, Thunderbird, 15249 N 59th Ave, Glendale AZ 85306 *Ph:* 602-978 7252 *Fax:* 602-978 7419 *E-mail:* haytond@t-bird.edu

---

0458
KENTUCKY INSTITUTE FOR INTERNATIONAL STUDIES (KIIS)
Athens/Rome
Site: Greece: Athens; Italy: Rome
Dates: 5 wks, late May-early Jul
Subjects: Classical studies, History, Literature
Eligibility: *Level:* fresh, sophs, jrs, srs, grads, adults, teachers, professionals *Requires:* 2.0 GPA, good acad standing, transcript, faculty recommendation *Age:* min 18
Credit: *Undergrad:* 3-6 *Grad:* 3-6 *Doc:* transcript *Transfer credit through:* Murray State Univ
Instruction: *In:* English *Format:* independent study, lecture, study tour *Students:* mainly US
Costs: About $3,530 for students at member schs, $3,830 for others *incl* tuition, housing, some meals, intl airfare, fees, excursions, ISIC *Nonrefundable fee*
Housing: *Arr by pgm:* hotels
Deadline: Feb 15 ($100 late fee)
Other info: *US accredited sponsor:* yes *Began:* 1998 *Orient:* in US & abroad *Activities:* excursions, cultural events *Financial aid:* scholarships *URL:* http://www.kiis.org
Contact: *See Index II for Members* Dr J Milton Grimes, Exec Dir, KIIS, Murray State Univ, PO Box 9, Murray KY 42071 *Ph:* 270-762 3091 *Fax:* 270-762 3434 *E-mail:* kiismsu@murraystate.edu
Or Contact: Nancy Martin, Coord, KIIS, Murray State Univ, PO Box 9, Murray KY 42071 *Ph:* 270-502 3091 *Fax:* 270-502 3434 *E-mail:* nancy.martin@murraystate.edu

---

0459
MADONNA UNIVERSITY
Comparative Cultures: Foreign Travel Study Program
Site: Various countries
Dates: 2 wks or longer, yr-round
Subjects: Civilization/culture, European studies, Government, History, Homestay, Spanish language
Eligibility: *Level:* fresh, sophs, jrs, srs, grads, precoll *Requires:* term paper or credit from a univ abroad
Credit: *Undergrad:* 3-15 *Grad:* 3-15
Instruction: *In:* English, Spanish *Format:* lecture *Students:* mainly US
Costs: About $2,500-$5,500 depending on pgm *incl* tuition, housing, all meals, intl airfare, fees, excursions, books/materials
Housing: *Arr by pgm:* residence halls, homestay
Deadline: Apply during fall term
Other info: *US accredited sponsor:* yes *Began:* 1974 *In coop with:* AIFS, Educ Travel, others *Orient:* in US & abroad *URL:* http://www.munet.edu
Contact: Dr Jonathan Swift, Dir, Ctr for Intl Studies, Madonna Univ, 36600 Schoolcraft Rd, Livonia MI 48150 *Ph:* 734-432 5636 *Fax:* 734-432 5393 *E-mail:* swift@smtp.munet.edu

---

0460
MICHIGAN STATE UNIVERSITY
Environmental Planning and Management
Site: Belgium: Brussels; France: Paris; Netherlands: Amsterdam
Dates: 3 wks, May
Subjects: Agriculture, Development administration/management, Natural resource management, Natural resources
Eligibility: *Level:* srs, grads, adults, professionals *Requires:* 2.00 GPA, good acad standing, major in natural resources *Age:* min 18
Credit: *Undergrad:* 3 *Grad:* 3 *Doc:* transcript
Instruction: *In:* English *Format:* lecture, seminar *Students:* mainly US
Costs: About $2,500 *incl* housing, some meals, insurance, excursions, books/materials, ground transport, support svcs *Nonrefundable fee*
Housing: *Arr by pgm:* hotels
Deadline: Mar 2
Other info: *US accredited sponsor:* yes *Orient:* in US *Activities:* excursions, field trips *Misc:* Loans avail. *Financial aid:* scholarships *URL:* http://studyabroad.msu.edu
Contact: Cheryl Benner, Study Abroad, Michigan State Univ, 109 Intl Ctr, East Lansing MI 48824 *Ph:* 517-353 8920 *Fax:* 517-432 2082 *E-mail:* bennerc@msu.edu ▲

0461
MICHIGAN STATE UNIVERSITY
Food, Agriculture and Environmental Systems
Site: England, Ireland, Scotland
Dates: 3 wks, May
Subjects: Agriculture, Animal sciences, Natural resources
Eligibility: *Level:* fresh, sophs, jrs, srs *Requires:* 2.0 GPA *Age:* min 18
Credit: *Undergrad:* avail *Grad:* none *Doc:* transcript
Instruction: *In:* English *Format:* directed field study, lecture *Students:* mainly US
Costs: About $2,200 *incl* housing, some meals, insurance, fees, excursions *Nonrefundable fee*
Housing: *Arr by pgm:* hotels
Deadline: Mar 2
Other info: *US accredited sponsor:* yes *Orient:* in US (1 day) *Activities:* excursions, field trips, program travel, cultural events *URL:* http://studyabroad.msu.edu
Contact: Cheryl Benner, Study Abroad, Michigan State Univ, 109 Intl Ctr, East Lansing MI 48824-1035 *Ph:* 517-353 8920 *Fax:* 517-432 2082 *E-mail:* bennerc@msu.edu ▲

0462
MICHIGAN STATE UNIVERSITY
History, Arts and Humanities
Site: England: London; Ireland: Dublin; Scotland: Edinburgh
Dates: 5 wks, Jul-Aug
Subjects: Arts, History, Humanities, Independent study
Eligibility: *Level:* sophs, jrs, srs, grads *Requires:* 2.0 GPA, good acad standing *Age:* min 18
Credit: *Undergrad:* 6 *Grad:* 6 *Doc:* transcript
Instruction: *In:* English *Format:* independent study, lecture *Students:* mainly US
Costs: About $2,700 *incl* housing, some meals, insurance, excursions, support svcs *Nonrefundable fee*
Housing: *Arr by pgm:* residence halls
Deadline: Mar 2
Other info: *US accredited sponsor:* yes *Began:* 1991 *Orient:* in US & abroad *Activities:* field trips *Misc:* Loans avail. May contact former participants. *Financial aid:* scholarships *URL:* http://studyabroad.msu.edu
Contact: Cheryl Benner, Study Abroad, Michigan State Univ, 109 Intl Ctr, East Lansing MI 48824-1035 *Ph:* 517-353 8920 *Fax:* 517-432 2082 *E-mail:* bennerc@msu.edu ▲

0463
MICHIGAN STATE UNIVERSITY
Interior Design and Architecture
Site: England: London; Italy: Milan
Dates: 4 wks, Jun-Jul
Subjects: Architectural history, Architecture, Environmental design, Interior design
Eligibility: *Level:* sophs, jrs, srs, grads *Requires:* 2.0 GPA, good acad standing *Age:* min 18
Credit: *Undergrad:* 6 *Grad:* avail *Doc:* transcript
Instruction: *In:* English *Format:* lecture *Students:* mainly US
Costs: About $2,600 *incl* housing, some meals, insurance, excursions, support svcs *Nonrefundable fee*
Housing: *Arr by pgm:* residence halls, hotels
Deadline: Mar 2
Other info: *US accredited sponsor:* yes *Began:* 1975 *Orient:* in US & abroad *Activities:* field trips *Misc:* Loans avail. May contact former participants. *Financial aid:* scholarships *URL:* http://studyabroad.msu.edu
Contact: Cheryl Benner, Study Abroad, Michigan State Univ, 109 Intl Ctr, East Lansing MI 48824-1035 *Ph:* 517-353 8920 *Fax:* 517-432 2082 *E-mail:* bennerc@msu.edu ▲

0464
MICHIGAN STATE UNIVERSITY
Is This a Postmodern World?
Site: France, Ireland, Netherlands
Dates: 4 wks, May-Jun
Subjects: Civilization/culture, Humanities
Eligibility: *Level:* jrs, srs *Requires:* 2.0 GPA, good acad standing, good physical condition, interview *Age:* min 18
Credit: *Undergrad:* avail *Grad:* none *Doc:* transcript
Instruction: *In:* English *Format:* lecture, seminar, study tour *Students:* mainly US
Costs: About $1,600 *incl* housing, insurance, excursions *Nonrefundable fee*
Housing: *Arr by pgm:* residence halls, pensions, hotels
Deadline: Mar 2
Other info: *US accredited sponsor:* yes *Began:* 1996 *Orient:* in US (1 day) *Activities:* excursions, field trips, program travel, cultural events *Misc:* Eurail pass required. *Financial aid:* scholarships *URL:* http://studyabroad.msu.edu
Contact: Cheryl Benner, Study Abroad, Michigan State Univ, 109 Intl Ctr, East Lansing MI 48824-1035 *Ph:* 517-353 8920 *Fax:* 517-432 2082 *E-mail:* bennerc@msu.edu ▲

0465
MICHIGAN STATE UNIVERSITY
Reporting in the British Isles
Site: England: London; Ireland: Dublin
Dates: 5 wks, May-Jun
Subjects: Communications, Independent study, Journalism
Eligibility: *Level:* sophs, jrs, srs, grads *Requires:* 2.0 GPA, journalism 200 *Age:* min 18
Credit: *Undergrad:* avail *Grad:* avail *Doc:* transcript
Instruction: *In:* English *Format:* independent study, lecture *Students:* mainly US
Costs: About $2,500 *incl* housing, some meals, insurance, excursions, support svcs
Housing: *Arr by pgm:* residence halls
Deadline: Mar 2
Other info: *US accredited sponsor:* yes *Orient:* in US (1 day) *Activities:* excursions *Financial aid:* scholarships *URL:* http://studyabroad.msu.edu
Contact: Cheryl Benner, Study Abroad, Michigan State Univ, 109 Intl Ctr, East Lansing MI 48824-1035 *Ph:* 517-353 8920 *Fax:* 517-432 2082 *E-mail:* bennerc@msu.edu ▲

0466
MICHIGAN STATE UNIVERSITY
Social Science
Site: Belgium: Brussels; England: London; France: Paris
Dates: 5 wks, Jul-Aug
Subjects: Political science/politics, Social sciences
Eligibility: *Level:* fresh, sophs, jrs, srs, grads *Requires:* 2.0 GPA, good acad standing *Age:* min 18
Credit: *Undergrad:* 8 *Grad:* 8 *Doc:* transcript
Instruction: *In:* English *Format:* lecture, seminar *Students:* mainly US
Costs: About $3,300 *incl* housing, some meals, insurance, excursions, support svcs *Nonrefundable fee*
Housing: *Arr by pgm:* residence halls
Deadline: Mar 2
Other info: *US accredited sponsor:* yes *Began:* 1970 *Orient:* in US & abroad *Activities:* excursions, field trips, cultural events *Misc:* Loans avail. May contact former participants. *Financial aid:* scholarships *URL:* http://studyabroad.msu.edu
Contact: Cheryl Benner, Study Abroad, Michigan State Univ, 109 Intl Ctr, East Lansing MI 48824-1035 *Ph:* 517-353 8920 *Fax:* 517-432 2082 *E-mail:* bennerc@msu.edu ▲

0467
MICHIGAN STATE UNIVERSITY
Telecommunications in Europe
Site: Belgium: Brussels; England: London; France: Paris; Germany: Bonn; Switzerland: Geneva *Host inst:* Natl des Telecommunications (INT)
Dates: 4 wks, Jul
Subjects: Telecommunications
Eligibility: *Level:* jrs, srs, grads *Requires:* 2.0 GPA, good acad standing, major in telecommunications *Age:* min 18
Credit: *Undergrad:* 4 *Grad:* 4 *Doc:* transcript
Instruction: *In:* English *Format:* lecture, seminar *Students:* mainly US
Costs: About $2,200 *incl* housing, insurance, excursions, books/materials, Eurostar pass, support svcs *Nonrefundable fee*
Housing: *Arr by pgm:* residence halls, hotels
Deadline: Mar 2
Other info: *US accredited sponsor:* yes *Began:* 1990 *Orient:* in US & abroad *Activities:* excursions, field trips *Misc:* Loans avail. *Financial aid:* scholarships *URL:* http://studyabroad.msu.edu
Contact: Cheryl Benner, Study Abroad, Michigan State Univ, 109 Intl Ctr, East Lansing MI 48824-1035 *Ph:* 517-353 8920 *Fax:* 517-432 2082 *E-mail:* bennerc@msu.edu ▲

0468
NEW YORK UNIVERSITY, SCHOOL OF EDUCATION
Arts Administration Utrecht, Paris, Berlin and Barcelona
Site: France: Paris; Germany: Berlin; Netherlands: Utrecht; Spain: Barcelona *Host inst:* Utrecht Sch of the Arts
Dates: Summer; next offered in 2002
Subjects: Arts management
Eligibility: *Level:* grads *Requires:* 3.0 GPA, previous study in field
Credit: *Undergrad:* none *Grad:* avail *Doc:* transcript
Instruction: *In:* English *Format:* directed field study, lecture, seminar *Students:* mainly US
Costs: Contact sponsor
Housing: *Arr by pgm:* hotels
Deadline: Contact sponsor
Other info: *US accredited sponsor:* yes *Began:* 1993 *Orient:* in US (1 day) *Activities:* field trips *Misc:* Pgm next offered in 2002. Please contact sponsor for full pgm details. May contact former participants. *URL:* http://www.nyu.edu/summer
Contact: Carlo Lamagna, Art & Art Professions, New York Univ, 34 Stuyvesant St, New York NY 10003 *Ph:* 212-998 9011 *Fax:* 212-995 4320 *E-mail:* carlo.lamagna@nyu.edu

Or Contact: Helen J Kelly, Dir of Special Pgms, New York Univ, 82 Washington Square E, Rm 62, New York NY 10003 *Ph:* 212-998 5090 *Fax:* 212-995 4923 ▲

0469
NORTHERN ILLINOIS UNIVERSITY
Design and Architecture in Northern Italy and Spain
Site: Italy, Spain
Dates: 3 wks, May-Jun
Subjects: Architecture, Art, Field study, Graphic arts/design
Eligibility: *Level:* jrs, srs, grads, adults, teachers, professionals *Requires:* 2.5 GPA, previous study in field *Age:* min 18, avg 21
Credit: *Undergrad:* 3-6 *Grad:* 3-6 *Doc:* transcript
Instruction: *In:* English *Format:* directed field study, lecture *Students:* mainly US
Costs: $3,100 *incl* tuition, housing, some meals, insurance, excursions
Housing: *Arr by pgm:* pensions, hotels
Deadline: Apr 15
Other info: *US accredited sponsor:* yes *Began:* 1985 *Orient:* in US *Misc:* Pgm incls 2 wks in Italy, 1 wk in Spain. May contact former participants. *URL:* http://www.niu.edu/niuabroad/
Contact: Anne Seitzinger, Pgm Coord, Study Abroad, Williston 417, Northern Illinois Univ, W1417, DeKalb IL 60115 *Ph:* 815-753 0700 *Fax:* 815-753 0825 *E-mail:* niuabroad@niu.edu
Or Contact: Prof Jon Ashmann, Sch of Art, Northern Illinois Univ, DeKalb IL 60115 *Ph:* 815-753 7884

0470
NORTHERN ILLINOIS UNIVERSITY
International Business Seminars
Site: Western Europe
Dates: Dec-Jan or May-Jun
Subjects: Administration, Business/management, Finance, International business, Marketing
Eligibility: *Level:* sophs, jrs, srs, grads, professionals *Requires:* 2.5 GPA, previous study in field, previous study or experience in bus admin, good acad standing *Age:* min 18, avg 21
Credit: *Undergrad:* 3-6 *Grad:* 3-6 *Doc:* transcript
Instruction: *In:* English *Format:* lecture, seminar *Students:* mainly US
Costs: About $3,800-$4,700 *incl* tuition, housing, some meals, intl airfare, insurance
Housing: *Arr by pgm:* hotels
Deadline: Nov 1 for winter; Apr 15 for summer
Other info: *US accredited sponsor:* yes *Orient:* in US & abroad *Misc:* May contact former participants. *URL:* http://www.niu.edu/niuabroad/
Contact: Anne Seitzinger, Pgm Coord, Study Abroad, Northern Illinois Univ, DeKalb IL 60115 *Ph:* 815-753 0700 *Fax:* 815-753 0825 *E-mail:* niuabroad@niu.edu

---

0471
OKLAHOMA STATE UNIVERSITY
Summer in Europe
Site: France, Switzerland
Dates: Jul 5-29
Subjects: Business administration, Marketing
Eligibility: *Level:* jrs, srs, grads, adults, teachers, professionals *Age:* min 18
Credit: *Undergrad:* avail *Grad:* avail
Instruction: *In:* English *Format:* study tour *Students:* mainly US
Costs: $3,800 *incl* tuition
Housing: *Arr by pgm:* residence halls, hotels
Deadline: May 1
Other info: *US accredited sponsor:* yes *Began:* 1999 *Orient:* abroad *Activities:* excursions, field trips, program travel, cultural events *Misc:* May contact former participants. *Financial aid:* scholarships *URL:* http://www.bus.okstate.edu/intbus/index.htm#study_abroad
Contact: Bus Extension, Oklahoma State Univ, 215 Coll of Bus Admin, Stillwater OK 74078 *Ph:* 405-744 5208 *Fax:* 405-744 6143 *E-mail:* nvickie@okstate.edu
Or Contact: Dr Steve Miller, Dir, Intl Bus Pgms, Oklahoma State Univ, 112 Coll of Bus Admin, Stillwater OK 74078 *Ph:* 405-744 5204 *Fax:* 405-744 6143 *E-mail:* stevejm@okstate.edu

---

0472
PENNSYLVANIA STATE UNIVERSITY
Holocaust and Its Aftermath
Site: Germany; Netherlands: Amsterdam *Host inst:* Anne Frank House
Dates: 3 wks, May-Jun
Subjects: Holocaust studies, Independent study, Jewish/judaic studies
Eligibility: *Level:* fresh, sophs, jrs, srs, grads *Requires:* 2.5 GPA
Credit: *Undergrad:* 6 *Grad:* none
Instruction: *In:* English *Format:* lecture, study tour *Students:* mainly US
Costs: Contact sponsor
Housing: *Arr by pgm:* residence halls
Deadline: Rolling admissions
Other info: *US accredited sponsor:* yes *Began:* 2000 *Orient:* in US & abroad *Activities:* excursions, field trips, program travel *Misc:* Incls visits to conentration camps. May contact former participants. *Financial aid:* scholarships, work study
Contact: Summer Abroad, Pennsylvania State Univ, 225 Penn State Conference Ctr, University Park PA 16802 *Ph:* 814-863 5170
Or Contact: Intl Pgm Adviser, Pennsylvania State Univ, 222 Boucke Bldg, University Park PA 16802 *Ph:* 814-865 7681 *Fax:* 814-865 3336

0473
RUTGERS UNIVERSITY
Rutgers Summer Study in Spain/Portugal
Site: Portugal: Coimbra; Spain: Salamanca *Host inst:* Univ de Salamanca, Univ of Coimbra
Dates: 5 wks, about Jun 28-Aug 4
Subjects: Civilization/culture, Literature, Portuguese language (int/adv), Portuguese studies, Spanish language (int/adv), Spanish studies
Eligibility: *Level:* sophs, jrs, srs, grads, adults, teachers, professionals *Requires:* 1 yr coll Spanish or equiv *Age:* min 18
Credit: *Undergrad:* 7 *Grad:* 6 *Doc:* transcript
Instruction: *In:* Spanish *Format:* lang study, lecture *Students:* mainly US
Costs: $4,095 for NJ residents, $4,295 for nonresidents & grads *incl* tuition, housing, all meals, intl airfare, insurance, excursions, books/materials *Nonrefundable fee*
Housing: *Arr by pgm:* residence halls
Deadline: Mar 1
Other info: *US accredited sponsor:* yes *Began:* 1983 *Orient:* in US (2 days) *Activities:* excursions, program travel, cultural events *Misc:* May contact former participants. *Financial aid:* scholarships *URL:* http://span-port.rutgers.edu
Contact: Flora Feldman, Spanish & Portuguese, Rutgers Univ, 105 George St, Carpender Hall, New Brunswick NJ 08903-1404 *Ph:* 732-932 9323 ext 11 *Fax:* 732-932 9837 *E-mail:* ffeldman@rci.rutgers.edu
Or Contact: Maribel Gill, Spanish & Portuguese, Rutgers Univ, 105 George St, Carpender Hall, New Brunswick NJ 08903-1414 *Ph:* 732-932 9323 ext 10 *Fax:* 732-932 9837 *E-mail:* maribelg@rci.rutgers.edu

---

0474
SOUND & FURIES PRODUCTIONS
Women's Magical Tours
Site: England, Greece
Dates: 2 wks each country: England, Apr-May; Greece, Oct
Subjects: Women's studies
Eligibility: *Level:* adults *Age:* min 18, avg 40
Credit: *Undergrad:* none *Grad:* none
Instruction: *In:* English *Format:* study tour *Students:* mainly US
Costs: About $1,300-$1,600 for 2 wks (sliding scale) *incl* housing, some meals, excursions, tour guides

Housing: *Arr by pgm:* bed & breakfasts
Deadline: Contact sponsor
Other info: *US accredited sponsor:* no *Began:* 1996 *Misc:* Tours are to pre-Christian goddess sites with local guides. Pay what you can afford (sliding scale).
Contact: Pat Hogan, Coord, Sounds & Furies, PO Box 21510, 1850 Commercial Dr, Vancouver, BC Canada *E-mail:* path@lynx.bc.ca

---

0475
SOUTHERN ILLINOIS UNIVERSITY AT CARBONDALE
Architectural Field Studies
Site: England, France, Germany, Greece, Italy, Turkey
Dates: 4 wks, May 13-Jun 10
Subjects: Architecture, Field study
Eligibility: *Level:* adults *Requires:* 2.75 GPA *Age:* min 18
Credit: *Undergrad:* 1-6 *Grad:* none *Doc:* transcript
Instruction: *In:* English *Format:* directed field study *Students:* mainly US
Costs: $5,000 *incl* housing, intl airfare, fees, excursions, books/materials, railpass *Nonrefundable fee*
Housing: *Arr by pgm:* hotels
Deadline: Apr 1
Other info: *US accredited sponsor:* yes *Began:* 1997 *Orient:* in US (1 day) *Activities:* excursions, field trips, program travel, cultural events *Misc:* Scholarships for own students only. May contact former participants. *Financial aid:* scholarships *URL:* http://www.siu.edu/departments/study_abroad/
Contact: Thomas A Saville, Study Abroad Pgms, Mailcode 6885, Southern Illinois Univ, Carbondale IL 62901-6885 *Ph:* 618-453 7670 *Fax:* 618-453 7647 *E-mail:* studyabr@siu.edu

---

0476
SOUTHWEST TEXAS STATE UNIVERSITY
SWT in Europe
Site: France: Paris; Italy: Milan, Pisa, Venice; Switzerland: Lugano, Zurich, St. Moritz
Dates: 3-1/2 wks, Jun
Subjects: European studies, Field study, Geography
Eligibility: *Level:* jrs, srs, grads *Requires:* previous study in field, one course in Geography, *Age:* min 18, avg 22
Credit: *Undergrad:* 6 *Grad:* 6 *Doc:* transcript
Instruction: *In:* English *Format:* study tour *Students:* mainly US
Costs: $3,500-$3,995 *incl* tuition, housing, intl airfare, excursions
Housing: *Arr by pgm:* residence halls, hotels
Deadline: Contact sponsor
Other info: *US accredited sponsor:* yes *Began:* 1999 *Orient:* in US *Activities:* excursions, field trips *Misc:* May contact former participants. *Financial aid:* scholarships *URL:* http://www.ideal.swt.edu/extension/study-abroad/
Contact: Dr Richard Earl, Southwest Texas State Univ, 601 Univ Dr, San Marcos TX 78666 *Ph:* 512-245 3204 *Fax:* 512-245 8353 *E-mail:* re02@swt.edu

Or Contact: Isis Gomez Extension Studies Coord, Southwest Texas State Univ, 601 Univ Dr, San Marcos TX 78666 *Ph:* 512-245 2322 *Fax:* 512-245 8934 *E-mail:* ig02@swt.edu

---

0477
SUMMER ACADEMY
Summer Academy: Study Holidays
Site: Ireland: Cork; United Kingdom: various sites
Dates: 1 wk, Jun 16-Aug 25
Subjects: Alternative medicine, Antiques, Archaeology, Art, Art history, Creative writing, Field study, Geology, Literature, Music, Natural history
Eligibility: *Level:* adults *Age:* min 16, avg 60
Credit: *Undergrad:* none *Grad:* none
Instruction: *In:* English *Format:* directed field study, lecture, seminar *Students:* intl & host country
Costs: UK 480-510 *incl* tuition, housing, all meals, fees, excursions *Nonrefundable fee*
Housing: *Arr by pgm:* residence halls, (all singles with private bath)
Deadline: Contact sponsor
Other info: *US accredited sponsor:* no *Began:* 1986 *Activities:* excursions, field trips *URL:* http://www.ukc.ac.uk/sa
Contact: *See Index II for Members* Andrea McDonnell or Louise Smith, Summer Acad, Keynes Coll, Univ of Kent, Kent CT2 7NP, UK *E-mail:* summeracademy@ukc.ac.uk

---

0478
SUNY COLLEGE AT BROCKPORT
Study of 19th and 20th Century British Writers
Site: England: London; Ireland: Dublin; Scotland: Edinburgh
Dates: 2 wks, Jul
Subjects: English literature
Eligibility: *Level:* jrs, srs *Requires:* 2.5 GPA
Credit: *Undergrad:* 3 *Grad:* 3 *Doc:* transcript
Instruction: *In:* English *Format:* study tour *Students:* mainly US
Costs: $3,360 *incl* housing, some meals, intl airfare, insurance, excursions
Housing: *Arr by pgm:* bed & breakfasts
Deadline: Mar 15
Other info: *US accredited sponsor:* yes *Began:* 1985 *Activities:* excursions, field trips, program travel *Misc:* Faculty dir. *URL:* http://www.brockport.edu/study_abroad
Contact: Dr John Perry, Intl Educ, 360 New Campus Dr, SUNY Brockport, Brockport NY 14420 *Ph:* 800-298 7869 *Fax:* 716-637 3218 *E-mail:* overseas@brockport.edu

---

0479
SUNY COLLEGE AT OSWEGO
Summer City Tour
Site: England: London; France: Paris; Ireland: Dublin; Italy: Rome
Dates: 2 wks, Jul
Subjects: British studies, English, French studies, History, Irish studies, Italian studies
Eligibility: *Level:* fresh, sophs, jrs, srs, precoll *Requires:* 2.5 GPA
Credit: *Undergrad:* 3 *Grad:* none
Instruction: *In:* English *Format:* independent study, study tour *Students:* mainly US
Costs: $3,500 *incl* tuition, housing, some meals, intl airfare, insurance, excursions
Housing: *Arr by pgm:* pensions, hostels
Deadline: Apr 1
Other info: *US accredited sponsor:* yes *Began:* 1997 *Orient:* in US *Activities:* excursions, field trips, program travel, cultural events *Misc:* May contact former participants. *Financial aid:* scholarships *URL:* http://www.oswego.edu/~intled
Contact: Susan Ansara, Dir, Intl Educ, SUNY Coll at Oswego, 102 Rich Hall, Oswego NY 13126 *Ph:* 888-467 9346; 315-341 2118 *Fax:* 315-341 2477 *E-mail:* intled@oswego.edu

---

0480
SUNY UNIVERSITY AT BUFFALO
Study Abroad Program in London and Paris
Site: England: London; France: Paris
Dates: 1 mo, Jul 8-Aug 5
Subjects: Business/management, Communications, European studies, Field study, Literature
Eligibility: *Level:* fresh, sophs, jrs, srs *Requires:* 2.67 GPA *Age:* min 18, avg 20
Credit: *Undergrad:* 6 *Grad:* none *Doc:* transcript
Instruction: *In:* English *Format:* directed field study *Students:* mainly US
Costs: $3,000 *incl* housing, some meals, excursions *Nonrefundable fee*
Housing: *Arr by pgm:* hotels, hostels
Deadline: Apr 1; rolling admissions
Other info: *US accredited sponsor:* yes *Began:* 1998 *Orient:* in US & abroad (1 day) *Activities:* field trips *Misc:* US pgm dir on-site. May contact former participants. *Financial aid:* scholarships *URL:* http://www.buffalo.edu/studyabroad/
Contact: Dr Sandra J Flash, Dir, Study Abroad Pgms, SUNY Univ at Buffalo, 210 Talbert Hall, Box 601604, Buffalo NY 14260-1604 *Ph:* 716-645 3912 *Fax:* 716-645 6197 *E-mail:* studyabroad@acsu.buffalo.edu

---

0481
SYRACUSE UNIVERSITY
Comparative Ethnic and Race Relations
Site: England: London; France: Strasbourg; Italy: Florence
Dates: 4 wks, Jun 2-30
Subjects: European studies, Independent study
Eligibility: *Level:* sophs, jrs, srs, grads, adults *Requires:* 2.5 GPA *Age:* min 18
Credit: *Undergrad:* 6 *Grad:* 6 *Doc:* transcript
Instruction: *In:* English *Format:* independent study, lecture, seminar *Students:* mainly US
Costs: $7,000 *incl* tuition, housing, some meals, intl airfare, fees, excursions
Housing: *Arr by pgm:* hotels
Deadline: Mar 15
Other info: *US accredited sponsor:* yes *Began:* 2001 *Orient:* abroad *Activities:* program travel *Financial aid:* scholarships *URL:* http://sumweb.syr.edu/dipa/summer
Contact: Daisy Fried, Assoc Dir, Intl Pgms Abroad, Syracuse Univ, 119 Euclid Ave, Syracuse NY 13244 *Ph:* 800-251 9674; 315-443 9419 *Fax:* 315-443 4593 *E-mail:* dsfried@summons3.sgr.edu ▲

0482
SYRACUSE UNIVERSITY
Drawing Architecture in Spain and Portugal
Site: Portugal, Spain
Dates: 6 wks, May 17-Jun 30
Subjects: Architecture
Eligibility: *Level:* sophs, jrs, srs, grads *Requires:* 2.7 GPA, previous study in field, 1 yr architecture design studio
Credit: *Undergrad:* 6 *Grad:* 6 *Doc:* transcript
Instruction: *In:* English *Format:* art studio, study tour *Students:* mainly US
Costs: $7,200 *incl* tuition, housing, some meals, excursions *Nonrefundable fee*
Housing: *Arr by pgm:* pensions, hotels
Deadline: Mar 15
Other info: *US accredited sponsor:* yes *Began:* 2000 *Orient:* avail (1 day) *Activities:* field trips, program travel, cultural events *Financial aid:* scholarships *URL:* http://sumweb.syr.edu/dipa/summer

Contact: Daisy Fried, Assoc Dir, Syracuse Univ, 119 Euclid Ave, Syracuse NY 13244-4170 *Ph:* 800-251 9674; 315-443 9419 *Fax:* 315-443 4593 *E-mail:* dsfried@summon3.syr.edu ▲

0483
SYRACUSE UNIVERSITY
Globalization: Race for the World
Site: Various European countries
Dates: 4 wks, Jun 4-Jul 3
Subjects: Business administration, Business/management, Field study, Independent study, Marketing
Eligibility: *Level:* sophs, jrs, srs, grads, adults *Requires:* 2.5 GPA *Age:* min 18
Credit: *Undergrad:* 6 *Grad:* 6 *Doc:* transcript
Instruction: *In:* English *Format:* directed field study, independent study, lecture *Students:* mainly US
Costs: $6,000 *incl* tuition, housing, some meals, fees, excursions *Nonrefundable fee*
Housing: *Arr by pgm:* hotels
Deadline: Mar 15
Other info: *US accredited sponsor:* yes *Began:* 2001 *Orient:* abroad *Activities:* program travel *Financial aid:* scholarships *URL:* http://sumweb.syr.edu/dipa/summer
Contact: Daisy Fried, Assoc Dir, Syracuse Univ, 119 Euclid Ave, Syracuse NY 13219 *Ph:* 800-251 9674; 315-443 9419 *Fax:* 315-443 4593 *E-mail:* dsfried@summon3.syr.edu ▲

0484
SYRACUSE UNIVERSITY
Human Sexuality in Europe
Site: England: London; Netherlands: Amsterdam; Sweden: Stockholm
Dates: 4 wks, Jun 8-Jul 6
Subjects: Civilization/culture, Gender studies, Sociology
Eligibility: *Level:* sophs, jrs, srs, grads, adults *Requires:* 2.5 GPA
Credit: *Undergrad:* 6 *Grad:* 6 *Doc:* transcript
Instruction: *In:* English *Format:* independent study, study tour *Students:* mainly US
Costs: $7,000 *incl* tuition, housing, some meals, excursions *Nonrefundable fee*
Housing: *Arr by pgm:* hotels
Deadline: Mar 15
Other info: *US accredited sponsor:* yes *Began:* 1999 *Orient:* abroad (2 days) *Activities:* excursions, field trips, program travel, cultural events *Misc:* May contact former participants. *Financial aid:* scholarships *URL:* http://sumweb.syr.edu/dipa/summer
Contact: Daisy Fried, Assoc Dir, Syracuse Univ, 119 Euclid Ave, Syracuse NY 13244-4170 *Ph:* 800-251 9674; 315-443 9419 *Fax:* 315-443 4593 *E-mail:* dsfried@summon3.syr.edu ▲

0485
UNIVERSITY OF ARIZONA
Summer Program in Greece and Italy: Art and Architecture
Site: Greece: Athens, various islands; Italy: Florence, Rome, Siena, other sites
Dates: 6 wks, Jun-Jul
Subjects: Creative writing, Drawing, Field study, Independent study, Painting, Photography
Eligibility: *Level:* sophs, jrs, srs, grads, adults, teachers, professionals, precoll *Age:* min 18
Credit: *Undergrad:* 6 *Grad:* 6 *Doc:* transcript
Instruction: *In:* English *Format:* independent study, lecture, seminar *Students:* mainly US
Costs: $4,400 *incl* tuition, housing, some meals, intl airfare, ground transport
Housing: *Sponsor assists:* hotels
Deadline: Apr 1
Other info: *US accredited sponsor:* yes *Orient:* in US *Activities:* program travel *Misc:* May contact former participants. *URL:* http://w3.arizona.edu/~ciss/
Contact: Renee Griggs, Ctr for Global Student Pgms, Univ of Arizona, 939 N Tyndall Ave, Tucson AZ 85721 *Ph:* 520-626 7180 *Fax:* 520-626 9004 *E-mail:* griggsr@u.arizona.edu
Or Contact: Prof Charles Albanese, Coll of Architecture, Univ of Arizona, Tucson AZ 87521 *Ph:* 520-621 6751 *Fax:* 520-621 8700 ▲

0486
UNIVERSITY OF DELAWARE
Winter Session in Europe
Site: England: London, York; France: Paris; Ireland: Dublin; Italy: Milan; Scotland: Edinburgh
Dates: 1 mo, Jan
Subjects: Economics, Human resources, Independent study
Eligibility: *Level:* fresh, sophs, jrs, srs *Requires:* 2.0 GPA
Credit: *Undergrad:* 7 *Grad:* none *Doc:* transcript
Instruction: *In:* English *Format:* independent study, lecture, study tour *Students:* mainly US
Costs: Contact sponsor
Housing: *Arr by pgm:* hotels
Deadline: Early Oct
Other info: *US accredited sponsor:* yes *Began:* 1993 *Activities:* excursions, field trips, program travel, cultural events *Misc:* Contact sponsor to arrange honors credit. Pgm offered even-numbered years. May contact former participants. *Financial aid:* scholarships *URL:* http://www.udel.edu/studyabroad/
Contact: Intl Pgms & Special Sessions, Univ of Delaware, 4 Kent Way, Newark DE 19716 *Ph:* 888-831 4685; 302-831 2852 *Fax:* 302-831 6042 *E-mail:* studyabroad@udel.edu

---

0487
UNIVERSITY OF DELAWARE
Winter Session in Scotland, England and Ireland
Site: England: London; Ireland: Dublin; Scotland: Edinburgh
Dates: 1 mo, Jan
Subjects: Education/teaching, Field study
Eligibility: *Level:* fresh, sophs, jrs, srs *Requires:* 2.0 GPA
Credit: *Undergrad:* 6 *Grad:* none *Doc:* transcript
Instruction: *In:* English *Format:* directed field study, lecture, seminar, study tour *Students:* mainly US
Costs: Contact sponsor
Housing: *Arr by pgm*
Deadline: Early Oct
Other info: *US accredited sponsor:* yes *Activities:* excursions, field trips, program travel *Misc:* Contact sponsor to arrange honors credit. Pgm offered even-numbered yrs. *Financial aid:* scholarships *URL:* http://www.udel.edu/studyabroad/
Contact: Intl Pgms, Univ of Delaware, 4 Kent Way, Newark DE 19716 *Ph:* 888-831 4685; 302-831 2852 *Fax:* 302-831 6042 *E-mail:* studyabroad@udel.edu

---

0488
UNIVERSITY OF MINNESOTA
Design in Europe
Site: England: London; France: Paris; Germany: Trier; Italy: Florence; Luxembourg
Dates: 4 wks, early Jun-early Jul
Subjects: Architecture, European studies, Interior design
Eligibility: *Level:* fresh, sophs, jrs, srs, grads, adults, teachers, professionals *Requires:* 2.5 GPA, previous study in field, helpful
Credit: *Undergrad:* 5 *Grad:* 5 *Doc:* transcript
Instruction: *In:* English *Format:* seminar, study tour *Students:* mainly US
Costs: About $3,850 for Univ of MN students, $4,100 for others *incl* tuition, housing, some meals, fees, excursions, railpass, local transport, admissions
Housing: *Arr by pgm:* hotels
Deadline: Mar 1
Other info: *US accredited sponsor:* yes *Began:* 1982 *Orient:* in US *Activities:* field trips, program travel, cultural events *Misc:*

Univ of Minnesota financial aid applies. Scholarships for own students only. May contact former participants. *URL:* http://www.UMabroad.umn.edu
Contact: Dr Denise Guerin, Interior Design in Europe, Univ of Minnesota, Housing & Apparel, 240 McNeal Hall, St Paul MN 55108 *Ph:* 612-626 1257 *Fax:* 612-624 2750 *E-mail:* queri001@tc.umn.edu
Or Contact: Interior Design in Europe, Global Campus, Univ of Minnesota, 102 Nicholson Hall, 216 Pillsbury Dr SE, Minneapolis MN 55455-0138 *Ph:* 612-626 9000 *Fax:* 612-626 8009 *E-mail:* umabroad@tc.umn.edu

---

0489
UNIVERSITY OF MONTANA
Group Study Abroad Summer Program in Germany and France
Site: France: Domain de la Tour; Germany: Heidelberg, Munich *Host inst:* Univ of Heidelberg
Dates: 3-1/2 wks, mid-May-mid-Jun
Subjects: Business/management, Civilization/culture, History, Homestay
Eligibility: Own students only. *Level:* sophs, jrs, srs *Requires:* 1 yr coll German preferred
Credit: *Undergrad:* 3 *Grad:* none
Instruction: *In:* English, German *Format:* directed field study, lecture, study tour *Students:* mainly US
Costs: About $2,000 *incl* housing, some meals, intl airfare, local transport
Housing: *Arr by pgm:* homestay
Deadline: Early spring
Other info: *US accredited sponsor:* yes *Orient:* in US *Activities:* excursions, field trips, program travel, cultural events *Misc:* Pgm has bus emphasis. *Financial aid:* scholarships *URL:* http://www.umt.edu/oip
Contact: Intl Pgms, Univ of Montana, Main Hall 022, Missoula MT 59812 *Ph:* 406-243 2288 *Fax:* 406-243 6194 *E-mail:* goabroad@selway.umt.edu

---

0490
UNIVERSITY OF NEBRASKA-LINCOLN
Winterim Study Abroad
Site: England: London; France: Paris
Dates: 2 wks, Dec 26-Jan 10
Subjects: Art history, Visual arts
Eligibility: *Level:* fresh, sophs, jrs, srs, grads *Requires:* 2.50 GPA *Age:* avg 20
Credit: *Undergrad:* 3 *Grad:* 3 *Doc:* transcript
Instruction: *In:* English *Format:* seminar, study tour *Students:* mainly US
Costs: $2,300-$2,400 *incl* housing, some meals, intl airfare, insurance, excursions *Nonrefundable fee*
Housing: *Arr by pgm:* hotels
Deadline: Oct 1
Other info: *US accredited sponsor:* yes *Began:* 1971 *Orient:* in US *URL:* http://www.iaffairs.unl.edu
Contact: Christa Joy, Study Abroad Coord, Intl Affairs, Univ of Nebraska-Lincoln, 420 University Terrace, Lincoln NE 68588-0286 *Ph:* 402-472 5358 *Fax:* 402-472 5383 *E-mail:* iaffairs@unl.edu

---

0491
UNIVERSITY OF SOUTHERN MISSISSIPPI
European Union/Business
Site: Belgium, England, France
Dates: 3 wks, Jun 17-Jul 7
Subjects: International business, International studies
Eligibility: *Level:* sophs, jrs, srs, grads, adults *Requires:* 2.0 GPA *Age:* min 18, max 50, avg 25
Credit: *Undergrad:* 4 *Grad:* 4 *Doc:* transcript
Instruction: *In:* English *Format:* lecture, seminar *Students:* mainly US
Costs: $2,999 for undergrads, $3,299 for grads *incl* tuition, housing, intl airfare, fees, excursions
Housing: *Arr by pgm:* residence halls, hotels, hostels
Deadline: Apr 30
Other info: *US accredited sponsor:* yes *Orient:* avail avail *Misc:* May contact former participants. *Financial aid:* scholarships *URL:* http://www.usm.edu
Contact: Dr Tim W Hudson, Dean, or Dir, European Union/Bus, Univ of Southern Mississippi, Box 10047, Hattiesburg MS 39406 *Ph:* 601-266 4344 *Fax:* 601-266 5699 *E-mail:* melissa.ravencraft@usm.edu

---

0492
UNIVERSITY OF UTAH
Psychology of Living Spaces: Eastern Mediterranean
Site: Greece; Turkey; Cyprus; Syria; Isreal; Egypt
Dates: 3 wks, Jun-Jul
Subjects: Architecture, Environmental design
Eligibility: *Level:* fresh, sophs, jrs, srs, grads, adults *Requires:* 2.5 GPA *Age:* min 18, avg 23
Credit: *Undergrad:* avail *Grad:* none *Doc:* transcript
Instruction: *In:* English *Format:* study tour *Students:* mainly US
Costs: About $3,600 *incl* tuition, housing, some meals, intl airfare *Nonrefundable fee*
Housing: *Arr by pgm:* hotels
Deadline: Mar 15
Other info: *US accredited sponsor:* yes *Began:* 1999 *Orient:* in US (1 day) *Activities:* excursions *Misc:* May contact former participants. *URL:* http://www.saff.utah.edu/inter/
Contact: Aaron Rose, Study Abroad, Univ of Utah, 159 University Union, Salt Lake City UT 84112 *Ph:* 801-581 5849 *Fax:* 801-581 5914 *E-mail:* arose@saff.utah.edu

---

0493
UNIVERSITY OF WISCONSIN-STEVENS POINT
Art, Architecture and Design in Europe
Site: Germany: Munich, Dessau Darmstadt, Marburg, & various sites; Czech Republic: Marienbad, Prague; France: Colmar, Ronchamp
Dates: Jul 24 - Aug 13
Subjects: Architecture, Art history, Graphic arts/design, Interior design
Eligibility: *Level:* fresh, sophs, jrs, srs, grads, adults *Requires:* architecture, art, art history or design majors
Credit: *Undergrad:* 3 *Grad:* avail *Doc:* transcript
Instruction: *In:* English *Format:* study tour *Students:* mainly US
Costs: $3,275 for WI residents *incl* tuition, housing, some meals, intl airfare, excursions, entrance fees, rail/bus transf
Housing: *Arr by pgm:* residence halls, hotels
Deadline: 10 wks before pgm (or when full)
Other info: *US accredited sponsor:* yes *Orient:* in US *Activities:* excursions, field trips *Financial aid:* scholarships *URL:* http://www.uwsp.edu/studyabroad
Contact: Dir, Intl Pgms, Univ of Wisconsin-Stevens Point, Stevens Point WI 54481 *Ph:* 715-346 2717 *Fax:* 715-346 3591
Or Contact: Dr Kathe Miller Stumpf, Interior Design, Univ of Wisconsin-Stevens Point, Stevens Point WI 54481 *Ph:* 715-346 3067 *E-mail:* kstumpf@uwsp.edu
Or Contact: Dr Larry Ball, Art, Univ of Wisconsin-Stevens Point, Stevens Point WI 54481 *Ph:* 715-346 2839 *E-mail:* lball@uwsp.edu

---

0494
UNIVERSITY OF WISCONSIN-STEVENS POINT
Music of the 19th Century and Opera
Site: Austria: Salzburg; Germany: Munich; Italy: Bologna,Florence, Milan, Padua, Venice
Dates: 3 wks, Jun 11-Jul 2
Subjects: Field study, Music, Music history
Eligibility: *Level:* grads, adults *Requires:* good physical condition
Credit: *Undergrad:* 3 *Grad:* avail *Doc:* transcript
Instruction: *In:* English *Format:* directed

field study, lecture, study tour *Students:* mainly US
Costs: $2,995 for WI residents *incl* tuition, housing, some meals, intl airfare, fees, excursions, railpass, entrance fees, bus svc *Nonrefundable fee*
Housing: *Arr by pgm:* hotels, hostels
Deadline: 10 wks before pgm or until filled
Other info: *US accredited sponsor:* yes *Began:* 1999 *Orient:* in US (1 day) *Activities:* excursions, program travel, cultural events *Misc:* Itinerant pgm. *URL:* http://www.uwsp.edu/acad/internat/
Contact: Intl Pgms, Univ of Wisconsin-Stevens Point, 108 CCC, Stevens Point WI 54481 *Ph:* 715-346 2717 *Fax:* 715-346 3591 *E-mail:* intlprog@uwsp.edu
Or Contact: Dr Patrick Miles, Music Dept, Univ of Wisconsin-Stevens Point, C-126 Fine Arts, Stevens Point WI 54481 *Ph:* 715-346 2027 *E-mail:* pmiles@uwsp.edu

0495
VIRGINIA POLYTECHNIC INSTITUTE & STATE UNIVERSITY
Interdisciplinary Environmental Semester
Site: France, Germany, Italy, Switzerland *Host inst:* Ctr for European Studies & Architecture (Riva San Vitale, Switzerland)
Dates: May 15-Aug 15
Subjects: Agriculture, Ecology/environmental studies, Natural resource management
Eligibility: *Level:* sophs, jrs, srs
Credit: *Undergrad:* 15 *Grad:* none *Doc:* transcript
Instruction: *In:* English *Format:* directed field study, independent study, lecture, practical training, seminar, study tour *Students:* mainly US
Costs: Contact sponsor
Housing: *Arr by pgm:* hotels, residence halls at CESA
Deadline: Feb 1
Other info: *US accredited sponsor:* yes *Began:* 1998 *In coop with:* European Univs *Orient:* abroad *Activities:* excursions, field trips, program travel, cultural events
Contact: Dr Waldon Kerns, Virginia Polytechnic Inst & State Univ, Blacksburg VA 24061-0401 *Ph:* 540-231 5995 *Fax:* 540-231 7417 *E-mail:* kernsw@vt.edu
Or Contact: Lyn Gray, Virginia Polytechnic Inst & State Univ, 134 Burruss Hall, Blacksburg VA 24061-0265 *Ph:* 540-231 5888 *Fax:* 540-231 5750 *E-mail:* vtabroad@vt.edu

0496
WESTERN CONNECTICUT STATE UNIVERSITY
Alps-2002
Site: Austria: Salzburg; Germany: Berchtesgaden, Munich
Dates: 10 days, Mar
Subjects: Education/teaching, History, Sociology
Eligibility: US citizens only. *Level:* adults *Requires:* 2.8 GPA, good health *Age:* min 18, max 60
Credit: *Undergrad:* 3 *Grad:* 3 *Doc:* transcript
Instruction: *In:* English *Format:* study tour *Students:* mainly US
Costs: $2,400 *incl* housing, some meals, intl airfare, fees, excursions *Nonrefundable fee*
Housing: *Arr by pgm:* hotels
Deadline: Nov 5
Other info: *US accredited sponsor:* yes *Began:* 1973 *Orient:* in US (1 day) *Activities:* excursions, field trips, program travel, cultural events *Misc:* May contact former participants. *URL:* http://www.wcsu.ctstateu.edu/homepage.html
Contact: Dr John Caruso Jr, Educ, Western Connecticut State Univ, 181 White St, Danbury CT 06810 *Ph:* 203-837 8517 *E-mail:* carusoj@wcsu.edu

0497
WHITWORTH COLLEGE
Core 250: Western Civilization
Site: England: London; France: Paris; Greece: Athens; Italy: Rome; Switzerland
Dates: 1 mo, Jan
Subjects: Art, Civilization/culture, Classical studies, European studies, Literature, Philosophy, Sciences
Eligibility: *Level:* sophs, jrs, srs *Requires:* 2.5 GPA
Credit: *Undergrad:* 4 *Grad:* none *Doc:* transcript
Instruction: *In:* English *Format:* study tour *Students:* mainly US
Costs: About $3,500 *incl* housing, some meals, intl airfare, ground transport
Housing: *Arr by pgm:* hotels, hostels
Deadline: Apr 1
Other info: *US accredited sponsor:* yes *Began:* 1990 *Activities:* program travel *Misc:* Pgm next offered in Jan 2003. May contact former participants. *URL:* http://www.whitworth.edu
Contact: Sue Jackson, Coord, Off-Campus Pgms, Ctr for Intl & Multicultural Educ, Whitworth Coll, Spokane WA 99251 *Ph:* 509-777 4596 *Fax:* 509-777 3723 *E-mail:* sjackson@whitworth.edu

0498
WHITWORTH COLLEGE
Jazz Workshop
Site: Germany: Munich; Italy: Rome
Dates: Jan
Subjects: Civilization/culture, Field study, Music, Music history
Eligibility: *Level:* fresh, sophs, jrs, srs *Requires:* audition
Credit: *Undergrad:* 3-4 *Grad:* none
Instruction: *In:* English *Format:* music lesson, study tour *Students:* mainly US
Costs: About $3,000 *incl* housing, all meals, intl airfare
Housing: *Arr by pgm*
Deadline: Sep 15
Other info: *US accredited sponsor:* yes *Began:* 1991 *Activities:* field trips *URL:* http://www.whitworth.edu
Contact: Sue Jackson, Coord, Off-Campus Pgms, Ctr for Intl & Multicultural Educ, Whitworth Coll, Spokane WA 99251 *Ph:* 509-777 4596 *Fax:* 509-777 3723 *E-mail:* sjackson@whitworth.edu

Austria

MORE THAN ONE CITY

0499
INTERNATIONAL COUNCIL FOR CULTURAL EXCHANGE (ICCE)
German Language and Austrian Culture: Music Programs
Site: Austria: Salzburg, Vienna, others *Host inst:* Regional univs
Dates: 3-6 wks, Jul-Aug
Subjects: Austrian studies, Civilization/culture, Field study, German language (beg/int/adv), Homestay, Master classes, Music
Eligibility: *Level:* fresh, sophs, jrs, srs, grads, adults, teachers, professionals, precoll
Credit: *Undergrad:* avail *Grad:* avail *Doc:* transcript, certificate
Instruction: *In:* English, German *Format:* directed field study, lab, lang study, lecture, music lesson, practical training, study tour *Students:* intl
Costs: Contact sponsor
Housing: *Sponsor assists:* residence halls, homestay, hotels
Deadline: 1 mo before pgm
Other info: *US accredited sponsor:* no *Began:* 1982 *Orient:* abroad *Activities:* excursions, program travel, cultural events, sports *Misc:* Yr-round pgms of 2 wks or longer for pre-arr groups.
Contact: Dr Stanley Gochman, ICCE, 5 Bellport Ln, Bellport NY 11713 *Ph:* 631-286 5228 ▲

0500
NATIONAL REGISTRATION CENTER FOR STUDY ABROAD (NRCSA)
German Language Study in Austria
Site: Austria: Kitzbuhel, Salzburg *Host inst:* Amadeus Acad, Deutsch Inst Tirol
Dates: 2 wks or longer, yr-round
Subjects: German language (beg/int/adv), Homestay
Eligibility: *Level:* adults *Age:* min 16
Credit: *Undergrad:* avail *Grad:* avail *Doc:* certificate
Instruction: *In:* German *Format:* lang study, lecture *Students:* intl
Costs: Contact sponsor
Housing: *Arr by pgm:* residence halls, apartments, homestay, pensions
Deadline: Contact sponsor
Other info: *US accredited sponsor:* no *Orient:* abroad *Activities:* excursions *URL:* http://www.nrcsa.com
Contact: Reuel Zielke, NRCSA, 823 N 2nd St, #206, Milwaukee WI 53203 *Ph:* 414-278 0631 *Fax:* 414-271 8884 *E-mail:* info@nrcsa.com

---

0501
SOUTHERN ILLINOIS UNIVERSITY AT CARBONDALE
International Social Work
Site: Austria: various sites
Dates: 2 wks, May 14-29
Subjects: Civilization/culture, Field study, Social work
Eligibility: *Level:* fresh, sophs, jrs, srs *Requires:* 2.75 GPA *Age:* min 18
Credit: *Undergrad:* avail *Grad:* avail *Doc:* transcript
Instruction: *In:* English *Format:* directed field study, lecture, study tour *Students:* mainly US
Costs: $2,000 *incl* housing, intl airfare, excursions, local transportation
Housing: *Arr by pgm*
Deadline: Mar 1
Other info: *US accredited sponsor:* yes *Began:* 1996 *Activities:* excursions, field trips, program travel, cultural events *URL:* http://www.siu.edu/departments/study_abroad/
Contact: Thomas Saville, Coord, Study Abroad Pgm, Mailcode 6885, Southern Illinois Univ, Carbondale IL 62901-6885 *Ph:* 618-453 7670 *Fax:* 618-453 7647 *E-mail:* studyabr@siu.edu

---

BRAUNAU

0502
ADVENTIST COLLEGES ABROAD
Summer German Language Program
Site: Austria: Braunau *Host inst:* Seminar Schloss Bogenhofen
Dates: 6 wks, Jun 12-Jul 24
Subjects: German language (beg/int/adv)
Eligibility: Students of member insts only. *Level:* adults *Requires:* 2.5 GPA *Age:* min 15
Credit: *Undergrad:* 9 qtr hrs *Grad:* none
Instruction: *In:* German *Format:* lab, lang study, lecture *Students:* intl
Costs: $2,096 *incl* tuition, housing, all meals, insurance, fees, excursions, books/materials *Nonrefundable fee*
Housing: *Arr by pgm:* residence halls
Deadline: May 31
Other info: *US accredited sponsor:* yes *Began:* 1992 *Orient:* abroad *Activities:* excursions, field trips, sports *URL:* http://www.nadadventist.org/aca
Contact: *See Index II for Members* Odette Ferreira, Dir, Adventist Colls Abroad, 12501 Old Columbia Pike, Silver Spring MD 20904-6600 *Ph:* 301-680 6444 *Fax:* 301-680 6463 *E-mail:* 104474.304@compuserve.com

---

BREGENZ

0503
KENTUCKY INSTITUTE FOR INTERNATIONAL STUDIES (KIIS)
Environmental Studies
Site: Austria: Bregenz
Dates: 2 wks, about Jul 5-20
Subjects: Ecology/environmental studies, Homestay
Eligibility: *Level:* grads, adults, teachers, professionals *Requires:* 2.0 GPA *Age:* min 18
Credit: *Undergrad:* none *Grad:* 3 *Doc:* transcript *Transfer credit through:* Murray State Univ
Instruction: *In:* English *Format:* directed field study, independent study, lecture *Students:* mainly US
Costs: About $2,190 *incl* tuition, housing, some meals, intl airfare, excursions, ISIC/ITIC
Housing: *Arr by pgm:* homestay
Deadline: Feb 15 ($100 late fee); Mar 15 for scholarships
Other info: *US accredited sponsor:* yes *Began:* 2000 *Orient:* in US & abroad *Activities:* excursions, field trips, program travel *Misc:* Topic: Special Problems in Environmental Educ: Comparing Austria, Germany & Switzerland with the US. *URL:* http://www.kiis.org
Contact: *See Index II for Members* Dr J Milton Grimes, Exec Dir, KIIS, Murray State Univ, PO Box 9, Murray KY 42071 *Ph:* 270-762 3091 *Fax:* 270-762 3434 *E-mail:* kiismsu@murraystate.edu

---

0504
KENTUCKY INSTITUTE FOR INTERNATIONAL STUDIES (KIIS)
Program in Bregenz, Austria
Site: Austria: Bregenz
Dates: 5 wks, late May-Jun
Subjects: Business/management, Communications, Economics, English, German language (beg/int/adv), Marketing, Political science/politics
Eligibility: *Level:* fresh, sophs, jrs, srs, grads, adults, teachers, professionals *Requires:* 2.0 GPA, good acad standing at home inst, faculty recommendations *Age:* min 18
Credit: *Undergrad:* 3-6 *Grad:* none *Doc:* transcript
Instruction: *In:* English, German *Format:* lang study, lecture *Students:* mainly US
Costs: $3,240 for students at member schs, $3,540 for others *incl* tuition, housing, some meals, intl airfare, fees, excursions, Eurail youth flexi pass, ISIC *Nonrefundable fee*
Housing: *Arr by pgm:* family-owned guest houses
Deadline: Feb 15 ($100 late fee)
Other info: *US accredited sponsor:* yes *Began:* 1975 *Orient:* in US & abroad *Misc:* Independent travel. May contact former participants. *Financial aid:* scholarships *URL:* http://www.kiis.org
Contact: *See Index II for Members* Dr J Milton Grimes, Exec Dir, KIIS, Murray State Univ, PO Box 9, Murray KY 42071-0009 *Ph:* 270-762 3091 *Fax:* 270-762 3434 *E-mail:* kiismsu@murraystate.edu

---

0505
MICHIGAN STATE UNIVERSITY
Opera on the Lake
Site: Austria: Bregenz
Dates: 4 wks, Jun-Jul
Subjects: German language (beg), Homestay, Humanities
Eligibility: *Level:* fresh, sophs, jrs, srs *Requires:* 2.0 GPA, 1 sem German *Age:* min 18
Credit: *Undergrad:* avail *Grad:* none *Doc:* transcript
Instruction: *In:* English *Format:* lecture *Students:* mainly US
Costs: About $1,500 *incl* housing, some meals, insurance, fees, excursions, opera tickets
Housing: *Arr by pgm:* homestay
Deadline: Mar 2
Other info: *US accredited sponsor:* yes *Began:* 1999 *Orient:* in US (1 day) *Activities:* excursions, field trips, cultural events *URL:* http://studyabroad.msu.edu
Contact: Cheryl Benner, Study Abroad, Michigan State Univ, 109 Intl Ctr, East Lansing MI 48824-1035 *Ph:* 517-353 8920 *Fax:* 517-432 2082 *E-mail:* bennerc@msu.edu ▲

FURTH

0506
EICHENDORFF'S RUH
Bassoon Ensemble and Introduction to Repair
Site: Austria: Furth *Host inst:* Eichendorff's Ruh Double Reed Ctr
Dates: 1 wk, Jul 6-12
Subjects: Music, Musical instrument repair, Woodwind instruments
Eligibility: *Level:* jrs, srs, grads, adults, teachers, professionals *Requires:* previous study in field *Age:* min 16, avg 20
Credit: *Undergrad:* none *Grad:* none *Doc:* certificate
Instruction: *In:* English, German *Format:* lecture, music lesson, practical training, seminar *Students:* intl
Costs: $700 *incl* tuition, housing, all meals, excursions, books/materials
Housing: *Arr by pgm:* pensions
Deadline: 1 mo before pgm
Other info: *US accredited sponsor:* no *Began:* 1970 *In coop with:* Breiteneich Courses *Orient:* abroad *Activities:* excursions, cultural events *Misc:* Emphasis on double reed, concentrating on bassoon & contra bassoon. May contact former participants.
Contact: Walter H Sallagar, Eichendorff's Ruh, A-2564 Furth, Austria
Or Contact: Fagottisten Treff Wien, Walter Hermann Sallagar, Fox Bassoon Svc, Neulinggasse 42, A-1030 Vienna, Austria

---

GRAZ

0507
EASTERN MICHIGAN UNIVERSITY
German Language Program
Site: Austria: Graz *Host inst:* Deutsch in Graz
Dates: Jul 7-Aug 18
Subjects: German language (int/adv)
Eligibility: *Level:* fresh, sophs, jrs, srs, grads, adults *Requires:* good acad standing, references *Age:* min 18
Credit: *Undergrad:* 6-9 *Grad:* 6-9 *Doc:* transcript
Instruction: *In:* German *Format:* lang study, lecture *Students:* US & intl
Costs: $3,495 *incl* tuition, housing, insurance, fees
Housing: *Arr by pgm:* apartments, homestay
Deadline: Mar 15
Other info: *US accredited sponsor:* yes *Began:* 1986 *Orient:* avail by mail *Activities:* excursions *Misc:* May contact former participants. *URL:* http://www.emich.edu/abroad
Contact: Acad Pgms Abroad, Eastern Michigan Univ, 127 Boone Hall, Ypsilanti MI 48197 *Ph:* 800-777 3541; 734-487 2424 *Fax:* 734-487 4377 *E-mail:* programs.abroad@emich.edu

---

0508
INDIANA UNIVERSITY
Summer Study in Graz
Site: Austria: Graz
Dates: 6 wks, mid-May-Jun
Subjects: Civilization/culture, German language
Eligibility: *Level:* fresh, sophs, jrs, srs, grads *Requires:* B avg, 3-4 sems coll German
Credit: *Undergrad:* 6 *Grad:* none *Doc:* transcript
Instruction: *In:* German *Format:* lang study, lecture *Students:* mainly US
Costs: $2,500-$3,700 *incl* tuition, housing, all meals, insurance, fees, excursions *Nonrefundable fee*
Housing: *Arr by pgm:* homestay
Deadline: Early Feb
Other info: *US accredited sponsor:* yes *Began:* 1981 *Orient:* in US *Activities:* excursions *Misc:* May contact former participants. *Financial aid:* scholarships *URL:* http://www.indiana.edu/~overseas
Contact: Overseas Study, Indiana Univ, Franklin Hall 303, Bloomington IN 47405 *Ph:* 812-855 9304 *Fax:* 812-855 6452 *E-mail:* overseas@indiana.edu

---

INNSBRUCK

0509
INNSBRUCKER HOCHSCHULKURSE DEUTSCH, UNIVERSITAET INNSBRUCK
Innsbrucker Hochschulkurse Deutsch
Site: Austria: Innsbruck
Dates: 3 or 6 wks, Jul 2-22, Jul 23-Aug 12 or Jul 2-Aug 12
Subjects: Austrian studies, German language (beg/int/adv)
Eligibility: *Level:* fresh, sophs, jrs, srs, grads, adults, teachers, professionals *Age:* min 17, avg 26
Credit: *Undergrad:* avail *Grad:* none *Doc:* certificate
Instruction: *In:* German *Format:* lang study *Students:* intl
Costs: AS 1,830 per wk *incl* tuition, fees, excursions, books/materials, library & sports ctr *Nonrefundable fee*
Housing: *Arr by pgm:* residence halls, hotels
Deadline: 1 day before pgm
Other info: *US accredited sponsor:* no *Began:* 1985 *Activities:* excursions, field trips, cultural events, sports *URL:* http://ihd.uibk.ac.at
Contact: Mag Claudia Mair-Gredler, IHD, Innrain 52, A-6020 Innsbruck, Austria *E-mail:* ihd-univ-innsbruck@uibk.ac.at
Or Contact: Dr Uta Maley, IHD, Innrain 52, 6020 Innsbruck, Austria *E-mail:* ihd-univ-innsbruck@uibk.ac.at

---

0510
UNIVERSITY OF NEW ORLEANS
European Center
Site: Austria: Innsbruck *Host inst:* Leopold-Franzens Univ
Dates: 3 wks, Jul
Subjects: Anthropology, Civilization/culture, Fine arts, History, Languages, Literature, Opera
Eligibility: *Level:* adults, teachers *Age:* min 30, avg 47
Credit: *Undergrad:* 3 *Grad:* 3 *Doc:* transcript, certificate
Instruction: *In:* English *Format:* lecture *Students:* mainly US
Costs: About $3,295 *incl* tuition, housing, most meals, insurance, fees, excursions
Housing: *Arr by pgm:* residence halls
Deadline: May 1 or until pgm filled
Other info: *US accredited sponsor:* yes *Began:* 1989 *Orient:* in US & abroad *Activities:* excursions, field trips *Misc:* Lang practice. May contact former participants. *URL:* http://www.uno.edu/~inst/Welcome.html
Contact: Irene Ziegler, Intl Study Pgms, Univ of New Orleans, PO Box 1340, New Orleans LA 70148 *Ph:* 504-280 7318 *Fax:* 504-280 7317 *E-mail:* iziegler@uno.edu

---

0511
UNIVERSITY OF NEW ORLEANS and **UNIVERSITY OF GEORGIA**
The International Summer School
Site: Austria: Innsbruck *Host inst:* Univ of Innsbruck
Dates: 6 wks, Jul-Aug
Subjects: Anthropology, Art history, Business/management, Communications, Drama/theater, Earth sciences, Economics, Finance, Fine arts, Geography, History, Music, Political science/politics, Sociology
Eligibility: *Level:* fresh, sophs, jrs, srs, grads, adults *Age:* min 17
Credit: *Undergrad:* 6-10 *Grad:* 6-9 *Doc:* transcript
Instruction: *In:* English *Format:* lang study, lecture *Students:* mainly US
Costs: $3,595 *incl* tuition, housing, some meals, insurance, fees, excursions
Housing: *Arr by pgm:* residence halls
Deadline: Apr 1 or until pgm filled
Other info: *US accredited sponsor:* yes *Began:* 1973 *Orient:* in US & abroad *Activities:* excursions, program travel *Misc:* May contact former participants. *URL:* http://www.uno.edu/~inst/Welcome.html

Contact: Mr Peter Alongia, Intl Study Pgms, Univ of New Orleans, Box 1315, New Orleans LA 70148 *Ph:* 504-280 7116 *Fax:* 504-280 7317 *E-mail:* palongia@uno.edu

KITZBUHEL

0512
DEUTSCH-INSTITUT TIROL
German Courses
Site: Austria: Kitzbuhel
Dates: 1 wk or longer, yr-round
Subjects: German language (beg/int/adv), Hiking/trekking, Skiing, Sports, Tennis
Eligibility: *Level:* adults, precoll *Age:* min 16, avg 25
Credit: *Undergrad:* avail *Grad:* avail *Doc:* certificate, diploma
Instruction: *In:* German *Format:* lang study, lecture, practical training *Students:* intl
Costs: About AS 6,000 per wk *incl* tuition, housing, some meals, books/materials
Housing: *Arr by pgm:* furnished rms
Deadline: None
Other info: *US accredited sponsor:* no *Began:* 1981 *Activities:* excursions, sports *Misc:* Small classes of 1-6. *URL:* http://www.deutschinstitut.com
Contact: Deutsch-Inst Tirol, Am Sandhugel 2, Kitzbuhel A-6370, Tirol, Austria *E-mail:* dit@kitz.netwing.at

KLAGENFURT

0513
EUROPEAN HERITAGE INSTITUTE
German Language and Culture in Austria
Site: Austria: Klagenfurt *Host inst:* Univ Klagenfurt
Dates: 1 or 2 mos, Jul 11-Aug 5 and/or Aug 8-Sep 2
Subjects: Austrian studies, Business language, German language (beg/int/adv), German studies, Literature
Eligibility: *Level:* fresh, sophs, jrs, srs, grads, adults, teachers, professionals *Age:* min 18
Credit: *Undergrad:* 6 *Grad:* 6 *Doc:* transcript, certificate
Instruction: *In:* German *Format:* lab, lang study, lecture, practical training, seminar *Students:* intl
Costs: $1,800 for 3 wks *incl* tuition, housing, some meals, fees, excursions
Housing: *Arr by pgm:* residence halls
Deadline: 2 mos before pgm
Other info: *US accredited sponsor:* no *Began:* 1993 *Orient:* in US & abroad *Activities:* excursions, cultural events, sports *Misc:* 12 students max per class. May contact former participants. *URL:* http://www.europeanheritage.org
Contact: Dr Antonio Masullo or Ms Barbara Cotter, European Heritage Inst, 2708 E Franklin St, Richmond VA 23223 *Ph:* 804-643 0661 *Fax:* 804-648 0826 *E-mail:* euritage@i2020.net ▲

0514
LANGUAGE LIAISON
German Language-Klagenfurt
Site: Austria: Klagenfurt
Dates: 2 wks or longer, yr-round
Subjects: Austrian studies, Business language, Foreign language teaching, German language (beg/int/adv), German studies, Humanities, Literature
Eligibility: *Level:* fresh, sophs, jrs, srs, grads, adults, teachers, professionals, precoll *Age:* min 18
Credit: *Undergrad:* avail *Grad:* avail *Doc:* transcript, certificate
Instruction: *In:* German *Format:* lab, lang study, lecture, practical training, seminar *Students:* intl
Costs: Contact sponsor
Housing: *Arr by pgm:* pensions, student dorms
Deadline: 30 days before pgm
Other info: *US accredited sponsor:* no *Activities:* excursions, cultural events, sports *Misc:* Scholarship research svc. *URL:* http://www.languageliaison.com
Contact: Nancy Forman, Dir, Lang Liaison, 4 Burnham Pkwy, Morristown NJ 07960 *Ph:* 800-284 4448 *Fax:* 973-898 1710 *E-mail:* learn@languageliaison.com

0515
UNIVERSITY OF ALABAMA
Alabama in Austria
Site: Austria: Klagenfurt *Host inst:* Univ of Klagenfurt
Dates: Jul 12-Aug 17
Subjects: Civilization/culture, German language (int/adv), German studies
Eligibility: *Level:* sophs, jrs, srs, grads, adults, teachers *Requires:* previous study in field
Credit: *Undergrad:* 6 *Grad:* 6 *Doc:* transcript
Instruction: *In:* German *Format:* lang study, lecture, study tour *Students:* mainly US
Costs: $2,800 *incl* tuition, housing, some meals, fees, excursions, ISIC
Housing: *Arr by pgm:* residence halls
Deadline: Feb 1
Other info: *US accredited sponsor:* yes *Began:* 1989 *Orient:* abroad *Activities:* program travel, cultural events *Misc:* May contact former participants. *URL:* http://www.ua.edu/international
Contact: Capstone Intl Pgm Ctr, Univ of Alabama, PO Box 870254, Tuscaloosa AL 35487-0254 *Ph:* 205-348 5256 *Fax:* 205-348 5298 *E-mail:* achannel@aalan.ua.edu
Or Contact: Christel Bell, German & Russian, Univ of Alabama, PO Box 870246, Tuscaloosa AL 35487 *Ph:* 205-348 9067 *Fax:* 205-348 5298

0516
UNIVERSITY OF NORTHERN IOWA
German Summer Institute
Site: Austria: Klagenfurt
Dates: 5 wks, late Jun-late Jul
Subjects: Civilization/culture, Education/teaching, Foreign language teaching, German language (adv), Homestay, Linguistics, Literature, Written composition
Eligibility: *Level:* fresh, sophs, jrs, srs, grads *Requires:* German lang background
Credit: *Undergrad:* 6 *Grad:* 6 *Doc:* transcript, diploma, degree
Instruction: *In:* German *Format:* lang study, lecture, seminar *Students:* mainly US
Costs: $2,760 *incl* tuition, housing, some meals, fees, excursions *Nonrefundable fee*
Housing: *Arr by pgm:* homestay
Deadline: Apr 15
Other info: *US accredited sponsor:* yes *Began:* 1968 *Orient:* abroad (intensive lang study) *Activities:* excursions, cultural events *Misc:* Participants can attend for lang & culture studies, professional improvement or earn MA by attending several summers. *URL:* http://www.uni.edu/modlangs/institutes-abroad
Contact: Prof Fritz Konig, Modern Langs, Univ of Northern Iowa, Cedar Falls IA 50614-0504 *Ph:* 319-273 2200 *Fax:* 319-273 2848 *E-mail:* mark.welty@uni.edu

PORTSCHACH

0517
LANGUAGE LIAISON
German Language-Portschach
Site: Austria: Portschach
Dates: 2 wks or longer, yr-round
Subjects: Austrian studies, Business language, Foreign language teaching, German language (beg/int/adv), History, Homestay, Humanities, Literature
Eligibility: *Level:* fresh, sophs, jrs, srs, grads, adults, teachers, professionals, precoll *Age:* min 16
Credit: *Undergrad:* avail *Grad:* avail *Doc:* transcript, certificate
Instruction: *In:* German *Format:* lab, lang study, lecture, seminar *Students:* intl
Costs: Contact sponsor
Housing: *Arr by pgm:* apartments, homestay

Deadline: 30 days before pgm
Other info: *US accredited sponsor:* no *Activities:* excursions, cultural events, sports *Misc:* Scholarship research svc. *URL:* http://www.languageliaison.com
Contact: Nancy Forman, Dir, Lang Liaison, 4 Burnham Pkwy, Morristown NJ 07960 *Ph:* 800-284 4448 *Fax:* 973-898 1710 *E-mail:* learn@languageliaison.com

SALZBURG

0518
BOWLING GREEN STATE UNIVERSITY
Summer Program in Salzburg
Site: Austria: Salzburg *Host inst:* IFK Deutschkurse Salzburg
Dates: 3 or 6 wks, Jul-Aug
Subjects: Austrian studies, Business language, Civilization/culture, Foreign language teaching, German language (beg/int/adv), Literature
Eligibility: *Level:* adults
Credit: *Undergrad:* avail *Grad:* avail *Doc:* transcript
Instruction: *In:* German *Format:* lang study, lecture *Students:* intl
Costs: $1,364-$1,464 for OH residents, $1,892 for others *incl* tuition, housing, some meals, fees, excursions, books/materials, for 3-wk pgm
Housing: *Arr by pgm:* residence halls, pensions
Deadline: May 20
Other info: *US accredited sponsor:* yes *Began:* 1967 *In coop with:* Univ of Salzburg *Activities:* excursions *Misc:* May contact former participants. *URL:* http://www.bgsu.edu/departments/greal
Contact: Dr Joseph Gray, German, Russian & East Asian Langs, Bowling Green State Univ, Bowling Green OH 43403-0219 *Ph:* 419-372 7140 *Fax:* 419-372 2571 *E-mail:* jgray@bgnet.bgsu.edu

0519
COLLEGE CONSORTIUM FOR INTERNATIONAL STUDIES and **TRUMAN STATE UNIVERSITY** and **MIAMI-DADE COMMUNITY COLLEGE**
Summer in Austria
Site: Austria: Salzburg *Host inst:* Salzburg Coll
Dates: 5 wks, about May 20-late Jun
Subjects: Art history, German language (beg/int/adv), Homestay, International business, Music history, Political science/politics
Eligibility: *Level:* fresh, sophs, jrs, srs, adults, teachers *Requires:* 2.7 GPA *Age:* min 18
Credit: *Undergrad:* 6-7 *Grad:* none *Doc:* transcript
Instruction: *In:* English, German *Format:* art studio, lang study, lecture, music lesson *Students:* mainly US
Costs: About $3,350 *incl* tuition, housing, all meals, excursions *Nonrefundable fee*
Housing: *Arr by pgm:* homestay
Deadline: Apr 15
Other info: *US accredited sponsor:* yes *Began:* 1998 *Orient:* abroad *Activities:* excursions, field trips *URL:* http://www.ccisabroad.org
Contact: *See Index II for Members* CCIS, 2000 P St NW, Ste 503, Washington DC 20036 *Ph:* 800-453 6956; 202-223 0330 *Fax:* 202-223 0999 *E-mail:* info@ccisabroad.org
Or Contact: Reinaldo Changsut, Study Abroad, Miami-Dade CC, 11011 SW 104th St, Miami FL 33176-3393 *Ph:* 305-237 2535, 305-237 2533 *Fax:* 305-237 2949 *E-mail:* rchangsu@mdcc.edu ▲

0520
INTERNATIONAL SUMMER ACADEMY OF FINE ARTS
International Summer Academy of Fine Arts
Site: Austria: Salzburg
Dates: 2-5 wks, Jul 24-Aug 28
Subjects: Architecture, Drawing, Etching, Fashion design, Graphic arts/design, Illustration, Jewelry/jewelry-making, Painting, Photography, Sculpture, Television/video, Visual arts
Eligibility: *Level:* adults *Requires:* previous study in field, German lang knowledge preferred *Age:* min 17
Credit: *Undergrad:* none *Grad:* none *Doc:* certificate
Instruction: *In:* English, German *Format:* art studio, lecture, workshop *Students:* intl
Costs: AS 6,462 for 2 wks, AS 8,669 for 3 wks, AS 13,572 for 5 wks *incl* tuition, insurance, fees
Housing: *Sponsor assists:* apartments, pensions, hotels, hostels
Deadline: Jun 15
Other info: *US accredited sponsor:* no *Misc:* Reduced fees for art & architecture students: AS 5,500 for 2 wks, 7,000 for 3 wks, 10,500 for 5 wks. *URL:* http://www.Land-sbg.gv.at/sommerakademie
Contact: Frau Dr Barbara Wally, or Frau Gabriele Winter, Intl Summer Acad, Kapitelgasse 5, POB 18, A-5010 Salzburg, Austria *E-mail:* soak.salzburg@magnet.at

0521
KENTUCKY INSTITUTE FOR INTERNATIONAL STUDIES (KIIS)
Program in Salzburg, Austria
Site: Austria: Salzburg
Dates: 5 wks, Jun-Jul
Subjects: Music, Music history
Eligibility: *Level:* fresh, sophs, jrs, srs, grads, adults, teachers, professionals *Requires:* 2.0 GPA, faculty recommendation letter, good standing at home inst *Age:* min 18
Credit: *Undergrad:* 3-6 *Grad:* none *Doc:* transcript
Instruction: *In:* English *Format:* lecture, seminar *Students:* mainly US
Costs: $3,090 for students at member schs, $3,390 for others *incl* tuition, housing, some meals, intl airfare, fees, excursions, ISIC *Nonrefundable fee*
Housing: *Arr by pgm:* hotels
Deadline: Feb 15 ($100 late fee)
Other info: *US accredited sponsor:* yes *Began:* 1990 *Orient:* in US & abroad *Activities:* excursions, cultural events *Misc:* Optional independent travel. May contact former participants. *Financial aid:* scholarships *URL:* http://www.kiis.org
Contact: *See Index II for Members* Dr J Milton Grimes, Exec Dir, KIIS, Murray State Univ, PO Box 9, Murray KY 42071-0009 *Ph:* 270-762 3091 *Fax:* 270-762 3434 *E-mail:* kiismsu@murraystate.edu

0522
LANGUAGES ABROAD
Language and Cultural Immersion Programs-Salzburg
Site: Austria: Salzburg
Dates: 2 wks or longer, yr-round
Subjects: Civilization/culture, German language (beg/int/adv)
Eligibility: *Level:* adults *Age:* min 17, max 65, avg 25
Credit: *Undergrad:* none *Grad:* none *Doc:* certificate
Instruction: *In:* German *Format:* lang study *Students:* intl
Costs: $2,800 for 4 wks *incl* tuition, housing, some meals, excursions, books/materials
Housing: *Arr by pgm:* apartments, homestay
Deadline: None
Other info: *US accredited sponsor:* no *Misc:* May contact former participants. *URL:* http://www.languagesabroad.com
Contact: Ms Jesse Philippe, Langs Abroad, 317 Adelaide St W, Ste 900, Toronto, Ontario M5V 1P9, Canada *Ph:* 800-219 9924; 416-925 7117 *E-mail:* info@languagesabroad.com

0523
UNIVERSITY OF NORTH CAROLINA AT CHAPEL HILL
Saltzburg Summer Program in Intl Environmental Risk Mgmt
Site: Austria: Salzburg *Host inst:* Univ of Salzburg
Dates: 5 wks, Jun 1-Jul 7

Subjects: Ecology/environmental studies
Eligibility: *Level:* sophs, jrs, srs, grads, adults, teachers, professionals *Requires:* 3.0 GPA *Age:* min 18
Credit: *Undergrad:* 6 *Grad:* 6 *Doc:* transcript
Instruction: *In:* English *Format:* lecture, seminar *Students:* intl
Costs: $3,000 *incl* tuition, housing, some meals, insurance, fees *Nonrefundable fee*
Housing: *Arr by pgm:* residence halls
Deadline: Feb 10
Other info: *US accredited sponsor:* yes *Began:* 2000 *Orient:* in US (1 day) *Activities:* field trips *Misc:* applications avail only on website. May contact former participants. *URL:* http://www.study-abroad.unc.edu
Contact: Paul Carlson, UNC-Chapel Hill, Study Abroad Office, CB #3130, Chapel Hill NC 27599-3130 *Ph:* 919-962 7001 *Fax:* 919-962 2262 *E-mail:* abroad@unc.edu
Or Contact: Kim Priebe, UNC-Chapel Hill, Study Abroad Office, CB #3130, Chapel Hill NC 27599-313- *Ph:* 919-962 7001 *Fax:* 919-962 2262 *E-mail:* abroad@unc.edu

---

0524
UNIVERSITY OF PORTLAND
Salzburg Summer Program
Site: Austria: Salzburg *Host inst:* Univ of Portland Ctr
Dates: 6 wks, Jun 21-Jul 29
Subjects: Fine arts, History, Sciences
Eligibility: *Level:* sophs, jrs, srs *Requires:* 3.00 GPA *Age:* min 18
Credit: *Undergrad:* 6 *Grad:* none *Doc:* transcript
Instruction: *In:* English *Format:* study tour *Students:* mainly US
Costs: $3,700 *incl* tuition, housing, excursions *Nonrefundable fee*
Housing: *Arr by pgm:* residence halls
Deadline: Oct 15
Other info: *US accredited sponsor:* yes *Began:* 1998 *Orient:* abroad *Activities:* excursions, field trips, cultural events
Contact: Rev Arthur Wheeler CSC, Univ of Portland, 5000 N Willamette Blvd, Portland OR 97203-5798 *Ph:* 503-943 7221 *Fax:* 503-943 7804 *E-mail:* wheeler@up.edu

---

STROBL

0525
UNIVERSITY OF MIAMI (FL)
European Studies Program in Strobl, Austria
Site: Austria: Strobl *Host inst:* Univ of Vienna
Dates: 4 wks, mid-Jul-mid-Aug
Subjects: European studies, German language, International relations, Political science/politics
Eligibility: *Level:* sophs, jrs, srs *Requires:* 3.0 GPA *Age:* min 18
Credit: *Undergrad:* 6 *Grad:* none *Doc:* transcript
Instruction: *In:* English, German *Format:* lang study, lecture *Students:* intl
Costs: $3,950 *incl* tuition, housing, all meals *Nonrefundable fee*
Housing: *Arr by pgm:* residence halls
Deadline: Apr 1
Other info: *US accredited sponsor:* yes *Began:* 1998 *Orient:* abroad (1 day) *Misc:* May contact former participants. *URL:* http://www.studyabroad.miami.edu/
Contact: Intl Educ & Exch Pgms, Allen Hall 212, 5050 Brunson Dr, PO Box 248005, Univ of Miami, Coral Gables FL 33124-1610 *Ph:* 800-557 5421; 305-284 3434 *Fax:* 305-284 6629 *E-mail:* ieep@miami.edu

---

0526
XAVIER UNIVERSITY
Xavier University Summer Program in Austria
Site: Austria: Strobl *Host inst:* Univ of Vienna
Dates: 4 wks, Jul 14-Aug 11
Subjects: European studies, German language (beg/int/adv)
Eligibility: *Level:* fresh, sophs, jrs, srs, grads, adults, teachers, professionals *Requires:* 2.5 GPA *Age:* min 18
Credit: *Undergrad:* 8 *Grad:* avail *Doc:* transcript
Instruction: *In:* English, German *Format:* lang study, lecture, seminar *Students:* intl
Costs: About $3,300 *incl* tuition, housing, all meals, excursions, books/materials *Nonrefundable fee*
Housing: *Arr by pgm:* residence halls
Deadline: May 8
Other info: *US accredited sponsor:* yes *Began:* 1982 *Orient:* in US *Activities:* excursions, field trips, cultural events, sports *Misc:* Pgm focus on econ, political, historical, legal & socio-cultural aspects of an emerging new Europe. May contact former participants. *URL:* http://www.xu.edu
Contact: Margaret McDiarmid, Xavier Univ, 3800 Victory Pkwy, Cincinnati OH 45207-5184 *Ph:* 800-344 4698; 513-745 3406 *Fax:* 513-745 1955 *E-mail:* mcdiarmi@xu.edu
Or Contact: Gerhard & Carol Neuzil, Xavier Univ, 3800 Victory Parkway, Cincinnati OH *Ph:* 513-459 9799 *Fax:* 513-459 1470 *E-mail:* GeCaNe@prodigy.net

---

VIENNA

0527
ACTILINGUA ACADEMY
German Courses in Vienna
Site: Austria: Vienna
Dates: 2-36 wks, yr-round
Subjects: Business/management, Civilization/culture, German language (beg/int/adv), Homestay, Internships, Music, Sports
Eligibility: *Level:* fresh, sophs, jrs, srs, grads, adults, teachers, precoll *Age:* min 16, avg 25
Credit: *Undergrad:* avail *Grad:* avail *Doc:* transcript, certificate
Instruction: *In:* German *Format:* internship, lang study, lecture, music lesson *Students:* intl
Costs: $1,100 for 4 wks *incl* tuition, housing, some meals, books/materials, cultural pgm
Housing: *Arr by pgm:* residence halls with local students, apartments, homestay, hotels
Deadline: 4 wks before pgm; Jun 1 for scholarships
Other info: *US accredited sponsor:* no *Began:* 1988 *Activities:* excursions, cultural events, sports *Financial aid:* scholarships *URL:* http://www.actilingua.at
Contact: Ms Y Ramser, Admissions, Actilingua Acad, Gloriettegasse 8, A-1130 Vienna, Austria *E-mail:* info@actilingua.at

---

0528
ALPHA SPRACHINSTITUT AUSTRIA
German for Foreigners
Site: Austria: Vienna
Dates: 4 wks, yr-round
Subjects: German language (beg/int/adv)
Eligibility: *Level:* fresh, sophs, jrs, srs, adults, teachers *Requires:* placement test *Age:* min 16
Credit: *Undergrad:* avail *Grad:* none *Doc:* certificate
Instruction: *In:* German *Format:* lang study *Students:* intl
Costs: AS 5,800 *incl* tuition
Housing: *Arr by pgm:* residence halls, apartments, homestay, pensions, hotels, hostels
Deadline: Rolling admissions
Other info: *US accredited sponsor:* no *Began:* 1946 *Activities:* excursions, cultural events, sports *URL:* http://www.alpha.at
Contact: Schwarzenbergplatz 16/ Canovagasse 5, Alpha Sprachinst Austria, 1010 Vienna, Austria *E-mail:* office@alpha.at

---

See "How To Use This Book" for definitions of terms used above. ▲ = See program sponsor's ad(s) in this book.

0529
CULTURA WIEN
German Language Courses in Vienna, Austria
Site: Austria: Vienna
Dates: 4 wks or longer, yr-round
Subjects: German language (beg/int/adv), Music (beg/int/adv)
Eligibility: *Level:* fresh, sophs, jrs, srs, grads, adults, teachers, professionals, precoll *Age:* min 15, avg 24
Credit: *Undergrad:* avail *Grad:* avail *Doc:* certificate *Transfer credit through:* Slippery Rock Univ
Instruction: *In:* German *Format:* lang study *Students:* intl
Costs: About $900 per mo *incl* tuition, housing, books/materials, lectures, cultural pgm
Housing: *Arr by pgm:* apartments with local students, residence halls with local students, homestay, pensions, hotels, hostels
Deadline: 1 mo before pgm
Other info: *US accredited sponsor:* no *Began:* 1987 *Activities:* excursions, cultural events, sports *Misc:* May contact former participants. *URL:* http://www.culturawien.at
Contact: Renate Schmid, Cultura Wien, Bauernmarkt 18, A-1010 Vienna, Austria *E-mail:* cultura@nextra.at

---

0530
EUROPEAN HERITAGE INSTITUTE
Music Master Classes in Vienna
Site: Austria: Vienna *Host inst:* Vienna Conservatory of Music
Dates: 2-wk terms, Jul 3-Aug 11
Subjects: Conducting, Master classes, Opera, Piano, Singing/voice, String instruments, Woodwind instruments
Eligibility: *Level:* fresh, sophs, jrs, srs, grads, adults *Requires:* portfolio & audition for master classes; recommended for adv courses *Age:* min 18, max 35
Credit: *Undergrad:* none *Grad:* avail *Doc:* certificate
Instruction: *In:* English, French, German, Italian, Spanish *Format:* music lesson, practical training, seminar *Students:* intl
Costs: $580 to audit, $820 *incl* tuition, fees
Housing: *Arr by pgm:* apartments, pensions, hotels
Deadline: Apr 1
Other info: *US accredited sponsor:* no *Began:* 1975 *Orient:* in US & abroad *Activities:* cultural events *Misc:* May contact former participants. *URL:* http://www.europeanheritage.org
Contact: Dr Antonio Masullo or Ms Barbara Cotter, European Heritage Inst, 2708 E Franklin St, Richmond VA 23223 *Ph:* 804-643 0661 *Fax:* 804-648 0826 *E-mail:* euritage@i2020.net ▲

0531
EUROPEAN HERITAGE INSTITUTE
Summer in Vienna
Site: Austria: Vienna *Host inst:* Univ of Vienna-Intl Univ
Dates: 2, 3 or 4 wks-3 mos, Jul 4-Sep 23
Subjects: German language (beg/int/adv), Linguistics, Literature, Music
Eligibility: *Level:* fresh, sophs, jrs, srs, grads, adults, teachers, professionals *Age:* min 18
Credit: *Undergrad:* avail *Grad:* avail *Doc:* transcript, certificate
Instruction: *In:* German *Format:* lab, lang study, lecture, practical training, seminar *Students:* intl
Costs: $1,150 for 4 wks *incl* tuition, housing, fees
Housing: *Arr by pgm:* residence halls
Deadline: Apr 15
Other info: *US accredited sponsor:* no

Began: 1952 *Orient:* in US & abroad *Activities:* excursions, cultural events, sports *Misc:* May contact former participants. *URL:* http://www.europeanheritage.org
Contact: Dr Antonio Masullo or Ms Barbara Cotter, European Heritage Inst, 2708 E Franklin St, Richmond VA 23223 *Ph:* 804-643 0661 *Fax:* 804-648 0826 *E-mail:* euritage@i2020.net ▲

0532
INTERNATIONALES KULTURINSTITUT (IKI)
IKI Deutschkurse
Site: Austria: Vienna
Dates: 1 mo or longer, yr-round
Subjects: German language (beg/int/adv)
Eligibility: *Level:* adults *Age:* min 16, avg 25
Credit: *Undergrad:* none *Grad:* none *Doc:* certificate
Instruction: *In:* German *Format:* lang study *Students:* intl
Costs: AS 4,800 for 1 mo, AS 4,400 for each addtl mo *incl* tuition, books/materials
Housing: *Arr by pgm:* residence halls, pensions
Deadline: 4 wks before pgm
Other info: *US accredited sponsor:* no *Began:* 1981 *Activities:* excursions, sports *Misc:* Parties in summer. May contact former participants. *URL:* http://www.ikivienna.at
Contact: Brigitte Resch, or Susanne Sedlaczek, IKI, Opernring 7, A-1010 Vienna, Austria *E-mail:* iki@friends.at

---

0533
LANGUAGE LIAISON
German Language-Vienna
Site: Austria: Vienna
Dates: 2 wks or longer, yr-round
Subjects: Business language, Civilization/culture, German language (beg/int/adv), Homestay, Humanities, Tourism
Eligibility: *Level:* fresh, sophs, jrs, srs, grads, adults, teachers, professionals, precoll *Age:* min 10
Credit: *Undergrad:* avail *Grad:* avail *Doc:* transcript, certificate
Instruction: *In:* German *Format:* internship, lang study *Students:* intl
Costs: Contact sponsor
Housing: *Arr by pgm:* residence halls, apartments, homestay, hotels
Deadline: 30 days before pgm
Other info: *US accredited sponsor:* no *Activities:* excursions, cultural events, sports *Misc:* Scholarship research svc. *URL:* http://www.languageliaison.com
Contact: Nancy Forman, Dir, Lang Liaison, 4 Burnham Pkwy, Morristown NJ 07960 *Ph:* 800-284 4448 *Fax:* 973-898 1710 *E-mail:* learn@languageliaison.com

---

0534
LANGUAGE STUDIES ABROAD, INC
Intensive German-Austria
Site: Austria: Vienna *Host inst:* LSA Vienna
Dates: 1 wk or longer, yr-round
Subjects: Business language, Composition, German language (beg/int/adv), Homestay, Music, Singing/voice
Eligibility: *Level:* fresh, sophs, jrs, srs, grads, adults, teachers, professionals, precoll *Age:* min 16
Credit: *Undergrad:* none *Grad:* none *Doc:* certificate, diploma
Instruction: *In:* German *Format:* lang study, music lesson *Students:* intl
Costs: $1,210 for 4 wks *incl* tuition, housing, some meals, excursions, books/materials *Nonrefundable fee*
Housing: *Sponsor assists:* apartments, homestay, hotels
Deadline: 4 wks before pgm
Other info: *US accredited sponsor:* no *Began:* 1988 *Orient:* abroad *Activities:* excursions, field trips, cultural events, sports *Misc:* Special German & wintersports package avail. May contact former participants. *Financial aid:* work study *URL:* http://www.languagestudiesabroad.com
Contact: Lang Studies Abroad, Inc, 103 Londonderry Ct, Reno NV 89511-2718 *Ph:* 800-424 5522; 775-849 9206 *Fax:* 775-849 9217 *E-mail:* info@languagestudiesabroad.com

---

0535
LANGUAGES ABROAD
Language and Culture-Vienna
Site: Austria: Vienna
Dates: 2 wks or longer, yr-round
Subjects: Austrian studies, Civilization/culture, German language (beg/int/adv), Homestay
Eligibility: *Level:* adults *Age:* min 17, max 65, avg 25
Credit: *Undergrad:* none *Grad:* none *Doc:* certificate
Instruction: *In:* German *Format:* lang study *Students:* intl
Costs: $1,390 per mo *incl* tuition, housing, some meals, fees, excursions, books/materials
Housing: *Arr by pgm:* residence halls, homestay
Deadline: None
Other info: *US accredited sponsor:* no *Began:* 1995 *Activities:* excursions, field trips, program travel, cultural events, sports *Misc:* May contact former participants. *URL:* http://www.languagesabroad.com
Contact: Ms Jesse Philippe, Langs Abroad, 317 Adelaide St W, Ste 900, Toronto, Ontario M5V 1P9, Canada *Ph:* 800-219 9924; 416-925 7117 *E-mail:* info@languagesabroad.com

---

0536
LINGUA SERVICE WORLDWIDE
Total Immersion/Intensive Language and Culture in Austria
Site: Austria: Vienna *Host inst:* Actilingua Acad
Dates: 1 wk-1 yr, yr-round
Subjects: Civilization/culture, German language (beg/int/adv), Homestay, Sports
Eligibility: *Level:* fresh, sophs, jrs, srs, grads, adults, teachers, professionals, precoll *Age:* min 14
Credit: *Undergrad:* avail *Grad:* avail *Doc:* transcript, certificate *Transfer credit through:* Univ of Southern Mississippi
Instruction: *In:* German *Format:* lang study, lecture *Students:* intl & host country
Costs: Contact sponsor
Housing: *Arr by pgm:* apartments with local students, residence halls with local students, homestay, pensions, hotels, hostels
Deadline: 45 days before pgm
Other info: *US accredited sponsor:* no *Began:* 1993 *Activities:* excursions, cultural events *Misc:* May contact former participants. *URL:* http://www.linguaserviceworldwide.com
Contact: Dir, Lingua Svc Worldwide, 75 Prospect St, Ste 4, Huntington NY 11743 *Ph:* 800-394 5327; 631-424 0777 *Fax:* 631-271 3441 *E-mail:* itctravel@worldnet.att.net ▲

0537
NATIONAL REGISTRATION CENTER FOR STUDY ABROAD (NRCSA)
Summer Study in Vienna
Site: Austria: Vienna *Host inst:* Univ of Vienna
Dates: 3-4 wks, Jul-Sep
Subjects: Austrian studies, Civilization/culture, German language (beg/int/adv), German studies, Homestay
Eligibility: *Level:* fresh, sophs, jrs, srs, grads, adults *Age:* min 18
Credit: *Undergrad:* none *Grad:* none
Instruction: *In:* German *Format:* lang study, lecture *Students:* intl
Costs: $853 for 3 wks, $990 for 4 wks *incl* tuition, housing, insurance, fees
Housing: *Arr by pgm:* residence halls,

apartments, homestay, pensions, hotels
Deadline: None
Other info: *US accredited sponsor:* no *Misc:* Optional excursions. *URL:* http://www.nrcsa.com
Contact: Reuel Zielke, NRCSA, 823 N 2nd St, #206, Milwaukee WI 53203 *Ph:* 414-278 0631 *Fax:* 414-271 8884 *E-mail:* info@nrcsa.com

---

0538
NEW YORK UNIVERSITY, TISCH SCHOOL OF THE ARTS
Post Production/Editing Workshop
Site: Austria: Vienna
Dates: 6 wks, Jun 25-Aug 3
Subjects: Austrian studies, Film studies, Media studies, Performing arts, Visual arts
Eligibility: *Level:* sophs, jrs, srs, grads, adults *Requires:* previous study in field *Age:* min 18
Credit: *Undergrad:* 8 per sem *Grad:* 8 per sem *Doc:* transcript
Instruction: *In:* English *Format:* lecture, practical training, seminar, tutorial, workshop *Students:* mainly US
Costs: $4,012 per sem *incl* tuition, fees *Nonrefundable fee*
Housing: *Arr by pgm:* residence halls, apartments
Deadline: Apr 15 priority deadline
Other info: *US accredited sponsor:* yes *Began:* 2001 *Orient:* in US & abroad *Activities:* field trips *Misc:* May contact former participants. *Financial aid:* scholarships, work study *URL:* http://www.nyu.edu/tisch/international
Contact: Linda Kow, Assoc Dir, New York Univ, Tisch Intl Pgms, 721 Broadway, 12th Fl, New York NY 10003 *Ph:* 212-998 9175 *Fax:* 212-995 4578 *E-mail:* tisch.international@nyu.edu

---

0539
NORTH CAROLINA STATE UNIVERSITY
Summer Program in Vienna, Austria
Site: Austria: Vienna
Dates: 4 wks, Jul
Subjects: Austrian studies, Central European studies, German language (beg/int/adv), History, International business, Political science/politics
Eligibility: *Level:* fresh, sophs, jrs, srs, grads
Credit: *Undergrad:* 6 *Grad:* none *Doc:* transcript
Instruction: *In:* English *Format:* lang study, lecture, seminar, study tour *Students:* mainly US
Costs: $2,200 *incl* tuition, housing, some meals, excursions, railpass, ISIC
Housing: *Arr by pgm:* pensions, hotels
Deadline: Feb
Other info: *US accredited sponsor:* yes *Orient:* in US *Activities:* excursions, field trips, program travel, cultural events *URL:* http://www.ncsu.edu/studyabroad
Contact: Anne Haberkern, North Carolina State Univ, 2118 Pullen Hall, Box 7344, Raleigh NC 27695-7344 *Ph:* 919-515 2087 *Fax:* 919-515 6021 *E-mail:* study_abroad@ncsu.edu

---

0540
UNIVERSITAET WIEN, WIENER INTERNATIONALE HOCHSCHULKURSE
German Language Course
Site: Austria: Vienna *Host inst:* Univ of Vienna
Dates: Jul 8-Aug 4, Aug 5-Sep 1, Sep 9-22
Subjects: Foreign language teaching, German language (beg/int/adv)
Eligibility: *Level:* fresh, sophs, jrs, srs, adults, teachers, precoll *Age:* min 16
Credit: *Undergrad:* none *Grad:* none *Doc:* certificate
Instruction: *In:* German *Format:* lang study, lecture *Students:* intl
Costs: About AS 10,800 *incl* tuition, housing
Housing: *Arr by pgm:* residence halls
Deadline: 2 wks before pgm
Other info: *US accredited sponsor:* no *Began:* 1922 *Activities:* excursions *Financial aid:* scholarships *URL:* http://www.univie.ac.at/WIHOK
Contact: Sigrun Inmann-Trojer, Wiener Intl Hochschulkurse Univ, A-1010 Vienna, Austria *E-mail:* wihok@univie.ac.at

---

0541
UNIVERSITY OF KENTUCKY
Summer Study Program, Vienna
Site: Austria: Vienna *Host inst:* Wirtschaftsuniv Wien (Econ Univ)
Dates: 3 wks, Aug 1-20
Subjects: Austrian studies, Business/management, Civilization/culture, Finance, International business, International marketing, International studies
Eligibility: *Level:* srs, grads *Requires:* previous study in field, good acad standing
Credit: *Undergrad:* 3-4 *Grad:* 3-4 *Doc:* transcript
Instruction: *In:* English *Format:* lecture *Students:* mainly US
Costs: About $1,250 *incl* tuition, housing, some meals, excursions
Housing: *Arr by pgm:* residence halls
Deadline: Apr 15
Other info: *US accredited sponsor:* yes *Began:* 1987 *Activities:* excursions *Misc:* May contact former participants. *URL:* http://gatton.uky.edu/abroad.htm
Contact: Diana Rast, Coll of Bus & Econ, Univ of Kentucky, 237 Gatton, Lexington KY 40506-0034 *Ph:* 800-456 0965; 606-257 3024 *Fax:* 606-257 3293 *E-mail:* derast01@pop.uky.edu

---

0542
UNIVERSITY OF SOUTHERN MISSISSIPPI
Austrian Studies Program
Site: Austria: Vienna
Dates: 3 wks, Jun 14-Jul 5
Subjects: Field study, History
Eligibility: *Level:* sophs, jrs, srs, grads *Requires:* 2.0 GPA, clear academic standing.
Credit: *Undergrad:* 4 *Grad:* 4 *Doc:* transcript
Instruction: *In:* English *Format:* directed field study, lecture, seminar *Students:* mainly US
Costs: $3,499 for undergrads, $3,799 for grads *incl* tuition, housing, some meals, intl airfare, fees, excursions *Nonrefundable fee*
Housing: *Arr by pgm*
Deadline: Feb 15
Other info: *US accredited sponsor:* yes *Began:* 1985 *Orient:* abroad *Activities:* excursions, field trips, program travel, cultural events *Misc:* Grants & loans avail. Optional trips to Budapest & Central Europe at an addtl fee. Pgm limited to 20 students. May contact former participants. *URL:* http://www.usm.edu
Contact: Dr Tim W Hudson, Intl & Continuing Educ, Univ of Southern Mississippi, Box 10047, Hattiesburg MS 39406 *Ph:* 601-266 4344 *Fax:* 601-266 5699
Or Contact: Dr G T Harper, Dir, Austrian Studies Pgm, Univ of Southern Mississippi, Box 5004, Hattiesburg MS 39406-0047 *Ph:* 601-266 4315 *Fax:* 601-266 5699 *E-mail:* melissa.ravencraft@usm.edu

---

0543
WEBSTER UNIVERSITY
Degree Programs
Site: Austria: Vienna *Host inst:* Webster Univ Vienna campus
Dates: 2, 4 or 8 wks, summer
Subjects: Accounting, Art history, Finance, Fine arts, German language (beg), International business, International relations, Marketing, Psychology
Eligibility: *Level:* sophs, jrs, srs, grads, adults *Requires:* 2.5 GPA, GMAT for MBA *Age:* avg 23
Credit: *Undergrad:* avail *Grad:* avail *Doc:* degree
Instruction: *In:* English *Format:* lecture, music lesson *Students:* intl
Costs: $1,149 per 3-credit course *incl* tuition

Housing: *Sponsor assists:* residence halls with local students
Deadline: Feb 15
Other info: *US accredited sponsor:* yes *Began:* 1981 *Orient:* in US & abroad *Activities:* excursions *Misc:* BA, MA & MBA avail. May contact former participants. *Financial aid:* scholarships *URL:* http://www.websteruniv.edu
Contact: Teresa Bruno, Study Abraod, Webster Univ, 470 E Lockwood, St Louis MO 63119 *Ph:* 800-984 6857; 314-968 6857 *Fax:* 314-968 7119 *E-mail:* worldview@webster.edu

---

0544
WEBSTER UNIVERSITY
Graduate Program in Vienna
Site: Austria: Vienna *Host inst:* Webster Univ Vienna campus
Dates: 2, 4, or 8 wks, summer
Subjects: Art, Business administration, Finance, International business, International relations, Marketing
Eligibility: *Level:* grads *Requires:* 2.5 GPA, bachelor's degree
Credit: *Undergrad:* none *Grad:* 3-6 *Doc:* transcript, diploma
Instruction: *In:* English *Format:* lecture, seminar *Students:* intl
Costs: $1,149 per 3-credit course *incl* tuition
Housing: *Sponsor assists:* residence halls, apartments
Deadline: 4 mos before pgm
Other info: *US accredited sponsor:* yes *Began:* 1981 *Orient:* in US & abroad *Financial aid:* scholarships *URL:* http://www.websteruniv.edu
Contact: Study Abroad Ctr, Webster Univ, 470 E Lockwood, St Louis MO 63119 *Ph:* 800-984 6857; 314-968 6988 *Fax:* 314-968 7119 *E-mail:* worldview@webster.edu

---

0545
WEBSTER UNIVERSITY
Undergraduate Program in Vienna
Site: Austria: Vienna *Host inst:* Webster Univ Vienna campus
Dates: 8 wks, summer
Subjects: Accounting, Art, Art history, Business/management, Central European studies, Computer sciences, East European studies, Economics, International relations, Marketing, Psychology
Eligibility: *Level:* sophs, jrs, srs *Requires:* 2.5 GPA
Credit: *Undergrad:* 3-9 *Grad:* none *Doc:* transcript, diploma
Instruction: *In:* English *Format:* lecture, seminar *Students:* intl
Costs: $1,149 per 3-credit course *incl* tuition
Housing: *Sponsor assists:* residence halls, apartments
Deadline: 6 mos before pgm
Other info: *US accredited sponsor:* yes *Began:* 1991 *Orient:* in US & abroad *Financial aid:* scholarships *URL:* http://www.websteruniv.edu
Contact: Study Abroad Ctr, Webster Univ, 470 E Lockwood, St Louis MO 63119 *Ph:* 800-984 6857; 314-968 6988 *Fax:* 314-968 7119 *E-mail:* worldview@webster.edu

---

0546
WIENER MEISTERKURSE
Vienna Master Courses in Music
Site: Austria: Vienna *Host inst:* Vienna Conservatory, Univ of Music & Arts
Dates: 2-wk courses, Jul 1-Aug 25
Subjects: Brass instruments, Chamber music, Conducting, Master classes, Opera, Piano, Singing/voice, String instruments, Woodwind instruments
Eligibility: *Requires:* adv music students, audition
Credit: *Undergrad:* none *Grad:* none *Doc:* diploma
Instruction: *In:* English, French, German *Format:* lecture, music lesson *Students:* intl
Costs: AS 6,500 for active participants, AS 4,000 for auditors/1 course *incl* tuition, fees
Housing: *Arr by pgm:* hostels
Deadline: Jun 1
Other info: *US accredited sponsor:* no *Began:* 1975 *Misc:* Activities incl concerts. *URL:* http://www.wiener-meisterkurse.music.at
Contact: Elisabeth Keschmann, or Dr Monica Wildauer, Wiener Meisterkurse, Reisnerstr 3, A-1030 Vienna, Austria *E-mail:* wiener-meisterkurse@music.at

Belgium

MORE THAN ONE CITY

0547
INTERNATIONAL MANAGEMENT INSTITUTE
Total European Experience
Site: Belgium: Antwerp, Brussels
Dates: 11 days, Jul-Aug
Subjects: Contemporary issues, European studies, International business
Eligibility: *Level:* fresh, sophs, jrs, srs, grads, adults, teachers, professionals, precoll
Credit: *Undergrad:* none *Grad:* none *Doc:* certificate
Instruction: *In:* English *Format:* lecture, seminar, study tour, workshop *Students:* intl
Costs: $1,495 *incl* tuition, housing, some meals, excursions
Housing: *Arr by pgm:* apartments, pensions, hotels
Deadline: 1 mo before pgm
Other info: *US accredited sponsor:* no *Began:* 1998 *Activities:* excursions, field trips, program travel, cultural events, sports *Misc:* May contact former participants. *URL:* http://www.timi.edu
Contact: Mr L Van Mele, IMI, J Jordaensstr 77, 2018 Antwerp, Belgium
Or Contact: IMI, rue de Livourne 116-120, 1000 Brussels, Belgium

---

0548
INTERNATIONAL MANAGEMENT INSTITUTE
Undergraduate Studies in Business Administration-Belgium
Site: Belgium: Antwerp, Brussels
Dates: Jul-Sep
Subjects: Accounting, Advertising, Business/management, Dutch language, Economics, Finance, French language, German language, Law, Marketing, Mathematics, Spanish language, Statistics
Eligibility: *Level:* fresh, sophs, jrs, srs
Credit: *Undergrad:* 20 per sem *Grad:* none
Instruction: *In:* Dutch, English, French *Format:* lang study, lecture *Students:* intl
Costs: Contact sponsor
Housing: *Sponsor assists*
Deadline: Late Jun
Other info: *US accredited sponsor:* no *Activities:* excursions, field trips *URL:* http://www.timi.edu
Contact: Mr L Van Mele, IMI, J Jordaensstr 77, 2018 Antwerp, Belgium *E-mail:* info@timi.edu
Or Contact: IMI, rue de Livourne 116-120, 1000 Brussels, Belgium *E-mail:* info@timi.edu

---

0549
INTERNATIONAL MANAGEMENT INSTITUTE
Undergraduate Studies in Business Communication-Belgium
Site: Belgium: Antwerp, Brussels
Dates: Jul-Sep
Subjects: Accounting, Advertising, Business/management, Dutch language, Economics, Finance, French language, German language, Law, Marketing, Media studies, Psychology, Public relations, Sociology, Statistics
Eligibility: *Level:* fresh, sophs, jrs, srs
Credit: *Undergrad:* 20 per sem *Grad:* none
Instruction: *In:* Dutch, English, French *Format:* lang study, lecture *Students:* intl
Costs: Contact sponsor
Housing: *Sponsor assists*
Deadline: Late Jun
Other info: *US accredited sponsor:* no *Activities:* excursions, field trips *Misc:* May

contact former participants. *URL:* http://www.timi.edu
Contact: Mr L Van Mele, IMI, J Jordaensstr 77, 2018 Antwerp, Belgium
Or Contact: IMI, rue de Livourne 116-120, 1000 Brussels, Belgium

---

0550
INTERNATIONAL MANAGEMENT INSTITUTE
Undergraduate Studies in Information Systems-Belgium
Site: Belgium: Antwerp, Brussels
Dates: Jul-Sep
Subjects: Business/management, Computer sciences, Dutch language (beg/int/adv), Economics, Finance, French language (beg/int/adv), German language (beg/int/adv), Information science/systems, Information technology, Law, Marketing, Mathematics, Spanish language (beg/int/adv), Statistics
Eligibility: *Level:* fresh, sophs, jrs, srs
Credit: *Undergrad:* 20 per sem *Grad:* none *Doc:* certificate
Instruction: *In:* Dutch, English, French *Format:* lang study, lecture, study tour, workshop *Students:* intl
Costs: Contact sponsor
Housing: *Sponsor assists*
Deadline: Late Jun
Other info: *US accredited sponsor:* no *Began:* 1977 *Activities:* excursions, field trips *Misc:* May contact former participants. *URL:* http://www.timi.edu
Contact: Mr L Van Mele, IMI, J Jordaenststr 77, 2018 Antwerp, Belgium *E-mail:* info@timi.edu
Or Contact: IMI, rue de Livourne 116-120, 1000 Brussels, Belgium *E-mail:* info@timi.edu

---

ANTWERP

0551
GEORGETOWN UNIVERSITY
Antwerp, the European Union
Site: Belgium: Antwerp *Host inst:* Univ of Antwerp
Dates: May 20-Jun 2
Subjects: Economics, European Union
Eligibility: *Level:* sophs, jrs, srs, grads *Requires:* previous study in field
Credit: *Undergrad:* 3 *Grad:* avail *Doc:* transcript
Instruction: *In:* English *Format:* directed field study, lecture, seminar, study tour *Students:* mainly US
Costs: About $2,250 *incl* tuition, housing, some meals, excursions *Nonrefundable fee*
Housing: *Arr by pgm:* hotels
Deadline: Mar 16
Other info: *US accredited sponsor:* yes *Activities:* excursions, field trips, program travel *Misc:* May contact former participants. *URL:* http://www.georgetown.edu/ssce/
Contact: Marianne Siemietkowski Needham, Antwerp Summer Pgm, Georgetown Univ, Poulton Hall, 2nd Fl, Box 571012, Washington DC 20057-1012 *Ph:* 202-687 6184 *Fax:* 202-687 8954 *E-mail:* sscefps@gunet.georgetown.edu

---

0552
MARQUETTE UNIVERSITY
Business in the EEC
Site: Belgium: Antwerp *Host inst:* Univ of Antwerp
Dates: 3 wks, May 21-Jun 10
Subjects: Business/management, European Union
Eligibility: *Level:* sophs, jrs, srs, grads *Requires:* 2.75 GPA
Credit: *Undergrad:* 3 *Grad:* 3 *Doc:* transcript
Instruction: *In:* English *Format:* lecture, seminar, study tour *Students:* mainly US
Costs: $3,195 for undergrads, $3,395 for grads *incl* tuition, housing, most meals, intl airfare, fees, excursions
Housing: *Arr by pgm:* hotels
Deadline: Mar 1
Other info: *US accredited sponsor:* yes *Began:* 1992 *Activities:* excursions, field trips, cultural events *Misc:* Incl trips to Common Market, Amsterdam, Brussels, Brugge, Ghent & 6 bus. May contact former participants. *URL:* http://www.busadm.mu.edu/international
Contact: Dr Jamshid Hosseini, Dir, Intl Studies, Marquette Univ, Straz Hall, PO Box 1881, Milwaukee WI 53201-1881 *Ph:* 414-288 3433 *Fax:* 414-288 1660 *E-mail:* jamshid.hosseini@marquette.edu

---

0553
UNIVERSITY OF ANTWERP-UFSIA
Dutch as a Foreign Language, Beginners to Advanced
Site: Belgium: Antwerp
Dates: 4 wks, Jul-Aug or Aug-Sep
Subjects: Dutch language (beg/int/adv)
Eligibility: *Level:* fresh, sophs, jrs, srs, grads, adults, teachers, professionals, precoll *Age:* min 18
Credit: *Undergrad:* none *Grad:* none *Doc:* certificate
Instruction: *In:* Dutch *Format:* lang study *Students:* intl
Costs: BFr 14,000 *incl* tuition, fees, books/materials
Housing: *Sponsor assists:* residence halls, apartments
Deadline: 2 wks before pgm; apply early
Other info: *US accredited sponsor:* no
Contact: Ms Ann Aertssen, UFSIA, ICTL, Prinsstr 13, B-2000 Antwerp, Belgium *E-mail:* ann.aertssen@ufsia.ac.be
Or Contact: Mr L Vandenberghe, Dienst voor Studieadvies, UFSIA, Prinsstr 13, 2000 Antwerp, Belgium *E-mail:* lionel.vandenberghe@ufsia.ac.be
Or Contact: Marie Anne Fivez, UFSIA, Prinsstr 13, 2000 Antwerp, Belgium *E-mail:* marieanne.fivez@ufsia.ac.be

---

0554
UNIVERSITY OF ANTWERP-UFSIA
French as a Foreign Language
Site: Belgium: Antwerp
Dates: Sep 3-27
Subjects: Civilization/culture, French language (beg/int)
Eligibility: *Level:* fresh, sophs, jrs, srs, grads, adults, professionals, precoll *Age:* min 18
Credit: *Undergrad:* none *Grad:* none *Doc:* certificate
Instruction: *In:* French *Format:* lang study *Students:* intl
Costs: BFr 14,000 *incl* tuition, books/materials
Housing: *Sponsor assists:* apartments with local students, residence halls with local students
Deadline: 2 wks before pgm; apply early
Other info: *US accredited sponsor:* no *Began:* 1992 *Activities:* excursions
Contact: Ms Ann Aertssen, UFSIA (ICTL), Prinsstr 13, B-2000 Antwerp, Belgium *E-mail:* ann.aertssen@ufsia.ac.be
Or Contact: Marie Anne Fivez, UFSIA, Prinsstr 13, 2000 Antwerp, Belgium *E-mail:* marieanne.fivez@ufsia.ac.be

---

0555
UNIVERSITY OF ANTWERP-UFSIA
German Language: Beginners and Intermediate Level
Site: Belgium: Antwerp
Dates: Oct 8-Dec 20 for beg, Jan 21-Mar 28 for int
Subjects: German language (beg/int)
Eligibility: *Level:* fresh, sophs, jrs, srs, grads, adults, teachers, professionals, precoll *Age:* min 18
Credit: *Undergrad:* none *Grad:* none *Doc:* certificate
Instruction: *In:* German *Format:* lang study, lecture *Students:* intl
Costs: BFr 10,000 *incl* tuition, books/materials
Housing: *Sponsor assists:* residence halls, apartments
Deadline: 2 wks before pgm; apply early
Other info: *US accredited sponsor:* no
Contact: Ms Ann Aertssen, ICTL-UFSIA, Prinsstr 13, B-2000 Antwerp, Belgium *E-mail:* ann.aertssen@ufsia.ac.be
Or Contact: Mrs M A Fivez, UFSIA, Prinsstr 31, B-2000 Antwerp, Belgium *E-mail:* marieanne.fivez@ufsia.ac.be

---

0556
UNIVERSITY OF ANTWERP-UFSIA
Spanish for Beginners
Site: Belgium: Antwerp
Dates: Jul 5-Aug 3
Subjects: Spanish language (beg)
Eligibility: *Level:* fresh, sophs, jrs, srs, grads, adults, teachers, professionals, precoll *Age:* min 18
Credit: *Undergrad:* none *Grad:* none *Doc:* certificate
Instruction: *In:* Spanish *Format:* lang study *Students:* intl
Costs: BFr 14,000 *incl* tuition, fees, books/materials
Housing: *Sponsor assists:* apartments with local students, residence halls with local students
Deadline: Contact sponsor
Other info: *US accredited sponsor:* no *Began:* 1993 *Orient:* abroad (intensive lang study)
Contact: Ms Ann Aertssen, UFSIA, Prinsstr 13, B-2000 Antwerp, Belgium *E-mail:* ann.aertssen@ufsia.ac.be
Or Contact: Mrs Marie-Anne Fivez, UFSIA, Prinsstr 13, B-2000 Antwerp, Belgium *E-mail:* marieanne.fivez@ufsia.ac.be

---

BRUSSELS

0557
EDUCATIONAL PROGRAMMES ABROAD (EPA)
Brussels Internship
Site: Belgium: Brussels *Host inst:* Free Univ
Dates: 8 wks, May 29-Jul 23
Subjects: Business/management, European law
Eligibility: *Level:* jrs, srs, grads *Requires:* 3.0 GPA *Age:* avg 21
Credit: *Undergrad:* avail *Grad:* avail
Instruction: *In:* Contact sponsor *Format:* internship *Students:* mainly US
Costs: $4,450 *incl* housing, some meals
Housing: *Sponsor assists:* apartments, homestay
Deadline: Mar 1
Other info: *US accredited sponsor:* no *Began:* 1993 *Orient:* abroad (3 days, intensive lang study) *Activities:* excursions, field trips, cultural events *Misc:* Students who work in the European Parliament may use any EU lang of proficiency. May contact former participants. *URL:* http://studyabroad.com/epa
Contact: Eleanor Krawutschke, US Dir, Educ Pgms Abroad, 137 N Park St, Kalamazoo MI 49007 *Ph:* 616-382 0139 *Fax:* 616-382 5222 *E-mail:* epainterns@aol.com

---

0558
GEORGIA INSTITUTE OF TECHNOLOGY
Brussels Summer Program
Site: Belgium: Brussels
Dates: 6 wks, Jun 4-Jul 14
Subjects: European studies, International relations
Eligibility: *Level:* fresh, sophs, jrs, srs, grads *Requires:* good acad standing
Credit: *Undergrad:* 6 *Grad:* avail *Doc:* transcript
Instruction: *In:* English *Format:* lecture, seminar *Students:* mainly US
Costs: $3,000 for GA residents, $3,250 for others *incl* tuition, housing, most meals, fees, excursions, books/materials *Nonrefundable fee*
Housing: *Arr by pgm:* homestay
Deadline: Mar
Other info: *US accredited sponsor:* yes *Began:* 1992 *Orient:* in US (1 day) *Activities:* excursions *Misc:* Students are responsible for travel arrangements.
Contact: Dr Vicki Birchfield, Georgia Inst of Technology, Atlanta GA 30332-0284 *Ph:* 404-385 0604 *E-mail:* vicki.birchfield@inta.gatech.edu
Or Contact: Study Abroad, Georgia Inst of Technology, J S Coon Bldg, Ste 203, Atlanta GA 30332-0284 *Ph:* 404-894 7475 *Fax:* 404-894 9682 *E-mail:* study.abroad@gatech.edu

---

0559
MICHIGAN STATE UNIVERSITY
International Relations
Site: Belgium: Brussels
Dates: 4 wks, Jul
Subjects: Economics, Political science/politics, Sociology
Eligibility: *Level:* fresh, sophs, jrs, srs *Requires:* 2.3 GPA, good acad standing *Age:* min 18
Credit: *Undergrad:* 2-4 *Grad:* none *Doc:* transcript
Instruction: *In:* English *Format:* lecture, seminar *Students:* mainly US
Costs: About $950 *incl* housing, insurance, excursions, support svcs *Nonrefundable fee*
Housing: *Arr by pgm:* residence halls
Deadline: Mar 2
Other info: *US accredited sponsor:* yes *Orient:* in US *Activities:* excursions, field trips *Misc:* Loans avail. *Financial aid:* scholarships *URL:* http://studyabroad.msu.edu
Contact: Cheryl Benner, Study Abroad, Michigan State Univ, 109 Intl Ctr, East Lansing MI 48824 *Ph:* 517-353 8920 *Fax:* 517-432 2082 *E-mail:* bennerc@msu.edu ▲

0560
UNIVERSITY OF KANSAS
European Studies in Brussels, Belgium
Site: Belgium: Brussels *Host inst:* Vrije Univ Brussel
Dates: Jun 11-25
Subjects: European studies, History, Political science/politics
Eligibility: *Level:* fresh, sophs, jrs, srs, grads, teachers *Requires:* previous study in field *Age:* avg 21
Credit: *Undergrad:* 3 *Grad:* none *Doc:* transcript
Instruction: *In:* English *Format:* lecture *Students:* mainly US
Costs: $1,900 *incl* tuition, housing, some meals, fees, excursions *Nonrefundable fee*
Housing: *Arr by pgm:* residence halls
Deadline: Rolling admissions
Other info: *US accredited sponsor:* yes *Began:* 1999 *Orient:* in US & abroad (1 day) *Activities:* excursions, field trips, cultural events *Misc:* Guest lecturers. *URL:* http://www.ukans.edu/~osa
Contact: Susan MacNally, Asst Dir, Study Abroad, Univ of Kansas, 108 Lippincott Hall, Lawrence KS 66045-1731 *Ph:* 785-864 3742 *Fax:* 785-864 5040 *E-mail:* osa@ukans.edu ▲

0561
UNIVERSITY OF ROCHESTER
Internships in Europe-Belgium
Site: Belgium: Brussels
Dates: 8 wks, May 28-Jul 22
Subjects: Business/management, Internships, Political science/politics
Eligibility: *Level:* jrs, srs, grads *Requires:* 3.0 GPA, 2 yrs coll French for bus interns *Age:* avg 20
Credit: *Undergrad:* 8 *Grad:* none *Doc:* transcript
Instruction: *In:* English, French *Format:* internship *Students:* mainly US
Costs: $5,290 *incl* tuition, housing, some meals, fees
Housing: *Sponsor assists:* apartments
Deadline: Mar 1
Other info: *US accredited sponsor:* yes *Began:* 1978 *Orient:* abroad (1 wk, intensive lang study) *Misc:* May contact former participants. *URL:* http://www.rochester.edu/College/study-abroad/sa/global.html
Contact: Jacqueline Levine, Ctr for Study Abroad, Univ of Rochester, Lattimore 206, PO Box 270376, Rochester NY 14627-0376 *Ph:* 716-275 7532 *Fax:* 716-461 5131 *E-mail:* csaip@cc.mail.edu

---

LEUVEN

0562
LEHIGH UNIVERSITY
Lehigh in Belgium
Site: Belgium: Leuven *Host inst:* Irish Inst for European Affairs
Dates: 5 wks, late May-early Jul
Subjects: History, Marketing
Eligibility: *Level:* sophs, jrs, srs *Requires:* 2.0 GPA
Credit: *Undergrad:* 6 *Grad:* none *Doc:* transcript
Instruction: *In:* English *Format:* study tour *Students:* mainly US
Costs: $4,650 *incl* tuition, housing, some meals, intl airfare, excursions, ISIC
Housing: *Arr by pgm:* residence halls
Deadline: Feb 1
Other info: *US accredited sponsor:* yes *Began:* 1991 *Orient:* in US *Activities:* excursions, field trips, program travel, cultural events *URL:* http://www.Lehigh.edu/~incis/incis.html
Contact: Dr Sandi Smith, Dir, Study Abroad, Lehigh Abroad, 5 E Packer Ave, Whitaker Lab 343, Lehigh Univ, Bethlehem PA 18015 *Ph:* 610-758 3351 *Fax:* 610-758 5156 *E-mail:* incis@lehigh.edu

---

LIEGE

0563
UNIVERSITY OF ALABAMA
Alabama in Belgium
Site: Belgium: Liege *Host inst:* Hautes Etudes Commerciales Inst
Dates: 10 days, May 15-25
Subjects: Civilization/culture, Economics, European Union, Social policy
Eligibility: *Level:* jrs, srs, grads *Requires:* 3.0 GPA, intro econ or instructor's permission
Credit: *Undergrad:* 3 *Grad:* none
Instruction: *In:* English *Format:* lecture, study tour *Students:* mainly US
Costs: $2,000 *incl* tuition, housing, some meals, fees, excursions
Housing: *Arr by pgm:* hostels
Deadline: Mar
Other info: *US accredited sponsor:* yes *Began:* 1996 *Orient:* in US (1 day) *Activities:* field trips, program travel *Misc:* May contact former participants. *Financial aid:* scholarships *URL:* http://www.ua.edu/international
Contact: Dr CB Hilton, Dir, Intl Bus Pgms, Coll of Commerce & Bus Admin, Univ of Alabama, Box 870225, Tuscaloosa AL 35487-0225 *Ph:* 205-348 9432 *Fax:* 205-348 6695 *E-mail:* chilton@cba.ua.edu
Or Contact: Angie Channell, Intl Pgms, Univ of Alabama, Box 870254, 135 BB Comer Hall, Tuscaloosa AL 34587-0250 *Ph:* 205-348 5256, 205-348 7024 *Fax:* 205-348 5298 *E-mail:* achannel@aalan.ua.edu

Denmark

COPENHAGEN

0564
DIS, DENMARK'S INTERNATIONAL STUDY PROGRAM
Architecture and Design Summer Semester
Site: Denmark: Copenhagen
Dates: 7 or 9 wks, mid-Jun-mid-Aug
Subjects: Architecture, Furnishings/furniture, Interior design
Eligibility: *Level:* jrs, srs, grads *Requires:* 3.0 GPA
Credit: *Undergrad:* 9-12 *Grad:* avail *Doc:* transcript, certificate
Instruction: *In:* English *Format:* art studio, directed field study, lecture, seminar, study tour *Students:* intl
Costs: About $5,500-$7,000 *incl* tuition, housing, insurance, fees, excursions, orient, local transport
Housing: *Arr by pgm:* residence halls, homestay
Deadline: Contact member insts
Other info: *US accredited sponsor:* yes *Began:* 1977 *Orient:* abroad *Activities:* program travel *Misc:* May contact former participants. *Financial aid:* scholarships, work study *URL:* http://www.disp.dk/
Contact: *See Index II for Members* Charlotte Simonsen, DiS, N Amer Off, Univ of Minnesota, 214 Heller Hall, 271 19th Ave S, Minneapolis MN 55455 *Ph:* 800-247 3477; 612-626 7679 *Fax:* 612-626 8009 *E-mail:* dis@umn.edu

---

0565
DIS, DENMARK'S INTERNATIONAL STUDY PROGRAM
International Business Summer Program
Site: Denmark: Copenhagen
Dates: 6 wks, early Jun-late Jul
Subjects: International business
Eligibility: *Level:* jrs, srs *Requires:* 3.0 GPA, previous study in field, bus or econ major
Credit: *Undergrad:* 6 *Grad:* none *Doc:* transcript
Instruction: *In:* English *Format:* lecture *Students:* mainly US
Costs: $4,385 *incl* tuition, housing, insurance, fees, excursions, books/materials, local transport
Housing: *Arr by pgm:* residence halls with local students
Deadline: Contact member insts
Other info: *US accredited sponsor:* yes *Began:* 1998 *Orient:* abroad (2 days) *Activities:* excursions *Financial aid:* scholarships *URL:* http://www.disp.dk/
Contact: *See Index II for Members* Charlotte Simonsen, Field Dir, DIS, 214 Heller Hall, 271 19th Ave S, Minneapolis MN 55455 *Ph:* 800-247 3477; 612-626 7679 *Fax:* 612-626 8009 *E-mail:* dis@umn.edu

---

0566
NATIONAL REGISTRATION CENTER FOR STUDY ABROAD (NRCSA)
Study Danish
Site: Denmark: Copenhagen *Host inst:* Home Lang Schs Intl
Dates: 1 wk or longer, yr-round
Subjects: Danish language, Homestay
Eligibility: *Level:* fresh, sophs, jrs, srs, grads, adults, teachers, professionals
Credit: *Undergrad:* none *Grad:* none
Instruction: *In:* Danish *Format:* lang study, tutorial *Students:* intl
Costs: $1,135 per wk *incl* tuition, housing, all meals, insurance *Nonrefundable fee*
Housing: *Arr by pgm:* homestay
Deadline: 6 wks before pgm
Other info: *US accredited sponsor:* no *Misc:* Student lives in teacher's home. *URL:* http://www.nrcsa.com
Contact: Reuel Zielke, NRCSA, 823 N 2nd St, #206, Milwaukee WI 53203 *Ph:* 414-278 0631 *Fax:* 414-871 8884 *E-mail:* info@nrcsa.com

---

0567
SUNY COLLEGE AT NEW PALTZ
Summer Study in Copenhagen, Denmark-Comparative Human Services
Site: Denmark: Copenhagen
Dates: 2 wks, May 25-Jun 5
Subjects: Field study, Homestay, Social welfare/services
Eligibility: *Level:* fresh, sophs, jrs, srs, grads *Requires:* good acad standing, *Age:* min 17
Credit: *Undergrad:* 3 *Grad:* 3 *Doc:* transcript
Instruction: *In:* English *Format:* directed field study, lecture *Students:* mainly US
Costs: $1,326 for undergrad, $1,556 for grad *incl* tuition, housing, intl airfare, insurance, fees, excursions *Nonrefundable fee*
Housing: *Arr by pgm:* homestay
Deadline: Mar 1
Other info: *US accredited sponsor:* yes *Orient:* in US *Activities:* excursions *Financial aid:* scholarships *URL:* http://www.newpaltz.edu/oie/

Contact: Ctr for Intl Pgm, SUNY New Paltz, 75 S Manheim Blvd, New Paltz NY 12561 *Ph:* 845-257 3125 *Fax:* 845-257 3120 *E-mail:* international@newpaltz.edu ▲

0568
UNIVERSITY OF HAWAII AT MANOA
Architecture, Landscape & Scandinavian Furniture Design
Site: Denmark: Copenhagen *Host inst:* Denmark's Intl Study Pgm
Dates: 7 wks, Jun-Jul
Subjects: Architecture, Field study, Immunology, Independent study
Eligibility: *Level:* sophs, jrs, srs *Requires:* 3.0 GPA
Credit: *Undergrad:* 6 *Grad:* none *Doc:* transcript
Instruction: *In:* English *Format:* art studio, directed field study, independent study *Students:* intl
Costs: $7,701 *incl* tuition, housing, intl airfare, insurance, fees, excursions, books/materials *Nonrefundable fee*
Housing: *Arr by pgm:* residence halls
Deadline: Feb 17
Other info: *US accredited sponsor:* yes *Began:* 1994 *Orient:* in US & abroad *Activities:* excursions, field trips *Financial aid:* scholarships, work study *URL:* http://www2.hawaii.edu/study-abroad
Contact: Sarita Mac Leod, Univ of Hawaii at Manoa, Study Abroad Center, Moore Hall 115, 1890 East-West Rd, Honolulu HI 96822 *Ph:* 808-956 5143 *Fax:* 808-956 9319 *E-mail:* uhmsac@hawaii.edu

---

0569
UNIVERSITY STUDIES ABROAD CONSORTIUM
Business and Economic Studies: Copenhagen, Denmark
Site: Denmark: Copenhagen *Host inst:* Copenhagen Bus Sch
Dates: 6 wks, Jun 25-Aug 10
Subjects: Accounting, Danish studies, Finance, Information technology, International business, International marketing, International planning, Internet, Sociology
Eligibility: *Level:* jrs, srs, grads, adults, teachers, professionals *Requires:* 2.5 GPA *Age:* min 18
Credit: *Undergrad:* 6 *Grad:* 6 *Doc:* transcript
Instruction: *In:* English *Format:* lecture *Students:* US & intl
Costs: $1,450 *incl* tuition, insurance, ISIC *Nonrefundable fee*
Housing: *Sponsor assists:* apartments with local students, residence halls with local students
Deadline: Apr 15
Other info: *US accredited sponsor:* yes *Began:* 2000 *Orient:* abroad *Misc:* May contact former participants. *Financial aid:* scholarships, work study
Contact: *See Index II for Members* Carmello Urza, Univ Studies Abroad Consortium, Univ of Nevada, USAC/323, Reno NV 89557-0993 *Ph:* 775-784 6569 *Fax:* 775-784 6010 *E-mail:* usac@unr.edu ▲

Finland

HELSINKI

0570
NATIONAL REGISTRATION CENTER FOR STUDY ABROAD (NRCSA)
Language Study in Finland
Site: Finland: Helsinki *Host inst:* Home Lang Schs Intl
Dates: 1 wk or longer, yr-round
Subjects: Finnish language, Homestay
Eligibility: *Level:* fresh, sophs, jrs, srs, grads, adults, teachers, professionals
Credit: *Undergrad:* none *Grad:* none *Doc:* certificate
Instruction: *In:* Finnish *Format:* lang study, tutorial *Students:* intl
Costs: $1,135 per wk *incl* tuition, housing, all meals, insurance *Nonrefundable fee*
Housing: *Arr by pgm:* homestay
Deadline: 6 wks before pgm
Other info: *US accredited sponsor:* no *Misc:* Student lives in teacher's home. *URL:* http://www.nrcsa.com
Contact: Reuel Zielke, NRCSA, 823 N 2nd St, #206, Milwaukee WI 53203 *Ph:* 414-278 0631 *Fax:* 414-871 8884 *E-mail:* info@nrcsa.com

---

JYVASKYLA

0571
UNIVERSITY OF JYVASKYLA and **FINNISH MINISTRY OF EDUCATION**
Tenth Jyvaskyla International Summer School
Site: Finland: Jyvaskyla
Dates: Jul 31-Aug 18
Subjects: Biology, Chemistry, Computer sciences, Ecology/environmental studies, Information science/systems, Mathematics, Physics, Statistics
Eligibility: *Level:* grads *Requires:* previous study in field
Credit: *Undergrad:* none *Grad:* avail *Doc:* transcript, certificate
Instruction: *In:* English *Format:* lab, lecture, seminar *Students:* intl & host country
Costs: Contact sponsor
Housing: *Arr by pgm:* residence halls, apartments
Deadline: May 26
Other info: *US accredited sponsor:* no *Began:* 1991 *Activities:* excursions, cultural events *Misc:* Subjects change every yr. *URL:* http://www.jyu.fi/summerschool/
Contact: Ms Anni Kekki, Maths & Scis, Univ of Jyvaskyla, PO Box 35, FIN-40351 Jyvaskyla, Finland *E-mail:* jss@cc.jyu.fi

---

KAUHAVA

0572
FINNISH SCHOOL OF SME BUSINESS ADMINISTRATION
Doing Business in Finland and Her Neighboring Areas
Site: Finland: Kauhava
Dates: 3 mos, Mar 1-May 30
Subjects: Baltic studies, Business/management, Civilization/culture, Finance, Finnish language (beg), Finnish studies, Geography, History, Political science/politics, Russian language (beg), Russian studies, Sociology
Eligibility: *Level:* fresh, sophs, jrs, srs, grads, adults *Age:* min 18
Credit: *Undergrad:* avail *Grad:* none *Doc:* certificate
Instruction: *In:* English *Format:* independent study, lang study, lecture, seminar, study tour *Students:* intl
Costs: $1,500 *incl* tuition, housing, excursions, books/materials
Housing: *Arr by pgm:* residence halls, apartments
Deadline: Nov 30
Other info: *US accredited sponsor:* no *Began:* 1994 *Orient:* abroad *Activities:* excursions, field trips, program travel, cultural events, sports *Misc:* May contact former participants. *URL:* http://www.smek.fi/syoamk/kansainv/gateway.htm
Contact: Marjo Arola or Minna Nyman, Finnish Sch of SME Bus Admin, Kauppatie 109, PO Box 11, 62200 Kauhava, Finland *E-mail:* mn@smek.fi

---

KILJAVA

0573
FINLAND SOCIETY
Seminar on Finnish Language and Culture
Site: Finland: Kiljava
Dates: 3 wks, Jul 16-Aug 3
Subjects: Civilization/culture, Finnish language (beg/int/adv), Finnish studies
Eligibility: *Level:* adults *Requires:* Finnish descent *Age:* min 18, max 30
Credit: *Undergrad:* none *Grad:* none
Instruction: *In:* English *Format:* lang study, lecture *Students:* intl
Costs: FIM 4,100 *incl* tuition, housing, all meals, excursions, books/materials

Housing: *Arr by pgm:* residence halls
Deadline: Apr 1
Other info: *US accredited sponsor:* no *Activities:* excursions, field trips *Financial aid:* scholarships *URL:* http://www.suomi-seura.fi
Contact: Mikko Harjulehto, Finland Socy, Mariankatu 8B, 00170 Helsinki, Finland *E-mail:* suomis@suomi-seura.fi

---

KUOPIO

0574
UNIVERSITY OF KUOPIO
Developing Research and Technology-Based Entrepreneurship
Site: Finland: Kuopio
Dates: Oct 18-22
Subjects: Information science/systems, Small business development, Small business management
Eligibility: *Level:* grads *Requires:* previous study in field, bachelor's degree in econ or related scis
Credit: *Undergrad:* none *Grad:* avail *Doc:* certificate
Instruction: *In:* English *Format:* lecture *Students:* mainly host country
Costs: Contact sponsor
Housing: *Arr by pgm:* residence halls
Deadline: Aug 31
Other info: *US accredited sponsor:* no *Began:* 1998 *Orient:* abroad (intensive lang study) *URL:* http://www.uku.fi/intl
Contact: Seija Partanen, Acad Adviser, Univ of Kuopio, PO Box 1627, FIN-70211 Kuopio, Finland *E-mail:* seija.partanen@uku.fi
Or Contact: Ms Anitta Etula, Univ of Kuopio, PO Box 1627, FIN-70211 Kuopio, Finland *E-mail:* anitta.etula@uku.fi

---

MIKKELI

0575
INDIANA UNIVERSITY
Summer Study in Finland
Site: Finland: Mikkeli *Host inst:* Helsinki Sch of Econ & Bus
Dates: 9 wks, mid-May-late Jul
Subjects: Business/management
Eligibility: Own students only. *Level:* sophs, jrs, srs *Requires:* 3.0 GPA, completion of bus integrative core
Credit: *Undergrad:* 9 *Grad:* none *Doc:* transcript
Instruction: *In:* English *Format:* lecture *Students:* mainly US
Costs: $2,900 or $5,000 *incl* tuition, housing, all meals, insurance *Nonrefundable fee*
Housing: *Arr by pgm:* apartments
Deadline: Mid-Feb
Other info: *US accredited sponsor:* yes *Began:* 1993 *Orient:* in US *Misc:* May contact former participants. *Financial aid:* scholarships *URL:* http://www.indiana.edu/~overseas
Contact: Overseas Study, Indiana Univ, Franklin Hall 303, Bloomington IN 47405 *Ph:* 812-855 9304 *Fax:* 812-855 6452 *E-mail:* overseas@indiana.edu

---

OULU

0576
UNIVERSITY OF OULU
Northern Nature and Environment Summer School
Site: Finland: Oulu *Host inst:* Univ of Oulu
Dates: 3 mos, Jun 1-Aug 31
Subjects: Ecology/environmental studies, Field study, Independent study, Natural sciences
Eligibility: *Level:* jrs, srs, grads, teachers *Requires:* previous study in field
Credit: *Undergrad:* 15 *Grad:* none *Doc:* transcript
Instruction: *In:* English *Format:* directed field study, independent study, lab, lecture, practical training, study tour *Students:* mainly host country
Costs: $1,300 *incl* tuition, housing, some meals, excursions
Housing: *Arr by pgm:* residence halls with local students
Deadline: Mar 31
Other info: *US accredited sponsor:* no *Began:* 1995 *Activities:* field trips *URL:* http://www.oulu.fi/
Contact: Dr Annamari Markkola, Univ of Oulu, Linnanmaa, PL 3000, FIN-90401 Oulu, Finland *E-mail:* annamari.markkola@oulu.fi
Or Contact: Anja Malaska, Intl Pgms Coord, Univ of Oulu, PO Box 8100, FIN-90401 Oulu, Finland *E-mail:* international.office@oulu.fi

France

MORE THAN ONE CITY

0577
BAYLOR UNIVERSITY
Summer Study Program in Paris and Burgundy
Site: France: Lyon, Paris
Dates: 5 wks, Jun 1-Jul 6
Subjects: Civilization/culture, Drama/theater, French language (int/adv), French studies, Homestay
Eligibility: *Level:* fresh, sophs, jrs, srs *Requires:* 2 sems coll French
Credit: *Undergrad:* 6 *Grad:* none
Instruction: *In:* French *Format:* lang study, lecture *Students:* mainly US
Costs: $3,400 *incl* housing, all meals, fees, excursions, theater outings
Housing: *Arr by pgm:* homestay
Deadline: Mar 15
Other info: *US accredited sponsor:* yes *Began:* 1978 *Orient:* in US & abroad (1 day) *Activities:* excursions, program travel, cultural events *Misc:* Final wk in Lyon. *URL:* http://www.baylor.edu/~French_Ital_Chinese/
Contact: Dr David M Uber, Summer Study in Paris, French & Italian, Baylor Univ, Waco TX 76798 *Ph:* 817-755 3711 *Fax:* 817-755 3799 *E-mail:* david_uber@baylor.edu

---

0578
CENTER FOR CULTURAL INTERCHANGE
Internship in France
Site: France: various sites
Dates: 1-3 mos, yr-round
Subjects: Business/management, Homestay, Humanities, Internships, Social sciences
Eligibility: *Level:* fresh, sophs, jrs, srs, grads *Requires:* 3.0 GPA, previous study in field, 2 yrs coll French *Age:* min 18, max 28, avg 21
Credit: *Undergrad:* none *Grad:* none *Doc:* certificate
Instruction: *In:* French *Format:* internship, practical training *Students:* mainly host country
Costs: $2,230 for 2 mos *incl* housing, some meals, insurance, fees, placement *Nonrefundable fee*
Housing: *Arr by pgm:* homestay
Deadline: 3 mos before pgm
Other info: *US accredited sponsor:* no *Began:* 1999 *Orient:* in US & abroad (1 day) *Misc:* Hosting discount avail. *URL:* http://www.cci-exchange.com
Contact: Karen Hindhede, Outbound Pgms Dir, Ctr for Cultural Interchange, 17 N 2nd Ave, St Charles IL 60174 *Ph:* 888-227 6231; 630-377 2272 *Fax:* 630-377 2307 *E-mail:* info@cci-exchange.com

---

0579
COLLEGE CONSORTIUM FOR INTERNATIONAL STUDIES and **MIAMI-DADE COMMUNITY COLLEGE**
Summer in France
Site: France: Aix-en-Provence, Paris *Host inst:* Inst for Amer Univs
Dates: 6 wks, mid-Jun-late Jul
Subjects: Art history, Arts, Drama/theater, French language (beg/int/adv), French studies, Homestay, Humanities, International business, International law,

International relations, Literature, Music history
Eligibility: *Level:* fresh, sophs, jrs, srs, teachers *Requires:* 2.5 GPA *Age:* min 18, avg 20
Credit: *Undergrad:* 6-10 *Grad:* none *Doc:* transcript
Instruction: *In:* English, French *Format:* lang study, lecture *Students:* mainly US
Costs: $3,795 *incl* tuition, housing, some meals, insurance, fees, excursions
Housing: *Arr by pgm:* homestay
Deadline: Jun 1
Other info: *US accredited sponsor:* yes *Began:* 1978 *Orient:* abroad *Activities:* excursions, program travel *Misc:* Last wk in Paris. *URL:* http://www.ccisabroad.org
Contact: *See Index II for Members* CCIS, 2000 P St NW, Ste 503, Washington DC 20036 *Ph:* 800-453 6956; 202-223 0330 *Fax:* 202-223 0999 *E-mail:* info@ccisabroad.org
Or Contact: Dr Robert Vitale or Reinaldo Changsut, Ctr for Foreign Langs & Intl Educ, Miami-Dade CC, 11011 SW 104th St, Miami FL 33176-3393 *Ph:* 305-237 2533, 305-237 2535 *Fax:* 305-237 2949 *E-mail:* rchangsu@mdcc.edu ▲

0580
EDUVACATIONS
French Language and Culture with Sports and Arts
Site: France: Alps, Antibes, Avignon, Bordeaux, Burgundy, Cannes, Nice, Paris, Provence
Dates: 1 wk-1 yr, yr-round
Subjects: Business language (beg/int/adv), Civilization/culture, Culinary arts, Cycling, Diving, Equestrian arts, Foreign language teaching, French language (beg/int/adv), Painting, Photography, Skiing, Sports, Tennis, Wine
Eligibility: *Level:* adults
Credit: *Undergrad:* avail *Grad:* none *Doc:* certificate
Instruction: *In:* French *Format:* art studio, directed field study, practical training, workshop *Students:* intl
Costs: Contact sponsor
Housing: *Arr by pgm:* apartments, homestay, hotels
Deadline: Contact sponsor
Other info: *US accredited sponsor:* no *Misc:* Custom-tailored pgms combine French lang study with sports, arts, cooking, wines & more for individuals & groups. May contact former participants. *URL:* http://www.eduvacations.com
Contact: Mary Ann Puglisi, eduVacations, 1431 21st St NW, Ste 302, Washington DC 20036 *Ph:* 202-857 8384 *Fax:* 202-463 8091

0581
INTERNATIONAL COUNCIL FOR CULTURAL EXCHANGE (ICCE)
French Language/Culture and Art/ Music on the French Riviera
Site: France: Paris, Riviera, other sites *Host inst:* regional univs
Dates: 2-4 wks, yr-round
Subjects: Art, Business language, Civilization/culture, Field study, French language (beg/int/adv), French studies, Homestay, Master classes, Music
Eligibility: *Level:* fresh, sophs, jrs, srs, grads, adults, teachers, professionals, precoll
Credit: *Undergrad:* avail *Grad:* avail *Doc:* transcript, certificate
Instruction: *In:* English, French *Format:* art studio, directed field study, lab, lang study, lecture, music lesson, practical training, study tour *Students:* intl
Costs: From $3,400 *incl* tuition, housing, some meals, intl airfare, fees, excursions, pgm travel
Housing: *Arr by pgm:* residence halls, homestay, hotels
Deadline: 1 mo before pgm
Other info: *US accredited sponsor:* no *Began:* 1982 *Orient:* abroad *Activities:* excursions, program travel, cultural events, sports *Misc:* Yr-round pgm of 2 wks or longer avail for pre-arr groups. Sem & yr pgms avail.
Contact: Dr Stanley Gochman, ICCE, 5 Bellport Ln, Bellport NY 11713 *Ph:* 631-286 5228 ▲

0582
LANGUAGE LIAISON
French Language
Site: France: Aix-en-Provence, Antibes, Avignon, Brest, Cannes, Hyeres, Lyons, Nice, Paris, Ville Franche
Dates: 2 wks or longer, yr-round
Subjects: Business language, Drama/ theater, Film studies, French language (beg/int/adv), Homestay, Humanities, Technical language
Eligibility: *Level:* fresh, sophs, jrs, srs, grads, adults, teachers, professionals, precoll *Age:* min 14
Credit: *Undergrad:* avail *Grad:* avail *Doc:* transcript, certificate
Instruction: *In:* French *Format:* lab, lang study, lecture, practical training, tutorial *Students:* intl
Costs: Contact sponsor
Housing: *Arr by pgm:* apartments, homestay, hotels
Deadline: 30 days before pgm
Other info: *US accredited sponsor:* no *Activities:* excursions, field trips, cultural events, sports *Misc:* Subjects offered vary by location. Youth pgm for 14-18 yrs avail. Scholarship researh svc. *URL:* http://www.languageliaison.com
Contact: Nancy Forman, Dir, Lang Liaison, 4 Burnham Pkwy, Morristown NJ 07960 *Ph:* 800-284 4448 *Fax:* 973-898 1710 *E-mail:* learn@languageliaison.com

---

0583
LANGUAGE LIAISON
French Saturation
Site: France: Aix-en-Provence, Bordeaux, Bretagne, Cote d'Azur, Haute Savoie, Loire Valley, Normandy, Paris *Host inst:* Live in Learn
Dates: 1 wk or longer, yr-round
Subjects: Civilization/culture, French language (beg/int/adv), Homestay
Eligibility: *Level:* fresh, sophs, jrs, srs, grads, adults, teachers, professionals, precoll *Age:* min 10
Credit: *Undergrad:* avail *Grad:* avail *Doc:* transcript, certificate
Instruction: *In:* French *Format:* lang study *Students:* intl
Costs: Contact sponsor
Housing: *Arr by pgm:* teacher's home
Deadline: 45 days before pgm
Other info: *US accredited sponsor:* no *Misc:* Live & learn in your teacher's home. Scholarship research svc. *URL:* http://www.languageliaison.com
Contact: Nancy Forman, Dir, Lang Liaison, 4 Burnham Pkwy, Morristown NJ 07960 *Ph:* 800-284 4448 *Fax:* 973-898 1710 *E-mail:* learn@languageliaison.com

---

0584
LANGUAGE STUDIES ABROAD, INC
Intensive French
Site: France: Hyeres, Nice, Paris *Host inst:* various LSA insts
Dates: 1 wk or longer, yr-round
Subjects: Business language, Business/ management, Culinary arts, French language (beg/int/adv), French studies, History, Homestay
Eligibility: *Level:* fresh, sophs, jrs, srs, grads, adults, teachers, professionals, precoll *Requires:* some French for Hyeres pgm
Credit: *Undergrad:* avail *Grad:* avail *Doc:* certificate
Instruction: *In:* French *Format:* lang study, tutorial *Students:* intl
Costs: From $1,350 for 4 wks *incl* tuition, housing, some meals
Housing: *Sponsor assists:* apartments, homestay, hotels
Deadline: 4 wks before pgm
Other info: *US accredited sponsor:* no *Orient:* abroad *Activities:* excursions, field trips, cultural events *Misc:* May contact former participants. *URL:* http://www.languagestudiesabroad.com

Contact: Lang Studies Abroad, Inc, 103 Londonderry Ct, Reno NV 89511-2718 *Ph:* 800-424 5522; 775-849 9206 *Fax:* 775-849 9217 *E-mail:* info@languagestudiesabroad.com

---

0585
LANGUAGES ABROAD
Language and Cultural Immersion Programs-France
Site: France: Nice, Paris
Dates: 2 wks or longer, yr-round
Subjects: Civilization/culture, French language (beg/int/adv)
Eligibility: *Level:* adults *Age:* min 17, max 65, avg 25
Credit: *Undergrad:* none *Grad:* none *Doc:* certificate
Instruction: *In:* French *Format:* lang study *Students:* intl
Costs: About $1,710 for 4 wks *incl* tuition, housing, some meals, excursions, books/materials
Housing: *Arr by pgm:* apartments, homestay
Deadline: None
Other info: *US accredited sponsor:* no *Misc:* May contact former participants. *URL:* http://www.languagesabroad.com
Contact: Ms Jesse Philippe, Langs Abroad, 317 Adelaide St W, Ste 900, Toronto, Ontario M5V 1P9, Canada *Ph:* 800-219 9924; 416-925 7117 *E-mail:* info@languagesabroad.com

---

0586
LINGUA SERVICE WORLDWIDE
Total Immersion/Intensive Language and Culture in France
Site: France: various sites *Host inst:* CELA, CELIA, Ctr Intl Antibes, Ctr Mediterraneen, CIEL, CLE, Coll Intl de Cannes, others
Dates: 1 wk-1 yr, yr-round
Subjects: Arts, Business language, Civilization/culture, Culinary arts, Economics, Foreign language teaching, French language (beg/int/adv), French studies, Homestay, International business, Literature, Media studies, Political science/politics, Social sciences, Sports
Eligibility: *Level:* fresh, sophs, jrs, srs, grads, adults, teachers, professionals, precoll *Age:* min 14
Credit: *Undergrad:* avail *Grad:* avail *Doc:* transcript, certificate *Transfer credit through:* Univ of Southern Mississippi
Instruction: *In:* French *Format:* lang study *Students:* intl
Costs: Contact sponsor
Housing: *Arr by pgm:* apartments with local students, residence halls with local students, homestay, pensions, hotels, hostels
Deadline: 45 days before pgm
Other info: *US accredited sponsor:* no *Began:* 1993 *Activities:* excursions, cultural events *Misc:* Addtl host insts: France Langue, IMEF, Inst Franco Europeen, IS Aix-en-Provence. May contact former participants. *URL:* http://www.linguaserviceworldwide.com
Contact: Dir, Lingua Svc Worldwide, 75 Prospect St, Ste 4, Huntington NY 11743 *Ph:* 800-394 5327; 631-424 0777 *Fax:* 631-271 3441 *E-mail:* itctravel@worldnet.att.net ▲

0587
LINGUA SERVICE WORLDWIDE
Total Immersion/Intensive Language and Culture-France
Site: France: Aix-en-Provence, Bordeaux, Bretagne, Cote d'Azur, Haute Savoie, Loire Valley, Normandy, Paris, Tours *Host inst:* Home Lang Intl
Dates: 1 wk-1 yr, yr-round
Subjects: Civilization/culture, French language (beg/int/adv), Homestay
Eligibility: *Level:* fresh, sophs, jrs, srs, grads, adults, teachers, professionals, precoll *Age:* min 14
Credit: *Undergrad:* avail *Grad:* avail *Doc:* transcript, certificate *Transfer credit through:* Univ of Southern Mississippi
Instruction: *In:* French *Format:* lang study *Students:* intl
Costs: Contact sponsor
Housing: *Arr by pgm:* apartments with local students, residence halls with local students, homestay, pensions, hotels, hostels
Deadline: 45 days before pgm
Other info: *US accredited sponsor:* no *Began:* 1993 *Activities:* excursions, cultural events *Misc:* Participate in teacher's family & social life. May contact former participants. *URL:* http://www.linguaserviceworldwide.com
Contact: Dir, Lingua Svc Worldwide, 75 Prospect St, Ste 4, Huntington NY 11743 *Ph:* 800-394 5327; 631-516 4240 *Fax:* 631-516 2713 *E-mail:* itctravel@worldnet.att.net ▲

0588
LIVE & LEARN
Live & Learn Ltd
Site: France: Paris, other sites
Dates: 1 wk or longer, yr-round
Subjects: Civilization/culture, French language, Homestay
Eligibility: *Level:* adults
Credit: *Undergrad:* none *Grad:* none
Instruction: *In:* French *Format:* lang study, tutorial *Students:* mainly US
Costs: $1,150 per wk *incl* tuition, housing, all meals *Nonrefundable fee*
Housing: *Arr by pgm:* homestay
Deadline: None
Other info: *US accredited sponsor:* no *Misc:* May contact former participants.
Contact: Sara S Monick, Live & Learn, 4215 Poplar Dr, Minneapolis MN 55422 *Ph:* 612-374 2444 *Fax:* 612-333 3554 *E-mail:* monick4215@aol.com

---

0589
MINNESOTA STATE UNIVERSITY, MANKATO
Summer Study in France Program
Site: France: La Rochelle, Normandy, Paris *Host inst:* Inst d'Etudes Francaises
Dates: Jun 24-Aug 6
Subjects: Business/management, Civilization/culture, Education/teaching, French language (beg/int/adv), French studies, Homestay
Eligibility: *Level:* fresh, sophs, jrs, srs, grads, precoll *Requires:* some knowledge of French
Credit: *Undergrad:* 9-12 *Grad:* 9-12 *Doc:* transcript, certificate
Instruction: *In:* French *Format:* lang study, lecture, seminar *Students:* intl
Costs: $3,800 *incl* tuition, housing, most meals, fees, excursions, local transport *Nonrefundable fee*
Housing: *Arr by pgm:* homestay, in La Rochelle, hostel in Paris, motel in Normandy
Deadline: Apr 15
Other info: *US accredited sponsor:* yes *Began:* 1981 *Activities:* field trips *Misc:* Pgm tape & handouts provided. *URL:* http://www.mankato.msus.edu/dept/ipo
Contact: Dr John J Janc, Summer Study in France Pgm, Minnesota State Univ, Mankato, 227AH, Mankato MN 56001 *Ph:* 507-389 2116, 507-389-1818 *Fax:* 507-389 5887 *E-mail:* john.janc@mankato.msus.edu

---

0590
NATIONAL REGISTRATION CENTER FOR STUDY ABROAD (NRCSA)
Study in France
Site: France: Angers, Avignon, Hyeres, Paris *Host inst:* Angers Catholic Univ, CELA, ELFCA, ELFE
Dates: 2 wks or longer, yr-round
Subjects: French language (beg/int/adv), Homestay
Eligibility: *Level:* fresh, sophs, jrs, srs, grads, adults, teachers *Age:* min 17
Credit: *Undergrad:* none *Grad:* none
Instruction: *In:* French *Format:* lab, lang study, lecture, seminar *Students:* intl
Costs: Contact sponsor
Housing: *Arr by pgm:* residence halls, apartments, homestay, pensions, hotels
Deadline: None
Other info: *US accredited sponsor:* no *Activities:* excursions *URL:* http://www.nrcsa.com
Contact: Reuel Zielke, NRCSA, 823 N 2nd St, #206, Milwaukee WI 53203 *Ph:* 414-278 0631 *Fax:* 414-271 8884 *E-mail:* info@nrcsa.com

---

0591
REMPART
Workcamps in France
Site: France: various sites
Dates: 2 wks, summer
Subjects: Archaeology, Community service projects, Historical preservation/restoration, Leadership
Eligibility: *Level:* fresh, sophs, jrs, grads, adults, teachers, precoll *Requires:* basic French *Age:* min 13, avg 22
Credit: *Undergrad:* none *Grad:* none
Instruction: *In:* French *Format:* volunteer/svc *Students:* mainly host country
Costs: Fr 340 plus about Fr 40 per day *incl* housing, all meals, insurance, fees, excursions *Nonrefundable fee*
Housing: *Arr by pgm*
Deadline: Contact sponsor
Other info: *US accredited sponsor:* no *Misc:* Participants need to bring sleeping bags. *URL:* http://www.rempart.com
Contact: Sabine Guilbert, Rempart, 1 Rue des Guillemites, Paris, France 75004 *E-mail:* contact@rempart.com

---

0592
SOUTHERN METHODIST UNIVERSITY
SMU in the South of France
Site: France: La Napoule, Cannes *Host inst:* Institut Grand Bleu
Dates: 5 wks, May 21-Jun 24
Subjects: Civilization/culture, French language (beg/int/adv)
Eligibility: *Level:* sophs, jrs, srs, grads *Requires:* 2.5 GPA
Credit: *Undergrad:* 6 *Grad:* none *Doc:* transcript
Instruction: *In:* French *Format:* lang study *Students:* mainly US
Costs: $5,100 *incl* tuition, housing, most meals, excursions, most meals *Nonrefundable fee*
Housing: *Arr by pgm:* residence halls
Deadline: Mar 1 or until pgm filled
Other info: *US accredited sponsor:* yes *Began:* 1993 *Orient:* avail (yes) *Activities:* excursions, cultural events, sports *Misc:* Scholarships for own students only. *Financial aid:* scholarships *URL:* http://www.smu.edu/studyabroad
Contact: Intl Pgms, Southern Methodist Univ, PO Box 750391, 3108 Fondren Dr, Dallas TX 75275 *Ph:* 214-768 2338 *Fax:* 214-768 1051 *E-mail:* intlpro@mail.smu.edu
Or Contact: Dr Rita Winandy, Foreign Langs, Southern Methodist Univ, Dallas TX 75275 *Ph:* 214-768 1423 *E-mail:* rwinandy@post.cis.smu.edu ▲

0593
SUNY COLLEGE AT OSWEGO
French Language and Civilization
Site: France: Paris, St Malo *Host inst:* Univ de Haute Bretagne de Rennes
Dates: 6 wks, late Jun-Aug
Subjects: Civilization/culture, French language (int/adv), French studies, Literature
Eligibility: *Level:* fresh, sophs, jrs, srs, grads, precoll *Requires:* 2.5 GPA, good acad standing

Credit: *Undergrad:* 6 *Grad:* none *Doc:* transcript
Instruction: *In:* French *Format:* lang study, lecture *Students:* mainly US
Costs: $4,500 *incl* tuition, housing, some meals, intl airfare, excursions, local transport *Nonrefundable fee*
Housing: *Arr by pgm:* residence halls, homestay
Deadline: Apr 1
Other info: *US accredited sponsor:* yes *Began:* 1971 *Orient:* abroad *Activities:* excursions *Misc:* 2 wks in Paris, 4 wks in St Malo. May contact former participants. *URL:* http://www.oswego.edu/~intled
Contact: Susan Ansara, Dir, Intl Educ, SUNY Coll at Oswego, 102 Rich Hall, Oswego NY 13126 *Ph:* 888-467 9346; 315-341 2118 *Fax:* 315-341 2477 *E-mail:* intled@oswego.edu

---

0594
THUNDERBIRD, THE AMERICAN GRADUATE SCHOOL OF INTERNATIONAL MANAGEMENT
Winterim in Europe
Site: France: Geneva, Valbonne, Rousset, Lyon
Dates: 3 wks, Jan 8-26
Subjects: Field study, Information technology, Telecommunications
Eligibility: *Level:* grads *Requires:* 3.0 GPA
Credit: *Undergrad:* none *Grad:* 3
Instruction: *In:* English *Format:* directed field study, study tour *Students:* intl
Costs: $2,625 *incl* tuition, off campus pgm fee *Nonrefundable fee*
Housing: *Arr by pgm:* hotels
Deadline: Dec 1
Other info: *US accredited sponsor:* yes *Activities:* program travel *URL:* http://www.t-bird.edu
Contact: James Scott, Thunderbird, 15249 North 59th Avenue, Glendale AZ 85306 *Ph:* 602-978 7251 *Fax:* 602-547 1356 *E-mail:* scottj@t-bird.edu

---

0595
TRUMAN STATE UNIVERSITY
Intensive French in Annecy or Chambery
Site: France: Annecy, Chambery *Host inst:* IFALPES
Dates: Jun 2-29, Jul 5-30, Aug 2-27 or Jun 2-Aug 27
Subjects: French language, Homestay
Eligibility: *Level:* sophs, jrs, srs, adults *Requires:* 2.5 GPA, 3 recommendation letters *Age:* min 18
Credit: *Undergrad:* 6 *Grad:* none *Doc:* transcript
Instruction: *In:* French *Format:* lecture, seminar *Students:* intl
Costs: About $1,765 per 4-wk term *incl* tuition, housing, all meals, books/materials *Nonrefundable fee*
Housing: *Sponsor assists:* apartments, homestay
Deadline: May 1
Other info: *US accredited sponsor:* yes *Began:* 1998 *Orient:* abroad *Activities:* field trips *Misc:* Scholarships for own student only. *Financial aid:* scholarships *URL:* http://www2.truman.edu/ciea/
Contact: Ctr for Intl Educ Abroad, Truman State Univ, Kirk Bldg, Rm 120, Kirksville MD 63501 *Ph:* 660-785 4076 *Fax:* 660-785 7473 *E-mail:* ciea@truman.edu

---

0596
UNIVERSITY OF DAYTON
Interdepartmental Summer Study Abroad Program (ISSAP)-France
Site: France: Aix-en-Provence, Paris
Dates: 1 mo, Jun 28-Jul 28
Subjects: Art history, Film studies, History, Interdisciplinary studies
Eligibility: *Level:* fresh, sophs, jrs, srs, grads, adults *Requires:* 2.0 GPA *Age:* min 18, avg 20
Credit: *Undergrad:* 7 *Grad:* none *Doc:* transcript
Instruction: *In:* English *Format:* lecture *Students:* mainly US
Costs: $3,595 *incl* tuition, housing, some meals, insurance, excursions *Nonrefundable fee*
Housing: *Arr by pgm:* residence halls, pensions
Deadline: Mar 1; Jan 15 for scholarships
Other info: *US accredited sponsor:* yes *Began:* 1972 *Orient:* in US & abroad (4 days) *Activities:* excursions, field trips, cultural events *Misc:* May contact former participants. *Financial aid:* scholarships
Contact: James W Stiles, Univ of Dayton, 300 College Park, Dayton OH 45469-1481 *Ph:* 937-229 3728 *Fax:* 937-229 2766 *E-mail:* stiles@udayton.edu

---

0597
UNIVERSITY STUDIES ABROAD CONSORTIUM
French Studies in Pau and Bayonne, France
Site: France: Bayonne, Pau
Dates: Three 4-wk sessions, May 26-Jun 30, Jun 25-Jul 29 and/or Jul 30-Aug 18
Subjects: Art history, Basque studies, Civilization/culture, Culinary arts, Economics, Folklore, French language (beg/int/adv), Geography, History, Homestay, Literature
Eligibility: *Level:* fresh, sophs, jrs, srs, grads, adults, teachers, professionals, precoll *Requires:* 2.5 GPA *Age:* min 18
Credit: *Undergrad:* 4-5 per session *Grad:* 5 per session *Doc:* transcript
Instruction: *In:* English, French *Format:* lang study, lecture *Students:* US & intl
Costs: $1,580-$1,880 per mo, $2,870-$3,480 for 2 sessions, $4,580 3 sessions *incl* tuition, housing, insurance, fees, excursions, ISIC
Housing: *Arr by pgm:* residence halls, homestay
Deadline: Apr 15
Other info: *US accredited sponsor:* yes *Began:* 1985 *Orient:* abroad *Activities:* excursions, field trips, program travel, cultural events, sports *Misc:* Optional Paris tour & pgm flights. May contact former participants. *URL:* http://www.usac.unr.edu
Contact: *See Index II for Members* Carmelo Urza, Univ Studies Abroad Consortium, Univ of Nevada Library 323, Reno NV 89557-0093 *Ph:* 775-784 6569 *Fax:* 775-784 6010 *E-mail:* usac@unr.edu
▲

0598
WEBSTER UNIVERSITY
Webster on Wheels in France
Site: Southern France: various sites
Dates: 2 wks, Jul 27-Aug 14
Subjects: French language (beg/int)
Eligibility: *Level:* fresh, sophs, jrs, srs, grads, adults, teachers *Requires:* 2.5 GPA, some knowledge of French, physical fitness to ride bike *Age:* min 18
Credit: *Undergrad:* 3 *Grad:* 3 *Doc:* transcript
Instruction: *In:* French *Format:* lang study, study tour *Students:* mainly US
Costs: $1,899 *incl* housing, some meals, intl airfare, excursions, railpass *Nonrefundable fee*
Housing: *Arr by pgm:* pensions, hostels, campsites
Deadline: Feb 1
Other info: *US accredited sponsor:* yes *Began:* 1998 *Orient:* in US (1 day) *Activities:* excursions, cultural events *URL:* http://www.websteruniv.edu/intl/sa/index.html
Contact: Brian Kennelly, Webster Univ, 470 E Lockwood Ave, St Louis MO 63119 *Ph:* 314-968 7054 *E-mail:* kennelly@pop.websteruniv.edu
Or Contact: Teresa Bruno, Webster Univ, 470 E Lockwood Ave, St Louis MO 63119 *Ph:* 800-984 6857 *Fax:* 314-968 7119 *E-mail:* brunote@webster.edu

---

AGEN

0599
NORTHERN ILLINOIS UNIVERSITY
Comparative and European Union Law in Agen, France
Site: France: Agen *Host inst:* Univ of Bordeaux-Juridical Studies Ctr of Agen
Dates: 4 wks, Jun-Jul
Subjects: Law
Eligibility: *Level:* grads, adults *Requires:* 2.5 GPA, previous study in field *Age:* min 18, avg 25
Credit: *Undergrad:* none *Grad:* 6 *Doc:* transcript
Instruction: *In:* English *Format:* lecture *Students:* mainly US
Costs: $3,900 *incl* tuition, housing, some meals, insurance, excursions
Housing: *Arr by pgm:* residence halls
Deadline: Apr 15
Other info: *US accredited sponsor:* yes *Began:* 1996 *Orient:* in US *Misc:* May contact former participants. *URL:* http://www.niu.edu/niuabroad/
Contact: Anne Seitzinger, Pgm Coord, Study Abroad Office, Williston 417, Northern Illinois Univ, DeKalb IL 60115 *Ph:* 815-753 0700 *Fax:* 815-753 0825 *E-mail:* niuabroad@niu.edu

---

AIX-EN-PROVENCE

0600
COLLEGE CONSORTIUM FOR INTERNATIONAL STUDIES and **MIAMI-DADE COMMUNITY COLLEGE**
Studio Art in Aix-en-Provence, France
Site: France: Aix-en-Provence *Host inst:* Marchutz Sch of Inst for Amer Univs
Dates: 6 wks, mid-Jun-late Jul
Subjects: Arts criticism, Drawing, Homestay, Painting, Studio arts
Eligibility: *Level:* fresh, sophs, jrs, srs, professionals *Requires:* 2.5 GPA *Age:* min 16, max 65
Credit: *Undergrad:* 6 *Grad:* none *Doc:* transcript
Instruction: *In:* English *Format:* art studio *Students:* mainly US
Costs: About $3,850 *incl* tuition, housing, some meals, insurance, fees
Housing: *Arr by pgm:* residence halls, homestay
Deadline: None
Other info: *US accredited sponsor:* yes *Began:* 1982 *Orient:* abroad *Activities:* excursions *Misc:* Supplies about $250. Optional post-pgm wk in Paris. *Financial aid:* scholarships *URL:* http://www.ccisabroad.org
Contact: *See Index II for Members* CCIS, 2000 P St NW, Ste 503, Washington DC 20036 *Ph:* 800-453 6956; 202-223 0330 *Fax:* 202-223 0999 *E-mail:* info@ccisabroad.org
Or Contact: Reinaldo Changsut, Study Abroad, Miami-Dade CC, 11011 SW 104th St, Miami FL 33176-3393 *Ph:* 305-237 2533 *Fax:* 305-237 2949 *E-mail:* rchangsu@mdcc.edu ▲

0601
CULTURAL EXPERIENCES ABROAD (CEA)
Study French Language and Culture in Southern France
Site: France: Aix-en-Provence *Host inst:* Univ of Aix-Marseille
Dates: 4-8 wks, Jun-Jul
Subjects: Civilization/culture, French language, French studies, Homestay, Independent study, Literature
Eligibility: *Level:* fresh, sophs, jrs, srs, grads, precoll *Requires:* 2.5 GPA, previous French study recommended, recommendation letter, transcript *Age:* min 17, avg 20
Credit: *Undergrad:* 4-8 per 4 wks *Grad:* 4-8 per 4 wks *Doc:* transcript, certificate, diploma
Instruction: *In:* French *Format:* independent study, lab, lang study, lecture, tutorial, workshop *Students:* intl
Costs: $3,295-$4,995 *incl* tuition, housing, some meals, insurance, fees, excursions, books/materials, railpass, orient, airport transfer *Nonrefundable fee*
Housing: *Arr by pgm:* residence halls, apartments, homestay
Deadline: Rolling admissions
Other info: *US accredited sponsor:* no *Orient:* abroad (1 day) *Activities:* excursions, field trips, program travel, cultural events, sports *Misc:* On-site staff. E-mail. May contact former participants. *Financial aid:* scholarships *URL:* http://www.travelabroad.com
Contact: CEA Study Abroad, 1400 E Southern Ave, Ste B-108, Tempe AZ 85282-8011 *Ph:* 480-557 7900 *Fax:* 480-557 7926 *E-mail:* france@travelabroad.com

---

0602
FRENCH-AMERICAN EXCHANGE
Intensive Summer Program in Aix
Site: France: Aix-en-Provence *Host inst:* Inst d'Etudes Francaises Pour Etudiants Etrangers at Univ d'Aix-Marseille III
Dates: 4 or 8 wks, Jun, Jul, Sep
Subjects: Civilization/culture, French language (beg/int/adv), French studies, Literature, Written composition
Eligibility: *Level:* sophs, jrs, srs, grads, adults, teachers, professionals *Requires:* 2.5 GPA, previous study in field, high sch diploma; previous lang study preferred *Age:* min 18, max 75, avg 20
Credit: *Undergrad:* 6 per mo *Grad:* 6 per mo *Doc:* transcript, certificate
Instruction: *In:* French *Format:* lab, lang study *Students:* intl
Costs: $1,775 for 4 wks *incl* tuition, housing, some meals, fees, excursions, books/materials *Nonrefundable fee*
Housing: *Arr by pgm:* apartments, homestay, bed & breakfasts
Deadline: 6 wks before pgm
Other info: *US accredited sponsor:* no *Began:* 1996 *Orient:* avail info packet *Activities:* excursions, field trips, cultural events, sports *Misc:* May contact former participants. *URL:* http://www.faetours.com
Contact: Jim Pondolfino, Exec Dir, French-Amer Exch, 111 Roberts Ct, Alexandria VA 22314 *Ph:* 800-995 5087; 703-549 5087 *Fax:* 703-549 2865 *E-mail:* faetours@erols.com

---

0603
INSTITUTE FOR AMERICAN UNIVERSITIES
Art in Provence
Site: France: Aix-en-Provence *Host inst:* Marchutz Sch
Dates: 6 wks, mid-Jun-late Jul
Subjects: Art history, Arts criticism, Drawing, French language, Homestay, Painting
Eligibility: *Level:* fresh, sophs, jrs, srs, adults *Age:* min 18
Credit: *Undergrad:* 6 *Grad:* none *Doc:* transcript
Instruction: *In:* English *Format:* art studio, lang study, lecture, seminar *Students:* mainly US
Costs: $3,385 *incl* tuition, housing, some meals, excursions
Housing: *Arr by pgm:* apartments, homestay
Deadline: Rolling admissions
Other info: *US accredited sponsor:* no *Began:* 1969 *Orient:* abroad *Activities:* field trips *Misc:* May contact former participants. *Financial aid:* scholarships *URL:* http://www.iau-univ.org
Contact: Giancarlo Taylor, Asst Dir, Admissions, IAU US Off, PO Box 592, 1830 Sherman Ave at University Pl, Evanston IL 60204 *Ph:* 800-224 2051 *Fax:* 847-864 6897 *E-mail:* iauusa2@univ-aix.fr
Or Contact: Coll Consortium for Intl Studies, c/o Miami-Dade CC, Foreign Lang, South Campus, 11011 SW 104th St, Miami FL 33176 *Ph:* 305-237 2533
Or Contact: Eckerd Coll, Intl Educ & Off-Campus Pgms, 4200 54th Ave S, St Petersburg FL 33711 *Ph:* 813-864 8381 ▲

0604
INSTITUTE FOR AMERICAN UNIVERSITIES
Le Centre d'Aix
Site: France: Aix-en-Provence
Dates: 6 wks, mid-Jun-late Jul
Subjects: Archaeology, Art, Drama/theater, French language (beg/int/adv), History, Homestay, International business, International relations, Literature, Political science/politics, Social sciences
Eligibility: *Level:* fresh, sophs, jrs, srs, adults *Age:* min 18
Credit: *Undergrad:* 3-9 *Grad:* none *Doc:* transcript
Instruction: *In:* English, French *Format:* lang study, lecture *Students:* intl & host country
Costs: $3,385 *incl* tuition, housing, some meals, excursions
Housing: *Arr by pgm:* homestay
Deadline: Rolling admissions
Other info: *US accredited sponsor:* no *Began:* 1969 *Orient:* abroad *Activities:* field trips, program travel *Misc:* Aix Music Festival. See also IAU French lang & literature in Avignon & the Marchutz Sch of Painting & Drawing. *Financial aid:* scholarships *URL:* http://www.iau-univ.org
Contact: Giancarlo Taylor, Asst Dir, Admissions, IAU US Off, PO Box 592, 1830 Sherman Ave at University Pl, Evanston IL 60204 *Ph:* 800-221 2051 *Fax:* 847-864 6897 *E-mail:* iauusa2@univ-aix.fr
Or Contact: Northern Illinois Univ, Study Abroad Off, Williston Hall 417, DeKalb IL 60115-2854 *Ph:* 815-753 1988
Or Contact: Coll Consortium for Intl Studies, c/o Miami-Dade CC, Foreign Langs, South Campus, 11011 SW 104th St, Miami FL 33176 *Ph:* 305-237 2533 ▲

0605
IS AIX-EN-PROVENCE/IFS
Discover Provence: Language and Culture (DP)
Site: France: Aix-en-Provence
Dates: 2 wks, beg Feb 12, May 7, Sep 10 or Nov 5
Subjects: Civilization/culture, Culinary arts, French language (int), Homestay, Wine
Eligibility: *Level:* adults *Requires:* beg French
Credit: *Undergrad:* none *Grad:* none *Doc:* certificate
Instruction: *In:* French *Format:* lang study, lecture, practical training, study tour *Students:* intl
Costs: Fr 4,400 *incl* tuition, excursions, books/materials *Nonrefundable fee*
Housing: *Arr by pgm:* apartments, homestay, pensions, hotels
Deadline: Contact sponsor
Other info: *US accredited sponsor:* no *Began:* 1998 *Activities:* excursions, cultural events *Misc:* May contact former participants. *URL:* http://www.is-aix.com
Contact: Ms A C Sainte-Rose, IS Aix-en-Provence, 9 Cours des Arts et Metiers, 13100 Aix-en-Provence, France *E-mail:* info@is-aix.com
Or Contact: Lingua Svc Worldwide, 75 Prospect St, Ste 4, Huntington NY 11743 *Ph:* 631-424 0777 *Fax:* 631-271 3441 *E-mail:* itctravel@worldnet.att.net
Or Contact: French-Amer Exch, 111 Roberts Ct, Alexandria VA 22314 *Ph:* 703-549 5087 *Fax:* 703-549 2865 *E-mail:* faetours@erols.com ▲

0606
IS AIX-EN-PROVENCE/IFS
French Language Course: Commercial French (FGFC)
Site: France: Aix-en-Provence
Dates: 2 wks, beg Feb 12, Mar 26, May 7, Jun 18, Jul 30, Sep 10, Oct 22 or Dec 3
Subjects: Business administration, Business language, Business/management, French language (int), Homestay, Industry, Trade
Eligibility: *Level:* adults *Requires:* int French *Age:* min 18, max 70, avg 30
Credit: *Undergrad:* none *Grad:* none *Doc:* certificate
Instruction: *In:* French *Format:* lang study, practical training *Students:* intl
Costs: Fr 5,500 *incl* tuition, books/materials
Housing: *Sponsor assists:* apartments, homestay, pensions, hotels
Deadline: 1st day of pgm
Other info: *US accredited sponsor:* no *Began:* 1994 *Orient:* abroad *Activities:* excursions, cultural events *Misc:* May contact former participants. *URL:* http://www.is-aix.com
Contact: IS Aix-en-Provence, 9 cours des Arts et Metiers, 13100 Aix-en-Provence, France *E-mail:* info@is-aix.com
Or Contact: Lingua Svc Worldwide, 75 Prospect St, Ste 4, Huntington NY 11743 *Ph:* 631-424 0777 *Fax:* 631-271 3441 *E-mail:* itctravel@workdnet.att.net
Or Contact: French-Amer Exch, 111 Roberts Ct, Alexandria VA 22314 *Ph:* 703-549 5087 *Fax:* 703-549 2865 *E-mail:* faetours@erols.com ▲

0607
IS AIX-EN-PROVENCE/IFS
French Language Courses: French for Executives
Site: France: Aix-en-Provence
Dates: 2 wks, beg Jan 29, Mar 12, Apr 23, Jun 4, Jul 16, Aug 27, Oct 8 or Nov 19
Subjects: Business language, Business/management, French language, Homestay
Eligibility: *Level:* adults, professionals *Requires:* lower int French *Age:* min 22, max 65, avg 38
Credit: *Undergrad:* none *Grad:* none *Doc:* certificate
Instruction: *In:* French *Format:* lang study, practical training *Students:* intl
Costs: Fr 9,500 *incl* tuition, books/materials
Housing: *Sponsor assists:* apartments, homestay, pensions, hotels
Deadline: 1st day of pgm
Other info: *US accredited sponsor:* no *Began:* 1980 *Orient:* abroad *Activities:* excursions, cultural events *URL:* http://www.is-aix.com
Contact: IS Aix-en-Provence, 9 cours des Arts et Metiers, 13100 Aix-en-Provence, France *E-mail:* info@is-aix.com
Or Contact: Lingua Svc Worldwide, 75 Prospect St, Ste 4, Huntington NY 11743 *Ph:* 631-424 0777 *Fax:* 631-271 3441 *E-mail:* itctravel@worldnet.att.net
Or Contact: French-Amer Exch, 111 Roberts Ct, Alexandria VA 22314 *Ph:* 703-549 5087 *Fax:* 703-549 2865 *E-mail:* faetours@erols.com ▲

0608
IS AIX-EN-PROVENCE/IFS
French Language Courses: General and Intensive French
Site: France: Aix-en-Provence
Dates: 1-10 wks, yr-round
Subjects: Civilization/culture, French language (beg/int/adv), Homestay
Eligibility: *Level:* adults, teachers, professionals *Age:* min 18, avg 31
Credit: *Undergrad:* none *Grad:* none *Doc:* certificate
Instruction: *In:* French *Format:* lang study, lecture, practical training *Students:* intl
Costs: Fr 3,500-5,075 for 2 wks *incl* tuition, books/materials
Housing: *Sponsor assists:* residence halls, apartments, homestay, pensions, hotels
Deadline: 1st day of class
Other info: *US accredited sponsor:* no *Began:* 1972 *Orient:* abroad *Activities:* excursions, cultural events *Misc:* May contact former participants. *URL:* http://www.is-aix.com
Contact: IS Aix-en-Provence, 9 cours des Arts et Metiers, 13100 Aix-en-Provence, France *E-mail:* info@is-aix.com
Or Contact: Lingua Svc Worldwide, 75 Prospect St, Ste 4, Huntington NY 11743 *Ph:* 631-424 0777 *Fax:* 631-271 3441 *E-mail:* itctravel@worldnet.att.net
Or Contact: French-Amer Exch, 111 Roberts Ct, Alexandria VA 22314 *Ph:* 703-549 5087 *Fax:* 703-549 2865 *E-mail:* faetours@erols.com ▲

0609
VANDERBILT UNIVERSITY
Vanderbilt in France Summer Session
Site: France: Aix-en-Provence
Dates: About May 30-Jul 21
Subjects: Civilization/culture, French language, French studies, Homestay, Independent study, Internships, Literature
Eligibility: *Level:* sophs, jrs, srs *Requires:* 2.7 GPA, 4 sems coll French with B avg, transcript, references, personal essay
Credit: *Undergrad:* 7 *Grad:* none
Instruction: *In:* French *Format:* independent study, lang study, lecture, study tour *Students:* mainly US
Costs: Contact sponsor
Housing: *Arr by pgm:* homestay
Deadline: Feb 15
Other info: *US accredited sponsor:* yes *Activities:* program travel
Contact: Ms Marci Hunt, Study Abroad Off, Vanderbilt Univ, Box 1573, Station B, Nashville TN 37235 *Ph:* 615-343 3139 *Fax:* 615-343 5774 *E-mail:* marcella.a.hunt@vanderbilt.edu

---

AMIENS

0610
SOUTHWEST TEXAS STATE UNIVERSITY
SWT in Amiens, France
Site: France: Amiens *Host inst:* Univ de Picardie Jules Verne
Dates: 4 wks, Jul
Subjects: French language (int/adv), Independent study, Marketing
Eligibility: *Level:* sophs, jrs, srs, adults, teachers *Requires:* 2.0 GPA, previous study in field *Age:* min 18
Credit: *Undergrad:* 6 *Grad:* none *Doc:* transcript
Instruction: *In:* English, French *Format:* independent study, lang study, lecture, practical training, seminar *Students:* mainly US
Costs: $2,500 *incl* tuition, housing, intl airfare, fees, excursions, books/materials

Housing: *Arr by pgm:* residence halls
Deadline: Contact sponsor
Other info: *US accredited sponsor:* yes *Began:* 1996 *Activities:* excursions, field trips, cultural events, sports *Misc:* May contact former participants. *Financial aid:* scholarships *URL:* http://www.ideal.swt.edu/extension/study_abroad/
Contact: Dr Robert Fischer, Modern Langs, Southwest Texas State Univ, 601 Univ Dr, San Marcos TX 78666 *Ph:* 512-245 2360 *Fax:* 512-245 8298 *E-mail:* rf02@swt.edu
Or Contact: Isis de la O Gomez, Extension Studies Coord, Southwest Texas State Univ, 601 Univ Dr, San Marcos TX 78666 *Ph:* 512-245 2322 *Fax:* 512-245 8934 *E-mail:* ig02@swt.edu

ANGERS

0611
FLORIDA INTERNATIONAL UNIVERSITY
FIU in Angers
Site: France: Angers *Host inst:* Ctr Intl d'Etudes Francaises (CIDEF)
Dates: 1 mo, Jun 29-Jul 31
Subjects: French language
Eligibility: *Level:* adults *Requires:* previous study in field, int French
Credit: *Undergrad:* avail *Grad:* avail *Doc:* transcript
Instruction: *In:* French *Format:* directed field study, lang study, study tour, tutorial *Students:* US & intl
Costs: $3,539 *incl* housing, some meals, intl airfare, fees, excursions *Nonrefundable fee*
Housing: *Arr by pgm:* homestay
Deadline: May 15
Other info: *US accredited sponsor:* yes *Began:* 1997 *Orient:* in US (1 day) *Activities:* excursions, field trips, program travel, cultural events *Misc:* May contact former participants. *URL:* http://www.fiu.edu/~intered
Contact: Intl Studies, Florida Intl Univ, 11200 SW 8th St, DM 300B, Miami FL 33199 *Ph:* 305-348 1913, 305-348 1918 *Fax:* 305-348 1941 *E-mail:* intered@fiu.edu

0612
ILLINOIS STATE UNIVERSITY
Summer Study in International Agriculture and Agribusiness
Site: France: Angers *Host inst:* Ecole Superieure d'Agriculture
Dates: 4 wks, Jun
Subjects: Agribusiness, Agriculture, Civilization/culture, French studies, History, Homestay, International business
Eligibility: *Level:* sophs, jrs, srs *Requires:* 2.5 GPA
Credit: *Undergrad:* 6 *Grad:* none *Doc:* transcript
Instruction: *In:* English *Format:* lecture, seminar, study tour *Students:* mainly US
Costs: $3,400 *incl* tuition, housing, some meals, intl airfare, insurance, fees, excursions, ground transport
Housing: *Arr by pgm:* homestay
Deadline: Feb 14
Other info: *US accredited sponsor:* yes

Orient: in US *Activities:* field trips, program travel *Misc:* Loans avail. *Financial aid:* scholarships *URL:* http://www.its.ilstu.edu/intlstudies/
Contact: Chairperson, Illinois State Univ, Campus Box 5020, Normal IL 61790-5020 *Ph:* 309-438 5654 *Fax:* 309-438 3987 *E-mail:* oisp@ilstu.edu
Or Contact: Intl Studies, Illinois State Univ, Campus Box 6120, Normal IL 61790-6120 *Ph:* 309-438 5365 *Fax:* 309-438 3987 *E-mail:* oisp@ilstu.edu

---

0613
ISA
Cours de Francais: Summer Program in Angers
Site: France: Angers *Host inst:* Univ Catholique de l'Ouest
Dates: Jun 27-Jul 28, Jul 28-Aug 27, Aug 30-Sep 29
Subjects: Civilization/culture, French language (int/adv), French studies, History, Homestay, Literature
Eligibility: *Level:* sophs, jrs, srs, grads *Requires:* 2.5 GPA, recommendation letter *Age:* min 17, avg 22
Credit: *Undergrad:* 6 sem hrs *Grad:* none *Doc:* transcript, certificate
Instruction: *In:* French *Format:* lang study, lecture, tutorial *Students:* intl
Costs: $3,850 *incl* tuition, housing, some meals, insurance, fees, excursions, tutoring, overnight stays
Housing: *Arr by pgm:* homestay
Deadline: Apr 5; Mar 10 for scholarships
Other info: *US accredited sponsor:* no *Began:* 1994 *Orient:* in US & abroad *Activities:* excursions, field trips, program travel, cultural events *Misc:* Resident dir incl in costs. May contact former participants. *Financial aid:* scholarships *URL:* http://www.studiesabroad.com
Contact: Gustavo Artaza, Exec Dir, ISA, 901 W 24th St, Austin TX 78705 *Ph:* 800-580 8826; 512-480 8522 *Fax:* 512-480 8866 *E-mail:* isa@studiesabroad.com ▲

0614
NORTHWEST COUNCIL ON STUDY ABROAD (NCSA) and AHA INTERNATIONAL
Summer French Language and Culture Studies in Angers
Site: France: Angers *Host inst:* Univ Catholique de l'Ouest
Dates: 4 wks, Jul, Aug or Sep
Subjects: French language, Homestay
Eligibility: *Level:* sophs, jrs, srs *Requires:* 2.5 GPA, previous study in field *Age:* min 18
Credit: *Undergrad:* avail *Grad:* none *Doc:* transcript *Transfer credit through:* Central Washington Univ
Instruction: *In:* French *Format:* lang study, lecture *Students:* intl
Costs: About $2,350 *incl* tuition, housing, all meals, insurance, excursions
Housing: *Arr by pgm:* residence halls, homestay
Deadline: 65 days before pgm
Other info: *US accredited sponsor:* yes *Began:* 1997 *In coop with:* Ctr Intl d'Etudes Francaises *Orient:* abroad (1 day) *Activities:* excursions *Misc:* May contact former participants. *URL:* http://www.aha-intl.org

Contact: *See Index II for Members* Carlotta Troy, AHA Intl, 741 SW Lincoln St, Portland OR 97201 *Ph:* 800-654 2051; 503-295 7730 *Fax:* 503-295 5969 *E-mail:* mail@aha-intl.org

---

0615
TRUMAN STATE UNIVERSITY
Intensive French in Angers
Site: France: Angers *Host inst:* Catholic Univ of Angers
Dates: Jul 2-29
Subjects: French language, Homestay
Eligibility: *Level:* fresh, sophs, jrs, srs, grads, adults *Requires:* 2.5 GPA *Age:* min 18
Credit: *Undergrad:* 6 *Grad:* none *Doc:* transcript
Instruction: *In:* French *Format:* lecture, seminar *Students:* intl
Costs: $2,120 *incl* tuition, housing, all meals, excursions, books/materials *Nonrefundable fee*
Housing: *Sponsor assists:* residence halls, homestay
Deadline: May 1
Other info: *US accredited sponsor:* yes *Began:* 1990 *Orient:* abroad *Activities:* field trips *Misc:* Scholarships for own students only. May contact former participants. *Financial aid:* scholarships *URL:* http://www2.truman.edu/ciea/
Contact: Ctr for Intl Educ Abroad, Truman State Univ, Kirk Bldg, Rm 120, Kirksville MD 63501 *Ph:* 660-785 4076 *Fax:* 660-785 7473 *E-mail:* ciea@truman.edu

---

0616
UNIVERSITY OF HAWAII AT MANOA
French Language and Culture in Angers
Site: France: Angers *Host inst:* Ctr Intl d'Etudes Francaises of Univ Catholique de L'Ouest
Dates: 5 wks, Jul
Subjects: French language (int/adv), Homestay
Eligibility: *Level:* sophs, jrs, srs *Requires:* 3.0 GPA, 1 yr coll French
Credit: *Undergrad:* 6 *Grad:* none *Doc:* transcript
Instruction: *In:* French *Format:* lang study *Students:* mainly US
Costs: $4,151 *incl* tuition, housing, some meals, intl airfare, insurance, fees, excursions
Housing: *Arr by pgm:* homestay
Deadline: Feb 17
Other info: *US accredited sponsor:* yes *Began:* 1992 *Orient:* in US & abroad *Activities:* excursions, field trips, cultural events *Misc:* UHM financial aid avail to eligible UHM students. *URL:* http://www2.hawaii.edu/study-abroad
Contact: Dir or Study Abroad Adviser, Study Abroad Ctr, Univ of Hawaii at Manoa, Moore Hall 115, 1890 East-West Rd, Honolulu HI 96822 *Ph:* 808-956 5143, 808-956 6958 *Fax:* 808-956 9319 *E-mail:* uhmsac@hawaii.edu

---

0617
UNIVERSITY OF NORTHERN IOWA
Summer Institute for Teachers of French
Site: France: Angers
Dates: Late Jun-early Aug
Subjects: Civilization/culture, French language (adv), Homestay, Linguistics, Literature
Eligibility: *Level:* grads, teachers *Requires:* BA, currently teaching French
Credit: *Undergrad:* none *Grad:* 6 *Doc:* transcript, diploma, degree
Instruction: *In:* French *Format:* lang study, lecture, seminar *Students:* mainly US
Costs: $2,300 *incl* tuition, housing, some meals, fees, excursions *Nonrefundable fee*
Housing: *Arr by pgm:* homestay
Deadline: Jan 1
Other info: *US accredited sponsor:* yes *Began:* 1967 *Orient:* abroad (intensive lang study) *Activities:* excursions, cultural events *Misc:* Participants can attend for professional improvement or earn MA by attending several summers. *URL:* http://www.uni.edu/modlangs/institutes-abroad
Contact: Prof Michael Oates, Modern Langs, Univ of Northern Iowa, Cedar Falls IA 50614-0504 *Ph:* 319-273 2200 *Fax:* 319-273 2848 *E-mail:* mark.welty@uni.edu

---

ANNECY

0618
MIAMI-DADE COMMUNITY COLLEGE and TRUMAN STATE UNIVERSITY
Summer in France
Site: France: Annecy *Host inst:* Inst Francais des Alpes (IFALPES)
Dates: 1 mo, Jul
Subjects: French language (beg/int/adv), French studies, Homestay, Literature
Eligibility: *Level:* fresh, sophs, jrs, srs, adults, teachers *Requires:* 2.5 GPA *Age:* min 18
Credit: *Undergrad:* avail *Grad:* none *Doc:* transcript
Instruction: *In:* English, French *Format:* lang study, lecture *Students:* intl
Costs: About $1,595 *incl* tuition, housing, some meals, fees, books/materials
Housing: *Arr by pgm:* homestay
Deadline: Rolling admissions
Other info: *US accredited sponsor:* yes *Began:* 1996 *Orient:* abroad *Activities:* excursions *Misc:* Under acad supervision of Univ Catholique de Lyon. *URL:* http://www.truman.edu.administration/ceia/abroad.html
Contact: Dr Robert Vitale, Dir, Intl Educ, Miami-Dade CC, 11011 SW 104th St, Miami FL 33176 *Ph:* 305-237 2533 *Fax:* 305-237 2949 *E-mail:* rvitale@mdcc.edu
Or Contact: Dr Patrick Lecaque, Dir, Intl Educ Abroad, Truman State Univ, Kirksville MO 63501 *Ph:* 660-785 4076 *Fax:* 660-785 7473

0619
TUFTS UNIVERSITY
Tufts in Annecy
Site: France: Annecy *Host inst:* Inst Francais d'Annecy (IFALPES)
Dates: Contact sponsor
Subjects: French language (beg/int)
Eligibility: *Level:* fresh, sophs, jrs, srs, grads, adults *Requires:* 2.0 GPA *Age:* min 18
Credit: *Undergrad:* 4 *Grad:* none *Doc:* transcript
Instruction: *In:* French *Format:* lang study *Students:* intl
Costs: $3,375 *incl* tuition, housing, all meals, fees, books/materials, airport transfers
Housing: *Arr by pgm:* homestay
Deadline: Contact sponsor
Other info: *US accredited sponsor:* yes *Began:* 1994 *Orient:* abroad *Activities:* excursions, cultural events, sports *Misc:* May contact former participants. *URL:* http://www.ase.tufts.edu/FrenchAlps
Contact: Sally Pym, Tufts Univ European Ctr, 108 Packard Ave, Medford MA 02155 *Ph:* 617-627 3290 *Fax:* 617-627 3457 *E-mail:* france@infonet.tufts.edu ▲

0620
UNIVERSITY OF COLORADO AT BOULDER
Summer Intensive French Program
Site: France: Annecy *Host inst:* Inst Francais des Alpes (IFALPES)
Dates: 4, 8 or 12 wks, Jun 1-Aug 31
Subjects: Civilization/culture, French language (beg/int/adv), Homestay
Eligibility: *Level:* sophs, jrs, srs, grads, adults *Requires:* 2.75 GPA, previous French study recommended
Credit: *Undergrad:* 4 or 8 or 12 *Grad:* none *Doc:* transcript
Instruction: *In:* French *Format:* lang study *Students:* intl
Costs: $1,779 per term for CO residents, $2,779 for others *incl* tuition, housing, some meals, insurance, bus pass *Nonrefundable fee*
Housing: *Arr by pgm:* residence halls, homestay
Deadline: Mar 1

Other info: *US accredited sponsor:* yes *Began:* 1991 *Orient:* in US *Misc:* May contact former participants. *URL:* http://www.colorado.edu/OIE/StudyAbroad
Contact: Intl Educ, Univ of Colorado, Campus Box 123, Boulder CO 80309-0123 *Ph:* 303-492 7741 *Fax:* 303-492 5185 *E-mail:* studyabr@colorado.edu

---

0621
UNIVERSITY OF HAWAII AT MANOA
French Language and Culture in Annecy
Site: France: Annecy *Host inst:* Inst Francais des Alpes (IFALPES)
Dates: 5 wks, late May-late Jun
Subjects: French language (beg/int/adv)
Eligibility: *Level:* sophs, jrs, srs *Requires:* 1 yr coll French
Credit: *Undergrad:* 6 *Grad:* none *Doc:* transcript
Instruction: *In:* French *Format:* lang study, lecture *Students:* intl
Costs: $4,179 *incl* tuition, housing, some meals, intl airfare, insurance, fees, excursions, books/materials
Housing: *Arr by pgm:* residence halls
Deadline: Feb 17
Other info: *US accredited sponsor:* yes *Began:* 1988 *Orient:* in US & abroad *Misc:* UHM financial aid avail for UHM students only. *URL:* http://www2.hawaii.edu/study-abroad
Contact: Dir or Study Abroad Adviser, Study Abroad Ctr, Univ of Hawaii at Manoa, Moore Hall 115, 1890 East-West Rd, Honolulu HI 96822 *Ph:* 808-956 5143, 808-956 6958 *Fax:* 808-956 9319 *E-mail:* uhmsac@hawaii.edu

---

ANTIBES

0622
COLLEGE INTERNATIONAL D'ANTIBES
College International d'Antibes
Site: France: Antibes
Dates: 2 wks or longer, yr-round
Subjects: Civilization/culture, French language (beg/int/adv), French studies
Eligibility: *Level:* fresh, sophs, jrs, srs, grads, adults, teachers, professionals, precoll *Age:* min 16, avg 25
Credit: *Undergrad:* avail *Grad:* none *Doc:* certificate
Instruction: *In:* French *Format:* lang study *Students:* intl
Costs: $2,700 per mo *incl* tuition, housing, some meals, airport transfers *Nonrefundable fee*
Housing: *Arr by pgm:* residence halls, apartments, homestay
Deadline: Contact sponsor
Other info: *US accredited sponsor:* no *Began:* 1985 *Activities:* excursions, cultural events *Misc:* May contact former participants. *Financial aid:* work study
Contact: Dr Janice E Ovadiah, US Rep, Coll Intl d'Antibes, 303 W 66th St, 4HE, New York NY 10023 *Ph:* 212-724 5823 *Fax:* 212-496 2264 *E-mail:* jovadiah@aol.com

---

ARCACHON

0623
UNIVERSITY OF IOWA
Iowa/Bordeaux Program in International and Comparative Law
Site: France: Arcachon (Gironde)
Dates: Mid-May-mid-Jun
Subjects: Law
Eligibility: *Level:* grads
Credit: *Undergrad:* none *Grad:* 6
Instruction: *In:* English *Format:* lecture *Students:* mainly US
Costs: $3,250 *incl* tuition, housing, fees, excursions, books/materials *Nonrefundable fee*
Housing: *Arr by pgm:* apartments
Deadline: Apr 1
Other info: *US accredited sponsor:* yes *Began:* 1984 *Activities:* program travel
Contact: Prof Adrien Wing, Coll of Law, Univ of Iowa, Iowa City IA 52242 *Ph:* 319-335 9129 *Fax:* 319-335 9098 *E-mail:* adrienwing@uiowa.edu

---

ARCHAMPS

0624
INTERNATIONAL CAMPUS CONSORTIUM and **THUNDERBIRD, THE AMERICAN GRADUATE SCHOOL OF INTERNATIONAL MANAGEMENT**
Thunderbird French Geneva Center
Site: France: Archamps
Dates: 14 wks, May 22-Aug 25
Subjects: Business/management, Finance, French language (int/adv), German language (int/adv), International business, International marketing, International studies, Italian language (int/adv), Spanish language (int/adv)
Eligibility: *Level:* grads *Requires:* 3.0 GPA, previous lang study recommended
Credit: *Undergrad:* none *Grad:* 9-12 *Doc:* certificate
Instruction: *In:* English *Format:* lang study, lecture *Students:* intl
Costs: $11,000 *incl* tuition, insurance, fees
Housing: *Sponsor assists:* residence halls, apartments, hotels
Deadline: Contact sponsor
Other info: *US accredited sponsor:* yes *Orient:* abroad *Activities:* field trips *Misc:* May contact former participants. *Financial aid:* scholarships *URL:* http://www.t-bird.edu
Contact: *See Index II for Members* Dr Earl Gibbons, Assoc VP, Overseas Pgms, Thunderbird, 15249 N 59th Ave, Glendale AZ 85306 *Ph:* 602-978 7252 *Fax:* 602-978 7419 *E-mail:* gibbonse@t-bird.edu
Or Contact: Diane Hayton, Coord, Overseas Pgms, Thunderbird, 15249 N 59th Ave, Glendale AZ 85306 *Ph:* 602-978 7252 *Fax:* 602-978 7419 *E-mail:* haytond@t-bird.edu

---

ARLES

0625
NORTHWESTERN UNIVERSITY
Northwestern University in Arles
Site: France: Arles *Host inst:* Coll St Charles Arles
Dates: 6 wks, Jun 16-Jul 29
Subjects: Art history, Classical studies, Drama/theater, French language, Photography, Political science/politics
Eligibility: *Level:* fresh, sophs, jrs, srs *Requires:* 3.0 GPA
Credit: *Undergrad:* 3 per course *Grad:* none *Doc:* transcript
Instruction: *In:* English, French *Format:* lecture, study tour *Students:* mainly US
Costs: $6,875 for 2 courses *incl* tuition, housing, some meals, intl airfare, fees, excursions *Nonrefundable fee*
Housing: *Arr by pgm:* hotels
Deadline: Mar 31
Other info: *US accredited sponsor:* yes *Began:* 1995 *Orient:* in US (1 day) *Activities:* excursions *Misc:* Students must take 2 courses. May contact former participants. *URL:* http://www.northwestern.edu/summersa
Contact: Christina Kyres, Asst Dir, Sch of Continuing Studies, Northwestern Univ, 339 E Chicago Ave, Chicago IL 60611-3008 *Ph:* 312-503 3021 *Fax:* 312-503 3003 *E-mail:* summersa@northwestern.edu

---

0626
SPEOS-PARIS PHOTOGRAPHIC INSTITUTE
Photography in Provence
Site: France: Arles
Dates: 5 days, late Jun
Subjects: Photography
Eligibility: *Level:* adults *Requires:* camera *Age:* min 18, max 77, avg 30
Credit: *Undergrad:* none *Grad:* none
Instruction: *In:* English, French *Format:* lab, lecture, practical training *Students:* intl
Costs: About $1,500 *incl* tuition, housing, some meals, fees, excursions, railpass
Housing: *Arr by pgm:* hotels

Deadline: Apply early
Other info: *US accredited sponsor:* no *Began:* 1999 *Misc:* Beg & int photography students, shooting visits in Provence. *URL:* http://www.photography-education.com
Contact: Sophie Malon, Dir, SPEOS, 8 rue Jules Valles, Paris, France 75011 *E-mail:* speos@speos.fr

---

0627
UNIVERSITY OF SOUTHERN MISSISSIPPI
Mediterranean France
Site: France: Arles
Dates: 2 wks, May 13-May 30
Subjects: International studies, Journalism
Eligibility: *Level:* sophs, jrs, srs, grads *Requires:* 2.0 GPA, good acad standing
Credit: *Undergrad:* 4 *Grad:* none *Doc:* transcript
Instruction: *In:* English *Format:* lecture, study tour *Students:* mainly US
Costs: $2,599 *incl* tuition, housing, some meals, intl airfare, fees, excursions
Housing: *Arr by pgm:* hotels
Deadline: Feb 15
Other info: *US accredited sponsor:* yes *Began:* 1999 *Orient:* abroad (1 day) *Activities:* excursions, field trips *Misc:* Grants & loans avail. *URL:* http://www.usm.edu
Contact: Dr Tim W Hudson, Intl & Continuing Educ, Univ of Southern Mississippi, Box 10047, Hattiesburg MS 39406 *Ph:* 601-266 4344 *Fax:* 601-266 5699 *E-mail:* melissa.ravencraft@usm.edu

---

AVIGNON

0628
COLLEGE CONSORTIUM FOR INTERNATIONAL STUDIES and **MIAMI-DADE COMMUNITY COLLEGE**
Summer in France: French Language and Literature
Site: France: Avignon *Host inst:* Ctr d'Avignon of Inst for Amer Univs
Dates: 6 wks, beg mid-Jun
Subjects: French language (int/adv), French studies, Homestay, Literature
Eligibility: *Level:* adults *Requires:* 2.5 GPA, previous study in field, 2 yrs coll or equiv *Age:* min 18
Credit: *Undergrad:* 6 *Grad:* none *Doc:* transcript
Instruction: *In:* French *Format:* lang study, lecture, seminar *Students:* mainly US
Costs: About $3,850 *incl* tuition, housing, some meals, insurance, fees, excursions, books/materials
Housing: *Arr by pgm:* homestay
Deadline: Contact sponsor
Other info: *US accredited sponsor:* yes *Began:* 1972 *Orient:* abroad *URL:* http://www.ccisabroad.org
Contact: *See Index II for Members* CCIS, 2000 P St NW, Ste 503, Washington DC 20036 *Ph:* 800-453 6956; 202-223 0330 *Fax:* 202-223 0999 *E-mail:* info@ccisabroad.org
Or Contact: Robert Vitale, Dir, Intl Educ, Miami-Dade CC, 11011 SW 104th St, Miami FL 33176-3393 *Ph:* 305-237 2533 *Fax:* 305-237 2949
Or Contact: Reinaldo Changsut, Study Abroad Adviser, Miami-Dade CC, 11011 SW 104th St, Miami FL 33176-3393 *Ph:* 305-237 2535 *Fax:* 305-237 2949 *E-mail:* rchangsu@mdcc.edu ▲

0629
INSTITUTE FOR AMERICAN UNIVERSITIES
Atelier D'Expression Theatrale
Site: France: Avignon
Dates: About 1 mo, Jul 1-30
Subjects: Acting, Drama/theater, Homestay
Eligibility: *Level:* jrs, srs, grads, adults, teachers, professionals *Requires:* previous study in field, adv French; theater experience preferred *Age:* min 18
Credit: *Undergrad:* avail *Grad:* avail *Doc:* certificate
Instruction: *In:* French *Format:* lecture, workshop *Students:* mainly US
Costs: $3,385 *incl* tuition, housing, some meals, excursions, theater tickets *Nonrefundable fee*
Housing: *Arr by pgm:* homestay
Deadline: Rolling admissions
Other info: *US accredited sponsor:* no *Began:* 1999 *Orient:* abroad (1 day) *Activities:* excursions, field trips, cultural events *URL:* http://www.iau-univ.org
Contact: Giancarlo Taylor, Asst Dir, Admissions, IAU US Off, PO Box 592, 1830 Sherman Ave at University Pl, Evanston IL 60204 *Ph:* 800-221 2051; 847-864 6876 *Fax:* 847-864 6897 *E-mail:* iauusa2@univ-aix.fr
Or Contact: Prof Bonnie Gould, Univ of Tennessee-Knoxville, Theater, Knoxville TN *Ph:* 423-974 7302 *Fax:* 423-974 4867 *E-mail:* bkgould@utk.edu ▲

0630
INSTITUTE FOR AMERICAN UNIVERSITIES
Le Centre d'Avignon
Site: France: Avignon *Host inst:* IAU, Chapelle St Antoine
Dates: 6 wks, mid-Jun-late Jul
Subjects: Business language, Civilization/culture, French language (adv), Homestay, International business, Literature, Theater arts
Eligibility: *Level:* jrs, srs, adults *Requires:* 2 yrs coll French *Age:* min 18
Credit: *Undergrad:* 6 *Grad:* none *Doc:* transcript
Instruction: *In:* French *Format:* lang study, lecture, workshop *Students:* mainly US
Costs: $3,385 *incl* tuition, housing, some meals, excursions
Housing: *Arr by pgm:* homestay
Deadline: Rolling admissions
Other info: *US accredited sponsor:* no *Began:* 1967 *Orient:* abroad *Activities:* field trips, program travel *Misc:* Atelier d'Expression Theatrale in Jul in conjunction with Avignon Theater Festival. May contact former participants. *Financial aid:* scholarships *URL:* http://www.iau-univ.org
Contact: Giancarlo Taylor, Asst Dir, Admissions, IAU US Off, PO Box 592, 1830 Sherman Ave at University Pl, Evanston IL 60204 *Ph:* 800-221 2051 *Fax:* 847-864 6897 *E-mail:* iauusa2@univ-aix.fr
Or Contact: Northern Illinois Univ, Study Abroad Off, Williston Hall 417, DeKalb IL 60115-2854 *Ph:* 815-753 1988
Or Contact: Coll Consortium for Intl Studies, c/o Miami-Dade CC, Foreign Langs, South Campus, 11011 SW 104th St, Miami FL 33176 *Ph:* 305-237 2533 ▲

0631
NORTHERN ILLINOIS UNIVERSITY
French Language and Literature in Avignon, France
Site: France: Avignon *Host inst:* Inst for Amer Univs
Dates: 6 wks, Jun-Jul
Subjects: Art history, Civilization/culture, French language (int), Homestay, Literature
Eligibility: *Level:* jrs, srs, grads *Requires:* 2.75 GPA, previous study in field, 2 yrs coll French, good acad standing *Age:* min 18, avg 20
Credit: *Undergrad:* 3-6 *Grad:* none *Doc:* transcript
Instruction: *In:* French *Format:* lang study, lecture *Students:* mainly US
Costs: About $3,700 *incl* tuition, housing, some meals, insurance, fees, excursions
Housing: *Arr by pgm:* homestay
Deadline: Apr 15 or until pgm filled
Other info: *US accredited sponsor:* yes *In coop with:* IAU *Orient:* abroad *URL:* http://www.niu.edu/niuabroad/
Contact: Anne Seitzinger, Pgm Coord, Study Abroad Office, Williston 417, Northern Illinois Univ, DeKalb IL 60115 *Ph:* 815-753 0700 *Fax:* 815-753 0825 *E-mail:* niuabroad@niu.edu

---

0632
UNIVERSITY OF GEORGIA
Avignon Study Abroad Program-UGA
Site: France: Avignon *Host inst:* Univ of Avignon, Univ Pays du Vaucluse
Dates: 7 wks, May 14-Jun 27
Subjects: Art history, Business/ management, Civilization/culture, Communications, Comparative literature, Drama/theater, French language, History, Literature, Philosophy, Translating/ interpreting
Eligibility: *Level:* sophs, jrs, srs, grads, adults, teachers, professionals *Requires:* 3.0 GPA, previous study in field, 1 yr coll French or equiv *Age:* min 18, avg 20
Credit: *Undergrad:* 6 *Grad:* 6 *Doc:* transcript
Instruction: *In:* English, French *Format:* tutorial *Students:* mainly US
Costs: $4,300 *incl* tuition, housing, some meals, fees, excursions
Housing: *Arr by pgm:* residence halls, hotels
Deadline: Feb 1
Other info: *US accredited sponsor:* yes *Began:* 1999 *Orient:* in US & abroad (1 day, intensive lang study) *Activities:* excursions, cultural events *Misc:* May contact former participants. *Financial aid:* scholarships *URL:* http://www.uga.edu/oie
Contact: Dr Mihai Spariosu, Dir, Univ of Georgia, 225 Joseph Brown Hall, Athens GA 30602-6204 *Ph:* 706-542 2297 *Fax:* 706-542 1878 *E-mail:* spariosu@arches.uga.edu
Or Contact: Cathy Roszell, Asst Dir, Univ of Georgia, 207 B Candler Hall, Athens GA 30602 *Ph:* 706-542 2423 *Fax:* 706-583 0805 *E-mail:* croszell@arches.uga.edu

---

BESANCON

0633
PENNSYLVANIA STATE UNIVERSITY
Summer Education Abroad French Language Studies
Site: France: Besancon *Host inst:* Ctr de Linguistique Appliquee
Dates: 2 mos, Jun-Jul
Subjects: French language (int), Homestay
Eligibility: *Level:* fresh, sophs, jrs, srs *Requires:* 2.5 GPA, previous study in field, French lang study, reference letter, transcript *Age:* min 18, avg 20
Credit: *Undergrad:* 8 *Grad:* none *Doc:* transcript
Instruction: *In:* French *Format:* lang study, practical training *Students:* intl
Costs: About $3,660 for PA residents, $6,028 for others *incl* tuition, railpass *Nonrefundable fee*
Housing: *Arr by pgm:* apartments, homestay
Deadline: Apr 1
Other info: *US accredited sponsor:* yes *Orient:* in US (1 day) *Misc:* May contact former participants. *URL:* http://www.outreach.psu.edu/PSSEA/
Contact: Summer Abroad, Pennsylvania State Univ, 225 Penn State Conference Ctr, University Park PA 16802 *Ph:* 814-863 5170 *Fax:* 814-863 5190 *E-mail:* SummerAbroad@outreach.psu.edu

---

BEZIERS

0634
ECOLE DE LANGUES HOBSON
French Courses for Foreigners
Site: France: Beziers

Dates: 2 wks-1 yr, yr-round
Subjects: Art history, Arts, Business language, Business/management, Crafts, Culinary arts, French language (beg/int/adv), German language (beg/int/adv), Italian language (beg/int/adv), Law, Literature, Russian language (beg/int/adv), Spanish language (beg/int/adv), Tourism, Translating/interpreting
Eligibility: *Level:* adults *Age:* min 15, max 65, avg 25
Credit: *Undergrad:* avail *Grad:* avail *Doc:* certificate, diploma
Instruction: *In:* French *Format:* lab, lang study, lecture, practical training, seminar, student teaching, study tour *Students:* intl
Costs: About Fr 750 for 10 hrs, Fr 3,000 for 40 hrs *incl* tuition, fees, books/materials, railpass *Nonrefundable fee*
Housing: *Sponsor assists:* apartments with local students, residence halls with local students, homestay, pensions, hotels, hostels
Deadline: 1 mo before pgm
Other info: *US accredited sponsor:* no *Began:* 1982 *In coop with:* CCI of Paris, Montpellier Univ *Activities:* excursions, field trips, program travel, cultural events, sports *Misc:* Courses avail in any foreign lang upon request. Small groups of 3-5 persons. Diplomas of CCIP, DELF, DALF. May contact former participants. *URL:* http://www.centre-hobson.com
Contact: Jacqueline Hobson, Dir, Ecole de Langues Hobson, 31 rue Pelisson, 34500 Beziers, France *E-mail:* horizon@centre-hobson.com

---

BIARRITZ

0635
LANGUAGE STUDIES ABROAD, INC
General French-Biarritz
Site: France: Biarritz
Dates: 2 wks or longer, Jun 25-Aug 26
Subjects: Civilization/culture, French language, French studies, Homestay
Eligibility: *Level:* adults *Age:* min 13, max 17
Credit: *Undergrad:* none *Grad:* none
Instruction: *In:* French *Format:* lang study *Students:* intl
Costs: $2,200 for 4 wks *incl* tuition, housing, all meals, excursions, books/materials
Housing: *Arr by pgm:* homestay
Deadline: 4 wks before pgm
Other info: *US accredited sponsor:* no *Orient:* abroad *Activities:* excursions, sports *Misc:* May contact former participants. *URL:* http://www.languagestudiesabroad.com
Contact: Lang Studies Abroad, Inc, 103 Londonderry Ct, Reno NV 89511 *Ph:* 800-424 5522; 775-849 9206 *Fax:* 775-849 9217 *E-mail:* info@languagestudiesabroad.com

---

BORDEAUX

0636
BLS-BORDEAUX LANGUAGE STUDIES
Bordeaux Language Studies
Site: France: Bordeaux
Dates: 2 wks or longer, yr-round; summer pgm for jrs; 2-4 wks summer pgms for precoll students
Subjects: Business language, Culinary arts, Foreign language teaching, French language (beg/int/adv), Homestay, Wine
Eligibility: *Level:* fresh, sophs, jrs, srs, grads, adults, teachers, professionals, precoll *Age:* min 18, avg 25
Credit: *Undergrad:* avail *Grad:* none *Doc:* certificate
Instruction: *In:* English, French *Format:* lab, lang study, seminar, tutorial *Students:* intl
Costs: $1,585 for 2 wks *incl* tuition, housing, some meals, books/materials
Housing: *Sponsor assists:* homestay, hotels
Deadline: 4 wks before pgm
Other info: *US accredited sponsor:* no *Activities:* excursions, cultural events, sports *Misc:* May contact former participants. *Financial aid:* work study
Contact: Janice E Ovadiah, 303 W 66th St, #4HE, New York NY 10023-6305 *Ph:* 212-724 5823 *Fax:* 212-496 2264 *E-mail:* jovadiah@aol.com

---

0637
BLS-BORDEAUX LANGUAGE STUDIES
General French Courses: 22 Lessons per Week
Site: France: Bordeaux
Dates: 2 wks, yr-round
Subjects: French language (beg/int/adv)
Eligibility: *Level:* fresh, sophs, adults *Age:* min 17, avg 25
Credit: *Undergrad:* none *Grad:* none *Doc:* certificate
Instruction: *In:* French *Format:* lang study *Students:* intl
Costs: $928 *incl* tuition, housing, some meals, fees *Nonrefundable fee*
Housing: *Arr by pgm:* apartments with local students, homestay
Deadline: 3 wks before pgm
Other info: *US accredited sponsor:* no *Began:* 1992 *In coop with:* SOUFFLE, Bordeaux Univ *Orient:* abroad *Activities:* excursions, cultural events *Misc:* May contact former participants. *URL:* http://www.bls-bordeaux.com
Contact: Corine Woodward, Marketing, BLS, 42 rue Lafaurie de Monbadon, 33000 Bordeaux, France *E-mail:* info@bls-frenchcourses.com
Or Contact: Veronique Durham, Students Liaison, BLS, 42 rue Lafaurie de Monbadon, 33000 Bordeaux, France *E-mail:* info@bls-frenchcourses.com

---

0638
BLS-BORDEAUX LANGUAGE STUDIES
Summer Course
Site: France: Bordeaux
Dates: 4 wks, Jun 4-29, Jul 2-27, Aug 6-31 or Sep 3-28
Subjects: French language (int)
Eligibility: *Level:* fresh, sophs, jrs, srs, adults *Age:* min 17, avg 25
Credit: *Undergrad:* none *Grad:* none *Doc:* certificate
Instruction: *In:* French *Format:* lang study *Students:* intl
Costs: $1,550 *incl* tuition, housing, some meals
Housing: *Arr by pgm:* residence halls with local students, apartments, homestay, hotels
Deadline: 3 wks before pgm
Other info: *US accredited sponsor:* no *Orient:* abroad *Activities:* excursions, cultural events *Misc:* May contact former participants. *URL:* http://www.bls-frenchcourses.com
Contact: Corinne Woodward, Marketing Mgr, 42 rue Lafaurie de Monbadon, Bordeaux, France 33000 *E-mail:* info@bls-frenchcourses.com
Or Contact: Veronique Durham, Student Liaison, 42 rue Lafaurie de Monbadon, Bordeaux, France 33000 *E-mail:* info@bls-frenchcourses.com

---

0639
EDUVACATIONS
Study in and Live in Your Teacher's Home-France
Site: France: Bordeaux
Dates: 1 wk or longer, yr-round
Subjects: Civilization/culture, Culinary arts, French language (beg/int/adv), Hiking/trekking, Homestay, Outdoor activities/education, Tennis, Wine
Eligibility: *Level:* adults, precoll *Age:* min 15
Credit: *Undergrad:* none *Grad:* none
Instruction: *In:* French *Format:* lang study *Students:* intl
Costs: Contact sponsor
Housing: *Arr by pgm:* homestay
Deadline: None
Other info: *US accredited sponsor:* no *Activities:* excursions, field trips, cultural

events, sports *Misc:* May contact former participants. *URL:* http://www.eduvacations.com
Contact: Mary Ann Puglisi, eduVacations, 1431 21st St NW, Ste 302, Washington DC 20036 *Ph:* 202-857 8384 *Fax:* 202-463 8091

0640
LANGUAGE STUDIES ABROAD, INC
General French-Bordeaux
Site: France: Bordeaux *Host inst:* LSA Bordeaux
Dates: 2 wks or longer, yr-round
Subjects: Civilization/culture, French language, French studies, Homestay, Wine
Eligibility: *Level:* adults *Age:* min 17
Credit: *Undergrad:* none *Grad:* none
Instruction: *In:* French *Format:* lang study *Students:* intl
Costs: $1,840 for 4 wks *incl* tuition, housing, some meals
Housing: *Arr by pgm:* homestay, pensions, hostels
Deadline: 4 wks before pgm
Other info: *US accredited sponsor:* no *Began:* 1992 *Orient:* abroad *Activities:* excursions, cultural events, sports *Misc:* May contact former participants. *URL:* http://www.languagestudiesabroad.com
Contact: Chris Cote, Lang Studies Abroad, Inc, 103 Londonderry Ct, Reno NV 89511 *Ph:* 800-424 5522; 775-849 9206 *Fax:* 775-849 9217 *E-mail:* info@languagestudiesabroad.com

---

0641
UNIVERSITY OF PENNSYLVANIA
Penn-in-Bordeaux
Site: France: Bordeaux *Host inst:* Univ of Bordeaux
Dates: 2-1/2 wks, mid-Jun-early Jul
Subjects: Anthropology
Eligibility: *Level:* fresh, sophs, jrs, srs, grads, professionals
Credit: *Undergrad:* 3 *Grad:* 3 *Doc:* transcript
Instruction: *In:* English *Students:* mainly US
Costs: About $2,200 *incl* tuition, housing, excursions *Nonrefundable fee*
Housing: *Arr by pgm:* residence halls
Deadline: Mar 15
Other info: *US accredited sponsor:* yes *Began:* 1993 *Orient:* in US & abroad *Activities:* field trips, cultural events *Misc:* May contact former participants. *URL:* http://www.sas.upenn.edu/CGS/
Contact: Elizabeth Sachs, Penn Summer Abroad, Univ of Pennsylvania, 3440 Market St, Ste 100, Philadelphia PA 19104-3335 *Ph:* 215-898 5738 *Fax:* 215-573 2053 *E-mail:* sdanti@mail.sas.upenn.edu

---

BREST

0642
EASTERN MICHIGAN UNIVERSITY
French Language Program
Site: France: Brest *Host inst:* CIEL
Dates: Jun 30-Aug 11
Subjects: French language (int/adv)
Eligibility: *Level:* fresh, sophs, jrs, srs, grads, adults *Requires:* good acad standing, references *Age:* min 18
Credit: *Undergrad:* 6-9 *Grad:* 6-9 *Doc:* transcript
Instruction: *In:* French *Format:* lang study, lecture *Students:* mainly US
Costs: $3,695 *incl* tuition, housing, all

meals, intl airfare, insurance, fees, ground transport
Housing: *Arr by pgm:* homestay
Deadline: Mar 1
Other info: *US accredited sponsor:* yes *Began:* 1992 *Orient:* avail by mail *Activities:* excursions *Misc:* May contact former participants. *URL:* http://www.emich.edu/abroad
Contact: Acad Pgms Abroad, Eastern Michigan Univ, 127 Boone Hall, Ypsilanti MI 48197 *Ph:* 800-777 3541; 734-487 2424 *Fax:* 734-487 4377 *E-mail:* programs.abroad@emich.edu

CAEN

0643
UNIVERSITY OF DELAWARE
Winter Session in Caen
Site: France: Caen *Host inst:* Univ of Caen
Dates: 1 mo, Jan
Subjects: Civilization/culture, French language (int), French studies, Homestay
Eligibility: *Level:* fresh, sophs, jrs, srs, adults *Requires:* 2.0 GPA, 4 yrs high sch or 2 sems coll French
Credit: *Undergrad:* 6-7 *Grad:* none *Doc:* transcript
Instruction: *In:* English, French *Format:* lang study, lecture, study tour *Students:* mainly US
Costs: Contact sponsor
Housing: *Arr by pgm:* homestay
Deadline: Early Oct
Other info: *US accredited sponsor:* yes *Began:* 1988 *Orient:* avail yes *Activities:* excursions, field trips, program travel, cultural events *Misc:* Contact sponsor to arrange honors credit. May contact former participants. *Financial aid:* scholarships *URL:* http://www.udel.edu/studyabroad/
Contact: Lisa Chieffo, Study Abroad Coord, Foreign Langs & Literatures, Univ of Delaware, 326 Smith Hall, Newark DE 19716 *Ph:* 302-831 6458 *Fax:* 302-831 0597 *E-mail:* lchieffo@udel.edu
Or Contact: Intl Pgms & Special Sessions, Univ of Delaware, 4 Kent Way, Newark DE 19716 *Ph:* 888-831 4685; 302-831 2852 *Fax:* 302-831 6042 *E-mail:* studyabroad@udel.edu

CANNES

0644
AMERICAN INSTITUTE FOR FOREIGN STUDY (AIFS)
College International de Cannes
Site: France: Cannes *Host inst:* Coll Intl de Cannes
Dates: 4 wks, Jun 30-Jul 28 or Jul 28-Aug 25, 6 wks, Jun 30-Aug 25 or 8 wks, Jun 30-Aug 25
Subjects: Civilization/culture, Culinary arts, Fine arts, French language, French studies, Sociology, Wine
Eligibility: *Level:* fresh, sophs, jrs, srs, adults, precoll *Requires:* 2.0 GPA
Credit: *Undergrad:* 9 max *Grad:* none *Doc:* transcript *Transfer credit through:* Chapman Coll
Instruction: *In:* English *Format:* lang study, lecture *Students:* intl
Costs: About $4,899 for 4 wks, $6,399 for 6 wks, $7,499 for 8 wks *incl* tuition, housing, all meals, excursions
Housing: *Arr by pgm:* residence halls
Deadline: Mar 15
Other info: *US accredited sponsor:* no *Began:* 1987 *Orient:* abroad *Activities:* excursions, cultural events *Misc:* Resident dir. May contact former participants. *Financial aid:* scholarships *URL:* http://www.aifsabroad.com
Contact: Solandy Meza, Coll Div, AIFS, River Plaza, 9 W Broad St, Stamford CT 06902 *Ph:* 800-727 2437 ext 5163 *E-mail:* college.info@aifs.com ▲

0645
COLLEGE INTERNATIONAL DE CANNES
Cours de Francais pour Etrangers
Site: France: Cannes
Dates: 4 wks or longer, Jul 2-Aug 26
Subjects: Business/management, Civilization/culture, French language (beg/int/adv), French studies, Homestay
Eligibility: *Level:* fresh, sophs, jrs, srs, grads, adults, teachers, professionals, precoll *Age:* min 16, avg 21
Credit: *Undergrad:* avail *Grad:* avail *Doc:* certificate, diploma
Instruction: *In:* French *Format:* lab, lang study, seminar *Students:* intl
Costs: About $2,040 per mo *incl* tuition, housing, all meals, books/materials
Housing: *Arr by pgm:* residence halls, apartments, homestay
Deadline: Until pgm filled; apply early
Other info: *US accredited sponsor:* no *Began:* 1931 *Activities:* excursions, cultural events, sports *Misc:* Test ctr for DELF (French TOEFL), Alliance Francaise, Certificat de Francais Commercial. May contact former participants. *URL:* http://www.french-in-cannes.com
Contact: Mr Andreas Schweitzer, Genl Secy, Coll Intl de Cannes, 1 Rue du Dr Pascal, Cannes, France 06400 *E-mail:* cic@imaginet.fr

0646
CSA, CENTER FOR STUDY ABROAD
French Language and Culture Studies-Cannes
Site: France: Cannes *Host inst:* Coll Intl de Cannes
Dates: 4 or 8 wks, Jul 2-Aug 26; qtr/sem/yr pgms also avail
Subjects: Art, Drama/theater, French language (beg/int/adv), French studies, History, Independent study, Literature, Music, Political science/politics, Translating/interpreting
Eligibility: *Level:* adults *Age:* min 17
Credit: *Undergrad:* avail *Grad:* avail *Doc:* transcript, certificate
Instruction: *In:* English, French *Format:* independent study, lang study, lecture *Students:* intl
Costs: $2,695 for 4 wks, $4,895 for 8 wks *incl* tuition, housing, all meals, insurance, fees *Nonrefundable fee*
Housing: *Sponsor assists:* residence halls, homestay
Deadline: None
Other info: *US accredited sponsor:* no *Began:* 1920 *Orient:* abroad *Activities:* excursions, field trips, program travel, cultural events, sports *URL:* http://www.studyabroad.com/csa
Contact: Alima Khan, Assoc Dir, CSA, Ctr for Study Abroad, 2802 E Madison St, MS #160, Seattle WA 98112 *Ph:* 206-726 1498 *Fax:* 206-583 8192 *E-mail:* virtuecsa@aol.com

0647
UNIVERSITY OF PENNSYLVANIA
Penn-in-Cannes
Site: France: Cannes
Dates: 2 wks, May
Subjects: Film studies
Eligibility: *Level:* fresh, sophs, jrs, srs, grads, professionals
Credit: *Undergrad:* 3 *Grad:* none *Doc:* transcript
Instruction: *In:* English *Format:* lecture *Students:* mainly US
Costs: About $2,200 *incl* tuition, housing *Nonrefundable fee*
Housing: *Arr by pgm:* hostels
Deadline: Feb 1
Other info: *US accredited sponsor:* yes *Began:* 1983 *Orient:* in US & abroad *Misc:* May contact former participants. *URL:* http://www.sas.upenn.edu/CGS/
Contact: Elizabeth Sachs, Penn Summer Abroad, Univ of Pennsylvania, 3440 Market St, Ste 100, Philadelphia PA 19104-3335 *Ph:* 215-898 5738 *Fax:* 215-573 2053 *E-mail:* sdanti@mail.sas.upenn.edu

0648
WAYNE STATE UNIVERSITY
Au Soleil with Wayne
Site: France: Cannes
Dates: 6 wks, Jun 21-Jul 28
Subjects: Civilization/culture, Independent study, Written composition
Eligibility: *Level:* sophs, adults, teachers *Requires:* 3.0 GPA, 3 sems French *Age:* min 18, max 50, avg 23
Credit: *Undergrad:* 12 *Grad:* 12
Instruction: *In:* French *Format:* lang study, study tour, workshop *Students:* mainly US
Costs: $4,000 *incl* tuition, housing, some meals, insurance, fees, excursions, books/ materials, concert, cruise *Nonrefundable fee*
Housing: *Arr by pgm:* residence halls
Deadline: May 1
Other info: *US accredited sponsor:* yes *Began:* 1997 *Activities:* excursions, field trips, program travel, cultural events *Misc:* May contact former participants. *URL:* http://www.langlab.wayne.edu/ studyabroad/soleilhome.html
Contact: Drr Fabienne S Chauderlot, Dir, Wayne State Univ, Romania Land & Lit, 487 Manogian, Detroit MI 48202 *Ph:* 313-577 6241 *Fax:* 734-214 9481 *E-mail:* fabienne@mich.com

COLLONGES-SOUS-SALEVE

0649
ADVENTIST COLLEGES ABROAD
Summer French Language Program
Site: France: Collonges-sous-Saleve *Host inst:* Ctr Univ et Pedagogique du Saleve
Dates: 6 wks, Jun 22-Jul 31
Subjects: French language (beg/int/adv)
Eligibility: Students of member insts only. *Level:* fresh, sophs, jrs, srs, grads, adults, teachers, professionals, precoll *Requires:* 2.5 GPA *Age:* min 15
Credit: *Undergrad:* 9 qtr hrs *Grad:* none *Doc:* transcript
Instruction: *In:* French *Format:* lab, lang study, lecture *Students:* intl
Costs: $1,996 *incl* tuition, housing, all meals, insurance, fees, excursions, books/ materials *Nonrefundable fee*
Housing: *Arr by pgm:* residence halls
Deadline: May 31
Other info: *US accredited sponsor:* yes *Began:* 1992 *Orient:* in US & abroad *Activities:* excursions, field trips, sports *URL:* http://www.nadadventist.org/aca
Contact: *See Index II for Members* Odette Ferreira, Dir, Adventist Colls Abroad, 12501 Old Columbia Pike, Silver Spring MD 20904-6600 *Ph:* 301-680 6444 *Fax:* 301-680 6463 *E-mail:* 104474. 304@compuserve.com

COMPIEGNE

0650
UNIVERSITY OF PENNSYLVANIA
Penn-in-Compiegne
Site: France: Compiegne *Host inst:* Univ de Technologie de Compiegne
Dates: 6 or 8 wks, late May-mid-Jul
Subjects: Business language, Economics, European Union, French language, Homestay, Internships, Sociology
Eligibility: *Level:* fresh, sophs, jrs, srs *Requires:* good knowledge of French
Credit: *Undergrad:* 6-7 *Grad:* none *Doc:* transcript
Instruction: *In:* French *Format:* internship, lang study, lecture *Students:* mainly US
Costs: About $4,300-$4,600 *incl* tuition, housing, all meals *Nonrefundable fee*
Housing: *Arr by pgm:* homestay
Deadline: Mar 15
Other info: *US accredited sponsor:* yes *Began:* 1983 *Orient:* in US & abroad *URL:* http://www.sas.upenn.edu/CGS/
Contact: Elizabeth Sachs, Penn Summer Abroad, Univ of Pennsylvania, 3440 Market St, Ste 100, Philadelphia PA 19104-3335 *Ph:* 215-898 5738 *Fax:* 215-573 2053 *E-mail:* sdanti@mail.sas.upenn.edu

DIJON

0651
CSA, CENTER FOR STUDY ABROAD
French Language and Culture Studies-University of Bourgogne
Site: France: Dijon *Host inst:* Univ de Bourgogne
Dates: Jul-Aug
Subjects: Art, Culinary arts, Economics, French language (beg/int/adv), History, Independent study, Literature, Music, Sociology
Eligibility: *Level:* adults *Age:* min 17
Credit: *Undergrad:* avail *Grad:* avail *Doc:* transcript, certificate
Instruction: *In:* French *Format:* independent study, lang study, lecture *Students:* intl
Costs: Contact sponsor
Housing: *Sponsor assists:* residence halls
Deadline: None
Other info: *US accredited sponsor:* no *Began:* 1985 *Orient:* abroad *Activities:* excursions *URL:* http://www.studyabroad. com/csa
Contact: Philip Virtue, Dir, or Alima Khan, Assoc Dir, CSA, Ctr for Study Abroad, 2802 E Madison St, MS #160, Seattle WA 98112 *Ph:* 206-726 1498 *Fax:* 206-583 8192 *E-mail:* virtuecsa@aol.com

0652
CULTURAL EXPERIENCES ABROAD (CEA)
Study French Language and Culture in Dijon
Site: France: Dijon *Host inst:* Univ of Burgundy
Dates: 4-8 wks, Jul-Aug
Subjects: Art history, Civilization/culture, Culinary arts, Dance, Drama/theater, French language (beg/int/adv), History, Independent study, International studies, Literature, Music, Philosophy, Political science/politics, Translating/interpreting, Wine
Eligibility: *Level:* fresh, sophs, jrs, srs, grads, precoll *Requires:* previous French study recommended *Age:* min 17, avg 20
Credit: *Undergrad:* 4-8 *Grad:* avail *Doc:* transcript, certificate
Instruction: *In:* French *Format:* independent study, lang study, lecture, study tour, tutorial *Students:* intl
Costs: $2,795 for 4 wks, $3,295 for 6 wks, $3,795 for 8 wks *incl* tuition, housing, some meals, insurance, fees, excursions, books/materials, orient, support svcs, e-mail *Nonrefundable fee*
Housing: *Arr by pgm:* residence halls, homestay
Deadline: Rolling admissions
Other info: *US accredited sponsor:* no *In coop with:* Univ of Burgundy (Dijon) *Orient:* abroad *Activities:* excursions, field trips, program travel, cultural events, sports *Misc:* Lang exch pgm. May contact former participants. *Financial aid:* scholarships *URL:* http://www. travelabroad.com
Contact: CEA Study Abroad, 1400 E Southern Ave, Ste B-108, Tempe AZ 85282-8011 *Ph:* 480-557 7900 *Fax:* 480-557 7926 *E-mail:* france@travelabroad.com

0653
TEXAS CHRISTIAN UNIVERSITY
Spring in France
Site: France: Dijon
Dates: 3 wks, May 15-Jun 2
Subjects: French language, French studies
Eligibility: *Level:* grads *Requires:* 2.75 GPA
Credit: *Undergrad:* none *Grad:* 3
Instruction: *In:* English *Format:* directed field study, lang study, study tour *Students:* mainly US
Costs: $3,200 *incl* tuition, housing, some meals, excursions, books/materials, railpass
Housing: *Arr by pgm:* hotels
Deadline: Mar 31
Other info: *US accredited sponsor:* yes *Began:* 2000 *Orient:* in US *Activities:* excursions, field trips, program travel, cultural events *URL:* http://www.neeley. tcu.edu

Contact: Kristi Dill, Asst Dean, Neeley Sch of Bus, TCU Box 298530, Ft Worth TX 76129 *Ph:* 817-257 7527 *Fax:* 817-257 6049 *E-mail:* k.dill@tcu.edu

---

0654
UNIVERSITE DE BOURGOGNE, CENTRE INTERNATIONAL D'ETUDES FRANCAISES
Course in September
Site: France: Dijon *Host inst:* Univ of Burgundy
Dates: 4 wks, Sep
Subjects: French language (beg/int/adv), Homestay
Eligibility: *Level:* adults *Age:* min 18
Credit: *Undergrad:* none *Grad:* none *Doc:* transcript, certificate
Instruction: *In:* French *Format:* lang study *Students:* intl
Costs: Fr 3,600
Housing: *Arr by student:* homestay, foyer with intl students
Deadline: None
Other info: *US accredited sponsor:* no *Activities:* excursions, field trips, program travel, cultural events, sports *URL:* http://www.u-bourgogne.fr/cief
Contact: CIEF, Maison de l'Univ, Esplanade Erasme, BP 87874, 21078 Dijon Cedex, France *E-mail:* cief@u-bourgogne.fr

---

0655
UNIVERSITE DE BOURGOGNE, CENTRE INTERNATIONAL D'ETUDES FRANCAISES
Intensive Spoken French
Site: France: Dijon *Host inst:* Univ of Burgundy
Dates: 4 wks, Jun
Subjects: Contemporary issues, Field study, French language (beg/int/adv), Homestay
Eligibility: *Level:* adults *Age:* min 18
Credit: *Undergrad:* none *Grad:* none
Instruction: *In:* French *Format:* directed field study, lang study, tutorial *Students:* intl
Costs: Fr 3,600 *incl* tuition, books/materials
Housing: *Arr by student:* homestay, foyer with intl students
Deadline: None
Other info: *US accredited sponsor:* no *Began:* 1999 *Activities:* excursions, field trips, program travel, cultural events, sports *Misc:* Lang Resource Ctr offers customized pgms to suit individual needs. *URL:* http://www.u-bourgogne.fr/cief
Contact: CIEF, Maison de l'Univ, Esplanade Erasme, BP 87874, 21078 Dijon Cedex, France *E-mail:* cief@u-bourgogne.fr

---

0656
UNIVERSITE DE BOURGOGNE, CENTRE INTERNATIONAL D'ETUDES FRANCAISES
Preparatory Course for the Chambre de Commerce et d'Industrie de Paris Exams
Site: France: Dijon *Host inst:* Univ of Burgundy
Dates: 8-10 wks, Jul-Aug or Oct-Dec
Subjects: French language
Eligibility: *Level:* adults *Requires:* 300 hrs of French or DELF *Age:* min 18
Credit: *Undergrad:* none *Grad:* none *Doc:* transcript, certificate, diploma
Instruction: *In:* French *Format:* lang study *Students:* intl
Costs: Fr 6,450 *incl* tuition
Housing: *Arr by pgm:* residence halls with local students, apartments, homestay
Deadline: None
Other info: *US accredited sponsor:* no *Began:* 2000 *In coop with:* CCIP *Activities:* excursions, field trips, program travel, cultural events, sports *URL:* http://www.u-bourgogne.fr/CIEF
Contact: Ctr Intl d'Etudes Francaises, Maison de l'Univ, Esplanade Erasme, BP 87874, 21078 Dijon Cedex, France *E-mail:* cief@u-bourgogne.fr

---

0657
UNIVERSITE DE BOURGOGNE, CENTRE INTERNATIONAL D'ETUDES FRANCAISES
Refresher Course for Teachers of French
Site: France: Dijon *Host inst:* Univ of Burgundy
Dates: 4 wks, Jul
Subjects: Civilization/culture, Homestay, Linguistics, Literature, Multimedia
Eligibility: *Level:* teachers *Requires:* French lang study *Age:* min 18
Credit: *Undergrad:* none *Grad:* none *Doc:* certificate
Instruction: *In:* French *Format:* seminar, workshop *Students:* intl
Costs: Fr 4,600 *incl* tuition, books/materials *Nonrefundable fee*
Housing: *Arr by pgm:* residence halls, apartments, homestay, pensions, foyer intl
Deadline: None
Other info: *US accredited sponsor:* no *Began:* 1902 *Activities:* excursions, field trips, program travel, cultural events, sports *Misc:* Pgm incl how to run a resource ctr. *URL:* http://www.u-bourgogne.fr/cief
Contact: CIEF, Maison de L'Univ, Esplanade Erasme, BP 87874, 21078 Dijon Cedex, France *E-mail:* cief@u-bourgogne.fr

---

0658
UNIVERSITE DE BOURGOGNE, CENTRE INTERNATIONAL D'ETUDES FRANCAISES
Summer Courses
Site: France: Dijon *Host inst:* Univ of Burgundy
Dates: 2, 3, 4, 6 or 8 wks, Jul-Aug
Subjects: French language (beg/int/adv), Homestay
Eligibility: *Level:* adults *Age:* min 18
Credit: *Undergrad:* none *Grad:* none *Doc:* transcript, certificate, diploma
Instruction: *In:* French *Format:* lang study *Students:* intl
Costs: Fr 2,250-5,150 *incl* tuition, books/materials *Nonrefundable fee*
Housing: *Arr by student:* residence halls, homestay, foyer with intl students
Deadline: Contact sponsor
Other info: *US accredited sponsor:* no *Activities:* excursions, field trips, program travel, cultural events, sports *URL:* http://www.u-bourgogne.fr/cief
Contact: CIEF, Maison de l'Univ, Esplanade Erasme, BP 87874, 21078 Dijon Cedex, France *E-mail:* cief@u-bourgogne.fr

---

0659
VIRGINIA POLYTECHNIC INSTITUTE & STATE UNIVERSITY
Marketing in the European Union
Site: France: Dijon *Host inst:* Ecole Superieure de Commerce de Dijon
Dates: 6 wks, May 15-Jun 30
Subjects: Civilization/culture, European studies, French language (beg), French studies, International business, International marketing
Eligibility: *Level:* jrs, srs, grads *Requires:* 2.0 GPA, previous study in field *Age:* min 20, avg 22
Credit: *Undergrad:* avail *Grad:* avail *Doc:* transcript
Instruction: *In:* English *Format:* directed field study, independent study, lang study, lecture, seminar, study tour *Students:* mainly US
Costs: About $4,000 *incl* tuition, housing, some meals, intl airfare, excursions, books/materials
Housing: *Arr by pgm:* residence halls with local students, hostels
Deadline: Jan 31
Other info: *US accredited sponsor:* yes *Began:* 1999 *Orient:* in US (1 day) *Financial aid:* scholarships *URL:* http://www.cob.vt.edu/market/faculty/sirgy/personal/dijon
Contact: M Joseph Sirgy, Virginia Tech, Dept of Marketing, Blacksburg VA 24061-0236 *Ph:* 504-231 5110 *Fax:* 540-231 3076 *E-mail:* sirgy@vt.edu

Or Contact: Marie-Jose Albert-Batt, Ecole Superieure de Commerce, 29 Rue Sambin-F, Dijon 21000,, France *E-mail:* m-j.albert-batt@wanadoo.fr

---

GRENOBLE

0660
ACADEMIC PROGRAMS INTERNATIONAL (API)
Academic Programs International-Grenoble
Site: France: Grenoble *Host inst:* Univ Stendhal Grenoble III
Dates: 6-8 wks, Jun 17-Jul 28, Jul 1-July 28
Subjects: Civilization/culture, Current events, French language (beg/int/adv), French studies, Homestay, Literature, Media studies, Theater arts, Translating/interpreting, Written composition
Eligibility: *Level:* fresh, sophs, jrs, srs, adults *Requires:* 2.75 GPA *Age:* min 18, avg 21
Credit: *Undergrad:* 4-6 *Grad:* none *Doc:* transcript, certificate
Instruction: *In:* French *Format:* tutorial *Students:* intl
Costs: $3,800 for short pgm, $7,300 for long pgm *incl* tuition, housing, all meals, insurance, excursions, books/materials, tutoring, ground transport
Housing: *Arr by pgm:* residence halls, homestay
Deadline: Apr 1
Other info: *US accredited sponsor:* no *Began:* 1997 *Orient:* in US & abroad (2 wks, intensive lang study) *Activities:* excursions, field trips, program travel, cultural events *Misc:* On-site dir. Airport reception. May contact former participants. *Financial aid:* scholarships *URL:* http://www.academicintl.com
Contact: Brittany Norman, Dir, Acad Pgms Intl, 129 E Hopkins, Ste 101, San Marcos TX 78666 *Ph:* 800-844 4124; 512-392 8520 *Fax:* 512-392 8420 *E-mail:* api@onr.com

---

0661
BOSTON UNIVERSITY
Summer Program in Grenoble
Site: France: Grenoble *Host inst:* Ctr Univ d'Etudes Francaises (CUEF), Univ de Grenoble
Dates: 6 wks, Jun-Jul
Subjects: Civilization/culture, French language (int/adv), French studies, Homestay
Eligibility: *Level:* sophs, jrs, srs *Requires:* 3.0 GPA, in major, 2 sems coll French, good acad standing
Credit: *Undergrad:* 8 *Grad:* none *Doc:* transcript
Instruction: *In:* French *Format:* lang study, lecture, seminar *Students:* mainly US
Costs: $4,550 *incl* tuition, housing, all meals, excursions
Housing: *Arr by pgm:* homestay
Deadline: Mar 1; Apr 1 for scholarships
Other info: *US accredited sponsor:* yes *Began:* 1994 *Orient:* in US & abroad *Misc:* Full-time resident dir. Pgm may be taken before joining Boston Univ French pgms in Sep. May contact former participants. *Financial aid:* scholarships *URL:* http://www.bu.edu/abroad/

Contact: Intl Pgms, Boston Univ, 232 Bay State Rd, Boston MA 02215 *Ph:* 617-353 9888 *Fax:* 617-353 5402 *E-mail:* abroad@bu.edu ▲

0662
COUNCIL ON INTERNATIONAL EDUCATIONAL EXCHANGE CONSORTIUM
University of Grenoble
Site: France: Grenoble *Host inst:* Univ de Grenoble
Dates: 4 or 8 wks, Jul-Aug
Subjects: Civilization/culture, Contemporary issues, French language (beg/int/adv), French studies, Homestay, Literature
Eligibility: *Level:* sophs, jrs, srs *Requires:* 2.75 GPA *Age:* min 18
Credit: *Undergrad:* avail *Grad:* none *Doc:* transcript
Instruction: *In:* English, French *Format:* lecture, seminar, tutorial *Students:* intl
Costs: $1,200 for 4 wks, $1,800 for 8 wks *incl* tuition, insurance, ISIC *Nonrefundable fee*
Housing: *Arr by pgm:* residence halls, homestay
Deadline: May 1
Other info: *US accredited sponsor:* yes *Began:* 1996 *Orient:* abroad (1 day) *Misc:* May contact former participants. *Financial aid:* scholarships *URL:* http://www.ciee.org/study
Contact: *See Index II for Members* Pgm Adviser, Council-ISP, 633 3rd Ave, 20th Fl, New York NY 10017-6706 *Ph:* 800-407 8839; 212-822 2600, 212-822 2772 *Fax:* 212-822 2779 *E-mail:* studyinfo@ciee.org

---

0663
CULTURAL EXPERIENCES ABROAD (CEA)
Study French Language and Culture in Grenoble
Site: France: Grenoble *Host inst:* Univ of Grenoble
Dates: 4-12 wks, Jun-Aug
Subjects: Business/management, Civilization/culture, French language, French studies, Homestay
Eligibility: *Level:* fresh, sophs, jrs, srs, precoll *Requires:* 2.5 GPA, previous study in field, previous lang study recommended, recommendation letter, transcipt *Age:* min 17, avg 20
Credit: *Undergrad:* avail *Grad:* none *Doc:* transcript, certificate, diploma
Instruction: *In:* English, French *Format:* lab, lecture, seminar, tutorial, workshop *Students:* intl & host country
Costs: $2,895 *incl* tuition, housing, some meals, insurance, fees, excursions, airport transfers *Nonrefundable fee*
Housing: *Arr by pgm:* residence halls, homestay
Deadline: Rolling admissions
Other info: *US accredited sponsor:* no *Orient:* abroad *Activities:* excursions, field trips, program travel, cultural events, sports *Misc:* Lang exch pgm. May contact former participants. *Financial aid:* scholarships *URL:* http://www.travelabroad.com
Contact: CEA Study Abroad, 1400 E Southern Ave, Ste B-108, Tempe AZ 85282-8011 *Ph:* 480-557 7900 *Fax:* 480-557 7926 *E-mail:* france@travelabroad.com

---

0664
ILLINOIS STATE UNIVERSITY
Program at the University of Grenoble
Site: France: Grenoble *Host inst:* Univ de Grenoble
Dates: 8 wks, mid-Jun-Aug 1
Subjects: Civilization/culture, Field study, French language, Literature
Eligibility: *Level:* sophs, jrs, srs *Requires:* 2.5 GPA, 1 yr coll French
Credit: *Undergrad:* 6 *Grad:* none
Instruction: *In:* French *Format:* directed field study, lang study, lecture *Students:* mainly US
Costs: About $5,350 *incl* housing, all meals, intl airfare, fees, excursions, overseas tuition
Housing: *Arr by pgm:* residence halls
Deadline: Feb 14
Other info: *US accredited sponsor:* yes *Began:* 1967 *Orient:* in US *Activities:* excursions *URL:* http://www.its.ilstu.edu/intlstudies/
Contact: Adviser, 4300 Foreign Langs, Illinois State Univ, Normal IL 61790-4300 *Ph:* 309-438 3604 *Fax:* 309-438 3987
Or Contact: Intl Studies, Illinois State Univ, Campus Box 6120, Normal IL 61761-6901 *Ph:* 309-438 5365 *Fax:* 309-438 3987 *E-mail:* oisp@ilstu.edu

---

0665
ISA
Cours de Langue et de Culture Francaises: Summer Program in Grenoble
Site: France: Grenoble *Host inst:* Univ de Stendahl Grenoble
Dates: 5 wks, late Jun-early Aug or mid-Jul-late Aug
Subjects: Business language, Civilization/culture, French language, French studies, Homestay, Literature, Written composition
Eligibility: *Level:* fresh, sophs, jrs, srs, adults, teachers, professionals *Requires:* 2.5 GPA, previous study in field, 2 sems coll French, recommendation letter
Credit: *Undergrad:* 5 sem hrs *Grad:* none *Doc:* transcript
Instruction: *In:* French *Format:* lecture *Students:* intl
Costs: $3,800 *incl* tuition, housing, all meals, insurance, fees, excursions, books/materials, resident dir *Nonrefundable fee*
Housing: *Arr by pgm:* apartments, homestay, hotels
Deadline: Apr 5
Other info: *US accredited sponsor:* no *Began:* 1999 *Orient:* in US & abroad (2 days) *Activities:* excursions, field trips, program travel, cultural events, sports *Misc:* May contact former participants. *Financial aid:* scholarships *URL:* http://www.studiesabroad.com
Contact: Gustavo Artaza, Intl Studies Abroad, 901 W 24th St, Austin TX 78705 *Ph:* 800-580 8826; 512-480 8522 *Fax:* 512-480 8866 *E-mail:* isa@studiesabroad.com ▲

0666
UNIVERSITY OF DELAWARE
Winter Session in Grenoble
Site: France: Grenoble
Dates: 1 mo, Jan
Subjects: Business/management, International business, International marketing
Eligibility: *Level:* fresh, sophs, jrs, srs *Requires:* previous study in field
Credit: *Undergrad:* 6 *Grad:* none *Doc:* transcript
Instruction: *In:* English *Format:* lecture, seminar, study tour *Students:* mainly US
Costs: Contact sponsor
Housing: *Arr by pgm*
Deadline: Early Oct
Other info: *US accredited sponsor:* yes *Activities:* excursions, field trips, program travel, cultural events *Misc:* Contact sponsor to arrange honors credit. May contact former participants. *Financial aid:* scholarships *URL:* http://www.udel.edu/studyabroad/
Contact: Intl Pgms, Univ of Delaware, 4 Kent Way, Newark DE 19716 *Ph:* 888-831 4685; 302-831 2852 *Fax:* 302-831 6042 *E-mail:* studyabroad@udel.edu

---

HYERES

0667
CSA, CENTER FOR STUDY ABROAD
French Language-Riviera
Site: France: Hyeres *Host inst:* ELFCA
Dates: 1 wk or longer, yr-round
Subjects: French language (beg/int/adv), Homestay
Eligibility: *Level:* adults *Age:* min 17
Credit: *Undergrad:* avail *Grad:* avail *Doc:* certificate
Instruction: *In:* French *Format:* lang study *Students:* intl
Costs: $2,395 for 1 mo *incl* tuition,

housing, all meals, insurance, fees, excursions, books/materials
Housing: *Sponsor assists:* homestay, hotels
Deadline: None
Other info: *US accredited sponsor:* no *Began:* 1975 *Orient:* abroad *Activities:* excursions, field trips, cultural events, sports *URL:* http://www.studyabroad.com/csa
Contact: Alima Khan, Pgm Dir, CSA, Ctr for Study Abroad, 2802 E Madison St, MS #160, Seattle WA 98112 *Ph:* 206-726 1498 *Fax:* 206-583 8192 *E-mail:* virtuecsa@aol.com

---

0668
ELFCA (INSTITUT INTL DE LANGUE FRANCAISE DE LA COTE D'AZUR)
ELFCA-Intensive French Language Study
Site: France: Hyeres
Dates: 2 wks or longer, yr-round
Subjects: Civilization/culture, French language (beg/int/adv), French studies
Eligibility: *Level:* fresh, sophs, jrs, srs, grads, adults, teachers, professionals, precoll *Age:* min 18, avg 25
Credit: *Undergrad:* avail *Grad:* none *Doc:* certificate
Instruction: *In:* French *Format:* lab, seminar, tutorial *Students:* intl
Costs: $1,300 for 2 wks *incl* tuition, housing, some meals
Housing: *Sponsor assists:* homestay, hotels
Deadline: 4 wks before pgm
Other info: *US accredited sponsor:* no *Began:* 1975 *Activities:* excursions, cultural events, sports *Misc:* May contact former participants. *Financial aid:* work study
Contact: Dr Janice E Ovadiah, USA Rep, 303 W 66th St, #4HE, New York NY 10023-6305 *Ph:* 212-724 5823 *Fax:* 212-496 2264 *E-mail:* jovadiah@aol.com

---

0669
SUNY COLLEGE AT NEW PALTZ, LANGUAGE IMMERSION INSTITUTE
Overseas Learning Vacation in France
Site: France: Hyeres *Host inst:* ELFCA
Dates: 2 wks or longer, yr-round
Subjects: French language, Homestay
Eligibility: *Level:* fresh, sophs, jrs, srs, adults, teachers, professionals *Requires:* min level Adv Beg French *Age:* min 18, avg 35
Credit: *Undergrad:* avail *Grad:* none *Doc:* certificate
Instruction: *In:* French *Format:* lang study, lecture, study tour *Students:* intl
Costs: About $1,028 for 2 wks *incl* housing, fees, deposit
Housing: *Arr by pgm:* apartments, homestay, hotels
Deadline: 8 wks before pgm
Other info: *US accredited sponsor:* yes *Began:* 1981 *Activities:* excursions, field trips, cultural events *URL:* http://www.newpaltz.edu/lii
Contact: Lang Immersion Inst, SUNY New Paltz, 75 S Manheim Blvd, New Paltz NY 12561-2499 *Ph:* 845-257 3500 *Fax:* 845-257 3569 *E-mail:* lii@newpaltz.edu ▲

LA NAPOULE

0670
UNIVERSITY OF MASSACHUSETTS AMHERST
Summer Program in Studio Art
Site: France: La Napoule *Host inst:* La Napoule Art Fdn
Dates: About Jun 26-Jul 28
Subjects: Studio arts
Eligibility: *Level:* fresh, sophs, jrs, srs, grads *Requires:* portfolio review & transcript
Credit: *Undergrad:* 9 *Grad:* 9
Instruction: *In:* English *Format:* art studio, lecture *Students:* mainly US
Costs: About $3,900 for UM students, $4,400 for others *incl* tuition, housing, some meals, excursions
Housing: *Arr by pgm:* residence halls
Deadline: Mar 15
Other info: *US accredited sponsor:* yes *Activities:* excursions, program travel *Misc:* Pgm offered in even-numbered yrs. *URL:* http://www.umass.edu/ipo/
Contact: Mike Coblyn, Fine Arts Ctr, Univ of Massachusetts, Amherst MA 01003 *Ph:* 413-545 1902 *E-mail:* mec@art.umass.edu

---

LA ROCHELLE

0671
SUNY COLLEGE AT CORTLAND
University of La Rochelle (Summer Program)
Site: France: La Rochelle
Dates: 4 wks, Jul 1-Jul 30
Subjects: Civilization/culture, French language, French studies
Eligibility: *Level:* adults *Requires:* 2.5 GPA, at least 1 sem coll level French or equiv *Age:* min 18
Credit: *Undergrad:* 6 per session *Grad:* none *Doc:* transcript
Instruction: *In:* French *Format:* lang study *Students:* intl
Costs: $2,000 *incl* housing, all meals, intl airfare, insurance, fees, excursions, books/materials *Nonrefundable fee*
Housing: *Arr by pgm:* residence halls, apartments
Deadline: Apr 1
Other info: *US accredited sponsor:* yes *Began:* 1999 *Orient:* in US & abroad (1 day) *Activities:* excursions, field trips, cultural events *Misc:* state of the art multi-media lang facilities May contact former participants. *URL:* http://www.studyabroad.com/suny/cortland
Contact: John Ogden, Dir, Off of Intl Pgms, PO Box 2000, B-15 Old Main, SUNY Cortland, Cortland NY 13045 *Ph:* 607-753 2209 *Fax:* 607-753 5989 ▲

0672
UNIVERSITY OF RICHMOND
Summer Study Abroad in La Rochelle
Site: France: La Rochelle *Host inst:* Inst d'Etudes Francaises
Dates: 5 wks, Jun-Jul
Subjects: French language (int/adv)
Eligibility: *Level:* sophs, jrs, srs, grads, adults
Credit: *Undergrad:* 6-9 *Grad:* 6-9
Instruction: *In:* French *Format:* lang study, lecture *Students:* mainly US
Costs: About $4,600 *incl* housing, all meals, intl airfare, excursions
Housing: *Arr by pgm:* homestay
Deadline: Rolling admissions
Other info: *US accredited sponsor:* yes *Began:* 1977 *Activities:* excursions
Contact: Barbara Baroody, La Rochelle Pgm Dir, Univ of Richmond, Richmond VA 23173 *Ph:* 804-287 6460
Or Contact: Jeanne Burkett, Univ of Richmond, Richmond VA 23173 *Ph:* 804-287 6835 *Fax:* 804-289 8138 *E-mail:* jburkett@richmond.edu

---

LILLE

0673
NORTH CAROLINA STATE UNIVERSITY
Intensive French Language and European Studies
Site: France: Lille *Host inst:* Univ Catholique de Lille
Dates: May-Jun
Subjects: Civilization/culture, European studies, French language (beg/int/adv), Homestay, Independent study
Eligibility: *Level:* fresh, sophs, jrs, srs, grads, adults, teachers, professionals
Credit: *Undergrad:* 6 *Grad:* none
Instruction: *In:* English, French *Format:* independent study, lab, lang study, lecture, seminar, study tour, tutorial *Students:* mainly US
Costs: $4,075 *incl* tuition, housing, all meals, intl airfare, insurance, excursions, local transport
Housing: *Arr by pgm:* homestay, hotels
Deadline: Feb
Other info: *US accredited sponsor:* yes

Began: 1994 *Orient:* in US *Activities:* excursions, cultural events *Misc:* 1 wk field study in Paris, Normandy, Loire Valley. May contact former participants. *Financial aid:* scholarships *URL:* http://www.ncsu.edu/studyabroad
Contact: Anne Haberkern, North Carolina State Univ, 2118 Pullen Hall, Box 7344, Raleigh NC 27695-7344 *Ph:* 919-515 2087 *Fax:* 919-515 6021 *E-mail:* study_abroad@ncsu.edu

---

LISIEUX

0674
FRENCH AMERICAN STUDY CENTER
A La Carte Vacation and Learning Program
Site: France: Lisieux
Dates: 1-10 wks, spring, summer & fall
Subjects: Civilization/culture, Education/teaching, Foreign language teaching, French language (beg/int/adv)
Eligibility: *Level:* fresh, sophs, jrs, srs, grads, adults, teachers, professionals, precoll *Age:* min 15, avg 30
Credit: *Undergrad:* avail *Grad:* none *Doc:* certificate
Instruction: *In:* French *Format:* lang study, lecture *Students:* US & intl
Costs: $746 per wk *incl* tuition, housing, some meals
Housing: *Arr by pgm:* homestay, furnished rms in chateau
Deadline: 1 mo before pgm
Other info: *US accredited sponsor:* no *Began:* 1975 *Activities:* field trips *URL:* http://perso.wanadoo.fr/centre.normandie/
Contact: Dr Philippe C Almeras, French Amer Study Ctr, BP h176, 14104 Lisieux Cedex, France *E-mail:* centre.normandie@wanadoo.fr

---

0675
FRENCH AMERICAN STUDY CENTER
Light Vacation Programs
Site: France: Lisieux
Dates: 1-10 wks, mid-May-mid-Oct
Subjects: Civilization/culture, Culinary arts, French language (beg/int/adv), History, Literature
Eligibility: *Level:* fresh, sophs, jrs, srs, grads, adults, teachers, professionals, precoll *Requires:* tape recorder; beginners must come at beg of given session (spring, summer, summer II & III, fall)
Credit: *Undergrad:* avail *Grad:* none *Doc:* certificate
Instruction: *In:* French *Format:* lang study, lecture, practical training *Students:* intl
Costs: $746 per wk *incl* tuition, housing, some meals, fees, excursions
Housing: *Arr by pgm:* residence halls, furnished rms
Deadline: 1 mo before pgm
Other info: *US accredited sponsor:* no *Began:* 1975 *Orient:* abroad *Activities:* excursions, field trips, sports *Misc:* 2 tracks (3 or 6 hrs/day) offered; all conversation in French; optional Sat excursions. May contact former participants. *URL:* http://perso.wanadoo.fr/centre.normandie/
Contact: Dr Philippe C Almeras or Dr Dimter, French Amer Study Ctr, BP h176, 14104 Lisieux Cedex, France *E-mail:* centre.normandie@wanadoo.fr
Or Contact: Dr Alan Farrell, Virginia Military Inst, Lexington VA 24450

LYON

0676
GEORGIA INSTITUTE OF TECHNOLOGY
Languages for Business and Technology (LBAT)-French
Site: France: Lyon
Dates: Jun 22-Aug 2
Subjects: French language (int/adv)
Eligibility: *Level:* fresh, sophs, jrs, srs *Requires:* previous study in field, good acad standing, 1 yr coll lang study
Credit: *Undergrad:* 9 *Grad:* none *Doc:* transcript
Instruction: *In:* French *Format:* lang study *Students:* mainly US
Costs: Contact sponsor
Housing: *Arr by pgm:* residence halls, hotels
Deadline: Mar 15
Other info: *US accredited sponsor:* yes *Began:* 1992 *Orient:* in US (1 day) *Activities:* excursions *Misc:* For students planning study in intl bus or tech expertise.
Contact: Dr Lionel Lemarchand, Modern Langs, Georgia Inst of Technology, Atlanta GA 30332-0375 *Ph:* 404-385 0194 *Fax:* 404-894 0955 *E-mail:* lionel.lemarchand@modlangs.gatech.edu
Or Contact: Intl Educ, Georgia Inst of Technology, J S Coon Bldg, Ste 203, Atlanta GA 30332-0284 *Ph:* 404-894 7475 *Fax:* 404-894 9682 *E-mail:* study.abroad@gatech.edu

---

0677
SOUTHERN ILLINOIS UNIVERSITY AT CARBONDALE
French Language and Culture
Site: France: Lyon *Host inst:* Catholic Univ of Lyon
Dates: 3 wks, Jul
Subjects: Civilization/culture, Field study, French language, French studies
Eligibility: *Level:* fresh, sophs, jrs, srs *Requires:* 2.75 GPA *Age:* min 18, avg 21
Credit: *Undergrad:* avail *Grad:* none *Doc:* transcript
Instruction: *In:* English *Format:* directed field study, lecture, study tour *Students:* mainly US
Costs: Contact sponsor
Housing: *Arr by pgm:* residence halls, homestay, hostels
Deadline: Apr 2
Other info: *US accredited sponsor:* yes *Began:* 1996 *Activities:* excursions, field trips, program travel, cultural events *URL:* http://www.siu.edu/departments/study_abroad/
Contact: Thomas Saville, Coord, Study Abroad Pgm, Mailcode 6885, Southern Illinois Univ, Carbondale IL 62901-6885 *Ph:* 618-453 7670 *Fax:* 618-453 7647 *E-mail:* studyabr@siu.edu

---

0678
UNIVERSITY OF MISSOURI-KANSAS CITY
UMKC Summer Study in Lyon, France
Site: France: Lyon *Host inst:* Univ of Lyon II
Dates: 6 wks, Jun-Jul
Subjects: Civilization/culture, Education/teaching, French language (beg/int/adv), French studies, Homestay
Eligibility: *Level:* sophs, jrs, srs, grads *Requires:* 2.7 GPA, previous study in field, French lang study, 2 recommendation letters
Credit: *Undergrad:* 9 *Grad:* 9 *Doc:* transcript
Instruction: *In:* French *Format:* lang study, lecture *Students:* intl
Costs: $3,800 *incl* tuition, housing, some meals, intl airfare, insurance, fees *Nonrefundable fee*
Housing: *Arr by pgm:* homestay
Deadline: Early Feb
Other info: *US accredited sponsor:* yes *Began:* 1995 *Orient:* abroad *Activities:* excursions, field trips, cultural events *Misc:* Scholarships for own students only. Pedagogy courses for grad students only. May contact former participants. *URL:* http://www.umkc.edu/international
Contact: Dr Kathy Krause, Foreign Langs, Univ of Missouri-Kansas City, 5100 Rockhill Rd, Kansas City MO 64110 *Ph:* 816-235 1316 *Fax:* 816-235 1312 *E-mail:* international@umkc.edu
Or Contact: Coord, Ctr for Intl Affairs, Univ of Missouri-Kansas City, 5100 Rockhill Rd, Kansas City MO 64110 *Ph:* 816-235 5759 *Fax:* 816-235 5610 *E-mail:* international@umkc.edu

---

0679
UNIVERSITY OF TEXAS AT AUSTIN
French Summer Program in Lyon
Site: France: Lyon *Host inst:* Univ Jean Moulin (Lyon III)
Dates: 6 wks, late May-early Jul
Subjects: Civilization/culture, French language (int), Homestay
Eligibility: *Level:* fresh, sophs, jrs, srs *Requires:* 2.5 GPA, 2-3 sems coll French or equiv
Credit: *Undergrad:* 6 *Grad:* none *Doc:* transcript
Instruction: *In:* French *Format:* lang study, lecture *Students:* mainly US
Costs: Contact sponsor
Housing: *Arr by pgm:* homestay
Deadline: Mar 1
Other info: *US accredited sponsor:* yes *Began:* 1996 *Orient:* avail in Paris (4 days) *Activities:* excursions, field trips *URL:* http://www.utexas.edu/student/abroad
Contact: Joy Williamson, Adviser, Study Abroad, Univ of Texas at Austin, Univ Station, Drawer A, Austin TX 78713 *Ph:* 512-471 6490 *Fax:* 512-232 4363 *E-mail:* studyabroadinfo@mozart.io.utexas.edu

---

MEGEVE

0680
CENTRE INTERNATIONAL DE FORMATION ET ECHANGES LINGUISTIQUES
Language-Sports-Cultural Discovery
Site: France: Megeve *Host inst:* CIFEL
Dates: 1 wk-2 mos yr round
Subjects: English (beg/int/adv), French language (beg/int/adv), German language (beg/int/adv), Hiking/trekking, Italian language (beg/int/adv), Japanese language (beg/int/adv), Russian language (beg/int/adv), Skiing, Spanish language (beg/int/adv), Sports, Tennis
Eligibility: *Level:* adults *Age:* avg 21
Credit: *Undergrad:* none *Grad:* none *Doc:* certificate
Instruction: *In:* French *Format:* lang study, lecture, study tour *Students:* intl
Costs: $2,100 for 2 wks, $1,000 for each addtl wk *incl* tuition, housing, all meals, books/materials *Nonrefundable fee*
Housing: *Arr by pgm:* pensions, hotels
Deadline: 2 wks before pgm
Other info: *US accredited sponsor:* no *Began:* 1996 *Activities:* excursions, field trips, cultural events, sports *Misc:* May contact former participants. *URL:* http://www.cifel.fr
Contact: Ada Djumisic Dir, CIFEL, 17 Pl Grenette, Albertville, France 73200 *Ph:* 310-305 3248 *Fax:* 310-305 3248 *E-mail:* info@cifel.fr
Or Contact: Jamie Schoenfeld, Dir, CIFEL, 4346 Redwood Ave, #202, Marina del Rey CA 90292 *Ph:* 310-305 3248 *Fax:* 310-305-3248 *E-mail:* trninic@gateway.net

---

METZ

0681
GEORGIA INSTITUTE OF TECHNOLOGY
Georgia Tech Lorraine: Undergraduate Summer Program
Site: France: Metz *Host inst:* Georgia Tech Lorraine
Dates: May 15-Aug 2
Subjects: Art history, Business/management, Electrical/electronic engineering, French language, Industrial engineering, International studies, Mechanical engineering
Eligibility: *Level:* sophs, jrs, srs *Requires:* previous study in field, good acad standing
Credit: *Undergrad:* 6-15 *Grad:* none *Doc:* transcript
Instruction: *In:* English *Format:* lecture *Students:* mainly US
Costs: $3,911 for GA residents, $4,161 for others *incl* tuition, housing, some meals *Nonrefundable fee*
Housing: *Arr by pgm:* residence halls
Deadline: Feb 15
Other info: *US accredited sponsor:* yes *Began:* 1990 *Orient:* in US *Activities:* excursions, field trips *Financial aid:* scholarships *URL:* http://www.georgiatech-metz.fr
Contact: Ms Florence Stoia, Electrical Engineering, Georgia Inst of Technology, Atlanta GA 30332-0250 *Ph:* 404-894 0076 *Fax:* 404-894 2997 *E-mail:* florence.stoia@ee.gatech.edu
Or Contact: Intl Educ, Georgia Inst of Technology, J S Coon Bldg, Ste 203, Atlanta GA 30332-0284 *Ph:* 404-894 7475 *Fax:* 404-894 9682 *E-mail:* study.abroad@gatech.edu

---

MONTPELLIER

0682
FRENCH-AMERICAN EXCHANGE
Intensive Summer Program in Montpellier
Site: France: Montpellier *Host inst:* Inst Linguistique du Peyrou
Dates: 4 or 8 wks, Jun-Sep
Subjects: Civilization/culture, French language (beg/int/adv), French studies, Literature, Written composition
Eligibility: *Level:* sophs, jrs, srs, grads, adults, teachers, professionals *Requires:* 2.5 GPA, some knowledge of French, high sch diploma *Age:* min 18, max 75, avg 21
Credit: *Undergrad:* 6 per 4-wk session *Grad:* 6 per 4-wk session *Doc:* transcript, certificate
Instruction: *In:* French *Format:* lab, lang study *Students:* intl
Costs: $1,700 per mo *incl* tuition, housing, some meals, fees, books/materials *Nonrefundable fee*
Housing: *Arr by pgm:* residence halls, apartments, homestay, bed & breakfasts
Deadline: 6 wks before pgm
Other info: *US accredited sponsor:* no *Began:* 1987 *Orient:* avail info packet *Activities:* excursions, cultural events, sports *Misc:* Montpellier hosts dance & music festival, Jun-Jul. Mediterranean beaches. May contact former participants. *URL:* http://www.faetours.com
Contact: Jim Pondolfino, Exec Dir, French-Amer Exch, 111 Roberts Ct, Alexandria VA 22314 *Ph:* 800-995 5087; 703-549 5087 *Fax:* 703-549 2865 *E-mail:* faetours@erols.com

---

0683
INSTITUT D'ADMINISTRATION DES ENTREPRISES, UNIVERSITE DE MONTPELLIER II
Institut Mediterraneen de Langues
Site: France: Montpellier
Dates: 1 mo or longer, yr-round
Subjects: Business/management, Community service projects, Field study, French language, Homestay
Eligibility: *Level:* fresh, sophs, jrs, srs *Requires:* previous French lang study
Credit: *Undergrad:* avail *Grad:* avail *Doc:* transcript, diploma
Instruction: *In:* English, French *Format:* directed field study, lang study, seminar, volunteer/svc *Students:* intl
Costs: Contact sponsor
Housing: *Arr by pgm:* apartments, homestay
Deadline: 1 mo before pgm
Other info: *US accredited sponsor:* no *Began:* 1990 *Orient:* abroad *Activities:* excursions *Misc:* May contact former participants. *URL:* http://www.sspfrance.com/iml
Contact: Chantal Thery, IAE, Univ Montpellier, Pl Eugene Bataillon, 34095 Montpellier, Cedex 5, France *E-mail:* thery@iae.univ-montp2.fr
Or Contact: IML, 4 Pl Jean Jaures, 34000 Montpellier, France *E-mail:* iml@cge-ol.fr

---

0684
INSTITUT LINGUISTIQUE ADENET (ILA)
French in the Mediterranean
Site: France: Montpellier
Dates: 1 wk or longer, yr-round
Subjects: French language (beg/int/adv)

Eligibility: *Level:* adults, precoll *Age:* min 16, avg 26
Credit: *Undergrad:* none *Grad:* none *Doc:* certificate
Instruction: *In:* French *Format:* lang study *Students:* intl
Costs: Fr 2,450 *incl* tuition, housing, some meals, fees, books/materials, airport meeting svc *Nonrefundable fee*
Housing: *Arr by pgm:* residence halls with local students, apartments, homestay, pensions, hotels, hostels
Deadline: None
Other info: *US accredited sponsor:* no *Began:* 1997 *Activities:* excursions, field trips, cultural events, sports *Misc:* May contact former participants. *URL:* http://www.ila-france.com
Contact: Mr Stefan Adenet, Dir, Inst Linguistique Adenet (ILA), 33 Grand Rue Jean Moulin, F-34000 Montpellier, France *E-mail:* ila.france@mnet.fr

---

0685
UNIVERSITY OF NEW ORLEANS
Glories of France
Site: France: Montpellier *Host inst:* Cours Intensif de Francais (CIF)
Dates: 4 wks, Jul
Subjects: Civilization/culture, French language (beg/int/adv), Literature
Eligibility: *Level:* fresh, sophs, jrs, srs *Requires:* good acad standing, some prerequisites *Age:* min 16, avg 20
Credit: *Undergrad:* 3-6 *Grad:* none
Instruction: *In:* French *Format:* directed field study, lang study, lecture *Students:* intl
Costs: About $2,995 *incl* tuition, housing, some meals, insurance, fees, excursions
Housing: *Arr by pgm:* residence halls
Deadline: Apr 1 or until pgm filled
Other info: *US accredited sponsor:* yes *Orient:* abroad abroad & through bulletins *Activities:* excursions *Misc:* Beach, leisure activities. Incl weekend in Paris. *URL:* http://www.uno.edu/~inst/Welcome.html
Contact: Ms Marie Kaposchyn, Coord, Intl Educ, Univ of New Orleans, PO Box 569, New Orleans LA 70148 *Ph:* 504-280 7455 *Fax:* 504-280 7317 *E-mail:* mkaposch@uno.edu

---

0686
UNIVERSITY OF NORTH CAROLINA AT CHAPEL HILL
Summer Session in Montpellier
Site: France: Montpellier *Host inst:* Univ Paul Valery (Montpellier III)
Dates: 4 wks, Jun 30-Jul 31
Subjects: Civilization/culture, Field study, French language, Written composition
Eligibility: *Level:* fresh, sophs, jrs, srs, adults, teachers, professionals *Requires:* 2.7 GPA, previous study in field, 3 sems coll French
Credit: *Undergrad:* 6 *Grad:* none *Doc:* transcript
Instruction: *In:* French *Format:* directed field study, lang study, lecture, study tour, workshop *Students:* intl
Costs: $3,900 *incl* tuition, housing, all meals, intl airfare, fees, excursions
Housing: *Arr by pgm:* residence halls
Deadline: Mar 15
Other info: *US accredited sponsor:* yes *Began:* 1999 *Orient:* abroad (1 day) *Activities:* excursions, field trips, program travel, cultural events, sports *Misc:* May contact former participants. *Financial aid:* scholarships *URL:* http://www.unc.edu/depts/mont
Contact: Dr C A Maley or Celeste Yowell, Pgm Asst, UNC Year at Montpellier, Univ of North Carolina-Chapel Hill, Romance Lang, 238 Dey, CB 3170, Chapel Hill NC 27599-3170 *Ph:* 919-962 0154 *Fax:* 919-962 4547 *E-mail:* cmaley@email.unc.edu

---

NANTES

0687
MICHIGAN STATE UNIVERSITY
Agriculture and Veterinary Science
Site: France: Nantes
Dates: 6 wks, May-Jun
Subjects: Field study, French language, Homestay, Humanities, Veterinary science
Eligibility: *Level:* fresh, sophs, jrs, srs *Requires:* 2.5 GPA, previous study in field, 1 yr coll French *Age:* min 18
Credit: *Undergrad:* 9 *Grad:* none *Doc:* transcript
Instruction: *In:* English *Format:* directed field study, lecture *Students:* intl
Costs: About $1,200 *incl* housing, all meals, insurance, fees, excursions *Nonrefundable fee*
Housing: *Arr by pgm:* homestay
Deadline: Mar 2
Other info: *US accredited sponsor:* yes *Began:* 2000 *Orient:* in US & abroad (2 days) *Activities:* excursions, field trips *Financial aid:* scholarships *URL:* http://studyabroad.msu.edu
Contact: Cheryl Benner, MSU Study Abroad, 109 Intl Ctr, East Lansing MI 448824-1035 *Ph:* 517-353 8920 *Fax:* 517-432 2082 *E-mail:* bennerc@msu.edu ▲

0688
UNIVERSITY OF CINCINNATI
ESCNA School of Management Summer School
Site: France: Nantes *Host inst:* ESCNA/Nantes
Dates: 6 wks, Jun 10-Jul 22
Subjects: Civilization/culture, French language, French studies, Homestay, International business
Eligibility: *Level:* sophs, jrs *Age:* min 18
Credit: *Undergrad:* 9-12 qtr hrs *Grad:* none *Doc:* transcript
Instruction: *In:* English, French *Format:* lang study, lecture *Students:* mainly US
Costs: $2,516 *incl* tuition, housing, excursions
Housing: *Arr by pgm:* homestay
Deadline: Mar 31
Other info: *US accredited sponsor:* yes *Began:* 1979 *Orient:* in US & abroad (3 days) *Activities:* excursions, field trips, program travel, cultural events *Misc:* Study tour to Brussels, Belgium. Scholarships for own students only. May contact former participants. *Financial aid:* scholarships *URL:* http://www.uc.edu/global/cbanantes.html
Contact: Arthur Neisberg, Educ Abroad Coord, 608 Swift Hall, Univ of Cincinnati, PO Box 210640, Cincinnati OH 45221-0640 *Ph:* 513-556 1363 *Fax:* 513-556 2990 *E-mail:* arthur.neisberg@uc.edu
Or Contact: Susan Sadlier, Intl Pgms Coord, Coll of Bus Admin, 102 Linder Hall, Univ of Cincinnati, PO Box 210020, Cincinnati OH 45221-0020 *Ph:* 513-556 0407 *Fax:* 513-556 4891 *E-mail:* susan.sadlier@uc.edu

---

NICE

0689
ALPHA B INSTITUT LINGUISTIQUE
French Language
Site: France: Nice
Dates: 2 wks-3 mos, Feb-Dec
Subjects: French language (beg/int/adv), Homestay
Eligibility: *Level:* fresh, sophs, srs, grads, adults, teachers, professionals *Age:* min 16, avg 25
Credit: *Undergrad:* none *Grad:* none *Doc:* certificate
Instruction: *In:* French *Format:* lang study *Students:* intl
Costs: Fr 2,450 for 2 wks *incl* tuition, fees, books/materials, VAT
Housing: *Arr by pgm:* apartments with local students, homestay, hotels
Deadline: None
Other info: *US accredited sponsor:* no *Began:* 1993 *Activities:* excursions, field trips, cultural events, sports *Misc:* 20 classes per wk, 6-10 students per class. *URL:* http://www.alpha-b.fr
Contact: Anja Denysiuk, Admin Dir, or Pascal Richez, Pgm Dir, Alpha B Inst Linguistique, 2 rue d'Angleterre, 06000 Nice, France *E-mail:* alpha.b@webstore.fr

---

0690
ALPHA B INSTITUT LINGUISTIQUE
Intensive French Course
Site: France: Nice
Dates: 2 wks-3 mos, Feb-Dec
Subjects: French language (beg/int/adv), Homestay
Eligibility: *Level:* fresh, sophs, srs, grads, adults, teachers, professionals *Age:* min 16, avg 25
Credit: *Undergrad:* none *Grad:* none *Doc:* certificate
Instruction: *In:* French *Format:* lang study *Students:* intl
Costs: Fr 3,150 for 2 wks *incl* tuition, fees, books/materials, VAT
Housing: *Arr by pgm:* apartments with local students, homestay, hotels
Deadline: None
Other info: *US accredited sponsor:* no *Began:* 1993 *Activities:* excursions, field trips, cultural events, sports *Misc:* 30 classes per wk, 6-10 students per class. *URL:* http://www.alpha-b.fr
Contact: Anja Denysiuk, Admin Dir, or Pascal Richez, Pgm Dir, Alpha B Inst Linguistique, 2 rue d'Angleterre, 06000 Nice, France *E-mail:* alpha.b@webstore.fr

---

0691
AZURLINGUA
Azurlingua
Site: France: Nice
Dates: 2-12 wks, yr-round
Subjects: Foreign language teaching, French language
Eligibility: *Level:* adults *Age:* min 18, avg 25
Credit: *Undergrad:* avail *Grad:* none *Doc:* certificate
Instruction: *In:* French *Format:* lab, seminar, tutorial *Students:* intl
Costs: About $1,500 for 2 wks, $2,200 per mo *incl* tuition
Housing: *Arr by pgm:* residence halls, apartments, homestay, hotels
Deadline: 4 wks before pgm
Other info: *US accredited sponsor:* no *Misc:* May contact former participants.
Contact: Janice E Ovadiah, Azurlingua, 303 W 66th St #4HE, New York NY 10023 *Ph:* 212-724 5823 *Fax:* 212-496 2264 *E-mail:* jovadiah@aol.com

---

0692
BABEL
French Audiovisual Courses
Site: France: Nice
Dates: 2 or 4 wks, Jul-Aug
Subjects: Business language, French language (beg/int/adv)
Eligibility: *Level:* adults *Age:* min 16, max 50, avg 25
Credit: *Undergrad:* none *Grad:* none *Doc:* certificate
Instruction: *In:* French *Format:* lang study *Students:* intl
Costs: Fr 2,600 for 2 wks *incl* tuition, fees, books/materials
Housing: *Arr by pgm:* apartments, hotels
Deadline: 5 wks before pgm
Other info: *US accredited sponsor:* no *Began:* 1977 *Orient:* abroad *Activities:* excursions *URL:* http://www.language-centres-world.com
Contact: Monique Broch, Babel, 22 ter rue de France, 06000 Nice, France *E-mail:* 101755.2404@compuserve.com

---

0693
BABEL
Intensive One-to-One French Classes for Students or Professionals
Site: France: Nice
Dates: Yr-round
Subjects: French language (beg/int/adv)
Eligibility: *Level:* sophs, jrs, srs, grads, adults, teachers, professionals, precoll *Requires:* previous study in field
Credit: *Undergrad:* none *Grad:* none *Doc:* certificate
Instruction: *In:* French *Format:* lab, lang study *Students:* intl
Costs: Contact sponsor
Housing: *Arr by pgm:* apartments
Deadline: 6 wks before pgm
Other info: *US accredited sponsor:* no *Began:* 1977 *Orient:* abroad (intensive lang study & assessment test) *Misc:* Located 1 block from beach. Experienced French lang specialists. Customized courses to meet specific needs.
Contact: BABEL, 22 ter rue de France, Nice, France 06000 *E-mail:* babel121@aol.com

---

0694
FRENCH-AMERICAN EXCHANGE
Intensive Summer Program in Nice
Site: France: Nice *Host inst:* Ecole France Langue
Dates: 4 or 8 wks, May-Sep
Subjects: Civilization/culture, French language (beg/int/adv), French studies, Literature, Written composition
Eligibility: *Level:* sophs, jrs, srs, grads, adults, teachers, professionals *Requires:* previous study in field *Age:* min 18, max 75, avg 20
Credit: *Undergrad:* 6 per mo *Grad:* 6 per mo *Doc:* transcript, certificate
Instruction: *In:* French *Format:* independent study, lab, lang study, workshop *Students:* intl
Costs: $1,795 per mo *incl* tuition, housing, some meals, fees, excursions *Nonrefundable fee*
Housing: *Arr by pgm:* apartments, homestay, bed & breakfasts
Deadline: 6 wks before pgm
Other info: *US accredited sponsor:* no *Began:* 1997 *Activities:* field trips, cultural events, sports *Misc:* May contact former participants. *URL:* http://www.faetours.com
Contact: Jim Pondolfino, Exec Dir, French-Amer Exch, 111 Roberts Ct, Alexandria VA 22314 *Ph:* 800-995 5087; 703-549 5087 *Fax:* 703-549 2865 *E-mail:* faetours@erols.com

---

0695
LANGUAGES PLUS
Language Immersion and Cultural Program-Nice
Site: France: Nice
Dates: 2 wks or longer, yr-round
Subjects: French language (beg/int/adv), Homestay
Eligibility: *Level:* adults *Age:* min 17, max 65, avg 24
Credit: *Undergrad:* none *Grad:* none *Doc:* certificate
Instruction: *In:* French *Format:* lang study *Students:* intl
Costs: From $810 for 2 wks *incl* tuition, housing, books/materials, cultural activities
Housing: *Arr by pgm:* apartments, homestay
Deadline: 2 wks before pgm
Other info: *US accredited sponsor:* no *Activities:* excursions, field trips *Misc:* May contact former participants. *URL:* http://www.languagesplus.com
Contact: Margot Haldenby, North Amer Enrollment, Langs Plus, 317 Adelaide St W, Ste 900, Toronto, Ontario M5V 1P9, Canada *Ph:* 888-526 4758; 416-925 7117 *Fax:* 416-925 5990 *E-mail:* info@languagesplus.com

---

ORLEANS

0696
UNIVERSITY OF MIAMI (FL)
Intensive French in Orleans, France
Site: France: Orleans *Host inst:* Univ d'Orleans
Dates: 4 wks, Jul
Subjects: French language (int/adv), French studies, Government, History, Homestay, Literature, Media studies, Political science/politics
Eligibility: *Level:* sophs, jrs, srs, grads *Requires:* 3.0 GPA, 1-2 yrs coll French, 2 faculty recommendation letters
Credit: *Undergrad:* 3 *Grad:* none *Doc:* transcript
Instruction: *In:* French *Format:* lang study, lecture, seminar *Students:* intl
Costs: $1,980 *incl* tuition
Housing: *Arr by pgm:* residence halls, homestay

Deadline: Mar 30
Other info: *US accredited sponsor:* yes *Began:* 1991 *Activities:* excursions *Financial aid:* scholarships *URL:* http://www.studyabroad.miami.edu
Contact: Intl Educ & Exch Pgms, Allen Hall 212, 5050 Brunson Dr, PO Box 248005, Univ of Miami, Coral Gables FL 33124-3300 *Ph:* 800-557 5421; 305-284 3434 *Fax:* 305-284 6629 *E-mail:* ieep@miami.edu

OTTROTT

0697
CHANTIERS D'ETUDES MEDIEVALES
Ottrott Castle Restoration
Site: France: Ottrott
Dates: 2 wks, Jul 15-30, Aug 1-15 or Aug 16-30
Subjects: Historical preservation/restoration
Eligibility: *Level:* adults *Requires:* parental approval for participants under 18 yrs of age *Age:* min 16
Credit: *Undergrad:* none *Grad:* none
Instruction: *In:* French *Format:* volunteer/svc *Students:* intl
Costs: Fr 555 *incl* housing, all meals, insurance
Housing: *Arr by pgm:* barracks
Deadline: Jun 15
Other info: *US accredited sponsor:* no *URL:* http://perso.wanadoo.fr/castrum
Contact: Mlle Rouviere Melanie, Chantiers d'Etudes Medievales, 4 rue du Tonnelat Rouge, 67000 Strasbourg, France *E-mail:* castrum@wanadoo.fr

PARIS

0698
ACADEMIC PROGRAMS ABROAD
Academic Programs Abroad-Summer Program in Paris
Site: France: Paris
Dates: 6 wks, Jun 10-Jul 22
Subjects: Art history, Civilization/culture, French language (beg/int), French studies, History, Homestay, Literature, Studio arts
Eligibility: *Level:* sophs, jrs, srs, grads *Requires:* 3.0 GPA, recommendation, 4 sems coll French *Age:* min 19, max 25
Credit: *Undergrad:* avail *Grad:* none *Doc:* transcript
Instruction: *In:* French *Format:* lang study, lecture, study tour *Students:* mainly US
Costs: Contact sponsor
Housing: *Arr by pgm:* homestay
Deadline: Apr 1
Other info: *US accredited sponsor:* no *Began:* 1997 *Orient:* abroad (2 days) *Activities:* excursions, cultural events *Misc:* May contact former participants. *URL:* http://www.apaparis.com
Contact: Dr Odile KORY Asst Dir, Acad Pgm Abroad, 330 E 33rd St, apt #17J, NEW YORK NY 10016 *Ph:* 212-686 8410 *Fax:* 212-448 1883 *E-mail:* apaparis@pipeline.com ▲

0699
ACCENT PARIS CONSORTIUM
Summer in Paris
Site: France: Paris *Host inst:* Univ de Paris IV (Sorbonne)
Dates: 4 wks, Jul
Subjects: Art history, Civilization/culture, French language (beg/int/adv), Homestay
Eligibility: *Level:* adults *Age:* min 16
Credit: *Undergrad:* 4-6 *Grad:* none *Doc:* transcript
Instruction: *In:* English, French *Format:* lang study, lecture, tutorial *Students:* mainly US
Costs: $2,800 *incl* tuition, housing, some meals, excursions
Housing: *Arr by pgm:* residence halls, homestay
Deadline: May 1
Other info: *US accredited sponsor:* yes *Began:* 1980 *Orient:* in US & abroad (intensive lang study) *Activities:* excursions, field trips, program travel, cultural events *Misc:* May contact former participants. *URL:* http://www.accentintl.com
Contact: *See Index II for Members* Accent, 870 Market St, Ste 1026, San Francisco CA 94102 *Ph:* 800-869 9291; 415-835 3744 *Fax:* 415-835 3749 *E-mail:* info@accentintl.com

0700
ACCORD ECOLE DE LANGUES
French Courses
Site: France: Paris
Dates: 2 wks or longer, yr-round
Subjects: Business language, Civilization/culture, Foreign language teaching, French language, French studies, Homestay
Eligibility: *Level:* adults *Age:* min 18, avg 25
Credit: *Undergrad:* avail *Grad:* none *Doc:* certificate
Instruction: *In:* French *Format:* lang study, tutorial, workshop *Students:* intl
Costs: $2,100 per mo *incl* tuition, housing, some meals
Housing: *Arr by pgm:* residence halls with local students, apartments, homestay, hotels
Deadline: Contact sponsor
Other info: *US accredited sponsor:* no *Began:* 1990 *Activities:* excursions, cultural events *Misc:* Theater workshop in French. May contact former participants. *URL:* http://www.accord-langues.com
Contact: Dr Janice E Ovadiah, USA Agent, 303 W 66th St, #4HE, New York NY 10023-6305 *Ph:* 212-724 5823 *Fax:* 212-496 2264 *E-mail:* jovadiah@aol.com

0701
ACTE INTERNATIONAL
French Language Study at University Campuses, La Sorbonne
Site: France: Paris
Dates: 4 wks-2 sems, yr-round
Subjects: Business language, French language (beg/int/adv), Homestay
Eligibility: *Level:* fresh, sophs, jrs, srs, grads, adults, teachers, precoll *Age:* min 18
Credit: *Undergrad:* none *Grad:* none *Doc:* certificate
Instruction: *In:* French *Format:* lang study *Students:* intl
Costs: $2,100 per mo *incl* tuition, housing, some meals, excursions *Nonrefundable fee*
Housing: *Sponsor assists:* residence halls, homestay
Deadline: 1 mo before pgm
Other info: *US accredited sponsor:* no *Began:* 1976 *Activities:* excursions, cultural events *Misc:* May contact former participants.
Contact: Dr Janice E Ovadiah, USA Agent, 303 W 66th St, New York NY 10023 *Ph:* 212-724 5823 *Fax:* 212-496 2173 *E-mail:* jovadiah@aol.com

0702
ALMA COLLEGE
Summer Program of Studies in France
Site: France: Paris *Host inst:* Alliance Francaise
Dates: 1-3 mos, May-Jul, Sep-May for intensive lang study; flexible schedules avail
Subjects: Art history, French language, Homestay
Eligibility: *Level:* sophs, jrs, srs *Requires:* 2.5 GPA, 2 faculty recommendations
Credit: *Undergrad:* 3-15 *Grad:* none *Doc:* transcript
Instruction: *In:* French *Format:* lab, lang study, lecture *Students:* mainly US
Costs: $3,147-$7,783 depending on pgm length *incl* tuition, housing, some meals, insurance, fees, excursions, railpass, e-mail
Housing: *Arr by pgm:* apartments, homestay
Deadline: 2 mos before pgm
Other info: *US accredited sponsor:* yes *Began:* 1962 *Orient:* abroad *Activities:* excursions *Misc:* Resident dir. May contact former participants. *URL:* http://www.alma.edu/academics/international

THE AMERICAN UNIVERSITY OF PARIS
THERE'S NO PLACE LIKE AUP.
The education is American.
The mix is international.
The setting is Paris.
The advantage is yours.
Paris: 31, avenue Bosquet, 75343 Paris cedex 07, France • (33/1) 40.62.07.20 • admissions@aup.edu
New York: 60 East 42nd Street, Ste. 1463, New York, NY 10017 • (212) 983-1414 • nyoffice@aup.edu • www.aup.edu

Contact: Chris Musick, Dir, Intl Educ, Alma Coll, Alma MI 48801-1599 *Ph:* 800-321 2562; 517-463 7055 *Fax:* 517-463 7126 *E-mail:* intl_studies@alma.edu

---

0703
AMERICAN INSTITUTE FOR FOREIGN STUDY (AIFS)
University of Paris IV
Site: France: Paris *Host inst:* Univ de Paris IV (Sorbonne)
Dates: 4 or 6 wks, Jun 30-Aug 15
Subjects: Art history, Culinary arts, Fashion design, French language, Homestay
Eligibility: *Level:* fresh, sophs, jrs, srs, adults, precoll *Requires:* 2.0 GPA
Credit: *Undergrad:* avail *Grad:* none *Doc:* transcript
Instruction: *In:* English *Format:* lang study, lecture, seminar *Students:* intl
Costs: $4,239 for 4 wks, $5,139 for 6 wks *incl* tuition, housing, some meals, intl airfare, excursions
Housing: *Arr by pgm:* residence halls, homestay
Deadline: Mar 15
Other info: *US accredited sponsor:* no *Began:* 1968 *Orient:* abroad *Activities:* excursions, cultural events *Misc:* Resident dir. May contact former participants. *Financial aid:* scholarships *URL:* http://www.aifsabroad.com
Contact: Solandy Meza, Coll Div, AIFS, River Plaza, 9 W Broad St, Stamford CT 06902 *Ph:* 800-727-2437 ext 5163 *E-mail:* college.info@aifs.com ▲

0704
ARIZONA STATE UNIVERSITY
France
Site: France: Paris
Dates: 4 wks, May 28-Jun 28
Subjects: Civilization/culture, French language (adv), French studies, Independent study
Eligibility: *Level:* fresh, sophs, jrs, srs, grads, adults, teachers, professionals *Requires:* 4 sems coll French or equiv
Credit: *Undergrad:* 7 *Grad:* none
Instruction: *In:* French *Format:* independent study, lang study, lecture, study tour *Students:* mainly US
Costs: $3,096 *incl* tuition, housing, some meals, fees, excursions, ISIC
Housing: *Arr by pgm:* apartments, hotels
Deadline: Early Mar
Other info: *US accredited sponsor:* yes *Began:* 1996 *Activities:* excursions, field trips, program travel, cultural events *Misc:* Loans avail. All students pay equiv of ASU resident tuition. *Financial aid:* scholarships *URL:* http://www.asu.edu/ssc/StudyAbroad
Contact: Ara Pachmayer, Pgm Coord, Summer Sessions, Arizona State Univ, PO Box 873003, Tempe AZ 85287-3003 *Ph:* 480-965 0101 *Fax:* 480-965 3851 *E-mail:* study.programs@asu.edu

---

0705
BOSTON UNIVERSITY
History, Art and Culture in Paris
Site: France: Paris
Dates: 6 wks, May-Jul
Subjects: Art history, Civilization/culture, History, Homestay
Eligibility: *Level:* sophs, jrs, srs *Requires:* 3.0 GPA, in major, good acad standing
Credit: *Undergrad:* 8 *Grad:* none *Doc:* transcript
Instruction: *In:* English *Format:* lecture, seminar *Students:* mainly US
Costs: $5,100 *incl* tuition, housing, excursions
Housing: *Arr by pgm:* residence halls, homestay
Deadline: Mar 1; Apr 1 for scholarships
Other info: *US accredited sponsor:* yes *Began:* 1996 *Orient:* in US & abroad *Activities:* excursions, field trips, cultural events *Misc:* May contact former participants. *Financial aid:* scholarships *URL:* http://www.bu.edu/abroad/
Contact: Intl Pgms, Boston Univ, 232 Bay State Rd, Boston MA 02215 *Ph:* 617-353 9888 *Fax:* 617-353 5402 *E-mail:* abroad@bu.edu ▲

0706
COUNCIL ON INTERNATIONAL EDUCATIONAL EXCHANGE CONSORTIUM
Institut Catholique de Paris
Site: France: Paris *Host inst:* Inst Catholique de Paris
Dates: 4 wks, Jul 1-31
Subjects: Business language, Civilization/culture, Foreign language teaching, French language, French studies, Written composition
Eligibility: *Level:* sophs, jrs, srs *Requires:* 2.5 GPA *Age:* min 18
Credit: *Undergrad:* 6 *Grad:* none *Doc:* transcript
Instruction: *In:* English, French *Format:* lang study, lecture *Students:* intl
Costs: $1,200 *incl* tuition, insurance, ISIC
Housing: *Arr by pgm:* residence halls
Deadline: May 1
Other info: *US accredited sponsor:* yes *Began:* 1996 *Orient:* abroad *Misc:* May contact former participants. *URL:* http://www.ciee.org/study
Contact: *See Index II for Members* Pgm Adviser, Council-ISP, 633 3rd Ave, 20th Fl, New York NY 10017-6706 *Ph:* 800-407 8839; 212-822 2600, 212-822 2772 *Fax:* 212-822 2779 *E-mail:* studyinfo@ciee.org

---

0707
CSA, CENTER FOR STUDY ABROAD
French Language and Culture Studies-Paris
Site: France: Paris *Host inst:* Univ de Paris IV (Sorbonne)
Dates: 4, 6 or 8 wks, Jul 1-Aug 31; sem/yr pgms avail
Subjects: Civilization/culture, French language (beg/int/adv), French studies, History, Independent study, Literature, Political science/politics
Eligibility: *Level:* adults *Age:* min 17
Credit: *Undergrad:* avail *Grad:* avail *Doc:* transcript, certificate
Instruction: *In:* French *Format:* independent study, lang study, lecture *Students:* intl
Costs: $995 for 4 wks, $1,395 for 6 wks, $1,695 for 8 wks *incl* tuition, insurance, fees *Nonrefundable fee*
Housing: *Sponsor assists:* residence halls, apartments, pensions, hotels, hostels
Deadline: None
Other info: *US accredited sponsor:* no *Orient:* abroad *Activities:* excursions *URL:* http://www.studyabroad.com/csa
Contact: Alima Khan, Assoc Dir, CSA, Ctr for Study Abroad, 2802 E Madison St, MS #160, Seattle WA 98112 *Ph:* 206-726 1498 *Fax:* 206-583 8192 *E-mail:* virtuecsa@aol.com

---

0708
CULTURAL EXPERIENCES ABROAD (CEA)
Study French Language and Culture in Paris (Sorbonne)
Site: France: Paris *Host inst:* Univ of Paris IV (Sorbonne)
Dates: 4-8 wks, Jun-Aug
Subjects: Art history, Civilization/culture, Communications, Culinary arts, French language (beg/int/adv), French studies, History, Homestay, Independent study, Literature, Political science/politics, Translating/interpreting
Eligibility: *Level:* fresh, sophs, jrs, srs, grads, precoll *Requires:* previous French lang study recommended *Age:* min 17
Credit: *Undergrad:* 5-9 *Grad:* avail *Doc:* transcript, certificate
Instruction: *In:* French *Format:* independent study, lang study, lecture, study tour, tutorial *Students:* intl
Costs: $3,295 for 4 wks, $4,095 for 6 wks, $4,995 for 8 wks *incl* tuition, housing, some meals, insurance, fees, excursions, orient, airport transfers *Nonrefundable fee*

Housing: *Arr by pgm:* residence halls, apartments, homestay
Deadline: Rolling admissions
Other info: *US accredited sponsor:* no *In coop with:* Univ of Paris IV (Sorbonne) *Orient:* abroad *Activities:* excursions, field trips, program travel, cultural events, sports *Misc:* On-site dir. E-mail. May contact former participants. *Financial aid:* scholarships *URL:* http://www.travelabroad.com
Contact: CEA Study Abroad, 1400 E Southern Ave, Ste B-108, Tempe AZ 85282-8011 *Ph:* 480-557 7900 *Fax:* 480-557 7926 *E-mail:* france@travelabroad.com

---

0709
DUKE UNIVERSITY
Duke in Paris
Site: France: Paris
Dates: Mid-May-late Jun
Subjects: Civilization/culture, French language (adv), French studies, Humanities, Literature
Eligibility: *Level:* fresh, sophs, jrs, srs *Requires:* good acad standing, 2 yrs coll French, transcript
Credit: *Undergrad:* 2 credits *Grad:* none *Doc:* transcript
Instruction: *In:* French *Format:* lang study, lecture *Students:* mainly US
Costs: $6,075 for 2 courses *incl* tuition, housing, all meals, excursions
Housing: *Arr by pgm:* residence halls, hotels
Deadline: Feb 16
Other info: *US accredited sponsor:* yes *Began:* 1983 *Activities:* excursions, program travel *URL:* http://www.aas.duke.edu/study_abroad/
Contact: Study Abroad, Duke Univ, 121 Allen Bldg, Box 9005, Durham NC 27708-0057 *Ph:* 919-684 2174 *Fax:* 919-684 3083 *E-mail:* abroad@asdean.duke.edu

---

0710
EASTERN MICHIGAN UNIVERSITY
Art History and Drawing
Site: France: Paris
Dates: May 5-26
Subjects: Art history, Drawing
Eligibility: *Level:* fresh, sophs, jrs, srs, grads, adults, teachers *Requires:* good acad standing *Age:* min 18
Credit: *Undergrad:* 6 *Grad:* 6 *Doc:* transcript
Instruction: *In:* English *Format:* art studio, lecture, seminar *Students:* mainly US
Costs: $3,550 *incl* tuition, housing, some meals, intl airfare, insurance, fees, excursions
Housing: *Arr by pgm:* hotels
Deadline: Jan 15
Other info: *US accredited sponsor:* yes *Began:* 1987 *Orient:* avail by mail *Activities:* excursions *Misc:* Pgm destination rotates annually. May contact former participants. *URL:* http://www.emich.edu/abroad
Contact: Acad Pgms Abroad, Eastern Michigan Univ, 212 Bus & Finance, Ypsilanti MI 48197 *Ph:* 800-777 3541; 734-487 2424 *Fax:* 734-487 4377 *E-mail:* programs.abroad@emich.edu

---

0711

ELFE (ECOLE DE LANGUE FRANCAISE POUR ETRANGERS)

French Language Program at ELFE

Site: France: Paris
Dates: 2 wks or longer, yr-round; 3-wk summer courses for teachers
Subjects: Business language, Foreign language teaching, French language (beg/int/adv), Technical language
Eligibility: *Level:* fresh, sophs, jrs, srs, adults, teachers, precoll *Age:* min 18
Credit: *Undergrad:* avail *Grad:* none *Doc:* certificate
Instruction: *In:* French *Format:* lang study, lecture *Students:* intl
Costs: $1,900 for 2 wks, $3,800 per mo *incl* tuition, housing, some meals, fees
Housing: *Arr by pgm:* homestay, pensions, hotels
Deadline: 1 mo before pgm
Other info: *US accredited sponsor:* no *Began:* 1973 *Orient:* abroad *Activities:* excursions *Misc:* Teacher certification avail. Preparation for Paris Chamber of Commerce exam. Refresher course for French teachers. May contact former participants.
Contact: Dr Janice Ovadiah, USA Rep, ELFE, 303 W 66th St, #4HE, New York NY 10023 *Ph:* 212-724 5823 *Fax:* 212-496 2264 *E-mail:* jovadiah@aol.com

---

0712

EUROPEAN HERITAGE INSTITUTE

Art in Paris

Site: France: Paris *Host inst:* Paris Amer Acad
Dates: 1-2 mos, Jan, Jun, Jul, Sep, Feb
Subjects: Drawing, Fashion design, French language (beg/int/adv), French studies, Interior design, Painting
Eligibility: *Level:* fresh, sophs, jrs, srs, grads, adults, professionals *Requires:* 2.0 GPA *Age:* min 18
Credit: *Undergrad:* 6-9 *Grad:* avail *Doc:* transcript, certificate, diploma
Instruction: *In:* English, French *Format:* art studio, lab, lang study, practical training, seminar *Students:* intl
Costs: $3,000 per mo *incl* tuition, housing, fees
Housing: *Arr by pgm:* apartments
Deadline: Apr 15
Other info: *US accredited sponsor:* no *Began:* 1996 *Orient:* in US & abroad *Activities:* excursions, field trips, cultural events *Misc:* May contact former participants. *URL:* http://www.europeanheritage.org
Contact: Dr Antonio Masullo or Ms Barbara Cotter, European Heritage Inst, 2708 E Franklin St, Richmond VA 23223 *Ph:* 804-643 0661 *Fax:* 804-648 0826 *E-mail:* euritage@i2020.net ▲

0713

EUROPEAN HERITAGE INSTITUTE

Graduate Summer Program in Paris

Site: France: Paris *Host inst:* Ctr Experimental d'Etude de la Civilization Francais, Univ de Paris IV (Sorbonne)
Dates: 6 wks, Jul 3-Aug 12
Subjects: Art, Civilization/culture, Economics, French language (adv), History, Literature
Eligibility: *Level:* grads, adults, teachers, professionals *Requires:* bachelor's in French or equiv *Age:* min 18
Credit: *Undergrad:* none *Grad:* 6-12 *Doc:* transcript, diploma
Instruction: *In:* French *Format:* lab, lang study, lecture, practical training, seminar *Students:* intl
Costs: $1,500 *incl* tuition, fees
Housing: *Arr by pgm:* residence halls, apartments, homestay, pensions, hotels, hostels
Deadline: Apr 15
Other info: *US accredited sponsor:* no *Began:* 1919 *Orient:* in US & abroad (intensive lang study) *Activities:* excursions, cultural events *Misc:* May contact former participants. *URL:* http://www.europeanheritage.org
Contact: Dr Antonio Masullo or Ms Barbara Cotter, European Heritage Inst, 2708 E Franklin St, Richmond VA 23223 *Ph:* 804-643 0661 *Fax:* 804-648 0826 *E-mail:* euritage@i2020.net ▲

0714

EUROPEAN HERITAGE INSTITUTE

Summer in Paris at La Sorbonne

Site: France: Paris *Host inst:* Univ de Paris IV (Sorbonne)
Dates: 1, 2 or 3 mos, Jun-Sep
Subjects: Art, Civilization/culture, Economics, French language (beg/int/adv), Literature
Eligibility: *Level:* fresh, sophs, jrs, srs, grads, adults, teachers, professionals *Age:* min 18
Credit: *Undergrad:* avail *Grad:* 15 *Doc:* transcript, certificate
Instruction: *In:* French *Format:* lab, lang study, lecture, seminar *Students:* intl
Costs: $1,100-$1,700 per mo *incl* tuition, fees
Housing: *Arr by pgm:* residence halls, apartments, homestay, pensions, hotels
Deadline: Apr 15
Other info: *US accredited sponsor:* no *Began:* 1919 *Orient:* in US & abroad (intensive lang study) *Activities:* excursions, cultural events *Misc:* May contact former participants. *URL:* http://www.europeanheritage.org
Contact: Dr Antonio Masullo or Ms Barbara Cotter, European Heritage Inst, 2708 E Franklin St, Richmond VA 23223 *Ph:* 804-643 0661 *Fax:* 804-648 0826 *E-mail:* euritage@i2020.net ▲

0715

EUROPEAN STUDIES ASSOCIATION (ESA)

Summer Study in Paris

Site: France: Paris
Dates: 1 mo, Jul 1-31
Subjects: Business language, Foreign language teaching, French language (beg/int/adv), French studies
Eligibility: *Level:* fresh, sophs, jrs, srs, grads, adults, teachers, professionals, precoll *Age:* min 16
Credit: *Undergrad:* 4 *Grad:* none *Doc:* transcript, diploma
Instruction: *In:* English, French *Format:* lang study, study tour *Students:* mainly US
Costs: $2,150 or $2,900 *incl* tuition, housing, some meals, insurance, fees, excursions, books/materials
Housing: *Arr by pgm:* residence halls with local students, homestay
Deadline: May 25
Other info: *US accredited sponsor:* yes *Began:* 1978 *Orient:* in US *Activities:* excursions, field trips, cultural events *Misc:* May contact former participants. *URL:* http://www.jps.net/tblair
Contact: *See Index II for Members* Dr Thomas Blair, Dir, European Studies Assn, 424 Dorado Terrace, San Francisco CA 94112-1753 *Ph:* 415-334 4222 *Fax:* 415-334 4222 *E-mail:* tblair@ccsf.org
Or Contact: Dr Yolanda Patterson, California State Univ Hayward, Hayward CA 94542 *Ph:* 510-885 3211 *Fax:* 510-885 4797 *E-mail:* guyyopat@aol.com

---

0716

FASHION INSTITUTE OF TECHNOLOGY

French Costume and Interiors: Baroque to Present

Site: France: Paris
Dates: 3 wks, Jun 1-21
Subjects: Architectural history, Art history, Costumes, Fashion design, Furnishings/furniture, Interdisciplinary studies, Interior design
Eligibility: *Level:* fresh, sophs, jrs, srs, grads, adults, teachers, professionals *Requires:* interview by faculty member teaching course
Credit: *Undergrad:* 3 *Grad:* none *Doc:* transcript
Instruction: *In:* English *Format:* study tour *Students:* mainly US
Costs: About $2,265 for NY residents,

See "How To Use This Book" for definitions of terms used above. ▲ = See program sponsor's ad(s) in this book.

$2,670 for others *incl* tuition, housing, intl airfare, fees
Housing: *Arr by pgm:* residence halls
Deadline: Mar 3
Other info: *US accredited sponsor:* yes *Began:* 1987 *Orient:* in US *Activities:* field trips *Misc:* May contact former participants. *URL:* http://www.fitnyc.suny.edu
Contact: Georgianna Appignani, Dir, Intl Educ, FIT, 7th Ave at 27th St, New York NY 10001-5992 *Ph:* 212-217 7633 *Fax:* 212-217 7010
Or Contact: Carole De Santis, Coord, FIT, 7th Ave at 27th St, New York NY 10001-5992 *Ph:* 212-217 7633 *Fax:* 212-217 7010 *E-mail:* desantca@sfitva.cc.fitsuny.edu

---

0717
FASHION INSTITUTE OF TECHNOLOGY
French in Paris
Site: France: Paris
Dates: 4 wks, Jun 1-Jul 1
Subjects: Civilization/culture, French language, French studies, History
Eligibility: *Level:* fresh, sophs, jrs, srs, grads, adults *Requires:* 3.5 GPA, 2 sems coll French, interview by faculty member teaching course *Age:* min 18
Credit: *Undergrad:* 3.5 *Grad:* none *Doc:* transcript
Instruction: *In:* French *Format:* lang study *Students:* mainly US
Costs: About $1,950 for NY residents, $2,423 for others *incl* tuition, housing, intl airfare, fees
Housing: *Arr by pgm:* residence halls
Deadline: Mar 3
Other info: *US accredited sponsor:* yes *Began:* 1987 *Orient:* in US *Activities:* field trips *Misc:* May contact former participants. *URL:* http://www.fitnyc.suny.edu
Contact: Georgianna Appignani, Dir, Intl Educ, FIT, 7th Ave at 27th St, New York NY 10001-5992 *Ph:* 212-217 7633 *Fax:* 212-217 7010
Or Contact: Carole De Santis, Coord, FIT, 7th Ave at 27th St, New York NY 10001-5992 *Ph:* 212-217 7633 *Fax:* 212-217 7010 *E-mail:* desantca@sfitva.cc.fitsuny.edu

---

0718
FLORIDA STATE UNIVERSITY
Paris Summer Program
Site: France: Paris
Dates: 6 wks, Jul 1-Aug 15
Subjects: Art, Business/management, Civilization/culture, Economics, European studies, French language, French studies, History, Liberal arts
Eligibility: *Level:* fresh, sophs, jrs, srs, grads, precoll *Requires:* 2.5 GPA
Credit: *Undergrad:* 10 *Grad:* avail
Instruction: *In:* English *Format:* lang study, lecture *Students:* mainly US
Costs: $4,575 *incl* tuition, housing, intl airfare
Housing: *Arr by pgm:* residence halls
Deadline: Jan 19
Other info: *US accredited sponsor:* yes *Began:* 1996 *Orient:* in US & abroad (2 days) *Activities:* excursions, field trips, program travel, cultural events *Misc:* May contact former participants. *URL:* http://www.international.fsu.edu
Contact: Elizabeth Trelenberg or Bonnie Snyder, Intl Pgms, Florida State Univ, 5500 UCA, Tallahassee FL 32306-2420 *Ph:* 800-374 8581; 850-644 3272 *Fax:* 850-644 8817 *E-mail:* intprog@www.fsu.edu

---

0719
FRENCH PIANO INSTITUTE
Annual Piano Festival
Site: France: Paris *Host inst:* Schola Cantorum
Dates: Jul 4-21

Subjects: French studies, Master classes, Music, Piano
Eligibility: *Level:* srs, grads, adults, teachers, professionals *Requires:* previous study in field, adv & professional performers *Age:* min 18, avg 30
Credit: *Undergrad:* none *Grad:* none *Doc:* diploma
Instruction: *In:* English *Format:* lecture, music lesson *Students:* intl
Costs: Contact sponsor
Housing: *Sponsor assists:* residence halls, hotels
Deadline: Apr 15
Other info: *US accredited sponsor:* no *Began:* 1993 *Orient:* avail avail *Activities:* field trips, program travel, cultural events *Misc:* Recitals by distinguished intl guest artists. Private lessons. Tours. *Financial aid:* scholarships, work study *URL:* http://www.fpiinc.org
Contact: Gail Delente, Artistic Dir, French Piano Inst, 9908 Old Spring Rd, Kensington MD 20895-3235 *Ph:* 301-929 8433 *Fax:* 301-929 0254 *E-mail:* gdelente@msn.com

---

0720
FRENCH-AMERICAN EXCHANGE
Intensive Summer Program in Paris
Site: France: Paris *Host inst:* Ecole France Langue
Dates: 4 or 8 wks, May-Sep
Subjects: Civilization/culture, French language (beg/int/adv), French studies, Literature, Written composition
Eligibility: *Level:* sophs, jrs, srs, grads, adults, teachers, professionals *Requires:* previous study in field *Age:* min 18, max 75, avg 20
Credit: *Undergrad:* 6 per mo *Grad:* 6 per mo *Doc:* transcript, certificate
Instruction: *In:* French *Format:* independent study, lab, lang study, workshop *Students:* intl
Costs: $1,875 per mo *incl* tuition, housing, some meals, fees, excursions *Nonrefundable fee*
Housing: *Arr by pgm:* apartments, homestay, bed & breakfasts
Deadline: 6 wks before pgm
Other info: *US accredited sponsor:* no *Began:* 1997 *Activities:* field trips, cultural events, sports *Misc:* May contact former participants. *URL:* http://www.faetours.com
Contact: Jim Pondolfino, Exec Dir, French-Amer Exch, 111 Roberts Ct, Alexandria VA 22314 *Ph:* 800-995 5087; 703-549 5087 *Fax:* 703-549 2865 *E-mail:* faetours@erols.com

---

0721
GEORGE WASHINGTON UNIVERSITY
Inside French Theatre
Site: France: Paris
Dates: 5 wks
Subjects: Dance, Theater arts
Eligibility: *Level:* sophs, jrs, srs, grads, adults, professionals *Age:* min 18
Credit: *Undergrad:* none *Grad:* none *Doc:* transcript
Instruction: *In:* English *Format:* lecture, seminar, study tour *Students:* US & intl
Costs: $3,695 *incl* tuition, housing, fees *Nonrefundable fee*
Housing: *Arr by pgm:* hostels
Deadline: Contact sponsor
Other info: *US accredited sponsor:* yes *Began:* 1999 *Orient:* abroad *Misc:* Summer pgms are updated in Dec. Contact sponsor for new info. *URL:* http://www.summer.gwu.edu
Contact: Summer, Special & Intl Programs, George Washington Univ, 609 22nd St NW, Washington DC 20052 *Ph:* 202-999 6360 *Fax:* 202-994 9133 *E-mail:* sumprogs@gwu.edu

---

0722
IES, INSTITUTE FOR THE INTERNATIONAL EDUCATION OF STUDENTS
IES Paris Summer
Site: France: Paris
Dates: Jun 4-Jul 20
Subjects: Art history, Civilization/culture, French language (int/adv), History, Homestay, Literature
Eligibility: *Level:* fresh, sophs, jrs, srs, grads, adults *Requires:* good acad standing *Age:* min 18
Credit: *Undergrad:* 6 *Grad:* none *Doc:* transcript
Instruction: *In:* French *Format:* directed field study, lang study, lecture *Students:* mainly US
Costs: $3,500 *incl* tuition, housing, some meals, excursions, health insurance, support svcs *Nonrefundable fee*
Housing: *Arr by pgm:* homestay
Deadline: Apr 1
Other info: *US accredited sponsor:* yes *Began:* 1972 *Activities:* field trips *Misc:* Field trips to chateaux de la Loire. *URL:* http://www.IESabroad.org
Contact: *See Index II for Members* IES, 33 N LaSalle St, 15th Fl, Chicago IL 60602-2602 *Ph:* 800-995 2300; 312-944 1750 *Fax:* 312-944 1448 *E-mail:* info@iesabroad.org ▲

0723
ILLINOIS STATE UNIVERSITY
Summer Communications Program in Paris
Site: France: Paris *Host inst:* Cite Univ
Dates: 4 wks, Jun-Jul
Subjects: Communications
Eligibility: *Level:* jrs, srs, grads *Requires:* 2.5 GPA, undergrad, 3.0 GPA grad, major or minor in communications, organizational communication & research methods courses
Credit: *Undergrad:* 6 *Grad:* 6 *Doc:* transcript
Instruction: *In:* English *Format:* lecture, seminar *Students:* mainly US
Costs: $4,120 *incl* tuition, housing, all meals, intl airfare, insurance, fees, excursions, books/materials
Housing: *Arr by pgm:* residence halls
Deadline: Mar 1
Other info: *US accredited sponsor:* yes *Orient:* in US *Activities:* excursions *Misc:* Excursions to Brussels, Chartres & Versailles. *URL:* http://www.its.ilstu.edu/intlstudies/
Contact: Dr Kenneth Levine, Illinois State Univ, Campus Box 4480, Normal IL 61790-4480 *Ph:* 309-438 8270 *Fax:* 309-438 3987 *E-mail:* oisp@ilstu.edu
Or Contact: Study Abroad Adviser, Illinois State Univ, Campus Box 6120, Normal IL 61790-6120 *Ph:* 309-438 5365 *Fax:* 309-438 3987 *E-mail:* oisp@ilstu.edu

---

0724
INSTITUT DE LANGUE FRANCAISE (ILF)
Francais Langue Etrangere
Site: France: Paris
Dates: 4 wks, 8 wks or trimester, yr-round
Subjects: French language (beg/int/adv)
Eligibility: *Level:* adults *Age:* min 18
Credit: *Undergrad:* none *Grad:* none *Doc:* certificate
Instruction: *In:* English, French, German, Spanish *Format:* lang study *Students:* intl
Costs: Contact sponsor
Housing: *Arr by pgm:* residence halls with local students, residence halls, homestay, hotels, hostels
Deadline: Contact sponsor
Other info: *US accredited sponsor:* no *Activities:* excursions, cultural events *URL:* http://www.inst-langue-fr.com
Contact: Inst de Langue Francaise, 3 Ave Bertie Albrecht, 75008 Paris, France *E-mail:* ilf@inst-langue-fr-com

---

0725
INSTITUT DE LANGUE FRANCAISE (ILF)
French Language and Civilization
Site: France: Paris
Dates: 1 wk or longer, yr-round
Subjects: Civilization/culture, Culinary arts, French language (beg/int/adv), French studies, History, Literature
Eligibility: *Level:* fresh, sophs, jrs, srs,

grads, adults, teachers, professionals *Age:* min 16
Credit: *Undergrad:* avail *Grad:* none *Doc:* certificate
Instruction: *In:* French *Format:* lang study, lecture *Students:* intl
Costs: Contact sponsor
Housing: *Arr by pgm:* residence halls, homestay, hotels
Deadline: Contact sponsor
Other info: *US accredited sponsor:* no *Began:* 1986 *Activities:* excursions, cultural events *Misc:* May contact former participants. *URL:* http://www.inst-langue-fr.com
Contact: Dr Janice Ovadiah, USA Agent, 303 W 66th St, #4HE NY 10023-6305 *Ph:* 212-724 5823 *E-mail:* jovadiah@aol.com

---

0726
ISA
Summer in Paris
Site: France: Paris *Host inst:* Univ de Paris IV - La Sorbonne
Dates: 4 wks, Jun, Jul or Aug
Subjects: French language, French studies
Eligibility: *Level:* fresh, sophs, jrs, srs, adults *Requires:* 2.5 GPA *Age:* min 18, avg 22
Credit: *Undergrad:* 12-15 per sem *Grad:* none *Doc:* transcript
Instruction: *In:* French *Format:* lang study *Students:* intl
Costs: $3,050-$4,250 *incl* tuition, housing, some meals, excursions *Nonrefundable fee*
Housing: *Arr by pgm:* homestay
Deadline: Apr 5
Other info: *US accredited sponsor:* no *Misc:* May contact former participants. *URL:* http://www.studiesabroad.com
Contact: Gustavo Artaza, Exec Dir, Intl Studies Abroad, 901 W 24th St, Austin TX 78705 *Ph:* 800-580 8826; 512-480 8522 *Fax:* 512-480 8866 *E-mail:* isa@studiesabroad.com ▲

0727
KENTUCKY INSTITUTE FOR INTERNATIONAL STUDIES (KIIS)
Program in France
Site: France: Paris
Dates: 5 wks, late May-Jul
Subjects: English, French language (int/adv), Humanities
Eligibility: *Level:* fresh, sophs, jrs, srs, grads, adults, teachers, professionals *Requires:* 2.0 GPA, good acad standing at home inst, faculty recommendation *Age:* min 18
Credit: *Undergrad:* 3-6 *Grad:* none *Doc:* transcript
Instruction: *In:* English, French *Format:* lang study, lecture *Students:* mainly US
Costs: $3,280 for students at member schs, $3,580 for others *incl* tuition, housing, some meals, intl airfare, fees, excursions, ISIC *Nonrefundable fee*
Housing: *Arr by pgm:* pensions
Deadline: Feb 15 ($100 late fee)
Other info: *US accredited sponsor:* yes *Began:* 1977 *Orient:* in US & abroad *Activities:* excursions *Misc:* Optional independent travel. May contact former participants. *Financial aid:* scholarships *URL:* http://www.kiis.org
Contact: *See Index II for Members* Dr J Milton Grimes, Exec Dir, KIIS, Murray State Univ, PO Box 9, Murray KY 42071-0009 *Ph:* 270-762 3091 *Fax:* 270-762 3434 *E-mail:* kiismsu@murraystate.edu

---

0728
LA CUISINE DE MARIE-BLANCHE
French Cooking Classes
Site: France: Paris
Dates: 1 wk, yr-round
Subjects: Culinary arts
Eligibility: *Level:* fresh, sophs, jrs, srs, grads, adults, teachers, professionals, precoll *Age:* min 18, avg 27
Credit: *Undergrad:* none *Grad:* none *Doc:* certificate
Instruction: *In:* English, French *Format:* practical training *Students:* intl
Costs: $750 *incl* tuition, some meals
Housing: *Arr by pgm:* hotels
Deadline: Contact sponsor
Other info: *US accredited sponsor:* no *Began:* 1975 *Misc:* Individual classes avail. May contact former participants.
Contact: Dr Janice E Ovadiah, USA Rep, La Cuisine de Marie-Blanche, 303 W 66th St, 4HE, New York NY 10023 *Ph:* 212-724 5823 *E-mail:* jovadiah@aol.com

---

0729
LANGUAGES PLUS
Language Immersion and Cultural Program-Paris
Site: France: Paris
Dates: 2 wks or longer, yr-round
Subjects: French language (beg/int/adv), Homestay
Eligibility: *Level:* adults *Age:* min 17, max 65, avg 24
Credit: *Undergrad:* none *Grad:* none *Doc:* certificate
Instruction: *In:* French *Format:* lang study *Students:* intl
Costs: From $930 for 2 wks *incl* tuition, housing, books/materials, cultural activities
Housing: *Arr by pgm:* apartments, homestay
Deadline: 2 wks before pgm
Other info: *US accredited sponsor:* no *Activities:* excursions, field trips *Misc:* May contact former participants. *URL:* http://www.languagesplus.com
Contact: Margot Haldenby, North Amer Enrollment, Langs Plus, 317 Adelaide St W, Ste 900, Toronto, Ontario M5V 1P9, Canada *Ph:* 888-526 4758 *E-mail:* info@languagesplus.com

---

0730
LEHIGH UNIVERSITY
Lehigh in Paris
Site: France: Paris *Host inst:* Cite Intl Univ de Paris (CIUP)
Dates: 4-5 wks, late Jun-late Jul
Subjects: Architectural history, Architecture
Eligibility: *Level:* fresh, sophs, jrs, srs *Requires:* 2.0 GPA
Credit: *Undergrad:* 6 *Grad:* none *Doc:* transcript
Instruction: *In:* English *Format:* lecture, study tour *Students:* mainly US
Costs: $3,300 *incl* tuition, housing, fees, metro, activities *Nonrefundable fee*
Housing: *Arr by pgm:* residence halls
Deadline: Feb 15
Other info: *US accredited sponsor:* yes *Began:* 1990 *Orient:* in US & abroad *Activities:* excursions, field trips, program travel, cultural events *Misc:* Pgm offered in alternate yrs. Excursions throughout Paris everyday. May contact former participants. *URL:* http://www.Lehigh.edu/~incis/incis.html
Contact: Dr Sandi Smith, Dir, Study Abroad, Lehigh Abroad, 5 E Packer Ave, Whitaker Lab 343, Lehigh Univ, Bethlehem PA 18015 *Ph:* 610-758 3351 *Fax:* 610-758 5156 *E-mail:* cms2@lehigh.edu

---

0731
LEXIA INTERNATIONAL
LEXIA Summer in Paris
Site: France: Paris *Host inst:* Univ of Paris
Dates: 8 wks, mid-Jun-mid-Aug
Subjects: Anthropology, Arts, Civilization/culture, Ecology/environmental studies, Economics, European studies, Fine arts, French language (beg/int/adv), History, Homestay, Independent study, Internships, Literature, Political science/politics, Sociology
Eligibility: *Level:* fresh, sophs, jrs, srs, grads *Requires:* 2.5 GPA, 1 yr postsecondary educ completed *Age:* min 18, avg 21
Credit: *Undergrad:* 8-10 *Grad:* 8-10 *Doc:* transcript *Transfer credit through:* Western Washington Univ
Instruction: *In:* English, French *Format:* independent study, internship, lang study, lecture, seminar, volunteer/svc *Students:* mainly US
Costs: $4,950 *incl* tuition, housing,

insurance, fees, excursions, ISIC, computer access *Nonrefundable fee*
Housing: *Arr by pgm:* residence halls with local students, homestay
Deadline: Apr 15; Apr 1 for scholarships
Other info: *US accredited sponsor:* no *Began:* 2000 *In coop with:* Western Washington Univ *Orient:* abroad (2 days, intensive lang study) *Activities:* excursions, field trips, program travel, cultural events, sports *Misc:* Student support svcs. May contact former participants. *Financial aid:* scholarships, work study *URL:* http://www.lexiaintl.org
Contact: LEXIA Intl, 25 S Main St, Hanover NH 03755 *Ph:* 800-755 3942; 603-643 9898 *Fax:* 603-643 9899 *E-mail:* info@lexiaintl.org
Or Contact: LEXIA Intl, West Coast, 378 Cambridge Ave, Palo Alto CA 94306 *Ph:* 650-327 9191 *Fax:* 650-327 9192

0732
LOUISIANA STATE UNIVERSITY
LSU in Paris
Site: France: Paris
Dates: 6 wks, early Jun-mid-Jul
Subjects: Civilization/culture, English, French language, Independent study, Political science/politics
Eligibility: *Level:* sophs, jrs, srs, grads, adults, teachers, professionals *Requires:* 2.5 GPA, for undergrads, 3.0 GPA for grads & those seeking 9 credit hrs
Credit: *Undergrad:* 6-9 *Grad:* avail *Doc:* transcript
Instruction: *In:* English, French *Format:* lang study, lecture *Students:* mainly US
Costs: About $2,995 *incl* tuition, housing, some meals, excursions
Housing: *Arr by pgm:* residence halls
Deadline: Mar 15
Other info: *US accredited sponsor:* yes *Began:* 1981 *Orient:* in US & abroad *Misc:* Loans avail. Scholarships for own students only. May contact former participants. *Financial aid:* scholarships *URL:* http://www.lsu.edu/studyabroad
Contact: Joseph Rosenbach, Acad Pgms Abroad, Louisiana State Univ, 113 Hatcher Hall, Baton Rouge LA 70803 *Ph:* 225-388 6801 *Fax:* 225-388 6806 *E-mail:* studyabroad@lsu.edu

---

0733
MIAMI-DADE COMMUNITY COLLEGE and **TRUMAN STATE UNIVERSITY**
Intensive French in Paris
Site: France: Paris *Host inst:* Inst Parisien
Dates: 1 mo or longer, yr-round
Subjects: Fashion design, French language (beg/int/adv), Homestay
Eligibility: *Level:* fresh, sophs, jrs, srs, adults, teachers *Requires:* 2.5 GPA *Age:* min 18
Credit: *Undergrad:* 6-8 per mo *Grad:* none *Doc:* transcript
Instruction: *In:* French *Format:* lang study *Students:* intl
Costs: About $1,495 *incl* tuition, fees
Housing: *Arr by pgm:* residence halls, homestay, hotels
Deadline: Rolling admissions
Other info: *US accredited sponsor:* yes *Began:* 1999 *Orient:* abroad (1 day) *Activities:* excursions, field trips, cultural events *Misc:* Apply through Miami-Dade CC.
Contact: Mr Reinaldo Changsut, S A Adviser, or Dr Robert Vitale, Intl Educ, Miami-Dade CC, 11011 SW 104th St, Miami FL 33143 *Ph:* 305-237 2533 *Fax:* 305-237 2949 *E-mail:* rvitale@mdcc.edu
Or Contact: Ms Alci Arias, Asst Dir, Intl Educ Abroad, Truman State Univ, Kirksville MO 63501 *Ph:* 660-785 4076 *Fax:* 660-785 7473 *E-mail:* alcidean@truman.edu

---

0734
MICHIGAN STATE UNIVERSITY
Modern Art
Site: France: Paris
Dates: 6 wks, May-Jun
Subjects: Civilization/culture, Drawing, Field study, Studio arts
Eligibility: *Level:* fresh, sophs, jrs, srs, grads *Requires:* 2.5 GPA *Age:* min 18
Credit: *Undergrad:* avail *Grad:* avail *Doc:* transcript
Instruction: *In:* English *Format:* directed field study *Students:* mainly US
Costs: About $2,600 *incl* housing, insurance, fees, excursions *Nonrefundable fee*
Housing: *Arr by pgm:* apartments
Deadline: Mar 2
Other info: *US accredited sponsor:* yes *Began:* 1999 *Orient:* in US (1 day) *Activities:* excursions, field trips, cultural events *URL:* http://studyabroad.msu.edu
Contact: Cheryl Benner, Study Abroad, Michigan State Univ, 109 Intl Ctr, East Lansing MI 48824-1035 *Ph:* 517-353 8920 *Fax:* 517-432 2082 *E-mail:* bennerc@msu.edu ▲

0735
NEW YORK UNIVERSITY, SCHOOL OF EDUCATION
Arts and Humanities: Art, Culture and Politics
Site: France: Paris
Dates: 3 wks, summer; next offered in 2002
Subjects: Humanities
Eligibility: *Level:* grads *Requires:* 3.0 GPA
Credit: *Undergrad:* none *Grad:* avail *Doc:* transcript
Instruction: *In:* English *Format:* lecture, seminar, tutorial *Students:* mainly US
Costs: $5,200 *incl* tuition, housing, some meals, excursions, books/materials *Nonrefundable fee*
Housing: *Arr by pgm:* residence halls
Deadline: Apr 1
Other info: *US accredited sponsor:* yes *Orient:* abroad *Activities:* field trips, cultural events *Misc:* May contact former participants. *URL:* http://www.nyu.edu/summer
Contact: Helen J Kelly, Dir, Special Pgms, New York Univ, 82 Washington Square E, Rm 62, New York NY 10003 *Ph:* 212-998 5090 *Fax:* 212-995 4923 ▲

0736
NEW YORK UNIVERSITY, TISCH SCHOOL OF THE ARTS
French Cinema & Culture
Site: France; Paris
Dates: 6 wks, Jun 25-Aug 3
Subjects: Film studies, French studies, Media studies, Performing arts, Visual arts
Eligibility: *Level:* adults *Age:* min 18
Credit: *Undergrad:* 8 per sem *Grad:* 8 per sem *Doc:* transcript
Instruction: *In:* English *Format:* lecture, seminar *Students:* mainly US
Costs: $4,012 *incl* tuition, fees
Housing: *Arr by pgm:* residence halls
Deadline: Apr 15 priority deadline
Other info: *US accredited sponsor:* yes *Began:* 2001 *Orient:* in US & abroad *Activities:* field trips *Misc:* May contact former participants. *Financial aid:* scholarships *URL:* http://www.nyu.edu/tisch/international
Contact: Linda Kow, Assoc Dir, Tisch Sch of the Arts, Intl Pgrms, 721 Broadway, 12th Fl, New York NY 10003 *Ph:* 212-998 9175 *Fax:* 212-995 4578 *E-mail:* tisch.international@nyu.edu

---

0737
NEW YORK UNIVERSITY, TISCH SCHOOL OF THE ARTS
Performance in Paris
Site: France: Paris
Dates: 6 wks, about Jun 25-Aug 3
Subjects: Acting, Civilization/culture, Performing arts, Theater arts
Eligibility: *Level:* adults *Requires:* prior acting training and/or experience or instructor's permission
Credit: *Undergrad:* 8 *Grad:* none *Doc:* transcript
Instruction: *In:* English *Format:* lecture, practical training, seminar, workshop *Students:* mainly US

Costs: About $5,733 *incl* tuition, housing, fees, excursions *Nonrefundable fee*
Housing: *Arr by pgm:* residence halls
Deadline: About Apr 15
Other info: *US accredited sponsor:* yes *Began:* 2001 *Orient:* in US & abroad *Activities:* excursions, field trips, cultural events *Misc:* Loans & scholarships for own students only. *Financial aid:* scholarships *URL:* http://www.nyu.edu/tisch/international/
Contact: Linda Kow, Assoc Dir, Tisch Intl Pgms, New York Univ, 721 Broadway, 12th Fl, New York NY 10003 *Ph:* 212-998 9175 *Fax:* 212-995 4578 *E-mail:* tisch.international@nyu.edu

---

0738
NEW YORK UNIVERSITY, TISCH SCHOOL OF THE ARTS
Video Production
Site: France: Paris
Dates: 6 wks, Jun 25-Aug 3
Subjects: Film studies, French studies, Media studies, Performing arts, Visual arts
Eligibility: *Level:* fresh, sophs, jrs, srs, grads, adults *Age:* min 18
Credit: *Undergrad:* 8 *Grad:* avail *Doc:* transcript
Instruction: *In:* English *Format:* lecture, seminar, workshop *Students:* mainly US
Costs: About $6,500 *incl* tuition, housing, fees, excursions *Nonrefundable fee*
Housing: *Arr by pgm:* residence halls
Deadline: Apr 15; rolling admissions
Other info: *US accredited sponsor:* yes *Began:* 2001 *Orient:* in US & abroad (1 day) *Activities:* excursions, cultural events *Misc:* Scholarships & loans for own students only. *Financial aid:* scholarships *URL:* http://www.nyu.edu/tisch/international/
Contact: Linda Kow, Assoc Dir, Tisch Intl Pgms, New York Univ, 721 Broadway, 12th Fl, New York NY 10003 *Ph:* 212-998 9175 *Fax:* 212-995 4578 *E-mail:* tisch.international@nyu.edu

---

0739
NEW YORK UNIVERSITY, TISCH SCHOOL OF THE ARTS
Workshop: Developing the Screenplay; Seminar: French Cinema and Culture
Site: France: Paris
Dates: 6 wks, Jul 5-Aug 15
Subjects: Creative writing, Film studies, French studies, Media studies, Screenwriting
Eligibility: *Level:* sophs, jrs, srs, grads, adults, teachers, professionals *Requires:* coll-level screenwriting or equiv, 1st act & synopsis of screenplay at application, completed screenplay 1 mo before pgm *Age:* min 18
Credit: *Undergrad:* 8 *Grad:* 8 *Doc:* transcript
Instruction: *In:* English *Format:* lecture, practical training, seminar, workshop *Students:* mainly US
Costs: $5,249 *incl* tuition, housing, some meals, fees, excursions *Nonrefundable fee*
Housing: *Arr by pgm:* residence halls
Deadline: Apr 15; rolling admissions
Other info: *US accredited sponsor:* yes *Began:* 1998 *Orient:* in US & abroad (1 day) *Activities:* excursions, cultural events *Misc:* Scholarships & loans for own students only. *Financial aid:* scholarships *URL:* http://www.nyu.edu/tisch/international/
Contact: Linda Kow, Assoc Dir, Tisch Intl Pgms, New York Univ, 721 Broadway, 12th Fl, New York NY 10003 *Ph:* 212-998 9175 *Fax:* 212-995 4578 *E-mail:* tisch.international@nyu.edu

---

0740
PARSONS SCHOOL OF DESIGN
Drawing/Painting in Paris
Site: France: Paris *Host inst:* Parsons Paris
Dates: Jul 3-28
Subjects: Art history, Drawing, Painting
Eligibility: *Level:* fresh, sophs, jrs, srs, grads, adults, teachers, professionals
Credit: *Undergrad:* 5 *Grad:* none *Doc:* transcript
Instruction: *In:* English *Format:* art studio, lecture *Students:* mainly US
Costs: $3,572 *incl* tuition
Housing: *Sponsor assists:* residence halls
Deadline: May 1
Other info: *US accredited sponsor:* yes *Activities:* excursions *URL:* http://www.parsons.edu/sis
Contact: Admissions, Parsons Sch of Design, 66 Fifth Ave, New York NY 10011 *Ph:* 800-252 0852

0741
PARSONS SCHOOL OF DESIGN
Fashion in Paris
Site: France: Paris *Host inst:* Parsons Paris
Dates: Jul 3-28
Subjects: Costumes, European studies, Fashion design, History, Illustration
Eligibility: *Level:* fresh, sophs, jrs, srs, teachers, professionals
Credit: *Undergrad:* 5 *Grad:* none *Doc:* transcript
Instruction: *In:* English *Format:* art studio, lecture *Students:* mainly US
Costs: $3,572 *incl* tuition
Housing: *Arr by pgm:* residence halls
Deadline: May 1
Other info: *US accredited sponsor:* yes *Began:* 1976 *Orient:* abroad *Activities:* excursions *URL:* http://www.parsons.edu/sis
Contact: Admissions, Parsons Sch of Design, 66 Fifth Ave, New York NY 10011 *Ph:* 800-252 0852; 212-229 8910

0742
PARSONS SCHOOL OF DESIGN
French Architecture and Interiors
Site: France: Paris *Host inst:* Parsons Paris
Dates: Jul 3-28
Subjects: Architectural history, Drafting, Drawing, Interior design
Eligibility: *Level:* fresh, sophs, jrs, srs, grads, adults, teachers, professionals *Age:* min 16
Credit: *Undergrad:* 5 *Grad:* none *Doc:* transcript
Instruction: *In:* English *Format:* art studio, lecture *Students:* mainly US
Costs: $3,572 *incl* tuition
Housing: *Arr by pgm:* residence halls
Deadline: May 1
Other info: *US accredited sponsor:* yes *Began:* 1976 *Orient:* abroad (1 day, intensive lang study) *Activities:* excursions, field trips, cultural events *Misc:* May contact former participants. *URL:* http://www.parsons.edu/sis
Contact: Admissions, Parsons Sch of Design, 66 Fifth Ave, New York NY 10011 *Ph:* 800-252 0852; 212-229 8910 *Fax:* 212-229 8975 *E-mail:* parsadm@newschool.edu

---

0743
PARSONS SCHOOL OF DESIGN
Parsons in Paris: Fine Arts
Site: France: Paris *Host inst:* Parsons Paris
Dates: Jul 5-30
Subjects: Art history, Drawing, French studies, Painting
Eligibility: *Level:* precoll *Age:* min 16
Credit: *Undergrad:* 5 *Grad:* none *Doc:* transcript
Instruction: *In:* English *Format:* art studio, lecture *Students:* mainly US
Costs: $3,370 *incl* tuition
Housing: *Arr by pgm:* residence halls
Deadline: May 1
Other info: *US accredited sponsor:* yes *Began:* 1976 *Orient:* abroad *URL:* http://www.parsons.edu/sis
Contact: Admissions, Parsons Sch of Design, 66 Fifth Ave, New York NY 10011 *Ph:* 212-229 8989

0744
PARSONS SCHOOL OF DESIGN
Photography in Paris
Site: France: Paris *Host inst:* Parsons Paris

Dates: Jul 3-28
Subjects: Photography
Eligibility: *Level:* fresh, sophs, jrs, srs, teachers, professionals, precoll *Age:* min 16
Credit: *Undergrad:* 5 *Grad:* none *Doc:* transcript
Instruction: *In:* English *Format:* art studio, lecture *Students:* mainly US
Costs: $3,572 *incl* tuition
Housing: *Arr by pgm:* residence halls
Deadline: May 1
Other info: *US accredited sponsor:* yes *Began:* 1976 *Orient:* abroad *Activities:* excursions *URL:* http://www.parsons.edu/sis
Contact: Admissions, Parsons Sch of Design, 66 Fifth Ave, New York NY 10011 *Ph:* 212-741 8989

0745
RUTGERS UNIVERSITY
Rutgers Summer Institute in Art History in Paris
Site: France: Paris
Dates: 6 wks, early Jun-mid-Jul
Subjects: Art history
Eligibility: *Level:* sophs, jrs, srs *Requires:* 2.5 GPA, 1 recommendation letter
Credit: *Undergrad:* 6 *Grad:* none *Doc:* transcript
Instruction: *In:* English *Format:* seminar *Students:* mainly US
Costs: $3,615 for NJ residents, $3,865 for others *incl* tuition, housing, insurance, excursions *Nonrefundable fee*
Housing: *Arr by pgm:* apartments
Deadline: May 1
Other info: *US accredited sponsor:* yes *Orient:* in US *Activities:* excursions *URL:* http://studyabroad.rutgers.edu
Contact: Dir, Study Abroad, Rutgers Univ, 102 College Ave, New Brunswick NJ 08901 *Ph:* 732-932 7787 *Fax:* 732-932 8659 *E-mail:* ru_abroad@email.rutgers.edu

---

0746
RUTGERS UNIVERSITY
Summer in Paris
Site: France: Paris
Dates: 6 wks, mid-Jun-late Jul
Subjects: Civilization/culture, Contemporary issues, French language (adv), French studies, Homestay, Literature
Eligibility: *Level:* fresh, sophs, jrs, srs *Requires:* previous study in field, 2 yr coll French or equiv *Age:* min 18, avg 21
Credit: *Undergrad:* 6-9 *Grad:* none
Instruction: *In:* French *Format:* lang study, lecture *Students:* mainly US
Costs: $3,500 for NJ residents, $3,900 for others *incl* tuition, housing, some meals, insurance, fees, excursions, ground transport *Nonrefundable fee*
Housing: *Arr by pgm:* homestay
Deadline: Until pgm filled
Other info: *US accredited sponsor:* yes *Began:* 1967 *Activities:* excursions, cultural events *Misc:* May contact former participants. *Financial aid:* scholarships *URL:* http://french.rutgers.edu/PARIS.HTM
Contact: French Dept, Rutgers Univ, 131 George St, New Brunswick NJ 08901-1414 *Ph:* 732-932 9030 *Fax:* 732-932 8327 *E-mail:* french1@rci.rutgers.edu

---

0747
SAINT JOHN'S UNIVERSITY (NY)
College Europa France
Site: France: Paris
Dates: 1 mo, May-Jun
Subjects: French language (beg/int/adv), Internships, Photography, Studio arts
Eligibility: *Level:* fresh, sophs, jrs, srs, grads *Requires:* 2.75 GPA, 2 recommendation letters *Age:* min 18
Credit: *Undergrad:* 6 per term *Grad:* none *Doc:* transcript
Instruction: *In:* English, French *Format:* lang study, lecture *Students:* mainly US
Costs: $2,295 *incl* housing, some meals, intl airfare, excursions
Housing: *Arr by pgm:* residence halls
Deadline: Feb 1
Other info: *US accredited sponsor:* yes *Began:* 1997 *Orient:* in US & abroad (1 day) *Activities:* field trips *Misc:* Field trips to Loire castles, Versailles; optional field trips.
Contact: Joyce Lawlor, Dean, Study Abroad Pgms, St John's Univ, Bent Hall, Rm 388, 8000 Utopia Pkwy, Jamaica NY 11439 *Ph:* 718-990 6105 *Fax:* 718-990 2321 *E-mail:* intled@stjohns.edu

---

0748
SAN FRANCISCO STATE UNIVERSITY
Summer Study in Paris
Site: France: Paris *Host inst:* Inst Catholique
Dates: Jul 1-Jul 30
Subjects: Civilization/culture, French language (beg/int/adv)
Eligibility: *Level:* adults *Age:* min 16
Credit: *Undergrad:* avail *Grad:* none *Doc:* certificate
Instruction: *In:* English, French *Format:* lang study, lecture *Students:* intl
Costs: About $3,000 *incl* tuition, housing, some meals, excursions, books/materials
Housing: *Arr by pgm:* residence halls, homestay, hotels
Deadline: May 1
Other info: *US accredited sponsor:* yes *Began:* 1978 *Orient:* in US (intensive lang study incl) *Activities:* field trips *Misc:* Course in survival French, 3-day trip to Brittany.
Contact: Mary Pieratt, Extended Educ, San Francisco State Univ, 1600 Halloway Ave, Adm 153, San Francisco CA 94132 *Ph:* 415-338 1372 *Fax:* 415-338 7290 *E-mail:* travel@sfsu.edu or maryp@sfsu.edu

---

0749
SCHOOL OF THE MUSEUM OF FINE ARTS, BOSTON
Paris Program
Site: France: Paris
Dates: Aug 4-Aug 25
Subjects: Studio arts (beg/int/adv)
Eligibility: *Level:* fresh, sophs, jrs, srs, grads, adults, teachers, professionals *Age:* min 18
Credit: *Undergrad:* avail *Grad:* none *Doc:* transcript
Instruction: *In:* English *Format:* art studio *Students:* mainly US
Costs: $2,450 *incl* tuition, housing, some meals, excursions, railpass, studio facilities *Nonrefundable fee*
Housing: *Arr by pgm:* residence halls
Deadline: May 4 or until pgm filled
Other info: *US accredited sponsor:* yes *Began:* 2001 *Activities:* excursions, program travel *Misc:* One hr info session at the Sch of the Museum of Fine Arts on Apr 30. *URL:* http://www.smfa.edu
Contact: Nathaniel Bradley, SMFA Continuing Educ, 230 The Fenway, Boston MA 02115 *Ph:* 617-267 1219 *Fax:* 617-369 3679 *E-mail:* coned@smfa.edu

---

0750
SOUTHERN METHODIST UNIVERSITY
SMU Summer-in-Paris
Site: France: Paris *Host inst:* Reid Hall
Dates: 5 wks, Jul 5- Aug 4
Subjects: Anthropology, History
Eligibility: *Level:* sophs, jrs, srs *Requires:* 2.5 GPA
Credit: *Undergrad:* 6 *Grad:* none *Doc:* transcript
Instruction: *In:* English *Format:* lecture *Students:* mainly US
Costs: $3,800 *incl* tuition, housing, some meals, excursions *Nonrefundable fee*
Housing: *Arr by pgm:* residence halls
Deadline: Mar 1
Other info: *US accredited sponsor:* yes *Began:* 1997 *Orient:* in US *Activities:* excursions, field trips, cultural events *Misc:* Scholarships for own students only. Loans avail. May contact former participants. *Financial aid:* scholarships *URL:* http://www.smu.edu/studyabroad
Contact: Intl Off, Southern Methodist Univ, PO Box 750391, 3108 Fondren Dr, Dallas TX 75275 *Ph:* 214-768 2338 *Fax:* 214-768 1051 *E-mail:* intlpro@mail.smu.edu

Or Contact: Carolyn Sargent, Anthropology, Southern Methodist Univ, 311 Heroy Hall, Dallas TX 75275 *Ph:* 214-768 2753 *E-mail:* csargent@mail.smu.edu ▲

0751

SPEOS-PARIS PHOTOGRAPHIC INSTITUTE

Summer Session

Site: France: Paris
Dates: Late-May-mid-Aug
Subjects: Advertising, Computer aided design, Computer graphics, Fashion design, Internet, Photography, Photojournalism
Eligibility: *Level:* fresh, sophs, jrs, srs, grads, adults, professionals *Age:* min 18, max 77, avg 30
Credit: *Undergrad:* avail *Grad:* avail *Doc:* transcript *Transfer credit through:* Rochester Inst of Technology
Instruction: *In:* English, French *Students:* intl
Costs: $570 per wk *incl* tuition, books/materials
Housing: *Arr by student*
Deadline: Apply early
Other info: *US accredited sponsor:* no *Began:* 1984 *Orient:* abroad *Activities:* excursions *Misc:* May contact former participants. *URL:* http://www.speos.fr
Contact: Sophie Malon, Speos-Paris Photographic Inst, 8 rue Jules Valles, 75011 Paris, France *Ph:* 800-258 8492 *E-mail:* speos@speos.fr

---

0752

SPEOS-PARIS PHOTOGRAPHIC INSTITUTE

Winter Session

Site: France: Paris
Dates: 5 wks, early Jan-early Feb
Subjects: Arts criticism, Photography
Eligibility: *Level:* fresh, sophs, jrs, srs, grads *Age:* avg 22
Credit: *Undergrad:* 3 *Grad:* none *Doc:* certificate
Instruction: *In:* English *Format:* independent study, lab, lecture, practical training *Students:* mainly US
Costs: $1,780 *incl* tuition
Housing: *Sponsor assists*
Deadline: Apply early
Other info: *US accredited sponsor:* no *Began:* 1990 *In coop with:* Rhode Island Sch of Design *Orient:* abroad *Activities:* excursions, field trips, cultural events *Misc:* Taught by Rhode Island Sch of Design faculty. May contact former participants. *URL:* http://www.speos.fr
Contact: Speos-Paris Photographic Inst, 8 rue Jules Valles, 75011 Paris, France *Ph:* 800-258 8492 *E-mail:* pymahe@speos.fr

---

0753

SUNY COLLEGE AT NEW PALTZ, LANGUAGE IMMERSION INSTITUTE

Language Immersion Institute-Paris

Site: France: Paris *Host inst:* SILC
Dates: 2, 4 or 6 wks, yr-round
Subjects: French language
Eligibility: *Level:* adults, teachers, professionals *Age:* min 18, avg 40
Credit: *Undergrad:* avail *Grad:* none *Doc:* certificate
Instruction: *In:* French *Format:* lang study, lecture *Students:* intl
Costs: Contact sponsor
Housing: *Arr by pgm:* residence halls, homestay, hotels
Deadline: 2 mos before pgm
Other info: *US accredited sponsor:* yes *URL:* http://www.newpaltz.edu/lii
Contact: Dr Henry Urbanski, Dir, Lang Immersion Inst, SUNY New Paltz, 75 S Manheim Blvd, New Paltz NY 12561-2499 *Ph:* 914-257 3500 *Fax:* 914-257 3569 *E-mail:* lii@newpaltz.edu ▲

0754

SUNY COLLEGE AT NEW PALTZ

Summer Study in Paris

Site: France: Paris
Dates: 5 wks, late Jun-early Aug
Subjects: French language (int/adv), French studies
Eligibility: *Level:* fresh, sophs, jrs, srs, grads, adults *Requires:* 1 yr coll or 2 yrs high sch French
Credit: *Undergrad:* 9 *Grad:* 9 *Doc:* transcript
Instruction: *In:* French *Format:* lang study, lecture *Students:* mainly US
Costs: $3,386 for NY resident undergrads *incl* tuition, housing, all meals, insurance, excursions
Housing: *Arr by pgm:* residence halls
Deadline: Mar 1 or until pgm filled
Other info: *US accredited sponsor:* yes *Began:* 1990 *Activities:* field trips, cultural events *Misc:* Loans avail. *Financial aid:* scholarships *URL:* http://www.newpaltz.edu/oie/
Contact: Ctr for Intl Pgms, SUNY New Paltz, 75 S Manheim Blvd, Ste 9, New Paltz NY 12561 *Ph:* 845-257 3125 *Fax:* 845-257 3129 *E-mail:* international@newpaltz.edu ▲

0755

SYRACUSE UNIVERSITY

Paris Noir/Black Paris

Site: France: Paris
Dates: Jun 2-Jul 2
Subjects: Civilization/culture, French language, Literature
Eligibility: *Level:* jrs, srs, grads, adults, teachers, professionals *Requires:* 2.5 GPA
Credit: *Undergrad:* 6 *Grad:* 6 *Doc:* transcript
Instruction: *In:* English *Format:* independent study, seminar *Students:* mainly US
Costs: $6,000 *incl* tuition, housing, some meals, fees, excursions
Housing: *Arr by pgm:* hotels
Deadline: Mar 15
Other info: *US accredited sponsor:* yes *Began:* 2001 *Orient:* abroad *Activities:* field trips, cultural events *Misc:* May contact former participants. *Financial aid:* scholarships *URL:* http://sumweb.syr.edu/dipa/summer
Contact: Daisy Fried, Assoc Dir, Syracuse Univ, 119 Euclid Ave, Syracuse NY 13244-4170 *Ph:* 800-251 9674; 315-443 9419 *Fax:* 315-443 4593 *E-mail:* dsfried@summon3.syr.edu ▲

0756

TEMPLE UNIVERSITY

Sorbonne Study Program

Site: France: Paris *Host inst:* Univ de Paris IV (Sorbonne)
Dates: 4 or 6 wks, Jul-Aug
Subjects: Civilization/culture, French language (beg/int/adv), French studies, Homestay
Eligibility: *Level:* fresh, sophs, jrs, srs, grads, adults, professionals, precoll
Credit: *Undergrad:* 4-6 *Grad:* 4-6
Instruction: *In:* French *Format:* lang study, lecture *Students:* intl
Costs: About $1,946-$3,868 *incl* tuition, housing, some meals, excursions
Housing: *Arr by pgm:* residence halls, homestay, pensions
Deadline: Apr 15 (Mar 1 for pension housing)
Other info: *US accredited sponsor:* yes *Began:* 1950 *Orient:* in US & abroad *Activities:* excursions *URL:* http://www.temple.edu/intlprog/
Contact: Intl Pgms, Temple Univ, 200 Tuttleman Learning Ctr, 1809 N 13th St, Philadelphia PA 19122 *Ph:* 215-204 0720 *Fax:* 215-204 0729 *E-mail:* intlprog@vm.temple.edu

---

0757

THUNDERBIRD, THE AMERICAN GRADUATE SCHOOL OF INTERNATIONAL MANAGEMENT

Winterim in Paris

Site: France: Paris
Dates: 3 wks, Jan 8-26
Subjects: Advertising, Business language, Business/management, Finance, French

language, Human resources, Marketing, Trade
Eligibility: *Level:* grads *Requires:* 3.0 GPA
Credit: *Undergrad:* none *Grad:* 3
Instruction: *In:* English *Format:* lang study, lecture *Students:* intl
Costs: $2,250, $375 off-campus fee *incl* tuition
Housing: *Sponsor assists:* hotels
Deadline: Contact sponsor
Other info: *US accredited sponsor:* yes *Orient:* abroad *Activities:* field trips *Misc:* Afternoons at industrial sites, corporate headquarters & political insts. *URL:* http://www.t-bird.edu
Contact: Dr Earl Gibbons, Assoc VP, Overseas Pgms, Thunderbird, 15249 N 59th Ave, Glendale AZ 85306 *Ph:* 602-978 7251 *Fax:* 602-547 1356 *E-mail:* scottj@t-bird.edu

---

0758
TULANE UNIVERSITY
Summer Abroad in Paris
Site: France: Paris
Dates: 4 wks, Jul
Subjects: Art, French language, French studies, Psychology
Eligibility: *Level:* fresh, sophs, jrs, srs, grads, adults *Requires:* good acad standing *Age:* min 18
Credit: *Undergrad:* 6-7 *Grad:* none
Instruction: *In:* English *Format:* lang study, lecture *Students:* mainly US
Costs: About $4,200 *incl* tuition, housing, some meals, insurance, fees, excursions *Nonrefundable fee*
Housing: *Arr by pgm:* hotels
Deadline: May 1
Other info: *US accredited sponsor:* yes *Began:* 1983 *Orient:* in US & abroad *Activities:* excursions *Misc:* Loans avail. May contact former participants. *URL:* http://www.Tulane.EDU/~summer/abroad/paris
Contact: Richard A Marksbury, Summer Sch, Tulane Univ, 125 Gibson Hall, New Orleans LA 70118-5698 *Ph:* 504-865 5555 *Fax:* 504-865 5562 *E-mail:* rmarksby@tulane.edu

---

0759
UNIVERSITY OF ARIZONA
Arizona in Paris
Site: France: Paris
Dates: 6 wks, Jun-Jul
Subjects: Civilization/culture, French language (int/adv), Homestay
Eligibility: *Level:* sophs, jrs, srs *Requires:* 1 yr coll French *Age:* min 18
Credit: *Undergrad:* 6 *Grad:* none *Doc:* transcript
Instruction: *In:* French *Format:* lang study, lecture *Students:* mainly US
Costs: $3,900 *incl* tuition, housing, some meals, excursions
Housing: *Arr by pgm:* homestay, furnished rms
Deadline: Mar 26
Other info: *US accredited sponsor:* yes *Began:* 1986 *Orient:* in US *Activities:* excursions, program travel, cultural events *Misc:* May contact former participants. *Financial aid:* scholarships *URL:* http://w3.arizona.edu/~ciss/
Contact: Renee Griggs, Ctr for Global Student Pgms, Univ of Arizona, 939 N Tyndall Ave, Tucson AZ 85721 *Ph:* 520-626 7180 *Fax:* 520-626 9004 *E-mail:* griggsr@u.arizona.edu ▲

0760
UNIVERSITY OF CALIFORNIA, SAN DIEGO EXTENSION
French Immersion Program: Paris, France
Site: France: Paris *Host inst:* Euroctrs Paris
Dates: 2-12 wks, yr-round
Subjects: French language (beg/int/adv)
Eligibility: *Level:* fresh, sophs, jrs, srs, grads, adults, teachers, precoll *Requires:* 1 French lang course for beg recommended *Age:* min 18
Credit: *Undergrad:* avail *Grad:* none *Doc:* transcript, certificate
Instruction: *In:* French *Format:* lang study, lecture, seminar *Students:* intl
Costs: $1,229 for 2 wks *incl* tuition, housing, some meals, books/materials *Nonrefundable fee*
Housing: *Sponsor assists:* homestay, hotels
Deadline: 4-6 wks before pgm
Other info: *US accredited sponsor:* yes *Began:* 1999 *Orient:* abroad *Activities:* excursions, field trips *Misc:* flexible, short-term pgm. Located in heart of Latin Quarter. May contact former participants. *URL:* http://www.extension.ucsd.edu/laip
Contact: Tanya Knebel, Pgm Rep, UCSD Extension, Liberal Arts & Intl Pgms 0176Z, 9500 Gilman Dr, La Jolla CA 92093-0176 *Ph:* 858-822 2747 *Fax:* 858-534 7385 *E-mail:* travelstduy@ucsd.edu

---

0761
UNIVERSITY OF DELAWARE
Summer Session in France
Site: France: Paris
Dates: 5 wks, Jun
Subjects: Art history, French language (int), Homestay, Music
Eligibility: *Level:* fresh, sophs, jrs, srs, adults *Requires:* 2.0 GPA
Credit: *Undergrad:* 6 *Grad:* none *Doc:* transcript
Instruction: *In:* English, French *Format:* lang study, lecture, study tour *Students:* mainly US
Costs: Contact sponsor
Housing: *Arr by pgm:* homestay
Deadline: Mid-Mar
Other info: *US accredited sponsor:* yes *Orient:* avail yes *Activities:* excursions, field trips, cultural events *Misc:* Contact sponsor to arrange honors credit. *Financial aid:* scholarships *URL:* http://www.udel.edu/studyabroad/
Contact: Lisa Chieffo, Foreign Langs & Literatures, Univ of Delaware, Newark DE 19716 *Ph:* 302-831 6458 *Fax:* 302-831 6459 *E-mail:* lchieffo@udel.edu
Or Contact: Intl Pgms & Special Sessions, Univ of Delaware, 4 Kent Way, Newark DE 19716-1450 *Ph:* 888-831 4685; 302-831 2852 *Fax:* 302-831 6042 *E-mail:* studyabroad@udel.edu

---

0762
UNIVERSITY OF DELAWARE
Winter Session in Paris
Site: France: Paris
Dates: 1 mo, Jan
Subjects: Fashion design, Fashion merchandising, Marketing
Eligibility: *Level:* fresh, sophs, jrs, srs *Requires:* 2.0 GPA
Credit: *Undergrad:* 6 *Grad:* none *Doc:* transcript
Instruction: *In:* English *Format:* lecture, seminar, study tour *Students:* mainly US
Costs: Contact Sponsor
Housing: *Arr by pgm*
Deadline: mid-Oct
Other info: *US accredited sponsor:* yes *Orient:* in US *Activities:* excursions, field trips, cultural events *Misc:* Contact sponsor to arrange honors credit. *Financial aid:* scholarships *URL:* http://www.udel.edu/studyabroad
Contact: Int Pgm & Special Sessions, Univ of Delaware, 4 Kent Way, Newark DE 19716 *Ph:* 888-831 4685; 302-831 2852 *Fax:* 302-831 6042 *E-mail:* studyabroad@udel.edu

---

0763
UNIVERSITY OF HAWAII AT MANOA
UHM Art in Paris
Site: France: Paris
Dates: 6 wks, mid-May-late Jun
Subjects: Art history, Civilization/culture
Eligibility: *Level:* sophs, jrs, srs *Requires:* 3.0 GPA
Credit: *Undergrad:* 6 *Grad:* none *Doc:* transcript
Instruction: *In:* English *Format:* lecture, seminar *Students:* mainly US
Costs: $4,943 *incl* tuition, housing, some meals, excursions, orient, museum & metro passes *Nonrefundable fee*
Housing: *Arr by pgm:* residence halls

Deadline: Feb 17
Other info: *US accredited sponsor:* yes *Began:* 1994 *Orient:* in US *Misc:* UHM financial aid for UHM students only. *URL:* http://www2.hawaii.edu/study-abroad
Contact: Dir or Study Abroad Adviser, Study Abroad Ctr, Univ of Hawaii at Manoa, Moore Hall 115, 1890 East-West Rd, Honolulu HI 96822 *Ph:* 808-956 5143 *Fax:* 808-956 9319 *E-mail:* uhmsac@hawaii.edu

---

0764
UNIVERSITY OF KANSAS
Summer Language and Culture Institute in Paris, France
Site: France: Paris *Host inst:* L'Etoile Lang Sch
Dates: 6 wks, mid-Jun-Aug
Subjects: Civilization/culture, French language (int/adv), French studies, Literature
Eligibility: *Level:* fresh, sophs, jrs, srs *Requires:* 2 sems coll French
Credit: *Undergrad:* 6 *Grad:* none *Doc:* transcript
Instruction: *In:* French *Format:* lang study, lecture, study tour *Students:* US & intl
Costs: $3,500 *incl* tuition, housing, some meals, fees, excursions, 12-day study tour
Housing: *Arr by pgm:* residence halls, hotels during tour
Deadline: Mar 1
Other info: *US accredited sponsor:* yes *Began:* 1960 *Activities:* program travel, cultural events *Misc:* 12-day tour of Normandy, Brittany, Touraine. All meals incl during study tour. *URL:* http://www.ukans.edu/~osa
Contact: Susan MacNally, Asst Dir, Study Abroad, Univ of Kansas, 108 Lippincott Hall, Lawrence KS 66045 *Ph:* 785-864 3742 *Fax:* 785-864 5040 *E-mail:* osa@ukans.edu ▲

0765
UNIVERSITY OF NORTH CAROLINA AT CHAPEL HILL
UNC-CH Summer Language Program in Paris, France
Site: France: Paris *Host inst:* Univ de Paris IV (Sorbonne)
Dates: 1 mo, late May-late Jun
Subjects: French language (beg/int/adv), French studies, History
Eligibility: *Level:* adults *Requires:* 2.5 GPA, 2 sems coll French
Credit: *Undergrad:* 6 *Grad:* none *Doc:* transcript, certificate
Instruction: *In:* English, French *Format:* lang study, seminar, study tour *Students:* US & intl
Costs: $2,842 *incl* tuition, housing, all meals, insurance, fees *Nonrefundable fee*
Housing: *Arr by pgm:* residence halls
Deadline: Early Feb
Other info: *US accredited sponsor:* yes *Began:* 1992 *Orient:* in US & abroad *Activities:* excursions, field trips, cultural events *Misc:* May contact former participants. *Financial aid:* scholarships *URL:* http://www.unc.edu/depts/abroad
Contact: Study Abroad, UNC Chapel Hill, 12 Caldwell Hall, CB-3130, Cameron Ave, Chapel Hill NC 27599-3130 *Ph:* 919-962 7001 *Fax:* 919-962 2262 *E-mail:* abroad@unc.edu

---

0766
UNIVERSITY OF PITTSBURGH
Pitt in Paris, France
Site: France: Paris
Dates: 2 wks, early Jul
Subjects: Architecture, Art, Independent study
Eligibility: *Level:* sophs, jrs, srs *Requires:* 2.75 GPA
Credit: *Undergrad:* 3-4 *Grad:* none *Doc:* transcript
Instruction: *In:* English *Format:* independent study, lecture, study tour *Students:* mainly US
Costs: $1,675 for Univ of Pitt students, $1,825 for others *incl* tuition, housing, excursions, museum visits *Nonrefundable fee*
Housing: *Arr by pgm:* hotels
Deadline: Feb 15
Other info: *US accredited sponsor:* yes *Began:* 1999 *Orient:* in US & abroad *Activities:* excursions, field trips *Misc:* Scholarships for own students only. Loans & grants avail. May contact former participants. *Financial aid:* scholarships *URL:* http://www.pitt.edu/~stdyabrd/
Contact: Jennifer Sill, Study Abroad, Univ of Pittsburgh, 802 William Pitt Union, Pittsburgh PA 15260 *Ph:* 412-648 2299 *Fax:* 412-383 7166 *E-mail:* jsill+@pitt.edu
Or Contact: Dr Aaron Sheon, History of Art & Architecture, Univ of Pittsburgh, Pittsburgh PA 15260 *Ph:* 412-648 2416 *Fax:* 412-648 2792 *E-mail:* ash2+@pitt.edu

---

0767
UNIVERSITY OF SAN DIEGO, SCHOOL OF LAW
Paris Institute on International and Comparative Law
Site: France: Paris *Host inst:* Univ de Paris I
Dates: Jul 2-Aug 3
Subjects: Comparative law, European Union, International business, International law, Internships
Eligibility: *Level:* grads, teachers, professionals *Requires:* law or bus students
Credit: *Undergrad:* none *Grad:* 6 *Doc:* certificate
Instruction: *In:* English *Format:* internship, lang study, seminar *Students:* mainly US
Costs: About $2,800 for classes, $3,950 for internship *incl* tuition, books/materials *Nonrefundable fee*
Housing: *Sponsor assists*
Deadline: Mar 11
Other info: *US accredited sponsor:* yes *Began:* 1973 *In coop with:* ESSEC, Inst Catholique, Univ of Paris I Law Sch *Orient:* abroad *Misc:* Legal trips, some tourist trips arranged by USD Paris off. Correspondence regarding pgm must be in English *URL:* http://www.acusd.edu/lawabroad
Contact: Cindy King, Law Pgms Abroad, Univ of San Diego, 5998 Alcala Park, San Diego CA 92110-2492 *Ph:* 619-260 7460 *Fax:* 619-260 2230 *E-mail:* cking@acusd.edu

---

0768
UNIVERSITY OF SOUTH FLORIDA
French Culture and Civilization in Paris
Site: France: Paris
Dates: 4 wks, Jun
Subjects: Civilization/culture, Field study, French language, French studies
Eligibility: *Level:* fresh, sophs, jrs, srs, grads, teachers *Requires:* 2.0 GPA, French lang study preferred *Age:* min 18
Credit: *Undergrad:* 3-6 *Grad:* 3 *Doc:* transcript
Instruction: *In:* English *Format:* directed field study *Students:* mainly US
Costs: About $1,800 *incl* tuition, housing, insurance, fees, excursions *Nonrefundable fee*
Housing: *Arr by pgm:* residence halls
Deadline: Mar 1
Other info: *US accredited sponsor:* yes *Began:* 2000 *Orient:* in US & abroad (1 day) *Activities:* excursions, field trips *URL:* http://www.usf.edu/~iac/paris.htm
Contact: Julie Hale, Overseas Study Pgms, Univ of South Florida, 4202 E Fowler Ave, CPR 107, Tampa FL 33620-5550 *Ph:* 813-974 3933, 813-974 4043 *Fax:* 813-974 4613 *E-mail:* jhale@iac.usf.edu
Or Contact: Dr Roberta Tucker, Langs & Linguistics, Univ of South Florida, 4202 E Fowler Ave, CPR 107, Tampa FL 33620-5550 *Ph:* 813-974 2762 *Fax:* 813-974 4613 *E-mail:* tucker@chumal.cas.usf.edu

---

0769
UNIVERSITY OF SOUTHERN MISSISSIPPI
Contemporary French History
Site: France: Paris
Dates: 3 wks, Jun 13-Jul 7

Subjects: Anthropology, Art, French studies, History, Sociology
Eligibility: *Level:* sophs, jrs, srs, grads *Requires:* 2.0 GPA *Age:* min 18
Credit: *Undergrad:* 4 *Grad:* 4 *Doc:* transcript
Instruction: *In:* English, French *Format:* lang study, lecture, seminar *Students:* mainly US
Costs: $2,899 for undergrads, $3,199 for grads *incl* tuition, housing, intl airfare *Nonrefundable fee*
Housing: *Arr by pgm:* hotels, hostels
Deadline: Apr 26
Other info: *US accredited sponsor:* yes *Began:* 1996 *Activities:* excursions, field trips *Misc:* May contact former participants. *Financial aid:* scholarships *URL:* http://www.usm.edu
Contact: Dr Tim Hudson, Dean, CICE, or Dir, Contemporary French History, Univ of Southern Mississippi, Box 10047, Hattiesburg MS 39406-0047 *Ph:* 601-266 4344 *Fax:* 601-266 5699 *E-mail:* melissa.ravencraft@usm.edu

RENNES

0770
UNIVERSITY OF ROCHESTER
French in France
Site: France: Rennes *Host inst:* Inst Franco-Americain, Rennes
Dates: 4 wks, late May-late Jun
Subjects: French language, Homestay
Eligibility: *Level:* fresh, sophs, jrs, srs, adults *Requires:* previous study in field, 3 yrs high sch or 1 yr coll French
Credit: *Undergrad:* 6 *Grad:* none *Doc:* transcript
Instruction: *In:* French *Format:* lang study *Students:* mainly US
Costs: About $2,750 *incl* tuition, housing, some meals, fees, excursions
Housing: *Arr by pgm:* homestay
Deadline: Mar 15
Other info: *US accredited sponsor:* yes *Activities:* cultural events *URL:* http://www.rochester.edu/College/study-abroad/sa/global.html
Contact: Anne Lutkus, Modern Langs & Cultures, Univ of Rochester, Lattimore 403, Rochester NY 14627-0082 *Ph:* 716-275 2235 *E-mail:* adlt@mail.rochester.edu

ROUEN

0771
LEHIGH UNIVERSITY
Lehigh in Rouen
Site: France: Rouen *Host inst:* Ecole Superieure d'Ingenieurs en Genie Electrique (ESIGELEC)
Dates: Late May-Jun 14
Subjects: Education/teaching, Electrical/electronic engineering, Electronics, French language, Technology
Eligibility: *Level:* fresh, sophs, jrs, srs *Requires:* 2.0 GPA
Credit: *Undergrad:* 3 *Grad:* none *Doc:* transcript
Instruction: *In:* English *Format:* study tour *Students:* mainly US
Costs: $2,450 *incl* tuition, housing, excursions, Paris-Rouen train *Nonrefundable fee*
Housing: *Arr by pgm:* residence halls
Deadline: Mar 1
Other info: *US accredited sponsor:* yes *Began:* 1998 *Orient:* in US & abroad *Activities:* field trips *Misc:* Field trips to area industry, historical sites & museums. May contact former participants. *URL:* http://www.Lehigh.edu/~incis/incis.html
Contact: Dr Sandi Smith, Dir of Study Abroad, Lehigh Univ, 5 E Packer Ave, Whitaker Lab 343, Bethlehem PA 18015 *Ph:* 610-758 3351 *Fax:* 610-758 5156 *E-mail:* incis@lehigh.edu

ROYAN

0772
UNIVERSITE DE POITIERS and **CENTRE AUDIO-VISUEL DE ROYAN (CAREL)**
French Intensive
Site: France: Royan *Host inst:* CAREL
Dates: 2 wks or longer, yr-round
Subjects: Business language, Education/teaching, French language, Homestay
Eligibility: Own students only. *Level:* fresh, sophs, jrs, srs, grads, adults, teachers, professionals, precoll *Age:* min 18, avg 32
Credit: *Undergrad:* avail *Grad:* avail *Doc:* transcript, certificate
Instruction: *In:* French *Format:* lang study *Students:* intl
Costs: Fr 2,270 for 2 wks *incl* tuition, housing, all meals, books/materials
Housing: *Sponsor assists:* apartments with local students, residence halls with local students, homestay, hotels
Deadline: Contact sponsor
Other info: *US accredited sponsor:* no *Began:* 1966 *Activities:* excursions, cultural events, sports *Misc:* Specialized French courses for the legal & bus professions. May contact former participants. *URL:* http://www.carel.org
Contact: Regis Gendre, Dir, CAREL, BP 219C, 17205 Royan Cedex, France *E-mail:* info@carel.org

SAINT MALO

0773
COUNCIL ON INTERNATIONAL EDUCATIONAL EXCHANGE CONSORTIUM
Universite Rennes Z Haute Bretagne a Saint Malo
Site: France: St Malo
Dates: Jul 3-22
Subjects: Civilization/culture, French language, French studies
Eligibility: *Level:* jrs, srs, grads, adults, teachers, professionals *Requires:* 2.75 GPA, previous study in field, high int-adv lang level *Age:* min 18
Credit: *Undergrad:* avail *Grad:* none *Doc:* transcript
Instruction: *In:* English *Format:* lang study *Students:* mainly US
Costs: $1,400 *incl* tuition, some meals, insurance, excursions, ISIC
Housing: *Arr by pgm:* residence halls, homestay
Deadline: Contact sponsor
Other info: *US accredited sponsor:* yes *Orient:* abroad *Activities:* excursions, field trips, program travel, cultural events *Misc:* May contact former participants. *URL:* http://www.ciee.org/study
Contact: *See Index II for Members* Council, 633 3rd Ave, 20th Fl, New York NY 10017 *Ph:* 800-407 8839; 212-822 2779 *Fax:* 212-822 2779 *E-mail:* studyinfo@ciee.org
Or Contact: Pgm Adviser, Council, 633 3rd Ave, 20th Fl, New York NY 10017-5706 *Ph:* 212-822 2772 *Fax:* 212-822 2779 *E-mail:* studyinfo@ciee.org

0774
UNIVERSITY OF MICHIGAN
Summer Study-France
Site: France: St Malo
Dates: 6 wks, early Jul-mid-Aug
Subjects: French language (int/adv), Homestay
Eligibility: *Level:* fresh, sophs, jrs, srs *Requires:* 3 sems coll French, enrollment in US or Canadian univ
Credit: *Undergrad:* 7 *Grad:* none
Instruction: *In:* French *Format:* lang study, lecture *Students:* mainly US
Costs: Contact sponsor
Housing: *Arr by pgm:* homestay
Deadline: Feb 16
Other info: *US accredited sponsor:* yes *Began:* 1974 *Orient:* avail in Paris *URL:* http://www.umich.edu/~iinet/oip/
Contact: Intl Pgms, Univ of Michigan, G513 Michigan Union, Ann Arbor MI 48109-1349 *Ph:* 734-764 4311 *Fax:* 734-764 3229 *E-mail:* oip@umich.edu

STRASBOURG

0775
GEORGE MASON UNIVERSITY
Intensive French Language and Culture
Site: France: Strasbourg
Dates: 4 wks, Jul 29-Aug 25
Subjects: Civilization/culture, French language (int/adv)
Eligibility: *Level:* fresh, sophs, jrs, srs, adults, teachers, professionals *Requires:* 2.25 GPA, previous study in field, 1 yr coll French *Age:* min 18
Credit: *Undergrad:* avail *Grad:* none *Doc:* transcript
Instruction: *In:* French *Format:* lang study *Students:* mainly US
Costs: About $2,750 for VA residents, $3,300 for others *incl* tuition, housing, some meals, insurance, fees, excursions, ISIC *Nonrefundable fee*
Housing: *Arr by pgm:* homestay
Deadline: Apr 10
Other info: *US accredited sponsor:* yes *Began:* 1996 *In coop with:* CIEL de Strasbourg *Orient:* in US (1 day) *Misc:* May contact former participants. *Financial aid:* scholarships, work study *URL:* http://www.gmu.edu/departments/cge
Contact: Ctr for Global Educ, George Mason Univ, Johnson Ctr, Rm 235, 4400 University Dr, Fairfax VA 22030-4444 *Ph:* 703-993 2154 *Fax:* 703-993 2153 *E-mail:* cge@gmu.edu

---

0776
HOOD COLLEGE (MD)
Short Term Courses
Site: France: Strasbourg *Host inst:* Univ of Strasbourg
Dates: Summer
Subjects: Full curriculum
Eligibility: *Level:* sophs, jrs, srs, adults *Requires:* 2.0 GPA *Age:* avg 22
Credit: *Undergrad:* 3 *Grad:* none *Doc:* transcript
Instruction: *In:* English *Format:* lecture, seminar *Students:* mainly US
Costs: $3,000-$3,500 *incl* tuition, housing, some meals, intl airfare, fees, excursions, books/materials
Housing: *Arr by pgm:* hostels
Deadline: Mar 15
Other info: *US accredited sponsor:* yes *Began:* 1994 *Orient:* abroad *Activities:* excursions, field trips *Misc:* May contact former participants. *URL:* http://www.hood.edu/academic/strasbourg/htm
Contact: Jennifer Boston, Dir, Study Abroad, Hood Coll, 401 Rosemont Ave, Frederick MD 21701-8575 *Ph:* 301-696 3420 *Fax:* 301-696 3952 *E-mail:* jboston@hood.edu

---

0777
SYRACUSE UNIVERSITY
European Human Rights and Language in Strasbourg
Site: France: Strasbourg
Dates: 6 wks, May 22-Jun 30
Subjects: Field study, French language, Homestay, Political science/politics
Eligibility: *Level:* fresh, sophs, jrs, srs *Requires:* 2.5 GPA
Credit: *Undergrad:* 6 *Grad:* none *Doc:* transcript
Instruction: *In:* English *Format:* directed field study, lang study, lecture, study tour *Students:* mainly US

Costs: $5,000 *incl* tuition, housing, some meals, fees, excursions
Housing: *Arr by pgm:* homestay
Deadline: Mar 15
Other info: *US accredited sponsor:* yes *Began:* 1999 *Orient:* abroad (2 days) *Activities:* excursions, cultural events *Misc:* May contact former participants. *Financial aid:* scholarships *URL:* http://sumweb.syr.edu/dipa/summer
Contact: Daisy Fried, Assoc Dir, Syracuse Univ, 119 Euclid Ave, Syracuse NY 13244-4170 *Ph:* 800-251 9674; 315-443 9419 *Fax:* 315-443 4593 *E-mail:* dsfried@summon3.syr.edu ▲

0778
UNIVERSITY OF KANSAS
Advanced French Language and Literature Studies in Strasbourg
Site: France: Strasbourg *Host inst:* Univ of Strasbourg
Dates: 4 wks, late Jun-late Jul
Subjects: French language, French studies, Literature
Eligibility: *Level:* sophs, jrs, srs, grads *Requires:* good acad standing, 4 sems French
Credit: *Undergrad:* 6 *Grad:* none *Doc:* transcript
Instruction: *In:* French *Format:* lecture, seminar, study tour *Students:* mainly US
Costs: $2,900 *incl* tuition, housing, some meals, fees, excursions
Housing: *Arr by pgm:* residence halls
Deadline: Rolling admissions
Other info: *US accredited sponsor:* yes *Began:* 1999 *Orient:* in US & abroad (1 day) *Activities:* excursions, field trips, program travel, cultural events *Misc:* May contact former participants. *URL:* http://www.ukans.edu/~osa
Contact: Susan MacNally, Asst Dir, Univ of Kansas, 108 Lippincott Hall, Lawrence KS 66045-1731 *Ph:* 785-864 3742 *Fax:* 785-864 5040 *E-mail:* osa@ukans.edu ▲

TALLOIRES

0779
TUFTS UNIVERSITY
Landscape Painting
Site: France: Talloires
Dates: Contact sponsor
Subjects: Applied arts, Drawing, Painting, Studio arts
Eligibility: *Level:* adults *Age:* min 18
Credit: *Undergrad:* none *Grad:* none *Doc:* certificate
Instruction: *In:* English *Format:* art studio *Students:* mainly US
Costs: $2,690 *incl* tuition, housing, all meals, excursions *Nonrefundable fee*
Housing: *Arr by pgm:* hotels
Deadline: Contact sponsor
Other info: *US accredited sponsor:* yes *Began:* 1996 *Orient:* abroad *Activities:* excursions, field trips, program travel, cultural events *Misc:* Individualized instruction to painters of all levels in this summer resort with lake & mountain scenery. *Financial aid:* work study *URL:* http://www.ase.tufts.edu/FrenchAlps
Contact: Sally Pym or Amy Shocker, Tufts Univ, 108 Packard Ave, Medford MA 02155 *Ph:* 617-627 3290 *Fax:* 617-627 3457 *E-mail:* france@infonet.tufts.edu ▲

0780
TUFTS UNIVERSITY
Tufts in Talloires
Site: France: Talloires *Host inst:* Tufts Univ European Campus
Dates: Contact sponsor
Subjects: Art, Art history, Botany, Economics, Film studies, French language, History, International relations, Natural sciences, Ornithology, Public health, Religion/theology
Eligibility: *Level:* fresh, sophs, jrs, srs, grads *Requires:* 2.0 GPA, good acad standing *Age:* min 18
Credit: *Undergrad:* 4-8 *Grad:* none *Doc:* transcript
Instruction: *In:* English, French *Format:* lang study, lecture *Students:* mainly US
Costs: $4,550 *incl* tuition, housing, all meals, fees, excursions
Housing: *Arr by pgm:* homestay
Deadline: Contact sponsor
Other info: *US accredited sponsor:* yes *Began:* 1979 *Orient:* in US & abroad . *Activities:* excursions, program travel, cultural events, sports *Misc:* Optional travel to Paris & Provence. Overnight hiking trips in the French Alps at addtl fee. May contact former participants. *URL:* http://www.ase.tufts.edu/FrenchAlps
Contact: Sally Pym, Tufts Univ European Ctr, 108 Packard Ave, Medford MA 02155 *Ph:* 617-627 3290 *Fax:* 617-627 3457 *E-mail:* france@infonet.tufts.edu ▲

TOULON

0781
CAMPUS INTERNATIONAL
French Language and Civilization
Site: France: Toulon
Dates: Varying pgm lengths, yr-round
Subjects: Culinary arts, French language (beg/int/adv), Photography, Serigraphy, Singing/voice
Eligibility: *Level:* fresh, sophs, jrs, srs, grads, adults *Age:* min 16, avg 25
Credit: *Undergrad:* none *Grad:* none *Doc:* certificate
Instruction: *In:* French *Format:* lang study, lecture, tutorial *Students:* intl
Costs: $1,550 for 2 wks *incl* tuition, housing, all meals, excursions, books/materials, workshops
Housing: *Arr by pgm:* residence halls, homestay
Deadline: 1 mo before pgm
Other info: *US accredited sponsor:* no *Began:* 1973 *Activities:* excursions, cultural events, sports *Misc:* May contact former participants. *Financial aid:* work study
Contact: Dr Janice E Ovadiah, 303 W 66th St, New York NY 10023-6305 *Ph:* 212-724 5823 *Fax:* 212-496 2264 *E-mail:* jovadiah@aol.com
Or Contact: Campus Intl, BP 133, 83957 La Garde Cedex, France

---

TOULOUSE

0782
ALLIANCE FRANCAISE TOULOUSE MIDI-PYRENEES
French Courses for Foreigners
Site: France: Toulouse
Dates: 4 wks, yr-round
Subjects: French language (beg/int/adv), Homestay
Eligibility: *Level:* adults *Age:* min 16, avg 25
Credit: *Undergrad:* none *Grad:* none *Doc:* certificate
Instruction: *In:* French *Format:* lab, lang study, lecture, practical training *Students:* intl
Costs: Fr 2,500 per mo *incl* tuition, fees, books/materials
Housing: *Arr by pgm:* apartments with local students, homestay
Deadline: 2 wks before pgm
Other info: *US accredited sponsor:* no *Activities:* excursions, field trips, cultural events *URL:* http://www.alliance-toulouse.org
Contact: Monique Tarabbia, Alliance Francaise Toulouse, 9 pl du Capitole, 31000 Toulouse, France *E-mail:* af.toulouse@wanadoo.fr

---

0783
DICKINSON COLLEGE
Studio Arts in Toulouse
Site: France: Toulouse
Dates: 6 wks, mid-Jun-late Jul
Subjects: Drawing, Painting
Eligibility: *Level:* fresh, sophs, jrs, srs, adults *Requires:* previous study in field
Credit: *Undergrad:* avail *Grad:* none
Instruction: *In:* English *Format:* art studio *Students:* mainly US
Costs: About $5,850 *incl* tuition, housing, all meals, intl airfare, fees, excursions *Nonrefundable fee*
Housing: *Arr by pgm:* homestay

Deadline: Mar 1
Other info: *US accredited sponsor:* yes *Began:* 1998 *Orient:* in US & abroad *Activities:* field trips *URL:* http://www.dickinson.edu/departments/ocs/abroad.html
Contact: Global Educ, Dickinson Coll, PO Box 1773, Carlisle PA 17013-2896 *Ph:* 717-245 1341 *Fax:* 717-245 1688 *E-mail:* ocs@dickinson.edu

---

0784
DICKINSON COLLEGE
Toulouse Summer Immersion Program
Site: France: Toulouse *Host inst:* Dickinson Study Ctr
Dates: 6 wks, late May-early Jul
Subjects: Civilization/culture, French language (int/adv)
Eligibility: *Level:* fresh, sophs *Requires:* 2 yrs coll French
Credit: *Undergrad:* 4 *Grad:* none
Instruction: *In:* French *Format:* lang study, lecture *Students:* mainly US
Costs: About $5,800 *incl* tuition, housing, all meals, intl airfare, excursions
Housing: *Arr by pgm:* homestay
Deadline: Mar 1
Other info: *US accredited sponsor:* yes *Began:* 1977 *Orient:* in US *Activities:* excursions *Misc:* Exclusive use of French during pgm. Offered alternate yrs. *URL:* http://www.dickinson.edu/departments/ocs/summer.html
Contact: Global Educ, Dickinson Coll, PO Box 1773, Carlisle PA 17013-2896 *Ph:* 717-245 1341 *Fax:* 717-245 1688 *E-mail:* ocs@dickinson.edu

---

TOURS

0785
BOWLING GREEN STATE UNIVERSITY
Summer Study in France
Site: France: Tours
Dates: 1 or 2 mos, Jun 1-Aug 29
Subjects: Field study, French language (beg/int/adv), Homestay, Independent study
Eligibility: *Level:* fresh, sophs, jrs, srs *Requires:* 2.5 GPA, good acad standing
Credit: *Undergrad:* avail *Grad:* none *Doc:* transcript
Instruction: *In:* French *Format:* directed field study, independent study, lang study, lecture, study tour *Students:* mainly US
Costs: $2,957 for 1 mo, $4,456 for 2 mos OH residents, $5,205/$7,495 others *incl* tuition, housing, all meals, fees, excursions, books/materials *Nonrefundable fee*
Housing: *Arr by pgm:* homestay
Deadline: Mar 15
Other info: *US accredited sponsor:* yes *Began:* 1966 *Orient:* in US (1 day) *Activities:* excursions, field trips *Misc:* May contact former participants. *URL:* http://www.bgsu.edu/departments/roml/homepage.htm
Contact: Dr Opportune Zongo, Romance Lang, Bowling Green State Univ, Bowling Green OH 43403 *Ph:* 419-372 7396 *Fax:* 419-372 7332 *E-mail:* ozongo@bgnet.bgsu.edu

---

0786
FRENCH-AMERICAN EXCHANGE
Intensive Summer Program in Tours
Site: France: Tours *Host inst:* Inst de Touraine
Dates: 4 or 8 wks, Jun-Sep
Subjects: Civilization/culture, French language (beg/int/adv), French studies, Literature, Written composition
Eligibility: *Level:* sophs, jrs, srs, grads, adults, teachers, professionals *Requires:* 2.5 GPA, previous study in field, high sch diploma; previous lang study preferred *Age:* min 18, max 75, avg 20
Credit: *Undergrad:* 6 per mo *Grad:* 6 per mo *Doc:* transcript, certificate
Instruction: *In:* French *Format:* lab, lang study *Students:* intl
Costs: $2,020 for 4 wks *incl* tuition, housing, some meals, fees, excursions, books/materials *Nonrefundable fee*
Housing: *Arr by pgm:* residence halls, apartments, homestay, bed & breakfasts
Deadline: 6 wks before pgm
Other info: *US accredited sponsor:* no *Began:* 1996 *Orient:* avail info packet *Activities:* excursions, field trips, cultural events, sports *Misc:* Located in Loire River Valley, chateaux country, 1-1/2 hrs outside Paris. May contact former participants. *URL:* http://www.faetours.com
Contact: Jim Pondolfino, Exec Dir, French-Amer Exch, 111 Roberts Ct, Alexandria VA 22314 *Ph:* 800-995 5087; 703-549 5087 *Fax:* 703-549 2865 *E-mail:* faetours@erols.com

---

0787
GEORGETOWN UNIVERSITY
Summer in Tours, France
Site: France: Tours *Host inst:* Inst de Touraine
Dates: 6 wks, mid-Jun-late Jul
Subjects: Civilization/culture (adv), French language (beg/int/adv), French studies (adv)
Eligibility: *Level:* fresh, sophs, jrs, srs, grads, precoll *Requires:* previous study in field, beg French *Age:* min 18
Credit: *Undergrad:* 6 *Grad:* none *Doc:* transcript
Instruction: *In:* French *Format:* lang study, lecture, seminar *Students:* mainly US
Costs: About $3,800 *incl* tuition, housing, some meals, insurance, fees, excursions, books/materials *Nonrefundable fee*
Housing: *Arr by pgm:* residence halls, homestay
Deadline: Mid-Mar
Other info: *US accredited sponsor:* yes *Orient:* in US (1 day) *Activities:* excursions *Misc:* On-site placement exam, 2-wks in residence halls & cultural workshops, the emainder at Inst de Touraine. May contact former participants. *Financial aid:* scholarships *URL:* http://www.georgetown.edu/ssce/
Contact: Dr Munzberg or Rachel Rubin, Intl Pgms, Georgetown Univ, Box 571013, Washington DC 20057-1013 *Ph:* 202-687 5620 *E-mail:* rubinr@georgetown.edu

---

0788
MICHIGAN STATE UNIVERSITY
French Language, Literature and Culture
Site: France: Tours
Dates: May-Jul
Subjects: Civilization/culture, French language (int/adv), French studies, Literature
Eligibility: *Level:* fresh, sophs, jrs, srs *Requires:* 2.5 GPA, 2 yrs coll French, good acad standing *Age:* min 18
Credit: *Undergrad:* 7 or more *Grad:* none *Doc:* transcript
Instruction: *In:* French *Format:* lang study, lecture *Students:* mainly US
Costs: About $2,200 *incl* housing, some meals, insurance, excursions, support svcs *Nonrefundable fee*
Housing: *Arr by pgm:* homestay
Deadline: Mar 2
Other info: *US accredited sponsor:* yes *Began:* 1976 *Orient:* in US *Misc:* Loans avail. May contact former participants. *Financial aid:* scholarships *URL:* http://studyabroad.msu.edu
Contact: Cheryl Benner, Study Abroad, Michigan State Univ, 109 Intl Ctr, East Lansing MI 48824-1035 *Ph:* 517-353 8920 *Fax:* 517-432 2082 *E-mail:* bennerc@msu.edu ▲

0789
RUTGERS UNIVERSITY
Rutgers Summer Institute in European Studies in Tours
Site: France: Tours *Host inst:* Univ Francois Rabelais
Dates: 4 wks, late Jun-late Jul
Subjects: European studies
Eligibility: *Level:* fresh, sophs, jrs, srs *Requires:* 2.5 GPA, recommendation letter
Credit: *Undergrad:* 6 *Grad:* none *Doc:* transcript
Instruction: *In:* English *Format:* seminar *Students:* mainly US

Costs: $2,384 for NJ residents, $2,634 for others *incl* tuition, housing, insurance, fees *Nonrefundable fee*
Housing: *Arr by pgm:* residence halls
Deadline: Apr 1
Other info: *US accredited sponsor:* yes *Began:* 1997 *Orient:* in US *URL:* http://studyabroad.rutgers.edu
Contact: Dir, Study Abroad, Rutgers Univ, 102 College Ave, New Brunswick NJ 08901 *Ph:* 732-932 7787 *Fax:* 732-932 8659 *E-mail:* ru_abroad@email.rutgers.edu
Or Contact: Melanie Andrich, Pgm Coord, Study Abroad, Rutgers Univ, 102 College Ave, New Brunswick NJ 08901 *Ph:* 732-932 7787 *Fax:* 732-932 8659 *E-mail:* mandrich@rci.rutgers.edu

---

0790
UNIVERSITY OF ALABAMA
Alabama Academic Summer Program in France
Site: France: Tours *Host inst:* Inst de Touraine
Dates: 4 1/2 wks, Jun 26-Jul 29
Subjects: Business language, Civilization/culture, French language (int/adv), Homestay
Eligibility: *Level:* fresh, sophs, jrs, srs, grads, teachers *Requires:* 2 sems coll French *Age:* avg 20
Credit: *Undergrad:* 6 *Grad:* 6
Instruction: *In:* French *Format:* lang study, lecture *Students:* intl
Costs: $3,800 *incl* tuition, housing, some meals, intl airfare, fees, excursions, ISIC
Housing: *Arr by pgm:* homestay
Deadline: Mar 1
Other info: *US accredited sponsor:* yes *Began:* 1974 *Activities:* excursions, program travel *Misc:* May contact former participants. *URL:* http://www.ua.edu/international
Contact: Capstone Intl Pgm Ctr, Univ of Alabama, PO Box 870254, Tuscaloosa AL 35487-0254 *Ph:* 205-348 5256 *Fax:* 205-348 5298 *E-mail:* achannel@aalan.ua.edu

---

0791
UNIVERSITY OF PENNSYLVANIA
Penn-in-Tours
Site: France: Tours
Dates: 6 wks, late May-mid-Jul
Subjects: Art history, Civilization/culture, French language (int/adv), Homestay, Literature
Eligibility: *Level:* fresh, sophs, jrs, srs, grads, professionals
Credit: *Undergrad:* 6-8 *Grad:* none *Doc:* transcript
Instruction: *In:* French *Format:* lang study, lecture *Students:* mainly US
Costs: About $4,900 *incl* tuition, housing, all meals, excursions *Nonrefundable fee*
Housing: *Arr by pgm:* homestay
Deadline: Feb 15
Other info: *US accredited sponsor:* yes *Began:* 1983 *Orient:* in US & abroad *URL:* http://www.sas.upenn.edu/CGS/
Contact: Elizabeth Sachs, Penn Summer Abroad, Univ of Pennsylvania, 3440 Market, Ste 100, Philadelphia PA 19104-3335 *Ph:* 215-898 5738 *Fax:* 215-573 2053 *E-mail:* sdanti@mail.sas.upenn.edu

---

VENASQUE

0792
HORIZONS TO GO
Horizons in Southern France: Provence
Site: France: Venasque
Dates: 1 wk, Apr 20-27 or Oct 7-14
Subjects: Painting, Photography, Printmaking, Textiles
Eligibility: *Level:* adults *Age:* min 19, max 85
Credit: *Undergrad:* none *Grad:* avail
Instruction: *In:* English *Format:* art studio, workshop *Students:* mainly US
Costs: $1,535 *incl* tuition, housing, all meals, excursions, books/materials *Nonrefundable fee*
Housing: *Arr by pgm:* bed & breakfasts
Deadline: Contact sponsor
Other info: *US accredited sponsor:* no *Activities:* excursions, field trips *Misc:* Field trips to vineyards, village markets & Avignon. May contact former participants. *URL:* http://www.horizons-art.org
Contact: Jane Sinauer, Horizons To Go, PO Box 2206, Amherst MA 01004 *Ph:* 413-549 2900 *Fax:* 413-549 5995 *E-mail:* horizons@horizons-art.org

---

VICHY

0793
CAVILAM VICHY
French Language and Culture in Vichy
Site: France: Vichy
Dates: 1 wk-1 yr, yr-round
Subjects: Business language, Civilization/culture, Foreign language teaching, French language (beg/int/adv), Homestay
Eligibility: *Level:* fresh, sophs, jrs, srs, grads, adults *Age:* min 16
Credit: *Undergrad:* avail *Grad:* none *Doc:* certificate
Instruction: *In:* French *Format:* lang study, lecture *Students:* intl
Costs: $1,500 for 2 wks *incl* tuition, housing, all meals
Housing: *Arr by pgm:* apartments, homestay, hotels
Deadline: None
Other info: *US accredited sponsor:* no *Began:* 1964 *Activities:* cultural events *Misc:* May contact former participants. *Financial aid:* work study
Contact: Dr Janice E Ovadiah, 303 W 66th St #4HE, New York NY 10023-6305 *Ph:* 212-724 5823 *Fax:* 212-496 2264 *E-mail:* jovadiah@aol.com
Or Contact: CAVILAM Vichy, 14 rue Marechal Foch, BP 164, Vichy Cedex 03206, France

Germany

MORE THAN ONE CITY

0794
CENTER FOR CULTURAL INTERCHANGE
Internship in Germany
Site: Germany: various sites *Host inst:* STEP IN
Dates: 1-3 mos, yr-round
Subjects: Business administration, German language, Homestay, Internships
Eligibility: *Level:* fresh, sophs, jrs, srs, grads *Requires:* 3.0 GPA, 2 yrs coll German *Age:* min 18, max 25, avg 20
Credit: *Undergrad:* none *Grad:* none *Doc:* certificate
Instruction: *In:* German *Format:* practical training *Students:* mainly host country
Costs: $1,930 per mo *incl* housing, some meals, insurance, fees, placement *Nonrefundable fee*
Housing: *Arr by pgm:* homestay
Deadline: 3 mos before pgm
Other info: *US accredited sponsor:* no *Began:* 1985 *In coop with:* STEP IN *Orient:* in US & abroad (1 day) *Misc:* Bus trainee pgm in a German co. May contact former participants. *URL:* http://www.cci-exchange.com
Contact: Karen Hindhede, Outbound Pgm Dir, Ctr for Cultural Interchange, 17 N 2nd Ave, St Charles IL 60174 *Ph:* 888-227 6231; 630-377 2272 *Fax:* 630-377 2307 *E-mail:* info@cci-exchange.com

---

0795
COUNCIL ON INTERNATIONAL EDUCATIONAL EXCHANGE (COUNCIL)
International Faculty Development Seminars-Germany
Site: Germany: Berlin, Dresden *Host inst:* Free Univ Berlin, Technical Univ of Dresden
Dates: 1 wk, Jun
Subjects: Contemporary issues, Economics, German studies, History, Political science/politics
Eligibility: *Level:* teachers, professionals *Requires:* must be full-time faculty at 2-yr or 4-yr insts

Credit: *Undergrad:* avail *Grad:* none
Instruction: *In:* English *Format:* lecture, seminar *Students:* mainly US
Costs: $1,900 *incl* tuition, housing, some meals, fees, excursions, books/materials, in-country transport, ITIC
Housing: *Arr by pgm:* hotels
Deadline: Mar 15
Other info: *US accredited sponsor:* no *Began:* 1990 *Orient:* abroad *Activities:* excursions, field trips, cultural events *Misc:* Seminar title: Facing Old & New Challenges: Germany in 2000. May contact former participants. *Financial aid:* scholarships *URL:* http://www.ciee.org/ifds
Contact: Jennifer Ley, Council, 633 3rd Ave, New York NY 10017 *Ph:* 212-822 2747 *Fax:* 212-822 2699 *E-mail:* ifds@ciee.org ▲

0796
DID DEUTSCH-INSTITUT
German Language and Educational Programs in Germany
Site: Germany: Berlin, Frankfurt, Munich, Wiesbaden
Dates: 2 wks or longer, yr-round
Subjects: German language (beg/int/adv)
Eligibility: *Level:* fresh, sophs, jrs, srs, adults *Age:* min 17
Credit: *Undergrad:* none *Grad:* none
Instruction: *In:* German *Format:* internship, lang study, student teaching, study tour *Students:* intl
Costs: Contact sponsor
Housing: *Sponsor assists:* apartments, homestay, pensions, hotels
Deadline: Contact sponsor
Other info: *US accredited sponsor:* no *Activities:* excursions, field trips, program travel, cultural events, sports *Misc:* Diploma exams. *Financial aid:* work study *URL:* http://www.did.de
Contact: Mr Koetter, Dir, did deutsch-inst, Hauptstr 26, D-63811 Stockstadt/ Main, Germany *E-mail:* office@did.de

---

0797
EDUCATIONAL PROGRAMMES ABROAD (EPA)
Bonn/Cologne Internship
Site: Germany: Bonn, Cologne
Dates: 8 wks, May 29-Jul 23
Subjects: Advertising, Art, Banking, Business/management, Drama/theater, Finance, Health sciences, Law, Political science/politics, Public relations, Social sciences
Eligibility: *Level:* jrs, srs, grads *Requires:* 3.0 GPA, int German *Age:* avg 21
Credit: *Undergrad:* avail *Grad:* none
Instruction: *In:* German *Format:* internship *Students:* mainly US
Costs: $4,400 *incl* housing, some meals
Housing: *Arr by pgm:* apartments, homestay
Deadline: Mar 1
Other info: *US accredited sponsor:* no *Began:* 1988 *Orient:* abroad (3 days, intensive lang study) *Activities:* excursions, field trips, cultural events *Misc:* Other internships avail. May contact former participants. *URL:* http://studyabroad.com/ epa
Contact: Eleanor Krawutschke, US Dir, Educ Pgms Abroad, 137 N Park St, Kalamazoo MI 49007 *Ph:* 616-382 0139 *Fax:* 616-382 5222 *E-mail:* epainterns@aol. com

---

0798
EDUVACATIONS
German Language Study, Arts and Culture
Site: Germany: Berlin, Munich
Dates: 1 wk or longer, yr-round
Subjects: Business language, Civilization/ culture, German language (beg/int/adv)
Eligibility: *Level:* adults *Age:* min 16
Credit: *Undergrad:* none *Grad:* none *Doc:* certificate
Instruction: *In:* German *Format:* lang study, lecture *Students:* intl
Costs: Contact sponsor
Housing: *Arr by pgm:* homestay, pensions, hotels, cottage
Deadline: Contact sponsor
Other info: *US accredited sponsor:* no *Activities:* excursions, cultural events, sports *Misc:* Custom-tailored pgms with lang classes for engineering, finance, banking & teaching. May contact former participants. *URL:* http://www. eduvacations.com
Contact: Mary Ann Puglisi, eduVacations, 1431 21st St NW, Ste 302, Washington DC 20036 *Ph:* 202-857 8384 *Fax:* 202-463 8091

0799
GEORGIA INSTITUTE OF TECHNOLOGY
Languages for Business and Technology (LBAT)-German
Site: Germany: Berlin, Dusseldorf
Dates: Jun 19-Aug 3
Subjects: German language
Eligibility: *Level:* fresh, sophs, jrs, srs *Requires:* previous German lang study, good acad standing
Credit: *Undergrad:* 9 *Grad:* none *Doc:* transcript
Instruction: *In:* German *Format:* lang study, lecture *Students:* mainly US
Costs: $3,684 for GA resident, $3,934 for others *incl* tuition, housing, some meals, intl airfare, excursions
Housing: *Arr by pgm*
Deadline: Mar 1
Other info: *US accredited sponsor:* yes *Activities:* excursions
Contact: Dr Bettina Cothran, Georgia Inst of Technology, Modern Langs, Atlanta GA 30332 *Ph:* 404-385 0192 *Fax:* 404-894 0955 *E-mail:* bettina.cothran@modlangs. gatech.edu
Or Contact: Intl Educ, Georgia Inst of Technology, J S Coon Bldg, Ste 203, Atlanta GA 30332-0284 *Ph:* 404-894 7475 *Fax:* 404-894 9682 *E-mail:* study. abroad@gatech.edu

---

0800
GOETHE INSTITUT
German Language and German Studies Course
Site: Germany: Berlin, Bonn, Bremen, Dresden, Dusseldorf, Frankfurt, Freiburg, Groettingen, Heidelberg, Konstanz, others
Dates: 2-12 wks, yr-round
Subjects: Civilization/culture, German studies, Homestay
Eligibility: *Level:* fresh, sophs, jrs, srs, grads, adults, teachers, professionals, precoll *Age:* min 18
Credit: *Undergrad:* avail *Grad:* avail *Doc:* transcript, certificate, diploma *Transfer credit through:* Millersville Univ
Instruction: *In:* German *Format:* lang study *Students:* intl
Costs: Contact sponsor
Housing: *Arr by pgm:* residence halls, homestay, pensions, hotels
Deadline: Until pgm filled; apply early
Other info: *US accredited sponsor:* no *Began:* 1951 *Activities:* excursions, field trips, program travel, cultural events, sports *Misc:* Scholarships for teachers of German & grad students of German/ German Studies. May contact former participants. *Financial aid:* scholarships *URL:* http://www.goethe.de/i/deiindex.htm
Contact: Dr Gabriele Landwehr, Goethe-Institut Inter Nationes eV, 1014 Fifth Ave, New York NY 10028 *Ph:* 888-446 3843; 212-439 8700 *Fax:* 212-439 8705 *E-mail:* lservice@goethe-newyork.org

---

0801
LANGUAGE LIAISON
German Language
Site: Germany: Berlin, Hamburg, Munich
Dates: 2 wks or longer, yr-round
Subjects: Civilization/culture, German language (beg/int/adv), Homestay, Humanities
Eligibility: *Level:* fresh, sophs, jrs, srs, grads, adults, teachers, professionals, precoll *Age:* min 16
Credit: *Undergrad:* avail *Grad:* avail *Doc:* transcript, certificate
Instruction: *In:* German *Format:* lang study *Students:* intl
Costs: Contact sponsor
Housing: *Arr by pgm:* residence halls with

local students, apartments, homestay, pensions, hotels, hostels
Deadline: 30 days before pgm
Other info: *US accredited sponsor:* no *Activities:* excursions, field trips, cultural events, sports *Misc:* Scholarship research svc. *URL:* http://www.languageliaison.com
Contact: Nancy Forman, Dir, Lang Liaison, 4 Burnham Pkwy, Morristown NJ 07960 *Ph:* 800-284 4448 *Fax:* 973-898 1710 *E-mail:* learn@languageliaison.com

---

0802
LANGUAGE LIAISON
German Saturation
Site: Germany: Berlin, Black Forest, Bonn, Frankfurt, Hannover, Heidelberg, Munich, Westphalia *Host inst:* Home Lang Intl
Dates: 1 wk or longer, yr-round
Subjects: Civilization/culture, German language (beg/int/adv), Homestay
Eligibility: *Level:* adults *Age:* min 10
Credit: *Undergrad:* none *Grad:* none *Doc:* certificate
Instruction: *In:* German *Format:* lang study *Students:* intl
Costs: Contact sponsor
Housing: *Arr by pgm:* teacher's home
Deadline: 45 days before pgm
Other info: *US accredited sponsor:* no *Misc:* Live & learn in your teacher's home. Scholarship research svc. *URL:* http://www.languageliaison.com
Contact: Nancy Forman, Dir, Lang Liaison, 4 Burnham Pkwy, Morristown NJ 07960 *Ph:* 800-284 4448 *Fax:* 973-898 1710 *E-mail:* learn@languageliaison.com

---

0803
LANGUAGE STUDIES ABROAD, INC
Intensive German
Site: Germany: Berlin, Gruen, Hamburg, Munich, Passau, Stuttgart *Host inst:* various LSA insts
Dates: 1 wk or longer Grun, Hamburg, Munich, Passau or Stuttgart/2 wks or longer Berlin, yr-round
Subjects: Business language, Dance, German language (beg/int/adv), Homestay, Hotel management, Music, Tourism
Eligibility: *Level:* fresh, sophs, jrs, srs, grads, adults, teachers, professionals, precoll *Age:* min 16, avg 30
Credit: *Undergrad:* avail *Grad:* avail *Doc:* certificate
Instruction: *In:* Chinese, Danish, English, French, German, Italian, Portuguese, Spanish, others *Format:* lang study, music lesson *Students:* intl
Costs: From $1,285 for 4 wks *incl* tuition
Housing: *Sponsor assists:* apartments, homestay, hotels, hostels
Deadline: 4 wks before pgm
Other info: *US accredited sponsor:* no *Orient:* abroad *Activities:* field trips, program travel, cultural events, sports *Misc:* May contact former participants. *URL:* http://www.languagestudiesabroad.com
Contact: Lang Studies Abroad, Inc, 103 Londonderry Ct, Reno NV 89511-2718 *Ph:* 800-424 5522; 775-849 9206 *Fax:* 775-849 9217 *E-mail:* info@languagestudiesabroad.com

---

0804
LINGUA SERVICE WORLDWIDE
Total Immersion/Intensive Language and Culture in Germany
Site: Germany: Berlin, Cologne, Frankfurt, Hamburg, Mainz, Munich, Stuttgart, Wiesbaden *Host inst:* AGI Delfin, Carl Duisberg Ctr, Colon Fremdsprachen Inst, Deutsch Inst, GLS Sprachenzentrum
Dates: 1 wk-1 yr, yr-round
Subjects: Civilization/culture, German language (beg/int/adv), Homestay
Eligibility: *Level:* fresh, sophs, jrs, srs, grads, adults, teachers, professionals, precoll *Age:* min 14
Credit: *Undergrad:* avail *Grad:* avail *Doc:* transcript, certificate *Transfer credit through:* Univ of Southern Mississippi
Instruction: *In:* German *Format:* lang study *Students:* intl
Costs: Contact sponsor
Housing: *Arr by pgm:* apartments with local students, residence halls with local students, homestay, pensions, hotels, hostels
Deadline: 45 days before pgm
Other info: *US accredited sponsor:* no *Began:* 1993 *Activities:* excursions, cultural events *Misc:* May contact former participants. *URL:* http://www.linguaserviceworldwide.com
Contact: Dir, Lingua Svc Worldwide, 75 Prospect St, Ste 4, Huntington NY 11743 *Ph:* 800-394 5327; 631-424 0777 *Fax:* 631-271 3441 *E-mail:* itctravel@worldnet.att.net ▲

0805
LINGUA SERVICE WORLDWIDE
Total Immersion/Intensive Language and Culture-Germany
Site: Germany: Berlin & region, Frankfurt & region, Hamburg, Hannover, Heidelberg *Host inst:* Home Lang Intl
Dates: 1 wk-1 yr, yr-round
Subjects: Civilization/culture, German language (beg/int/adv), Homestay
Eligibility: *Level:* fresh, sophs, jrs, srs, grads, adults, teachers, professionals, precoll *Age:* min 14
Credit: *Undergrad:* avail *Grad:* avail *Doc:* transcript, certificate *Transfer credit through:* Univ of Southern Mississippi
Instruction: *In:* German *Format:* lang study *Students:* intl
Costs: Contact sponsor
Housing: *Arr by pgm:* teacher's home
Deadline: 45 days before pgm
Other info: *US accredited sponsor:* no *Began:* 1993 *Activities:* excursions, cultural events *Misc:* Participate in teacher's family & social life. May contact former participants. *URL:* http://www.linguaserviceworldwide.com
Contact: Dir, Lingua Svc Worldwide, 75 Prospect St, Ste 4, Huntington NY 11743 *Ph:* 800-394 5327; 631-424 0777 *Fax:* 631-271 3441 *E-mail:* itctravel@worldnet.att.net ▲

0806
NATIONAL REGISTRATION CENTER FOR STUDY ABROAD (NRCSA)
German Language Study
Site: Germany: Berlin, Regensburg *Host inst:* GLS Sprachenzentrum, Horizonte
Dates: 2-8 wks, yr-round
Subjects: German language (beg/int/adv), Homestay
Eligibility: *Level:* fresh, sophs, jrs, srs, grads, adults, teachers, precoll *Age:* min 18
Credit: *Undergrad:* avail *Grad:* avail *Doc:* certificate
Instruction: *In:* German *Format:* lang study *Students:* intl
Costs: About $2,400 for 2 wks *incl* tuition, housing, some meals, insurance, books/materials
Housing: *Arr by pgm:* residence halls, homestay
Deadline: 6 wks before pgm
Other info: *US accredited sponsor:* no *Orient:* abroad (intensive lang study) *Activities:* field trips, cultural events *URL:* http://www.nrcsa.com
Contact: Reuel Zielke, NRCSA, 823 N 2nd St, #206, Milwaukee WI 53203 *Ph:* 414-278 0631 *Fax:* 414-271 8884 *E-mail:* info@nrcsa.com

---

0807
NATIONAL REGISTRATION CENTER FOR STUDY ABROAD (NRCSA)
German Lingua
Site: Germany: Munich, Passau *Host inst:* German Lingua
Dates: 2 wks or longer, yr-round/Munich; Jun 15-Sep 19/Passau
Subjects: Art, German language, Homestay, Music
Eligibility: *Level:* adults
Credit: *Undergrad:* none *Grad:* none
Instruction: *In:* German *Format:* lang study *Students:* intl
Costs: $794 for 2 wks, $2,982 for 8 wks *incl* tuition, housing, some meals, insurance *Nonrefundable fee*
Housing: *Arr by pgm:* homestay

Deadline: Rolling admissions
Other info: *US accredited sponsor:* no *Activities:* field trips *URL:* http://www.nrcsa.com
Contact: Reuel Zielke, NRCSA, 823 N 2nd St, #206, Milwaukee WI 53203 *Ph:* 414-278 0631 *Fax:* 414-271 8884 *E-mail:* info@nrcsa.com

---

0808
PENNSYLVANIA STATE UNIVERSITY
Flight Program in Germany
Site: Germany: Berlin, Flensburg *Host inst:* Univ of Flensburg
Dates: 3 mo, Jun-Aug
Subjects: German language, German studies
Eligibility: CIC students only *Level:* fresh, sophs *Requires:* 2.5 GPA *Age:* min 18
Credit: *Undergrad:* 11 *Grad:* none
Instruction: *In:* English, German *Format:* lang study, lecture *Students:* mainly US
Costs: Contact sponsor
Housing: *Arr by pgm:* residence halls
Deadline: Rolling admissions
Other info: *US accredited sponsor:* yes *Began:* 1999 *Orient:* in US & abroad *Activities:* excursions, field trips *Misc:* Begins with study in University Park, PA. May contact former participants. *Financial aid:* scholarships
Contact: Summer Abroad, Pennsylvania State Univ, 225 Penn State Conference Ctr, University Park PA 16802 *Ph:* 814-863 5170
Or Contact: Intl Pgm Adviser, Pennsylvania State Univ, 222 Boucke Bldg, University Park PA 16802 *Ph:* 814-865 7681 *Fax:* 814-865 3336

0809
SAINT RUPERT ORDEN ZU SALZBURG
Aquarelle and Music
Site: Germany: Konigsee, Schonau *Host inst:* Mentenlehen
Dates: 10 days, Sep 4-14
Subjects: Chamber music, Painting, String instruments, Woodwind instruments
Eligibility: *Level:* adults *Requires:* adv level musician for chamber music course, painting all levels *Age:* min 18, max 80, avg 30
Credit: *Undergrad:* none *Grad:* none
Instruction: *In:* English, German *Format:* art studio, practical training, workshop *Students:* intl
Costs: EUR 900 *incl* tuition, housing, all meals, all painting materials
Housing: *Arr by pgm:* homestay
Deadline: 1 mo before pgm
Other info: *US accredited sponsor:* no *Began:* 1999 *Activities:* excursions, field trips, cultural events *Misc:* May contact former participants.
Contact: Walter Hermann Sallagar, CSRO, Neulinggasse 42/10, A-1030 Vienna, Austria

---

0810
SUNY COLLEGE AT NEW PALTZ
Summer Study in Germany
Site: Germany: Berlin, Hamburg, Stade
Dates: 7 wks, mid-Jun-early Aug
Subjects: Civilization/culture, German language (int/adv), German studies
Eligibility: *Level:* fresh, sophs, jrs, srs, grads, adults *Requires:* 1 yr coll or 2 yrs high sch German
Credit: *Undergrad:* 9 *Grad:* 6 *Doc:* transcript
Instruction: *In:* German *Format:* lang study, lecture *Students:* mainly US
Costs: $3,400 for NY resident undergrads (9 credits) *incl* tuition, housing, all meals, insurance, excursions *Nonrefundable fee*
Housing: *Arr by pgm:* homestay
Deadline: Mar 1 or until pgm filled
Other info: *US accredited sponsor:* yes *Began:* 1971 *Orient:* abroad *Activities:* field trips, program travel *Misc:* Loans avail. *Financial aid:* scholarships *URL:* http://www.newpaltz.edu/oie/
Contact: Ctr for Intl Pgms, SUNY New Paltz, 75 S Manheim Blvd, Ste 9, New Paltz NY 12561 *Ph:* 914-257 3125 *Fax:* 914-257 3129 *E-mail:* international@newpaltz.edu ▲

0811
UNIVERSITY OF ROCHESTER
Internships in Europe-Germany
Site: Germany: Berlin, Bonn, Cologne
Dates: 8 wks, May 28-Jul 22
Subjects: Business/management, Homestay, Internships, Law, Museology, Political science/politics, Psychology, Social sciences, Theater arts
Eligibility: *Level:* jrs, srs, grads *Requires:* 3.0 GPA, 2 yrs coll German *Age:* avg 20
Credit: *Undergrad:* 8 *Grad:* none *Doc:* transcript
Instruction: *In:* German *Format:* internship *Students:* mainly US
Costs: $5,290 *incl* tuition, housing, some meals, fees
Housing: *Sponsor assists:* apartments, homestay
Deadline: Mar 1
Other info: *US accredited sponsor:* yes *Began:* 1981 *Orient:* abroad (1 wk, intensive lang study) *Activities:* excursions *Misc:* May contact former participants. *URL:* http://www.rochester.edu/College/study-abroad/sa/global.html
Contact: Jacqueline Levine, Ctr for Study Abroad, Univ of Rochester, Lattimore 206, PO Box 270376, Rochester NY 14627-0376 *Ph:* 716-275 7532 *Fax:* 716-461 5131 *E-mail:* csaip@cc.mail.edu

---

AUGSBURG

0812
UNIVERSITY OF PITTSBURGH
Pitt in Germany
Site: Germany: Augsburg *Host inst:* Univ of Augsburg
Dates: 3 mos, early May-late Jul
Subjects: Civilization/culture, German language, German studies
Eligibility: Own students only. *Level:* sophs, jrs, srs *Requires:* 3.0 GPA, previous study in field, 2 yrs coll German
Credit: *Undergrad:* 6-8 credits *Grad:* none *Doc:* transcript
Instruction: *In:* German *Format:* lab, lang study, lecture, seminar, tutorial *Students:* mainly host country
Costs: About $3,610 *incl* tuition, housing, all meals, intl airfare, insurance, fees, books/materials *Nonrefundable fee*
Housing: *Arr by pgm:* residence halls with local students
Deadline: Oct 13
Other info: *US accredited sponsor:* yes *Orient:* in US *Misc:* Scholarships for own students only. Loans & grants avail. May contact former participants. *Financial aid:* scholarships *URL:* http://www.pitt.edu/~stdyabrd/
Contact: Jennifer Sill, Study Abroad, Univ of Pittsburgh, Pittsburgh PA 15260 *Ph:* 412-648 2299 *Fax:* 412-383 7166 *E-mail:* jsill+@pitt.edu

---

BAYREUTH

0813
UNIVERSITY OF DELAWARE
Winter Session in Bayreuth
Site: Germany: Bayreuth *Host inst:* Univ of Bayreuth
Dates: 1 mo, Jan
Subjects: Civilization/culture, German language (int), Homestay
Eligibility: *Level:* fresh, sophs, jrs, srs, adults *Requires:* 2.0 GPA, 1 sem coll German or equiv
Credit: *Undergrad:* 6-7 *Grad:* none *Doc:* transcript
Instruction: *In:* English, German *Format:* lang study, lecture, study tour *Students:* mainly US
Costs: Contact sponsor
Housing: *Arr by pgm:* homestay
Deadline: Early Oct
Other info: *US accredited sponsor:* yes

Began: 1988 *Orient:* avail yes *Activities:* excursions, field trips, program travel, cultural events *Misc:* Contact sponsor to arrange honors credit. May contact former participants. *Financial aid:* scholarships *URL:* http://www.udel.edu/studyabroad/
Contact: Lisa Chieffo, Study Abroad Coord, Foreign Langs & Literatures, Univ of Delaware, 326 Smith Hall, Newark DE 19716 *Ph:* 302-831 6458 *Fax:* 302-831 0597 *E-mail:* lchieffo@udel.edu
Or Contact: Intl Pgms & Special Sessions, Univ of Delaware, 4 Kent Way, Newark DE 19716 *Ph:* 888-831 4685; 302-831 2852 *Fax:* 302-831 6042 *E-mail:* studyabroad@udel.edu

---

BERLIN

0814
DIE NEUE SCHULE
German Language Courses
Site: Germany: Berlin
Dates: 2 wks or longer, yr-round
Subjects: German language (beg/int)
Eligibility: *Level:* adults *Age:* min 15, max 60, avg 25
Credit: *Undergrad:* none *Grad:* none *Doc:* certificate
Instruction: *In:* German *Format:* lang study *Students:* intl
Costs: Contact sponsor
Housing: *Arr by pgm:* homestay
Deadline: Contact sponsor
Other info: *US accredited sponsor:* no *Began:* 1986 *Activities:* excursions *Misc:* May contact former participants. *URL:* http://www.neueschule.de
Contact: Ms Ulrike Laule, Dir, Die Neue Schule, Gieselerstr 30A, 10713 Berlin, Germany *E-mail:* info@neueschule.de

---

0815
FREIE UNIVERSITAET BERLIN
International Summer University - FUBIS
Site: Germany: Berlin
Dates: 4 wks, Jul 21-Aug 17
Subjects: Architectural history, Art history, Creative writing, Environmental law, Film studies, German language (beg/int/adv), German studies, History, Law, Literature, Political science/politics, Social history, Urban studies
Eligibility: *Level:* sophs, jrs, srs, grads, adults, teachers *Requires:* 2.5 GPA, 2 yrs coll
Credit: *Undergrad:* avail *Grad:* avail *Doc:* transcript
Instruction: *In:* English *Format:* lecture, seminar, study tour *Students:* US & intl
Costs: About DM 2,500 for 1 course, DM 3,700 for 2 courses *incl* tuition, housing, all meals, fees, excursions, books/materials *Nonrefundable fee*
Housing: *Arr by pgm:* apartments
Deadline: May 15
Other info: *US accredited sponsor:* no *Began:* 1998 *Orient:* abroad *Activities:* excursions, field trips, cultural events, sports *Misc:* May contact former participants. *Financial aid:* scholarships *URL:* http://www.fu-berlin.de/summeruniversity/
Contact: Jens Westerfeld, Freie Univ Berlin, Intl Off, Kaiserswerther Str, 16 - 18, Berlin, Germany 14195 *E-mail:* fusummer@zedat.fu-berlin.de

---

0816
GLS SPRACHENZENTRUM
German Language Course and Work Experience in Berlin
Site: Germany: Berlin *Host inst:* Bosch, Deutsche Welle TV, Lufthansa Servicegesellschaft, others
Dates: 8 wks, yr-round
Subjects: German language, Internships
Eligibility: Own students only. *Level:* sophs, grads, adults, professionals *Age:* min 20, max 35, avg 23
Credit: *Undergrad:* none *Grad:* none *Doc:* certificate
Instruction: *In:* German *Format:* lang study, practical training *Students:* intl
Costs: Contact sponsor
Housing: *Arr by pgm:* apartments with local students, homestay
Deadline: Contact sponsor
Other info: *US accredited sponsor:* no *Began:* 1996 *Orient:* abroad *Misc:* Pgm begins with 4-wk min German lang course. Interview at host company. *URL:* http://www.german-courses.com

---

0817
GLS SPRACHENZENTRUM
Learn German and Discover Berlin Language Programs/Internships
Site: Germany: Berlin
Dates: 1 wk or longer, yr-round
Subjects: Business language, German language (beg/int/adv), Internships
Eligibility: *Level:* jrs, srs, adults, teachers, professionals *Age:* min 16, avg 25
Credit: *Undergrad:* none *Grad:* none *Doc:* certificate
Instruction: *In:* German *Format:* directed field study, independent study, lang study, practical training *Students:* intl
Costs: About $510 for 2 wks, $950 for 1 mo *incl* tuition, housing, books/materials, activities
Housing: *Arr by pgm:* residence halls with local students, apartments, homestay, pensions, hotels, bed & breakfasts
Deadline: None
Other info: *US accredited sponsor:* no *Began:* 1983 *Orient:* abroad *Activities:* excursions *Misc:* Some Univ may grant credit. May contact former participants. *URL:* http://www.gls-berlin.com
Contact: Barbara Jaeschke, Managing Dir, or Susanne Thiessen, GLS Sprachenzentrum, Kolonnenstr 26, 10829 Berlin, Germany *E-mail:* gls.berlin@t-online.de

---

0818
LEXIA INTERNATIONAL
LEXIA Summer in Berlin
Site: Germany: Berlin *Host inst:* Freie Univ Berlin
Dates: 8 wks, mid-Jun-mid-Aug
Subjects: Anthropology, Arts, Civilization/culture, Ecology/environmental studies, Economics, Fine arts, German language (beg/int/adv), German studies, History, Homestay, Internships, Literature, Political science/politics, Sociology
Eligibility: *Level:* fresh, sophs, jrs, srs, grads, adults *Requires:* 2.5 GPA *Age:* min 18, avg 21
Credit: *Undergrad:* 8-10 *Grad:* 8-10 *Doc:* transcript *Transfer credit through:* Western Washington Univ
Instruction: *In:* English, German *Format:* internship, lang study, lecture, seminar, volunteer/svc *Students:* mainly US
Costs: $4,950 *incl* tuition, housing, insurance, fees, excursions, ISIC *Nonrefundable fee*
Housing: *Arr by pgm:* apartments, homestay
Deadline: Apr 15; Apr 1 for scholarships
Other info: *US accredited sponsor:* no *Began:* 1995 *In coop with:* Western Washington Univ *Orient:* abroad *Activities:* excursions, field trips, program travel, cultural events, sports *Misc:* Student support svcs. May contact former participants. *Financial aid:* scholarships, work study *URL:* http://www.lexiaintl.org
Contact: LEXIA Intl, 25 S Main St, Hanover NH 03755 *Ph:* 800-775 3942; 603-643 9898 *Fax:* 603-643 9899 *E-mail:* info@lexiaintl.org
Or Contact: LEXIA Intl, West Coast, 378 Cambridge Ave, Palo Alto CA 94306-1544 *Ph:* 650-327 9191 *Fax:* 650-327 9192

0819
NATIONAL REGISTRATION CENTER FOR STUDY ABROAD (NRCSA)
German in Berlin
Site: Germany: Berlin *Host inst:* GLS Sprachen Zentrum
Dates: 8 wks, Jan-Oct
Subjects: German language (beg/int/adv)
Eligibility: *Level:* fresh, sophs, jrs, srs, grads, adults, teachers, professionals *Age:* min 18

Credit: *Undergrad:* avail *Grad:* avail *Doc:* certificate
Instruction: *In:* German *Format:* lang study, lecture *Students:* intl
Costs: $2,077 *incl* tuition, housing, insurance *Nonrefundable fee*
Housing: *Arr by pgm:* apartments with local students
Deadline: 6 wks before pgm
Other info: *US accredited sponsor:* no *Activities:* field trips *Misc:* May contact former participants. *URL:* http://www.nrcsa.com
Contact: Reuel Zielke, NRCSA, 823 N 2nd St, #206, Milwaukee WI 53203 *Ph:* 414-278 0631 *Fax:* 414-271 8884 *E-mail:* info@nrcsa.com

---

0820
STUDIENFORUM BERLIN
Intensive German Language in Berlin
Site: Germany: Berlin
Dates: 4-8 wks, beg Apr 29
Subjects: German language (beg/int/adv), Homestay
Eligibility: *Level:* sophs, jrs, srs, grads *Requires:* 2.5 GPA, 2 sems coll German *Age:* min 18
Credit: *Undergrad:* none *Grad:* none *Doc:* certificate
Instruction: *In:* English, German *Format:* lang study *Students:* intl
Costs: $1,800 per mo *incl* tuition, housing, some meals, insurance, fees, excursions, books/materials, local transport *Nonrefundable fee*
Housing: *Arr by pgm:* homestay, pensions, hostels
Deadline: 10 wks before pgm
Other info: *US accredited sponsor:* no *Began:* 1998 *In coop with:* Die Neue Sch Berlin *Orient:* abroad (1 day, intensive lang study) *Activities:* excursions, field trips, cultural events *URL:* http://www.studienforum-berlin.de
Contact: Prof Hanns D Jacobsen, Studienforum Berlin, Haupstr 74, D-12159 Berlin-Friedenau, Germany *E-mail:* jacobsfb@zedat.fu-berlin.de

---

0821
UNIVERSITY OF HAWAII AT MANOA
German Language and Culture in Berlin
Site: Germany: Berlin *Host inst:* Studienforum Berlin
Dates: 5 wks, mid-Jul-mid-Aug
Subjects: Civilization/culture, German language (int/adv)
Eligibility: *Level:* sophs, jrs, srs *Requires:* 3.0 GPA, 1 yr German
Credit: *Undergrad:* 6 *Grad:* none *Doc:* transcript
Instruction: *In:* German *Format:* lang study, lecture *Students:* US & intl
Costs: $4,813 *incl* tuition, housing, some meals, intl airfare, fees, excursions, metro pass *Nonrefundable fee*
Housing: *Arr by pgm:* residence halls
Deadline: Feb 17
Other info: *US accredited sponsor:* yes *Began:* 1994 *Orient:* in US & abroad *Activities:* excursions, field trips, cultural events *Misc:* UHM financial aid avail to eligible UHM students. *URL:* http://www2.hawaii.edu/study-abroad
Contact: Dir or Study Abroad Adviser, Study Abroad Ctr, Univ of Hawaii at Manoa, Moore Hall 115, 1890 East-West Rd, Honolulu HI 96822 *Ph:* 808-956 5143, 808-956 6958 *Fax:* 808-956 9319 *E-mail:* uhmsac@hawaii.edu

---

0822
UNIVERSITY OF ROCHESTER
German in Germany
Site: Germany: Berlin *Host inst:* Studienforum Berlin
Dates: 4 wks, Jun 1-30
Subjects: German language
Eligibility: *Level:* fresh, sophs, jrs, srs, adults *Requires:* previous study in field, 3 yrs high sch or 1 yr coll German
Credit: *Undergrad:* 6 *Grad:* none *Doc:* transcript
Instruction: *In:* German *Format:* lang study *Students:* mainly US
Costs: About $3,000 *incl* tuition, housing, some meals, excursions
Housing: *Arr by pgm:* hostels
Deadline: Mar 15
Other info: *US accredited sponsor:* yes *Activities:* cultural events *URL:* http://www.rochester.edu/College/study-abroad/sa/global.html
Contact: Anne Lutkus, Modern Langs & Cultures, Univ of Rochester, Lattimore 403, Rochester NY 14627 *Ph:* 716-275 2235 *E-mail:* adlt@mail.cc.rochester.edu

---

0823
UNIVERSITY OF SOUTH FLORIDA
USF in Berlin
Site: Germany: Berlin
Dates: 4 wks, Jul-Aug
Subjects: Civilization/culture, German language, German studies
Eligibility: *Level:* fresh, sophs, jrs, srs, adults, teachers, professionals *Requires:* 2.0 GPA *Age:* min 18, avg 25
Credit: *Undergrad:* 6 *Grad:* none *Doc:* transcript, certificate
Instruction: *In:* English, German *Format:* directed field study, lang study, lecture *Students:* mainly US
Costs: $2,100 *incl* tuition, housing, insurance, fees, excursions, books/materials, local trasportation pass *Nonrefundable fee*
Housing: *Arr by pgm:* apartments with local students
Deadline: Apr 30
Other info: *US accredited sponsor:* yes *Began:* 2000 *In coop with:* GLS-Sprachenzentrum *Orient:* in US & abroad *Activities:* excursions, field trips *Misc:* May contact former participants.
Contact: James Pulos, USF Overseas St;udy Pgms, 4202 E Fowler Ave, CPR 107, Tampa FL 33620-5550 *Ph:* 813-974 4043 *Fax:* 813-974 4613 *E-mail:* jpulos@iac.usf.edu
Or Contact: Brendan Calandra, USF Overseas St;udy Pgms, 4202 E Fowler Ave, CPR 107, Tampa 33620-5550 *Ph:* 813-974 4043 *Fax:* 813-974 4613 *E-mail:* bcalaldr@luna.cas.usf.edu

---

0824
UNIVERSITY OF UTAH
Free University of Berlin International Summer University
Site: Germany: Berlin *Host inst:* Free Univ Berlin
Dates: 4 wks, Jul-Aug
Subjects: Architecture, Art history, Film studies, History, Literature, Political science/politics
Eligibility: *Level:* sophs, jrs, srs, adults, teachers, professionals *Requires:* 3.0 GPA *Age:* min 18, avg 22
Credit: *Undergrad:* avail *Grad:* none *Doc:* transcript
Instruction: *In:* English *Format:* lecture *Students:* mainly US
Costs: $2,400 *incl* tuition, housing, fees, excursions
Housing: *Arr by pgm:* residence halls
Deadline: Mar 15
Other info: *US accredited sponsor:* yes *Began:* 2000 *Orient:* in US *Activities:* excursions, field trips *Misc:* Financial aid for own students only. May contact former participants. *Financial aid:* scholarships *URL:* http://www.saff.utah.edu/inter
Contact: Aaron Rose, Univ of Utah, 200 S Central Campus Dr #159, Salt Lake City UT 84112 *Ph:* 801-581 5849 *Fax:* 801-581 5914 *E-mail:* arose@saff.utah.edu

---

BRAUNSCHWEIG

0825
SUNY UNIVERSITY AT ALBANY
Language and Cultural Studies in Braunschweig
Site: Germany: Braunschweig *Host inst:* Technische Univ Carolo-Wilhelmina
Dates: 6 wks, Jul-Aug
Subjects: Civilization/culture, German language (int/adv), Homestay
Eligibility: *Level:* fresh, sophs, jrs, srs,

grads *Requires:* high sch degree, very good acad standing, 1 yr coll German
Credit: *Undergrad:* 6 *Grad:* none *Doc:* transcript
Instruction: *In:* German *Students:* mainly US
Costs: About $2,012 for NY residents *incl* tuition, housing, all meals, insurance, student support svcs *Nonrefundable fee*
Housing: *Arr by pgm:* residence halls, homestay
Deadline: April 1 or until pgm filled
Other info: *US accredited sponsor:* yes *Began:* 1981 *Orient:* in US *Misc:* May contact former participants. *URL:* http://www.albany.edu/intled
Contact: Joan N Savitt, Intl Pgms, SUNY Univ at Albany, LI-66, Albany NY 12222 *Ph:* 518-442 3525 *Fax:* 518-442 3338 *E-mail:* intled@uamail.albany.edu

---

0826
TECHNISCHE UNIVERSITAET BRAUNSCHWEIG, SPRACHENZENTRUM
International Summer Course A: German Language and Culture
Site: Germany: Braunschweig
Dates: 6 wks, Jul 16-Aug 24
Subjects: Civilization/culture, German language, German studies
Eligibility: *Level:* fresh, sophs, jrs, srs, grads, adults, teachers, professionals *Requires:* previous study in field, basic knowledge of German *Age:* min 18, avg 23
Credit: *Undergrad:* avail *Grad:* none *Doc:* certificate
Instruction: *In:* German *Format:* lang study, lecture, study tour *Students:* intl
Costs: DM 2,190 *incl* tuition, housing, fees, excursions, books/materials *Nonrefundable fee*
Housing: *Arr by pgm:* apartments with local students, residence halls with local students, homestay
Deadline: May 31
Other info: *US accredited sponsor:* no *Began:* 1982 *Activities:* excursions, field trips *Misc:* 20th anniversary of pgm with special events & activities. *URL:* http://www.tu-bs.de/sz/
Contact: Christina Neidert, Sprachenzentrum der TU, Pockelsstr 4, D-38106 Braunschweig, Germany *E-mail:* sommerkurs@tu-bs.de

---

0827
TECHNISCHE UNIVERSITAET BRAUNSCHWEIG, SPRACHENZENTRUM
International Summer Course B: German Language and Culture
Site: Germany: Braunschweig
Dates: 3 wks, Jul 16 - Aug 3
Subjects: Civilization/culture, German language, German studies, History, Political science/politics, Sociology
Eligibility: *Level:* fresh, sophs, jrs, srs, grads, adults, teachers, professionals *Age:* min 18, avg 23
Credit: *Undergrad:* avail *Grad:* none *Doc:* certificate *Transfer credit through:* SUNY Univ at Albany
Instruction: *In:* German *Format:* lang study, lecture, study tour *Students:* intl
Costs: DM 1,250 *incl* tuition, housing, fees, excursions, books/materials
Housing: *Arr by pgm:* apartments with local students, residence halls with local students, homestay
Deadline: May 31
Other info: *US accredited sponsor:* no *Began:* 1982 *Misc:* 20th anniversary of the summer courses with a special jubilee pgm & special events, parties. *URL:* http://www.tu-bs.de/sz/
Contact: Christina Neidert, Coord, Sprachenzentrum der TU, Pockelsstr 4, D-38106 Braunschweig, Germany *E-mail:* sommerkurs@tu-bs.de

---

0828
TECHNISCHE UNIVERSITAET BRAUNSCHWEIG, SPRACHENZENTRUM
International Summer Course C: German Language and Culture
Site: Germany: Braunschweig
Dates: 3 wks, Aug 6-24
Subjects: Civilization/culture, German language
Eligibility: *Level:* fresh, sophs, jrs, srs, grads, adults, teachers, professionals *Requires:* beg German *Age:* min 18, avg 23
Credit: *Undergrad:* avail *Grad:* none
Instruction: *In:* German *Format:* lang study, lecture, study tour *Students:* intl
Costs: DM 1,250 *incl* tuition, housing, fees, excursions, books/materials
Housing: *Arr by pgm:* apartments with local students, residence halls with local students, homestay
Deadline: May 31
Other info: *US accredited sponsor:* no *Began:* 1982 *Misc:* 20th anniversary of the Intl Summer courses. Special pgm, special events. *URL:* http://www.tu-bs.de/sz/
Contact: Christina Neidert, Coord, Sprachenzentrum der TU, Pockelsstr 4, D-38106 Braunschweig, Germany *E-mail:* c.neidert@tu-bs.de

---

0829
TECHNISCHE UNIVERSITAET BRAUNSCHWEIG, SPRACHENZENTRUM
International Summer Course D: German in Science/Technology
Site: Germany: Braunschweig
Dates: 4 wks, Sep 17-Oct 12
Subjects: Civilization/culture, German language, Technical language
Eligibility: *Level:* fresh, sophs, jrs, srs, grads, adults, teachers, professionals *Requires:* basic knowledge of German *Age:* min 18, avg 23
Credit: *Undergrad:* avail *Grad:* none *Doc:* certificate
Instruction: *In:* German *Format:* lang study, lecture, study tour *Students:* intl
Costs: DM 1,620 *incl* tuition, housing, fees, excursions, books/materials *Nonrefundable fee*
Housing: *Arr by pgm:* residence halls with local students, homestay
Deadline: Jun 30
Other info: *US accredited sponsor:* no *Began:* 1991 *Activities:* excursions, field trips, cultural events, sports *URL:* http://www.tu-bs.de/sz/
Contact: Christina Neidert, Sprachenzentrum der TU, Pockelsstr 4, D-38106 Braunschweig, Germany *E-mail:* c.neidert@tu-bs.de

---

BREMEN

0830
DICKINSON COLLEGE
Bremen Physics Program
Site: Germany: Bremen *Host inst:* Univ Bremen
Dates: 5 wks, late May-late Jun
Subjects: Physics
Eligibility: *Level:* fresh, sophs, jrs *Requires:* beg German, completion of PHYS 131 & 132
Credit: *Undergrad:* avail *Grad:* none
Instruction: *In:* English *Format:* seminar *Students:* intl
Costs: About $3,950 *incl* tuition, housing, all meals, intl airfare, fees, excursions *Nonrefundable fee*
Housing: *Arr by pgm:* homestay
Deadline: Mar 1
Other info: *US accredited sponsor:* yes *Began:* 2000 *In coop with:* Univ Bremen *Orient:* in US & abroad *Activities:* excursions *URL:* http://www.dickinson.edu/departments/ocs/abroad.html
Contact: Global Educ, Dickinson Coll, PO Box 1773, Carlisle PA 17013-2896 *Ph:* 717-245 1341 *Fax:* 717-245 1688 *E-mail:* ocs@dickinson.edu

---

0831
DICKINSON COLLEGE
Bremen Summer Immersion Program
Site: Germany: Bremen *Host inst:* Univ of Bremen
Dates: 5 wks, late May-early Jul
Subjects: Civilization/culture, German language (int/adv)

Eligibility: *Level:* fresh, sophs *Requires:* 2 yrs coll German
Credit: *Undergrad:* 4 *Grad:* none
Instruction: *In:* German *Format:* lang study, lecture *Students:* mainly US
Costs: About $3,950 *incl* tuition, housing, all meals, intl airfare, fees, excursions
Housing: *Arr by pgm:* homestay
Deadline: Mar 1
Other info: *US accredited sponsor:* yes *Began:* 1984 *Orient:* in US *Activities:* excursions *Misc:* Exclusive use of German during pgm. *URL:* http://www.dickinson.edu/departments/ocs/summer.html
Contact: Global Educ, Dickinson Coll, PO Box 1773, Carlisle PA 17013-2896 *Ph:* 717-245 1341 *Fax:* 717-245 1688 *E-mail:* ocs@dickinson.edu

COLOGNE

0832
TEXAS CHRISTIAN UNIVERSITY
TCU Summer in Germany
Site: Germany: Cologne
Dates: Jun 1-30
Subjects: German language (beg), Homestay, International business
Eligibility: *Level:* jrs, srs, grads *Requires:* 2.75 GPA, for undergrads, 3.0 GPA for grads; bus majors/minors preferred
Credit: *Undergrad:* 6 *Grad:* 6
Instruction: *In:* English *Format:* lang study, lecture, study tour *Students:* mainly US
Costs: About $4,600 *incl* tuition, housing, some meals, insurance, fees, excursions, Eurailpass
Housing: *Arr by pgm:* homestay
Deadline: Mar 15
Other info: *US accredited sponsor:* yes *Began:* 1969 *In coop with:* Carl Duisberg Socy *Orient:* in US *Activities:* field trips *Misc:* May contact former participants. *URL:* http://www.neeley.tcu.edu
Contact: Jan Titsworth, Asst Dean, Neeley Sch of Bus, Texas Christian Univ, PO Box 298530, Ft Worth TX 76129 *Ph:* 817-257 7527 *Fax:* 817-257 6049 *E-mail:* k.dill@tcu.edu

DUSSELDORF

0833
LANGUAGES PLUS
Language Immersion and Cultural Program-Dusseldorf
Site: Germany: Dusseldorf
Dates: 2 wks or longer, summer
Subjects: German language (beg/int/adv), Homestay
Eligibility: *Level:* adults *Age:* min 17, max 65, avg 24
Credit: *Undergrad:* none *Grad:* none *Doc:* certificate
Instruction: *In:* German *Format:* lang study *Students:* intl
Costs: From $700 for 2 wks *incl* tuition, housing, books/materials, cultural activities
Housing: *Arr by pgm:* apartments, homestay
Deadline: 2 wks before pgm
Other info: *US accredited sponsor:* no *Activities:* excursions, field trips *Misc:* May contact former participants. *URL:* http://www.languagesplus.com
Contact: Margot Haldenby, North Amer Enrollment, Langs Plus, 317 Adelaide St W, Ste 900, Toronto, Ontario M5V 1P9, Canada *Ph:* 888-526 4758; 416-925 7117 *Fax:* 416-925 5990 *E-mail:* info@languagesplus.com

ERLANGEN

0834
DUKE UNIVERSITY
Duke in Erlangen
Site: Germany: Erlangen (Nuernberg) *Host inst:* Friedrich-Alexander-Univ
Dates: Mid-May-late Jun
Subjects: Civilization/culture, German language (int/adv)
Eligibility: *Level:* fresh, sophs, jrs, srs *Requires:* 2 sems coll German, good acad standing, transcript
Credit: *Undergrad:* 2 credits *Grad:* none *Doc:* transcript
Instruction: *In:* German *Format:* lang study, lecture *Students:* mainly US
Costs: $4,825 for 2 courses *incl* tuition, housing, all meals, excursions
Housing: *Arr by pgm:* homestay
Deadline: Feb 16
Other info: *US accredited sponsor:* yes *Began:* 1981 *Activities:* excursions, program travel *URL:* http://www.aas.duke.edu/study_abroad/
Contact: Study Abroad, Duke Univ, 121 Allen Bldg, Box 90057, Durham NC 27708-0057 *Ph:* 919-684 2174 *Fax:* 919-684 3083 *E-mail:* abroad@asdean.duke.edu

EUTIN

0835
UNIVERSITY OF KANSAS
Summer Language and Culture Institute in Eutin, Germany
Site: Germany: Eutin
Dates: 8 wks, late May-mid-Jul
Subjects: Civilization/culture, German language (int)
Eligibility: *Level:* fresh, sophs, jrs, srs, grads *Requires:* 2 sems coll German
Credit: *Undergrad:* 9 *Grad:* none *Doc:* transcript
Instruction: *In:* German *Format:* lang study, lecture, study tour *Students:* mainly US
Costs: $3,250 *incl* tuition, housing, all meals, fees, excursions, cultural events, tour
Housing: *Arr by pgm:* homestay, hotels during tour
Deadline: Rolling admissions
Other info: *US accredited sponsor:* yes *Began:* 1963 *Activities:* program travel, cultural events *Misc:* Study tour incl visits to Berlin, Hamburg, Kiel, Lubeck, Mainz, Munich. *URL:* http://www.ukans.edu/~osa
Contact: Susan MacNally, Asst Dir, Study Abroad, Univ of Kansas, 108 Lippincott Hall, Lawrence KS 66045 *Ph:* 785-864 3742 *Fax:* 785-864 5040 *E-mail:* osa@ukans.edu ▲

FRANKFURT

0836
LANGUAGES ABROAD
Language and Cultural Immersion Programs-Frankfurt
Site: Germany: Frankfurt
Dates: 2 wks or longer, yr-round
Subjects: Civilization/culture, German language (beg/int/adv)
Eligibility: *Level:* adults *Age:* min 17, max 65, avg 25
Credit: *Undergrad:* none *Grad:* none *Doc:* certificate
Instruction: *In:* German *Format:* lang study *Students:* intl
Costs: $1,315 for 4 wks *incl* tuition, housing, some meals, excursions, books/materials
Housing: *Arr by pgm:* apartments, homestay
Deadline: None
Other info: *US accredited sponsor:* no *Misc:* May contact former participants. *URL:* http://www.languagesabroad.com
Contact: Ms Jesse Philippe, Langs Abroad, 317 Adelaide St W, Ste 900, Toronto, Ontario M5V 1P9, Canada *Ph:* 800-219 9924; 416-925 7117 *E-mail:* info@languagesabroad.com

0837
LANGUAGES PLUS
Language Immersion and Cultural Program-Frankfurt
Site: Germany: Frankfurt
Dates: 2 wks or longer, yr-round
Subjects: German language (beg/int/adv), Homestay
Eligibility: *Level:* adults *Age:* min 17, max 65, avg 24

Credit: *Undergrad:* none *Grad:* none *Doc:* certificate
Instruction: *In:* German *Format:* lang study *Students:* intl
Costs: From $700 for 2 wks *incl* tuition, housing, books/materials, cultural activities
Housing: *Arr by pgm:* apartments, homestay
Deadline: 2 wks before pgm
Other info: *US accredited sponsor:* no *Activities:* excursions, field trips *Misc:* May contact former participants. *URL:* http://www.languagesplus.com
Contact: Margot Haldenby, North Amer Enrollment, Langs Plus, 317 Adelaide St W, Ste 900, Toronto, Ontario M5V 1P9, Canada *Ph:* 888-526 4758; 416-925 7117 *Fax:* 416-925 5990 *E-mail:* info@languagesplus.com

FREIBURG

0838
UNIVERSITY OF PENNSYLVANIA
Penn-in-Germany
Site: Germany: Freiburg
Dates: 5-1/2 wks, late Jul-Aug
Subjects: German language (int)
Eligibility: *Level:* fresh, sophs, jrs, srs, professionals *Requires:* beg German
Credit: *Undergrad:* 6-8 *Grad:* avail *Doc:* transcript
Instruction: *In:* German *Format:* lang study, lecture *Students:* mainly US
Costs: About $4,500 *incl* tuition, housing, excursions *Nonrefundable fee*
Housing: *Arr by pgm:* residence halls
Deadline: Apr 1
Other info: *US accredited sponsor:* yes *Began:* 1977 *Orient:* in US & abroad *Misc:* May contact former participants. *URL:* http://www.sas.upenn.edu/CGS/
Contact: Elizabeth Sachs, Penn Summer Abroad, Univ of Pennsylvania, 3440 Market St, Ste 100, Philadelphia PA 19104-3335 *Ph:* 215-898 5738 *Fax:* 215-573 2053 *E-mail:* sdanti@mail.sas.upenn.edu

HAMBURG

0839
NATIONAL REGISTRATION CENTER FOR STUDY ABROAD (NRCSA)
Study German in Hamburg
Site: Germany: Hamburg *Host inst:* Colon Lang Ctr
Dates: 2 wks or longer, yr-round
Subjects: German language, Homestay
Eligibility: *Level:* fresh, sophs, jrs, srs, grads, adults, teachers, professionals
Credit: *Undergrad:* none *Grad:* none *Doc:* certificate
Instruction: *In:* German *Format:* lang study, lecture, tutorial *Students:* intl
Costs: $1,449 for 4 wks *incl* tuition, housing, some meals, insurance *Nonrefundable fee*
Housing: *Arr by pgm:* homestay
Deadline: 6 wks before pgm
Other info: *US accredited sponsor:* no *Misc:* May contact former participants. *URL:* http://www.nrcsa.com
Contact: Reuel Zielke, NRCSA, 823 N 2nd St, #206, Milwaukee WI 53203 *Ph:* 414-278 0631 *Fax:* 414-271 8884 *E-mail:* info@nrcsa.com

HAMMINKELN

0840
AKADEMIE KLAUSENHOF
German as a Foreign Language
Site: Germany: Hamminkeln
Dates: 2-6 mos, yr-round
Subjects: German language (beg/int)
Eligibility: *Level:* adults, precoll *Age:* min 18, avg 25
Credit: *Undergrad:* none *Grad:* none *Doc:* certificate
Instruction: *In:* German *Format:* lang study *Students:* intl
Costs: DM 3,240 for 2 mos *incl* tuition, housing, all meals, books/materials
Housing: *Arr by pgm:* residence halls
Deadline: None
Other info: *US accredited sponsor:* no *Began:* 1959 *Activities:* excursions, cultural events, sports *URL:* http://www.akademie-klausenhof.de
Contact: Claudia Schottler, Akad Klausenhof, Klausenhofstr 100, D-46499 Hamminkeln-Dingden, Germany *E-mail:* akademie.klausenhof@t-online.de

HANNOVER

0841
SOUTHWEST TEXAS STATE UNIVERSITY
SWT in Hannover, Germany Exchange Program
Site: Germany: Hannover *Host inst:* Univ Hannover
Dates: 4 wks, summer
Subjects: German studies
Eligibility: *Level:* adults
Credit: *Undergrad:* 6 *Grad:* none
Instruction: *In:* German *Format:* lecture, seminar *Students:* mainly US
Costs: $2,300 *incl* tuition, housing, intl airfare, books/materials, ground transport
Housing: *Arr by pgm:* apartments with local students
Deadline: Contact sponsor
Other info: *US accredited sponsor:* yes *Began:* 1991 *Orient:* in US *Activities:* excursions, field trips *Misc:* May contact former participants. *Financial aid:* scholarships *URL:* http://www.ideal.swt.edu/extension/study_abroad/
Contact: Stephanie Ortega, Modern Langs, Southwest Texas State Univ, 601 University Dr, San Marcos TX 78666 *Ph:* 512-245 2360 *Fax:* 512-245 8298
Or Contact: Isis de la O Gomez, Extension Studies Coord, Southwest Texas State Univ, 601 University Dr, San Marcos TX 78666 *Ph:* 512-245 2322 *Fax:* 512-245 8934 *E-mail:* jp11@swt.edu

HEIDELBERG

0842
COLLEGE CONSORTIUM FOR INTERNATIONAL STUDIES and **OCEAN COUNTY COLLEGE**
Summer Intensive German Language Program
Site: Germany: Heidelberg *Host inst:* Collegium Palatinum
Dates: Two 8-wk terms, May-Jun & Jun-Aug
Subjects: German language (beg/int/adv)
Eligibility: *Level:* fresh, sophs, jrs, srs, grads *Requires:* 3.0 GPA, 2 recommendations *Age:* min 18
Credit: *Undergrad:* 12 per term *Grad:* none *Doc:* transcript, certificate
Instruction: *In:* German *Format:* lang study, lecture *Students:* intl
Costs: About $3,595 for 8 wks *incl* tuition, housing, fees, excursions
Housing: *Arr by pgm:* residence halls
Deadline: 45 days before pgm
Other info: *US accredited sponsor:* yes *Began:* 1977 *Orient:* abroad *Activities:* field trips *Misc:* Loans & federal financial aid. *URL:* http://www.ccisabroad.org
Contact: *See Index II for Members* CCIS, 2000 P St NW, Ste 503, Washington DC 20036 *Ph:* 800-453 6956; 202-223 0330 *Fax:* 202-223 0999 *E-mail:* info@ccisabroad.org
Or Contact: Dr William Lavundi, Dir, Intl Educ, Ocean CC, College Dr, PO Box 2001, Toms River NJ 08754-2001 *Ph:* 877-588 4324 *Fax:* 732-255 0524 *E-mail:* wlavundi@ocean.cc.nj.us ▲

0843
INTERNATIONAL COUNCIL FOR CULTURAL EXCHANGE (ICCE)
German Language and Culture
Site: Germany: Heidelberg *Host inst:* Univ of Heidelberg
Dates: 3-6 wks, Jul & Aug
Subjects: Civilization/culture, Field study, German language (beg/int/adv), Homestay
Eligibility: *Level:* fresh, sophs, jrs, srs,

grads, adults, teachers, professionals, precoll
Credit: *Undergrad:* avail *Grad:* avail *Doc:* transcript, certificate
Instruction: *In:* English, German *Format:* directed field study, lab, lang study, lecture, practical training, study tour *Students:* intl
Costs: Contact sponsor
Housing: *Sponsor assists:* residence halls, homestay, hotels, hostels
Deadline: 1 mo before pgm
Other info: *US accredited sponsor:* no *Began:* 1982 *Orient:* abroad *Activities:* excursions, program travel, cultural events, sports
Contact: Dr Stanley Gochman, ICCE, 5 Bellport Ln, Bellport NY 11713 *Ph:* 631-286 5228 ▲

0844
UNIVERSITY OF HEIDELBERG
Summer School of German Language & Culture
Site: Germany: Heidelberg *Host inst:* Univ of Heidelberg
Dates: 4 wks, mid-Jul-mid-Aug
Subjects: Business language, Civilization/culture, German language (beg/int/adv), German studies, Literature
Eligibility: *Level:* fresh, sophs, jrs, srs, grads, adults, teachers, professionals *Age:* min 18
Credit: *Undergrad:* 1-3 *Grad:* none *Doc:* certificate
Instruction: *In:* German *Format:* lang study, lecture, seminar *Students:* intl
Costs: DM 860 *incl* tuition, fees
Housing: *Arr by pgm:* residence halls, apartments, furnished rms
Deadline: Jun 1
Other info: *US accredited sponsor:* no *Began:* 1926 *Activities:* excursions, cultural events *Misc:* Social activities. *URL:* http://www.zuv.uni-heidelberg.de/aaa/ifk/Ferienku.
Contact: Univ of Heidelberg, Akademisches Auslandsamt, Seminarstr 2, Postfach 105 760, D-69047 Heidelberg, Germany *E-mail:* ferienkurs@zuv.uni-heidelberg.de

---

HEIDELBURG

0845
UNIVERSITY OF ARIZONA
Summer in Germany
Site: Germany: Heidelburg
Dates: 4 wks, Jul-mid-Aug
Subjects: German language (int/adv), Independent study
Eligibility: *Level:* sophs, jrs, srs *Requires:* 2.5 GPA, 1 yr German
Credit: *Undergrad:* avail *Grad:* none
Instruction: *In:* German *Format:* lang study, lecture *Students:* mainly US
Costs: $1,500 *incl* tuition, housing, fees, excursions *Nonrefundable fee*
Housing: *Arr by pgm:* residence halls, apartments
Deadline: Jun 1
Other info: *US accredited sponsor:* yes *Began:* 1999 *Orient:* abroad *Misc:* May contact former participants. *URL:* http://w3.arizona.edu/~ciss/
Contact: Caroline Patrick, Univ of Arizona, 939 N Tyndall Ave, Tucson AZ 85721 *Ph:* 520-626 9211 *Fax:* 520-626 9004 *E-mail:* cpatrick@u.arizona.edu ▲

HOLZKIRCHEN

0846
UNIVERSITY OF KANSAS
Advanced Summer Language Institute in Holzkirchen, Germany
Site: Germany: Holzkirchen *Host inst:* Volkschochsch Holzkirchen
Dates: 8 wks, Jun 1-Jul 27
Subjects: Civilization/culture, German language (int/adv), Literature, Written composition
Eligibility: *Level:* fresh, sophs, jrs, srs, grads *Requires:* good overall acad avg, 4 sems coll German
Credit: *Undergrad:* 9 *Grad:* avail *Doc:* transcript
Instruction: *In:* German *Format:* lang study, lecture, study tour *Students:* mainly US
Costs: $3,450 *incl* tuition, housing, all meals, excursions, cultural events, tour
Housing: *Arr by pgm:* homestay, hotels during tour
Deadline: Rolling admissions
Other info: *US accredited sponsor:* yes *Began:* 1963 *Activities:* excursions, program travel, cultural events *Misc:* Study tour incl visits to Cologne, Heidelburg, Nuernburg, Rothenburg, Wurzburg, others. *URL:* http://www.ukans.edu/~osa
Contact: Susan MacNally, Asst Dir, Study Abroad, Univ of Kansas, 108 Lippincott Hall, Lawrence KS 66045 *Ph:* 785-864 3742 *Fax:* 785-864 5040 *E-mail:* osa@ukans.edu ▲

KASSEL

0847
ALMA COLLEGE
Summer Program of Studies in Germany
Site: Germany: Kassel *Host inst:* Europa-Kolleg
Dates: 3-15 wks, Jun-Sep/4-11 wks, Aug-May
Subjects: German language (beg/int/adv), German studies, Homestay
Eligibility: *Level:* sophs, jrs, srs *Requires:* 2.5 GPA, 2 faculty recommendations
Credit: *Undergrad:* 3-15 *Grad:* none *Doc:* transcript
Instruction: *In:* German *Format:* lab, lang study, lecture *Students:* mainly US
Costs: $2,609-$7,668 depending on pgm length *incl* tuition, housing, some meals, most meals, fees, excursions, books/materials
Housing: *Arr by pgm:* homestay
Deadline: 2 mos before pgm
Other info: *US accredited sponsor:* yes *Began:* 1980 *Orient:* abroad *Activities:* excursions, cultural events, sports *Misc:* Resident dir. May contact former participants. *URL:* http://www.alma.edu/academics/international
Contact: Chris Musick, Intl Educ, Alma Coll, 614 W Superior St, Alma MI 48801-1599 *Ph:* 800-321 2562; 517-463 7055 *Fax:* 517-463 7126 *E-mail:* intl_studies@alma.edu

---

0848
UNIVERSITY OF COLORADO AT BOULDER
Study German in Germany
Site: Germany: Kassel *Host inst:* Europa-Kolleg
Dates: 3, 4, 7 or 8 wks, Jun-Aug
Subjects: German language (beg/int/adv), Homestay
Eligibility: *Level:* sophs, jrs, srs, adults, teachers, professionals *Requires:* 2.75 GPA *Age:* avg 20
Credit: *Undergrad:* 3-8 *Grad:* none *Doc:* transcript
Instruction: *In:* German *Format:* lang study *Students:* intl
Costs: $1,824-$5,165 for CO residents, $2,829-$6,165 for others *incl* tuition, housing, all meals, insurance, fees, books/materials
Housing: *Arr by pgm:* homestay
Deadline: Mar 1
Other info: *US accredited sponsor:* yes *Began:* 1982 *Orient:* in US *Activities:* field trips, cultural events, sports *Misc:* May contact former participants. *URL:* http://www.colorado.edu/OIE/StudyAbroad
Contact: Intl Educ, Univ of Colorado, Campus Box 123, Boulder CO 80309-0123 *Ph:* 303-492 7741 *Fax:* 303-492 5185 *E-mail:* studyabr@colorado.edu

---

KIEL

0849
UNIVERSITY OF UTAH
Study in Kiel, Germany
Site: Germany: Kiel *Host inst:* Christian Albrechts Univ
Dates: 4 wks, Jul-Aug
Subjects: German language (beg/int/adv)
Eligibility: *Level:* fresh, sophs, jrs, srs, grads, adults *Requires:* 2.5 GPA *Age:* min 18
Credit: *Undergrad:* avail *Grad:* none *Doc:* transcript
Instruction: *In:* German *Format:* lang study *Students:* mainly US
Costs: About $1,840 *incl* tuition, housing, excursions
Housing: *Arr by pgm:* residence halls
Deadline: Mar 15
Other info: *US accredited sponsor:* yes *Orient:* in US *Activities:* excursions *Misc:* Scholarships for Univ of UT students only. *URL:* http://www.saff.utah.edu/inter/
Contact: Laura Ashton, Study Abroad Adviser, Univ of Utah, 159 University Union, Salt Lake City UT 84112 *Ph:* 801-581 5849 *Fax:* 801-581 5914 *E-mail:* lashton@saff.utah.edu

---

KONSTANZ

0850
GERMAN LANGUAGE SCHOOL CONFERENCE
Summer Study/Travel in Germany and Switzerland
Site: Germany: Konstanz
Dates: 4 wks, Jul 27-Aug 23
Subjects: German studies (beg/int/adv)
Eligibility: *Level:* fresh, sophs, jrs, srs, grads, adults, precoll *Age:* min 16
Credit: *Undergrad:* none *Grad:* none *Doc:* certificate
Instruction: *In:* English *Format:* lang study, study tour *Students:* mainly US
Costs: $1,495 *incl* tuition, housing, all meals, excursions
Housing: *Arr by pgm:* residence halls
Deadline: Apr 1
Other info: *US accredited sponsor:* no *Began:* 1990 *URL:* http://www.germanschool.org/summerprg.htm
Contact: Peter Schroeck, GLSC, 1 Hiram Sq, New Brunswick NJ 08901 *Ph:* 732-249 9785 *Fax:* 732-249 9785 *E-mail:* germanschools@yahoo.com

---

0851
RUTGERS UNIVERSITY
Rutgers Summer Study in Konstanz
Site: Germany: Konstanz *Host inst:* Univ Konstanz
Dates: 6 wks, mid-Jul-late Aug
Subjects: Art history, Civilization/culture, German language (beg/int/adv), German studies, History
Eligibility: *Level:* sophs, jrs, srs *Requires:* 2.5 GPA, recommendation letter
Credit: *Undergrad:* avail *Grad:* none *Doc:* transcript
Instruction: *In:* English, German *Format:* lang study, lecture *Students:* mainly US
Costs: $2,627 for NJ residents, $2,877 for others *incl* tuition, housing, insurance, fees, excursions *Nonrefundable fee*
Housing: *Arr by pgm:* residence halls
Deadline: Mar 15
Other info: *US accredited sponsor:* yes *Began:* 1978 *Orient:* in US *Activities:* excursions *Misc:* May contact former participants. *URL:* http://studyabroad.rutgers.edu
Contact: Dir, Study Abroad, Rutgers Univ, 102 College Ave, New Brunswick NJ 08901 *Ph:* 732-932 7787 *Fax:* 732-932 8659 *E-mail:* ru_abroad@email.rutgers.edu

---

LUNEBURG

0852
UNIVERSITY STUDIES ABROAD CONSORTIUM
German Studies-Luneburg
Site: Germany: Luneburg *Host inst:* Univ of Luneburg
Dates: Two 4-wk sessions, May 22-Jun 24 and/or Jun 20-Jul 21
Subjects: Civilization/culture, Economics, German language (beg/int/adv), History, Homestay, Literature, Political science/politics
Eligibility: *Level:* fresh, sophs, jrs, srs, grads, adults, teachers, precoll *Requires:* 2.5 GPA *Age:* min 18, avg 21
Credit: *Undergrad:* 4-5 per session *Grad:* 4-5 per session *Doc:* transcript
Instruction: *In:* English, German *Format:* lang study, lecture, seminar *Students:* US & intl
Costs: $1,980 for 1 session, $3,680 for 2 sessions *incl* tuition, housing, insurance, excursions, ISIC
Housing: *Arr by pgm:* residence halls with local students, homestay
Deadline: Apr 1
Other info: *US accredited sponsor:* yes *Began:* 1994 *Orient:* abroad *Activities:* excursions, field trips, program travel, cultural events, sports *Misc:* Pgm organized flights. Berlin tour. May contact former participants. *URL:* http://www.usac.unr.edu
Contact: *See Index II for Members* Carmelo Urza, Univ Studies Abroad Consortium, Univ of Nevada Library 323, Reno NV 89557-0093 *Ph:* 775-784 6569 *Fax:* 775-784 6010 *E-mail:* usac@unr.edu ▲

MAYEN

0853
MICHIGAN STATE UNIVERSITY
German Language and Culture
Site: Germany: Mayen
Dates: 6 wks, May-Jul
Subjects: Civilization/culture, German language, Homestay
Eligibility: *Level:* sophs, jrs, srs *Requires:* 2.0 GPA, 2 yrs coll German, good acad standing, interview *Age:* min 18
Credit: *Undergrad:* 7 or more *Grad:* none *Doc:* transcript
Instruction: *In:* English, German *Format:* lang study, lecture, seminar *Students:* mainly US
Costs: About $1,500 *incl* housing, some meals, insurance, excursions, support svcs *Nonrefundable fee*
Housing: *Arr by pgm:* homestay
Deadline: Mar 2
Other info: *US accredited sponsor:* yes *Began:* 1974 *Orient:* in US & abroad *Misc:* Loans avail. *Financial aid:* scholarships *URL:* http://studyabroad.msu.edu
Contact: Cheryl Benner, Study Abroad, Michigan State Univ, 109 Intl Ctr, East Lansing MI 48824-1035 *Ph:* 517-353 8920 *Fax:* 517-432 2082 *E-mail:* bennerc@msu.edu ▲

MUNICH

0854
BWS GERMANLINGUA
Learning German in Munich
Site: Germany: Munich *Host inst:* Iwanson Dance Center, Atelier Project College of Munich Univs
Dates: yr-round, 2-48 wks
Subjects: German language (beg/int/adv), Homestay
Eligibility: *Level:* adults, teachers, professionals, precoll *Age:* min 16, avg 30
Credit: *Undergrad:* avail *Grad:* avail *Doc:* certificate
Instruction: *In:* German *Format:* lang study *Students:* intl
Costs: DM 1,450 *incl* tuition, books/materials
Housing: *Arr by pgm:* residence halls, apartments, homestay
Other info: *US accredited sponsor:* no *Began:* 1984 *Activities:* cultural events,

sports *URL:* http://www.bws-germanlingua.de
Contact: BWS Germanlingua, Bayerstr. 13, D-80335 Munchen *E-mail:* info@bws-germanlingua.de

---

0855
EDUVACATIONS
Study in and Live in Your Teacher's Home-Germany
Site: Germany: Munich countryside
Dates: 1 wk or longer, yr-round
Subjects: German language (beg/int/adv), Homestay
Eligibility: *Level:* adults *Age:* min 15
Credit: *Undergrad:* none *Grad:* none
Instruction: *In:* German *Format:* lang study, study tour *Students:* intl
Costs: Contact sponsor
Housing: *Arr by pgm:* apartments, homestay, cottage
Deadline: Contact sponsor
Other info: *US accredited sponsor:* no *Activities:* excursions, field trips *Misc:* Hiking, cycling, cultural activities also avail. May contact former participants. *URL:* http://www.eduvacations.com
Contact: Mary Ann Puglisi, eduVacations, 1431 21st St NW, Ste 302, Washington DC 20036 *Ph:* 202-857 8384 *Fax:* 202-463 8091

0856
KENTUCKY INSTITUTE FOR INTERNATIONAL STUDIES (KIIS) and **MURRAY STATE UNIVERSITY**
Summer Program in Germany
Site: Germany: Munich
Dates: 6 wks, mid-Jun-early Aug
Subjects: German language (int/adv), German studies, Homestay, Literature
Eligibility: *Level:* fresh, sophs, jrs, srs, grads *Requires:* 2.0 GPA, 1 yr coll German, good acad standing at home inst, faculty recommendation *Age:* min 18
Credit: *Undergrad:* 3-6 *Grad:* avail *Doc:* transcript
Instruction: *In:* German *Format:* lang study, lecture *Students:* mainly US
Costs: $2,790 for students at member schs, $3,090 for others *incl* tuition, housing, all meals, intl airfare, fees, excursions, U-Bahn & S-Bahn pass, ISIC *Nonrefundable fee*
Housing: *Arr by pgm:* homestay
Deadline: Feb 15 ($100 late fee)
Other info: *US accredited sponsor:* yes *Began:* 1988 *Orient:* in US & abroad *Activities:* excursions *Misc:* May contact former participants. *Financial aid:* scholarships *URL:* http://www.kiis.org
Contact: *See Index II for Members* Dr J Milton Grimes, Exec Dir, KIIS, Murray State Univ, PO Box 9, Murray KY 42071-0009 *Ph:* 270-762 3091 *Fax:* 270-762 3434 *E-mail:* kiismsu@murraystate.edu

---

0857
LUDWIG-MAXIMILIANS-UNIVERSITAET MUNCHEN
German Language Courses for Foreign Students
Site: Germany: Munich *Host inst:* Univ of Munich
Dates: 2-mo courses, Jan, Mar, May, Jul, Sep, Nov
Subjects: German language (beg/int/adv)
Eligibility: *Level:* jrs, srs, adults *Requires:* high sch grad, 16 acad units
Credit: *Undergrad:* avail *Grad:* none
Instruction: *In:* German *Format:* lang study, lecture *Students:* intl

Costs: $620 for 2 mo *incl* tuition
Housing: *Arr by student*
Deadline: 2 mos before pgm
Other info: *US accredited sponsor:* no *Began:* 1964 *URL:* http://www.lrz.de/~deutschkurse
Contact: Dr Bernd Wintermann, Deutschkurse fuer Auslaender, Univ Muenchen, Adelheidstr 13, D-80798 Munich, Germany *E-mail:* deutschkurse@extern.lrz-muenchen.de

---

0858
UNIVERSITY OF CINCINNATI
University of Cincinnati Munich Summer Program
Site: Germany: Munich
Dates: 3 wks, Jun 15-Jul 18
Subjects: Civilization/culture, Field study, German language, German studies
Eligibility: *Level:* fresh, sophs, jrs, srs *Requires:* previous study in field, 2 yrs coll German *Age:* min 18
Credit: *Undergrad:* 6 qtr hrs *Grad:* none *Doc:* transcript
Instruction: *In:* German *Format:* directed field study, lang study, lecture, study tour *Students:* mainly US
Costs: $2,100 for OH resident undergrads *incl* tuition, housing, some meals, fees, excursions *Nonrefundable fee*
Housing: *Arr by pgm:* hostels
Deadline: Mar 1
Other info: *US accredited sponsor:* yes *Began:* 1998 *Orient:* in US & abroad (3 days) *Activities:* excursions, field trips, program travel, cultural events *Misc:* Scholarships for own students only. May contact former participants. *Financial aid:* scholarships *URL:* http://www.uc.edu/global
Contact: Arthur Neisberg, Educ Abroad Coord, 608 Swift Hall, Univ of Cincinnati, PO Box 210640, Cincinnati OH 45221-0640 *Ph:* 513-556 1363 *Fax:* 513-556 2990 *E-mail:* arthur.neisberg@uc.edu

---

0859
UNIVERSITY OF ILLINOIS URBANA-CHAMPAIGN, SCHOOL OF ARCHITECTURE
Graduate Student Exchange
Site: Germany: Munich *Host inst:* Technische Univ Munchen
Dates: May 1-Jul 31
Subjects: Architecture, German studies, Independent study
Eligibility: *Level:* grads *Requires:* previous study in field *Age:* avg 24
Credit: *Undergrad:* none *Grad:* avail
Instruction: *In:* English, German *Format:* art studio, independent study *Students:* mainly US
Costs: $4,000 *incl* tuition, housing, all meals, insurance, fees *Nonrefundable fee*
Housing: *Arr by pgm:* residence halls with local students
Deadline: Nov 15
Other info: *US accredited sponsor:* yes *Began:* 1999 *Orient:* in US (2 days) *Activities:* excursions, field trips *Misc:* May contact former participants. *Financial aid:* scholarships *URL:* http://www.arch.uiuc.edu
Contact: Johannes Albrecht, Sch of Architecture, Univ of Illinois, 611 Taft Dr, Champaign IL 61820 *Ph:* 217-333 1330 *Fax:* 217-244 2900
Or Contact: Alejandro Lapunzina, Univ of Illinois, 611 Taft Dr, Champaign IL 61820 *Ph:* 217-244 7774 *Fax:* 217-244 2900 *E-mail:* alejlapu@uiuc.edu

---

REGENSBURG

0860
ARIZONA STATE UNIVERSITY
Germany
Site: Germany: Regensburg
Dates: 4 wks, May 28-Jun 30
Subjects: Civilization/culture, German language, German studies, Homestay, Independent study
Eligibility: *Level:* adults *Requires:* 1 yr German or equiv *Age:* min 18
Credit: *Undergrad:* avail *Grad:* none
Instruction: *In:* German *Format:* independent study, lang study, lecture, study tour *Students:* mainly US
Costs: $2,125 *incl* tuition, housing, excursions, ISIC *Nonrefundable fee*
Housing: *Arr by pgm:* residence halls, apartments, homestay
Deadline: Early Mar
Other info: *US accredited sponsor:* yes *Began:* 1994 *Orient:* in US *Activities:* excursions, field trips *Misc:* Loans avail. All students pay equiv of ASU resident tuition. *Financial aid:* scholarships *URL:* http://www.asu.edu/ssc/StudyAbroad
Contact: Ara Pachmayer, Pgm Coord, Arizona State Univ, PO Box 873003, Tempe AZ 85287-3003 *Ph:* 480-965 0101 *Fax:* 480-965 3851 *E-mail:* study.programs@asu.edu

---

SPEYER

0861
NATIONAL SCHOOL OF PUBLIC ADMINISTRATION
Complementary Training in Administrative Sciences
Site: Germany: Speyer
Dates: 3 mos, May 1-Jul 31 or Nov 1-Jan 31
Subjects: Administration, Economics, Finance, Human resources, Information technology, International relations, Organizational behavior, Political science/politics, Public administration
Eligibility: *Level:* grads *Requires:* good knowledge of German; degree in law, econ or soc scis
Credit: *Undergrad:* none *Grad:* none *Doc:* certificate
Instruction: *In:* German *Format:* lang study, lecture, practical training, seminar, tutorial *Students:* mainly host country
Costs: Contact sponsor
Housing: *Arr by pgm:* residence halls with local students, residence halls, homestay
Deadline: Mar 1 or Sep 1
Other info: *US accredited sponsor:* no *Began:* 1976 *URL:* http://www.dhv-speyer.de
Contact: Rainer Pitschas, Natl Sch of Public Admin, DHV Speyer, Freiherr-von-Stein-Str 2, D-67346 Speyer, Germany *E-mail:* rpitschas@dhv-speyer.de

---

TRIER

0862
GEORGETOWN UNIVERSITY
Georgetown at Universitaet Trier
Site: Germany: Trier *Host inst:* Univ Trier
Dates: 5 wks, early Jun-mid-Jul
Subjects: Business language, Civilization/culture, German language (int/adv), German studies, Internships, Literature, Written composition
Eligibility: *Level:* fresh, sophs, jrs, srs, grads, adults, teachers, professionals, precoll *Requires:* previous study in field
Credit: *Undergrad:* 3-6 *Grad:* none *Doc:* transcript
Instruction: *In:* German *Format:* internship, lang study, lecture, seminar *Students:* mainly US
Costs: About $3,550 *incl* tuition, housing, some meals, insurance, fees, excursions, books/materials
Housing: *Arr by pgm:* homestay
Deadline: Mid-Mar
Other info: *US accredited sponsor:* yes *Began:* 1973 *Orient:* in US *Activities:* field trips *Misc:* May contact former participants. *URL:* http://www.georgetown.edu/programs/oip/os
Contact: Peter C Pfeiffer, Intl Pgms, Georgetown Univ, Box 571013, Washington DC 20057-1013 *Ph:* 202-687 5693 *Fax:* 202-687 7568 *E-mail:* pfeiffep@georgetown.edu
Or Contact: Rachel Rubin, Intl Pgms, Georgetown Univ, Box 571013, Washington DC 20057-1013 *Ph:* 202-687 5620 *Fax:* 202-687 5944 *E-mail:* rubinr@georgetown.edu

---

0863
PENNSYLVANIA STATE UNIVERSITY
German Language and Studies, Trier, Germany
Site: Germany: Trier
Dates: 4 wks, May 14-Jun 13
Subjects: German language
Eligibility: *Level:* adults *Requires:* 2 sems coll German or equiv
Credit: *Undergrad:* 4 *Grad:* none *Doc:* transcript
Instruction: *In:* German *Format:* lang study *Students:* mainly US
Costs: Contact Sponsor
Housing: *Arr by pgm:* residence halls
Deadline: Mar 1; Apr 1 for scholarships
Other info: *US accredited sponsor:* yes *Began:* 1996 *Activities:* excursions, cultural events *Misc:* May contact former participants. *Financial aid:* scholarships
Contact: Dr Steven de Hart, Behrend Coll, Penn State Univ, Erie PA 16563-1501 *Ph:* 814-898 6032 *E-mail:* sad2@psu.edu

---

0864
UNIVERSITAET TRIER
Summer Session in German Language, Literature and Culture
Site: Germany: Trier
Dates: 4 wks, Aug-Sep
Subjects: Art, Civilization/culture, German language (int/adv), History, Homestay, Literature, Social sciences
Eligibility: *Level:* adults, teachers *Requires:* basic knowledge of German *Age:* min 18, avg 25
Credit: *Undergrad:* none *Grad:* none *Doc:* certificate
Instruction: *In:* German *Format:* lang study, lecture *Students:* intl
Costs: About DM 800 *incl* tuition, fees, excursions, books/materials *Nonrefundable fee*
Housing: *Arr by pgm:* residence halls, apartments, homestay, furnished rms
Deadline: Jun 15
Other info: *US accredited sponsor:* no *Began:* 1971 *URL:* http://www.uni-trier.de/uni/aaa/ifk/ferienku.htm
Contact: Gretlies Haungs, Akademisches Auslandsamt, Univ Trier, D-54286 Trier, Tarforst, Germany *E-mail:* ifk@uni-trier.de

---

TUBINGEN

0865
UNIVERSITY OF MARYLAND
Summer in Tubingen
Site: Germany: Tubingen *Host inst:* Univ of Tubingen
Dates: Aug 1 -Aug 26
Subjects: Civilization/culture, German language (int/adv)
Eligibility: *Level:* fresh, sophs, jrs, srs *Requires:* 1 yr German with 3.0 GPA
Credit: *Undergrad:* 6 *Grad:* none *Doc:* certificate
Instruction: *In:* German *Format:* lang study, lecture *Students:* intl
Costs: $750 *incl* tuition, fees, excursions
Housing: *Arr by pgm:* residence halls
Deadline: Mar 15
Other info: *US accredited sponsor:* yes *Began:* 2000 *Orient:* in US & abroad *Activities:* excursions *Misc:* May contact former participants. *URL:* http://www.inform.umd.edu/INTL/studyabroad
Contact: Christine Bodziak, Adviser, Study Abroad, Univ of Maryland, 3125 Mitchell Bldg, College Park MD 20742 *Ph:* 301-314 7746 *Fax:* 301-314 9347 *E-mail:* studyabr@deans.umd.edu

---

0866
UNIVERSITY OF NORTH CAROLINA AT CHAPEL HILL
UNC-CH Summer Language Program at Sprachinstitut Tubingen
Site: Germany: Tubingen *Host inst:* Sprachinst Tubingen
Dates: Three 4 wk sessions, May-Aug
Subjects: Civilization/culture, Field study, German language (beg/int/adv), German studies, History, Homestay
Eligibility: *Level:* adults *Requires:* 2.5 GPA
Credit: *Undergrad:* 6 *Grad:* none *Doc:* transcript
Instruction: *In:* English, German *Format:* directed field study, lang study, seminar *Students:* intl
Costs: $1,939 *incl* tuition, housing, all meals, insurance, fees, excursions *Nonrefundable fee*
Housing: *Arr by pgm:* residence halls, homestay
Deadline: Early Feb
Other info: *US accredited sponsor:* yes *Began:* 1994 *Orient:* in US & abroad *Activities:* excursions, field trips, cultural events *Misc:* May contact former participants. *Financial aid:* scholarships *URL:* http://www.unc.edu/depts/abroad
Contact: Study Abroad, UNC Chapel Hill, 12 Caldwell Hall, CB-3130, Cameron Ave, Chapel Hill NC 27599-3130 *Ph:* 919-962 7001 *Fax:* 919-962 2262 *E-mail:* abroad@unc.edu

---

WILHELMSHAVEN

0867
OHIO UNIVERSITY
Geography in Germany
Site: Germany: Wilhelmshaven *Host inst:* FH Wilhelmshaven
Dates: 5 wks, late Jul-late Aug
Subjects: Field study, Geography, German language, Homestay
Eligibility: *Level:* sophs, jrs, srs *Requires:* 3.0 GPA
Credit: *Undergrad:* 8 qtr hrs *Grad:* none *Doc:* transcript
Instruction: *In:* English, German *Format:* directed field study, lang study, lecture *Students:* mainly US
Costs: $3,629 yr *incl* tuition, housing, some meals, intl airfare, fees, excursions, books/materials *Nonrefundable fee*
Housing: *Arr by pgm:* homestay, pensions
Deadline: Apr 1
Other info: *US accredited sponsor:* yes *Began:* 1998 *Orient:* in US & abroad (2 days) *Activities:* excursions, field trips, program travel, cultural events *Misc:* May contact former participants. *URL:* http://www.ohiou.edu
Contact: Prof Timothy Anderson, Ohio Univ, Clippinger 122, Athens OH 45701 *Ph:* 740-593 1148 *E-mail:* anderst1@ohiou.edu
Or Contact: Connie Perdreau, Dir, Educ Abroad, Ohio Univ, Gordy Hall 107, Athens OH 45701 *Ph:* 740-593 4583 *Fax:* 740-593 9758 *E-mail:* perdreau@ohiou.edu

---

WURZBURG

0868
SUNY UNIVERSITY AT ALBANY
Language and Cultural Studies at the University of Wurzburg
Site: Germany: Wurzburg *Host inst:* Univ Wurzburg
Dates: 10 wks, May-Jul
Subjects: German language
Eligibility: *Level:* sophs, jrs, srs, grads, adults *Requires:* 2.5 GPA, 1 yr coll German
Credit: *Undergrad:* 6 *Grad:* none *Doc:* transcript
Instruction: *In:* German *Format:* lang study, lecture *Students:* mainly US
Costs: $4,029 for NY residents *incl* tuition, housing, all meals, fees, excursions, student support svcs *Nonrefundable fee*
Housing: *Arr by pgm:* apartments, homestay
Deadline: Mar 1; late applications considered
Other info: *US accredited sponsor:* yes *In coop with:* Univ of Texas at Austin *Orient:* in US *Misc:* May contact former participants. *URL:* http://www.albany.edu/intled
Contact: Joan N Savitt, Intl Pgms, SUNY Univ at Albany, LI 66, Albany NY 12222 *Ph:* 518-442 3525 *Fax:* 518-442 3338 *E-mail:* intled@uamail.albany.edu

---

0869
UNIVERSITY OF TEXAS AT AUSTIN
Wurzburg Summer Program
Site: Germany: Wurzburg *Host inst:* Univ Wurzburg
Dates: 10 wks, mid-May-late Jul
Subjects: Art history, Economics, German language, German studies, Government, History, Homestay, Literature
Eligibility: *Level:* sophs, jrs, srs *Requires:* 1 yr coll German or equiv
Credit: *Undergrad:* 9 *Grad:* none *Doc:* transcript, certificate
Instruction: *In:* English, German *Format:* lang study, lecture *Students:* mainly US
Costs: Contact sponsor
Housing: *Arr by pgm:* homestay
Deadline: Mar 1
Other info: *US accredited sponsor:* yes *Began:* 1991 *Orient:* abroad *Activities:* excursions, cultural events *Misc:* May contact former participants. *URL:* http://www.utexas.edu/student/abroad
Contact: Joy Williamson, Adviser, Study Abroad, Univ of Texas at Austin, Drawer A, Univ Station, Austin TX 78713-7206 *Ph:* 512-471 6490 *Fax:* 512-232 4363 *E-mail:* studyabroadinfo@mozart.io.utexas.edu

Greece

MORE THAN ONE CITY

0870
ALEXANDER THE GREAT HELLENIC LANGUAGE SCHOOL
Greek Language Courses: Compact
Site: Greece: Athens, Chania, Thessaloniki *Host inst:* Hellenic British Coll
Dates: 2 wks, yr-round
Subjects: Field study, Greek language (beg/int/adv), Homestay, Student teaching
Eligibility: *Level:* adults *Age:* min 15
Credit: *Undergrad:* none *Grad:* none
Instruction: *In:* English *Format:* directed field study, independent study, lab, lang study, lecture, music lesson, practical training, seminar, student teaching, study tour, tutorial, workshop *Students:* intl
Costs: GRD 150,000-160,000 *incl* tuition, some meals, fees, excursions, books/materials *Nonrefundable fee*
Housing: *Arr by pgm:* apartments, homestay, hotels
Deadline: 2 wks before pgm
Other info: *US accredited sponsor:* no *Began:* 1972 *Financial aid:* scholarships
Contact: Kanellopoulou Nektaria, Dir, Alexander the Great, Makrigianni 20, 17342 Agios Dimitrios, Athens, Greece *E-mail:* alexander@bhc.gr
Or Contact: Sekertzi Kyriaki, Teacher, Alexander the Great, Thiras 111, 10446 Athens, Greece

0871
ALEXANDER THE GREAT HELLENIC LANGUAGE SCHOOL
Greek Language Courses: Extended
Site: Greece: Athens, Chania, Thessaloniki *Host inst:* Hellenic British Coll
Dates: 4 wks, yr-round
Subjects: Field study, Greek language (beg/int/adv), Homestay, Student teaching
Eligibility: *Level:* adults *Age:* min 15
Credit: *Undergrad:* none *Grad:* none
Instruction: *In:* English *Format:* directed field study, independent study, lab, lang study, lecture, music lesson, practical training, seminar, student teaching, study tour, tutorial, workshop *Students:* intl
Costs: GRD 270,000-280,000 *incl* tuition, some meals, fees, excursions, books/materials *Nonrefundable fee*
Housing: *Arr by pgm:* apartments, homestay, hotels
Deadline: 2 wks before pgm start-date
Other info: *US accredited sponsor:* no *Began:* 1972 *Financial aid:* scholarships
Contact: Kanellopoulou Nektaria, Dir, Alexander the Great, Makrigianni 20, 17342 Agios Dimitrios, Athens, Greece *E-mail:* alexander@bhc.gr
Or Contact: Sekertzi Kyriaki, Teacher, Alexander the Great, Thiras 111, 10446 Athens, Greece

0872
ALEXANDER THE GREAT HELLENIC LANGUAGE SCHOOL
Greek Language Courses: Regular
Site: Greece: Athens, Chania, Thessaloniki *Host inst:* Hellenic British Coll
Dates: 10 wks, yr-round
Subjects: Field study, Greek language (beg/int/adv), Homestay, Student teaching
Eligibility: *Level:* adults *Age:* min 15
Credit: *Undergrad:* none *Grad:* none
Instruction: *In:* English *Format:* directed field study, independent study, lab, lang study, lecture, music lesson, practical training, seminar, student teaching, study tour, tutorial, workshop *Students:* intl
Costs: GRD 115,000 *incl* tuition, fees, books/materials *Nonrefundable fee*
Housing: *Arr by pgm:* apartments, homestay, hotels
Deadline: 2 wks before pgm
Other info: *US accredited sponsor:* no *Began:* 1972 *Financial aid:* scholarships
Contact: Kanellopoulou Nektaria, Dir, Alexander the Great, Makrigianni 20, 17342 Agios Dimitrios, Athens, Greece *E-mail:* alexander@bhc.gr
Or Contact: Sekertzi Kyriaki, Teacher, Alexander the Great, Thiras 111, 10446 Athens, Greece

0873
BEAVER COLLEGE, CENTER FOR EDUCATION ABROAD
On the Trail of Alexander the Great
Site: Greece: Athens and surrounding countryside
Dates: Jun 18-Jul 8
Subjects: Art history, Greek/Hellenic studies
Eligibility: *Level:* sophs, jrs, srs *Requires:* 3.0 GPA
Credit: *Undergrad:* 3 *Grad:* none *Doc:* transcript
Instruction: *In:* English *Format:* directed field study, lecture *Students:* mainly US
Costs: $2,950 *incl* tuition, housing, some meals, insurance, excursions, ISIC, orient, transcript *Nonrefundable fee*
Housing: *Arr by pgm:* apartments, hotels
Deadline: Mar 31
Other info: *US accredited sponsor:* yes *Orient:* abroad *Misc:* Program incltravel to Athens, Macedonia, the Greek islands of Mykonos, Delos & Samos, and Turkey. May contact former participants. *URL:* http://www.arcadia.edu/cea
Contact: Ctr for Educ Abroad, Beaver Coll, 450 S Easton Rd, Glenside PA 19038 *Ph:* 888-232 8379 *Fax:* 215-572 2174 *E-mail:* cea@beaver.edu ▲

0874
COLLEGE YEAR IN ATHENS
Intensive Summer Programs
Site: Greece: Athens, Paros, Santorini
Dates: May-Jul
Subjects: Greek/Hellenic studies, History, Humanities, Religion/theology
Eligibility: *Level:* fresh, sophs, jrs, srs, adults *Age:* min 18
Credit: *Undergrad:* 3-4 *Grad:* none
Instruction: *In:* English *Format:* art studio, lang study, seminar, study tour *Students:* mainly US
Costs: Contact sponsor
Housing: *Arr by pgm:* apartments, hotels
Deadline: Apr 1
Other info: *US accredited sponsor:* no *Began:* 1962 *Orient:* abroad *Misc:* Contact Coord of Admissions & Recruitment for info on credit transfer. May contact former participants.
Contact: Coll Yr in Athens, PO Box 390890, Cambridge MA 02139 *Ph:* 617-868 8200 *Fax:* 617-868 8207 *E-mail:* cyathens@aol.com ▲

0875
DUKE UNIVERSITY
Duke in Greece
Site: Greece: Athens, Olympia, Pylos, Sparta, other classical sites
Dates: Mid-May-mid-Jun, even-numbered yrs
Subjects: Classical studies, History

Eligibility: *Level:* fresh, sophs, jrs, srs *Requires:* good acad standing, transcript
Credit: *Undergrad:* 1 credit *Grad:* none *Doc:* transcript
Instruction: *In:* English *Format:* lecture *Students:* mainly US
Costs: $5,295 for 1 course *incl* tuition, housing, all meals, excursions
Housing: *Arr by pgm:* hotels
Deadline: Feb 16
Other info: *US accredited sponsor:* yes *Began:* 1984 *Activities:* program travel *Misc:* Pgm next offered in 2002. *URL:* http://www.aas.duke.edu/study_abroad/
Contact: Study Abroad, Duke Univ, 121 Allen Bldg, Box 90057, Durham NC 27708-0057 *Ph:* 919-684 2174 *Fax:* 919-684 3083 *E-mail:* abroad@asdean.duke.edu

---

0876
FUND FOR AMERICAN STUDIES
International Institute for Political and Economic Studies
Site: Greece: various sites *Host inst:* Greek Assn for Atlantic & European Coop
Dates: 3 wks, Jul
Subjects: Business/management, Conflict studies, Economics, International relations, Political science/politics
Eligibility: *Level:* jrs, srs, grads *Requires:* recommendation letters, essays, transcript, resume *Age:* avg 23
Credit: *Undergrad:* 3 *Grad:* 3 *Doc:* certificate *Transfer credit through:* Georgetown Univ
Instruction: *In:* English *Format:* lecture, seminar, workshop *Students:* intl
Costs: $2,500 *incl* tuition, housing, some meals, excursions, books/materials
Housing: *Arr by pgm:* residence halls
Deadline: Mar 15
Other info: *US accredited sponsor:* no *Began:* 1996 *In coop with:* Georgetown Univ *Orient:* abroad (1 day) *Activities:* excursions, cultural events, sports *Misc:* All students receive scholarships. May contact former participants. *Financial aid:* scholarships *URL:* http://www.iipes.org
Contact: Leslie Berlin, Dir, Intl Pgms, Fund for Amer Studies, 1706 New Hampshire Ave NW, Washington DC 20009 *Ph:* 800-741 6964; 202-986 0384 *Fax:* 202-986 0390 *E-mail:* iipes@tfas.org

---

0877
GEORGETOWN UNIVERSITY
Life and Thought in Ancient Greece
Site: Greece: Athens, Attica, Central Greece, the Peloponnese, various Greek Islands
Dates: 2 wks, late May/early Jun-mid/late Jun
Subjects: Archaeology, Classical studies, History
Eligibility: *Level:* adults
Credit: *Undergrad:* 3 *Grad:* none *Doc:* transcript
Instruction: *In:* English *Format:* lecture, seminar, study tour *Students:* mainly US
Costs: About $4,200 *incl* tuition, housing, some meals, intl airfare, insurance, fees, excursions, books/materials *Nonrefundable fee*
Housing: *Arr by pgm:* hotels
Deadline: Mid-Mar
Other info: *US accredited sponsor:* yes *Orient:* in US (1 day) *Activities:* program travel *Misc:* May contact former participants. *URL:* http://www.georgetown.edu/programs/oip/os/sites/summer
Contact: Dr Alexander Sens or Rachel Rubin, Intl Pgms, Georgetown Univ, Box 571013, Washington DC 20057-1013 *Ph:* 202-687 5620 *E-mail:* rubinr@georgetown.edu

---

0878
HIPHAISTIA
Greek Summer Cultural Seminars
Site: Greece: various villages & towns
Dates: 10-day sessions, Jul 1-Aug 31
Subjects: Dance, Folk dance, Folk music, Greek language (beg/int), Greek/Hellenic studies, Music history
Eligibility: *Level:* fresh, sophs, jrs, srs, adults
Credit: *Undergrad:* none *Grad:* none *Doc:* certificate
Instruction: *In:* English, Greek *Format:* lang study, lecture, practical training, seminar *Students:* intl
Costs: $650-$675 per session *incl* tuition, housing, some meals, excursions *Nonrefundable fee*
Housing: *Arr by pgm:* hotels, spas
Deadline: May 31
Other info: *US accredited sponsor:* no *Began:* 1983 *In coop with:* Hellenic Amer Union *Activities:* excursions, field trips, cultural events *Misc:* Instruction in traditional Greek dance. Village visits. May contact former participants.
Contact: Mrs Yvonne Hunt, Hiphaistia, 4837 38th Ave NE, Seattle WA 98105-3020 *Ph:* 206-523 2477 *Fax:* 206-523 2477 *E-mail:* bg901@scn.org

---

0879
LANGUAGE LIAISON
Greek Language
Site: Greece: Athens, Chania (Crete)
Dates: 2 wks or longer, yr-round
Subjects: Civilization/culture, Greek language (beg/int/adv), Homestay
Eligibility: *Level:* fresh, sophs, jrs, srs, grads, adults, teachers, professionals, precoll *Age:* min 14
Credit: *Undergrad:* avail *Grad:* avail *Doc:* transcript, certificate
Instruction: *In:* Greek *Format:* lang study *Students:* intl
Costs: Contact sponsor
Housing: *Arr by pgm:* homestay, hotels
Deadline: 30 days before pgm
Other info: *US accredited sponsor:* no *Activities:* excursions, cultural events *Misc:* Scholarship research svc. *URL:* http://www.languageliaison.com
Contact: Nancy Forman, Dir, Lang Liaison, 4 Burnham Pkwy, Morristown NJ 07960 *Ph:* 800-284 4448 *Fax:* 973-898 1017 *E-mail:* learn@languageliaison.com

---

0880
LINGUA SERVICE WORLDWIDE
Total Immersion/Intensive Language and Culture in Greece
Site: Greece: Athens, Chania (Crete) *Host inst:* Hellenic Lang Sch Alexander the Great
Dates: 1 wk-1 yr, yr-round
Subjects: Civilization/culture, Greek language (beg/int/adv), Homestay
Eligibility: *Level:* adults
Credit: *Undergrad:* avail *Grad:* avail *Doc:* transcript, certificate
Instruction: *In:* Greek *Format:* lang study *Students:* intl
Costs: Contact sponsor
Housing: *Arr by pgm:* homestay, hotels
Deadline: 45 days before pgm
Other info: *US accredited sponsor:* no *Activities:* cultural events *URL:* http://www.linguaserviceworldwide.com
Contact: Dir, Lingua Svc Worldwide, 75 Prospect St, Ste 4, Huntington NY 11743 *Ph:* 800-394 5327; 631-424 0777 *Fax:* 631-271 3441 *E-mail:* itctravel@worldnet.att.net ▲

0881
RAMAPO COLLEGE OF NEW JERSEY
Greece Study Abroad
Site: Greece: Athens, Ikaria, Lesvos, Mytilini, Samos
Dates: 3 wks, Jul
Subjects: Field study, Greek/Hellenic studies
Eligibility: *Level:* fresh, sophs, jrs, srs, grads *Requires:* 2.0 GPA *Age:* min 18, avg 24
Credit: *Undergrad:* 3 *Grad:* none
Instruction: *In:* English *Format:* directed field study *Students:* mainly US
Costs: $3,000 for Ramapo students, $3,200 for others *incl* tuition, housing, some meals, intl airfare, fees, excursions *Nonrefundable fee*
Housing: *Arr by pgm:* pensions, hotels
Deadline: May 1
Other info: *US accredited sponsor:* yes *Began:* 1999 *Orient:* in US 1 day *Misc:* May contact former participants.

Contact: Ms Robyn Perricelli, Coord, Study Abroad, Ramapo Coll, 505 Ramapo Valley Rd, Mahwah NJ 07430 *Ph:* 201-684 7030 *Fax:* 201-684 7651 *E-mail:* rperrice@ramapo.edu

---

0882
SCHOOL OF VISUAL ARTS (SVA)
The Art, Myth and History of Ancient Greece
Site: Greece: Athens to Mikonos
Dates: 3 wks, May 30-Jun 20
Subjects: Architecture, Art, History, Mythology
Eligibility: *Level:* sophs, jrs, srs, grads, adults, teachers *Requires:* 1 yr coll
Credit: *Undergrad:* 3 *Grad:* none *Doc:* transcript
Instruction: *In:* English *Format:* lecture, study tour *Students:* US & intl
Costs: $3,100 *incl* tuition, housing, some meals, intl airfare, fees, excursions
Housing: *Arr by pgm:* hotels
Deadline: Apr 25
Other info: *US accredited sponsor:* yes
Contact: Dora Riomayor, Intl Studies, Sch of Visual Arts, 209 E 23rd St, New York NY 10010 *Ph:* 212-592 2543 *Fax:* 212-592 2545 *E-mail:* morariomayor@schoolofvisualarts.edu

---

0883
SOUTHERN ILLINOIS UNIVERSITY AT CARBONDALE
Myth and Cosmos in Greece
Site: Greece: various sites
Dates: 2 or 4 wks, May 25-Jun 10
Subjects: Archaeology, Classical studies, Interdisciplinary studies, Philosophy
Eligibility: *Level:* fresh, sophs, jrs, srs, grads, teachers *Requires:* faculty approval
Credit: *Undergrad:* 1-3 *Grad:* 1-3 *Doc:* transcript
Instruction: *In:* English *Format:* directed field study, lecture, seminar *Students:* mainly US
Costs: $2,500 *incl* tuition, housing, some meals, fees, excursions
Housing: *Arr by pgm:* hotels
Deadline: Apr 1
Other info: *US accredited sponsor:* yes *Began:* 1984 *Orient:* in US *Activities:* excursions *Misc:* Interdisciplinary seminar with primary focus on origins of philosophy. *URL:* http://www.siu.edu/departments/study_abroad/
Contact: Thomas A Saville, Study Abroad Pgms, Mailcode 6885, Southern Illinois Univ, Carbondale IL 62901-6885 *Ph:* 618-453 7670 *Fax:* 618-453 7647 *E-mail:* studyabr@siu.edu

---

0884
SUNY COLLEGE AT BROCKPORT
Greek Mythology
Site: Greece: Athens, Crete
Dates: 3 wks, late Jun-early Jul
Subjects: Classical studies, Greek/Hellenic studies, History, Literature, Mythology
Eligibility: *Level:* fresh, sophs, jrs, srs, grads, teachers
Credit: *Undergrad:* 3 *Grad:* none *Doc:* transcript
Instruction: *In:* English *Format:* study tour *Students:* mainly US
Costs: About $3,350 *incl* tuition, housing, all meals, intl airfare, fees, excursions, books/materials
Housing: *Arr by pgm:* hotels
Deadline: May 1
Other info: *US accredited sponsor:* yes *Began:* 1972 *Orient:* in US *Activities:* excursions, cultural events *URL:* http://www.brockport.edu/study_abroad
Contact: Dr John Perry, Dir, Intl Educ, 350 New Campus Dr, SUNY Coll at Brockport, Brockport NY 14420 *Ph:* 800-298 7869 *Fax:* 716-637 3218 *E-mail:* overseas@brockport.edu

---

0885
UNIVERSITY OF ALABAMA
Alabama in Greece
Site: Greece: Athens, Delphi, Dion, Epidauros, Litohoro, Olympia, Sounion, others
Dates: 3 wks, May 30-Jun 19
Subjects: Classical studies, Field study
Eligibility: *Level:* sophs, jrs, srs, grads, adults, teachers, professionals
Credit: *Undergrad:* 6 *Grad:* none *Doc:* transcript
Instruction: *In:* English *Format:* directed field study *Students:* mainly US
Costs: $2,500 *incl* tuition, housing, some meals, intl airfare, excursions
Housing: *Arr by pgm:* hotels
Deadline: Feb 1
Other info: *US accredited sponsor:* yes *Began:* 1997 *Orient:* in US *Activities:* excursions, field trips, program travel *URL:* http://www.ua.edu/international
Contact: Capstone Intl Pgm Ctr, Univ of Alabama, PO Box 870254, Tuscaloosa AL 35487 *Ph:* 205-348 5256 *Fax:* 205-348 5298 *E-mail:* achannel@aalan.ua.edu
Or Contact: Dr Kirk Summers, Univ of Alabama, PO Box 870246, Tuscaloosa AL 35487 *Ph:* 205-348 5059 *Fax:* 205-348 5298 *E-mail:* ksummers@woodsquad.as.ua.edu

---

0886
UNIVERSITY OF ARIZONA
Art and Archaeology in Greece
Site: Greece: various sites
Dates: 4 wks, May 14-Jun 8
Subjects: Classical studies, Humanities, Independent study
Eligibility: *Level:* sophs, jrs, srs, adults, teachers *Requires:* 2.5 GPA *Age:* min 18
Credit: *Undergrad:* 3 *Grad:* none *Doc:* transcript
Instruction: *In:* English *Format:* independent study, lecture *Students:* mainly US
Costs: Contact sponsor
Housing: *Arr by pgm:* pensions, hotels, hostels
Deadline: Apr 1
Other info: *US accredited sponsor:* yes *Began:* 1996 *Orient:* in US *Activities:* excursions, program travel *Misc:* May contact former participants. *Financial aid:* scholarships *URL:* http://w3.arizona.edu/~ciss/
Contact: Ctr for Global Student Pgms, Univ of Arizona, 939 N Tyndall Ave, Tucson AZ 85721 *Ph:* 520-626 9211 *Fax:* 520-626 9004 *E-mail:* cpatrick@u.arizona.edu ▲

0887
UNIVERSITY OF RICHMOND
Land of Hellas: Ancient Topography-Modern Legacy
Site: Greece: Crete, Peloponnesus, sites on the mainland
Dates: 4 wks, May-Jun
Subjects: Classical studies, Greek/Hellenic studies
Eligibility: *Level:* fresh, sophs, jrs, srs, adults *Requires:* 2.0 GPA *Age:* min 18
Credit: *Undergrad:* 3 *Grad:* none *Doc:* transcript
Instruction: *In:* English *Format:* study tour *Students:* mainly US
Costs: About $3,200 *incl* tuition, housing, some meals *Nonrefundable fee*
Housing: *Arr by pgm:* hotels
Deadline: Rolling admissions
Other info: *US accredited sponsor:* yes *Began:* 1992 *Orient:* abroad *Activities:* excursions, field trips
Contact: Prof Stuart L Wheeler, Univ of Richmond, Richmond VA 23173 *Ph:* 804-289 8426 *E-mail:* swheeler@richmond.edu
Or Contact: Jeanne Burkett, Sch of Continuing Studies, Univ of Richmond, Richmond VA 23173 *Ph:* 804-289 8133 *Fax:* 804-289 8138 *E-mail:* jburkett@richmond.edu

---

0888
UNIVERSITY OF WISCONSIN-RIVER FALLS
Experience Greece Study Tour
Site: Greece: Athens, Chania, Delphi, Iraklion, Mykonos, Nauplia, Olympia, Santorini
Dates: Varies, end of May to early Jun

See "How To Use This Book" for definitions of terms used above. ▲ = See program sponsor's ad(s) in this book.

Subjects: Art history, Field study, Geography, History, Mythology
Eligibility: *Level:* sophs, jrs, srs, grads, adults, teachers, professionals *Requires:* 2.0 GPA *Age:* min 18
Credit: *Undergrad:* 3 credits *Grad:* by request *Doc:* transcript
Instruction: *In:* English *Format:* directed field study, study tour *Students:* mainly US
Costs: About $3,000 for Univ of Wisconsin-River Falls students *incl* tuition, housing, most meals, intl airfare, fees, excursions
Housing: *Arr by pgm:* hotels
Deadline: About Apr 1
Other info: *US accredited sponsor:* yes *Began:* 1985 *Orient:* in US *Activities:* excursions, field trips, program travel, cultural events *Misc:* Grants avail, if eligible. May contact former participants.
Contact: Dr Nicholas Karolides, Univ of Wisconsin-River Falls, 410 S 3rd St, River Falls WI 54022 *Ph:* 715-425 3366/3537 *Fax:* 715-425 3367 *E-mail:* nicholas.karolides@uwrf.edu
Or Contact: Dr Yolanda Dewar, Univ of Wisconsin-River Falls, 410 S 3rd St, River Falls WI 54022 *Ph:* 715-425 4891 *Fax:* 715-425 3185 *E-mail:* yolanda.a.dewar@uwrf.edu
Or Contact: Dr Barbara Rebhuhn, Univ of Wisconsin-River Falls, 410 S 3rd St, River Falls WI 54022 *Ph:* 715-425 4891 *Fax:* 715-425 3185 *E-mail:* barbara.a.rebhuhn

---

ATHENS

0889
ARTIS-ART RESEARCH TOURS AND INTERNATIONAL STUDIOS
Greece-Cradle of Western Civilization
Site: Greece: Athens
Dates: 2-4 wks, yr-round
Subjects: Art history, Drawing, Photography
Eligibility: *Level:* fresh, sophs, jrs, srs, grads, adults, teachers, professionals, precoll *Requires:* good physical & mental health *Age:* min 18, max 78, avg 25
Credit: *Undergrad:* 3-6 *Grad:* none *Doc:* transcript
Instruction: *In:* English *Format:* directed field study, lecture, study tour, workshop *Students:* mainly US
Costs: $3,585 *incl* housing, some meals, intl airfare, insurance, fees, excursions *Nonrefundable fee*
Housing: *Arr by pgm:* hotels
Deadline: Contact sponsor
Other info: *US accredited sponsor:* no *Began:* 1999 *Orient:* abroad (2 days) *Activities:* excursions, field trips, program travel, cultural events *Misc:* Workshop instructors have MFAs. May contact former participants. *Financial aid:* scholarships *URL:* http://www.artis-tours.org
Contact: Robert Renfrow, ARTIS, 1102 W Huron St, Tucson AZ 85745 *Ph:* 800-232 6893; 520-620 6613 *E-mail:* dfro@socket.net
Or Contact: David Renfrow, ARTIS, 1616 Pioneer Dr, Columbia MO *Ph:* 573-447 3495 *Fax:* 573-447 3495 *E-mail:* dfro@socket.net

---

0890
ATHENS CENTRE
Modern Greek Language Program
Site: Greece: Athens
Dates: 3, 4, 7 or 10 wks, yr-round
Subjects: Greek language (beg/int/adv)
Eligibility: *Level:* fresh, sophs, jrs, srs, adults, precoll *Age:* min 16
Credit: *Undergrad:* avail *Grad:* none *Doc:* certificate
Instruction: *In:* English, Greek *Format:* lang study, lecture *Students:* intl

Costs: $500 per 60-hr course *incl* tuition, fees
Housing: *Arr by pgm:* apartments, pensions
Deadline: 1 wk before pgm
Other info: *US accredited sponsor:* no *Began:* 1976 *URL:* http://www.athenscentre.gr
Contact: Rosemary C Donnelly, Athens Ctr, 48 Archimidous St, GR-11636 Athens, Greece *E-mail:* athenscr@compulink.gr

---

0891
ATHENS CENTRE
Summer Classical Performing Theatre Program in Greece
Site: Greece: Athens
Dates: 1 mo, Jun 12-Jul 11
Subjects: Acting, Drama/theater, Greek/Hellenic studies, Singing/voice
Eligibility: *Level:* adults *Age:* min 16, max 70, avg 22
Credit: *Undergrad:* avail *Grad:* none *Doc:* certificate *Transfer credit through:* Univ of Detroit Mercy
Instruction: *In:* English *Format:* practical training, study tour, workshop *Students:* mainly US
Costs: $3,500-$4,000 *incl* tuition, housing, some meals, intl airfare, fees, excursions, books/materials
Housing: *Arr by pgm:* residence halls, hotels
Deadline: May 15
Other info: *US accredited sponsor:* no *Began:* 1975 *Orient:* abroad (1 day) *Misc:* May contact former participants. *URL:* http://www.athenscentre.gr
Contact: Dr Arthur Beer, Univ of Detroit Mercy, PO Box 19900, Detriot MI 48219-3599 *Ph:* 313-993 1130 *Fax:* 313-993 6465 *E-mail:* beeraj@udmercy.edu

---

0892
BEAVER COLLEGE, CENTER FOR EDUCATION ABROAD
Of Gods and the City
Site: Greece: Athens
Dates: May 25-Jun 16
Subjects: Archaeology, Art history, Classical studies, Greek/Hellenic studies, History
Eligibility: *Level:* sophs, jrs, srs, grads *Requires:* 3.0 GPA
Credit: *Undergrad:* 3 *Grad:* none *Doc:* transcript
Instruction: *In:* English *Format:* directed field study, seminar *Students:* mainly US
Costs: $2,550 *incl* tuition, housing, some meals, insurance, excursions, ISIC, transcript, orient *Nonrefundable fee*
Housing: *Arr by pgm:* apartments, hostels
Deadline: Mar 31
Other info: *US accredited sponsor:* yes *Began:* 1995 *Orient:* abroad *Activities:* excursions, field trips, program travel *Misc:* May contact former participants. *URL:* http://www.arcadia.edu/cea/
Contact: Ctr for Educ Abroad, Beaver Coll, 450 S Easton Rd, Glenside PA 19038 *Ph:* 888-232 8379 *E-mail:* cea@beaver.edu ▲

0893
CALIFORNIA STATE UNIVERSITY, LONG BEACH
The Greek World
Site: Greece: Athens
Dates: 3 wks, Dec 30-Jan 20
Subjects: Art history, Classical studies, Greek/Hellenic studies, History, Literature
Eligibility: *Level:* jrs, srs, grads, adults, teachers, professionals
Credit: *Undergrad:* 3 *Grad:* none *Doc:* transcript
Instruction: *In:* English *Format:* study tour *Students:* mainly US
Costs: $2,665 *incl* tuition, housing, some meals, intl airfare, excursions
Housing: *Arr by pgm:* hotels
Deadline: Oct 1
Other info: *US accredited sponsor:* yes *Began:* 1989 *Orient:* in US (1 day) *Activities:* excursions, field trips, program travel *Misc:* Pgm travel to Delphi, Naupkion, Oympia & Sparta. *URL:* http://www.uces.csulb.edu/winter
Contact: Prof David Hood, History, California State Univ Long Beach, 1250 Bellflower Blvd, Long Beach CA 90840 *Ph:* 562-985 4420 *Fax:* 562-985 5431 *E-mail:* dhood@csulb.edu

---

0894
COLLEGE YEAR IN ATHENS
Summer Academic Study-Travel
Site: Greece: Athens
Dates: 6 wks, Jun-Jul
Subjects: Archaeology, Classical studies, Mythology, Religion/theology
Eligibility: *Level:* fresh, sophs, jrs, srs, teachers, precoll *Requires:* high sch diploma *Age:* min 18
Credit: *Undergrad:* avail *Grad:* none *Doc:* transcript
Instruction: *In:* English *Format:* study tour *Students:* mainly US
Costs: $3,600 *incl* tuition, housing, excursions, books/materials
Housing: *Arr by pgm:* apartments
Deadline: Apr 1
Other info: *US accredited sponsor:* no *Began:* 1962 *Orient:* abroad *Activities:* excursions, field trips *Misc:* Contact Coord of Admissions & Recruitment for info on credit transfer. May contact former participants. *Financial aid:* scholarships *URL:* http://www.cyathens.org
Contact: Coll Yr in Athens, PO Box 390890, N Amer Off, Dept V, Cambridge MA 02139-0010 *Ph:* 617-868 8200 *Fax:* 617-868 8207 *E-mail:* cyathens@aol.com ▲

0895
GREEK DANCES THEATRE
Greek Dance and Folk Culture
Site: Greece: Athens
Dates: 1 wk, summer; 1-6 mos, yr-round
Subjects: Civilization/culture, Costumes, Dance, Folk dance, Folk music, Folklore, Music
Eligibility: *Level:* adults
Credit: *Undergrad:* none *Grad:* none *Doc:* certificate
Instruction: *In:* English *Format:* volunteer/svc, workshop *Students:* intl & host country
Costs: $120 per wk *incl* tuition
Housing: *Sponsor assists:* hotels, hostels
Deadline: None
Other info: *US accredited sponsor:* no *Began:* 1989 *In coop with:* Ministry of Culture *Activities:* field trips, cultural events *URL:* http://users.hol.gr/~grdance
Contact: Adamantia Angeli, Greek Dances Theater, 8 Scholiou Str, GR-10558 Athens, Greece *E-mail:* grdance@hol.gr

---

0896
LANGUAGES ABROAD
Language and Cultural Immersion Programs-Athens
Site: Greece: Athens
Dates: 2 wks or longer, yr-round
Subjects: Civilization/culture, Greek language (beg/int/adv)
Eligibility: *Level:* adults *Age:* min 17, max 65, avg 25
Credit: *Undergrad:* none *Grad:* none *Doc:* certificate
Instruction: *In:* Greek *Format:* lang study *Students:* intl
Costs: From $2,250 for 4 wks *incl* tuition, housing, some meals, excursions, books/materials
Housing: *Arr by pgm:* apartments, homestay
Deadline: None
Other info: *US accredited sponsor:* no *Misc:* May contact former participants. *URL:* http://www.languagesabroad.com
Contact: Ms Jesse Philippe, Langs Abroad, 317 Adelaide St W, Ste 900, Toronto, Ontario M5V 1P9, Canada *Ph:* 800-219 9924; 416-925 7117 *E-mail:* info@languagesabroad.com

---

See "How To Use This Book" for definitions of terms used above. ▲ = See program sponsor's ad(s) in this book.

0897
NATIONAL REGISTRATION CENTER FOR STUDY ABROAD (NRCSA)
Hellenic Language School Alexander the Great
Site: Greece: Athens *Host inst:* Hellenic Lang Sch Alexander the Great
Dates: 2-4 wks, yr-round
Subjects: Greek language (beg/int/adv), Homestay
Eligibility: *Level:* fresh, sophs, jrs, srs, grads, adults, teachers *Age:* min 17
Credit: *Undergrad:* none *Grad:* none *Doc:* certificate
Instruction: *In:* Greek *Format:* lang study *Students:* intl
Costs: $995 for 2 wks, $1,923 for 4 wks *incl* tuition, housing, some meals, insurance
Housing: *Arr by pgm:* homestay, hotels
Deadline: Contact sponsor
Other info: *US accredited sponsor:* no *Began:* 1983 *Orient:* abroad (intensive lang study) *URL:* http://www.nrcsa.com
Contact: June Domoe, NRCSA, 823 N 2nd St, #206, Milwaukee WI 53203 *Ph:* 414-278 0631 *Fax:* 414-271 8884 *E-mail:* info@nrcsa.com

---

0898
SUNY COLLEGE AT NEW PALTZ
Summer Study in Athens, Greece
Site: Greece: Athens
Dates: 6 wks, Jun 13-Jul 26
Subjects: Full curriculum
Eligibility: *Level:* fresh, sophs, jrs, srs, precoll *Requires:* good acad standing *Age:* min 17
Credit: *Undergrad:* 6 per term *Grad:* none *Doc:* transcript
Instruction: *In:* English *Format:* lecture *Students:* intl
Costs: $3,592 for NY residents, $4,846 for others *incl* tuition, housing, insurance, fees, excursions *Nonrefundable fee*
Housing: *Arr by pgm:* apartments
Deadline: Mar 1
Other info: *US accredited sponsor:* yes *Orient:* abroad *Activities:* field trips, program travel *Financial aid:* scholarships *URL:* http://www.newpaltz.edu/oie/
Contact: Ctr for Intl Pgm, SUNY New Paltz, 75 S Manheim Blvd, New Paltz NY 12561 *Ph:* 845-257 3125 *Fax:* 845-527 3129 *E-mail:* international@newpaltz.edu ▲

0899
TEMPLE UNIVERSITY SCHOOL OF LAW
Temple Law Summer Session in Greece
Site: Greece: Athens *Host inst:* Univ of Athens
Dates: 4 wks, Jun 9-Jul 11
Subjects: Criminal law, European law, Human rights, International law, Law, Trade law
Eligibility: Own students preferred. *Level:* grads, grads *Requires:* 1 yr law sch, good acad standing
Credit: *Undergrad:* none *Grad:* 6 *Doc:* transcript, certificate
Instruction: *In:* English, English *Format:* lecture, lecture, seminar, seminar *Students:* US & US & intl & intl
Costs: About $5,650-$6,990 *incl* tuition, tuition, housing, housing, all meals, all meals, intl airfare, intl airfare, fees, fees, excursions, excursions, books/materials, books/materials, personal expenses *Nonrefundable fee*
Housing: *Arr by pgm, Arr by pgm:* hotels, hotels
Deadline: April 15
Other info: *US accredited sponsor:* yes *Began:* 1977 *Orient:* abroad (1 day) *Activities:* field trips, field trips, cultural

events, cultural events *Misc:* May contact former participants. *URL:* http://www.temple.edu/lawschool
Contact: Adelaide Ferguson, Asst Dean, or Karen McMichael, Temple Univ Law Sch, Klein Law Bldg, Rm 710, Philadelphia PA 19122 *Ph:* 215-204 1448 *Fax:* 215-204 2282 *E-mail:* intl-law@vm.temple.edu

---

0900
UNIVERSITY OF INDIANAPOLIS ATHENS
Odyssey in Athens-Summer Program
Site: Greece: Athens
Dates: 1 mo, Jun 20-Jul 19
Subjects: Anthropology, Archaeology, Greek language
Eligibility: *Level:* fresh, sophs, jrs, srs, grads, adults *Requires:* good acad standing *Age:* min 17
Credit: *Undergrad:* avail *Grad:* avail *Doc:* transcript
Instruction: *In:* English *Format:* seminar *Students:* mainly host country
Costs: $2,000 *incl* tuition, housing, fees, excursions
Housing: *Arr by pgm:* apartments
Deadline: Rolling admissions
Other info: *US accredited sponsor:* yes *Began:* 1999 *Orient:* abroad (2 days) *Activities:* excursions, cultural events *URL:* http://www.star.net/People/~odyssey
Contact: Barbara Tsairis, Odyssey in Athens, PO Box 5666, Portsmouth NH 03802-5666 *Ph:* 603-431 4999 *Fax:* 603-431 4999 *E-mail:* odyssey@star.net
Or Contact: Dina Skias, Univ of Indianapolis Athens, 29 Voulis St, Athens 105 57, Greece *E-mail:* odyds@hotmail.com

---

0901
UNIVERSITY OF LA VERNE
Summer in Greece
Site: Greece: Athens (Kifissia)
Dates: 6 wks, Jun-Jul
Subjects: Anthropology, Art, Behavioral sciences, Biology, Business/management, Chemistry, Computer sciences, Economics, Education/teaching, Greek language (beg), Mathematics, Philosophy, Photography, Political science/politics, Psychology
Eligibility: *Level:* fresh, sophs, jrs, srs, grads, teachers
Credit: *Undergrad:* 4 *Grad:* 3 *Doc:* transcript
Instruction: *In:* English *Format:* art studio, lab, lecture, seminar *Students:* US & intl
Costs: About $950 per course for grads, $1,200 for undergrads *incl* tuition
Housing: *Arr by pgm:* residence halls
Deadline: Rolling admissions
Other info: *US accredited sponsor:* yes *Began:* 1975 *In coop with:* La Verne Coll of Athens *Orient:* abroad *Activities:* excursions *Misc:* May contact former participants. *URL:* http://www.laverne.edu.gr
Contact: Dr Rahavia Yakovee, La Verne Coll of Athens, PO Box 51105, Kifissia, 14510 Athens, Greece *E-mail:* ryako@laverne.edu.gr
Or Contact: Dr Alfred Clark, Univ of La Verne, 1950 Third St, La Verne CA 91750 *Ph:* 909-593 3511ext 4240 *Fax:* 909-392 2709 *E-mail:* clarka@ulv.edu

---

CHALKIDIKI

0902
FLORIDA STATE UNIVERSITY
The Greece Program
Site: Greece: Chalkidiki
Dates: 4 wks, May 11-Jun 4
Subjects: Art, Civilization/culture, Gender studies, Greek/Hellenic studies, Humanities, Mythology, Psychology
Eligibility: *Level:* fresh, sophs, jrs, srs, grads *Requires:* 2.50 GPA
Credit: *Undergrad:* avail *Grad:* avail
Instruction: *In:* English *Format:* lecture, seminar *Students:* mainly US
Costs: Contact Sponsor
Housing: *Arr by pgm:* hotels
Deadline: Jan 19
Other info: *US accredited sponsor:* yes
Contact: Bonnie Snyder ofrLiz Johnson, Florida State Univ, A5500 Univ Ctr, Tallahassee FL 32306-2420 *Ph:* 800-375 8581; 850-644 3272 *Fax:* 850-644 8817 *E-mail:* intprog@www.fsu.edu

---

CRETE

0903
ARIADNE INSTITUTE
Goddess Pilgrimage to Crete with Carol Christ
Site: Greece: Crete *Host inst:* California Inst of Integral Studies
Dates: 15 days, May 26-Jun 9 or Sep 29-Oct 13
Subjects: Civilization/culture, Greek/Hellenic studies, Independent study, Mythology, Religion/theology, Women's studies
Eligibility: *Level:* fresh, sophs, jrs, srs, grads, adults, teachers, professionals
Credit: *Undergrad:* avail *Grad:* avail *Transfer credit through:* California Inst of Integral Studies
Instruction: *In:* English *Format:* independent study *Students:* intl
Costs: $2,275 *incl* tuition, housing, some meals, fees, excursions *Nonrefundable fee*
Housing: *Arr by pgm:* pensions
Deadline: None; apply early
Other info: *US accredited sponsor:* no *Began:* 1993 *Activities:* excursions, field trips, program travel, cultural events *Misc:* Exploration of ancient goddess sites. Loans avail. May contact former participants. *Financial aid:* scholarships *URL:* http://www.goddessariadne.org
Contact: Jana Ruble, Co-Dir, Ariadne Inst, 1306 Crestview Dr, Blacksburg VA 24060 *Ph:* 540-951 3070 *Fax:* 540-951 3070 *E-mail:* institute@goddessariadne.org

---

0904
NATIONAL REGISTRATION CENTER FOR STUDY ABROAD (NRCSA)
Greek Language Study in Crete
Site: Greece: Crete *Host inst:* Hellenic Lang Sch
Dates: 2 or 4 wks, yr-round
Subjects: Greek language (beg/int/adv)
Eligibility: *Level:* fresh, sophs, jrs, srs, grads, adults, teachers, professionals *Age:* min 18
Credit: *Undergrad:* none *Grad:* none *Doc:* certificate
Instruction: *In:* Greek *Format:* lang study, lecture *Students:* intl
Costs: $1,355 for 2 wks, $2,636 for 4 wks *incl* tuition, housing, some meals, insurance *Nonrefundable fee*
Housing: *Arr by pgm:* hotels
Deadline: 6 wks before pgm
Other info: *US accredited sponsor:* no *URL:* http://www.nrcsa.com
Contact: June Domoe, NRCSA, 823 N 2nd St, #206, Milwaukee WI 53203 *Ph:* 414-278 0631 *Fax:* 414-271 8884 *E-mail:* info@nrcsa.com

---

KATOHI

0905
UNIVERSITY OF KANSAS
Summer Theater in Greece
Site: Greece: Katohi
Dates: 6 wks, mid-Jun-late Jul
Subjects: Architectural history, Civilization/culture, Dance, Greek/Hellenic studies, History, Singing/voice, Theater arts
Eligibility: *Level:* fresh, sophs, jrs, srs, grads, professionals
Credit: *Undergrad:* avail *Grad:* avail *Doc:* transcript
Instruction: *In:* English *Format:* study tour, volunteer/svc, workshop *Students:* mainly US
Costs: About $2,500 *incl* tuition, housing, some meals, fees, excursions
Housing: *Arr by pgm:* residence halls
Deadline: Mar 1
Other info: *US accredited sponsor:* yes *Orient:* in US *Activities:* excursions, field trips, cultural events *Misc:* Students will

prepare & perform a Greek tragedy during the Summer Theatre Festival in Katohi. *URL:* http://www.ukans.edu/~osa
Contact: Study Abroad, Univ of Kansas, 108 Lippincott Hall, Lawrence KS 66045 *Ph:* 785-864 3742 *Fax:* 785-864 5040 *E-mail:* osa@ukans.edu ▲

LESVOS

0906
CALIFORNIA INSTITUTE OF INTEGRAL STUDIES
Women's Quest in Lesvos, Greece
Site: Greece: Lesvos *Host inst:* Ariadne Inst
Dates: 2 wks, Jun 24-Jul 9
Subjects: Art, Field study, Music, Women's studies, Written composition
Eligibility: *Level:* adults
Credit: *Undergrad:* 3 *Grad:* 3
Instruction: *In:* English *Format:* art studio, directed field study, lecture, music lesson, seminar, study tour *Students:* intl
Costs: $2,150 *incl* tuition, housing, some meals, fees, excursions, books/materials *Nonrefundable fee*
Housing: *Arr by pgm:* hotels
Deadline: None; apply early
Other info: *US accredited sponsor:* yes *Began:* 1993 *Activities:* excursions, field trips, program travel, cultural events *Misc:* Loans avail. May contact former participants. *Financial aid:* scholarships *URL:* http://www.goddessariadne.org
Contact: Jana Ruble, Ariadne Inst, 1306 Crestview Dr, Blacksburg VA 24060 *Ph:* 540-951 3070 *Fax:* 540-951 3070 *E-mail:* institute@goddessariadne.org

---

PAROS

0907
COLLEGE YEAR IN ATHENS
Intensive Modern Greek Studies
Site: Greece: Paros
Dates: 3 week programs 6/11/01-6/30/01, and 7/2/01-7/21/01
Subjects: Art history, Drama/theater, Greek language (beg/int/adv), Greek/Hellenic studies, History, Italian studies, Literature, Performing arts, Visual arts
Eligibility: *Level:* fresh, sophs, jrs, srs, grads, adults, teachers *Age:* min 18
Credit: *Undergrad:* 8 *Grad:* 8 *Doc:* transcript
Instruction: *In:* English, Greek, Modern Greek Language *Students:* US & US
Costs: $1,700-$1,900 per 3 week course *incl* tuition, housing, excursions, books/materials
Housing: *Arr by pgm:* residence halls, apartments, hotels
Deadline: Apr 15
Other info: *US accredited sponsor:* no *Began:* 2000 *In coop with:* Contact Coordinator of Admissions and Recruitment for more information 617-868-8200 *Activities:* excursions, field trips, cultural events *Misc:* May contact former participants. *URL:* http://www.cyathens.org
Contact: College Year in Athens, PO Box 390890, Cambridge MA 02139 *Ph:* 617-868 8200 *Fax:* 617-868 8207 *E-mail:* cyathens@aol.com ▲

SAMOS

0908
ART SCHOOL OF THE AEGEAN
Art School of the Aegean
Site: Greece: Samos
Dates: 3-4 wks, Jun 15-Jul 15
Subjects: Civilization/culture, Painting, Photography, Sculpture, Tile making
Eligibility: *Level:* fresh, sophs, jrs, srs, adults, teachers, professionals *Age:* min 18, max 70, avg 35
Credit: *Undergrad:* none *Grad:* none *Doc:* certificate
Instruction: *In:* Greek *Format:* art studio, independent study, lecture, workshop *Students:* US & intl
Costs: $2,050 for 3 wks *incl* tuition, housing, some meals *Nonrefundable fee*
Housing: *Arr by pgm:* pensions
Deadline: Apr 10
Other info: *US accredited sponsor:* no *Began:* 1991 *Activities:* excursions, field trips, cultural events *Misc:* May contact former participants. *URL:* http://www.artschool-aegean.com
Contact: Susan Trovas, Dir, Art Sch of the Aegean, PO Box 1375, Sarasota FL 34230 *Ph:* 941-351 5597 *E-mail:* susan1615@home.com

---

SPETSES ISLAND

0909
ATHENS CENTRE
Summer Greek Language Program
Site: Greece: Spetses Island
Dates: 3 wks, Jun 24-Jul 14
Subjects: Greek language (beg/int/adv)
Eligibility: *Level:* fresh, sophs, jrs, srs, grads, adults *Age:* min 16, avg 30
Credit: *Undergrad:* avail *Grad:* none *Doc:* certificate *Transfer credit through:* San Francisco State Univ
Instruction: *In:* English, Greek *Format:* lang study *Students:* intl
Costs: $1,600 *incl* tuition, housing, excursions
Housing: *Arr by pgm:* pensions
Deadline: Jun 20
Other info: *US accredited sponsor:* no *Began:* 1994 *Orient:* abroad *Activities:* excursions, cultural events *Misc:* May contact former participants. *URL:* http://www.athenscentre.gr
Contact: Rosemary Donnelly, Athens Ctr, 48 Archimidous St, 11636 Athens, Greece *E-mail:* athenscr@compulink.gr

---

0910
UNIVERSITY OF DETROIT MERCY
Classic Theatre & Drama
Site: Greece: Spetses Island *Host inst:* Athens Centre
Dates: 4 wks, Jun-Jul
Subjects: Acting, Dance, Drama/theater, Greek language, History, Mythology, Singing/voice
Eligibility: *Level:* fresh, sophs, jrs, srs, grads, adults, teachers, professionals, precoll *Requires:* previous study in field, good health; audition for acting roles, resume & interview for tech positions *Age:* min 16, max 75, avg 22
Credit: *Undergrad:* 6 *Grad:* 6 *Doc:* transcript, certificate
Instruction: *In:* English *Format:* lab, lecture, music lesson, practical training, study tour *Students:* mainly US
Costs: $4,000 without credit, $5,000 with credit *incl* tuition, housing, some meals, intl airfare, insurance, fees, excursions, books/materials *Nonrefundable fee*
Housing: *Arr by pgm:* residence halls, hotels
Deadline: Apr 15
Other info: *US accredited sponsor:* yes *Began:* 1975 *Orient:* in US 1 day *Activities:* excursions, field trips, program travel, cultural events *Misc:* students work with professionals for Comedy/tragedy perfs on tour. May contact former participants. *Financial aid:* work study *URL:* http://www.udmercy.edu/
Contact: Dr Arthur J Beer, Univ Detroit Mercy, 112 Marian, Outer Dr. Campus, Detroit MI 48219 *Ph:* 810-264 2611, 313-993 6463 *Fax:* 313-993 6465 *E-mail:* beeraj@udmercy.edu
Or Contact: Mary F Bremner, Assoc Dir, 4201 Chicago Rd, Warren MI 48092 *Ph:* 810-264 2611

THESSALONIKI

0911
ARISTOTLE UNIVERSITY OF THESSALONIKI, SCHOOL OF MODERN GREEK LANGUAGE
Modern Greek Language
Site: Greece: Thessaloniki
Dates: 1 mo, Aug 16-Sep 15, Sep 15-Oct 14 or Feb 1-28
Subjects: Greek language
Eligibility: *Level:* adults, precoll *Requires:* high sch diploma *Age:* min 18
Credit: *Undergrad:* avail *Grad:* none *Doc:* certificate
Instruction: *In:* English *Format:* lang study, lecture *Students:* intl
Costs: EUR 200 *incl* tuition, fees
Housing: *Sponsor assists:* residence halls
Deadline: May 31; Aug 16; Dec 31; Apr 30 for scholarships
Other info: *US accredited sponsor:* no *Activities:* excursions, cultural events *Financial aid:* scholarships *URL:* http://www.auth.gr/smgl
Contact: Theodora Kaldi-Koulikidou, Aristotle Univ of Thessaloniki, Sch of Modern Greek Lang, 54006 Thessaloniki, Greece *E-mail:* thkaldi@auth.gr

Iceland

REYKJAVIK

0912
DIS, DENMARK'S INTERNATIONAL STUDY PROGRAM
Arctic Biology Summer Program
Site: Iceland: Reykjavik *Host inst:* Univ of Iceland
Dates: 6 wks, mid-Jun-late Jul
Subjects: Area studies, Biology, Ecology/environmental studies, Geology, Marine biology
Eligibility: *Level:* sophs, jrs, srs, grads *Requires:* 3.0 GPA, 1 yr biology, 1 chemistry course
Credit: *Undergrad:* 8 *Grad:* none *Doc:* transcript
Instruction: *In:* English *Format:* directed field study, lab, lecture, study tour *Students:* mainly US
Costs: $4,580 *incl* tuition, housing, fees, excursions, books/materials
Housing: *Arr by pgm:* furnished rms
Deadline: Contact member insts
Other info: *US accredited sponsor:* yes *Orient:* abroad *Activities:* excursions, field trips, cultural events *Misc:* May contact former participants. *Financial aid:* scholarships *URL:* http://www.disp.dk/
Contact: *See Index II for Members* Charlotte Simonsen, Field Dir, Univ of Minnesota, 214 Heller Hall, 271 19th Ave S, Minneapolis MN 55455 *Ph:* 800-247 3477; 612-626 7679 *Fax:* 612-626 8009 *E-mail:* dis@umn.edu

---

0913
DIS, DENMARK'S INTERNATIONAL STUDY PROGRAM
Geology of Iceland Summer Program
Site: Iceland: Reykjavik *Host inst:* Univ of Iceland
Dates: 6 wks, mid-Jun-late Jul
Subjects: Biology, Geology, Geophysics, Geoscience, Mineral exploration, Volcanology
Eligibility: *Level:* sophs, jrs, srs, grads *Requires:* 3.0 GPA, 1 yr geology, 1 chemistry course
Credit: *Undergrad:* 8 *Grad:* none *Doc:* transcript, certificate
Instruction: *In:* English *Format:* directed field study, lab, lecture, study tour *Students:* US & intl
Costs: $4,580 *incl* tuition, housing, some meals, excursions, books/materials

Housing: *Arr by pgm:* furnished rms
Deadline: Contact member insts
Other info: *US accredited sponsor:* yes *Began:* 1997 *Orient:* abroad *Activities:* excursions, field trips, cultural events *Misc:* May contact former participants. *Financial aid:* scholarships *URL:* http://www.disp.dk/
Contact: *See Index II for Members* Charlotte Simonsen, Field Dir, DIS, Univ of Minnesota, 214 Heller Hall, 271 19th Ave S, Minneapolis MN 55455 *Ph:* 800-247 3477; 612-626 7679 *Fax:* 612-626 8009 *E-mail:* dis@umn.edu

---

0914
SIGURDUR NORDAL INSTITUTE
Icelandic Summer Course
Site: Iceland: Reykjavik *Host inst:* Univ of Iceland
Dates: 4 wks, Jul 2-27
Subjects: Homestay, Icelandic language (beg/int/adv)
Eligibility: *Level:* adults *Requires:* foreign lang study & some background in Icelandic preferred *Age:* min 20
Credit: *Undergrad:* avail *Grad:* none
Instruction: *In:* English, Icelandic *Format:* lab, lang study, lecture *Students:* intl
Costs: $450 *incl* tuition, excursions *Nonrefundable fee*
Housing: *Arr by pgm:* residence halls, apartments, homestay
Deadline: Mar 1
Other info: *US accredited sponsor:* no *Activities:* excursions, cultural events *URL:* http://www.nordals.hi.is
Contact: Ulfar Bragason, Sigurdur Nordal Inst, PO Box 1220, 121 Reykjavik, Iceland *E-mail:* ulfarb@hi.is

Ireland

MORE THAN ONE CITY

0915
ACHILL ARCHAEOLOGICAL SUMMER FIELD SCHOOL
Archaeological Field Study Program
Site: Ireland: various sites
Dates: 4 wks, May 25-Jun 15
Subjects: Archaeology, Field study, Folklore, Homestay, Surveying
Eligibility: *Level:* srs, grads, adults, teachers, professionals, precoll *Age:* min 17, max 60
Credit: *Undergrad:* avail *Grad:* none *Doc:* transcript, certificate
Instruction: *In:* English *Format:* directed field study, lecture, practical training, seminar, study tour, workshop *Students:* intl
Costs: Contact sponsor
Housing: *Arr by pgm:* apartments, homestay, hotels
Deadline: Feb 28
Other info: *US accredited sponsor:* no *Began:* 2001 *Orient:* abroad *Activities:* excursions, field trips, program travel *Misc:* May contact former participants. *URL:* http://achill-fieldschool.com
Contact: Theresa McDonald, Achille Folklife Ctr, Dodagh, Achill Island, Co Mayo, Ireland *E-mail:* achill-fieldschool@iol.ie
Or Contact: Elizabeth Davis, Univ of MN, 2018 55th St, Des Moines IA 50310 *Ph:* 515-279 4841 *E-mail:* davis173@tc.umn.edu

---

0916
COOPERATIVE CENTER FOR STUDY ABROAD
Ireland Early Summer Program
Site: Ireland: Dublin, Galway
Dates: 2 wks, May 16-31
Subjects: Accounting, Education/teaching, History, Homestay, Literature
Eligibility: *Level:* fresh, sophs, jrs, srs, grads, adults, teachers, professionals *Requires:* 2.0 GPA, recommendation *Age:* min 18, avg 25
Credit: *Undergrad:* 3 *Grad:* 3 *Doc:* transcript
Instruction: *In:* English *Format:* lecture, seminar, study tour, tutorial *Students:* mainly US
Costs: $2,295 *incl* housing, some meals, intl airfare, excursions, ISIC/ITIC *Nonrefundable fee*
Housing: *Arr by pgm:* residence halls, homestay, budget accommodations
Deadline: Mar 1
Other info: *US accredited sponsor:* yes *Began:* 1992 *Orient:* in US & abroad *Activities:* excursions, field trips, program travel, cultural events *Misc:* May contact former participants. *Financial aid:* scholarships *URL:* http://www.nku.edu/ccsa
Contact: *See Index II for Members* Dr Michael A Klembara or Robin Byerly, Coop Ctr for Study Abroad, Northern Kentucky Univ, BEP 301, Highland Heights KY 41099 *Ph:* 800-319 6015; 859-572 6512 *Fax:* 859-572 6650 *E-mail:* ccsa@nku.edu

---

0917
COOPERATIVE CENTER FOR STUDY ABROAD
Ireland Late Summer Program
Site: Ireland: Dublin, Galway
Dates: 2 wks, Jul 16-31
Subjects: Art, History, Homestay, Literature, Music
Eligibility: *Level:* fresh, sophs, jrs, srs, grads, adults, teachers, professionals *Requires:* 2.0 GPA, recommendation *Age:* min 18
Credit: *Undergrad:* 3 *Grad:* 3 *Transfer credit through:* Northern Kentucky Univ
Instruction: *In:* English *Format:* lecture, study tour *Students:* mainly US
Costs: $2,495 *incl* housing, some meals, intl airfare, excursions, airport transfers, ISIC/ITIC *Nonrefundable fee*
Housing: *Arr by pgm:* residence halls, homestay, budget accommodations
Deadline: Mar 1
Other info: *US accredited sponsor:* yes *Began:* 1997 *Orient:* in US & abroad *Activities:* excursions, field trips, program travel, cultural events *Misc:* May contact former participants. *Financial aid:* scholarships *URL:* http://www.nku.edu/ccsa
Contact: *See Index II for Members* Dr Michael Klembara, or Robin Byerly, Coop Ctr for Study Abroad, Northern Kentucky Univ, BEP 301 Nunn Dr, Highland Heights KY 41099 *Ph:* 800-319 6015; 859-572 6512 *Fax:* 859-572 6650 *E-mail:* ccsa@nku.edu

---

0918
GAEL-LINN
Courses in Spoken Irish for Adults
Site: Ireland: Dublin, Gweedore (Co Donegal)
Dates: 6 wks, yr-round for Dublin; 8 days, Jul 8-15 & Jul 29-Aug 5 for Donegal
Subjects: Irish language/Gaelic (beg/int/adv), Music, Poetry
Eligibility: *Level:* adults *Age:* min 21
Credit: *Undergrad:* none *Grad:* none *Doc:* certificate
Instruction: *In:* Gaelic *Format:* lang study *Students:* intl
Costs: IR 140 for Dublin courses, IR 125 for Donegal *incl* tuition *Nonrefundable fee*
Housing: *Arr by student*
Deadline: 1 mo before a pgm
Other info: *US accredited sponsor:* no *Activities:* excursions, cultural events *Misc:* Donegal course incl lectures on cultural background, poetry readings, music. Lang only in Dublin.
Contact: Aine O Cuireain, Gael-Linn, 26 Cearnog Mhuirfean, Baile Atha Cliath 2, Ireland *E-mail:* gaellinn@circom.net

---

0919
NATIONAL REGISTRATION CENTER FOR STUDY ABROAD (NRCSA)
Language Study in Ireland
Site: Ireland: Cork, Dublin, Galway *Host inst:* Home Lang Schs Intl
Dates: 1 wk or longer, yr-round
Subjects: Homestay, Irish language/Gaelic
Eligibility: *Level:* fresh, sophs, jrs, srs, grads, adults, teachers, professionals
Credit: *Undergrad:* none *Grad:* none *Doc:* certificate
Instruction: *In:* Gaelic *Format:* lang study, tutorial *Students:* intl

Costs: $1,006 per wk *incl* tuition, housing, all meals, insurance *Nonrefundable fee*
Housing: *Arr by pgm:* homestay
Deadline: 6 wks before pgm
Other info: *US accredited sponsor:* no *Misc:* Student lives in teacher's home. *URL:* http://www.nrcsa.com
Contact: Reuel Zielke, NRCSA, 823 N 2nd St, #206, Milwaukee WI 53203 *Ph:* 414-278 0631 *Fax:* 414-271 8884 *E-mail:* info@nrcsa.com

---

0920
OIDEAS GAEL, ULSTER CULTURAL CENTRE
Irish Language, Culture, Music, Arts and Dance for Adults
Site: Ireland: Glencolmcille, Glenfin (Gaelic-speaking regions of Co Donegal) *Host inst:* Ulster Cultural Inst
Dates: 1-wk courses, Mar 15-Oct 30
Subjects: Archaeology, Crafts, Field study, Folk dance, Hiking/trekking, Homestay, Irish language/Gaelic (beg/int/adv), Irish studies, Music, Painting
Eligibility: *Level:* fresh, sophs, jrs, srs, adults, precoll *Age:* min 16, avg 30
Credit: *Undergrad:* avail *Grad:* none
Instruction: *In:* English, Gaelic *Format:* directed field study, lang study, lecture, seminar, study tour, tutorial *Students:* intl
Costs: $300 *incl* tuition, housing, some meals, insurance, excursions, books/ materials
Housing: *Arr by pgm:* homestay, furnished rms
Deadline: 4 wks before pgm; Feb 1 for scholarship
Other info: *US accredited sponsor:* no *Began:* 1984 *In coop with:* Govt Educ Dept *Activities:* excursions, cultural events *Misc:* May contact former participants. *Financial aid:* scholarships *URL:* http://www.Oideas-Gael.com
Contact: Liam O'Cuinneagain, Oideas Gael, Ulster Cultural Ctr, Glencolmcille, Co Donegal, Ireland *E-mail:* oidsgael@iol.ie

---

0921
PENNSYLVANIA STATE UNIVERSITY
Flight Program in Ireland
Site: Ireland: Dublin, Galway
Dates: 6 wks, Jun-Aug
Subjects: Civilization/culture, Communications, Irish language/Gaelic, Irish studies, Speech/debate/forensics
Eligibility: CIC students only *Level:* fresh, sophs *Requires:* 2.5 GPA *Age:* min 18
Credit: *Undergrad:* 9 *Grad:* none
Instruction: *In:* English *Format:* lecture, study tour *Students:* mainly US
Costs: Contact Sponsor
Housing: *Arr by pgm:* residence halls
Deadline: Rolling admissions
Other info: *US accredited sponsor:* yes *Began:* 1999 *Orient:* in US & abroad *Misc:* May contact former participants. *Financial aid:* scholarships
Contact: Summer Abroad, Pennsylvania State Univ, 225 Penn State Conference Ctr, University Park PA 16802 *Ph:* 814-863 5170
Or Contact: Intl Pgm Adviser, Pennsylvania State Univ, 222 Boucke Bldg, University Park PA 16802 *Ph:* 814-865 7681 *Fax:* 814-865 3336

0922
PENNSYLVANIA STATE UNIVERSITY
Writing and Painting the Irish Landscape
Site: Ireland: Achill Island, Allihies (Beara Peninsula), Dublin *Host inst:* Allihies Lang & Arts Ctr, Trinity Coll, Dublin
Dates: 3 wks, May-Jun
Subjects: Creative writing, Homestay, Painting
Eligibility: *Level:* sophs, jrs, srs *Requires:* 2.5 GPA *Age:* min 18
Credit: *Undergrad:* 9 *Grad:* none
Instruction: *In:* English *Format:* art studio, lecture *Students:* mainly US
Costs: About $4,000 for PA residents, $6,650 for others *incl* tuition, housing, most meals, all meals, books/materials
Housing: *Arr by pgm:* residence halls, homestay
Deadline: Mar 17
Other info: *US accredited sponsor:* yes *Began:* 1999 *Orient:* in US & abroad *URL:* http://www.outreach.psu.edu/PSSEA/
Contact: Summer Abroad, Pennsylvania State Univ, 225 Penn State Conference Ctr, University Park PA 16802 *Ph:* 814-863 5170 *Fax:* 814-863 5190 *E-mail:* SummerAbroad@outreach.psu.edu

---

0923
SYRACUSE UNIVERSITY
Irish Drama: Politics and War
Site: Ireland: Cashel, Dublin, Galway
Dates: 4 wks, Jul 4-27
Subjects: Drama/theater, English
Eligibility: *Level:* fresh, sophs, jrs, srs, grads, adults, teachers *Requires:* 2.5 GPA *Age:* min 18, avg 21
Credit: *Undergrad:* 6 *Grad:* 6
Instruction: *In:* English *Format:* study tour *Students:* mainly US
Costs: $5,100 *incl* tuition, housing, some meals, fees, excursions, books/materials *Nonrefundable fee*
Housing: *Arr by pgm:* residence halls
Deadline: Mar 15
Other info: *US accredited sponsor:* yes *Began:* 1994 *Orient:* abroad *Activities:* excursions, field trips, program travel, cultural events *Misc:* May contact former participants. *Financial aid:* scholarships *URL:* http://sumweb.syr.edu/dipa/summer
Contact: Daisy Fried, Assoc Dir, Syracuse Univ, 119 Euclid Ave, Syracuse NY 13244-4170 *Ph:* 800-251 9674; 315-443 9419 *Fax:* 315-443 4593 *E-mail:* dsfried@summon3.syr.edu ▲

0924
UNIVERSITY OF SOUTH FLORIDA
USF Irish Summer School
Site: Ireland: Limerick, various sites *Host inst:* Univ of Limerick
Dates: 3 wks, Jun
Subjects: Creative writing, Irish studies, Literature, Written composition
Eligibility: *Level:* fresh, sophs, jrs, srs, grads, adults, teachers, professionals *Requires:* 2.5 GPA *Age:* min 18
Credit: *Undergrad:* 6 *Grad:* 6 *Doc:* transcript, certificate
Instruction: *In:* English *Format:* lecture, study tour, workshop *Students:* mainly host country
Costs: About $2,100 *incl* tuition, housing, most meals, intl airfare, fees, excursions *Nonrefundable fee*
Housing: *Arr by pgm:* residence halls, bed & breakfasts during study tour
Deadline: Mar 1
Other info: *US accredited sponsor:* yes *Began:* 1998 *In coop with:* Univ of Limerick *Orient:* in US (1 day) *Activities:* excursions, program travel *Misc:* About 7-day study tour with 2-wk sch in professional writing. *URL:* http://www.usf.edu/~iac/
Contact: Dr Richard Wilber, Pgm Dir, Mass Communications, Univ of South Florida, 4202 E Fowler Ave, CIS 1040, Tampa FL 33620 *Ph:* 813-974 6792 *Fax:* 813-974 4613
Or Contact: Julie Hale, Coord, Overseas Study Pgm, Univ of South Florida, 4202 E Fowler Ave, CPR 107, Tampa FL 33620 *Ph:* 813-974 3933, 813-974 4043 *Fax:* 813-974 4613 *E-mail:* jhale@iac.usf.edu

---

ACHILL ISLAND

0925
ACHILL ARCHAEOLOGICAL SUMMER FIELD SCHOOL
Achill Archaeological Summer Field School
Site: Ireland: Achill Island
Dates: 10 wks, Jun 25-Aug 31
Subjects: Anthropology, Archaeology, Botany, Field study, Folklore, Geology, Geophysics, Irish language/Gaelic, Surveying
Eligibility: *Level:* srs, grads, adults, teachers, precoll *Age:* min 17
Credit: *Undergrad:* avail *Grad:* none *Doc:* transcript, certificate
Instruction: *In:* English *Format:* directed

field study, lecture, seminar, workshop *Students:* intl
Costs: $3,500 *incl* tuition, housing, books/materials, local transport
Housing: *Arr by pgm:* apartments
Deadline: Apr 30
Other info: *US accredited sponsor:* no *In coop with:* Mayo Co Council *Orient:* abroad *Activities:* excursions, field trips, cultural events *Misc:* May contact former participants. *URL:* http://achill-fieldschool.com
Contact: Theresa McDonald, Achill Archaeological Field Sch, St O'Hara's Hill, Tullamore, Co Offaly, Ireland *E-mail:* theresa@iol.ie

BALLYVAUGHAN

0926
BURREN COLLEGE OF ART
Burren College of Art, Ireland Summer Program
Site: Ireland: Ballyvaughan
Dates: 4 wks, Jun 3-30 or 6 wks, Jul 1-Aug 11
Subjects: Creative writing, Drawing, Independent study, Irish studies, Painting, Photography, Sculpture
Eligibility: *Level:* adults *Requires:* previous study in field, portfolio review
Credit: *Undergrad:* avail *Grad:* none *Doc:* transcript, certificate
Instruction: *In:* English *Format:* art studio, lecture, seminar, study tour, tutorial *Students:* intl
Costs: $2,500 for 4 wks, $3,500 for 6 wks *incl* tuition, housing, excursions, some materials *Nonrefundable fee*
Housing: *Arr by pgm:* cottages
Deadline: Mar 30
Other info: *US accredited sponsor:* no *Began:* 1995 *Orient:* abroad *Activities:* excursions, program travel, cultural events, sports *Financial aid:* work study *URL:* http://www.burrencollege.com
Contact: Mary Hawkes-Greene, Dir, Burren Coll of Art, Ballyvaughan, Cty Clare, Ireland *E-mail:* mhg@burrencollege.com

0927
SCHOOL OF THE MUSEUM OF FINE ARTS, BOSTON
Painting and Drawing in the Burren
Site: Ireland: Ballyvaughan *Host inst:* Burren Coll of Art
Dates: Aug 4-Aug 25
Subjects: Studio arts (beg/int/adv)
Eligibility: *Level:* fresh, sophs, jrs, srs, grads, adults, teachers, professionals *Age:* min 18
Credit: *Undergrad:* avail *Grad:* none *Doc:* transcript
Instruction: *In:* English *Format:* art studio *Students:* mainly US
Costs: $2,360 *incl* tuition, housing, some meals, fees, excursions, host facilities *Nonrefundable fee*
Housing: *Arr by pgm:* cottages
Deadline: May 4 or until pgm filled
Other info: *US accredited sponsor:* yes *Began:* 1980 *Activities:* excursions, cultural events *Misc:* One hr info session at Sch of the Museum of Fine Arts on Apr 18. *URL:* http://www.smfa.edu
Contact: Nathaniel Bradley, SMFA Continuing Educ, 230 The Fenway, Boston MA 02115 *Ph:* 617-267 1219 *Fax:* 617-369 3679 *E-mail:* coned@smfa.edu

CORK

0928
NORTH AMERICAN INSTITUTE FOR STUDY ABROAD
Summer Study in Ireland-Cork
Site: Ireland: Cork *Host inst:* Univ Coll Cork
Dates: 4 wks, Jul
Subjects: Archaeology, Art, Celtic studies, History, Irish studies, Literature, Religion/theology, Sociology
Eligibility: *Level:* adults *Age:* min 18, avg 20
Credit: *Undergrad:* 6 *Grad:* 6 *Doc:* transcript
Instruction: *In:* English *Format:* lecture, seminar, tutorial *Students:* intl
Costs: $3,075 *incl* tuition, housing, fees, ISIC, orient, handbook *Nonrefundable fee*
Housing: *Arr by pgm:* residence halls
Deadline: May 30; Apr 1 for scholarships
Other info: *US accredited sponsor:* no *Began:* 1989 *Orient:* abroad *Misc:* May contact former participants. *Financial aid:* scholarships *URL:* http://www.naisa.com
Contact: Operations Mgr, North Amer Inst for Study Abroad, 129 Mill St, Danville PA 17821 *Ph:* 570-275 5099 *Fax:* 570-275 1644 *E-mail:* naisa@naisa.com

0929
SUNY COLLEGE AT CORTLAND
Summer Courses in Irish Studies
Site: Ireland: Cork *Host inst:* Univ Coll Cork
Dates: 4 wks, Jul
Subjects: History, Irish studies, Literature
Eligibility: *Level:* fresh, sophs, jrs, srs
Credit: *Undergrad:* 6 *Grad:* none *Doc:* transcript
Instruction: *In:* English *Format:* lecture, seminar *Students:* mainly US
Costs: $3,400 *incl* housing, all meals, intl airfare, insurance, excursions, books/materials, passport *Nonrefundable fee*
Housing: *Arr by pgm:* apartments
Deadline: Apr 1
Other info: *US accredited sponsor:* yes *Orient:* in US *Activities:* field trips *Misc:* Intro course in Irish lang. Loans avail. *URL:* http://www.studyabroad.com/suny/cortland
Contact: Dr John Ogden, Dir, Intl Pgms, SUNY Coll at Cortland, PO Box 2000, Cortland NY 13045 *Ph:* 607-753 2209 *Fax:* 607-753 5989 *E-mail:* studyabroad@snycorva.cortland.edu ▲

DONEGAL

0930
OIDEAS GAEL, ULSTER CULTURAL CENTRE
Archaeology-5,000 Years in Stone
Site: Ireland: Donegal
Dates: 1 wk, Aug 1-8
Subjects: Archaeology, Field study, Homestay
Eligibility: *Level:* srs, grads, adults, teachers, professionals *Age:* min 16, max 80, avg 30
Credit: *Undergrad:* avail *Grad:* avail
Instruction: *In:* English *Format:* directed field study, lecture, workshop *Students:* intl
Costs: $150 *incl* tuition
Housing: *Arr by pgm:* apartments, homestay, hotels, hostels
Deadline: 4 wks before pgm
Other info: *US accredited sponsor:* no *Began:* 1987 *Orient:* abroad *Activities:* field trips, cultural events *URL:* http://www.Oideas-Gael.com
Contact: Liam O'Cuinneagain, Oideas Gael, Glencolmcille, Co Donegal, Ireland *E-mail:* oidsgael@iol.ie

DUBLIN

0931
BEAVER COLLEGE, CENTER FOR EDUCATION ABROAD
Summer in Dublin
Site: Ireland: Dublin *Host inst:* Inst of Public Admin
Dates: Jun 27-Aug 10
Subjects: History, Irish studies, Literature, Political science/politics
Eligibility: *Level:* sophs, jrs, srs *Requires:* 3.0 GPA
Credit: *Undergrad:* 6 *Grad:* none *Doc:* transcript
Instruction: *In:* English *Format:* directed field study, lecture, seminar *Students:* mainly US
Costs: $3,390 *incl* tuition, housing, insurance, excursions, ISIC, orient, transcript *Nonrefundable fee*

Housing: *Arr by pgm:* apartments
Deadline: Mar 31
Other info: *US accredited sponsor:* yes *Began:* 1995 *Orient:* abroad (2 days) *Misc:* May contact former participants. *URL:* http://www.arcadia.edu/cea
Contact: Ctr for Educ Abroad, Beaver Coll, 450 S Easton Rd, Glenside PA 19038 *Ph:* 888-232 8379 *E-mail:* cea@beaver.edu ▲

0932
BRAM STOKER PROJECT
Bram Stoker International Summer School
Site: Ireland: Dublin
Dates: 1 wk, Jul
Subjects: Gothic studies, Literature
Eligibility: *Level:* adults
Credit: *Undergrad:* none *Grad:* none *Doc:* certificate
Instruction: *In:* English *Format:* lecture, seminar, workshop *Students:* intl
Costs: Contact Sponsor
Housing: *Arr by student*
Deadline: None
Other info: *US accredited sponsor:* no *Began:* 1991 *Activities:* excursions, field trips, cultural events
Contact: Dennis McIntyre, Bram Stoker Sch, 101 Foxfield Grove, Raheny, Dublin 5, Ireland *E-mail:* dmcintyre@ireland.com

---

0933
CENTER FOR CULTURAL INTERCHANGE
Internship in Ireland
Site: Ireland: Dublin
Dates: 1-3 mos, yr-round
Subjects: Business/management, Health/health education, Homestay, Humanities, Internships, Social sciences
Eligibility: *Level:* fresh, sophs, jrs, srs, grads *Requires:* 3.0 GPA *Age:* min 18, max 28, avg 21
Credit: *Undergrad:* none *Grad:* none *Doc:* certificate
Instruction: *In:* English *Format:* internship, practical training *Students:* mainly host country
Costs: $1,980 per mo *incl* housing, some meals, insurance, fees, placement *Nonrefundable fee*
Housing: *Arr by pgm:* homestay
Deadline: 3 mos before pgm
Other info: *US accredited sponsor:* no *Began:* 1999 *In coop with:* Dublin Sch of English *Orient:* in US & abroad (1 day) *Misc:* May contact former participants. *URL:* http://www.cci-exchange.com
Contact: Karen Hindhede, Outbound Pgms Dir, Ctr for Cultural Interchange, 17 N 2nd Ave, St Charles IL 60174 *Ph:* 888-227 6231; 630-377 2272 *Fax:* 630-377 2307 *E-mail:* info@cci-exchange.com

---

0934
COUNCIL ON INTERNATIONAL EDUCATIONAL EXCHANGE (COUNCIL)
Trinity College, Dublin/USIT NOW (Summer)
Site: Ireland: Dublin *Host inst:* Trinity Coll Dublin
Dates: Jun 22-Aug 10
Subjects: Irish studies
Eligibility: *Level:* sophs, jrs, srs *Requires:* 2.5 GPA *Age:* min 18
Credit: *Undergrad:* 6 *Grad:* none *Doc:* transcript
Instruction: *In:* English *Format:* lecture, seminar, tutorial *Students:* mainly US
Costs: $4,800 *incl* tuition, housing, all meals, insurance, excursions, ISIC *Nonrefundable fee*
Housing: *Arr by pgm:* residence halls, homestay
Deadline: May 1
Other info: *US accredited sponsor:* no *Began:* 1959 *In coop with:* USIT *Orient:* abroad (1-2 days) *Activities:* field trips *Misc:* Field trip to Northern Ireland. May contact former participants. *URL:* http://www.ciee.org/study
Contact: Pgm Adviser, Council-ISP, 633 3rd Ave, 20th Fl, New York NY 10017 *Ph:* 800-407 8839; 212-822 2600, 212-822 2772 *Fax:* 212-822 2779 *E-mail:* studyinfo@ciee.org ▲

0935
CREIGHTON UNIVERSITY
Creighton University Summer School in Ireland
Site: Ireland: Dublin *Host inst:* Trinity Coll Dublin
Dates: 4 wks, Jun 26-Jul 21
Subjects: Civilization/culture, History, Irish studies, Literature
Eligibility: *Level:* sophs, jrs, srs, grads, adults
Credit: *Undergrad:* 6 *Grad:* 6 *Doc:* transcript
Instruction: *In:* English *Format:* lecture, seminar, study tour *Students:* mainly US
Costs: $2,550 *incl* tuition, housing, some meals
Housing: *Sponsor assists:* residence halls
Deadline: Mar 31
Other info: *US accredited sponsor:* yes *Began:* 1992 *Activities:* field trips, cultural events *Financial aid:* scholarships *URL:* http://mentor.creighton.edu/human/English/Irish.htm
Contact: English Dept, Creighton Univ, 2500 California Plaza, Omaha NE 68178 *Ph:* 402-280 2822 *Fax:* 402-280 2143 *E-mail:* micsun@creighton.edu

---

0936
DICKINSON COLLEGE
Business Internship in Dublin
Site: Ireland: Dublin
Dates: 6 wks, late May-late Jun
Subjects: Finance, Internships
Eligibility: *Level:* fresh, sophs, jrs
Credit: *Undergrad:* 8 *Grad:* none
Instruction: *In:* English *Format:* internship, practical training *Students:* mainly US
Costs: About $4,500 *incl* tuition, housing, intl airfare, excursions *Nonrefundable fee*
Housing: *Arr by pgm:* apartments
Deadline: Mar
Other info: *US accredited sponsor:* yes *Began:* 2000 *Orient:* in US & abroad *Activities:* excursions *URL:* http://www.dickinson.edu/departments/ocs/abroad.html
Contact: Global Educ, Dickinson Coll, PO Box 1773, Carlisle PA 17013-2896 *Ph:* 717-245 1341 *Fax:* 717-245 1688 *E-mail:* ocs@dickinson.edu

---

0937
DUBLIN INTERNSHIPS
Dublin International Internships
Site: Ireland: Dublin
Dates: 10 wks, summer
Subjects: Full curriculum, Internships
Eligibility: *Level:* jrs, srs, grads *Requires:* previous study in field
Credit: *Undergrad:* avail *Grad:* avail
Instruction: *In:* English *Format:* internship, seminar *Students:* mainly US
Costs: Contact sponsor
Housing: *Sponsor assists:* apartments, homestay
Deadline: 3 mos before pgm recommended
Other info: *US accredited sponsor:* no *Orient:* abroad *Activities:* cultural events *Misc:* Credit via student's coll. *URL:* http://homepage.eircom.net/~dublinternships
Contact: Mary H Rieke, MA, Dublin Internships, Scholarstown Rd, Dublin 16, Ireland *E-mail:* mhrieke@eircom.net

---

0938
ENGLISH LITERATURE SUMMER SCHOOL
Irish Literature Summer School
Site: Ireland: Dublin *Host inst:* Trinity Coll Dublin
Dates: 1 wk, Jul 30-Aug 4
Subjects: Irish studies, Literature
Eligibility: *Level:* adults *Age:* min 16, avg 40

 See "How To Use This Book" for definitions of terms used above. ▲ = See program sponsor's ad(s) in this book.

Credit: *Undergrad:* none *Grad:* none *Doc:* certificate
Instruction: *In:* English *Format:* lecture, study tour *Students:* intl
Costs: UK 485 *incl* tuition, housing, all meals, fees, excursions *Nonrefundable fee*
Housing: *Arr by pgm:* residence halls
Deadline: Contact sponsor
Other info: *US accredited sponsor:* no *Began:* 2000 *URL:* http://www.webmarketing.co.uk/ess/
Contact: Irish Literature Summer Sch, English Literature Summer Schs, 10 Victoria Rd, Sheffield S10 2DL, UK *E-mail:* arthurmeakin@netscape.net

---

0939
FLORIDA INTERNATIONAL UNIVERSITY
Creative Writing in Dublin
Site: Ireland: Dublin *Host inst:* Trinity Coll
Dates: 1 mo, Jun 26-Jul 27
Subjects: Creative writing, Poetry
Eligibility: *Level:* fresh, sophs, jrs, srs, grads, adults, teachers, professionals
Credit: *Undergrad:* 3 *Grad:* avail *Doc:* transcript
Instruction: *In:* English *Format:* practical training, study tour, workshop *Students:* US & intl
Costs: $2,975 *incl* housing, some meals, intl airfare, excursions, books/materials, railpass
Housing: *Arr by pgm:* residence halls
Deadline: May 15
Other info: *US accredited sponsor:* yes *Began:* 1997 *Orient:* in US (1 day) *Activities:* excursions, field trips, program travel, cultural events *Misc:* May contact former participants. *URL:* http://www.fiu.edu/~intered
Contact: Intl Studies, Florida Intl Univ, 11200 SW 8th St, DM 300B, Miami FL 33199 *Ph:* 305-348 1913, 305-348 1918 *Fax:* 305-348 1941 *E-mail:* intered@fiu.edu

---

0940
GAIETY SCHOOL OF ACTING
Irish Theater Summer School/Irish Theater January Term
Site: Ireland: Dublin
Dates: 3 wks, Jan 2-19 or 4 wks, Jul 2-23
Subjects: Acting, Drama/theater
Eligibility: *Level:* fresh, sophs, jrs, srs, grads, adults *Age:* min 18, avg 25
Credit: *Undergrad:* avail *Grad:* avail *Transfer credit through:* Gustavus Adolphus Coll
Instruction: *In:* English *Format:* lecture, seminar, workshop *Students:* US & intl
Costs: $2,500 for 3 wks Jan, $2,900-$3,300 for 4 wks summer *incl* tuition, housing, some meals, fees, excursions
Housing: *Arr by pgm:* homestay, hostels
Deadline: Contact sponsor
Other info: *US accredited sponsor:* no *Began:* 1998 *In coop with:* Gustavus Adolphus Coll, Univ of Utah *Activities:* field trips, cultural events *Misc:* Transfer credit avail through Univ of Utah for summer session. May contact former participants. *Financial aid:* scholarships *URL:* http://www.gaietyschool.com
Contact: Patrick Sutton, or Elaine Comyn, Gaiety Sch of Acting, Meeting House Sq, Temple Bar, Dublin 2, Ireland *E-mail:* gaiety.school@indigo.ie

---

0941
IES, INSTITUTE FOR THE INTERNATIONAL EDUCATION OF STUDENTS
IES Dublin Summer
Site: Ireland: Dublin
Dates: About 6 wks, Jun 7-Jul 21
Subjects: Business/management, Economics, Field study, History, Literature, Political science/politics
Eligibility: *Level:* fresh, sophs, jrs, srs, grads, adults *Requires:* 3.0 GPA *Age:* min 18
Credit: *Undergrad:* 6 *Grad:* none *Doc:* transcript
Instruction: *In:* English *Format:* directed field study, lecture *Students:* mainly US
Costs: About $3,800 *incl* tuition, housing, some meals, insurance, field trips to Galway
Housing: *Sponsor assists:* residence halls
Deadline: Apr 1
Other info: *US accredited sponsor:* yes *Began:* 1999 *Orient:* abroad (2 days) *Activities:* field trips, cultural events *Misc:* May contact former participants. *URL:* http://www.IESabroad.org
Contact: *See Index II for Members* IES, 33 N LaSalle St, 15th Fl, Chicago IL 60602-2602 *Ph:* 800-995 2300; 312-944 1750 *Fax:* 312-944 1448 *E-mail:* info@iesabroad.org ▲

0942
NEW YORK UNIVERSITY, TISCH SCHOOL OF THE ARTS
Arts in Dublin
Site: Ireland: Dublin *Host inst:* Trinity Coll Dublin
Dates: 6 wks, about Jun 25-Aug 3
Subjects: Acting, Civilization/culture, Film studies, Irish studies, Theater arts
Eligibility: *Level:* fresh, sophs, jrs, srs, adults, teachers, professionals *Age:* min 18
Credit: *Undergrad:* 8 *Grad:* 8 *Doc:* transcript
Instruction: *In:* English *Format:* lecture, practical training, seminar, workshop *Students:* mainly US
Costs: $5,494-$5,994 *incl* tuition, housing, fees, excursions *Nonrefundable fee*
Housing: *Arr by pgm:* apartments
Deadline: About Apr 15; rolling admissions
Other info: *US accredited sponsor:* yes *Began:* 1998 *Orient:* in US & abroad *Activities:* excursions, field trips, cultural events *Misc:* Loans & scholarships for own students only. *URL:* http://www.nyu.edu/tisch/international/
Contact: Linda Kow, Assoc Dir, Tisch Intl Pgms, New York Univ, 721 Broadway, 12th Fl, New York NY 10003 *Ph:* 212-998 9175 *Fax:* 212-995 4578 *E-mail:* tisch.international@nyu.edu

0943
NORTH AMERICAN INSTITUTE FOR STUDY ABROAD
Academy for Irish Studies
Site: Ireland: Dublin *Host inst:* Acad for Irish Studies
Dates: 4 wks, July
Subjects: Archaeology, Art, English, Film studies, History, Media studies, Political science/politics
Eligibility: *Level:* fresh, sophs, jrs, srs, grads *Requires:* 2.5 GPA *Age:* min 18, avg 20
Credit: *Undergrad:* 6 *Grad:* none *Doc:* transcript
Instruction: *In:* English *Format:* lecture, seminar, study tour, tutorial *Students:* US & intl
Costs: $3,190 *incl* tuition, housing, insurance, fees, ISIC *Nonrefundable fee*
Housing: *Sponsor assists:* residence halls
Deadline: Apr 30; Nov 30 for scholarships
Other info: *US accredited sponsor:* no *Began:* 1995 *In coop with:* IPA *Orient:* abroad (1 day) *Activities:* excursions, field trips, program travel, cultural events *Misc:* May contact former participants. *Financial aid:* scholarships *URL:* http://www.naisa.com
Contact: Dr Michael Currio, NAISA, 129 Mill St, Danville PA 17821 *Ph:* 570-275 5099 *Fax:* 570-275 1644 *E-mail:* naisa@naisa.com
Or Contact: Dr Tony Wilson, Acad for Irish Studies, Bearna Park, Sandyford, Dublin Ireland *E-mail:* wilsontj@tinet.ie

0944
NORTH AMERICAN INSTITUTE FOR STUDY ABROAD
Summer in Dublin
Site: Ireland: Dublin *Host inst:* Inst of Public Admin
Dates: 6 wks, early Jul-mid-Aug
Subjects: History, Irish studies, Literature, Political science/politics
Eligibility: *Level:* fresh, sophs, jrs, srs, grads, precoll *Requires:* 2.7 GPA *Age:* min 18, avg 20
Credit: *Undergrad:* 6 *Grad:* 6 *Doc:* transcript
Instruction: *In:* English *Format:* lecture, seminar, study tour *Students:* mainly US
Costs: $3,450 *incl* tuition, housing, ISIC *Nonrefundable fee*
Housing: *Sponsor assists:* residence halls, apartments, homestay
Deadline: Apr 30; Nov 30 for scholarships
Other info: *US accredited sponsor:* no *Began:* 1999 *Orient:* abroad (1 day) *Activities:* field trips, cultural events *Misc:* May contact former participants. *Financial aid:* scholarships *URL:* http://www.naisa.com
Contact: Dr Michael Currid, NAISA, 129 Mill St, Danville PA 17868 *Ph:* 570-275 5099 *Fax:* 570-275 1644 *E-mail:* naisa@naisa.com

0945
NORTH AMERICAN INSTITUTE FOR STUDY ABROAD
Summer School of Irish Studies
Site: Ireland: Dublin *Host inst:* Univ Coll Dublin
Dates: 2-3 wks, early Jul
Subjects: Civilization/culture, Irish studies, Political science/politics
Eligibility: *Level:* adults *Age:* min 18, avg 20
Credit: *Undergrad:* 3 *Grad:* avail *Doc:* transcript
Instruction: *In:* English *Format:* lecture, seminar, tutorial *Students:* intl
Costs: $1,750 *incl* tuition, housing, fees, ISIC, orient, handbook *Nonrefundable fee*
Housing: *Arr by pgm:* residence halls
Deadline: May 30; Apr 1 for scholarships
Other info: *US accredited sponsor:* no *Began:* 1991 *Orient:* abroad *Misc:* May contact former participants. *Financial aid:* scholarships *URL:* http://www.naisa.com
Contact: Operations Mgr, North Amer Inst for Study Abroad, 129 Mill St, Danville PA 17821 *Ph:* 570-275 5099 *Fax:* 570-275 1644 *E-mail:* naisa@naisa.com

0946
NORTH AMERICAN INSTITUTE FOR STUDY ABROAD
Summer Study in Ireland: James Joyce Annual Summer School
Site: Ireland: Dublin *Host inst:* Univ Coll Dublin
Dates: 2 wks, mid-Jul
Subjects: Literature
Eligibility: *Level:* adults *Age:* min 18, avg 20
Credit: *Undergrad:* 3 *Grad:* avail *Doc:* transcript
Instruction: *In:* English *Format:* lecture, seminar, tutorial *Students:* intl
Costs: $1,850 *incl* tuition, housing, fees, ISIC, orient, handbook *Nonrefundable fee*
Housing: *Arr by pgm:* bed & breakfast
Deadline: May 30; Apr 1 for scholarships
Other info: *US accredited sponsor:* no *Began:* 1991 *Orient:* abroad *Misc:* Guest lectures, poetry readings, concerts of Joycean music, theater productions, visits to Joyce's Dublin haunts. May contact former participants. *Financial aid:* scholarships *URL:* http://www.naisa.com
Contact: Operations Mgr, North Amer Inst for Study Abroad, 129 Mill St, Danville PA 17821 *Ph:* 570-275 5099 *Fax:* 570-275 1644 *E-mail:* naisa@naisa.com

0947
NORTHERN ILLINOIS UNIVERSITY
Media and Culture in Ireland
Site: Ireland: Dublin *Host inst:* Dublin City Univ
Dates: 4 wks, Jun-Jul
Subjects: Communications, Film studies, Homestay, Literature, Media studies
Eligibility: *Level:* sophs, jrs, srs, grads *Requires:* 2.5 GPA *Age:* min 18, avg 21
Credit: *Undergrad:* 6 *Grad:* 6 *Doc:* transcript
Instruction: *In:* English *Format:* directed field study, lecture *Students:* mainly US
Costs: $2,600 *incl* tuition, housing, some meals, insurance, excursions
Housing: *Arr by pgm:* homestay
Deadline: May 1 or until pgm filled
Other info: *US accredited sponsor:* yes *Began:* 1991 *Orient:* in US & abroad *Misc:* May contact former participants. *Financial aid:* scholarships *URL:* http://www.niu.edu/niuabroad/
Contact: Anne Seitzinger, Pgm Coord, Study Abroad Office, Williston 417, Northern Illinois Univ, DeKalb IL 60115 *Ph:* 815-753 0700 *Fax:* 815-753 0825 *E-mail:* niuabroad@niu.edu

---

0948
SCHOOL OF PRACTICAL CHILD CARE
Childcare Training
Site: Ireland: Dublin
Dates: Multiple pgm lengths, Sep-Jun
Subjects: Child care, Child development, First aid training, Learning disabilities, Preschool education, TEFL/TESL
Eligibility: *Level:* adults *Age:* min 17, avg 20
Credit: *Undergrad:* none *Grad:* none *Doc:* certificate
Instruction: *In:* English *Format:* practical training *Students:* intl & host country
Costs: IR 300-2,000 *incl* tuition
Housing: *Arr by pgm:* homestay
Deadline: Aug
Other info: *US accredited sponsor:* no *Began:* 1986 *Misc:* Montessori studies, care for older people. Correspondence & Internet training avail. *URL:* http://www.practicalchildcare.com
Contact: Anne Clinch, Principal, Sch of Practical Childcare, Carysfort Ave, Blackrock, Cty Dublin, Ireland

---

0949
SUNY COLLEGE AT CORTLAND
Internships in Dublin
Site: Ireland: Dublin
Dates: Summer term
Subjects: Full curriculum, Homestay, Internships
Eligibility: *Level:* jrs, srs *Requires:* 2.5 GPA, previous study in field
Credit: *Undergrad:* 10 *Grad:* none *Doc:* transcript
Instruction: *In:* English *Format:* internship *Students:* mainly US
Costs: About $4,360 *incl* housing, all meals, intl airfare, insurance, fees, passport, bus pass *Nonrefundable fee*
Housing: *Sponsor assists:* apartments, homestay
Deadline: Apr 1
Other info: *US accredited sponsor:* yes *Began:* 1993 *In coop with:* Inst of Public Admin (IPA), Dublin Internships *Orient:* in US *URL:* http://www.studyabroad.com/suny/cortland
Contact: John Ogden, Intl Pgms, SUNY Coll at Cortland, PO Box 2000, Cortland NY 13045 *Ph:* 607-753 2209 *Fax:* 607-753 5989 *E-mail:* studyabroad@cortland.edu ▲

0950
UNIVERSITY OF DAYTON
Interdepartmental Summer Study Abroad Program (ISSAP)-Dublin
Site: Ireland: Dublin *Host inst:* Trinity Coll
Dates: 1 mo, Jun 28-Jul 28
Subjects: Education/teaching, Literature, Music, Philosophy, Religion/theology
Eligibility: *Level:* fresh, sophs, jrs, srs, grads, adults *Requires:* 2.0 GPA *Age:* min 18, avg 20
Credit: *Undergrad:* 7 *Grad:* none *Doc:* transcript
Instruction: *In:* English *Format:* lecture *Students:* mainly US
Costs: $3,595 *incl* tuition, housing, some meals, insurance, excursions *Nonrefundable fee*
Housing: *Arr by pgm:* residence halls
Deadline: Mar 1; Jan 15 for scholarships
Other info: *US accredited sponsor:* yes *Began:* 1972 *Orient:* in US & abroad (4 days) *Activities:* excursions, field trips, cultural events *Misc:* May contact former participants. *Financial aid:* scholarships
Contact: James W Stiles, Univ of Dayton, 300 College Park, Dayton OH 45469-1481 *Ph:* 937-229 3728 *Fax:* 937-229 2766 *E-mail:* stiles@udayton.edu

---

0951
UNIVERSITY OF IOWA
The Irish Writing Program
Site: Ireland: Dublin *Host inst:* Trinity Coll Dublin
Dates: 7 wks, late Jun-mid-Aug
Subjects: Creative writing, Literature
Eligibility: *Level:* fresh, sophs, jrs, srs, grads, adults *Requires:* 2.5 GPA, writing sample *Age:* min 18, avg 22
Credit: *Undergrad:* 5 *Grad:* 5 *Doc:* transcript
Instruction: *In:* English *Format:* seminar, workshop *Students:* mainly US
Costs: $4,250 for UI students, $4,450 for others *incl* tuition, housing, some meals, fees *Nonrefundable fee*
Housing: *Arr by pgm:* residence halls
Deadline: Mar 15
Other info: *US accredited sponsor:* yes *Began:* 1997 *Orient:* in US & abroad (2 days) *Activities:* cultural events *Misc:* May contact former participants. *URL:* http://www.uiowa.edu/~irishwp
Contact: Study Abroad, Univ of Iowa, 120 Intl Ctr, Iowa City IA 52242 *Ph:* 319-335 0353 *Fax:* 319-353 2033 *E-mail:* irishwp@uiowa.edu

---

0952
UNIVERSITY OF SAN DIEGO, SCHOOL OF LAW
Dublin Institute on International and Comparative Law
Site: Ireland: Dublin *Host inst:* Trinity Coll Dublin
Dates: About Jul 2-Aug 3
Subjects: Criminal justice, Human rights, International law
Eligibility: *Level:* grads, teachers, professionals *Requires:* law or bus students
Credit: *Undergrad:* none *Grad:* 6 *Doc:* certificate
Instruction: *In:* English *Format:* seminar *Students:* mainly US
Costs: $2,800, $1,200 for housing *incl* tuition, housing, books/materials *Nonrefundable fee*
Housing: *Arr by pgm:* residence halls
Deadline: Mar 11
Other info: *US accredited sponsor:* yes *Began:* 1983 *In coop with:* Trinity Coll *Orient:* abroad *Misc:* $1,200 - housing. Legal visits & some tourist visits arr from site. Correspondence regarding pgm must be in English. Loan for US students only *URL:* http://www.acusd.edu/lawabroad
Contact: Cindy King, Law Pgms Abroad, Univ of San Diego, 5998 Alcala Park, San Diego CA 92110-2492 *Ph:* 619-260 7460 *Fax:* 619-260 2230 *E-mail:* cking@acusd.edu

---

0953
UNIVERSITY OF SOUTHERN MISSISSIPPI
Irish Studies Program
Site: Ireland: Dublin
Dates: 3 wks, Jun 14-Jul 5
Subjects: Anthropology, English, Sociology
Eligibility: *Level:* fresh, sophs, jrs, srs, grads *Requires:* 2.00 GPA, good acad standing *Age:* min 18, avg 22
Credit: *Undergrad:* 4 *Grad:* 4 *Doc:* transcript
Instruction: *In:* English *Format:* directed field study, lecture *Students:* mainly US
Costs: $3,499 for undergrads, $3,799 for grads *incl* tuition, housing, intl airfare

Housing: *Arr by pgm:* bed & breakfast
Deadline: Apr 24
Other info: *US accredited sponsor:* yes *Began:* 1995 *Activities:* field trips *Financial aid:* scholarships *URL:* http://www.usm.edu
Contact: Dr Tim W Hudson, Intl & Continuing Educ, Univ of Southern Mississippi, Box 10047, Hattiesburg MS 39406-0047 *Ph:* 601-266 4344 *Fax:* 601-266 5699 *E-mail:* melissa.ravencraft@usm.edu
Or Contact: Dr James Flanagan, Chair, Anthropology & Sociology, Univ of Southern Mississippi, Hattiesburg MS 39406-0047 *Ph:* 601-266 4306 *Fax:* 601-266 5699

0954
USIT
Ireland in Europe: Trinity Summer School
Site: Ireland: Dublin *Host inst:* Trinity Coll Dublin
Dates: Jul 15-28
Subjects: Art history, Civilization/culture, Drama/theater, History, Irish studies, Literature, Political science/politics, Sociology
Eligibility: *Level:* fresh, sophs, jrs, srs, grads, adults, teachers, professionals *Age:* min 18, max 80
Credit: *Undergrad:* none *Grad:* none *Doc:* certificate
Instruction: *In:* English *Format:* seminar *Students:* intl
Costs: IR 900 *incl* tuition, housing, some meals, fees, excursions, bus pass, tickets *Nonrefundable fee*
Housing: *Arr by pgm:* residence halls, apartments, homestay, hotels, hostels
Deadline: Contact sponsor
Other info: *US accredited sponsor:* no *Began:* 1989 *Activities:* excursions, field trips, cultural events *Misc:* May contact former participants. *URL:* http://www.usitnow.ie
Contact: Seona MacReamoinn, USIT, Aston Quay, Dublin 2, Ireland *E-mail:* smacreamoinn@usit.ie

---

ENNIS

0955
CALIFORNIA STATE UNIVERSITY, LONG BEACH
Archaeological Field School
Site: Ireland: near Ennis (Co Clare) *Host inst:* Burren Archaeology Research
Dates: 4 wks, early Jul-late Aug
Subjects: Archaeology, Field study, Irish studies
Eligibility: *Level:* fresh, sophs, jrs, srs, grads, adults *Age:* min 17
Credit: *Undergrad:* 3 *Grad:* 3 *Doc:* transcript
Instruction: *In:* English *Format:* directed field study *Students:* mainly US
Costs: $2,687 *incl* tuition, housing, all meals, excursions, books/materials *Nonrefundable fee*
Housing: *Arr by pgm:* holiday cottages
Deadline: Until pgm filled
Other info: *US accredited sponsor:* yes *Began:* 1998 *Activities:* field trips *Misc:* May contact former participants. *URL:* http://www.burrenarch.com
Contact: Alix Gilmer, Dir, Burren Archaeology Research, 82 Cowleigh Rd, Malvern, Worcester WR141QN, UK *E-mail:* burrenarch@hotmail.com
Or Contact: Wendy Rayburn, Coord, Summer Sessions, Univ Coll & Extension Svcs, California State Univ-Long Beach, 6300 State Univ Dr, Ste 104, Long Beach CA 90815 *Ph:* 800-963 2250 ext 57754; 562-985 7754 *Fax:* 562-985 8449 *E-mail:* wrayburn@uces.csulb.edu

---

GALWAY

0956
COLLEGE CONSORTIUM FOR INTERNATIONAL STUDIES and **SAINT BONAVENTURE UNIVERSITY** and **TRUMAN STATE UNIVERSITY**
Summer in Ireland
Site: Ireland: Galway *Host inst:* Natl Univ of Ireland, Galway
Dates: 1 mo, Jun 28-Jul 28
Subjects: Gaelic language (beg/int), History, Literature, Written composition
Eligibility: *Level:* sophs, jrs, srs *Requires:* 3.0 GPA, 2 recommendations *Age:* min 18
Credit: *Undergrad:* 6 *Grad:* none *Doc:* transcript
Instruction: *In:* English *Format:* lang study, lecture, seminar, tutorial
Costs: $1,500-$2,000 *incl* tuition, fees
Housing: *Arr by pgm:* apartments with local students, residence halls with local students, homestay
Deadline: Apr 1
Other info: *US accredited sponsor:* yes *Began:* 2000 *Misc:* 3 sessions avail: Irish Studies, Irish Language, Irish Writing. May contact former participants. *URL:* http://www.ccisabroad.org
Contact: *See Index II for Members* Alice Sayegh, Dir, Intl Studies, St Bonaventure Univ, St Bonaventure NY 14778 *Ph:* 716-375 2574 *Fax:* 716-375 7882 *E-mail:* asayegh@sbu.edu
Or Contact: Ctr for Intl Education Abroad, Truman State Univ, Kirk Bldg 120, Kirksville MO 63501 *Ph:* 660-785 4076 *Fax:* 660-785 7473 *E-mail:* ciea@truman.edu ▲

0957
GEORGE MASON UNIVERSITY
Ireland and Its Cultures
Site: Ireland: Galway *Host inst:* Univ Coll Galway
Dates: 2 wks, Jun 26-Jul 11
Subjects: Civilization/culture, English, History, Irish studies
Eligibility: *Level:* fresh, sophs, jrs, srs, grads, adults, teachers, professionals *Requires:* 2.25 GPA *Age:* min 18
Credit: *Undergrad:* 3 *Grad:* 3 *Doc:* transcript
Instruction: *In:* English *Format:* study tour *Students:* mainly US
Costs: About $1,900 for VA residents, $2,500 for others *incl* tuition, housing, insurance, fees, excursions, ISIC *Nonrefundable fee*
Housing: *Arr by pgm:* apartments
Deadline: Apr 10
Other info: *US accredited sponsor:* yes *Began:* 1996 *Orient:* in US (1 day) *Misc:* May contact former participants. *Financial aid:* scholarships, work study *URL:* http://www.gmu.edu/departments/cge
Contact: Ctr for Global Educ, George Mason Univ, Johnson Ctr, Rm 235, 4400 University Dr, Fairfax VA 22030-4444 *Ph:* 703-993 2154 *Fax:* 703-993 2153 *E-mail:* cge@gmu.edu

---

0958
NORTH AMERICAN INSTITUTE FOR STUDY ABROAD
Summer Study in Ireland-Galway
Site: Ireland: Galway *Host inst:* Natl Univ of Ireland
Dates: 4-5 wks, Jun-Jul
Subjects: Archaeology, Civilization/culture, Film studies, History, Irish studies, Literature, Sociology
Eligibility: *Level:* adults *Age:* min 18, avg 20
Credit: *Undergrad:* 6 *Grad:* avail *Doc:* transcript
Instruction: *In:* English *Format:* lecture, seminar, tutorial *Students:* intl
Costs: $3,390 *incl* tuition, housing, fees, ISIC, orient, handbook *Nonrefundable fee*
Housing: *Arr by pgm:* residence halls, apartments
Deadline: May 30; Apr 1 for scholarships
Other info: *US accredited sponsor:* no *Began:* 1991 *Orient:* abroad *Misc:* May contact former participants. *Financial aid:* scholarships *URL:* http://www.naisa.com
Contact: Operations Mgr, North Amer Inst for Study Abroad, 129 Mill St, Danville PA 17821 *Ph:* 570-275 5099 *Fax:* 570-275 1644 *E-mail:* naisa@naisa.com

---

0959
RAMAPO COLLEGE OF NEW JERSEY
Summer Study in Ireland
Site: Ireland: Galway *Host inst:* Univ Coll Galway
Dates: 3-1/2 wks, Jun-Jul
Subjects: International marketing, Irish studies
Eligibility: *Level:* sophs, jrs, srs *Requires:* good acad standing *Age:* min 18
Credit: *Undergrad:* 3 *Grad:* none
Instruction: *In:* English *Format:* lecture *Students:* mainly US
Costs: $2,800 for Ramapo students, $3,000 for others *incl* tuition, housing, most meals, intl airfare, excursions, most meals *Nonrefundable fee*
Housing: *Arr by pgm:* residence halls
Deadline: May 1
Other info: *US accredited sponsor:* yes *Began:* 1998 *Orient:* in US *Activities:* excursions, cultural events *URL:* http://www.ramapo.edu/Academics/Abroad/
Contact: Robyn Perricelli, Ramapo Coll of New Jersey, 505 Ramapo Valley Rd, Mahwah NJ 07430 *Ph:* 201-684 7030 *Fax:* 201-684 7651 *E-mail:* rperrice@ramapo.edu

---

0960
SOUTHWEST TEXAS STATE UNIVERSITY
SWT in Ireland
Site: Ireland: Galway *Host inst:* Univ Coll Galway
Dates: 5 wks, Jul
Subjects: Independent study, Literature, Written composition
Eligibility: *Level:* sophs, jrs, srs, grads, adults *Requires:* 2.5 GPA *Age:* min 19
Credit: *Undergrad:* 6 *Grad:* 6
Instruction: *In:* English *Format:* directed field study, independent study, study tour, workshop *Students:* mainly US
Costs: $2,800 *incl* tuition, housing, intl airfare, fees, excursions
Housing: *Arr by pgm:* apartments
Deadline: Jan
Other info: *US accredited sponsor:* yes *Began:* 1999 *Orient:* in US *Activities:* excursions, field trips, program travel, cultural events *Financial aid:* scholarships *URL:* http://www.English.swt.edu/ireland/index.html
Contact: Steve Wilson, Co-Dir, English, Southwest Texas State Univ, San Marcos TX 78666 *Ph:* 512-245 2163 *Fax:* 512-245 8546 *E-mail:* sw13@swt.edu
Or Contact: John Blair, Co-Dir, English, Southwest Texas State Univ, San Marcos TX 78666 *Ph:* 512-245 2163 *Fax:* 512-245 8546 *E-mail:* ig02@swt.edu

---

0961
SUNY UNIVERSITY AT ALBANY
Irish Studies Program
Site: Ireland: Galway
Dates: 4 wks, Jun 29-Jul 29
Subjects: Architecture, Civilization/culture, Film studies, History, Irish studies, Literature
Eligibility: *Level:* fresh, sophs, jrs, srs, adults *Requires:* 2.5 GPA
Credit: *Undergrad:* 6 per sem *Grad:* none *Doc:* transcript
Instruction: *In:* English *Format:* lecture *Students:* intl
Costs: $3,292 for NY residents *incl* tuition, housing, all meals, fees, student support svcs *Nonrefundable fee*
Housing: *Arr by pgm:* residence halls
Deadline: Mar 15; late applications considered
Other info: *US accredited sponsor:* yes *Began:* 2000 *Orient:* abroad *Activities:* excursions, field trips, cultural events *Misc:* May contact former participants. *URL:* http://www.albany.edu/intled
Contact: Joan N Savitt, SUNY Univ at Albany, LI 66, Off of Intl Edu, Albany NY 12222 *Ph:* 518-442 3525 *Fax:* 518-442 3338 *E-mail:* ubtked@uamail.albany.edu

---

0962
TRUMAN STATE UNIVERSITY and **SAINT BONAVENTURE UNIVERSITY**
Summer Study in Ireland
Site: Ireland: Galway *Host inst:* Univ Coll Galway
Dates: 4 wks, Jun 30-Jul 30 or Jul 15-Aug 12
Subjects: Creative writing, Education/teaching, Irish studies
Eligibility: *Level:* jrs, srs, grads, adults, teachers, professionals *Requires:* 2.9 GPA *Age:* min 18
Credit: *Undergrad:* 6 per session *Grad:* none *Doc:* transcript
Instruction: *In:* English *Format:* lecture, seminar *Students:* intl
Costs: $1,840 per term *incl* tuition *Nonrefundable fee*
Housing: *Sponsor assists:* apartments with local students
Deadline: May 5
Other info: *US accredited sponsor:* yes *Began:* 2000 *Orient:* abroad (1 day) *Misc:* May contact former participants.
Contact: Ctr Intl Educ Abroad, Truman State Univ, 120 Kirk Bldg, Kirksville MO 63501 *Ph:* 660-785 4076 *Fax:* 660-785 7473 *E-mail:* ciea@truman.edu
Or Contact: Alice Soyegh, Dir, St. Bonaventure Univ, RC 221 B, St. Bonaventure NY 14778 *Ph:* 660-785 4076 *Fax:* 660-785 7473 *E-mail:* asoycgh@sbu.edu

---

0963
UNIVERSITY OF ARKANSAS and **UNIVERSITY COLLEGE GALWAY**
International Writers' Course
Site: Ireland: Galway
Dates: 4 wks, Jun 28-Jul 28
Subjects: Creative writing, Irish studies, Literature, Poetry
Eligibility: *Level:* jrs, srs, grads, adults, teachers *Requires:* 2.7 GPA, submission of sample manuscript of poetry or fiction *Age:* avg 24
Credit: *Undergrad:* 6 *Grad:* 6 *Doc:* transcript
Instruction: *In:* English *Format:* seminar, workshop *Students:* mainly US
Costs: $2,900 *incl* tuition, housing, some meals, fees, excursions
Housing: *Arr by pgm:* residence halls
Deadline: Mar 15 or until pgm filled
Other info: *US accredited sponsor:* yes *Began:* 1990 *Orient:* abroad *Activities:* excursions, cultural events *Misc:* Guest lectures & workshops with Irish writers. May contact former participants. *URL:* http://www.uark.edu/~studyabr
Contact: Skip Hays, English, Univ of Arkansas, 333 Kimpel Hall, Fayetteville AR 72701 *Ph:* 501-575 4301 *Fax:* 501-575 5919 *E-mail:* english@cavern.uark.edu
Or Contact: Michelle Morris, 722 W Maple St, Univ of Arkansas, Fayetteville AR 72701 *Ph:* 501-575 7785, 501-575 7785

GLENCOLMCILLE

0964
OIDEAS GAEL, ULSTER CULTURAL CENTRE
Intensive Irish Language for Beginners
Site: Ireland: Glencolmcille (Co Donegal)
Dates: 2 wks, Nov 2-16, Feb 3-17
Subjects: Archaeology, Dance, Folklore, Homestay, Irish language/Gaelic (beg), Music, Singing/voice
Eligibility: *Level:* adults
Credit: *Undergrad:* none *Grad:* none
Instruction: *In:* English, Gaelic *Format:* lang study, lecture, seminar, study tour *Students:* intl
Costs: $750 *incl* tuition, housing, all meals, fees, books/materials
Housing: *Arr by pgm:* homestay, pensions
Deadline: Feb 10
Other info: *US accredited sponsor:* no *Began:* 1984 *In coop with:* Govt Dept Educ *Orient:* abroad *Activities:* field trips, cultural events *Misc:* May contact former participants. *URL:* http://www.Oideas-Gael.com
Contact: Liam O'Cuinneagain, Oideas Gael, Glencolmcille, Co Donegal, Ireland *E-mail:* oidsgael@iol.ie

---

0965
OIDEAS GAEL, ULSTER CULTURAL CENTRE
Landscape and Marine Painting
Site: Ireland: Glencolmcille (Co Donegal)
Dates: 1 wk, Jul 13-20 or Sep 7-14
Subjects: Field study, Homestay, Painting, Studio arts
Eligibility: *Level:* adults *Age:* min 17, avg 35
Credit: *Undergrad:* avail *Grad:* avail
Instruction: *In:* English, Gaelic *Format:* art studio, directed field study, lecture, practical training, tutorial *Students:* intl & host country
Costs: $200 *incl* tuition, housing *Nonrefundable fee*
Housing: *Arr by pgm:* homestay, pensions, hostels
Deadline: Jun 15; Apr 1 for scholarships
Other info: *US accredited sponsor:* no *Began:* 1991 *Activities:* field trips, cultural events *Misc:* Sch dirs are leading Irish artists. May contact former participants. *Financial aid:* scholarships *URL:* http://www.Oideas-Gael.com
Contact: Liam O'Cuinneagain, Oideas Gael, Ulster Cultural Ctr, Glencolmcille, Co Donegal, Ireland *E-mail:* owsgael@iol.ie

KINSALE

0966
HORIZONS TO GO
An Irish Idyll/From Dublin to Bantry Bay
Site: Ireland: Kinsale
Dates: 1 wk, May 19-26 or Sep 15-22
Subjects: Glassmaking, Jewelry/jewelry-making, Painting, Photography, Printmaking, Sculpture
Eligibility: *Level:* adults *Age:* min 19, max 85
Credit: *Undergrad:* none *Grad:* avail
Instruction: *In:* English *Format:* art studio, workshop *Students:* mainly US
Costs: $1,445 *incl* tuition, housing, all meals, excursions, books/materials *Nonrefundable fee*
Housing: *Arr by pgm:* bed & breakfasts
Deadline: Contact sponsor
Other info: *US accredited sponsor:* no *Activities:* excursions, field trips *Misc:* Field trips to Dublin, the west coast & Irish villages *URL:* http://www.horizons-art.org
Contact: Jane Sinauer, Horizons To Go, 108 N Main St T, Amherst MA 01004 *Ph:* 413-549 2900 *Fax:* 413-549 5995 *E-mail:* horizons@horizons-art.org

LISDOONVARNA

0967
BURREN PAINTING CENTER
Landscape Painting
Site: Ireland: Lisdoonvarna
Dates: 2-6 days, May 1-Sep 1
Subjects: Painting
Eligibility: *Level:* adults *Age:* min 18, avg 55
Credit: *Undergrad:* avail *Grad:* none
Instruction: *In:* English *Format:* tutorial, workshop *Students:* mainly host country
Costs: $450 per wk *incl* tuition, housing, some meals
Housing: *Arr by pgm:* bed & breakfast
Deadline: None
Other info: *US accredited sponsor:* no *Began:* 1974 *Activities:* field trips, cultural events *Misc:* Landscape painting en plein air in watercolor, oils, gouache, acrylics, pastels & silk painting. May contact former participants. *URL:* http://indigo.ie/~isclo
Contact: Christine O'Neill, Burren Painting Ctr, Lisdoonvarna, Co Clare, Ireland *E-mail:* isclo@indigo.ie

MAYNOOTH

0968
PENNSYLVANIA STATE UNIVERSITY
Administration of Justice in Ireland
Site: Ireland: Maynooth *Host inst:* St Patrick's Coll
Dates: 4 wks, late Jun-late Jul
Subjects: Criminal justice
Eligibility: *Level:* jrs, srs, grads *Requires:* 2.5 GPA
Credit: *Undergrad:* 4 *Grad:* 4
Instruction: *In:* English *Format:* lecture, seminar *Students:* mainly US
Costs: Contact sponsor
Housing: *Arr by pgm:* residence halls
Deadline: Apr 1
Other info: *US accredited sponsor:* yes *Began:* 1995 *Orient:* in US *Activities:* excursions *Misc:* May contact former participants. *Financial aid:* scholarships *URL:* http://www.cde.psu.edu/PSSEA/
Contact: Kristin Owens, Conference & Insts, Penn State Univ, University Park PA 16802 *Ph:* 814-863 5170 *Fax:* 814-863 5190 *E-mail:* conferenceinfo1@cde.psu.edu
Or Contact: Kristi Wormhoudt, Asst Dir, Educ Abroad Pgms, Penn State Univ, 222 Boucke Bldg, University Park PA 16802 *Ph:* 814-865 7681 *Fax:* 814-865 3336

STROKESTOWN

0969
ILLINOIS STATE UNIVERSITY
Strokestown, County Roscommon, Ireland Summer
Site: Ireland: Strokestown
Dates: 3, 4, 5 or 6 wks, Jun 26-Aug 4
Subjects: Archaeology, Field study, Independent study, Irish studies
Eligibility: *Level:* sophs, jrs, srs, grads, professionals *Requires:* 2.5 GPA, previous study in field
Credit: *Undergrad:* 6 *Grad:* 6 *Doc:* transcript
Instruction: *In:* English *Format:* directed field study, independent study *Students:* mainly US
Costs: $4,003 *incl* housing, some meals, intl airfare, fees, excursions
Housing: *Arr by pgm:* hotels, bed & breakfasts
Deadline: Feb 14
Other info: *US accredited sponsor:* yes *Orient:* in US *Activities:* field trips *URL:* http://www.its.ilstu.edu/intlstudies/
Contact: Dr Charles Orser, Illinois State Univ, Campus Box 4640, Normal IL 61790-4640 *Ph:* 309-438 2271 *E-mail:* ceorser@ilstu.edu
Or Contact: Intl Studies, Illinois State Univ, Campus Box 6120, Normal IL 61790-6120 *Ph:* 309-438 5365 *Fax:* 309-438 3987 *E-mail:* oisp@cmp.ilstu.edu

TRALEE

0970
IRISH COLLEGE FOR THE HUMANITIES
Irish College for the Humanities
Site: Ireland: Tralee
Dates: 4 wks, Jun
Subjects: Art history, Fine arts, History, Homestay, Irish studies, Literature, Social sciences
Eligibility: *Level:* fresh, sophs, jrs, srs, adults, teachers *Age:* min 18, avg 20
Credit: *Undergrad:* 3-6 *Grad:* none *Doc:* transcript *Transfer credit through:* Randolph-Macon Coll
Instruction: *In:* English *Format:* art studio, directed field study, independent study, internship, lecture, seminar, study tour, tutorial, workshop *Students:* mainly US
Costs: $3,600 *incl* tuition, housing, some meals, fees, excursions, site visits, social pgm *Nonrefundable fee*
Housing: *Arr by pgm:* residence halls, homestay
Deadline: Apr 15
Other info: *US accredited sponsor:* no *Orient:* abroad *Activities:* excursions, field trips, program travel, cultural events,

sports *Misc:* Guest lecturers. May contact former participants. *Financial aid:* scholarships *URL:* http://www.iol.ie/~ichkerry
Contact: Kathryn Kissane, Irish Coll for the Humanities, Kilteely Hse, Ballyard, Tralee, Co Kerry, Ireland *Ph:* 800-610-2858 *E-mail:* ichkerry@iol.ie

Italy

MORE THAN ONE CITY

0971
ARTE/VITA
Travel Art Workshops
Site: Italy: Tuscany region
Dates: 2-4 wks, Jul 1-30
Subjects: Art history, Book arts, Bookbinding, Drawing, Independent study, Modern art, Painting, Renaissance studies, Studio arts
Eligibility: *Level:* adults, precoll *Age:* min 18, max 75
Credit: *Undergrad:* avail *Grad:* avail *Doc:* certificate
Instruction: *In:* English *Format:* art studio *Students:* intl
Costs: $2,500 for 2 wks *incl* tuition, housing, all meals, fees, excursions, books/materials, railpass, local transport, studio space
Housing: *Arr by pgm:* villa
Deadline: Jun 1; Apr 1 for scholarships
Other info: *US accredited sponsor:* no *Began:* 1999 *Activities:* excursions, field trips, program travel *Misc:* May contact former participants. *Financial aid:* work study *URL:* http://www.artevita.net
Contact: Jessica Houston, Cofounder, Arte/Vita, 180 Riverside Blvd 12L, New York NY 10069 *Ph:* 212-726 1379 *E-mail:* info@artevita.net
Or Contact: Marcia Teusink, Cofounder, Arte/Vita, Florastrasse 30, CH-8008 Zurich, Switzerland *E-mail:* info@artevita.net

---

0972
BOSTON UNIVERSITY
Summer Program in Padova and Venice
Site: Italy: Padova, Venice *Host inst:* Ctr Studi
Dates: 7 wks, May-Jul
Subjects: Art history, History, Homestay, Italian language (beg/int)
Eligibility: *Level:* sophs, jrs, srs *Requires:* 3.0 GPA, in major, good acad standing
Credit: *Undergrad:* 8 *Grad:* none *Doc:* transcript
Instruction: *In:* English, Italian *Format:* lang study, lecture, seminar *Students:* mainly US
Costs: $4,550 *incl* tuition, housing, all meals, excursions
Housing: *Arr by pgm:* homestay
Deadline: Mar 1; Apr 1 for scholarships
Other info: *US accredited sponsor:* yes *Began:* 1992 *Orient:* in US & abroad *Activities:* excursions, field trips, cultural events *Misc:* Full-time resident dir. Program may be taken before joining Boston Univ Padova pgm in Sep. May contact former participants. *Financial aid:* scholarships *URL:* http://www.bu.edu/abroad/

Contact: Intl Pgms, Boston Univ, 232 Bay State Rd, Boston MA 02215 *Ph:* 617-353 9888 *Fax:* 617-353 5402 *E-mail:* abroad@bu.edu ▲

0973
CENTRO FIORENZA LINGUA E CULTURA ITALIANA PER STRANIERI
50 Plus
Site: Italy: Elba, Florence
Dates: 2-wk terms, May-Oct
Subjects: Art history, Civilization/culture, Culinary arts, Italian language (beg/int/adv), Italian studies
Eligibility: *Level:* adults *Age:* min 50
Credit: *Undergrad:* none *Grad:* none
Instruction: *In:* Italian *Format:* lang study, study tour *Students:* intl
Costs: $500 per term *incl* tuition, excursions, books/materials
Housing: *Sponsor assists:* residence halls, apartments, homestay, pensions, hotels
Deadline: 4 wks before pgm
Other info: *US accredited sponsor:* no *Began:* 1995 *Orient:* avail *Activities:* excursions, cultural events *Misc:* May contact former participants. *URL:* http://www.centrofiorenza.com
Contact: Ms S Merlini-Seiwald, Ctr Fiorenza, Via Santo Spirito 14, 50125 Florence, Italy *E-mail:* fiorenza@centrofiorenza.com

---

0974
CITY COLLEGE OF SAN FRANCISCO
Summer in Italy
Site: Italy: Florence, Rome, Venice *Host inst:* Scuola Leonardo da Vinci
Dates: 3 wks, Jun 10-Jul 4
Subjects: Art history, Ecology/environmental studies
Eligibility: *Level:* fresh, sophs, jrs, srs, grads, adults, teachers, professionals *Requires:* 2.0 GPA *Age:* min 18, avg 30
Credit: *Undergrad:* 6 *Grad:* none *Doc:* transcript
Instruction: *In:* English *Format:* study tour *Students:* mainly US
Costs: $2,600 *incl* tuition, housing, insurance, fees, excursions *Nonrefundable fee*
Housing: *Arr by pgm:* apartments, hotels
Deadline: Apr 1
Other info: *US accredited sponsor:* yes *Began:* 1997 *In coop with:* ACCENT *Orient:* in US & abroad (2 days) *Activities:* excursions, field trips, cultural events *Misc:* Loans & grants avail. May contact former participants. *Financial aid:* scholarships *URL:* http://www.ccsf.org/studyabroad
Contact: Jill Heffron, Study Abroad Coord, CCSF, 50 Phelan Ave, Box C212, San Francisco CA 94110 *Ph:* 415-239 3778 *Fax:* 415-239 3804 *E-mail:* jheffron@ccsf.org
Or Contact: ACCENT, 870 Market St, Ste 1026, San Francisco CA 94102 *Ph:* 800-869 9291; 415-835 3744 *Fax:* 415-835-3744 *E-mail:* info@accentintl.com

---

0975
CSA, CENTER FOR STUDY ABROAD
Italian Language and Culture Studies
Site: Italy: Florence, Perugia, Rome, Siena *Host inst:* Ctr Dante Alighieri, Ist Michelangelo, Italian Univ for Foreigners, Torre di Babele
Dates: 4-12 wks, yr-round
Subjects: Art, History, Homestay, Independent study, Italian language, Italian studies, Literature, Political science/politics
Eligibility: *Level:* adults *Age:* min 17
Credit: *Undergrad:* avail *Grad:* avail *Doc:* transcript, certificate
Instruction: *In:* Italian *Format:* independent study, lang study *Students:* intl
Costs: $1,495-$1,995 per mo depending on sch *incl* tuition, housing, some meals, insurance, fees, books/materials *Nonrefundable fee*
Housing: *Sponsor assists:* apartments, homestay, hotels
Deadline: None
Other info: *US accredited sponsor:* no *Orient:* abroad *Activities:* excursions, field trips, program travel, cultural events, sports *URL:* http://www.studyabroad.com/csa
Contact: Alima Khan, Assoc Dir, CSA, Ctr for Study Abroad, 2802 E Madison St, MS #160, Seattle WA 98112 *Ph:* 206-726 1498 *Fax:* 206-583 8192 *E-mail:* virtuecsa@aol.com

---

0976
EDUVACATIONS
Arts Restoration Courses and Programs
Site: Italy: Como, Florence
Dates: 2 wks or longer, yr-round
Subjects: Art conservation, Art history, Art restoration, Chemistry, Drawing, Furnishings/furniture
Eligibility: *Level:* adults *Age:* min 18
Credit: *Undergrad:* avail *Grad:* avail *Doc:* certificate
Instruction: *In:* English, Italian *Format:* art studio, directed field study, practical training, seminar, workshop *Students:* intl
Costs: Contact sponsor
Housing: *Arr by pgm:* apartments, homestay, hotels, hostels
Deadline: Contact sponsor
Other info: *US accredited sponsor:* no *Activities:* excursions, cultural events *Misc:* Non-participating partners of participants welcome. 3-yr pgm avail. May contact former participants. *URL:* http://www.eduvacations.com
Contact: Mary Ann Puglisi, eduVacations, 1431 21st St NW, Ste 302, Washington DC 20036 *Ph:* 202-857 8384 *Fax:* 202-463 8091

0977
EDUVACATIONS
Study in and Live in Your Teacher's Home-Italy
Site: Italy: Florence, Naples, Rome, Siena, Tuscany, Vico Equense
Dates: 1 wk or longer, yr-round
Subjects: Art, Art history, Business language, Culinary arts, History, Homestay, Italian language (beg/int/adv), Literature, Music, Wine
Eligibility: *Level:* adults, precoll *Age:* min 15
Credit: *Undergrad:* none *Grad:* none
Instruction: *In:* Italian *Format:* lang study *Students:* intl
Costs: Contact sponsor
Housing: *Arr by pgm:* homestay
Deadline: None
Other info: *US accredited sponsor:* no *Began:* 1969 *Activities:* excursions, field trips, cultural events, sports *Misc:* May contact former participants. *URL:* http://www.eduvacations.com
Contact: Mary Ann Puglisi, eduVacations, 1431 21st St NW, Ste 302, Washington DC 20036 *Ph:* 202-857 8384 *Fax:* 202-463 8091

0978
FASHION INSTITUTE OF TECHNOLOGY
Decorative Arts, Architecture and Interior Design in Italy
Site: Italy: Florence, Rome, Venice
Dates: 3 wks, Jan or Jun 30-Jul 22
Subjects: Architectural history, Art history, Baroque studies, Classical studies, Furnishings/furniture, Interior design, Textiles
Eligibility: *Level:* fresh, sophs, jrs, srs, grads, adults, teachers, professionals *Requires:* interview by faculty member teaching course *Age:* min 18
Credit: *Undergrad:* 3 *Grad:* none *Doc:* transcript
Instruction: *In:* English *Format:* study tour *Students:* mainly US
Costs: About $2,790 for NY residents, $2,979 for others *incl* tuition, housing, intl airfare, fees, excursions
Housing: *Arr by pgm:* hotels
Deadline: Mar 3
Other info: *US accredited sponsor:* yes *Began:* 1986 *Orient:* in US *Activities:* excursions, field trips, program travel

See "How To Use This Book" for definitions of terms used above. ▲ = See program sponsor's ad(s) in this book.

Misc: May contact former participants. *URL:* http://www.fitnyc.suny.edu
Contact: Georgianna Appignani, Dir, Intl Educ, FIT, 7th Ave at 27th St, New York NY 10001-5992 *Ph:* 212-217 7633 *Fax:* 212-217 7010
Or Contact: Carole De Santis, Coord, FIT, 7th Ave at 27th St, New York NY 10001-5992 *Ph:* 212-217 7633 *Fax:* 212-217 7010 *E-mail:* desantca@fitsuny.edu

---

0979
FASHION INSTITUTE OF TECHNOLOGY
Fabric Styling in Italy
Site: Italy: Como, Florence, Milan, Prato, San Gimignano, Siena
Dates: 3 wks, May 30-Jun 21
Subjects: Fashion design, Textiles
Eligibility: *Level:* fresh, sophs, jrs, srs, grads, adults *Requires:* interview by faculty member teaching course *Age:* min 18
Credit: *Undergrad:* 3 *Grad:* none *Doc:* transcript
Instruction: *In:* English *Format:* study tour *Students:* mainly US
Costs: $3,350 for NY residents, $3,845 for others *incl* tuition, housing, intl airfare
Housing: *Arr by pgm:* pensions, hotels
Deadline: Mar 3
Other info: *US accredited sponsor:* yes *Began:* 1996 *Orient:* in US *Activities:* program travel *URL:* http://www.fitnyc.suny.edu
Contact: Georgianna Appignani, Dir, Intl Educ, FIT, 7th Ave at 27th St, New York NY 10001-5992 *Ph:* 212-217 7633 *Fax:* 212-217 7010
Or Contact: Carole De Santis, Coord, FIT, 7th Ave at 27th St, New York NY 10001-5992 *Ph:* 212-217 7633 *Fax:* 212-217 7010 *E-mail:* desantca@sfitva.cc.fitsuny.edu

---

0980
FLORIDA INTERNATIONAL UNIVERSITY
Looking for the Future-The Case of Italy
Site: Italy: various sites
Dates: 1 mo, Apr 27-May 23
Subjects: Civilization/culture, Italian studies, Literature
Eligibility: *Level:* sophs, jrs, srs, adults, teachers, professionals *Requires:* honors students, some Italian
Credit: *Undergrad:* avail *Grad:* avail *Doc:* transcript
Instruction: *In:* English, Italian *Format:* lang study, study tour *Students:* US & intl
Costs: $3,500 *incl* housing, some meals, intl airfare, excursions, railpass *Nonrefundable fee*
Housing: *Arr by pgm:* hotels
Deadline: May 15
Other info: *US accredited sponsor:* yes *Began:* 1999 *Orient:* in US (1 day) *Activities:* excursions, field trips, program travel *Misc:* May contact former participants. *URL:* http://www.fiu.edu/~intered
Contact: Intl Studies, Florida Intl Univ, 11200 SW 8th St, DM 300B, Miami FL 33199 *Ph:* 305-348 1913, 305-348 1918 *Fax:* 305-348 1941 *E-mail:* intered@fiu.edu

---

0981
GEORGIA INSTITUTE OF TECHNOLOGY
Summer Study in Italy
Site: Italy: Florence, Rome, Venice
Dates: May 22-Jun 23
Subjects: Architectural history, Architecture, Art, Art history, Field study, Independent study
Eligibility: *Level:* fresh, sophs, jrs, srs, grads *Requires:* good acad standing
Credit: *Undergrad:* 6-12 *Grad:* avail *Doc:* transcript
Instruction: *In:* English *Format:* directed field study, independent study, study tour *Students:* mainly US
Costs: $5,082 for GA residents, $5,332 for others *incl* housing, all meals, intl airfare, insurance, fees, books/materials
Housing: *Arr by pgm:* hotels
Deadline: Mid-Jan
Other info: *US accredited sponsor:* yes *Began:* 1993 *Orient:* in US *Activities:* excursions
Contact: Dr Betty Dowling, Coll of Architecture, Georgia Inst of Technology, Atlanta GA 30332-0155 *Ph:* 404-894 3803 *Fax:* 404-894 0572 *E-mail:* betty.dowling@arch.gatech.edu
Or Contact: Intl Educ, Georgia Inst of Technology, J S Coon Bldg, Ste 203, Atlanta GA 30332-0284 *Ph:* 404-894 7475 *Fax:* 404-894 9682 *E-mail:* study.abroad@gatech.edu

---

0982
INSTITUTE OF ITALIAN LANGUAGE GALILEO GALILEI
One-to-One and Small Group Italian Language Courses
Site: Italy: Florence, branches in Elba & Chianti countryside
Dates: 1-52 wks, yr-round
Subjects: Art history, Business language, Culinary arts, Drawing, History, Homestay, Independent study, Italian language (beg/int/adv), Italian studies, Painting, Technical language, Translating/interpreting
Eligibility: *Level:* fresh, sophs, jrs, srs, grads, adults, teachers, professionals
Credit: *Undergrad:* avail *Grad:* none *Doc:* certificate, diploma
Instruction: *In:* English, French, German, Italian *Format:* independent study, lang study, lecture, tutorial *Students:* intl
Costs: About $365-$1,690 per wk *incl* tuition, some meals, insurance, fees, books/materials, exams, certificates
Housing: *Arr by pgm:* apartments, homestay, pensions, hotels, furnished rms
Deadline: 15 days before pgm
Other info: *US accredited sponsor:* no *Began:* 1985 *Activities:* excursions *Misc:* Sch serves personnel from major companies throughout the world. Guided visits to museums & churches. *URL:* http://www.galilei.it
Contact: Ms Alexandra Schmitz, Inst of Italian Lang Galileo Galilei, via degli Alfani 68, 50121 Florence, Italy *E-mail:* info@galilei.it

---

0983
INTERNATIONAL COUNCIL FOR CULTURAL EXCHANGE (ICCE)
Summer Programs in Italy
Site: Italy: Pisa, Viareggio, Italian Riviera, other sites *Host inst:* Univ of Pisa, others
Dates: 2-4 wks or longer, summer
Subjects: Arts, Civilization/culture, Culinary arts, Field study, Homestay, Italian language (beg/int/adv), Music, Opera, Painting, Political science/politics, Psychology, Social sciences
Eligibility: *Level:* fresh, sophs, jrs, srs, grads, adults, professionals, precoll
Credit: *Undergrad:* avail *Grad:* avail *Doc:* transcript, certificate
Instruction: *In:* English, Italian *Format:* art studio, directed field study, lab, lang study, lecture, practical training, study tour *Students:* US & intl
Costs: From $3,219 for 4 wks *incl* tuition, housing, some meals, intl airfare, fees, excursions, transfers, pgm travel
Housing: *Sponsor assists:* residence halls, homestay, hotels
Deadline: 1 mo before pgm
Other info: *US accredited sponsor:* no *Began:* 1982 *Orient:* abroad *Activities:* excursions, program travel, cultural events, sports *Misc:* Yr-round pgms of 2 wks or longer avail for pre-arr groups. Local coord assistance.
Contact: Dr Stanley Gochman, ICCE, 5 Bellport Ln, Bellport NY 11713 *Ph:* 631-286 5228 ▲

0984
KENTUCKY INSTITUTE FOR INTERNATIONAL STUDIES (KIIS)
Program in Italy
Site: Italy: Florence, Rome
Dates: 5 wks, late May-Jul
Subjects: Art history, Italian language (beg), Studio arts
Eligibility: *Level:* fresh, sophs, jrs, srs,

grads, adults, teachers, professionals *Requires:* 2.0 GPA, good acad standing at home inst, faculty recommendation *Age:* min 18
Credit: *Undergrad:* 3-6 *Grad:* none *Doc:* transcript
Instruction: *In:* English, Italian *Format:* art studio, lang study, lecture *Students:* mainly US
Costs: $3,460 for students at member schs, $3,760 for others *incl* tuition, housing, some meals, intl airfare, fees, excursions, ISIC *Nonrefundable fee*
Housing: *Arr by pgm:* pensions, hotels
Deadline: Feb 15 ($100 late fee)
Other info: *US accredited sponsor:* yes *Began:* 1984 *Orient:* in US & abroad *Activities:* excursions *Misc:* Optional travel in Italy. May contact former participants. *Financial aid:* scholarships *URL:* http://www.kiis.org
Contact: *See Index II for Members* Dr J Milton Grimes, Exec Dir, KIIS, Murray State Univ, PO Box 9, Murray KY 42071-0009 *Ph:* 270-762 3091 *Fax:* 270-762 3434 *E-mail:* kiismsu@murraystate.edu

---

0985
LANGUAGE LIAISON
Italian Language
Site: Italy: Florence, Naples, Sicily
Dates: 2 wks-1 yr, yr-round
Subjects: Art, Art history, Business language, Civilization/culture, Culinary arts, Drama/theater, Fashion design, Homestay, Humanities, Italian language, Italian studies, Literature, Music, Wine
Eligibility: *Level:* adults *Age:* min 14
Credit: *Undergrad:* avail *Grad:* avail *Doc:* transcript, certificate
Instruction: *In:* Italian *Format:* lang study, lecture *Students:* intl
Costs: Contact sponsor
Housing: *Arr by pgm:* apartments, homestay, pensions, hotels, hostels
Deadline: 30 days before pgm
Other info: *US accredited sponsor:* no *Activities:* excursions, field trips, cultural events, sports *Misc:* Scholarship research svc. *URL:* http://www.languageliaison.com
Contact: Nancy Forman, Dir, Lang Liaison, 4 Burnham Pkwy, Morristown NJ 07960 *Ph:* 800-284 4448 *Fax:* 973-898 1710 *E-mail:* learn@languageliaison.com

---

0986
LANGUAGE LIAISON
Italian Saturation
Site: Italy: Michaelangelo, Milan, Rimini, Rome, Sienna, Venice *Host inst:* Live in Learn
Dates: 1 wk or longer, yr-round
Subjects: Civilization/culture, Homestay, Italian language (beg/int/adv)
Eligibility: *Level:* fresh, sophs, jrs, srs, grads, adults, teachers, professionals, precoll *Age:* min 10
Credit: *Undergrad:* none *Grad:* none *Doc:* transcript, certificate
Instruction: *In:* Italian *Format:* lang study *Students:* intl
Costs: Contact sponsor
Housing: *Arr by pgm:* teacher's home
Deadline: 45 days before pgm
Other info: *US accredited sponsor:* no *Misc:* Live & learn in your teacher's home. Scholarship research svc. *URL:* http://www.languageliaison.com
Contact: Nancy Forman, Dir, Lang Liaison, 4 Burnham Pkwy, Morristown NJ 07960 *Ph:* 800-284 4448 *Fax:* 973-898 1710 *E-mail:* learn@languageliaison.com

---

0987
LANGUAGE STUDIES ABROAD, INC
Intensive Italian Language and Culture
Site: Italy: Florence, Rimini, Rome, Siena *Host inst:* various LSA insts
Dates: 2 wks or longer, yr-round
Subjects: Art, Art history, Culinary arts, Drama/theater, Drawing, History, Italian language (beg/int/adv), Italian studies, Literature, Music, Painting, Photography, Sculpture, Tourism, Wine
Eligibility: *Level:* fresh, sophs, jrs, srs, grads, adults, teachers, professionals, precoll *Age:* min 18
Credit: *Undergrad:* avail *Grad:* avail *Doc:* certificate
Instruction: *In:* Italian *Format:* art studio, independent study, lang study, lecture, seminar, study tour *Students:* intl
Costs: From $945 for 4 wks *incl* tuition
Housing: *Sponsor assists:* apartments, homestay, pensions, hotels, hostels
Deadline: 4 wks before pgm
Other info: *US accredited sponsor:* no *Orient:* abroad *Activities:* excursions, field trips, cultural events, sports *Misc:* Scholarships for Siena pgm only. May contact former participants. *URL:* http://www.languagestudiesabroad.com
Contact: Lang Studies Abroad, Inc, 103 Londonderry Ct, Reno NV 89511-2718 *Ph:* 800-424 5522; 775-849 9206 *Fax:* 775-849 9217 *E-mail:* info@languagestudiesabroad.com

---

0988
LINGUA SERVICE WORLDWIDE
Total Immersion/Intensive Language and Culture Courses-Italy
Site: Italy: Asti, Florence, Milan, Naples, Rome, Venice *Host inst:* Home Lang Intl
Dates: 1 wk-1 yr, yr-round
Subjects: Culinary arts, Homestay, Italian language (beg/int/adv)
Eligibility: *Level:* adults *Age:* min 14
Credit: *Undergrad:* avail *Grad:* avail *Doc:* transcript, certificate
Instruction: *In:* Italian *Format:* lang study *Students:* intl
Costs: Contact sponsor
Housing: *Arr by pgm:* teacher's home
Deadline: 45 days before pgm
Other info: *US accredited sponsor:* no *Began:* 1993 *Activities:* excursions, cultural events *Misc:* Participate in teacher's family & social life. May contact former participants. *URL:* http://www.linguaserviceworldwide.com
Contact: Dir, Lingua Svc Worldwide, 75 Prospect St, Ste 4, Huntington NY 11743 *Ph:* 800-394 5327; 631-424 0777 *Fax:* 631-271 3441 *E-mail:* itctravel@worldnet.att.net ▲

0989
LINGUA SERVICE WORLDWIDE
Total Immersion/Intensive Language and Culture in Italy
Site: Italy: Florence, Rimini, Rome, Siena *Host inst:* Ctr Dante Alighieri, Ctr di Lingua e Cultura Italiana, I Malatesta, Ist Italiano, others
Dates: 1 wk-1 yr, yr-round
Subjects: Art history, Civilization/culture, Culinary arts, Drawing, History, Homestay, Italian language (beg/int/adv), Italian studies, Literature, Music, Painting, Wine
Eligibility: *Level:* fresh, sophs, jrs, srs, grads, adults, teachers, professionals, precoll *Age:* min 14
Credit: *Undergrad:* avail *Grad:* avail *Doc:* transcript, certificate *Transfer credit through:* Univ of Southern Mississippi
Instruction: *In:* Italian *Format:* lang study, lecture *Students:* intl
Costs: Contact sponsor
Housing: *Arr by pgm:* residence halls, apartments, homestay, pensions, hotels, hostels
Deadline: 45 days before pgm
Other info: *US accredited sponsor:* no *Activities:* excursions, field trips, cultural events *Misc:* May contact former participants. *URL:* http://www.linguaserviceworldwide.com
Contact: Dir, Lingua Svc Worldwide, 75 Prospect St, Ste 4, Huntington NY 11743 *Ph:* 800-394 5327; 631-424 0777 *Fax:* 631-271 3441 *E-mail:* itctravel@worldnet.att.net ▲

0990
LOUISIANA STATE UNIVERSITY
LSU in Italy
Site: Italy: Florence, Rome, Venice
Dates: 6 wks, May-Jul
Subjects: Art history, Independent study, Italian language (int/adv)
Eligibility: *Level:* fresh, sophs, jrs, srs,

grads, adults, teachers, professionals *Requires:* 2.5 GPA, for undergrads, 3.0 for grads & those seeking 9 credit hrs
Credit: *Undergrad:* 6-9 *Grad:* 6-9 *Doc:* transcript
Instruction: *In:* English, Italian *Format:* independent study, lang study, lecture *Students:* mainly US
Costs: $3,400 *incl* tuition, housing, some meals, excursions
Housing: *Arr by pgm:* pensions
Deadline: Mar 15
Other info: *US accredited sponsor:* yes *Orient:* in US & abroad *Activities:* excursions, field trips, cultural events *Misc:* Loans avail. Scholarships for own students only. May contact former participants. *Financial aid:* scholarships *URL:* http://www.lsu.edu/studyabroad
Contact: Joseph Rosenbach, Acad Pgms Abroad, Louisiana State Univ, 113 Hatcher Hall, Baton Rouge LA 70803 *Ph:* 225-388 6801 *Fax:* 225-388 6806 *E-mail:* studyabroad@lsu.edu

---

0991
NATIONAL REGISTRATION CENTER FOR STUDY ABROAD (NRCSA)
Study in Italy
Site: Italy: Livorno, Portico di Romagna, Rimini, Siena, Viareggio *Host inst:* Ctrs Culturale Giacomo Puccini & L'Olmo, I Malatesta, Ist Linguistico Mediterraneo, Siena Lang
Dates: 2 wks or longer, yr-round
Subjects: Civilization/culture, Homestay, Italian language (beg/int/adv), Italian studies
Eligibility: *Level:* fresh, sophs, jrs, srs, grads, adults *Age:* min 18
Credit: *Undergrad:* none *Grad:* none *Doc:* certificate
Instruction: *In:* Italian *Format:* lang study, lecture *Students:* intl
Costs: Contact sponsor
Housing: *Arr by pgm:* residence halls, apartments, homestay, pensions, hotels
Deadline: 6 wks before pgm
Other info: *US accredited sponsor:* no *Activities:* excursions *URL:* http://www.nrcsa.com
Contact: Reuel Zielke, NRCSA, 823 N 2nd St, #206, Milwaukee WI 53203 *Ph:* 414-278 0631 *Fax:* 414-271 8884 *E-mail:* info@nrcsa.com

---

0992
NORTHERN ILLINOIS UNIVERSITY
Archaeological Field School in Sicily
Site: Italy: various sites
Dates: May 21-Jun 15
Subjects: Anthropology, Archaeology, Field study
Eligibility: *Level:* jrs, srs, grads *Requires:* 2.5 GPA, previous study in field *Age:* min 18, avg 21
Credit: *Undergrad:* 3-6 *Grad:* 3
Instruction: *In:* English *Format:* directed field study, lecture, practical training *Students:* mainly US
Costs: $2,900 *incl* tuition, housing, some meals, insurance
Housing: *Arr by pgm:* residence halls
Deadline: Mar 1 or until pgm filled
Other info: *US accredited sponsor:* yes *Began:* 1999 *Orient:* in US *Misc:* Goal of pgm is to teach practical archaeological skills in a research environment. May contact former participants. *URL:* http://www.niu.edu/niuabroad/
Contact: Anne Seitzinger, Study Abroad, Williston 417, Northern Illinois Univ, DeKalb IL 60115 *Ph:* 815-753 0700 *Fax:* 815-753 0825 *E-mail:* niuabroad@niu.edu
Or Contact: Professor Michael Kolb, Anthropology, Northern Illinois Univ, DeKalb IL 60115 *Ph:* 815-753 7037 *E-mail:* aloha@niu.edu

---

0993
OHIO UNIVERSITY
Art History in Italy
Site: Italy: Florence, Rome
Dates: 5 wks, summer
Subjects: Art, Civilization/culture, Italian studies, Photography, Renaissance studies
Eligibility: *Level:* sophs, jrs, srs
Credit: *Undergrad:* 15 qtr hrs *Grad:* 15 qtr hrs *Doc:* transcript
Instruction: *In:* English *Format:* lecture, practical training *Students:* mainly US
Costs: Contact Sponsor
Housing: *Arr by pgm:* hotels
Deadline: Mar 5
Other info: *US accredited sponsor:* yes *URL:* http://www.ohiou.edu
Contact: Marilyn Bradshaw, Assoc Dean, Fine Arts, Ohio Univ, Jennings House, Athens OH 45701 *Ph:* 740-593 1811, 740-593 4288

0994
PENNSYLVANIA STATE UNIVERSITY
Italian Language, Art History and Visual Art
Site: Italy: Todi, Rome
Dates: May-Jul
Subjects: Art history, Homestay, Independent study, Italian language, Visual arts
Eligibility: CIC students only. *Level:* fresh, sophs, jrs, srs *Requires:* 2.5 GPA
Credit: *Undergrad:* 10 *Grad:* none
Instruction: *In:* English, Italian *Format:* independent study, study tour *Students:* mainly US
Costs: Contact Sponsor
Housing: *Arr by pgm:* homestay
Deadline: Rolling admissions
Other info: *US accredited sponsor:* yes *Orient:* in US & abroad *Activities:* excursions, field trips *Misc:* May contact former participants. *Financial aid:* scholarships
Contact: Summer Abroad, Pennsylvania State Univ, 225 Penn State Conference Ctr, University Park PA 16802 *Ph:* 814-863 5170
Or Contact: Intl Pgm Adviser, Pennsylvania State Univ, 222 Boucke Bldg, University Park PA 16802 *Ph:* 814-865 7681 *Fax:* 814-865 3336

0995
SETON HALL UNIVERSITY, SCHOOL OF LAW
Law in Italy
Site: Italy: Milan, Nervi-Genoa, Parma *Host inst:* Univ of Milan, Univ of Parma
Dates: Contact sponsor
Subjects: Business/management, Comparative law, Constitutional law, European Union, History, International law, Law
Eligibility: *Level:* grads, professionals *Requires:* 2.00 GPA, previous study in field, must have completed min 1 yr law sch
Credit: *Undergrad:* none *Grad:* 6 *Doc:* transcript
Instruction: *In:* English *Format:* lecture *Students:* mainly US
Costs: About $3,000 *incl* tuition, fees
Housing: *Arr by pgm:* residence halls, hotels
Deadline: Contact sponsor
Other info: *US accredited sponsor:* yes *Began:* 1988 *Orient:* abroad *Activities:* field trips *Misc:* May contact former participants. *URL:* http://law.shu.edu
Contact: Prof Terence Blackburn, Seton Hall Law Sch, 1 Newark Ctr, Newark NJ 07102-5210 *Ph:* 973-642 8586 *Fax:* 973-642 8194 *E-mail:* blackbte@shu.edu
Or Contact: Gina Fondetto, Mgr of Special Pgms, Seton Hall Law Sch, 1 Newark Ctr, Newark NJ 07102-5210 *Ph:* 973-642 8587 *Fax:* 973-642 8377 *E-mail:* fondetgi@shu.edu

---

0996
SOUTHERN ILLINOIS UNIVERSITY AT CARBONDALE
Ancient Romans in Italy
Site: Italy: Rome, Naples
Dates: 3 wks, May 12-Jun 3
Subjects: Classical studies, Field study
Eligibility: *Level:* adults *Requires:* 2.75 GPA *Age:* min 18
Credit: *Undergrad:* 3 *Grad:* none *Doc:* transcript
Instruction: *In:* English *Format:* directed field study, seminar *Students:* mainly US
Costs: $3,200 *incl* housing, intl airfare,

excursions, books/materials, ISIC, support svcs
Housing: *Arr by pgm:* apartments
Deadline: Apr 15
Other info: *US accredited sponsor:* yes *Began:* 1997 *Orient:* abroad *Activities:* excursions, field trips, program travel *Misc:* Scholarships for own students only. *Financial aid:* scholarships *URL:* http://www.siu.edu/departments/study_abroad/
Contact: Thomas Saville, Coord, Study Abroad Pgms, Mailcode 6885, Southern Illinois Univ at Carbondale, Carbondale IL 62901-6885 *Ph:* 618-453 7670 *Fax:* 618-453 7647 *E-mail:* studyabroad@siu.edu

---

0997
SOUTHERN METHODIST UNIVERSITY
SMU in Italy
Site: Italy: Florence, Orvieto, Rome *Host inst:* Loyola Univ Rome campus
Dates: May 30-Jul 3
Subjects: Art, Art history, Drawing, Italian studies
Eligibility: *Level:* sophs, jrs, srs, grads *Requires:* 2.5 GPA, priority given to students interested in art history & Italian studies
Credit: *Undergrad:* 6 *Grad:* none *Doc:* transcript
Instruction: *In:* English *Format:* art studio, lecture *Students:* mainly US
Costs: About $3,950 *incl* tuition, housing, fees, excursions *Nonrefundable fee*
Housing: *Arr by pgm:* residence halls, hotels
Deadline: Mar 1 or until pgm filled
Other info: *US accredited sponsor:* yes *Began:* 1985 *Orient:* in US & abroad *Activities:* excursions, field trips, program travel *Misc:* Scholarships for own students only. Loans avail. May contact former participants. *Financial aid:* scholarships *URL:* http://www.smu.edu/studyabroad
Contact: Intl Pgms, Southern Methodist Univ, PO Box 0391, 3108 Fondren Dr, Dallas TX 75275-0391 *Ph:* 214-768 2338 *Fax:* 214-768 1051 *E-mail:* intlpro@mail.smu.edu ▲

0998
SOUTHERN METHODIST UNIVERSITY
SMU in Rome and Siena
Site: Italy: Rome, Siena *Host inst:* Loyola Univ
Dates: 5 wks, Jul 6-Aug 6
Subjects: Civilization/culture, Italian language (beg/int/adv), Italian studies
Eligibility: *Level:* sophs, jrs, srs *Requires:* 2.5 GPA
Credit: *Undergrad:* 6 *Grad:* none *Doc:* transcript
Instruction: *In:* Italian *Format:* lang study *Students:* mainly US
Costs: $3,950 *incl* tuition, housing, some meals, excursions, railpass *Nonrefundable fee*
Housing: *Arr by pgm:* residence halls, pensions
Deadline: Mar 1
Other info: *US accredited sponsor:* yes *Began:* 1997 *Orient:* in US & abroad *Activities:* excursions, field trips *Misc:* Scholarships for own students only. May contact former participants. *Financial aid:* scholarships *URL:* http://www.smu.edu/studyabroad
Contact: Intl Off, Southern Methodist Univ, PO Box 0391, 3108 Fondren Dr, Dallas TX 75275 *Ph:* 214-768 2338 *Fax:* 214-768 1051 *E-mail:* intlpro@mail.smu.edu
Or Contact: Dr Vincenzo De Nardo, Foreign Langs, Southern Methodist Univ, Box 236, Dallas TX 75275 *Ph:* 214-768 1418 *E-mail:* vdenardo@mail.smu.edu ▲

0999
SUNY COLLEGE AT NEW PALTZ, LANGUAGE IMMERSION INSTITUTE
Overseas Learning Vacation to Italy
Site: Italy: Florence, Portico, Rome, Siena, Viareggio *Host inst:* Scuola Leonardo da Vinci
Dates: 2 wks or longer, yr-round
Subjects: Italian language
Eligibility: *Level:* adults *Age:* min 18, avg 40
Credit: *Undergrad:* avail *Grad:* none
Instruction: *In:* Italian *Format:* lang study *Students:* intl
Costs: About $1030 for 2 wks *incl* tuition, housing, fees
Housing: *Arr by pgm:* residence halls with local students, homestay, hotels
Deadline: 2 mos before pgm
Other info: *US accredited sponsor:* yes *Misc:* May contact former participants. *URL:* http://www.newpaltz.edu/lii
Contact: Lang Immersion Inst, SUNY New Paltz, 75 S Manheim Blvd, New Paltz NY 12561-2499 *Ph:* 845-257 3500 *Fax:* 845-257 3569 *E-mail:* lii@newpaltz.edu ▲

1000
SUNY COLLEGE AT NEW PALTZ
Art History Abroad
Site: Italy: Rome, other sites
Dates: 3 wks, Jun
Subjects: Art history
Eligibility: *Level:* fresh, sophs, jrs, srs, grads
Credit: *Undergrad:* 3 *Grad:* 3 *Doc:* transcript
Instruction: *In:* English *Format:* lecture *Students:* mainly US
Costs: $2,879 *incl* tuition, housing, some meals, insurance, excursions
Housing: *Arr by pgm:* hotels
Deadline: Mar 1 or until pgm filled
Other info: *US accredited sponsor:* yes *Began:* 1978 *Orient:* in US *Activities:* program travel *Misc:* All instruction takes place on-site. Loans avail. *Financial aid:* scholarships *URL:* http://www.newpaltz.edu/oie/
Contact: Ctr for Intl Pgms, SUNY at New Paltz, 75 S Manheim Blvd, Ste 9, New Paltz NY 12561 *Ph:* 845-257 3125 *Fax:* 845-257 3129 *E-mail:* international@newpaltz.edu ▲

1001
SUNY ROCKLAND COMMUNITY COLLEGE
Italian Renaissance: Presence of the Past
Site: Italy: Florence, Rome
Dates: 2 wks, May 29-Jun 12
Subjects: Art history, Humanities, Literature, Music
Eligibility: *Level:* fresh, sophs, jrs, srs, adults, teachers, professionals *Age:* min 18
Credit: *Undergrad:* 3 *Grad:* none *Doc:* transcript
Instruction: *In:* English *Format:* seminar, study tour *Students:* mainly US
Costs: About $2,800 *incl* tuition, housing, some meals, intl airfare, fees, excursions
Housing: *Arr by pgm:* hotels
Deadline: Apr 1
Other info: *US accredited sponsor:* yes *Began:* 1994 *Orient:* abroad *Activities:* excursions, field trips, program travel, cultural events *Financial aid:* scholarships *URL:* http://www.studyabroad.com/suny/rockland
Contact: Jody Dudderar, Rockland CC, SUNY Rockland, 145 College Rd, Suffern NY 10901 *Ph:* 845-574 4205 *Fax:* 845-574 4423 *E-mail:* study-abroad@sunyrockland.edu

---

1002
SYRACUSE UNIVERSITY
Education in Italy
Site: Italy: Florence, Parma, Rome, Venice
Dates: 4 wks, May 17-Jun 11
Subjects: Field study, Special education
Eligibility: *Level:* grads, adults, teachers, professionals *Requires:* previous study in field
Credit: *Undergrad:* none *Grad:* 6
Instruction: *In:* English *Format:* directed field study, lecture, study tour *Students:* mainly US
Costs: $6,000 *incl* tuition, housing, some meals, excursions *Nonrefundable fee*
Housing: *Arr by pgm:* hotels
Deadline: Mar 15
Other info: *US accredited sponsor:* yes

Began: 1990 *Orient:* abroad *Activities:* field trips, program travel, cultural events *Misc:* May contact former participants. *Financial aid:* scholarships *URL:* http://sumweb.syr.edu/dipa/summer
Contact: Summer Pgms, Intl Pgms Abroad, Syracuse Univ, 119 Euclid Ave, Syracuse NY 13244-4170 *Ph:* 800-251 9674; 315-443 9420 *Fax:* 315-443 4593 *E-mail:* dipasum@summon3.syr.edu ▲

1003
SYRACUSE UNIVERSITY
Humanism & the Arts in Renaissance Italy: Traveling Seminar
Site: Italy: Assisi, Florence, Naples, Pisa, Prato, Ravenna, Rome, Siena, Urbino, Venice
Dates: Jun 4-Jul 8
Subjects: Art, Humanism, Italian studies, Literature, Philosophy, Renaissance studies
Eligibility: *Level:* fresh, sophs, jrs, srs, grads, adults, professionals
Credit: *Undergrad:* 6 *Grad:* 6
Instruction: *In:* English *Format:* lecture, seminar *Students:* mainly US
Costs: About $7,400 *incl* tuition, housing, some meals, fees, excursions *Nonrefundable fee*
Housing: *Arr by pgm:* hotels
Deadline: Mar 15
Other info: *US accredited sponsor:* yes *Began:* 1975 *Orient:* abroad *Activities:* excursions *Misc:* Guest lectures by Italian Renaissance scholars. *Financial aid:* scholarships *URL:* http://sumweb.syr.edu/dipa/summer
Contact: Summer Pgms, Intl Pgms Abroad, Syracuse Univ, 119 Euclid Ave, Syracuse NY 13244-4170 *Ph:* 800-251 9674; 315-443 9420 *Fax:* 315-443 4593 *E-mail:* dipasum@summon3.syr.edu ▲

1004
UNIVERSITY OF CINCINNATI
Study Abroad in Italy
Site: Italy: Bologna, Florence, Milan, Siena, Venice
Dates: 2 wks, Sep 6-19
Subjects: Architecture, Art, Civilization/culture, Field study, History, Italian studies, Music, Urban planning
Eligibility: Own students only. *Level:* fresh, precoll *Requires:* 3.0 GPA
Credit: *Undergrad:* 4 qtr hrs *Grad:* none *Doc:* transcript
Instruction: *In:* English *Format:* directed field study, lecture, study tour *Students:* mainly US
Costs: $2,400 *incl* housing, some meals, intl airfare, excursions
Housing: *Arr by pgm:* hotels
Deadline: Apr 1
Other info: *US accredited sponsor:* yes *Began:* 1996 *Orient:* in US & abroad (1 day) *Activities:* excursions, field trips, program travel, cultural events *Misc:* Scholarships for own students only. May contact former participants. *Financial aid:* scholarships *URL:* http://www.uc.edu/global
Contact: Prof Robert Zierolf, Univ of Cincinnati, PO Box 210003, Cincinnati OH 45221-0003 *Ph:* 513-556 6046 *Fax:* 513-556 0202 *E-mail:* robert.zierolf@uc.edu
Or Contact: Arthur Neisberg, Educ Abroad, Univ of Cincinatti, PO Box 210640, Swift 608, Cincinatti OH 45221-0640 *Ph:* 513-556 1363 *Fax:* 513-556 2990 *E-mail:* arthur.neisberg@uc.edu

---

1005
UNIVERSITY OF COLORADO AT BOULDER
Art History in Italy
Site: Italy: Florence, Rome
Dates: Late May-end Jun
Subjects: Art history, Field study
Eligibility: *Level:* jrs, srs, grads, teachers, professionals *Requires:* background in art history or humanities
Credit: *Undergrad:* 6 *Grad:* 6 *Doc:* transcript
Instruction: *In:* English *Format:* directed field study, lecture, seminar *Students:* mainly US
Costs: About $4,040 for CO residents, $5,040 for others *incl* tuition, housing, some meals, insurance, fees, in-country travel
Housing: *Arr by pgm:* pensions, hotels
Deadline: Mar 1
Other info: *US accredited sponsor:* yes *Began:* 1970 *Orient:* in US *Activities:* program travel *Misc:* May contact former participants. *URL:* http://www.colorado.edu/OIE/StudyAbroad
Contact: Intl Educ, Univ of Colorado, Campus Box 123, Boulder CO 80309-0123 *Ph:* 303-492 7741 *Fax:* 303-492 5185 *E-mail:* studyabr@colorado.edu

---

1006
UNIVERSITY OF DELAWARE
Winter Session in Italy-Education
Site: Italy: various sites
Dates: 1 mo, Jan
Subjects: Education/teaching
Eligibility: *Level:* fresh, sophs, jrs, srs *Requires:* 2.0 GPA
Credit: *Undergrad:* 6 *Grad:* none *Doc:* transcript
Instruction: *In:* English *Format:* directed field study, lecture, seminar, study tour *Students:* mainly US
Costs: Contact sponsor
Housing: *Arr by pgm:* hotels
Deadline: Mid-Oct
Other info: *US accredited sponsor:* yes *Orient:* in US *Activities:* excursions, field trips, program travel, cultural events *Misc:* Contact sponsor to arr honors credit. May contact former participants. *Financial aid:* scholarships *URL:* http://www.udel.edu/studyabroad
Contact: Intl Pgms & Special Sessions, Univ of Delaware, 4 Kent Way, Newark DE 19716 *Ph:* 888-831 4685; 302-831 2852 *Fax:* 302-831 6042 *E-mail:* studyabroad@udel.edu

---

1007
UNIVERSITY OF DELAWARE
Winter Session in Italy-Political Science
Site: Italy: various sites
Dates: 1 mo, Jan
Subjects: Political science/politics
Eligibility: *Level:* fresh, sophs, jrs, srs *Requires:* 2.0 GPA
Credit: *Undergrad:* 6 *Grad:* none *Doc:* transcript
Instruction: *In:* English *Format:* lecture, seminar, study tour *Students:* mainly US
Costs: Contact sponsor
Housing: *Arr by pgm:* hotels
Deadline: Mid-Oct
Other info: *US accredited sponsor:* yes *Orient:* in US *Activities:* excursions, field trips, program travel, cultural events *Misc:* Contact sponsors to arr honors credit. *Financial aid:* scholarships *URL:* http://www.udel.edu/studyabroad
Contact: Intl Pgms & Special Sessions, Univ of Delaware, 4 Kent Way, Newark DE 19716 *Ph:* 888-831 4685; 302-831 2852 *Fax:* 302-831 6042 *E-mail:* studyabroad@udel.edu

---

1008
UNIVERSITY OF UTAH
Study in Siena, Italy
Site: Italy: Siena, Viterbo *Host inst:* Ctr Linguistico Italiano Dante Alighieri
Dates: 4 wks, Jun-Jul
Subjects: Art, Civilization/culture, Culinary arts, Homestay, Italian language (beg/int/adv), Italian studies
Eligibility: *Level:* fresh, sophs, jrs, srs, grads, adults *Requires:* 2.50 GPA, one semester Italian *Age:* min 18
Credit: *Undergrad:* avail *Grad:* none *Doc:* transcript
Instruction: *In:* Italian *Format:* lang study, workshop *Students:* intl
Costs: About $2,200 *incl* tuition, housing, some meals, fees
Housing: *Arr by pgm:* apartments, homestay
Deadline: Mar 15
Other info: *US accredited sponsor:* yes *Orient:* in US *Activities:* excursions *Misc:* Scholarships for Univ of UT students only.

Financial aid: scholarships *URL:* http://www.saff.utah.edu/inter/
Contact: Aaron Rose, Study Abroad Adviser, Univ of Utah, 159 University Union, Salt Lake City UT 84112 *Ph:* 801-581 5849 *Fax:* 801-581 5914 *E-mail:* lashton@saff.utah.edu

ALTOMONTE

1009
SUNY COLLEGE AT OSWEGO
Italian Language, Art and Civilization
Site: Italy: Altomonte
Dates: 4 wks, mid-Jul-mid-Aug
Subjects: Art, International studies, Italian language (beg/int/adv)
Eligibility: *Level:* fresh, sophs, jrs, srs, adults, teachers, professionals, precoll *Requires:* good acad standing, previous study in field desirable
Credit: *Undergrad:* 6 *Grad:* none *Doc:* transcript
Instruction: *In:* English, Italian *Format:* lang study, lecture *Students:* mainly US
Costs: $3,600 *incl* tuition, housing, all meals, intl airfare, excursions, local transport *Nonrefundable fee*
Housing: *Arr by pgm:* apartments
Deadline: Apr 1
Other info: *US accredited sponsor:* yes *Began:* 1992 *Orient:* abroad *Activities:* excursions, field trips, cultural events *Misc:* May contact former participants. *URL:* http://www.oswego.edu/~intled
Contact: Susan Ansara, Dir, Intl Educ, SUNY Coll at Oswego, 102 Rich Hall, Oswego NY 13126 *Ph:* 888-467 9346; 315-341 2118 *Fax:* 315-341 2477 *E-mail:* intled@oswego.edu

AREZZO

1010
CENTRO DI CULTURA ITALIANA
Centro di Cultura Italiana Arezzo
Site: Italy: Arezzo
Dates: 2-8 wks, yr-round
Subjects: Italian language (beg/int/adv), Italian studies
Eligibility: *Level:* adults *Age:* min 18
Credit: *Undergrad:* avail *Grad:* avail *Doc:* certificate
Instruction: *In:* Italian *Format:* lang study, lecture *Students:* intl
Costs: EUR 301 for 2 wks *incl* tuition, fees
Housing: *Arr by pgm:* residence halls, apartments, homestay
Deadline: 2 wks before pgm
Other info: *US accredited sponsor:* no *Began:* 1995 *Orient:* abroad *Activities:* excursions, cultural events *Misc:* Discount for those under 30 & extended stays. May contact former participants. *Financial aid:* scholarships *URL:* http://www.culturaitaliana.it
Contact: Cultura Italiana, Via Roma 2, I-52100 Arezzo, Italy *E-mail:* culturait@iol.it

1011
UNIVERSITY OF NORTH CAROLINA AT CHARLOTTE
Architectural Design Studio and Field Study in Italy
Site: Italy: Arezzo
Dates: 6 wks, late May-early Aug
Subjects: Architecture, Field study, Studio arts
Eligibility: *Level:* sophs, jrs, srs, grads *Requires:* previous study in field, instructor approval
Credit: *Undergrad:* 8 *Grad:* none *Doc:* transcript
Instruction: *In:* English *Format:* practical training, study tour *Students:* mainly US
Costs: $3,700 for summer *incl* tuition, housing, insurance, fees, excursions, books/materials *Nonrefundable fee*
Housing: *Arr by pgm:* pensions, castello
Deadline: Nov 4
Other info: *US accredited sponsor:* yes *Began:* 1988 *Orient:* in US *Activities:* excursions, field trips *Misc:* May contact former participants. *URL:* http://www.uncc.edu/oip/edabroad.htm
Contact: Joel A Gallegos, Dir, Educ Abroad/Intl Pgms, UNC Charlotte, 9201 University City Blvd, Charlotte NC 28223-0001 *Ph:* 704-687 2464 *Fax:* 704-687 3168 *E-mail:* stennies@email.uncc.edu
Or Contact: Italy Pgm Dir, Coll of Architecture, UNC Charlotte, 9201 University City Blvd, Charlotte NC 28223-0001 *Ph:* 704-687 2358 *Fax:* 704-687 3353 *E-mail:* aar00alb@email.uncc.edu

ASSISI

1012
EUROPEAN HERITAGE INSTITUTE
Summer in Assisi
Site: Italy: Assisi *Host inst:* Italian Lang Acad
Dates: 1-3 mos, Jun 1-Aug 31
Subjects: Civilization/culture, Italian language (beg/int/adv), Italian studies
Eligibility: *Level:* adults *Age:* min 18
Credit: *Undergrad:* 3-6 *Grad:* none *Doc:* certificate
Instruction: *In:* Italian *Format:* lang study, seminar *Students:* intl
Costs: $1,200 per mo *incl* tuition, housing, fees
Housing: *Arr by pgm:* apartments, pensions
Deadline: Apr 1
Other info: *US accredited sponsor:* no *Began:* 1994 *Orient:* in US & abroad *Activities:* excursions, field trips, cultural events *Misc:* May contact former participants. *URL:* http://www.europeanheritage.org
Contact: Dr Antonio Masullo or Ms Barbara Cotter, European Heritage Inst, 2708 E Franklin St, Richmond VA 23223 *Ph:* 804-643 0661 *Fax:* 804-648 0826 *E-mail:* euritage@i2020.net ▲

1013
GEORGE MASON UNIVERSITY
The Italian City: Function, Form and Fantasy
Site: Italy: Assisi
Dates: 2 wks, Jul 4-Jul 17
Subjects: Art history
Eligibility: *Level:* fresh, sophs, jrs, srs, adults, teachers, professionals *Requires:* 2.25 GPA, previous study in field *Age:* min 18
Credit: *Undergrad:* 3 *Grad:* none *Doc:* transcript
Instruction: *In:* English *Format:* lecture, seminar *Students:* mainly US
Costs: $2,779 for GMU, $3,379 for others *incl* tuition, housing, some meals, insurance, fees, excursions *Nonrefundable fee*
Housing: *Arr by pgm:* hotels
Deadline: Apr 15
Other info: *US accredited sponsor:* yes *Orient:* in US (1 day) *Financial aid:* scholarships, work study *URL:* http://www.gmu.edu/departments/cge
Contact: Ctr for Global Educ, George Mason Univ, Johnson Ctr, Rm 235, 4400 University Dr, Fairfax VA 22030-4444 *Ph:* 703-993 2154 *Fax:* 703-993 2153 *E-mail:* cge@gmn.edu

BAGNO DI ROMAGNA

1014
SCUOLA PALAZZO MALVISI
Italian for Foreign Students
Site: Italy: Bagno di Romagna (Forli)
Dates: 1 mo, yr-round
Subjects: Art history, Culinary arts, Italian language (beg/int/adv), Literature
Eligibility: *Level:* adults *Age:* min 16
Credit: *Undergrad:* none *Grad:* none
Instruction: *In:* Italian *Format:* lang study, lecture *Students:* intl
Costs: About $950 *incl* tuition, housing, fees, books/materials
Housing: *Arr by pgm:* apartments, hotels, furnished rms
Deadline: 1 mo before pgm; 2 mos for scholarships
Other info: *US accredited sponsor:* no

Began: 1981 *In coop with:* AIL, ASILS, ELITE *Activities:* excursions, cultural events *Misc:* Wine & cooking classes. May contact former participants. *URL:* http://www.scuolapalazzomalvisi.com
Contact: Dr Cesare Portolani, Scuola Palazzo Malvisi, via Fiorentina 36, 47021 Bagno di Romagna (Forli), Italy *E-mail:* malvisi@infuturo.it
Or Contact: Matilde Portolani, Scuola Palazzo Malvisi, via Salara 31, 48100 Ravenna, Italy *E-mail:* malvisi@infuturo.it

BOLOGNA

1015
CENTRO DI CULTURA ITALIANA
Centro di Cultura Italiana Bologna
Site: Italy: Bologna
Dates: 2-10 wks, yr-round
Subjects: Italian language (beg/int/adv), Literature
Eligibility: *Level:* fresh, sophs, jrs, srs, grads, adults, teachers, professionals *Age:* min 18
Credit: *Undergrad:* avail *Grad:* avail *Doc:* certificate
Instruction: *In:* Italian *Format:* lang study, lecture *Students:* intl
Costs: EUR 301 for 2 wks, EUR 540 for 4 wks *incl* tuition, fees
Housing: *Arr by pgm:* residence halls, apartments, homestay, furnished rms
Deadline: 2 wks before pgm
Other info: *US accredited sponsor:* no *Began:* 1980 *Activities:* excursions *Misc:* Discounts for participants under 30 & for extended stays. May contact former participants. *Financial aid:* scholarships *URL:* http://www.culturaitaliana.it
Contact: Cultura Italiana, via Castiglione 4, I-40124 Bologna, Italy *E-mail:* culturait@iol.it

1016
DICKINSON COLLEGE
Bologna Summer Immersion Program
Site: Italy: Bologna
Dates: 5 wks, about late May-late Jun
Subjects: Art history, Civilization/culture, Intercultural studies, Italian language (int/adv)
Eligibility: *Level:* fresh, sophs *Requires:* 3 sems coll Italian
Credit: *Undergrad:* 4 *Grad:* none
Instruction: *In:* Italian *Format:* lang study, lecture *Students:* mainly US
Costs: About $4,400 *incl* tuition, housing, all meals, intl airfare, fees, excursions
Housing: *Arr by pgm:* homestay
Deadline: Mar 1
Other info: *US accredited sponsor:* yes *Began:* 1984 *Orient:* in US *Activities:* excursions, program travel *URL:* http://www.dickinson.edu/departments/ocs/summer.html
Contact: Global Educ, Dickinson Coll, PO Box 1773, Carlisle PA 17013-2896 *Ph:* 717-245 1341 *Fax:* 717-245 1688 *E-mail:* ocs@dickinson.edu

1017
KOINE CENTER
Italian Language and Culture-Bologna
Site: Italy: Bologna
Dates: 2 wks-5 mos, yr-round
Subjects: Art history, Civilization/culture, Culinary arts, Homestay, Italian language (beg/int/adv)
Eligibility: *Level:* adults *Age:* min 15, max 90
Credit: *Undergrad:* none *Grad:* none *Doc:* certificate
Instruction: *In:* English, Italian *Format:* lang study, lecture *Students:* intl
Costs: $690 for 2 wks, $1,320 for 4 wks *incl* tuition, housing, some meals, excursions, books/materials
Housing: *Arr by pgm:* homestay, pensions, hotels, hostels
Deadline: Contact sponsor
Other info: *US accredited sponsor:* no *Began:* 1992 *In coop with:* Modern Langs sch *Orient:* in US *Activities:* excursions *Misc:* 12 participants max per group. May contact former participants. *URL:* http://www.koinecenter.com
Contact: Linda Larson & Anja Schultz, Koine, via Pandolfini 27, 50122 Florence, Italy *E-mail:* koine@firenze.net

CAPO VATICANO

1018
LANGUAGES PLUS
Language Immersion and Cultural Program-Capo Vaticano
Site: Italy: Capo Vaticano
Dates: 2 wks or longer, summer only
Subjects: Homestay, Italian language (beg/int/adv)
Eligibility: *Level:* adults *Age:* min 17, max 65, avg 24
Credit: *Undergrad:* none *Grad:* none *Doc:* certificate
Instruction: *In:* Italian *Format:* lang study *Students:* intl
Costs: From $700 for 2 wks *incl* tuition, housing, books/materials, cultural activities
Housing: *Arr by pgm:* apartments, homestay
Deadline: 2 wks before pgm
Other info: *US accredited sponsor:* no *Activities:* excursions, field trips *Misc:* May contact former participants. *URL:* http://www.languagesplus.com
Contact: Margot Haldenby, North Amer Enrollment, Langs Plus, 317 Adelaide St W, Ste 900, Toronto, Ontario M5V 1P9, Canada *Ph:* 888-526 4758; 416-925 7117 *Fax:* 416-925 5990 *E-mail:* info@languagesplus.com

CARMIGNANO

1019
CAPEZZANA WINE AND CULINARY CENTER
Wine and Culinary Arts
Site: Italy: Carmignano
Dates: 5 days, fall and/or spring
Subjects: Culinary arts, Wine
Eligibility: *Level:* adults, professionals *Age:* min 18
Credit: *Undergrad:* none *Grad:* none *Doc:* certificate
Instruction: *In:* English *Format:* practical training, study tour, workshop *Students:* US & intl
Costs: $2,300-$3,000 *incl* tuition, housing, all meals, fees, excursions, books/materials *Nonrefundable fee*
Housing: *Arr by pgm:* hotels, estate
Deadline: Contact sponsor
Other info: *US accredited sponsor:* no *Orient:* abroad *Activities:* excursions, cultural events *Misc:* May contact former participants. *URL:* http://www.capezzana.it
Contact: Lili Rollins, Booking Agent, Capezzana Wine-Culinary Ctr, 1607 Pearl St, Alameda CA 94501 *Ph:* 510-865 8191 *Fax:* 510-865 8191 *E-mail:* lrrol@pacbell.net

CASTELFIORENTINO

1020
HORIZONS TO GO
Horizons in Italy/Glorious Tuscany
Site: Italy: Castelfiorentino
Dates: 1 wk, Apr 28-May 5 or Oct 13-20
Subjects: Book arts, Glassmaking, Jewelry/jewelry-making, Painting, Photography
Eligibility: *Level:* fresh, sophs, jrs, srs, grads, adults, teachers, professionals *Age:* min 19, max 85
Credit: *Undergrad:* none *Grad:* avail
Instruction: *In:* English *Format:* art studio, workshop *Students:* mainly US
Costs: $1,445 *incl* tuition, housing, all meals, excursions, books/materials *Nonrefundable fee*
Housing: *Arr by pgm:* bed & breakfasts
Deadline: Contact sponsor
Other info: *US accredited sponsor:* no *Activities:* excursions, field trips *Misc:* Field trips to Florence, Siena & Tuscan

villages. May contact former participants. *URL:* http://www.horizons-art.org
Contact: Jane Sinauer, Horizons To Go, 108 N Main St T, Amherst MA 01004 *Ph:* 413-549 2900 *Fax:* 413-549 5995 *E-mail:* horizons@horizons-art.org

CORTONA

1021
KOINE CENTER
Italian Language and Culture-Cortona
Site: Italy: Cortona
Dates: 2 wks-5 mos, mid-Mar-mid-Oct
Subjects: Art history, Civilization/culture, Culinary arts, Italian language (beg/int/adv)
Eligibility: *Level:* adults *Age:* min 15, max 90
Credit: *Undergrad:* none *Grad:* none *Doc:* certificate
Instruction: *In:* English, Italian *Format:* lang study, lecture *Students:* intl
Costs: $690 for 2 wks, $1,320 for 4 wks *incl* tuition, housing, some meals, excursions, books/materials
Housing: *Arr by pgm:* pensions, hotels, hostels
Deadline: 2 wks before pgm
Other info: *US accredited sponsor:* no *Began:* 1981 *In coop with:* Municipality of Cortona *Orient:* in US *Activities:* excursions *Misc:* Max 12 participants per group. May contact former participants. *URL:* http://www.koinecenter.com
Contact: Linda Larson or Anja Schultz, Koine, via Pandolfini 27, 50122 Florence, Italy *E-mail:* koine@firenze.net

ELBA

1022
CENTRO FIORENZA LINGUA E CULTURA ITALIANA PER STRANIERI
Intensive Group and Individual Courses-Elba
Site: Italy: Elba
Dates: 2 wks or longer, May-Oct
Subjects: Italian language (beg/int/adv)
Eligibility: *Level:* fresh, sophs, jrs, srs, grads, adults, teachers, professionals *Age:* min 18
Credit: *Undergrad:* avail *Grad:* none
Instruction: *In:* Italian *Format:* lang study, lecture *Students:* intl
Costs: About $1,000-$1,500 *incl* tuition, housing, some meals, fees
Housing: *Arr by pgm:* apartments, hotels
Deadline: 4 wks before pgm
Other info: *US accredited sponsor:* no *Began:* 1983 *Orient:* in US *Activities:* excursions *Misc:* May contact former participants. *URL:* http://www.centrofiorenza.com
Contact: Mrs S Merlini-Seiwald, Ctr Fiorenza, via Santo Spirito 14, I-50125 Florence, Italy *E-mail:* fiorenza@centrofiorenza.com

FAENZA

1023
SUNY COLLEGE AT BROCKPORT
Art History and Ceramics in Faenza
Site: Italy: Faenza *Host inst:* Ist Statale d'Arte per la Ceramica
Dates: 2 wks, Jul
Subjects: Art history, Ceramics/pottery
Eligibility: *Level:* sophs, jrs, srs *Requires:* 2.5 GPA
Credit: *Undergrad:* 3 *Grad:* none *Doc:* transcript
Instruction: *In:* English *Format:* art studio, directed field study, lecture *Students:* mainly US
Costs: $3,000 *incl* tuition, housing, some meals, intl airfare, insurance
Housing: *Arr by pgm:* hotels
Deadline: May 1
Other info: *US accredited sponsor:* yes *Began:* 1988 *Orient:* in US *Activities:* excursions, field trips *Misc:* Faculty dir. Pgm offered in even-numbered yrs. *Financial aid:* scholarships *URL:* http://www.brockport.edu/study_abroad
Contact: Dr John Perry, Dir, Intl Educ, SUNY Coll at Brockport, 360 New Campus Dr, Rakov Ctr, Brockport NY 14420 *Ph:* 800-298 7869 *Fax:* 716-637 3218 *E-mail:* overseas@brockport.edu

FLORENCE

1024
ACCADEMIA DEL GIGLIO
Language, Art and Culture
Site: Italy: Florence
Dates: Multiple pgm lengths, yr-round
Subjects: Art history, Costumes, Film studies, Fine arts, Graphic arts/design, Homestay, Italian language (beg/int/adv), Italian studies, Literature, Music history, Painting, Student teaching
Eligibility: *Level:* adults *Age:* min 15, avg 25
Credit: *Undergrad:* avail *Grad:* none *Doc:* certificate
Instruction: *In:* Italian *Format:* lang study, practical training, student teaching *Students:* intl
Costs: Lit 850,000 per mo *incl* tuition, books/materials
Housing: *Sponsor assists:* apartments, homestay, pensions, hotels
Deadline: 1 mo before pgm
Other info: *US accredited sponsor:* no *Began:* 1994 *Activities:* excursions, cultural events *URL:* http://www.adg.it
Contact: Cecilia Pontenani, Dir, Accad del Giglio, via Ghibellina 116, 50122 Florence, Italy *E-mail:* info@adg.it

1025
ACCENT
Summer in Florence
Site: Italy: Florence *Host inst:* Scuola Leonardo da Vinci
Dates: 4 wks, Jul
Subjects: Art history, Civilization/culture, Italian language (beg/int/adv)
Eligibility: *Level:* fresh, sophs, jrs, srs, grads, adults, teachers, professionals, precoll
Credit: *Undergrad:* 4 *Grad:* none *Doc:* transcript *Transfer credit through:* San Francisco State Univ
Instruction: *In:* English, Italian *Format:* lang study, lecture *Students:* mainly US
Costs: $2,750 *incl* tuition, housing, excursions, activities
Housing: *Arr by pgm:* homestay, student apts
Deadline: May 1
Other info: *US accredited sponsor:* no *Began:* 1983 *Orient:* in US & abroad *Activities:* excursions, field trips, program travel, cultural events *Misc:* May contact former participants. *URL:* http://www.accentintl.com
Contact: Accent, 870 Market St, Ste 1026, San Francisco CA 94102 *Ph:* 800-869 9291; 415-835 3744 *Fax:* 415-835 3749 *E-mail:* info@accentintl.com
Or Contact: Mary Pieratt, San Francisco State Univ, Coll of Extended Learning, 1600 Holloway Ave, ADM 153, San Francisco CA 94132 *Ph:* 415-338 1372

1026
ADVENTIST COLLEGES ABROAD
Summer Italian Language Program
Site: Italy: Florence *Host inst:* Ist Avventista Villa Aurora
Dates: 6 wks, Jun 26-Aug 2
Subjects: Italian language (beg/int)
Eligibility: Students of member insts only. *Level:* adults *Requires:* 2.5 GPA *Age:* min 15
Credit: *Undergrad:* 9 qtr hrs *Grad:* none *Doc:* transcript
Instruction: *In:* Italian *Format:* lang study, lecture *Students:* intl
Costs: $2,055 *incl* tuition, housing, all meals, insurance, fees, excursions, books/materials *Nonrefundable fee*
Housing: *Arr by pgm:* residence halls
Deadline: May 31
Other info: *US accredited sponsor:* yes *Began:* 1993 *Orient:* in US & abroad

Activities: excursions, field trips, sports *URL:* http://www.nadadventist.org/aca
Contact: *See Index II for Members* Odette Ferreira, Dir, Adventist Colls Abroad, 12501 Old Columbia Pike, Silver Spring MD 20904-6600 *Ph:* 301-680 6444 *Fax:* 301-680 6463 *E-mail:* 104474.304@compuserve.com

---

1027
AMERICAN INSTITUTE FOR FOREIGN STUDY (AIFS) and **RICHMOND, THE AMERICAN INTERNATIONAL UNIVERSITY IN LONDON**
Richmond in Florence
Site: Italy: Florence *Host inst:* Richmond in Florence
Dates: 4 wks, May 31-Jul 3
Subjects: Art history, History, Homestay, Italian language, Literature, Sociology, Studio arts
Eligibility: *Level:* fresh, sophs, jrs, srs, adults, precoll *Requires:* 2.0 GPA
Credit: *Undergrad:* avail *Grad:* none *Doc:* transcript
Instruction: *In:* English, Italian *Format:* art studio, lang study, lecture *Students:* mainly US
Costs: $4,499 *incl* tuition, housing, most meals, intl airfare
Housing: *Arr by pgm:* apartments, homestay
Deadline: Mar 15
Other info: *US accredited sponsor:* yes *Began:* 1969 *Orient:* abroad *Activities:* excursions, cultural events *Misc:* Resident dir. May contact former participants. *Financial aid:* scholarships *URL:* http://www.aifsabroad.com
Contact: Solandy Meza, Coll Div, AIFS, River Plaza, 9 W Broad St, Stamford CT 06902 *Ph:* 800-727 2437 ext 5163 *E-mail:* college.info@aifs.com ▲

1028
ARTIS-ART RESEARCH TOURS AND INTERNATIONAL STUDIOS
Study Art in Florence
Site: Italy: Florence
Dates: 2-4 wks, summer
Subjects: Art history, Batik, Drawing, Jewelry/jewelry-making, Photography, Serigraphy, Textiles
Eligibility: *Level:* fresh, sophs, jrs, srs, grads, adults, teachers, professionals *Requires:* good physical & mental health *Age:* min 18, max 78, avg 25
Credit: *Undergrad:* 3-6 *Grad:* none *Doc:* transcript
Instruction: *In:* English *Format:* art studio, directed field study, independent study, lecture, study tour, workshop *Students:* mainly US
Costs: $3,585 *incl* tuition, housing, some meals, intl airfare, insurance, fees, excursions, art workshops, museum fees *Nonrefundable fee*
Housing: *Arr by pgm:* residence halls, apartments
Deadline: Contact sponsor
Other info: *US accredited sponsor:* no *Began:* 1993 *Orient:* abroad (2 days) *Activities:* excursions, field trips, program travel, cultural events *Misc:* Excursions to Rome, Venice, Pisa, Siena. Workshop instructors have MFA degrees. May contact former participants. *URL:* http://www.artis-tours.org
Contact: David Renfrow, ARTIS, 1616 Princeton Dr, Columbia MO 65203 *Ph:* 800-232 6893; 573-447 3495 *Fax:* 573-234 2926 *E-mail:* dfro@socket.net

---

1029
BENTLEY COLLEGE
Summer Program in Florence, Italy
Site: Italy: Florence *Host inst:* Lorenzo de' Medici Inst
Dates: 4 wks, May-Jun
Subjects: Art history, History, Italian language, Political science/politics
Eligibility: *Level:* fresh, sophs, jrs, srs *Requires:* 2.7 GPA, faculty reference
Credit: *Undergrad:* 6 *Grad:* none *Doc:* transcript
Instruction: *In:* English, Italian *Format:* lang study, seminar *Students:* mainly US
Costs: $2,500 *incl* tuition, housing, ISIC *Nonrefundable fee*
Housing: *Arr by pgm:* apartments
Deadline: Mar 1
Other info: *US accredited sponsor:* yes *Orient:* in US & abroad *Misc:* May contact former participants. *URL:* http://ecampus.bentley.edu/dept/sa
Contact: Jill A Perry Redin, Dir, Study Abroad, Intl Ctr, Bentley Coll, 175 Forest St, Waltham MA 02452-4705 *Ph:* 781-891 3474 *Fax:* 781-891 2819 *E-mail:* study_abroad@bentley.edu

---

1030
BRYN MAWR COLLEGE and **UNIVERSITY OF PENNSYLVANIA**
Italian Studies Summer Institute
Site: Italy: Florence
Dates: 6 wks, early Jun-mid-Jul
Subjects: Art history, Civilization/culture, Italian language (beg/int/adv), Literature
Eligibility: *Level:* fresh, sophs, jrs, srs, grads, professionals
Credit: *Undergrad:* 6-8 *Grad:* avail *Doc:* transcript
Instruction: *In:* English, Italian *Format:* lang study, lecture *Students:* mainly US
Costs: About $6,500 *incl* tuition, housing, some meals, intl airfare, excursions *Nonrefundable fee*
Housing: *Arr by pgm:* pensions, hotels
Deadline: Mar 15
Other info: *US accredited sponsor:* yes *Began:* 1981 *Orient:* in US & abroad *Activities:* excursions *Financial aid:* scholarships *URL:* http://www.sas.upenn.edu/CGS/
Contact: Elizabeth Sachs, Penn Summer Abroad, Univ of Pennsylvania, 3440 Market St, Ste 100, Philadelphia PA 19104-3335 *Ph:* 215-898 5738 *Fax:* 215-573 2053 *E-mail:* sdanti@mail.sas.upenn.edu

---

1031
CENTRO FIORENZA LINGUA E CULTURA ITALIANA PER STRANIERI
Intensive Group and Individual Courses-Florence
Site: Italy: Florence
Dates: 2-32 wks, yr-round
Subjects: Art history, Business language, Ceramics/pottery, Civilization/culture, Culinary arts, Italian language (beg/int/adv), Italian studies, Literature
Eligibility: *Level:* adults *Age:* min 18
Credit: *Undergrad:* avail *Grad:* none
Instruction: *In:* Italian *Format:* lang study, lecture *Students:* intl
Costs: About $320 for 2 wks, $560 for 4 wks, $1,100 for 8 wks *incl* tuition, fees, excursions, conference
Housing: *Arr by pgm:* residence halls, apartments, homestay, pensions, hotels, furnished rms
Deadline: 1 mo before pgm
Other info: *US accredited sponsor:* no *Began:* 1983 *Orient:* in US *Activities:* excursions, field trips, cultural events, sports *Misc:* May contact former participants. *Financial aid:* scholarships *URL:* http://www.centrofiorenza.com
Contact: Mrs S Merlini-Seiwald, Ctr Fiorenza, via Santo Spirito 14, I-50125 Florence, Italy *E-mail:* fiorenza@centrofiorenza.com
Or Contact: Michele Cacciottolo, 7-13 River Rd, Fair Lawn NJ 07410 *Ph:* 201-398 0693 *Fax:* 201-398 0694 *E-mail:* michelecac@aol.com
Or Contact: Paola Servino, 31 Caughey St, Waltham MA 02154 *Ph:* 781-893 3218 *Fax:* 781-647 7065 *E-mail:* servino@binah.cc.brandeis.edu

---

1032
CENTRO LINGUISTICO ITALIANO DANTE ALIGHIERI
Italian Language and Culture
Site: Italy: Florence
Dates: 2-4 wks, yr-round
Subjects: Art, Culinary arts, Drama/theater, Film studies, Geography, History, Italian language (beg/int/adv), Literature, Music, Opera, Political science/politics
Eligibility: *Level:* adults

Credit: *Undergrad:* none *Grad:* none *Doc:* certificate, diploma
Instruction: *In:* Italian *Format:* lang study *Students:* intl
Costs: $670 for 4 wks *incl* tuition
Housing: *Arr by pgm:* apartments, homestay, hotels
Deadline: 4 wks before pgm
Other info: *US accredited sponsor:* no *Began:* 1966 *Orient:* abroad (1 day) *Activities:* excursions, field trips, program travel, cultural events, sports *Misc:* May contact former participants. *Financial aid:* scholarships *URL:* http://www.clida.it
Contact: Dr Alberto Materassi, CLI Dante Alighieri, Piazza della Repubblica 5, I-50123 Florence, Italy *E-mail:* study@clida.it

---

1033
CENTRO PONTEVECCHIO
Italian Language and Culture for Foreigners
Site: Italy: Florence
Dates: 2 wks or longer, yr-round
Subjects: Art history, Civilization/culture, Culinary arts, Foreign language teaching, Italian language (beg/int/adv), Italian studies, Music history, Tourism, Trade
Eligibility: *Level:* adults *Age:* min 16, max 85, avg 23
Credit: *Undergrad:* none *Grad:* none *Doc:* certificate, diploma
Instruction: *In:* Italian *Format:* lang study *Students:* intl
Costs: Contact sponsor
Housing: *Arr by pgm:* apartments, homestay, pensions, hotels
Deadline: 1 mo before pgm
Other info: *US accredited sponsor:* no *Began:* 1986 *Orient:* abroad *Activities:* excursions, field trips, cultural events *Financial aid:* scholarships *URL:* http://www.cpv.it
Contact: Paola De Mari, Ctr Pontevecchio, Piazza della Signoria 4A, 50122 Florence, Italy *E-mail:* info@cpv.it

---

1034
COLLEGE CONSORTIUM FOR INTERNATIONAL STUDIES and **COLLEGE OF STATEN ISLAND, CITY UNIVERSITY OF NEW YORK**
CSI Program in Florence, Italy: Liberal Arts and Studio Art
Site: Italy: Florence *Host inst:* Scuola Lorenzo de' Medici
Dates: 4 or 8 wks, May 23-Jun 23, Jun 27-Jul 28 and/or Aug 1-Sep 1
Subjects: Art history, Art restoration, Civilization/culture, Drawing, Graphic arts/design, Italian language (beg/int/adv), Italian studies, Painting, Photography, Studio arts
Eligibility: *Level:* fresh, sophs, jrs, srs *Requires:* 2.5 GPA, recommendation letter, essay, transcript *Age:* min 18
Credit: *Undergrad:* 6 per session *Grad:* none *Doc:* transcript
Instruction: *In:* English, Italian *Format:* art studio, lang study, lecture, seminar *Students:* intl
Costs: $2,070 4 wks/$3,545 8 wks NY res & CCIS members, $2,070/$3,640 others *incl* tuition, fees, ISIC *Nonrefundable fee*
Housing: *Arr by pgm:* apartments, residential hotel
Deadline: Mar 15 for Jun; Apr 1 for Jul & Aug
Other info: *US accredited sponsor:* yes *Began:* 1992 *Orient:* in US & abroad *Activities:* excursions, field trips *Misc:* Optional trips to Siena, Venice, Assisi, Rome. Walking tours. May contact former participants. *URL:* http://www.ccisabroad.org
Contact: *See Index II for Members* CCIS, 2000 P St NW, Ste 503, Washington DC 20036 *Ph:* 800-453 6956; 202-223 0330 *Fax:* 202-223 0999 *E-mail:* info@ccisabroad.org
Or Contact: Coord, Italy Pgms, Ctr for Intl Svc, Coll of Staten Island/CUNY, Bldg 2A, Rm 206, 2800 Victory Blvd, Staten Island NY 10314 *Ph:* 718-982 2100 *Fax:* 718-982 2108 *E-mail:* studyab@postbox.csi.cuny.edu ▲

1035
COLLEGE CONSORTIUM FOR INTERNATIONAL STUDIES and **COLLEGE OF STATEN ISLAND, CITY UNIVERSITY OF NEW YORK**
CSI Program in Florence, Italy: Super-Intensive Italian
Site: Italy: Florence *Host inst:* Scuola Lorenzo de' Medici
Dates: 4 or 8 wks, May 23-Jun 23, Jun 27-Jul 28 and/or Aug 1-Sep 1
Subjects: Italian language (beg/int/adv)
Eligibility: *Level:* fresh, sophs, jrs, srs *Requires:* 2.5 GPA, recommendation letter, essay, transcript *Age:* min 18
Credit: *Undergrad:* 6 per session *Grad:* none *Doc:* transcript
Instruction: *In:* Italian *Format:* lang study, seminar *Students:* intl
Costs: $1,370 4 wks/$2,395 8 wks NY res & CCIS members, $1,820/$3,640 others *incl* tuition, fees, ISIC *Nonrefundable fee*
Housing: *Arr by pgm:* apartments, residential hotel
Deadline: Mar 15 for Jun; Apr 1 for Jul & Aug
Other info: *US accredited sponsor:* yes *Began:* 1992 *Orient:* in US & abroad *Activities:* excursions, field trips *Misc:* Walking tours. Optional trips to Siena, Venice, Assisi, Rome. May contact former participants. *URL:* http://www.ccisabroad.org
Contact: *See Index II for Members* CCIS, 2000 P St NW, Ste 503, Washington DC 20036 *Ph:* 800-453 6956; 202-223 0330 *Fax:* 202-223 0999 *E-mail:* info@ccisabroad.org
Or Contact: Coord, Italy Pgms, Ctr for Intl Svc, Coll of Staten Island/CUNY, Bldg 2A, Rm 206, 2800 Victory Blvd, Staten Island NY 10314 *Ph:* 718-982 2100 *Fax:* 718-982 2108 *E-mail:* studyab@postbox.csi.cuny.edu ▲

1036
COLLEGE OF WILLIAM & MARY
Summer in Florence
Site: Italy: Florence *Host inst:* Linguaviva Sch of Italian
Dates: May 25-Jun 22
Subjects: Art history, Italian language (beg/int/adv), Literature
Eligibility: *Level:* fresh, sophs, jrs, srs, adults, teachers, professionals *Requires:* good acad standing
Credit: *Undergrad:* 6 *Grad:* none *Doc:* transcript
Instruction: *In:* English, Italian *Format:* lang study, lecture *Students:* intl
Costs: $3,350 *incl* tuition, housing, some meals, fees, excursions, books/materials *Nonrefundable fee*
Housing: *Arr by pgm:* homestay
Deadline: Feb 15
Other info: *US accredited sponsor:* yes *Began:* 1980 *Activities:* excursions *Misc:* Scholarships for own students only. Resident dir. *URL:* http://www.wm.edu/academics/reves/programs_abroad/
Contact: Guru Ghosh, Reves Ctr for Intl Studies, Coll of William & Mary, PO Box 8795, Williamsburg VA 23187-8795 *Ph:* 757-221 3595 *Fax:* 757-221 3597 *E-mail:* gxghos@wm.edu

---

1037
DOMINICAN UNIVERSITY
Summer Study in Florence
Site: Italy: Florence
Dates: 6 wks, Jun 17-Jul 28
Subjects: Art history, History, Italian language (beg/int/adv), Literature, Political science/politics, Studio arts
Eligibility: *Level:* sophs, jrs, srs, adults *Requires:* 2.5 GPA, 3 recommendation letters, medical report *Age:* min 18, avg 21
Credit: *Undergrad:* 7 *Grad:* none *Doc:* transcript
Instruction: *In:* English, Italian *Format:* art studio, independent study, lang study, lecture, seminar *Students:* mainly US
Costs: $2,900 *incl* tuition, housing, some meals, fees, excursions *Nonrefundable fee*
Housing: *Arr by pgm:* hotels
Deadline: Feb 1
Other info: *US accredited sponsor:* yes *Began:* 1980 *Orient:* in US & abroad (2

days) *Activities:* excursions *Misc:* May contact former participants. *Financial aid:* scholarships *URL:* http://www.dom.edu/academic/studyabroad/florence.html
Contact: Sue Ponremy, Dir, or, Ms Pat Klbecka, Adjunct Dir, Intl Studies, Dominican Univ, 7900 W Division St, River Forest IL 60305 *Ph:* 708-524 6965 *Fax:* 708-366 5360 *E-mail:* intstudy@email.dom.edu

---

1038
DRAKE UNIVERSITY and **INSTITUTE OF ITALIAN STUDIES**
Summer in Florence
Site: Italy: Florence *Host inst:* Art Inst of Florence, Ctr Lorenzo de' Medici
Dates: 4, 8 or 12 wks, May-Aug
Subjects: Art history, Humanities, Italian language (beg/int/adv), Photography, Studio arts
Eligibility: *Level:* sophs, jrs, srs, adults *Requires:* 2.75 GPA *Age:* min 19
Credit: *Undergrad:* 6-12 *Grad:* avail *Doc:* transcript
Instruction: *In:* English, Italian *Format:* art studio, directed field study, lang study, lecture *Students:* intl
Costs: Contact sponsor
Housing: *Sponsor assists:* apartments, pensions
Deadline: Apr 15
Other info: *US accredited sponsor:* yes *Began:* 1985 *Orient:* abroad *Activities:* excursions, field trips, cultural events *Misc:* Intl faculty. *Financial aid:* scholarships *URL:* http://www.mac.drake.edu/iis
Contact: Dr Mario Soria, Dir, or Rick Soria, Assoc Dir, Ctr for Intl Pgms, Drake Univ, Box 51, 2507 University Ave, Des Moines IA 50311 *Ph:* 800-443 7253 ext 3984; 515-225 2998 *Fax:* 515-225 0196 *E-mail:* drakeiis@acad.drake.edu

---

1039
EUROPEAN HERITAGE INSTITUTE
Art in Italy: Florence
Site: Italy: Florence *Host inst:* Lorenzo de' Medici Inst
Dates: 1, 2 or 3 mos, May 1-Aug 28
Subjects: Architecture, Art history, Art restoration, Drawing, Fashion design, Graphic arts/design, Italian language (beg/int/adv), Jewelry/jewelry-making, Liberal arts, Painting, Photography, Sculpture, Television/video
Eligibility: *Level:* fresh, sophs, jrs, srs, grads, adults, teachers, professionals *Age:* min 18
Credit: *Undergrad:* 3-6 *Grad:* 3-6 *Doc:* transcript, certificate
Instruction: *In:* English, Italian *Format:* art studio, independent study, lab, lang study, lecture, practical training, seminar, study tour *Students:* intl
Costs: $1,050 for 1 course, $1,750 for 2 courses *incl* tuition, fees
Housing: *Arr by pgm:* residence halls, apartments, hotels
Deadline: 60 days before pgm
Other info: *US accredited sponsor:* no *Began:* 1993 *Orient:* in US & abroad *Activities:* excursions, field trips, cultural events *Misc:* May contact former participants. *URL:* http://www.europeanheritage.org
Contact: Dr Antonio Masullo or Ms Barbara Cotter, European Heritage Inst, 2708 E Franklin St, Richmond VA 23223 *Ph:* 804-643 0661 *Fax:* 804-648 0826 *E-mail:* euritage@i2020.net ▲

1040
EUROPEAN HERITAGE INSTITUTE
Fashion and Interior Design at Accademia Italiana-Summer
Site: Italy: Florence *Host inst:* Accad Italiana
Dates: 1-2 mos, Jun-Jul
Subjects: Fashion design, Interior design, Italian language
Eligibility: *Level:* fresh, sophs, jrs, srs, grads, adults, teachers, professionals *Requires:* 2.5 GPA *Age:* min 18
Credit: *Undergrad:* 6 *Grad:* 6
Instruction: *In:* English *Format:* art studio, lab, practical training, workshop *Students:* mainly host country
Costs: From $1,000 per mo *incl* tuition
Housing: *Sponsor assists*
Deadline: Mar 15
Other info: *US accredited sponsor:* no *Began:* 1998 *Orient:* abroad *Misc:* May contact former participants. *URL:* http://www.europeanheritage.org
Contact: Dr Antonio Masullo or Ms Barbara Cotter, European Heritage Inst, 2708 E Franklin St, Richmond VA 23223 *Ph:* 804-643 0661 *Fax:* 804-648 0826 *E-mail:* euritage@i2020.net ▲

1041
FAIRFIELD UNIVERSITY
Summer Campus in Florence
Site: Italy: Florence *Host inst:* Lorenzo de' Medici Inst
Dates: 1-2 mos, Jun and/or Jul
Subjects: Architecture, Art history, Communications, Culinary arts, Fine arts, History, Italian language (beg/int/adv), Literature, Media studies, Music history, Social sciences, Studio arts
Eligibility: *Level:* fresh, sophs, jrs, srs, grads, adults, teachers, professionals, precoll *Requires:* recommendation letters *Age:* min 17, avg 21
Credit: *Undergrad:* 6 per session *Grad:* none *Doc:* transcript
Instruction: *In:* English *Format:* art studio, lang study, lecture, seminar, study tour *Students:* intl
Costs: $3,375-$5,510 per mo *incl* tuition, housing, some meals, intl airfare
Housing: *Arr by pgm:* apartments, hotels
Deadline: Mar 1 for Jun; Apr 1 for Jul; or until pgm filled
Other info: *US accredited sponsor:* yes *Began:* 1986 *Orient:* in US & abroad *Activities:* excursions, field trips, cultural events *Misc:* May contact former participants. *URL:* http://www.fairfield.edu/sce/studyabroad/florence.htm
Contact: Ms Christine Bowers, Study Abroad Coord, Fairfield Univ, Dolan House, Fairfield CT 06430-5195 *Ph:* 888-254 1566; 203-254 4220 *Fax:* 203-254 4106 *E-mail:* cbbowers@fair1.fairfield.edu

---

1042
FASHION INSTITUTE OF TECHNOLOGY
Italian in Florence
Site: Italy: Florence
Dates: 4 wks, Jun
Subjects: Italian language, Italian studies
Eligibility: *Level:* sophs, jrs, srs *Requires:* 3.0 GPA, one year Italian or approval of instructor *Age:* min 18
Credit: *Undergrad:* 3.5 *Grad:* none *Doc:* transcript
Instruction: *In:* Italian *Format:* directed field study *Students:* mainly US
Costs: About $2,200 for NY residents, $3,000 for others *incl* tuition, housing, some meals, intl airfare, fees
Housing: *Arr by pgm:* pensions, hotels
Deadline: Mar 3
Other info: *US accredited sponsor:* no *Began:* 2001 *Activities:* excursions, field trips
Contact: Georgianna Appignani, Dir, FIT, 7th Ave at 27th St, New York NY 10001-5992 *Ph:* 212-217 7633 *Fax:* 212-217 7010
Or Contact: Carole De Santis, Coord, FIT, 7th Ave at 27th St, New York NY 10001-5992 *E-mail:* desantca@fitsuyn.edu

---

1043
FASHION INSTITUTE OF TECHNOLOGY
Restoration: Gilded Objects in Florence
Site: Italy: Florence
Dates: 4 wks, May 31-Jun 26
Subjects: Art restoration
Eligibility: *Level:* fresh, sophs, jrs, srs, grads, adults, teachers, professionals *Requires:* interview by faculty member teaching course *Age:* min 18
Credit: *Undergrad:* 1.5 *Grad:* none *Doc:* transcript
Instruction: *In:* English *Format:* study tour *Students:* mainly US

Costs: $2,265 for NY residents, $2,512 for others *incl* tuition, housing, intl airfare, excursions
Housing: *Arr by pgm:* pensions
Deadline: Mar 3
Other info: *US accredited sponsor:* yes *Began:* 1996 *Orient:* in US *Activities:* field trips, program travel *URL:* http://www.fitnyc.suny.edu
Contact: Georgianna Appignani, Dir, Intl Educ, FIT, 7th Ave at 27th St, New York NY 10001-5992 *Ph:* 212-217 7633 *Fax:* 212-217 7010
Or Contact: Carole De Santis, Coord, FIT, 7th Ave at 27th St, New York NY 10001-5992 *Ph:* 212-217 7633 *Fax:* 212-217 7010 *E-mail:* desantca@sfitva.cc.fitsuny.edu

---

1044
FASHION INSTITUTE OF TECHNOLOGY
The Italian Way: Lessons from the Masters for Our Time
Site: Italy: Florence
Dates: 4 wks, May 31-Jun 28
Subjects: Art, Civilization/culture, Italian studies
Eligibility: *Level:* fresh, sophs, jrs, srs, grads, adults *Requires:* interview by faculty member teaching course *Age:* min 18
Credit: *Undergrad:* 2.5 *Grad:* none *Doc:* transcript
Instruction: *In:* English *Format:* lang study, lecture *Students:* mainly US
Costs: About $2,400 for NY residents, $2,290 for others *incl* tuition, housing, some meals, intl airfare, insurance, fees, airport transfers
Housing: *Arr by pgm:* pensions
Deadline: Mar 3
Other info: *US accredited sponsor:* yes *Began:* 1989 *Orient:* in US *Activities:* field trips *Misc:* May contact former participants. *URL:* http://www.fitnyc.suny.edu
Contact: Georgianna Appignani, Dir, Intl Educ, FIT, 7th Ave at 27th St, New York NY 10001-5992 *Ph:* 212-217 7633 *Fax:* 212-217 7010
Or Contact: Carole De Santis, Coord, FIT, 7th Ave at 27th St, New York NY 10001-5992 *Ph:* 212-217 7633 *Fax:* 212-217 7010 *E-mail:* desantca@svitva.cc.fitsuny.edu

---

1045
FLORENCE ACADEMY OF ART
Summer Session
Site: Italy: Florence
Dates: 1 mo, Jul 1-31
Subjects: Drawing, Painting, Sculpture
Eligibility: *Level:* fresh, sophs, jrs, srs, grads, adults, teachers, professionals, precoll
Credit: *Undergrad:* none *Grad:* none
Instruction: *In:* English *Format:* art studio, lecture, study tour *Students:* intl
Costs: $1,150 *incl* tuition, museum admissions
Housing: *Sponsor assists:* apartments, pensions
Deadline: Jun 30
Other info: *US accredited sponsor:* no *Began:* 1995 *Activities:* excursions, field trips, program travel, cultural events *Misc:* 45-60 hrs model time provided. *URL:* http://www.florenceacademyofart.com
Contact: Susan Tintori, Florence Acad of Art, via delle Casine 21/r, 50122 Florence, Italy *E-mail:* florenceacademy@dada.it

---

1046
FLORIDA STATE UNIVERSITY
Florence Summer Program
Site: Italy: Florence
Dates: 4 or 6 wks, May 10-Jun 21 or Jul 5-Aug 2
Subjects: Art history, English, History, Humanities, Italian language (beg)
Eligibility: *Level:* fresh, sophs, jrs, srs, grads, adults *Requires:* 2.5 GPA
Credit: *Undergrad:* 10 *Grad:* 3
Instruction: *In:* English, Italian *Format:* lang study, lecture *Students:* mainly US
Costs: $2,995 for 4 wks, $3,995 for 6 wks *incl* tuition, housing, insurance, excursions, ISIC
Housing: *Arr by pgm:* pensions
Deadline: Jan 19
Other info: *US accredited sponsor:* yes *Began:* 1966 *Orient:* abroad *Activities:* excursions, program travel *Misc:* May contact former participants. *URL:* http://www.international.fsu.edu
Contact: Bonnie Snyder, Intl Pgms, Study Abroad, Florida State Univ, 5500 UCA, Tallahassee FL 32306-2420 *Ph:* 800-374 8581; 850-644 3272 *Fax:* 850-644 8817 *E-mail:* intprog@www.fsu.edu

---

1047
GONZAGA UNIVERSITY
Gonzaga in Florence
Site: Italy: Florence
Dates: 7 wks, May 15-Jun 28
Subjects: Art, Communications, History, Italian language, Philosophy, Religion/theology
Eligibility: *Level:* fresh, sophs, jrs, srs, grads, adults, teachers, professionals
Credit: *Undergrad:* 6 *Grad:* none *Doc:* transcript
Instruction: *In:* English *Format:* art studio, lang study, lecture *Students:* mainly US
Costs: $5,000 *incl* tuition, housing, some meals, pgm travel, opening tour
Housing: *Arr by pgm:* pensions
Deadline: Contact sponsor
Other info: *US accredited sponsor:* yes *Began:* 1963 *Orient:* in US *Activities:* excursions *Misc:* May contact former participants. *URL:* http://www.gonzaga.edu/studiesabroad/florence
Contact: Wanda Reynolds, Dir, Studies Abroad, Gonzaga Univ, Spokane WA 99258 *Ph:* 800-440 5391 *Fax:* 509-323 5987 *E-mail:* reynolds@gu.gonzaga.edu

---

1048
IL BISONTE
Courses in Printmaking
Site: Italy: Florence *Host inst:* Il
Dates: Oct 15-Jun
Subjects: Art history, Bookbinding, Etching, Lithography, Photography, Serigraphy
Eligibility: *Level:* adults
Credit: *Undergrad:* none *Grad:* none *Doc:* certificate
Instruction: *In:* Italian *Format:* art studio, independent study, lab, lecture, practical training, seminar *Students:* intl
Costs: Lit 8,000 *incl* tuition, insurance, fees, books/materials *Nonrefundable fee*
Housing: *Arr by student:* apartments with local students, homestay, pensions, hotels, hostels
Deadline: Late Sep
Other info: *US accredited sponsor:* no *Began:* 1982 *Activities:* excursions, field trips, cultural events *Misc:* May contact former participants. *URL:* http://www.ilbisonte.it
Contact: Costanza Piccinini or Simone Guaita, Il Bisonte, Via San Niccolo 24 R, 50125 Florence, Italy *E-mail:* info@ilbisonte.it

---

1049
INDIANA UNIVERSITY
Summer Study in Florence
Site: Italy: Florence
Dates: 6 wks, about May 15-Jun 30
Subjects: Civilization/culture, Drawing, Italian language
Eligibility: *Level:* fresh, sophs, jrs, srs, grads *Requires:* 3.0 GPA
Credit: *Undergrad:* 6 *Grad:* 6 *Doc:* transcript
Instruction: *In:* English, Italian *Format:* art studio, lang study, lecture *Students:* mainly US
Costs: $3,300 or $4,800 *incl* tuition, housing, all meals, insurance, fees, excursions *Nonrefundable fee*
Housing: *Arr by pgm:* pensions
Deadline: Early Feb
Other info: *US accredited sponsor:* yes *Began:* 1976 *Orient:* in US *Activities:* excursions *Misc:* May contact former participants. *Financial aid:* scholarships *URL:* http://www.indiana.edu/~overseas

Contact: Overseas Study, Indiana Univ, Franklin Hall 303, Bloomington IN 47405 *Ph:* 812-855 9304 *Fax:* 812-855 6452 *E-mail:* overseas@indiana.edu

---

1050
ISTITUTO DI LINGUA E CULTURA ITALIANA DONATELLO
Italian Language for Foreign Students
Site: Italy: Florence
Dates: Yr-round
Subjects: Italian language
Eligibility: *Level:* adults *Age:* min 18, max 80, avg 25
Credit: *Undergrad:* none *Grad:* none
Instruction: *In:* Italian *Format:* art studio, lang study *Students:* intl
Costs: Contact Sponsor
Housing: *Arr by pgm:* apartments with local students, residence halls with local students, residence halls, apartments, homestay, pensions, hotels, hostels
Deadline: Contact sponsor
Other info: *US accredited sponsor:* no *Began:* 2000 *Orient:* abroad *Activities:* excursions, field trips, program travel, cultural events *Misc:* May contact former participants. *Financial aid:* scholarships *URL:* http://www.istitutodonatello.com

Contact: Dr Gianluca Mugnai, Ist Donatello, Via Galliano 1, Florence, Italy *Fax:* 39-055-355 686 *E-mail:* donatello@istitutodonatello.com

---

1051
JAMES MADISON UNIVERSITY
Summer Semester in Florence
Site: Italy: Florence
Dates: 6 wks, late May-mid-Jul
Subjects: Art history, History, Homestay, Italian language (beg/int/adv), Literature
Eligibility: *Level:* fresh, sophs, jrs, srs
Credit: *Undergrad:* 9-12 *Grad:* none *Doc:* transcript
Instruction: *In:* English, Italian *Format:* lang study, lecture *Students:* mainly US
Costs: $3,750 for VA residents, $5,400 for others *incl* tuition, housing, excursions, books/materials, orient *Nonrefundable fee*
Housing: *Arr by pgm:* homestay
Deadline: Feb 1
Other info: *US accredited sponsor:* yes *Began:* 1993 *Activities:* excursions, program travel, cultural events *Misc:* May contact former participants. *URL:* http://www.jmu.edu/international/

Contact: Intl Pgms, James Madison Univ, Harrisonburg VA 22807 *Ph:* 540-568 6419 *Fax:* 540-568 8080 *E-mail:* international@jmu.edu

---

1052
KOINE CENTER and **ENOTECA DE' GIRALDI**
Bread, Wine and Language
Site: Italy: Florence
Dates: 2 wks, yr-round
Subjects: Civilization/culture, Culinary arts, Italian language (beg/int/adv), Wine
Eligibility: *Level:* adults *Age:* min 16, max 90
Credit: *Undergrad:* none *Grad:* none *Doc:* certificate
Instruction: *In:* English, Italian *Format:* lang study, lecture, practical training, seminar *Students:* intl
Costs: $1,270 *incl* tuition, housing, some meals, fees, excursions, books/materials, wines *Nonrefundable fee*
Housing: *Arr by pgm:* apartments, homestay, pensions, hotels
Deadline: Contact sponsor
Other info: *US accredited sponsor:* no *Began:* 1995 *Activities:* excursions, field trips *Misc:* Connection between culture, lang & wine in Tuscany. Farm excursions.

Max 12 participants per group. *URL:* http://www.koinecenter.com/code/enoteca.html
Contact: Andrea Moradei, Enoteca de' Giraldi, Via de' Giraldi 4/r, 50122 Florence, Italy *E-mail:* koine@firenze.net
Or Contact: Linda Larson & Anja Schultz, Koine, via Pandolfini 27, 50122 Florence, Italy *E-mail:* koine@firenze.net

---

1053
KOINE CENTER
Course for Teachers of Italian as a Foreign Language
Site: Italy: Florence
Dates: 3 wks, Apr-Nov
Subjects: Education/teaching, Foreign language teaching, Homestay, Italian language
Eligibility: *Level:* teachers *Requires:* adv Italian
Credit: *Undergrad:* none *Grad:* none
Instruction: *In:* Italian *Format:* lang study, practical training, seminar *Students:* intl
Costs: $335 per wk *incl* tuition, housing, some meals, insurance, fees, excursions, books/materials
Housing: *Arr by pgm:* apartments with local students, homestay, pensions, hotels
Deadline: Contact sponsor
Other info: *US accredited sponsor:* no *Began:* 1985 *URL:* http://www.koinecenter.com
Contact: Moradei Andrea, Koine Ctr, via Pandolfini 27, 50122 Florence, Italy *E-mail:* koine@firenze.net

---

1054
KOINE CENTER
Italian Language and Culture-Florence
Site: Italy: Florence
Dates: 1-5 mos, yr-round
Subjects: Art history, Civilization/culture, Culinary arts, Homestay, Italian language (beg/int/adv)
Eligibility: *Level:* adults *Age:* min 15, max 90
Credit: *Undergrad:* none *Grad:* none *Doc:* certificate
Instruction: *In:* English, Italian *Format:* lang study, lecture *Students:* intl
Costs: $690 for 2 wks, $1,320 for 4 wks *incl* tuition, housing, excursions, books/materials
Housing: *Arr by pgm:* apartments, homestay, pensions, hotels
Deadline: 2 wks before pgm
Other info: *US accredited sponsor:* no *Began:* 1980 *In coop with:* Municipality of Florence *Orient:* in US *Activities:* excursions *Misc:* 12 participants max per group. May contact former participants. *URL:* http://www.koinecenter.com
Contact: Linda Larson or Anja Schultz, Koine, via Pandolfini 27, 50122 Florence, Italy *E-mail:* koine@firenze.net

---

1055
LANGUAGE LIAISON
Art or Italian Language Study
Site: Italy: Florence
Dates: 2 wks or longer, yr-round
Subjects: Architecture, Art history, Business language, Fashion design, Graphic arts/design, Homestay, Interior design, Italian language, Jewelry/jewelry-making, Painting, Photography, Sculpture
Eligibility: *Level:* fresh, sophs, jrs, srs, grads, adults, teachers, professionals, precoll
Credit: *Undergrad:* avail *Grad:* avail *Doc:* transcript, certificate
Instruction: *In:* Italian *Format:* art studio, lang study, lecture, seminar *Students:* intl
Costs: Contact sponsor
Housing: *Arr by pgm:* apartments, homestay
Deadline: 30 days before pgm
Other info: *US accredited sponsor:* no *Activities:* excursions, field trips, cultural events *Misc:* Scholarship research svc. *URL:* http://www.languageliaison.com
Contact: Nancy Forman, Dir, Lang Liaison, 4 Burnham Pkwy, Morristown NJ 07960 *Ph:* 800-284 4448 *Fax:* 973-898 1710 *E-mail:* learn@languageliaison.com

---

1056
LANGUAGE LIAISON
Summer Course-Florence
Site: Italy: Florence
Dates: 4 wks, May-Jul
Subjects: Architecture, Art history, Art restoration, Drawing, Homestay, Italian language, Jewelry/jewelry-making, Painting, Photography, Sculpture, Studio arts
Eligibility: *Level:* fresh, sophs, jrs, srs *Requires:* high sch diploma or equiv *Age:* min 18
Credit: *Undergrad:* none *Grad:* none *Doc:* certificate
Instruction: *In:* English, Italian *Format:* art studio, lang study *Students:* intl
Costs: Contact sponsor
Housing: *Sponsor assists:* apartments, homestay, pensions, boarding house
Deadline: 4 wks before pgm
Other info: *US accredited sponsor:* no *Began:* 1997 *Misc:* Only painting & drawing offered in Aug. Scholarship research svc. *URL:* http://www.languageliaison.com
Contact: Nancy Forman, Dir, Lang Liaison, 4 Burnham Pkwy, Morristown NJ 07960 *Ph:* 800-284 4448 *Fax:* 973-898 1710 *E-mail:* learn@languageliaison.com

---

1057
LANGUAGES PLUS
Language Immersion and Cultural Program-Florence
Site: Italy: Florence
Dates: 2 wks or longer, yr-round
Subjects: Homestay, Italian language (beg/int/adv)
Eligibility: *Level:* adults *Age:* min 17, max 65, avg 24
Credit: *Undergrad:* none *Grad:* none *Doc:* certificate
Instruction: *In:* Italian *Format:* lang study *Students:* intl
Costs: From $795 for 2 wks *incl* tuition, housing, books/materials, cultural activities
Housing: *Arr by pgm:* apartments, homestay
Deadline: 2 wks before pgm
Other info: *US accredited sponsor:* no *Activities:* excursions, field trips *Misc:* May contact former participants. *URL:* http://www.languagesplus.com
Contact: Margot Haldenby, North Amer Enrollment, Langs Plus, 317 Adelaide St W, Ste 900, Toronto, Ontario M5V 1P9, Canada *Ph:* 888-526 4758; 416-925 7117 *Fax:* 416-925 5990 *E-mail:* info@languagesplus.com

---

1058
L'ATELIER
Fashion-Jewelry-Interior Design
Site: Italy: Florence
Dates: 2 or 4 wks, Jun 1-Jul 31
Subjects: Fashion design, Interior design, Jewelry/jewelry-making
Eligibility: *Level:* sophs, jrs, adults *Requires:* 2.8 GPA *Age:* min 16, avg 20
Credit: *Undergrad:* 6 *Grad:* none
Instruction: *In:* English *Format:* study tour *Students:* intl
Costs: $1,000 per mo *incl* tuition
Housing: *Sponsor assists:* apartments, homestay, pensions, hotels
Deadline: 1 mo before pgm
Other info: *US accredited sponsor:* no *Began:* 1998 *In coop with:* Lorenzo de' Medici *Orient:* abroad (1 day) *Activities:* excursions, field trips, program travel, cultural events, sports *URL:* http://www.atelierfirenze.it
Contact: Melissa Rossi, L'Atelier, Via dei Bardi 46, Florence, Italy *E-mail:* info@atelierfirenze.it

---

1059
LINGUAVIVA
Italian Language and Culture Courses
Site: Italy: Florence
Dates: 1 mo, yr-round
Subjects: Art history, Business language, Fine arts, Graphic arts/design, Homestay, Internships, Italian language (beg/int/adv), Studio arts
Eligibility: *Level:* adults, teachers, professionals, precoll *Age:* min 16, avg 22
Credit: *Undergrad:* none *Grad:* none *Doc:* certificate
Instruction: *In:* Italian *Format:* art studio, internship, lang study *Students:* intl
Costs: Lit 1,000,000 per mo *incl* tuition, activities *Nonrefundable fee*
Housing: *Arr by pgm:* apartments with local students, homestay, pensions, hotels
Deadline: 4 wks before pgm
Other info: *US accredited sponsor:* no *Began:* 1976 *Orient:* abroad *Activities:* excursions, cultural events, sports *Misc:* May contact former participants. *URL:* http://www.linguaviva.it
Contact: Alessandro Vidoni, Linguaviva, Via Fiume 17, 50123 Florence, Italy *E-mail:* info@linguaviva.it

1060
MICHIGAN STATE UNIVERSITY
Italian Language, Literature and Culture
Site: Italy: Florence
Dates: 6 wks, May-Jun
Subjects: Art, Civilization/culture, Homestay, Italian language (beg/int/adv), Italian studies, Literature
Eligibility: *Level:* sophs, jrs, srs *Requires:* 2.0 GPA, good acad standing *Age:* min 18
Credit: *Undergrad:* 8 *Grad:* none *Doc:* transcript
Instruction: *In:* English, Italian *Format:* lang study, lecture *Students:* mainly US
Costs: About $3,100 *incl* housing, most meals, insurance, excursions, support svcs *Nonrefundable fee*
Housing: *Arr by pgm:* homestay
Deadline: Mar 2
Other info: *US accredited sponsor:* yes *Began:* 1976 *Orient:* in US & abroad *Misc:* Loans avail. *Financial aid:* scholarships *URL:* http://studyabroad.msu.edu
Contact: Cheryl Benner, Study Abroad, Michigan State Univ, 109 Intl Ctr, East Lansing MI 48824-1035 *Ph:* 517-353 8920 *Fax:* 517-432 2082 *E-mail:* bennerc@msu.edu ▲

1061
NEW YORK UNIVERSITY, GALLATIN SCHOOL OF INDIVIDUALIZED STUDY
Gallatin Abroad: Humanities Seminar in Italy
Site: Italy: Florence
Dates: 3 wks, Jun 5-25
Subjects: Art, Art history, Literature, Renaissance studies
Eligibility: *Level:* fresh, sophs, jrs, srs, grads, adults, teachers, professionals *Age:* min 18
Credit: *Undergrad:* 4 *Grad:* 4 *Doc:* transcript
Instruction: *In:* English *Format:* lecture, seminar *Students:* mainly US
Costs: $3,000 *incl* tuition, housing, some meals, fees
Housing: *Arr by pgm:* apartments, villa
Deadline: Mar 1
Other info: *US accredited sponsor:* yes *Began:* 1986 *Orient:* in US *Activities:* excursions, field trips, cultural events *Misc:* Grad-level class open to undergrads. May contact former participants. *Financial aid:* scholarships *URL:* http://www.nyu.edu/gallatin
Contact: Prof Bella Mirabella, NYU Gallatin Sch, 715 Broadway, New York NY 10003 *Ph:* 212-998 7371 *Fax:* 212-995 4509 *E-mail:* bella.mirabella@nyu.edu

1062
NEW YORK UNIVERSITY, TISCH SCHOOL OF THE ARTS
Acting Workshop: Comedia Del Arte
Site: Italy: Florence
Dates: 6 wks, Jun 25-Aug 3
Subjects: Art history, Arts, Italian studies, Performing arts
Eligibility: *Level:* fresh, sophs, jrs, srs, adults *Requires:* prior acting training or experience or permission of instructor
Credit: *Undergrad:* 8 per sem *Grad:* 8 per sem *Doc:* transcript
Instruction: *In:* English *Format:* lecture, seminar, tutorial *Students:* mainly US
Costs: $4,012 *incl* tuition *Nonrefundable fee*
Housing: *Arr by pgm:* residence halls, apartments
Deadline: Apr 15 priority deadline
Other info: *US accredited sponsor:* yes *Began:* 2000 *Orient:* in US & abroad *Activities:* field trips *Misc:* Loans avail. May contact former participants. *Financial aid:* scholarships *URL:* http://www.nyu.edu/tisch/international
Contact: Linda Kow, Assoc Dir, New York Univ, Tisch Intl Pgms, 721 Broadway, 12th Fl, New York NY 10003 *Ph:* 212-998 9175 *Fax:* 212 975 4578 *E-mail:* tisch.international@nyu.edu

1063
NEW YORK UNIVERSITY, TISCH SCHOOL OF THE ARTS
Children's Television
Site: Italy: Florence
Dates: 3 wks, Jun 4-Jun 22
Subjects: Film studies, Media studies, Sociology, Telecommunications
Eligibility: *Level:* fresh, sophs, jrs, srs, grads, adults *Age:* min 18
Credit: *Undergrad:* 4 per sem *Grad:* 4 per sem *Doc:* transcript
Instruction: *In:* English *Format:* lecture, seminar, tutorial *Students:* mainly US
Costs: $2,730 per sem *incl* tuition, housing, fees *Nonrefundable fee*
Housing: *Arr by pgm:* residence halls, apartments
Deadline: Mar 31 priority deadline
Other info: *US accredited sponsor:* yes *Began:* 2000 *Orient:* in US & abroad *Activities:* excursions, field trips *Misc:* May contact former participants. *Financial aid:* scholarships *URL:* http://www.nyu.edu/tisch/international
Contact: Linda Kow, Assoc Dir, New York Univ, Tisch Intl Pgms, 721 Broadway, 12th Fl, New York NY 10003 *Ph:* 212-995 9175 *Fax:* 212-995 4578 *E-mail:* tisch.international@nyu.edu

1064
NEW YORK UNIVERSITY, TISCH SCHOOL OF THE ARTS
Directed Projects in Photography: Art, Culture, Landscape
Site: Italy: Florence *Host inst:* La Pietra, Studio Marangoni
Dates: 6 wks, May 14-Jun 22
Subjects: Civilization/culture, Field study, Fine arts, Photography
Eligibility: *Level:* sophs, jrs, srs, grads, adults, teachers, professionals *Requires:* coll-level coursework in photography or equiv, portfolio of 20 slides or prints, instructor's permission *Age:* min 18
Credit: *Undergrad:* 4 *Grad:* avail *Doc:* transcript
Instruction: *In:* English *Format:* art studio, directed field study, lab, lecture, practical training *Students:* mainly US
Costs: About $3,699 *incl* tuition, housing, fees, excursions *Nonrefundable fee*
Housing: *Arr by pgm:* residence halls, apartments, La Pietra estate
Deadline: Mar 15; rolling admissions
Other info: *US accredited sponsor:* yes *Began:* 1998 *Orient:* in US & abroad (1 day) *Activities:* excursions, field trips *Misc:* Loans & scholarships for own students only. *Financial aid:* scholarships *URL:* http://www.nyu.edu/tisch/international/
Contact: Linda Kow, Assoc Dir, Tisch Intl Pgms, 721 Broadway, 12th Fl, New York NY 10003 *Ph:* 212-998 9175 *Fax:* 212-995 4578 *E-mail:* tisch.international@nyu.edu

1065
NEW YORK UNIVERSITY, TISCH SCHOOL OF THE ARTS
Directing Actors for Film and Television
Site: Italy: Florence *Host inst:* La Pietra
Dates: 4 wks, May 28-Jun 22
Subjects: Acting, Directing, Drama/theater, Film studies, Television/video
Eligibility: *Level:* fresh, sophs, jrs, srs, grads, adults, teachers, professionals *Requires:* coll-level coursework in acting or equiv or instructor's permission *Age:* min 18
Credit: *Undergrad:* 4 *Grad:* none *Doc:* transcript
Instruction: *In:* English *Format:* lecture, practical training, workshop *Students:* mainly US
Costs: $3,032-$3232 *incl* tuition, housing, fees, excursions *Nonrefundable fee*
Housing: *Arr by pgm:* residence halls, apartments, La Pietra estate
Deadline: Mar 15; rolling admissions
Other info: *US accredited sponsor:* yes *Began:* 1998 *Orient:* avail avail *Activities:* excursions, field trips *Misc:* Scholarships & loans for own students only. *URL:* http://www.nyu.edu/tisch/international/
Contact: Linda Kow, Assoc Dir, Tisch Intl Pgms, New York Univ, 721 Broadway, 12th Fl, New York NY 10003 *Ph:* 212-998 9175 *Fax:* 212-995 4578 *E-mail:* tisch.international@nyu.edu

---

1066
NEW YORK UNIVERSITY, TISCH SCHOOL OF THE ARTS
Film Directing Workshop
Site: Italy: Florence
Dates: 6 wks, Jun 25-Aug 3
Subjects: Film studies, Media studies
Eligibility: *Level:* fresh, sophs, jrs, srs, grads, adults *Age:* avg 35
Credit: *Undergrad:* 8 per sem *Grad:* 8 per sem *Doc:* transcript
Instruction: *In:* English *Format:* lecture, practical training, seminar, tutorial, workshop *Students:* mainly US
Costs: $5,912-$6,412 *incl* tuition, housing, some meals, fees, excursions, equipment *Nonrefundable fee*
Housing: *Arr by pgm:* residence halls, apartments, hotels
Deadline: Apr 15 priority deadline
Other info: *US accredited sponsor:* yes *Began:* 2000 *Orient:* in US *Activities:* excursions, field trips *Misc:* May contact former participants. *Financial aid:* scholarships *URL:* http://www.nyu.edu/tisch/international
Contact: Linda Kow, Assoc Dir, New York Univ, Tisch Intl Pgms, 721 Broadway, 12th Fl, New York NY 10003 *Ph:* 212-998 9175 *Fax:* 212-995 4578 *E-mail:* tisch.international@nyu.edu

---

1067
NEW YORK UNIVERSITY, TISCH SCHOOL OF THE ARTS
Film Music: An Italian Perspective
Site: Italy: Florence *Host inst:* La Pietra
Dates: 3 wks, Jun 25-Jul 13
Subjects: Film studies, Music
Eligibility: *Level:* fresh, sophs, jrs, srs, grads, adults, teachers, professionals *Age:* min 18
Credit: *Undergrad:* 4 *Grad:* avail *Doc:* transcript
Instruction: *In:* English *Format:* lecture, practical training, seminar *Students:* mainly US
Costs: About $2,782-$3032 depending on housing *incl* tuition, housing, fees, excursions *Nonrefundable fee*
Housing: *Arr by pgm:* residence halls, apartments, La Pietra estate
Deadline: Apr 15; rolling admissions
Other info: *US accredited sponsor:* yes *Began:* 1998 *Orient:* in US & abroad (1 day) *Activities:* excursions, field trips *Misc:* Scholarships & loans for own students only. *Financial aid:* scholarships *URL:* http://www.nyu.edu/tisch/international/
Contact: Linda Kow, Assoc Dir, Tisch Intl Pgms, New York Univ, 721 Broadway, 12th Fl, New York NY 10003 *Ph:* 212-998 9175 *Fax:* 212-995 4578 *E-mail:* tisch.international@nyu.edu

---

1068
NEW YORK UNIVERSITY, TISCH SCHOOL OF THE ARTS
Writing Florence
Site: Italy: Florence *Host inst:* La Pietra
Dates: 4 wks, May 19-Jun 22
Subjects: Creative writing, Drama/theater, Film studies, Interdisciplinary studies, Italian studies, Literature, Media studies, Playwriting, Screenwriting
Eligibility: *Level:* fresh, sophs, jrs, srs, grads, adults *Age:* min 18
Credit: *Undergrad:* 8 *Grad:* avail *Doc:* transcript
Instruction: *In:* English *Format:* lecture, practical training, seminar, workshop *Students:* mainly US
Costs: $5,512-$6,012 depending on housing *incl* tuition, housing, fees, excursions *Nonrefundable fee*
Housing: *Arr by pgm:* residence halls, apartments, La Pietra estate
Deadline: Mar 15; rolling admissions
Other info: *US accredited sponsor:* yes *Began:* 1997 *Orient:* in US & abroad *Activities:* excursions, field trips *Misc:* Scholarships & loans for own students only. *URL:* http://www.nyu.edu/tisch/international/
Contact: Linda Kow, Assoc Dir, Tisch Intl Pgms, New York Univ, 721 Broadway, 12th Fl, New York NY 10003 *Ph:* 212-998 9175 *Fax:* 212-995 4578 *E-mail:* tisch.international@nyu.edu

---

1069
NORTH CAROLINA STATE UNIVERSITY
Florence Summer Program
Site: Italy: Florence *Host inst:* Lorenzo de Medici
Dates: 4 wks, Jun-Jul
Subjects: Art, Art history, Italian language (beg/int/adv), Italian studies, Renaissance studies
Eligibility: *Level:* sophs, jrs, srs, adults, teachers *Requires:* 2.0 GPA *Age:* min 18
Credit: *Undergrad:* 6 *Grad:* none *Doc:* transcript
Instruction: *In:* English *Format:* art studio, lang study, lecture *Students:* mainly US
Costs: $2,800 *incl* tuition, housing, insurance, fees, excursions
Housing: *Arr by pgm:* apartments
Deadline: Feb 20
Other info: *US accredited sponsor:* yes *Began:* 2000 *Orient:* abroad *Activities:* excursions, cultural events *URL:* http://www.ncsu.edu/studyabroad
Contact: Anne Haberkern, North Carolina State Univ, 2118 Pullen Hall, Box 7344, Raleigh NC 27695-7344 *Ph:* 919-515 2087 *Fax:* 919-515 6021 *E-mail:* study_abroad@ncsu.edu

---

1070
SCHOOL OF VISUAL ARTS (SVA)
Painting in Florence
Site: Italy: Florence
Dates: 3 wks, May 31-Jun 23
Subjects: Drawing, Painting
Eligibility: *Level:* sophs, jrs, srs, grads, adults, professionals *Requires:* previous study in field, slide portfolio *Age:* min 19
Credit: *Undergrad:* 3 *Grad:* none *Doc:* transcript
Instruction: *In:* English *Students:* mainly US
Costs: $3,400 *incl* tuition, housing, some meals, intl airfare *Nonrefundable fee*
Housing: *Arr by pgm:* residence halls
Deadline: Apr 25
Other info: *US accredited sponsor:* yes *Began:* 1999 *Orient:* abroad *Activities:* field trips *Misc:* Museum visits.
Contact: Dora Riomayor, Sch of Visual Arts, 209 E 23rd St, New York NY 10010 *Ph:* 212-592 2543 *Fax:* 212-592 2545 *E-mail:* dorariomayor@schoolofvisualarts.edu

---

Studio Art Centers International Florence
SACI
Summer Art Studies in Florence
Late Spring Term
May 17 - June 25
(5 weeks)
Summer Term
June 28 - July 30
(4 weeks)
SACI is now celebrating its 25th anniversary as Italy's most complete art program for Summer Studies, Undergraduate Semester/A Year Abroad Study and Graduate Studies. Located in the historic landmark (fully air conditioned) "Palazzo dei Cartelloni" in the center of Florence, SACI provides a stimulating educational experience that draws upon the rich cultural resources of both past and present Italy.
For information, contact:
SACI Coordinator
Institute of International Education
809 United Nations Plaza
New York, NY 10017-3580
Tel: 1-800-344-9186
(212) 984-5548
Fax: (212) 984-5325
E-mail: saci@iie.org
or Studio Art Centers International
Via Sant'Antonino, 11
Florence 50123, Italy
Tel: (39) 055289948
Fax: (39) 0552776408
For complete information about any of SACI's programs please visit our website
www.saci-florence.org

1071
SCHOOL OF VISUAL ARTS (SVA)
Photography in Florence
Site: Italy: Florence *Host inst:* Studio Marangoni
Dates: 3 wks, May 31- Jun 23
Subjects: Photography
Eligibility: *Level:* sophs, jrs, srs, grads, adults, professionals *Requires:* previous study in field, slide portfolio *Age:* min 19
Credit: *Undergrad:* 3 *Grad:* none
Instruction: *In:* English *Students:* mainly US
Costs: $3,650 *incl* tuition, housing, some meals, excursions *Nonrefundable fee*
Housing: *Arr by pgm:* residence halls
Deadline: Apr 25
Other info: *US accredited sponsor:* yes *Began:* 1999 *Orient:* abroad *Activities:* field trips *Misc:* Museum visits.
Contact: Dora Riomayor, Sch of Visual Arts, 209 E 23rd St, New York NY 10010 *Ph:* 212-592 2543 *Fax:* 212-592 2545 *E-mail:* dorariomayor@schoolofvisualarts.edu

---

1072
SCUOLA PALAZZO MALVISI
Italian Language Courses-Florence
Site: Italy: Florence
Dates: 1 mo, Jan-Dec
Subjects: Art history, Culinary arts, Film studies, Homestay, Italian language (beg/int/adv), Italian studies, Literature, Wine
Eligibility: *Level:* adults
Credit: *Undergrad:* none *Grad:* none *Doc:* certificate
Instruction: *In:* Italian *Format:* lang study, lecture *Students:* intl
Costs: $580 *incl* tuition, insurance, fees, books/materials
Housing: *Arr by pgm:* apartments, homestay, pensions, hotels
Deadline: 1 mo before pgm
Other info: *US accredited sponsor:* no *Began:* 1981 *Orient:* abroad *Activities:* field trips, cultural events *URL:* http://www.scuolapallazzomalvisi.com
Contact: Dr Cesare Portolani, Scuola Palazzo Malvisi, via Fiorentina 36, 47021 Bagno di Romagna (Forli), Italy *E-mail:* malvisi@infuturo.it
Or Contact: Matilde Portolani, Scuola Palazzo Malvisi, via Salara 31, 48100 Ravenna, Italy *E-mail:* malvisi@infuturo.it
Or Contact: Mrs Luisa Brunello, Scuola Palazzo Malvisi, Via dei Rustiti 7, 50122 Florence, Italy

---

1073
SOUTHERN METHODIST UNIVERSITY
Poggio Colla Field School and Mugello Valley Archaeology
Site: Italy: Florence, (Poggia Colla Excavation at Vicchio)
Dates: 6 wks, Jun 24-Aug 10
Subjects: Archaeology, Art history
Eligibility: *Level:* sophs, jrs, srs, grads *Requires:* 2.5 GPA, priority to students of archaeology, Italian studies
Credit: *Undergrad:* 6 *Grad:* 3 *Doc:* transcript
Instruction: *In:* English *Format:* directed field study, lecture *Students:* mainly US
Costs: $4,000 *incl* tuition, housing, most meals, most meals *Nonrefundable fee*
Housing: *Arr by pgm*
Deadline: Mar 1
Other info: *US accredited sponsor:* yes *Began:* 1995 *Misc:* Scholarships for own students only. Grad credits for own students only. Loans avail. *Financial aid:* scholarships *URL:* http://www.smu.edu/~poggio/
Contact: Intl Off, Southern Methodist Univ, PO Box 0391, 3108 Fondren Dr, Dallas TX 75275-0391 *Ph:* 214-768 2338 *Fax:* 214-768 1051 *E-mail:* intlpro@mail.smu.edu
Or Contact: Dr Greg Warden, Art History, Southern Methodist Univ, Dallas TX 75275 *Ph:* 214-768 2880 *E-mail:* gwarden@mail.smu.edu ▲

1074
STUDIO ART CENTERS INTERNATIONAL (SACI)
Studio Art Centers International
Site: Italy: Florence
Dates: 4 or 5 wks, May-Jun and/or Jun-Jul
Subjects: Art history, Art restoration, Ceramics/pottery, Drawing, Fiber art, Graphic arts/design, Italian language, Jewelry/jewelry-making, Painting, Photography, Printmaking, Sculpture
Eligibility: *Level:* adults *Requires:* 2.5 GPA
Credit: *Undergrad:* 6 (3 per course) *Grad:* none *Doc:* transcript *Transfer credit through:* Bowling Green State Univ
Instruction: *In:* English *Format:* art studio, lang study, lecture *Students:* US & intl
Costs: $4,450-$4,690 *incl* tuition, housing, fees, refundable damage deposit
Housing: *Arr by pgm:* apartments
Deadline: Rolling admissions
Other info: *US accredited sponsor:* no *Began:* 1975 *Orient:* abroad *Activities:* excursions, field trips *Financial aid:* scholarships *URL:* http://www.saci-florence.org
Contact: SACI Coord, US Student Pgms, IIE, 809 United Nations Plaza, New York NY 10017 *Ph:* 800-344 9186; 212-984 5548 *Fax:* 212-984 5325 *E-mail:* saci@iie.org ▲

1075
SYRACUSE UNIVERSITY
Architecture in Florence
Site: Italy: Florence
Dates: 9 wks, May 24-Jul 31
Subjects: Architecture, Italian language (beg)
Eligibility: *Level:* jrs, srs, grads, teachers, professionals *Requires:* 3 yrs undergrad or 2 yrs grad study in architecture
Credit: *Undergrad:* 9 *Grad:* 9
Instruction: *In:* English, Italian *Students:* mainly US
Costs: About $8,900 *incl* tuition, housing, fees, excursions *Nonrefundable fee*
Housing: *Arr by pgm:* apartments
Deadline: Mar 15
Other info: *US accredited sponsor:* yes *Began:* 1988 *Orient:* abroad *Activities:* excursions *Financial aid:* scholarships *URL:* http://sumweb.syr.edu/dipa/summer
Contact: Summer Pgms, Intl Pgms Abroad, Syracuse Univ, 119 Euclid Ave, Syracuse NY 13244-4170 *Ph:* 800-251 9674; 315-443 9420 *Fax:* 315-443 4593 *E-mail:* dipasum@summon3.syr.edu ▲

1076
SYRACUSE UNIVERSITY
Discovering Italy: The Language, the Culture
Site: Italy: Florence
Dates: May 31-Jul 17
Subjects: Art history, Homestay, Italian language (beg/int/adv)
Eligibility: *Level:* fresh, sophs, jrs, srs
Credit: *Undergrad:* 6 *Grad:* none
Instruction: *In:* English, Italian *Format:* lang study, lecture *Students:* mainly US
Costs: $6,750 *incl* tuition, housing, some meals, fees, excursions *Nonrefundable fee*
Housing: *Arr by pgm:* homestay
Deadline: Mar 15
Other info: *US accredited sponsor:* yes *Began:* 1977 *Orient:* abroad *Financial aid:* scholarships *URL:* http://sumweb.syr.edu/dipa/summer
Contact: Summer Pgms, Intl Pgms Abroad, Syracuse Univ, 119 Euclid Ave, Syracuse NY 13244-4170 *Ph:* 800-251 9674; 315-443 9420 *Fax:* 315-443 4593 *E-mail:* dipasum@summon3.syr.edu ▲

1077
SYRACUSE UNIVERSITY
Environmental Design in Florence
Site: Italy: Florence
Dates: May 31-Jul 31

Subjects: Art history, Environmental design, Field study, Italian language (beg), Italian studies
Eligibility: *Level:* sophs, jrs, srs, grads *Requires:* 2.5 GPA, previous study in field
Credit: *Undergrad:* 6 *Grad:* 6 *Doc:* transcript
Instruction: *In:* English *Format:* art studio, directed field study, lecture *Students:* mainly US
Costs: About $6,700 *incl* tuition, housing, some meals, fees, excursions *Nonrefundable fee*
Housing: *Arr by pgm:* apartments
Deadline: Mar 15
Other info: *US accredited sponsor:* yes *Began:* 1986 *Orient:* abroad *Activities:* excursions, field trips, program travel, cultural events *Misc:* May contact former participants. *Financial aid:* scholarships *URL:* http://sumweb.syr.edu/dipa/summer
Contact: Summer Pgms, Intl Pgms Abroad, Syracuse Univ, 119 Euclid Ave, Syracuse NY 13244-4170 *Ph:* 800-251 9674; 315-443 9420 *Fax:* 315-443 4593 *E-mail:* dipasum@summon3.syr.edu ▲

1078
SYRACUSE UNIVERSITY
Pre-Architecture in Florence
Site: Italy: Florence
Dates: May 31-Jul 31
Subjects: Architecture, Drawing, Graphic arts/design, Italian language (beg), Studio arts
Eligibility: *Level:* fresh, sophs, jrs, srs
Credit: *Undergrad:* 6 *Grad:* none
Instruction: *In:* English *Format:* art studio, lecture *Students:* mainly US
Costs: About $7,000 *incl* tuition, housing, fees, excursions *Nonrefundable fee*
Housing: *Arr by pgm:* apartments
Deadline: Mar 15
Other info: *US accredited sponsor:* yes *Began:* 1985 *Orient:* abroad *Activities:* excursions *Financial aid:* scholarships *URL:* http://sumweb.syr.edu/dipa/summer
Contact: Summer Pgms, Intl Pgms Abroad, Syracuse Univ, 119 Euclid Ave, Syracuse NY 13244-4170 *Ph:* 800-251 9674; 315-443 9420 *Fax:* 315-443 4593 *E-mail:* dipasum@summon3.syr.edu ▲

1079
SYRACUSE UNIVERSITY
Visual Arts in Florence
Site: Italy: Florence
Dates: May 31-Jul 17
Subjects: Art history, Fibers, Homestay, Italian language (beg), Metalworking, Painting, Photography
Eligibility: *Level:* jrs, adults
Credit: *Undergrad:* 6 *Grad:* 6
Instruction: *In:* English *Format:* art studio, lecture *Students:* mainly US
Costs: $6,700 *incl* tuition, housing, fees, excursions *Nonrefundable fee*
Housing: *Arr by pgm:* apartments, homestay
Deadline: Mar 15
Other info: *US accredited sponsor:* yes *Began:* 1988 *Orient:* abroad *Activities:* excursions *Financial aid:* scholarships *URL:* http://sumweb.syr.edu/dipa/summer
Contact: Summer Pgms, Intl Pgms Abroad, Syracuse Univ, 119 Euclid Ave, Syracuse NY 13244-4170 *Ph:* 800-251 9674; 315-443 9420 *Fax:* 315-443 4593 *E-mail:* dipasum@summon3.syr.edu ▲

1080
UNIVERSITY OF ALABAMA
Alabama in Italy
Site: Italy: Florence
Dates: May 24-Jun 24
Subjects: Art, Civilization/culture, Homestay, Italian language (beg/int/adv), Literature, Political science/politics, Social policy
Eligibility: *Level:* fresh, sophs, jrs, srs, grads, teachers *Requires:* 2.5 GPA *Age:* min 18, avg 25
Credit: *Undergrad:* avail *Grad:* none *Doc:* transcript
Instruction: *In:* English, Italian *Format:* art studio, lang study, lecture, seminar *Students:* intl
Costs: About $2,950 *incl* tuition, housing, some meals, fees, excursions, books/ materials, ISIC
Housing: *Arr by pgm:* apartments, homestay
Deadline: Feb 1
Other info: *US accredited sponsor:* yes *Began:* 1993 *Orient:* in US & abroad *Activities:* excursions *URL:* http://www.ua.edu/international
Contact: Capstone Intl Pgm Ctr, Univ of Alabama, PO Box 870254, Tuscaloosa AL 35487 *Ph:* 205-348 5256 *Fax:* 205-348 5998 *E-mail:* achannel@aalan.ua.edu
Or Contact: Dr Gary Taylor, Univ of Alabama, PO Box 870244, Tuscaloosa AL 35487 *Ph:* 205-348 6538 *Fax:* 205-348 5298 *E-mail:* gtaylor@english.as.ua.edu

---

1081
UNIVERSITY OF CALIFORNIA, SAN DIEGO EXTENSION
Italian Immersion Program: Florence, Italy
Site: Italy: Florence *Host inst:* Euroctrs Florence
Dates: 2-12 wks, yr-round
Subjects: Italian language (beg/int/adv)
Eligibility: *Level:* fresh, sophs, jrs, srs, grads, adults, teachers, professionals, precoll *Age:* min 18
Credit: *Undergrad:* none *Grad:* none *Doc:* transcript, certificate
Instruction: *In:* Italian *Format:* lang study, lecture, seminar *Students:* intl
Costs: $903 for 2 wks *incl* tuition, housing, some meals, books/materials *Nonrefundable fee*
Housing: *Sponsor assists:* homestay, hotels
Deadline: 4-6 wks before pgm
Other info: *US accredited sponsor:* yes *Began:* 1999 *Orient:* abroad *Activities:* excursions, field trips *Misc:* Located in the oldest part of Florence, pgm is ideal for novices to adv. May contact former participants. *URL:* http://www.extension.ucsd.edu/laip
Contact: Tanya Knebel, Pgm Rep, UCSD Extension, Liberal Arts & International Pgms 0176Z, 9500 Gilman Dr, La Jolla CA 92093-0176 *Ph:* 858-822 2747 *Fax:* 858-534 7385 *E-mail:* travelstudy@ucsd.edu

---

1082
UNIVERSITY OF CINCINNATI
Study of Italian in Firenze
Site: Italy: Florence *Host inst:* Ist M S Frances-Cane di Maria
Dates: 4 wks, Jun 11-Jul 6
Subjects: Architectural history, Art history, Civilization/culture, History, Italian language, Italian studies
Eligibility: *Level:* sophs, jrs, srs, grads, adults, teachers *Requires:* previous study in field, 2 yrs Italian lang study *Age:* min 18
Credit: *Undergrad:* 4 qtr hrs *Grad:* none *Doc:* transcript
Instruction: *In:* English, Italian *Format:* lang study, lecture, practical training, study tour *Students:* mainly US
Costs: $2,200 for OH resident undergrads *incl* tuition, housing, some meals, excursions, books/materials
Housing: *Arr by pgm:* residence halls
Deadline: Mar 13
Other info: *US accredited sponsor:* yes *Began:* 1996 *Orient:* in US & abroad (4 days, intensive lang study) *Activities:* excursions, program travel, cultural events *Misc:* May contact former participants. *Financial aid:* scholarships *URL:* http://www.uc.edu/global
Contact: Prof Nettine Eckert, Adjunct Asst Prof, Univ of Cincinnati, ML 377, Cincinnati OH 45221-0377 *Ph:* 513-556 1833, 513-556 1950 *Fax:* 513-556 2577 *E-mail:* nettina.eckert@uc.edu

---

1083
UNIVERSITY OF DAYTON
Interdepartmental Summer Study Abroad Program (ISSAP)-Florence
Site: Italy: Florence
Dates: 1 mo, May 24-Jun 24
Subjects: Architecture, Art, English,

Italian studies, Music, Philosophy, Religion/theology
Eligibility: *Level:* fresh, sophs, jrs, srs, grads, adults *Requires:* 2.0 GPA *Age:* min 18, avg 20
Credit: *Undergrad:* 7 *Grad:* none *Doc:* transcript
Instruction: *In:* English *Format:* lecture *Students:* mainly US
Costs: $3,595 *incl* tuition, housing, some meals, insurance, excursions *Nonrefundable fee*
Housing: *Arr by pgm:* pensions
Deadline: Mar 1; Jan 15 for scholarships
Other info: *US accredited sponsor:* yes *Began:* 1972 *Orient:* in US & abroad (4 days) *Activities:* excursions, field trips, cultural events *Misc:* May contact former participants. *Financial aid:* scholarships
Contact: James W Stiles, Univ of Dayton, 300 College Park, Dayton OH 45469-1481 *Ph:* 937-229 3728 *Fax:* 937-229 2766 *E-mail:* stiles@udayton.edu

---

1084
UNIVERSITY OF HAWAII AT MANOA
Italian Language and Culture in Italy
Site: Italy: Florence *Host inst:* Ctr Linguistico Italiano Dante Alighieri
Dates: 4 wks, late May-late Jun
Subjects: Homestay, Italian language
Eligibility: *Level:* sophs, jrs, srs *Requires:* 3.0 GPA
Credit: *Undergrad:* 6-8 *Grad:* none *Doc:* transcript, certificate
Instruction: *In:* Italian *Format:* lang study, lecture, seminar *Students:* mainly US
Costs: $4,311 *incl* tuition, housing, some meals, intl airfare, insurance, fees, books/materials, ground transport *Nonrefundable fee*
Housing: *Arr by pgm:* homestay
Deadline: Feb 17
Other info: *US accredited sponsor:* yes *Began:* 1995 *Orient:* in US & abroad *Activities:* excursions, cultural events *Misc:* UHM financial aid avail to eligible UHM students. *URL:* http://www2.hawaii.edu/study-abroad
Contact: Dir or Study Abroad Adviser, Study Abroad Ctr, Univ of Hawaii at Manoa, Moore Hall 115, 1890 East-West Rd, Honolulu HI 96822 *Ph:* 808-956 5143, 808-956 6958 *Fax:* 808-956 9319 *E-mail:* uhmsac@hawaii.edu

---

1085
UNIVERSITY OF KANSAS
Summer Language and Culture Institute in Florence, Italy
Site: Italy: Florence *Host inst:* Ctr Linguistico Italiano Dante Alighieri
Dates: 1 or 2 mos, Jun and/or Jul
Subjects: Civilization/culture, Culinary arts, Homestay, Italian language (beg/int/adv), Italian studies, Literature
Eligibility: *Level:* sophs, jrs, srs, grads *Requires:* 1 yr coll Italian recommended
Credit: *Undergrad:* 5-10 *Grad:* none *Doc:* transcript
Instruction: *In:* Italian *Format:* lang study, lecture *Students:* US & intl
Costs: $2,650 for 1 mo, $4,370 for 2 mos *incl* tuition, housing, all meals, fees, medical evacuation svcs
Housing: *Arr by pgm:* homestay
Deadline: Mar 1
Other info: *US accredited sponsor:* yes *Began:* 1978 *Misc:* Optional excursions. Tuscan Cooking Sch. *URL:* http://www.ukans.edu/~osa
Contact: Susan MacNally, Asst Dir, Study Abroad, Univ of Kansas, 108 Lippincott Hall, Lawrence KS 66045 *Ph:* 785-864 3742 *Fax:* 785-864 5040 *E-mail:* osa@ukans.edu ▲

1086
UNIVERSITY OF MICHIGAN
Spring Program in Florence
Site: Italy: Florence
Dates: 6 wks, early May-mid-Jun
Subjects: Architecture, Art, Art history, History, Music, Studio arts
Eligibility: *Level:* sophs, jrs, srs *Requires:* good acad standing
Credit: *Undergrad:* 6 *Grad:* none
Instruction: *In:* English *Format:* art studio, lecture *Students:* mainly US
Costs: Contact Sponsor
Housing: *Arr by pgm:* villa with single, double or triple rms
Deadline: Feb 16
Other info: *US accredited sponsor:* yes *Began:* 1997 *Orient:* in US & abroad *Activities:* field trips, cultural events *Misc:* May contact former participants. *Financial aid:* scholarships
Contact: Intl Pgms, Univ of Michigan, G513 Michigan Union, Ann Arbor MI 48109-1349 *Ph:* 734-764 4311 *Fax:* 734-764 3229 *E-mail:* oip@umich.edu

---

1087
UNIVERSITY OF MICHIGAN
Summer Program in Florence
Site: Italy: Florence
Dates: 6 wks, late Jun-early Aug
Subjects: Architecture, Art history, Civilization/culture, Italian language (beg/int), Studio arts
Eligibility: *Level:* sophs, jrs, srs *Requires:* good acad standing, enrollment at US or Canadian univ
Credit: *Undergrad:* 6 *Grad:* none
Instruction: *In:* English *Format:* lang study, lecture *Students:* mainly US
Costs: Contact Sponsor
Housing: *Arr by pgm:* villa with single, double or triple rms
Deadline: Feb 16
Other info: *US accredited sponsor:* yes *Began:* 1966 *Orient:* in US & abroad *Activities:* excursions *URL:* http://www.umich.edu/~iinet/oip/
Contact: Intl Pgms, Univ of Michigan, G513 Michigan Union, Ann Arbor MI 48109-1349 *Ph:* 734-764 4311 *Fax:* 734-764 3229 *E-mail:* oip@umich.edu

---

1088
UNIVERSITY OF NORTH CAROLINA AT CHAPEL HILL
UNC-CH Summer Program in Florence
Site: Italy: Florence *Host inst:* Lorenzo de' Medici Inst
Dates: Two 4-wk sessions, May 24-Jun 23 and/or Jun 28-Jul 28
Subjects: Art history, Art restoration, Ceramics/pottery, Civilization/culture, History, Homestay, Italian language (beg/int/adv), Italian studies, Jewelry/jewelry-making, Literature, Social sciences, Studio arts
Eligibility: *Level:* adults *Requires:* 2.7 GPA
Credit: *Undergrad:* 6 *Grad:* none *Doc:* transcript, certificate
Instruction: *In:* English, Italian *Format:* art studio, lang study, lecture, seminar *Students:* intl
Costs: $2,306 *incl* tuition, housing, insurance, fees *Nonrefundable fee*
Housing: *Arr by pgm:* apartments, homestay, pensions
Deadline: Early Feb
Other info: *US accredited sponsor:* yes *Began:* 1994 *Orient:* in US & abroad *Activities:* excursions, field trips *Misc:* May contact former participants. *Financial aid:* scholarships *URL:* http://www.unc.edu/depts/abroad
Contact: Dir, Study Abroad, UNC-Chapel Hill, 12 Caldwell Hall CB-3130, Cameron Ave, Chapel Hill NC 27599-2262 *Ph:* 919-962 7001 *Fax:* 919-962 2262 *E-mail:* abroad@unc.edu

---

1089
UNIVERSITY OF PITTSBURGH
Pitt in Italy
Site: Italy: Florence *Host inst:* Ctrs for Acad Pgms Abroad
Dates: 6 wks, May 18-Jun 30
Subjects: Civilization/culture, Homestay, Italian language, Italian studies
Eligibility: *Level:* sophs, jrs, srs *Requires:* 2.75 GPA, previous study in field, 1 yr coll Italian or equiv
Credit: *Undergrad:* 7 *Grad:* none *Doc:* transcript
Instruction: *In:* English, Italian *Format:*

lang study, lecture, seminar, study tour *Students:* mainly US
Costs: About $4,525 for Univ of Pitt students, $4,695 for others *incl* tuition, housing, intl airfare, excursions, social events *Nonrefundable fee*
Housing: *Arr by pgm:* apartments, homestay
Deadline: Feb 15
Other info: *US accredited sponsor:* yes *Began:* 1991 *Orient:* in US & abroad *Activities:* excursions, field trips, cultural events *Misc:* Scholarships for own students only. Loans & grants avail. May contact former participants. *Financial aid:* scholarships *URL:* http://www.pitt.edu/~stdyabrd/
Contact: Jennifer Sill, Study Abroad, Univ of Pittsburgh, 802 William Pitt Union, Pittsburgh PA 15260 *Ph:* 412-648 2299 *Fax:* 412-383 7166 *E-mail:* jsill+@pitt.edu

---

1090
UNIVERSITY OF SAN DIEGO, SCHOOL OF LAW
Florence Institute of International and Comparative Law
Site: Italy: Florence *Host inst:* ABC Scuola Palazzo Malvisi
Dates: May 28-Jun 22
Subjects: International law
Eligibility: *Level:* grads, teachers, professionals *Requires:* law or bus students
Credit: *Undergrad:* none *Grad:* 4 *Doc:* certificate
Instruction: *In:* English *Format:* lang study, seminar *Students:* mainly US
Costs: $2,200 *incl* tuition, books/materials *Nonrefundable fee*
Housing: *Sponsor assists*
Deadline: Mar 11
Other info: *US accredited sponsor:* yes *Began:* 1996 *Orient:* in US & abroad *Misc:* Correspondence to pgm must be in English. Legal & some tourist visits arr from site. Loans avail for US students only. *URL:* http://www.acusd.edu/lawabroad
Contact: Cindy King, Law Pgms Abroad, Univ of San Diego, 5998 Alcala Park, San Diego CA 92110-2492 *Ph:* 619-260 7460 *Fax:* 619-260 2230 *E-mail:* cking@acusd.edu

---

1091
VIRGINIA COMMONWEALTH UNIVERSITY
Italy: Art in Florence
Site: Italy: Florence *Host inst:* Lorenzo de' Medici Inst
Dates: 1 mo, Jul
Subjects: Art history, Drawing, Painting
Eligibility: *Level:* sophs, jrs, srs, grads, adults, teachers, professionals *Requires:* 2.0 GPA *Age:* min 18
Credit: *Undergrad:* 6 *Grad:* 6 *Doc:* transcript
Instruction: *In:* English *Format:* art studio, lang study, lecture, study tour *Students:* mainly US
Costs: $2,400 *incl* tuition, housing *Nonrefundable fee*
Housing: *Arr by pgm:* apartments
Deadline: Contact sponsor
Other info: *US accredited sponsor:* yes *Began:* 1996 *Financial aid:* scholarships *URL:* http://www.vcu.edu/cspweb/cspdocs/stdyabrd.html
Contact: Tina Murray, Asst Dir, Ctr for Intl Pgms, Virginia Commonwealth Univ, 916 W Franklin St, Box 843043, Richmond VA 23284-3043 *Ph:* 804-828 8471 *Fax:* 804-828 2552

GUBBIO

1092
NORTH CAROLINA STATE UNIVERSITY
School of Design Program in Italy
Site: Italy: Gubbio
Dates: 5 wks, Jun 27-Aug 2
Subjects: Architecture, Fine arts, Interdisciplinary studies, Landscape architecture
Eligibility: *Level:* sophs, jrs, srs, grads, adults, teachers, professionals
Credit: *Undergrad:* 6 *Grad:* 6 *Doc:* transcript
Instruction: *In:* English *Format:* art studio, independent study *Students:* mainly US
Costs: $3,900 *incl* tuition, housing, some meals, intl airfare, insurance, excursions *Nonrefundable fee*
Housing: *Arr by pgm:* hotels
Deadline: Contact sponsor
Other info: *US accredited sponsor:* yes *Began:* 1996 *Orient:* in US & abroad *Activities:* excursions, field trips *Misc:* On-site examinations of Italian art, culture & civilization. May contact former participants. *URL:* http://www2.ncsu.edu/ncsu/stud-affairs
Contact: Anne Haberkern, North Carolina State Univ, 2118 Pullen Hall, Box 7344, Raleigh NC 27695-7344 *Ph:* 919-515 2087 *Fax:* 919-515 6021 *E-mail:* study-abroad@ncsu.edu

---

L'AQUILA

1093
UNIVERSITY OF MIAMI (FL)
Italian and Humanities in L'Aquila, Italy
Site: Italy: L'Aquila *Host inst:* Univ degli Studi dell'Aquila
Dates: Early Jun-mid-Jul
Subjects: Humanities, Italian studies, Theater arts
Eligibility: *Level:* fresh, sophs, jrs, srs *Requires:* 2.5 GPA *Age:* min 18
Credit: *Undergrad:* 6 *Grad:* none *Doc:* transcript
Instruction: *In:* English, Italian *Format:* lecture *Students:* mainly US
Costs: $4,900 *incl* tuition, housing, some meals
Housing: *Arr by pgm:* apartments
Deadline: Mar 30
Other info: *US accredited sponsor:* yes *Began:* 2001 *URL:* http://www.studyabroad.miami.edu
Contact: Intl Educ & Exch Pgms, Allen Hall 212, 5050 Brunson Dr, PO Box 248005, Univ of Miami, Coral Gables FL 33124-1610 *Ph:* 800-557 5421; 305-284 3434 *Fax:* 305-284 6629 *E-mail:* ieep@miami.edu

---

LECCHI

1094
CENTRO PONTEVECCHIO
Chianti in Tuscany
Site: Italy: Gaiole in Chianti (Lecchi)
Dates: 1 wk, Apr-Oct
Subjects: Culinary arts, Italian language, Wine
Eligibility: *Level:* adults *Age:* min 18, max 70, avg 35
Credit: *Undergrad:* none *Grad:* none
Instruction: *In:* English, Italian *Format:* lang study, practical training *Students:* intl
Costs: Contact sponsor
Housing: *Sponsor assists:* apartments, homestay, hotels
Deadline: 1 mo before pgm
Other info: *US accredited sponsor:* no *Began:* 1989 *Orient:* abroad *Misc:* Special wkly package non-vocational/vacation cooking pgm. *URL:* http://www.cpv.it/chianti
Contact: Simonetta de Mari, Ctr Pontevecchio, Piazza della Signoria 4A, 50122 Florence, Italy *E-mail:* info@cpv.it

---

LUCCA

1095
KOINE CENTER
Italian Language and Culture-Lucca
Site: Italy: Lucca
Dates: 1-5 mos, yr-round
Subjects: Art history, Civilization/culture, Culinary arts, Homestay, Italian language (beg/int/adv)
Eligibility: *Level:* adults *Age:* min 15, max 90
Credit: *Undergrad:* none *Grad:* none *Doc:* certificate
Instruction: *In:* English, Italian *Format:* lang study, lecture *Students:* intl
Costs: $690 for 2 wks, $1,320 for 4 wks *incl* tuition, housing, excursions, books/materials
Housing: *Arr by pgm:* apartments, homestay, pensions, hotels, hostels
Deadline: 2 wks before pgm
Other info: *US accredited sponsor:* no *Began:* 1988 *In coop with:* Municipality of Lucca *Orient:* in US *Activities:* excursions, field trips, cultural events *Misc:* 12 participants max per group. May contact former participants. *URL:* http://www.koinecenter.com
Contact: Linda Larson or Anja Schultz, Koine, via Pandolfini 27, 50122 Florence, Italy *E-mail:* koine@firenze.net
Or Contact: Stefano Allegrini, Secy, Koine, via Mordini, 55100 Lucca, Italy *E-mail:* koinelu@tin.it

---

1096
STUDIO CAMNITZER
Summer Printmaking in Italy, Residency Program
Site: Italy: Valdottavo (Lucca)
Dates: 2 wk min, May 15-Oct 15
Subjects: Computer aided design, Etching, Independent study, Photography, Printmaking
Eligibility: *Level:* adults, precoll *Requires:* working knowledge in printmaking *Age:* min 18, avg 30
Credit: *Undergrad:* none *Grad:* none *Doc:* certificate
Instruction: *In:* English, German, Italian, Spanish *Format:* art studio, independent study *Students:* intl
Costs: $380 per wk *incl* housing, studio, some materials
Housing: *Arr by pgm:* residence halls
Deadline: Mar 25
Other info: *US accredited sponsor:* no *Began:* 1975 *Misc:* May contact former participants. *URL:* http://www.studio-camnitzer.com
Contact: Luis Camnitzer, Studio Camnitzer, 124 Susquehanna Ave, Great Neck NY 11021 *Ph:* 516-466 6975 *Fax:* 516-487 8244 *E-mail:* camnitzer@aol.com

---

1097
UNIVERSITY OF CINCINNATI
Opera Theater of Lucca
Site: Italy: Lucca
Dates: 5 wks, Jun 19-Jul 21
Subjects: Chamber music, Costumes, Homestay, Italian language (beg), Opera, Orchestra, Singing/voice, Theater arts, Theater design
Eligibility: *Level:* fresh, sophs, jrs, srs, grads, adults, teachers, professionals, precoll *Requires:* previous study in field, audition
Credit: *Undergrad:* 15 qtr hrs *Grad:* 15 qtr hrs *Doc:* transcript
Instruction: *In:* English *Format:* lang study, music lesson *Students:* mainly US
Costs: $1,400-$1,700 for OH residents, $3,442-$4,046 for others *incl* tuition, fees *Nonrefundable fee*
Housing: *Arr by pgm:* residence halls, homestay
Deadline: Apr 1
Other info: *US accredited sponsor:* yes *Began:* 1996 *Orient:* in US & abroad *Activities:* excursions, field trips, program travel, cultural events, sports *Misc:* Scholarships for own students only. Pgm for singers, instrumentalists, designers & technicians. May contact former participants. *Financial aid:* scholarships *URL:* http://www.uc.edu/global
Contact: General Mgr, Opera Theatre of Lucca, Coll-Conservatory of Music, Univ of Cincinnati, PO Box 210077, Cincinnati OH 45221-0077 *Ph:* 513-556 5662 *Fax:* 513-556 1028 *E-mail:* operalucca@uc.edu
Or Contact: Dr Arthur Neisberg, Educ Abroad Coord, Univ of Cincinnati, PO Box 210640, Cincinnati OH 45221-0640 *Ph:* 513-556 1363 *Fax:* 513-556 2990 *E-mail:* arthur.neisberg@uc.edu

---

MANCIANO

1098
CENTRO DI CULTURA ITALIANA
Centro di Cultura Italiana Maremma
Site: Italy: Manciano (Tuscany)
Dates: 1-4 wks, Mar-Dec
Subjects: Civilization/culture, Italian language (beg/int/adv), Literature
Eligibility: *Level:* adults *Age:* min 18
Credit: *Undergrad:* avail *Grad:* avail *Doc:* certificate
Instruction: *In:* Italian *Format:* lang study, lecture *Students:* intl
Costs: EUR 301 for 2 wks *incl* tuition, fees
Housing: *Arr by pgm:* residence halls, apartments, homestay, furnished rms
Deadline: 2 wks before pgm
Other info: *US accredited sponsor:* no *Began:* 1980 *Activities:* excursions *Misc:* Extended stay discounts. May contact former participants. *Financial aid:* scholarships *URL:* http://www.culturaitaliana.it
Contact: Cultura Italiana, via Castiglione 4, I-40124 Bologna, Italy *E-mail:* culturait@iol.it

---

MERANO

1099
UNIVERSITY OF NEW ORLEANS
UNO Field School in Anthropology
Site: Italy: near Merano (South Tyrolean Alps) *Host inst:* Castle Brunnenberg
Dates: 1 mo, Jun
Subjects: Anthropology
Eligibility: *Level:* sophs, jrs, srs, adults
Credit: *Undergrad:* 6 *Grad:* none
Instruction: *In:* English *Format:* directed field study, lecture *Students:* mainly US
Costs: $1,995 *incl* tuition, housing, some meals, insurance, fees, excursions
Housing: *Arr by pgm:* furnished rms, castle
Deadline: Apr 1 or until pgm filled
Other info: *US accredited sponsor:* yes *Began:* 1983 *Orient:* in US & abroad *Activities:* excursions *Misc:* May contact former participants. *URL:* http://www.uno.edu/~inst/Welcome.html
Contact: Peter Alongia, Intl Study Pgms, Univ of New Orleans, PO Box 1315, New Orleans LA 70148 *Ph:* 504-280 7116 *Fax:* 504-280 7317 *E-mail:* palongia@uno.edu

---

MILAN

1100
IES, INSTITUTE FOR THE INTERNATIONAL EDUCATION OF STUDENTS
IES Milan Summer
Site: Italy: Milan
Dates: About 6 wks, Jun 4-Jul 20
Subjects: Italian language (beg/int), Italian studies, Music history, Political science/politics
Eligibility: *Level:* fresh, sophs, jrs, srs, grads, adults *Requires:* good acad standing *Age:* min 18
Credit: *Undergrad:* 7 *Grad:* none *Doc:* transcript
Instruction: *In:* English, Italian *Format:* directed field study, lang study, lecture *Students:* mainly US
Costs: About $3,600 *incl* tuition, housing, insurance, excursions, orient, cell phone
Housing: *Sponsor assists:* apartments with local students
Deadline: Apr 1
Other info: *US accredited sponsor:* yes *Began:* 2000 *Orient:* abroad (1 wk, intensive lang study) *Activities:* field trips, cultural events *Misc:* May contact former

participants. *URL:* http://www.IESabroad.org
Contact: *See Index II for Members* Bruce Broerman, IES, 33 N LaSalle St, 15th Fl, Chicago IL 60602-2602 *Ph:* 800-995 2300; 312-944-1750 *Fax:* 312-944 1448 *E-mail:* bbroerman@iesabroad.org ▲

1101
LANGUAGE LIAISON
Italian Design School-Milan
Site: Italy: Milan
Dates: 4 wks, Jul 3-28
Subjects: Fashion design, Fashion merchandising, Graphic arts/design, Interior design, Italian studies, Packaging
Eligibility: *Level:* fresh, sophs, jrs, srs *Age:* min 17
Credit: *Undergrad:* none *Grad:* none
Instruction: *In:* Italian *Format:* art studio, practical training *Students:* intl
Costs: Contact sponsor
Housing: *Sponsor assists:* double rms
Deadline: May 15
Other info: *US accredited sponsor:* no *Began:* 1997 *Misc:* Scholarship research svc. *URL:* http://www.languageliaison.com
Contact: Nancy Forman, Dir, Lang Liaison, 4 Burnham Pkwy, Morristown NJ 07960 *Ph:* 800-284 4448 *Fax:* 973-898 1710 *E-mail:* learn@languageliaison.com

---

1102
LINGUADUE
Italian Language and Culture Courses
Site: Italy: Milan
Dates: 2 wks or longer, Jan 8-Dec 21
Subjects: Au pair, Business language, Homestay, Internships, Italian language (beg/int/adv)
Eligibility: *Level:* adults, teachers, professionals, precoll *Age:* min 18, avg 24
Credit: *Undergrad:* none *Grad:* none *Doc:* certificate
Instruction: *In:* Italian *Format:* internship, lang study *Students:* intl
Costs: Lit 1,080,000 per mo *incl* tuition, activities *Nonrefundable fee*
Housing: *Arr by pgm:* apartments with local students, homestay, pensions, hotels
Deadline: 4 wks before pgm
Other info: *US accredited sponsor:* no *Began:* 1990 *Orient:* abroad *Activities:* excursions, cultural events, sports *Misc:* May contact former participants. *URL:* http://www.linguadue.com
Contact: Mrs Marialuisa Comini, or Mrs Marilena Motta, Linguadue, Corso Buenos Aires 43, 20124 Milan, Italy *E-mail:* info@linguadue.com

---

MONSUMMANO TERME

1103
UNIVERSITY OF CONNECTICUT
Carlo Rossi Academy Graduate Seminar
Site: Italy: Monsummano Terme (PT) *Host inst:* Carlo Rossi Acad
Dates: 6 wks, May-Jul
Subjects: Italian studies, Literature
Eligibility: *Level:* srs, grads, teachers *Requires:* previous study in field, undergrad degree in Italian studies or related field, adv Italian
Credit: *Undergrad:* none *Grad:* 3 *Doc:* transcript
Instruction: *In:* Italian *Format:* lecture *Students:* intl
Costs: About $3,300 *incl* tuition, fees
Housing: *Sponsor assists:* apartments
Deadline: Mar 30
Other info: *US accredited sponsor:* yes *Began:* 1995 *Activities:* excursions *Misc:* May contact former participants. *Financial aid:* scholarships *URL:* http://www.studyabroad.uconn.edu
Contact: Study Abroad Pgms, Univ of Connecticut, U-207, 843 Bolton Rd, Storrs CT 06269-1207 *Ph:* 860-486 5022 *Fax:* 860-486 2976 *E-mail:* sabadm03@uconnum.uconn.edu

---

MONTECASTELLO DI VIBIO

1104
INTERNATIONAL SCHOOL OF ART IN UMBRIA, ITALY
International School of Art in Umbria
Site: Italy: Montecastello di Vibio
Dates: 2-13 wks, May-Oct
Subjects: Drawing, Painting, Sculpture
Eligibility: *Level:* grads, adults, teachers, professionals *Requires:* previous study in field, slides, recommendations
Credit: *Undergrad:* avail *Grad:* avail *Doc:* transcript
Instruction: *In:* English *Format:* art studio, independent study, workshop *Students:* mainly US
Costs: Lit 7,000,000 *incl* tuition, housing, all meals, excursions, studio space, airport transfer
Housing: *Arr by pgm:* residence halls, apartments
Deadline: 2 mos before pgm
Other info: *US accredited sponsor:* no *Began:* 1988 *Orient:* abroad *Activities:* excursions, field trips, cultural events *Misc:* Intensive studio pgms for developing painters & sculptors. Lectures by visiting artists & scholars. May contact former participants. *URL:* http://www.giotto.org/
Contact: Helaine Treitman or Marc Servin, Co-Dirs, Intl Sch of Art, 06057 Montecastello di Vibio PG, Italy *Ph:* 212-386 2705 *Fax:* 323-402 1223 ext. 4156 *E-mail:* mservin@giotto.org

---

ORBETELLO

1105
KOINE CENTER
Italian Language and Culture-Orbetello
Site: Italy: Orbetello
Dates: 2 wks-5 mos, mid-Mar-Nov
Subjects: Art history, Civilization/culture, Culinary arts, Italian language (beg/int/adv), Oenology/Wine science
Eligibility: *Level:* adults *Age:* min 15, max 90
Credit: *Undergrad:* none *Grad:* none *Doc:* certificate
Instruction: *In:* Italian *Format:* lang study, lecture *Students:* intl
Costs: $690 for 2 wks *incl* tuition, housing, excursions, books/materials
Housing: *Arr by pgm:* apartments, pensions, hotels
Deadline: 2 wks before pgm
Other info: *US accredited sponsor:* no *Began:* 1984 *In coop with:* Municipality of Orbetello *Orient:* in US *Activities:* excursions *Misc:* 12 participants max per group. May contact former participants. *URL:* http://www.koinecenter.com
Contact: Linda Larson & Anja Schultz, Koine, via Pandolfini 27, 50122 Florence, Italy *E-mail:* koine@firenze.net

---

PADOVA

1106
UNIVERSITY OF ROCHESTER
Italian in Italy
Site: Italy: Padova
Dates: 4 wks, late May-late Jun
Subjects: Homestay, Italian language
Eligibility: *Level:* fresh, sophs, jrs, srs, adults *Requires:* previous study in field, 3 yrs high sch or 1 yr coll Italian
Credit: *Undergrad:* 6 *Grad:* none *Doc:* transcript
Instruction: *In:* Italian *Format:* lang study *Students:* mainly US
Costs: About $2,800 *incl* tuition, housing, some meals, fees, excursions
Housing: *Arr by pgm:* homestay
Deadline: Mar 15
Other info: *US accredited sponsor:* yes *Activities:* cultural events *URL:* http://www.rochester.edu/College/study-abroad/sa/global.html

Contact: Anne Lutkus, Modern Langs & Cultures, Univ of Rochester, Lattimore 403, Rochester NY 14627-0082 *Ph:* 716-275 2235 *E-mail:* adlt@mail.rochester.edu

PERUGIA

1107
COMITATO LINGUISTICO
Italian Language Courses for Foreigners
Site: Italy: Perugia
Dates: 4 wks or longer, Jan 8-Dec 21
Subjects: Homestay, Italian language (beg/int/adv)
Eligibility: *Level:* srs, grads, adults *Age:* min 16, avg 23
Credit: *Undergrad:* none *Grad:* none *Doc:* certificate
Instruction: *In:* Italian *Format:* lang study *Students:* intl
Costs: Lit 960,000 *incl* tuition, fees
Housing: *Sponsor assists:* apartments with local students, homestay
Deadline: 3 wks before pgm
Other info: *US accredited sponsor:* no *Began:* 1986 *Orient:* abroad *Activities:* excursions, field trips, cultural events *Misc:* May contact former participants. *URL:* http://www.edisons.it/homepages/ctlingua
Contact: Kernberger Christa, Comitato Linguistico, via XIV Settembre 57, 06122 Perugia, Italy *E-mail:* ctlingua@edisons.it

1108
EUROPEAN HERITAGE INSTITUTE
Summer in Italy
Site: Italy: Perugia *Host inst:* Univ Italiana per Stranieri
Dates: Jun 1-30, Jul 1-31, Aug 1-31
Subjects: Art history, Civilization/culture, Film studies, Italian language (beg/int/adv), Italian studies, Literature, Music history
Eligibility: *Level:* fresh, sophs, jrs, srs, grads, adults, teachers, professionals *Age:* min 18
Credit: *Undergrad:* avail *Grad:* avail *Doc:* certificate
Instruction: *In:* Italian *Format:* lab, lang study, seminar, study tour *Students:* intl
Costs: $1,100 *incl* tuition, housing, fees
Housing: *Arr by pgm:* apartments, hotels
Deadline: 2 mos before pgm
Other info: *US accredited sponsor:* no *Began:* 1987 *Activities:* excursions, field trips, program travel, cultural events, sports *URL:* http://www.europeanheritage.org
Contact: Dr Antonio Masullo or Ms Barbara Cotter, European Heritage Inst, 2708 E Franklin St, Richmond VA 23223 *Ph:* 804-643 0661 *Fax:* 804-648 0826 *E-mail:* euritage@i2020.net ▲

1109
GEORGE MASON UNIVERSITY
Intensive Italian Language and Culture
Site: Italy: Perugia *Host inst:* Univ Italiana per Stranieri
Dates: 8 wks, Jun 1-Jul 31
Subjects: Italian language
Eligibility: *Level:* fresh, sophs, jrs, srs *Requires:* 2.25 GPA *Age:* min 18
Credit: *Undergrad:* 12 *Grad:* none *Doc:* transcript
Instruction: *In:* Italian *Format:* lang study *Students:* intl
Costs: About $3,720 for VA residents, $4,370 for others *incl* tuition, housing, insurance, fees, excursions, ISIC *Nonrefundable fee*
Housing: *Arr by pgm:* homestay
Deadline: Apr 10
Other info: *US accredited sponsor:* yes *Began:* 1996 *Orient:* in US (1 day) *Misc:* May contact former participants. *Financial aid:* scholarships, work study *URL:* http://www.gmu.edu/departments/cge
Contact: Ctr for Global Educ, George Mason Univ, Johnson Ctr, Rm 235, 4400 University Dr, Fairfax VA 22030-4444 *Ph:* 703-993 2154 *Fax:* 703-993 2153 *E-mail:* cge@gmu.edu

1110
UNIVERSITY OF SOUTH FLORIDA
USF in Italy
Site: Italy: Perugia *Host inst:* Univ Italiana per Stranieri
Dates: Jul 1-31
Subjects: Art, Civilization/culture, History, Independent study, Italian language (beg/int/adv), Italian studies
Eligibility: *Level:* adults *Requires:* 2.5 GPA *Age:* min 18
Credit: *Undergrad:* 8-12 *Grad:* 3 *Doc:* transcript
Instruction: *In:* English, Italian *Format:* independent study, lecture, seminar *Students:* intl
Costs: $1,450 for FL residents *incl* tuition, housing, fees, excursions *Nonrefundable fee*
Housing: *Arr by pgm:* apartments, homestay
Deadline: 90 days before pgm
Other info: *US accredited sponsor:* yes *Began:* 1983 *Orient:* in US & abroad *Activities:* excursions, field trips, program travel *Misc:* May contact former participants. *Financial aid:* scholarships *URL:* http://www.usf.edu/~iac/
Contact: Dr Domenico Ierardo, Lang Dept, CPR 107, Univ of South Florida, Tampa FL 33620-5550 *Ph:* 813-974 2783 *Fax:* 813-974 4613
Or Contact: James Pulos, Overseas Study Pgms, CPR 107, Univ of South Florida, Tampa FL 33620-5550 *Ph:* 813-974 4043, 813-974 3933 *Fax:* 813-974 4613 *E-mail:* jpulos@iac.usf.edu

1111
UNIVERSITY OF WISCONSIN-MADISON
Summer in Perugia, Italy
Site: Italy: Perugia *Host inst:* Univ Italiana per Stranieri
Dates: 8 wks, Jun-Jul
Subjects: Art, Civilization/culture, Film studies, History, Italian language (beg/int/adv), Italian studies, Music, Renaissance studies
Eligibility: *Level:* sophs, jrs, srs *Requires:* 2.5 GPA
Credit: *Undergrad:* 9 *Grad:* none *Doc:* transcript
Instruction: *In:* English, Italian *Format:* lang study, lecture, seminar *Students:* intl
Costs: $5,100 for WI residents, $5,200 for others *incl* tuition, housing, all meals, intl airfare, fees, books/materials, local transport, area travel *Nonrefundable fee*
Housing: *Sponsor assists:* apartments, boardinghouse
Deadline: 1st Fri in Mar
Other info: *US accredited sponsor:* yes *Began:* 1994 *Orient:* in US *Misc:* Loans for qualifying degree-seeking undergrads. May contact former participants. *Financial aid:* scholarships *URL:* http://www.wisc.edu/studyabroad
Contact: Intl Studies & Pgms, Univ of Wisconsin-Madison, 261 Bascom Hall, 500 Lincoln Dr, Madison WI 53706 *Ph:* 608-265 6329 *Fax:* 608-262 6998 *E-mail:* peeradvisor@bascom.wisc.edu

1112
VIRGINIA COMMONWEALTH UNIVERSITY
Romancing Italy in Enchanting Perugia-Intensive Language
Site: Italy: Perugia *Host inst:* Univ Italiana per Stranieri
Dates: 1 mo, Jul
Subjects: Homestay, Italian language, Literature
Eligibility: *Level:* sophs, adults *Requires:* 2.0 GPA *Age:* min 18
Credit: *Undergrad:* 3-6 *Grad:* none *Doc:* transcript
Instruction: *In:* Italian *Format:* lang study, lecture *Students:* mainly US
Costs: $1,495 *incl* tuition, housing *Nonrefundable fee*

Housing: *Arr by pgm:* apartments, homestay
Deadline: Contact sponsor
Other info: *US accredited sponsor:* yes *Began:* 1974 *Activities:* excursions, field trips *URL:* http://www.vcu.edu/cspweb/cspdocs/stdyabrd.html
Contact: Tina Murray, Asst Dir, Ctr for Intl Pgms, Virginia Commonwealth Univ, 916 W Franklin St, Box 843043, Richmond VA 23284-3043 *Ph:* 804-828 8471 *Fax:* 804-828 2552

PISA

1113
NATIONAL REGISTRATION CENTER FOR STUDY ABROAD (NRCSA)
Italian in Pisa
Site: Italy: Pisa *Host inst:* Ist Linguistico Mediterraneo
Dates: 2 or 4 wks, yr-round
Subjects: Homestay, Italian language (beg/int/adv)
Eligibility: *Level:* fresh, sophs, jrs, srs, grads, adults, teachers, professionals *Age:* min 18
Credit: *Undergrad:* none *Grad:* none *Doc:* certificate
Instruction: *In:* Italian *Format:* lang study, tutorial *Students:* intl
Costs: $651 for 2 wks, $1,026 for 4 wks *incl* tuition, housing, some meals, insurance *Nonrefundable fee*
Housing: *Arr by pgm:* homestay
Deadline: 6 wks before pgm
Other info: *US accredited sponsor:* no *URL:* http://www.nrcsa.com
Contact: Reuel Zielke, NRCSA, 823 N 2nd St, #206, Milwaukee WI 53203 *Ph:* 414-278 0631 *Fax:* 414-271 8884 *E-mail:* info@nrcsa.com

1114
NEW YORK UNIVERSITY, SCHOOL OF EDUCATION
Music and Dance Program
Site: Italy: Pisa *Host inst:* Univ of Pisa
Dates: 3 wks, Jul 2-21
Subjects: Composition, Dance, Music, Performing arts
Eligibility: *Level:* grads *Requires:* 3.0 GPA, previous study in field
Credit: *Undergrad:* none *Grad:* avail *Doc:* transcript
Instruction: *In:* English *Format:* lecture, seminar *Students:* mainly US
Costs: $5,500 *incl* tuition, housing, some meals *Nonrefundable fee*
Housing: *Arr by pgm:* residence halls
Deadline: Apr 1
Other info: *US accredited sponsor:* yes *Activities:* cultural events *Misc:* May contact former participants. *URL:* http://www.nyu.edu/summer
Contact: Dr Esther Lamneck, Music & Performing Arts, New York Univ, 35 W 4th St, Rm 777, New York NY 10012-1172 *Ph:* 212-998 5441 *Fax:* 212-995 4043 *E-mail:* lamneck@is3.nyu.edu
Or Contact: Helen J Kelly, Dir of Special Pgms, Sch of Educ, New York Univ, 82 Washington Square E, New York NY 10003-6680 *Ph:* 212-998 5090 *Fax:* 212-995 4923 ▲

RAVENNA

1115
SCUOLA PALAZZO MALVISI
Italian Language Courses-Ravenna
Site: Italy: Ravenna
Dates: 1-mo courses, Feb-Dec
Subjects: Art history, Italian language (beg/int/adv), Literature, Mosaics
Eligibility: *Level:* adults *Age:* min 16
Credit: *Undergrad:* none *Grad:* none
Instruction: *In:* Italian *Format:* lang study, lecture *Students:* intl
Costs: $600 *incl* tuition, insurance, fees, books/materials
Housing: *Arr by pgm:* apartments, homestay, hotels
Deadline: 1 mo before pgm
Other info: *US accredited sponsor:* no *Began:* 1986 *Activities:* excursions *Misc:* May contact former participants. *URL:* http://www.scuolapalazzomalvisi.com
Contact: Matilde Portolani, Scuola Palazzo Malvisi, via Salara 31, 48100 Ravenna, Italy *E-mail:* malvisi@infuturo.it
Or Contact: Dr Cesare Portolani, Scuola Palazzo Malvisi, via Fiorentina 36, 47021 Bagno di Romagna (Forli), Italy

ROME

1116
ACADEMIC PROGRAMS INTERNATIONAL (API)
Academic Programs International at John Cabot University
Site: Italy: Rome
Dates: 6 wks, yr-round
Subjects: Art history, Civilization/culture, Field study, Geography, Geology, History, Independent study, Italian language, Literature
Eligibility: *Level:* fresh, sophs, jrs, srs, grads, adults, teachers, professionals *Requires:* 2.75 GPA, recommendation letter *Age:* min 18, avg 22
Credit: *Undergrad:* avail *Grad:* none *Doc:* transcript
Instruction: *In:* English, Italian *Format:* directed field study, independent study, lab, lang study, lecture, practical training, study tour, tutorial, workshop *Students:* mainly US
Costs: $4,000 per summer *incl* tuition, housing, all meals, insurance, fees, excursions, books/materials, ground transport, tutoring *Nonrefundable fee*
Housing: *Arr by pgm:* apartments
Deadline: Contact sponsor
Other info: *US accredited sponsor:* no *Began:* 1997 *Orient:* in US & abroad (2 wks, intensive lang study) *Activities:* excursions, field trips, program travel, cultural events *Misc:* Airport reception. On-site dir. May contact former participants. *Financial aid:* scholarships *URL:* http://www.academicintl.com
Contact: Jennifer Allen, Dir, Acad Pgms Intl, 129 E Hopkins St, Ste 101, San Marcos TX 78666 *Ph:* 800-844 4124; 512-392 8520 *Fax:* 512-392 8420 *E-mail:* api@onr.com

1117
CALIFORNIA STATE UNIVERSITY, LONG BEACH
The Roman World
Site: Italy: Rome
Dates: 3 wks, Jan 2-22
Subjects: Art history, Classical studies, History, Italian studies, Literature
Eligibility: *Level:* jrs, srs, grads, adults, teachers, professionals
Credit: *Undergrad:* 3 *Grad:* none *Doc:* transcript
Instruction: *In:* English *Format:* study tour *Students:* mainly US
Costs: $2,665 *incl* tuition, housing, some meals, intl airfare, excursions
Housing: *Arr by pgm:* hotels
Deadline: Oct 1
Other info: *US accredited sponsor:* yes *Began:* 1989 *Orient:* in US (1 day) *Activities:* excursions, field trips, program travel *Misc:* Excursions to Florence, Herculaneum, Naples, Pompeii, Tivoli. *URL:* http://www.uces.csulb.edu/winter
Contact: Prof David Hood, History, California State Univ Long Beach, 1250 Bellflower Blvd, Long Beach CA 90840 *Ph:* 562-985 4420 *Fax:* 562-985 5431 *E-mail:* dhood@csulb.edu

1118
COLLEGE CONSORTIUM FOR INTERNATIONAL STUDIES and **COLLEGE OF STATEN ISLAND, CITY UNIVERSITY OF NEW YORK**
CSI Program in Rome, Italy
Site: Italy: Rome *Host inst:* Amer Univ of Rome
Dates: 4 wks, about May 31-Jun 30
Subjects: Art history, Business/management, Italian language (beg/int), Political science/politics, Studio arts

Eligibility: *Level:* fresh, sophs, jrs, srs *Requires:* 2.5 GPA, recommendation letter, essay, transcript *Age:* min 18
Credit: *Undergrad:* 6 *Grad:* none *Doc:* transcript
Instruction: *In:* English, Italian *Format:* lang study, lecture, seminar *Students:* intl & host country
Costs: $1,905 *incl* tuition, fees, ISIC *Nonrefundable fee*
Housing: *Arr by pgm:* apartments
Deadline: Mar 15
Other info: *US accredited sponsor:* yes *Began:* 1992 *Orient:* in US & abroad *Activities:* field trips, cultural events *Misc:* May contact former participants. *URL:* http://www.ccisabroad.org
Contact: *See Index II for Members* CCIS, 2000 P St NW, Ste 503, Washington DC 20036 *Ph:* 800-453 6956; 202-223 0330 *Fax:* 202-223 0999 *E-mail:* info@ccisabroad.org
Or Contact: Coord, Italy Pgms, Ctr for Intl Svc, Coll of Staten Island/CUNY, Bldg 2A, Rm 206, 2800 Victory Blvd, Staten Island NY 10314 *Ph:* 718-982 2100 *Fax:* 718-982 2108 *E-mail:* studyab@postbox.csi.cuny.edu ▲

1119
DUKE UNIVERSITY
Duke in Rome
Site: Italy: Rome
Dates: Mid-May-Jun, odd-numbered yrs
Subjects: Archaeology, Art history, Civilization/culture, Classical studies
Eligibility: *Level:* fresh, sophs, jrs, srs *Requires:* good acad standing, transcript
Credit: *Undergrad:* 1 credit *Grad:* none *Doc:* transcript
Instruction: *In:* English *Format:* lecture *Students:* mainly US
Costs: $4,520 *incl* tuition, housing, some meals, excursions
Housing: *Arr by pgm:* residence halls
Deadline: Feb 16
Other info: *US accredited sponsor:* yes *Began:* 1982 *Activities:* excursions, field trips *Misc:* Next offered summer 2001. *URL:* http://www.aas.duke.edu/study_abroad/
Contact: Study Abroad, Duke Univ, 121 Allen Bldg Box 90057, Durham NC 27708-0057 *Ph:* 919-684 2174 *Fax:* 919-684 3083 *E-mail:* abroad@asdean.duke.edu

---

1120
IONA COLLEGE and **PENNSYLVANIA STATE UNIVERSITY**
Iona in Italy
Site: Italy: Rome *Host inst:* Penn State Rome Ctr
Dates: 5 wks, May 22-Jun 22
Subjects: Business/management, Fine arts, History, Religion/theology
Eligibility: *Level:* fresh, sophs, jrs, srs *Requires:* 2.5 GPA
Credit: *Undergrad:* 6 *Grad:* none *Doc:* transcript
Instruction: *In:* English *Format:* lecture *Students:* mainly US
Costs: $3,370 *incl* tuition, intl airfare
Housing: *Arr by pgm:* apartments
Deadline: Contact sponsor
Other info: *US accredited sponsor:* yes *Began:* 1991 *Activities:* field trips *Misc:* Pgm incl wkend in Tuscany. 2 courses max per student.
Contact: John Mahon, Dir, Study Abroad, Iona Coll, New Rochelle NY 10801 *Ph:* 914-633 2060 *E-mail:* jmahon@iona.edu

---

1121
ITALIAIDEA
Italian Language and Culture Courses for Foreigners
Site: Italy: Rome
Dates: 2-12 wks, yr-round
Subjects: Art history, Business language, Civilization/culture, Film studies, History, Italian language (beg/int/adv), Literature
Eligibility: *Level:* fresh, sophs, jrs, srs, adults *Age:* min 16
Credit: *Undergrad:* avail *Grad:* none *Doc:* certificate
Instruction: *In:* Italian *Format:* lang study, lecture *Students:* intl
Costs: About Lit 850,000 per mo *incl* tuition, fees, activities
Housing: *Sponsor assists:* apartments with local students, homestay
Deadline: 3 wks before pgm
Other info: *US accredited sponsor:* no *Began:* 1984 *Orient:* avail avail *Activities:* excursions, cultural events *Misc:* Videoteque, library. *URL:* http://www.italiaidea.com
Contact: Ms D Curioso or Mrs C Ciampaglia, Italiaidea, Piazza della Cancelleria 85, 00186 Rome, Italy *E-mail:* italiaidea@italiaidea.com

---

1122
LEXIA INTERNATIONAL
LEXIA Summer in Rome
Site: Italy: Rome *Host inst:* Ist Italiano, Ctr di Lingua e Cultura
Dates: 8 wks, mid-Jun-mid-Aug
Subjects: Anthropology, Arts, Civilization/culture, Ecology/environmental studies, Economics, European studies, Fine arts, History, Homestay, Independent study, Internships, Italian language (beg/int/adv), Literature, Political science/politics, Sociology
Eligibility: *Level:* fresh, sophs, jrs, srs, grads *Requires:* 2.5 GPA, 1 yr postsecondary educ completed *Age:* min 18, avg 21
Credit: *Undergrad:* 8-10 *Grad:* 8-10 *Doc:* transcript *Transfer credit through:* Western Washington Univ
Instruction: *In:* English, Italian *Format:* independent study, internship, lang study, lecture, seminar, volunteer/svc *Students:* mainly US
Costs: $4,950 *incl* tuition, housing, insurance, fees, excursions, ISIC *Nonrefundable fee*
Housing: *Arr by pgm:* residence halls with local students, homestay
Deadline: Apr 15; Apr 1 for scholarships
Other info: *US accredited sponsor:* no *Began:* 2000 *In coop with:* Western Washington Univ *Orient:* abroad (2 days, intensive lang study) *Activities:* excursions, field trips, program travel, cultural events, sports *Misc:* Student support svcs. May contact former participants. *Financial aid:* scholarships, work study *URL:* http://www.lexiaintl.org
Contact: LEXIA Intl, 25 S Main St, Hanover NH 03755 *Ph:* 800-775 3942; 603-643 9898 *Fax:* 603-643 9899 *E-mail:* info@lexiaintl.org
Or Contact: LEXIA Intl, West Coast, 378 Cambridge Ave, Palo Alto CA 94306 *Ph:* 650-327 9191 *Fax:* 650-327 9192

1123
LOYOLA UNIVERSITY OF CHICAGO
Rome Summer Program
Site: Italy: Rome *Host inst:* Loyola Univ Chicago Rome Ctr
Dates: About May 26-Jun 30
Subjects: Civilization/culture, Film studies, History, Italian language, Literature
Eligibility: *Level:* fresh, sophs, jrs, srs, grads, adults, teachers, professionals
Credit: *Undergrad:* 6 *Grad:* none
Instruction: *In:* English, Italian *Format:* lang study, seminar, tutorial *Students:* mainly US
Costs: About $3,500 *incl* tuition, housing, some meals, excursions
Housing: *Arr by pgm:* residence halls
Deadline: About Mar 15
Other info: *US accredited sponsor:* yes *Began:* 1992 *Orient:* abroad *Activities:* excursions, field trips *URL:* http://www.luc.edu/depts/modern_lang/
Contact: North Amer Enrollment, Modern Langs & Literature, Loyola Univ Chicago, 820 N Michigan, Ste 903, Chicago IL 60626 *Ph:* 773-508 2850 *E-mail:* pgiorda@luc.edu
Or Contact: Dr Sergio Corsi, Modern Langs & Literature, Loyola Univ Chicago, 820 N Michigan, Ste 903, Chicago IL 60611 *Ph:* 312-915 6097, 312-915 6097 *Fax:* 312-915 8553

1124
MICHIGAN STATE UNIVERSITY
History and Art History
Site: Italy: Rome
Dates: 6 wks, May-Jul
Subjects: Art history, History, Italian language
Eligibility: *Level:* fresh, sophs, jrs, srs, grads *Requires:* 2.0 GPA, good acad standing, letter of interest *Age:* min 18
Credit: *Undergrad:* 6 *Grad:* 6 *Doc:* transcript
Instruction: *In:* English *Format:* lang study, lecture, seminar *Students:* mainly US
Costs: About $3,000 *incl* housing, insurance, excursions, 1-mo bus pass, support svcs *Nonrefundable fee*
Housing: *Arr by pgm:* apartments
Deadline: Mar 2
Other info: *US accredited sponsor:* yes *Began:* 1990 *Orient:* in US & abroad *Activities:* field trips *Misc:* Loans avail. May contact former participants. *Financial aid:* scholarships *URL:* http://studyabroad.msu.edu
Contact: Cheryl Benner, Study Abroad, Michigan State Univ, 109 Intl Ctr, East Lansing MI 48824-1035 *Ph:* 517-353 8920 *Fax:* 517-432 2082 *E-mail:* bennerc@msu.edu ▲

1125
MICHIGAN STATE UNIVERSITY
Social Science-Italy
Site: Italy: Rome
Dates: 5 wks, May-Jul
Subjects: Political science/politics, Social sciences
Eligibility: *Level:* sophs, jrs, srs *Requires:* 2.0 GPA, good acad standing *Age:* min 18
Credit: *Undergrad:* 8 *Grad:* none *Doc:* transcript
Instruction: *In:* English *Format:* lecture *Students:* mainly US
Costs: About $3,000 *incl* housing, insurance, excursions, support svcs *Nonrefundable fee*
Housing: *Arr by pgm:* pensions
Deadline: Mar 2
Other info: *US accredited sponsor:* yes *Began:* 1986 *Orient:* in US *Activities:* excursions *Misc:* Loans avail. *Financial aid:* scholarships *URL:* http://studyabroad.msu.edu
Contact: Cheryl Benner, Study Abroad, Michigan State Univ, 109 Intl Ctr, East Lansing MI 48824-1035 *Ph:* 517-353 8920 *Fax:* 517-432 2082 *E-mail:* bennerc@msu.edu ▲

1126
NORTHERN ILLINOIS UNIVERSITY
Art and Architecture: From Caesars to Mussolini
Site: Italy: Rome *Host inst:* Amer Univ of Rome
Dates: 3 wks, May-Jun
Subjects: Architecture, Art history
Eligibility: *Level:* sophs, jrs, srs, grads, adults, teachers, professionals *Requires:* 2.75 GPA, previous study in field, helpful
Credit: *Undergrad:* 3-6 *Grad:* 3-6 *Doc:* transcript
Instruction: *In:* English *Format:* directed field study, lecture *Students:* mainly US
Costs: About $1,700 *incl* tuition, housing, some meals, insurance, fees, excursions
Housing: *Sponsor assists:* pensions
Deadline: Feb 12
Other info: *US accredited sponsor:* yes *Began:* 1995 *Orient:* in US *Misc:* May contact former participants. *Financial aid:* scholarships *URL:* http://www.niu.edu/niuabroad
Contact: Anne Seitzinger, Study Abroad, Williston Hall 417, DeKalb, Northern Illinois Univ IL *Ph:* 815-753 0700 *Fax:* 815-753 0825 *E-mail:* niuabroad@niu.edu
Or Contact: Judith Testa, Pgm Dir, Art, Northern Illinois Univ, Art Bldg 201C, DeKalb IL 60115 *Ph:* 815-753 8392 *E-mail:* judyt@niu.edu

---

1127
OHIO UNIVERSITY
Ancient Rome: Development of a City
Site: Italy: Rome
Dates: 3 wks, late Nov-mid-Dec
Subjects: Field study, History, Italian studies
Eligibility: *Level:* sophs, jrs, srs *Requires:* 3.0 GPA, previous study in field
Credit: *Undergrad:* 4 qtr hrs *Grad:* none
Instruction: *In:* English *Format:* directed field study, lecture, study tour *Students:* mainly US
Costs: Contact Sponsor
Housing: *Arr by pgm:* pensions
Deadline: Oct 15
Other info: *US accredited sponsor:* yes *Began:* 1998 *Orient:* in US & abroad (2 days) *Activities:* excursions, field trips, program travel *URL:* http://www.ohiou.edu
Contact: Prof Thomas Carpenter, Classics, Ohio Univ, Ellis Hall, Athens OH 45701 *Ph:* 740-593 2741 *E-mail:* carpentt@ohiou.edu
Or Contact: Connie Perdreau, Dir, Educ Abroad, Ohio Univ, Gordy Hall 107, Athens OH 45701 *Ph:* 740-593 4583 *Fax:* 740-593 9758 *E-mail:* perdreau@ohiou.edu

---

1128
RAMAPO COLLEGE OF NEW JERSEY
Rome-Italy
Site: Italy: Rome *Host inst:* St John's Univ Rome campus
Dates: 4 wks, Jun
Subjects: Art history, Drawing, Italian language (beg/int/adv), Painting
Eligibility: *Level:* fresh, sophs, jrs, srs *Requires:* 2.0 GPA *Age:* min 18, max 24, avg 22
Credit: *Undergrad:* avail *Grad:* none
Instruction: *In:* Italian *Format:* art studio, lang study *Students:* mainly US
Costs: Contact sponsor
Housing: *Arr by pgm:* apartments
Deadline: Apr 1
Other info: *US accredited sponsor:* yes *Orient:* in US *Activities:* excursions, field trips, cultural events *Misc:* May contact former participants.
Contact: Ms Robyn Perricelli, Coord, Study Abroad, Ramapo Coll of New Jersey, 505 Ramapo Valley Rd, Mahwah NJ 07430 *Ph:* 201-684 7030 *Fax:* 201-684 7651

1129
SAINT JOHN'S UNIVERSITY (NY)
College Europa Italy
Site: Italy: Rome
Dates: 1 mo, Jun-Jul
Subjects: Art history, International business, Internships, Italian language (int/adv), Italian studies, Political science/politics, Studio arts
Eligibility: *Level:* fresh, sophs, jrs, srs, grads, adults, teachers *Requires:* 2.75 GPA, 2 recommendation letters, interview *Age:* min 18
Credit: *Undergrad:* 6 per term *Grad:* none *Doc:* transcript
Instruction: *In:* English, Italian *Format:* art studio, lang study, lecture *Students:* mainly US
Costs: $2,484 *incl* housing, some meals, intl airfare, excursions
Housing: *Arr by pgm:* residence halls, apartments
Deadline: Feb 1
Other info: *US accredited sponsor:* yes *Began:* 1996 *Orient:* in US & abroad (1 day) *Activities:* field trips *Misc:* Field trips to Florence, Pompeii/Paestum, Turin, Venice. May contact former participants.
Contact: Joyce Lawlor, Dean, Study Abroad Pgms, St John's Univ, Bent Hall, Rm 388, 8000 Utopia Pkwy, Jamaica NY 11439 *Ph:* 718-990 6105 *Fax:* 718-990 2321 *E-mail:* intled@stjohns.edu
Or Contact: Dr Annalisa Sacca, Modern Foreign Langs, St John's Univ, 8000 Utopia Pkwy, Jamaica NY 11439 *Ph:* 718-990 6161 ext 5115 *Fax:* 718-990 1870 *E-mail:* saccaa@stjohns.edu

---

1130
TEMPLE UNIVERSITY SCHOOL OF LAW
Temple Law Summer Session in Italy
Site: Italy: Rome *Host inst:* Temple Univ Rome
Dates: 6 wks, Jun-Jul
Subjects: Conflict studies, European law, European Union, International business, International law
Eligibility: *Level:* grads *Requires:* 1 yr law sch, good acad standing
Credit: *Undergrad:* none *Grad:* avail *Doc:* transcript, certificate
Instruction: *In:* English *Format:* art studio, lecture *Students:* US & host country
Costs: About $5,812-$7,141 *incl* tuition, housing, all meals, intl airfare, fees, personal expenses *Nonrefundable fee*
Housing: *Arr by pgm:* apartments
Deadline: Apr 15
Other info: *US accredited sponsor:* yes *Began:* 1973 *Orient:* abroad (1 day) *Activities:* excursions, field trips, cultural events *Misc:* May contact former participants. *URL:* http://www.temple.edu/lawschool
Contact: Adelaide Ferguson, Asst Dean, Temple Law Sch, Intl Pgms, 1719 N Broad St Rm 710, Philadelphia PA 19122 *Ph:* 215-204 1448 *Fax:* 215-204 2282 *E-mail:* intl-law@vm.temple.edu

---

1131
TEMPLE UNIVERSITY
Art and Culture Seminar
Site: Italy: Rome
Dates: 4 wks, Jun
Subjects: Aesthetics, Arts criticism, Civilization/culture, Field study, Film studies, Italian studies, Literary criticism, Literature
Eligibility: *Level:* jrs, srs, grads *Requires:* 3.0 GPA
Credit: *Undergrad:* none *Grad:* 6 *Doc:* transcript
Instruction: *In:* English *Format:* directed field study *Students:* mainly US
Costs: $3,050-$3,850 depending on PA residency *incl* tuition, housing, fees
Housing: *Arr by pgm:* apartments
Deadline: Mar 1
Other info: *US accredited sponsor:* yes *Began:* 1989 *Activities:* excursions, cultural events *Misc:* Scholarships avail for Temple students only May contact former participants. *URL:* http://www.temple.edu/intlprog/
Contact: Intl Pgms, Temple Univ, 200 Tuttleman Learning Ctr, 1809 N 13th St, Philadelphia PA 19122 *Ph:* 215-204 0720 *Fax:* 215-204 0729 *E-mail:* intlprog@vm.temple.edu

---

1132
TEMPLE UNIVERSITY
International Business in Rome
Site: Italy: Rome
Dates: 5 wks, May-Jun
Subjects: Business/management, International business, International marketing
Eligibility: *Level:* jrs, srs, grads *Requires:* 2.5 GPA
Credit: *Undergrad:* 6 *Grad:* 6
Instruction: *In:* English *Format:* lecture, seminar *Students:* mainly US
Costs: About $2,700-$4,000 *incl* tuition, housing, fees
Housing: *Arr by pgm:* apartments
Deadline: Mar 1
Other info: *US accredited sponsor:* yes *Activities:* field trips *URL:* http://www.temple.edu/intlprog/
Contact: Intl Pgms, Temple Univ, Tuttleman Learning Ctr, 1809 N 13th St, Philadelphia PA 19122 *Ph:* 215-204 4684 *Fax:* 215-204 5735 *E-mail:* intlprog@vm.temple.edu ▲

1133
TEMPLE UNIVERSITY
Temple University Rome Summer Program
Site: Italy: Rome
Dates: 6 wks, mid-May-Jul
Subjects: Art history, Business/management, Classical studies, Finance, History, International marketing, Italian language, Sociology, Visual arts
Eligibility: *Level:* jrs, srs *Requires:* 2.5 GPA
Credit: *Undergrad:* 6 *Grad:* none *Doc:* transcript
Instruction: *In:* English *Format:* art studio, directed field study, lang study, lecture, seminar *Students:* mainly US
Costs: $2,900-$3,800 depending on PA residency *incl* tuition, housing, fees, excursions *Nonrefundable fee*
Housing: *Arr by pgm:* apartments
Deadline: Mar 1
Other info: *US accredited sponsor:* yes *Began:* 1992 *Orient:* abroad *Activities:* excursions, field trips, cultural events *URL:* http://www.temple.edu/intlprog/
Contact: Intl Pgms, Temple Univ, 200 Tuttleman Learning Ctr, 1809 N 13th St, Philadelphia PA 19122 *Ph:* 215-204 0720 *Fax:* 215-204 0729 *E-mail:* intlprog@vm.temple.edu ▲

1134
TRINITY COLLEGE (CT)
Trinity College in Rome
Site: Italy: Rome *Host inst:* Trinity Coll Rome Campus
Dates: 2 mos, Jun-Jul
Subjects: Art, Baroque studies, Drawing, History, Italian language (beg/int), Italian studies, Renaissance studies
Eligibility: *Level:* sophs, jrs, srs *Requires:* 3.0 GPA *Age:* avg 20
Credit: *Undergrad:* avail *Grad:* none *Doc:* transcript
Instruction: *In:* Italian *Format:* lecture *Students:* mainly US
Costs: About $4,100 *incl* tuition, housing, some meals, excursions, books/materials *Nonrefundable fee*
Housing: *Arr by pgm:* hotels
Deadline: Last wk in Feb
Other info: *US accredited sponsor:* yes *Began:* 1970 *Orient:* abroad *Activities:* excursions *Misc:* May contact former participants. *URL:* http://www.trincoll.edu/depts/rome/summer.html
Contact: Ms Sandra Andrews, Trinity Coll, 300 Summit St, Hartford CT 06106-3100 *Ph:* 860-297 2562 *E-mail:* sandra.andrews@mail.tricoll.edu

---

1135
UNIVERSITY OF KANSAS
Art and Architecture of Ancient Rome
Site: Italy: Rome
Dates: 3 wks, Jun 6-30
Subjects: Architectural history, Art history, Baroque studies, Renaissance studies
Eligibility: *Level:* fresh, sophs, jrs, srs, grads, adults, teachers, professionals
Credit: *Undergrad:* 3 *Grad:* avail *Doc:* transcript
Instruction: *In:* English *Format:* lecture, study tour *Students:* mainly US
Costs: $3,100 *incl* tuition, housing, some meals, fees, excursions
Housing: *Arr by pgm:* pensions
Deadline: Rolling admissions
Other info: *US accredited sponsor:* yes *Began:* 1996 *Activities:* excursions, field trips, cultural events *Misc:* Visits to Palestrina, Tivoli. *URL:* http://www.ukans.edu/~osa
Contact: Susan MacNally, Asst Dir, Study Abroad, Univ of Kansas, 108 Lippincott Hall, Lawrence KS 66045 *Ph:* 785-864 3742 *Fax:* 785-864 5040 *E-mail:* osa@ukans.edu ▲

1136
UNIVERSITY OF MONTANA
Group Study Abroad Intersession Program in Rome
Site: Italy: Rome
Dates: 3 wks, Jan
Subjects: Art history, Civilization/culture, Classical studies, History, Italian language (beg), Italian studies, Literature
Eligibility: Own students only. *Level:* fresh, sophs, jrs, srs
Credit: *Undergrad:* 6-9 *Grad:* none *Doc:* transcript

Instruction: *In:* English *Format:* lang study, lecture, study tour *Students:* mainly US
Costs: Contact sponsor
Housing: *Arr by pgm:* residence halls
Deadline: Oct
Other info: *US accredited sponsor:* yes *Began:* 1995 *Orient:* in US *Activities:* excursions, field trips, program travel, cultural events *Financial aid:* scholarships *URL:* http://www.umt.edu/oip
Contact: Intl Pgms, Univ of Montana, Main Hall 022, Missoula MT 59812 *Ph:* 406-243 2288 *Fax:* 406-243 6194 *E-mail:* goabroad@selway.umt.edu

---

1137
UNIVERSITY OF TEXAS AT AUSTIN
Rome Study Program
Site: Italy: Rome
Dates: 6 wks, late May-early Jul
Subjects: Civilization/culture, Italian language (int/adv), Italian studies, Theater arts
Eligibility: *Level:* sophs, jrs, srs, grads *Requires:* 1 yr coll Italian or equiv
Credit: *Undergrad:* 3-6 *Grad:* avail
Instruction: *In:* Italian *Format:* lecture *Students:* mainly US
Costs: Contact sponsor
Housing: *Arr by pgm:* homestay
Deadline: Mar 1
Other info: *US accredited sponsor:* yes *Began:* 1996 *Misc:* Excursion to Tivoli. *URL:* http://www.utexas.edu/student/abroad
Contact: Joy Williamson, Adviser, Study Abroad, Univ of Texas at Austin, Univ Station, Drawer A, Austin TX 78713-7208 *Ph:* 512-471 6490 *Fax:* 512-232 4363 *E-mail:* studyabroadinfo@mozart.io.utexas.edu

---

SAN GIOVANNI VALDARNO

1138
IL SILLABO
Italian Language and Culture School
Site: Italy: San Giovanni Valdarno
Dates: 2-20 wks, Jan 29-Dec 14
Subjects: Archaeology, Culinary arts (beg/int/adv), Drawing, Italian language, Painting
Eligibility: *Level:* grads, adults, teachers, professionals, precoll *Age:* min 14, avg 30
Credit: *Undergrad:* none *Grad:* none *Doc:* certificate
Instruction: *In:* Italian *Format:* internship, lang study *Students:* intl
Costs: EUR 263-481 per wk depending on length of stay *incl* tuition, housing, some meals, fees, books/materials, some school activities
Housing: *Arr by pgm:* apartments, homestay, hotels
Deadline: Rolling admissions
Other info: *US accredited sponsor:* no *Activities:* excursions, cultural events *Misc:* May contact former participants. *Financial aid:* scholarships *URL:* http://www.sillabo.it

---

SIENA

1139
CENTRO INTERNAZIONALE DANTE ALIGHIERI
Intensive Italian Language Courses
Site: Italy: Siena
Dates: 1 wk or longer, Jan 8-Dec 14
Subjects: Civilization/culture, Culinary arts, Homestay, Italian language (beg/int/adv), Italian studies
Eligibility: *Level:* fresh, sophs, jrs, srs, grads, adults *Age:* min 17, avg 25
Credit: *Undergrad:* none *Grad:* none *Doc:* transcript, certificate
Instruction: *In:* Italian *Format:* lang study *Students:* intl
Costs: Lit 980,000 per mo *incl* tuition
Housing: *Arr by pgm:* apartments, homestay, pensions, hotels, hostels
Deadline: 30 days before pgm
Other info: *US accredited sponsor:* no *Began:* 1979 *Orient:* abroad (1 day) *Activities:* excursions, field trips, program travel, cultural events, sports *Financial aid:* scholarships *URL:* http://www.dantealighieri.com
Contact: Mr Luca Bonomi or Ms Emma Thorley, C I Dante Alighieri, Piazza la Lizza 10, 53100 Siena, Italy *E-mail:* info@dantealighieri.com

---

1140
CET ACADEMIC PROGRAMS
History of Art Program in Siena, Italy
Site: Italy: Siena *Host inst:* Univ of Siena for Foreigners
Dates: Jun 3-Jul 22
Subjects: Art, Art history, Independent study, Italian language (beg/int/adv), Italian studies
Eligibility: *Level:* fresh, sophs, jrs, srs, grads, adults, professionals
Credit: *Undergrad:* avail *Grad:* avail *Doc:* transcript, certificate
Instruction: *In:* English, Italian *Format:* independent study, lang study, lecture, seminar, study tour *Students:* mainly US
Costs: $5,690 per sem *incl* tuition, housing, some meals, intl airfare, insurance, excursions, books/materials *Nonrefundable fee*
Housing: *Arr by pgm:* apartments with local students
Deadline: Mar 1; Apr 1 for scholarships
Other info: *US accredited sponsor:* no *Began:* 2001 *Orient:* abroad (3 days) *Misc:* May contact former participants. *Financial aid:* scholarships *URL:* http://www.cetacademicprograms.com
Contact: Katie Smithson, Pgm Development, CET Acad Pgms, 1000 16th Street, NW, Ste 350, Washington DC 20036 *Ph:* 800-225 4262; 202-530 0800 *Fax:* 202-342 0317 *E-mail:* cet@academic-travel.com

---

1141
MONTCLAIR STATE UNIVERSITY
Montclair in Siena
Site: Italy: Siena *Host inst:* Univ of Siena
Dates: 5 wks, mid-Jul-late Aug
Subjects: Art history, Broadcasting, Civilization/culture, History, Italian language (beg/int/adv), Italian studies, Literature
Eligibility: *Level:* fresh, sophs, jrs, srs, precoll *Age:* avg 20
Credit: *Undergrad:* 6-9 *Grad:* none *Doc:* transcript
Instruction: *In:* English, Italian *Format:* independent study, lang study, lecture, seminar, study tour *Students:* mainly US
Costs: About $2,500 *incl* housing, some meals, intl airfare, fees, excursions
Housing: *Arr by pgm:* residence halls, hotels
Deadline: Jun 1
Other info: *US accredited sponsor:* yes *Orient:* in US (2 days) *Misc:* May contact former participants.
Contact: Global Educ Ctr, Montclair State Univ, 22 Normal Ave, Upper Montclair NJ 07043 *Ph:* 973-655 4185 *Fax:* 973-655 7654
Or Contact: Dr Vincenzo Bollettino, Montclair State Univ, Upper Montclair NJ 07043 *Ph:* 973-655 7510

1142
NORTHWEST COUNCIL ON STUDY ABROAD (NCSA)
Fall Intensive Italian Language Session in Siena
Site: Italy: Siena *Host inst:* Univ per Stranieri di Siena
Dates: Sep 7-28
Subjects: Italian language
Eligibility: *Level:* sophs, jrs, srs *Requires:* 2.5 GPA, good acad standing
Credit: *Undergrad:* avail *Grad:* none *Doc:* transcript *Transfer credit through:* Central Washington Univ
Instruction: *In:* Italian *Format:* lang study *Students:* mainly US
Costs: $1,830 *incl* tuition, housing, some meals, insurance *Nonrefundable fee*
Housing: *Arr by pgm:* apartments
Deadline: 65 days before pgm
Other info: *US accredited sponsor:* yes *Began:* 1988 *In coop with:* Univ per

Stranieri di Siena *Orient:* abroad *Misc:* May contact former participants. *URL:* http://www.aha-intl.org
Contact: *See Index II for Members* Gail Lavin, Assoc Dir, AHA Intl, 741 SW Lincoln St, Portland OR 97201-3178 *Ph:* 800-654 2051; 503-295 7730 *Fax:* 503-295 5969 *E-mail:* mail@aha-intl.org

1143
UNIVERSITA PER STRANIERI DI SIENA
Italian Language Courses in Siena
Site: Italy: Siena
Dates: 3-4 wks, Jan, Mar, Jun-Jul, Aug, Sep
Subjects: Homestay, Italian language (beg/int/adv), Italian studies
Eligibility: *Level:* fresh, sophs, jrs, srs, grads, adults, teachers, professionals *Age:* min 16
Credit: *Undergrad:* none *Grad:* none *Doc:* transcript, certificate
Instruction: *In:* Italian *Format:* lab, lang study, lecture *Students:* intl
Costs: About $520 per course *incl* tuition, fees
Housing: *Sponsor assists:* apartments with local students, residence halls, homestay
Deadline: 20 days before pgm
Other info: *US accredited sponsor:* no *Began:* 1917 *Activities:* excursions, field trips *Financial aid:* scholarships *URL:* http://www.unistrasi.it
Contact: Secretariat, Univ per Stranieri di Siena, via Pantaneto 45, 53100 Siena, Italy *E-mail:* info@unistrasi.it

1144
UNIVERSITY OF DELAWARE
Winter Session in Siena
Site: Italy: Siena *Host inst:* Univ per Stranieri di Siena
Dates: 1 mo, Jan
Subjects: Civilization/culture, Italian language (beg/int)
Eligibility: *Level:* fresh, sophs, jrs, srs, adults *Requires:* 2.0 GPA
Credit: *Undergrad:* 6-7 *Grad:* none *Doc:* transcript
Instruction: *In:* English, Italian *Format:* lecture, study tour *Students:* mainly US
Costs: Contact sponsor
Housing: *Arr by pgm:* hotels
Deadline: Early Oct
Other info: *US accredited sponsor:* yes *Began:* 1990 *Orient:* avail yes *Activities:* excursions, field trips, program travel, cultural events *Misc:* Contact sponsor to arrange honors credit. *Financial aid:* scholarships *URL:* http://www.udel.edu/studyabroad/
Contact: Lisa Chieffo, Study Abroad Coord, Foreign Langs & Literatures, Univ of Delaware, 326 Smith Hall, Newark DE 19716 *Ph:* 302-831 6458 *Fax:* 302-831 0597 *E-mail:* lchieffo@udel.edu
Or Contact: Intl Pgms & Special Sessions, Univ of Delaware, 4 Kent Way, Newark DE 19716 *Ph:* 888-831 4685; 302-831 2585 *Fax:* 302-831 6042 *E-mail:* studyabroad@udel.edu

TODI

1145
PENNSYLVANIA STATE UNIVERSITY
Summer Abroad Italian Language, Art History and Visual Arts
Site: Italy: Todi *Host inst:* The Lang Ctr
Dates: 7 wks, May-Jul
Subjects: Architectural history, Art history, Drawing, Homestay, Independent study, Italian language (beg/int), Italian studies
Eligibility: *Level:* fresh, sophs, jrs, srs *Requires:* 2.5 GPA *Age:* min 18, avg 20
Credit: *Undergrad:* 9-10 *Grad:* none *Doc:* transcript
Instruction: *In:* Italian *Format:* independent study, lang study, lecture, study tour *Students:* mainly US
Costs: About $5,200 for PA residents, $8,000 for others *incl* tuition, housing, some meals, excursions *Nonrefundable fee*
Housing: *Arr by pgm:* homestay, hotels
Deadline: Apr 1
Other info: *US accredited sponsor:* yes *Orient:* in US & abroad (1 day) *Activities:* field trips, program travel *Misc:* May contact former participants. *URL:* http://www.outreach.psu.edu/PSSEA/
Contact: Summer Abroad, Pennsylvania State Univ, 225 Penn State Conference Ctr, University Park PA 16802 *Ph:* 814-863 5170 *Fax:* 814-863 5190 *E-mail:* SummerAbroad@outreach.psu.edu

TURIN

1146
UNIVERSITY STUDIES ABROAD CONSORTIUM
International Business, Italian Studies and Architecture
Site: Italy: Turin *Host inst:* Univ of Turin
Dates: Two 4-wk sessions, Jun 4-Jul 7 and/or Jul 3-Aug 4
Subjects: Business administration, Civilization/culture, Economics, Finance, Homestay, Italian language (beg/int/adv), Italian studies, Marketing
Eligibility: *Level:* fresh, jrs, srs, grads *Requires:* 2.5 GPA *Age:* min 18, avg 21
Credit: *Undergrad:* 4 per session *Grad:* 4 per session *Doc:* transcript
Instruction: *In:* English, Italian *Format:* lecture, seminar *Students:* US & intl
Costs: $1,980 for 1 session, $3,680 for 2 sessions *incl* tuition, housing, insurance, fees, excursions
Housing: *Arr by pgm:* apartments, homestay
Deadline: Apr 15
Other info: *US accredited sponsor:* yes *Began:* 1993 *Orient:* abroad *Activities:* excursions, field trips *Misc:* Pgm organized flights. Florence tour. May contact former participants. *URL:* http://www.usac.unr.edu
Contact: *See Index II for Members* Carmelo Urza, Univ Studies Abroad Consortium, Univ of Nevada Library 323, Reno NV 89557-0093 *Ph:* 775-784 6569 *Fax:* 775-784 6010 *E-mail:* usac@unr.edu ▲

URBINO

1147
SUNY COLLEGE AT NEW PALTZ
Dance in Italy
Site: Italy: Urbino *Host inst:* Univ di Urbino
Dates: 3 wks, Jun-Jul
Subjects: Modern dance
Eligibility: *Level:* fresh, sophs, jrs, srs *Requires:* prior dance experience
Credit: *Undergrad:* 3 *Grad:* none *Doc:* transcript
Instruction: *In:* English *Format:* practical training *Students:* US & host country
Costs: $2,386 for NY resident undergrads *incl* tuition, housing, some meals, insurance, excursions
Housing: *Arr by pgm:* residence halls
Deadline: Mar 1 or until pgm filled
Other info: *US accredited sponsor:* yes *Began:* 1989 *Activities:* field trips, program travel, cultural events *Misc:* Intensive dance workshop. Loans avail. *Financial aid:* scholarships *URL:* http://www.newpaltz.edu/oie/
Contact: Ctr for Intl Pgms, SUNY New Paltz, 75 S Manheim Blvd, Ste 9, New Paltz NY 12561 *Ph:* 845-257 3125 *Fax:* 845-257 3129 *E-mail:* international@newpaltz.edu ▲

1148
SUNY COLLEGE AT NEW PALTZ
Summer Study in Italy
Site: Italy: Urbino *Host inst:* Univ di Urbino
Dates: 4 wks, early Jul-early Aug
Subjects: Area studies, Italian language (beg/int/adv)

Eligibility: *Level:* fresh, sophs, jrs, srs *Requires:* 1 sem coll Italian
Credit: *Undergrad:* 6 *Grad:* none *Doc:* transcript
Instruction: *In:* Italian *Format:* lang study, lecture *Students:* US & host country
Costs: $3,832 for NY resident undergrads *incl* tuition, housing, some meals, insurance, excursions
Housing: *Arr by pgm:* residence halls
Deadline: Mar 1 or until pgm filled
Other info: *US accredited sponsor:* yes *Activities:* field trips, program travel, cultural events *Misc:* Loans avail. *Financial aid:* scholarships *URL:* http://www.newpaltz.edu/oie/
Contact: Ctr for Intl Pgms, SUNY New Paltz, 75 S Manheim Blvd, Ste 9, New Paltz NY 12561 *Ph:* 845-257 3125 *Fax:* 845-257 3129 *E-mail:* international@newpaltz.edu ▲

VENICE

1149
DUKE UNIVERSITY
Duke in Venice
Site: Italy: Venice *Host inst:* Venice Intl Univ
Dates: 6 wks, mid-May-early Jul
Subjects: Art history, Classical studies, History, Literature
Eligibility: *Level:* sophs, jrs, srs *Requires:* good acad standing, transcript
Credit: *Undergrad:* 2 credits *Grad:* none
Instruction: *In:* English *Format:* lecture, seminar, study tour *Students:* mainly US
Costs: $5,375 *incl* tuition, housing, all meals, excursions
Housing: *Arr by pgm:* residence halls
Deadline: Feb 16
Other info: *US accredited sponsor:* yes *Began:* 1998 *Activities:* excursions, cultural events *Misc:* May contact former participants. *URL:* http://www.aas.duke.edu/study_abroad/
Contact: Study Abroad, Duke Univ, 121 Allen Bldg, Box 90057, Durham NC 27708-0057 *Ph:* 919-684 2174 *Fax:* 919-684 3083 *E-mail:* abroad@asdean.duke.edu

1150
LEXIA INTERNATIONAL
LEXIA Summer in Venice
Site: Italy: Venice *Host inst:* Univ of Venice, Venice Inst
Dates: 8 wks, mid-Jun-mid-Aug
Subjects: Anthropology, Arts, Civilization/culture, Community service projects, Ecology/environmental studies, Economics, European studies, Fine arts, History, Homestay, Internships, Italian language (beg/int/adv), Literature, Political science/politics, Sociology
Eligibility: *Level:* fresh, sophs, jrs, srs, grads, adults *Requires:* 2.5 GPA *Age:* min 18, avg 21
Credit: *Undergrad:* 8-10 *Grad:* 8-10 *Doc:* transcript *Transfer credit through:* Western Washington Univ
Instruction: *In:* English, Italian *Format:* internship, lang study, lecture, seminar, volunteer/svc *Students:* mainly US

Costs: $4,950 *incl* tuition, housing, insurance, fees, excursions, ISIC, computer access *Nonrefundable fee*
Housing: *Arr by pgm:* apartments, homestay
Deadline: Apr 15; Apr 1 for scholarships
Other info: *US accredited sponsor:* no *Began:* 1991 *In coop with:* Western Washington Univ *Orient:* abroad *Activities:* excursions, field trips, program travel, cultural events, sports *Misc:* Student support svcs. May contact former participants. *Financial aid:* scholarships, work study *URL:* http://www.lexiaintl.org
Contact: LEXIA Intl, 25 S Main St, Hanover NH 03755 *Ph:* 800-775 3942; 603-643 9898 *Fax:* 603-643 9899 *E-mail:* info@lexiaintl.org
Or Contact: LEXIA Intl, West Coast, 378 Cambridge Ave, Palo Alto CA 94306-1544 *Ph:* 650-327 9191 *Fax:* 650-327 9192

1151
NEW YORK UNIVERSITY, SCHOOL OF EDUCATION
Studio Art
Site: Italy: Venice *Host inst:* Inst Univ d'Architettura di Venezia
Dates: 8 wks, Jul 2-Aug 24
Subjects: Studio arts
Eligibility: *Level:* grads *Requires:* 3.0 GPA
Credit: *Undergrad:* none *Grad:* avail *Doc:* transcript
Instruction: *In:* English *Format:* lecture, seminar *Students:* mainly US
Costs: $9,700 *incl* tuition, housing, excursions *Nonrefundable fee*
Housing: *Arr by pgm:* apartments
Deadline: Apr 1
Other info: *US accredited sponsor:* yes *Began:* 1974 *Orient:* in US & abroad (1 day) *Activities:* field trips, cultural events *Misc:* May contact former participants. *URL:* http://www.nyu.edu/summer
Contact: Dr Angiola Churchill, New York Univ, 34 Stuyvesant St, 6th Fl, New York NY 10003-7599 *Ph:* 212-998 5754 *Fax:* 212-995 4320
Or Contact: Helen J Kelly, Dir of Special Pgms, New York Univ, 82 Washington Sq E, Rm 62, New York NY 10003-6680 *Ph:* 212-998 5090 *Fax:* 212-995 4923 ▲

1152
SCHOOL OF THE MUSEUM OF FINE ARTS, BOSTON
Venice through Painting, Drawing and Collage
Site: Italy: Venice *Host inst:* Scuola Intl di Grafica
Dates: Jun 2-Jun 23
Subjects: Studio arts
Eligibility: *Level:* fresh, sophs, jrs, srs, grads, adults, teachers, professionals *Age:* min 18
Credit: *Undergrad:* avail *Grad:* none *Doc:* transcript
Instruction: *In:* English *Format:* art studio *Students:* mainly US
Costs: $2,485 *incl* tuition, housing, some meals, fees, excursions, host facilities *Nonrefundable fee*
Housing: *Arr by pgm:* apartments
Deadline: Until pgm filled
Other info: *US accredited sponsor:* yes *Began:* 1997 *Activities:* excursions, cultural events *URL:* http://www.smfa.edu
Contact: Nathaniel Bradley, SMFA Continuing Educ, 230 The Fenway, Boston MA 02115 *Ph:* 617-267 1219 *Fax:* 617-369 3679 *E-mail:* coned@smfa.edu

---

1153
UNIVERSITY OF IOWA
Printmaking and Drawing in Venice
Site: Italy: Venice *Host inst:* Scuola Intl di Grafica
Dates: 4 wks, early Jul-early Aug
Subjects: Drawing, Printmaking
Eligibility: *Level:* sophs, jrs, srs, grads, adults, teachers, professionals *Requires:* previous study in field *Age:* avg 25
Credit: *Undergrad:* 6 *Grad:* 6 *Doc:* transcript
Instruction: *In:* English *Format:* art studio *Students:* mainly US
Costs: About $3,100 *incl* tuition, housing, some meals, fees, excursions, cultural activities
Housing: *Arr by pgm:* apartments
Deadline: Mar 15
Other info: *US accredited sponsor:* yes *Began:* 1995 *Activities:* excursions, cultural events *Misc:* Museum visits, expositions, festivals & opera. *URL:* http://www.uiowa.edu/~uiabroad
Contact: Study Abroad, Univ of Iowa, 28 Intl Ctr, Iowa City IA 52242 *Ph:* 319-335 0353 *Fax:* 319-353 2021 *E-mail:* study-abroad@uiowa.edu

---

VERONA

1154
NORTHWESTERN UNIVERSITY
Northwestern University in Verona
Site: Italy: Verona *Host inst:* Univ of Verona
Dates: Jun 15-Jul 29
Subjects: Civilization/culture, Film studies, Italian language (int), Italian studies, Media studies, Opera
Eligibility: *Level:* fresh, sophs, jrs, srs *Requires:* 3.0 GPA
Credit: *Undergrad:* 3 per course *Grad:* none *Doc:* transcript
Instruction: *In:* English, Italian *Format:* lecture, study tour *Students:* mainly US
Costs: $6,875 for 2 courses *incl* tuition, housing, some meals, intl airfare, fees, excursions
Housing: *Arr by pgm*
Deadline: Mar 31
Other info: *US accredited sponsor:* yes *Began:* 1996 *Orient:* in US (1 day) *Activities:* excursions *Misc:* Students must take 2 courses. May contact former participants. *URL:* http://www.northwestern.edu/summersa
Contact: Christina Kyres, Asst Dir, Sch of Continuing Studies, Northwestern Univ, 339 E Chicago Ave, Chicago IL 60611-3008 *Ph:* 312-503 3021 *Fax:* 312-503 3003 *E-mail:* summersa@northwestern.edu

---

VIAREGGIO

1155
BOROUGH OF MANHATTAN COMMUNITY COLLEGE (CUNY)
Field Experience in Italy
Site: Italy: Viareggio (Tuscany) *Host inst:* Coll C Colombo, Univ of Pisa
Dates: 4 wks, late Jul-Aug
Subjects: Civilization/culture, Field study, Italian language (beg/int/adv)
Eligibility: *Level:* fresh, sophs, jrs, srs *Requires:* 2.5 GPA, some knowledge of Italian recommended *Age:* min 18
Credit: *Undergrad:* 3 social sci credits *Grad:* none *Doc:* certificate, diploma
Instruction: *In:* English *Format:* directed field study, lang study, lecture *Students:* mainly US
Costs: About $2,600 *incl* tuition, housing, most meals, intl airfare, fees, excursions *Nonrefundable fee*
Housing: *Arr by pgm:* residence halls
Deadline: Mar 15
Other info: *US accredited sponsor:* yes *Orient:* in US & abroad (1 wk) *Activities:* excursions, cultural events, sports *Misc:* Scholarships for BMCC students only, beach access. *Financial aid:* scholarships
Contact: Prof Michael Giammarella, Coord, Italy Study Abroad Pgm, Borough of Manhattan CC, 199 Chambers St, New York NY 10007 *Ph:* 212-346 8138 *Fax:* 212-346 4755 *E-mail:* mgiammarella@bmcc.cuny.edu

---

1156
CENTRO CULTURALE GIACOMO PUCCINI
Italian Language Courses at the Seaside
Site: Italy: Viareggio
Dates: 2-16 wks, Apr 2-Oct 19
Subjects: Italian language (beg/int/adv)
Eligibility: *Level:* adults *Age:* min 16, avg 26
Credit: *Undergrad:* avail *Grad:* none *Doc:*

certificate *Transfer credit through:* SUNY College at New Paltz
Instruction: *In:* Italian *Format:* lang study *Students:* intl
Costs: Lit 460,000 per wk *incl* tuition, housing, fees *Nonrefundable fee*
Housing: *Arr by pgm:* apartments with local students, pensions, hotels
Deadline: 1 mo before pgm; 2 mos before pgm for scholarships
Other info: *US accredited sponsor:* no *Began:* 1999 *In coop with:* AIL, ASILS, ELITE *Orient:* abroad (1 day) *Activities:* excursions, field trips, cultural events, sports *Misc:* May contact former participants. *Financial aid:* scholarships *URL:* http://www.centropuccini.it
Contact: Mr Giovanni Poggi, Dir, Ctr Culturale Giacomo Puccini, Via Ugo Foscolo 36, Viareggio, Italy 55049 *E-mail:* info@centropuccini.it
Or Contact: Mr Guido Poggi, Marketing Asst, Scuola Leonardo da Vinci, Via Brunelleschi 4, Florence, Italy 50123 *E-mail:* g.poggi@agora.stm.it

---

VICENZA

1157
LEHIGH UNIVERSITY
Lehigh in Italy
Site: Italy: Vicenza *Host inst:* Terrafirma Cultural Inst
Dates: 5 wks, late May-late Jun
Subjects: Architecture
Eligibility: *Level:* sophs, jrs, srs *Requires:* 2.0 GPA, previous study in field, previous study in architecture
Credit: *Undergrad:* 6 *Grad:* none *Doc:* transcript
Instruction: *In:* English *Format:* study tour *Students:* mainly US
Costs: $4,080 *incl* tuition, housing, some meals, excursions
Housing: *Arr by pgm:* residence halls with local students
Deadline: Mar 1
Other info: *US accredited sponsor:* yes *Began:* 1995 *Orient:* in US *Activities:* excursions, field trips, cultural events *Misc:* Pgm offered in alternate yrs. May contact former participants. *URL:* http://www.Lehigh.edu/~incis/incis.html
Contact: Dr Sandi Smith, Dir, Study Abroad, Lehigh Abroad, 5 E Packer Ave, Whitaker Lab 343, Lehigh Univ, Bethlehem PA 18015 *Ph:* 610-758 3351 *Fax:* 610-758 5156 *E-mail:* cms2@lehigh.edu

Luxembourg

MORE THAN ONE CITY

1158
LANGUAGE LIAISON
German and French Language
Site: Luxembourg: various sites
Dates: 2 wks or longer, yr-round
Subjects: Business language, French language (beg/int/adv), German language (beg/int/adv), Homestay
Eligibility: *Level:* fresh, sophs, jrs, srs, grads, adults, teachers, professionals, precoll
Credit: *Undergrad:* avail *Grad:* avail *Doc:* transcript, certificate
Instruction: *In:* French, German *Format:* lang study *Students:* intl
Costs: Contact sponsor
Housing: *Arr by pgm:* apartments with local students, residence halls with local students, homestay, pensions, hotels, hostels
Deadline: 30 days before pgm
Other info: *US accredited sponsor:* no *Misc:* Scholarship research svc. *URL:* http://www.languageliaison.com
Contact: Nancy Forman, Dir, Lang Liaison, 4 Burnham Pkwy, Morristown NJ 07960 *Ph:* 800-284 4448 *Fax:* 973-898 1710 *E-mail:* learn@languageliaison.com

Malta

MARSAXLOKK

1159
JAMES MADISON UNIVERSITY
Summer in Malta
Site: Malta: Marsaxlokk *Host inst:* Inst for Energy Technology, Univ of Malta
Dates: 4 wks, mid-May-mid-Jun
Subjects: Energy sciences, Technology
Eligibility: *Level:* jrs, srs *Requires:* 2.8 GPA, previous study in field *Age:* min 18
Credit: *Undergrad:* 3 *Grad:* none *Doc:* transcript
Instruction: *In:* English *Format:* directed field study *Students:* mainly US
Costs: $2,300 for VA residents, $2,900 for others *incl* tuition, housing, some meals, fees, excursions, books/materials
Housing: *Arr by pgm:* residence halls
Deadline: Nov 15
Other info: *US accredited sponsor:* yes *Began:* 1998 *Orient:* in US (3 days) *Activities:* excursions, field trips *Misc:* May contact former participants. *URL:* http://www.jmu.edu/international/
Contact: Dr Jonathan Miles, James Madison Univ, Harrisonburg VA 22807 *Ph:* 540-568 3044 *Fax:* 540-568 8080 *E-mail:* milesjj@jmu.edu
Or Contact: Intl Pgms, James Madison Univ, Harrisonburg VA 22807 *Ph:* 540-568 6419 *Fax:* 540-568 8080 *E-mail:* international@jmu.edu

---

1160
UNIVERSITY OF MALTA
Summer School in Archaeology
Site: Malta: Marsaxlokk (Tas-silg)
Dates: 2-6 wks, Jun 18-Jul 27
Subjects: Archaeology, Mediterranean studies
Eligibility: *Level:* adults *Age:* min 18
Credit: *Undergrad:* 2-3 *Grad:* none *Doc:* certificate
Instruction: *In:* English *Format:* directed field study, lecture, volunteer/svc *Students:* intl
Costs: $2,100 for 6 wks *incl* tuition, housing, some meals, excursions, airport transfer, transport
Housing: *Arr by pgm:* hotels
Deadline: May 18
Other info: *US accredited sponsor:* no *Began:* 1996 *Activities:* excursions, field trips *URL:* http://www.um.edu.mt
Contact: Daphne P De Guara, or Rachelle Mifsud, Intl Off,Univ of Malta, St Paul St, Valletta VLT 07, Malta *E-mail:* summerabroad@um.edu.mt ▲

MSIDA

1161
GEORGE MASON UNIVERSITY
Contemporary Societies and Politics in the Mediterranean
Site: Malta: Msida *Host inst:* Univ of Malta
Dates: 4 wks, Jul-Aug
Subjects: Anthropology, Economics, History, International business, Political science/politics, Sociology
Eligibility: *Level:* fresh, sophs, jrs, srs, grads *Requires:* 2.25 GPA *Age:* min 18
Credit: *Undergrad:* avail *Grad:* avail *Doc:* transcript
Instruction: *In:* English *Format:* directed field study, lecture, seminar *Students:* intl & host country
Costs: About $2,400 for VA residents, $3,000 for others *incl* tuition, housing, some meals, insurance, fees, excursions, ISIC *Nonrefundable fee*
Housing: *Arr by pgm:* residence halls with local students
Deadline: Apr 12
Other info: *US accredited sponsor:* yes *Began:* 1994 *Orient:* in US *Activities:* excursions *Misc:* Min 10 students for pgm. May contact former participants. *URL:* http://www.gmu.edu/departments/cge

Contact: Ctr for Global Educ, George Mason Univ, Johnson Ctr, Rm 235, 4400 University Dr, Fairfax VA 22030-4444 *Ph:* 703-993 2154 *Fax:* 703-993 2153 *E-mail:* cge@gmu.edu

---

1162
UNIVERSITY OF MALTA
Cell Culture Techniques and Cytotoxity Testing
Site: Malta: Msida *Host inst:*
Dates: 3 wks, Jul-Aug
Subjects: Anatomy, Biology, Molecular biology
Eligibility: *Level:* fresh, sophs, jrs, srs, grads *Requires:* previous study in field *Age:* min 18
Credit: *Undergrad:* none *Grad:* none *Doc:* certificate
Instruction: *In:* English *Format:* lab, lecture *Students:* intl
Costs: About $735 *incl* tuition, housing, excursions, airport transfer
Housing: *Arr by pgm:* apartments
Deadline: Jun 15
Other info: *US accredited sponsor:* no *Began:* 2000 *Activities:* excursions *URL:* http://www.um.edu.mt
Contact: Daphne P DeGuara, or Rachelle Mifsud, Intl Off, Univ of Malta, St Paul St, Valletta VLT 07, Malta *E-mail:* summerabroad@um.edu.mt ▲

1163
UNIVERSITY OF MALTA
Introduction to Mediterranean Studies
Site: Malta: Msida
Dates: 3 wks, late May-early Jun
Subjects: Mediterranean studies
Eligibility: *Level:* adults *Age:* min 18
Credit: *Undergrad:* none *Grad:* none *Doc:* certificate
Instruction: *In:* English *Format:* lecture, study tour *Students:* intl
Costs: Contact Sponsor
Housing: *Arr by pgm:* hotels
Deadline: May 11
Other info: *US accredited sponsor:* no *Began:* 2000 *Activities:* excursions *URL:* http://www.um.edu.mt
Contact: Daphne P DeGuara, or Rachelle Mifsud, Intl Off, Univ of Malta, St Paul St, Valletta VLT 07, Malta *E-mail:* summerabroad@um.edu.mt ▲

1164
UNIVERSITY OF MALTA
Summer School on Heat Treatment and Surface Engineering
Site: Malta: Msida
Dates: 3 wks, Jun-Jul
Subjects: Engineering
Eligibility: *Level:* fresh, sophs, jrs, srs *Requires:* previous study in field, engineering major *Age:* min 18
Credit: *Undergrad:* 3 *Grad:* none *Doc:* transcript, certificate
Instruction: *In:* English *Format:* lecture *Students:* intl
Costs: About $1,230 *incl* tuition, housing, some meals, excursions, airport transfer, transport
Housing: *Arr by pgm:* residence halls, hotels
Deadline: May 11
Other info: *US accredited sponsor:* no *Began:* 2000 *Activities:* excursions *URL:* http://www.um.edu.mt
Contact: Daphne P DeGuara, or Rachelle Mifsud, Intl Off, Univ of Malta, St Paul St, Valletta VLT 07, Malta *E-mail:* summerabroad@um.edu.mt ▲

VALLETTA

1165
UNIVERSITY OF MALTA
Mediterranean Environment: An Overview
Site: Malta: Valletta
Dates: 1 wk, early Jun
Subjects: Ecology/environmental studies, Mediterranean studies
Eligibility: *Level:* adults *Age:* min 18
Credit: *Undergrad:* none *Grad:* none *Doc:* certificate
Instruction: *In:* English *Format:* lecture, seminar *Students:* intl
Costs: $500 *incl* tuition, housing, some meals, excursions, airport transfer, transport
Housing: *Arr by pgm:* residence halls, hotels
Deadline: May 31
Other info: *US accredited sponsor:* no *In coop with:* Intl Environment Inst *Activities:* excursions, field trips *URL:* http://www.um.edu.mt
Contact: Daphne P DeGuara, or Rachelle Mifsud, Intl Off, Univ of Malta, St Paul St, Valletta VLT 07, Malta *E-mail:* summerabroad@um.edu.mt ▲

1166
UNIVERSITY OF MALTA
Training Seminar on the Mediterranean Environment
Site: Malta: Valletta
Dates: 3 wks, Jun
Subjects: Ecology/environmental studies, Mediterranean studies, Natural sciences
Eligibility: *Level:* adults *Age:* min 18
Credit: *Undergrad:* 3 *Grad:* none *Doc:* transcript, certificate
Instruction: *In:* English *Format:* directed field study, independent study, lecture, seminar *Students:* intl
Costs: $1,400 *incl* tuition, housing, some meals, fees, excursions, airport transfer, transport
Housing: *Arr by pgm:* hotels
Deadline: May 18
Other info: *US accredited sponsor:* no *Began:* 2000 *Activities:* excursions, field trips *URL:* http://www.um.edu.mt
Contact: Daphne P DeGuara, or Rachelle Mifsud, Intl Off, Univ of Malta, St Paul St, Valletta VLT 07, Malta *E-mail:* summerabroad@um.edu.mt ▲

Monaco

MONTE CARLO

1167
NATIONAL REGISTRATION CENTER FOR STUDY ABROAD (NRCSA)
Study in Monaco
Site: Monaco: Monte Carlo *Host inst:* Regency Sch of French
Dates: 1 wk or longer, yr-round
Subjects: French language, Homestay
Eligibility: *Level:* fresh, sophs, jrs, srs, grads, adults, teachers, professionals
Credit: *Undergrad:* none *Grad:* none *Doc:* certificate
Instruction: *In:* French *Format:* lang study, lecture, seminar *Students:* intl
Costs: $742 per wk *incl* tuition, housing, some meals, insurance, local transport *Nonrefundable fee*
Housing: *Arr by pgm:* homestay, hotels
Deadline: None
Other info: *US accredited sponsor:* no *URL:* http://www.nrcsa.com
Contact: Reuel Zielke, NRCSA, 823 N 2nd St, #206, Milwaukee WI 53203 *Ph:* 414-278 0631 *Fax:* 414-871 8884 *E-mail:* info@nrcsa.com

Netherlands

MORE THAN ONE CITY

1168
PENNSYLVANIA STATE UNIVERSITY
European Criminal Justice: The Dutch Model
Site: Netherlands: Leiden, others *Host inst:* Univ of Leiden
Dates: 5 wks, Jun-Jul
Subjects: Criminal justice, Field study, Independent study
Eligibility: CIC students only *Level:* fresh, sophs, jrs, srs, grads *Requires:* 2.5 GPA
Credit: *Undergrad:* 9 *Grad:* none
Instruction: *In:* English *Format:* independent study, lecture, study tour *Students:* mainly US
Costs: Contact Sponsor

See "How To Use This Book" for definitions of terms used above. ▲ = See program sponsor's ad(s) in this book.

Housing: *Arr by pgm:* residence halls
Deadline: Rolling admissions
Other info: *US accredited sponsor:* yes *Began:* 2000 *Orient:* in US & abroad *Activities:* excursions, field trips *Misc:* May contact former participants. *Financial aid:* scholarships
Contact: Summer Abroad, Pennsylvania State Univ, 225 Penn State Conference Ctr, University Park PA 16802 *Ph:* 814-863 5170
Or Contact: Intl Pgm Adviser, Pennsylvania State Univ, 222 Boucke Bldg, University Park PA 16802 *Ph:* 814-865 7681 *Fax:* 814-865 3336

AMSTERDAM

1169
IBFD INTERNATIONAL TAX ACADEMY
Principles of International and Comparative Taxation
Site: Netherlands: Amsterdam
Dates: 2 wks Aug 21-Sep 1
Subjects: International business, Taxation
Eligibility: *Level:* jrs, srs, grads, professionals *Age:* min 20
Credit: *Undergrad:* none *Grad:* none *Doc:* certificate
Instruction: *In:* English *Format:* workshop *Students:* intl
Costs: Dfl 5,900 *incl* tuition, some meals, fees, books/materials *Nonrefundable fee*
Housing: *Sponsor assists:* pensions, hotels, hostels
Deadline: Aug 7
Other info: *US accredited sponsor:* no *Began:* 1992 *Orient:* abroad *URL:* http://www.ibfd.nl
Contact: IBFD, PO Box 20237, 1000 HE Amsterdam, Netherlands *E-mail:* ita@ibfd.nl
Or Contact: G Goede, IBFD, PO Box 20237, 1000 HE Amsterdam, Netherlands *E-mail:* gg@ibfd.nl

---

1170
IBFD INTERNATIONAL TAX ACADEMY
Spring Course: International Taxation and Tax Planning Issues
Site: Netherlands: Amsterdam
Dates: 5 days, May 7-11
Subjects: International business, Taxation
Eligibility: *Level:* srs, grads, professionals *Requires:* previous study in field *Age:* min 20
Credit: *Undergrad:* none *Grad:* none *Doc:* certificate
Instruction: *In:* English *Format:* tutorial, workshop *Students:* intl
Costs: Dfl 4,950 *incl* tuition, some meals, fees, books/materials
Housing: *Sponsor assists:* pensions, hotels, hostels
Deadline: Apr 25
Other info: *US accredited sponsor:* no *Began:* 1999 *Orient:* abroad *URL:* http://www.ibfd.nl
Contact: IBFD Intl Tax Acad, Sarphatistraat 500, PO Box 20237, 1000 HE Amsterdam, Netherlands *E-mail:* ita@ibfd.nl

---

1171
IBFD INTERNATIONAL TAX ACADEMY
Winter Course: Selected Issues in International Taxation
Site: Netherlands: Amsterdam
Dates: 5 days, Feb 5-9
Subjects: International business, Taxation
Eligibility: *Level:* jrs, srs, grads, professionals *Requires:* previous study in field *Age:* min 20
Credit: *Undergrad:* none *Grad:* none *Doc:* certificate
Instruction: *In:* English *Format:* tutorial, workshop *Students:* intl
Costs: Dfl 4,750 *incl* tuition, some meals, fees, books/materials
Housing: *Sponsor assists:* pensions, hotels, hostels
Deadline: Jan 24
Other info: *US accredited sponsor:* no *Began:* 1993 *Orient:* abroad *URL:* http://www.ibfd.nl
Contact: IBFD Intl Tax Acad, Sarphatistraat 500, PO Box 20237, 1000 HE Amsterdam, Netherlands *E-mail:* ita@ibfd.nl

---

1172
ITW-INTERNATIONAL TRAINING CENTER FOR WOMEN
Gender MBA/Professional Management Training
Site: Netherlands: Amsterdam
Dates: Contact sponsor
Subjects: Business/management, Gender studies
Eligibility: *Level:* srs, grads, adults, professionals *Age:* min 20, max 60
Credit: *Undergrad:* none *Grad:* none
Instruction: *In:* English *Format:* practical training, seminar, study tour, tutorial, workshop *Students:* intl
Costs: $2,500 per sem *incl* tuition *Nonrefundable fee*
Housing: *Arr by pgm:* apartments
Deadline: Jan 9
Other info: *US accredited sponsor:* no
Contact: Dir, Intl Studies, Intl Training Ctr for Women, Herengracht 213, PO Box 3611, Amsterdam, 1001 AK Netherlands *E-mail:* itw@euronet.nl

---

1173
LANGUAGE LIAISON
Dutch Saturation
Site: Netherlands: Amsterdam region *Host inst:* Live in Learn
Dates: 1 wk or longer, yr-round
Subjects: Civilization/culture, Dutch language (beg/int/adv), Homestay
Eligibility: *Level:* adults, precoll *Age:* min 10
Credit: *Undergrad:* none *Grad:* none *Doc:* certificate
Instruction: *In:* Dutch *Format:* lang study, tutorial *Students:* intl
Costs: Contact sponsor
Housing: *Arr by pgm:* teacher's home
Deadline: 45 days before pgm
Other info: *US accredited sponsor:* no *Misc:* Scholarship research svc. *URL:* http://www.languageliaison.com
Contact: Nancy Forman, Dir, Lang Liaison, 4 Burham Pkwy, Morristown NJ 07960 *Ph:* 800-284 4448 *Fax:* 973-898 1710 *E-mail:* learn@languageliaison.com

---

1174
LINGUA SERVICE WORLDWIDE
Intensive Language and Culture in Holland
Site: Netherlands: Amsterdam *Host inst:* Home Lang Intl
Dates: 1 wk-1 yr, yr-round
Subjects: Civilization/culture, Dutch language (beg/int/adv), Homestay
Eligibility: *Level:* adults
Credit: *Undergrad:* avail *Grad:* avail *Doc:* transcript, certificate
Instruction: *In:* Dutch *Format:* lang study, lecture *Students:* intl
Costs: Contact sponsor
Housing: *Arr by pgm:* homestay
Deadline: 45 days before pgm
Other info: *US accredited sponsor:* no *Activities:* excursions, field trips *Misc:* May contact former participants. *URL:* http://www.linguaserviceworldwide.com
Contact: Dir, Lingua Svc Worldwide, 75 Prospect St, Ste 4, Huntington NY 11743 *Ph:* 800-394 5327; 631-424 0777 *Fax:* 631-271 3441 *E-mail:* itctravel@worldnet.att.net ▲

1175
NATIONAL REGISTRATION CENTER FOR STUDY ABROAD (NRCSA)
Dutch in Amsterdam
Site: Netherlands: Amsterdam *Host inst:* Home Lang Schs Intl
Dates: 1 wk or longer, yr-round
Subjects: Dutch language, Homestay
Eligibility: *Level:* fresh, sophs, jrs, srs, grads, adults, teachers, professionals
Credit: *Undergrad:* none *Grad:* none *Doc:* certificate
Instruction: *In:* Dutch *Format:* lang study *Students:* intl
Costs: $1,135 per wk *incl* tuition, housing, all meals, insurance *Nonrefundable fee*
Housing: *Arr by pgm:* homestay
Deadline: 6 wks before pgm
Other info: *US accredited sponsor:* no *Misc:* Student lives in teacher's home. *URL:* http://www.nrcsa.com
Contact: Reuel Zielke, NRCSA, 823 N 2nd St, #206, Milwaukee WI 53203 *Ph:* 414-278 0631 *Fax:* 414-871 8884 *E-mail:* info@nrcsa.com

---

1176
NEW YORK UNIVERSITY, SCHOOL OF EDUCATION
Communication Studies
Site: Netherlands: Amsterdam *Host inst:* Univ of Amsterdam
Dates: May 25-Jun 27
Subjects: Communications
Eligibility: *Level:* srs *Requires:* 3.00 GPA, previous study in field
Credit: *Undergrad:* 6 *Grad:* none *Doc:* transcript
Instruction: *In:* English *Format:* directed field study, lecture, seminar *Students:* mainly US
Costs: $4,000 *incl* tuition, housing, some meals, insurance, excursions, books/materials *Nonrefundable fee*
Housing: *Arr by pgm:* residence halls with local students, residence halls
Deadline: Apr 1
Other info: *US accredited sponsor:* yes *Began:* 1999 *Orient:* abroad *Activities:* excursions *Misc:* May contact former participants. *URL:* http://www.nyu.edu/summer
Contact: Ted Magder, Dir, Communication Studies, New York Univ, 239 Greene St, Ste 737, New York NY 10003 *Ph:* 212-998 5015
Or Contact: Helen J Kelly, Dir, Special Pgms, New York Univ, 82 Washington Square E, Rm 62, New York NY 10003 *Ph:* 212-998 5090 *Fax:* 212-995 4923 ▲

1177
NEW YORK UNIVERSITY, TISCH SCHOOL OF THE ARTS
International Theater Workshop in Amsterdam
Site: Netherlands: Amsterdam *Host inst:* Amsterdam Theater Sch
Dates: 6-7 wks, Jun 24-Aug 12
Subjects: Acting, Dance, Drama/theater, Performing arts, Playwriting, Singing/voice
Eligibility: *Level:* sophs, jrs, srs, grads, adults *Requires:* previous study in field, audition or interview, prior acting training and/or experience, instructor's permission *Age:* min 18
Credit: *Undergrad:* 8 *Grad:* none *Doc:* transcript
Instruction: *In:* English *Format:* practical training, seminar, tutorial, workshop *Students:* mainly US
Costs: $6,990 *incl* tuition, housing, fees, excursions *Nonrefundable fee*
Housing: *Arr by pgm:* apartments
Deadline: Feb 15
Other info: *US accredited sponsor:* yes

Began: 1992 *Orient:* avail avail *Activities:* excursions, cultural events *Misc:* Scholarships & loans for own students only. *URL:* http://www.nyu.edu/tisch/international/
Contact: Nanc Allen, Dir, Intl Theater Workshop, Drama, Tisch Sch of the Arts, New York Univ, 721 Broadway, Rm 211, New York NY 10003 *Ph:* 212-998 1865 *Fax:* 212-995 4572 *E-mail:* nanc.allen@nyu.edu
Or Contact: Linda Kow, Assoc Dir, Tisch Intl Pgms, New York Univ, 721 Broadway, 12th Fl, New York NY 10003 *Ph:* 212-998 9175 *Fax:* 212-995 4578 *E-mail:* tisch.international@nyu.edu

---

1178
ROYAL TROPICAL INSTITUTE (KIT)
Training Workshop on Gender, Citizenship and Good Governance
Site: Netherlands: Amsterdam
Dates: 3 wks, Sep
Subjects: Gender studies, Government
Eligibility: *Level:* grads, adults, professionals *Requires:* 1 yr professional experience in gender & development issues
Credit: *Undergrad:* none *Grad:* none *Doc:* certificate
Instruction: *In:* English *Format:* lecture, seminar, workshop *Students:* intl
Costs: About Dfl 7,000 *incl* tuition, excursions, books/materials
Housing: *Sponsor assists:* hotels
Deadline: Jul
Other info: *US accredited sponsor:* no *Began:* 1998 *Activities:* excursions *Financial aid:* scholarships *URL:* http://www.kit.nl
Contact: Ms M Mukhopadyay or Ms Marguerite Appel, Royal Tropical Inst, PO Box 95001, 1090 HA Amsterdam, Netherlands *E-mail:* cmo@kit.nl

---

BARNEVELD

1179
IPC LIVESTOCK BARNEVELD COLLEGE
Professional Training Programs
Site: Netherlands: Barneveld
Dates: 2 wks, May-Jun
Subjects: Agricultural economics, Animal production, Animal sciences, Farm management, Food production, Veterinary science, Zoology
Eligibility: *Level:* grads, adults, teachers, professionals *Requires:* previous study in field *Age:* min 18
Credit: *Undergrad:* avail *Grad:* avail *Doc:* certificate
Instruction: *In:* English *Format:* lecture, practical training, study tour, workshop *Students:* intl
Costs: Contact sponsor
Housing: *Sponsor assists:* residence halls, hostels
Deadline: 1 mo before pgm
Other info: *US accredited sponsor:* no *Began:* 1990 *Misc:* May contact former participants. *URL:* http://www.ipc-training.nl
Contact: Head, Intl Training & Projects, IPC Barneveld, PO Box 64, 3772 AB Barneveld, Netherlands *E-mail:* barneveld@ipc-training.nl

---

LEIDEN

1180
LEIDEN UNIVERSITY
Undergraduate Summer Research Exchange Program in Chemistry
Site: Netherlands: Leiden
Dates: Jun 1-Aug 16
Subjects: Biochemistry, Chemistry
Eligibility: *Level:* jrs, srs *Requires:* 3.0 GPA, chemistry major *Age:* avg 20
Credit: *Undergrad:* avail *Grad:* none *Doc:* certificate
Instruction: *In:* English *Format:* lab, practical training, tutorial *Students:* mainly host country
Costs: Scholarship paid by sponsor *incl* tuition, housing, all meals, intl airfare, fees, excursions
Housing: *Arr by pgm:* residence halls with local students
Deadline: Mar 1
Other info: *US accredited sponsor:* no *Began:* 1985 *Activities:* excursions *Misc:* Exch pgm with 7 US univs in which host inst pays scholarship.
Contact: Mrs drs A A van Kalleveen, Gorlaeus Lab, Leiden Univ, Leiden, Netherlands, PO Box 9502 2300 RA *E-mail:* kalleveen@fwnbur.leidenuniv.nl
Or Contact: Prof A van der Gen, Gorlaeus Lab, Leiden Univ, PO Box 9502, Leiden, Netherlands 2300 RA *E-mail:* a.gen@chem.leidenuniv.nl

---

1181
PENNSYLVANIA STATE UNIVERSITY
Summer Abroad European Criminal Justice: The Dutch Model
Site: Netherlands: Leiden *Host inst:* Univ of Leiden
Dates: 1 mo, Jul-Aug
Subjects: Criminal justice, European studies, Field study, Independent study, Internships
Eligibility: *Level:* fresh, sophs, jrs, srs *Requires:* 2.5 GPA, previous study in field, reference letter, transcript, goal statement *Age:* min 18, avg 20
Credit: *Undergrad:* 6-9 *Grad:* none *Doc:* transcript
Instruction: *In:* English *Format:* independent study, internship, lecture, seminar *Students:* mainly US
Costs: About $4,043 for PA residents, $5,069 for others *incl* tuition, housing, some meals, books/materials *Nonrefundable fee*
Housing: *Arr by pgm:* residence halls, apartments
Deadline: Apr 1
Other info: *US accredited sponsor:* yes *Orient:* avail (1 day) *Misc:* May contact former participants. *URL:* http://www.outreach.psu.edu/PSSEA/
Contact: Summer Abroad, Pennsylvania State Univ, 225 Penn State Conference Ctr, University Park PA 16802 *Ph:* 814-863 5170 *Fax:* 814-863 5190 *E-mail:* SummerAbroad@outreach.psu.edu

---

1182
SUNY COLLEGE AT BROCKPORT
Netherlands Social Policy
Site: Netherlands: Leiden
Dates: 2 wks, Jun
Subjects: Criminal justice, Health administration/planning, Public administration, Social work, Women's studies
Eligibility: *Level:* jrs, srs, grads *Requires:* 2.5 GPA, previous study in field *Age:* min 18
Credit: *Undergrad:* 6 *Grad:* none *Doc:* transcript
Instruction: *In:* English *Format:* lecture, seminar, study tour *Students:* mainly US
Costs: $2,250 *incl* housing, all meals, fees, excursions *Nonrefundable fee*
Housing: *Arr by pgm:* hotels
Deadline: Apr 1
Other info: *US accredited sponsor:* yes *Began:* 1999 *Activities:* excursions, field trips, program travel *Misc:* Faculty dir. May contact former participants. *URL:* http://www.brockport.edu/study_abroad
Contact: Dr John Perry, Dir, Intl Educ, SUNY Coll at Brockport, 350 New Campus Dr, Brockport NY 14420-2914 *Ph:* 800-298 7869; 716-395 2119 *Fax:* 716-637 3218 *E-mail:* overseas@brockport.edu

---

1183
WEBSTER UNIVERSITY
Degree Programs
Site: Netherlands: Leiden *Host inst:* Webster Univ Leiden campus
Dates: 2 or 8 wks, summer
Subjects: Business administration, Communications, Computer sciences, International relations, Psychology
Eligibility: *Level:* sophs, jrs, srs, grads, adults *Requires:* 2.5 GPA, GMAT for MBA
Credit: *Undergrad:* avail *Grad:* avail *Doc:* degree

Instruction: *In:* English *Format:* lecture, seminar *Students:* intl
Costs: $1,149 per 3-credit course *incl* tuition
Housing: *Arr by pgm:* residence halls
Deadline: Feb 15
Other info: *US accredited sponsor:* yes *Began:* 1983 *Orient:* in US & abroad *Misc:* BA, MA & MBA avail. May contact former participants. *Financial aid:* scholarships *URL:* http://www.websteruniv.edu
Contact: Teresa Bruno, Study Abroad, Webster Univ, 470 E Lockwood, St Louis MO 63119 *Ph:* 800-984 6857; 314-968 6988 *Fax:* 314-968 7119 *E-mail:* worldview@webster.edu

---

1184
WEBSTER UNIVERSITY
Graduate Program in Leiden
Site: Netherlands: Leiden *Host inst:* Webster Univ Leiden campus
Dates: 2 wks & 8 wks, summer
Subjects: Business administration, Business/management, Finance, International business, International relations
Eligibility: *Level:* grads *Requires:* 2.5 GPA, bachelor's degree
Credit: *Undergrad:* none *Grad:* 3-6 *Doc:* transcript, diploma
Instruction: *In:* English *Format:* lecture, seminar *Students:* intl
Costs: $1,149 per 3-credit course *incl* tuition
Housing: *Sponsor assists:* residence halls
Deadline: 6 mos before pgm
Other info: *US accredited sponsor:* yes *Began:* 1983 *Orient:* in US & abroad *Financial aid:* scholarships *URL:* http://www.websteruniv.edu
Contact: Study Abroad Ctr, Webster Univ, 470 E Lockwood, St Louis MO 63119 *Ph:* 800-984 6857; 314-968 6988 *Fax:* 314-968 7119 *E-mail:* worldview@webster.edu

---

1185
WEBSTER UNIVERSITY
Undergraduate Program in Leiden
Site: Netherlands: Leiden
Dates: 8 wks, summer
Subjects: Business/management, International business, International relations, Marketing, Psychology
Eligibility: *Level:* sophs, jrs, srs *Requires:* 2.5 GPA
Credit: *Undergrad:* 3-9 *Grad:* none *Doc:* transcript, diploma
Instruction: *In:* English *Format:* lecture, seminar *Students:* intl
Costs: $1,149 per 3-credit course *incl* tuition
Housing: *Sponsor assists:* residence halls
Deadline: 6 mos before pgm
Other info: *US accredited sponsor:* yes *Began:* 1983 *Orient:* in US & abroad *Misc:* May contact former participants. *Financial aid:* scholarships *URL:* http://www.websteruniv.edu
Contact: Study Abroad Ctr, Webster Univ, 470 E Lockwood, St Louis MO 63119 *Ph:* 800-984 6857; 314-968 6988 *Fax:* 314-968 7119 *E-mail:* worldview@webster.edu

---

MAASTRICHT

1186
INDIANA UNIVERSITY
Summer Study in Maastricht
Site: Netherlands: Maastricht *Host inst:* Ctr for European Studies
Dates: About Jul 1-Aug 15
Subjects: Economics, European Union, Intercultural studies
Eligibility: Own students only. *Level:* jrs, srs *Requires:* 3.0 GPA, bus major, completion of integrative core in bus sch
Credit: *Undergrad:* 6 *Grad:* none *Doc:* transcript
Instruction: *In:* English *Format:* lecture *Students:* mainly US
Costs: $3,500 or $4,500 *incl* tuition, housing, all meals, fees, excursions, books/materials
Housing: *Arr by pgm:* residence halls
Deadline: Mid-Feb
Other info: *US accredited sponsor:* yes *Began:* 1992 *Orient:* in US *Activities:* excursions *Misc:* May contact former participants. *Financial aid:* scholarships *URL:* http://www.indiana.edu/~overseas
Contact: Overseas Study, Indiana Univ, Franklin Hall 303, Bloomington IN 47405 *Ph:* 812-855 9304 *Fax:* 812-855 6452 *E-mail:* overseas@indiana.edu

---

1187
PENNSYLVANIA STATE UNIVERSITY
European Integration
Site: Netherlands: Maastricht
Dates: 6 wks, Jun-Jul
Subjects: Political science/politics
Eligibility: *Level:* fresh, sophs, jrs, srs *Requires:* 2.5 GPA, previous study in field
Credit: *Undergrad:* 7 *Grad:* none
Instruction: *In:* English *Format:* lecture, study tour *Students:* mainly US
Costs: Contact Sponsor
Housing: *Arr by pgm*
Deadline: Rolling admissions
Other info: *US accredited sponsor:* no *Orient:* in US & abroad *Activities:* excursions, field trips *Misc:* May contact former participants. *Financial aid:* scholarships
Contact: Summer Abroad, Pennsylvania State Univ, 225 Penn State Conference Ctr, University Park PA 16802 *Ph:* 814-863 5170
Or Contact: Intl Pgm Adviser, Pennsylvania State Univ, 222 Boucke Bldg, University Park PA 16802 *Ph:* 814-865 7681 *Fax:* 814-865 3336

1188
PENNSYLVANIA STATE UNIVERSITY
Maastricht
Site: Netherlands: Maastricht *Host inst:* Univ of Maastricht
Dates: 5 wks, Jun
Subjects: Economics, European studies, European Union, Political science/politics
Eligibility: *Level:* sophs, jrs, srs *Requires:* 2.5 GPA *Age:* min 18
Credit: *Undergrad:* 7 *Grad:* none *Doc:* transcript
Instruction: *In:* English *Format:* directed field study, independent study, lecture, study tour *Students:* mainly US
Costs: $3,440 for PA residents, $5,512 for others *incl* tuition, housing, excursions *Nonrefundable fee*
Housing: *Arr by pgm:* residence halls
Deadline: Apr 1
Other info: *US accredited sponsor:* yes *Began:* 2000 *In coop with:* PSU/Maastricht Univ *Orient:* in US & abroad (2 days) *Activities:* field trips, program travel *Misc:* May contact former participants. *Financial aid:* scholarships *URL:* http://www.outreach.psu.edu/PSSEA/
Contact: Judith Meder. Conference Planner, Pennsylvania State Univ, 225 Penn State Conference Ctr, University Park PA 16802 *Ph:* 814-863 5170 *Fax:* 814-863 5190 *E-mail:* summerabroad@outreach.psu.edu

---

1189
UNIVERSITY OF NORTH CAROLINA AT CHARLOTTE
European Approach: Adolescent Sexual Behavior/Responsibility
Site: Netherlands: Maastricht *Host inst:* Univ of Maastricht
Dates: 3 wks, late Jul-mid-Aug
Subjects: Field study, Health/health education
Eligibility: *Level:* grads, adults, teachers, professionals *Requires:* previous study in field
Credit: *Undergrad:* none *Grad:* avail *Doc:* transcript
Instruction: *In:* English *Format:* directed field study, lecture, seminar, study tour, workshop *Students:* mainly US
Costs: $3,300 *incl* tuition, housing, some meals, intl airfare, insurance, fees, excursions *Nonrefundable fee*
Housing: *Arr by pgm:* hotels, hostels
Deadline: Feb 15
Other info: *US accredited sponsor:* yes *Began:* 1998 *In coop with:* Advocates for Youth, Washington DC *Orient:* in US (1

day) *Activities:* excursions, field trips, program travel, cultural events *Misc:* Students will be matched up with professionals. May contact former participants. *URL:* http://www.uncc.edu/oip/edabroad.htm
Contact: Joel A Gallegos, Dir, Educ Abroad, UNC Charlotte, 9201 University City Blvd, Charlotte NC 28223-0001 *Ph:* 704-687 2464 *Fax:* 704-687 3168 *E-mail:* stennies@email.uncc.edu

---

1190
UNIVERSITY OF NORTH CAROLINA AT CHARLOTTE
Summer Institute: Health Care Systems in the Netherlands
Site: Netherlands: Maastricht
Dates: 2 wks, May 16-30
Subjects: Health administration/planning, Health/health education, Nursing
Eligibility: *Level:* sophs, jrs, srs, grads, professionals *Requires:* 3.0 GPA, previous study in field *Age:* min 21
Credit: *Undergrad:* 3 *Grad:* 3 *Doc:* transcript
Instruction: *In:* English *Format:* lecture, seminar, study tour *Students:* mainly US
Costs: $3,000 *incl* tuition, housing, some meals, intl airfare, insurance, fees, excursions *Nonrefundable fee*
Housing: *Arr by pgm:* pensions, hotels
Deadline: Feb 15
Other info: *US accredited sponsor:* yes *Began:* 1999 *In coop with:* European Orient Ctr *Orient:* abroad *Activities:* excursions, field trips, cultural events *Misc:* May contact former participants. *URL:* http://www.uncc.edu/oip/edabroad.htm
Contact: Joel A Gallegos, Educ Abroad, UNC Charlotte, 9201 University Blvd, Charlotte NC 28223-0001 *Ph:* 704-687 2464 *Fax:* 704-687 3168 *E-mail:* stennies@email.uncc.edu

---

ROTTERDAM

1191
ERASMUS UNIVERSITY ROTTERDAM
Erasmus Summer Program
Site: Netherlands: Rotterdam
Dates: 3 wks, Aug 13-31
Subjects: Epidemiology, Genetics, Health sciences, Public health
Eligibility: *Level:* professionals *Requires:* previous study in field
Credit: *Undergrad:* none *Grad:* none *Doc:* certificate
Instruction: *In:* English *Format:* lecture, practical training, workshop *Students:* intl
Costs: Dfl 3,950 *incl* tuition, some meals, books/materials *Nonrefundable fee*
Housing: *Arr by pgm:* residence halls, hotels
Deadline: Jun 1
Other info: *US accredited sponsor:* no *Began:* 1990 *In coop with:* NIHES *Activities:* excursions *Financial aid:* scholarships *URL:* http://www.eur.nl/fgg/emco/esp
Contact: M L Bot, EMCO, PO Box 1738, 3000 DR, Rotterdam, Netherlands *E-mail:* info@emco.fgg.eur.nl

---

1192
FAIRFIELD UNIVERSITY
Summer in Rotterdam
Site: Netherlands: Rotterdam *Host inst:* Intl Sch of Econ Rotterdam (ISER)
Dates: 1 mo, about May 21-Jun 17
Subjects: International business
Eligibility: *Level:* sophs, jrs, srs *Requires:* previous study in field, intro bus courses *Age:* min 18, avg 20
Credit: *Undergrad:* 6 *Grad:* none *Doc:* transcript
Instruction: *In:* English *Format:* lecture, seminar *Students:* mainly US
Costs: $3,710 *incl* tuition, housing, some meals, intl airfare, excursions
Housing: *Arr by pgm:* hostels
Deadline: Mar 1
Other info: *US accredited sponsor:* yes *Began:* 2000 *Orient:* abroad (1 day) *Activities:* field trips, program travel *Misc:* May contact former participants. *URL:* http://www.fairfield.edu/sce/studyabroad
Contact: Christine Bowers, Study Abroad Coord, Fairfield Univ, Dolan House, Fairfield CT 06430 *Ph:* 888-254 1566; 203-254 4220 *Fax:* 203-254 4106 *E-mail:* cbbowers@mail.fairfield.edu

---

VENLO

1193
LANGUAGES ABROAD
Language and Culture-Venlo
Site: Netherlands: Venlo
Dates: 2 wks or longer, yr-round
Subjects: Civilization/culture, Dutch language (beg/int/adv), Dutch studies, Homestay
Eligibility: *Level:* adults *Age:* min 17, max 65, avg 25
Credit: *Undergrad:* none *Grad:* none *Doc:* certificate
Instruction: *In:* Dutch *Format:* lang study *Students:* intl
Costs: $2,000 for 4 wks *incl* tuition, housing, some meals, fees, books/materials
Housing: *Arr by pgm:* residence halls, homestay
Deadline: None
Other info: *US accredited sponsor:* no *Began:* 1995 *Activities:* excursions, field trips, program travel, cultural events, sports *Misc:* May contact former participants. *URL:* http://www.languagesabroad.com
Contact: Ms Jesse Philippe, Langs Abroad, 317 Adelaide St W, Ste 900, Toronto, Ontario M5V 1P9, Canada *Ph:* 800-219 9924; 416-925 7117 *E-mail:* info@languagesabroad.com

---

WAGENINGEN

1194
INTERNATIONAL INSTITUTE ON LAND RECLAMATION AND IMPROVEMENT
Computer Applications in Irrigation (ICCAI)
Site: Netherlands: Wageningen
Dates: Mar 12-Apr 20
Subjects: Computer sciences, Environmental system analysis, Water management
Eligibility: *Level:* professionals *Requires:* BSc or equiv, practical experience with computers & irrigation *Age:* min 25, max 45
Credit: *Undergrad:* none *Grad:* none *Doc:* certificate
Instruction: *In:* English *Format:* lecture, practical training *Students:* intl
Costs: $7,000 *incl* tuition, housing, all meals, insurance, fees, excursions, books/materials *Nonrefundable fee*
Housing: *Arr by pgm:* hostels
Deadline: Jan 31
Other info: *US accredited sponsor:* no *Began:* 1997 *In coop with:* Inst Irrigation Studies, UK *Misc:* May contact former participants. *URL:* http://www.ILRI.NL/
Contact: Registrar, ILRI, PO Box 45, 6700 AA Wageningen, Netherlands *E-mail:* ilri@ilri.nl

---

1195
INTERNATIONAL INSTITUTE ON LAND RECLAMATION AND IMPROVEMENT
Drainage Execution and Maintenance (ICDEM)
Site: Netherlands: Wageningen
Dates: 5 wks, Aug 14-Sep 15
Subjects: Field study, Water management
Eligibility: *Level:* professionals *Requires:* experience in land drainage projects with installation drain pipes *Age:* min 25, max 45
Credit: *Undergrad:* none *Grad:* none *Doc:* certificate
Instruction: *In:* English *Format:* directed field study, lecture, practical training *Students:* intl
Costs: $6,500 *incl* tuition, housing, all

meals, insurance, fees, excursions, books/ materials
Housing: *Arr by pgm:* hotels
Deadline: May 15
Other info: *US accredited sponsor:* no *Began:* 1997 *URL:* http://www.ILRI.NL/
Contact: Registrar, ILRI, PO Box 45, 6700 AA Wageningen, Netherlands *E-mail:* ilri@ilri.nl

---

1196
INTERNATIONAL INSTITUTE ON LAND RECLAMATION AND IMPROVEMENT
Institutions for Water Management
Site: Netherlands: Wageningen
Dates: Contact Sponsor
Subjects: Field study, Water management
Eligibility: *Level:* professionals
Credit: *Undergrad:* none *Grad:* none *Doc:* certificate
Instruction: *In:* English *Format:* directed field study, workshop *Students:* intl
Costs: $5,000 *incl* tuition, housing, all meals, fees, books/materials
Housing: *Arr by pgm:* hotels
Deadline: Feb 15
Other info: *US accredited sponsor:* no *URL:* http://www.ILRI.NL/
Contact: ILRI, PO Box 45, 6700 AA Wageningen, Netherlands *E-mail:* ilri@ilri.agro.nl

---

1197
INTERNATIONAL INSTITUTE ON LAND RECLAMATION AND IMPROVEMENT
Microcomputer Applications in Land Drainage (ICMALD)
Site: Netherlands: Wageningen
Dates: 2 wks, Apr 9-20
Subjects: Computer sciences, Environmental system analysis, Water management
Eligibility: *Level:* professionals *Requires:* working experience in land drainage, BSc or equiv experience with computer pgms *Age:* min 30, max 45
Credit: *Undergrad:* none *Grad:* none *Doc:* certificate
Instruction: *In:* English *Format:* lecture, practical training *Students:* intl
Costs: $4,500 *incl* tuition, housing, all meals, insurance, fees, excursions, books/ materials *Nonrefundable fee*
Housing: *Arr by pgm:* hostels
Deadline: Feb 1
Other info: *US accredited sponsor:* no *Began:* 1997 *In coop with:* Wageningen Agricultural Univ *Misc:* May contact former participants. *URL:* http://www.ILRI.NL/
Contact: Registrar, ILRI, PO Box 45, 6700 AA Wageningen, Netherlands *E-mail:* ilri@ilri.nl

Norway

MORE THAN ONE CITY

1198
SCANDINAVIAN SEMINAR
Ambassadors for the Environment
Site: Norway: Bergen, Oslo, Tordal
Dates: Jul 8-26
Subjects: Agriculture, Area studies, Civilization/culture, Ecology/environmental studies, Field study, International studies, Marine sciences, Mountaineering, Natural sciences, Norwegian studies, Rural studies, Scandinavian studies, Sustainable development
Eligibility: *Level:* fresh, sophs, jrs, srs, teachers, precoll *Age:* min 15
Credit: *Undergrad:* avail *Grad:* none *Doc:* certificate
Instruction: *In:* English *Format:* directed field study, independent study, lecture, practical training, study tour *Students:* US & intl
Costs: $1,600-$2,600 *incl* tuition, housing, all meals, intl airfare, excursions *Nonrefundable fee*
Housing: *Arr by pgm:* residence halls, hostels, platform tents
Deadline: Mar 1
Other info: *US accredited sponsor:* no *Began:* 1999 *Activities:* excursions, field trips, program travel, cultural events, sports *Financial aid:* scholarships *URL:* http://www.scandinavianseminar.com
Contact: Leslie Evans, Scandinavian Seminar, 24 Dickinson St, Amherst MA 01002 *Ph:* 800-316 9833; 413-253 9736 *Fax:* 413-253 5282 *E-mail:* study@scandinavianseminar.com

---

MOSS

1199
UNIVERSITY OF NORTH DAKOTA
UND-American College of Norway Exchange
Site: Norway: Moss
Dates: 4 wks, May-Jun
Subjects: Norwegian language, Peace studies
Eligibility: *Level:* fresh, sophs, jrs, srs, grads, adults, teachers, professionals, precoll *Requires:* 2.7 GPA *Age:* min 18, avg 22
Credit: *Undergrad:* avail *Grad:* none *Doc:* transcript
Instruction: *In:* English, Norwegian *Format:* lang study *Students:* mainly US
Costs: $1,800 *incl* tuition, housing, some meals, fees, excursions *Nonrefundable fee*
Housing: *Arr by pgm:* residence halls
Deadline: Apr 1
Other info: *US accredited sponsor:* yes *Began:* 1994 *Orient:* in US & abroad (1 day) *Activities:* excursions, field trips, cultural events *Misc:* May contact former participants. *Financial aid:* scholarships *URL:* http://www.und.edu/dept/oip
Contact: Barry L Stinson, Dir, Univ of North Dakota, Intl Pgms, 2908 University Ave, Grand Forks ND 58203 *Ph:* 800-225 5863 ext 3301; 701-777 3301 *Fax:* 701-777 4773 *E-mail:* barry_stinson@mail.und.nodak.edu
Or Contact: Marilyn L Wilkens, Admin Asst, Univ of North Dakota, Intl Pgms, 2908 Univ Ave, Grand Forks ND 58203 *Ph:* 800-225 5863 ext 6438; 701-777 6438 *Fax:* 701-777 4773 *E-mail:* marilyn_wilkens@mail.und.nodak.edu

---

OSLO

1200
NATIONAL REGISTRATION CENTER FOR STUDY ABROAD (NRCSA)
Language Study in Oslo
Site: Norway: Oslo *Host inst:* Home Lang Schs Intl
Dates: 1 wk or longer, yr-round
Subjects: Homestay, Norwegian language
Eligibility: *Level:* fresh, sophs, jrs, srs, grads, adults, teachers, professionals
Credit: *Undergrad:* none *Grad:* none *Doc:* certificate
Instruction: *In:* Norwegian *Format:* lang study, tutorial *Students:* intl
Costs: $1,135 per wk *incl* tuition, housing, all meals, insurance *Nonrefundable fee*
Housing: *Arr by pgm:* homestay
Deadline: 6 wks before pgm
Other info: *US accredited sponsor:* no *Misc:* Student lives in teacher's home. *URL:* http://www.nrcsa.com
Contact: Reuel Zielke, NRCSA, 823 N 2nd St, #206, Milwaukee WI 53203 *Ph:* 414-278 0631 *Fax:* 414-871 8884 *E-mail:* info@nrcsa.com

---

1201
UNIVERSITY OF OSLO
International Summer School
Site: Norway: Oslo
Dates: 6 wks, late Jun-Aug
Subjects: Art history, Civilization/culture, Economics, Folklore, History, International relations, Literature, Norwegian language, Political science/politics, Public administration, Social sciences
Eligibility: *Level:* sophs, jrs, srs
Credit: *Undergrad:* 6 *Grad:* avail *Doc:* transcript
Instruction: *In:* English *Format:* lang study, lecture *Students:* intl
Costs: $2,395-$3,050 *incl* tuition, housing, all meals, insurance, fees, excursions
Housing: *Arr by pgm:* residence halls

Deadline: Feb 1
Other info: *US accredited sponsor:* no *Began:* 1947 *Activities:* excursions *Misc:* Listed as an approved foreign study pgm at the Univ of Washington in Seattle. Optional pgm travel. *Financial aid:* scholarships *URL:* http://www.uio.no/iss/iss.html
Contact: Torild Homstad, N Amer Admissions, Oslo Summer Sch, St Olaf Coll, 1520 St Olaf Ave, Northfield MN 55057-1098 *Ph:* 800-639 0058; 507-646 3269 *Fax:* 507-646 3732 *E-mail:* iss@stolaf.edu
Or Contact: Intl Summer Sch, Univ of Oslo, PO Box 3, Blindern, 0313 Oslo, Norway *E-mail:* iss@admin.uio.no

SKOGN

1202
SONS OF NORWAY
Camp Norway
Site: Norway: Skogn near Trondhelm
Dates: 1 mo, Jul
Subjects: Civilization/culture, Norwegian language (beg/int)
Eligibility: *Level:* fresh, sophs, jrs, srs, grads, adults, precoll *Requires:* 3.0 GPA *Age:* min 16
Credit: *Undergrad:* avail *Grad:* none *Transfer credit through:* Augsburg Coll, Ctr for Global Educ
Instruction: *In:* English, Norwegian *Format:* lang study, lecture *Students:* mainly US
Costs: About $2,600 *incl* tuition, housing, all meals, excursions
Housing: *Arr by pgm:* residence halls
Deadline: About Mar 1 for scholarships
Other info: *US accredited sponsor:* no *Orient:* abroad *Activities:* excursions, field trips, program travel, cultural events *Misc:* May contact former participants. *Financial aid:* scholarships *URL:* http://www.sofn.com
Contact: Liv Dahl, Heritage Pgms, Sons of Norway, 1455 W Lake St, Minneapolis MN 55408 *Ph:* 612-827 3611

STAVANGER

1203
MICHIGAN STATE UNIVERSITY
Service Management
Site: Norway: Stavanger
Dates: 4 wks, Jul-Aug
Subjects: Field study, Hospitality management, Hotel management, Independent study, Restaurant management
Eligibility: *Level:* sophs, jrs, srs, grads *Requires:* 2.0 GPA, good acad standing, interview *Age:* min 18
Credit: *Undergrad:* avail *Grad:* none *Doc:* transcript
Instruction: *In:* English *Format:* directed field study, independent study, practical training, seminar *Students:* mainly US
Costs: About $2,300 *incl* housing, some meals, insurance, excursions, support svcs *Nonrefundable fee*
Housing: *Arr by pgm:* residence halls
Deadline: Mar 2
Other info: *US accredited sponsor:* yes *Began:* 1997 *Orient:* in US & abroad *Activities:* excursions, field trips *Misc:* Loans avail. *Financial aid:* scholarships *URL:* http://studyabroad.msu.edu
Contact: Cheryl Benner, Study Abroad, Michigan State Univ, 109 Intl Ctr, East Lansing MI 48824 *Ph:* 517-353 8920 *Fax:* 517-432 2082 *E-mail:* bennerc@msu.edu ▲

Portugal

MORE THAN ONE CITY

1204
COLLEGE CONSORTIUM FOR INTERNATIONAL STUDIES and CAPE COD COMMUNITY COLLEGE
Summer Study in Portugal
Site: Portugal: Faro, Lisbon, Porto *Host inst:* CIAL Ctr de Linguas
Dates: 4-wk sessions, summer
Subjects: Homestay, Portuguese language (beg/int/adv), Portuguese studies
Eligibility: *Level:* fresh, sophs, jrs, srs, grads, adults, teachers, professionals *Requires:* 2.0 GPA *Age:* min 18
Credit: *Undergrad:* 3 *Grad:* none *Doc:* transcript
Instruction: *In:* English, Portuguese *Format:* lang study, lecture *Students:* intl
Costs: $1,710 *incl* tuition, housing, some meals, fees, excursions, books/materials
Housing: *Arr by pgm:* apartments, homestay, pensions, hotels
Deadline: 1 mo before pgm
Other info: *US accredited sponsor:* yes *Began:* 1987 *Orient:* abroad (intensive lang study) *Activities:* excursions, field trips *Misc:* May contact former participants. *URL:* http://www.ccisabroad.org
Contact: *See Index II for Members* CCIS, 2000 P St NW, Ste 503, Washington DC 20036 *Ph:* 800-453 6956; 202-223 0330 *Fax:* 202-223 0999 *E-mail:* info@ccisabroad.org
Or Contact: Gretchen Farnham, Cape Cod CC, 2240 Iyanough Rd, West Barnstable MA 02668 *Ph:* 508-375 4016 *Fax:* 508-375 4085 *E-mail:* gfarnham@capecod.mass.edu ▲

1205
EDUVACATIONS
Learn Portuguese in Portugal
Site: Portugal: Faro, Lisbon, Portimao
Dates: 1 wk or longer, yr-round
Subjects: Ceramics/pottery, Culinary arts, Dance, Portuguese language (beg/int/adv), Sports, Tennis
Eligibility: *Level:* adults *Age:* min 16
Credit: *Undergrad:* none *Grad:* none
Instruction: *In:* Portuguese *Format:* lang study, lecture *Students:* intl
Costs: Contact sponsor
Housing: *Arr by pgm:* apartments, homestay, hotels, guest houses
Deadline: Contact sponsor
Other info: *US accredited sponsor:* no *Activities:* excursions, field trips, cultural events, sports *Misc:* Max 6 students per class. May contact former participants. *URL:* http://www.eduvacations.com
Contact: Mary Ann Puglisi, eduVacations, 1431 21st St NW, Ste 302, Washington DC 20036 *Ph:* 202-857 8384 *Fax:* 202-463 8091

1206
LANGUAGE STUDIES ABROAD, INC
Intensive Portuguese-Portugal
Site: Portugal: Faro, Lisbon, Porto *Host inst:* CIAL Ctr de Linguas
Dates: 1 wk or longer, yr-round
Subjects: Homestay, Portuguese language (beg/int/adv)
Eligibility: *Level:* fresh, sophs, jrs, srs, grads, adults, teachers, professionals, precoll
Credit: *Undergrad:* avail *Grad:* avail
Instruction: *In:* Portuguese *Format:* lang study *Students:* intl
Costs: $1,320 for 4 wks *incl* tuition, housing, some meals *Nonrefundable fee*
Housing: *Sponsor assists:* homestay, hotels
Deadline: 4 wks before pgm
Other info: *US accredited sponsor:* no *Began:* 1959 *Orient:* abroad *Activities:* excursions, field trips, cultural events, sports *Misc:* May contact former participants. *URL:* http://www.languagestudiesabroad.com
Contact: Lang Studies Abroad, Inc, 103 Londonderry Ct, Reno NV 89511-2718 *Ph:* 800-424 5522; 775-849 9206 *Fax:* 775-849 9217 *E-mail:* info@languagestudiesabroad.com

1207
LANGUAGES ABROAD
Language and Cultural Immersion-Portugal
Site: Portugal: Faro, Porto
Dates: 2 wks or longer, yr-round
Subjects: Civilization/culture, Portuguese language (beg/int/adv), Portuguese studies

Eligibility: *Level:* adults *Age:* min 17, max 65, avg 25
Credit: *Undergrad:* none *Grad:* none *Doc:* certificate
Instruction: *In:* Portuguese *Format:* lang study *Students:* intl
Costs: From $1,390 for 4 wks *incl* tuition, housing, some meals, books/materials, cultural activities
Housing: *Arr by pgm:* residence halls, homestay
Deadline: None
Other info: *US accredited sponsor:* no *Began:* 1995 *Activities:* excursions, field trips, program travel, cultural events, sports *Misc:* May contact former participants. *URL:* http://www.languagesabroad.com
Contact: Ms Jesse Philippe, Langs Abroad, 317 Adelaide St W, Ste 900, Toronto, Ontario M5 V 1P9, Canada *Ph:* 800-219 9924; 416-925 7117 *E-mail:* info@languagesabroad.com

---

1208
LINGUA SERVICE WORLDWIDE
Total Immersion and Culture in Portugal/Intensive Language
Site: Portugal: Faro, Lisbon, Porto *Host inst:* CIAL Ctr de Linguas
Dates: 1 wk or longer, yr-round
Subjects: Civilization/culture, Homestay, Portuguese language (beg/int/adv), Portuguese studies
Eligibility: *Level:* fresh, sophs, jrs, srs, grads, adults, teachers, professionals, precoll *Age:* min 18
Credit: *Undergrad:* avail *Grad:* avail *Doc:* transcript, certificate *Transfer credit through:* Univ of Southern Mississippi
Instruction: *In:* Portuguese *Format:* lang study, lecture *Students:* intl
Costs: Contact sponsor
Housing: *Arr by pgm:* apartments, homestay, pensions, hotels
Deadline: 45 days before pgm
Other info: *US accredited sponsor:* no *Activities:* excursions, cultural events *Misc:* May contact former participants. *URL:* http://www.linguaserviceworldwide.com
Contact: Dir, Lingua Svc Worldwide, 75 Prospect St, Ste 4, Huntington NY 11743 *Ph:* 800-394 5327; 631-424 0777 *Fax:* 631-271 3441 *E-mail:* itctravel@worldnet.att.net ▲

1209
NATIONAL REGISTRATION CENTER FOR STUDY ABROAD (NRCSA)
Study in Portugal
Site: Portugal: Faro, Lisbon, Porto *Host inst:* CIAL Ctr de Linguas
Dates: 1 wk or longer, yr-round
Subjects: Civilization/culture, Homestay, Portuguese language (beg/int/adv), Portuguese studies
Eligibility: *Level:* fresh, sophs, jrs, srs, grads, adults *Age:* min 18
Credit: *Undergrad:* avail *Grad:* avail
Instruction: *In:* Portuguese *Format:* lang study, lecture, tutorial *Students:* intl
Costs: $970 for 2 wks, $389 for each addtl wk *incl* tuition, housing, some meals, insurance, fees
Housing: *Arr by pgm:* apartments, homestay, pensions, hotels
Deadline: 6 wks before pgm
Other info: *US accredited sponsor:* no *Misc:* Optional excursions. *URL:* http://www.nrcsa.com
Contact: June Domoe, NRCSA, 823 N 2nd St, #206, Milwaukee WI 53203 *Ph:* 414-278 0631 *Fax:* 414-271 8884 *E-mail:* info@nrcsa.com

---

LISBON

1210
LANGUAGE LIAISON
Portuguese Language-Portugal
Site: Portugal: Lisbon
Dates: 2 wks or longer, yr-round
Subjects: Civilization/culture, Homestay, Portuguese language (beg/int/adv), Portuguese studies
Eligibility: *Level:* fresh, sophs, jrs, srs, grads, adults, teachers, professionals, precoll *Age:* min 16
Credit: *Undergrad:* avail *Grad:* avail *Doc:* transcript, certificate
Instruction: *In:* Portuguese *Format:* lang study, lecture *Students:* intl
Costs: Contact sponsor
Housing: *Arr by pgm:* homestay, hotels
Deadline: 30 days before pgm
Other info: *US accredited sponsor:* no *Misc:* Scholarship research svc. *URL:* http://www.languageliaison.com
Contact: Nancy Forman, Dir, Lang Liaison, 4 Burnham Pkwy, Morristown NJ 07960 *Ph:* 800-284 4448 *Fax:* 973-898 1710 *E-mail:* learn@languageliaison.com

---

1211
LANGUAGES ABROAD
Language and Cultural Immersion Programs-Lisbon
Site: Portugal: Lisbon
Dates: 2 wks or longer, yr-round
Subjects: Civilization/culture, Portuguese language (beg/int/adv)
Eligibility: *Level:* adults *Age:* min 17, max 65, avg 25
Credit: *Undergrad:* none *Grad:* none *Doc:* certificate
Instruction: *In:* Portuguese *Format:* lang study *Students:* intl
Costs: From $2,250 for 4 wks *incl* tuition, housing, some meals, excursions, books/materials
Housing: *Arr by pgm:* apartments, homestay
Deadline: None
Other info: *US accredited sponsor:* no *Misc:* May contact former participants. *URL:* http://www.languagesabroad.com
Contact: Ms Jesse Philippe, Langs Abroad, 317 Adelaide St W, Ste 900, Toronto, Ontario M5V 1P9, Canada *Ph:* 800-219 9924; 416-925 7117 *E-mail:* info@languagesabroad.com

---

PORTO

1212
SCHOOL OF THE MUSEUM OF FINE ARTS, BOSTON
Porto, Portugal: Making Art in a European Capital of Culture
Site: Portugal: Porto
Dates: Jul 14-Aug 4
Subjects: Studio arts (beg/int/adv)
Eligibility: *Level:* fresh, sophs, jrs, srs, grads, adults, teachers, professionals *Age:* min 18
Credit: *Undergrad:* avail *Grad:* none *Doc:* transcript
Instruction: *In:* English *Format:* art studio *Students:* mainly US
Costs: $2,060 *incl* tuition, housing, some meals, fees, excursions *Nonrefundable fee*
Housing: *Arr by pgm:* pensions
Deadline: Apr 13 or until pgm filled
Other info: *US accredited sponsor:* yes *Began:* 2001 *Misc:* One hr info session at the Sch of the Museum of Fine Arts on Apr 5. *URL:* http://www.smfa.edu
Contact: Nathaniel Bradley, SMFA Continuing Educ, 230 The Fenway, Boston MA 02115 *Ph:* 617-267 1219 *Fax:* 617-369 3679 *E-mail:* nbradley@mfa.org

Spain

MORE THAN ONE CITY

1213
AMERISPAN UNLIMITED
Spanish Study and Homestay in Spain
Site: Spain: Barcelona, Granada, Madrid, Marbella, Salamanca, Seville
Dates: 1 wk-1 yr, yr-round
Subjects: Civilization/culture, Current events, Folk dance, History, Homestay, Literature, Music, Spanish language (beg/int/adv)
Eligibility: *Level:* fresh, sophs, jrs, srs, grads, adults, teachers, professionals, precoll *Age:* min 16
Credit: *Undergrad:* avail *Grad:* avail *Doc:* transcript, certificate *Transfer credit through:* Univ of Southern Mississippi

Instruction: *In:* Spanish *Format:* lang study, lecture, music lesson, study tour, tutorial, workshop *Students:* intl
Costs: $1,050-$1,295 per mo *incl* tuition, housing, some meals, insurance, books/materials *Nonrefundable fee*
Housing: *Arr by pgm:* apartments with local students, residence halls with local students, homestay, hotels
Deadline: 4 wks before pgm
Other info: *US accredited sponsor:* no *Began:* 1991 *Orient:* abroad *Activities:* excursions, field trips, cultural events, sports *Misc:* Transfer credit also avail through Seattle Central CC. May contact former participants. *URL:* http://www.amerispan.com/
Contact: Amerispan Unltd, PO Box 40007, Philadelphia PA 19106 *Ph:* 800-879 6640; 215-751 1100 *Fax:* 215-751 1986 *E-mail:* info@amerispan.com

---

1214
BOSTON UNIVERSITY
Archaeological Field School
Site: Spain: various sites
Dates: 6 wks, late May-early Jul
Subjects: Archaeology, Field study
Eligibility: *Level:* sophs, jrs, srs, grads, adults *Requires:* 3.0 GPA, in major, good acad standing
Credit: *Undergrad:* 8 *Grad:* 8 *Doc:* transcript
Instruction: *In:* English *Format:* directed field study, lecture, seminar *Students:* mainly US
Costs: $5,100 *incl* tuition
Housing: *Arr by pgm:* pensions, hotels, field station
Deadline: Mar 1; Apr 1 for scholarships
Other info: *US accredited sponsor:* yes *Began:* 1996 *Orient:* in US & abroad *Activities:* field trips *Misc:* Full-time resident dir. May contact former participants. *Financial aid:* scholarships *URL:* http://www.bu.edu/abroad/
Contact: Intl Pgms, Boston Univ, 232 Bay State Rd, Boston MA 02215 *Ph:* 617-353 9888 *Fax:* 617-353 5402 *E-mail:* abroad@bu.edu ▲

1215
CSA, CENTER FOR STUDY ABROAD
Spanish Language and Culture Studies
Site: Spain: Barcelona, El Puerto de Santa Maria, Las Palmas de Gran Canaria, Madrid, Salamanca, Seville *Host inst:* Estudio Intl Sampere, Gran Canaria Sch, Intl House, Linguaviva
Dates: 2 wks or longer, yr-round
Subjects: Civilization/culture, Homestay, Independent study, Spanish language (beg/int/adv)
Eligibility: *Level:* adults *Age:* min 17
Credit: *Undergrad:* avail *Grad:* avail *Doc:* transcript, certificate
Instruction: *In:* Spanish *Format:* independent study, lang study, lecture *Students:* intl
Costs: $1,695-$1,895 per mo depending on sch *incl* tuition, housing, all meals, insurance, fees, books/materials *Nonrefundable fee*
Housing: *Sponsor assists:* residence halls, homestay, hotels
Deadline: None
Other info: *US accredited sponsor:* no *Began:* 1956 *Orient:* abroad *Activities:* excursions, field trips, program travel,

cultural events, sports *URL:* http://www.studyabroad.com/csa
Contact: Alima Khan, Assoc Dir, CSA, Ctr for Study Abroad, 2802 E Madison St, MS #160, Seattle WA 98112 *Ph:* 206-726 1498 *Fax:* 206-583 8192 *E-mail:* virtuecsa@aol.com

---

1216
DUKE UNIVERSITY
Duke in Spain
Site: Spain: Madrid, Seville
Dates: Late May-early Jul
Subjects: Art, Civilization/culture, Literature, Political science/politics, Spanish language (int/adv)
Eligibility: *Level:* fresh, sophs, jrs, srs *Requires:* 2 yrs coll Spanish or equiv, transcript, good acad standing
Credit: *Undergrad:* 2 credits *Grad:* none *Doc:* transcript
Instruction: *In:* Spanish *Format:* lang study, lecture *Students:* mainly US
Costs: $4,425 for 2 courses *incl* tuition, housing, all meals, excursions, books/materials, cultural activities
Housing: *Arr by pgm:* homestay
Deadline: Feb 16
Other info: *US accredited sponsor:* yes *Began:* 1974 *Activities:* excursions *Misc:* 2 wks in Malaga, 4 wks in Madrid. Excursions to Barcelona, Seville, Granada, Cordoba, Toledo, Salamanca. *URL:* http://www.aas.duke.edu/study_abroad/
Contact: Prof Miguel Garci-Gomez, Romance Studies, Duke Univ, 203 Lang Bldg, Box 90257, Durham NC 27708-0257 *Ph:* 919-660 3111 *Fax:* 919-684 4029 *E-mail:* garci@acpub.duke.edu
Or Contact: Study Abroad, Duke Univ, 121 Allen Bldg, Box 90057, Durham NC 27708-0057 *Ph:* 919-684 2174 *Fax:* 919-684 3083 *E-mail:* abroad@asdean.duke.edu

---

1217
EDUVACATIONS
Spanish Language and Culture with Sports and Arts
Site: Spain: Barcelona, Granada, Madrid, Malaga, Marbella, Salamanca, Seville
Dates: 1 wk or longer, yr-round
Subjects: Business language, Civilization/culture, Culinary arts, Cycling, Equestrian arts, Folk dance, Hiking/trekking, Painting, Skiing, Spanish language (beg/int/adv), Spanish studies, Sports, Tennis, Wine
Eligibility: *Level:* adults
Credit: *Undergrad:* avail *Grad:* avail *Doc:* certificate
Instruction: *In:* Spanish *Format:* art studio, lang study, study tour, workshop *Students:* intl
Costs: Contact sponsor
Housing: *Arr by pgm:* residence halls, apartments, homestay, hotels
Deadline: Contact sponsor
Other info: *US accredited sponsor:* no *Activities:* excursions, field trips, cultural events, sports *Misc:* Custom-tailored pgms combine French lang study with sports, arts, cooking, wines & more for individual & groups. May contact former participants. *URL:* http://www.eduvacations.com
Contact: Mary Ann Puglisi, eduVacations, 1431 21st St NW, Ste 302, Washington DC 20036 *Ph:* 202-857 8384 *Fax:* 202-463 8091

1218
EDUVACATIONS
Study in and Live in Your Teacher's Home-Spain
Site: Spain: Barcelona, Seville
Dates: 1 wk or longer, yr-round
Subjects: Civilization/culture, Culinary arts, Cycling, Dance, Equestrian arts, Hiking/trekking, Homestay, Painting, Spanish language (beg/int/adv), Sports, Tennis
Eligibility: *Level:* adults
Credit: *Undergrad:* avail *Grad:* none *Doc:* certificate
Instruction: *In:* Spanish *Format:* lang study *Students:* intl
Costs: Contact sponsor
Housing: *Arr by pgm:* homestay
Deadline: Contact sponsor
Other info: *US accredited sponsor:* no *Activities:* excursions, field trips, cultural events, sports *Misc:* May contact former participants. *URL:* http://www.eduvacations.com
Contact: Mary Ann Puglisi, eduVacations, 1431 21st St NW, Ste 302, Washington DC 20036 *Ph:* 202-857 8384 *Fax:* 202-463 8091

1219
ENFOREX SPANISH LANGUAGE SCHOOL
Christmas Course (22 Lessons/Week)
Site: Spain: Barna, Madrid, Marbella
Dates: 2 wks, Christmas-time
Subjects: Spanish language (beg/int/adv)
Eligibility: *Level:* adults *Age:* min 16
Credit: *Undergrad:* avail *Grad:* avail *Doc:* certificate, diploma
Instruction: *In:* Spanish *Format:* lang study *Students:* intl
Costs: $250 *incl* tuition, housing, all meals, fees, excursions, books/materials
Housing: *Arr by pgm:* apartments with local students, residence halls with local students, homestay, hotels
Deadline: Until pgm filled; 4 mos before pgm for scholarships
Other info: *US accredited sponsor:* no *Began:* 1989 *Orient:* abroad (intensive lang study) *Activities:* excursions, field trips, program travel, cultural events, sports *Misc:* May contact former participants. *Financial aid:* scholarships *URL:* http://www.enforex.es
Contact: Antonio Anadon, ENFOREX, Alberto Aguilera 26, 28015 Madrid, Spain *E-mail:* spanish@enforex.es ▲

1220
ENFOREX SPANISH LANGUAGE SCHOOL
Intensive General Spanish-Long Duration Courses
Site: Spain: Barcelona, Madrid, Marbella, Salamanca
Dates: 12 wks or longer, yr-round
Subjects: Spanish language (beg/int/adv)
Eligibility: *Level:* adults *Age:* min 16, max 65, avg 22
Credit: *Undergrad:* avail *Grad:* avail *Doc:* certificate
Instruction: *In:* Spanish *Format:* lang study *Students:* intl
Costs: $1,200 for 12 wks, $100 for each addtl wk *incl* tuition, housing, all meals, fees, books/materials *Nonrefundable fee*
Housing: *Arr by pgm:* residence halls with local students, apartments, homestay, hotels
Deadline: 2 wks before pgm
Other info: *US accredited sponsor:* no *Began:* 1994 *Orient:* abroad *Activities:* excursions, field trips, program travel, cultural events, sports *Misc:* 22 lessons per wk, avg 5 students per class. May contact former participants. *URL:* http://www.enforex.es
Contact: Mr Antonio Anadon, Main Dir, or Mr Jose-Manuel Martin, ENFOREX-Spanish Lang Sch, Alberto Aguilera 26, 28015 Madrid, Spain *E-mail:* spanish@enforex.es ▲

1221
ENFOREX SPANISH LANGUAGE SCHOOL
Intensive Spanish
Site: Spain: Barcelona, Madrid, Marbella, Salamanca
Dates: 2 wks-8 mos, yr-round
Subjects: Civilization/culture, Spanish language
Eligibility: *Level:* adults *Age:* min 16, avg 25
Credit: *Undergrad:* avail *Grad:* avail *Doc:* certificate, diploma
Instruction: *In:* Spanish *Format:* lang study *Students:* intl
Costs: $100-$280 per wk depending on number of lessons per wk *incl* tuition, housing, all meals, fees, books/materials
Housing: *Arr by pgm:* apartments with local students, residence halls with local students, homestay, hotels

Deadline: 2 wks before pgm; 4 mos before pgm for scholarships
Other info: *US accredited sponsor:* no *Began:* 1989 *Orient:* abroad (intensive lang study) *Activities:* excursions, field trips, program travel, cultural events, sports *Misc:* Beginners must begin on major start dates; contact sponsor. 12, 22 or 30 lessons per wk. May contact former participants. *Financial aid:* scholarships *URL:* http://www.enforex.es
Contact: Antonio Anadon, Main Dir, ENFOREX Spanish Lang Sch, Alberto Aguilera 26, 28015 Madrid, Spain *E-mail:* spanish@enforex.es ▲

1222
ENFOREX SPANISH LANGUAGE SCHOOL
Learn Spanish Traveling (Combined Course)
Site: Spain: Barcelona, Madrid, Marbella, Salamanca
Dates: 12 wks or longer, yr-round
Subjects: Business language, Internships, Spanish language (beg/int/adv), Technical language
Eligibility: *Level:* adults *Requires:* CV, letter describing area for internship *Age:* min 16, max 65, avg 25
Credit: *Undergrad:* none *Grad:* none *Doc:* certificate
Instruction: *In:* Spanish *Format:* internship, lang study, practical training *Students:* intl
Costs: $1,200 for 12 wks, $100 for each addtl wk *incl* tuition, housing, all meals, fees, books/materials *Nonrefundable fee*
Housing: *Arr by pgm:* residence halls with local students, apartments, homestay, hotels
Deadline: 2 wks before pgm
Other info: *US accredited sponsor:* no *Began:* 1994 *Orient:* abroad *Activities:* excursions, field trips, program travel, cultural events, sports *Misc:* 20 lessons in technical Spanish per wk plus work experience. May contact former participants. *URL:* http://www.enforex.es
Contact: Mr Antonio Anadon, Main Dir, ENFOREX Spanish Lang Sch, Alberto Aguilera 26, 28015 Madrid, Spain *E-mail:* spanish@enforex.es ▲

1223
ENFOREX SPANISH LANGUAGE SCHOOL
One to One Course
Site: Spain: Barcelona, Madrid, Marbella, Salamanca
Dates: 4 wks, beg every Mon yr-round
Subjects: Spanish language (beg/int/adv)
Eligibility: *Level:* adults *Age:* min 16
Credit: *Undergrad:* avail *Grad:* avail
Instruction: *In:* Spanish *Format:* lang study *Students:* intl
Costs: $335 for 10 hrs, $600 for 20 hrs, $785 for 30 hrs *incl* tuition, housing, all meals, fees, excursions, books/materials
Housing: *Arr by pgm:* apartments with local students, residence halls with local students, homestay, hotels
Deadline: Until pgm filled; 4 mos before pgm for scholarships
Other info: *US accredited sponsor:* no *Began:* 1989 *Orient:* abroad (intensive lang study) *Activities:* excursions, field trips, program travel, cultural events, sports *Misc:* Test preparation course. May contact former participants. *Financial aid:* scholarships *URL:* http://www.enforex.es
Contact: Antonio Anadon, Main Dir, ENFOREX Spanish Lang Sch, Alberto Aguilera 26, 28015 Madrid, Spain *E-mail:* spanish@enforex.es ▲

1224
ENFOREX SPANISH LANGUAGE SCHOOL
Preparation Course for the DELE Exam
Site: Spain: Barcelona, Madrid
Dates: 4 or 6 wks, beg Jan 3, Jan 17, Apr 3, Apr 17, Jul 6, Jul 20, Oct 2 or Oct 16
Subjects: Spanish language
Eligibility: *Level:* adults *Age:* min 16
Credit: *Undergrad:* avail *Grad:* avail
Instruction: *In:* Spanish *Format:* lang study *Students:* intl
Costs: $750 for 4 wks, $1,000 for 6 wks *incl* tuition, housing, all meals, fees, excursions, books/materials
Housing: *Arr by pgm:* apartments with local students, residence halls with local students, homestay, hotels
Deadline: Until pgm filled; 4 mos before pgm for scholarships
Other info: *US accredited sponsor:* no *Began:* 1989 *Orient:* abroad (intensive lang study) *Activities:* excursions, field trips, program travel, cultural events, sports *Misc:* May contact former participants. *Financial aid:* scholarships *URL:* http://www.enforex.es
Contact: Antonio Anadon, Main Dir, ENFOREX Spanish Lang Sch, Alberto Aguilera 26, 28015 Madrid, Spain *E-mail:* spanish@enforex.es ▲

1225
ENFOREX SPANISH LANGUAGE SCHOOL
Spanish Language and Business
Site: Spain: Barcelona, Madrid
Dates: 4 wks, beg Jan 3, Jan 31, Jul 3, Oct 2
Subjects: Business language, Spanish language (int/adv), Technical language
Eligibility: *Level:* jrs, srs, grads, adults, professionals, precoll *Requires:* int or adv Spanish *Age:* min 18, max 65, avg 25
Credit: *Undergrad:* avail *Grad:* none
Instruction: *In:* Spanish *Format:* lang study *Students:* intl
Costs: $740 *incl* tuition, housing, all meals, fees, books/materials *Nonrefundable fee*
Housing: *Arr by pgm:* residence halls with local students, apartments, homestay, hotels
Deadline: Until pgm filled
Other info: *US accredited sponsor:* no *Began:* 1989 *Orient:* abroad *Activities:* excursions, field trips, program travel, cultural events, sports *Misc:* 20 lessons per wk. May contact former participants. *Financial aid:* scholarships *URL:* http://www.enforex.es
Contact: Mr Antonio Anadon, Main Dir, ENFOREX Spanish Lang Sch, Alberto Aguilera 26, 28015 Madrid, Spain *E-mail:* spanish@enforex.es ▲

1226
ENFOREX SPANISH LANGUAGE SCHOOL
Spanish Language, Art, History and Literature
Site: Spain: Barcelona, Madrid
Dates: 4 wks, beg Jan 3, Jan 31, Jul 3 or Oct 2
Subjects: Art, Civilization/culture, History, Literature, Spanish language, Spanish studies
Eligibility: *Level:* jrs, srs, grads, adults, teachers, professionals, precoll *Requires:* high int-adv Spanish *Age:* min 16, avg 22
Credit: *Undergrad:* avail *Grad:* avail *Doc:* certificate
Instruction: *In:* Spanish *Format:* lang study *Students:* intl
Costs: $740 *incl* tuition, housing, all meals, fees, books/materials
Housing: *Arr by pgm:* residence halls with local students, apartments, homestay, hotels
Deadline: Until pgm filled
Other info: *US accredited sponsor:* no *Began:* 1989 *Orient:* abroad *Activities:* excursions, field trips, program travel, cultural events *Misc:* May contact former participants. *URL:* http://www.enforex.es
Contact: Mr Antonio Anadon, Main Dir, or Ms Beatriz Cuerda, ENFOREX-Spanish Lang Sch, Alberto Aguilera 26, 28015 Madrid, Spain *E-mail:* spanish@enforex.es ▲

1227
ENFOREX SPANISH LANGUAGE SCHOOL
Study Tour
Site: Spain: Barcelona, Madrid
Dates: 2 wks, beg Jan 3, Jan 17, Feb 7,

Feb 21, Mar 27, Jun 12, Jun 26, Jul 13, Jul 27, Aug 10, Aug 24
Subjects: Spanish language (beg/int/adv), Spanish studies
Eligibility: *Level:* adults *Age:* min 16, avg 22
Credit: *Undergrad:* avail *Grad:* none *Doc:* certificate
Instruction: *In:* Spanish *Format:* lang study, study tour *Students:* intl
Costs: $365 *incl* tuition, housing, some meals, insurance, fees, excursions, books/materials *Nonrefundable fee*
Housing: *Arr by pgm:* apartments with local students, residence halls with local students, homestay, hotels
Deadline: 1 mo before pgm
Other info: *US accredited sponsor:* no *Began:* 1989 *Orient:* abroad *Activities:* excursions, field trips, program travel, cultural events, sports *Misc:* 12 lessons per wk, cultural activities, walking tours. May contact former participants. *Financial aid:* scholarships, work study *URL:* http://www.enforex.es
Contact: Mr Antonio Anadon, Main Dir, ENFOREX Spanish Lang Sch, Alberto Aguilera 26, 28015 Madrid, Spain *E-mail:* spanish@enforex.es ▲

1228
ESCUELA INTERNACIONAL
Intensive Spanish Course
Site: Spain: Madrid, Malaga, Salamanca
Dates: 2 wks or longer, yr-round
Subjects: Civilization/culture, Spanish language (beg/int/adv), Spanish studies
Eligibility: *Level:* adults *Age:* min 17, avg 22
Credit: *Undergrad:* avail *Grad:* none *Doc:* certificate
Instruction: *In:* Spanish *Format:* lang study *Students:* intl
Costs: 215,000-220,000 ptas per mo *incl* tuition, housing, all meals, fees, books/materials *Nonrefundable fee*
Housing: *Arr by pgm:* apartments, homestay, hotels, hostels
Deadline: 1 wk before pgm
Other info: *US accredited sponsor:* no *Began:* 1988 *Orient:* abroad *Activities:* excursions, cultural events, sports *Misc:* May contact former participants. *URL:* http://www.escuelai.com
Contact: Midori Ishizaka, Escuela Intl, c/ Talamanca 10, 28807 Alcala de Henares, Madrid, Spain *E-mail:* info@escuelai.com ▲

1229
ESCUELA INTERNACIONAL
Spanish Courses in Spain
Site: Spain: Madrid, Malaga, Salamanca
Dates: 2 wks-1 yr, yr-round
Subjects: Spanish language (beg/int/adv)
Eligibility: *Level:* fresh, sophs, jrs, srs, grads, adults, teachers, professionals, precoll *Age:* min 17, avg 22
Credit: *Undergrad:* avail *Grad:* none *Doc:* certificate
Instruction: *In:* Spanish *Format:* independent study, lab, lang study, lecture, student teaching, study tour *Students:* intl
Costs: 185,000-195,000 ptas for 4 wks *incl* tuition, housing, all meals, fees, books/materials
Housing: *Arr by pgm:* apartments, homestay, pensions, hotels, hostels
Deadline: 1 wk before pgm
Other info: *US accredited sponsor:* no

Began: 1988 *Activities:* excursions, program travel, cultural events, sports *Misc:* May contact former participants. *URL:* http://www.escuelai.com
Contact: Midori Ishizaka, Escuela Intl, c/Talamanca 10, 28807 Alcala de Henares, Madrid, Spain *E-mail:* info@escuelai.com ▲

1230
EUROPEAN HERITAGE INSTITUTE
Spain
Site: Spain: Barcelona, Granada, Madrid, Salamanca, Tenerife *Host inst:* Don Quijote
Dates: 2 wks-3 mos, Jun 1-Sep 30
Subjects: Civilization/culture, History, Spanish language (beg/int/adv), Spanish studies
Eligibility: *Level:* fresh, sophs, jrs, srs, grads, adults, teachers, professionals, precoll *Age:* min 18
Credit: *Undergrad:* 3-9 *Grad:* 3-9 *Doc:* certificate
Instruction: *In:* Spanish *Format:* lang study, seminar *Students:* intl
Costs: $1,460 per mo *incl* tuition, housing, fees
Housing: *Arr by pgm:* apartments, homestay
Deadline: Apr 15
Other info: *US accredited sponsor:* no *Began:* 1995 *Orient:* in US & abroad *Activities:* excursions, field trips, cultural events *Misc:* May contact former participants. *URL:* http://www.europeanheritage.org
Contact: Dr Antonio Masullo or Ms Barbara Cotter, European Heritage Inst, 2708 E Franklin St, Richmond VA 23223 *Ph:* 804-643 0661 *Fax:* 804-648 0826 *E-mail:* euritage@i2020.net ▲

1231
GEORGE MASON UNIVERSITY
Spanish Language and Culture
Site: Spain: Madrid, Seville *Host inst:* Estudios Univ de Andalucia, Univ Complutense
Dates: 8 wks, Jun 4-Jul 29
Subjects: Spanish language (int/adv)
Eligibility: *Level:* sophs, jrs, srs, grads, adults, teachers, professionals *Requires:* 1 yr coll Spanish *Age:* min 18
Credit: *Undergrad:* 12 *Grad:* 6 *Doc:* transcript
Instruction: *In:* Spanish *Format:* lang study *Students:* intl
Costs: About $5,984 for VA residents, $7,184 for others *incl* tuition, housing, all meals, insurance, excursions, ISIC *Nonrefundable fee*
Housing: *Sponsor assists:* residence halls, homestay
Deadline: Apr 10
Other info: *US accredited sponsor:* yes *Began:* 1993 *Orient:* in US *Activities:* excursions, field trips, program travel, cultural events *Misc:* May contact former participants. *URL:* http://www.gmu.edu/departments/cge
Contact: Ctr for Global Educ, George Mason Univ, Fairfax VA 22030 *Ph:* 703-993 2154 *Fax:* 703-993 2153 *E-mail:* cge@gmu.edu

---

1232
GEORGE WASHINGTON UNIVERSITY
Models of Education Service Delivery in Spain
Site: Spain: Andalucia, Madrid, Seville, others
Dates: 2 wks, Jul 15-Jul 30
Subjects: Bilingualism, Education/teaching, Special education
Eligibility: *Level:* grads, adults, teachers, professionals *Requires:* 3.0 GPA *Age:* min 21
Credit: *Undergrad:* none *Grad:* 3 *Doc:* transcript
Instruction: *In:* English *Format:* lecture, seminar, study tour *Students:* mainly US
Costs: $4,600 *incl* tuition, housing, some meals, intl airfare, fees *Nonrefundable fee*
Housing: *Arr by pgm:* hotels
Deadline: Contact Sponsor
Other info: *US accredited sponsor:* yes *Began:* 2000 *Orient:* abroad (1 day) *Activities:* excursions, field trips, program travel *Misc:* Summer pgms are updated in Dec. Contact sponsor for new info. *URL:* http://www.summer.gwu.edu
Contact: Summer, Special & Int'l Programs, George Washington Univ, 609 22nd St NW, Washington DC 20052 *Ph:* 202-994 6360 *Fax:* 202-994 9133 *E-mail:* sumprogs@gwu.edu

---

1233
IH ESPANA
Combined Courses in: Barcelona, Madrid, San Sebastian and Seville
Site: Spain: Barcelona, Madrid, San Sebastian, Seville
Dates: 2 wks or longer, yr-round
Subjects: Spanish language (beg/int/adv)
Eligibility: *Level:* adults *Age:* min 16
Credit: *Undergrad:* avail *Grad:* avail *Doc:* certificate
Instruction: *In:* Spanish *Format:* lang study *Students:* intl
Costs: About $1,200 for 4 wks *incl* tuition
Housing: *Arr by pgm:* residence halls, apartments, homestay, pensions, hotels, hostels
Deadline: Until pgm filled
Other info: *US accredited sponsor:* no *Orient:* avail *Activities:* excursions *Misc:* Pgm incl 2 wks in each city. *URL:* http://www.ihspain.com
Contact: *See Index II for Members* IH Espana, Trafalgar 14, 08010 Barcelona, Spain *E-mail:* ihspain@ihspain.com ▲

1234
INTERNATIONAL COUNCIL FOR CULTURAL EXCHANGE (ICCE)
Spanish Language and Culture
Site: Spain: Costa del Sol, other sites *Host inst:* Regional univs
Dates: 2-4 wks or longer, yr-round
Subjects: Business language, Civilization/culture, Field study, Homestay, Spanish language (beg/int/adv), Spanish studies
Eligibility: *Level:* fresh, sophs, jrs, srs, grads, adults, teachers, professionals, precoll
Credit: *Undergrad:* avail *Grad:* avail *Doc:* transcript, certificate
Instruction: *In:* English, Spanish *Format:* directed field study, lab, lang study, lecture, practical training, study tour *Students:* intl
Costs: From $3,200 for 4 wks *incl* tuition, housing, some meals, intl airfare, fees, excursions, transfers, pgm travel
Housing: *Sponsor assists:* residence halls, homestay, hotels
Deadline: 1 mo before pgm
Other info: *US accredited sponsor:* no *Began:* 1982 *Activities:* excursions, program travel, cultural events, sports *Misc:* Yr-round pgm avail for 2 wks or longer for pre-arr groups. Sem & yr pgms avail. Local coord assistance.
Contact: Dr Stanley Gochman, ICCE, 5 Bellport Ln, Bellport NY 11713 *Ph:* 631-286 5228 ▲

1235
KENTUCKY INSTITUTE FOR INTERNATIONAL STUDIES (KIIS)
Program in Spain
Site: Spain: Madrid, Segovia
Dates: 5 wks, Jul-Aug
Subjects: Business language, Civilization/culture, Homestay, Literature, Spanish language (int/adv)
Eligibility: *Level:* fresh, sophs, jrs, srs, grads, adults, teachers, professionals *Requires:* 2.0 GPA, good acad standing at home inst, 2 yrs coll Spanish, faculty recommendations *Age:* min 18
Credit: *Undergrad:* 3-6 *Grad:* none *Doc:* transcript
Instruction: *In:* Spanish *Format:* lang study, lecture *Students:* mainly US
Costs: $2,920 for students at member schs, $3,220 for others *incl* tuition, housing, all meals, intl airfare, fees, excursions *Nonrefundable fee*
Housing: *Arr by pgm:* residence halls, homestay
Deadline: Feb 15 ($100 late fee)
Other info: *US accredited sponsor:* yes

Began: 1979 *Orient:* in US & abroad *Activities:* excursions *Misc:* Optional travel. Homestay in Segovia. *Financial aid:* scholarships *URL:* http://www.kiis.org
Contact: *See Index II for Members* Dr J Milton Grimes, Exec Dir, KIIS, Murray State Univ, PO Box 9, Murray KY 42071-0009 *Ph:* 270-762 3091 *Fax:* 270-762 3434 *E-mail:* kiismsu@murraystate.edu

---

1236
KENTUCKY INSTITUTE FOR INTERNATIONAL STUDIES (KIIS)
Spain for Teachers
Site: Spain: Madrid, Segovia
Dates: 4 wks, Jun-Jul
Subjects: Education/teaching, Homestay, Spanish language (adv)
Eligibility: *Level:* teachers *Requires:* Spanish teaching experience *Age:* min 21
Credit: *Undergrad:* none *Grad:* 6 *Doc:* transcript *Transfer credit through:* Murray State Univ
Instruction: *In:* Spanish *Format:* lang study, lecture, seminar *Students:* mainly US
Costs: About $2,880 *incl* tuition, housing, all meals, intl airfare, excursions, ISIC *Nonrefundable fee*
Housing: *Arr by pgm:* homestay
Deadline: Feb 15
Other info: *US accredited sponsor:* yes *Began:* 1998 *Orient:* in US & abroad (1 day) *Activities:* excursions, field trips *Misc:* Homestay in Segovia. May contact former participants. *URL:* http://www.kiis.org
Contact: *See Index II for Members* Dr J Milton Grimes, Exec Dir, KIIS, Murray State Univ, PO Box 9, Murray KY 42071-0009 *Ph:* 270-762 3091 *Fax:* 270-762 3434 *E-mail:* kiismsu@murraystate.edu
Or Contact: Nancy Martin, Coord, KIIS, Murray State Univ, PO Box 9, Murray KY 42071 *Ph:* 270-762 3423 *Fax:* 270-762 3434 *E-mail:* nancy.martin@murraystate.edu

---

1237
LANGUAGE LIAISON
Spanish Language
Site: Spain: Barcelona, Madrid, Malaga, Marbella
Dates: 2 wks or longer, yr-round
Subjects: Business administration, Business language, Civilization/culture, Computer sciences, History, Humanities, Literature, Office/secretarial studies, Spanish language (beg/int/adv), Spanish studies
Eligibility: *Level:* fresh, sophs, jrs, srs, grads, adults, teachers, professionals, precoll *Age:* min 14
Credit: *Undergrad:* avail *Grad:* avail *Doc:* transcript, certificate
Instruction: *In:* Spanish *Format:* independent study, lang study, practical training, study tour *Students:* intl
Costs: Contact sponsor
Housing: *Arr by pgm:* residence halls, apartments, homestay, pensions, hotels, hostels, student-shared flat
Deadline: 30 days before pgm
Other info: *US accredited sponsor:* no *Activities:* excursions, field trips, cultural events, sports *Misc:* Scholarship research svc. *URL:* http://www.languageliaison.com
Contact: Nancy Forman, Dir, Lang Liaison, 4 Burnham Pkwy, Morristown NJ 07960 *Ph:* 800-284 4448 *Fax:* 973-898 1710 *E-mail:* learn@languageliaison.com

---

1238
LANGUAGE LIAISON
Spanish Saturation
Site: Spain: Granada, Nerja, Salamanca, San Sebastian, Seville, Valencia *Host inst:* Live in Learn
Dates: 2 wks or longer, yr-round
Subjects: Civilization/culture, Homestay, Spanish language (beg/int/adv)
Eligibility: *Level:* fresh, sophs, jrs, srs, grads, adults, teachers, professionals, precoll *Age:* min 14
Credit: *Undergrad:* avail *Grad:* avail *Doc:* transcript, certificate
Instruction: *In:* Spanish *Format:* lang study *Students:* intl
Costs: Contact sponsor
Housing: *Arr by pgm:* homestay
Deadline: 30 days before pgm
Other info: *US accredited sponsor:* no *Misc:* Live & learn in your teacher's home. Scholarship research svc. *URL:* http://www.languageliaison.com
Contact: Nancy Forman, Dir, Lang Liaison, 4 Burnham Pkwy, Morristown NJ 07960 *Ph:* 800-284 4448 *Fax:* 973-898 1710 *E-mail:* learn@languageliaison.com

---

1239
LANGUAGE STUDIES ABROAD, INC
Intensive Spanish-Spain
Site: Spain: El Puerto de Santa Maria, Las Palmas de Gran Canaria, Madrid, Malaga, Nerja, Salamanca, Seville, Valencia, others *Host inst:* various LSA insts
Dates: 1-2 wks or longer, yr-round
Subjects: Business language, Business/management, Civilization/culture, History, Homestay, Humanities, Spanish language (beg/int/adv), Spanish studies
Eligibility: *Level:* fresh, sophs, jrs, srs, grads, adults, teachers, professionals, precoll
Credit: *Undergrad:* avail *Grad:* avail *Doc:* certificate, diploma
Instruction: *In:* Spanish *Format:* lab, lang study, tutorial *Students:* intl
Costs: Contact sponsor
Housing: *Sponsor assists:* residence halls, apartments, homestay, hotels
Deadline: 4 wks before pgm
Other info: *US accredited sponsor:* no *Orient:* abroad *Activities:* excursions, field trips, program travel, cultural events, sports *Misc:* May contact former participants. *URL:* http://www.languagestudiesabroad.com
Contact: Lang Studies Abroad, Inc, 103 Londonderry Ct, Reno NV 89511-2718 *Ph:* 800-424 5522; 775-849 9206 *Fax:* 775-849 9217 *E-mail:* info@languagestudiesabroad.com

---

1240
LANGUAGES ABROAD
Language and Cultural Immersion Programs-Spain
Site: Spain: Madrid, Malaga
Dates: 2 wks or longer, yr-round
Subjects: Civilization/culture, Spanish language (beg/int/adv)
Eligibility: *Level:* adults *Age:* min 17, max 65, avg 25
Credit: *Undergrad:* none *Grad:* none *Doc:* certificate
Instruction: *In:* Spanish *Format:* lang study *Students:* intl
Costs: $1,040 for 4 wks *incl* tuition, housing, some meals, excursions, books/materials
Housing: *Arr by pgm:* apartments, homestay
Deadline: None
Other info: *US accredited sponsor:* no *Misc:* May contact former participants. *URL:* http://www.languagesabroad.com
Contact: Ms Jesse Philippe, Langs Abroad, 317 Adelaide St W, Ste 900, Toronto, Ontario M5V 1P9, Canada *Ph:* 800-219 9924; 416-925 7117 *E-mail:* info@languagesabroad.com

---

1241
LINGUA SERVICE WORLDWIDE
Total Immersion/Intensive Language and Culture in Spain
Site: Spain: Barcelona, Canary Islands, Madrid, Malaga, Salamanca, Valencia *Host inst:* Home Lang Intl
Dates: 1 wk-1 yr, yr-round
Subjects: Civilization/culture, Homestay, Spanish language (beg/int/adv)
Eligibility: *Level:* adults *Age:* min 14
Credit: *Undergrad:* avail *Grad:* avail *Doc:* transcript, certificate
Instruction: *In:* Spanish *Format:* lang study *Students:* intl
Costs: Contact sponsor
Housing: *Arr by pgm:* homestay, with teacher
Deadline: 45 days before pgm
Other info: *US accredited sponsor:* no *Began:* 1993 *Activities:* excursions, cultural events *Misc:* Participate in teacher's family & social life. May contact former participants. *URL:* http://www.linguaserviceworldwide.com
Contact: Dir, Lingua Svc Worldwide, 75 Prospect St, Ste 4, Huntington NY 11743 *Ph:* 800-394 5327; 631-424 0777 *Fax:* 631-271 3441 *E-mail:* itctravel@worldnet.att.net ▲

1242
LINGUA SERVICE WORLDWIDE
Total Immersion/Intensive Language and Culture-Spain
Site: Spain: Alicante, Barcelona, Canary Islands, Granada, Madrid, Malaga, Nerja, Salamanca, San Sebastian, others *Host inst:* CILCE, CLIC, EIS, Escuela de Idiomas Nerja, Gran Canaria Sch, Inst Alhambra, Lacunza Ctr de Idiomas
Dates: 1 wk-1 yr, yr-round
Subjects: Civilization/culture, Homestay, Humanities, Spanish language (beg/int/adv)
Eligibility: *Level:* fresh, sophs, jrs, srs, grads, adults, teachers, professionals, precoll *Age:* min 14
Credit: *Undergrad:* avail *Grad:* avail *Doc:* transcript, certificate *Transfer credit through:* Univ of Southern Mississippi
Instruction: *In:* Spanish *Format:* lang study, lecture *Students:* intl
Costs: Contact sponsor
Housing: *Arr by pgm:* apartments with local students, residence halls with local students, homestay, pensions, hotels, hostels
Deadline: 45 days before pgm
Other info: *US accredited sponsor:* no *Began:* 1993 *Activities:* excursions, cultural events *Misc:* May contact former participants. *URL:* http://www.linguaserviceworldwide.com
Contact: Dir, Lingua Svc Worldwide, 75 Prospect St, Ste 4, Huntington NY 11743 *Ph:* 800-394 5327; 631-424 0777 *Fax:* 631-271 3441 *E-mail:* itctravel@worldnet.att.net ▲

1243
MICHIGAN STATE UNIVERSITY
Packaging-Spain
Site: Spain: Barcelona, Valencia
Dates: 2 wks, May
Subjects: Field study, Packaging
Eligibility: *Level:* fresh, sophs, jrs, srs, grads *Requires:* 2.0 GPA, previous study in field *Age:* min 18
Credit: *Undergrad:* avail *Grad:* avail *Doc:* transcript
Instruction: *In:* English *Format:* directed field study, lecture *Students:* mainly US
Costs: About $1,300 *incl* housing, some meals, insurance, fees, excursions *Nonrefundable fee*
Housing: *Arr by pgm:* hotels
Deadline: Mar 2
Other info: *US accredited sponsor:* yes *Began:* 1999 *Orient:* in US (1 day) *Activities:* excursions, field trips, program travel *URL:* http://studyabroad.msu.edu
Contact: Cheryl Benner, Study Abroad, Michigan State Univ, 109 Intl Ctr, East Lansing MI 48824-1035 *Ph:* 517-353 8920 *Fax:* 517-432 2082 *E-mail:* bennerc@msu.edu ▲

1244
NATIONAL REGISTRATION CENTER FOR STUDY ABROAD (NRCSA)
Study in Spain
Site: Spain: various sites *Host inst:* CILCE, CLIC, Col Maravillas, Don Quijote, EIS, Escuela de Idiomas Nerja, others
Dates: 2 wks or longer, yr-round
Subjects: Civilization/culture, Homestay, Humanities, Spanish language (beg/int/adv), Spanish studies
Eligibility: *Level:* fresh, sophs, jrs, srs, grads, adults, teachers, professionals, precoll *Age:* min 18
Credit: *Undergrad:* avail *Grad:* avail *Doc:* certificate
Instruction: *In:* Spanish *Format:* lang study, lecture, seminar, tutorial *Students:* intl
Costs: Contact sponsor
Housing: *Arr by pgm:* residence halls, apartments, homestay, pensions, hotels
Deadline: 6 wks before pgm
Other info: *US accredited sponsor:* no *Activities:* cultural events *Misc:* Addtl host insts: Malaca Inst, Euroctr Santander, SEC. Optional excursions. May contact former participants. *URL:* http://www.nrcsa.com
Contact: Reuel Zielke or June Domoe, NRCSA, 823 N 2nd St, #206, Milwaukee WI 53203 *Ph:* 414-278 0631 *Fax:* 414-271 8884 *E-mail:* info@nrcsa.com

---

1245
SEVEN CONTINENTS' EXCHANGE PROGRAM
Seven Continents' Exchange Programs
Site: Spain: Cordoba, Granada, Seville *Host inst:* Univ of Granada
Dates: 2 wks-8 mos, winter, spring or summer
Subjects: Art history, Civilization/culture, Culinary arts, Dance, Geography, History, Literature, Music, Political science/politics, Religion/theology, Spanish language (beg/int/adv), Spanish studies, Wine
Eligibility: *Level:* adults *Age:* min 16
Credit: *Undergrad:* avail *Grad:* avail *Doc:* transcript, certificate
Instruction: *In:* English, Spanish *Format:* lab, lecture, practical training, study tour, tutorial *Students:* intl
Costs: Contact sponsor
Housing: *Arr by pgm:* apartments, homestay
Deadline: 40 days before pgm
Other info: *US accredited sponsor:* no *Began:* 1992 *Orient:* abroad (5-7 days) *Activities:* excursions, field trips, cultural events, sports *Misc:* Special lang exch with native speakers. Personalized pgms for groups or individuals. *URL:* http://www.moebius.es/sevencontinents/
Contact: Domenico M Vene, Dir, Seven Continents' Exch Pgms, PO Box 8163, Paramus NJ 07653-8163 *Ph:* 201-444 8687 *Fax:* 201-444 8687 *E-mail:* sevencontinents@worldnet.att.net

---

1246
SUNY COLLEGE AT NEW PALTZ, LANGUAGE IMMERSION INSTITUTE
Overseas Learning Vacations in Spain
Site: Spain: Barcelona, Granada, Madrid, Malaga, Salamanca, Tenerife *Host inst:* Don Quijote
Dates: 2 wks-9 mos, yr-round
Subjects: Business language, Foreign language teaching, Homestay, Spanish language (beg/int/adv), Spanish studies, Tourism
Eligibility: *Level:* adults, teachers, professionals *Age:* min 18, avg 26
Credit: *Undergrad:* avail *Grad:* none *Doc:* certificate
Instruction: *In:* Spanish *Format:* lang study, lecture, practical training, study tour *Students:* intl
Costs: About $920 for 2 wks *incl* tuition, housing, fees, books/materials
Housing: *Arr by pgm:* apartments with local students, homestay
Deadline: 2 mos before pgm
Other info: *US accredited sponsor:* yes *Activities:* excursions, cultural events *Misc:* Preparation for DELE exam, refresher course for teachers, World Wise Exec training in Salamanca in summer. *URL:* http://www.newpaltz.edu/lii
Contact: Lang Immersion Inst, SUNY New Paltz, 75 S Manheim Blvd, New Paltz NY 12561-2499 *Ph:* 914-257 3500 *Fax:* 914-257 3569 *E-mail:* lii@newpaltz.edu ▲

1247
SUNY COLLEGE AT NEW PALTZ
Summer Study in Spain
Site: Spain: Oviedo, Seville
Dates: 4 wks, Jul
Subjects: Area studies, Civilization/culture, Spanish language (beg/int/adv)
Eligibility: *Level:* fresh, sophs, jrs, srs, grads
Credit: *Undergrad:* 6 *Grad:* 6 *Doc:* transcript
Instruction: *In:* Spanish *Format:* lang study, lecture *Students:* mainly US
Costs: $2,654 for NY resident undergrads *incl* tuition, housing, all meals, insurance, excursions
Housing: *Arr by pgm:* hotels
Deadline: Mar 1 or until pgm filled
Other info: *US accredited sponsor:* yes *Began:* 1968 *Activities:* field trips, program travel *Misc:* Loans avail. *Financial aid:* scholarships *URL:* http://www.newpaltz.edu/oie/
Contact: Ctr for Intl Pgms, SUNY New Paltz, 75 S Manheim Blvd, Ste 9, New Paltz NY 12561 *Ph:* 845-257 3125 *Fax:* 845-257 3129 *E-mail:* international@newpaltz.edu ▲

1248
UNIVERSITY OF ARIZONA
Summer in Spain
Site: Spain: El Puerto de Santa Maria, Madrid, Salamanca *Host inst:* Estudio Intl Sampere (EIS)
Dates: Jun 6-Jul 7 and/or Jul 11-Aug 10
Subjects: Civilization/culture, Homestay, Literature, Spanish language (beg/int/adv), Spanish studies
Eligibility: *Level:* sophs, jrs, srs *Requires:* 2.5 GPA, 1 sem coll Spanish
Credit: *Undergrad:* 6-7 per term *Grad:* none *Doc:* transcript
Instruction: *In:* English, Spanish *Format:* lang study, lecture *Students:* intl
Costs: $2,800 *incl* tuition, housing, all meals, insurance, fees, excursions, books/materials
Housing: *Arr by pgm:* homestay
Deadline: Contact sponsor
Other info: *US accredited sponsor:* yes *Orient:* in US & abroad *Activities:* excursions, field trips *Misc:* May contact former participants. *Financial aid:* scholarships *URL:* http://w3.arizona.edu/~ciss/
Contact: Renee Griggs, Ctr for Global Student Pgms, Univ of Arizona, 939 N Tyndall Ave, Tucson AZ 85721 *Ph:* 520-626 7180 *Fax:* 520-626 9004 *E-mail:* griggsr@u.arizona.edu ▲

1249
UNIVERSITY OF MARYLAND
University of Maryland Summer in Madrid and San Roque, Spain
Site: Spain: Madrid, San Roque *Host inst:* Intl Inst
Dates: May 26-Jul 11
Subjects: Civilization/culture, Communications, Homestay, International studies, Literature, Spanish language (adv)
Eligibility: *Level:* sophs, jrs, srs *Requires:* 2.5 GPA, 2 yrs coll Spanish with B avg
Credit: *Undergrad:* 6 *Grad:* none *Doc:* transcript
Instruction: *In:* Spanish *Format:* lang study, lecture, study tour *Students:* mainly US
Costs: $3,700 *incl* tuition, housing, most meals, excursions, some transport
Housing: *Arr by pgm:* residence halls, homestay
Deadline: Mar 1
Other info: *US accredited sponsor:* yes *Began:* 1990 *Orient:* abroad *Activities:* excursions, field trips *Misc:* May contact

former participants. *URL:* http://www.inform.umd.edu/INTL/studyabroad
Contact: Christine Bodziak, Adviser, Study Abroad, Univ of Maryland, 3125 Mitchell Bldg, College Park MD 20742 *Ph:* 301-314 7746 *Fax:* 301-314 9347 *E-mail:* studyabr@deans.umd.edu
Or Contact: Prof Jose Naharro, Spanish & Portuguese, Univ of Maryland, 2215 Jimenez Hall, College Park MD 20742 *Ph:* 301-405 6455 *Fax:* 301-314 9752 *E-mail:* jn3@umail.umd.edu

---

1250
UNIVERSITY OF RICHMOND
Salamanca Summer Study Abroad
Site: Spain: Madrid, Salamanca *Host inst:* Col de Espana
Dates: 6 wks, Jun 26-Aug 3
Subjects: Art history, Civilization/culture, Literature, Spanish language (int/adv), Written composition
Eligibility: *Level:* fresh, sophs, jrs, srs *Requires:* 2.0 GPA, int Spanish, strong interest in Spanish major *Age:* min 18, avg 20
Credit: *Undergrad:* 6 *Grad:* none *Doc:* transcript
Instruction: *In:* Spanish *Format:* lang study, lecture, study tour *Students:* mainly US
Costs: About $4,600 *incl* tuition, housing, some meals, intl airfare, excursions
Housing: *Arr by pgm:* homestay
Deadline: Rolling admissions
Other info: *US accredited sponsor:* yes *Began:* 1992 *Orient:* in US & abroad *Activities:* excursions, field trips, cultural events
Contact: Jeanne Burkett, Sch of Continuing Studies, Univ of Richmond, Richmond VA 23173 *Ph:* 804-287 6835 *Fax:* 804-289 8138 *E-mail:* jburkett@richmond.edu

---

1251
UNIVERSITY OF SOUTH FLORIDA
USF in Spain
Site: Spain: Andalucia, Barcelona, Madrid *Host inst:* Forspro
Dates: Jun-Jul
Subjects: Civilization/culture, History, Literature, Spanish language (beg/int/adv), Spanish studies
Eligibility: *Level:* adults *Requires:* 2.5 GPA *Age:* min 18
Credit: *Undergrad:* 3-6 *Grad:* 3 *Doc:* transcript
Instruction: *In:* English, Spanish *Format:* lang study, lecture, study tour *Students:* mainly US
Costs: From $3,000 *incl* tuition, housing, all meals, intl airfare, insurance, fees, excursions *Nonrefundable fee*
Housing: *Arr by pgm:* residence halls, hotels
Deadline: Apr 1
Other info: *US accredited sponsor:* yes *In coop with:* Forspro *Orient:* in US & abroad *Activities:* excursions, field trips *Misc:* 3 wks in Madrid, 1 wk in Barcelona or Andalucia. May contact former participants. *Financial aid:* scholarships *URL:* http://www.usf.edu/~iac/
Contact: James Pulos, Overseas Study Pgms, Univ of South Florida, 4202 E Fowler Ave, CPR 107, Tampa FL 33620-5550 *Ph:* 813-974 4613, 813-974 3933 *Fax:* 813-974 4613 *E-mail:* jpulos@iac.usf.edu
Or Contact: Dr Carlos Cano, Modern Langs & Linguistics, Univ of South Florida, 4202 E Fowler Ave, CPR 107, Tampa FL 33620-5550 *Ph:* 813-974 2077 *Fax:* 813-974 4613 *E-mail:* cano@chuma1.cas.usf.edu

---

1252
UNIVERSITY OF SOUTHERN MISSISSIPPI
Business in Spain
Site: Spain: Madrid, Marbella
Dates: Jun 11-Jul 6
Subjects: International business, Spanish language

Eligibility: *Level:* jrs, srs, grads *Requires:* 2.0 GPA, grads must have 3.0 GPA
Credit: *Undergrad:* 4-6 *Grad:* 3-6 *Doc:* transcript
Instruction: *In:* English, Spanish *Format:* lecture, seminar *Students:* mainly US
Costs: $3,599 for undergrads, $3,899 for grads *incl* tuition, housing, some meals, intl airfare, fees, excursions, pgm transport *Nonrefundable fee*
Housing: *Arr by pgm*
Deadline: May 1
Other info: *US accredited sponsor:* yes *Activities:* field trips *Misc:* May contact former participants. *URL:* http://www.usm.edu
Contact: Dr Tim Hudson, Dean, CICE, or Dir, Bus in Spain, Univ of Mississippi, Box 10047, Hattiesburg MS 39406-0047 *Ph:* 601-266 4344 *Fax:* 601-266 5699 *E-mail:* melissa.ravencraft@usm.edu

---

1253
UNIVERSITY OF SOUTHERN MISSISSIPPI
Spanish in Spain
Site: Spain: Madrid, Nerja *Host inst:* ENFOREX, Escuela de Idiomas Nerja
Dates: 5 wks, May 19-Jun 24
Subjects: Spanish language
Eligibility: *Level:* fresh, sophs, jrs, srs, grads, adults, teachers, professionals *Requires:* 2.0 GPA, good acad standing, Spanish lang study recommended *Age:* min 18, max 30, avg 23
Credit: *Undergrad:* 6 *Grad:* 6 *Doc:* transcript
Instruction: *In:* Spanish *Format:* lang study *Students:* mainly US
Costs: $3,599 for undergrads, $3,899 for grads *incl* tuition, housing, some meals, intl airfare, fees
Housing: *Arr by pgm:* homestay
Deadline: Apr 3
Other info: *US accredited sponsor:* yes *Began:* 1998 *Orient:* avail *Activities:* excursions *Misc:* May contact former participants. *URL:* http://www.usm.edu
Contact: Dr Tim W Hudson, Dean, or Dir, Spanish in Spain, Univ of Southern Mississippi, Box 10047, Hattiesburg MS 39406 *Ph:* 601-266 4344 *Fax:* 601-266 5699 *E-mail:* melissa.ravencraft@usm.edu

---

1254
WESTERN CONNECTICUT STATE UNIVERSITY
Spain Program
Site: Spain: Cordoba, Granada, Madrid, Segovia, Seville, Toledo
Dates: Mar 16-25
Subjects: Education/teaching, History, Sociology
Eligibility: *Level:* srs, grads, teachers, professionals *Requires:* 2.8 GPA *Age:* min 18, max 60
Credit: *Undergrad:* 3 *Grad:* 3
Instruction: *In:* English *Format:* seminar, study tour *Students:* mainly US
Costs: $2,100 *incl* housing, some meals, intl airfare, fees, excursions
Housing: *Arr by pgm:* hotels
Deadline: Nov 5
Other info: *US accredited sponsor:* yes *Began:* 1973 *Orient:* in US *Activities:*

excursions, field trips *Misc:* May contact former participants. *URL:* http://www.wcsu.ctstateu.edu/homepage.html
Contact: Dr John Caruso, Jr, Educ, Western Connecticut State Univ, 181 White St, Danbury CT 06810 *Ph:* 203-837 8510 *E-mail:* caruso@wcsu.ctstateu.edu

ALCALA DE HENARES

1255
BOWLING GREEN STATE UNIVERSITY
Summer Cluster Program in Spain
Site: Spain: Alcala de Henares *Host inst:* Univ de Alcala de Henares
Dates: 2 mos, about May 26-Jul 28
Subjects: Civilization/culture, Homestay, Spanish language (beg/int), Spanish studies
Eligibility: *Level:* fresh, sophs, jrs, srs *Requires:* 2.0 GPA, some Spanish recommended
Credit: *Undergrad:* 13-15 *Grad:* none
Instruction: *In:* Spanish *Format:* lang study, lecture *Students:* mainly US
Costs: About $4,521 for OH residents, $7,470 for others *incl* tuition, housing, all meals, fees, excursions *Nonrefundable fee*
Housing: *Arr by pgm:* homestay
Deadline: Feb 28
Other info: *US accredited sponsor:* yes *Began:* 1962 *Orient:* in US & abroad (2 days) *Activities:* excursions *Financial aid:* scholarships *URL:* http://www.bgsu.edu/departments/roml/AYA_Spain
Contact: Cynthia Phelps, AYA Spain Dir, Romance Langs, Bowling Green State Univ, Bowling Green OH 43403 *Ph:* 419-372 8053 *Fax:* 419-372 7332 *E-mail:* ayaspain@bgnet.bgsu.edu

1256
BOWLING GREEN STATE UNIVERSITY
Summer Regular Program in Spain
Site: Spain: Alcala de Henares *Host inst:* Univ de Alcala de Henares
Dates: 2 mos, about May 26-Jul 28
Subjects: Business language, Civilization/culture, Drama/theater, Homestay, Poetry, Spanish language (int/adv), Spanish studies, Written composition
Eligibility: *Level:* fresh, sophs, jrs, srs *Requires:* 2.0 GPA, 2.5 in Spanish
Credit: *Undergrad:* 12-14 *Grad:* none
Instruction: *In:* Spanish *Format:* lang study, lecture, seminar *Students:* mainly US
Costs: About $4,521 for OH residents, $7,470 for others *incl* tuition, housing, all meals, fees, excursions *Nonrefundable fee*
Housing: *Arr by pgm:* homestay
Deadline: Feb 28
Other info: *US accredited sponsor:* yes *Began:* 1962 *Orient:* in US & abroad (2 days) *Activities:* excursions *Financial aid:* scholarships *URL:* http://www.bgsu.edu/departments/roml/AYA_Spain
Contact: Cynthia Phelps, AYA Spain Dir, Romance Langs, Bowling Green State Univ, Bowling Green OH 43403 *Ph:* 419-372 8053 *Fax:* 419-372 7332 *E-mail:* ayaspain@bgnet.bgsu.edu

1257
COUNCIL ON INTERNATIONAL EDUCATIONAL EXCHANGE (COUNCIL)
Spain Today and European Integration
Site: Spain: Alcala de Henares *Host inst:* Univ of Alcala
Dates: 13 days, Jun
Subjects: Economics, Immigration, Political science/politics, Sociology, Spanish studies
Eligibility: *Level:* teachers, professionals
Credit: *Undergrad:* none *Grad:* none
Instruction: *In:* English *Format:* lecture *Students:* intl
Costs: $1,995 *incl* tuition, housing, some meals, insurance, fees, excursions, books/materials *Nonrefundable fee*
Housing: *Arr by pgm:* hotels
Deadline: Mar 15
Other info: *US accredited sponsor:* no *Began:* 2001 *Misc:* May contact former participants.
Contact: Jennifer Ley, Dir, Faculty Pgms, Council, 633 3rd Ave, New York NY 10017 *Ph:* 212-822 2746 *Fax:* 212-822 2779 *E-mail:* jley@ciee.org ▲

1258
ESCUELA INTERNACIONAL
Business Spanish Course
Site: Spain: Alcala de Henares
Dates: 2-16 wks, yr-round
Subjects: Business language, Spanish language (int/adv)
Eligibility: *Level:* sophs, jrs, srs, grads, adults, professionals *Requires:* adv Spanish *Age:* min 17, avg 25
Credit: *Undergrad:* avail *Grad:* none *Doc:* certificate
Instruction: *In:* Spanish *Format:* lang study *Students:* intl
Costs: 113,000 ptas for 4 wks *incl* tuition, fees, books/materials *Nonrefundable fee*
Housing: *Arr by pgm:* apartments, homestay, hotels, hostels
Deadline: 1 wk before pgm
Other info: *US accredited sponsor:* no *Began:* 1988 *Orient:* abroad *Activities:* excursions, cultural events, sports *Misc:* May contact former participants. *URL:* http://www.escuelai.com
Contact: Midori Ishizaka, Escuela Intl, c/ Talamanca 10, 28807 Alcala de Henares, Madrid, Spain *E-mail:* info@escuelai.com ▲

1259
ESCUELA INTERNACIONAL
Spanish Course for Teachers
Site: Spain: Alcala de Henares
Dates: 2 or 4 wks, Jul
Subjects: Foreign language teaching, Spanish language (adv)
Eligibility: *Level:* teachers *Requires:* adv Spanish *Age:* min 20, avg 30
Credit: *Undergrad:* none *Grad:* none *Doc:* certificate
Instruction: *In:* Spanish *Format:* lang study, lecture, practical training, seminar, workshop *Students:* intl
Costs: 72,000 ptas for 2 wks *incl* tuition, fees, books/materials *Nonrefundable fee*
Housing: *Arr by pgm:* apartments, homestay, hotels, hostels
Deadline: 2 wks before pgm
Other info: *US accredited sponsor:* no *Began:* 1988 *Orient:* abroad *Activities:* excursions, cultural events, sports *Misc:* May contact former participants. *URL:* http://www.escuelai.com
Contact: Midori Ishizaka, Escuela Intl, c/ Talamanca 10, 28807 Alcala de Henares, Madrid, Spain *E-mail:* info@escuelai.com ▲

1260
LOYOLA UNIVERSITY OF CHICAGO
Summer Program in Alcala
Site: Spain: Alcala de Henares *Host inst:* Univ de Alcala de Henares
Dates: 4 wks, May 28-Jun 30
Subjects: Civilization/culture, Literature, Spanish language, Spanish studies
Eligibility: *Level:* fresh, sophs, jrs, srs, grads, adults, teachers, professionals
Credit: *Undergrad:* 6 *Grad:* none
Instruction: *In:* English, Spanish *Format:* lang study, seminar, tutorial *Students:* mainly US
Costs: About $3,500 *incl* tuition, housing, some meals, excursions *Nonrefundable fee*
Housing: *Arr by pgm:* residence halls
Deadline: About Mar 15
Other info: *US accredited sponsor:* yes *Began:* 1999 *Activities:* excursions, field trips, program travel, cultural events *URL:* http://www.luc.edu/depts/modern_lang/
Contact: Dr Paolo Giordano, Chair, Loyola Univ Chicago, Modern Langs & Literatures, 6525 N Sheridan Rd, Chicago IL 60626 *Ph:* 773-508 2850 *Fax:* 773-508 2893 *E-mail:* pgiorda@luc.edu

Or Contact: Ms Patricia Clemente, Loyola Univ Chicago, Modern Langs & Literatures, 6525 N Sheridan Rd, Chicago IL 60626 *Ph:* 773-508 2850 *Fax:* 773-508 2893 *E-mail:* pclemen@luc.edu

---

1261
MICHIGAN STATE UNIVERSITY
Spanish Language, Literature and Culture
Site: Spain: Alcala de Henares
Dates: 9 wks, May-Jul
Subjects: Field study, Homestay, Independent study, Literature, Spanish language
Eligibility: *Level:* fresh, sophs, jrs, srs *Requires:* 2.5 GPA, 2 yrs Spanish, good acad standing, interview *Age:* min 18
Credit: *Undergrad:* 12 *Grad:* none *Doc:* transcript
Instruction: *In:* English, Spanish *Format:* directed field study, independent study, lang study, lecture *Students:* mainly US
Costs: About $2,100 *incl* housing, all meals, insurance, excursions, support svcs *Nonrefundable fee*
Housing: *Arr by pgm:* homestay
Deadline: Mar 2
Other info: *US accredited sponsor:* yes *Began:* 1976 *Orient:* in US & abroad *Activities:* field trips, cultural events *Misc:* Loans avail. May contact former participants. *Financial aid:* scholarships *URL:* http://studyabroad.msu.edu
Contact: Cheryl Benner, Study Abroad, Michigan State Univ, 109 Intl Ctr, East Lansing MI 48824 *Ph:* 517-353 8920 *Fax:* 517-432 2082 *E-mail:* bennerc@msu.edu ▲

1262
UNIVERSIDAD DE ALCALA
Spanish Studies
Site: Spain: Alcala de Henares
Dates: 1 mo, Jun 1-30 or Jul 1-31
Subjects: Art, Business/management, Civilization/culture, Economics, Film studies, Geography, History, International relations, Languages (beg/int/adv), Literature, Political science/politics, Sociology
Eligibility: *Level:* fresh, sophs, jrs, srs, grads *Requires:* 2.75 GPA
Credit: *Undergrad:* avail *Grad:* avail *Doc:* transcript
Instruction: *In:* English, Spanish *Format:* directed field study, independent study, lang study, lecture, practical training, seminar, student teaching, study tour, tutorial *Students:* mainly US
Costs: $350 for 1 mo *incl* tuition, fees
Housing: *Arr by pgm:* residence halls with local students, homestay
Deadline: Contact sponsor
Other info: *US accredited sponsor:* no *Began:* 1988 *Orient:* abroad (4 days, intensive lang study) *Activities:* excursions, field trips, program travel, cultural events, sports *URL:* http://www2.alcala.es/cenva/spanish/spanstud.htm
Contact: Arturo Jarque, Coord, Univ de Alcala (CENUA), Trinitarios 1, 28801, Alcala de Henares, Madrid, Spain *E-mail:* arturo.jarque@uah.es
Or Contact: Rocio Martin, Asst, Univ of Alcala (CENUA), Trinitarios 1, 28801, Alcala de Henares, Madrid, Spain *E-mail:* reden@cenuah.alcala.es

---

1263
UNIVERSITY OF ALABAMA
Alabama in Spain
Site: Spain: Alcala de Henares
Dates: May 30-Jul 3
Subjects: Civilization/culture, Homestay, Literature, Spanish language (int/adv), Spanish studies
Eligibility: *Level:* jrs, srs, grads, adults *Requires:* previous study in field, Spanish
Credit: *Undergrad:* avail *Grad:* avail *Doc:* transcript
Instruction: *In:* Spanish *Format:* lecture, study tour *Students:* mainly US
Costs: $3,800 *incl* tuition, housing, some meals, intl airfare, excursions, ISIC
Housing: *Arr by pgm:* homestay
Deadline: Mar 1
Other info: *US accredited sponsor:* yes *Began:* 1994 *In coop with:* Univ de Alcala de Henares *Activities:* excursions, field trips, program travel, cultural events *Misc:* May contact former participants. *URL:* http://www.ua.edu/international
Contact: José Cano, Univ of Alabama, 200 BB Comer, Tuscaloosa AL 35487 *Ph:* 205-348 8477 *Fax:* 205-348 5298 *E-mail:* jcano@woodsquad.as.ua.edu
Or Contact: Capstone Intl Pgm Ctr, Univ of Alabama, PO Box 870254, Tuscaloosa AL 35487 *Ph:* 205-348 5256 *Fax:* 205-348 5298 *E-mail:* achannel@aalan.ua.edu

---

ALICANTE

1264
COUNCIL ON INTERNATIONAL EDUCATIONAL EXCHANGE CONSORTIUM
Spanish Mediterranean: Language and Area Studies
Site: Spain: Alicante *Host inst:* Univ of Alicante
Dates: 6 wks, mid-Jun-late Jul
Subjects: Art history, Civilization/culture, Homestay, Mediterranean studies, Spanish language (beg/int/adv), Spanish studies
Eligibility: *Level:* fresh, sophs, jrs, srs, grads, adults, teachers, professionals *Requires:* 2.75 GPA, completion of 1 coll sem
Credit: *Undergrad:* 7 *Grad:* none
Instruction: *In:* English, Spanish *Format:* lang study, lecture *Students:* mainly US
Costs: $3,475 *incl* tuition, housing, all meals, insurance, excursions, ISIC *Nonrefundable fee*
Housing: *Arr by pgm:* homestay
Deadline: Apr 1
Other info: *US accredited sponsor:* yes *Began:* 1992 *Orient:* avail in Madrid *Activities:* excursions, field trips, cultural events *Misc:* Full-time resident dir. Faculty from host country univs. Grade report. May contact former participants. *Financial aid:* scholarships *URL:* http://www.ciee.org/study
Contact: *See Index II for Members* Alicante Pgm Adviser, Council-ISP, 633 3rd Ave, 20th Fl, New York NY 10017-6706 *Ph:* 800-407 8839; 212-822 2600 *Fax:* 212-822 2779 *E-mail:* studyinfo@ciee.org

---

1265
CULTURAL EXPERIENCES ABROAD (CEA)
Study Spanish Language and Culture in Alicante
Site: Spain: Alicante *Host inst:* Univ of Alicante
Dates: 4-8 wks, Jul-Aug
Subjects: Arts, Composition, History, Homestay, Independent study, Internships, Literature, Media studies, Spanish language, Spanish studies
Eligibility: Recommendation letter and unofficial transcripts *Level:* fresh, sophs, jrs, srs, grads, precoll *Requires:* 2.5 GPA, recommendation letter, transcripts *Age:* min 17, avg 20
Credit: *Undergrad:* avail *Grad:* none *Doc:* transcript
Instruction: *In:* Spanish *Format:* independent study, lang study, lecture, seminar *Students:* intl
Costs: $2,995-$4,000 *incl* tuition, housing, all meals, insurance, fees, excursions, on-site staff *Nonrefundable fee*
Housing: *Arr by pgm:* residence halls, apartments, homestay, independent housing
Deadline: Rolling admissions
Other info: *US accredited sponsor:* no *Began:* 2001 *Orient:* abroad (1 day) *Activities:* excursions, field trips, program travel, cultural events, sports *Misc:* Lang exch pgm. City tour. May contact former participants. *Financial aid:* scholarships *URL:* http://www.travelabroad.com
Contact: CEA Study Abroad, 1400 E Southern Ave, Ste B-108, Tempe AZ 85282-8011 *Ph:* 480-557 7900 *Fax:* 480-557 7926 *E-mail:* spanish@travelabroad.com

---

1266
UNIVERSITY OF PENNSYLVANIA
Penn-in-Alicante
Site: Spain: Alicante
Dates: 5 wks, late Jun-Jul
Subjects: Civilization/culture, Homestay, Literature, Spanish language (beg/int/adv)
Eligibility: *Level:* fresh, sophs, jrs, srs, grads, professionals
Credit: *Undergrad:* 6-8 *Grad:* none *Doc:* transcript
Instruction: *In:* Spanish *Format:* lang study, lecture *Students:* mainly US
Costs: About $4,900 *incl* tuition, housing, all meals, excursions *Nonrefundable fee*
Housing: *Arr by pgm:* homestay
Deadline: Apr 1
Other info: *US accredited sponsor:* yes *Began:* 1981 *Orient:* in US & abroad *Activities:* excursions *URL:* http://www.sas.upenn.edu/CGS/
Contact: Elizabeth Sachs, Penn Summer Abroad, Univ of Pennsylvania, 3440 Market St, Ste 100, Philadelphia PA 19104-3335 *Ph:* 215-898 5738 *Fax:* 215-573 2053 *E-mail:* sdanti@mail.sas.upenn.edu

---

BARCELONA

1267
ACADEMIC PROGRAMS INTERNATIONAL (API)
API in Barcelona, Spain
Site: Spain: Barcelona *Host inst:* Univ of Barcelona
Dates: 6-9 wks, May 21-Jul 28, Jun 19-Jul 28
Subjects: Civilization/culture, Homestay, Spanish language, Spanish studies
Eligibility: *Level:* fresh, sophs, jrs, srs, grads, adults, professionals, precoll *Requires:* 2.75 GPA, recommendation letter *Age:* min 18
Credit: *Undergrad:* 6-8 *Grad:* none *Doc:* transcript
Instruction: *In:* Spanish *Format:* lang study, lecture *Students:* intl
Costs: $3,200 for 6 wks, $6,000 for 9 wks *incl* tuition, housing, all meals, insurance, fees, excursions, books/materials, local transport, on-site dir *Nonrefundable fee*
Housing: *Arr by pgm:* residence halls, homestay
Deadline: Apr 1; Mar 1 for scholarships
Other info: *US accredited sponsor:* no *Began:* 1999 *Orient:* in US & abroad (2 wks, intensive lang study) *Activities:* excursions, field trips, program travel, cultural events, sports *Misc:* May contact former participants. *Financial aid:* scholarships *URL:* http://www.academicintl.com
Contact: Jennifer C Allen, Dir, Acad Pgms Intl, 129 E Hopkins St, Ste 101, San Marcos TX 78666 *Ph:* 800-844 4124; 512-392 8520 *Fax:* 512-392 8420 *E-mail:* api@onr.com

---

1268
DIALOGUE IDIOMAS
One-to-One Residential Spanish
Site: Spain: near Barcelona
Dates: 1 wk or longer, yr-round
Subjects: Spanish language
Eligibility: *Level:* grads, adults, teachers, professionals *Age:* min 18, avg 35
Credit: *Undergrad:* none *Grad:* none *Doc:* certificate
Instruction: *In:* Spanish *Format:* lang study *Students:* intl
Costs: EUR 1,125-1,750 per wk *incl* tuition, housing, all meals, books/materials
Housing: *Arr by pgm:* homestay
Deadline: Contact sponsor
Other info: *US accredited sponsor:* no *Misc:* May contact former participants. *URL:* http://www.dialogue-languages.com
Contact: Elliot Essman, Dialogue Idiomas, PO Box 901, Larchmont NY 10538 *Ph:* 800-474 7416; 914-834 5412 *E-mail:* dialogue@buildingyourself.com
Or Contact: Julian Melbourne, Dialogue Idiomas, Bonavista 5, 08635 Sant Esteve, Barcelona, Spain *E-mail:* dialogue@retemail.es

---

1269
DON QUIJOTE
DELE Preparation Course-Barcelona
Site: Spain: Barcelona
Dates: 2, 3 or 4 wks, special starting dates in May & Nov
Subjects: Spanish language (adv)
Eligibility: *Level:* adults *Requires:* int Spanish *Age:* min 18, avg 26
Credit: *Undergrad:* none *Grad:* none *Doc:* diploma
Instruction: *In:* Spanish *Format:* lang study *Students:* intl
Costs: $522 for 2 wks, $722 for 3 wks, $922 for 4 wks *incl* tuition, housing, books/materials, activities
Housing: *Arr by pgm:* apartments, homestay, pensions
Deadline: Rolling admissions
Other info: *US accredited sponsor:* no *Began:* 1990 *Activities:* excursions, field trips, program travel, cultural events, sports *Misc:* Official diploma preparation. 25% discount if combined with standard course. *URL:* http://www.donquijote.org
Contact: Area Mgr/USA, Don Quijote-Central Promotion, Apdo de Correos 333, Ref: USII98, 37080 Salamanca, Spain *E-mail:* amusa@donquijote.org

---

1270
DON QUIJOTE
Intensive Business Course
Site: Spain: Barcelona
Dates: 2 or 4 wks, yr-round; special starting dates
Subjects: Accounting, Business/management, Finance, International business
Eligibility: *Level:* adults *Age:* min 18, avg 26
Credit: *Undergrad:* none *Grad:* none *Doc:* certificate
Instruction: *In:* Spanish *Format:* lang study, practical training *Students:* intl
Costs: $328 for 2 wks, $616 for 4 wks *incl* tuition, housing, books/materials, activities
Housing: *Sponsor assists:* homestay, pensions, apts with intl students
Deadline: Rolling admissions
Other info: *US accredited sponsor:* no *Began:* 1996 *Activities:* excursions, field trips, program travel, cultural events, sports *Misc:* 25% discount if combined with standard course. May contact former participants. *URL:* http://www.donquijote.org
Contact: Area Mgr/USA, Don Quijote-Central Promotion, Apdo de Correos 333, Ref: USII98, Salamanca 37080, Spain *E-mail:* amusa@donquijote.org

---

1271
DON QUIJOTE
Refresher Courses for Teachers of Spanish/Repaso-Barcelona
Site: Spain: Barcelona
Dates: 2 wks, yr-round; special starting dates
Subjects: Foreign language teaching, Spanish language (adv)
Eligibility: *Level:* teachers *Requires:* adv Spanish *Age:* min 18
Credit: *Undergrad:* none *Grad:* none *Doc:* certificate
Instruction: *In:* Spanish *Format:* lang study, lecture, practical training *Students:* intl
Costs: $694 for group, $1,184 for individual *incl* tuition, housing, books/materials, activities
Housing: *Arr by pgm:* homestay
Deadline: Rolling admissions
Other info: *US accredited sponsor:* no *Began:* 1992 *Activities:* excursions, field trips, program travel, cultural events, sports *Misc:* Pgm examines theoretical & practical methods of teaching Spanish, incl workshops, lectures, discussions. May contact former participants. *URL:* http://www.donquijote.org
Contact: Area Mgr/USA, Don Quijote-Central Promotion, Apdo de Correos 333, Ref: USII98, 37080 Salamanca, Spain *E-mail:* amusa@donquijote.org

---

1272
DON QUIJOTE
Spanish in Spain Short-Term Courses: Barcelona
Site: Spain: Barcelona
Dates: 1-11 wks, yr-round
Subjects: Spanish language (beg/int/adv)
Eligibility: *Level:* adults *Age:* min 18, avg 26
Credit: *Undergrad:* 3 for 60 hrs *Grad:* none *Doc:* certificate, diploma
Instruction: *In:* Spanish *Format:* lang study, lecture *Students:* intl
Costs: $842 for 4 wks *incl* tuition, housing, books/materials, activities
Housing: *Arr by pgm:* apartments, homestay, hotels, hostels
Deadline: Rolling admissions
Other info: *US accredited sponsor:* no *Began:* 1991 *Activities:* excursions, field trips, program travel, cultural events, sports *Misc:* May contact former participants. *URL:* http://www.donquijote.org
Contact: Area Mgr/USA, Don Quijote-Central Promotion, Apdo de Correos 333, Ref: USII98, 37080 Salamanca, Spain *E-mail:* amusa@donquijote.org

---

1273
DON QUIJOTE
Super Intensive Course-Barcelona
Site: Spain: Barcelona
Dates: 1-36 wks, yr-round
Subjects: Civilization/culture, Spanish language (beg/int/adv)
Eligibility: *Level:* adults *Age:* min 18, avg 26
Credit: *Undergrad:* none *Grad:* none *Doc:* certificate, diploma
Instruction: *In:* Spanish *Format:* independent study, lang study, lecture, study tour, tutorial *Students:* intl
Costs: $581 for 2 wks *incl* tuition, housing, fees, books/materials, activities
Housing: *Sponsor assists:* apartments, homestay, hotels, hostels
Deadline: Contact sponsor
Other info: *US accredited sponsor:* no *Began:* 1990 *Activities:* excursions, field trips, program travel, cultural events, sports *Misc:* Costs incl homestay housing option only. May contact former participants. *URL:* http://www.donquijote.org
Contact: Area Mgr/USA, Don Quijote, Placentinos No 2, Apdo 333, 37080 Salamanca, Spain *E-mail:* amusa@donquijote.org

---

1274
GEORGIA INSTITUTE OF TECHNOLOGY
Summer Program in Barcelona
Site: Spain: Barcelona *Host inst:* Univ Politecnica de Cataluna
Dates: May 24-Jul 26
Subjects: Architecture, Computer sciences, Spanish language
Eligibility: *Level:* fresh, sophs, jrs, srs *Requires:* good acad standing
Credit: *Undergrad:* 9 *Grad:* none *Doc:* transcript
Instruction: *In:* English *Format:* lecture *Students:* mainly US
Costs: About $4,059 for GA residents, $4,309 for others *incl* tuition, housing, some meals, intl airfare, insurance, fees, excursions *Nonrefundable fee*
Housing: *Arr by pgm:* residence halls
Deadline: About Feb 1
Other info: *US accredited sponsor:* yes *Began:* 1999 *Orient:* in US (1 day) *URL:* http://www.cc.gatech.edu/programs/SA-Barcelona
Contact: Intl Educ, Georgia Inst of Technology, JS Coon Bldg, Ste 203, Atlanta GA 30332-0284 *Ph:* 404-894 7475 *Fax:* 404-894 9682 *E-mail:* study.abroad@gatech.edu

---

1275
IH ESPANA and INTERNATIONAL HOUSE BARCELONA
Business Spanish Course
Site: Spain: Barcelona
Dates: 4 wks, Feb, May, Jul, Nov
Subjects: Business language, Homestay, Spanish language (int/adv)
Eligibility: *Level:* adults *Requires:* previous study in field, int-adv Spanish *Age:* min 16
Credit: *Undergrad:* none *Grad:* none *Doc:* certificate
Instruction: *In:* Spanish *Format:* lang study *Students:* intl
Costs: About $1,300 *incl* tuition, housing, pgm activities
Housing: *Arr by pgm:* residence halls, apartments, homestay, pensions, hotels, hostels
Deadline: Until pgm filled
Other info: *US accredited sponsor:* no *Orient:* abroad *Activities:* excursions *Misc:* May take exam in bus Spanish given by Madrid Chamber of Commerce. Exam fees not incl. *URL:* http://www.ihes.com/bcn
Contact: *See Index II for Members* Intl House Barcelona, Trafalgar 14, 08010 Barcelona, Spain *E-mail:* spanish@bcn.ihes.com ▲

1276
IH ESPANA and INTERNATIONAL HOUSE BARCELONA
Courses in Spanish Culture
Site: Spain: Barcelona
Dates: 1 wk or longer, yr-round
Subjects: Art history, Civilization/culture, Folk dance, History, Literature, Media studies, Social work, Spanish studies
Eligibility: *Level:* adults *Requires:* int Spanish *Age:* min 16
Credit: *Undergrad:* none *Grad:* none *Doc:* certificate
Instruction: *In:* Spanish *Format:* lang study, lecture, workshop *Students:* intl
Costs: About $45 per wk *incl* tuition, fees
Housing: *Arr by pgm:* residence halls, apartments, homestay, pensions, hotels, hostels
Deadline: Until pgm filled
Other info: *US accredited sponsor:* no *Began:* 1993 *Orient:* abroad *Activities:* excursions *Misc:* Pgm designed to be combined with Intl House Barcelona intensive Spanish course. Course focuses on a different aspect of Spanish culture each wk. May contact former participants. *URL:* http://www.ihes.com/bcn
Contact: *See Index II for Members* Spanish, Intl House Barcelona, Trafalgar 14, 08010 Barcelona, Spain *E-mail:* spanish@bcn.ihes.com ▲

1277
IH ESPANA and INTERNATIONAL HOUSE BARCELONA
Curso de Metodologia y Cultura para Profesores-Barcelona
Site: Spain: Barcelona
Dates: 2 wks, Jan or Jul
Subjects: Civilization/culture, Spanish language, Spanish studies
Eligibility: *Level:* adults *Requires:* adv Spanish *Age:* min 18
Credit: *Undergrad:* none *Grad:* none *Doc:* certificate
Instruction: *In:* Spanish *Format:* lang study, lecture, practical training, seminar, student teaching, tutorial *Students:* intl
Costs: About $600 *incl* tuition, housing, fees, books/materials
Housing: *Arr by pgm:* residence halls, apartments, homestay, pensions, hotels, hostels
Deadline: 2 wks before pgm
Other info: *US accredited sponsor:* no *Began:* 1995 *Orient:* abroad *Misc:* May contact former participants. *URL:* http://www.ihes.com/bcn
Contact: *See Index II for Members* Intl House Barcelona, Trafalgar 14, Barcelona E-08010, Spain *E-mail:* formacio@bcn.ihes.com ▲

1278
IH ESPANA and **INTERNATIONAL HOUSE BARCELONA**
Cursos de Formacion para Profesores de Espanol-Barcelona
Site: Spain: Barcelona
Dates: 3 wks, Sep 4, Nov 6, Jan 31, Mar 27, Jun 7, Jul 3, Aug 7
Subjects: Foreign language teaching, Spanish language (beg/int/adv)
Eligibility: *Level:* adults *Requires:* adv Spanish *Age:* min 18
Credit: *Undergrad:* none *Grad:* none *Doc:* certificate
Instruction: *In:* Spanish *Format:* lang study, lecture, practical training, seminar, student teaching *Students:* intl
Costs: About $950 *incl* tuition, housing, books/materials
Housing: *Sponsor assists:* residence halls, apartments, homestay, pensions, hotels, hostels
Deadline: 2 wks before pgm
Other info: *US accredited sponsor:* no *Began:* 1987 *In coop with:* Intl Teacher Training Inst, Les Heures-Univ of Barcelona *Misc:* May contact former participants. *URL:* http://www.ihes.com/bcn
Contact: *See Index II for Members* Begona Montmany or Belen Rosado, Intl House Barcelona, Trafalgar 14, 08010 Barcelona, Spain *E-mail:* formacio@bcn.ihes.com ▲

1279
IH ESPANA and **INTERNATIONAL HOUSE BARCELONA**
Cursos Intensivos de Espanol en Barcelona
Site: Spain: Barcelona
Dates: 2-4 wks or longer, yr-round
Subjects: Spanish language (beg/int/adv)
Eligibility: *Level:* adults, adults *Age:* min 16
Credit: *Undergrad:* none *Grad:* none
Instruction: *In:* Spanish, Spanish *Format:* lang study, lang study *Students:* intl & intl
Costs: About $1,000 for 4 wks *incl* tuition, tuition, housing, housing, some meals, some meals, fees, fees, excursions, excursions, books/materials, books/materials
Housing: *Arr by pgm, Arr by pgm:* residence halls, residence halls, apartments, apartments, homestay, homestay, pensions, pensions, hotels, hotels, hostels, hostels
Deadline: Until pgm filled
Other info: *US accredited sponsor:* no *Began:* 1972 *Orient:* in US *Activities:* excursions, excursions *Misc:* May contact former participants. *URL:* http://www.ihes.com/bcn
Contact: *See Index II for Members* Registrations (Spanish Pgm), Intl House Barcelona, Trafalgar 14, 08010 Barcelona, Spain *E-mail:* spanish@bcn.ihes.com ▲

1280
IH ESPANA and **INTERNATIONAL HOUSE BARCELONA**
DELE Preparation Course-Barcelona
Site: Spain: Barcelona
Dates: 9 wks, Mar & Sep
Subjects: Spanish language (beg/int/adv)
Eligibility: *Level:* adults *Age:* min 16
Credit: *Undergrad:* none *Grad:* none *Doc:* certificate
Instruction: *In:* Spanish *Format:* lang study *Students:* intl
Costs: About $2,400 *incl* tuition, housing, pgm activities
Housing: *Arr by pgm:* residence halls, apartments, homestay, pensions, hotels, hostels
Deadline: Until pgm filled
Other info: *US accredited sponsor:* no *Orient:* abroad *Activities:* excursions *Misc:* Exam fees not incl. *URL:* http://www.ihes.com/bcn
Contact: *See Index II for Members* Intl House Barcelona, Trafalgar 14, 08010 Barcelona, Spain *E-mail:* spanish@bcn.ihes.com ▲

1281
IH ESPANA and **INTERNATIONAL HOUSE BARCELONA**
Executive Plus Course
Site: Spain: Barcelona
Dates: Yr-round
Subjects: Business language, Business/management, Spanish language
Eligibility: *Level:* adults *Age:* min 18
Credit: *Undergrad:* none *Grad:* none *Doc:* certificate
Instruction: *In:* Spanish *Format:* lang study, tutorial *Students:* intl
Costs: Contact sponsor
Housing: *Arr by pgm:* apartments, homestay, hotels
Deadline: Contact sponsor
Other info: *US accredited sponsor:* no *Misc:* One-on-one instruction & visits to companies. *URL:* http://www.ihes.com/bcn
Contact: *See Index II for Members* Spanish, Intl House Barcelona, Trafalgar 14, 08010 Barcelona, Spain *E-mail:* spanish@bcn.ihes.com ▲

1282
INSTITUTE FOR SOCIAL & INTERNATIONAL STUDIES (ISIS) and **PORTLAND STATE UNIVERSITY**
ISIS-Architectural Studies: City and Space-Barcelona
Site: Spain: Barcelona
Dates: 4 wks, Jul
Subjects: Architectural history, Architecture, Field study, Spanish language (beg/int/adv), Urban planning
Eligibility: *Level:* sophs, jrs, srs, grads *Requires:* 3.0 GPA, previous study in field
Credit: *Undergrad:* 8 *Grad:* none *Doc:* transcript
Instruction: *In:* English *Format:* directed field study, lecture *Students:* mainly US
Costs: $3,250 *incl* tuition, housing, some meals, insurance, fees, excursions, books/materials *Nonrefundable fee*
Housing: *Arr by pgm:* homestay
Deadline: May 15
Other info: *US accredited sponsor:* yes *Began:* 2000 *Orient:* abroad (2 days) *Activities:* excursions, field trips *Misc:* May contact former participants. *URL:* http://isis.pdx.edu
Contact: Teresa Taylor, ISIS at Portland State Univ, Intl Educ Svcs, PO Box 751, Portland OR 97207-0751 *Ph:* 800-547 8887 ext 4029; 503-725 4029 *Fax:* 503-725 5320 *E-mail:* isis@pdx.edu

---

1283
PORTLAND STATE UNIVERSITY and **INSTITUTE FOR SOCIAL & INTERNATIONAL STUDIES (ISIS)**
ISIS Professional Development Program for Teachers of Spanish
Site: Spain: Barcelona
Dates: 3 wks, Jul 5-30
Subjects: Education/teaching, Foreign language teaching, Spanish language (adv), Spanish studies
Eligibility: *Level:* grads, teachers *Requires:* previous study in field, Spanish fluency, Spanish teaching experience
Credit: *Undergrad:* none *Grad:* 8 *Doc:* transcript
Instruction: *In:* Spanish *Format:* directed field study, independent study, lang study, lecture, practical training *Students:* mainly US
Costs: $2,850 *incl* tuition, housing, some meals, insurance, fees, excursions, ITIC
Housing: *Arr by pgm:* homestay
Deadline: May 31
Other info: *US accredited sponsor:* yes *Began:* 1996 *Orient:* abroad *Activities:* excursions *Misc:* May contact former participants. *URL:* http://www.isis.pdx.edu
Contact: Dean Teresa Taylor, ISIS, c/o Portland State Univ, Intl Educ Svcs, PO Box 751, Portland OR 97207 *Ph:* 800-547 8887 ext 4029; 503-725 4029 *Fax:* 503-725 5320 *E-mail:* isis@pdx.edu

---

1284
PORTLAND STATE UNIVERSITY and **INSTITUTE FOR SOCIAL & INTERNATIONAL STUDIES (ISIS)**
ISIS Program in Barcelona: Summer Session
Site: Spain: Barcelona *Host inst:* ISIS
Dates: 4 wks, Jul 3-31
Subjects: Architecture, Art history, Geography, History, Sociology, Spanish language (beg/int/adv), Spanish studies
Eligibility: *Level:* sophs, jrs, srs, grads *Requires:* B avg, references, dr's statement
Credit: *Undergrad:* 8 *Grad:* none *Doc:* transcript
Instruction: *In:* English, Spanish *Format:* lang study, lecture, seminar, tutorial *Students:* mainly US
Costs: $3,375 *incl* tuition, housing, some meals, insurance, fees, excursions, books/materials, ISIC
Housing: *Arr by pgm:* homestay
Deadline: May 15; rolling admissions
Other info: *US accredited sponsor:* yes *Began:* 1988 *Orient:* abroad (intensive lang study) *Activities:* field trips *Misc:* May contact former participants. *Financial aid:* scholarships *URL:* http://www.isis.pdx.edu
Contact: ISIS, Portland State Univ, Intl Educ Svcs, PO Box 751, Portland OR 97207 *Ph:* 800-547 8887 ext 4029; 503-725 4029 *Fax:* 503-725 5320 *E-mail:* isis@pdx.edu

---

1285
SCHOOL OF VISUAL ARTS (SVA)
Painting in Barcelona
Site: Spain: Barcelona *Host inst:* Escola d'Arts Aplicades i d'Oficis Artistics Llotja
Dates: 3 wks, Jun 21-Jul 14
Subjects: Painting, Studio arts
Eligibility: *Level:* sophs, jrs, srs, grads, adults, teachers, professionals *Requires:* portfolio review/slides
Credit: *Undergrad:* avail *Grad:* none
Instruction: *In:* English *Format:* art studio *Students:* intl & host country
Costs: $3,200 *incl* tuition, housing, some meals, intl airfare *Nonrefundable fee*
Housing: *Arr by pgm:* hotels
Deadline: May 15
Other info: *US accredited sponsor:* yes *Began:* 1989 *Orient:* abroad *Misc:* May contact former participants.
Contact: Dora Riomayor, Intl Studies, Sch of Visual Arts, 209 E 23rd St, New York NY 10010 *Ph:* 212-592 2543 *Fax:* 212-592 2545 *E-mail:* dorariomayor@schoolofvisualarts.edu

---

1286
SOUTHERN ILLINOIS UNIVERSITY AT CARBONDALE
Summer Workshop in Barcelona
Site: Spain: Barcelona *Host inst:* La Rectoria Ctr d'Arts
Dates: 3 wks, May 18-Jun 7
Subjects: Ceramics/pottery, Furnishings/furniture, Photography, Printmaking
Eligibility: *Level:* sophs, jrs, srs, grads, adults, teachers, professionals *Requires:* 2.5 GPA, previous study in field, arts background *Age:* min 18
Credit: *Undergrad:* 3 *Grad:* none *Doc:* transcript
Instruction: *In:* English *Students:* mainly US
Costs: $1,900 *incl* housing, all meals, intl airfare, excursions
Housing: *Arr by pgm:* residence halls
Deadline: Apr 1
Other info: *US accredited sponsor:* yes *Began:* 1997 *In coop with:* La Rectoria Ctr d'Arts *Orient:* in US & abroad (1 day) *Activities:* field trips, cultural events *URL:* http://www.siu.edu/departments/study_abroad/
Contact: Thomas A Saville, Study Abroad Pgms, Mailcode 6885, Southern Illinois Univ, Carbondale IL 62901-6885 *Ph:* 618-453 7670 *Fax:* 618-453 7647 *E-mail:* studyabr@siu.edu

---

1287
SUNY COLLEGE AT OSWEGO
Barcelona Summer
Site: Spain: Barcelona *Host inst:* Univ of Barcelona
Dates: 4 wks, Jul
Subjects: Homestay, Spanish language
Eligibility: *Level:* jrs, srs *Requires:* 2.5 GPA, Spanish lang study
Credit: *Undergrad:* 6 *Grad:* none *Doc:* transcript
Instruction: *In:* Spanish *Format:* lang study *Students:* intl
Costs: $3,700 *incl* tuition, housing, all meals, intl airfare, insurance, fees, books/materials *Nonrefundable fee*
Housing: *Arr by pgm:* homestay
Deadline: Apr 1
Other info: *US accredited sponsor:* yes *Began:* 1999 *Orient:* abroad *Activities:* field trips *URL:* http://www.oswego.edu/~intled
Contact: Intl Educ, SUNY Oswego, 102 Rich Hall, Oswego NY 13126 *Ph:* 888-467 9346; 315-341 2118 *Fax:* 315-341 2477 *E-mail:* intled@oswego.edu

---

1288
UNIVERSITY OF KANSAS
Summer Language and Culture Institute in Barcelona, Spain
Site: Spain: Barcelona
Dates: 8 wks, mid-Jun-early Aug
Subjects: Civilization/culture, Literature, Spanish language, Spanish studies
Eligibility: *Level:* fresh, sophs, jrs, srs *Requires:* 2 sems coll Spanish
Credit: *Undergrad:* 7 *Grad:* none *Doc:* transcript
Instruction: *In:* Spanish *Format:* lang study, lecture, study tour *Students:* mainly US
Costs: $2,700 *incl* tuition, housing, all meals, fees, excursions, study tour, cultural events
Housing: *Arr by pgm:* residence halls, hotels during tour
Deadline: Feb 15
Other info: *US accredited sponsor:* yes *Began:* 1963 *Activities:* field trips, program travel *Misc:* 10-day study tour incl visits to Alicante, Cordoba, Granada, Madrid, Peniscola, Segovia, Toledo. *URL:* http://www.ukans.edu/~osa
Contact: Renee Bergene, Coord, Study Abroad, Univ of Kansas, 108 Lippincott Hall, Lawrence KS 66045 *Ph:* 785-864 3742 *Fax:* 785-864 5040 *E-mail:* osa@ukans.edu ▲

1289
UNIVERSITY OF SAN DIEGO, SCHOOL OF BUSINESS ADMINISTRATION
Graduate Business Study Abroad in Barcelona
Site: Spain: Barcelona *Host inst:* ESADE
Dates: Jun-early Jul (3 wks distance learning, 2 wks in country)
Subjects: Business/management, European studies, Finance, Homestay, Human resources, International business, International marketing, Organizational behavior
Eligibility: *Level:* grads, professionals *Requires:* enrollment in or graduation from grad bus or related grad pgm, good acad standing
Credit: *Undergrad:* none *Grad:* 3 per course *Doc:* transcript
Instruction: *In:* English *Format:* lecture, seminar *Students:* US & intl
Costs: $1,450 for 1 course, $2,400 for 2 courses *incl* tuition, intl airfare *Nonrefundable fee*
Housing: *Sponsor assists:* apartments, homestay, hotels
Deadline: None
Other info: *US accredited sponsor:* yes *Began:* 1999 *Orient:* abroad (1 day) *Activities:* excursions, field trips, program travel, cultural events *Misc:* Company visits. May contact former participants. *URL:* http://business.acusd.edu/ib/spain.html

Contact: Kira Mendez, Coord, or Amanda Ryan, Admin Asst, Ahlers Ctr for Intl Bus, Univ of San Diego Sch of Bus Admin, 5998 Alcala Park, San Diego CA 92110-2492 *Ph:* 800-248 4873; 619-260 4896 *Fax:* 619-260 4891 *E-mail:* ib@acusd.edu

---

1290
UNIVERSITY OF SAN DIEGO, SCHOOL OF LAW
Barcelona Institute on International and Comparative Law
Site: Spain: Barcelona *Host inst:* Univ of Barcelona
Dates: May 28-Jun 22
Subjects: Business law, European law, International law, Internships
Eligibility: *Level:* grads, teachers, professionals *Requires:* law or bus students
Credit: *Undergrad:* none *Grad:* 4 *Doc:* certificate
Instruction: *In:* English *Format:* internship, lang study *Students:* mainly US
Costs: $2,200 for classes, $3,950 for internship *incl* tuition, books/materials *Nonrefundable fee*
Housing: *Sponsor assists*
Deadline: Mar 11
Other info: *US accredited sponsor:* yes *Began:* 1996 *In coop with:* Mayor of Barcelona, General Dir of Catalan Univs *Orient:* in US & abroad *Misc:* Correspondence re:pgm must be in English. Legal & some tourist visits arr from site. Loans avail to US students only. *URL:* http://www.acusd.edu/lawabroad
Contact: Cindy King, Law Pgms Abroad, Univ of San Diego, 5998 Alcala Park, San Diego CA 92110-2492 *Ph:* 619-260 7460 *Fax:* 619-260 2230 *E-mail:* cking@acusd.edu

---

CADIZ

1291
ACADEMIC PROGRAMS INTERNATIONAL (API)
Academic Programs International-Cadiz
Site: Spain: Cadiz *Host inst:* Univ de Cadiz
Dates: 6 wks, Jun-Jul
Subjects: Business/management, Civilization/culture, Homestay, Literature, Spanish language (beg/int/adv), Spanish studies
Eligibility: *Level:* fresh, sophs, jrs, srs, adults *Requires:* 2.75 GPA *Age:* min 18, avg 21
Credit: *Undergrad:* 6 *Grad:* none *Doc:* transcript, certificate
Instruction: *In:* Spanish *Format:* lab, lang study, lecture, seminar, tutorial *Students:* intl
Costs: $3,150 *incl* tuition, housing, all meals, insurance, excursions, books/materials, tutoring, ground transport
Housing: *Arr by pgm:* homestay
Deadline: Apr 1
Other info: *US accredited sponsor:* no *Began:* 1997 *Orient:* in US & abroad (2 wks, intensive lang study) *Activities:* excursions, field trips, program travel, cultural events *Misc:* On-site dir. Airport reception. May contact former participants. *Financial aid:* scholarships *URL:* http://www.academicintl.com
Contact: Jennifer Allen or Dr Sharon Foerster, Acad Pgms Intl, 129 E Hopkins, Ste 101, San Marcos TX 78666 *Ph:* 800-844 4124; 512-392 8520 *Fax:* 512-392 8420 *E-mail:* api@onr.com

---

1292
SAINT JOHN'S UNIVERSITY (NY)
College Europa Spain
Site: Spain: Cadiz
Dates: 1 mo, Aug-Sep
Subjects: Spanish language (beg/int/adv)
Eligibility: *Level:* fresh, sophs, jrs, srs, grads *Requires:* 2.75 GPA, 2 recommendation letters, interview *Age:* min 18
Credit: *Undergrad:* 3 per term *Grad:* none *Doc:* transcript
Instruction: *In:* Spanish *Format:* lang study, lecture, study tour *Students:* mainly US
Costs: Contact Sponsor
Housing: *Arr by pgm:* residence halls, apartments, hotels
Deadline: Apr 1
Other info: *US accredited sponsor:* yes *Began:* 1997 *Orient:* in US (1 day) *Activities:* excursions, field trips *Misc:* Field trips to Madrid, Segovia, Toledo, Seville, Escorial & the Valley of the Fallen. May contact former participants.
Contact: Joyce Lawlor, Dean, Study Abroad Pgms, St John's Univ, Bent Hall, Rm 388, 8000 Utopia Pkwy, Jamaica NY 11439 *Ph:* 718-990 6105 *Fax:* 718-990 2321 *E-mail:* intled@stjohns.edu
Or Contact: Dr Nicholas Toscano, Modern Foreign Langs, St John's Univ, 8000 Utopia Pkwy, Jamaica NY 11439 *Ph:* 718-990 6161 ext 5112 *Fax:* 718-990 1870

CAMINO DE SANTIAGO

1293
COUNCIL ON INTERNATIONAL EDUCATIONAL EXCHANGE (COUNCIL)
International Faculty Development Seminars-Camino de Santiago
Site: Spain: Camino de Santiago *Host inst:* Univs of Leon, Navarra, Santiago
Dates: 12 days, Jun
Subjects: Architecture, Art, Economics, History, Religion/theology, Spanish studies
Eligibility: *Level:* teachers, professionals *Requires:* must be faculty at 2-yr or 4-yr inst
Credit: *Undergrad:* avail *Grad:* none
Instruction: *In:* English *Format:* lecture, seminar *Students:* mainly US
Costs: $1,950 *incl* tuition, housing, some meals, fees, excursions, books/materials *Nonrefundable fee*
Housing: *Arr by pgm:* hotels
Deadline: Mar 15
Other info: *US accredited sponsor:* no *Began:* 1999 *Orient:* abroad *Activities:* excursions, field trips, program travel, cultural events *Misc:* Seminar title: Spain: Past & Present: Camino de Santiago. May contact former participants. *Financial aid:* scholarships *URL:* http://www.ciee.org/ifds
Contact: Jennifer Ley, Pgm Mgr, Intl Faculty Development Seminars, Council, 633 3rd Ave, New York NY 10017-5706 *Ph:* 212-822 2747 *Fax:* 212-822 2699 *E-mail:* ifds@ciee.org ▲

CORDOBA

1294
WILLIAM JEWELL COLLEGE
Summer in Spain
Site: Spain: Cordoba *Host inst:* Col Mayor Univ Mixto Nuestra Senora de la Asuncion
Dates: Late May-early Jul
Subjects: Spanish language (beg/int/adv), Spanish studies
Eligibility: *Level:* fresh, sophs, jrs, srs, adults *Age:* min 16
Credit: *Undergrad:* 2-10 *Grad:* none
Instruction: *In:* Spanish *Format:* lang study, lecture *Students:* mainly US
Costs: $2,900 *incl* tuition, housing, all meals, excursions
Housing: *Arr by pgm:* residence halls
Deadline: Mar 15
Other info: *US accredited sponsor:* yes *Began:* 1983 *Orient:* in US *Activities:* excursions *Misc:* Pgm offered in even-numbered yrs only. *URL:* http://www.jewell.edu/overseas/

Contact: Tami Lewis Jones, Evening Div, Summer Sch, William Jewell Coll, Liberty MO 64068 *Ph:* 816-415 5001 *Fax:* 816-415 5015 *E-mail:* jonest@william.jewell.edu

EL PUERTO DE SANTA MARIA

1295
ESTUDIO INTERNACIONAL SAMPERE
Curso y Lengua de Civilizacion
Site: Spain: El Puerto de Santa Maria
Dates: 1 wk-1 yr, yr-round
Subjects: Spanish language (beg/int/adv)
Eligibility: *Level:* grads, adults, teachers, professionals, precoll *Age:* min 16, max 65, avg 21
Credit: *Undergrad:* avail *Grad:* none *Doc:* certificate, diploma *Transfer credit through:* Nicholls State Univ
Instruction: *In:* Spanish *Format:* lang study, lecture *Students:* intl
Costs: $350 per wk *incl* tuition, housing, all meals, fees, excursions, books/materials
Housing: *Arr by pgm:* apartments, homestay, pensions
Deadline: Contact sponsor
Other info: *US accredited sponsor:* no *Began:* 1987 *Activities:* excursions, field trips *Misc:* Transfer credit also avail through Univ of Arizona. May contact former participants.
Contact: Cristina Sampere, EIS, Pagador 18, E-11500 Pto Sta Maria, Spain *E-mail:* puerto@eisampere.es

1296
TRINITY SCHOOL, ACADEMIA DE IDIOMAS
Spanish in Spain
Site: Spain: El Puerto de Santa Maria
Dates: 2 wks or longer, yr-round
Subjects: Spanish language (beg/int/adv)
Eligibility: *Level:* fresh, sophs, jrs, srs, grads, adults, teachers, professionals, precoll *Age:* min 18, avg 25
Credit: *Undergrad:* none *Grad:* none *Doc:* certificate
Instruction: *In:* Spanish *Format:* lang study, lecture *Students:* intl
Costs: 36,000-51,500 ptas for 2 wks *incl* tuition, excursions, books/materials *Nonrefundable fee*
Housing: *Arr by pgm:* apartments, homestay, pensions, hotels, hostels, campsites
Deadline: 1-2 wks before pgm
Other info: *US accredited sponsor:* no *Began:* 1986 *Activities:* excursions, cultural events *Misc:* May contact former participants. *URL:* http://www.spa.es/~trinity
Contact: Mr Ian Walsh or Maria Lopez Rodriguez, Trinity Sch, Apdo de Correos 720, Calle Ave del Paraiso 6, El Puerto de Santa Maria, Cadiz, Spain 11500 *E-mail:* trinity@spa.es

GIRONA

1297
TEMPLE UNIVERSITY
Temple in Spain
Site: Spain: Girona *Host inst:* Univ of Girona
Dates: 6 wks, Jun-Jul
Subjects: Homestay, Literature, Spanish language, Spanish studies
Eligibility: *Level:* jrs, srs *Requires:* I yr coll level Spanish
Credit: *Undergrad:* 6 *Grad:* none
Instruction: *In:* Spanish *Format:* lang study, lecture *Students:* mainly US
Costs: $2,800-$3,600 *incl* tuition, housing, some meals, fees, excursions, 5-7 day trip through Central & *Nonrefundable fee*
Housing: *Arr by pgm:* homestay
Deadline: Mar 1
Other info: *US accredited sponsor:* yes *Orient:* in US & abroad *Activities:* excursions *Misc:* Scholarships avail for Temple students only May contact former participants. *URL:* http://www.temple.edu/intlprog/
Contact: Intl Pgms, Temple Univ, 200 Tuttleman Learning Ctr, 1809 N 13th St, Philadelphia PA 19122 *Ph:* 215-204 0720 *Fax:* 215-204 0729 *E-mail:* intlprog@vm.temple.edu

GRANADA

1298
ACADEMIC PROGRAMS INTERNATIONAL (API)
Academic Programs International at University of Granada
Site: Spain: Granada *Host inst:* Univ of Granada
Dates: 6 wks, May 23-Jun 30, Jun 20-Jul 28 or Jul 22-Aug 31
Subjects: Civilization/culture, Homestay, Literature, Spanish language, Spanish studies
Eligibility: *Level:* fresh, sophs, jrs, srs, adults, teachers, professionals *Requires:* 2.75 GPA, recommendation letter *Age:* min 18, avg 21
Credit: *Undergrad:* 6-8 *Grad:* none *Doc:* transcript
Instruction: *In:* Spanish *Format:* lang study, lecture, study tour, tutorial *Students:* intl
Costs: $3,100 *incl* tuition, housing, all meals, insurance, fees, excursions, books/materials, airport transfer, tutoring
Housing: *Arr by pgm:* homestay, residencia
Deadline: Apr 1; Mar 1 for scholarships
Other info: *US accredited sponsor:* no *Began:* 1998 *Orient:* in US & abroad (2 wks, intensive lang study) *Activities:* excursions, field trips, program travel, cultural events *Misc:* Resident dir. May contact former participants. *Financial aid:* scholarships *URL:* http://www.academicintl.com
Contact: Jennifer C Allen, Dir, Acad Pgms Intl, 129 E Hopkins St, Ste 101, San Marcos TX 78666 *Ph:* 800-844 4124; 512-392 8520 *Fax:* 512-392 8420 *E-mail:* api@onr.com

1299
CULTURAL EXPERIENCES ABROAD (CEA)
Study Spanish Language and Culture in Granada
Site: Spain: Granada *Host inst:* Univ of Granada
Dates: 4-8 wks, Jun-Aug
Subjects: Civilization/culture, Homestay, Independent study, Liberal arts, Linguistics, Spanish language (beg/int/adv)
Eligibility: *Level:* fresh, sophs, jrs, srs, grads, precoll *Requires:* previous Spanish lang study recommended *Age:* min 17, avg 20
Credit: *Undergrad:* 4-5 per 4 wks *Grad:* avail *Doc:* transcript, certificate
Instruction: *In:* Spanish *Format:* independent study, lang study, lecture, study tour, tutorial *Students:* intl
Costs: $3,000-4,000 per session *incl* tuition, housing, all meals, insurance, fees, excursions, orient, airport transfers *Nonrefundable fee*
Housing: *Arr by pgm:* residence halls, apartments, homestay
Deadline: Rolling admissions
Other info: *US accredited sponsor:* no *In coop with:* Univ of Granada *Orient:* abroad *Activities:* excursions, field trips, program travel, cultural events, sports *Misc:* Exch pgm with native speakers. Support svcs, tutoring, on-site dir. May contact former participants. *Financial aid:* scholarships *URL:* http://www.travelabroad.com
Contact: CEA Study Abroad, 1400 E Southern Ave, Ste B-108, Tempe AZ 85282-8011 *Ph:* 480-557 7900 *Fax:* 480-557 7926 *E-mail:* spanish@travelabroad.com

1300
DON QUIJOTE
DELE Preparation Course-Granada
Site: Spain: Granada
Dates: 2, 3 or 4 wks, May or Nov
Subjects: Spanish language (int/adv)

Eligibility: *Level:* adults *Requires:* previous study in field *Age:* min 18, avg 26
Credit: *Undergrad:* none *Grad:* none *Doc:* diploma
Instruction: *In:* Spanish *Format:* lang study, lecture *Students:* intl
Costs: $522 for 2 wks, $722 for 3 wks, $922 for 4 wks *incl* tuition, housing, books/materials, activities
Housing: *Arr by pgm:* residence halls, apartments, homestay, hotels, hostels
Deadline: Rolling admissions
Other info: *US accredited sponsor:* no *Began:* 1992 *Orient:* abroad *Activities:* excursions, program travel, cultural events, sports *Misc:* Diploma preparation. 25discount if combined with standard course. *URL:* http://www.donquijote.org
Contact: Area Mgr/USA, Don Quijote-Central Promotion, Apdo de Correos 333, Ref: USII98, 37080 Salamanca, Spain *E-mail:* amusa@donquijote.org

---

1301
DON QUIJOTE
Refresher Course for Teachers of Spanish/Curso de Repaso-Granada
Site: Spain: Granada
Dates: 2 wks, yr-round; special starting dates
Subjects: Foreign language teaching, Spanish language (adv)
Eligibility: *Level:* teachers *Requires:* adv Spanish *Age:* min 18, avg 40
Credit: *Undergrad:* none *Grad:* none *Doc:* certificate
Instruction: *In:* Spanish *Format:* directed field study, independent study, internship, lang study, lecture, practical training, seminar, student teaching *Students:* intl
Costs: $694 for group, $1,184 for individual *incl* tuition, housing, books/materials, activities
Housing: *Arr by pgm:* residence halls, homestay
Deadline: Rolling admissions
Other info: *US accredited sponsor:* no *Began:* 1992 *Orient:* abroad (intensive lang study) *Activities:* excursions, field trips, cultural events *Misc:* Pgm examines theoretical & practical methods of teaching Spanish. May contact former participants. *URL:* http://www.donquijote.org
Contact: Area Mgr/USA, Don Quijote-Central Promotion, Apdo de Correos 333, Ref: USII98, Salamanca 37080, Spain *E-mail:* amusa@donquijote.org

---

1302
DON QUIJOTE
Spanish in Spain Short-Term Courses: Granada
Site: Spain: Granada
Dates: 1-12 wks, yr-round
Subjects: Spanish language (beg/int/adv)
Eligibility: *Level:* adults *Age:* min 18, avg 26
Credit: *Undergrad:* 3 for 60 hrs *Grad:* none *Doc:* certificate, diploma
Instruction: *In:* Spanish *Format:* lang study, lecture *Students:* intl
Costs: $842 for 4 wks *incl* tuition, housing, books/materials, activities
Housing: *Arr by pgm:* residence halls, apartments, homestay, hotels, hostels
Deadline: Rolling admissions
Other info: *US accredited sponsor:* no *Began:* 1991 *Activities:* excursions, field trips, program travel, cultural events, sports *Misc:* May contact former participants. *URL:* http://www.donquijote.org
Contact: Area Mgr/USA, Don Quijote-Central Promotion, Apdo de Correos 333, Ref: USII98, 37080 Salamanca, Spain *E-mail:* amusa@donquijote.org

---

1303
DON QUIJOTE
Super Intensive Course-Granada
Site: Spain: Granada
Dates: 1-36 wks, yr-round
Subjects: Civilization/culture, Spanish language (beg/int/adv)
Eligibility: *Level:* adults *Age:* min 18, avg 26
Credit: *Undergrad:* none *Grad:* none *Doc:* certificate, diploma
Instruction: *In:* Spanish *Format:* independent study, lang study, lecture, study tour, tutorial *Students:* intl
Costs: Contact sponsor
Housing: *Sponsor assists:* apartments, homestay, hotels, hostels
Deadline: Contact sponsor
Other info: *US accredited sponsor:* no *Began:* 1990 *Activities:* excursions, field trips, program travel, cultural events, sports *Misc:* Costs incl homestay housing option only. May contact former participants. *URL:* http://www.donquijote.org
Contact: Area Mgr/USA, Don Quijote, Placentinos No 2, Apdo 333, 37080 Salamanca, Spain *E-mail:* amusa@donquijote.org

---

1304
ISA
Cursos Intesivo de Lengua Espanola: Summer Program in Granada
Site: Spain: Granada *Host inst:* Univ of Granada
Dates: 5 wks, May 24-Jun 30, Jun 22-Jul 28 or Jul 25-Aug 31, or 4 wks, Jan, May or Sep
Subjects: Civilization/culture, Homestay, Literature, Spanish language (beg/int/adv)
Eligibility: *Level:* fresh, sophs, jrs, srs, grads, adults *Requires:* 2.5 GPA, recommendation letter *Age:* min 18, avg 21
Credit: *Undergrad:* 5 sem hrs /8 qtr hrs *Grad:* none *Doc:* transcript, certificate
Instruction: *In:* Spanish *Format:* lab, lang study, lecture, tutorial *Students:* intl
Costs: $2,225 for 4 wks, $3,225 for 5 wks *incl* tuition, housing, all meals, insurance, fees, excursions, laundry, tutoring, ISIC
Housing: *Arr by pgm:* apartments, homestay, hotels
Deadline: Apr 5; Mar 10 for scholarships
Other info: *US accredited sponsor:* no *Began:* 1994 *Orient:* in US & abroad *Activities:* excursions, field trips, cultural events *Misc:* Resident dir incl in costs. May contact former participants. *Financial aid:* scholarships *URL:* http://www.studiesabroad.com
Contact: Gustavo Artaza, Exec Dir, ISA, 901 W 24th St, Austin TX 78705 *Ph:* 800-580 8826; 512-480 8522 *Fax:* 512-480 8866 *E-mail:* isa@studiesabroad.com ▲

1305
UNIVERSITY OF DELAWARE
Summer Session in Spain
Site: Spain: Granada *Host inst:* Univ of Granada
Dates: 1 mo, beg Jun
Subjects: Art history, Civilization/culture, Homestay, Music, Spanish language, Spanish studies (int)
Eligibility: *Level:* fresh, sophs, jrs, srs, adults *Requires:* 2.0 GPA
Credit: *Undergrad:* 6-7 *Grad:* none *Doc:* transcript
Instruction: *In:* English, Spanish *Format:* lang study, lecture, study tour *Students:* mainly US
Costs: Contact sponsor
Housing: *Arr by pgm:* homestay
Deadline: Mid-Mar
Other info: *US accredited sponsor:* yes *Orient:* avail yes *Activities:* excursions, field trips, program travel, cultural events *Misc:* Contact sponsor to arrange honors credit. *Financial aid:* scholarships *URL:* http://www.udel.edu/studyabroad/
Contact: Lisa Chieffo, Foreign Langs & Literatures, Univ of Delaware, 326 Smith Hall, Newark DE 19716 *Ph:* 302-831 6458 *Fax:* 302-831 6459 *E-mail:* lchieffo@udel.edu
Or Contact: Intl Pgms & Special Sessions, Univ of Delaware, 4 Kent Way, Newark DE 19716-1450 *Ph:* 888-831 4685; 302-831 2852 *Fax:* 302-831 6042 *E-mail:* studyabroad@udel.edu

---

1306
UNIVERSITY OF DELAWARE
Winter Session in Granada
Site: Spain: Granada *Host inst:* Univ of Granada
Dates: 1 mo, Jan

Subjects: Civilization/culture, Homestay, Spanish language (int)
Eligibility: *Level:* fresh, sophs, jrs, srs, adults *Requires:* 2.0 GPA, 2 sems coll Spanish or 4 yrs high sch
Credit: *Undergrad:* 6-7 *Grad:* none *Doc:* transcript
Instruction: *In:* English, Spanish *Format:* lang study, lecture, study tour *Students:* mainly US
Costs: Contact sponsor
Housing: *Arr by pgm:* homestay
Deadline: Early Oct
Other info: *US accredited sponsor:* yes *Began:* 1988 *Orient:* avail yes *Activities:* excursions, field trips, program travel, cultural events *Misc:* Contact sponsor to arrange honors credit. *Financial aid:* scholarships *URL:* http://www.udel.edu/studyabroad/
Contact: Lisa Chieffo, Study Abroad Coord, Foreign Langs & Literatures, Univ of Delaware, 326 Smith Hall, Newark DE 19716 *Ph:* 302-831 6458 *Fax:* 302-831 0597 *E-mail:* lchieffo@udel.edu
Or Contact: Intl Pgms & Special Sessions, Univ of Delaware, 4 Kent Way, Newark DE 19716 *Ph:* 888-831 4685; 302-831 2852 *Fax:* 302-831 6042 *E-mail:* studyabroad@udel.edu

---

ISLA CRISTINA

1307
IH ESPANA and CLIC INTERNATIONAL HOUSE SEVILLA
Spanish Intensive Courses at the Beach
Site: Spain: Isla Cristina
Dates: 4-wk sessions, Jul-Sep 1
Subjects: Civilization/culture, Spanish language (beg/int/adv), Spanish studies
Eligibility: *Level:* adults *Age:* min 16, avg 22
Credit: *Undergrad:* none *Grad:* none *Doc:* certificate
Instruction: *In:* Spanish *Format:* lang study *Students:* intl
Costs: About $1,030 per mo *incl* tuition, housing, some meals, fees, excursions, books/materials, cultural pgm
Housing: *Arr by pgm:* apartments with local students, apartments, homestay, hotels
Deadline: 3 wks before pgm
Other info: *US accredited sponsor:* no *Began:* 1993 *In coop with:* FIYTO, ALTO, ACEIA, OLE, INTERNATIONAL HOUSE *Activities:* excursions, field trips, program travel, cultural events, sports *Misc:* May contact former participants. *URL:* http://www.clic.es
Contact: *See Index II for Members* Bernhard Roters, Dir or Eva White, CLIC, Calle Albareda 19, 41001 Seville, Spain *E-mail:* clic@clic.es ▲

LAS PALMAS

1308
GRAN CANARIA SCHOOL OF LANGUAGES
Intensive Spanish Courses
Site: Spain: Las Palmas de Gran Canaria
Dates: 2-24 wks, yr-round
Subjects: Spanish language (beg/int/adv)
Eligibility: *Level:* fresh, sophs, jrs, srs,

grads, adults, teachers, professionals, precoll *Age:* min 16
Credit: *Undergrad:* avail *Grad:* none
Instruction: *In:* Spanish *Format:* lang study, lecture, student teaching *Students:* intl
Costs: EUR 313 per wk *incl* tuition, housing, some meals *Nonrefundable fee*
Housing: *Arr by pgm:* residence halls
Deadline: 1 mo before pgm
Other info: *US accredited sponsor:* no *Began:* 1964 *Orient:* in US *Activities:* excursions, cultural events *Misc:* Teacher certification avail. May contact former participants. *URL:* http://usuarios.intercom.es/gcschool
Contact: Oliver Belz, Gran Canaria Sch of Langs, Grau Bassas 27, Las Palmas de Gran Canaria E-35007, Spain *E-mail:* gcschool@intercom.es
Or Contact: Ms Lorraine Haber, Study Abroad, CES, 330 7th Ave, 6th Fl, New York NY 10001 *Ph:* 212-629 7300 *Fax:* 212-736 7950 *E-mail:* ces_newyork@cescorp.com

---

1309
STUDY ABROAD/A LIFE EXPERIENCE
Spanish Language-Las Palmas
Site: Spain: Las Palmas *Host inst:* Univ de Las Palmas de Gran Canaria
Dates: 6 wks
Subjects: Civilization/culture, History, Literature, Spanish language (beg/int/adv), Spanish studies
Eligibility: *Level:* fresh, sophs, jrs, srs *Requires:* 2.5 GPA
Credit: *Undergrad:* 6-8 *Grad:* none
Instruction: *In:* Spanish *Format:* lang study, lecture, study tour, tutorial *Students:* intl
Costs: Contact sponsor
Housing: *Arr by pgm:* residence halls
Deadline: Contact sponsor
Other info: *US accredited sponsor:* no *Began:* 2000 *Orient:* abroad *Activities:* excursions, field trips *Misc:* May contact former participants. *URL:* http://www.foreignstudies.net
Contact: Clayton Murphy, Study Abroad/A Life Experience, 4513 Albatross Dr, Seabrook TX 77586 *Ph:* 888-722 5346; 281-291 7344 *Fax:* 281-291 7355 *E-mail:* moreinfo@foreignstudies.net

---

LEON

1310
UNIVERSIDAD DE LEON and HAMILTON COLLEGE
Summer Institute of Hispanic Studies (SIHS)
Site: Spain: Leon *Host inst:* Summer Inst of Hispanic Studies
Dates: 6 wks, Jun 19-Aug 2
Subjects: Anthropology, Art, Civilization/culture, Dance, Economics, Ethnography, Field study, History, Homestay, Independent study, Literature, Political science/politics, Spanish language (int/adv), Spanish studies
Eligibility: *Level:* fresh, sophs, jrs, srs, grads, adults, teachers, professionals *Requires:* previous study in field, 2 sems coll lang study for Tier 1, 3-4 sems for Tier 2 *Age:* avg 20
Credit: *Undergrad:* 6 *Grad:* none *Doc:* transcript, certificate
Instruction: *In:* Spanish *Format:* directed field study, independent study, lang study, lecture, practical training, seminar, study tour *Students:* mainly US
Costs: $4,675 or $4,875 *incl* tuition, housing, all meals, fees, excursions, dance lessons, entertainment *Nonrefundable fee*
Housing: *Arr by pgm:* homestay
Deadline: Apr 15; Feb 29 for early decision
Other info: *US accredited sponsor:* yes *Began:* 1993 *Orient:* avail in Andalusia, Extremadura & Nerja (1 wk, intensive lang study) *Activities:* excursions, field trips, program travel, cultural events, sports *Misc:* Excursions throughout Northern Spain, Segovia, Madrid, Extremadura & Andalusia. Univ of Leon sports facilities. May contact former participants. *URL:* http://www.hamilton.edu/academics/programs_abroad/
Contact: Prof Jeremy T Medina, Dir, Summer Inst Hispanic Studies, Romance Langs, Hamilton Coll, PO Box 165, 13 Stryker La, Clinton NY 13323 *Ph:* 315-859 4213, 315-853 1616 *Fax:* 315-859 4969 *E-mail:* jmedina@hamilton.edu
Or Contact: Santiago Tejerina-Canal, Dir of SIHS in Leon, Head of Spanish, Hamilton Coll, Clinton NY 13323 *Ph:* 315-859 4145 *Fax:* 315-859 4969 *E-mail:* stejerin@hamilton.edu

---

LLANCA

1311
LANGUAGES PLUS
Language Immersion and Cultural Program-Llanca
Site: Spain: Llanca
Dates: 2 wks or longer, summer only
Subjects: Homestay, Spanish language (beg/int/adv)
Eligibility: *Level:* adults *Age:* min 17, max 65, avg 24
Credit: *Undergrad:* none *Grad:* none *Doc:* certificate
Instruction: *In:* Spanish *Format:* lang study *Students:* intl
Costs: From $625 for 2 wks *incl* tuition, housing, books/materials, cultural activities
Housing: *Arr by pgm:* apartments, homestay
Deadline: 2 wks before pgm
Other info: *US accredited sponsor:* no *Activities:* excursions, field trips *Misc:* May contact former participants. *URL:* http://www.languagesplus.com
Contact: Margot Haldenby, North Amer Enrollment, Langs Plus, 317 Adelaide St W, Ste 900, Toronto, Ontario M5V 1P9, Canada *Ph:* 888-526 4758; 416-925 7117 *Fax:* 416-925 5990 *E-mail:* info@languagesplus.com

---

MADRID

1312
ALMA COLLEGE
Summer Program of Studies in Madrid, Spain
Site: Spain: Madrid *Host inst:* ENFOREX
Dates: 1-4 mos, May-Aug, flexible schedules avail
Subjects: Art, Business/management, Civilization/culture, Dance, Education/teaching, Homestay, Literature, Spanish language (beg/int/adv)
Eligibility: *Level:* sophs, jrs, srs *Requires:* 2.5 GPA, faculty recommendations
Credit: *Undergrad:* 3-15 *Grad:* none *Doc:* transcript
Instruction: *In:* Spanish *Format:* lang study, lecture *Students:* intl
Costs: $3,096-$8,985 depending on pgm length *incl* tuition, housing, all meals, insurance, fees, excursions, railpass, e-mail
Housing: *Arr by pgm:* apartments, homestay
Deadline: 2 mos before pgm
Other info: *US accredited sponsor:* yes *Orient:* abroad *Activities:* excursions, field trips, cultural events *Misc:* Structured lang partnerships with Spaniards. Resident dir. *URL:* http://www.alma.edu/academics/international
Contact: Chris Musick, Intl Educ, Alma Coll, 614 W Superior St, Alma MI 48801-1599 *Ph:* 800-321 2562; 517-463 7055 *Fax:* 517-463 7126 *E-mail:* intl_studies@alma.edu

---

1313
BENTLEY COLLEGE
Summer Program in Madrid, Spain
Site: Spain: Madrid *Host inst:* Coll for Intl Studies
Dates: 4 wks, May-Jun
Subjects: Business/management, Civilization/culture, Homestay, Spanish language, Spanish studies
Eligibility: *Level:* fresh, sophs, jrs, srs *Requires:* 2.7 GPA, faculty reference
Credit: *Undergrad:* 6 *Grad:* none *Doc:* transcript
Instruction: *In:* English *Format:* seminar *Students:* mainly US
Costs: $2,500 *incl* tuition, housing, some meals *Nonrefundable fee*
Housing: *Arr by pgm:* homestay
Deadline: Mar 1
Other info: *US accredited sponsor:* yes *Orient:* in US & abroad *Misc:* May contact former participants. *URL:* http://ecampus.bentley.edu/dept/sa
Contact: Jill A Perry Redin, Dir, Study Abroad, Intl Ctr, Bentley Coll, 175 Forest St, Waltham MA 02452-4705 *Ph:* 781-891 3474 *Fax:* 781-891 2819 *E-mail:* study_abroad@bentley.edu

---

1314
BOSTON UNIVERSITY
Madrid Internship Program
Site: Spain: Madrid *Host inst:* Intl Inst en Espana
Dates: 7 wks, May-Jul
Subjects: Civilization/culture, Homestay, Internships, Literature
Eligibility: *Level:* jrs, srs *Requires:* 3.0 GPA, in major, 5 sems coll Spanish, good acad standing
Credit: *Undergrad:* 8 *Grad:* none *Doc:* transcript
Instruction: *In:* Spanish *Format:* internship, lecture *Students:* mainly US
Costs: $5,100 *incl* tuition, housing, all meals, excursions
Housing: *Arr by pgm:* homestay
Deadline: Mar 1; Apr 1 for scholarships
Other info: *US accredited sponsor:* yes *Began:* 1993 *Orient:* in US & abroad *Activities:* excursions *Misc:* Full-time resident dir. Pgm may be taken before joining Boston Univ Madrid pgms in Sep. May contact former participants. *Financial aid:* scholarships *URL:* http://www.bu.edu/abroad/
Contact: Intl Pgms, Boston Univ, 232 Bay State Rd, Boston MA 02215 *Ph:* 617-353 9888 *Fax:* 617-353 5402 *E-mail:* abroad@bu.edu ▲

1315
BOSTON UNIVERSITY
Summer Program in Madrid
Site: Spain: Madrid *Host inst:* Intl Inst en Espana
Dates: 6 wks, May-Jul
Subjects: Art history, Civilization/culture, Homestay, Literature, Spanish language (int/adv)
Eligibility: *Level:* sophs, jrs, srs *Requires:* 3.0 GPA, in major, 2 sems coll Spanish, good acad standing
Credit: *Undergrad:* 8 *Grad:* none *Doc:* transcript
Instruction: *In:* Spanish *Format:* lang

study, lecture, seminar *Students:* mainly US
Costs: $4,550 *incl* tuition, housing, all meals, excursions
Housing: *Arr by pgm:* homestay
Deadline: Mar 1; Apr 1 for scholarships
Other info: *US accredited sponsor:* yes *Began:* 1991 *Orient:* in US & abroad *Activities:* excursions *Misc:* Full-time resident dir. Program may be taken before joining Boston Univ Madrid pgms in Sep. May contact former participants. *Financial aid:* scholarships *URL:* http://www.bu.edu/abroad/
Contact: Intl Pgms, Boston Univ, 232 Bay State Rd, Boston MA 02215 *Ph:* 617-353 9888 *Fax:* 617-353 5402 *E-mail:* abroad@bu.edu ▲

1316
CULTURAL EXPERIENCES ABROAD (CEA)
Study Spanish Language and Culture in Madrid
Site: Spain: Madrid *Host inst:* Complutense Univ of Madrid
Dates: Jul
Subjects: Civilization/culture, Drawing, Homestay, Independent study, Liberal arts, Literature, Spanish language, Spanish studies
Eligibility: *Level:* fresh, sophs, jrs, srs, grads *Requires:* 2.5 GPA, previous study in field *Age:* min 17, avg 20
Credit: *Undergrad:* 4-5 *Grad:* none *Doc:* transcript, certificate
Instruction: *In:* Spanish *Format:* independent study, lang study, lecture, study tour, tutorial *Students:* intl
Costs: $3,000-$4,000 *incl* tuition, housing, all meals, insurance, fees, excursions, orient, airport transfers *Nonrefundable fee*
Housing: *Arr by pgm:* residence halls, apartments, homestay
Deadline: Rolling admissions
Other info: *US accredited sponsor:* no *Orient:* abroad *Activities:* excursions, field trips, program travel, cultural events, sports *Misc:* Lang exch pgm with native speakers. Support svcs, on-site dir. May contact former participants. *Financial aid:* scholarships *URL:* http://www.travelabroad.com
Contact: CEA Study Abroad, 1400 E Southern Ave, Ste B-108, Tempe AZ 85282-8011 *Ph:* 480-557 7900 *Fax:* 480-557 7926 *E-mail:* spain@travelabroad.com

---

1317
EDUCATIONAL PROGRAMMES ABROAD (EPA)
Madrid Internship
Site: Spain: Madrid *Host inst:* Univ Antonio Nebrija
Dates: 8 wks, May 29-Jul 23
Subjects: Art, Business/management, History, Internships, Law, Literature, Political science/politics, Spanish language
Eligibility: *Level:* jrs, srs, grads *Requires:* 3.0 GPA, int Spanish *Age:* min 18, avg 20
Credit: *Undergrad:* avail *Grad:* none
Instruction: *In:* Spanish *Format:* internship, lecture *Students:* mainly US
Costs: $4,400 *incl* tuition, housing, some meals, fees *Nonrefundable fee*
Housing: *Arr by pgm:* homestay
Deadline: Mar 1
Other info: *US accredited sponsor:* no *Began:* 1988 *In coop with:* Univ of Rochester *Orient:* abroad (3 days, intensive lang study) *Activities:* excursions, field trips, cultural events *Misc:* May contact former participants. *URL:* http://studyabroad.com/epa
Contact: Eleanor Krawutschke, US Dir, Educ Pgms Abroad, 137 N Park St, Kalamazoo MI 49007 *Ph:* 616-382 0139 *Fax:* 616-382 5222 *E-mail:* epainterns@aol.com

---

1318
ENFOREX SPANISH LANGUAGE SCHOOL
Specialized Spanish Course for Tourist Guides
Site: Spain: Madrid
Dates: 3 wks, beg Mar 27, Jul 10 or Jul 31
Subjects: Homestay, Spanish language
Eligibility: *Level:* adults *Requires:* adv Spanish *Age:* min 22
Credit: *Undergrad:* avail *Grad:* avail *Doc:* certificate, diploma
Instruction: *In:* Spanish *Format:* lang study *Students:* intl
Costs: $1,900 *incl* tuition, housing, all meals, fees, excursions, books/materials
Housing: *Arr by pgm:* apartments with local students, residence halls with local students, homestay, hotels
Deadline: Until pgm filled; 4 mos before pgm for scholarships
Other info: *US accredited sponsor:* no *Began:* 1989 *Orient:* abroad (intensive lang study) *Activities:* excursions, field trips, program travel, cultural events, sports *Misc:* May contact former participants. *Financial aid:* scholarships *URL:* http://www.enforex.es
Contact: Antonio Anadon, Enforex, Alberto Aguilera 26, 28015 Madrid, Spain *E-mail:* spanish@enforex.es ▲

1319
ENFOREX SPANISH LANGUAGE SCHOOL
Teachers of Spanish as a Foreign Language Training Course
Site: Spain: Madrid
Dates: 2 or 4 wks, Jan 3, Jan 17, Jul 3, Jul 17 or Jul 31
Subjects: Foreign language teaching
Eligibility: *Level:* srs, grads, teachers *Requires:* adv Spanish *Age:* min 22
Credit: *Undergrad:* avail *Grad:* avail *Doc:* certificate, diploma
Instruction: *In:* Spanish *Format:* lang study *Students:* intl
Costs: $500 for 2 wks, $875 for 4 wks *incl* tuition, housing, all meals, fees, books/materials
Housing: *Arr by pgm:* apartments with local students, residence halls with local students, homestay, hotels
Deadline: Until pgm filled; 4 mos before pgm for scholarships
Other info: *US accredited sponsor:* no *Began:* 1989 *Orient:* abroad (intensive lang study) *Activities:* excursions, field trips, program travel, cultural events, sports *Misc:* May contact former participants. *Financial aid:* scholarships *URL:* http://www.enforex.es
Contact: Antonio Anadon, Main Dir, ENFOREX Spanish Lang Sch, Alberto Aguilera 26, 28015 Madrid, Spain *E-mail:* spanish@enforex.es ▲

1320
ESTUDIO INTERNACIONAL SAMPERE
Curso de Lengua y Civilizacion Espanolas-Madrid
Site: Spain: Madrid
Dates: 1 mo or sem, yr-round
Subjects: Bilingualism, Business language, Film studies, Literature, Office/secretarial studies, Spanish language, Translating/interpreting
Eligibility: *Level:* grads, adults, teachers, professionals *Age:* min 17, max 65, avg 23
Credit: *Undergrad:* avail *Grad:* none *Doc:* certificate, diploma *Transfer credit through:* Nicholls State Univ
Instruction: *In:* Spanish *Format:* lang study, study tour *Students:* intl & host country
Costs: $1,900 per mo, $5,800 per sem *incl* tuition, housing, all meals, insurance, fees, excursions, books/materials
Housing: *Arr by pgm:* residence halls, homestay, pensions
Deadline: 4 wks before pgm
Other info: *US accredited sponsor:* no *Began:* 1956 *Activities:* excursions, field trips, cultural events *Misc:* Transfer credit also avail through Univ of Arizona. *URL:* http://www.sampere.com
Contact: Juan Manuel Sampere, EIS, Lagasca 16, E-28001 Madrid, Spain *E-mail:* madrid@eisampere.es

---

1321
FLORIDA ATLANTIC UNIVERSITY
Business in Madrid
Site: Spain: Madrid *Host inst:* Escuela Superior de Gestion Comercial y Marketing
Dates: 2 or 4 wks, mid-Jun-mid-Jul
Subjects: Business/management, International business, Marketing
Eligibility: *Level:* jrs, srs, grads *Requires:* 2.5 GPA, previous study in field *Age:* min 18
Credit: *Undergrad:* 3 per 2 wks *Grad:* 3 per 2 wks *Doc:* transcript
Instruction: *In:* English, Spanish *Format:* lecture *Students:* intl & host country
Costs: $1,300 for 2 wks, $2,075 for 4 wks *incl* tuition, housing, some meals, fees, excursions, books/materials, ISIC *Nonrefundable fee*
Housing: *Arr by pgm:* hostels
Deadline: May 15; Apr 15 for scholarships
Other info: *US accredited sponsor:* yes *Began:* 1994 *Orient:* in US & abroad *Activities:* excursions *Misc:* Single rm avail for addtl fee. *Financial aid:* scholarships *URL:* http://www.fau.edu/madrid
Contact: Intl Pgms, Florida Atlantic Univ, 777 Glades Rd, GCS 259, Boca Raton FL 33431-0991 *Ph:* 800-935 5734; 561-297 2580, 561-297 3282 *Fax:* 561-297 2850 *E-mail:* goabroad@fau.edu

---

1322
GEORGE MASON UNIVERSITY
Spanish Language and Culture
Site: Spain: Madrid *Host inst:* Univ Complutense de Madrid
Dates: Jul 2-29
Subjects: Spanish language (beg/int/adv)
Eligibility: *Level:* sophs, jrs, srs, grads, adults, teachers, professionals *Requires:* 2.25 GPA, previous study in field, 1 yr coll Spanish *Age:* min 18
Credit: *Undergrad:* 6 *Grad:* 6 *Doc:* transcript
Instruction: *In:* Spanish *Format:* lang study *Students:* intl
Costs: About $3,050 for VA residents, $3,650 for others *incl* tuition, housing, all meals, insurance, fees, excursions, ISIC *Nonrefundable fee*
Housing: *Sponsor assists:* residence halls
Deadline: Apr 10
Other info: *US accredited sponsor:* yes *Began:* 1993 *Orient:* in US *Activities:* excursions, field trips, program travel, cultural events *Misc:* May contact former participants. *URL:* http://www.gmu.edu/departments/cge
Contact: Ctr for Global Educ, George Mason Univ, Fairfax VA 22030 *Ph:* 703-993 2154 *Fax:* 703-993 2153 *E-mail:* cge@gmu.edu

---

1323
GEORGIA INSTITUTE OF TECHNOLOGY
Languages for Business and Technology (LBAT)-Spanish
Site: Spain: Madrid
Dates: Jun 19-30 in Atlanta, Jul 3-31 in Spain
Subjects: Business language, Civilization/culture, Economics, Government, Spanish language, Spanish studies, Technical language
Eligibility: *Level:* fresh, sophs, jrs, srs *Requires:* 2 yrs high sch Spanish or coll equiv, good acad standing
Credit: *Undergrad:* 9 *Grad:* none *Doc:* transcript
Instruction: *In:* Spanish *Format:* lang study, lecture *Students:* mainly US
Costs: About $2,895 for 4 wks in Spain, addtl cost for 2 wks in Atlanta *incl* tuition, intl airfare, insurance, excursions, housing in Spain
Housing: *Arr by pgm:* hotels
Deadline: Mar 1
Other info: *US accredited sponsor:* yes *Began:* 1992 *Activities:* excursions *Misc:* 3 credit hrs in Atlanta, 6 credit hrs in Spain.
Contact: Dr Angela Labarca, Georgia Inst of Technology, Modern Langs, Atlanta GA 30332-0375 *Ph:* 404-894 7327, 404-385 0193 *Fax:* 404-894 0955 *E-mail:* angela.labarca@modlangs.gatech.edu
Or Contact: Intl Educ, Georgia Inst of Technology, J S Coon Bldg, Ste 203, Atlanta GA 30332-0284 *Ph:* 404-894 7475 *Fax:* 404-894 9682 *E-mail:* study.abroad@gatech.edu

---

1324
IES, INSTITUTE FOR THE INTERNATIONAL EDUCATION OF STUDENTS
IES Madrid Summer
Site: Spain: Madrid
Dates: May 31-Jul 14, May 24-Jul 14 for internships
Subjects: Art history, Economics, Field study, Film studies, History, Homestay, Internships, Literature, Spanish language (beg/int/adv)
Eligibility: *Level:* fresh, sophs, jrs, srs, grads, adults *Requires:* good acad standing *Age:* min 18
Credit: *Undergrad:* 6 *Grad:* none *Doc:* transcript
Instruction: *In:* Spanish *Format:* directed field study, internship, lang study, lecture *Students:* mainly US
Costs: $3,400 *incl* tuition, housing, some meals, excursions, health insurance, support svcs *Nonrefundable fee*
Housing: *Arr by pgm:* homestay
Deadline: Apr 1; Mar 1 for internships
Other info: *US accredited sponsor:* yes *Began:* 1970 *Orient:* abroad (2 days) *Activities:* excursions *Misc:* Excursions to Granada, Cuenca, Bilbao, Segovia & Pedraza. *URL:* http://www.IESabroad.org
Contact: *See Index II for Members* IES, 33 N LaSalle St, 15th Fl, Chicago IL 60602-2602 *Ph:* 800-955 2300; 312-944 1750 *Fax:* 312-944 1448 *E-mail:* info@iesabroad.org ▲

1325
IH ESPANA and **INTERNATIONAL HOUSE MADRID**
Curso de Metodologia y Cultura Espanola
Site: Spain: Madrid
Dates: 2 wks, Feb, Apr, or Aug
Subjects: Foreign language teaching, Spanish language (beg/int/adv)
Eligibility: *Level:* adults *Age:* min 18
Credit: *Undergrad:* none *Grad:* none *Doc:* certificate
Instruction: *In:* Spanish *Format:* lang study, lecture, practical training, seminar, student teaching *Students:* intl
Costs: About $600 *incl* tuition, housing, books/materials
Housing: *Arr by pgm:* apartments, homestay, hotels, hostels
Deadline: 2 wks before pgm
Other info: *US accredited sponsor:* no *Orient:* abroad *Misc:* Min number of candidates required 6, max 18. *URL:* http://www.ihmadrid.es
Contact: *See Index II for Members* Intl House Madrid, Zurbano, 8 28010 Madrid, Spain *E-mail:* spanish@ihmadrid.es ▲

1326
IH ESPANA and **INTERNATIONAL HOUSE MADRID**
Cursos de Formacion para Profesores de Espanol-Madrid
Site: Spain: Madrid
Dates: 3 wks, Feb, Mar, May, Jul, Aug, Sept, Nov, Dec
Subjects: Spanish language (adv)
Eligibility: *Level:* srs, grads, adults, teachers, professionals *Requires:* adv Spanish *Age:* min 21
Credit: *Undergrad:* avail *Grad:* avail *Doc:* certificate
Instruction: *In:* Spanish *Format:* lang study, practical training, seminar, student teaching *Students:* intl
Costs: About $950 *incl* tuition, housing, books/materials
Housing: *Arr by pgm:* apartments, homestay, pensions, hotels, hostels
Deadline: 2 wks before pgm
Other info: *US accredited sponsor:* no *URL:* http://www.ihmadrid.es
Contact: *See Index II for Members* Berta Sarralde, Intl House Madrid, Zurbano, 8 28010 Madrid, Spain *E-mail:* spanish@ihmadrid.es ▲

1327
IH ESPANA and **INTERNATIONAL HOUSE MADRID**
DELE Preparation Course-Madrid
Site: Spain: Madrid
Dates: 8 wks, Mar & Sep
Subjects: Spanish language (beg/int/adv)
Eligibility: *Level:* adults *Age:* min 16
Credit: *Undergrad:* none *Grad:* none *Doc:* certificate
Instruction: *In:* Spanish *Format:* lang study *Students:* intl
Costs: About $2,000 *incl* tuition, housing, pgm activities
Housing: *Arr by pgm:* residence halls, apartments, homestay, pensions, hotels, hostels
Deadline: Until pgm filled
Other info: *US accredited sponsor:* no *Orient:* abroad *Activities:* excursions *Misc:* Exam fees not incl. *URL:* http://www.ihmadrid.es
Contact: *See Index II for Members* Intl House Madrid, Zurbano 8, 28010 Madrid, Spain *E-mail:* spanish@ihmadrid.es ▲

1328
IH ESPANA and **INTERNATIONAL HOUSE MADRID**
Intensive Spanish Courses in Madrid
Site: Spain: Madrid
Dates: 2 wks or longer, yr-round
Subjects: Spanish language (beg/int/adv)
Eligibility: *Level:* adults *Age:* min 16
Credit: *Undergrad:* none *Grad:* none *Doc:* certificate
Instruction: *In:* Spanish *Format:* lang study *Students:* intl
Costs: About $1,000 for 4 wks *incl* tuition, housing, pgm activities
Housing: *Arr by pgm:* residence halls, apartments, homestay, pensions, hotels, hostels
Deadline: Until pgm filled
Other info: *US accredited sponsor:* no *Orient:* abroad *Activities:* excursions *URL:* http://www.ihmadrid.es
Contact: *See Index II for Members* Intl House Madrid, Zurbano 8, 28010 Madrid, Spain *E-mail:* spanish@ihmadrid.es ▲

1329
IH ESPANA and **INTERNATIONAL HOUSE MADRID**
Spanish and Culture
Site: Spain: Madrid
Dates: 2 wks, yr-round
Subjects: Civilization/culture, Spanish language (beg/int/adv)
Eligibility: *Level:* adults *Age:* min 16
Credit: *Undergrad:* none *Grad:* none *Doc:* certificate
Instruction: *In:* Spanish *Format:* lang study *Students:* intl
Costs: $900 *incl* tuition, housing, excursions, pgm activities
Housing: *Arr by pgm:* student housing
Deadline: Until pgm filled
Other info: *US accredited sponsor:* no *Orient:* abroad *Activities:* excursions, field trips *URL:* http://www.ihmadrid.es
Contact: *See Index II for Members* Intl House Madrid, Zurbano 8, 28010 Madrid, Spain *E-mail:* spanish@ihmadrid.es ▲

1330
IH ESPANA and **INTERNATIONAL HOUSE MADRID**
Specialized Courses
Site: Spain: Madrid
Dates: Yr-round
Subjects: Art, Business/management, Civilization/culture, History, Spanish language
Eligibility: *Level:* adults *Age:* min 16
Credit: *Undergrad:* none *Grad:* none *Doc:* certificate
Instruction: *In:* Spanish *Format:* lang study *Students:* intl
Costs: Contact Sponsor
Housing: *Arr by pgm:* residence halls, apartments, homestay, pensions, hotels, hostels
Deadline: 2 wks before pgm
Other info: *US accredited sponsor:* no *Orient:* abroad *URL:* http://www.ihmadrid.es
Contact: *See Index II for Members* Intl House Madrid, Zurbano 8, 28010 Madrid, Spain *E-mail:* spanish@ihmadrid.es ▲

1331
ISA
Cursos de Lengua y Cultura Espanola: Summer Program in Madrid
Site: Spain: Madrid *Host inst:* Univ Complutense de Madrid
Dates: 6 wks, Jun 26-Aug 1
Subjects: Civilization/culture, Drama/theater, Homestay, Music, Sociology, Spanish language (beg/int/adv)
Eligibility: *Level:* fresh, sophs, jrs, srs, adults *Requires:* 2.5 GPA, recommendation letter *Age:* min 18, avg 23
Credit: *Undergrad:* 6 sem hrs *Grad:* none *Doc:* transcript
Instruction: *In:* Spanish *Format:* lang study *Students:* intl
Costs: $3,400 *incl* tuition, housing, all meals, insurance, fees, excursions, resident dir
Housing: *Arr by pgm:* homestay
Deadline: Apr 5; Mar 10 for scholarships
Other info: *US accredited sponsor:* no *Began:* 1998 *Activities:* excursions, cultural events *Misc:* May contact former participants. *Financial aid:* scholarships *URL:* http://www.studiesabroad.com
Contact: Gustavo J Artaza, Intl Studies Abroad, 901 W 24th St, Austin TX 78705 *Ph:* 800-580 8826; 512-480 8522 *Fax:* 512-480 8866 *E-mail:* isa@studiesabroad.com ▲

1332
LANGUAGE LINK and **FORMULA SI OF MADRID**
Learn Spanish in Madrid, Spain
Site: Spain: Madrid
Dates: 2-16 wks, yr-round
Subjects: Spanish language
Eligibility: *Level:* fresh, sophs, jrs, srs, grads, adults, teachers, professionals, precoll *Age:* min 18, avg 30
Credit: *Undergrad:* 12 *Grad:* 6 *Doc:* transcript
Instruction: *In:* Spanish *Format:* lang study, tutorial *Students:* intl
Costs: $338 per wk *incl* tuition, housing, some meals, insurance, fees *Nonrefundable fee*
Housing: *Arr by pgm:* residence halls, apartments, homestay, hotels
Deadline: None
Other info: *US accredited sponsor:* no *Began:* 2000 *In coop with:* Austin Peay State Univ *Orient:* abroad *Activities:* field trips, cultural events, sports *Misc:* May contact former participants. *URL:* http://www.langlink.com
Contact: Kay Rafool, Dir, Lang Link, PO Box 3006, Peoria IL 61612 *Ph:* 800-552 2051; 309-692 2961 *Fax:* 309-692 2926 *E-mail:* info@langlink.com

---

1333
LANGUAGES PLUS
Language Immersion and Cultural Program-Madrid
Site: Spain: Madrid
Dates: 2 wks or longer, yr-round
Subjects: Homestay, Spanish language (beg/int/adv)
Eligibility: *Level:* adults *Age:* min 17, max 65, avg 24
Credit: *Undergrad:* none *Grad:* none *Doc:* certificate
Instruction: *In:* Spanish *Format:* lang study *Students:* intl
Costs: From $710 for 2 wks *incl* tuition, housing, books/materials, cultural activities
Housing: *Arr by pgm:* apartments, homestay
Deadline: 2 wks before pgm
Other info: *US accredited sponsor:* no *Activities:* excursions, field trips *Misc:* May contact former participants. *URL:* http://www.languagesplus.com

Contact: Margot Haldenby, North Amer Enrollment, Langs Plus, 317 Adelaide St W, Ste 900, Toronto, Ontario M5V 1P9, Canada *Ph:* 888-526 4758; 416-925 7117 *Fax:* 416-925 5990 *E-mail:* info@languagesplus.com

---

1334
MONTCLAIR STATE UNIVERSITY
Montclair in Madrid
Site: Spain: Madrid *Host inst:* Univ of Madrid
Dates: 4 wks, early Jul-early Aug
Subjects: Civilization/culture, History, Spanish language (beg/int/adv), Spanish studies
Eligibility: *Level:* fresh, sophs, jrs, srs, grads, teachers
Credit: *Undergrad:* 6 *Grad:* 6 *Doc:* transcript
Instruction: *In:* English, Spanish *Format:* lang study, lecture, seminar, study tour *Students:* mainly US
Costs: About $2,600 *incl* housing, all meals, intl airfare, fees, excursions
Housing: *Arr by pgm:* residence halls
Deadline: Jun 1
Other info: *US accredited sponsor:* yes *Orient:* in US (1 day) *Misc:* May contact former participants.
Contact: Global Educ Ctr, Montclair State Univ, Upper Montclair NJ 07043 *Ph:* 973-655 4185 *Fax:* 973-655 7654
Or Contact: Dr John Hwang, Montclair State Univ, Upper Montclair NJ 07043 *Ph:* 973-655 7508

1335
ROLLINS COLLEGE
Verano Espanol
Site: Spain: Madrid *Host inst:* Tandem Sch Intl
Dates: 6 wks, Jul 2-Aug 10
Subjects: Homestay, Spanish language
Eligibility: *Level:* fresh, sophs, jrs, srs *Requires:* 2.5 GPA, previous study in field, 1 yr Spanish for 1st yr students *Age:* min 18, avg 20
Credit: *Undergrad:* 8 *Grad:* none *Doc:* transcript
Instruction: *In:* Spanish *Format:* lang study *Students:* mainly US
Costs: $3,100 *incl* tuition, housing, all meals, fees, excursions *Nonrefundable fee*
Housing: *Arr by pgm:* homestay
Deadline: Mar 9
Other info: *US accredited sponsor:* yes *Began:* 1964 *Orient:* abroad (3 days) *Activities:* excursions, field trips, cultural events *Misc:* Resident dir. Group flight arranged. May contact former participants. *URL:* http://www.rollins.edu/int-programs
Contact: Dr Alberto Prieto-Calixto, Rollins Coll, Box 2752, 1000 Holt Ave, Winter Park FL 32789 *Ph:* 407-646 2217 *Fax:* 407-646 2595 *E-mail:* apcalixto@rollins.edu
Or Contact: Donna O'Connor, Dir, Intl Pgm, Rollins Coll, Box 2759, 1000 Holt Ave, Winter Park FL 32789 *Ph:* 407-646 2466 *Fax:* 407-646 2595 *E-mail:* intprog@rollins.edu ▲

1336
SUFFOLK UNIVERSITY (MA)
Madrid Campus
Site: Spain: Madrid *Host inst:* Suffolk Univ Madrid Campus
Dates: May 28-Jul 6
Subjects: Business/management, Communications, Computer sciences, Economics, English literature, Government, History, Homestay, Independent study, Journalism, Mathematics, Spanish language (beg/int/adv), Spanish studies
Eligibility: some spanish recommended *Level:* fresh, sophs, jrs, srs *Requires:* good acad standing, essay, letter of recommendation, some Spanish is recommended
Credit: *Undergrad:* avail *Grad:* none *Doc:* transcript
Instruction: *In:* English *Format:*

independent study, lecture, seminar, tutorial *Students:* intl
Costs: $3,850 per term *incl* tuition, housing, some meals, excursions, books/materials, airport pickup *Nonrefundable fee*
Housing: *Arr by pgm:* residence halls with local students, residence halls, homestay
Deadline: Apr 25
Other info: *US accredited sponsor:* yes *Began:* 1995 *Orient:* abroad In Madrid *Activities:* excursions, field trips, cultural events, sports *Misc:* World-wide faculty; also offers a Madrid-Boston degree pgm. May contact former participants. *URL:* http://www.suffolk.es
Contact: Megan Jones, Suffolk Univ Madrid, Calle de la Vina, 3, Madrid 28003 Spain *E-mail:* megan@suffolk.edu
Or Contact: Karen Karidoyonas, Suffolk Univ, 8 Ashburton Pl, Boston MA 02108 *Ph:* 800-678 3365 ext 8647; 617-573 8647 *Fax:* 617-742 2651 *E-mail:* kkaridoy@admin.suffolk.edu

---

1337
SYRACUSE UNIVERSITY
Spanish Language and Culture
Site: Spain: Madrid
Dates: 6 wks, May 21-Jul 7
Subjects: Anthropology, Homestay, Spanish language (beg/int/adv)
Eligibility: *Level:* fresh, sophs, jrs, srs *Requires:* previous study in field
Credit: *Undergrad:* 6 *Grad:* none
Instruction: *In:* English, Spanish *Format:* lang study, lecture, seminar, study tour *Students:* mainly US
Costs: $6,000 *incl* tuition, housing, some meals, excursions *Nonrefundable fee*
Housing: *Arr by pgm:* homestay
Deadline: Mar 15
Other info: *US accredited sponsor:* yes *Began:* 1992 *Orient:* abroad *Misc:* May contact former participants. *Financial aid:* scholarships *URL:* http://sumweb.syr.edu/dipa/summer
Contact: Summer Pgms, Intl Pgms Abroad, Syracuse Univ, 119 Euclid Ave, Syracuse NY 13244-4170 *Ph:* 800-251 9674; 315-443 9420 *Fax:* 315-443 4593 *E-mail:* dipasum@summon3.syr.edu ▲

1338
SYRACUSE UNIVERSITY
Summer Internships in Spain
Site: Spain: Madrid
Dates: 7 wks, May 20-Jul 7
Subjects: Homestay, Internships, Spanish studies
Eligibility: *Level:* sophs, jrs, srs, grads, adults *Requires:* 2.5 GPA
Credit: *Undergrad:* 6 *Grad:* 6 *Doc:* transcript
Instruction: *In:* English *Format:* internship *Students:* mainly US
Costs: $6,000 *incl* tuition, housing, some meals, fees, excursions
Housing: *Arr by pgm:* homestay
Deadline: Mar 15
Other info: *US accredited sponsor:* yes *Began:* 2001 *Orient:* abroad *Activities:* field trips *Misc:* May contact former participants. *Financial aid:* scholarships *URL:* http://sumweb.syr.edu/dipa/summer
Contact: Daisy Fried, Assoc Dir, Syracuse Univ, 119 Euclid Ave, Syracuse NY 13244-4170 *Ph:* 800-251 9674; 315-443 9419 *Fax:* 315-443 4593 *E-mail:* dsfried@summon3.syr.edu ▲

1339
UNIVERSIDAD COMPLUTENSE DE MADRID and **MODERN LANGUAGE STUDIES ABROAD**
Summer Study in Spain
Site: Spain: Madrid *Host inst:* Univ Complutense de Madrid (MLSA)
Dates: 2, 3 & 4 wks, May 19-Jun 18 or Jul 1-30
Subjects: Full curriculum, Art, Civilization/culture, International business, Internships, Literature, Philosophy, Spanish language (beg/int/adv), Trade
Eligibility: *Level:* fresh, sophs, jrs, srs, grads, adults, teachers, professionals *Age:* min 17
Credit: *Undergrad:* 5-9 *Grad:* 5-9 *Doc:* transcript, certificate, diploma
Instruction: *In:* Spanish *Format:* internship, lang study, lecture *Students:* intl
Costs: $1,985 for 2 wks, $2,575 for 3 wks, $2,785 for 4 wks *incl* tuition, housing, all meals, intl airfare, excursions, sports facilities *Nonrefundable fee*
Housing: *Arr by pgm:* residence halls, homestay
Deadline: Apr 15 or until pgm filled
Other info: *US accredited sponsor:* no *Began:* 1954 *Orient:* in US *Activities:* excursions *Misc:* May contact former participants. *URL:* http://www.mlsa.com
Contact: Modern Lang Studies Abroad, Univ Complutense de Madrid, PO Box 548, Frankfort IN 60423 *Ph:* 815-464 1800 *Fax:* 815-464 9458 *E-mail:* mlsa@sprintmail.com ▲

1340
UNIVERSITY OF CALIFORNIA, SAN DIEGO EXTENSION
Spanish Immersion Program: Madrid, Spain
Site: Spain: Madrid *Host inst:* Euroctrs Madrid
Dates: 2-12 wks, yr-round
Subjects: Art, Business language, Culinary arts, Spanish language (beg/int/adv), Spanish studies
Eligibility: *Level:* fresh, sophs, jrs, srs, grads, adults, teachers, professionals, precoll *Age:* min 18
Credit: *Undergrad:* none *Grad:* none *Doc:* transcript, certificate
Instruction: *In:* Spanish *Format:* lang study, lecture, seminar *Students:* intl
Costs: $891 for 2 wks *incl* tuition, housing, some meals, books/materials *Nonrefundable fee*
Housing: *Sponsor assists:* residence halls, homestay, hotels
Deadline: Contact sponsor
Other info: *US accredited sponsor:* yes *Began:* 1998 *Orient:* abroad *Activities:* excursions, field trips *Misc:* May contact former participants. *URL:* http://www.extension.ucsd.edu/laip
Contact: Tanya Knebel, Pgm Rep, UCSD Extension, Liberal Arts & Intl Pgms 0176Z, 9500 Gilman Dr, La Jolla CA 92093-0176 *Ph:* 858-822 2747 *Fax:* 858-534 7385 *E-mail:* travelstudy@ucsd.edu

---

1341
UNIVERSITY OF MINNESOTA
Summer Program for Spanish Teachers/King Juan Carlos Fellowships
Site: Spain: Madrid *Host inst:* Jose Ortega y Gasset Fdn
Dates: 3 wks, Jul 5-24
Subjects: Civilization/culture, Field study, Foreign language teaching, Homestay, Spanish language (adv)
Eligibility: *Level:* grads, teachers, professionals *Requires:* ACTFL int Spanish proficiency
Credit: *Undergrad:* none *Grad:* 4
Instruction: *In:* Spanish *Format:* directed field study, lang study, lecture *Students:* mainly US
Costs: $2,300 for fellowship recipients, $3,300 for others *incl* tuition, housing, all meals, insurance, fees, excursions *Nonrefundable fee*
Housing: *Arr by pgm:* residence halls, homestay
Deadline: May 31
Other info: *US accredited sponsor:* yes *Began:* 1989 *Orient:* in US & abroad *Activities:* excursions *Financial aid:* scholarships *URL:* http://www.UMabroad.umn.edu
Contact: Summer Pgm for Spanish Teachers, Global Campus, Univ of Minnesota, Study Abroad, 230 Heller Hall, 271 19th Ave S, Minneapolis MN 55455-0138 *Ph:* 612-626 9000 *Fax:* 612-626 8009 *E-mail:* UMabroad@tc.umn.edu

---

1342
UNIVERSITY OF ROCHESTER
Internships in Europe-Spain
Site: Spain: Madrid
Dates: 8 wks, May 29-Jul 23
Subjects: Business/management, Internships, Law, Media studies, Museology, Political science/politics
Eligibility: *Level:* jrs, srs, grads *Requires:* 3.0 GPA, 2 yrs coll Spanish *Age:* avg 20
Credit: *Undergrad:* 8 *Grad:* none *Doc:* transcript
Instruction: *In:* Spanish *Format:* internship *Students:* mainly US
Costs: $5,150 *incl* tuition, housing, some meals, fees, orient *Nonrefundable fee*
Housing: *Sponsor assists:* apartments, homestay
Deadline: Apr 1
Other info: *US accredited sponsor:* yes *Began:* 1971 *Orient:* abroad (1 wk, intensive lang study) *Misc:* May contact former participants. *URL:* http://www.rochester.edu/College/study-abroad/euro
Contact: Jacqueline Levine, Ctr for Study Abroad, Univ of Rochester, Lattimore 206, PO Box 270376, Rochester NY 14627-0376 *Ph:* 716-275 7532 *Fax:* 716-461 5131 *E-mail:* csaip@cc.rochester.edu

1343
VANDERBILT UNIVERSITY
Vanderbilt in Spain Summer Session
Site: Spain: Madrid
Dates: About May 24-Jul 12
Subjects: Art history, Civilization/culture, Homestay, Independent study, Literature, Spanish language (adv), Spanish studies
Eligibility: *Level:* sophs, jrs, srs *Requires:* 2.7 GPA, 2 yrs coll Spanish with B avg, transcript, references, personal essay
Credit: *Undergrad:* 7 *Grad:* none
Instruction: *In:* Spanish *Format:* independent study, lang study, lecture *Students:* mainly US
Costs: Contact sponsor
Housing: *Arr by pgm:* homestay
Deadline: Feb 15
Other info: *US accredited sponsor:* yes *Began:* 1977 *In coop with:* Univ of Madrid
Contact: Ms Marci Hunt, Study Abroad Off, Vanderbilt Univ, Box 1573, Station B, Nashville TN 37235 *Ph:* 615-343 3139 *Fax:* 615-343 5774 *E-mail:* marcella.a.hunt@vanderbilt.edu

MALAGA

1344
ACADEMIA CILE
Spanish Exam Preparation Courses in Andalucia
Site: Spain: Malaga
Dates: 4-16 wks, Jan 10-Dec 8
Subjects: Business language, Homestay, Spanish language
Eligibility: *Level:* adults *Age:* min 16, avg 24
Credit: *Undergrad:* none *Grad:* none *Doc:* certificate, diploma
Instruction: *In:* Spanish *Format:* lang study *Students:* intl
Costs: EUR 594 for 4 wks *incl* tuition, books/materials
Housing: *Arr by pgm:* apartments, homestay, pensions, hotels
Deadline: None
Other info: *US accredited sponsor:* no *Began:* 1988 *In coop with:* Chamber of Commerce & Industry of Madrid *Orient:* abroad *Activities:* excursions, field trips, cultural events, sports *Misc:* Exams in Spanish for bus & Spanish for tourism of the Chamber of Commerce held at CILE 2 times/yr. May contact former participants. *URL:* http://academia-cile.com

Contact: Mrs Barbara Reik, Secy, Acad CILE, c/Cister 4, 29015 Malaga, Spain *E-mail:* cile@vnet.es
Or Contact: Mr. Matthias Roskoschek, Acad CILE, c/Cister 4, 29015 Malaga, Spain *E-mail:* cile@vnet.es

---

1345
ACADEMIA CILE
Spanish Language and Hispanic Studies in Andalucia
Site: Spain: Malaga
Dates: 2 wks or longer, Jan 10-Dec 8
Subjects: Art history, Business language, History, Homestay, Literature, Spanish language, Sports
Eligibility: *Level:* adults *Age:* min 16, avg 24
Credit: *Undergrad:* none *Grad:* none *Doc:* certificate, diploma
Instruction: *In:* Spanish *Format:* lang study *Students:* intl
Costs: EUR 377 for 4 wks *incl* tuition, books/materials
Housing: *Arr by pgm:* apartments, homestay, pensions, hotels
Deadline: None
Other info: *US accredited sponsor:* no *Began:* 1988 *Orient:* abroad *Activities:* excursions, field trips, cultural events, sports *Misc:* CILE is official exam ctr for Chamber of Commerce exams (Spanish for bus & tourism). May contact former participants. *URL:* http://academia-cile.com
Contact: Mrs Barbara Reik, Secy, Acad CILE, c/Cister 4, 29015 Malaga, Spain *E-mail:* cile@vnet.es
Or Contact: Mr Matthias Roskoschek, Acad CILE, c/Cister 4, 29015 Malaga, Spain *E-mail:* cile@vnet.es

---

1346
DICKINSON COLLEGE
Malaga Summer Immersion Program
Site: Spain: Malaga
Dates: 4-1/2 wks, late May-late Jun
Subjects: Civilization/culture, Spanish language (int/adv)
Eligibility: *Level:* fresh, sophs *Requires:* 2 yrs coll Spanish
Credit: *Undergrad:* 4 *Grad:* none
Instruction: *In:* Spanish *Format:* lang study, lecture *Students:* mainly US
Costs: About $4,100 *incl* tuition, housing, all meals, intl airfare, fees, excursions
Housing: *Arr by pgm:* homestay
Deadline: Mar 1
Other info: *US accredited sponsor:* yes *Began:* 1984 *Orient:* in US *Activities:* excursions *Misc:* Exclusive use of Spanish during pgm. *URL:* http://www.dickinson.edu/departments/ocs/summer.html
Contact: Global Educ, Dickinson Coll, PO Box 1773, Carlisle PA 17013-2896 *Ph:* 717-245 1341 *Fax:* 717-245 1688 *E-mail:* ocs@dickinson.edu

---

1347
LANGUAGES PLUS
Language Immersion and Cultural Program-Malaga
Site: Spain: Malaga
Dates: 2 wks or longer, yr-round
Subjects: Homestay, Spanish language (beg/int/adv)
Eligibility: *Level:* adults *Age:* min 17, max 65, avg 24
Credit: *Undergrad:* none *Grad:* none *Doc:* certificate
Instruction: *In:* Spanish *Format:* lang study *Students:* intl
Costs: From $595 for 2 wks *incl* tuition, housing, books/materials, cultural activities
Housing: *Arr by pgm:* apartments, homestay
Deadline: 2 wks before pgm
Other info: *US accredited sponsor:* no *Activities:* excursions, field trips *Misc:* May contact former participants. *URL:* http://www.languagesplus.com
Contact: Margot Haldenby, North Amer Enrollment, Langs Plus, 317 Adelaide St W, Ste 900, Toronto, Ontario M5V 1P9, Canada *Ph:* 888-526 4758; 416-925 7117 *Fax:* 416-925 5990 *E-mail:* info@languagesplus.com

---

1348
MALACA INSTITUTO INTERNACIONAL DE ESTUDIOS DE ESPANOL
Spanish as a Foreign Language
Site: Spain: Malaga
Dates: 2 wks-5 mos, yr-round
Subjects: Spanish language (beg/int/adv), Spanish studies
Eligibility: *Level:* fresh, sophs, jrs, srs, grads, adults, teachers, professionals, precoll *Age:* min 18, avg 25
Credit: *Undergrad:* avail *Grad:* none *Doc:* transcript, certificate, diploma *Transfer credit through:* Santa Barbara City Coll
Instruction: *In:* Spanish *Format:* lang study *Students:* intl
Costs: 140,000 ptas per mo *incl* tuition, housing, fees, books/materials, fiestas
Housing: *Arr by pgm:* residence halls, apartments, homestay
Deadline: 2 wks before pgm
Other info: *US accredited sponsor:* yes *Began:* 1999 *In coop with:* Santa Barbara City Coll *Activities:* excursions, field trips, cultural events, sports *Misc:* Min age in summer is 16. May contact former participants. *URL:* http://www.malacainst-ch.es
Contact: Ida Willadsen, Dir, or Bob Burger, Marketing Dir, Malaca Inst, c/Cortada 6, Cerrado de Calderon, Malaga, Spain 29018 *E-mail:* espanol@malacainst-ch.es

---

MARBELLA

1349
ENFOREX SPANISH LANGUAGE SCHOOL
Golden Age Course (Senior +50 Years Old)
Site: Spain: Marbella
Dates: 2 wks, beg Mar 6, Mar 20, Apr 3, Apr 17, Sep 18, Oct 16, Nov 6, or Nov 20
Subjects: Spanish language (beg/int/adv)
Eligibility: *Level:* adults *Age:* min 50
Credit: *Undergrad:* avail *Grad:* avail *Doc:* certificate, diploma
Instruction: *In:* Spanish *Format:* lang study *Students:* intl
Costs: $525 *incl* tuition, housing, all meals, fees, excursions, books/materials
Housing: *Arr by pgm:* apartments with local students, residence halls with local students, homestay, hotels
Deadline: Until pgm filled; 4 mos before pgm for scholarships
Other info: *US accredited sponsor:* no *Began:* 1989 *Orient:* abroad (intensive lang study) *Activities:* excursions, field trips, program travel, cultural events, sports *Misc:* May contact former participants. *Financial aid:* scholarships *URL:* http://www.enforex.es
Contact: Antonio Anadon, ENFOREX, Alberto Aguilera 26, 28015 Madrid, Spain *E-mail:* spanish@enforex.es ▲

1350
SANTA BARBARA CITY COLLEGE
Intensive Spanish Language Program
Site: Spain: Marbella *Host inst:* Inst Intl de Idiomas
Dates: 4 wks, Jun-Jul
Subjects: Spanish language (beg/int/adv)
Eligibility: *Level:* adults *Age:* min 18
Credit: *Undergrad:* avail *Grad:* none *Doc:* transcript
Instruction: *In:* Spanish *Format:* lang study *Students:* mainly US
Costs: About $1,850 *incl* housing, some meals, insurance, excursions *Nonrefundable fee*
Housing: *Arr by pgm:* homestay
Deadline: Mar
Other info: *US accredited sponsor:* yes *Began:* 1997 *Orient:* in US & abroad (2 days) *Activities:* excursions, field trips, cultural events *Financial aid:* scholarships *URL:* http://www.sbcc.cc.ca.us/academic/StudyAbroad/

See "How To Use This Book" for definitions of terms used above. ▲ = See program sponsor's ad(s) in this book.

Contact: Naomi Sullwold, Santa Barbara City Coll, 721 Cliff Dr, Santa Barbara CA 93109 *Ph:* 805-965 0581 ext 2494 *Fax:* 805-963 7222 *E-mail:* sullwold@sbcc.net
Or Contact: Carola Smith, Dir, Study Abroad, Santa Barbara City Coll, 721 Cliff Dr, Sant Barbara CA 93109 *Ph:* 805-965 0581 ext 2243 *Fax:* 805-963 7222 *E-mail:* smithc@sbcc.net

OVIEDO

1351
NORTHWEST COUNCIL ON STUDY ABROAD (NCSA) and AHA INTERNATIONAL
Summer Spanish Language and Culture Studies in Oviedo
Site: Spain: Oviedo *Host inst:* Univ of Oviedo
Dates: 4 wks, Jul or Aug
Subjects: Spanish language
Eligibility: *Level:* sophs, jrs, srs *Requires:* 2.5 GPA *Age:* min 18
Credit: *Undergrad:* avail *Grad:* none *Doc:* transcript *Transfer credit through:* Central Washington Univ
Instruction: *In:* Spanish *Format:* lang study, lecture *Students:* intl
Costs: $1,865 per session *incl* tuition, housing, all meals, insurance, fees, excursions, orient *Nonrefundable fee*
Housing: *Arr by pgm:* residence halls
Deadline: 65 days before pgm
Other info: *US accredited sponsor:* yes *Began:* 1990 *Orient:* abroad (2 days) *Activities:* field trips, cultural events, sports *Misc:* May contact former participants. *URL:* http://www.aha-intl.org
Contact: *See Index II for Members* Carlotta Troy, Assoc Dir, AHA Intl, 741 SW Lincoln St, Portland OR 97201 *Ph:* 800-654 2051; 503-295 7730 *Fax:* 503-295 5969 *E-mail:* mail@aha-intl.org

RONDA

1352
CENTRAL COLLEGE ABROAD
Doing Business in Spain
Site: Spain: Ronda *Host inst:* Fundacion Publica para las Ensenanzas Univs in Ronda, Univ of Malaga
Dates: 4 wks, Jun; offered in alternate yrs
Subjects: Business language, Business/management, European studies, Spanish studies
Eligibility: *Level:* sophs, jrs, srs *Requires:* 2.5 GPA, 2 yrs coll Spanish, high int ACTFL, proficiency in Spanish *Age:* min 18
Credit: *Undergrad:* 7 *Grad:* none *Doc:* transcript
Instruction: *In:* Spanish *Format:* lang study, lecture *Students:* mainly US
Costs: $1,500 *incl* tuition, housing, some meals, excursions, ISIC *Nonrefundable fee*
Housing: *Arr by pgm:* homestay
Deadline: Mar 15
Other info: *US accredited sponsor:* yes *Began:* 1999 *Orient:* abroad (2 days) *Activities:* excursions, cultural events *Misc:* May contact former participants. *URL:* http://www.studyabroad.com/central
Contact: Central Coll Abroad, Central Coll, 812 University St, Pella IA 50219 *Ph:* 800-831 3629 *E-mail:* studyabroad@central.edu

1353
FUNDACION P ENSENANZAS UNIVERSITARIAS RONDA
Programa Internacional de Estudios de Espanol
Site: Spain: Ronda
Dates: 2 wks or longer, yr-round
Subjects: Art, Folklore, History, Literature, Music, Spanish language, Spanish studies
Eligibility: *Level:* fresh, sophs, jrs, srs, grads, adults, professionals, precoll *Age:* min 16, avg 23
Credit: *Undergrad:* avail *Grad:* none *Doc:* transcript, certificate
Instruction: *In:* Spanish *Format:* lang study *Students:* intl
Costs: About $1,636 for 1 yr *incl* tuition, fees *Nonrefundable fee*
Housing: *Arr by pgm:* apartments, homestay, pensions, hotels
Deadline: 3 wks before pgm
Other info: *US accredited sponsor:* no *Began:* 1991 *Orient:* abroad (2 days) *Activities:* excursions, field trips, program travel, cultural events, sports *Misc:* May contact former participants. *URL:* http://www.rondapiee.com
Contact: Joaquin Hita, Pgm Intl de Estudios de Espanol, Palacio de Mondragon, PO Box 332, E-29400 Ronda, Spain *E-mail:* info@rondapiee.com

SAGUNTO

1354
ADVENTIST COLLEGES ABROAD
Summer Spanish Language Program
Site: Spain: Sagunto *Host inst:* Col Adventista de Sagunto
Dates: 6 wks, Jun 19-Aug 2
Subjects: Spanish language (beg/int/adv)
Eligibility: Students of member insts only. *Level:* fresh, sophs, jrs, srs, grads, adults, teachers, professionals, precoll *Requires:* 2.5 GPA *Age:* min 15
Credit: *Undergrad:* 9 qtr hrs *Grad:* none *Doc:* transcript
Instruction: *In:* Spanish *Format:* lab, lang study, lecture, study tour, tutorial *Students:* intl
Costs: $2,164 *incl* tuition, housing, all meals, insurance, fees, excursions, books/materials *Nonrefundable fee*
Housing: *Arr by pgm:* residence halls
Deadline: May 31
Other info: *US accredited sponsor:* yes *Began:* 1992 *Orient:* in US & abroad *Activities:* excursions, field trips, program travel, cultural events, sports *URL:* http://www.nadadventist.org/aca
Contact: *See Index II for Members* Odette Ferrieira, Dir, Adventist Colls Abroad, 12501 Old Columbia Pike, Silver Spring MD 20904-8600 *Ph:* 301-680 6444 *Fax:* 301-680 6463 *E-mail:* 104474.304@compuserve.com

SALAMANCA

1355
ACADEMIC PROGRAMS INTERNATIONAL (API)
Academic Programs International-Salamanca
Site: Spain: Salamanca *Host inst:* Univ de Salamanca
Dates: 6 wks, May-Jun, Jun-Jul, Jul-Aug
Subjects: Art history, Business/management, Civilization/culture, History, Homestay, Literature, Spanish language (beg/int/adv), Translating/interpreting, Written composition
Eligibility: *Level:* fresh, sophs, jrs, srs, adults *Requires:* 2.75 GPA *Age:* min 18, avg 21
Credit: *Undergrad:* 6-8 *Grad:* none *Doc:* transcript, certificate
Instruction: *In:* Spanish *Format:* lab, lang study, lecture, seminar, tutorial *Students:* intl
Costs: $3,250 *incl* tuition, housing, all meals, insurance, excursions, tutoring, ground transport
Housing: *Arr by pgm:* homestay, residencia
Deadlinc: Apr 1
Other info: *US accredited sponsor:* no *Began:* 1997 *Orient:* in US & abroad (2 wks, intensive lang study) *Activities:* excursions, field trips, program travel, cultural events *Misc:* On-site dir. Airport reception. May contact former participants. *Financial aid:* scholarships *URL:* http://www.academicintl.com
Contact: Jennifer Allen or Dr Sharon Foerster, Acad Pgms Intl, 129 E Hopkins, Ste 101, San Marcos TX 78666 *Ph:* 800-844 4124; 512-392 8520 *Fax:* 512-392 8420 *E-mail:* jca@onr.com

1356
AMERICAN INSTITUTE FOR FOREIGN STUDY (AIFS)
University of Salamanca
Site: Spain: Salamanca
Dates: 4 wks, Jun 24-Jul 28 or 6 wks, Jun 24-Aug 11
Subjects: Art history, Economics, History, Homestay, Literature, Spanish language
Eligibility: *Level:* fresh, sophs, jrs, srs, adults, precoll *Requires:* 2.0 GPA
Credit: *Undergrad:* avail *Grad:* none *Doc:* transcript
Instruction: *In:* English, Spanish *Format:* lang study, lecture *Students:* mainly US
Costs: $3,699 for 4 wks, $4,359 for 6 wks *incl* tuition, housing, all meals, intl airfare, fees, excursions
Housing: *Arr by pgm:* residence halls, homestay
Deadline: Mar 15
Other info: *US accredited sponsor:* no *Began:* 1969 *Activities:* excursions, cultural events *Misc:* Resident dir. May contact former participants. *Financial aid:* scholarships *URL:* http://www.aifsabroad.com
Contact: Solandy Meza, Coll Div, AIFS, River Plaza, 9 W Broad St, Stamford CT 06902 *Ph:* 800-727 2437 ext 5163 *E-mail:* college.info@aifs.com ▲

1357
CSA, CENTER FOR STUDY ABROAD
Spanish Language and Culture Studies-Salamanca
Site: Spain: Salamanca *Host inst:* Univ de Salamanca
Dates: 4-8 wks, Jul 1-Aug 30; qtr/yr pgm also avail
Subjects: History, Homestay, Independent study, Literature, Political science/politics, Sociology, Spanish language (beg/int/adv), Spanish studies
Eligibility: *Level:* adults *Age:* min 17
Credit: *Undergrad:* avail *Grad:* avail *Doc:* transcript, certificate
Instruction: *In:* Spanish *Format:* independent study, lang study, lecture *Students:* intl
Costs: $1,795-$3,195 for summer sessions *incl* tuition, housing, all meals, insurance, fees, books/materials *Nonrefundable fee*
Housing: *Sponsor assists:* residence halls, homestay
Deadline: None
Other info: *US accredited sponsor:* no *Orient:* abroad *Activities:* excursions, field trips, program travel, cultural events, sports *URL:* http://www.studyabroad.com/csa
Contact: Alima Khan, Assoc Dir, CSA, Ctr for Study Abroad, 2802 E Madison St, MS #160, Seattle WA 98112 *Ph:* 206-726 1498 *Fax:* 206-583 8192 *E-mail:* virtuecsa@aol.com

1358
DON QUIJOTE
DELE Preparation Course-Salamanca
Site: Spain: Salamanca
Dates: 2, 3 or 4 wks, May or Nov
Subjects: Spanish language (int/adv)
Eligibility: *Level:* adults *Requires:* previous study in field *Age:* min 18, avg 26
Credit: *Undergrad:* none *Grad:* none *Doc:* diploma
Instruction: *In:* Spanish *Format:* lang study, lecture *Students:* intl
Costs: $522 for 2 wks, $722 for 3 wks, $922 for 4 wks *incl* tuition, housing, books/materials, activities
Housing: *Arr by pgm:* apartments, homestay, hotels, hostels
Deadline: Rolling admissions
Other info: *US accredited sponsor:* no *Began:* 1992 *Orient:* abroad *Activities:* excursions, program travel, cultural events, sports *Misc:* Diploma preparation. 25discount if combined with standard course. *URL:* http://www.donquijote.org
Contact: Area Mgr/USA, Don Quijote-Central Promotion, Apdo de Correos 333, Ref: USII98, 37080 Salamanca, Spain *E-mail:* amusa@donquijote.org

1359
DON QUIJOTE
Flight Attendants
Site: Spain: Salamanca
Dates: 2 wks, Feb, Aug or Sep
Subjects: Civilization/culture, Spanish language (beg/int/adv)
Eligibility: *Level:* adults *Age:* min 18, avg 26
Credit: *Undergrad:* none *Grad:* none *Doc:* certificate, diploma
Instruction: *In:* Spanish *Format:* independent study, lang study, lecture, study tour, tutorial *Students:* intl
Costs: $701 *incl* tuition, housing, fees, books/materials, activities
Housing: *Sponsor assists:* apartments, homestay, hotels, hostels
Deadline: Contact sponsor
Other info: *US accredited sponsor:* no *Began:* 1990 *Activities:* excursions, field trips, program travel, cultural events, sports *Misc:* Costs incl homestay housing option only. May contact former participants. *URL:* http://www.donquijote.org
Contact: Area Mgr/USA, Don Quijote, Placentinos No 2, Apdo 333, 37080 Salamanca, Spain *E-mail:* amusa@donquijote.org

1360
DON QUIJOTE
Refresher Course for Teachers of Spanish/Curso de Repaso-Salamanca
Site: Spain: Salamanca
Dates: 2 wks, yr-round; special starting dates
Subjects: Foreign language teaching, Spanish language (adv)
Eligibility: *Level:* teachers *Requires:* adv Spanish *Age:* min 18, avg 40
Credit: *Undergrad:* none *Grad:* none *Doc:* certificate
Instruction: *In:* Spanish *Format:* directed field study, independent study, internship, lang study, lecture, practical training, seminar, student teaching *Students:* intl
Costs: $694 for group, $1,184 for individual *incl* tuition, housing, books/materials, activities
Housing: *Arr by pgm:* homestay
Deadline: Rolling admissions
Other info: *US accredited sponsor:* no *Began:* 1992 *Orient:* abroad (intensive lang study) *Activities:* excursions, cultural events *Misc:* Pgm examines theoretical & practical methods of teaching Spanish, incl workshops, lectures. May contact former participants. *URL:* http://www.donquijote.org
Contact: Area Mgr/USA, Don Quijote-Central Promotion, Apdo de Correos 333, Ref: USII98, 37080 Salamanca, Spain *E-mail:* amusa@donquijote.org

1361
DON QUIJOTE
Spanish in Spain Short-Term Courses-Salamanca
Site: Spain: Salamanca
Dates: 1-12 wks, yr-round
Subjects: Spanish language (beg/int/adv)
Eligibility: *Level:* adults *Age:* min 18, avg 26
Credit: *Undergrad:* 3 for 60 hrs *Grad:* none *Doc:* certificate, diploma
Instruction: *In:* Spanish *Format:* lang study, lecture *Students:* intl
Costs: $842 for 4 wks *incl* tuition, housing, books/materials, activities
Housing: *Arr by pgm:* apartments, homestay, hotels, hostels
Deadline: Rolling admissions
Other info: *US accredited sponsor:* no *Began:* 1991 *Activities:* excursions, field trips, program travel, cultural events, sports *Misc:* May contact former participants. *URL:* http://www.donquijote.org
Contact: Area Mgr/USA, Don Quijote-Central Promotion, Apdo de Correos 333, Ref: USII98, 37080 Salamanca, Spain *E-mail:* amusa@donquijote.org

1362
DON QUIJOTE
Summer School
Site: Spain: Salamanca
Dates: 1-8 wks, summer

Subjects: Spanish language (beg/int/adv), Speech/debate/forensics
Eligibility: *Level:* adults *Age:* min 16, avg 20
Credit: *Undergrad:* none *Grad:* none *Doc:* certificate
Instruction: *In:* Spanish *Format:* lang study *Students:* intl
Costs: $400 for 2 wks *incl* tuition, housing, books/materials, activities *Nonrefundable fee*
Housing: *Arr by pgm:* apartments, homestay, pensions, hostels
Deadline: Rolling admissions
Other info: *US accredited sponsor:* no *Began:* 1988 *Activities:* excursions, cultural events, sports *Misc:* Conversation, interviews, role-playing, songs, discussions. May contact former participants. *URL:* http://www.donquijote.org
Contact: Area Mgr/USA, Don Quijote-Central Promotion, Apdo de Correos 333, Ref: USII98, 37080 Salamanca, Spain *E-mail:* amusa@donquijote.org

---

1363
DON QUIJOTE
Super Intensive Course-Salamanca
Site: Spain: Salamanca
Dates: 1-36 wks, yr-round
Subjects: Civilization/culture, Spanish language (beg/int/adv)
Eligibility: *Level:* adults *Age:* min 18, avg 26
Credit: *Undergrad:* none *Grad:* none *Doc:* certificate, diploma
Instruction: *In:* Spanish *Format:* independent study, lang study, lecture, study tour, tutorial *Students:* intl
Costs: Contact sponsor
Housing: *Sponsor assists:* apartments, homestay, hotels, hostels
Deadline: Contact sponsor
Other info: *US accredited sponsor:* no *Began:* 1990 *Activities:* excursions, field trips, program travel, cultural events, sports *Misc:* Costs incl homestay housing option only. May contact former participants. *URL:* http://www.donquijote.org
Contact: Area Mgr/USA, Don Quijote, Placentinos No 2, Apdo 333, 37080 Salamanca, Spain *E-mail:* amusa@donquijote.org

---

1364
ESTUDIO INTERNACIONAL SAMPERE
Curso de Lengua y Civilizacion Espanolas
Site: Spain: Salamanca
Dates: 1 mo or longer, yr-round
Subjects: Spanish language (beg/int/adv)
Eligibility: *Level:* adults *Age:* min 17, max 65, avg 21
Credit: *Undergrad:* avail *Grad:* none *Doc:* certificate, diploma *Transfer credit through:* Nicholls State Univ
Instruction: *In:* Spanish *Format:* lang study, practical training, study tour *Students:* intl
Costs: $1,400 per mo *incl* tuition, housing, all meals, insurance, fees, excursions, books/materials
Housing: *Sponsor assists:* apartments with local students, homestay, pensions, hostels
Deadline: 3 wks before pgm
Other info: *US accredited sponsor:* no *Began:* 1992 *Orient:* abroad *Activities:* excursions, field trips, cultural events *Misc:* Transfer credit also avail through Univ of Arizona. May contact former participants. *URL:* http://www.sampere.com
Contact: Juan Manuel Sampere, EIS, Lagasca 16, Madrid E-28001, Spain *E-mail:* madrid@eisampere.es

---

1365
FLORIDA ATLANTIC UNIVERSITY
Spanish Language and Culture in Salamanca
Site: Spain: Salamanca *Host inst:* Escuela Superior de Gestion Comercial y Marketing
Dates: 5 wks, late May-late Jun or early Jul-early Aug
Subjects: Architecture, Art, European studies, International business, Spanish studies
Eligibility: *Level:* fresh, sophs, jrs, srs, grads, adults, teachers, professionals *Requires:* 2.5 GPA *Age:* min 18
Credit: *Undergrad:* 7 *Grad:* none *Doc:* transcript
Instruction: *In:* English, Spanish *Format:* lang study, lecture *Students:* mainly US
Costs: $3,070 *incl* tuition, housing, all meals, excursions, books/materials, ISIC *Nonrefundable fee*
Housing: *Arr by pgm:* hostels
Deadline: May 15; Apr 15 for scholarships
Other info: *US accredited sponsor:* yes *Began:* 1999 *Orient:* in US & abroad *Activities:* excursions *Misc:* Single rm avail for addtl fee. *Financial aid:* scholarships
Contact: Intl Pgms, Florida Atlantic Univ, 777 Glades Rd, GCS 259, Boca Raton FL 33431-0991 *Ph:* 800-935 5734; 561-297 2580, 561-297 3282 *Fax:* 561-297 2850 *E-mail:* goabroad@fau.edu

---

1366
FLORIDA INTERNATIONAL UNIVERSITY
FIU in Spain
Site: Spain: Salamanca *Host inst:* Univ de Salamanca
Dates: 1 mo, Jun 28-Jul 29
Subjects: Business language, Literature, Spanish language, Spanish studies
Eligibility: *Level:* jrs, srs, adults, teachers, professionals *Requires:* previous study in field, Spanish lang study
Credit: *Undergrad:* 6 *Grad:* avail *Doc:* transcript
Instruction: *In:* Spanish *Format:* directed field study, practical training, study tour *Students:* US & intl
Costs: $3,450 *incl* housing, some meals, intl airfare, excursions, railpass
Housing: *Arr by pgm:* hotels
Deadline: May 15
Other info: *US accredited sponsor:* yes *Began:* 1993 *Orient:* in US (1 day) *Activities:* excursions, field trips, program travel, cultural events *Misc:* Pgm travel to Leon, Madrid, Santander, Segovia, Toledo, others. May contact former participants. *URL:* http://www.fiu.edu/~intered
Contact: Intl Studies, Florida Intl Univ, 11200 SW 8th St, DM 300B, Miami FL 33199 *Ph:* 305-348 1913, 305-348 1918 *Fax:* 305-348 1941 *E-mail:* intered@fiu.edu

---

1367
IES, INSTITUTE FOR THE INTERNATIONAL EDUCATION OF STUDENTS
IES Salamanca Summer
Site: Spain: Salamanca *Host inst:* Univ de Salamanca
Dates: 4 wks, Jun 3-30 or Jul 31-Aug 30
Subjects: Civilization/culture, Homestay, Spanish language
Eligibility: *Level:* fresh, sophs, jrs, srs *Requires:* good acad standing
Credit: *Undergrad:* 6 *Grad:* none *Doc:* transcript
Instruction: *In:* Spanish *Format:* lang study *Students:* mainly US
Costs: $2,400 *incl* tuition, housing, all meals, insurance, excursions, student support svcs *Nonrefundable fee*
Housing: *Sponsor assists:* homestay
Deadline: Apr 1
Other info: *US accredited sponsor:* yes *Activities:* field trips *Misc:* May contact former participants. *URL:* http://www.IESabroad.org
Contact: *See Index II for Members* IES, 33 N LaSalle St, 15th Fl, Chicago IL 60602-2602 *Ph:* 800-995 2300; 312-944 1750 *Fax:* 312-944 1448 *E-mail:* info@iesabroad.org
▲

1368
INDIANA UNIVERSITY
Summer Study in Salamanca
Site: Spain: Salamanca *Host inst:* Univ de Salamanca
Dates: 6 wks, Jul 1-Aug 15
Subjects: Homestay, Spanish language (int/adv)
Eligibility: Own students only. *Level:* fresh, sophs, jrs, srs, teachers *Requires:* 5 sems Spanish
Credit: *Undergrad:* 6 *Grad:* 6 *Doc:* transcript
Instruction: *In:* Spanish *Format:* lang study *Students:* intl
Costs: $2,600 or $3,800 *incl* tuition, housing, all meals, insurance, excursions, books/materials *Nonrefundable fee*
Housing: *Arr by pgm:* homestay
Deadline: Mid-Feb
Other info: *US accredited sponsor:* yes *Began:* 1991 *Orient:* in US *Activities:* excursions *Misc:* May contact former participants. *Financial aid:* scholarships *URL:* http://www.indiana.edu/~overseas
Contact: Overseas Study, Indiana Univ, Franklin Hall 303, Bloomington IN 47405 *Ph:* 812-855 9304 *Fax:* 812-855 6452 *E-mail:* overseas@indiana.edu

---

1369
ISA
Cursos de Lengua y Cultura Espanola: Summer Session in Salamanca
Site: Spain: Salamanca *Host inst:* Univ de Salamanca
Dates: 4 or 6 wks, May 23-Jun 30, Jun 20-Jul 28 or Jul 26-Aug 30
Subjects: Art history, Business/management, Civilization/culture, History, Homestay, Literature, Spanish language (beg/int/adv), Translating/interpreting
Eligibility: *Level:* fresh, sophs, jrs, srs, grads, adults, teachers *Requires:* 2.5 GPA, recommendation letter *Age:* min 18, avg 21
Credit: *Undergrad:* 6-8 sem hrs *Grad:* none *Doc:* transcript, certificate
Instruction: *In:* Spanish *Format:* lang study, lecture *Students:* US & intl
Costs: $2,225 for 4 wks, $3,425 for 6 wks *incl* tuition, housing, all meals, insurance, fees, excursions, ground transport, tutoring
Housing: *Arr by pgm:* homestay
Deadline: Apr 5; Mar 10 for scholarships
Other info: *US accredited sponsor:* no *Began:* 1988 *Orient:* in US & abroad *Activities:* excursions, field trips, cultural events *Misc:* Resident dir incl in costs. May contact former participants. *Financial aid:* scholarships *URL:* http://www.studiesabroad.com
Contact: Gustavo Artaza, Exec Dir, ISA, 901 W 24th St, Austin TX 78705 *Ph:* 800-580 8826; 512-480 8522 *Fax:* 512-480 8866 *E-mail:* isa@studiesabroad.com ▲

1370
JAMES MADISON UNIVERSITY
Summer Semester in Salamanca
Site: Spain: Salamanca *Host inst:* Univ de Salamanca
Dates: 9 wks, late May-late Jul
Subjects: Art history, Communications, Economics, Homestay, Spanish language (adv), Spanish studies
Eligibility: *Level:* sophs, jrs, srs *Requires:* 2.8 GPA, previous study in field, int Spanish *Age:* min 18, max 26, avg 20
Credit: *Undergrad:* 9-12 *Grad:* none *Doc:* transcript
Instruction: *In:* Spanish *Format:* lang study, lecture *Students:* mainly US
Costs: $5,100 for VA residents, $6,700 for others *incl* tuition, housing, some meals, excursions, books/materials *Nonrefundable fee*
Housing: *Arr by pgm:* homestay
Deadline: Feb 1
Other info: *US accredited sponsor:* yes *Began:* 1995 *Orient:* abroad (1 wk, intensive lang study) *Activities:* excursions, field trips, program travel, cultural events *Misc:* May contact former participants. *URL:* http://www.jmu.edu/international/
Contact: Dr Carmenza Kline, Dir, Intl Pgms, James Madison Univ, Harrisonburg VA 22807 *Ph:* 540-568 6419 *Fax:* 540-568 8080 *E-mail:* klineca@jmu.edu

---

1371
LOUISIANA STATE UNIVERSITY
LSU in Spain
Site: Spain: Salamanca *Host inst:* Col de Espana
Dates: 6 wks, May-Jul
Subjects: Civilization/culture, Homestay, Independent study, Literature, Spanish language (int/adv), Spanish studies
Eligibility: *Level:* sophs, jrs, srs, grads, teachers *Requires:* 2.5 GPA, for undergrads, 3.0 for grads & those seeking 9 credit hrs, 1 yr coll Spanish
Credit: *Undergrad:* 6-9 *Grad:* 6-9 *Doc:* transcript
Instruction: *In:* Spanish *Format:* lang study *Students:* mainly US
Costs: $2,600 *incl* tuition, housing, some meals, excursions, ground transport
Housing: *Sponsor assists:* homestay
Deadline: Mar 15
Other info: *US accredited sponsor:* yes *Began:* 1992 *Orient:* in US & abroad *Activities:* excursions, field trips, cultural events *Misc:* Loans avail. Scholarships for own students only. May contact former participants. *Financial aid:* scholarships *URL:* http://www.lsu.edu/studyabroad
Contact: Joseph Rosenbach, Acad Pgms Abroad, Louisiana State Univ, 113 Hatcher Hall, Baton Rouge LA 70803-1522 *Ph:* 225-388 6801 *Fax:* 225-388 6806 *E-mail:* studyabroad@lsu.edu

---

1372
SUNY UNIVERSITY AT BUFFALO and SUNY COLLEGE AT BUFFALO
Programa de Estudios Hispanicos (Spanish Language & Culture)
Site: Spain: Salamanca *Host inst:* Univ de Salamanca
Dates: 5 wks, Jun 27-Jul 31
Subjects: Civilization/culture, Literature, Spanish language (int/adv), Spanish studies
Eligibility: *Level:* sophs, jrs, srs, grads *Requires:* 1 yr coll Spanish, good acad standing; grad students must submit proof of grad status
Credit: *Undergrad:* 6 *Grad:* 6 *Doc:* transcript
Instruction: *In:* Spanish *Format:* lang study, lecture *Students:* mainly US
Costs: $2,504 *incl* tuition, housing, most meals, excursions, local transport
Housing: *Arr by pgm:* homestay
Deadline: Apr 1; rolling admissions
Other info: *US accredited sponsor:* yes *Began:* 1969 *Orient:* in US & abroad *Activities:* excursions, program travel, cultural events *Misc:* Pgm incl 4-5 days in Madrid. US resident dir on-site. *Financial aid:* scholarships *URL:* http://www.buffalo.edu/studyabroad/
Contact: Dr Sandra J Flash, Dir, Study Abroad Pgms, SUNY Univ at Buffalo, 210 Talbert Hall, Buffalo NY 14260-1604 *Ph:* 716-645 3912 *Fax:* 716-645 6197 *E-mail:* studyabroad@buffalo.edu
Or Contact: Dr Lee Ann Grace, Dir, Intl Educ, SUNY Coll at Buffalo, 1300 Elmwood Ave, Buffalo NY 14222-1095 *Ph:* 716-878 4620 *Fax:* 716-878 3054 *E-mail:* intleduc@buffalostate.edu

---

1373
UNIVERSITY OF CALIFORNIA, SAN DIEGO EXTENSION
Spanish Immersion Program: Salamanca, Spain
Site: Spain: Salamanca *Host inst:* Euroctrs Salamanca
Dates: 2 wks or longer, yr-round
Subjects: Civilization/culture, Contemporary issues, Spanish language (beg/int/adv), Spanish studies
Eligibility: *Level:* fresh, sophs, jrs, srs, grads, adults, teachers, professionals, precoll *Age:* min 18
Credit: *Undergrad:* none *Grad:* none *Doc:* transcript, certificate
Instruction: *In:* Spanish *Format:* lecture, seminar *Students:* intl
Costs: $716 for 2 wks *incl* tuition, housing, all meals, books/materials *Nonrefundable fee*
Housing: *Sponsor assists:* homestay, hotels
Deadline: 4-6 wks before pgm
Other info: *US accredited sponsor:* yes *Began:* 1999 *Orient:* abroad *Activities:* excursions, field trips *Misc:* May contact

former participants. *URL:* http://www.extensions.ucsd/laip
Contact: Tanya Knebel, Pgm Rep, UCSD Extension, Liberal Arts & Intl Pgms 0176Z, 9500 Gilman Dr, La Jolla CA 92093-0176 *Ph:* 858-822 2747 *Fax:* 858-534 7385 *E-mail:* travelstudy@ucsd.edu

---

1374
UNIVERSITY OF MASSACHUSETTS AMHERST
Summer Program in Spain
Site: Spain: Salamanca *Host inst:* Col Hispano Continental
Dates: About Jul 1-31
Subjects: Civilization/culture, Homestay, Linguistics, Literature, Spanish language
Eligibility: *Level:* fresh, sophs, jrs, srs, grads, precoll *Requires:* 1 sem coll Spanish for lang/culture, 6 sems for lang/literature or equiv
Credit: *Undergrad:* 6-9 *Grad:* 6
Instruction: *In:* Spanish *Format:* lang study, lecture *Students:* intl
Costs: About $1,800-$2,000 depending on pgm *incl* tuition, housing, all meals, excursions, cultural activities
Housing: *Arr by pgm:* residence halls, homestay
Deadline: May 15
Other info: *US accredited sponsor:* yes *Began:* 1976 *Activities:* excursions, cultural events *Financial aid:* scholarships *URL:* http://www.umass.edu/spanport
Contact: Dir, Summer Pgm in Spain, Spanish & Portuguese, Univ of Massachusetts, Amherst MA 01003 *Ph:* 413-545 2887 *Fax:* 413-545 3178 *E-mail:* ornelas@spanport.umass.edu

---

1375
UNIVERSITY OF MICHIGAN
Summer Program in Salamanca
Site: Spain: Salamanca *Host inst:* Univ de Salamanca
Dates: 6 wks, late Jun-late Jul
Subjects: Civilization/culture, Literature, Spanish language (int/adv), Spanish studies
Eligibility: *Level:* jrs, srs *Requires:* 2.5 GPA, 3 sems coll Spanish
Credit: *Undergrad:* 6-7 *Grad:* none
Instruction: *In:* Spanish *Format:* lang study, lecture *Students:* mainly US
Costs: Contact Sponsor
Housing: *Arr by pgm:* apartments, homestay
Deadline: Feb 23
Other info: *US accredited sponsor:* yes *Orient:* abroad (1 wk) *URL:* http://www.umich.edu/~iinet/oip/
Contact: Intl Pgms, Univ of Michigan, G513 Michigan Union, Ann Arbor MI 48109-1349 *Ph:* 734-764 4311 *Fax:* 734-764 3229 *E-mail:* oip@umich.edu

---

1376
UNIVERSITY OF RHODE ISLAND
URI Summer Study Program
Site: Spain: Salamanca *Host inst:* Colegio Hispano Continental
Dates: 4-1/2 wks, Jul 1-31
Subjects: Business language, Civilization/culture, History, Homestay, Linguistics, Literature, Spanish language (beg/int/adv)
Eligibility: *Level:* fresh, sophs, jrs, srs, grads, adults, teachers *Requires:* 1 sem coll Spanish preferred
Credit: *Undergrad:* 6-9 *Grad:* 6
Instruction: *In:* Spanish *Format:* lang study, lecture, seminar *Students:* US & intl
Costs: $1,800-$2,000 *incl* tuition, housing, all meals, insurance, fees, excursions
Housing: *Arr by pgm:* residence halls, homestay
Deadline: May 5
Other info: *US accredited sponsor:* yes *Began:* 1984 *Orient:* abroad *Activities:* excursions *Misc:* Lang practicum, literary colloquium offered. May contact former participants. *Financial aid:* scholarships *URL:* http://www.uri.edu/univcol/intl_ed.htm
Contact: Prof Mario F Trubiano, Langs, Univ of Rhode Island, 306B Independence Hall, Kingston RI 02881 *Ph:* 401-874 4717, 401-789 9501 *Fax:* 401-874 4694 *E-mail:* trubim@uri.edu

---

SAN SEBASTIAN

1377
CENTRAL COLLEGE ABROAD
Basque Ethnographic Research Project
Site: Spain: San Sebastian
Dates: 1 mo, Jun; offered in alternate yrs
Subjects: Anthropology, Basque studies, Political science/politics, Sociology
Eligibility: *Level:* sophs, jrs, srs *Requires:* 2.5 GPA, int Spanish or French
Credit: *Undergrad:* 6 *Grad:* none *Doc:* transcript
Instruction: *In:* English, Spanish *Format:* lang study, lecture *Students:* mainly US
Costs: About $1,500 *incl* tuition, housing, all meals, excursions, ISIC *Nonrefundable fee*
Housing: *Arr by pgm:* pensions, hotels
Deadline: Mar 15
Other info: *US accredited sponsor:* yes *Began:* 1995 *Orient:* abroad *Activities:* excursions, field trips, cultural events *Misc:* Intro to Basque culture & ethnographic research methods. Participation in group research project. May contact former participants.
Contact: Central Coll Abroad, Central Coll, Pella, 812 University IA 50219 *Ph:* 800-831 3629

1378
IH ESPANA and **LACUNZA INTERNATIONAL HOUSE SAN SEBASTIAN**
Course on the Basque Language and Culture
Site: Spain: San Sebastian
Dates: 2 wks, Apr & Sep
Subjects: Basque language, Basque studies
Eligibility: *Level:* adults *Requires:* adv Spanish *Age:* min 17
Credit: *Undergrad:* none *Grad:* none
Instruction: *In:* Spanish *Format:* lang study *Students:* intl
Costs: About $500 *incl* tuition, housing
Housing: *Arr by pgm:* apartments, homestay, hotels, hostels
Deadline: Until pgm filled
Other info: *US accredited sponsor:* no *Orient:* abroad *URL:* http://www.lacunza.com
Contact: *See Index II for Members* Lacunza Intl House San Sebastian, Fuenterrabia 19, 1st Fl, 20006 San Sebastian, Spain *E-mail:* info@lacunza.com ▲

1379
IH ESPANA and **LACUNZA INTERNATIONAL HOUSE SAN SEBASTIAN**
Courses Made to Measure
Site: Spain: San Sebastian
Dates: Yr-round
Subjects: Spanish language (beg/int/adv)
Eligibility: *Level:* adults *Age:* min 17
Credit: *Undergrad:* none *Grad:* none *Doc:* certificate
Instruction: *In:* Spanish *Format:* lang study *Students:* intl
Costs: Contact sponsor
Housing: *Arr by pgm:* apartments, homestay, pensions, hotels, hostels
Deadline: 2 wks before pgm
Other info: *US accredited sponsor:* no *Orient:* abroad *Activities:* excursions *URL:* http://www.lacunza.com
Contact: *See Index II for Members* Lacunza Intl House San Sebastian, Fuenterrabia 19, 1st Fl, 20006 San Sebastian, Spain *E-mail:* info@lacunza.com ▲

1380
IH ESPANA and **LACUNZA INTERNATIONAL HOUSE SAN SEBASTIAN**
Curso de Metodologia y Cultura para Profesores-San Sebastian
Site: Spain: San Sebastian
Dates: 2 wks, Sep
Subjects: Foreign language teaching, Spanish language (beg/int/adv)
Eligibility: *Level:* adults *Age:* min 18
Credit: *Undergrad:* none *Grad:* none *Doc:* certificate
Instruction: *In:* Spanish *Format:* lang study, lecture, practical training, seminar, student teaching *Students:* intl
Costs: About $500 *incl* tuition, housing, books/materials
Housing: *Arr by pgm:* apartments, homestay, hotels, hostels
Deadline: 2 wks before pgm
Other info: *US accredited sponsor:* no *Orient:* abroad *URL:* http://www.lacunza.com
Contact: *See Index II for Members* Yolanda Chimeno, Lacunza Intl House San Sebastian, Fuenterrabia 19, 1st Fl, 20006 San Sebastian, Spain *E-mail:* info@lacunza.com ▲

1381
IH ESPANA and **LACUNZA INTERNATIONAL HOUSE SAN SEBASTIAN**
Cursos de Formacion para Profesores de Espanol-San Sebastian
Site: Spain: San Sebastian
Dates: 3 wks, May, Jun, Oct
Subjects: Foreign language teaching, Spanish language (beg/int/adv)
Eligibility: *Level:* srs, grads, adults, teachers, professionals *Requires:* Adv Spanish *Age:* min 21
Credit: *Undergrad:* avail *Grad:* avail *Doc:* certificate
Instruction: *In:* Spanish *Format:* lang study, lecture, practical training, seminar, student teaching *Students:* intl
Costs: About $950 *incl* tuition, housing, books/materials
Housing: *Arr by pgm:* apartments, homestay, hotels, hostels
Deadline: 2 wks before pgm
Other info: *US accredited sponsor:* no *Orient:* abroad *URL:* http://www.lacunza.com
Contact: *See Index II for Members* Yolanda Chimeno, Lacunza Intl House San Sebastian, Fuenterrabia 19, 1st Fl, 20006 San Sebastian, Spain *E-mail:* info@lacunza.com ▲

1382
IH ESPANA and **LACUNZA INTERNATIONAL HOUSE SAN SEBASTIAN**
DELE Preparation Course-San Sebastian
Site: Spain: San Sebastian
Dates: 6 wks, Apr & Oct
Subjects: Spanish language (beg/int/adv)
Eligibility: *Level:* adults *Age:* min 17
Credit: *Undergrad:* none *Grad:* none *Doc:* certificate
Instruction: *In:* Spanish *Format:* lang study *Students:* intl
Costs: About $250 *incl* tuition
Housing: *Arr by student*
Deadline: Until pgm filled
Other info: *US accredited sponsor:* no *Orient:* abroad *Misc:* Exam fees not incl. *URL:* http://www.lacunza.com
Contact: *See Index II for Members* Lacunza Intl House San Sebastian, Fuenterrabia 19 1st Fl, 20006 San Sebastian, Spain *E-mail:* info@lacunza.com ▲

1383
IH ESPANA and **LACUNZA INTERNATIONAL HOUSE SAN SEBASTIAN**
Intensive Spanish Courses in San Sabastian
Site: Spain: San Sebastian
Dates: 2 wks or longer, yr-round
Subjects: Spanish language (beg/int/adv)
Eligibility: *Level:* fresh, sophs, jrs, srs, adults *Age:* min 17
Credit: *Undergrad:* avail *Grad:* none *Doc:* certificate
Instruction: *In:* Spanish *Format:* lang study *Students:* intl
Costs: About $1,000 for 4 wks *incl* tuition, housing, pgm activities
Housing: *Arr by pgm:* residence halls, apartments, homestay, pensions, hotels, hostels
Deadline: Until pgm filled
Other info: *US accredited sponsor:* no *Orient:* abroad *Activities:* excursions *URL:* http://www.lacunza.com
Contact: *See Index II for Members* Lacunza Intl House San Sebastian, Fuenterrabia 19, 1st Fl, 20006 San Sebastian, Spain *E-mail:* info@lacunza.com ▲

1384
UNIVERSITY STUDIES ABROAD CONSORTIUM
Spanish and Basque Studies in Spain
Site: Spain: San Sebastian *Host inst:* Univ of the Basque Country
Dates: Jun 1-Jul 3, Jun 30-Jul 28, Aug 1-29
Subjects: Anthropology, Basque language (beg), History, Literature, Political science/politics, Spanish language (beg/int/adv)
Eligibility: *Level:* fresh, sophs, jrs, srs, grads *Requires:* 2.5 GPA, good acad standing
Credit: *Undergrad:* 4-5 per term *Grad:* 4-5 per term *Doc:* transcript
Instruction: *In:* English, Spanish *Format:* lang study, lecture *Students:* US & intl
Costs: $2,165 Jun or Jul, $1,760 Aug, $3,490-$3,980 for 2 mos, $5,110 for all *incl* tuition, housing, insurance, fees, excursions, ISIC
Housing: *Arr by pgm:* apartments with local students, residence halls, homestay
Deadline: Apr 15
Other info: *US accredited sponsor:* yes *Began:* 1984 *Orient:* abroad *Activities:* excursions, field trips, program travel, cultural events, sports *Misc:* Hiking, beaches. Madrid segment. Pgm organized flights. May contact former participants. *Financial aid:* scholarships *URL:* http://www.usac.unr.edu
Contact: *See Index II for Members* Carmelo Urza, Univ Studies Abroad Consortium, Univ of Nevada Library 323, Reno NV 89557-0093 *Ph:* 775-784 6569 *Fax:* 775-784 6010 *E-mail:* usac@unr.edu ▲

SANTANDER

1385
SIMMONS COLLEGE
Simmons Summer Study in Spain
Site: Spain: Santander *Host inst:* Univ Intl Menendez Pelayo
Dates: 4 wks, Jul
Subjects: Civilization/culture, Spanish language (int/adv)
Eligibility: *Level:* grads, teachers *Requires:* good acad standing, 1 yr coll Spanish
Credit: *Undergrad:* 4 *Grad:* 4
Instruction: *In:* Spanish *Format:* lang study, lecture *Students:* intl
Costs: $3,215 *incl* tuition, housing, all meals *Nonrefundable fee*
Housing: *Arr by pgm:* residence halls
Deadline: Apr 1
Other info: *US accredited sponsor:* yes *Began:* 1989 *Activities:* excursions, cultural events *Misc:* May contact former participants. *URL:* http://www.simmons.edu
Contact: Prof Dolores Pelaez, Modern Langs & Literatures, Simmons Coll, 300 The Fenway, Boston MA 02115 *Ph:* 617-521 2234 *Fax:* 617-521 3199 *E-mail:* dpelaez@simmons.edu

---

1386
UNIVERSITY OF MIAMI (FL)
Intensive Spanish in Cantabria
Site: Spain: Santander *Host inst:* Univ de Cantabria
Dates: 1 mo, Jul-Aug
Subjects: Spanish language (beg/int/adv)
Eligibility: *Level:* sophs, jrs, srs *Requires:* 2.75 GPA, 2 faculty recommendation letters
Credit: *Undergrad:* 6 *Grad:* none *Doc:* certificate
Instruction: *In:* Spanish *Format:* lang study *Students:* intl
Costs: $3,850 *incl* tuition, housing, fees
Housing: *Arr by pgm:* residence halls
Deadline: Mar 30
Other info: *US accredited sponsor:* yes *Began:* 1989 *Orient:* abroad *Activities:* excursions *Misc:* May contact former participants. *URL:* http://www.studyabroad.miami.edu
Contact: Intl Educ & Exch Pgms, Allen Hall 212, 5050 Brunson Dr, PO Box 248005, Univ of Miami, Coral Gables FL 33124-1610 *Ph:* 800-557 5421; 305-284 3434 *Fax:* 305-284 6629 *E-mail:* ieep@miami.edu

---

1387
UNIVERSITY OF NORTH CAROLINA AT CHARLOTTE
Architecture and Landscape Architecture in Spain
Site: Spain: Santander
Dates: 6 wks, mid-May-Jul
Subjects: Architecture, Field study, Landscape architecture
Eligibility: *Level:* sophs, jrs, srs, grads *Requires:* completion of 4 sems in architectural design & history, instructor's approval
Credit: *Undergrad:* 8 *Grad:* 8 *Doc:* transcript
Instruction: *In:* English *Format:* directed field study, practical training *Students:* mainly US
Costs: About $3,700 *incl* tuition, housing, insurance, fees, excursions, books/materials *Nonrefundable fee*
Housing: *Arr by pgm:* residence halls
Deadline: Oct 30
Other info: *US accredited sponsor:* yes *Began:* 1990 *Orient:* in US *Activities:* excursions, field trips *Misc:* May contact former participants. *URL:* http://www.uncc.edu/oip/edabroad.htm
Contact: Joel A Gallegos, Dir, Educ Abroad/Intl Pgms, UNC Charlotte, 9201 University City Blvd, Charlotte NC 28223-0001 *Ph:* 704-687 2464 *Fax:* 704-687 3168 *E-mail:* stennies@email.uncc.edu
Or Contact: 1998 Spain Pgm Dir, Coll of Architecture, UNC Charlotte, 9201 University City Blvd, Charlotte NC 28223-0001 *Ph:* 704-687 2358 *Fax:* 704-687 3353 *E-mail:* aar00alb@email.uncc.edu

---

SANTIAGO DE COMPOSTELA

1388
AMERICAN INSTITUTE FOR FOREIGN STUDY (AIFS)
University of Santiago de Compostela, Spain
Site: Spain: Santiago de Compostela
Dates: 4 wks, Jun 25-Jul 28
Subjects: Art history, History, Homestay, Literature, Sociology, Spanish language
Eligibility: *Level:* sophs, jrs, srs, adults, precoll *Requires:* 2.0 GPA
Credit: *Undergrad:* avail *Grad:* none *Doc:* transcript
Instruction: *In:* English, Spanish *Format:* lang study, lecture, seminar *Students:* intl
Costs: $3,699 *incl* tuition, housing, most meals, intl airfare, excursions *Nonrefundable fee*
Housing: *Arr by pgm:* residence halls, homestay
Deadline: Mar 15
Other info: *US accredited sponsor:* no *Began:* 2000 *Orient:* abroad *Activities:* excursions, cultural events *Misc:* May contact former participants. *Financial aid:* scholarships *URL:* http://www.aifsabroad.com
Contact: Solandy Meza, Coll Div, AIFS, River Plaza, 9 W Broad St, Stamford CT 06902 *Ph:* 800-727 2437 ext 5163 *E-mail:* college.info@aifs.com ▲

1389
UNIVERSITY OF NORTHERN IOWA
UNISSIST in Spain
Site: Spain: Santiago de Compostela
Dates: 7-8 wks, late Jun-early Aug
Subjects: Civilization/culture, Homestay, Literature, Spanish language (adv), Written composition
Eligibility: *Level:* grads, teachers *Requires:* BA *Age:* avg 30
Credit: *Undergrad:* none *Grad:* 9 *Doc:* transcript, diploma, degree
Instruction: *In:* Spanish *Format:* lang study, lecture, seminar *Students:* mainly US
Costs: About $2,740 *incl* tuition, housing, all meals, fees, excursions *Nonrefundable fee*
Housing: *Arr by pgm:* homestay, pensions
Deadline: Jan 1
Other info: *US accredited sponsor:* yes *Began:* 1971 *Orient:* abroad (intensive lang study) *Activities:* excursions, cultural events *Misc:* Participants can attend for professional improvement or earn MA by attending several summers. *URL:* http://www.uni.edu/modlangs/institutes-abroad
Contact: Prof Nile Vernon, Modern Langs, Univ of Northern Iowa, Cedar Falls IA 50614-0504 *Ph:* 319-273 2200 *Fax:* 319-273 2848 *E-mail:* mark.welty@uni.edu

SEGOVIA

1390
AULA MAGNA CASTELLANA
Academic Vacation
Site: Spain: Segovia
Dates: 1 mo, yr-round
Subjects: Homestay, Spanish language, Student teaching
Eligibility: *Level:* adults, precoll *Age:* min 18, avg 25
Credit: *Undergrad:* none *Grad:* none *Doc:* certificate, diploma
Instruction: *In:* Spanish *Format:* lang study, lecture, music lesson, student teaching, study tour, tutorial, workshop *Students:* intl
Costs: $1,375 *incl* tuition, housing, all meals, fees, excursions, books/materials, airport transfer
Housing: *Arr by pgm:* apartments with local students, residence halls with local students, homestay
Deadline: 45 days before pgm
Other info: *US accredited sponsor:* no *Began:* 1997 *Orient:* abroad (1 day) *Activities:* excursions, field trips, program travel, cultural events, sports *Misc:* Conversation exch with Spanish students. Job database. *Financial aid:* work study *URL:* http://www.aulamagnacastellana.com
Contact: Aurora Garcia, Dir, Aula Magna Castellana, Santo Tomas 1, 3D, 40002 Segovia, Spain
E-mail: amagnac@arrakis.es

1391
AULA MAGNA CASTELLANA
Individual Courses
Site: Spain: Segovia
Dates: 1 wk or longer, yr-round
Subjects: Homestay, Spanish language
Eligibility: *Level:* adults, precoll *Age:* min 18, avg 25
Credit: *Undergrad:* none *Grad:* none *Doc:* certificate
Instruction: *In:* Spanish *Format:* tutorial *Students:* intl
Costs: $690 per wk *incl* tuition, housing, all meals, airport transfer *Nonrefundable fee*
Housing: *Arr by pgm:* homestay
Deadline: 45 days before pgm
Other info: *US accredited sponsor:* no *Began:* 1997 *Orient:* abroad (1 day) *Activities:* excursions, field trips, program travel, cultural events, sports *Financial aid:* work study *URL:* http://www.aulamagnacastellana.com
Contact: Aurora Garcia, Dir, Aula Magna Castellana, Santo Tomas 1, 3D, 40002 Segovia, Spain
E-mail: amagnac@arrakis.es

1392
AULA MAGNA CASTELLANA
Intensive Courses
Site: Spain: Segovia
Dates: 1 mo, yr-round
Subjects: Current events, Homestay, Spanish language, Spanish studies
Eligibility: *Level:* adults, precoll *Age:* min 18, avg 25
Credit: *Undergrad:* none *Grad:* none *Doc:* certificate, diploma
Instruction: *In:* Spanish *Format:* lang study, lecture, music lesson, seminar, study tour, tutorial *Students:* intl
Costs: $1,680 *incl* tuition, housing, all meals, fees, excursions, books/materials, airport transfer *Nonrefundable fee*
Housing: *Arr by pgm:* apartments with local students, residence halls with local students, homestay
Deadline: 45 days before pgm
Other info: *US accredited sponsor:* no *Began:* 1997 *Orient:* avail (1 day) *Activities:* excursions, field trips, cultural events, sports *Misc:* Conversation exch with Spanish students. Job database. *Financial aid:* work study *URL:* http://www.aulamagnacastellana.com
Contact: Aurora Garcia, Dir, Aula Magna Castellana, Santo Tomas 1, 3D, 40002 Segovia, Spain
E-mail: amagnac@arrakis.es

1393
AULA MAGNA CASTELLANA
Summer Specialized Courses
Site: Spain: Segovia
Dates: 1 mo, Jul 15-Aug 11 or Aug 5-Sep 1
Subjects: Art history, Business language, Business/management, Ecology/environmental studies, Field study, History, Homestay, Literature, Spanish language, Spanish studies, Technology
Eligibility: *Level:* fresh, sophs, srs, grads, adults, teachers, professionals, precoll *Requires:* 2 yrs Spanish *Age:* min 18, avg 25
Credit: *Undergrad:* avail *Grad:* none *Doc:* certificate, diploma
Instruction: *In:* Spanish *Format:* art studio, directed field study, lang study, lecture, seminar, study tour, tutorial *Students:* intl
Costs: $1,990 per mo *incl* tuition, housing, all meals, fees, excursions, books/materials, airport transfer *Nonrefundable fee*
Housing: *Arr by pgm:* apartments with local students, residence halls with local students, homestay
Deadline: 45 days before pgm
Other info: *US accredited sponsor:* no *Began:* 1997 *Orient:* abroad (1 day) *Activities:* excursions, field trips, cultural events, sports *Misc:* Conversation exch with Spanish students. Job database. *Financial aid:* work study *URL:* http://www.aulamagnacastellana.com

Contact: Aurora Garcia, Dir, Aula Magna Castellana, Santo Tomas 1, 3D, 40002 Segovia, Spain
E-mail: amagnac@arrakis.es

1394
MIDWEST CONSORTIUM FOR STUDY ABROAD and AHA INTERNATIONAL
Summer Spanish Language and Culture Studies in Segovia
Site: Spain: Segovia
Dates: 6 wks, Jun-Jul
Subjects: Art, Business language, Civilization/culture, Homestay, Literature, Media studies, Spanish language, Spanish studies
Eligibility: *Level:* sophs, jrs, srs, adults, professionals *Requires:* 2 yrs coll Spanish
Credit: *Undergrad:* avail *Grad:* none *Doc:* transcript
Instruction: *In:* Spanish *Format:* lang study, lecture *Students:* mainly US
Costs: $3,030 *incl* tuition, housing, all meals, insurance, fees, excursions, books/materials
Housing: *Arr by pgm:* homestay
Deadline: 65 days before pgm
Other info: *US accredited sponsor:* yes *Began:* 1969 *Orient:* abroad (1 day) *Activities:* excursions, field trips *Misc:* May contact former participants. *URL:* http://www.aha-intl.org
Contact: *See Index II for Members* Carlotta Troy, AHA Intl, 741 SW Lincoln St, Portland OR 97201 *Ph:* 800-654 2051; 503-295 7730 *Fax:* 503-295 5969 *E-mail:* mail@aha-intl.org

---

1395
UNIVERSITY OF ARIZONA
Summer in Segovia
Site: Spain: Segovia
Dates: 5 wks, Jul-Aug
Subjects: Homestay, Literature, Spanish language (beg/int/adv), Speech correction
Eligibility: *Level:* sophs, jrs, srs *Requires:* 2.5 GPA, 1 sem of spanish
Credit: *Undergrad:* 6-8 *Grad:* none *Doc:* transcript
Instruction: *In:* Spanish *Format:* lang study, lecture *Students:* mainly US
Costs: $3,000 *incl* tuition, housing, all meals, fees, excursions *Nonrefundable fee*
Housing: *Arr by pgm:* homestay
Deadline: May 15
Other info: *US accredited sponsor:* yes *Began:* 2000 *Orient:* in US & abroad *Misc:* May contact former participants. *URL:* http://w3.arizona.edu/~ciss/
Contact: Caroline Patrick, Undergrad Pgms, 939 N Tyndall Ave, Tucson AZ 85721 *Ph:* 520-626 9211 *Fax:* 520-626 9004 *E-mail:* cpatrick@u.arizona.edu ▲

SEVILLE

1396
ACADEMIC PROGRAMS INTERNATIONAL (API)
API in Seville, Spain
Site: Spain: Seville *Host inst:* Univ of Pablo de Olavide
Dates: 6 wks, May 23-Jun 30
Subjects: Civilization/culture, Homestay, Spanish language, Spanish studies
Eligibility: *Level:* fresh, sophs, jrs, srs, adults, teachers, professionals *Requires:* 2.75 GPA, previous study in field, 1 yr Spanish, 1 recommendation letter *Age:* min 18
Credit: *Undergrad:* 6 *Grad:* none *Doc:* transcript
Instruction: *In:* Spanish *Format:* lang study, lecture *Students:* mainly US
Costs: $3,200 *incl* tuition, housing, all meals, insurance, fees, excursions, local transport
Housing: *Arr by pgm:* residence halls, homestay
Deadline: Apr 1; Mar 1 for scholarships
Other info: *US accredited sponsor:* no *Began:* 1999 *Orient:* in US & abroad (2 wks, intensive lang study) *Activities:* excursions, field trips, program travel, cultural events, sports *Misc:* On-site dir. May contact former participants. *Financial aid:* scholarships *URL:* http://www.academicintl.com
Contact: Jennifer C Allen, Dir, Acad Pgms Intl, 129 E Hopkins St, Ste 101, San Marcos TX 78666 *Ph:* 800-844 4124; 512-392 8520 *Fax:* 512-392 8420 *E-mail:* api@onr.com

---

1397
CENTER FOR CROSS-CULTURAL STUDY
Summer Business Program in Seville, Spain
Site: Spain: Seville
Dates: 3-1/2 wks, Jul 1-25
Subjects: Business/management, Homestay
Eligibility: *Level:* sophs, jrs, srs, grads, adults, professionals *Requires:* previous study in field *Age:* min 16
Credit: *Undergrad:* 3 *Grad:* 3 *Doc:* transcript *Transfer credit through:* Russell Sage College
Instruction: *In:* English *Format:* directed field study, lecture, seminar, study tour *Students:* mainly US
Costs: $2,135 *incl* housing, all meals, insurance, fees, excursions, laundry, orient, e-mail
Housing: *Arr by pgm:* homestay
Deadline: May 1
Other info: *US accredited sponsor:* yes *Began:* 1996 *Orient:* abroad *Activities:* excursions, field trips, program travel, cultural events *Misc:* Visits to local multinatl companies. May contact former participants. *URL:* http://www.studyinspain.org
Contact: *See Index II for Members* Dr Judith Ortiz, Dir, US, CC-CS, Dept S, 446 Main St, Amherst MA 01002 *Ph:* 800-377 2621; 413-256 0011 *Fax:* 413-256 1968 *E-mail:* iie@cccs.com
Or Contact: Resident Dir, CC-CS, Calle Harinas 18, 41001 Seville, Spain *E-mail:* admin@cccs.es ▲

1398
CENTER FOR CROSS-CULTURAL STUDY
Summer Study in Seville, Spain
Site: Spain: Seville
Dates: 3-1/2 or 7 wks, Jun 3-28, Jul 1-25 or Jun 3-Jul 25
Subjects: Art history, Civilization/culture, Drama/theater, History, Homestay, Literature, Spanish language (beg/int/adv), Spanish studies
Eligibility: *Level:* fresh, sophs, jrs, srs, grads, adults
Credit: *Undergrad:* 3-6 *Grad:* 3-6 *Doc:* transcript
Instruction: *In:* Spanish *Format:* lang study, lecture, study tour, tutorial *Students:* mainly US
Costs: $1,935 for 3-1/2 wks, $3,585 for 7 wks *incl* tuition, housing, all meals, insurance, fees, excursions, laundry, orient, computer labs
Housing: *Arr by pgm:* homestay, student boarding houses
Deadline: Apr 15 or until pgm filled
Other info: *US accredited sponsor:* yes *Began:* 1969 *Orient:* abroad *Activities:* excursions, program travel, cultural events *Misc:* Courses in 35-rm mansion in historic ctr of Seville. Outings with Spanish students. May contact former participants. *URL:* http://www.studyinspain.org
Contact: *See Index II for Members* Dr Judith Ortiz, Dir, US, CC-CS, Dept S, 446 Main St, Amherst MA 01002-2314 *Ph:* 800-377 2621; 413-256 0011 *Fax:* 413-256 1968 *E-mail:* iie@cccs.com
Or Contact: Resident Dir, CC-CS, Calle Harinas 18, 41001 Seville, Spain *E-mail:* admin@cccs.es ▲

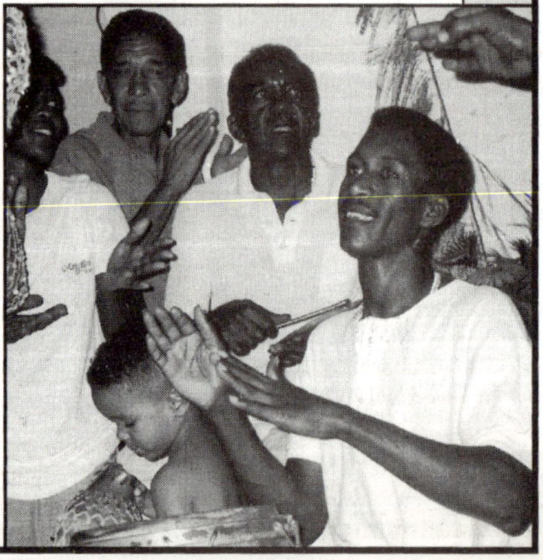

1399
COLLEGE CONSORTIUM FOR INTERNATIONAL STUDIES and **SAINT BONAVENTURE UNIVERSITY** and **BROWARD COMMUNITY COLLEGE**
Summer Program in Spain
Site: Spain: Seville *Host inst:* Inst of Intl Studies
Dates: 4 wks, late Jun-late Jul
Subjects: Civilization/culture, Spanish language (beg/int/adv), Spanish studies
Eligibility: *Level:* fresh, sophs, jrs, srs, grads, adults *Requires:* 2.5 GPA
Credit: *Undergrad:* 6 *Grad:* none *Doc:* transcript
Instruction: *In:* English, Spanish *Format:* lang study, lecture *Students:* intl
Costs: $1,950 *incl* tuition, housing, all meals, insurance, fees, excursions
Housing: *Arr by pgm:* apartments, homestay
Deadline: May 1
Other info: *US accredited sponsor:* yes *Began:* 1995 *Orient:* in US & abroad *Activities:* excursions, field trips *URL:* http://www.ccisabroad.org
Contact: *See Index II for Members* CCIS, 2000 P St NW, Ste 503, Washington DC 20036 *Ph:* 800-453 6956; 202-223 0330 *Fax:* 202-223 0999 *E-mail:* info@ccisabroad.org
Or Contact: Intl Educ Inst, Broward CC, 1000 Coconut Creek Blvd, Coconut Creek FL 33066 *Ph:* 954-973 2206 *Fax:* 954-973 2389 *E-mail:* wgreene@broward.cc.fl.us
Or Contact: Study Abroad Pgms, St Bonaventure Univ, St Bonaventure NY 14778 *Ph:* 716-375 2574 *Fax:* 716-375 2381 *E-mail:* asayegh@sbu.edu ▲

1400
COUNCIL ON INTERNATIONAL EDUCATIONAL EXCHANGE CONSORTIUM
Spanish Art History and Art Restoration
Site: Spain: Seville
Dates: 6 wks, early Jun-late Jul
Subjects: Art history, Art restoration, Homestay, Spanish language (beg/int/adv)
Eligibility: *Level:* fresh, sophs, jrs, srs, grads, adults, teachers, professionals *Requires:* 2.75 GPA, completion of 1 coll sem
Credit: *Undergrad:* 6 *Grad:* none
Instruction: *In:* English, Spanish *Format:* lab, lang study, lecture, practical training *Students:* mainly US
Costs: $3,400 *incl* tuition, housing, all meals, insurance, excursions, ISIC, orient
Housing: *Arr by pgm:* homestay, pensions
Deadline: Apr 1
Other info: *US accredited sponsor:* yes *Orient:* abroad *Activities:* excursions, field trips *Misc:* Full-time resident staff. Grade report. May contact former participants. *Financial aid:* scholarships *URL:* http://www.ciee.org/study
Contact: *See Index II for Members* Seville Pgm Adviser, Council-ISP, 633 3rd Ave, 20th Fl, New York NY 10017-6706 *Ph:* 800-407 8839 *Fax:* 212-822 2779 *E-mail:* studyinfo@ciee.org

---

1401
GEORGE MASON UNIVERSITY
Spanish Language and Culture
Site: Spain: Seville *Host inst:* Estudias Univ y Superiores de Andalucia

Dates: Jun 4-30
Subjects: Spanish language
Eligibility: *Level:* sophs, jrs, srs, adults, teachers, professionals *Requires:* 2.25 GPA, previous study in field, 1 yr coll Spanish *Age:* min 18
Credit: *Undergrad:* 6 *Grad:* none *Doc:* transcript
Instruction: *In:* Spanish *Format:* lang study *Students:* mainly US
Costs: About $2,934 for VA residents, $3,534 for others *incl* tuition, housing, all meals, insurance, fees, excursions, ISIC
Housing: *Arr by pgm:* homestay
Deadline: Apr 10
Other info: *US accredited sponsor:* yes *Began:* 1996 *Activities:* excursions, field trips *Misc:* May contact former participants. *Financial aid:* scholarships, work study *URL:* http://www.gmu.edu/departments/cge
Contact: Ctr for Global Educ, George Mason Univ, Johnson Ctr, Rm 235, 4400 University Dr, Fairfax VA 22030-4444 *Ph:* 703-993 2154 *Fax:* 703-993 2153 *E-mail:* cge@gmu.edu

---

1402
HORIZONS TO GO
Andalucia: Seville, Cordoba, Granada
Site: Spain: Seville
Dates: 1 wk, Jan 20-27
Subjects: Ceramics/pottery, Painting, Spanish language (beg/int), Tile making
Eligibility: *Level:* sophs, jrs, srs, grads, adults, teachers, professionals
Credit: *Undergrad:* none *Grad:* none
Instruction: *In:* English *Format:* workshop *Students:* mainly US
Costs: $1,465 *incl* tuition, housing, all meals, excursions, books/materials
Housing: *Arr by pgm:* hotels
Deadline: None
Other info: *US accredited sponsor:* no *Began:* 1983 *Activities:* excursions, field trips *Misc:* May contact former participants. *URL:* http://www.horizons-art.org
Contact: Jane Sinauer or Karen Totman-Gale, Horizons To Go, 108 N Main St, Sunderland MA 01375 *Ph:* 413-665 0300 *Fax:* 413-665 4141 *E-mail:* horizons@horizons-art.org

---

1403
IH ESPANA and **CLIC INTERNATIONAL HOUSE SEVILLA**
Business Spanish
Site: Spain: Seville
Dates: 8 wks, May 2-Jun 23
Subjects: Business language, Spanish language (int/adv)
Eligibility: *Level:* adults *Requires:* int Spanish *Age:* min 17, avg 30
Credit: *Undergrad:* avail *Grad:* none *Doc:* diploma *Transfer credit through:* Nicholls State Univ
Instruction: *In:* Spanish *Format:* lang study, lecture *Students:* intl
Costs: About $1,320 *incl* tuition, fees
Housing: *Arr by pgm:* apartments with local students, residence halls, apartments, homestay, pensions, hotels, hostels
Deadline: 2 wks before pgm
Other info: *US accredited sponsor:* no *Began:* 1994 *In coop with:* ALTO, FIYTO, Intl House, OLE, *Activities:* excursions, field trips, cultural events, sports *Misc:* May contact former participants. *URL:* http://www.clic.es
Contact: *See Index II for Members* Bernhard Roters, Dir or Eva White, CLIC, Calle Albareda 19, 41001 Seville, Spain *E-mail:* clic@clic.es ▲

1404
IH ESPANA and **CLIC INTERNATIONAL HOUSE SEVILLA**
Certificado Superior de Espanol de Negocios
Site: Spain: Seville
Dates: 4 wks, Jul 31 or Oct 30
Subjects: Business language, Spanish language (int/adv)
Eligibility: *Level:* adults *Requires:* int-adv Spanish *Age:* min 17
Credit: *Undergrad:* none *Grad:* none *Doc:* certificate
Instruction: *In:* Spanish *Format:* lang study *Students:* intl
Costs: About $1,143 *incl* tuition, housing, some meals, fees
Housing: *Arr by pgm:* residence halls, apartments, homestay, pensions, hotels, hostels
Deadline: Until pgm filled
Other info: *US accredited sponsor:* no *Orient:* abroad *Activities:* excursions *Misc:* May take exam in bus Spanish given by Madrid Chamber of Commerce. *URL:* http://www.clic.es
Contact: *See Index II for Members* CLIC Intl House Sevilla, Albareda 19, 41001 Seville, Spain *E-mail:* clic@clic.es ▲

1405
IH ESPANA and **CLIC INTERNATIONAL HOUSE SEVILLA**
Cursos de Formacion para Profesores de Espanol-Seville
Site: Spain: Seville
Dates: 3 wks, each mo
Subjects: Foreign language teaching, Spanish language (adv)
Eligibility: *Level:* srs, grads, adults, teachers, professionals *Requires:* adv Spanish *Age:* min 18
Credit: *Undergrad:* avail *Grad:* avail *Doc:* certificate
Instruction: *In:* Spanish *Format:* lang study, lecture, practical training, seminar, student teaching *Students:* intl
Costs: About $950 *incl* tuition, housing, books/materials
Housing: *Arr by pgm:* apartments, homestay, hotels, hostels
Deadline: Until pgm filled
Other info: *US accredited sponsor:* no *Orient:* abroad *Activities:* excursions *URL:* http://www.clic.es
Contact: *See Index II for Members* Antonio Orta, CLIC Intl House Sevilla, Albareda 19, 41001 Seville, Spain *E-mail:* clic@clic.es ▲

1406
IH ESPANA and **CLIC INTERNATIONAL HOUSE SEVILLA**
DELE Preparation Course-Seville
Site: Spain: Seville
Dates: 11 wks, fall & spring
Subjects: Spanish language (beg/int/adv)
Eligibility: *Level:* adults *Age:* min 17
Credit: *Undergrad:* none *Grad:* none *Doc:* certificate
Instruction: *In:* Spanish *Format:* lang study *Students:* intl
Costs: About $2,500 *incl* tuition, housing, some meals, fees
Housing: *Arr by pgm:* residence halls, apartments, homestay, pensions, hotels, hostels
Deadline: Until pgm filled
Other info: *US accredited sponsor:* no *Orient:* abroad *Activities:* excursions *Misc:* Exam fees not incl. *URL:* http://www.clic.es
Contact: *See Index II for Members* CLIC Intl House Sevilla, Albareda 19, 41001 Seville, Spain *E-mail:* clic@clic.es ▲

1407
IH ESPANA and **CLIC INTERNATIONAL HOUSE SEVILLA**
Intensive Spanish Courses in Seville
Site: Spain: Seville
Dates: 2 wks or longer, yr-round
Subjects: Spanish language (beg/int/adv)
Eligibility: *Level:* fresh, sophs, jrs, srs, grads, precoll *Age:* min 17
Credit: *Undergrad:* avail *Grad:* none *Doc:* certificate
Instruction: *In:* Spanish *Format:* lang study *Students:* intl
Costs: About $800 for 4 weeks *incl* tuition, housing, pgm activities
Housing: *Arr by pgm:* residence halls, apartments, homestay, pensions, hotels, hostels
Deadline: Until pgm filled
Other info: *US accredited sponsor:* no *Orient:* abroad *Activities:* excursions *URL:* http://www.clic.es

Contact: *See Index II for Members* CLIC Intl House Sevilla, Albareda 19, 41001 Seville, Spain *E-mail:* clic@clic.es ▲

1408
IH ESPANA and CLIC INTERNATIONAL HOUSE SEVILLA
Masterclass
Site: Spain: Seville
Dates: 2 wks, Feb, Mar, May, Oct
Subjects: Spanish language
Eligibility: *Level:* adults, adults
Credit: *Undergrad:* none *Grad:* none *Doc:* certificate
Instruction: *In:* Spanish, Spanish *Format:* lang study, lang study *Students:* intl & intl
Costs: About $700 *incl* tuition, tuition, housing, housing, some meals, some meals, cultural pgms
Housing: *Arr by pgm, Arr by pgm:* residence halls, residence halls, apartments, apartments, homestay, homestay, pensions, pensions, hotels, hotels, hostels, hostels
Deadline: Until pgm filled
Other info: *US accredited sponsor:* no *Orient:* abroad *Activities:* cultural events, cultural events *URL:* http://www.clic.es
Contact: *See Index II for Members* CLIC Intl House Sevilla, Albareda 19, 41001 Seville, Spain *E-mail:* clic@clic.es ▲

1409
IH ESPANA and CLIC INTERNATIONAL HOUSE SEVILLA
Spanish Intensive Courses
Site: Spain: Seville
Dates: 2 wks or longer, yr-round
Subjects: Civilization/culture, Folklore, History, Spanish language (beg/int/adv), Spanish studies
Eligibility: *Level:* fresh, sophs, jrs, srs, grads, adults, teachers, professionals, precoll *Age:* min 17, avg 30
Credit: *Undergrad:* none *Grad:* none *Doc:* certificate, diploma *Transfer credit through:* Nicholls State Univ
Instruction: *In:* Spanish *Format:* lang study *Students:* intl
Costs: About $870 per mo *incl* tuition, housing, some meals, fees, excursions, books/materials, cultural pgm, student exch
Housing: *Arr by pgm:* apartments with local students, residence halls, apartments, homestay, pensions, hotels
Deadline: 2 wks before pgm
Other info: *US accredited sponsor:* no *Began:* 1983 *In coop with:* ACEIA, ALTO, FECEI, FIYTO, Intl House, OLE *Activities:* excursions, field trips, program travel, cultural events, sports *URL:* http://www.clic.es

Contact: *See Index II for Members* Bernhard Roters, Dir or Eva White, CLIC, Calle Albareda 19, 41001 Seville, Spain *E-mail:* clic@clic.es ▲

1410
IH ESPANA and CLIC INTERNATIONAL HOUSE SEVILLA
Super Intensive Program
Site: Spain: Seville
Dates: 2 wks, yr-round
Subjects: Spanish language (int/adv)
Credit: *Undergrad:* none *Grad:* none *Doc:* certificate
Instruction: *In:* Spanish *Format:* lang study *Students:* intl
Costs: About $725 *incl* tuition, housing, some meals
Housing: *Arr by pgm:* residence halls, apartments, homestay, pensions, hotels, hostels
Deadline: Until pgm filled
Other info: *US accredited sponsor:* no *Orient:* abroad *Activities:* excursions *URL:* http://www.clic.es
Contact: *See Index II for Members* CLIC Intl House Sevilla, Albareda 19, 41001 Seville, Spain *E-mail:* clic@clic.es ▲

1411
INSTITUTO DE ESTUDIOS DE LA LENGUA ESPANOLA (IELE)
Business Spanish Course
Site: Spain: Seville
Dates: 4 wks, yr-round
Subjects: Business language, Independent study, Spanish language (int/adv)
Eligibility: *Level:* grads, adults, professionals *Age:* avg 30
Credit: *Undergrad:* none *Grad:* none
Instruction: *In:* Spanish *Format:* independent study, lang study *Students:* intl
Costs: 83,000 ptas *incl* tuition, fees, books/materials
Housing: *Arr by pgm:* apartments with local students, residence halls with local students, homestay, pensions, hotels, hostels
Deadline: 15 days before pgm
Other info: *US accredited sponsor:* no *Began:* 1994 *Activities:* excursions, cultural events *Misc:* May contact former participants. *URL:* http://www.iele.com
Contact: Macarena Hidalgo, IELE, c/ Garcia de Vinuesa 29, 41001 Seville, Spain *E-mail:* info@iele.com

---

1412
INSTITUTO DE ESTUDIOS DE LA LENGUA ESPANOLA (IELE)
Course for Teachers of Spanish/Spring and Summer
Site: Spain: Seville
Dates: 2 wks, Apr 3-14 or Jul 17-28
Subjects: Education/teaching, Foreign language teaching, Independent study, Spanish language (adv)
Eligibility: *Level:* srs, grads, adults, teachers *Age:* min 18, avg 25
Credit: *Undergrad:* none *Grad:* none
Instruction: *In:* Spanish *Format:* independent study, lang study, student teaching *Students:* intl
Costs: 65,000 ptas *incl* tuition, books/materials
Housing: *Arr by pgm:* apartments with local students, residence halls with local students, homestay, pensions, hotels, hostels
Deadline: 1 mo before pgm
Other info: *US accredited sponsor:* no *Began:* 1994 *Misc:* May contact former participants. *URL:* http://www.iele.com
Contact: Macarena Hidalgo, IELE, c/ Garcia de Vinuesa 29, 41001 Seville, Spain *E-mail:* info@iele.com

---

1413
INSTITUTO DE ESTUDIOS DE LA LENGUA ESPANOLA (IELE)
Course in the Teacher's Home
Site: Spain: Seville
Dates: 1 wk, yr-round
Subjects: Civilization/culture, Homestay, Literature, Spanish language, Spanish studies
Eligibility: *Level:* adults, precoll
Credit: *Undergrad:* none *Grad:* none
Instruction: *In:* Spanish *Format:* independent study, lang study *Students:* intl
Costs: 145,000 ptas *incl* tuition, housing, all meals, excursions, books/materials, transfer
Housing: *Arr by pgm:* homestay, (teacher's home)
Deadline: 15 days before pgm
Other info: *US accredited sponsor:* no *Began:* 1994 *Activities:* excursions, cultural events, sports *Misc:* May contact former participants. *URL:* http://www.iele.com
Contact: Macarena Hidalgo, IELE, c/ Garcia de Vinuesa 29, 41001 Seville, Spain *E-mail:* info@iele.com

---

1414
INSTITUTO DE ESTUDIOS DE LA LENGUA ESPANOLA (IELE)
DELE Course (Diploma de Espanol como Lengua Extranjera)
Site: Spain: Seville
Dates: 4 wks, yr-round

Subjects: Homestay, Independent study, Spanish language (int/adv)
Eligibility: *Level:* grads, adults *Age:* avg 25
Credit: *Undergrad:* none *Grad:* none
Instruction: *In:* Spanish *Format:* independent study, lang study *Students:* intl
Costs: 83,000 ptas *incl* tuition, fees, books/materials
Housing: *Arr by pgm:* apartments with local students, residence halls with local students, homestay, pensions, hotels, hostels
Deadline: 15 days before pgm
Other info: *US accredited sponsor:* no *Began:* 1994 *Activities:* excursions, cultural events *Misc:* May contact former participants. *URL:* http://www.iele.com
Contact: Macarena Hidalgo, IELE, c/ Garcia de Vinuesa 29, 41001 Seville, Spain *E-mail:* info@iele.com

---

1415
INSTITUTO DE ESTUDIOS DE LA LENGUA ESPANOLA (IELE)
General Course
Site: Spain: Seville
Dates: 4 wks, yr-round
Subjects: Civilization/culture, Independent study, Literature, Spanish language, Spanish studies
Eligibility: *Level:* fresh, sophs, jrs, grads, adults, precoll *Age:* avg 25
Credit: *Undergrad:* none *Grad:* none
Instruction: *In:* Spanish *Format:* independent study, lang study *Students:* intl
Costs: 60,000 ptas *incl* tuition, fees, books/materials
Housing: *Arr by pgm:* apartments with local students, residence halls with local students, homestay, pensions, hotels, hostels
Deadline: 15 days before pgm
Other info: *US accredited sponsor:* no *Began:* 1994 *Activities:* excursions, cultural events *Misc:* May contact former participants. *URL:* http://www.iele.com
Contact: Macarena Hidalgo, IELE, c/ Garcia de Vinuesa 29, 41001 Seville, Spain *E-mail:* info@iele.com

---

1416
INSTITUTO DE ESTUDIOS DE LA LENGUA ESPANOLA (IELE)
Senior Course
Site: Spain: Seville
Dates: 2 wks, May 8-21 or Sep 11-24
Subjects: Civilization/culture, Independent study, Literature, Spanish language, Spanish studies
Eligibility: *Level:* adults *Age:* min 40, avg 50
Credit: *Undergrad:* none *Grad:* none
Instruction: *In:* Spanish *Format:* independent study, lang study *Students:* intl
Costs: 220,000 ptas *incl* tuition, housing, all meals, fees, excursions, books/materials, transfer
Housing: *Arr by pgm:* hotels, country house
Deadline: 1 mo before pgm
Other info: *US accredited sponsor:* no *Began:* 1994 *Activities:* excursions, program travel, cultural events *Misc:* May contact former participants. *URL:* http://www.iele.com
Contact: Macarena Hidalgo, IELE, c/ Garcia de Vinuesa 29, 41001 Seville, Spain *E-mail:* info@iele.com

---

1417
LANGUAGE LINK
Spanish Study in Seville
Site: Spain: Seville *Host inst:* CLIC
Dates: 2 wks or longer, yr-round
Subjects: Spanish language
Eligibility: *Level:* fresh, sophs, jrs, srs, grads, adults, teachers, professionals, precoll *Age:* min 15, avg 28
Credit: *Undergrad:* 12 *Grad:* 6 *Doc:* transcript
Instruction: *In:* Spanish *Format:* lang study, tutorial *Students:* intl
Costs: $305 per wk *incl* tuition, housing, some meals, insurance, books/materials *Nonrefundable fee*
Housing: *Arr by pgm:* apartments with local students, residence halls, apartments, homestay
Deadline: None
Other info: *US accredited sponsor:* no *Began:* 1985 *In coop with:* Austin Peay State Univ *Orient:* abroad *Activities:* excursions, field trips, cultural events, sports *Misc:* May contact former participants. *URL:* http://www.langlink.com
Contact: Kay G Rafool, Dir, Lang Link, PO Box 3006, Peoria IL 61612-3006 *Ph:* 800-552 2051; 309-692 2961 *Fax:* 309-692 2926 *E-mail:* info@langlink.com

---

1418
TRINITY CHRISTIAN COLLEGE
Semester in Spain: Short-Term Programs
Site: Spain: Seville *Host inst:* Windsor Sch
Dates: 4-7 wks, May 29-Jun 22 and/or Jun 26-Jul 21
Subjects: Art history, Homestay, Spanish language (beg/int/adv), Spanish studies
Eligibility: *Level:* fresh, sophs, jrs, srs, grads, adults *Requires:* 2.0 GPA, high sch grad *Age:* avg 22
Credit: *Undergrad:* 4-8 *Grad:* none *Doc:* transcript
Instruction: *In:* Spanish *Format:* lang study, lecture, study tour *Students:* US & intl
Costs: $2,000 for 1 term, $4,000 for both terms *incl* tuition, housing, all meals, fees, excursions, books/materials *Nonrefundable fee*
Housing: *Arr by pgm:* homestay
Deadline: Apr 1
Other info: *US accredited sponsor:* yes *Began:* 1977 *Orient:* abroad *Activities:* field trips *Misc:* May contact former participants. *URL:* http://www.trnty.edu/spain
Contact: Debra Veenstra, Coord, Sem in Spain, Trinity Christian Coll, 6601 W College Dr, Palos Heights IL 60463 *Ph:* 800-748 0087; 708-396 7440 *Fax:* 708-239 3986 *E-mail:* spain@trnty.edu ▲

1419
UNIVERSITY OF WISCONSIN-PLATTEVILLE
Summer Session in Seville
Site: Spain: Seville *Host inst:* Spanish-Amer Inst
Dates: 4 wks, May 29-Jun 29
Subjects: History, Homestay, Literature, Spanish language (int/adv), Spanish studies
Eligibility: *Level:* fresh, sophs, jrs, srs, adults, teachers *Requires:* 2.0 GPA, 1 yr coll Spanish, good acad standing, 2 recommendations *Age:* min 18, avg 20
Credit: *Undergrad:* 6 *Grad:* none *Doc:* transcript
Instruction: *In:* English, Spanish *Format:* lang study, lecture, study tour *Students:* mainly US
Costs: $2,975 for WI/MN residents, $3,275 for others *incl* tuition, housing, most meals, fees, excursions, books/materials, ISIC *Nonrefundable fee*
Housing: *Arr by pgm:* homestay
Deadline: Apr 1
Other info: *US accredited sponsor:* yes *Began:* 1993 *Orient:* in US & abroad *Activities:* excursions, field trips, program travel, cultural events *Misc:* Each student assigned Spanish intercambio partner. May contact former participants. *URL:* http://www.uwplatt.edu/~studyabroad
Contact: Dr William Spofford, Dir, or Dr Julia Davis, Asst Dir, Study Abroad, Univ of Wisconsin-Platteville, 308 Warner Hall, Platteville WI 53818-3099 *Ph:* 800-342 1725; 608-342 1726 *Fax:* 608-342 1736 *E-mail:* studyabroad@uwplatt.edu

---

TOLEDO

1420
BEAVER COLLEGE, CENTER FOR EDUCATION ABROAD
Summer in Spain
Site: Spain: Toledo *Host inst:* Fundacion Jose Ortega y Gasset
Dates: Mid-Jun-late Jul
Subjects: Art history, History, Literature, Sociology, Spanish language (beg/int)
Eligibility: *Level:* sophs, jrs, srs, grads *Requires:* 3.0 GPA, 1 yr Spanish lang
Credit: *Undergrad:* 6 *Grad:* none *Doc:* transcript
Instruction: *In:* English, Spanish *Format:* lang study, lecture *Students:* US & Intl
Costs: $3,765 *incl* tuition, housing, some meals, insurance, excursions, ISIC, transcript, orient *Nonrefundable fee*
Housing: *Arr by pgm:* homestay
Deadline: Mar 31
Other info: *US accredited sponsor:* yes *Began:* 2000 *Orient:* abroad *Misc:* May contact former participants. *URL:* http://www.beaver.edu
Contact: Beaver Coll, Ctr for Educ Abroad, 450 S Easton Rd, Glenside PA 19038 *Ph:* 888-232 8379 *E-mail:* cea@beaver.edu ▲

1421
NORTHERN ILLINOIS UNIVERSITY
Spanish Language and Culture in Toledo, Spain
Site: Spain: Toledo
Dates: Jul 1-Aug 3
Subjects: Spanish language (int), Spanish studies (int)
Eligibility: *Level:* sophs, jrs, srs, grads *Requires:* 2.75 GPA, previous study in field *Age:* min 18, avg 21
Credit: *Undergrad:* 3-6 *Grad:* 3-6 *Doc:* transcript
Instruction: *In:* Spanish *Format:* lang study *Students:* mainly US
Costs: $2,100 *incl* tuition, housing, all meals, insurance, excursions
Housing: *Arr by pgm:* residence halls, homestay
Deadline: May 1; or until pgm filled
Other info: *US accredited sponsor:* yes *Began:* 2000 *In coop with:* Cursos de Espanol en Toledo (ESTO) *Orient:* in US & abroad *Misc:* Courses for non-natives, under auspices of Univ of Castilla-La Mancha & the sponsorship of the Patronato Univ. May contact former participants. *URL:* http://www.niu.edu/niuabroad/
Contact: Anne Seitzinger, Pgm Cood, Study Abroad, Williston 417, Northern Illinois Univ, DeKalb IL 60115 *Ph:* 815-753-0700 *Fax:* 815-753-0825 *E-mail:* niuabroad@niu.edu
Or Contact: Prof Pablo Virumbrales, Foreign Langs & Literatures, Northern Illinois Univ, DeKalb IL 60115 *Ph:* 815-758 7116

1422
UNIVERSITY OF MINNESOTA
International Program in Toledo, Spain
Site: Spain: Toledo *Host inst:* Jose Ortega y Gasset Fdn
Dates: Jun 16-Jul 28
Subjects: Anthropology, Archaeology, Art history, Civilization/culture, Drama/theater, Economics, European studies,

Field study, Geography, History, Latin American studies, Linguistics, Literature, Political science/politics, Spanish language (int/adv)
Eligibility: *Level:* fresh, sophs, jrs, srs, grads, adults, teachers, professionals, precoll *Requires:* 2.50 GPA, 1 yr Spanish (2 or more yrs preferred) *Age:* min 18
Credit: *Undergrad:* 6-9 *Grad:* avail
Instruction: *In:* Spanish *Format:* directed field study, lang study, lecture *Students:* US & intl
Costs: About $3,775 *incl* tuition, housing, all meals, insurance, fees, excursions *Nonrefundable fee*
Housing: *Arr by pgm:* residence halls, homestay
Deadline: Apr 30
Other info: *US accredited sponsor:* yes *Began:* 1982 *Orient:* in US & abroad *Activities:* program travel *Misc:* Addtl fee for homestay. Scholarships for own students only. *URL:* http://www.UMabroad.umn.edu
Contact: Toledo Pgm, Global Campus, Univ of Minnesota, 230 Heller Hall, 271 19th Ave S, Minneapolis MN 55455-0138 *Ph:* 612-626 9000 *Fax:* 612-626 8009 *E-mail:* UMabroad@tc.umn.edu

---

VALENCIA

1423
FLORIDA STATE UNIVERSITY
Valencia Summer Program
Site: Spain: Valencia
Dates: 6 or 12 wks, May 11-Jun 22 and/or Jun 22-Aug 3
Subjects: Civilization/culture, Humanities, Liberal arts, Literature
Eligibility: *Level:* fresh, sophs, jrs, srs, grads, precoll *Requires:* 2.5 GPA
Credit: *Undergrad:* avail *Grad:* avail
Instruction: *In:* English *Format:* lecture *Students:* mainly US
Costs: $4,200 for 6 wks, $6,995 for 12 wks *incl* tuition, housing, some meals, intl airfare, insurance
Housing: *Arr by pgm:* hotels
Deadline: Jan 19
Other info: *US accredited sponsor:* yes *Began:* 1994 *Orient:* in US & abroad (2 days) *Activities:* excursions, field trips, program travel, cultural events *Misc:* May contact former participants. *URL:* http://www.international.fsu.edu
Contact: Elizabeth Trelenberg or Bonnie Snyder, Intl Pgms, Florida State Univ, 5500 UCA, Tallahassee FL 32306-2420 *Ph:* 800-374 8581; 850-644 3272 *Fax:* 850-644 8817 *E-mail:* intprog@www.fsu.edu

---

1424
INSTITUTE OF SPANISH STUDIES
Summer Sessions Abroad
Site: Spain: Valencia
Dates: May 29-Jun 30 and/or Jul 3-Aug 4
Subjects: Art history, Civilization/culture, Contemporary issues, Drama/theater, Field study, Geography, History, Homestay, Literature, Spanish language (beg/int/adv), Translating/interpreting
Eligibility: *Level:* fresh, sophs, jrs, srs, grads, adults, teachers, professionals, precoll *Age:* min 17
Credit: *Undergrad:* 9 per session *Grad:* 9 per session *Doc:* transcript *Transfer credit through:* Longwood Coll (VA)
Instruction: *In:* Spanish *Format:* directed field study, independent study, lang study, lecture, practical training, study tour, tutorial *Students:* mainly US
Costs: $2,600 for 1 session, $4,900 for both sessions *incl* tuition, housing, all meals, insurance, excursions
Housing: *Arr by pgm:* homestay
Deadline: None
Other info: *US accredited sponsor:* no *Began:* 1950 *Orient:* abroad *Activities:* excursions, field trips, cultural events *Misc:* Optional tour of Spain. *URL:* http://www.spanish-studies.com
Contact: Inst of Spanish Studies, 17303 SW 80 Pl, Miami FL 33157 *Ph:* 888-454 6777; 305-971-5353 *Fax:* 305-971 5354 *E-mail:* institut@spanish-studies.com
Or Contact: Dr Lind Goff, Longwood Coll, 201 High St, Farmville VA 23909-1899 *Ph:* 804-395 2823 *Fax:* 804-395 2141 *E-mail:* lgoff@longwood.lwc.edu ▲

1425
LONGWOOD COLLEGE (VA)
Summer Study Abroad Program in Valencia, Spain
Site: Spain: Valencia *Host inst:* Inst of Spanish Studies
Dates: 4 wks, May 22-Jun 24 or Jun 26-Jul 29
Subjects: Art history, Business language, Civilization/culture, Drama/theater, Geography, History, Homestay, Linguistics, Literature, Spanish language (int/adv), Spanish studies, Translating/interpreting
Eligibility: *Level:* fresh, sophs, jrs, srs, grads, teachers *Requires:* 2.5 GPA *Age:* min 17
Credit: *Undergrad:* 6-9 *Grad:* 6 *Doc:* transcript
Instruction: *In:* Spanish *Format:* lang study, lecture *Students:* mainly US
Costs: $2,850 *incl* tuition, housing, all meals, insurance, excursions, activities *Nonrefundable fee*
Housing: *Arr by pgm:* homestay
Deadline: Apr 1
Other info: *US accredited sponsor:* yes *Began:* 1993 *Orient:* in US & abroad *Activities:* excursions, field trips, program travel, cultural events *Misc:* May contact former participants. *URL:* http://www.lwc.edu
Contact: Dr Linda Goff, Intl Affairs, Longwood Coll, Farmville VA 23909-1899 *Ph:* 804-395 2172 *Fax:* 804-395 2141 *E-mail:* lgoff@longwood.lwc.edu

---

1426
SUNY UNIVERSITY AT ALBANY
Language and Cultural Studies in Valencia
Site: Spain: Valencia *Host inst:* AIP Language Institute
Dates: 6 wks undergrad, 3 or 6 wks grad, late Jun-early Aug
Subjects: Civilization/culture, Spanish language (beg/int/adv)
Eligibility: *Requires:* 2.5 GPA
Credit: *Undergrad:* 6 *Grad:* 3-6 *Doc:* transcript
Instruction: *In:* English, Spanish *Format:* lang study, lecture *Students:* mainly US
Costs: $1,667 for 3 wks, $3,150 for 6 wks for NY residents *incl* tuition, housing, all meals, fees, student support svcs *Nonrefundable fee*
Housing: *Arr by pgm:* homestay
Deadline: Apr 15, late applications considered
Other info: *US accredited sponsor:* yes *Began:* 2000 *Orient:* in US & abroad *Activities:* excursions, field trips, program travel, cultural events *Misc:* May contact former participants.
Contact: Joan N Savitt, Intl Pgms, SUNY Univ at Albany LI 66, Albany NY 12222 *Ph:* 518-442 3325 *Fax:* 5180442 3338 *E-mail:* intled@usmail.albany.edu

---

1427
UNIVERSITY OF VIRGINIA and **UNIVERSITY OF RICHMOND** and **COLLEGE OF WILLIAM & MARY**
Hispanic Studies in Spain (Summer Program)
Site: Spain: Valencia *Host inst:* Univ de Valencia
Dates: May 31-Jul 6
Subjects: Art, History, Homestay, Literature, Spanish language (beg/int/adv)
Eligibility: *Level:* fresh, sophs, jrs, srs *Requires:* 2.5 GPA
Credit: *Undergrad:* avail *Grad:* none *Doc:* transcript
Instruction: *In:* Spanish *Format:* lang study, lecture *Students:* mainly US
Costs: $3,420 *incl* tuition, housing, all meals, intl airfare, insurance, fees, excursions *Nonrefundable fee*
Housing: *Arr by pgm:* homestay
Deadline: Apr 10
Other info: *US accredited sponsor:* yes *Began:* 1986 *Orient:* in US & abroad *Activities:* excursions *Misc:* Optional trips to Barcelona, Madrid & Ibiza. *Financial*

aid: scholarships *URL:* http://www.virginia.edu/~spitpo/spanish/valencia/summer.html
Contact: Fernando Opere, Spanish, Univ of Virginia, 115 Wilson Hall, Charlottesville VA 22903 *Ph:* 804-924 7155 *Fax:* 804-924 4025 *E-mail:* hispanicstudies@virginia.edu

---

1428
UNIVERSITY OF VIRGINIA
Summer Program for High School Teachers of Spanish
Site: Spain: Valencia *Host inst:* Univ de Valencia
Dates: 4 wks, summer
Subjects: Civilization/culture, Spanish language (adv), Spanish studies
Eligibility: *Level:* grads, teachers, professionals *Requires:* previous study in field, bachelor's in Spanish or equiv *Age:* min 22, avg 25
Credit: *Undergrad:* none *Grad:* 6 *Doc:* transcript
Instruction: *In:* Spanish *Format:* lang study *Students:* mainly US
Costs: $2,325 *incl* tuition, housing, intl airfare, fees *Nonrefundable fee*
Housing: *Arr by pgm:* apartments
Deadline: May 1
Other info: *US accredited sponsor:* yes *Began:* 1995 *Orient:* abroad *Misc:* May contact former participants. *URL:* http://www.virginia.edu/~spitpo/spanish/valencia/teacher.
Contact: Fernando Opere, Dir, Hispanic Studies, Univ of Virginia, 115 Wilson Hall, Charlottesville VA 22903 *Ph:* 804-924 7155 *Fax:* 804-924 4025 *E-mail:* hispanicstudies@virginia.edu

---

VALLADOLID

1429
CONSULTANTS FOR GLOBAL PROGRAMS
Spanish Language and Culture Program
Site: Spain: Valladolid *Host inst:* Fundacion San Pablo Castilla y Leon, CEU
Dates: 4 or 8 wks, Jun 30-Jul 24 or Jun 30-Aug 21
Subjects: Art, Civilization/culture, Field study, Homestay, Literature, Spanish language (int), Spanish studies
Eligibility: *Level:* fresh, sophs, jrs, srs, grads *Requires:* 2.75 GPA, previous study in field *Age:* min 20
Credit: *Undergrad:* avail *Grad:* none *Doc:* transcript
Instruction: *In:* English, Spanish *Format:* directed field study, lab, lang study, lecture, study tour *Students:* mainly host country
Costs: $2,550 for 4 wks, $3,550 for 8 wks *incl* tuition, housing, all meals, intl airfare, insurance, fees, excursions, books/materials, local transport *Nonrefundable fee*
Housing: *Arr by pgm:* homestay
Deadline: Apr 30
Other info: *US accredited sponsor:* no *Began:* 1998 *Orient:* in US (1-2 days) *Activities:* excursions, field trips, program travel, cultural events, sports *Financial aid:* scholarships, work study *URL:* http://www.globalprograms.com

Contact: Larry Kavich, Pres, Consultants for Global Pgms, 2019 Central Ave, McKinleyville CA 95519 *Ph:* 800-270 6870; 707-839 0478 *Fax:* 707-839 2991 *E-mail:* cgpusa@aol.com

---

1430
FUNDACION SAN PABLO CASTILLA Y LEON CEU
Summer Courses: July, August
Site: Spain: Valladolid
Dates: Jul 2-21 or Aug 6-24
Subjects: Art, Civilization/culture, History, Spanish language (beg/int/adv), Spanish studies
Eligibility: *Level:* fresh, sophs, jrs, srs, grads, adults, teachers, professionals, precoll *Requires:* 1 sem Spanish *Age:* min 16
Credit: *Undergrad:* none *Grad:* avail *Doc:* transcript, certificate, diploma
Instruction: *In:* Spanish *Format:* independent study, lang study, tutorial *Students:* intl
Costs: 60,000 ptas *incl* tuition *Nonrefundable fee*
Housing: *Arr by pgm:* residence halls, homestay
Deadline: 15 days before pgm; 1 mo before pgm for scholarships
Other info: *US accredited sponsor:* no *Began:* 1998 *Activities:* excursions, field trips, cultural events *Misc:* May contact former participants. *Financial aid:* scholarships *URL:* http://www.ceu.es
Contact: Manuel J Perucho Diaz, Fundacion San Pablo CEU, Fray Luis de Leon 3, 1 B-1, Valladolid 47002, Spain *E-mail:* ceu@cyl.com
Or Contact: Miguel Um Chi Phui, Fundacion San Pablo CEU, Fray Luis de Leon 3, 1 B-1, Valladolid 47002, Spain *E-mail:* infoceu@cyl.com

---

1431
IOWA REGENTS INSTITUTIONS
Iowa Hispanic Institute
Site: Spain: Valladolid
Dates: About May 20-Jun 30
Subjects: Civilization/culture, Homestay, Independent study, Literature, Spanish language (int/adv)
Eligibility: *Level:* fresh, sophs, jrs, srs *Requires:* 2 yrs coll Spanish, regular Iowa Regents' admission requirements
Credit: *Undergrad:* 7 *Grad:* none
Instruction: *In:* Spanish *Format:* independent study, lang study, lecture *Students:* mainly US
Costs: About $2,700 *incl* tuition, housing, all meals, fees, excursions, books/materials *Nonrefundable fee*
Housing: *Arr by pgm:* homestay
Deadline: Apr 1
Other info: *US accredited sponsor:* yes *Began:* 1990 *In coop with:* Col Univ Integrado & Univ of Valladolid *Orient:* abroad *Activities:* program travel *URL:* http://www.uni.edu/modlangs/institutes-abroad
Contact: *See Index II for Members* Dr Roslyn Frank, Spanish & Portuguese, Univ of Iowa, 111 Phillips Hall, Iowa City IA 52242 *Ph:* 319-335 2229, 319-335 2244
Or Contact: Iowa Regents Hispanic Inst, Modern Langs, Univ of Northern Iowa, Cedar Falls IA 50614-0504 *Ph:* 319-273 2200 *Fax:* 319-273 2848 *E-mail:* welty@uni.edu

---

1432
SOUTHWEST TEXAS STATE UNIVERSITY
SWT in Spain
Site: Spain: Valladolid *Host inst:* Univ Castellae
Dates: 6 wks, May-Jun
Subjects: Homestay, Literature, Spanish language (adv), Spanish studies
Eligibility: *Level:* jrs, srs, grads *Requires:* previous study in field, Spanish lang
Credit: *Undergrad:* 3 *Grad:* 6 *Doc:* transcript
Instruction: *In:* Spanish *Format:* lang study, lecture, seminar, tutorial *Students:* mainly US
Costs: $3,500 *incl* tuition, housing, all meals, intl airfare, fees, excursions, books/materials
Housing: *Arr by pgm:* homestay
Deadline: Contact sponsor
Other info: *US accredited sponsor:* yes *Began:* 2000 *Orient:* in US *Activities:* excursions, cultural events *Misc:* May contact former participants. *Financial aid:* scholarships *URL:* http://www.ideal.swt.edu/extensions/study_abroad/
Contact: Dr Antonio Candau, Modern Langs, Southwest Texas State Univ, 601 University Dr, San Marcos TX 78666 *Ph:* 512-245 2079 *Fax:* 512-245 8298 *E-mail:* ac06@swt.edu

---

VEJER DE LA FRONTERA

1433
LANGUAGE LINK
Learn Spanish in Small-Town Moorish Spain
Site: Spain: Vejer de la Frontera *Host inst:* La Janda
Dates: 1-16 wks, yr-round
Subjects: Dance, Music, Spanish language, Spanish studies
Eligibility: *Level:* fresh, sophs, jrs, srs, grads, adults, teachers, professionals, precoll *Age:* min 15, avg 30
Credit: *Undergrad:* avail *Grad:* avail *Doc:* certificate *Transfer credit through:* Austin Peay State Univ
Instruction: *In:* Spanish *Format:* lang study, music lesson, seminar *Students:* intl
Costs: $250 per wk *incl* tuition, housing, some meals, insurance
Housing: *Arr by pgm:* apartments with local students, apartments
Deadline: Contact sponsor
Other info: *US accredited sponsor:* no *Began:* 2000 *In coop with:* Austin Peay State Univ *Orient:* abroad *Misc:* Small Moorish town located next to beach. *URL:* http://www.langlink.com
Contact: Kay Rafool, Dir, Lang Link, PO Box 3006, Peoria IL 61612-3006 *Ph:* 800-552 2051; 309-692 2961 *Fax:* 309-692 2926 *E-mail:* info@langlink.com

Sweden

LUND

1434
LANGUAGES ABROAD
Language and Cultural Immersion-Sweden
Site: Sweden: Lund
Dates: 2 wks or longer, yr-round
Subjects: Civilization/culture, Swedish language (beg/int/adv), Swedish studies
Eligibility: *Level:* adults *Age:* min 17, max 65, avg 25
Credit: *Undergrad:* none *Grad:* none *Doc:* certificate
Instruction: *In:* English *Format:* lang study *Students:* intl
Costs: $2,000 per mo *incl* tuition, some meals, fees, excursions, books/materials
Housing: *Arr by pgm:* residence halls, homestay
Deadline: None
Other info: *US accredited sponsor:* no *Began:* 1995 *Activities:* excursions, field trips, program travel, cultural events, sports *Misc:* May contact former participants. *URL:* http://www.languagesabroad.com
Contact: Ms Jesse Philippe, Langs Abroad, 317 Adelaide St W, Ste 900, Toronto, Ontario M5V 1P9, Canada *Ph:* 800-219 9924; 416-925 7117 *E-mail:* info@languagesabroad.com

---

1435
MICHIGAN STATE UNIVERSITY
Packaging-Sweden
Site: Sweden: Lund
Dates: 2 wks, May-Jun
Subjects: Field study, Independent study, Packaging
Eligibility: *Level:* fresh, sophs, jrs, srs, grads *Requires:* 2.3 GPA, good acad standing, major in packaging *Age:* min 18

Credit: *Undergrad:* 5 *Grad:* 5 *Doc:* transcript
Instruction: *In:* English *Format:* directed field study, independent study, lecture *Students:* mainly US
Costs: About $1,300 *incl* housing, some meals, insurance, excursions, support svcs *Nonrefundable fee*
Housing: *Arr by pgm:* residence halls
Deadline: Mar 2
Other info: *US accredited sponsor:* yes *Orient:* in US & abroad *Activities:* field trips, cultural events *Misc:* Loans avail. May contact former participants. *Financial aid:* scholarships *URL:* http://studyabroad.msu.edu
Contact: Cheryl Benner, Study Abroad, Michigan State Univ, 109 Intl Ctr, East Lansing MI 48824 *Ph:* 517-353 8920 *Fax:* 517-432 2082 *E-mail:* bennerc@msu.edu ▲

1436
NEW YORK UNIVERSITY, SCHOOL OF EDUCATION
Speech Language Pathology
Site: Sweden: Lund *Host inst:* Lund Univ
Dates: 4 wks, May 28-Jun 29
Subjects: Speech pathology/therapy
Eligibility: *Level:* grads *Requires:* 3.0 GPA, previous study in field
Credit: *Undergrad:* none *Grad:* avail *Doc:* transcript
Instruction: *In:* English *Format:* lecture, seminar, tutorial *Students:* mainly US
Costs: $4,500 *incl* tuition, housing, fees, excursions, books/materials *Nonrefundable fee*
Housing: *Arr by pgm:* apartments
Deadline: Apr 1
Other info: *US accredited sponsor:* yes *Began:* 1997 *Orient:* in US *Activities:* excursions *Misc:* May contact former participants. *URL:* http://www.nyu.edu/summer
Contact: Asst Prof Celia Stewart, New York Univ, 719 Broadway, 2nd Fl, New York NY 10003-6060 *Ph:* 212-998 5230
Or Contact: Helen J Kelly, Dir, Special Pgms, NYU, 82 Washington Sq E, Rm 62, New York NY 10003-6680 *Ph:* 212-998 5090 *Fax:* 212-995 4923 ▲

STOCKHOLM

1437
LANGUAGE LIAISON
Swedish Saturation
Site: Sweden: Stockholm region *Host inst:* Live in Learn
Dates: 1 wk or longer, yr-round
Subjects: Civilization/culture, Homestay, Swedish language (beg/int/adv)
Eligibility: *Level:* fresh, sophs, jrs, srs, grads, adults, teachers, professionals, precoll *Age:* min 10
Credit: *Undergrad:* none *Grad:* none *Doc:* transcript, certificate
Instruction: *In:* Swedish *Format:* lang study *Students:* intl
Costs: Contact sponsor
Housing: *Arr by pgm:* teacher's home
Deadline: 45 days before pgm
Other info: *US accredited sponsor:* no *Misc:* Live & learn in your teacher's home. Scholarship research svc. *URL:* http://www.languageliaison.com
Contact: Nancy Forman, Dir, Lang Liaison, 4 Burnham Pkwy, Morristown NJ 07960 *Ph:* 800-284 4448 *Fax:* 973-898 1710 *E-mail:* learn@language.liaison.com

---

1438
LINGUA SERVICE WORLDWIDE
Intensive Language and Culture in Sweden
Site: Sweden: Stockholm *Host inst:* Home Lang Intl
Dates: 1 wk-1 yr, yr-round
Subjects: Civilization/culture, Homestay, Swedish language (beg/int/adv)
Eligibility: *Level:* adults
Credit: *Undergrad:* avail *Grad:* avail *Doc:* transcript, certificate
Instruction: *In:* Swedish *Format:* lang study, lecture *Students:* intl
Costs: Contact sponsor
Housing: *Arr by pgm:* homestay
Deadline: 45 days before pgm
Other info: *US accredited sponsor:* no *Activities:* excursions, field trips *Misc:* May contact former participants. *URL:* http://www.linguaserviceworldwide.com
Contact: Dir, Lingua Svc Worldwide, 75 Prospect St, Ste 4, Huntington NY 11743 *Ph:* 800-394 5327; 631-424 0777 *Fax:* 631-271 3441 *E-mail:* itctravel@worldnet.att.net ▲

1439
NATIONAL REGISTRATION CENTER FOR STUDY ABROAD (NRCSA)
Language Study in Stockholm
Site: Sweden: Stockholm *Host inst:* Home Lang Schs Intl
Dates: 1 wk or longer, yr-round
Subjects: Homestay, Swedish language
Eligibility: *Level:* fresh, sophs, jrs, srs, grads, adults, teachers, professionals
Credit: *Undergrad:* none *Grad:* none
Instruction: *In:* Swedish *Format:* lang study, tutorial *Students:* intl
Costs: $1,135 per wk *incl* tuition, housing, all meals, insurance *Nonrefundable fee*
Housing: *Arr by pgm:* homestay
Deadline: 6 wks before pgm
Other info: *US accredited sponsor:* no *Misc:* Student lives in teacher's home. *URL:* http://www.nrcsa.com
Contact: Reuel Zielke, NRCSA, 823 N 2nd St, #206, Milwaukee WI 53203 *Ph:* 414-278 0631 *Fax:* 414-871 8884 *E-mail:* info@nrcsa.com

---

UPPSALA

1440
FOLKUNIVERSITETET
Summer Courses in Swedish
Site: Sweden: Uppsala
Dates: Jun 11-22, Jul 9-27, Aug 13-24
Subjects: Swedish language
Eligibility: *Level:* jrs, srs, grads, adults, teachers, professionals, precoll
Credit: *Undergrad:* none *Grad:* none *Doc:* certificate
Instruction: *In:* Swedish *Format:* lang study *Students:* intl
Costs: About $800-$1,075 *incl* tuition, excursions, books/materials, lang lab *Nonrefundable fee*
Housing: *Sponsor assists:* apartments, homestay, student rms
Deadline: 1 mo before pgm
Other info: *US accredited sponsor:* no *Began:* 1985 *Activities:* field trips *URL:* http://www.folkuniversitetet.se/uppsala
Contact: Marlene Walivara, Folkuniversitetet, Box 386, Uppsala S-75106, Sweden *E-mail:* info.uppsala@folkuniversitetet.se

---

1441
UPPSALA UNIVERSITY
Uppsala International Summer Session
Site: Sweden: Uppsala
Dates: 2, 4, 6 or 8 wks, Jun 17-Aug 10
Subjects: Arts, Film studies, History, Literature, Music, Poetry, Singing/voice, Social administration, Social welfare/services, Swedish language (beg/int/adv), Swedish studies
Eligibility: *Level:* fresh, sophs, jrs, srs, adults *Requires:* univ eligibility *Age:* min 18, avg 30
Credit: *Undergrad:* 7 per 4-wk course *Grad:* none *Doc:* transcript
Instruction: *In:* English, Swedish *Students:* intl
Costs: About Skr 12,200-22,400 depending on pgm length *incl* tuition, housing, some meals, fees, excursions
Housing: *Arr by pgm:* residence halls, apts on request
Deadline: May 15 for Jun; Jun 15 for Jul; Mar 15 for scholarships
Other info: *US accredited sponsor:* no *Began:* 1963 *Activities:* excursions, cultural events, sports *Misc:* 2 & 6-wk courses for non-beginners. 3-wk courses for interpreters & translators. *Financial aid:* scholarships *URL:* http://www.uiss.org

Contact: Nelleke van Oevelen-Dorrestijn, Dir, Uppsala Univ Intl Summer Session, Box 1972, SE-751 49 Uppsala, Sweden *E-mail:* nelleke.vanoevelen@uiss.org

Switzerland

MORE THAN ONE CITY

1442
PENNSYLVANIA STATE UNIVERSITY
Summer Education Abroad Hospitality Studies in Switzerland
Site: Switzerland: Bluche, Montreux *Host inst:* Hotel Inst Montreux, Hotel Mgmt Sch Les Roches
Dates: 5 wks, Jun-Jul
Subjects: Hospitality management, Restaurant management
Eligibility: *Level:* sophs, jrs, srs *Requires:* 2.5 GPA, previous study in field *Age:* min 18
Credit: *Undergrad:* 6 per course *Grad:* none
Instruction: *In:* English *Format:* lecture, study tour *Students:* mainly US
Costs: About $4,200 for PA residents, $6,000 for others *incl* tuition, housing, some meals
Housing: *Arr by pgm:* residence halls
Deadline: Mar 15
Other info: *US accredited sponsor:* yes *Began:* 1999 *Orient:* in US *Activities:* excursions, field trips *Misc:* May contact former participants. *URL:* http://www.outreach.psu.edu/PSSEA/
Contact: Summer Abroad, Pennsylvania State Univ, 225 Penn State Conference Ctr, University Park PA 16802 *Ph:* 814-863 5170 *Fax:* 814-863 5190 *E-mail:* SummerAbroad@outreach.psu.edu
Or Contact: William Andrew, Pennsylvania State Univ, 201-H Mateer Bldg, University Park PA 16802 *Ph:* 814-863 0272 *Fax:* 814-863 4257 *E-mail:* wpa@psu.edu

---

CHUR

1443
UNIVERSITY OF DELAWARE
Swiss Hospitality Summer Session
Site: Switzerland: Chur *Host inst:* Swiss Sch of Hotel & Tourism Mgmt
Dates: 5 wks, beg Jun
Subjects: Field study, German language (beg), Hotel management, Restaurant management
Eligibility: *Level:* fresh, sophs, jrs, srs *Requires:* 2.0 GPA
Credit: *Undergrad:* 5 *Grad:* none *Doc:* transcript
Instruction: *In:* English *Format:* directed field study, lang study, lecture *Students:* mainly US
Costs: Contact sponsor
Housing: *Arr by pgm:* residence halls
Deadline: Mid-Mar
Other info: *US accredited sponsor:* yes *Began:* 1996 *Orient:* avail *Activities:* excursions, field trips *Misc:* Contact sponsor to arrange honors credit. *Financial aid:* scholarships *URL:* http://www.udel.edu/studyabroad/
Contact: Intl Pgms & Special Sessions, Univ of Delaware, 4 Kent Way, Newark DE 19716-1450 *Ph:* 888-831 4685; 302-831 2852 *Fax:* 302-831 6042 *E-mail:* studyabroad@udel.edu

---

GENEVA

1444
NEW YORK UNIVERSITY, SCHOOL OF CONTINUING AND PROFESSIONAL STUDIES
UN in Geneva Study Tour
Site: Switzerland: Geneva *Host inst:* United Nations Off in Geneva
Dates: 8 days, Jun 17-25
Subjects: Development studies, Health/health education, HIV/AIDS education, Human rights, International studies, Peace studies, Refugee studies, Trade
Eligibility: *Level:* jrs, srs, grads, adults, teachers, professionals *Age:* min 18, avg 28
Credit: *Undergrad:* avail *Grad:* none
Instruction: *In:* English *Format:* lecture, seminar, study tour *Students:* mainly US
Costs: $1,695 for noncredit, $1,995 for credit *incl* tuition, housing, some meals, excursions, books/materials *Nonrefundable fee*
Housing: *Sponsor assists:* hotels
Deadline: May 22
Other info: *US accredited sponsor:* yes *Began:* 1994 *Orient:* abroad (1 day) *Activities:* excursions *URL:* http://www.scps.nyu.edu
Contact: Vera Jelinek, NYU Sch of Continuing & Prof Studies, Intl Pgms, 48 Cooper Sq, Rm 101, New York NY 10003 *Ph:* 212-998 7133 *Fax:* 212-995 4134 *E-mail:* vera.jelinek@nyu.edu
Or Contact: Amber Devlin, NYU Sch of Continuing & Prof Studies, Intl Pgms, 48 Cooper Sq, Rm 101, New York NY 10003 *Ph:* 212-998 7133 *Fax:* 212-995 4134 *E-mail:* amber.devlin@nyu.edu

---

1445
NEW YORK UNIVERSITY, SCHOOL OF EDUCATION
Developmental Psychology
Site: Switzerland: Geneva *Host inst:* Univ de Geneve
Dates: 2-1/2 wks, Jul 8-26
Subjects: Psychology
Eligibility: *Level:* grads *Requires:* 3.0 GPA, previous study in field
Credit: *Undergrad:* none *Grad:* avail *Doc:* transcript
Instruction: *In:* English *Format:* lecture, seminar, study tour *Students:* mainly US
Costs: $4,600 *incl* tuition, housing, some meals, books/materials *Nonrefundable fee*
Housing: *Arr by pgm:* residence halls
Deadline: Apr 1
Other info: *US accredited sponsor:* yes *Began:* 1999 *Orient:* in US (1 day) *Activities:* field trips *Misc:* Loans avail. May contact former participants. *URL:* http://www.nyu.edu/summer
Contact: Prof Lawrence Balter, Applied Psychology, New York Univ, 239 Greene St, Rm 537E, New York NY 10003 *Ph:* 212-998 5368 *Fax:* 212-995 4358 *E-mail:* lb9@is2.nyu.edu
Or Contact: Helen J Kelly, Dir, Special Pgms, New York Univ, 82 Washington Square E, Rm 62, New York NY 10003 *Ph:* 212-998 5090 *Fax:* 212-995 4923 ▲

1446
SYRACUSE UNIVERSITY
Geneva: Graduate Internship in International Organizations
Site: Switzerland: Geneva
Dates: May 29-Jul 28
Subjects: International relations, Internships
Eligibility: *Level:* grads *Requires:* enrollment in grad degree pgm in intl relations or related field
Credit: *Undergrad:* none *Grad:* 6
Instruction: *In:* English *Format:* internship, lecture, practical training *Students:* mainly US
Costs: About $5,500 *incl* tuition, housing, fees, excursions *Nonrefundable fee*
Housing: *Arr by pgm:* conference ctr
Deadline: Feb 15
Other info: *US accredited sponsor:* yes *Began:* 1989 *Orient:* abroad *Activities:* excursions *Financial aid:* scholarships *URL:* http://sumweb.syr.edu/dipa/summer
Contact: Summer Pgms, Intl Pgms Abroad, Syracuse Univ, 119 Euclid Ave, Syracuse NY 13244-4170 *Ph:* 800-251 9674; 315-443 9420 *Fax:* 315-443 4593 *E-mail:* dipasum@summon3.syr.edu ▲

1447
UNIVERSITE DE GENEVE
Summer Courses in French Language and Culture
Site: Switzerland: Geneva
Dates: 3-12 wks, Jul 16-Oct 5
Subjects: Civilization/culture, French language (beg/int/adv), Homestay, Literature, Music, Word processing
Eligibility: *Level:* fresh, sophs, jrs, srs,

grads, adults, teachers, professionals, precoll *Age:* min 17
Credit: *Undergrad:* none *Grad:* none *Doc:* certificate
Instruction: *In:* French *Format:* lab, lang study, lecture, seminar, student teaching *Students:* intl
Costs: SFr 470 for 3 wks *incl* tuition, books/materials
Housing: *Sponsor assists:* residence halls, homestay, pensions
Deadline: None
Other info: *US accredited sponsor:* no *Orient:* abroad *Activities:* excursions, cultural events *URL:* http://www.unige.ch/lettres/elcf/coursete/cournet.html
Contact: Secretariat, Cours d'Ete, Univ de Geneve, 3 rue de Candolle, CH-1211 Geneve 4, Switzerland *E-mail:* elcfete@uni2a.unige.ch

---

1448
UNIVERSITY OF DELAWARE
Winter Session in Geneva
Site: Switzerland: Geneva
Dates: 1 mo, Jan
Subjects: Economics, French language (beg), Independent study, International business, International relations, Political science/politics
Eligibility: *Level:* fresh, sophs, jrs, srs *Requires:* 2.0 GPA
Credit: *Undergrad:* 7 *Grad:* none *Doc:* transcript
Instruction: *In:* English *Format:* independent study, lang study, lecture, study tour *Students:* mainly US
Costs: Contact sponsor
Housing: *Arr by pgm:* hotels
Deadline: Early Oct
Other info: *US accredited sponsor:* yes *Began:* 1993 *Orient:* in US & abroad yes *Activities:* excursions, field trips, program travel, cultural events *Misc:* Contact sponsor to arrange honors credit. May contact former participants. *Financial aid:* scholarships *URL:* http://www.udel.edu/studyabroad/
Contact: Intl Pgms & Special Sessions, Univ of Delaware, 4 Kent Way, Newark DE 19716 *Ph:* 888-831 4685; 302-831 2852 *Fax:* 302-831 6042 *E-mail:* studyabroad@udel.edu

---

1449
WEBSTER UNIVERSITY
Degree Programs
Site: Switzerland: Geneva *Host inst:* Webster Univ Geneva campus
Dates: 8 wks, summer
Subjects: Finance, French language (beg), International law, International organizations, Social history
Eligibility: *Level:* sophs, jrs, srs, grads, adults *Requires:* 2.5 GPA, GMAT for MBA *Age:* avg 23
Credit: *Undergrad:* avail *Grad:* avail *Doc:* degree
Instruction: *In:* English *Format:* lecture, seminar *Students:* intl
Costs: $1,104 per 3-credit course *incl* tuition
Housing: *Arr by pgm:* Apts in Geneva
Deadline: Feb 15
Other info: *US accredited sponsor:* yes *Began:* 1978 *Orient:* in US & abroad *Misc:* BA, MA & MBA avail. May contact former participants. *URL:* http://www.websteruniv.edu

Contact: Teresa Bruno, Study Abroad, Webster Univ, 470 E Lockwood, St Louis MO 63119 *Ph:* 800-984 6857; 314-968 6988 *Fax:* 314-968 7119 *E-mail:* worldview@webster.edu

---

1450
WEBSTER UNIVERSITY
Graduate Program in Geneva
Site: Switzerland: Geneva *Host inst:* Webster Univ Geneva campus
Dates: 8 wks, summer
Subjects: Business/management, Health care/hospitals, Human resources, International business, International relations, Internships, Real estate
Eligibility: *Level:* grads *Requires:* 2.5 GPA, bachelor's degree
Credit: *Undergrad:* none *Grad:* 3-6 *Doc:* transcript, diploma
Instruction: *In:* English *Format:* internship, lecture, seminar *Students:* intl
Costs: $1,149 per 3-credit course *incl* tuition
Housing: *Sponsor assists:* studio apts in Geneva
Deadline: 6 mos before pgm
Other info: *US accredited sponsor:* yes *Began:* 1978 *Orient:* in US & abroad *Misc:* Internship coord. Optional ski excursions. *Financial aid:* scholarships *URL:* http://www.websteruniv.edu
Contact: Study Abroad Ctr, Webster Univ, 470 E Lockwood, St Louis MO 63119 *Ph:* 800-984 6857; 314-968 6988 *Fax:* 314-968 7119 *E-mail:* worldview@webster.edu

---

1451
WEBSTER UNIVERSITY
Undergraduate Program in Geneva
Site: Switzerland: Geneva *Host inst:* Webster Univ Geneva campus
Dates: 8 wks, summer
Subjects: Accounting, Business/management, Computer sciences, Economics, Human resources, International relations, Internships, Marketing, Psychology, Refugee studies, Sociology
Eligibility: *Level:* sophs, jrs, srs *Requires:* 2.5 GPA
Credit: *Undergrad:* 3-9 *Grad:* none *Doc:* transcript, diploma
Instruction: *In:* English *Format:* internship, lecture, seminar *Students:* intl
Costs: $1,149 per class *incl* tuition
Housing: *Sponsor assists:* studio apts
Deadline: 4 mos before pgm
Other info: *US accredited sponsor:* yes *Began:* 1978 *Orient:* in US & abroad *Activities:* excursions *Misc:* Internship coord. *Financial aid:* scholarships *URL:* http://www.websteruniv.edu
Contact: Study Abroad Ctr, Webster Univ, 470 E Lockwood, St Louis MO 63119 *Ph:* 800-984 6857; 314-984 6988 *Fax:* 314-968 7119 *E-mail:* worldview@webster.edu

---

LAUSANNE

1452
IMD INTERNATIONAL
Accelerating International Growth
Site: Switzerland: Lausanne
Dates: 1 wk, Nov 4-9
Subjects: Human resources, International business
Eligibility: *Level:* professionals *Requires:* 10-15 yrs bus experience *Age:* min 35, max 60, avg 40
Credit: *Undergrad:* none *Grad:* none *Doc:* certificate
Instruction: *In:* English *Format:* seminar *Students:* intl
Costs: SFr 9,000 *incl* tuition, some meals, books/materials
Housing: *Arr by pgm:* hotels
Deadline: 2 mos before pgm
Other info: *US accredited sponsor:* no *Began:* 1996 *Misc:* For mgrs involved in intl expansion. *URL:* http://www.imd.ch
Contact: David forster, Pgm Adviser, IMD, PO Box 915, CH-1001 Lausanne, Switzerland *E-mail:* info@imd.ch

---

1453
IMD INTERNATIONAL
Breakthrough Program for Senior Executives
Site: Switzerland: Lausanne
Dates: 2 wks, Jun 5-16 or Oct 9-Nov 20
Subjects: Business/management, International business, Leadership
Eligibility: *Level:* professionals *Requires:* intl bus execs *Age:* min 40, max 60, avg 47
Credit: *Undergrad:* none *Grad:* none *Doc:* certificate
Instruction: *In:* English *Format:* seminar *Students:* intl
Costs: SFr 22,500 *incl* tuition, some meals, books/materials
Housing: *Arr by pgm:* hotels
Deadline: 2 mos before pgm
Other info: *US accredited sponsor:* no *Began:* 1966 *Orient:* abroad *URL:* http://www.imd.ch
Contact: David Forster, Pgm Adviser, IMD, PO Box 915, CH-1001 Lausanne, Switzerland *E-mail:* info@imd.ch

---

1454
IMD INTERNATIONAL
Building on Talent
Site: Switzerland: Lausanne
Dates: 3 wks, Dec 2-14 & Feb 25-Mar 1
Subjects: Business/management, Finance, Human resources, Leadership, Marketing, Organizational behavior, Technology
Eligibility: *Level:* professionals *Requires:* 5-10 yrs bus experience *Age:* min 28, max 38
Credit: *Undergrad:* none *Grad:* none *Doc:* certificate
Instruction: *In:* English *Format:* seminar *Students:* intl
Costs: SFr 19,000 *incl* tuition, some meals, books/materials
Housing: *Arr by pgm:* hotels
Deadline: 2 mos before pgm
Other info: *US accredited sponsor:* no *Began:* 1997 *Misc:* Pgm for high potential young mgrs. *URL:* http://www.imd.ch
Contact: David Forster, Pgm Adviser, IMD, PO Box 915, CH-1001 Lausanne, Switzerland *E-mail:* info@imd.ch

---

1455
IMD INTERNATIONAL
e-Business
Site: Switzerland: Lausanne
Dates: 1 wk, Nov 11-16
Subjects: Business/management, Information technology, Leadership
Eligibility: *Level:* professionals *Requires:* 12 yrs mgmt experience *Age:* min 38, max 60
Credit: *Undergrad:* none *Grad:* none *Doc:* certificate
Instruction: *In:* English *Format:* seminar *Students:* intl
Costs: SFr 9,000 *incl* tuition, some meals, books/materials
Housing: *Arr by pgm:* hotels
Deadline: 2 mos before pgm
Other info: *US accredited sponsor:* no *Began:* 1999 *Misc:* Provides genl mgrs with capabilities to evaluate investments in info & info technology. *URL:* http://www.imd.ch
Contact: David Forster, Pgm Adviser, IMD, PO Box 915, CH-1001 Lausanne, Switzerland *E-mail:* info@imd.ch

---

1456
IMD INTERNATIONAL
e-Commerce
Site: Switzerland: Lausanne
Dates: 4 days, Apr 30-May 3
Subjects: Business/management, Information technology, Internet
Eligibility: *Level:* professionals *Age:* min 30, max 50
Credit: *Undergrad:* none *Grad:* none *Doc:* certificate
Instruction: *In:* English *Format:* seminar *Students:* intl
Costs: SFr 7,500 *incl* tuition, some meals, books/materials
Housing: *Arr by pgm:* hotels
Deadline: 2 mos before pgm

Other info: *US accredited sponsor:* no *Began:* 2001 *Orient:* abroad *Misc:* Pgm designed for mgrs in consumer, bus or svc industries. May contact former participants. *URL:* http://www.imd.ch
Contact: David Forster, Pgm Adviser, IMD, chemin de Bellerive 23 PO Box 915, CH-1001 Lausanne, Switzerland *E-mail:* info@imd.ch

---

1457
IMD INTERNATIONAL
HR Leadership in Global Organizations
Site: Switzerland: Lausanne
Dates: 1 wk, Mar 18-Mar 23
Subjects: Business/management, Human resources, International business
Eligibility: *Level:* professionals *Age:* min 35, max 55
Credit: *Undergrad:* none *Grad:* none *Doc:* certificate
Instruction: *In:* English *Format:* seminar *Students:* intl
Costs: SFr 9,000 *incl* tuition, some meals, books/materials
Housing: *Arr by pgm:* hotels
Deadline: 2 mos before pgm
Other info: *US accredited sponsor:* no *Began:* 2000 *Orient:* abroad *Misc:* Pgm designed for human resource mgrs reponsible for developing intl HR strategies. May contact former participants. *URL:* http://www.imd.ch
Contact: David Forster, Pgm Adviser, IMD, Chemin de Bellerive, PO Box 915, CH-1001 Lausanne, Switzerland *E-mail:* info@imd.ch

---

1458
IMD INTERNATIONAL
International Program for Board Members
Site: Switzerland: Lausanne
Dates: 3 days, May 2-4
Subjects: Business/management, International business
Eligibility: *Level:* professionals *Age:* min 33, max 70
Credit: *Undergrad:* none *Grad:* none *Doc:* certificate
Instruction: *In:* English *Format:* seminar *Students:* intl
Costs: SFr 9,000 *incl* tuition, some meals, books/materials
Housing: *Arr by pgm:* hotels
Deadline: 2 mos before pgm
Other info: *US accredited sponsor:* no *Began:* 1993 *Orient:* abroad *Misc:* Pgm designed for members of the board, experienced & newly appointed. May contact former participants. *URL:* http://www.imd.ch
Contact: David Forster, Pgm Adviser, IMD, Chemin de Bellerive 23, PO Box 915, CH-1001 Lausanne, Switzerland *E-mail:* info@imd.ch

---

1459
IMD INTERNATIONAL
Leading Corporate Renewal
Site: Switzerland: Lausanne
Dates: 2 wks, Aug 27-Sep 7
Subjects: Accounting, Business/management, Finance, Human resources, Leadership, Organizational behavior
Eligibility: *Level:* professionals *Age:* min 35, max 55, avg 43
Credit: *Undergrad:* none *Grad:* none *Doc:* certificate
Instruction: *In:* English *Format:* seminar *Students:* intl
Costs: SFr 15,000 *incl* tuition, some meals, books/materials
Housing: *Arr by pgm:* hotels
Deadline: 2 mos before pgm
Other info: *US accredited sponsor:* no *Began:* 1963 *Orient:* abroad *URL:* http://www.imd.ch
Contact: David Forster, Pgm Adviser, IMD Intl, 23 chemin de Bellerive, PO Box 915, CH-1001 Lausanne, Switzerland *E-mail:* info@imd.ch

---

1460
IMD INTERNATIONAL
Leading the Family Business
Site: Switzerland: Lausanne
Dates: 4-1/2 days, May 6-10 or Sep 23-27
Subjects: Business/management
Eligibility: *Level:* professionals *Requires:* family bus *Age:* min 20, max 65, avg 47
Credit: *Undergrad:* none *Grad:* none *Doc:* certificate
Instruction: *In:* English *Format:* seminar *Students:* intl
Costs: SFr 8,000 *incl* tuition, some meals, books/materials
Housing: *Arr by pgm:* hotels
Deadline: 2 mos before pgm
Other info: *US accredited sponsor:* no *Began:* 1988 *Misc:* Several members of same family bus encouraged to participate as a team. *URL:* http://www.imd.ch
Contact: David Forster, Pgm Adviser, IMD, PO Box 915, CH-1001 Lausanne, Switzerland *E-mail:* info@imd.ch

---

1461
IMD INTERNATIONAL
Managing Corporate Resources
Site: Switzerland: Lausanne
Dates: 3 wks, May 8-May 26 or Oct 29-Nov 18
Subjects: Business/management, Finance, Human resources, Industrial management, International business, Leadership, Marketing
Eligibility: *Level:* professionals *Requires:* avg of 12 yrs experience in mgmt, marketing, finance, operations, R&D or human resources *Age:* min 38, max 60, avg 42
Credit: *Undergrad:* none *Grad:* none *Doc:* certificate
Instruction: *In:* English *Format:* seminar *Students:* intl
Costs: SFr 25,000 *incl* tuition, some meals, books/materials
Housing: *Arr by pgm:* hotels
Deadline: 2 mos before pgm
Other info: *US accredited sponsor:* no *Began:* 1981 *Orient:* abroad *URL:* http://www.imd.ch
Contact: David Forster, Pgm Adviser, IMD, PO Box 915, CH-1001 Lausanne, Switzerland *E-mail:* info@imd.ch

---

1462
IMD INTERNATIONAL
Managing for Marketing Success
Site: Switzerland: Lausanne
Dates: 2 wks, Jun 11-22
Subjects: Industrial management, Marketing
Eligibility: *Level:* professionals *Age:* min 30, max 55, avg 39
Credit: *Undergrad:* none *Grad:* none *Doc:* certificate
Instruction: *In:* English *Format:* seminar *Students:* intl
Costs: SFr 14,000 *incl* tuition, some meals, books/materials
Housing: *Arr by pgm:* hotels
Deadline: 2 mos before pgm
Other info: *US accredited sponsor:* no *Began:* 1988 *Misc:* Pgm for mgrs who integrate marketing as part of their company activities. *URL:* http://www.imd.ch
Contact: David Forster, Pgm Adviser, IMD, PO Box 915, CH-1001, Switzerland *E-mail:* info@imd.ch

---

1463
IMD INTERNATIONAL
Managing Manufacturing: Transforming Manufacturing Process
Site: Switzerland: Lausanne
Dates: Oct 28-Nov 9
Subjects: Business/management, Industrial management, Information science/systems, Manufacturing, Organizational behavior
Eligibility: *Level:* professionals *Requires:* 10 yrs bus experience *Age:* min 30, max 60, avg 40
Credit: *Undergrad:* none *Grad:* none *Doc:* certificate
Instruction: *In:* English *Format:* seminar *Students:* intl

Costs: SFr 14,000 *incl* tuition, some meals, books/materials
Housing: *Arr by pgm:* hotels
Deadline: 2 mos before pgm
Other info: *US accredited sponsor:* no *Began:* 1983 *URL:* http://www.imd.ch
Contact: David Forster, Pgm Adviser, IMD, PO Box 915, CH-1001 Lausanne, Switzerland *E-mail:* info@imd.ch

---

1464
IMD INTERNATIONAL
Managing the Innovation Process
Site: Switzerland: Lausanne
Dates: 1 wk, Oct 1-6
Subjects: Business/management, Leadership, Marketing, Technology
Eligibility: *Level:* professionals *Age:* min 35, max 60, avg 41
Credit: *Undergrad:* none *Grad:* none *Doc:* certificate
Instruction: *In:* English *Format:* lecture, seminar *Students:* intl
Costs: SFr 9,000 *incl* tuition, some meals, books/materials
Housing: *Arr by pgm:* hotels
Deadline: 2 mos before pgm
Other info: *US accredited sponsor:* no *Orient:* abroad *URL:* http://www.imd.ch
Contact: David Forster, Pgm Adviser, IMD Intl, 23 chemin de Bellerive, PO Box 915, CH-1001 Lausanne, Switzerland *E-mail:* info@imd.ch

---

1465
IMD INTERNATIONAL
Mastering Technology Enterprise
Site: Switzerland: Lausanne
Dates: 9 wks, Jan 14-Feb 2, May 6-25, Sep 2-21
Subjects: Business/management, Information technology, Leadership
Eligibility: *Level:* professionals *Age:* min 31, max 44
Credit: *Undergrad:* none *Grad:* none *Doc:* certificate
Instruction: *In:* English *Format:* seminar *Students:* intl
Costs: SFr 38,000 *incl* tuition, some meals, books/materials
Housing: *Arr by pgm:* hotels
Deadline: 2 mos before pgm
Other info: *US accredited sponsor:* no *Misc:* Pgm designed for technically trained mgrs with leadership potential. *URL:* http://www.imd.ch
Contact: David Forster, Pgm Adviser, IMD, chemin de Bellerive 23, PO Box 915, CH-1001 Lausanne, Switzerland *E-mail:* info@imd.cj

---

1466
IMD INTERNATIONAL
Mobilizing People
Site: Switzerland: Lausanne
Dates: 2 wks, May 13-24 or Sep 23-Oct 4
Subjects: Business/management, Communications, Leadership
Eligibility: *Level:* professionals *Requires:* 10 yrs bus experience *Age:* min 35, max 60, avg 40
Credit: *Undergrad:* none *Grad:* none *Doc:* certificate
Instruction: *In:* English *Format:* seminar *Students:* intl
Costs: SFr 16,000 *incl* tuition, some meals, books/materials
Housing: *Arr by pgm:* hotels
Deadline: 4 mos before pgm
Other info: *US accredited sponsor:* no *Began:* 1987 *Misc:* For all mgrs faced with the challenge of mobilizing people & leading successful teams. *URL:* http://www.imd.ch
Contact: David Forster, Pgm Adviser, IMD, PO Box 915, CH-1001 Lausanne, Switzerland *E-mail:* info@imd.ch

---

1467
IMD INTERNATIONAL
Orchestrating Winning Performance
Site: Switzerland: Lausanne
Dates: 6 days, Jun 27-Jul 2
Subjects: Business/management, Finance, International business, Manufacturing, Technology
Eligibility: *Level:* professionals *Age:* min 30, max 60, avg 45
Credit: *Undergrad:* none *Grad:* none *Doc:* certificate
Instruction: *In:* English *Format:* seminar *Students:* intl
Costs: SFr 10,000 *incl* tuition, some meals, books/materials
Housing: *Arr by pgm:* hotels
Deadline: 2 mos before pgm
Other info: *US accredited sponsor:* no *Began:* 1995 *Misc:* Multiple electives. Pgm for individual execs or teams. Pgm content changes each yr. May contact former participants. *URL:* http://www.imd.ch
Contact: David Forster, Pgm Adviser, IMD, PO Box 915, CH-1001 Lausanne, Switzerland *E-mail:* info@imd.ch

---

1468
IMD INTERNATIONAL
PRISM
Site: Switzerland, Lausanne
Dates: 10 days, Mar 26-31 &Jun 19-22 or Sep 10-15 & Dec 4-7
Subjects: Business administration, Business/management, Organizational behavior
Eligibility: *Level:* professionals *Age:* min 35, max 55
Credit: *Undergrad:* none *Grad:* none *Doc:* certificate
Instruction: *In:* English *Format:* seminar *Students:* intl
Costs: SFr 13,000 *incl* tuition, some meals, books/materials
Housing: *Arr by pgm:* hotels
Deadline: 2 mos before pgm
Other info: *US accredited sponsor:* no *Misc:* Pgm designed for mgmt or corporate teams of a bus. *URL:* http://www.imd.ch
Contact: David Forster, Pgm Adviser, IMD, 23 chemin de Bellerive, PO Box 915, CH-1001 Lausanne, Switzerland *E-mail:* inro@imd.ch

---

1469
IMD INTERNATIONAL
Senior Executive Forum
Site: Switzerland: Lausanne
Dates: 3 days, Feb 20-23 or Oct 2-5
Subjects: Business/management, Contemporary issues, Internet
Eligibility: *Level:* professionals *Age:* min 35, max 61
Credit: *Undergrad:* none *Grad:* none *Doc:* certificate
Instruction: *In:* English *Format:* seminar *Students:* intl
Costs: SFr 9,000 *incl* tuition, some meals, books/materials
Housing: *Arr by pgm:* hotels
Deadline: 2 mos before pgm
Other info: *US accredited sponsor:* no *Began:* 1998 *Misc:* Pgm designed for sr. execs. May contact former participants. *URL:* http://www.imd.cn
Contact: David Forster, Pgm Adviser, IMD, Chemin de Bellerive. PO Box 915, CH-1001 Lausanne, Switzerland *E-mail:* info@imd.ch

---

1470
IMD INTERNATIONAL
Strategic Finance
Site: Switzerland: Lausanne
Dates: 1 wk, Aug 19-24
Subjects: Business administration, Finance, Organizational behavior
Eligibility: *Level:* professionals *Requires:* 10 yrs bus experience *Age:* min 35, max 60, avg 38
Credit: *Undergrad:* none *Grad:* none *Doc:* certificate
Instruction: *In:* English *Format:* seminar *Students:* intl
Costs: SFr 9,000 *incl* tuition, some meals, books/materials
Housing: *Arr by pgm:* hotels
Deadline: 2 mos before pgm
Other info: *US accredited sponsor:* no *Began:* 1974 *Misc:* Pgm designed for sr financial professionals & genl mgrs. May contact former participants. *URL:* http://www.imd.ch

Contact: David Forster, Pgm Adviser, IMD, PO Box 915, CH-1001 Lausanne, Switzerland *E-mail:* info@imd.ch

---

1471
LANGUAGE LIAISON
German/French Language
Site: Switzerland: Lausanne
Dates: 2 wks or longer, yr-round
Subjects: French language (beg/int/adv), German language (beg/int/adv), Hotel management, Humanities
Eligibility: *Level:* fresh, sophs, jrs, srs, grads, adults, teachers, professionals, precoll
Credit: *Undergrad:* avail *Grad:* avail *Doc:* transcript, certificate
Instruction: *In:* French, German *Format:* lab, lang study *Students:* intl
Costs: Contact sponsor
Housing: *Arr by pgm:* residence halls, apartments, homestay, hotels
Deadline: 30 days before pgm
Other info: *US accredited sponsor:* no *Began:* 1992 *Activities:* excursions, field trips, cultural events *Misc:* Scholarship research svc. *URL:* http://www.languageliaison.com
Contact: Nancy Forman, Dir, Lang Liaison, 4 Burnham Pkwy, Morristown NJ 07960 *Ph:* 800-284 4448 *E-mail:* learn@languageliaison.com

---

1472
LANGUAGE STUDIES ABROAD, INC
Intensive French-Lausanne
Site: Switzerland: Lausanne *Host inst:* Diavox
Dates: 4 -11 wks, yr-round
Subjects: French language (beg/int/adv), Homestay, Hotel management, Tourism
Eligibility: *Level:* fresh, sophs, jrs, srs, grads, adults, teachers, professionals, precoll *Age:* min 16
Credit: *Undergrad:* avail *Grad:* avail *Doc:* certificate, diploma
Instruction: *In:* English, French *Format:* lang study *Students:* intl
Costs: $2,013 for 4 wks *incl* tuition, housing, some meals, books/materials *Nonrefundable fee*
Housing: *Sponsor assists:* apartments, homestay, hotels
Deadline: 4 wks before pgm
Other info: *US accredited sponsor:* no *Began:* 1969 *Orient:* abroad *Misc:* May contact former participants. *URL:* http://www.languagestudiesabroad.com
Contact: Lang Studies Abroad, Inc, 103 Londonderry Ct, Reno NV 89511-2718 *Ph:* 800-424 5522; 775-849 9206 *Fax:* 775-849 9217 *E-mail:* info@languagestudiesabroad.com

---

1473
LINGUA SERVICE WORLDWIDE
Total Immersion/Intensive Language and Culture in Lausanne
Site: Switzerland: Lausanne *Host inst:* Diavox
Dates: 1 wk-1 yr, yr-round
Subjects: Civilization/culture, French language (beg/int/adv), Homestay
Eligibility: *Level:* adults *Age:* min 14
Credit: *Undergrad:* avail *Grad:* avail *Doc:* transcript, certificate
Instruction: *In:* French *Format:* lang study *Students:* intl
Costs: Contact sponsor
Housing: *Arr by pgm:* apartments with local students, residence halls with local students, homestay, pensions, hotels, hostels
Deadline: 45 days before pgm
Other info: *US accredited sponsor:* no *Began:* 1993 *Activities:* excursions, cultural events *Misc:* May contact former participants. *URL:* http://www.linguaserviceworldwide.com
Contact: Dir, Lingua Svc Worldwide, 75 Prospect St, Ste 4, Huntington NY 11743 *Ph:* 800-394 5327; 631-424 0777 *Fax:* 631-271 3441 *E-mail:* itctravel@worldnet.att.net ▲

1474
NATIONAL REGISTRATION CENTER FOR STUDY ABROAD (NRCSA)
Study in Switzerland
Site: Switzerland: Lausanne *Host inst:* Euroctr
Dates: 3 wks or longer, yr-round
Subjects: Civilization/culture, French language, German language (beg/int/adv), German studies, Homestay, Swiss studies
Eligibility: *Level:* fresh, sophs, jrs, srs, grads, adults, teachers *Age:* min 18
Credit: *Undergrad:* none *Grad:* none *Doc:* certificate
Instruction: *In:* French, German *Format:* lang study, lecture *Students:* intl
Costs: $1,592 for 3 wks *incl* tuition, housing, most meals, insurance
Housing: *Arr by pgm:* apartments, homestay
Deadline: Contact sponsor
Other info: *US accredited sponsor:* no *Misc:* Optional excursions. *URL:* http://www.nrcsa.com
Contact: Reuel Zielke, NRCSA, 823 N 2nd St, #206, Milwaukee WI 53203 *Ph:* 414-278 0631 *Fax:* 414-271 8884 *E-mail:* info@nrcsa.com

---

1475
UNIVERSITE DE LAUSANNE
Cours de Vacances at the University of Lausanne
Site: Switzerland: Lausanne
Dates: 3 or 6 wks, Jul 9-Sep 27
Subjects: Civilization/culture, Film studies, French language (int/adv), Homestay, Literature
Eligibility: *Level:* adults, precoll *Age:* min 16
Credit: *Undergrad:* none *Grad:* none
Instruction: *In:* French *Format:* lang study, lecture *Students:* intl
Costs: SFr 470 for 3 wks, SFr 1,050 for 6-wk beg pgm *incl* tuition
Housing: *Arr by pgm:* residence halls, homestay, furnished rms, student houses
Deadline: Apply early
Other info: *US accredited sponsor:* no *Activities:* excursions, field trips *URL:* http://www.unil.ch/cvac
Contact: Cours de Vacances, Univ de Lausanne, BFSH 2, CH-1015 Lausanne, Switzerland *E-mail:* CoursDeVacances@cvac.unil.ch

---

1476
UNIVERSITY OF MIAMI (FL)
Intensive French in Lausanne, Switzerland
Site: Switzerland: Lausanne *Host inst:* Univ de Lausanne
Dates: 6 wks, early Jul-mid-Aug
Subjects: French language
Eligibility: *Level:* sophs, jrs, srs *Requires:* 3.0 GPA, 1 yr of French *Age:* min 18
Credit: *Undergrad:* 6 *Grad:* none *Doc:* transcript
Instruction: *In:* French *Format:* lang study *Students:* intl
Costs: $4,010 *incl* tuition, housing, some meals *Nonrefundable fee*
Housing: *Arr by pgm:* residence halls
Deadline: Mar 30
Other info: *US accredited sponsor:* yes *Began:* 2000 *Orient:* abroad (1 day) *Misc:* May contact former participants. *URL:* http://www.studyabroad.miami.edu
Contact: Intl Educ Exch Pgms, Allen Hall 212, 5050 Brunson Dr, PO Box 248005, Univ of Miami, Coral Gables FL 33124-1610 *Ph:* 800-557 5421; 305-284 3434 *Fax:* 305-284 6629 *E-mail:* ieep@miami.edu

---

LUGANO

1477
COLLEGE CONSORTIUM FOR INTERNATIONAL STUDIES and EMPIRE STATE COLLEGE
Summer Program in Switzerland
Site: Switzerland: Lugano *Host inst:* Franklin Coll
Dates: 4 wks, May 24-Jun 24 for session I or Jun 28-Jul 29 for session II
Subjects: Art history, Business/management, Economics, History, International business, Languages (beg/

int/adv), Literature, Political science/ politics
Eligibility: *Level:* fresh, sophs, jrs, srs *Requires:* 2.5 GPA
Credit: *Undergrad:* avail *Grad:* none *Doc:* transcript
Instruction: *In:* English *Format:* lang study, lecture
Costs: $2,175-$3,455 for 1 session, $4,357-$7,350 for 2 sessions *incl* tuition, housing, fees
Housing: *Arr by pgm:* apartments
Deadline: May 1
Other info: *US accredited sponsor:* yes *URL:* http://www.ccisabroad.org
Contact: *See Index II for Members* CCIS, 2000 P St NW, Ste 503, Washington DC 20036 *Ph:* 800-453 6956; 202-233 0330 *Fax:* 202-223 0999 *E-mail:* info@ccisabroad.org
Or Contact: Dr Kenneth Abrams, Intl Pgms, Empire State Coll/SUNY, 28 Union Ave, 3rd Fl, Saratoga Springs NY 12866 *Ph:* 518-587 2100 ext 231, 518-587 2100 ext 215 *Fax:* 518-580 0287 *E-mail:* international@esc.edu ▲

1478
LANGUAGES ABROAD
Language and Cultural Immersion-Switzerland
Site: Switzerland: Lugano
Dates: 2 wks or longer, yr-round
Subjects: Civilization/culture, Italian language (beg/int/adv), Swiss studies
Eligibility: *Level:* adults *Age:* min 17, max 65, avg 25
Credit: *Undergrad:* none *Grad:* none *Doc:* certificate
Instruction: *In:* Italian *Format:* lang study *Students:* intl
Costs: $2,700 for 4 wks *incl* tuition, housing, some meals, insurance, fees, excursions, books/materials
Housing: *Arr by pgm:* residence halls, homestay
Deadline: None
Other info: *US accredited sponsor:* no *Began:* 1995 *Activities:* excursions, field trips, program travel, cultural events, sports *Misc:* May contact former participants. *URL:* http://www.languagesabroad.com
Contact: Ms Jesse Philippe, Langs Abroad, 317 Adelaide St W, Ste 900, Toronto, Ontario M5V 1P9, Canada *Ph:* 800-219 9924; 416-925 7117 *E-mail:* info@languagesabroad.com

---

MONTREUX

1479
INTERNATIONAL ACADEMY OF BROADCASTING
International Broadcasting Management Program
Site: Switzerland: Montreux
Dates: 4 wks, Feb-Mar
Subjects: Advertising, Broadcasting, Business/management, Marketing, Public relations, Technology
Eligibility: *Level:* grads, professionals
Credit: *Undergrad:* none *Grad:* none *Doc:* certificate
Instruction: *In:* English *Format:* lecture, seminar, workshop *Students:* intl
Costs: SFr 8,000 *incl* tuition, housing, all meals, books/materials
Housing: *Arr by pgm:* hotels
Deadline: Dec 15
Other info: *US accredited sponsor:* no *Began:* 1998 *URL:* http://www.iab.ch
Contact: Aleksandar Todorovic, Dir & Dean, IAB, 11 Ave de Florimont, 1820 Montreux, Switzerland *E-mail:* atodorovic@iab.ch
Or Contact: Constance Amoakohene, Admin, IAB, 11 Ave de Florimont, 1820 Montreux, Switzerland *E-mail:* seretariat@iab.ch

---

1480
LANGUAGES ABROAD
Language and Cultural Immersion Programs-Montreux
Site: Switzerland: Montreux
Dates: 2 wks or longer, yr-round
Subjects: Civilization/culture, French language (beg/int/adv), German language (beg/int/adv)
Eligibility: *Level:* adults *Age:* min 17, max 65, avg 25
Credit: *Undergrad:* none *Grad:* none *Doc:* certificate
Instruction: *In:* French, German *Format:* lang study *Students:* intl
Costs: From $2,950 for 4 wks *incl* tuition, housing, some meals, excursions, books/materials
Housing: *Arr by pgm:* apartments, homestay
Deadline: None
Other info: *US accredited sponsor:* no *Misc:* May contact former participants. *URL:* http://www.languagesabroad.com
Contact: Ms Jesse Philippe, Langs Abroad, 317 Adelaide St W, Ste 900, Toronto, Ontario M5V 1P9, Canada *Ph:* 800-219 9924; 416-925 7117 *E-mail:* info@languagesabroad.com

---

NEUCHATEL

1481
UNIVERSITE DE NEUCHATEL
Summer Course
Site: Switzerland: Neuchatel
Dates: Contact sponsor
Subjects: Civilization/culture, Field study, French language, History, Homestay, Independent study, Literature, Singing/voice, Sports, Theater arts
Eligibility: *Level:* adults *Age:* min 17
Credit: *Undergrad:* none *Grad:* none *Doc:* certificate
Instruction: *In:* French *Format:* directed field study, independent study, lab, lang study, lecture, practical training, study tour, volunteer/svc, workshop *Students:* intl
Costs: SFr 650 *incl* tuition, fees, books/materials *Nonrefundable fee*
Housing: *Sponsor assists:* apartments with local students, residence halls with local students, homestay, pensions
Deadline: Late Jun; late Mar for scholarships
Other info: *US accredited sponsor:* no *Orient:* avail avail (intensive lang study) *Activities:* excursions, field trips, program travel, cultural events, sports *Misc:* Daily lectures by specialists. Theatre & choral activity incl. *Financial aid:* scholarships *URL:* http://www.unine.ch/sfm/
Contact: Cours d'été de Langue et Literature Francaises, Univ dc Neuchatel, Ave du 1er, Mars 26, CH-2000 Neuchatel, Switzerland *E-mail:* sfm.cv@lettres.unine.ch

---

1482
UNIVERSITY OF UTAH
Intensive French Language Program
Site: Switzerland: Neuchatel *Host inst:* Univ de Neuchatel
Dates: 4 wks, Jul
Subjects: French language (beg/int/adv), Homestay
Eligibility: *Level:* fresh, sophs, jrs, srs, grads, adults *Requires:* 2.5 GPA, 1 sem French *Age:* min 18, avg 20
Credit: *Undergrad:* avail *Grad:* none *Doc:* transcript
Instruction: *In:* French *Format:* lang study *Students:* intl
Costs: $2,200 *incl* tuition, housing, some meals, fees, excursions, local bus pass
Housing: *Arr by pgm:* residence halls, homestay
Deadline: Mar 15
Other info: *US accredited sponsor:* yes *Began:* 1980 *Orient:* in US & abroad *Activities:* excursions *Misc:* May contact former participants. *URL:* http://www.saff.utah.edu/inter/

Contact: Aaron Rose, Univ of Utah, 200 S Central Campus Dr, Rm 159, Salt Lake City UT 84112 *Ph:* 801-581 5849 *Fax:* 801-581 5914 *E-mail:* lashton@saff.utah.edu

ZURICH

1483
MICHIGAN STATE UNIVERSITY
Population Biology Studies
Site: Switzerland: Zurich
Dates: 3 wks, Jul
Subjects: Field study, Zoology
Eligibility: *Level:* fresh, sophs, jrs, srs, grads *Requires:* 2.5 GPA, previous study in field *Age:* min 18
Credit: *Undergrad:* avail *Grad:* avail *Doc:* transcript
Instruction: *In:* English *Format:* directed field study *Students:* mainly US
Costs: About $1,400 *incl* housing, insurance, fees, excursions *Nonrefundable fee*
Housing: *Arr by pgm:* hostels
Deadline: Mar 2
Other info: *US accredited sponsor:* yes *Began:* 1999 *Orient:* in US (1 day) *Activities:* excursions, field trips *URL:* http://studyabroad.msu.edu
Contact: Cheryl Benner, Study Abroad, Michigan State Univ, 109 Intl Ctr, East Lansing MI 48824-1035 *Ph:* 517-353 8920 *Fax:* 517-432 2082 *E-mail:* bennerc@msu.edu ▲

United Kingdom

MORE THAN ONE CITY

1484
COLLEGE CONSORTIUM FOR STUDY ABROAD
Summer Session in England
Site: England: Bath, London *Host inst:* Univ of Bath
Dates: 6 wks, Jun 27-Jul 26
Subjects: British studies, English literature, History, Political science/politics, Theater arts
Eligibility: *Level:* fresh, sophs, jrs, srs, grads, adults, teachers *Requires:* 2.0 GPA *Age:* min 19
Credit: *Undergrad:* 6 *Grad:* none *Doc:* transcript
Instruction: *In:* English *Format:* study tour *Students:* mainly US
Costs: $2,695 *incl* tuition, housing, some meals, fees, excursions, theater
Housing: *Arr by pgm:* residence halls
Deadline: Apr 24
Other info: *US accredited sponsor:* yes *Began:* 1983 *Orient:* abroad *Activities:* excursions, field trips, program travel *Misc:* Group airfare avail. May contact former participants. *URL:* http://ntas-k1.sv.cc.va.us/bath/
Contact: *See Index II for Members* Dr Al Yoder, 200 Daniel Rd, Keysville VA 23947 *Ph:* 804-736 2033 *Fax:* 804-736 2082 *E-mail:* bath@sv.cc.va.us
Or Contact: Dr Judie Wise *Ph:* 937-864 7077 *E-mail:* england@instruction.com

1485
CONSERVATION VOLUNTEERS NORTHERN IRELAND
Natural Breaks
Site: Northern Ireland: various sites
Dates: 1 wk or longer, yr-round
Subjects: Community service projects, Conservation, Outdoor activities/education
Eligibility: *Level:* adults *Age:* min 18
Credit: *Undergrad:* none *Grad:* none
Instruction: *In:* English *Format:* volunteer/svc *Students:* intl
Costs: UK 66-99 per wk *incl* housing, all meals, insurance
Housing: *Arr by pgm:* hostels
Deadline: None
Other info: *US accredited sponsor:* no *Began:* 1986 *Activities:* excursions, field trips, cultural events *URL:* http://www.btcv.org.uk
Contact: Maddy Kelly, CVNI, 159 Ravenhill Rd, Belfast, Northern Ireland, UK BT90BP *E-mail:* m.kelly@btcu.org.uk
Or Contact: Working Holidays Coord, CVNI, 159 Ravenhill Rd, Belfast, Northern Ireland, UK BT90BP *E-mail:* cvni@cvni.org

1486
COOPERATIVE CENTER FOR STUDY ABROAD
Scotland/England Program
Site: England: London; Scotland: Edinburgh, Glasgow
Dates: 2-1/2 wks, Jun 14-Jul 2
Subjects: Business/management, Education/teaching, English, History, Law, Literature, Mathematics, Occupational therapy, Political science/politics, Social work
Eligibility: *Level:* fresh, sophs, jrs, srs, grads, adults, teachers, professionals *Requires:* 2.0 GPA, recommendation *Age:* min 18
Credit: *Undergrad:* 3 *Grad:* 3 *Transfer credit through:* Northern Kentucky Univ
Instruction: *In:* English *Format:* lecture, seminar, study tour, tutorial *Students:* mainly US
Costs: $2,895 *incl* housing, some meals, intl airfare, excursions, airport transfers, ISIC/ITIC *Nonrefundable fee*
Housing: *Arr by pgm:* residence halls, hotels
Deadline: Mar 1
Other info: *US accredited sponsor:* yes *Began:* 1984 *Orient:* in US & abroad *Activities:* excursions, field trips, program travel, cultural events *Misc:* May contact former participants. *Financial aid:* scholarships *URL:* http://www.nku.edu/ccsa
Contact: *See Index II for Members* Dr Michael Klembara, or Robin Byerly, Coop Ctr for Study Abroad, Northern Kentucky Univ, BEP 301 Nunn Dr, Highland Heights KY 41099 *Ph:* 800-319 6015; 859-572 6512 *Fax:* 859-572 6650 *E-mail:* ccsa@nku.edu

1487
DICKINSON COLLEGE
Fieldwork in Classical Archaeology
Site: England, Scotland
Dates: 4-6 wks, mid-Jul-mid-Aug
Subjects: Archaeology, Classical studies
Eligibility: *Level:* fresh, sophs, jrs
Credit: *Undergrad:* 4 *Grad:* none
Instruction: *In:* English *Format:* directed field study *Students:* intl
Costs: About $3,900 *incl* tuition, housing, all meals, intl airfare, local transport *Nonrefundable fee*
Housing: *Arr by pgm*
Deadline: Mar 1
Other info: *US accredited sponsor:* yes *Began:* 1990 *Orient:* avail avail *Activities:* field trips *Misc:* Co-sponsored by Dept of Archaeology, Durham Univ, England *URL:* http://www.dickinson.edu/departments/ocs/abroad.html
Contact: Global Educ, Dickinson Coll, PO Box 1773, Carlisle PA 17013-2896 *Ph:* 717-245 1341 *Fax:* 717-245 1688 *E-mail:* ocs@dickinson.edu

1488
INDIANA UNIVERSITY-PURDUE UNIVERSITY AT INDIANAPOLIS
Literary Landscape in England
Site: England: Ambleside, London, Portsmouth, Stratford
Dates: 2-3 wks, Jul 4-25
Subjects: Independent study, Literature, Written composition
Eligibility: *Level:* jrs, srs, grads, adults, teachers, professionals *Requires:* 3.0 GPA *Age:* min 21, max 75, avg 37
Credit: *Undergrad:* 3-6 *Grad:* 4 *Doc:* transcript
Instruction: *In:* English *Format:* study tour *Students:* mainly US
Costs: $2,900 *incl* housing, some meals, intl airfare, fees, excursions, books/materials, railpass, theater tickets *Nonrefundable fee*
Housing: *Arr by pgm:* residence halls, bed & breakfast in Stratford
Deadline: Feb 28
Other info: *US accredited sponsor:* yes *Began:* 1987 *Orient:* in US (1 day) *Activities:* excursions, field trips, program travel, cultural events *Misc:* May contact

former participants. *URL:* http://www.universitycollege.iupui.edu/cw
Contact: Dr Sharon J Hamilton, IUPUI, 755 West Michigan St, Rm 1140, Indianapolis IN 46202 *Ph:* 317-278 1846, 317-274 5647 *Fax:* 317-278 3602 *E-mail:* shamilto@iupui.edu

---

1489
INTERNATIONAL ACADEMIC PROJECTS
2001 Professional Development Program
Site: England: Durham, London; Scotland: Glasgow
Dates: 1 day-1 wk, Jun-Oct
Subjects: Archaeology, Art conservation, Art history, Historical preservation/restoration, Materials science/technology, Museology
Eligibility: *Level:* fresh, sophs, jrs, srs, grads, adults, professionals *Age:* min 18, avg 35
Credit: *Undergrad:* none *Grad:* avail *Doc:* certificate
Instruction: *In:* English *Format:* lecture, practical training, seminar, study tour, workshop *Students:* intl
Costs: $100 per day, $800 per wk *incl* tuition, fees, books/materials *Nonrefundable fee*
Housing: *Sponsor assists:* residence halls, hotels, bed & breakfasts
Deadline: Contact sponsor
Other info: *US accredited sponsor:* no *Began:* 1983 *Activities:* excursions, field trips *URL:* http://www.academicprojects.co.uk
Contact: James Black, Intl Acad Projects, 6 Fitzroy Sq, London W1P 6DX, England, UK *E-mail:* iap@archetype.co.uk

---

1490
INTERNATIONAL ACADEMIC PROJECTS
Archaeology, Conservation of Antiquities and Museum Studies
Site: England: Durham, London; Scotland: Glasgow
Dates: 1 day-1 wk, mid-Jun-mid-Aug
Subjects: Archaeology, Art history, Art restoration, Conservation, Historical preservation/restoration, Materials science/technology, Museology
Eligibility: *Level:* fresh, sophs, jrs, srs, grads, adults, professionals
Credit: *Undergrad:* avail *Grad:* avail
Instruction: *In:* English *Format:* lecture, practical training *Students:* mainly host country
Costs: $200-$800 *incl* tuition
Housing: *Sponsor assists:* residence halls, hotels, bed & breakfasts
Deadline: Contact sponsor
Other info: *US accredited sponsor:* no *Began:* 1983 *Orient:* abroad *Activities:* excursions *URL:* http://www.academicprojects.co.uk
Contact: James Black, Intl Acad Projects, 6 Fitzroy Sq, London W1P 6DX, England, UK *E-mail:* iap@archetype.co.uk

---

1491
MICHIGAN STATE UNIVERSITY
Archaeology
Site: England: Yorkshire Dales National Park
Dates: 4 wks, Jul-Aug
Subjects: Anthropology
Eligibility: *Level:* sophs, jrs, srs, grads *Requires:* 2.0 GPA, good acad standing, good health *Age:* min 18
Credit: *Undergrad:* 7 *Grad:* 7 *Doc:* transcript
Instruction: *In:* English *Format:* lecture *Students:* mainly US
Costs: About $1,700 *incl* housing, all meals, insurance, excursions, support svcs, equipment *Nonrefundable fee*
Housing: *Arr by pgm:* house
Deadline: Mar 2
Other info: *US accredited sponsor:* yes *Began:* 1980 *Orient:* in US & abroad *Activities:* excursions *Misc:* Loans avail. *Financial aid:* scholarships *URL:* http://studyabroad.msu.edu
Contact: Cheryl Benner, Study Abroad, Michigan State Univ, 109 Intl Ctr, East Lansing MI 48824-1035 *Ph:* 517-353 8920 *Fax:* 517-432 2082 *E-mail:* bennerc@msu.edu ▲

1492
MICHIGAN STATE UNIVERSITY
Comparative Criminal Justice
Site: England: Cambridge, London
Dates: 4 wks, Jul-Aug
Subjects: Criminal justice
Eligibility: *Level:* sophs, jrs, srs, grads *Requires:* 2.0 GPA, good acad standing, major in criminal justice *Age:* min 18
Credit: *Undergrad:* 8 *Grad:* avail *Doc:* transcript
Instruction: *In:* English *Format:* lecture *Students:* mainly US
Costs: About $3,200 *incl* housing, some meals, insurance, excursions, support svcs *Nonrefundable fee*
Housing: *Arr by pgm:* residence halls
Deadline: Mar 2
Other info: *US accredited sponsor:* yes *Began:* 1970 *Orient:* in US *Activities:* field trips *Misc:* Loans avail. *Financial aid:* scholarships *URL:* http://studyabroad.msu.edu
Contact: Cheryl Benner, Study Abroad, Michigan State Univ, 109 Intl Ctr, East Lansing MI 48824-1035 *Ph:* 517-353 8920 *Fax:* 517-432 2082 *E-mail:* bennerc@msu.edu ▲

1493
MICHIGAN STATE UNIVERSITY
Film in Britain
Site: England: London; Scotland: Edinburgh
Dates: 5 wks, Jul-Aug
Subjects: Film studies
Eligibility: *Level:* sophs, jrs, srs, grads *Requires:* 2.0 GPA, good acad standing *Age:* min 18
Credit: *Undergrad:* 6 *Grad:* 6 *Doc:* transcript
Instruction: *In:* English *Format:* lecture *Students:* mainly US
Costs: About $2,900 *incl* housing, insurance, excursions, support svcs *Nonrefundable fee*
Housing: *Arr by pgm:* residence halls
Deadline: Mar 2
Other info: *US accredited sponsor:* yes *Began:* 1986 *Orient:* in US & abroad *Activities:* excursions *Misc:* Loans avail. May contact former participants. *Financial aid:* scholarships *URL:* http://studyabroad.msu.edu
Contact: Cheryl Benner, Study Abroad, Michigan State Univ, 109 Intl Ctr, East Lansing MI 48824-1035 *Ph:* 517-353 8920 *Fax:* 517-432 2082 *E-mail:* bennerc@msu.edu ▲

1494
MICHIGAN STATE UNIVERSITY
Forensic Anthropology and Human Identification
Site: England: Cambridge, London
Dates: 4 wks, Jun-Jul
Subjects: Criminal justice, Field study, Forensic anthropology, Independent study
Eligibility: *Level:* jrs, srs, grads *Requires:* 2.5 GPA, good acad standing *Age:* min 18
Credit: *Undergrad:* 8 *Grad:* 8 *Doc:* transcript
Instruction: *In:* English *Format:* directed field study, independent study, lab, practical training, seminar *Students:* mainly US
Costs: About $2,600 *incl* housing, some meals, insurance, excursions, support svcs *Nonrefundable fee*
Housing: *Arr by pgm:* residence halls
Deadline: Mar 2
Other info: *US accredited sponsor:* yes *Began:* 1986 *Orient:* in US & abroad *Activities:* field trips, cultural events *Misc:* Loans avail. *Financial aid:* scholarships *URL:* http://studyabroad.msu.edu

Contact: Cheryl Benner, Study Abroad, Michigan State Univ, 109 Intl Ctr, East Lansing MI 48824 *Ph:* 517-353 8920 *Fax:* 517-432 2082 *E-mail:* bennerc@msu.edu ▲

1495
MICHIGAN STATE UNIVERSITY
Mass Media
Site: England: London; Scotland: Edinburgh; Wales
Dates: 5 wks, Jul-Aug
Subjects: Communications, Journalism, Media studies
Eligibility: *Level:* jrs, srs, grads *Requires:* 2.5 GPA, good acad standing *Age:* min 18
Credit: *Undergrad:* 6 *Grad:* 6 *Doc:* transcript
Instruction: *In:* English *Format:* lecture *Students:* mainly US
Costs: About $2,300 *incl* housing, some meals, insurance, excursions, support svcs *Nonrefundable fee*
Housing: *Arr by pgm:* residence halls
Deadline: Mar 2
Other info: *US accredited sponsor:* yes *Began:* 1982 *Orient:* in US *Misc:* Loans avail. May contact former participants. *Financial aid:* scholarships *URL:* http://studyabroad.msu.edu
Contact: Cheryl Benner, Study Abroad, Michigan State Univ, 109 Intl Ctr, East Lansing MI 48824-1035 *Ph:* 517-353 8920 *Fax:* 517-432 2082 *E-mail:* bennerc@msu.edu ▲

1496
MICHIGAN STATE UNIVERSITY
Political Science
Site: England: London; Scotland: Edinburgh
Dates: 5 wks, Jul-Aug
Subjects: Political science/politics, Social sciences
Eligibility: *Level:* fresh, sophs, jrs, srs *Requires:* 2.0 GPA, good acad standing *Age:* min 18
Credit: *Undergrad:* 9 *Grad:* none *Doc:* transcript
Instruction: *In:* English *Format:* lecture *Students:* mainly US
Costs: About $3,400 *incl* housing, some meals, insurance, excursions, support svcs *Nonrefundable fee*
Housing: *Arr by pgm:* residence halls
Deadline: Mar 2
Other info: *US accredited sponsor:* yes *Began:* 1966 *Orient:* in US & abroad *Misc:* Loans avail. May contact former participants. *Financial aid:* scholarships *URL:* http://studyabroad.msu.edu
Contact: Cheryl Benner, Study Abroad, Michigan State Univ, 109 Intl Ctr, East Lansing MI 48824-1035 *Ph:* 517-353 8920 *Fax:* 517-432 2082 *E-mail:* bennerc@msu.edu ▲

1497
MICHIGAN STATE UNIVERSITY
Visual Communication
Site: England: Bath-Lacock Abbey, Bradford, London, York; Scotland: Edinburgh
Dates: 6 wks, Jul-Aug
Subjects: Communications, Field study, Journalism, Photography
Eligibility: *Level:* sophs, jrs, srs, grads *Requires:* 2.0 GPA, good acad standing *Age:* min 18
Credit: *Undergrad:* 6 *Grad:* 6 *Doc:* transcript
Instruction: *In:* English *Format:* directed field study, lecture *Students:* mainly US
Costs: About $2,700 *incl* housing, some meals, insurance, excursions, support svcs *Nonrefundable fee*
Housing: *Arr by pgm:* residence halls
Deadline: Mar 2
Other info: *US accredited sponsor:* yes *Began:* 1985 *Orient:* in US *Activities:* program travel *Misc:* Loans avail. May contact former participants. *Financial aid:* scholarships *URL:* http://studyabroad.msu.edu
Contact: Cheryl Benner, Study Abroad, Michigan State Univ, 109 Intl Ctr, East Lansing MI 48824-1035 *Ph:* 517-353 8920 *Fax:* 517-432 2082 *E-mail:* bennerc@msu.edu ▲

1498
MONTCLAIR STATE UNIVERSITY
Montclair in London: A Summer Institute on Shakespeare
Site: England: London, Stratford
Dates: 12 days, Jul 27-Aug 9
Subjects: Field study, Independent study, Theater arts
Eligibility: *Level:* sophs, jrs, srs, grads, teachers, professionals *Requires:* 2.5 GPA
Credit: *Undergrad:* 3 *Grad:* 3 *Doc:* transcript
Instruction: *In:* English *Format:* directed field study, independent study *Students:* mainly US
Costs: About $2,200 *incl* housing, some meals, intl airfare, excursions
Housing: *Arr by pgm:* residence halls, pensions
Deadline: May 26
Other info: *US accredited sponsor:* yes *Began:* 1999 *Orient:* in US 3 days *Activities:* excursions, cultural events *Misc:* Incl 7 theatre performances plus workshops & lectures. May contact former participants. *URL:* http://www.montclair.edu/pages/globaled/students.html
Contact: Wendy Gilbert-Simon, Montclair State Univ, Global Educ Ctr, 22 Normal Ave, Upper Montclair NJ 07043 *Ph:* 973-655 4185 *Fax:* 973-655 7654 *E-mail:* simonw@mail.montclair.edu
Or Contact: Susan Kerner, Montclair State Univ, Theatre, Upper Mountclair NJ 07043 *Ph:* 973-655 4378

1499
NEW YORK UNIVERSITY, SCHOOL OF EDUCATION
Educational Theater
Site: England: London, Newcastle
Dates: Jul 1-22 (London), Jul 27-Aug 18 (Newcastle)
Subjects: Education/teaching, Theater arts
Eligibility: *Level:* grads *Requires:* 3.0 GPA, previous study in field
Credit: *Undergrad:* none *Grad:* avail *Doc:* transcript
Instruction: *In:* English *Format:* lecture, seminar *Students:* mainly US
Costs: $7,800 for London, $7,650 for Newcastle, $14,000 for both *incl* tuition, housing, some meals, books/materials *Nonrefundable fee*
Housing: *Arr by pgm*
Deadline: Contact sponsor
Other info: *US accredited sponsor:* yes *Began:* 1973 *Activities:* field trips *Misc:* Loans avail. May contact former participants. *URL:* http://www.nyu.edu/summer
Contact: Nancy Swortzell, Assoc Prof, Sch of Educ, Pless Annex 23, NYU, 82 Washington Sq E, Rm 23, New York NY 10003-6680 *Ph:* 212-998 5868 *Fax:* 212-995 4569
Or Contact: Helen J Kelly, Dir, Special Pgms, NYU, 82 Washington Sq E, Rm 62, New York NY 10003 *Ph:* 212-998 5090 *Fax:* 212-995 4923 ▲

1500
OHIO UNIVERSITY
Art and Art History in Great Britain
Site: England: London; Scotland: Edinburgh
Dates: 4 wks, Jun-Jul
Subjects: Art history, Independent study, Studio arts
Eligibility: *Level:* fresh, sophs, jrs, srs, grads
Credit: *Undergrad:* 20 qtr hrs *Grad:* 18 qtr hrs *Doc:* transcript
Instruction: *In:* English *Format:* art studio, independent study, lecture, practical training *Students:* mainly US
Costs: Contact Sponsor
Housing: *Arr by pgm:* residence halls, hotels

Deadline: Contact sponsor
Other info: *US accredited sponsor:* yes *Began:* 1979 *Activities:* field trips, cultural events *Misc:* All art history at site. No classroom teaching. *URL:* http://www.ohiou.edu
Contact: Jody Lamb, Sch of Art, Ohio Univ, 436 Seigfred Hall, Athens OH 45701 *Ph:* 740-593 4283 *Fax:* 740-593 0457 *E-mail:* lambj@ohiou.edu

---

1501
PENNSYLVANIA STATE UNIVERSITY
Drama in Britain
Site: England: London, Stratford-upon-Avon
Dates: 2 mos, May-Jul
Subjects: Drama/theater, English, Field study
Eligibility: *Level:* fresh, sophs, jrs, srs, grads *Requires:* 2.5 GPA
Credit: *Undergrad:* 6 *Grad:* avail
Instruction: *In:* English *Format:* directed field study, lecture, study tour *Students:* mainly US
Costs: Contact Sponsor
Housing: *Arr by pgm:* pensions
Deadline: Rolling admissions
Other info: *US accredited sponsor:* yes *Orient:* in US & abroad *Activities:* excursions, field trips, cultural events *Misc:* 1 mo in PA, 1 mo in UK. May contact former participants. *Financial aid:* scholarships
Contact: Summer Abroad, Penn State Univ, 225 Penn State Conference Ctr, University Park PA 16802 *Ph:* 814-863 5170
Or Contact: Intl Pgm Adviser, Penn State, 222 Boucke Bldg, University Park PA 16802 *Ph:* 814-865 7681 *Fax:* 814-865 3336

1502
PENNSYLVANIA STATE UNIVERSITY
Western Economies in Transition: A European Perspective
Site: England: Oxford, Torquay
Dates: 3 wks, May-Jun
Subjects: Economics, European studies
Eligibility: *Level:* sophs, jrs, srs, grads, adults *Requires:* 2.5 GPA, previous study in field *Age:* min 18
Credit: *Undergrad:* 3 per course *Grad:* 3 per course
Instruction: *In:* English *Format:* lecture, study tour *Students:* mainly US
Costs: About $3,214 for PA residents, $4,098 for others *incl* tuition, housing, some meals, excursions
Housing: *Arr by pgm:* hotels
Deadline: Mar 1
Other info: *US accredited sponsor:* yes *Orient:* in US (1 day) *Activities:* excursions, cultural events *Misc:* May contact former participants. *URL:* http://www.outreach.psu.edu/PSSEA/
Contact: Summer Abroad, Penn State Univ, 225 Penn State Conference Ctr, University Park PA 16802 *Ph:* 814-863 5170 *Fax:* 814-863 5190 *E-mail:* SummerAbroad@outreach.psu.edu
Or Contact: Dr Philip Klein, Pennsylvania State Univ, 516 Kern Bldg, University Park PA 16802 *Ph:* 814-865 5781 *Fax:* 814-863 4775 *E-mail:* pklein@psu.edu

---

1503
RAMAPO COLLEGE OF NEW JERSEY
London and Scotland Theater Program
Site: England: London; Scotland: Edinburgh *Host inst:* Regent's Coll
Dates: 3 wks, July/Aug
Subjects: Drama/theater
Eligibility: *Level:* fresh, sophs, jrs, srs, grads, adults *Requires:* 2.0 GPA
Credit: *Undergrad:* 3 *Grad:* none
Instruction: *In:* English *Format:* lecture, study tour *Students:* mainly US
Costs: $3,000 for Ramapo students, $3,200 for others *incl* tuition, housing, some meals, intl airfare, fees, excursions
Housing: *Arr by pgm:* residence halls
Deadline: May 1
Other info: *US accredited sponsor:* yes *Began:* 1999 *Orient:* avail (avail 1 day) *Misc:* May contact former participants.
Contact: Ms Robyn Perricelli, Coord, Study Abroad, Ramapo Coll, 505 Ramapo Valley Rd, Mahwah NJ 07430 *Ph:* 201-684 7030 *Fax:* 201-684 7651 *E-mail:* rperrice@ramapo.edu

---

1504
SOUTHERN ILLINOIS UNIVERSITY AT CARBONDALE
Global Broadcasting in London
Site: England: Bristol, London
Dates: 2 wks, late May-early Jun
Subjects: Broadcasting, Communications, Field study, Journalism, Radio, Television/video
Eligibility: *Level:* sophs, jrs, srs, grads, professionals *Requires:* instructor's approval
Credit: *Undergrad:* 2-4 *Grad:* 2-4 *Doc:* transcript
Instruction: *In:* English *Format:* directed field study, lecture *Students:* mainly US
Costs: About $1,995 *incl* housing, some meals, intl airfare, books/materials, ground transport *Nonrefundable fee*
Housing: *Arr by pgm:* apartments, hotels
Deadline: Mar 4 or until pgm filled
Other info: *US accredited sponsor:* yes *Began:* 1986 *Orient:* in US *Activities:* excursions, field trips *URL:* http://www.siu.edu/departments/study_abroad/
Contact: Thomas A Saville, Study Abroad Pgms, Mailcode 6885, Southern Illinois Univ, Carbondale IL 62901-6885 *Ph:* 618-453 7670 *Fax:* 618-453 7647 *E-mail:* studyabr@siu.edu

---

1505
SUNY COLLEGE AT OSWEGO
Historical and Cultural Study Tour in The United Kingdom
Site: Varies each year
Dates: 3 wks, late May-early Jun or late Jul-early Aug
Subjects: Field study, History, International studies
Eligibility: *Level:* fresh, sophs, jrs, srs, grads *Requires:* good acad standing
Credit: *Undergrad:* 3 *Grad:* avail
Instruction: *In:* English *Format:* lecture, study tour *Students:* mainly US
Costs: $3,500 *incl* housing, some meals, intl airfare, excursions, passes to historical sites *Nonrefundable fee*
Housing: *Arr by pgm:* bed & breakfasts
Deadline: Apr 1
Other info: *US accredited sponsor:* yes *Began:* 1983 *Orient:* in US *Activities:* excursions *Misc:* Second session especially for adult learners. *URL:* http://www.oswego.edu/~intled
Contact: Susan Ansara, Dir, Intl Educ, SUNY Coll at Oswego, 102 Rich Hall, Oswego NY 13126 *Ph:* 888-467 9346; 315-341 2118 *Fax:* 315-341 2477 *E-mail:* intled@oswego.edu

---

1506
TEMPLE UNIVERSITY, TYLER SCHOOL OF ART
Art in Scotland
Site: England: London; Scotland: Arbroath, Glasgow, Scottish Highlands *Host inst:* Glasgow Sch of Art
Dates: 4 wks, mid-Jun-mid-Jul, pgm offered in odd-numbered yrs
Subjects: Studio arts
Eligibility: *Level:* sophs, jrs, srs, grads *Requires:* previous course in studio art
Credit: *Undergrad:* 6 *Grad:* 3
Instruction: *In:* English *Format:* art studio, lecture *Students:* US & host country
Costs: $4,400-$4,500 *incl* tuition, housing, some meals, intl airfare, fees, excursions, books/materials
Housing: *Arr by pgm:* pensions, furnished rms
Deadline: Mar 15
Other info: *US accredited sponsor:* yes *Began:* 1986 *Activities:* program travel *Misc:* Scholarships avail for Temple students only May contact former participants. *URL:* http://www.temple.edu/intlprog/

See "How To Use This Book" for definitions of terms used above. ▲ = See program sponsor's ad(s) in this book.

Contact: Intl Pgms, Temple Univ, Tuttleman Learning Ctr, 1809 N 13th St, Philadelphia PA 19122 *Ph:* 215-204 4684 *Fax:* 215-204 5735 *E-mail:* intlprog@vm.temple.edu

---

1507
UNIVERSITY OF ARKANSAS
Cambridge/Oxford Communication Seminar
Site: England: Cambridge, Oxford
Dates: Jul 8-28
Subjects: Communications, Constitutional law, Film studies
Eligibility: *Level:* jrs, srs, grads *Requires:* 3.0 GPA *Age:* avg 22
Credit: *Undergrad:* 3 *Grad:* 3 *Doc:* transcript
Instruction: *In:* English *Format:* seminar *Students:* mainly US
Costs: $3,800 *incl* tuition, housing, insurance, fees, excursions
Housing: *Arr by pgm:* residence halls
Deadline: Apr 1
Other info: *US accredited sponsor:* yes *Began:* 1998 *Orient:* in US *Activities:* field trips *Misc:* Time divided between Cambridge & Oxford. *URL:* http://www.uark.edu/~studyabr
Contact: Michelle Morris, 722 W Maple St, Univ of Arkansas, Fayetteville AR 72701 *Ph:* 501-575 7582 *Fax:* 501-575 7582 *E-mail:* studyabr@cavern.uark.edu

---

1508
UNIVERSITY OF IOWA
Civil Infrastructure in Europe: A Slice Through Time
Site: England, Scotland, Wales
Dates: May 17-Jun 1
Subjects: Civil engineering, Field study, Mechanical engineering, Urban planning
Eligibility: Own students preferred. *Level:* fresh, sophs, jrs, srs, grads *Requires:* engineering majors preferred
Credit: *Undergrad:* 3 *Grad:* 3
Instruction: *In:* English *Format:* directed field study, lecture *Students:* mainly US
Costs: $2,000 for Univ of Iowa students, $2,200 for others *incl* housing, some meals, fees, excursions
Housing: *Arr by pgm:* hotels
Deadline: Apr 1
Other info: *US accredited sponsor:* yes *Began:* 1999 *Orient:* in US & abroad (3 days) *Activities:* program travel, cultural events *URL:* http://www.uiowa.edu/~uiabroad
Contact: Study Abroad, Univ of Iowa, 28 Intl Ctr, Iowa City IA 52242-1802 *Ph:* 319-335 2021 *Fax:* 319-353 2033 *E-mail:* study-abroad@uiowa.edu

---

1509
UNIVERSITY OF KANSAS
British Summer Institute
Site: England: Cambridge, Exeter, Lancaster, Leicester, London
Dates: 5 wks, Jun 14-Jul 18
Subjects: Art history, English literature, History
Eligibility: *Level:* fresh, sophs, jrs, srs, grads *Requires:* 2.5 GPA, previous study in field, preferred
Credit: *Undergrad:* 6-9 *Grad:* avail *Doc:* transcript
Instruction: *In:* English *Format:* lecture, study tour *Students:* mainly US
Costs: About $3,995 *incl* tuition, housing, some meals, fees, excursions
Housing: *Arr by pgm:* residence halls, hotels
Deadline: Rolling admissions
Other info: *US accredited sponsor:* yes *Began:* 1973 *Activities:* field trips, program travel, cultural events *URL:* http://www.ukans.edu/~osa
Contact: Susan MacNally, Asst Dir, Study Abroad, Univ of Kansas, 108 Lippincott Hall, Lawrence KS 66045 *Ph:* 785-864 3742 *Fax:* 785-864 5040 *E-mail:* osa@ukans.edu ▲

1510
UNIVERSITY OF NORTH CAROLINA AT CHARLOTTE
Shakespeare in Performance Summer Institute
Site: England: London, Stratford-upon-Avon *Host inst:* Shakespeare Ctr
Dates: 4 wks, mid-Jul-Aug
Subjects: Drama/theater, English literature, Field study, Shakespeare studies
Eligibility: *Level:* adults
Credit: *Undergrad:* 6 *Grad:* 3-6 *Doc:* transcript
Instruction: *In:* English *Format:* directed field study *Students:* mainly US
Costs: $3,300 *incl* tuition, housing, some meals, intl airfare, insurance, fees, excursions, books/materials, theater tickets *Nonrefundable fee*
Housing: *Arr by pgm:* residence halls, bed & breakfasts
Deadline: Apr 15
Other info: *US accredited sponsor:* yes *Began:* 1980 *Orient:* in US *Activities:* excursions *Misc:* May contact former participants. *URL:* http://www.uncc.edu/oip/edabroad.htm
Contact: Educ Abroad/Intl Pgms, UNC Charlotte, 9201 University City Blvd, Charlotte NC 28223-0001 *Ph:* 704-687 2464 *Fax:* 704-687 3168 *E-mail:* stennies@email.uncc.edu
Or Contact: Dr John McNair, English, UNC Charlotte, 9201 University City Blvd, Charlotte NC 28223-0001 *Ph:* 704-687 4208 *Fax:* 704-687 3168 *E-mail:* jrmcnair@email.uncc.edu

---

1511
VIRGINIA POLYTECHNIC INSTITUTE & STATE UNIVERSITY
Virginia Tech Summer Study in England and Scotland
Site: England: Brighton, London; Scotland: Edinburgh
Dates: About May 19-Jul 3
Subjects: English literature, Homestay, Scottish studies, Shakespeare studies
Eligibility: *Level:* sophs, jrs, srs, grads
Credit: *Undergrad:* 9 *Grad:* 3 (independent study) *Doc:* transcript
Instruction: *In:* English *Format:* lecture, study tour *Students:* mainly US
Costs: Contact sponsor
Housing: *Arr by pgm:* residence halls, homestay, hotels
Deadline: Mar 1
Other info: *US accredited sponsor:* yes *Began:* 1972 *Orient:* in US *Activities:* excursions, field trips, cultural events *Misc:* Optional travel. *URL:* http://www.english.vt.edu/7Eabroad/StudyAbroad.ht
Contact: Charles E Modlin, English, Virginia Polytechnic Inst & State Univ, Blacksburg VA 24061-0112 *Ph:* 540-231 6513 *E-mail:* cmodlin@vt.edu

---

ALNWICK

1512
SAINT CLOUD STATE UNIVERSITY
Center for British Studies
Site: England: Alnwick *Host inst:* Alnwick Castle
Dates: 8-10 wks, early Jun-early Aug
Subjects: Education/teaching, History, Social sciences, Speech/debate/forensics
Eligibility: *Level:* fresh, sophs, jrs, srs *Requires:* 2.25 GPA *Age:* min 18
Credit: *Undergrad:* 12 *Grad:* none
Instruction: *In:* English *Format:* lecture *Students:* mainly US
Costs: $4,425 for MN residents *incl* tuition, housing, some meals, intl airfare, excursions *Nonrefundable fee*
Housing: *Arr by pgm:* residence halls
Deadline: Feb 1; Apr 1 for scholarships
Other info: *US accredited sponsor:* yes *Began:* 1999 *Orient:* in US & abroad *Financial aid:* scholarships, work study
Contact: Ctr for Intl Studies, St Cloud State Univ, 720 4th Ave S, St Cloud MN 56301-4498 *Ph:* 320-255 4287 *Fax:* 320-255 4223 *E-mail:* intstudy@stcloudstate.edu

---

AMBLESIDE

1513
LOUISIANA STATE UNIVERSITY
Library Science
Site: England: Ambleside *Host inst:* Rydall Hall
Dates: 2 wks, Jul 16-30
Subjects: Children's literature, Independent study, Library science
Eligibility: *Level:* grads *Requires:* 3.0 GPA, major in library sci *Age:* min 21, avg 21
Credit: *Undergrad:* none *Grad:* 3 *Doc:* transcript
Instruction: *In:* English *Format:* independent study, lecture *Students:* mainly US
Costs: About $2,000 *incl* tuition, housing, all meals, excursions *Nonrefundable fee*
Housing: *Arr by pgm:* residence halls
Deadline: Mar 15
Other info: *US accredited sponsor:* yes *Began:* 1987 *Orient:* in US (1 day) *Activities:* excursions, field trips, cultural events *Misc:* Scholarships for own students only. May contact former participants. *URL:* http://www.lsu.edu/studyabroad
Contact: Joseph Rosenbach, Louisiana State Univ, 113 Hatcher Hall, Baton Rouge LA 70803 *Ph:* 225-388 6801 *Fax:* 225-388 6806 *E-mail:* studyabroad@lsu.edu
Or Contact: Prof Patsy Perritt, Louisiana State Univ, Sch of Library & Info Sci, Baton Rouge LA 70803 *Ph:* 225-388 1460 *Fax:* 225-388 4581 *E-mail:* esperr@unix1.sncc.lsu.edu

ARBROATH

1514
SOUTHERN ILLINOIS UNIVERSITY AT CARBONDALE
Art and Culture in the Scottish Landscape
Site: Scotland: Arbroath *Host inst:* Hospitalfield Trust
Dates: 3 wks, late May-early Jun
Subjects: Art history, Independent study, Painting
Eligibility: *Level:* sophs, jrs, srs, grads, adults, teachers, professionals *Requires:* faculty approval *Age:* min 18
Credit: *Undergrad:* 1-3 *Grad:* 1-3 *Doc:* transcript
Instruction: *In:* English *Format:* art studio, independent study, lecture, seminar *Students:* mainly US
Costs: $2,600 *incl* housing, some meals, intl airfare, excursions, books/materials
Housing: *Arr by pgm:* residence halls
Deadline: Apr 1
Other info: *US accredited sponsor:* yes *Began:* 1993 *Orient:* in US & abroad *Activities:* excursions, field trips, cultural events *Misc:* Hospitalfield Trust is housed in Gaelic revival castle. May contact former participants. *URL:* http://www.siu.edu/departments/study_abroad/
Contact: Thomas A Saville, Study Abroad Pgms, Mailcode 6885, Southern Illinois Univ, Carbondale IL 62901-6885 *Ph:* 618-453 7670 *Fax:* 618-453 7647 *E-mail:* studyabr@siu.edu

BATH

1515
ADVANCED STUDIES IN ENGLAND
Advanced Studies in England Summer School
Site: England: Bath
Dates: 5 wks, Jun 10-Jul 15
Subjects: British studies, Civilization/culture, English literature, History, Medieval studies
Eligibility: *Level:* sophs, jrs, srs, grads *Requires:* 3.0 GPA, 2 current faculty references *Age:* avg 20
Credit: *Undergrad:* avail *Grad:* avail *Doc:* transcript
Instruction: *In:* English *Format:* lecture, seminar, tutorial, workshop *Students:* mainly US
Costs: $3,000 *incl* tuition, housing, some meals, fees, excursions *Nonrefundable fee*
Housing: *Arr by pgm:* apartments, houses
Deadline: May 1
Other info: *US accredited sponsor:* no *Began:* 1998 *Orient:* abroad (3 days) *Activities:* excursions, field trips, program travel, cultural events *Misc:* May contact former participants. *URL:* http://www.studyabroadbath.org
Contact: Mrs Ann Nunes, Dir, Advanced Studies in England, 2 Pierrepont St, Bath BA1 1LB, UK *E-mail:* ase_bath@compuserve.com
Or Contact: Patti Brown, ASE Coord, Denison Univ, Granville OH 43023 *Ph:* 740-587 6667 *Fax:* 740-587 6411 *E-mail:* brownp@cc.denison.edu

1516
MICHIGAN STATE UNIVERSITY
Law and Economics
Site: England: Bath *Host inst:* Univ of Bath
Dates: 8 wks, Jun-Aug
Subjects: Economics, Law
Eligibility: *Level:* fresh, sophs, jrs, srs *Requires:* 2.5 GPA, previous study in field, microecon (EC 201) *Age:* min 18
Credit: *Undergrad:* avail *Grad:* none *Doc:* transcript
Instruction: *In:* English *Format:* lecture *Students:* intl
Costs: About $2,000 *incl* housing, insurance, fees, excursions *Nonrefundable fee*
Housing: *Arr by pgm:* residence halls
Deadline: Mar 2
Other info: *US accredited sponsor:* yes *Began:* 1999 *Orient:* in US (1 day) *Activities:* excursions, field trips, program travel *URL:* http://studyabroad.msu.edu
Contact: Cheryl Benner, Study Abroad, Michigan State Univ, 109 Intl Ctr, East Lansing MI 48824-1035 *Ph:* 517-353 8920 *Fax:* 517-432 2082 *E-mail:* bennerc@msu.edu ▲

1517
UNIVERSITY OF RHODE ISLAND
URI in England Summer Program
Site: England: Bath *Host inst:* Univ of Bath
Dates: 4 wks, Jul 8-Aug 5
Subjects: British studies, English literature, Field study, History, Literary sites
Eligibility: *Level:* fresh, sophs, jrs, srs, grads, adults, teachers, professionals *Age:* min 18, max 90, avg 28
Credit: *Undergrad:* 6 *Grad:* 6 *Doc:* transcript
Instruction: *In:* English *Format:* study tour *Students:* mainly US
Costs: $1,830 *incl* tuition, housing, fees, excursions *Nonrefundable fee*
Housing: *Arr by pgm:* residence halls with local students
Deadline: Mar 15
Other info: *US accredited sponsor:* yes *Began:* 1980 *Orient:* in US *Activities:* excursions, field trips, program travel, cultural events *Misc:* May contact former participants. *Financial aid:* scholarships *URL:* http://www.uri.edu/artsci/uriuk.html
Contact: R B Reaves, English, Univ of Rhode Island, Independence Hall, Kingston RI 02881 *Ph:* 401-874 5931 *Fax:* 401-874 2580 *E-mail:* rbreaves@uriacc.uri.edu
Or Contact: Robert Gutchen, History, Univ of Rhode Island, Independence Hall, Kingston RI 02881 *Ph:* 401-874 4073, 401-783 8851 *Fax:* 401-874 2595

1518
WILLIAM JEWELL COLLEGE
British Teacher Education Program
Site: England: Bath
Dates: 4 wks, mid-Jun-early Jul; plus spring sem intro seminar on-campus
Subjects: Elementary education, Field study
Eligibility: *Level:* jrs, srs, grads, teachers *Requires:* jr status in teacher educ pgm or valid teaching certificate *Age:* min 18
Credit: *Undergrad:* 6 *Grad:* 5
Instruction: *In:* English *Students:* mainly US

Costs: $2,195-$2,345 *incl* tuition, housing, some meals, excursions
Housing: *Arr by pgm:* bed & breakfasts
Deadline: Jan 15
Other info: *US accredited sponsor:* yes *Began:* 1985 *Orient:* in US & abroad *URL:* http://www.jewell.edu/overseas/
Contact: Dr Mary Ellen Bleakley, Prof Ronilue Garrison or Dr Faye More, Educ, William Jewell Coll, Liberty MO 64068 *Ph:* 816-781 7700 ext 5498 *Fax:* 816-415 5027 *E-mail:* garrisonr@william.jewell.edu

BEDFORDSHIRE

1519
ROYAL SOCIETY FOR THE PROTECTION OF BIRDS (RSPB)
Residential Voluntary Wardening Scheme
Site: England: Bedfordshire
Dates: Up to 4 wks, yr-round
Subjects: Birdwatching, Community service projects, Conservation
Eligibility: *Level:* adults *Age:* min 18
Credit: *Undergrad:* none *Grad:* none
Instruction: *In:* English *Format:* volunteer/svc *Students:* intl
Costs: No fees
Housing: *Arr by pgm:* at or near nature reserve
Deadline: Contact sponser
Other info: *US accredited sponsor:* no *Misc:* Contact RSPB for info & application form. *URL:* http://www.rspb.org.uk
Contact: Royal Society for Protection of Birds, The Lodge, Sandy, Bedfordshire SG19 2DL, UK

BRIGHTON

1520
EASTERN MICHIGAN UNIVERSITY
Social Work Practicum in England
Site: England: Brighton *Host inst:* Univ of Brighton
Dates: 6 wks, May 3-Jun 15
Subjects: Health care/hospitals, Social work
Eligibility: *Level:* sophs, jrs, srs, grads, adults, professionals *Requires:* 2.0 GPA, references *Age:* min 18
Credit: *Undergrad:* 9 *Grad:* 8 *Doc:* transcript
Instruction: *In:* English *Format:* lecture, practical training *Students:* mainly US
Costs: $3,095 *incl* tuition, housing, all meals, insurance, fees, excursions
Housing: *Arr by pgm:* hostels
Deadline: Feb 1
Other info: *US accredited sponsor:* yes *Began:* 1996 *Orient:* in US & abroad *Activities:* excursions, field trips *Misc:* Clinical experience in & visits to British health care orgs. May contact former participants. *URL:* http://www.emich.edu/abroad
Contact: Acad Pgms Abroad, Eastern Michigan Univ, 127 Boone Hall, Ypsilanti MI 48197 *Ph:* 800-777 3541; 734-487 2424 *Fax:* 734-487 4377 *E-mail:* programs.abroad@emich.edu

1521
UNIVERSITY OF SUSSEX
International Summer School
Site: England: Brighton *Host inst:* Univ of Sussex
Dates: 4 or 8 wks, early Jul end Aug
Subjects: Art education, Biology, Chemistry, Ecology/environmental studies, Economics, Engineering, English literature, History, Independent study, International relations, Mathematics, Media studies, Philosophy, Physics, Sociology
Eligibility: *Level:* fresh, sophs, jrs, srs, adults, precoll *Requires:* 3.0 GPA, previous study required for some subjects, *Age:* min 17
Credit: *Undergrad:* avail *Grad:* none *Doc:* transcript
Instruction: *In:* English *Format:* independent study, lab, lang study, lecture, music lesson, seminar, tutorial, workshop *Students:* intl
Costs: UK 860 for 4 wks, UK1,650 for 8 wks *incl* tuition, fees *Nonrefundable fee*
Housing: *Sponsor assists:* residence halls
Deadline: May 1
Other info: *US accredited sponsor:* yes *Began:* 1999 *Orient:* abroad (1 day) *Activities:* excursions, cultural events, sports *Misc:* May contact former participants. *URL:* http://www.sussex.ac.uk/publications/summer00
Contact: Dr Penny Chaloner, Univ of Sussex, Intl Summer Schl, Falmer, Brighton, BNI 9QJ, UK *E-mail:* summer@sussex.ac.uk

BRISTOL

1522
ILLINOIS STATE UNIVERSITY
Summer Program in Bristol, England
Site: England: Bristol *Host inst:* Univ of the West of England (UWE)
Dates: 4 wks, mid-May-mid-Jun
Subjects: British studies, Civilization/culture, History, Homestay, International business
Eligibility: *Level:* jrs, srs *Requires:* 2.5 GPA, 60 credit hrs, 3 hrs coll econ for non-bus students
Credit: *Undergrad:* 6 *Grad:* none *Doc:* transcript
Instruction: *In:* English *Format:* lecture, seminar, study tour *Students:* mainly US
Costs: $3,832 *incl* tuition, housing, all meals, intl airfare, insurance, fees, excursions, ground transport
Housing: *Arr by pgm:* homestay
Deadline: Feb 14
Other info: *US accredited sponsor:* yes *Began:* 1991 *Orient:* in US *Activities:* excursions, field trips, program travel *URL:* http://www.its.ilstu.edu/intlstudies/
Contact: Intl Studies & Pgms, Illinois State Univ, Campus Box 6120, Normal IL 61790-6120 *Ph:* 309-438 5365 *Fax:* 309-438 3987 *E-mail:* oisp@ilstu.edu

CAMBRIDGE

1523
COLLEGE OF WILLIAM & MARY
Summer in Cambridge
Site: England: Cambridge *Host inst:* Christ's Coll of Univ of Cambridge
Dates: 5 wks, early Jul-early Aug
Subjects: Full curriculum
Eligibility: *Level:* fresh, sophs, jrs, srs, teachers, professionals *Requires:* good acad standing
Credit: *Undergrad:* 6 *Grad:* none *Doc:* transcript
Instruction: *In:* English *Format:* lecture *Students:* mainly US
Costs: $3,650 *incl* tuition, housing, some meals, fees, excursions *Nonrefundable fee*
Housing: *Arr by pgm:* residence halls
Deadline: Mar 1
Other info: *US accredited sponsor:* yes *Began:* 1974 *Activities:* excursions *Misc:* Must take 1 course min. Scholarships for own students only. Resident dir and W & M faculty. *URL:* http://www.wm.edu/academics/reves/programs_abroad/
Contact: Guru Ghosh, Reves Ctr for Intl Studies, Coll of William & Mary, Williamsburg VA 23187-8795 *Ph:* 757-221 3595 *Fax:* 757-221 3597 *E-mail:* gxghos@wm.edu

1524
DUKE UNIVERSITY
Duke in Cambridge
Site: England: Cambridge *Host inst:* Univ of Cambridge
Dates: Late Jun-early Aug
Subjects: Literature, Political science/politics
Eligibility: *Level:* fresh, sophs, jrs, srs *Requires:* good acad standing, transcript *Age:* min 19
Credit: *Undergrad:* 2 course credits *Grad:* none *Doc:* transcript
Instruction: *In:* English *Format:* lecture, seminar *Students:* mainly US

Costs: $5,140 *incl* tuition, housing, some meals, excursions
Housing: *Arr by pgm:* residence halls
Deadline: Feb 11
Other info: *US accredited sponsor:* yes *Orient:* in US & abroad *Activities:* excursions, cultural events *URL:* http://www.aas.duke.edu/study_abroad/
Contact: Study Abroad, Duke Univ, 121 Allen Bldg, Box 90057, Durham NC 27708-0057 *Ph:* 919-684 2174 *Fax:* 919-684 3083 *E-mail:* abroad@asdean.duke.edu

---

1525
GEORGE MASON UNIVERSITY
Cambridge University: 21st Century Business in Europe
Site: England: Cambridge
Dates: 2 wks, Jun 21-Jul 3
Subjects: International business
Eligibility: *Level:* grads, adults, professionals *Requires:* 2.25 GPA, previous study in field *Age:* min 18
Credit: *Undergrad:* none *Grad:* 3 *Doc:* transcript
Instruction: *In:* English *Format:* study tour *Students:* mainly US
Costs: About $3,000 for VA residents, $3,500 for others *incl* tuition, housing, some meals, insurance, fees, excursions, railpass, ISIC *Nonrefundable fee*
Housing: *Arr by pgm:* hotels
Deadline: Apr 10
Other info: *US accredited sponsor:* yes *Began:* 1996 *Orient:* in US (1 day) *Misc:* May contact former participants. *Financial aid:* scholarships, work study *URL:* http://www.gmu.edu/dcpartments/cge
Contact: Ctr for Global Educ, George Mason Univ, Johnson Ctr, Rm 235, 4400 University Dr, Fairfax VA 22030-4444 *Ph:* 703-993 2154 *Fax:* 703-993 2153 *E-mail:* cge@gmu.edu

---

1526
MICHIGAN STATE UNIVERSITY
Public Affairs
Site: England: Cambridge
Dates: 4 wks, Jun-Jul
Subjects: Political science/politics
Eligibility: *Level:* fresh, sophs, jrs, srs *Requires:* 3.0 GPA, good acad standing *Age:* min 18
Credit: *Undergrad:* 6 *Grad:* none *Doc:* transcript
Instruction: *In:* English *Format:* lecture, seminar *Students:* mainly US
Costs: About $2,200 *incl* housing, most meals, insurance, excursions, support svcs *Nonrefundable fee*
Housing: *Arr by pgm:* residence halls
Deadline: Mar 2
Other info: *US accredited sponsor:* yes *Began:* 1983 *Orient:* in US *Misc:* Loans avail. May contact former participants. *Financial aid:* scholarships *URL:* http://studyabroad.msu.edu
Contact: Cheryl Benner, Study Abroad, Michigan State Univ, 109 Intl Ctr, East Lansing MI 48824-1035 *Ph:* 517-353 8920 *Fax:* 517-432 2082 *E-mail:* bennerc@msu.edu ▲

1527
SUNY ROCKLAND COMMUNITY COLLEGE
SUNY Rockland MTS/Honors International
Site: England: Cambridge *Host inst:* Cambridge Univ
Dates: 3 wks, contact sponsor
Subjects: Art history, English literature, Sciences, Shakespeare studies
Eligibility: *Level:* sophs, jrs, srs *Requires:* 3.3 GPA *Age:* min 18
Credit: *Undergrad:* 4 *Grad:* none *Doc:* transcript
Instruction: *In:* English *Format:* lecture, seminar, tutorial *Students:* mainly US
Costs: About $2,800 *incl* tuition, housing, some meals *Nonrefundable fee*
Housing: *Sponsor assists:* residence halls
Deadline: Apr 1
Other info: *US accredited sponsor:* yes *Began:* 1998 *Orient:* in US & abroad *Activities:* cultural events *Misc:* May contact former participants. *Financial aid:* scholarships *URL:* http://www.studyabroad.com/suny/rockland
Contact: Judy Dudderar, SUNY Rockland, 145 College Rd, Suffern NY 10901 *Ph:* 845-574 4205 *Fax:* 845-574 4425 *E-mail:* studyabroad@sunyrockland.edu

---

1528
UNIVERSITY OF CAMBRIDGE
Art History Summer School
Site: England: Cambridge
Dates: 3 wks, Jul 8-28
Subjects: Art history
Eligibility: *Level:* fresh, sophs, jrs, srs, grads, adults, teachers, professionals *Age:* min 18
Credit: *Undergrad:* none *Grad:* none *Doc:* certificate
Instruction: *In:* English *Format:* lecture, seminar *Students:* intl
Costs: UK 1,360 *incl* tuition, housing, some meals *Nonrefundable fee*
Housing: *Arr by pgm:* residence halls
Deadline: None; apply early
Other info: *US accredited sponsor:* no *Began:* 1987 *Activities:* excursions, cultural events *Misc:* Intensive honors option avail. Students can combine 2 Cambridge summer courses for 6 wks study. *URL:* http://www.cont-ed.cam.ac.uk/IntSummer
Contact: Student Relations Officer, Intl Div, Univ of Cambridge, Madingley Hall, Madingley, Cambridge CB3 8AQ, UK *E-mail:* intenq@cont.ed.cam.ac.uk

---

1529
UNIVERSITY OF CAMBRIDGE
English Literature Summer School
Site: England: Cambridge
Dates: 3 wks, Jul 29-Aug 18
Subjects: English literature
Eligibility: *Level:* fresh, sophs, jrs, srs, grads, adults, teachers, professionals *Age:* min 18
Credit: *Undergrad:* none *Grad:* none *Doc:* certificate
Instruction: *In:* English *Format:* lecture, seminar *Students:* intl
Costs: UK 1,360 *incl* tuition, housing, some meals *Nonrefundable fee*
Housing: *Arr by pgm:* residence halls
Deadline: None; apply early
Other info: *US accredited sponsor:* no *Began:* 1986 *Activities:* excursions, cultural events *Misc:* Intensive honors option avail. Students can combine 2 Cambridge summer courses for 6 wks study. *URL:* http://www.cont-ed.cam.ac.uk/IntSummer
Contact: Intl Div, Univ of Cambridge, Madingley Hall, Madingley, Cambridge CB3 8AQ, UK *E-mail:* intenq@cont.ed.cam.ac.uk

---

1530
UNIVERSITY OF CAMBRIDGE
History Summer School
Site: England: Cambridge
Dates: 3 wks, Jul 8-28
Subjects: History
Eligibility: *Level:* fresh, sophs, jrs, srs, grads, adults, teachers, professionals *Age:* min 18
Credit: *Undergrad:* none *Grad:* none *Doc:* certificate
Instruction: *In:* English *Format:* lecture, seminar *Students:* intl
Costs: UK 1,360 *incl* tuition, housing, some meals *Nonrefundable fee*
Housing: *Arr by pgm:* residence halls
Deadline: None; apply early
Other info: *US accredited sponsor:* no *Began:* 1990 *Activities:* excursions, cultural events *Misc:* Intensive honors option avail. Students can combine 2 Cambridge summer courses for 6 wks study. *URL:* http://www.cont-ed.cam-ac-uk/IntSummer
Contact: Student Relations Officer, Intl Div, Univ of Cambridge, Madingley Hall, Madingley, Cambridge CB3 8AQ, UK *E-mail:* intenq@cont.ed.cam.ac.uk

---

See "How To Use This Book" for definitions of terms used above. ▲ = See program sponsor's ad(s) in this book.

1531
UNIVERSITY OF CAMBRIDGE
International Summer School Term I
Site: England: Cambridge
Dates: 4 wks, Jul 9-Aug 3
Subjects: Full curriculum, Art history, Economics, History, Literature, Philosophy, Political science/politics, Sciences
Eligibility: *Level:* fresh, sophs, jrs, srs, grads, adults, teachers, professionals *Age:* min 18
Credit: *Undergrad:* none *Grad:* none *Doc:* certificate
Instruction: *In:* English *Format:* lecture, seminar *Students:* intl
Costs: UK 1,659 *incl* tuition, housing, some meals *Nonrefundable fee*
Housing: *Arr by pgm:* residence halls
Deadline: None; apply early
Other info: *US accredited sponsor:* no *Began:* 1923 *Activities:* excursions, cultural events *Misc:* Intensive honors option avail. Students can combine 2 Cambridge summer courses for 6 wks study. *URL:* http://www.cont-ed.cam.ac.uk/IntSummer
Contact: Intl Div, Univ of Cambridge, Madingley Hall, Madingley, Cambridge CB3 8AQ, UK *E-mail:* intenq@cont.ed.cam.ac.uk

---

1532
UNIVERSITY OF CAMBRIDGE
International Summer School Term II
Site: England: Cambridge
Dates: 2 wks, Aug 5-18
Subjects: Full curriculum, Art history, Economics, History, Literature, Philosophy, Political science/politics, Sciences
Eligibility: *Level:* fresh, sophs, jrs, srs, grads, adults, teachers, professionals *Age:* min 18
Credit: *Undergrad:* none *Grad:* none *Doc:* certificate
Instruction: *In:* English *Format:* lecture, seminar *Students:* intl
Costs: UK 1,015 *incl* tuition, housing, some meals *Nonrefundable fee*
Housing: *Arr by pgm:* residence halls
Deadline: None; apply early
Other info: *US accredited sponsor:* no *Began:* 1923 *Activities:* excursions, cultural events *Misc:* Intensive honors option avail. Students can combine 2 Cambridge summer courses for 6 wks study. *URL:* http://www.cont-ed.cam.ac.uk/IntSummer
Contact: Intl Div, Univ of Cambridge, Madingley Hall, Madingley, Cambridge CB3 8AQ, UK *E-mail:* intenq@cont-ed.cam.ac.uk

---

1533
UNIVERSITY OF CAMBRIDGE
Medieval Studies Summer School
Site: England: Cambridge
Dates: 3 wks, Jul 29-Aug 18
Subjects: Architectural history, History, Literature, Medieval studies, Political science/politics, Social history
Eligibility: *Level:* fresh, sophs, jrs, srs, grads, adults, teachers, professionals *Age:* min 18
Credit: *Undergrad:* none *Grad:* none *Doc:* certificate
Instruction: *In:* English *Format:* lecture, seminar *Students:* intl
Costs: UK 1,360 *incl* tuition, housing, some meals *Nonrefundable fee*
Housing: *Arr by pgm:* residence halls
Deadline: None; apply early
Other info: *US accredited sponsor:* no *Began:* 1996 *Activities:* excursions, cultural events *Misc:* Intensive honors option avail. Students can combine 2 Cambridge summer courses for 6 wks study. *URL:* http://www.cont-ed.cam-ac-uk/IntSummer
Contact: Intl Div, Univ of Cambridge, Madingley Hall, Madingley, Cambridge CB3 8AQ, UK *E-mail:* intenq@cont.ed.cam.ac.uk

---

1534
UNIVERSITY OF CAMBRIDGE
Science Summer School
Site: England: Cambridge
Dates: 3 wks, Jul 15-Aug 4
Subjects: Astronomy, Biology, Botany, Ecology/environmental studies, History, Interdisciplinary studies, Philosophy, Zoology
Eligibility: *Level:* fresh, sophs, jrs, srs, grads, adults, teachers, professionals *Age:* min 18
Credit: *Undergrad:* none *Grad:* none *Doc:* certificate
Instruction: *In:* English *Format:* lecture, seminar *Students:* intl
Costs: UK 1,360 *incl* tuition, housing, some meals
Housing: *Arr by pgm:* residence halls
Deadline: None; apply early
Other info: *US accredited sponsor:* no *Began:* 1999 *Activities:* excursions, field trips, cultural events *URL:* http://www.cont-ed.cam.ac.uk/IntSummer
Contact: Intl Div, Univ of Cambridge, Madingley Hall, Madingley, Cambridge CB3 8AQ, UK *E-mail:* intenq@cont.ed.cam.ac.uk

---

1535
UNIVERSITY OF CAMBRIDGE
Shakespeare Summer School
Site: England: Cambridge
Dates: 3 wks, Jul 8-28
Subjects: Shakespeare studies
Eligibility: *Level:* fresh, sophs, jrs, srs, grads, adults, teachers, professionals *Age:* min 18
Credit: *Undergrad:* none *Grad:* none *Doc:* certificate
Instruction: *In:* English *Format:* lecture, seminar *Students:* intl
Costs: UK 1,360 *incl* tuition, housing, some meals *Nonrefundable fee*
Housing: *Arr by pgm:* residence halls
Deadline: None; apply early
Other info: *US accredited sponsor:* no *Began:* 1994 *Activities:* excursions, cultural events *Misc:* Intensive honors option avail. Students can combine 2 Cambridge summer courses for 6 wks study. *URL:* http://www.cont-ed.cam-ac-uk/IntSummer
Contact: Intl Div, Univ of Cambridge, Madingley Hall, Madingley, Cambridge CB3 8AQ, UK *E-mail:* intenq@cont.ed.cam.ac.uk

---

1536
UNIVERSITY OF KANSAS
Legal History in Cambridge, England
Site: England: Cambridge *Host inst:* Univ of Cambridge
Dates: 1 mo, Jul 2-29
Subjects: History, Law
Eligibility: *Level:* fresh, sophs, jrs, srs, grads, adults *Requires:* good acad standing *Age:* min 18
Credit: *Undergrad:* 6 *Grad:* avail *Doc:* transcript
Instruction: *In:* English *Format:* lecture, seminar, tutorial *Students:* mainly US
Costs: $3,000 *incl* tuition, housing, some meals, excursions, medical evacuation svcs
Housing: *Arr by pgm:* residence halls with local students
Deadline: Rolling admissions
Other info: *US accredited sponsor:* yes *Began:* 1995 *Orient:* in US (1 day) *URL:* http://www.ukans.edu/~osa
Contact: Susan MacNally, Asst Dir, Study Abroad, 108 Lippincott, Lawrence KS 66045 *Ph:* 785-864 3742 *Fax:* 785-864 5040 *E-mail:* osa@ukans.edu ▲

1537
UNIVERSITY OF NEW HAMPSHIRE
UNH Cambridge Summer Program
Site: England: Cambridge *Host inst:* Univ of Cambridge
Dates: Jul 9-Aug 17
Subjects: English, History, Humanities
Eligibility: *Level:* sophs, jrs, srs, grads, adults *Requires:* good acad standing
Credit: *Undergrad:* 8 *Grad:* 8 *Doc:* transcript
Instruction: *In:* English *Format:* lecture, seminar *Students:* mainly US
Costs: $4,850 *incl* tuition, housing, most meals, fees, excursions
Housing: *Arr by pgm:* residence halls
Deadline: Mar 15 or until pgm filled
Other info: *US accredited sponsor:* yes *Began:* 1977 *Activities:* excursions, cultural events *Misc:* Loans avail. Guest speakers,

artists. *Financial aid:* scholarships *URL:* http://www.unh.edu/cambridge/
Contact: Prof Margaret-Love Denman, UNH Cambridge Summer Pgm, Hamilton Smith Hall, 95 Main St, Durham NH 03824-3574 *Ph:* 604-862 3962 *Fax:* 603-862 3962 *E-mail:* cambridge.program@unh.edu

---

1538
UNIVERSITY OF NORTH CAROLINA AT CHAPEL HILL
UNC-CH Summer Study at Cambridge University Summer Schools
Site: England: Cambridge *Host inst:* Madingley Hall, Cambridge
Dates: 4-8 wks, Jun-Jul
Subjects: Art history, Drama/theater, English literature, History, Medieval studies
Eligibility: Own students only. *Level:* sophs, jrs, srs, adults, teachers *Requires:* 2.8 GPA
Credit: *Undergrad:* avail *Grad:* avail *Doc:* transcript
Instruction: *In:* English *Format:* lecture, tutorial *Students:* intl
Costs: $1,948-$2,565 *incl* tuition, housing, all meals, insurance *Nonrefundable fee*
Housing: *Arr by pgm:* residence halls
Deadline: Early Feb
Other info: *US accredited sponsor:* yes *Began:* 1993 *Orient:* in US & abroad *Activities:* excursions, field trips *Financial aid:* scholarships *URL:* http://www.unc.edu/depts/abroad
Contact: Study Abroad, UNC-Chapel Hill, 12 Caldwell Hall CB-3130, Chapel Hill NC 27599-3130 *Ph:* 919-962 7001 *Fax:* 919-962 2262 *E-mail:* abroad@unc.edu

---

1539
UNIVERSITY OF UTAH and **UNIVERSITY OF CAMBRIDGE**
University of Cambridge International Summer School
Site: England: Cambridge *Host inst:* Univ of Cambridge
Dates: 2, 3, 4 or 6 wks, Jul-Aug
Subjects: Architecture, Art history, Civilization/culture, Economics, History, Literature, Political science/politics, Sociology
Eligibility: *Level:* jrs, srs, grads, adults, teachers, professionals *Requires:* 3.0 GPA *Age:* min 18, avg 23
Credit: *Undergrad:* avail *Grad:* none *Doc:* certificate
Instruction: *In:* English *Format:* lecture *Students:* intl
Costs: $1,895-$5,680 *incl* tuition, housing, all meals, local transport
Housing: *Arr by pgm:* residence halls
Deadline: Feb 15
Other info: *US accredited sponsor:* yes *Began:* 1983 *Orient:* in US & abroad *Activities:* excursions, cultural events *Misc:* Certificate awarded through Univ of Cambridge. May contact former participants. *URL:* http://www.saff.utah.edu/inter/
Contact: Laura Ashton, Study Abroad Adviser, Intl Ctr, Univ of Utah, 159 University Union, Salt Lake City UT 84112 *Ph:* 801-581 5849 *Fax:* 801-581 5914 *E-mail:* lashton@saff.utah.edu

---

CANTERBURY

1540
SOUTHWEST TEXAS STATE UNIVERSITY
SWT in England
Site: England: Canterbury *Host inst:* Univ of Kent, Canterbury
Dates: 5 wks, early Jul-early Aug
Subjects: Art, Art history, British studies, Creative writing, English literature, Government, Graphic arts/design, History, Independent study, International marketing, Law, Poetry, Political science/politics, Psychology
Eligibility: *Level:* adults *Requires:* 2.0 GPA *Age:* min 18, avg 25
Credit: *Undergrad:* 6 *Grad:* 6 *Doc:* transcript
Instruction: *In:* English *Format:* independent study, lecture, seminar, workshop *Students:* mainly US
Costs: $3,799 *incl* tuition, housing, some meals, intl airfare, fees, excursions *Nonrefundable fee*
Housing: *Arr by pgm:* residence halls
Deadline: Contact sponsor
Other info: *US accredited sponsor:* yes *Began:* 1992 *Orient:* in US (1 day) *Activities:* excursions, field trips, program travel, cultural events *Misc:* Combines coursework, on-site activities & excursions. May contact former participants. *Financial aid:* scholarships *URL:* http://www.history.swt.edu/canterbury/index.html
Contact: Dr Gene Bourgeois, Dir, History, Southwest Texas State Univ, San Marcos TX 78666-4616 *Ph:* 512-245 2142 *Fax:* 512-245 3043 *E-mail:* eb04@swt.edu

---

COLERAINE

1541
COUNCIL ON INTERNATIONAL EDUCATIONAL EXCHANGE (COUNCIL)
International Faculty Development Seminars-Coleraine
Site: Northern Ireland: Coleraine *Host inst:* Univ of Ulster
Dates: 8 days, Jun
Subjects: Conflict studies, Current events, Irish studies, Peace studies
Eligibility: *Level:* teachers, professionals *Requires:* must be full-time faculty at 2-yr or 4-yr inst
Credit: *Undergrad:* none *Grad:* none
Instruction: *In:* English *Format:* lecture, seminar *Students:* mainly US
Costs: $1,750 *incl* tuition, housing, most meals, fees, excursions, ITIC
Housing: *Arr by pgm:* hotels
Deadline: Mar 15
Other info: *US accredited sponsor:* no *Began:* 1991 *Orient:* abroad *Activities:* excursions, field trips, cultural events *Misc:* Seminar title: Peace & Conflict in Northern Ireland. May contact former participants. *URL:* http://www.ciee.org/ifds
Contact: Jennifer Ley, Council, 633 3rd Ave, New York NY 10017 *Ph:* 212-822 2747 *Fax:* 212-822 2779 *E-mail:* ifds@ciee.org ▲

CURSHAM

1542
PENNSYLVANIA STATE UNIVERSITY
Summer Abroad Sustainable Design
Site: England: Cursham
Dates: 6 wks, Jun-Jul
Subjects: Homestay, Horticulture, Landscape architecture
Eligibility: *Level:* fresh, sophs, jrs, srs *Requires:* 2.5 GPA, previous study in field *Age:* min 18
Credit: *Undergrad:* 6 *Grad:* none *Doc:* transcript
Instruction: *In:* English *Format:* art studio, lecture *Students:* mainly US
Costs: $3,615 for PA residents, $5,391 for others *incl* tuition, housing, some meals, excursions *Nonrefundable fee*
Housing: *Arr by pgm:* homestay
Deadline: Mar 1
Other info: *US accredited sponsor:* yes *Began:* 2001 *Orient:* in US (1 day) *Activities:* excursions, field trips *Financial aid:* scholarships *URL:* http://www.outreach.psu.edu/pssea/
Contact: Summer Abroad, Pennsylvania State Univ, 225 Penn State Conference Ctr, University Park PA 16802 *Ph:* 814-863 5170 *Fax:* 814-863 5190 *E-mail:* summerabroad@outreach.psu.edu

---

DALKEITH

1543
SUNY COLLEGE AT CORTLAND
Summer in Dalkeith, Scotland
Site: Scotland: Dalkeith *Host inst:* Newbattle Abbey
Dates: 5 wks, Jun 10-Jul 15

Subjects: Art history, Government, History, Political science/politics
Eligibility: *Level:* sophs, jrs, srs *Requires:* 2.5 GPA *Age:* min 18
Credit: *Undergrad:* avail *Grad:* none *Doc:* transcript
Instruction: *In:* English *Format:* lecture, seminar *Students:* mainly US
Costs: $3,100 *incl* tuition, housing, all meals, intl airfare, insurance, fees, excursions, books/materials, orient, airport transfer *Nonrefundable fee*
Housing: *Arr by pgm:* residence halls
Deadline: Apr 1
Other info: *US accredited sponsor:* yes *Began:* 1999 *Orient:* in US (1 day) *Activities:* excursions, field trips *Misc:* May contact former participants. *URL:* http://www.studyabroad.com/suny/cortland
Contact: Dr Del Janik, Pgm Coord, Intl Pgms, SUNY Coll at Cortland, PO Box 2000, Cortland NY 13045 *Ph:* 607-753 2209 *Fax:* 607-753 5989 *E-mail:* janikd@cortland.edu ▲

EASTBOURNE

1544
ILLINOIS STATE UNIVERSITY
University of Brighton's Summer School Program in England
Site: England: Eastbourne *Host inst:* Univ of Brighton
Dates: 4 wks, mid-May-mid-Jun
Subjects: Education/teaching, Field study
Eligibility: *Level:* sophs, jrs, srs, grads, adults, teachers, professionals *Requires:* 2.5 GPA, previous study in field, educ major
Credit: *Undergrad:* 6 *Grad:* 6 *Doc:* transcript
Instruction: *In:* English *Format:* directed field study, lecture, seminar *Students:* US & host country
Costs: $4,200 *incl* tuition, housing, all meals, intl airfare, insurance, fees, excursions
Housing: *Arr by pgm:* residence halls
Deadline: Feb 14
Other info: *US accredited sponsor:* yes *Orient:* in US *Activities:* excursions, field trips *URL:* http://www.its.ilstu.edu/intlstudies/
Contact: Dr Kay Moss, Illinois State Univ, Campus Box 5440, Normal IL 61790-5440 *Ph:* 309-438 5365 *Fax:* 309-438 3987 *E-mail:* rkmoss@ilstu.edu
Or Contact: Intl Studies, Illinois State Univ, Campus Box 6120, Normal IL 61790-6120 *Ph:* 309-438 5365 *Fax:* 309-438 3987 *E-mail:* oisp@ilstu.edu

EDINBURGH

1545
BEAVER COLLEGE, CENTER FOR EDUCATION ABROAD
Literature in Scotland
Site: Scotland: Edinburgh *Host inst:* Univ of Edinburgh
Dates: 3 or 6 wks, early to late Jul
Subjects: British studies, English literature
Eligibility: *Level:* sophs, jrs, srs, grads *Requires:* 3.0 GPA
Credit: *Undergrad:* 3 per session *Grad:* none *Doc:* transcript
Instruction: *In:* English *Format:* lecture, seminar *Students:* intl
Costs: $2,450 for 1 session, $3,975 for 2 sessions *incl* tuition, housing, some meals, insurance, ISIC, orient, transcripts *Nonrefundable fee*
Housing: *Arr by pgm:* residence halls
Deadline: Mar 31; apply early
Other info: *US accredited sponsor:* yes *Began:* 1992 *In coop with:* Consortium of Scottish Univs *Orient:* abroad (1 day) *Activities:* cultural events *Misc:* May contact former participants. *URL:* http://www.arcadia.edu/cea/
Contact: Ctr for Educ Abroad, Beaver Coll, 450 S Easton Rd, Glenside PA 19038 *Ph:* 888-232 8379 *E-mail:* cea@beaver.edu ▲

1546
EDUCATIONAL PROGRAMMES ABROAD (EPA)
International Internships
Site: Scotland: Edinburgh *Host inst:* Univ of Edinburgh
Dates: 8 wks, May 29-Jul 23
Subjects: Banking, Business/management, Conference/meetings management, Dance, Drama/theater, Education/teaching, Internships, Media studies, Museology, Political science/politics, Tourism
Eligibility: *Level:* jrs, srs, grads *Requires:* 3.0 GPA *Age:* avg 21
Credit: *Undergrad:* 8 *Grad:* none
Instruction: *In:* English *Format:* internship, lecture *Students:* mainly US
Costs: $4,250 *incl* tuition, housing, some meals *Nonrefundable fee*
Housing: *Arr by pgm:* apartments, homestay
Deadline: Mar 1
Other info: *US accredited sponsor:* no *Began:* 1996 *Orient:* abroad (3 days) *Activities:* excursions, field trips, cultural events *Misc:* Other internships avail. *URL:* http://www.studyabroad.com/epa
Contact: Eleanor Krawutschke, US Dir, Educ Pgms Abroad, 137 N Park St, Kalamazoo MI 49007 *Ph:* 616-382 0139 *Fax:* 616-382 5222 *E-mail:* epainterns@aol.com

1547
NORTH AMERICAN INSTITUTE FOR STUDY ABROAD
Literature in Scotland
Site: Scotland: Edinburgh *Host inst:* Univ of Edinburgh
Dates: 3 wks, Jul or Aug
Subjects: Civilization/culture, Literature
Eligibility: *Level:* fresh, sophs, jrs, srs *Requires:* 2.8 GPA *Age:* min 18, avg 20
Credit: *Undergrad:* 3 *Grad:* none *Doc:* transcript
Instruction: *In:* English *Format:* lecture, seminar, tutorial *Students:* intl
Costs: $2,490 for 3 weeks, $3,990 for 6 weeks *incl* tuition, housing, some meals, insurance, fees, ISIC
Housing: *Sponsor assists:* residence halls
Deadline: Apr 30; Nov 30 for scholarships
Other info: *US accredited sponsor:* no *Began:* 1998 *Orient:* abroad *Activities:* field trips, cultural events *Misc:* May contact former participants. *Financial aid:* scholarships *URL:* http://www.naisa.com
Contact: Dr Michael Currid, NAISA, 129 Mill St, Danville PA 17821 *Ph:* 570-275 5099 *Fax:* 570-275 1644 *E-mail:* naisa@naisa.com

1548
OHIO UNIVERSITY, COLLEGE OF OSTEOPATHIC MEDICINE
Charles J Cannon Edinburgh Geriatric Tutorial
Site: Scotland: Edinburgh *Host inst:* Univ of Edinburgh Geriatric Medicine Unit
Dates: 4 wks, Aug 6-31
Subjects: Medicine
Eligibility: Own students only. *Level:* grads *Requires:* previous study in field, 2 yrs medical sch, mini research project *Age:* avg 24
Credit: *Undergrad:* none *Grad:* avail *Doc:* transcript, certificate
Instruction: *In:* English *Format:* tutorial *Students:* mainly host country
Costs: Stipend awarded *incl* housing, all meals, intl airfare
Housing: *Sponsor assists:* residence halls
Deadline: Jun 30 of yr before pgm
Other info: *US accredited sponsor:* yes *Began:* 1985 *Orient:* in US & abroad (1 day) *Activities:* field trips *Misc:* May contact former participants. *Financial aid:* scholarships *URL:* http://www.tcom.ohiou.edu/oucom/

Contact: Barbara A Pfeiffer, Admin, Geriatric Medicine/Gerontology, Ohio Univ, Coll of Osteopathic Medicine, 357 Grosvenor Hall, Athens OH 45701 *Ph:* 740-593 2266 *Fax:* 740-593 2205 *E-mail:* pfeiffer@exchange.oucom.ohiou.edu

---

1549
OHIO UNIVERSITY
School of Visual Communication Photographic Field School
Site: Scotland: Edinburgh
Dates: 5 wks, mid-Jul-mid-Aug
Subjects: Field study, Photography
Eligibility: *Level:* jrs, srs, grads, teachers, professionals *Requires:* 2.0 GPA, previous study in field, portfolio review or completion of soph photography, 2 cameras & assorted lenses *Age:* min 20, avg 23
Credit: *Undergrad:* 15 qtr hrs *Grad:* 15 qtr hrs *Doc:* transcript
Instruction: *In:* English *Format:* directed field study, lecture *Students:* mainly US
Costs: About $5,000 for undergrads *incl* tuition, housing, intl airfare, railpass, film processing
Housing: *Arr by pgm:* residence halls
Deadline: Mar 1; Feb 15 for scholarships
Other info: *US accredited sponsor:* yes *Began:* 1986 *Orient:* in US *Activities:* field trips *Misc:* May contact former participants. *URL:* http://www.viscom.ohiou.edu
Contact: Prof Terry Eiler, Dir, VisCom in Scotland, Sch of Visual Communication, Ohio Univ, Rm 301 Seigfred, Athens OH 45701 *Ph:* 740-593 4895 *Fax:* 740-593 0190 *E-mail:* eiler@ohiou.edu

---

1550
UNIVERSITY OF ARIZONA
Summer in Edinburgh
Site: Scotland: Edinburgh
Dates: 4 wks, Jul 9-Aug 5
Subjects: Animation, Ceramics/pottery, Drawing, Graphic arts/design, Illustration, Independent study, Painting, Photography
Eligibility: *Level:* jrs, srs, grads
Credit: *Undergrad:* 3-6 *Grad:* 3-6 *Doc:* transcript
Instruction: *In:* English *Format:* art studio, independent study *Students:* mainly US
Costs: $2,600 *incl* tuition, housing, fees *Nonrefundable fee*
Housing: *Arr by student:* residence halls, apartments
Deadline: Jun 1
Other info: *US accredited sponsor:* yes *Began:* 1998 *Orient:* abroad *Misc:* May contact former participants. *Financial aid:* scholarships *URL:* http://w3.arizona.edu/~ciss/
Contact: Caroline Patrick, Univ of Arizona, 939 N Tyndall Ave, Tucson AZ 85721 *Ph:* 520-626 7180 *Fax:* 520-626 9004 *E-mail:* cpatrick@u.arizona.edu ▲

1551
UNIVERSITY OF EDINBURGH
Archaeology
Site: Scotland: Edinburgh *Host inst:* Univ of Edinburgh
Dates: Jun 23-Jul 6
Subjects: Archaeology, Field study, Homestay
Eligibility: *Level:* fresh, sophs, jrs, srs, grads, adults, teachers, professionals *Age:* min 18, avg 35
Credit: *Undergrad:* avail *Grad:* none *Doc:* certificate
Instruction: *In:* English *Format:* directed field study, lecture, seminar, tutorial *Students:* intl & host country
Costs: UK 435 *incl* tuition, excursions, books/materials
Housing: *Arr by pgm:* residence halls, apartments, homestay
Deadline: Jun 1
Other info: *US accredited sponsor:* no *Began:* 1967 *Activities:* excursions, field trips, cultural events *URL:* http://www.cce.ed.ac.uk/summer
Contact: Bridget Stevens, Intl Summer Schs, Ctr for Continuing Educ, Univ of Edinburgh, 11 Buccleuch Pl, Edinburgh EH8 9LW, Scotland, UK *E-mail:* b.stevens@ed.ac.uk

---

1552
UNIVERSITY OF EDINBURGH
Creative Writing
Site: Scotland: Edinburgh
Dates: 3 wks, Jun 30-Jul 20
Subjects: Creative writing, Homestay, Playwriting
Eligibility: *Level:* fresh, sophs, jrs, srs, grads, adults, teachers, professionals *Age:* min 18, avg 35
Credit: *Undergrad:* avail *Grad:* none *Doc:* certificate
Instruction: *In:* English *Format:* seminar, tutorial *Students:* intl & host country
Costs: UK 215 per wk *incl* tuition, books/materials
Housing: *Arr by pgm:* residence halls, apartments, homestay
Deadline: May 26
Other info: *US accredited sponsor:* no *Began:* 1967 *Activities:* excursions, field trips, cultural events *URL:* http://www.cce.ed.ac.uk/summer
Contact: Bridget Stevens, Intl Summer Schs, Ctr for Continuing Educ, Univ of Edinburgh, 11 Buccleuch Pl, Edinburgh EH8 9LW, Scotland, UK *E-mail:* b.stevens@ed.ac.uk

---

1553
UNIVERSITY OF EDINBURGH
Drama
Site: Scotland: Edinburgh
Dates: 3 wks, Jul 28-Aug 17
Subjects: Drama/theater, Field study, Homestay
Eligibility: *Level:* fresh, sophs, jrs, srs, grads, adults, teachers, professionals *Age:* min 18, avg 35
Credit: *Undergrad:* avail *Grad:* none *Doc:* certificate
Instruction: *In:* English *Format:* directed field study, lecture, practical training, seminar, tutorial *Students:* intl & host country
Costs: UK 400 *incl* tuition, excursions, books/materials, theater tickets
Housing: *Arr by pgm:* residence halls, apartments, homestay
Deadline: Jun 22
Other info: *US accredited sponsor:* no *Began:* 1967 *Activities:* excursions, field trips, cultural events *URL:* http://www.cce.ed.ac.uk/summer
Contact: Bridget Stevens, Intl Summer Schs, Ctr for Continuing Educ, Univ of Edinburgh, 11 Buccleuch Pl, Edinburgh EH8 9LW, Scotland, UK *E-mail:* b.stevens@ed.ac.uk

---

1554
UNIVERSITY OF EDINBURGH
Festival Arts Summer School
Site: Scotland: Edinburgh
Dates: Aug 11-31
Subjects: Civilization/culture, Dance, Drama/theater, Homestay, Music, Painting, Scottish studies
Eligibility: *Level:* adults *Age:* min 18, avg 35
Credit: *Undergrad:* avail *Grad:* none *Doc:* certificate
Instruction: *In:* English *Format:* lecture, seminar, tutorial *Students:* intl & host country
Costs: About UK 255 per wk *incl* tuition, theater & concert tickets
Housing: *Arr by pgm:* residence halls, apartments, homestay
Deadline: Jul 12
Other info: *US accredited sponsor:* no *Began:* 1967 *Activities:* field trips, cultural events *Misc:* Edinburgh Festival events. *URL:* http://www.cce.ed.ac.uk/summer

Contact: Bridget M Stevens, Ctr for Continuing Educ, Univ of Edinburgh, 11 Buccleuch Pl, Edinburgh EH8 9JT, Scotland, UK *E-mail:* b.stevens@ed.ac.uk

---

1555
UNIVERSITY OF EDINBURGH and **EDINBURGH FILMHOUSE**
Film Studies
Site: Scotland: Edinburgh *Host inst:* Univ of Edinburgh
Dates: 3 wks, Jul 28-Aug 17
Subjects: Film studies
Eligibility: *Level:* adults *Age:* min 18
Credit: *Undergrad:* avail *Grad:* none *Doc:* certificate
Instruction: *In:* English *Format:* lecture, seminar, tutorial *Students:* intl & host country
Costs: UK 370 *incl* tuition, cinema tickets
Housing: *Sponsor assists*
Deadline: Jun 29
Other info: *US accredited sponsor:* no *Began:* 1987 *Misc:* Video & film screenings. *URL:* http://www.cce.ed.ac.uk/summer
Contact: Bridget M Stevens, Ctr for Continuing Educ, Univ of Edinburgh, 11 Buccleuch Pl, Edinburgh EH8 9JT, Scotland, UK *E-mail:* b.stevens@ed.ac.uk

---

1556
UNIVERSITY OF EDINBURGH
Geology of Southeast Scotland
Site: Scotland: Edinburgh
Dates: 1 wk, Jul 7-14
Subjects: Field study, Geology, Homestay, Independent study
Eligibility: *Level:* fresh, sophs, jrs, srs, grads, adults, teachers, professionals *Age:* min 18, avg 35
Credit: *Undergrad:* avail *Grad:* none *Doc:* certificate
Instruction: *In:* English *Format:* directed field study, independent study, lecture, seminar, tutorial *Students:* intl
Costs: UK 205 *incl* tuition
Housing: *Arr by pgm:* residence halls, apartments, homestay
Deadline: May 24
Other info: *US accredited sponsor:* no *Began:* 1999 *Activities:* excursions, field trips, cultural events *URL:* http://www.cce.ed.ac.uk/summer
Contact: Bridget M Stevens, Dir, Intl Summer Courses, Ctr for Continuing Educ, Univ of Edinburgh, 11 Buccleuch Pl, Edinburgh EH8 9LW, Scotland, UK *E-mail:* b.stevens@ed.ac.uk

---

1557
UNIVERSITY OF EDINBURGH
International Summer Courses
Site: Scotland: Edinburgh *Host inst:* Univ of Edinburgh
Dates: Lat Jun-early Sep
Subjects: Archaeology, Creative writing, Drama/theater, Ecology/environmental studies, Film studies, Gaelic language, Geology, History, Literature, Music, Performing arts, Scottish studies, Visual arts
Eligibility: *Level:* adults *Age:* min 18
Credit: *Undergrad:* none *Grad:* none *Doc:* transcript
Instruction: *In:* English *Format:* directed field study, lang study, lecture, seminar, tutorial *Students:* intl

Costs: About UK 200 per wk *incl* excursions
Housing: *Arr by pgm:* residence halls, apartments
Deadline: None
Other info: *US accredited sponsor:* no *Activities:* excursions, field trips, cultural events *Financial aid:* scholarships *URL:* http://www.cce.ed.ac.uk/summer
Contact: Ursula Michels, CCE, Univ of Edinburgh, 11 Buccleuch Pl, Edinburgh, Scotland *E-mail:* ccesummer@ed.ac.uk

---

1558
UNIVERSITY OF EDINBURGH
Nature Conservation
Site: Scotland: Edinburgh
Dates: Jul 14-20
Subjects: Conservation, Ecology/ environmental studies, Homestay
Eligibility: *Level:* fresh, sophs, jrs, srs, grads, adults, teachers, professionals *Age:* min 18, avg 35
Credit: *Undergrad:* avail *Grad:* none *Doc:* certificate
Instruction: *In:* English *Format:* seminar, tutorial *Students:* intl & host country
Costs: UK 205 *incl* tuition, excursions, books/materials
Housing: *Arr by pgm:* residence halls, apartments, homestay
Deadline: Jun 15
Other info: *US accredited sponsor:* no *Began:* 1967 *Activities:* excursions, field trips, cultural events *URL:* http://www.cce.ed.ac.uk/summer
Contact: Bridget Stevens, Intl Summer Schs, Ctr for Continuing Educ, Univ of Edinburgh, 11 Buccleuch Pl, Edinburgh EH8 9LW, Scotland, UK *E-mail:* b.stevens@ed.ac.uk

---

1559
UNIVERSITY OF EDINBURGH
New Writing in English: Poetry, Short Stories
Site: Scotland: Edinburgh
Dates: 2 wks, Aug 18-31
Subjects: Drama/theater, English literature, Homestay, Poetry, Scottish studies
Eligibility: *Level:* fresh, sophs, jrs, srs, grads, adults, teachers, professionals *Age:* min 18, avg 30
Credit: *Undergrad:* avail *Grad:* none *Doc:* certificate
Instruction: *In:* English *Format:* seminar, tutorial *Students:* intl & host country
Costs: UK 240 *incl* tuition, excursions, books/materials
Housing: *Arr by pgm:* residence halls, apartments, homestay
Deadline: Jul 19
Other info: *US accredited sponsor:* no *Began:* 1967 *Activities:* excursions, field trips, cultural events *URL:* http://www.cce.ed.ac.uk/summer
Contact: Bridget Stevens, Intl Summer Schs, Ctr for Continuing Educ, Univ of Edinburgh, 11 Buccleuch Pl, Edinburgh EH8 9LW, Scotland, UK *E-mail:* b.stevens@ed.ac.uk

---

1560
UNIVERSITY OF EDINBURGH
Our Global Environment
Site: Scotland: Edinburgh
Dates: 1 wk, Jul 21-27
Subjects: Conservation, Ecology/ environmental studies, Field study, Homestay
Eligibility: *Level:* fresh, sophs, jrs, srs, grads, adults, teachers, professionals *Age:* min 18, avg 35
Credit: *Undergrad:* avail *Grad:* none *Doc:* certificate
Instruction: *In:* English *Format:* directed field study, lecture *Students:* intl & host country
Costs: UK 165
Housing: *Arr by pgm:* residence halls, apartments, homestay
Deadline: Jun 22; May 23 for scholarships
Other info: *US accredited sponsor:* no *Began:* 1998 *Activities:* excursions, field trips, cultural events *Financial aid:* scholarships *URL:* http://www.cce.ed.ac.uk/summer
Contact: Bridget Stevens, Ctr for Continuing Educ, Univ of Edinburgh, 11 Buccleuch Pl, Edinburgh EH8 9JT, Scotland, UK *E-mail:* b.stevens@ed.ac.uk

---

1561
UNIVERSITY OF EDINBURGH
Piano Workshop
Site: Scotland: Edinburgh
Dates: Aug 6-24
Subjects: Homestay, Piano
Eligibility: *Level:* adults *Requires:* previous study in field
Credit: *Undergrad:* none *Grad:* none *Doc:* certificate
Instruction: *In:* English *Format:* lecture, music lesson, practical training *Students:* intl & host country
Costs: UK 465
Housing: *Arr by pgm:* residence halls, apartments, homestay, furnished rms
Deadline: None
Other info: *US accredited sponsor:* no *Began:* 1965 *Misc:* Final public concert. Optional excursions in Scotland. *URL:* http://www.cce.ed.ac.uk/summer
Contact: Bridget M Stevens, Ctr for Continuing Educ, Univ of Edinburgh, 11 Buccleuch Pl, Edinburgh EH8 9JT, Scotland, UK *E-mail:* b.stevens@ed.ac.uk

---

1562
UNIVERSITY OF EDINBURGH
Presentation Skills: Oral Communication
Site: Scotland: Edinburgh
Dates: 1 wk, Jul 14-20
Subjects: Homestay, Speech/debate/ forensics
Eligibility: *Level:* fresh, sophs, jrs, srs, grads, adults, teachers, professionals *Age:* min 18, avg 35
Credit: *Undergrad:* avail *Grad:* none *Doc:* certificate
Instruction: *In:* English *Format:* lecture, practical training, workshop *Students:* mainly host country
Costs: UK 180
Housing: *Arr by pgm:* residence halls, homestay
Deadline: Jun 15; May 15 for scholarships
Other info: *US accredited sponsor:* no *Began:* 1998 *Activities:* cultural events *Financial aid:* scholarships *URL:* http://www.cce.ed.ac.uk/summer
Contact: Bridget Stevens, Ctr for Continuing Educ, Univ of Edinburgh, 11 Buccleuch Pl, Edinburgh EH8 9JT, Scotland, UK *E-mail:* b.stevens@ed.ac.uk

---

1563
UNIVERSITY OF EDINBURGH
Radio Reportage at the Edinburgh Fringe
Site: Scotland: Edinburgh
Dates: 1 wk, Aug 4-10
Subjects: Field study, Homestay, Independent study, Journalism, Media studies, Radio
Eligibility: *Level:* fresh, sophs, jrs, srs, grads, adults, teachers, professionals *Age:* min 18, avg 35
Credit: *Undergrad:* avail *Grad:* none *Doc:* certificate
Instruction: *In:* English *Format:* directed field study, independent study, lecture, seminar, tutorial *Students:* intl
Costs: UK 255 *incl* tuition
Housing: *Arr by pgm:* residence halls, apartments, homestay
Deadline: Jul 5
Other info: *US accredited sponsor:* no *Began:* 1999 *Activities:* excursions, field trips, cultural events *URL:* http://www.cce.ed.ac.uk/summer

Contact: Bridget M Stevens, Dir, Intl Summer Courses, Ctr for Continuing Educ, Univ of Edinburgh, 11 Buccleuch Pl, Edinburgh EH8 9LW, Scotland, UK *E-mail:* b.stevens@ed.ac.uk

---

1564
UNIVERSITY OF EDINBURGH
Scotland Through the Ages
Site: Scotland: Edinburgh
Dates: Jul 7-Aug 3
Subjects: Architecture, Art, Civilization/culture, Field study, History, Homestay, Literature, Scottish studies
Eligibility: *Level:* adults *Age:* min 18
Credit: *Undergrad:* avail *Grad:* none *Doc:* certificate
Instruction: *In:* English *Format:* directed field study, lecture, seminar, tutorial *Students:* intl & host country
Costs: UK 740 *incl* tuition, excursions
Housing: *Arr by pgm:* residence halls, apartments, homestay
Deadline: Jul 8
Other info: *US accredited sponsor:* no *Began:* 1989 *Activities:* excursions *URL:* http://www.cce.ed.ac.uk/summer
Contact: Bridget M Stevens, Ctr for Continuing Educ, Univ of Edinburgh, 11 Buccleuch Pl, Edinburgh EH8 9JT, Scotland, UK *E-mail:* b.stevens@ed.ac.uk

---

1565
UNIVERSITY OF EDINBURGH
Scottish Architecture
Site: Scotland: Edinburgh
Dates: 2 wks, Jul 7-20
Subjects: Architectural history, Field study, Homestay
Eligibility: *Level:* fresh, sophs, jrs, srs, grads, adults, teachers, professionals *Age:* min 18, avg 35
Credit: *Undergrad:* avail *Grad:* none *Doc:* certificate
Instruction: *In:* English *Format:* directed field study, lecture, seminar, tutorial *Students:* intl & host country
Costs: UK 375 *incl* tuition, excursions, books/materials
Housing: *Arr by pgm:* residence halls, apartments, homestay
Deadline: Jul 8
Other info: *US accredited sponsor:* no *Began:* 1967 *Activities:* excursions, field trips, cultural events *Misc:* 10 SCOTCAT points and/or certificate of attendance awarded. *URL:* http://www.cce.ed.ac.uk/summer
Contact: Bridget Stevens, Intl Summer Schs, Ctr for Continuing Educ, Univ of Edinburgh, 11 Buccleuch Pl, Edinburgh EH8 9LW, Scotland, UK *E-mail:* b.stevens@ed.ac.uk

---

1566
UNIVERSITY OF EDINBURGH
Scottish Gaelic Language and Culture
Site: Scotland: Edinburgh
Dates: Jun 30-Jul 20
Subjects: Civilization/culture, Gaelic language (beg/int/adv), Homestay, Literature
Eligibility: *Level:* adults *Age:* min 18, avg 35
Credit: *Undergrad:* avail *Grad:* none *Doc:* certificate
Instruction: *In:* English, Gaelic *Format:* lang study, lecture, tutorial *Students:* intl & host country
Costs: About UK 95 per wk *incl* tuition, excursions, books/materials
Housing: *Arr by pgm:* residence halls, apartments, homestay
Deadline: Jun 1
Other info: *US accredited sponsor:* no *Began:* 1979 *Activities:* excursions, cultural events *URL:* http://www.cce.ed.ac.uk/summer
Contact: Bridget M Stevens, Ctr for Continuing Educ, Univ of Edinburgh, 11 Buccleuch Pl, Edinburgh EH8 9JT, Scotland, UK *Fax:* 44-131-667-6097 *E-mail:* b.stevens@ed.ac.uk

---

1567
UNIVERSITY OF EDINBURGH
Scottish Philosophy
Site: Scotland: Edinburgh
Dates: 1 wk, Jul 7-13
Subjects: Civilization/culture, Homestay, Philosophy, Scottish studies
Eligibility: *Level:* fresh, sophs, jrs, srs, grads, adults, teachers, professionals *Age:* min 18, avg 35
Credit: *Undergrad:* avail *Grad:* none *Doc:* certificate
Instruction: *In:* English *Format:* tutorial *Students:* intl & host country
Costs: About UK 200 *incl* tuition, excursions, books/materials
Housing: *Arr by pgm:* residence halls, apartments, homestay
Deadline: Jun 7
Other info: *US accredited sponsor:* no *Began:* 2000 *Financial aid:* scholarships *URL:* http://www.cce.ed.ac.uk/summer
Contact: Bridget M Stevens, Ctr for Contining Educ, Univ of Edinburgh EH8 9JT, Scotland, UK *E-mail:* b.stevens@ed.ac.uk

---

1568
UNIVERSITY OF SOUTHERN MISSISSIPPI
Scotland Program
Site: Scotland: Edinburgh
Dates: 2 wks, Aug 7-22
Subjects: Dance, Drama/theater, Music
Eligibility: *Level:* sophs, jrs, srs, grads *Requires:* 2.0 GPA
Credit: *Undergrad:* 3 *Grad:* 3 *Doc:* transcript
Instruction: *In:* English *Format:* directed field study, lecture *Students:* mainly US
Costs: $2,545 for undergrads, $2,845 for grads *incl* tuition, housing, intl airfare, excursions *Nonrefundable fee*
Housing: *Arr by pgm:* apartments
Deadline: Jun 23
Other info: *US accredited sponsor:* yes *Began:* 1993 *Orient:* in US & abroad *Activities:* excursions, field trips, cultural events *Financial aid:* scholarships *URL:* http://www.usm.edu
Contact: Dr Tim Hudson or Frances Sudduth, Intl & Continuing Educ, Univ of Southern Mississippi, Box 10047, Hattiesburg MS 39406 *Ph:* 601-266 4344 *Fax:* 601-266 5699 *E-mail:* melissa.ravencraft@usm.edu

---

ESKDALE

1569
UNIVERSITY OF WISCONSIN-STOUT
Low Birker Archaeological Field School in England
Site: England: Eskdale
Dates: 5 wks, Jul 7-Aug 10
Subjects: Anthropology, Archaeology
Eligibility: *Level:* sophs, jrs, srs, grads, adults, teachers *Requires:* 2.5 GPA, reference letter
Credit: *Undergrad:* 4 *Grad:* none *Doc:* transcript
Instruction: *In:* English *Format:* directed field study, lecture *Students:* mainly US
Costs: $2,900 *incl* tuition, housing, all meals, fees *Nonrefundable fee*
Housing: *Arr by pgm:* hostels
Deadline: Apr 1
Other info: *US accredited sponsor:* yes *Began:* 1988 *In coop with:* Univ of Minnesota SMELT Project *Orient:* in US & abroad (1 day) *Misc:* May contact former participants. *URL:* http://www.uwstout.edu/intlpro
Contact: Karen Kundy, Pgm Asst, Univ of Wisconsin-Stout, 400 Bowman Hall, Menomonie WI 54751 *Ph:* 715-232 1896 *Fax:* 715-232 2500 *E-mail:* kundyk@uwstout.edu
Or Contact: Stephen Snyder, Dir, Intl Pgms, Univ of Wisconsin-Stout, 400 Bowman Hall, Menomonie WI 54751 *Ph:* 715-232 1896 *Fax:* 715-232 2500 *E-mail:* snyders@uwstout.edu

---

FROME

1570
COOKERY AT THE GRANGE
The Essential Cookery Course
Site: England: Frome (Somerset)
Dates: 4 wks, yr-round
Subjects: Culinary arts
Eligibility: *Level:* adults *Age:* min 17
Credit: *Undergrad:* none *Grad:* none *Doc:* certificate
Instruction: *In:* English *Format:* practical training *Students:* mainly host country
Costs: UK 1,990-2,390 *incl* tuition, housing, all meals, fees
Housing: *Arr by pgm:* twin rms & some single rms avail
Deadline: Contact sponsor
Other info: *US accredited sponsor:* no *URL:* http://www.hi-media.co.uk/grange-cookery
Contact: Mrs Jane Averill, Cookery at the Grange, The Grange, Whatley, Frome, Somerset BA11 3JU, UK *E-mail:* info@cookery-grange.co.uk

---

GRANTHAM

1571
UNIVERSITY OF CINCINNATI
Raymond Walters College British Study Program
Site: England: Grantham *Host inst:* Harlaxton Coll, Univ of Evansville
Dates: About 4 wks, Jun 13-Jul 9
Subjects: Biology, British studies, Drawing, Ecology/environmental studies, English literature, History, Literature, Painting, Social sciences
Eligibility: *Level:* sophs, jrs, srs, grads, adults, teachers, professionals *Requires:* completion of coll fresh English *Age:* min 18
Credit: *Undergrad:* 6 qtr hrs *Grad:* none *Doc:* transcript
Instruction: *In:* English *Format:* lecture, study tour *Students:* mainly US
Costs: $2,600 *incl* housing, all meals, intl airfare, fees, excursions
Housing: *Arr by pgm:* residence halls
Deadline: Feb 15
Other info: *US accredited sponsor:* yes *Began:* 1997 *Orient:* in US (1 day) *Activities:* field trips, cultural events *Misc:* Courses taught by Raymond Walters English faculty. May contact former participants. *URL:* http://www.uc.edu/global
Contact: Michael Ross, English, Raymond Walter Coll, Univ of Cincinnati, 9555 Plainfield Rd, Cincinnati OH 45236 *Ph:* 513-745 5764 *Fax:* 513-745 8315 *E-mail:* roosme@ucrwcu.rwc.uc.edu

---

1572
UNIVERSITY OF EVANSVILLE
Harlaxton College
Site: England: Grantham
Dates: 5 wks, May 15-Jun 16
Subjects: Business/management, Education/teaching, European studies, History, Languages, Music, Theater arts
Eligibility: *Level:* sophs, jrs, srs, adults, teachers *Requires:* good acad standing *Age:* min 18
Credit: *Undergrad:* 3-6 *Grad:* none
Instruction: *In:* English *Format:* lecture *Students:* mainly US
Costs: $260 per sem hr, $1150 room & board *incl* tuition
Housing: *Arr by pgm:* English manor house
Deadline: Mar 1
Other info: *US accredited sponsor:* yes *Began:* 1971 *Orient:* in US & abroad *Activities:* excursions, field trips, cultural events, sports *Misc:* May contact former participants. *URL:* http://www.ueharlax.ac.uk
Contact: Suzy Lantz, Univ of Evansville, 1800 Lincoln Ave, Evansville IN 47722 *Ph:* 800-856 2667; 812-488 1040 *Fax:* 812-475 6389 *E-mail:* sl5@evansville.edu

---

GREENOCK

1573
COLLEGE CONSORTIUM FOR INTERNATIONAL STUDIES and **BROOKDALE COMMUNITY COLLEGE**
Summer Program in Scotland
Site: Scotland: Greenock *Host inst:* James Watt Coll
Dates: 4 wks, Jun 4-29 or 8 wks, Jun 4-Jul 27
Subjects: European Union, International business, Internships
Eligibility: *Level:* fresh, sophs, jrs, srs, grads *Requires:* 2.5 GPA, 2 recommendation letters, transcript, essay, application for internship, 15 credits prior to application *Age:* min 18
Credit: *Undergrad:* 6-9 *Grad:* none *Doc:* transcript
Instruction: *In:* English *Format:* lecture *Students:* mainly US
Costs: $1,750 session 1 (no internship), $2,300 session 2 (internship) *incl* tuition, housing, some meals, fees, excursions
Housing: *Arr by pgm:* residence halls
Deadline: Apr 2 (internship); May 14 (no internship)
Other info: *US accredited sponsor:* yes *Orient:* in US & abroad *Activities:* excursions, field trips, cultural events *Misc:* Loans avail. May contact former participants. *Financial aid:* scholarships *URL:* http://www.ccisabroad.org
Contact: *See Index II for Members* CCIS, 2000 P St NW, Ste 503, Washington DC 20036 *Ph:* 800-453 6956; 202-223 0330 *Fax:* 202-223 0999 *E-mail:* info@ccisabroad.org
Or Contact: Emily Hagadorn, Mgr, Intl Ctr, Brookdale CC, 765 Newman Springs Rd, Lincroft NJ 07738-1597 *Ph:* 732-224 2174 *Fax:* 732-224 2980 *E-mail:* ehagadorn@brookdale.cc.nj.us ▲

LANCASTER

1574
LANCASTER UNIVERSITY
Changing Places-Lancaster and the Lake District
Site: England: Lancaster
Dates: Aug 16-Sep 15
Subjects: British studies, Civilization/culture, Field study, Geography, History, Literature, Tourism
Eligibility: *Level:* sophs, jrs, srs, grads, adults, teachers, professionals *Requires:* good acad standing
Credit: *Undergrad:* 4 *Grad:* none *Doc:* transcript
Instruction: *In:* English *Format:* directed field study, lecture, seminar, tutorial *Students:* intl
Costs: UK 1,070 *incl* tuition, housing, excursions, orient, assessment
Housing: *Arr by pgm:* residence halls
Deadline: Jul 10
Other info: *US accredited sponsor:* no *Began:* 1998 *Orient:* abroad *Activities:* excursions, field trips *Misc:* Students may participate in this course separately or as an intro to fall/yr at Lancaster or British univ. May contact former participants. *URL:* http://www.lancs.ac.uk/users/conted/suindex.htm
Contact: Ethel Sussman, North Amer Off, Lancaster Univ, 111 E 10th St, New York NY 10003 *Ph:* 212-228 0321 *E-mail:* ethelsussman@compuserve.com
Or Contact: Gerry Cotter, Lancaster Summer Univ, Lancaster Univ, Lancaster LA1 4YN, UK *E-mail:* summer.university@lancaster.ac.uk

---

1575
LANCASTER UNIVERSITY
This Scepter'd Isle: Aspects of British History and Culture
Site: England: Lancaster
Dates: Aug 16-Sep 15
Subjects: British studies, Civilization/culture, Field study, History, Literature, Political science/politics, Religion/theology
Eligibility: *Level:* sophs, jrs, srs, grads, adults, teachers, professionals *Requires:* good acad standing

Credit: *Undergrad:* 4 *Grad:* none *Doc:* transcript
Instruction: *In:* English *Format:* directed field study, lecture, seminar, tutorial *Students:* intl
Costs: UK 1,070 *incl* tuition, housing, excursions, orient, assessment *Nonrefundable fee*
Housing: *Arr by pgm:* residence halls
Deadline: Aug 6
Other info: *US accredited sponsor:* no *Began:* 1994 *Orient:* abroad *Activities:* excursions, field trips *Misc:* Students may participate in this course separately or as an intro to fall/yr at Lancaster or other British univs. May contact former participants. *URL:* http://www.lancs.ac.uk/users/conted/suindex.htm
Contact: Ethel Sussman, N Amer Off, Lancaster Univ, 111 E 10th St, New York NY 10003 *Ph:* 212-228 0321 *E-mail:* ethelsussman@compuserve.com
Or Contact: Gerry Cotter, Lancaster Summer Univ, Lancaster Univ, Lancaster LA1 1YN, UK *E-mail:* summer.university@lancaster.ac.uk

---

1576
LANCASTER UNIVERSITY
World About Us: Explorations in the History, Principles & Application of Science
Site: England: Lancaster
Dates: Aug 16-Sep 15
Subjects: Full curriculum, Classical languages, Ecology/environmental studies, Field study, Geology, Humanities, Medicine, Sciences, Social sciences
Eligibility: *Level:* sophs, jrs, srs, grads, adults, teachers, professionals *Requires:* good acad standing *Age:* avg 21
Credit: *Undergrad:* 4 *Grad:* none *Doc:* transcript
Instruction: *In:* English *Format:* directed field study, lab, lecture, seminar *Students:* intl
Costs: UK 1,070 *incl* tuition, housing, excursions, orient, assessment *Nonrefundable fee*
Housing: *Arr by pgm:* residence halls
Deadline: Jun 13
Other info: *US accredited sponsor:* no *Began:* 2001 *Orient:* abroad *Activities:* excursions, field trips *Misc:* Students may participate in this course separately or as an intro to fall/yr at Lancaster or British univ. May contact former participants. *Financial aid:* scholarships *URL:* http://www.lancs.ac.uk/users/conted/suindex.htm
Contact: Ethel Sussman, N Amer Off, Lancaster Univ, 111 E 10th St, New York NY 10003 *Ph:* 212-228 0321 *E-mail:* ethelsussman@compuserve.com
Or Contact: Gerry Cotter, Lancaster Summer Univ, Lancaster Univ, Lancaster LA1 4YN, UK *E-mail:* summer.university@lancaster.ac.uk

---

1577
UNIVERSITY OF KENTUCKY
Summer Study Program, England
Site: England: Lancaster *Host inst:* Lancaster Univ
Dates: 3 wks, Jul 6-24
Subjects: Accounting, Finance
Eligibility: *Level:* jrs, srs, grads *Requires:* previous study in field, good acad standing *Age:* min 19
Credit: *Undergrad:* 3-4 *Grad:* 3-4 *Doc:* transcript
Instruction: *In:* English *Format:* lecture *Students:* mainly US
Costs: $1,250 *incl* housing, some meals, railpass *Nonrefundable fee*
Housing: *Arr by pgm:* residence halls
Deadline: Apr 15
Other info: *US accredited sponsor:* yes *Began:* 1996 *Orient:* in US *Activities:* excursions, field trips, program travel, cultural events *Misc:* May contact former participants. *URL:* http://gatton.uky.edu/abroad.htm
Contact: Diana Rast, Bus & Econ, Univ of Kentucky, 237 Gatton, Lexington KY 40506-0034 *Ph:* 800-456 0965; 606-257 3865 *Fax:* 606-323 1920

LIVERPOOL

1578
UNIVERSITY OF LIVERPOOL
Liverpool's Black Roots
Site: England: Liverpool *Host inst:* Univ of Liverpool
Dates: 3 wks, Jun-Jul
Subjects: African-American studies, British studies, History, Music history, Sociology
Eligibility: *Level:* jrs, srs, grads, adults, teachers, professionals *Requires:* good acad standing
Credit: *Undergrad:* 3 *Grad:* none *Doc:* transcript
Instruction: *In:* English *Format:* directed field study, independent study, lecture, seminar, study tour, tutorial, workshop *Students:* intl
Costs: About UK 525 *incl* tuition, fees, excursions
Housing: *Arr by pgm:* residence halls
Deadline: Apr 30
Other info: *US accredited sponsor:* no *Began:* 1998 *Orient:* abroad (1 day) *Activities:* field trips, program travel *URL:* http://www.liv.ac.uk/ipm/summer.htm
Contact: Lindsay Davies, UKSRO, Sir Alastair Pilkington Bldg, Univ of Liverpool, Mulberry St, Liverpool L69 7SH, UK *E-mail:* summer.school@liverpool.ac.uk

---

LONDON

1579
AMERICAN INSTITUTE FOR FOREIGN STUDY (AIFS)
London Summer Art and Design Program
Site: England: London *Host inst:* Central St Martins Coll of Art & Design, Chelsea Coll of Art & Design, London Inst
Dates: 3 wks, Jul 6-28, 4 wks, Jul 27-Aug 18 or 6 wks, Jul 6-Aug 18
Subjects: Arts, British studies, Computer graphics, Drawing, Fashion design, Graphic arts/design, Humanities, Illustration, Interior design, Painting, Photography, Printmaking, Studio arts, Theater design
Eligibility: *Level:* fresh, sophs, jrs, srs, grads, professionals *Requires:* 2.0 GPA, previous study in field
Credit: *Undergrad:* avail *Grad:* avail *Doc:* transcript
Instruction: *In:* English *Format:* art studio, lecture *Students:* intl
Costs: $4,299 for 3 wks, $6,999 for 6 wks *incl* tuition, housing, some meals, intl airfare, resident dir
Housing: *Arr by pgm:* residence halls, apartments
Deadline: Mar 15
Other info: *US accredited sponsor:* no *Began:* 1991 *Orient:* abroad *Activities:* excursions, cultural events *Misc:* May contact former participants. *Financial aid:* scholarships *URL:* http://www.aifsabroad.com
Contact: Solandy Meza, Coll Div, AIFS, River Plaza, 9 W Broad St, Stamford CT 06902 *Ph:* 800-727 2437 ext 5163 *E-mail:* college.info@aifs.com ▲

1580
AMERICAN INSTITUTE FOR FOREIGN STUDY (AIFS) and RICHMOND, THE AMERICAN INTERNATIONAL UNIVERSITY IN LONDON
Richmond International Internship Program
Site: England: London
Dates: 12 wks, May 25-Aug 18
Subjects: Education/teaching, Finance, International business, International relations, Marketing, Media studies, Museology, Political science/politics, Social welfare/services, Theater arts
Eligibility: *Level:* jrs, srs, grads *Requires:*

2.5 GPA, previous study in field, good acad standing
Credit: *Undergrad:* 12 *Grad:* none *Doc:* transcript
Instruction: *In:* English *Format:* internship, lecture *Students:* mainly US
Costs: $7,479 *incl* tuition, housing, all meals, intl airfare, fees, resident dir
Housing: *Arr by pgm:* residence halls, homestay
Deadline: Mar 15
Other info: *US accredited sponsor:* yes *Began:* 1989 *Orient:* abroad *Activities:* excursions, cultural events *Misc:* May contact former participants. *Financial aid:* scholarships *URL:* http://www.aifs.com
Contact: Solandy Meza, Coll Div, AIFS, River Plaza, 9 W Broad St, Stamford CT 06902 *Ph:* 800-727 2437 ext 5163 *E-mail:* college.info@aifs.com ▲

1581
AMERICAN INSTITUTE FOR FOREIGN STUDY (AIFS) and **RICHMOND, THE AMERICAN INTERNATIONAL UNIVERSITY IN LONDON**
Richmond International Summer Session
Site: England: London
Dates: 3, 6 or 9 wks, May 25-Jul 28
Subjects: Full curriculum, Administration, Art history, Business/management, Computer sciences, Economics, English, Fine arts, History, Homestay, Performing arts, Philosophy, Religion/theology, Social sciences, Studio arts
Eligibility: *Level:* fresh, sophs, jrs, srs, grads, adults *Requires:* 2.0 GPA
Credit: *Undergrad:* avail *Grad:* none *Doc:* transcript
Instruction: *In:* English *Format:* lecture *Students:* intl
Costs: $3,779 for 3 wks, $5,139 for 6 wks, $6,399 for 9 wks *incl* tuition, housing, all meals, intl airfare, resident dir
Housing: *Arr by pgm:* residence halls, apartments, homestay
Deadline: Mar 15
Other info: *US accredited sponsor:* yes *Began:* 1968 *Orient:* abroad *Activities:* excursions, cultural events *Misc:* May contact former participants. *Financial aid:* scholarships *URL:* http://www.aifsabroad.com
Contact: Solandy Meza, Coll Div, AIFS, River Plaza, 9 W Broad St, Stamford CT 06902 *Ph:* 800-727 2437 ext 5163 *E-mail:* college.info@aifs.com ▲

1582
AMERICAN INTERCONTINENTAL UNIVERSITY
London Program
Site: England: London
Dates: 4-wk sessions, Jun & Jul, 8-wk sessions, May-Jul, Jul-Sep
Subjects: Advertising, Business administration, Commercial art, Communications, Fashion design, Fine arts, Graphic arts/design, Intercultural studies, Interior design, International business, Liberal arts, Marketing, Media studies, Photography, Public relations
Eligibility: *Level:* fresh, sophs, jrs, srs, grads, adults *Requires:* good acad standing, approval by acad adviser & dean/dept head, coll transcripts
Credit: *Undergrad:* 3-12 (5-20 qtr hrs) *Grad:* 3-9 (5-15 qtr hrs) *Doc:* transcript
Instruction: *In:* English *Format:* art studio, independent study, internship, lecture, seminar *Students:* intl
Costs: About $3,700 for 4 wks, $3,850-$7,295 for 8 wks *incl* tuition, housing
Housing: *Arr by pgm:* apartments
Deadline: None; 6 mos before pgm recommended
Other info: *US accredited sponsor:* yes *Began:* 1970 *Orient:* in US & abroad *Activities:* excursions, field trips, program travel, cultural events, sports *Misc:* Central London location. May contact former participants. *Financial aid:* scholarships *URL:* http://studyabroad.aiuniv.edu
Contact: Study Abroad Pgms, Amer InterContinental Univ, 6600 Peachtree-Dunwoody Rd, 500 Embassy Row, Atlanta GA 30328 *Ph:* 800-255 6839; 404-965 5300 *Fax:* 404-965 8006 *E-mail:* studyabroad@aiuniv.edu ▲

1583
BEAVER COLLEGE, CENTER FOR EDUCATION ABROAD
London Summer Internship
Site: England: London
Dates: 7 wks, early Jun-late Jul
Subjects: Internships
Eligibility: *Level:* jrs, srs *Requires:* 3.0 GPA, previous study in field
Credit: *Undergrad:* 6 *Grad:* none *Doc:* transcript
Instruction: *In:* English *Format:* directed field study, internship *Students:* mainly host country
Costs: $4,250 *incl* tuition, housing, insurance, ISIC, orient, transcript *Nonrefundable fee*
Housing: *Arr by pgm:* apartments, student houses
Deadline: Mar 10
Other info: *US accredited sponsor:* yes *Began:* 1991 *Orient:* abroad *Misc:* May contact former participants. *URL:* http://www.arcadia.edu/cea
Contact: Ctr for Educ Abroad, Beaver Coll, 450 S Easton Rd, Glenside PA 19038 *Ph:* 888-232 8379 *E-mail:* cea@beaver.edu ▲

1584
BEAVER COLLEGE, CENTER FOR EDUCATION ABROAD
Summer in London
Site: England: London
Dates: Jun 3-Jul 28
Subjects: Art, British studies, Drama/theater, Literature, Political science/politics
Eligibility: *Level:* sophs, jrs, srs, adults, precoll *Requires:* 3.0 GPA
Credit: *Undergrad:* 3-6 *Grad:* none *Doc:* transcript
Instruction: *Format:* directed field study, lecture, tutorial *Students:* mainly US
Costs: $2,750 for 1 course, $3,750 for 2 courses *incl* tuition, housing, insurance, excursions, ISIC, orient, transcript *Nonrefundable fee*
Housing: *Arr by pgm:* student housing
Deadline: Mar 31
Other info: *US accredited sponsor:* yes *Began:* 1999 *Orient:* abroad (2 days) *Activities:* excursions *Misc:* May contact former participants. *URL:* http://www.arcadia.edu/cea/
Contact: Ctr for Educ Abroad, Beaver Coll, 450 S Easton Rd, Glenside PA 19083 *Ph:* 888-232 8379 *E-mail:* cea@beaver.edu ▲

1585
BENTLEY COLLEGE
Summer Program in London, England
Site: England: London *Host inst:* Middlesex Univ
Dates: 6 wks, Jul-Aug
Subjects: Business/management, Marketing
Eligibility: *Level:* sophs, jrs, srs *Requires:* 2.7 GPA, faculty reference
Credit: *Undergrad:* 4-8 *Grad:* none *Doc:* transcript
Instruction: *In:* English *Format:* lecture *Students:* mainly host country
Costs: $3,700 *incl* tuition, housing, fees, excursions, ISIC *Nonrefundable fee*
Housing: *Arr by pgm:* residence halls with local students
Deadline: Mar 1
Other info: *US accredited sponsor:* yes *Orient:* in US & abroad *Activities:* excursions, field trips, cultural events *Misc:* May contact former participants. *URL:* http://ecampus.bentley.edu/dept/sa

Contact: Jill A Perry Redin, Dir, Study Abroad, Intl Ctr, Bentley Coll, 175 Forest St, Waltham MA 02452-4705 *Ph:* 781-891 3474 *Fax:* 781-891 2819 *E-mail:* study_abroad@bentley.edu

---

1586
BOSTON UNIVERSITY
Graduate Mass Communications Internships in London
Site: England: London
Dates: 14 wks, May-Aug
Subjects: Communications, International marketing, Internships, Media studies, Political science/politics
Eligibility: *Level:* grads *Requires:* 3.0 GPA, in major, current enrollment in MS/MA communication pgm or BS/BA in communications, good acad standing
Credit: *Undergrad:* none *Grad:* 16 *Doc:* transcript
Instruction: *In:* English *Format:* internship, lecture, seminar *Students:* mainly US
Costs: $13,950 *incl* tuition, housing, intl airfare
Housing: *Arr by pgm:* apartments
Deadline: Feb 15; Apr 1 for scholarships
Other info: *US accredited sponsor:* yes *Began:* 1994 *Orient:* in US & abroad *Misc:* May contact former participants. *Financial aid:* scholarships *URL:* http://www.bu.edu/abroad/
Contact: Intl Pgms, Boston Univ, 232 Bay State Rd, Boston MA 02215 *Ph:* 617-353 9888 *Fax:* 617-353 5402 *E-mail:* abroad@bu.edu ▲

1587
BOSTON UNIVERSITY
London Internship Program
Site: England: London
Dates: 14 wks, May-Aug
Subjects: Art history, Business/management, Communications, Comparative law, Drama/theater, Economics, Film studies, International relations, Internships, Journalism, Marketing, Media studies, Political science/politics, Psychology, Social policy
Eligibility: *Level:* sophs, jrs, srs *Requires:* 3.0 GPA, in major, good acad standing
Credit: *Undergrad:* 16 *Grad:* none *Doc:* transcript
Instruction: *In:* English *Format:* internship, lecture, seminar *Students:* mainly US
Costs: $10,100 *incl* tuition, housing
Housing: *Arr by pgm:* apartments
Deadline: Mar 1; Apr 1 for scholarships
Other info: *US accredited sponsor:* yes *Began:* 1983 *Orient:* in US & abroad *Misc:* Full-time resident dir. May contact former participants. *Financial aid:* scholarships *URL:* http://www.bu.edu/abroad/
Contact: Intl Pgms, Boston Univ, 232 Bay State Rd, Boston MA 02215 *Ph:* 617-353 9888 *Fax:* 617-353 5402 *E-mail:* abroad@bu.edu ▲

1588
BOSTON UNIVERSITY
Political Communication in the US and UK
Site: England: London
Dates: 6 wks, May-Jun
Subjects: Advertising, Communications, Political science/politics
Eligibility: *Level:* sophs, jrs, srs *Requires:* 3.0 GPA, in major, good acad standing
Credit: *Undergrad:* 8 *Grad:* none *Doc:* transcript

Instruction: *In:* English *Format:* lecture, seminar *Students:* mainly US
Costs: $5,100 *incl* tuition, housing, excursions *Nonrefundable fee*
Housing: *Arr by pgm:* apartments
Deadline: Mar 1; Apr 1 for scholarships
Other info: *US accredited sponsor:* yes *Began:* 1999 *Orient:* in US & abroad *Activities:* excursions *Misc:* Full-time resident dir. May contact former participants. *Financial aid:* scholarships *URL:* http://www.bu.edu/abroad/
Contact: Intl Pgms, Boston Univ, 232 Bay State Rd, Boston MA 02215 *Ph:* 617-353 9888 *Fax:* 617-353 5402 *E-mail:* abroad@bu.edu ▲

1589
BOSTON UNIVERSITY
Summer Program in London
Site: England: London
Dates: 6 wks, May-Jul
Subjects: Advertising, Art history, Civilization/culture, Comparative law, Economics, Film studies, Journalism, Media studies, Psychology, Social policy
Eligibility: *Level:* sophs, jrs, srs *Requires:* 3.0 GPA, in major, good acad standing
Credit: *Undergrad:* 8 *Grad:* none *Doc:* transcript
Instruction: *In:* English *Format:* lecture, seminar *Students:* mainly US
Costs: $5,100 *incl* tuition, housing, excursions
Housing: *Arr by pgm:* apartments
Deadline: Mar 1; Apr 1 for scholarships
Other info: *US accredited sponsor:* yes *Began:* 1990 *Orient:* in US & abroad *Activities:* excursions, field trips *Misc:* Full-time resident dir. May contact former participants. *Financial aid:* scholarships *URL:* http://www.bu.edu/abroad/
Contact: Intl Pgms, Boston Univ, 232 Bay State Rd, Boston MA 02215 *Ph:* 617-353 9888 *Fax:* 617-353 5402 *E-mail:* abroad@bu.edu ▲

1590
CAMBERWELL COLLEGE OF ARTS
Summer School
Site: England: London
Dates: 1-12 wks, Jul-Sep
Subjects: Art history, Bookbinding, Calligraphy, Ceramics/pottery, Conservation, Drawing, Fiber art, Graphic arts/design, Illustration, Metalworking, Painting, Photography, Printmaking, Television/video, Textiles
Eligibility: *Level:* adults *Age:* min 16
Credit: *Undergrad:* none *Grad:* none *Doc:* certificate
Instruction: *In:* English *Format:* art studio, directed field study, lecture, practical training, workshop *Students:* intl
Costs: UK 250 per wk *incl* tuition, fees
Housing: *Arr by pgm:* residence halls, apartments, hotels, hostels
Deadline: None
Other info: *US accredited sponsor:* no *Began:* 1986 *URL:* http://www.camb.linst.ac.uk
Contact: Jane Coyle, Camberwell Coll of Arts, Dali at Camberwell & Chelsea, Peckham Rd, London SE5 8UF, UK *E-mail:* dali@camb.linst.ac.uk

---

1591
CENTER FOR CULTURAL INTERCHANGE
Internship in UK
Site: England: London *Host inst:* TWIN

Dates: 1-3 mos, yr-round
Subjects: Homestay, Internships
Eligibility: *Level:* fresh, sophs, jrs, srs, grads *Requires:* 3.0 GPA *Age:* min 18, max 28, avg 20
Credit: *Undergrad:* none *Grad:* none *Doc:* certificate
Instruction: *In:* English *Format:* practical training *Students:* mainly host country
Costs: $2,850 for 2 mos *incl* tuition, housing, some meals, insurance, fees *Nonrefundable fee*
Housing: *Arr by pgm:* homestay
Deadline: 3 mos before pgm
Other info: *US accredited sponsor:* no *Began:* 1985 *In coop with:* TWIN *Orient:* in US & abroad (1 day) *Misc:* May contact former participants. *URL:* http://www.cci-exchange.com
Contact: Karen Hindhede Dir, or Kim Coyne, Outbound Pgm, Ctr for Cultural Interchange, 17 N 2nd Ave, St Charles IL 60174 *Ph:* 888-227 6231; 630-377 2272 *Fax:* 630-377 2307 *E-mail:* info@cci-exchange.com

---

1592
CENTRAL SAINT MARTINS COLLEGE OF ART & DESIGN
Summer School
Site: England: London
Dates: 1 wk, Jul-Sep
Subjects: Fashion design, Film studies, Fine arts, Graphic arts/design, Photography, Textiles
Eligibility: *Level:* fresh, sophs, jrs, srs, grads, adults *Age:* min 16
Credit: *Undergrad:* none *Grad:* none
Instruction: *In:* English *Format:* art studio, practical training, workshop *Students:* intl
Costs: UK 160-580 *incl* tuition
Housing: *Sponsor assists:* residence halls
Deadline: Contact sponsor
Other info: *US accredited sponsor:* no *Began:* 1989 *Activities:* cultural events *URL:* http://www.csm.linst.ac.uk/shortcourse
Contact: Short Course Coord, Central St Martins Coll of Art & Design, Southampton Row, London WC1B 4AP, UK WC1B 4AP

1593
CHELSEA COLLEGE OF ART AND DESIGN
Summer School
Site: England: London
Dates: 1-12 wks, Jul-Sep
Subjects: Art history, Computer aided design, Drawing, Fiber art, Field study, Illustration, Interior design, Painting, Photography, Television/video, Textiles
Eligibility: *Level:* adults *Age:* min 16
Credit: *Undergrad:* none *Grad:* none *Doc:* certificate
Instruction: *In:* English *Format:* art studio, directed field study, lecture, practical training, workshop *Students:* intl
Costs: UK 250 per wk *incl* tuition, fees
Housing: *Arr by student:* residence halls, apartments, hotels, hostels
Deadline: Until pgm filled
Other info: *US accredited sponsor:* no *Began:* 1986 *URL:* http://www.chelsea.linst.ac.uk
Contact: Jane Coyle, Dali at Chelsea & Camberwell, Camberwell Coll of Arts, Peckham Rd, London SE5 8UF, UK *E-mail:* dali@chelsea.linst.ac.uk

---

1594
COLLEGE CONSORTIUM FOR INTERNATIONAL STUDIES and **MONTANA STATE UNIVERSITY** and **SUNY ROCKLAND COMMUNITY COLLEGE**
Summer Session at Kingston University, London, England
Site: England: London *Host inst:* Kingston Univ
Dates: 5 wks, Jun 29-Aug 3
Subjects: British studies, Civilization/ culture, Literature, Social sciences
Eligibility: *Level:* sophs, jrs, srs *Requires:* 2.5 GPA *Age:* min 18
Credit: *Undergrad:* 6 *Grad:* none *Doc:* transcript
Instruction: *In:* English *Format:* lecture, seminar *Students:* intl
Costs: About $2,750 *incl* tuition, housing, excursions
Housing: *Arr by pgm:* residence halls
Deadline: Apr 1
Other info: *US accredited sponsor:* yes *Began:* 2001 *Orient:* abroad *Activities:* excursions, field trips *Financial aid:* scholarships *URL:* http://www.ccisabroad.org
Contact: *See Index II for Members* Jody Dudderar, SUNY Rockland CC, 145 College Rd, Suffern NY 10901 *Ph:* 845-574 4205 *Fax:* 845-574 4423 *E-mail:* study-abroad@sunyrockland.edu
Or Contact: Kevin Hood, Montana State Univ, 400 Culbertson Hall, PO Box 172260, Bozeman MT 59717 *Ph:* 406-994 4031 *Fax:* 406-994 1619 *E-mail:* khood@montana.edu
Or Contact: CCIS, 2000 P St NW, Ste 503, Washington DC 20036 *Ph:* 800-453 6956; 202-223 0330 *Fax:* 202-223 0999 *E-mail:* info@ccisabroad.org ▲

1595
COLLEGE CONSORTIUM FOR INTERNATIONAL STUDIES and **SUNY ROCKLAND COMMUNITY COLLEGE** and **MONTANA STATE UNIVERSITY**
Summer Session at Thames Valley University, London
Site: England: London *Host inst:* Thames Valley Univ
Dates: 1 mo, Jun 6-Jul 6
Subjects: Art, British studies, Drama/ theater, European studies, History, Homestay, Psychology
Eligibility: *Level:* fresh, sophs, jrs, srs *Requires:* 2.5 GPA, good acad standing *Age:* min 18
Credit: *Undergrad:* 6 *Grad:* none *Doc:* transcript
Instruction: *In:* English *Format:* lecture, seminar *Students:* mainly US
Costs: $2,250 *incl* tuition, housing, some meals, fees, excursions, books/materials, ISIC, transport pass *Nonrefundable fee*
Housing: *Arr by pgm:* homestay
Deadline: Apr 1
Other info: *US accredited sponsor:* yes *Began:* 1989 *Activities:* excursions, field trips *Misc:* May contact former participants. *Financial aid:* scholarships *URL:* http://www.ccisabroad.org
Contact: *See Index II for Members* Jody Dudderar, Dir, Ctr for Intl Studies, SUNY Rockland CC, 145 College Rd, Suffern NY 10901 *Ph:* 845-574 4205 *Fax:* 845-574 4423 *E-mail:* study-abroad@sunyrockland.edu
Or Contact: Kevin Hood, Study Abroad Adviser, Intl Pgms, Montana State Univ, 400 Culbertson Hall, Bozeman MT 59717 *Ph:* 406-994 4031 *Fax:* 406-994 1619 *E-mail:* khood@montana.edu
Or Contact: Coll Consortium for Intl Studies (CCIS), 2000 P St NW, Ste 503, Washington DC 20036 *Ph:* 800-453 6956 *Fax:* 202-223 0999 *E-mail:* info@ccisabroad.org ▲

1596
COMMITTEE ON INSTITUTIONAL COOPERATION/AESOP LONDON INTERNSHIPS
Parliamentary and Other Political Internships in London
Site: England: London *Host inst:* EPA
Dates: Late May-Late Jul
Subjects: Homestay, Internships, Political science/politics
Eligibility: Students of member insts only. *Level:* jrs, srs *Requires:* 3.0 GPA, background in politics, course in British politics
Credit: *Undergrad:* avail *Grad:* none *Doc:* certificate
Instruction: *In:* English *Format:* internship, seminar *Students:* mainly US
Costs: $4,800 *incl* tuition, housing, some meals, fees, medical evacuation insurance
Housing: *Arr by pgm:* apartments, homestay
Deadline: Dec 15
Other info: *US accredited sponsor:* yes *Orient:* in US & abroad *Misc:* Internships avail in the British Parliament & other political agencies. May contact former participants. *Financial aid:* scholarships *URL:* http://www.server.ips.uiuc.edu/ips/sao/index.html
Contact: *See Index II for Members* Study Abroad, Univ of Illinois, 115 Intl Studies Bldg, 910 S Fifth, Champaign IL 61820 *Ph:* 217-333 6322 *Fax:* 217-244 0249 *E-mail:* sao@uiuc.edu

---

1597
COOPERATIVE CENTER FOR STUDY ABROAD
London Summer Program
Site: England: London
Dates: Jul 5-Aug 6
Subjects: Anthropology, Art, Business/ management, Criminology, Drama/theater, English, History, Journalism, Literature, Marketing, Music, Photography, Psychology, Religion/theology, Social work
Eligibility: *Level:* fresh, sophs, jrs, srs, grads, adults, teachers, professionals *Requires:* 2.0 GPA, recommendation *Age:* min 18
Credit: *Undergrad:* 3-6 *Grad:* 3-6 *Doc:* transcript
Instruction: *In:* English *Format:* lecture, seminar, tutorial *Students:* mainly US
Costs: $3,595 *incl* housing, some meals, intl airfare, excursions, railpass, bus/ subway pass, ISIC/ITIC *Nonrefundable fee*
Housing: *Arr by pgm:* residence halls
Deadline: Mar 1
Other info: *US accredited sponsor:* yes *Began:* 1983 *Orient:* in US & abroad *Activities:* field trips, cultural events *Misc:* Excursions to Salisbury & Stonehenge, London City tour. Optional trips to Edinburgh, Paris. *Financial aid:* scholarships *URL:* http://www.nku.edu/ccsa
Contact: *See Index II for Members* Dr Michael A Klembara or Robin Byerly, Coop Ctr for Study Abroad, Northern Kentucky Univ, BEP 301, Highland Heights KY 41099 *Ph:* 800-319 6015; 859-572 6512 *Fax:* 859-572 6650 *E-mail:* ccsa@nku.edu

---

1598
COOPERATIVE CENTER FOR STUDY ABROAD
London Winter Program
Site: England: London
Dates: Dec 26-Jan 8
Subjects: Accounting, Art, Business/ management, Communications, Drama/ theater, English, Finance, Geology, Hospitality management, Journalism, Literature, Marketing, Photography
Eligibility: *Level:* fresh, sophs, jrs, srs, grads, adults, teachers, professionals *Requires:* 2.0 GPA, recommendation *Age:* min 18
Credit: *Undergrad:* 3 *Grad:* 3 *Doc:* transcript
Instruction: *In:* English *Format:* lecture, study tour, tutorial *Students:* mainly US
Costs: $2,595 *incl* housing, some meals, intl airfare, excursions, transit pass, theater tickets *Nonrefundable fee*
Housing: *Arr by pgm:* hotels
Deadline: Oct 6
Other info: *US accredited sponsor:* yes *Began:* 1973 *Orient:* in US & abroad *Activities:* field trips, cultural events *Misc:* Excursions to Stratford, Stonehenge, Bath, Canterbury, Dover. ISIC/ITIC. *Financial aid:* scholarships *URL:* http://www.nku.edu/ccsa

Contact: *See Index II for Members* Dr Michael A Klembara or Robin Byerly, Coop Ctr for Study Abroad, Northern Kentucky Univ, BEP 301, Highland Heights KY 41099 *Ph:* 800-319 6015; 859-572 6512 *Fax:* 859-572 6650 *E-mail:* ccsa@nku.edu

---

1599
CULTURAL EXPERIENCES ABROAD (CEA)
Study Liberal Arts and Sciences in London
Site: England: London *Host inst:* Middlesex Univ
Dates: Jun, Jul, Aug
Subjects: Art history, British studies, Business/management, Civilization/culture, Communications, Computer sciences, Drama/theater, Ecology/environmental studies, Education/teaching, English literature, History, International relations, Journalism, Liberal arts, Political science/politics
Eligibility: *Level:* fresh, sophs, jrs, srs, grads, precoll *Requires:* 2.5 GPA, recommendation letter, transcript *Age:* min 17, avg 20
Credit: *Undergrad:* 3-10 per term *Grad:* 3-10 per term *Doc:* transcript
Instruction: *In:* English *Format:* art studio, independent study, internship, lab, lecture, study tour, tutorial, volunteer/svc *Students:* intl
Costs: $4,000-$5,000 per session *incl* tuition, housing, insurance, fees, excursions, orient, airport transfers *Nonrefundable fee*
Housing: *Arr by pgm:* residence halls with local students
Deadline: Rolling admissions
Other info: *US accredited sponsor:* no *Orient:* abroad *Activities:* excursions, field trips, program travel, cultural events, sports *Misc:* Excursions to Scotland, France, throughout England. Support svcs. E-mail. May contact former participants. *Financial aid:* scholarships *URL:* http://www.travelabroad.com
Contact: CEA Study Abroad, 1400 E Southern Ave, Ste B-108 AZ 85282-8011 *Ph:* 480-557 7900 *Fax:* 480-557 7926 *E-mail:* england@travelabroad.com

---

1600
DICKINSON COLLEGE
Summer Session in England
Site: England: London
Dates: 6 wks, late May-early Jul
Subjects: Art history, Drama/theater, Literature, Music history
Eligibility: *Level:* sophs, jrs, srs *Requires:* 2.5 GPA
Credit: *Undergrad:* 8 *Grad:* none
Instruction: *In:* English *Format:* directed field study, lecture *Students:* mainly US
Costs: About $5,900 *incl* tuition, housing, all meals, intl airfare, fees, excursions
Housing: *Arr by pgm:* residence halls, hotels
Deadline: Mar 1
Other info: *US accredited sponsor:* yes *Began:* 1976 *Orient:* in US *Activities:* excursions, cultural events *URL:* http://www.dickinson.edu/departments/ocs/summer.html
Contact: Global Educ, Dickinson Coll, PO Box 1773, Carlisle PA 17013-2896 *Ph:* 717-245 1341 *Fax:* 717-245 1688 *E-mail:* ocs@dickinson.edu

---

1601
DIS, DENMARK'S INTERNATIONAL STUDY PROGRAM
Summer Internship in London
Site: England: London
Dates: 6 wks, May 27-Jul 6
Subjects: Architecture, Arts, Banking, Biology, Business/management, Communications, Education/teaching, Graphic arts/design, Health sciences, Hotel management, International relations, Law, Media studies, Political science/politics, Tourism
Eligibility: Own students only. *Level:* sophs, jrs, srs, grads *Requires:* 3.0 GPA, fall/spring/summer sem at DIS
Credit: *Undergrad:* none *Grad:* none *Doc:* transcript, certificate
Instruction: *In:* English *Format:* internship *Students:* mainly US
Costs: $3,880 *incl* tuition, housing, insurance, fees, excursions, books/materials, railpass, internship placement *Nonrefundable fee*
Housing: *Arr by pgm:* residence halls with local students
Deadline: Rolling admissions
Other info: *US accredited sponsor:* yes *Began:* 2001 *Orient:* abroad (2 days) *Activities:* excursions, cultural events, sports *Financial aid:* scholarships *URL:* http://www.disp.dk
Contact: *See Index II for Members* Charlotte Simonsen, DIS N Amer Off, 214 Heller Hall, 271 19th Ave S, Minneapolis MN 55455 *Ph:* 800-247 3477; 612-626 7679 *Fax:* 612-626 8009 *E-mail:* dis@umn.edu
Or Contact: DIS, Vestergade 7, 1456 Copenhagen, Denmark *E-mail:* dis@disp.dk

---

1602
DREXEL UNIVERSITY
Drexel in London
Site: England: London
Dates: 6 or 12 wks, mid-Jun-late Aug
Subjects: Business/management, Culinary arts, Economics, Fashion design, Fashion merchandising, Finance, Graphic arts/design, Hospitality management, Hotel management, International business, Marketing, Photography, Restaurant management, Retailing, Textiles
Eligibility: *Level:* fresh, sophs, jrs, srs, adults *Requires:* 3.0 GPA *Age:* avg 20
Credit: *Undergrad:* 3 per course *Grad:* none *Doc:* transcript
Instruction: *In:* English *Format:* directed field study, independent study, internship, lecture, practical training, seminar, tutorial *Students:* mainly US
Costs: $4,100 for 6 wks, $8,200 for 12 wks *incl* tuition, housing *Nonrefundable fee*
Housing: *Arr by pgm:* residence halls
Deadline: Apr 15
Other info: *US accredited sponsor:* yes *Began:* 1998 *Orient:* in US & abroad (3 days) *Activities:* excursions, field trips, cultural events *Misc:* May contact former participants. *Financial aid:* scholarships *URL:* http://www.drexel.edu/International
Contact: Study Abroad, Drexel Univ, 3141 Chestnut St, 2-230, Philadelphia PA 19104 *Ph:* 215-895 1704 *Fax:* 215-895 6184 *E-mail:* studyabroad@drexel.edu

---

1603
DREXEL UNIVERSITY
Drexel in London: International Business
Site: England: London
Dates: 6 or 12 wks, mid-Jun-late Aug
Subjects: Business/management, Culinary arts, Economics, Fashion design, Fashion merchandising, Finance, Graphic arts/design, International business, Marketing, Photography, Restaurant management, Retailing
Eligibility: *Level:* fresh, sophs, jrs, srs, adults *Requires:* 3.0 GPA *Age:* avg 20
Credit: *Undergrad:* 3 per course *Grad:* none *Doc:* transcript
Instruction: *In:* English *Format:* independent study, internship, lecture, practical training, seminar, tutorial *Students:* mainly US
Costs: $4,100 for 6 wks, $8,200 for 12 wks *incl* tuition, housing *Nonrefundable fee*
Housing: *Arr by pgm:* residence halls
Deadline: Apr 15
Other info: *US accredited sponsor:* yes *Began:* 1998 *Orient:* in US & abroad (3 days) *Activities:* excursions, field trips, cultural events *Misc:* May contact former participants. *Financial aid:* scholarships *URL:* http://www.drexel.edu/international/studyabroad
Contact: Study Abroad, Drexel Univ, 3141 Chestnut St, 2-230, Philadelphia PA 19104 *Ph:* 215-895 1704 *Fax:* 215-895 6184 *E-mail:* studyabroad@drexel.edu

---

1604
DUKE UNIVERSITY
Duke in London-Drama
Site: England: London *Host inst:* Univ Coll London
Dates: Late Jun-early Aug
Subjects: Drama/theater
Eligibility: *Level:* fresh, sophs, jrs, srs *Requires:* good acad standing, transcript
Credit: *Undergrad:* 2 credits *Grad:* none *Doc:* transcript
Instruction: *In:* English *Format:* lecture *Students:* mainly US
Costs: $6,725 *incl* tuition, housing, all meals, excursions, theater entrance fees
Housing: *Arr by pgm:* residence halls
Deadline: Feb 16
Other info: *US accredited sponsor:* yes *Began:* 1987 *Activities:* excursions, cultural events *URL:* http://www.aas.duke.edu/study_abroad/
Contact: Study Abroad, Duke Univ, 121 Allen Bldg, Box 90057, Durham NC 27708-0057 *Ph:* 919-684 2174 *Fax:* 919-684 3083 *E-mail:* abroad@asdean.duke.edu

---

1605
DUKE UNIVERSITY
Duke in London-Media
Site: England: London *Host inst:* LSE
Dates: Early Jul-mid-Aug
Subjects: British studies, Media studies, Political science/politics
Eligibility: *Level:* sophs, jrs, srs *Requires:* good acad standing
Credit: *Undergrad:* 2 credits *Grad:* none *Doc:* transcript
Instruction: *In:* English *Format:* internship, lecture, seminar *Students:* mainly US
Costs: $6,725 *incl* tuition, housing, all meals, fees, excursions
Housing: *Arr by pgm:* residence halls
Deadline: Feb 16
Other info: *US accredited sponsor:* yes *Began:* 1988 *Orient:* in US (1 day) *Activities:* excursions, program travel, cultural events *Misc:* May contact former participants. *URL:* http://www.aas.duke.edu/study_abroad/
Contact: Study Abroad, Duke Univ, 121 Allen Bldg, Box 90057, Durham NC 27708-0057 *Ph:* 919-684 2174 *Fax:* 919-684 3083 *E-mail:* abroad@asdean.duke.edu

---

1606
EDUCATIONAL PROGRAMMES ABROAD (EPA)
London Internships
Site: England: London *Host inst:* Birkbeck Coll
Dates: 8 wks, May 29-Jul 23 or Jun 12-Aug 6
Subjects: Advertising, Architecture, Art, Arts management, Business/management, Drama/theater, Ecology/environmental studies, Education/teaching, Graphic arts/design, Health sciences, Law, Media studies, Political science/politics, Publishing, Sociology
Eligibility: *Level:* jrs, srs, grads *Requires:* 3.0 GPA *Age:* avg 21
Credit: *Undergrad:* avail *Grad:* none
Instruction: *In:* English *Format:* internship *Students:* mainly US
Costs: $4,300 *incl* tuition, housing, some meals *Nonrefundable fee*
Housing: *Sponsor assists:* apartments, homestay
Deadline: Mar 1
Other info: *US accredited sponsor:* no *Began:* 1975 *Orient:* abroad (3 days) *Activities:* excursions, field trips *Misc:* Other internships avail. May contact former participants. *URL:* http://studyabroad.com/epa

Contact: Eleanor Krawutschke, US Dir, Educ Pgms Abroad, 137 N Park St, Kalamazoo MI 49007 *Ph:* 616-382 0139 *Fax:* 616-382 5222 *E-mail:* epainterns@aol.com

---

1607
FASHION INSTITUTE OF TECHNOLOGY
Domestic Arts and Architecture in Britain: 1500-1830
Site: England: London
Dates: 3 wks, Aug 2-24
Subjects: Antiques, Architectural history, British studies, Furnishings/furniture, Interior design, Medieval studies, Renaissance studies
Eligibility: *Level:* fresh, sophs, jrs, srs, grads, adults, professionals *Requires:* interview by faculty member teaching course *Age:* min 18
Credit: *Undergrad:* 3 *Grad:* none *Doc:* transcript
Instruction: *In:* English *Format:* study tour *Students:* mainly US
Costs: About $2,465 for NY residents, $2,654 for others *incl* tuition, housing, intl airfare, fees, excursions
Housing: *Arr by pgm:* hotels
Deadline: Mar 3
Other info: *US accredited sponsor:* yes *Began:* 1978 *Orient:* in US *Activities:* excursions, field trips, program travel *Misc:* May contact former participants. *URL:* http://www.fitnyc.suny.edu
Contact: Georgianna Appignani, Dir, Intl Educ, FIT, 7th Ave at 27th St, New York NY 10001-5992 *Ph:* 212-217 7633 *Fax:* 212-217 7010
Or Contact: Carole De Santis, Coord, FIT, 7th Ave at 27th St, New York NY 10001-5992 *Ph:* 212-217 7633 *Fax:* 212-217 7010 *E-mail:* desantca@sfitva.cc.fitsuny.edu

---

1608
FASHION INSTITUTE OF TECHNOLOGY
Marketing Communications: An International Perspective
Site: England: London
Dates: 4 wks, Jun-Jul
Subjects: British studies, Interdisciplinary studies, International relations, Linguistics, Media studies, Psychology, Public relations, Social anthropology, Sociology
Eligibility: *Level:* sophs, jrs, srs *Requires:* interview by faculty member teaching course *Age:* min 18
Credit: *Undergrad:* 4 *Grad:* none *Doc:* transcript
Instruction: *In:* English *Format:* lecture *Students:* mainly US
Costs: About $2,200 for NY residents, $2,710 for others *incl* tuition, housing, intl airfare, fees
Housing: *Arr by pgm:* residence halls
Deadline: Mar 3
Other info: *US accredited sponsor:* yes *Began:* 1984 *Orient:* in US *Activities:* field trips *Misc:* May contact former participants. *URL:* http://www.fitnyc.suny.edu
Contact: Georgianna Appignani, Dir, Intl Educ, FIT, 7th Ave at 27th St, New York NY 10001-5992 *Ph:* 212-217 7633 *Fax:* 212-217 7010
Or Contact: Carole De Santis, Coord, FIT, 7th Ave at 27th St, New York NY 10001-5992 *Ph:* 212-217 7633 *Fax:* 212-217 7010 *E-mail:* desantca@sfitva.cc.fitsuny.edu

---

1609
FASHION INSTITUTE OF TECHNOLOGY
Summer Internship: Fashion Merchandising in London
Site: England: London
Dates: 4 wks, May 23-Jun 23
Subjects: Industrial studies, International business, Internships, Retailing
Eligibility: *Level:* sophs, jrs, srs *Requires:* interview by faculty member teaching course *Age:* min 18
Credit: *Undergrad:* 4 *Grad:* none *Doc:* transcript
Instruction: *In:* English *Format:* internship *Students:* mainly US
Costs: $2,320 for NY residents, $2,980 for others *incl* tuition, housing, some meals, intl airfare, fees, excursions
Housing: *Arr by pgm:* residence halls
Deadline: Mar 3
Other info: *US accredited sponsor:* yes *Began:* 1992 *Orient:* in US *Activities:* excursions *Misc:* May contact former participants. *URL:* http://www.fitnyc.suny.edu
Contact: Georgianna Appignani, Dir, Intl Educ, FIT, 7th Ave at 27th St, New York NY 10001-5992 *Ph:* 212-217 7633 *Fax:* 212-217 7010
Or Contact: Carole De Santis, Coord, FIT, 7th Ave at 27th St, New York NY 10001-5992 *Ph:* 212-217 7633 *Fax:* 212-217 7010 *E-mail:* desantca@sfitva.cc.fitsuny.edu

---

1610
FLORIDA STATE UNIVERSITY
London Summer Program
Site: England: London
Dates: 4 or 8 wks, May-Aug
Subjects: Anthropology, Art history, Drama/theater, English literature, Film studies, History, Music, Political science/politics, Sciences, Sociology
Eligibility: *Level:* fresh, sophs, jrs, srs *Requires:* 2.5 GPA, 1 sem coll completed
Credit: *Undergrad:* 9 *Grad:* none *Doc:* certificate
Instruction: *In:* English *Format:* internship, lecture *Students:* mainly US
Costs: Contact sponsor
Housing: *Arr by pgm:* flats in study ctr
Deadline: Jan 19 or until pgm filled
Other info: *US accredited sponsor:* yes *Began:* 1971 *Orient:* abroad *Activities:* excursions *Misc:* May contact former participants. *Financial aid:* scholarships, work study *URL:* http://www.international.fsu.edu
Contact: Bonnie Snyder, Intl Pgms, Study Abroad, Florida State Univ, 5500 UCA, Tallahassee FL 32306-2420 *Ph:* 800-374 8581; 850-644 3272 *Fax:* 850-644 8817 *E-mail:* intprog@www.fsu.edu

---

1611
GEORGIA INSTITUTE OF TECHNOLOGY
Chemical Engineering in London
Site: England: London *Host inst:* Univ Coll London
Dates: 5 wks, Jun 25-Jul 29
Subjects: Chemical engineering
Eligibility: *Level:* sophs, jrs, srs *Requires:* previous study in field, good acad standing, major in chemical engineering
Credit: *Undergrad:* 8 *Grad:* none *Doc:* transcript
Instruction: *In:* English *Format:* lab, lecture, study tour *Students:* mainly US
Costs: About $4,158 for GA residents, $4,408 for others *incl* tuition, housing, some meals, fees, excursions, travel to Wales
Housing: *Arr by pgm:* residence halls
Deadline: Contact sponsor
Other info: *US accredited sponsor:* yes *Began:* 1973 *Orient:* abroad *Activities:* excursions, program travel *Financial aid:* scholarships *URL:* http://www.chemeng.ucl.ac.uk/SummerSchool/
Contact: Dr Mark G White, Sch of Chemical Engineering, Georgia Inst of Technology, Atlanta GA 30332-0100 *Ph:* 404-894 2822 *E-mail:* mark.white@che.gatech.edu
Or Contact: Intl Educ, Georgia Inst of Technology, J S Coon Bldg, Ste 203, Atlanta GA 30332-0284 *Ph:* 404-894 7477 *Fax:* 404-894 9682 *E-mail:* study.abroad@gatech.edu

---

1612
HANSARD SOCIETY FOR PARLIAMENTARY GOVERNMENT and LONDON SCHOOL OF ECONOMICS AND POLITICAL SCIENCE
Hansard Scholars Program
Site: England: London *Host inst:* London Sch of Econ & Political Sci

Dates: 10 wks, May-late Jul
Subjects: Internships, Political science/politics, Public policy, Social sciences
Eligibility: *Level:* sophs, jrs, srs, grads *Requires:* 3.0 GPA
Credit: *Undergrad:* 15 *Grad:* 15 *Doc:* certificate
Instruction: *In:* English *Format:* independent study, internship, lecture, seminar, study tour, tutorial *Students:* mainly US
Costs: UK 4,600 *incl* tuition, housing, fees, excursions, London transport pass
Housing: *Arr by pgm:* apartments
Deadline: None
Other info: *US accredited sponsor:* no *Began:* 1985 *Orient:* abroad *Activities:* excursions, field trips, program travel, cultural events *Misc:* Internships in Parliament and in political & media orgs. 3-day study visit to Bruges, Belgium. May contact former participants. *URL:* http://www.hansardsociety.org.uk/scholars.htm
Contact: Melanie Rimmer, Hansard Socy, St Philips Bldg, Sheffield St, London WC2A 2EX, UK *E-mail:* study@hansard.lse.ac.uk

---

1613
IES, INSTITUTE FOR THE INTERNATIONAL EDUCATION OF STUDENTS
London Summer IES
Site: England: London
Dates: Jun 12-Jul 28, Jun 6-Jul 28 for internships
Subjects: Art history, Drama/theater, History, Internships, Journalism, Literature, Political science/politics, Sociology
Eligibility: *Level:* fresh, sophs, jrs, srs, grads, adults *Requires:* good acad standing *Age:* min 18
Credit: *Undergrad:* 6 *Grad:* none *Doc:* transcript
Instruction: *In:* English *Format:* directed field study, internship, lecture, seminar *Students:* mainly US
Costs: $3,550, $3,200 for Internships *incl* tuition, housing, excursions, health insurance, support svcs
Housing: *Arr by pgm:* residence halls, furnished apts
Deadline: Apr 1; Mar 1 for internships
Other info: *US accredited sponsor:* yes *Began:* 1972 *Orient:* abroad *Activities:* excursions *Misc:* BUNAC blue card for internship pgm participants. Student support svcs. *URL:* http://www.IESabroad.org
Contact: *See Index II for Members* IES, 33 N LaSalle St, 15th Fl, Chicago IL 60602-2602 *Ph:* 800-995 2300; 312-944 1750 *Fax:* 312-944 1448 *E-mail:* info@iesabroad.org ▲

1614
ILLINOIS STATE UNIVERSITY
British Culture and Institutions
Site: England: London
Dates: Jul 22-Aug 12
Subjects: British studies, Independent study, Philosophy, Political science/politics
Eligibility: Students enrolled for credit preferred. *Level:* fresh, sophs, jrs, srs, grads, adults, teachers, professionals *Requires:* 2.0 GPA, preparatory reading
Credit: *Undergrad:* 3-6 *Grad:* 3-6 *Doc:* transcript
Instruction: *In:* English *Format:* independent study, lecture, seminar, study tour *Students:* mainly US
Costs: About $5,700 *incl* housing, all meals, intl airfare, fees, excursions, books/materials, railpass, buses, theater tickets, subway *Nonrefundable fee*
Housing: *Arr by pgm:* apartments
Deadline: Feb 26 or until pgm filled; apply early
Other info: *US accredited sponsor:* yes *Began:* 1988 *Orient:* in US (1 day) *Activities:* excursions, field trips, program travel, cultural events *URL:* http://www.its.ilstu.edu/intlstudies/
Contact: Prof Walter B Mead, Dir, Illinois State Univ, Campus Box 4600, Normal IL 61790-4600 *Ph:* 309-829 7009 *Fax:* 309-438 5310 *E-mail:* wbmead@ilstu.edu

---

1615
INSTITUTE FOR READERS THEATRE and UNIVERSITY OF SOUTHERN MAINE
International Summer Workshop
Site: England: London *Host inst:* Wellington Hall, King's Coll
Dates: 2 wks, Jul 15-27
Subjects: Drama/theater, Independent study, Playwriting, Reading, Screenwriting, Storytelling
Eligibility: *Level:* fresh, sophs, jrs, srs, grads, adults, teachers, professionals, precoll *Age:* min 18, avg 35
Credit: *Undergrad:* 3-6 *Grad:* 3-12 *Doc:* transcript, certificate
Instruction: *In:* English *Format:* independent study, lab, lecture, practical training, seminar *Students:* mainly US
Costs: $1,395 *incl* housing, some meals, fees
Housing: *Arr by pgm:* residence halls
Deadline: Jun 1
Other info: *US accredited sponsor:* yes *In coop with:* San Diego State U, Kent State U, others *Activities:* excursions, field trips, cultural events *Misc:* Morning classes, guest lecturers, large expert faculty. *URL:* http://www.readerstheatre.net
Contact: Dr William Adams, Inst for Readers Theatre, PO Box 17193, San Diego CA 92177 *Ph:* 619-276 1948 *Fax:* 858-576 7369 *E-mail:* rtinst@aol.com

---

1616
JAMES MADISON UNIVERSITY
Summer Semester in London
Site: England: London
Dates: 8 wks, early Jun-mid-Jul
Subjects: Art history, Business/management, Drama/theater, English, History, Literature
Eligibility: *Level:* fresh, sophs, jrs, srs, grads
Credit: *Undergrad:* 9-12 *Grad:* none *Doc:* transcript
Instruction: *In:* English *Format:* lecture *Students:* mainly US
Costs: $3,600 for VA residents, $5,300 for others *incl* tuition, housing, some meals, excursions, books/materials
Housing: *Arr by pgm:* residence halls
Deadline: Feb 1
Other info: *US accredited sponsor:* yes *Began:* 1992 *Activities:* excursions, program travel, cultural events *Misc:* May contact former participants. *URL:* http://www.jmu.edu/international/
Contact: Intl Pgms, James Madison Univ, Harrisonburg VA 22807 *Ph:* 540-568 6419 *Fax:* 540-568 8080 *E-mail:* international@jmu.edu

---

1617
LABAN CENTRE LONDON
Easter School
Site: England: London
Dates: Mar 26-30
Subjects: Ballet, Choreography, Modern dance, Pilates
Eligibility: *Level:* fresh, sophs, jrs, srs, grads, adults, teachers, professionals, precoll *Age:* min 16
Credit: *Undergrad:* none *Grad:* none *Doc:* certificate
Instruction: *In:* English *Format:* practical training, workshop *Students:* intl
Costs: UK 165 per course *incl* tuition *Nonrefundable fee*
Housing: *Arr by student:* hotels, hostels, bed & breakfasts
Deadline: Mar 9
Other info: *US accredited sponsor:* no *Began:* 1996 *URL:* http://www.laban.co.uk
Contact: Mr Peter Curtis, Laban Ctr London, Laurie Grove, New Cross, London SE14 6NH, UK *E-mail:* p.curtis@laban.co.uk

---

1618
LABAN CENTRE LONDON
Summer School
Site: England: London
Dates: 2 wks, Jul 16-27
Subjects: Dance therapy, Education/teaching, Modern dance
Eligibility: *Level:* fresh, sophs, jrs, srs, grads, adults, teachers, professionals, precoll *Age:* min 16

Credit: *Undergrad:* none *Grad:* none *Doc:* certificate
Instruction: *In:* English *Format:* practical training, workshop *Students:* intl
Costs: UK 290-690 *incl* tuition, housing
Housing: *Arr by pgm:* residence halls
Deadline: Mid-Jun
Other info: *US accredited sponsor:* no *Began:* 1975 *Misc:* Age min 20 for dance therapy course. *URL:* http://www.laban.co.uk
Contact: Mr Peter Curtis, Admin, Laban Ctr London, Laurie Grove, New Cross, London SE14 6NH, UK *E-mail:* p.curtis@laban.co.uk

---

1619
LEHIGH UNIVERSITY
Lehigh in London
Site: England: London
Dates: 6 wks, Jul 4-Aug 16
Subjects: Internships, Political science/politics
Eligibility: *Level:* sophs, jrs, srs *Requires:* 2.0 GPA, work experience
Credit: *Undergrad:* 6 *Grad:* none *Doc:* transcript
Instruction: *In:* English *Format:* internship, lecture *Students:* mainly US
Costs: $3,960 *incl* tuition, housing, fees, underground pass, museum fees *Nonrefundable fee*
Housing: *Sponsor assists:* apartments
Deadline: Dec 16
Other info: *US accredited sponsor:* yes *Began:* 1997 *Orient:* in US (2 days) *Activities:* excursions, field trips, cultural events *Misc:* Students take 1 course in Political Sci (choose from two options) & work 120 hrs at an internship site. May contact former participants. *URL:* http://www.Lehigh.edu/~incis/incis.html
Contact: Dr Sandi Smith, Dir, Study Abroad, Lehigh Abroad, 5 E Packer Ave, Whitaker Lab 343, Lehigh Univ, Bethlehem PA 18015 *Ph:* 610-758 3351 *Fax:* 610-758 5156 *E-mail:* incis@lehigh.edu

---

1620
LONDON COLLEGE OF FASHION
European Fashion Summer Schools
Site: England: London
Dates: Two 6-wk sessions, May-Sep
Subjects: Computer aided design, Embroidery, Fashion design, Fashion merchandising, Illustration, Internships, Journalism, Marketing, Public relations, Retailing, Textiles
Eligibility: *Level:* fresh, sophs, jrs, srs, grads, adults, teachers, professionals, precoll *Requires:* 2.8 GPA *Age:* min 17
Credit: *Undergrad:* 2-16 *Grad:* none *Doc:* transcript, certificate
Instruction: *In:* English *Format:* art studio, directed field study, independent study, internship, lab, lecture, practical training, seminar, study tour, tutorial, workshop *Students:* intl
Costs: UK 995-5725 *incl* tuition, housing, fees, excursions, books/materials, travel to Paris *Nonrefundable fee*
Housing: *Arr by pgm:* apartments with local students, residence halls with local students, homestay, hotels, Contact sponsor
Deadline: Contact sponsor
Other info: *US accredited sponsor:* no *Began:* 1994 *Orient:* abroad *Activities:* excursions, field trips, cultural events *Misc:* Pgms in Fashion Merchandising, Fashion Design & various specialized areas. *URL:* http://www.lcf.linst.ac.uk/dali
Contact: Catherine Fuller, Study Abroad Dir, DALI at London Coll of Fashion, 20 John Princes St, London W1G 0BJ, UK *E-mail:* c.fuller@dali.linst.ac.uk

---

1621
LONDON LANGUAGE AND DRAMA SCHOOL, STAR TEK ASSOCIATES
Intensive Summer Drama Course A & B
Site: England: London
Dates: 4 wks, Jul-Aug
Subjects: Acting, Business administration, Business/management, Dance, Drama/theater, Homestay, Shakespeare studies, Singing/voice, Speech correction, Speech/debate/forensics, Television/video, Theater arts
Eligibility: *Level:* fresh, sophs, srs, grads, adults, teachers, professionals, precoll *Requires:* previous study in field, must have some acting experience for Course B *Age:* min 16, max 60, avg 30
Credit: *Undergrad:* none *Grad:* none *Doc:* certificate
Instruction: *In:* English *Format:* practical training *Students:* intl
Costs: UK 750 *incl* tuition, excursions, books/materials *Nonrefundable fee*
Housing: *Sponsor assists:* apartments with local students, residence halls, homestay
Deadline: Jun 30
Other info: *US accredited sponsor:* no *Began:* 1994 *Activities:* excursions, cultural events *Misc:* Course A ends with in-house performance; Course B showcases at Fortune Theatre Covent Gdn. May contact former participants. *Financial aid:* scholarships *URL:* http://www.startek-uk.com
Contact: Sarah Mann or Michelle Newman, London Drama & Lang Sch, 30 Brondesbury Pk, London, NW6 7DN, UK *E-mail:* enquiries@startek-uk.com

---

1622
LONDON LANGUAGE AND DRAMA SCHOOL, STAR TEK ASSOCIATES
Saturday Drama Workshops
Site: England: London
Dates: 4, 8 or 12 wks, Sep-Jun, 1st Sat of each mo
Subjects: Full curriculum, Drama/theater, Homestay, Shakespeare studies, Singing/voice, Speech correction, Speech/debate/forensics, Theater arts
Eligibility: *Level:* fresh, sophs, srs, grads, adults, teachers, professionals, precoll *Age:* min 16, max 60, avg 30
Credit: *Undergrad:* none *Grad:* none
Instruction: *In:* English *Format:* practical training, workshop *Students:* intl
Costs: UK 180 for 4 wks, UK 340 for 8 wks, UK 495 for 12 wks *incl* tuition *Nonrefundable fee*
Housing: *Sponsor assists:* apartments with local students, residence halls, homestay
Deadline: None
Other info: *US accredited sponsor:* no *Began:* 1994 *Misc:* May contact former participants. *URL:* http://www.startek-uk.com
Contact: Sarah Mann or Michelle Newman, London Drama & Lang Sch, 30 Brondesbury Pk, London, NW6 7DN, UK *E-mail:* enquiries@startek-uk.com

---

1623
LONDON LANGUAGE AND DRAMA SCHOOL, STAR TEK ASSOCIATES
Three-Day TV Acting Course
Site: England: London
Dates: 3 days, Sep-Jun
Subjects: Full curriculum, Acting, Broadcasting, Drama/theater, Film studies, Homestay, Media studies, Television/video
Eligibility: *Level:* fresh, sophs, srs, grads, adults, teachers, professionals, precoll *Age:* min 16, max 60, avg 30
Credit: *Undergrad:* none *Grad:* none
Instruction: *In:* English *Format:* practical training, workshop *Students:* intl
Costs: UK 450 *incl* tuition, books/materials
Housing: *Sponsor assists:* apartments with local students, residence halls, homestay
Deadline: None
Other info: *US accredited sponsor:* no *Began:* 1995 *Misc:* Students receive 15 min showreel at end of course. Max 8 students per class. May contact former participants. *URL:* http://www.startek-uk.com
Contact: Sarah Mann or Michelle Newman, London Drama & Lang Sch, 30 Brondesbury Pk, London, NW6 7DN, UK *E-mail:* enquiries@startek-uk.com

---

1624
LOUISIANA STATE UNIVERSITY
British Political Communication
Site: England: London *Host inst:* Goldsmiths' Coll
Dates: 6 wks, mid-Jul-mid-Aug
Subjects: Communications, Field study, Independent study, Media studies
Eligibility: *Level:* fresh, sophs, jrs, srs, grads *Requires:* 2.5 GPA, 3.0 for students seeking 9 hrs credit *Age:* min 19, avg 19
Credit: *Undergrad:* 6 *Grad:* none *Doc:* transcript
Instruction: *In:* English *Format:* directed field study, independent study, lecture, seminar *Students:* mainly US
Costs: $1,400 *incl* tuition, housing, some meals, excursions *Nonrefundable fee*
Housing: *Arr by pgm:* residence halls
Deadline: Apr
Other info: *US accredited sponsor:* yes *Began:* 1998 *Orient:* in US (1 day) *Activities:* excursions, field trips, program travel *Misc:* Scholarships for own students only. May contact former participants. *URL:* http://www.lsu.edu/studyabroad
Contact: Joseph Rosenbach, Louisiana State Univ, 113 Hatcher Hall, Baton Rouge LA 70803 *Ph:* 225-388 6801 *Fax:* 225-388 6806 *E-mail:* studyabroad@lsu.edu
Or Contact: Dr Ken Zagacki, Speech Communication, Louisiana State Univ, 136 Coates Hall, Baton Rouge LA 70803 *Ph:* 225-388 6812 *Fax:* 225-388 4828 *E-mail:* kzaga@unix1.sncc.lsu.edu

---

1625
LOUISIANA STATE UNIVERSITY
Health Care in London
Site: England: London
Dates: 3 wks, mid-Jul-early Aug
Subjects: Health care/hospitals
Eligibility: *Level:* sophs, jrs, srs, grads *Requires:* 2.5 GPA, for undergrads, 3.0 GPA for grads *Age:* min 20
Credit: *Undergrad:* 6 *Grad:* none *Doc:* transcript
Instruction: *In:* English *Format:* lecture *Students:* mainly US
Costs: $1,455 *incl* tuition
Housing: *Arr by pgm:* residence halls
Deadline: Mar 15
Other info: *US accredited sponsor:* yes *Began:* 1997 *Orient:* in US (1 day) *Activities:* excursions *Misc:* Scholarships for own students only. May contact former participants. *URL:* http://www.lsu.edu/studyabroad
Contact: Joseph Rosenbach, Louisiana State Univ, 113 Hatcher Hall, Baton Rouge LA 70803 *Ph:* 225-388 6801 *Fax:* 225-388 6816 *E-mail:* studyabroad@lsu.edu
Or Contact: Margo Abadie, Preprofession Studies, Louisiana State Univ, 150 Himes Hall, Baton Rouge LA 70803 *Ph:* 255-388 8281 *Fax:* 225-388 6806 *E-mail:* mabadie@lsu.edu

---

1626
LOUISIANA STATE UNIVERSITY
LSU in London
Site: England: London
Dates: 6 wks, Jul-Aug
Subjects: Drama/theater, English literature, Independent study, Political science/politics
Eligibility: *Level:* fresh, sophs, jrs, srs, grads, teachers, professionals *Requires:* 2.5 GPA, for undergrads, 3.0 GPA for grads & those seeking 9 credit hrs
Credit: *Undergrad:* 6-9 *Grad:* avail *Doc:* transcript
Instruction: *In:* English *Format:* independent study, lecture *Students:* mainly US
Costs: About $2,400 *incl* tuition, housing, fees, excursions, cultural events
Housing: *Arr by pgm:* residence halls
Deadline: Mar 15
Other info: *US accredited sponsor:* yes *Began:* 1974 *Activities:* excursions, cultural events *Misc:* Optional travel. Loans avail. Scholarships for own students only. May contact former participants. *Financial aid:* scholarships *URL:* http://www.lsu.edu/studyabroad
Contact: Joseph Rosenbach, Acad Pgms Abroad, Louisiana State Univ, 113 Hatcher Hall, Baton Rouge LA 70803 *Ph:* 225-388 6801 *Fax:* 225-388 6806 *E-mail:* studyabroad@lsu.edu

---

1627
MARYMOUNT COLLEGE
Actor in Training
Site: England: London
Dates: Jun 10-Jul 21
Subjects: Full curriculum, Acting, Dance, Shakespeare studies, Singing/voice, Speech/debate/forensics
Eligibility: *Level:* sophs, jrs, srs, grads *Requires:* 2.8 GPA *Age:* min 19, avg 20
Credit: *Undergrad:* 6 *Grad:* none *Doc:* transcript
Instruction: *In:* English *Format:* practical training, seminar, workshop *Students:* mainly US
Costs: $6,700 *incl* tuition, housing, all meals, fees, excursions, tube pass *Nonrefundable fee*
Housing: *Arr by pgm:* apartments, homestay
Deadline: Apr 15
Other info: *US accredited sponsor:* yes *Began:* 2000 *Orient:* abroad 3 days *Activities:* excursions, field trips, cultural events *Misc:* Workshop at Global Theatre. May contact former participants. *URL:* http://www.marymt.edu/~studyab/shorterm/sum2000.html
Contact: Hannah McChesney, Co Dir, Study Abroad, Marymount Coll, Tarrytown NY 10591 *Ph:* 888-662 4685; 914-332 8222 *Fax:* 914-631 3261 *E-mail:* studyab@mmc.martmt.edu

---

1628
MARYMOUNT COLLEGE
Summer Fashion Program
Site: England: London *Host inst:* London Coll of Fashion
Dates: Jun 10-Jul 21
Subjects: Fashion design, Fashion merchandising, Homestay, Internships, Marketing
Eligibility: *Level:* sophs, jrs, srs, grads *Requires:* 2.8 GPA *Age:* min 19, avg 20
Credit: *Undergrad:* 6 *Grad:* none *Doc:* transcript
Instruction: *In:* English *Format:* internship, lecture, practical training, seminar *Students:* mainly US
Costs: $7,000 *incl* tuition, housing, all meals, fees, tube pass *Nonrefundable fee*
Housing: *Arr by pgm:* apartments, homestay
Deadline: Apr 15
Other info: *US accredited sponsor:* yes *Began:* 2000 *Orient:* abroad (3 days) *Activities:* field trips, cultural events *Misc:* May contact former participants. *URL:* http://www.marymt.edu/~studyab/shorterm/sum2000.html
Contact: Hannah McChesney, Co Dir, Study Abroad, Marymount Coll, Tarrytown NY 10591 *Ph:* 888-662 4685; 914-332 8222 *Fax:* 914-631 3261 *E-mail:* studyab@mmc.martmt.edu

---

1629
MICHIGAN STATE UNIVERSITY
American Thought and Language
Site: England: London
Dates: 5 wks, Jul-Aug
Subjects: Creative writing
Eligibility: *Level:* sophs, jrs, srs *Requires:* 2.5 GPA, good acad standing *Age:* min 18
Credit: *Undergrad:* 8 *Grad:* none *Doc:* transcript
Instruction: *In:* English *Format:* lecture *Students:* mainly US
Costs: About $2,700 *incl* housing, some meals, insurance, excursions, support svcs *Nonrefundable fee*
Housing: *Arr by pgm:* residence halls
Deadline: Mar 2
Other info: *US accredited sponsor:* yes *Began:* 1989 *Orient:* in US & abroad *Activities:* excursions *Misc:* Loans avail. May contact former participants. *Financial aid:* scholarships *URL:* http://studyabroad.msu.edu

Contact: Cheryl Benner, Study Abroad, Michigan State Univ, 109 Intl Ctr, East Lansing MI 48824-1035 *Ph:* 517-353 8920 *Fax:* 517-432 2082 *E-mail:* bennerc@msu.edu ▲

1630
MICHIGAN STATE UNIVERSITY
Communication Disorders
Site: England: London
Dates: 5 wks, Jul-Aug
Subjects: Audiology, Speech pathology/therapy
Eligibility: *Level:* jrs, srs, grads *Requires:* 3.0 GPA, audiology & speech scis majors, good acad standing *Age:* min 18
Credit: *Undergrad:* 6 *Grad:* avail *Doc:* transcript
Instruction: *In:* English *Format:* lecture *Students:* mainly US
Costs: About $2,700 *incl* housing, some meals, insurance, excursions, support svcs *Nonrefundable fee*
Housing: *Arr by pgm:* residence halls
Deadline: Mar 2
Other info: *US accredited sponsor:* yes *Began:* 1985 *Orient:* in US & abroad *Activities:* program travel *Misc:* Loans avail. May contact former participants. *Financial aid:* scholarships *URL:* http://studyabroad.msu.edu
Contact: Cheryl Benner, Study Abroad, Michigan State Univ, 109 Intl Ctr, East Lansing MI 48824-1035 *Ph:* 517-353 8920 *Fax:* 517-432 2082 *E-mail:* bennerc@msu.edu ▲

1631
MICHIGAN STATE UNIVERSITY
English Literature-England
Site: England: London
Dates: 5 wks, Jul-Aug
Subjects: English literature
Eligibility: *Level:* sophs, jrs, srs, grads *Requires:* 2.0 GPA, good acad standing *Age:* min 18
Credit: *Undergrad:* 6 or more *Grad:* avail *Doc:* transcript
Instruction: *In:* English *Format:* lecture *Students:* mainly US
Costs: About $3,500 *incl* housing, some meals, insurance, excursions, support svcs *Nonrefundable fee*
Housing: *Arr by pgm:* residence halls
Deadline: Mar 2
Other info: *US accredited sponsor:* yes *Began:* 1973 *Orient:* in US *Misc:* Loans avail. May contact former participants. *Financial aid:* scholarships *URL:* http://studyabroad.msu.edu
Contact: Cheryl Benner, Study Abroad, Michigan State Univ, 109 Intl Ctr, East Lansing MI 48824-1035 *Ph:* 517-353 8920 *Fax:* 517-432 2082 *E-mail:* bennerc@msu.edu ▲

1632
MICHIGAN STATE UNIVERSITY
Medical Ethics and History of Health Care
Site: England: London
Dates: 5 wks, Jun-Jul
Subjects: Health care/hospitals, History, Philosophy
Eligibility: *Level:* sophs, jrs, srs, grads *Requires:* 2.0 GPA, good acad standing *Age:* min 18
Credit: *Undergrad:* 6 *Grad:* avail *Doc:* transcript
Instruction: *In:* English *Format:* lecture *Students:* mainly US
Costs: About $2,400 *incl* housing, insurance, excursions, support svcs *Nonrefundable fee*

Housing: *Arr by pgm:* residence halls
Deadline: Mar 2
Other info: *US accredited sponsor:* yes *Began:* 1986 *Orient:* in US & abroad *Activities:* program travel *Misc:* Loans avail. May contact former participants. *Financial aid:* scholarships *URL:* http://studyabroad.msu.edu
Contact: Cheryl Benner, Study Abroad, Michigan State Univ, 109 Intl Ctr, East Lansing MI 48824-1035 *Ph:* 517-353 8920 *Fax:* 517-432 2082 *E-mail:* bennerc@msu.edu ▲

1633
MICHIGAN STATE UNIVERSITY
Nursing
Site: England: London *Host inst:* Royal Coll of Nursing
Dates: 4 wks, Jun-Jul
Subjects: Nursing
Eligibility: *Level:* jrs, srs, grads, professionals *Requires:* 2.5 GPA, undergrads, 3.0 GPA grads, good acad standing, major in nursing *Age:* min 18
Credit: *Undergrad:* 6 *Grad:* avail *Doc:* transcript
Instruction: *In:* English *Format:* lecture *Students:* mainly US
Costs: About $2,100 *incl* housing, some meals, insurance, excursions, support svcs *Nonrefundable fee*
Housing: *Arr by pgm:* residence halls
Deadline: Mar 2
Other info: *US accredited sponsor:* yes *Began:* 1980 *Orient:* in US & abroad *Misc:* Optional pgm travel. Loans avail. May contact former participants. *Financial aid:* scholarships *URL:* http://studyabroad.msu.edu
Contact: Cheryl Benner, Study Abroad, Michigan State Univ, 109 Intl Ctr, East Lansing MI 48824-1035 *Ph:* 517-353 8920 *Fax:* 517-432 2082 *E-mail:* bennerc@msu.edu ▲

1634
MICHIGAN STATE UNIVERSITY
Packaging-England
Site: England: London
Dates: 5 wks, Jul
Subjects: Field study, Independent study, Packaging
Eligibility: *Level:* fresh, sophs, jrs, srs *Requires:* 2.0 GPA, good acad standing, packaging majors *Age:* min 18
Credit: *Undergrad:* 4 *Grad:* avail *Doc:* transcript
Instruction: *In:* English *Format:* directed field study, independent study, lecture *Students:* mainly US
Costs: About $2,400 *incl* housing, some meals, insurance, excursions, support svcs *Nonrefundable fee*
Housing: *Arr by pgm:* residence halls
Deadline: Mar 2
Other info: *US accredited sponsor:* yes *Orient:* in US & abroad *Activities:* field trips, cultural events *Misc:* Loans avail. May contact former participants. *Financial aid:* scholarships *URL:* http://studyabroad.msu.edu
Contact: Cheryl Benner, Study Abroad, Michigan State Univ, 109 Intl Ctr, East Lansing MI 48824 *Ph:* 517-353 8920 *Fax:* 517-432 2082 *E-mail:* bennerc@msu.edu ▲

1635
MICHIGAN STATE UNIVERSITY
Philosophy of Love and Art
Site: England: London
Dates: 5 wks, Jul-Aug
Subjects: Arts, Humanities, Philosophy
Eligibility: *Level:* fresh, sophs, jrs, srs *Requires:* 2.0 GPA *Age:* min 18
Credit: *Undergrad:* avail *Grad:* none *Doc:* transcript
Instruction: *In:* English *Format:* lecture, seminar *Students:* mainly US
Costs: About $3,000 *incl* housing, some meals, insurance, excursions, support svcs *Nonrefundable fee*
Housing: *Arr by pgm:* residence halls
Deadline: Mar 2
Other info: *US accredited sponsor:* yes *Orient:* in US (1 day) *Activities:* excursions, field trips, cultural events *Financial aid:* scholarships *URL:* http://studyabroad.msu.edu
Contact: Cheryl Benner, Study Abroad, Michigan State Univ, 109 Intl Ctr, East Lansing MI 48824-1035 *Ph:* 517-353 8920 *Fax:* 517-432 2082 *E-mail:* bennerc@msu.edu ▲

1636
MICHIGAN STATE UNIVERSITY
Women's Studies
Site: England: London
Dates: 5 wks, Jul-Aug
Subjects: Independent study, Women's studies
Eligibility: *Level:* sophs, jrs, srs *Requires:* 2.0 GPA, good acad standing *Age:* min 18
Credit: *Undergrad:* 8 *Grad:* 8 *Doc:* transcript
Instruction: *In:* English *Format:* independent study, lecture, seminar *Students:* mainly US
Costs: About $3,000 *incl* housing, some meals, insurance, excursions, support svcs *Nonrefundable fee*
Housing: *Arr by pgm:* residence halls
Deadline: Mar 2
Other info: *US accredited sponsor:* yes *Began:* 1994 *Orient:* in US & abroad *Activities:* excursions, field trips, cultural events *Misc:* Loans avail. *Financial aid:* scholarships *URL:* http://studyabroad.msu.edu
Contact: Cheryl Benner, Study Abroad, Michigan State Univ, 109 Intl Ctr, East Lansing MI 48824-1035 *Ph:* 517-353 8920 *Fax:* 517-432 2082 *E-mail:* bennerc@msu.edu ▲

1637
MIDDLESEX UNIVERSITY
Summer School
Site: England: London
Dates: Early Jul-mid-Aug
Subjects: Business administration, Business/management, Computer sciences, Crafts, Dance, Social sciences
Eligibility: *Level:* fresh, sophs, jrs *Requires:* 2.5 GPA *Age:* min 17
Credit: *Undergrad:* avail *Grad:* none *Doc:* transcript, certificate
Instruction: *In:* English *Format:* independent study, internship, lecture, seminar, tutorial *Students:* mainly host country
Costs: UK 2,200 *incl* tuition, housing, some meals, excursions
Housing: *Arr by pgm:* residence halls with local students
Deadline: May 30
Other info: *US accredited sponsor:* no *Began:* 1995 *Orient:* abroad (3 days) *Activities:* excursions, field trips, cultural events *Misc:* May contact former participants. *URL:* http://www.summer.mdx.ac.uk
Contact: Anita Mascarenhas, Admissions & Marketing, Middlesex Univ, Trent Park, Bramley Rd, London N14 4YZ, UK

1638
NEW YORK UNIVERSITY, TISCH SCHOOL OF THE ARTS
Arts in London
Site: England: London *Host inst:* Inst of Contemporary Art (ICA)
Dates: Jul 5-Aug 15
Subjects: Art history, British studies, Film studies, Interdisciplinary studies, Performing arts, Playwriting, Screenwriting, Shakespeare studies, Theater arts
Eligibility: *Level:* fresh, sophs, jrs, srs, grads, adults, teachers *Age:* min 18
Credit: *Undergrad:* 8 *Grad:* none *Doc:* transcript
Instruction: *In:* English *Format:* lecture, practical training, seminar, study tour, tutorial, workshop *Students:* mainly US
Costs: $5,712-$5,912 *incl* tuition, housing, some meals, fees, excursions, theater tickets *Nonrefundable fee*
Housing: *Arr by pgm:* residence halls
Deadline: Apr 15; rolling admissions
Other info: *US accredited sponsor:* yes *Began:* 1986 *Orient:* in US (1 day) *Activities:* excursions, field trips, cultural events *Misc:* Scholarships & loans for own

students only. *URL:* http://www.nyu.edu/tisch/international/
Contact: Linda Kow, Assoc Dir, Tisch Intl Pgms, New York Univ, 721 Broadway, 12th Fl, New York NY 10003 *Ph:* 212-998 9175 *Fax:* 212-995 4578 *E-mail:* tisch.international@nyu.edu

---

1639
NORTH CAROLINA STATE UNIVERSITY
London Experience
Site: England: London
Dates: 4 wks, Jul
Subjects: Arts, British studies, History, Political science/politics
Eligibility: *Level:* fresh, sophs, jrs, srs, grads
Credit: *Undergrad:* 6 *Grad:* 6 *Doc:* transcript
Instruction: *In:* English *Format:* lecture, seminar, study tour *Students:* mainly US
Costs: $2,600 *incl* tuition, housing, some meals, insurance, excursions
Housing: *Arr by pgm:* residence halls
Deadline: Feb
Other info: *US accredited sponsor:* yes *Began:* 1986 *Orient:* in US *Activities:* excursions, field trips, program travel, cultural events *Misc:* Wkend excursion to Paris. *URL:* http://www.ncsu.edu/studyabroad
Contact: Anne Haberkern, North Carolina State Univ, 2118 Pullen Hall, Box 7344, Raleigh NC 27695-7344 *Ph:* 919-515 2087 *Fax:* 919-515 6021 *E-mail:* study_abroad@ncsu.edu

---

1640
OHIO UNIVERSITY
London Summer Study Program: History and Drama
Site: England: London
Dates: 3 wks, Jun 14-Jul 5
Subjects: Drama/theater, English literature, History
Eligibility: *Level:* sophs, jrs, srs *Requires:* 3.0 GPA
Credit: *Undergrad:* 4 qtr hrs *Grad:* 4 qtr hrs *Doc:* transcript
Instruction: *In:* English *Format:* lecture, study tour *Students:* mainly US
Costs: Contact sponsor
Housing: *Arr by pgm:* apartments
Deadline: Jan 22
Other info: *US accredited sponsor:* yes *Began:* 1990 *Orient:* in US *Activities:* excursions, field trips, program travel, cultural events *Misc:* May contact former participants. *URL:* http://www.ohiou.edu
Contact: Dr Loreen Giese, English, Ohio Univ, Ellis Hall 358, Athens OH 45701 *Ph:* 740-593 2838
Or Contact: Connie Perdreau, Dir, Educ Abroad, Ohio Univ, 107 Gordy Hall, Athens OH 45701 *Ph:* 740-593 4583 *Fax:* 740-593 9758

1641
OKLAHOMA STATE UNIVERSITY
Summer in London
Site: England: London *Host inst:* Regent's Coll
Dates: 4 wks, Jun 1-30
Subjects: Accounting, Business administration, Finance, Marketing
Eligibility: *Level:* sophs, jrs, srs, grads *Requires:* 2.0 GPA, approval from acad adviser *Age:* min 18
Credit: *Undergrad:* 6 *Grad:* 6
Instruction: *In:* English *Format:* study tour *Students:* mainly US
Costs: $4,300 *incl* tuition, housing, some meals, intl airfare, books/materials, subway pass *Nonrefundable fee*
Housing: *Arr by pgm:* residence halls
Deadline: Mar 30
Other info: *US accredited sponsor:* yes *Began:* 1990 *Orient:* in US *Activities:* excursions, field trips, program travel, cultural events *Financial aid:* scholarships *URL:* http://www.bus.okstate.edu/intbus/index.htm#study_abroad
Contact: Business Extension, Oklahoma State Univ, 215 Coll of Bus Admin, Stillwater OK 74078 *Ph:* 405-744 5208 *Fax:* 405-744 6143 *E-mail:* nvickie@okstate.edu

---

1642
PENNSYLVANIA STATE UNIVERSITY
Summer Abroad Education Drama in Britain
Site: England: London *Host inst:* Goldsmith's Coll
Dates: 8 wks, May-Jul
Subjects: British studies, Drama/theater, Shakespeare studies
Eligibility: *Level:* sophs, jrs, srs, grads *Requires:* 2.5 GPA *Age:* min 18
Credit: *Undergrad:* 9 *Grad:* 9
Instruction: *In:* English *Format:* lecture, study tour *Students:* mainly US
Costs: About $3,020 for PA residents, $4,796 for others *incl* tuition, housing
Housing: *Arr by pgm:* apartments
Deadline: Mar 1
Other info: *US accredited sponsor:* yes *Activities:* field trips, cultural events *Misc:* May contact former participants. *URL:* http://www.outreach.psu.edu/PSSEA/
Contact: Summer Abroad, Penn State Univ, 225 Penn State Conference Ctr, University Park PA 16802 *Ph:* 814-863 5170 *Fax:* 814-863 5190 *E-mail:* SummerAbroad@outreach.psu.edu
Or Contact: William Kelly, Penn State Univ, 215 Wagner Bldg, University Park PA 16802 *Ph:* 814-865 1750 *Fax:* 814-863 8706

1643
RAMAPO COLLEGE OF NEW JERSEY
Winter Session in London
Site: England: London *Host inst:* Regent's Coll
Dates: 3 wks, Jan
Subjects: British studies, English literature, European studies
Eligibility: *Level:* fresh, sophs, jrs, srs, grads *Requires:* 2.0 GPA
Credit: *Undergrad:* 3 *Grad:* none
Instruction: *In:* English *Format:* lecture *Students:* mainly US
Costs: $2,000 for Ramapo students, $2,200 for others *incl* tuition, housing, most meals, intl airfare, fees, excursions, most meals
Housing: *Arr by pgm:* residence halls, hotels
Deadline: Nov 1
Other info: *US accredited sponsor:* yes *Began:* 1994 *Orient:* in US *Activities:* excursions, field trips, cultural events *Misc:* Stafford Loan avail. *URL:* http://www.ramapo.edu/Academics/Abroad/
Contact: Ms Robyn Perricelli, Ramapo Coll of New Jersey, 505 Ramapo Valley Rd, Mahwah NJ 07430 *Ph:* 201-684 7463 *Fax:* 201-684 7651 *E-mail:* studabrd@ramapo.edu

---

1644
SANTA BARBARA CITY COLLEGE
Theater and Philosophy in London
Site: England: London *Host inst:* ACCENT
Dates: 5 wks, Jun-Jul
Subjects: Drama/theater, Philosophy
Eligibility: *Level:* fresh, sophs, adults *Age:* min 16
Credit: *Undergrad:* avail *Grad:* none *Doc:* transcript
Instruction: *In:* English *Format:* lecture *Students:* mainly US
Costs: About $3,000 *incl* housing, some meals, intl airfare, insurance, fees, excursions *Nonrefundable fee*
Housing: *Arr by pgm:* residence halls
Deadline: Mar
Other info: *US accredited sponsor:* yes *Began:* 1998 *Orient:* in US & abroad (2 days) *Activities:* excursions, field trips, cultural events *Financial aid:* scholarships *URL:* http://www.sbcc.cc.ca.us/academic/StudyAbroad
Contact: Naomi Sullwold, Santa Barbara City Coll, 721 Cliff Dr, Santa Barbara CA 93109 *Ph:* 805-965 0581ext 2494 *Fax:* 805-963 7222 *E-mail:* sullwold@sbcc.net

Or Contact: Carola Smith, Dir, Study Abroad, Santa Barbara City Coll, 721 Cliff Dr, Santa Barbara CA 93109 *Ph:* 805-965 0581ext 2243 *Fax:* 805-963 7222 *E-mail:* smithc@sbcc.net

---

1645
SCHOOL FOR LIFE PAINTING AND DRAWING
Life Painting and Drawing
Site: England: London
Dates: 1, 2 or 5 days, Feb-Dec
Subjects: Drawing, Painting
Eligibility: *Level:* adults *Age:* min 17, avg 30
Credit: *Undergrad:* none *Grad:* none
Instruction: *In:* English *Format:* art studio *Students:* mainly host country
Costs: UK 80 per day, UK 150 for wkend, UK 285 per wk *incl* tuition, models *Nonrefundable fee*
Housing: *Arr by student*
Deadline: 10 days before pgm begins
Other info: *US accredited sponsor:* no *Began:* 1976 *Misc:* Individual instruction by arrangement, UK 33 per hr.
Contact: Rachel Clark, 25 Limehouse Cut, 46 Morris Rd, London E14 6NQ, UK *E-mail:* clark@ch.ctvt.easynet.co.uk

---

1646
SOTHEBY'S INSTITUTE
Decorative Art Summer Workshop
Site: England: London
Dates: 2 wks, Aug
Subjects: Ceramics/pottery, Decorative arts, Furnishings/furniture, Glassmaking, Metalworking
Eligibility: *Level:* adults *Age:* min 18, avg 25
Credit: *Undergrad:* none *Grad:* none *Doc:* certificate
Instruction: *In:* English *Format:* lecture, practical training, seminar, tutorial, workshop *Students:* intl
Costs: UK 900 *incl* tuition, fees, excursions, books/materials
Housing: *Arr by student:* accommodation list avail
Deadline: Contact sponsor
Other info: *US accredited sponsor:* no *Began:* 1999 *URL:* http://www.sothebys.com
Contact: Admissions or Registrar, Sotheby's Inst, 30 Oxford St, London W1N 9FL, UK *E-mail:* education@sothebys-institute.edu

---

1647
SOTHEBY'S INSTITUTE
Fine Art Summer Workshop
Site: England: London
Dates: 2 wks, Jul
Subjects: Drawing, Fine arts, Painting, Printmaking
Eligibility: *Level:* fresh, sophs, jrs, srs, grads, adults, professionals *Age:* min 18, avg 25
Credit: *Undergrad:* none *Grad:* none *Doc:* certificate
Instruction: *In:* English *Format:* lecture, practical training, seminar, tutorial, workshop *Students:* intl
Costs: UK 900 *incl* tuition, fees, excursions, books/materials
Housing: *Arr by student*
Deadline: Contact sponsor
Other info: *US accredited sponsor:* no *Began:* 1999 *Activities:* excursions *URL:* http://www.sothebys.com
Contact: Admissions or Registrar, Sotheby's Inst, 30 Oxford St, London W1N 9FL, UK *E-mail:* education@sothebys-institute.edu

---

1648
SOUTHERN METHODIST UNIVERSITY
SMU in London: Communications
Site: England: London *Host inst:* Regent's Coll
Dates: Jul 1-29
Subjects: Journalism, Media studies, Public relations
Eligibility: *Level:* sophs, jrs, srs *Requires:* 2.5 GPA
Credit: *Undergrad:* 6 *Grad:* none *Doc:* transcript
Instruction: *In:* English *Format:* lecture *Students:* mainly US
Costs: $4,300 *incl* tuition, housing, all meals, fees, excursions, railpass *Nonrefundable fee*
Housing: *Arr by pgm:* residence halls
Deadline: Mar 1 or until pgm filled
Other info: *US accredited sponsor:* yes *Orient:* in US *Activities:* excursions, field trips, program travel *Misc:* Scholarships for own students only. Loans avail. May contact former participants. *Financial aid:* scholarships *URL:* http://www.smu.edu/syudyabroad
Contact: Karen Westergaard, Intl Off, Southern Methodist Univ, PO Box 0395, 3108 Fondren Dr, Dallas TX 75275-0391 *Ph:* 214-768 2338 *Fax:* 214-768 1051 *E-mail:* intlpro@mail.smu.edu ▲

1649
SOUTHWESTERN UNIVERSITY
Arts in London
Site: England: London
Dates: Contact sponsor
Subjects: Art history, Drama/theater, Internships, Music history
Eligibility: *Level:* fresh, sophs, jrs, srs *Requires:* 2.5 GPA *Age:* min 18, avg 21
Credit: *Undergrad:* 4-6 *Grad:* none *Doc:* transcript
Instruction: *In:* English *Format:* seminar *Students:* mainly US
Costs: $3,800-$4,750 *incl* tuition, housing, intl airfare, insurance, fees, excursions, books/materials, subway pass
Housing: *Arr by pgm:* residence halls
Deadline: Contact sponsor
Other info: *US accredited sponsor:* no *Began:* 1972 *Orient:* in US & abroad (spring sem sessions in US, 1 day abroad) *Activities:* excursions, field trips, cultural events *Misc:* Option for 4-wk acad pgm or 6-wk combination acad/internship pgm. May contact former participants. *Financial aid:* scholarships *URL:* http://www.southwestern.edu/academic/
Contact: Sue Mennicke, Dir, Study Abroad, Southwestern Univ, PO Box 770, Georgetown TX 78627-0770 *Ph:* 512-863 1857 *Fax:* 512-863 1535 *E-mail:* mennicks@southwestern.edu

---

1650
SUNY COLLEGE AT CORTLAND
London Summer Teachers Institute
Site: England: London *Host inst:* Univ of North London
Dates: 4 wks, Jul 1-30
Subjects: Art, Drama/theater, Education/teaching, Government, History, Music, Political science/politics
Eligibility: *Level:* adults, teachers, professionals *Requires:* previous study in field, bachelor's degree
Credit: *Undergrad:* none *Grad:* avail *Doc:* certificate
Instruction: *In:* English *Format:* lecture, seminar *Students:* mainly US
Costs: $3,700 *incl* tuition, housing, all meals, intl airfare, insurance, fees, excursions, books/materials, airport transfer *Nonrefundable fee*
Housing: *Arr by pgm:* residence halls
Deadline: Apr 1
Other info: *US accredited sponsor:* yes *Began:* 1999 *Orient:* in US (1 day) *Activities:* excursions, field trips, cultural events *Misc:* Out-of-state incentives. May contact former participants. *Financial aid:* scholarships *URL:* http://www.studyabroad.com/suny/cortland
Contact: Dr Del Janik, Pgm Coord, Intl Pgms, SUNY Coll at Cortland, PO Box 2000, Cortland NY 13045 *Ph:* 607-753 2209 *Fax:* 607-753 5989 *E-mail:* janikd@cortland.edu ▲

1651
SUNY COLLEGE AT NEW PALTZ
London Art Seminar
Site: England: London
Dates: About Jan 2-16
Subjects: Art, Art education, Art history

See "How To Use This Book" for definitions of terms used above. ▲ = See program sponsor's ad(s) in this book.

Eligibility: *Level:* fresh, sophs, jrs, srs, grads
Credit: *Undergrad:* 3 *Grad:* none
Instruction: *In:* English *Format:* lecture *Students:* mainly US
Costs: $2,200 for NY residents *incl* tuition, housing, some meals, intl airfare, insurance, excursions, orient *Nonrefundable fee*
Housing: *Arr by pgm:* hotels
Deadline: Oct 1
Other info: *US accredited sponsor:* yes *Activities:* excursions, field trips *Misc:* Loans avail. *Financial aid:* scholarships *URL:* http://www.newpaltz.edu/oie/
Contact: Ctr for Intl Pgms, SUNY New Paltz, 75 S Manheim Blvd, Ste 9, New Paltz NY 12561 *Ph:* 914-257 3125 *Fax:* 914-257 3129
E-mail: international@newpaltz.edu ▲

1652
SUNY COLLEGE AT NEW PALTZ
London Theater Seminar
Site: England: London
Dates: 2 wks, Jan
Subjects: Theater arts
Eligibility: *Level:* fresh, sophs, jrs, srs, grads *Requires:* above avg acad record
Credit: *Undergrad:* 3 *Grad:* none
Instruction: *In:* English *Format:* lecture, seminar *Students:* mainly US
Costs: $1,624 for NY resident undergrads *incl* housing, some meals, intl airfare, insurance, excursions
Housing: *Arr by pgm:* hotels
Deadline: Oct 1 or until pgm filled
Other info: *US accredited sponsor:* yes *Began:* 1984 *Orient:* in US *Activities:* cultural events *Misc:* Workshops by Amer & British profs, actors, dirs & playwrights. Loans avail. *Financial aid:* scholarships *URL:* http://www.newpaltz.edu/oie/
Contact: Ctr for Intl Pgms, SUNY New Paltz, 75 S Manheim Blvd, Ste 9, New Paltz NY 12561 *Ph:* 845-257 3125 *Fax:* 845-257 3129
E-mail: international@newpaltz.edu ▲

1653
SUNY COLLEGE AT NEW PALTZ
Summer London Internship Program
Site: England: London *Host inst:* Middlesex Univ
Dates: 6 wks, early Jul-mid-Aug
Subjects: Business administration, Community service projects, Ecology/environmental studies, Government, Internships, Journalism, Medicine, Political science/politics
Eligibility: *Level:* fresh, sophs, jrs, srs *Requires:* good acad standing *Age:* min 17
Credit: *Undergrad:* 6 *Grad:* none *Doc:* transcript
Instruction: *In:* English *Format:* internship *Students:* mainly US
Costs: $3,700 *incl* tuition, housing, some meals, excursions, 1 acad course *Nonrefundable fee*
Housing: *Arr by pgm:* residence halls
Deadline: Mar 1
Other info: *US accredited sponsor:* yes *Orient:* abroad *Activities:* excursions *Misc:* Loans & scholarships for own students only. May contact former participants. *Financial aid:* scholarships *URL:* http://www.newpaltz.edu/oie/
Contact: Ctr for Intl Pgms, SUNY New Paltz, 75 S Manheim Blvd, Ste 9, New Paltz NY 12561 *Ph:* 845-257 3125 *Fax:* 845-257 3129
E-mail: international@newpaltz.edu ▲

1654
SUNY COLLEGE AT NEW PALTZ
Summer Studies in London, England
Site: England: London *Host inst:* Middlesex Univ
Dates: Mid-Jul-mid-Aug
Subjects: Full curriculum
Eligibility: *Level:* fresh, sophs, jrs, srs
Credit: *Undergrad:* 6 *Grad:* none *Doc:* transcript
Instruction: *In:* English *Format:* lecture, seminar *Students:* mainly host country
Costs: $3,792 for NY resident undergrads *incl* tuition, housing, most meals, insurance, excursions, most meals
Housing: *Arr by pgm:* residence halls
Deadline: Mar 1 or until pgm filled
Other info: *US accredited sponsor:* yes *Began:* 1995 *Orient:* abroad *Activities:* excursions, field trips *Misc:* Loans avail. *Financial aid:* scholarships *URL:* http://www.newpaltz.edu/oie/
Contact: Ctr for Intl Pgms, SUNY New Paltz, 75 S Manheim Blvd, Ste 9, New Paltz NY 12561 *Ph:* 845-257 3125 *Fax:* 845-257 3129
E-mail: international@newpaltz.edu ▲

1655
SUNY COLLEGE AT OSWEGO
London Summer Program
Site: England: London *Host inst:* Huron Univ
Dates: 6 wks, late May-Jul
Subjects: Business/management, Communications, Drama/theater, English, History, International studies, Internships, Political science/politics, Psychology
Eligibility: *Level:* fresh, sophs, jrs, srs *Requires:* 2.5 GPA
Credit: *Undergrad:* 6 *Grad:* none *Doc:* transcript
Instruction: *In:* English *Format:* lecture *Students:* mainly US
Costs: $5,800 *incl* tuition, housing, some meals, intl airfare, excursions *Nonrefundable fee*
Housing: *Arr by pgm:* residence halls
Deadline: Mar 1
Other info: *US accredited sponsor:* yes *Began:* 1994 *Orient:* abroad *Activities:* excursions, field trips, cultural events, sports *Misc:* May contact former participants. *URL:* http://www.oswego.edu/~intled
Contact: Susan Ansara, Dir, Intl Educ, SUNY Coll at Oswego, 102 Rich Hall, Oswego NY 13126 *Ph:* 888-467 9346; 315-341 2118 *Fax:* 315-341 2477 *E-mail:* intled@oswego.edu

---

1656
SUNY ROCKLAND COMMUNITY COLLEGE
Wintersession in London
Site: England: London
Dates: 2 wks, Jan 3-17
Subjects: Art history, Broadcasting, Criminal justice, Culinary arts, Drama/theater, History, International business, Literature, Nursing, Performing arts, Psychology
Eligibility: *Level:* fresh, sophs, jrs, srs, adults *Requires:* 2.5 GPA *Age:* min 18
Credit: *Undergrad:* 3 *Grad:* none *Doc:* transcript
Instruction: *In:* English *Format:* seminar, study tour *Students:* mainly US
Costs: $1,725 *incl* tuition, housing, some meals, intl airfare, fees, excursions
Housing: *Arr by pgm:* hotels
Deadline: Nov 1
Other info: *US accredited sponsor:* yes *Began:* 1977 *Activities:* excursions, field trips *Misc:* May contact former participants. *Financial aid:* scholarships *URL:* http://www.studyabroad.com/suny/rockland
Contact: Jody A Dudderar, Wintersession in London, Rockland CC, 145 College Rd, Suffern NY 10901 *Ph:* 845-574 4205 *Fax:* 845-574 4423 *E-mail:* study-abroad@sunyrockland.edu

---

1657
SYRACUSE UNIVERSITY
British Life and Culture
Site: England: London
Dates: Jul 2-28
Subjects: British studies, Civilization/culture
Eligibility: *Level:* sophs, jrs, srs, grads, adults *Requires:* 2.5 GPA
Credit: *Undergrad:* 6 *Grad:* 6 *Doc:* transcript
Instruction: *In:* English *Format:* directed field study, independent study *Students:* mainly US
Costs: $6,000 *incl* tuition, housing, some meals, fees, excursions *Nonrefundable fee*

Housing: *Arr by pgm:* hotels
Deadline: Mar 15
Other info: *US accredited sponsor:* yes *Began:* 2000 *Orient:* abroad (1 day) *Activities:* excursions, field trips, cultural events *Financial aid:* scholarships *URL:* http://sumweb.syr.edu/dipa/summer
Contact: Daisy Fried, Assoc Dir, Syracuse Univ, 119 Euclid Ave, Syracuse NY 13244-4170 *Ph:* 800-251 9674; 315-443 9419 *Fax:* 315-443 4593 *E-mail:* dsfried@summon3.syr.edu ▲

1658
SYRACUSE UNIVERSITY
Film in Britain
Site: England: London
Dates: 4 wks, Jul 2-28
Subjects: British studies, Civilization/culture, Film studies
Eligibility: *Level:* fresh, sophs, jrs, srs, adults *Requires:* 2.5 GPA *Age:* min 18
Credit: *Undergrad:* 6 *Grad:* 6 *Doc:* transcript
Instruction: *In:* English *Format:* directed field study, independent study, lecture *Students:* mainly US
Costs: $5,000 *incl* tuition, housing, some meals, fees, excursions *Nonrefundable fee*
Housing: *Arr by pgm:* residence halls
Deadline: Mar 15
Other info: *US accredited sponsor:* yes *Began:* 2001 *Orient:* abroad *Activities:* excursions *Misc:* May contact former participants. *Financial aid:* scholarships *URL:* http://sumweb.syr.edu/dipa/summer
Contact: Daisy Fried, Assoc Dir, Intl Pgms Abroad, Syracuse Univ, 119 Euclid Ave, Syracuse NY 13244 *Ph:* 800-251 9674; 315-443 9419 *Fax:* 315-443 4593 *E-mail:* dsfried@summons3.syr.edu ▲

1659
SYRACUSE UNIVERSITY
Law in London: Clinical Internships
Site: England: London
Dates: 7 wks, May 30-Jul 21
Subjects: Internships, Law
Eligibility: *Level:* grads *Requires:* 1 yr law sch, currently enrolled
Credit: *Undergrad:* 6 *Grad:* 6
Instruction: *In:* English *Format:* internship, lecture, seminar *Students:* mainly US
Costs: $4,800 *incl* tuition, some meals, excursions, books/materials *Nonrefundable fee*
Housing: *Arr by student*
Deadline: Feb 15
Other info: *US accredited sponsor:* yes *Began:* 1977 *Orient:* abroad *Misc:* May contact former participants. *Financial aid:* scholarships *URL:* http://sumweb.syr.edu/dipa/summer
Contact: Summer Pgms, Intl Pgms Abroad, Syracuse Univ, 119 Euclid Ave, Syracuse NY 13244-4170 *Ph:* 800-251 9674; 315-443 9420 *Fax:* 315-443 4593 *E-mail:* dipasum@summon3.syr.edu ▲

1660
SYRACUSE UNIVERSITY
Management Internships in London
Site: England: London
Dates: 7 wks, May 30-Jul 14
Subjects: Business/management, Internships
Eligibility: *Level:* jrs, srs, grads *Requires:* previous study in field
Credit: *Undergrad:* 6 *Grad:* 6
Instruction: *In:* English *Format:* internship, lecture, seminar *Students:* mainly US
Costs: $4,400 *incl* tuition, some meals, excursions *Nonrefundable fee*
Housing: *Arr by student*
Deadline: Feb 15
Other info: *US accredited sponsor:* yes *Orient:* abroad *Misc:* May contact former participants. *Financial aid:* scholarships *URL:* http://sumweb.syr.edu/dipa/summer
Contact: Summer Pgms, Intl Pgms Abroad, Syracuse Univ, 119 Euclid Ave, Syracuse NY 13244-4170 *Ph:* 800-251 9674; 315-443 9420 *Fax:* 315-443 4593 *E-mail:* dipasum@summon3.syr.edu ▲

1661
SYRACUSE UNIVERSITY
Politics and Media in England
Site: England: London
Dates: May 31-Jul 7
Subjects: Political science/politics
Eligibility: *Level:* sophs, jrs, srs, grads
Credit: *Undergrad:* 6 *Grad:* 6
Instruction: *In:* English *Format:* lecture *Students:* mainly US
Costs: $4,300 *incl* tuition, some meals, fees, excursions *Nonrefundable fee*
Housing: *Arr by student*
Deadline: Mar 15
Other info: *US accredited sponsor:* yes *Began:* 1984 *Orient:* abroad *Activities:* excursions *Misc:* Sessions with British political leaders. Meetings with experts on British issues. *Financial aid:* scholarships *URL:* http://sumweb.syr.edu/dipa/summer
Contact: Summer Pgms, Intl Pgms Abroad, Syracuse Univ, 119 Euclid Ave, Syracuse NY 13244-4170 *Ph:* 800-251 9674; 315-443 9420 *Fax:* 315-443 4593 *E-mail:* dipasum@summon3.syr.edu ▲

1662
SYRACUSE UNIVERSITY
Women in Contemporary London
Site: England: London
Dates: 4 wks, May 29-Jun 29
Subjects: Field study, Independent study, Sociology, Women's studies
Eligibility: *Level:* fresh, sophs, jrs, srs, grads, adults *Age:* min 18
Credit: *Undergrad:* 6 *Grad:* 6 *Doc:* transcript
Instruction: *In:* English *Format:* directed field study, independent study, lecture *Students:* mainly US
Costs: $5,000 *incl* tuition, housing, some meals, fees, excursions *Nonrefundable fee*
Housing: *Sponsor assists:* apartments
Deadline: Mar 15
Other info: *US accredited sponsor:* yes *Began:* 2001 *Orient:* abroad *Activities:* excursions *Misc:* May contact former participants. *Financial aid:* scholarships *URL:* http://sumweb.syr.edu/dipa/summer
Contact: Daisy Fried, Assoc Dir, Syracuse Univ, 119 Euclid Ave, Syracuse NY 13244 *Ph:* 800-251 9674; 315-251 9419 *Fax:* 315-443 4593 *E-mail:* dsfried@summon3.syr.edu ▲

1663
TEMPLE UNIVERSITY
British Mass Media Summer Seminar
Site: England: London
Dates: 4-1/2 wks, Jul-Aug
Subjects: Communications, Media studies, Telecommunications
Eligibility: *Level:* jrs, srs, grads *Requires:* previous study in field, or background in communications
Credit: *Undergrad:* 6 *Grad:* 6
Instruction: *In:* English *Format:* lecture, seminar *Students:* mainly US
Costs: $3,800-$4,300 *incl* tuition, housing, all meals, intl airfare
Housing: *Arr by pgm:* apartments
Deadline: May 1
Other info: *US accredited sponsor:* yes *Orient:* in US *Activities:* field trips *Misc:* Briefings by British journalists & media reps. *URL:* http://www.scat.temple.edu/london/
Contact: Coord of the London Pgm, Sch of Communications & Theater, Temple Univ, Philadelphia PA 19122 *Ph:* 215-204 1902 *E-mail:* augusta@astro.temple.edu

---

1664
THOMAS HEATHERLEY EDUCATIONAL TRUST
Part-Time Courses
Site: England: London *Host inst:* Heatherley Sch of Art
Dates: Varying pgm lengths, yr-round
Subjects: Drawing, Painting, Printmaking, Sculpture, Studio arts
Eligibility: *Level:* fresh, sophs, jrs, srs, grads, adults, teachers, professionals *Age:* min 17
Credit: *Undergrad:* avail *Grad:* avail

See "How To Use This Book" for definitions of terms used above. ▲ = See program sponsor's ad(s) in this book.

Instruction: *In:* English *Format:* art studio, music lesson, practical training, seminar, tutorial *Students:* intl
Costs: UK 120 for 25 hrs, UK 145 for 30 hrs, UK 290 for 60 hrs *incl* tuition
Nonrefundable fee
Housing: *Arr by student:* accommodation lists provided
Deadline: Rolling admissions
Other info: *US accredited sponsor:* no *Activities:* cultural events *Misc:* Gallery visits & open studio. *URL:* http://www.heatherleys.org
Contact: Registrar, Heatherley Sch of Fine Art, 80 Upcerne Rd, Chelsea, London SW10 0SH, UK
E-mail: heatherlys@hotmail.com

1665
UNIVERSITY OF ARIZONA
Gender Issues in Education
Site: England: London *Host inst:* Ctr for Acad Pgms Abroad (CAPA)
Dates: 6 wks, Jun 1-Jul 15
Subjects: Education/teaching, Gender studies, Secondary education
Eligibility: *Level:* jrs, srs, grads, adults, teachers, professionals *Requires:* 2.75 GPA
Credit: *Undergrad:* 3-6 *Grad:* 3-6 *Doc:* transcript
Instruction: *In:* English *Format:* independent study, lecture, study tour *Students:* mainly US
Costs: Contact sponsor
Housing: *Arr by pgm:* apartments
Deadline: Mar 1
Other info: *US accredited sponsor:* yes *Began:* 1998 *Orient:* in US *Activities:* excursions, field trips, program travel, cultural events *Misc:* May contact former participants. *URL:* http://w3.arizona.edu/-ciss/
Contact: Caroline Patrick, Study Abroad Adviser, Univ of Arizona, 939 N Tyndall Ave, Tucson AZ 85721 *Ph:* 520-626 7171 *Fax:* 520-626 9004 *E-mail:* cpatrick@u.arizona.edu ▲

1666
UNIVERSITY OF ARKANSAS
Theater in London Program
Site: England: London
Dates: 4 wks, Jul 8-Aug 8
Subjects: Drama/theater, Fine arts, Literature
Eligibility: *Level:* sophs, jrs, srs, grads, adults *Requires:* 2.5 GPA *Age:* avg 25
Credit: *Undergrad:* 6 *Grad:* 6 *Doc:* transcript
Instruction: *In:* English *Format:* lecture, seminar *Students:* mainly US
Costs: About $3,800 *incl* tuition, housing, intl airfare, fees, excursions, theater tickets
Housing: *Arr by pgm:* hotels, with kitchenettes
Deadline: Mar 1
Other info: *US accredited sponsor:* yes *Began:* 1985 *Orient:* in US *Activities:* excursions, field trips, cultural events *Misc:* May contact former participants. *URL:* http://www.uark.edu/~studyabr
Contact: Joseph Candido, Univ of Arkansas, Kimpel Hall 333, Fayetteville AR 72701 *Ph:* 501-575 4301
Or Contact: Michelle Morris, Study Abroad, Fulbright Inst, Univ of Arkansas, Fayetteville AR 72701 *Ph:* 501-575 7582 *Fax:* 501-575 7402 *E-mail:* studyabr@cavern.uark.edu

---

1667
UNIVERSITY OF COLORADO AT BOULDER
Field Seminar in International Finance and Business
Site: England: London
Dates: 1 mo, Jul
Subjects: Field study, Finance, International business
Eligibility: *Level:* jrs, srs, grads, professionals *Requires:* 2.75 GPA, previous study in intl econ or bus
Credit: *Undergrad:* 6 *Grad:* 6 *Doc:* transcript
Instruction: *In:* English *Format:* directed field study, lecture, seminar *Students:* mainly US
Costs: About $3,792 for CO residents, $4,792 for others *incl* tuition, housing, some meals, insurance, fees
Housing: *Arr by pgm:* apartments
Deadline: Rolling admissions from Nov 25
Other info: *US accredited sponsor:* yes *Began:* 1982 *Orient:* in US & abroad *Activities:* field trips *Misc:* Focus on European integration. May contact former participants. *URL:* http://www.colorado.edu/OIE/StudyAbroad
Contact: Intl Educ, Univ of Colorado, Campus Box 123, Boulder CO 80309-0123 *Ph:* 303-492 7741 *Fax:* 303-492 5185 *E-mail:* studyabr@colorado.edu

---

1668
UNIVERSITY OF DAYTON
Interdepartmental Summer Study Abroad Program (ISSAP)-London
Site: England: London
Dates: 1 mo, May 24-Jun 23
Subjects: Education/teaching, Liberal arts
Eligibility: *Level:* fresh, sophs, jrs, srs, grads, adults, teachers *Requires:* 2.0 GPA *Age:* min 18, avg 20
Credit: *Undergrad:* 7 *Grad:* none *Doc:* transcript
Instruction: *In:* English *Format:* lecture *Students:* mainly US
Costs: $3,595 *incl* tuition, housing, some meals, insurance, excursions
Nonrefundable fee
Housing: *Arr by pgm:* apartments
Deadline: Mar 1; Jan 15 for scholarships
Other info: *US accredited sponsor:* yes *Began:* 1972 *Orient:* in US & abroad (4 days) *Activities:* excursions, field trips, cultural events *Misc:* May contact former participants. *Financial aid:* scholarships
Contact: James W Stiles, Univ of Dayton, 300 College Park, Dayton OH 45469-1481 *Ph:* 937-229 3728 *Fax:* 937-229 2766
E-mail: stiles@udayton.edu

1669
UNIVERSITY OF DAYTON
Interdepartmental Summer Study Abroad Program (ISSAP)-University of London
Site: England: London *Host inst:* Univ of London
Dates: 1 mo, Jun 28-Jul 28
Subjects: Communications
Eligibility: *Level:* fresh, sophs, jrs, srs, grads, adults *Requires:* 2.5 GPA *Age:* min 18, avg 20
Credit: *Undergrad:* 7 *Grad:* none *Doc:* transcript
Instruction: *In:* English *Format:* lecture *Students:* mainly US
Costs: $3,595 *incl* tuition, housing, some meals, insurance, excursions
Nonrefundable fee
Housing: *Arr by pgm:* residence halls
Deadline: Dec 1
Other info: *US accredited sponsor:* yes *Began:* 1972 *Orient:* in US & abroad (4 days) *Activities:* excursions, field trips, cultural events *Misc:* May contact former participants. *Financial aid:* scholarships
Contact: James W Stiles, Univ of Dayton, 300 College Park, Dayton OH 45469-1481 *Ph:* 937-229 3728 *Fax:* 937-229 2766
E-mail: stiles@udayton.edu

1670
UNIVERSITY OF DELAWARE
Summer Session in England
Site: England: London
Dates: 5 wks, beg Jun
Subjects: Art history, English, Internships, Political science/politics, Sociology
Eligibility: *Level:* fresh, sophs, jrs, srs *Requires:* 2.0 GPA
Credit: *Undergrad:* 6 *Grad:* none *Doc:* transcript
Instruction: *In:* English *Format:* lecture *Students:* mainly US
Costs: Contact sponsor
Housing: *Arr by pgm:* apartments
Deadline: Mid-Mar
Other info: *US accredited sponsor:* yes *Orient:* avail yes *Activities:* excursions, field trips, cultural events *Misc:* Contact

sponsor to arrange honors credit. *Financial aid:* scholarships *URL:* http://www.udel.edu/studyabroad/
Contact: Intl Pgms & Special Sessions, Univ of Delaware, 4 Kent Way, Newark DE 19716-1450 *Ph:* 888-831 4685; 302-831 2852 *Fax:* 302-831 6042 *E-mail:* studyabroad@udel.edu

---

1671
UNIVERSITY OF DELAWARE
Winter Session in England - London Theater
Site: England: London
Dates: 1 mo, Jan
Subjects: Drama/theater, Independent study
Eligibility: *Level:* fresh, sophs, jrs, srs *Requires:* 2.0 GPA
Credit: *Undergrad:* 3-6 *Grad:* none *Doc:* transcript
Instruction: *In:* English *Format:* independent study, lecture, study tour *Students:* mainly US
Costs: Contact sponsor
Housing: *Arr by pgm:* apartments
Deadline: Early Oct
Other info: *US accredited sponsor:* yes *Began:* 1993 *Orient:* avail yes *Activities:* excursions, field trips, program travel, cultural events *Misc:* Contact sponsor to arrange honors credit. May contact former participants. *Financial aid:* scholarships *URL:* http://www.udel.edu/studyabroad/
Contact: Intl Pgms & Special Sessions, Univ of Delaware, 4 Kent Way, Newark DE 19716 *Ph:* 888-831 4685; 302-831 2852 *Fax:* 302-831 6042 *E-mail:* studyabroad@udel.edu

---

1672
UNIVERSITY OF DELAWARE
Winter Session in England/ Communication
Site: England: London
Dates: 1 mo, Jan
Subjects: Communications, Psychology, Women's studies
Eligibility: *Level:* fresh, sophs, jrs, srs *Requires:* 2.0 GPA
Credit: *Undergrad:* 6 *Grad:* none *Doc:* transcript
Instruction: *In:* English *Format:* lecture, seminar, study tour *Students:* mainly US
Costs: Contact sponsor
Housing: *Arr by pgm:* apartments
Deadline: Early Oct
Other info: *US accredited sponsor:* yes *Began:* 2001 *Orient:* avail yes *Activities:* excursions, field trips *Misc:* Contact sponsor to arrange honors credit. *Financial aid:* scholarships *URL:* http://www.udel.edu/studyabroad/
Contact: Intl Pgms & Special Sessions, Univ of Delaware, 4 Kent Way, Newark DE 19716-1450 *Ph:* 888-831 4685; 302-831 2852 *Fax:* 302-831 6042 *E-mail:* studyabroad@udel.edu

---

1673
UNIVERSITY OF DELAWARE
Winter Session in England/ Comparative Literature
Site: England: London
Dates: 1 mo, Jan
Subjects: Comparative literature, Women's studies
Eligibility: *Level:* fresh, sophs, jrs, srs *Requires:* 2.0 GPA
Credit: *Undergrad:* 3 *Grad:* none *Doc:* transcript
Instruction: *In:* English *Format:* lecture, seminar, study tour *Students:* mainly US
Costs: Contact sponsor
Housing: *Arr by pgm:* apartments
Deadline: Early Oct
Other info: *US accredited sponsor:* yes *Began:* 2001 *Orient:* avail yes *Activities:* excursions, field trips, program travel, cultural events *Misc:* Contact sponsor to arrange honors credit. *Financial aid:* scholarships *URL:* http://www.udel.edu/studyabroad/
Contact: Intl Pgms & Special Sessions, Univ of Delaware, 4 Kent way, Newark DE 19716-1450 *Ph:* 888-831 4685; 302-831 2852 *Fax:* 302-831 6042 *E-mail:* studyabroad@udel.edu

---

1674
UNIVERSITY OF DELAWARE
Winter Session in England/Geography
Site: England: London
Dates: 1 mo, Jan
Subjects: Geography
Eligibility: *Level:* fresh, sophs, jrs, srs *Requires:* 2.0 GPA
Credit: *Undergrad:* 4 *Grad:* none *Doc:* transcript
Instruction: *In:* English *Format:* lecture, seminar, study tour *Students:* mainly US
Costs: Contact sponsor
Housing: *Arr by pgm:* apartments
Deadline: Early Oct
Other info: *US accredited sponsor:* yes *Began:* 2000 *Orient:* abroad *Activities:* excursions, field trips, program travel, cultural events *Misc:* Contact sponsor to arrange honors credit. *Financial aid:* scholarships *URL:* http://www.udel.edu/studyabroad/
Contact: Intl Pgms & Special Sessions, Univ of Delaware, 4 Kent Way, Newark DE 19716-1450 *Ph:* 888-831 4685; 302-831 2852 *Fax:* 302-831 6042 *E-mail:* studyabroad@udel.edu

---

1675
UNIVERSITY OF DELAWARE
Winter Session in England/Philosophy
Site: England: London
Dates: 1 mo, Jan
Subjects: Philosophy
Eligibility: *Level:* fresh, sophs, jrs, srs *Requires:* 2.0 GPA
Credit: *Undergrad:* 3 *Grad:* none *Doc:* transcript
Instruction: *In:* English *Format:* lecture, seminar, study tour *Students:* mainly US
Costs: Contact sponsor
Housing: *Arr by pgm:* apartments
Deadline: Early Oct
Other info: *US accredited sponsor:* yes *Began:* 2000 *Activities:* excursions, field trips *Misc:* Contact sponser to arrange honors credit. Pgm offered even-numbered years. *Financial aid:* scholarships *URL:* http://www.udel.edu/studyabroad/
Contact: Intl Pgms & Special Sessions, Univ of Delaware, 4 Kent Way, Newark DE 19716-1450 *Ph:* 888-831 4685; 302-831 2852 *Fax:* 302-831 6042 *E-mail:* studyabroad@udel.edu

---

1676
UNIVERSITY OF DELAWARE
Winter Session in English Literature
Site: England: London
Dates: 1 mo, Jan
Subjects: English literature
Eligibility: *Level:* fresh, sophs, jrs, srs, adults *Requires:* 2.0 GPA
Credit: *Undergrad:* 3-6 *Grad:* none *Doc:* transcript
Instruction: *In:* English *Format:* lecture *Students:* mainly US
Costs: Contact sponsor
Housing: *Arr by pgm:* apartments
Deadline: Early Oct
Other info: *US accredited sponsor:* yes *Orient:* avail yes *Activities:* excursions, field trips, program travel, cultural events *Misc:* Contact sponsor to arrange honors credit. may be arranged. for info. *Financial aid:* scholarships *URL:* http://www.udel.edu/studyabroad/
Contact: Intl Pgms & Special Sessions, Univ of Delaware, 4 Kent Way, Newark DE 19716-1450 *Ph:* 888-831 4685; 302-831 2852 *Fax:* 302-831 6042 *E-mail:* studyabroad@udel.edu

---

1677
UNIVERSITY OF GEORGIA
Drama and Theatre in London
Site: England: London
Dates: 6 wks, mid-May-late Jun
Subjects: Acting, Drama/theater
Eligibility: *Level:* sophs, jrs, srs, grads *Requires:* 2.0 GPA *Age:* min 18
Credit: *Undergrad:* 9 *Grad:* 9
Instruction: *In:* English *Format:* directed

field study, independent study, lecture, practical training, seminar, study tour *Students:* mainly US
Costs: $6,000-$6,500 *incl* tuition, housing, some meals, intl airfare, insurance, fees, excursions, books/materials, tour of Stratford *Nonrefundable fee*
Housing: *Sponsor assists:* bedsits
Deadline: Late Feb
Other info: *US accredited sponsor:* yes *Began:* 2000 *In coop with:* AIFS *Orient:* in US & abroad (1 day) *Activities:* excursions, field trips, cultural events *Misc:* Incl 10+ theatre tickets to West End, Stratford & experimental venues. May contact former participants. *URL:* http://www.uga.edu/oie
Contact: Farley Richmond, Drama & Theatre, Univ of Georgia, Athens GA 30602 *Ph:* 706-542 2089 *Fax:* 706-542 2080 *E-mail:* richmond@arches.uga.edu

---

1678
UNIVERSITY OF IOWA
London Performance Study
Site: England: London
Dates: 4 wks, late May-late Jun
Subjects: Drama/theater, English
Eligibility: *Level:* fresh, sophs, jrs, srs *Requires:* 2.5 GPA
Credit: *Undergrad:* 3 *Grad:* none *Doc:* transcript
Instruction: *In:* English *Format:* lecture, seminar, workshop *Students:* mainly US
Costs: About $2,900 *incl* tuition, housing, fees, excursions, performances
Housing: *Arr by pgm:* apartments
Deadline: Feb 1
Other info: *US accredited sponsor:* yes *Began:* 1996 *Orient:* abroad *Activities:* excursions, cultural events *Misc:* Intensive intro to London theater incl 12 performances in London & Stratford. *URL:* http://www.uiowa.edu/~uiabroad
Contact: Study Abroad, Univ of Iowa, 120 Intl Ctr, Iowa City IA 52242 *Ph:* 319-335 0353 *Fax:* 319-353 2021 *E-mail:* study-abroad@uiowa.edu

---

1679
UNIVERSITY OF MICHIGAN
Summer Program in London
Site: England: London
Dates: 6 wks, early Jul-mid-Aug
Subjects: Drama/theater, Film studies, History, Literature, Social sciences
Eligibility: *Level:* sophs, jrs, srs, grads *Requires:* good acad standing, enrollment at US or Canadian univ
Credit: *Undergrad:* 8 *Grad:* none
Instruction: *In:* English *Format:* lecture *Students:* mainly US
Costs: Contact Sponsor
Housing: *Arr by pgm:* residence halls
Deadline: Feb 16
Other info: *US accredited sponsor:* yes *Began:* 1967 *Activities:* excursions, cultural events *URL:* http://www.umich.edu/~iinet/oip/
Contact: Intl Pgms, Univ of Michigan, G513 Michigan Union, Ann Arbor MI 48109-1349 *Ph:* 734-764 4311 *Fax:* 734-764 3229 *E-mail:* oip@umich.edu

---

1680
UNIVERSITY OF MINNESOTA
Summer Study in London
Site: England: London
Dates: Jun 7-Jul 22
Subjects: Architecture, British studies, Civilization/culture, Drama/theater, History, International marketing, Internships, Literature, Political science/politics, Shakespeare studies
Eligibility: *Level:* fresh, sophs, jrs, srs, precoll *Requires:* 2.5 GPA, letter of recommendation from faculty; jr or sr for internship *Age:* min 18
Credit: *Undergrad:* 6 *Grad:* none
Instruction: *In:* English *Format:* directed field study, internship, lecture, seminar *Students:* mainly US
Costs: $3,250 for U of MN students, $3,500 for others *incl* tuition, housing, insurance, fees, excursions *Nonrefundable fee*
Housing: *Arr by pgm:* apartments
Deadline: Apr 15
Other info: *US accredited sponsor:* yes *Began:* 1994 *Orient:* in US & abroad (1 day) *Activities:* excursions, field trips *Misc:* Internships for jrs & srs. Scholarships for own students only. May contact former participants. *Financial aid:* scholarships *URL:* http://www.UMabroad.umn.edu
Contact: Global Campus, Study Abroad, Univ of Minnesota, 230 Heller Hall, 271 19th Ave S, Minneapolis MN 55455 *Ph:* 612-626 9000 *Fax:* 612-626 8009 *E-mail:* UMabroad@umn.edu

---

1681
UNIVERSITY OF NORTH CAROLINA AT CHARLOTTE
Summer Study of International Business and British Culture
Site: England: London *Host inst:* Kingston Univ
Dates: 4 wks, Jul 10-Aug 4
Subjects: Accounting, History, International business
Eligibility: *Level:* fresh, sophs, jrs, srs, grads *Requires:* 2.5 GPA *Age:* avg 20
Credit: *Undergrad:* 3-6 *Grad:* none
Instruction: *In:* English *Format:* lecture *Students:* mainly US
Costs: $3,400 *incl* tuition, housing, intl airfare, insurance, fees, excursions, airport transfers *Nonrefundable fee*
Housing: *Arr by pgm:* residence halls
Deadline: Feb 17
Other info: *US accredited sponsor:* yes *Orient:* in US & abroad (1 day) *Activities:* excursions *Misc:* May contact former participants. *URL:* http://www.uncc.edu/oip/edabroad.htm
Contact: Joel A Gallegos, Dir, Educ Abroad, UNC Charlotte, 9201 University City Blvd, Charlotte NC 28223-0001 *Ph:* 704-687 2464 *Fax:* 704-687 3168 *E-mail:* stennies@email.uncc.edu
Or Contact: Mike Cornick, Accounting Dept, UNC Charlotte, 9201 University City Blvd, Charlotte NC 28223-0001 *Ph:* 704-547 4486 *Fax:* 704-687 3123 *E-mail:* fac00mfc@email.uncc.edu

---

1682
UNIVERSITY OF PENNSYLVANIA
Penn-in-London
Site: England: London
Dates: 5 wks, early Jul-early Aug
Subjects: Drama/theater, Literature
Eligibility: *Level:* fresh, sophs, jrs, srs, grads, professionals
Credit: *Undergrad:* 6 *Grad:* none *Doc:* transcript
Instruction: *In:* English *Format:* lecture *Students:* mainly US
Costs: About $4,800 *incl* tuition, housing, theater tickets *Nonrefundable fee*
Housing: *Arr by pgm:* residence halls
Deadline: Mar 15
Other info: *US accredited sponsor:* yes *Began:* 1976 *Orient:* in US & abroad *URL:* http://www.sas.upenn.edu/CGS/
Contact: Elizabeth Sachs, Penn Summer Abroad, Univ of Pennsylvania, 3440 Market St, Ste 100, Philadelphia PA 19104-3335 *Ph:* 215-898 5738 *Fax:* 215-573 2053 *E-mail:* sdanti@mail.sas.upenn.edu

---

1683
UNIVERSITY OF PORTLAND
London Program
Site: England: London *Host inst:* Scholar Svcs
Dates: May 10-Jun 15
Subjects: Finance, Literature, Psychology, Sciences, Zoology
Eligibility: *Level:* sophs, jrs, srs *Requires:* 3.0 GPA, recommendation letters
Credit: *Undergrad:* 6 *Grad:* none *Doc:* transcript
Instruction: *In:* English *Format:* study tour *Students:* mainly US
Costs: $3,900 *incl* tuition, housing, fees, excursions
Housing: *Arr by pgm:* apartments
Deadline: Oct 15
Other info: *US accredited sponsor:* yes *Began:* 1989 *Orient:* in US & abroad *Activities:* excursions

Contact: Rev Arthur Wheeler, CSC, Univ of Portland, 5000 N Willamette Blvd, Portland OR 97203-5798 *Ph:* 503-943 7221 *Fax:* 503-943 7804 *E-mail:* wheeler@up.edu

---

1684
UNIVERSITY OF ROCHESTER
Internships in London
Site: England: London
Dates: Early Jun-late Jul or mid-Jun-early Aug
Subjects: Accounting, Advertising, Business/management, Drama/theater, Health administration/planning, Health care/hospitals, Homestay, Internships, Law, Museology, Political science/politics, Public relations
Eligibility: *Level:* jrs, srs *Requires:* 3.0 GPA
Credit: *Undergrad:* 8 *Grad:* none *Doc:* transcript
Instruction: *In:* English *Format:* internship *Students:* mainly US
Costs: $5,290 *incl* tuition, housing, some meals
Housing: *Arr by pgm:* apartments, homestay
Deadline: Mar 1
Other info: *US accredited sponsor:* yes *Began:* 1975 *Orient:* abroad *URL:* http://www.rochester.edu/College/study-abroad/sa/global.html
Contact: Jacqueline Levine, Study Abroad Dir, Univ of Rochester, Lattimore 206, PO Box 270376, Rochester NY 14627-0376 *Ph:* 716-275 7532 *Fax:* 716-461 5131 *E-mail:* csaip@cc.mail.edu

---

1685
UNIVERSITY OF SAN DIEGO, SCHOOL OF LAW
London Institute on International and Comparative Law
Site: England: London *Host inst:* King's Coll London
Dates: About Jul 2-Aug 4
Subjects: Business law, European Union, International law, Internships
Eligibility: *Level:* grads, teachers, professionals *Requires:* law or bus students
Credit: *Undergrad:* none *Grad:* 6 *Doc:* certificate
Instruction: *In:* English *Format:* internship, seminar *Students:* mainly US
Costs: About $2,800 for classes, $3,950 for internship, $2,000 for housing *incl* tuition, housing, books/materials *Nonrefundable fee*
Housing: *Arr by pgm:* residence halls
Deadline: Mar 11
Other info: *US accredited sponsor:* yes *Began:* 1979 *Orient:* in US & abroad *Misc:* Legal visits, some tourist visits arr at site. Correspondence re: pgm must be in English. Loans avail for US students only. *URL:* http://www.acusd.edu/lawabroad
Contact: Cindy King, Law Pgms Abroad, Univ of San Diego, 5998 Alcala Park, San Diego CA 92110-2492 *Ph:* 619-260 7460 *Fax:* 619-260 2230 *E-mail:* cking@acusd.edu

---

1686
UNIVERSITY OF SOUTHERN MISSISSIPPI BRITISH STUDIES CONSORTIUM
British Studies Program
Site: England: London *Host inst:* King's Coll London
Dates: 5 wks, Jul 5-Aug 6
Subjects: Anthropology, Art, Business/management, Computer sciences, Criminal justice, Drama/theater, English literature, Fashion design, Finance, Geography, Insurance, Library science, Marketing, Political science/politics, Speech pathology/therapy
Eligibility: *Level:* sophs, jrs, srs, grads, teachers, professionals *Requires:* 2.0 GPA, for undergrads with clear academic standing *Age:* min 18
Credit: *Undergrad:* 6 *Grad:* 6
Instruction: *In:* English *Format:* directed field study, lecture *Students:* mainly US
Costs: $4,399 for undergrads, $4,699 for grads *incl* tuition, housing, intl airfare, fees *Nonrefundable fee*
Housing: *Arr by pgm:* residence halls
Deadline: May 19
Other info: *US accredited sponsor:* yes *Began:* 1976 *Activities:* excursions *Misc:* Accompanied by US faculty. Lectures by British experts. May contact former participants. *Financial aid:* scholarships *URL:* http://www.usm.edu
Contact: *See Index II for Members* Dr Tim Hudson or Frances Sudduth, Univ of Southern Mississippi, Box 10047, Hattiesburg MS 39406 *Ph:* 601-266 4344 *Fax:* 601-266 5699 *E-mail:* melissa.ravencaft@usm.edu

---

1687
UNIVERSITY OF WISCONSIN-PLATTEVILLE
Summer Session in London
Site: England: London *Host inst:* Thames Valley Univ
Dates: 4 wks, Jun 5-Jul 6
Subjects: Art, Civilization/culture, Drama/theater, History, Homestay, Psychology
Eligibility: *Level:* fresh, sophs, jrs, srs, adults, teachers *Requires:* 2.0 GPA, good acad standing, 2 recommendations *Age:* min 18, avg 20
Credit: *Undergrad:* 6 *Grad:* none *Doc:* transcript
Instruction: *In:* English *Format:* lecture, seminar, study tour *Students:* mainly US
Costs: $2,450 for WI/MN residents, $2,750 for others *incl* tuition, housing, some meals, fees, excursions, books/materials, railpass, ISIC *Nonrefundable fee*
Housing: *Arr by pgm:* homestay
Deadline: Apr 1
Other info: *US accredited sponsor:* yes *Began:* 1988 *In coop with:* Rockland Ctr for Intl Studies *Orient:* in US & abroad *Activities:* excursions, field trips, program travel *Misc:* May contact former participants. *URL:* http://www.uwplatt.edu/~studyabroad
Contact: Dr William Spofford, Dir, or Dr Julia Davis, Asst Dir, Study Abroad, Univ of Wisconsin-Platteville, 308 Warner Hall, Platteville WI 53818-3099 *Ph:* 800-342 1725; 608-342 1726 *Fax:* 608-342 1736 *E-mail:* studyabroad@uwplatt.edu

---

1688
UNIVERSITY OF WISCONSIN-STEVENS POINT
Mysterious Britain: British Mystery and Crime Writers
Site: England: London
Dates: 3 wks, Jun 14-Jul 5
Subjects: English literature, Field study, Literary sites
Eligibility: *Level:* fresh, sophs, jrs, srs, grads, adults, teachers, professionals *Age:* min 18
Credit: *Undergrad:* 3-6 *Grad:* avail *Doc:* transcript
Instruction: *In:* English *Format:* directed field study, study tour *Students:* mainly US
Costs: $2,750 *incl* tuition, housing, all meals, intl airfare, fees, excursions *Nonrefundable fee*
Housing: *Arr by pgm:* residence halls, hotels
Deadline: 10 wks befors pgm (or when full)
Other info: *US accredited sponsor:* yes *Orient:* in US *Activities:* excursions, field trips, cultural events *Misc:* Pgm next offered in 2001. *Financial aid:* scholarships *URL:* http://www.uwsp.edu/acad/internat/
Contact: Prof Kathy Ackley, Univ of Wisconsin-Stevens Point, Stevens Point WI 54481 *Ph:* 715-346 4347, 715-346 4131

1689
UNIVERSITY OF WISCONSIN-STEVENS POINT
Theater in London
Site: England: London
Dates: 3 wks, Jul 1-22
Subjects: Drama/theater, English, Field study
Eligibility: *Level:* adults *Age:* min 18
Credit: *Undergrad:* 3 *Grad:* avail *Doc:* transcript

Instruction: *In:* English *Format:* directed field study, lecture, seminar *Students:* mainly US
Costs: About $2,995 for WI residents *incl* tuition, housing, all meals, intl airfare, excursions, theater tickets, entrance fees
Housing: *Arr by pgm:* residence halls
Deadline: 10 wks before pgm or when full
Other info: *US accredited sponsor:* yes *Began:* 1994 *Orient:* in US *Activities:* excursions, cultural events *Misc:* May contact former participants. *Financial aid:* scholarships *URL:* http://www.uwsp.edu/studyabroad
Contact: Intl Pgms, Univ of Wisconsin-Stevens Point, Stevens Point WI 54481 *Ph:* 715-346 2717 *Fax:* 715-346 3951 *E-mail:* intlprog@uwsp.edu

---

1690
VANDERBILT UNIVERSITY
Humanities in London
Site: England: London
Dates: 5-1/2 wks, Jul 8-Aug 14
Subjects: Drama/theater, English literature, Fine arts, History
Eligibility: *Level:* sophs, jrs, srs *Requires:* 2.7 GPA, transcript, references *Age:* avg 20
Credit: *Undergrad:* 6 *Grad:* none *Doc:* transcript
Instruction: *In:* English *Format:* lecture *Students:* mainly US
Costs: Contact sponsor
Housing: *Arr by pgm:* apartments
Deadline: Contact sponsor
Other info: *US accredited sponsor:* yes *Activities:* field trips *Misc:* Guest lecturers. May contact former participants.
Contact: Ms Ann Oslin, Box 1806, Station B, Vanderbilt Univ, Nashville TN 37235 *Ph:* 615-322 2527 *Fax:* 615-322 2305 *E-mail:* oslinva@cfrvax.vanderbilt.edu

---

1691
VANDERBILT UNIVERSITY
International Studies in London
Site: England: London
Dates: 5-1/2 wks, Jul 8-Aug 14
Subjects: Economics, Political science/politics
Eligibility: *Level:* sophs, jrs, srs *Requires:* 2.7 GPA, previous study in field, transcript, references *Age:* avg 20
Credit: *Undergrad:* 6 *Grad:* none *Doc:* transcript
Instruction: *In:* English *Format:* lecture *Students:* mainly US
Costs: Contact sponsor
Housing: *Arr by pgm:* apartments
Deadline: Contact sponsor
Other info: *US accredited sponsor:* yes *Activities:* field trips *Misc:* May contact former participants.
Contact: Prof Derek Waller, Box 27, Station B, Vanderbilt Univ, Nashville TN 37235 *Ph:* 615-322 6226 *Fax:* 615-322 2305 *E-mail:* oslinva@cfrvax.vanderbilt.edu

---

1692
VIRGINIA POLYTECHNIC INSTITUTE & STATE UNIVERSITY
Finance & Technology in the UK
Site: England: London *Host inst:* IES-London
Dates: 7-1/2 wks, May 14-Jul 4
Subjects: Banking, Finance (beg/int), International business, Sciences, Technology
Eligibility: *Level:* srs, grads *Requires:* 2.0 GPA, previous study in field *Age:* min 18, max 65, avg 21
Credit: *Undergrad:* 9 *Grad:* 9 *Doc:* transcript
Instruction: *In:* English *Format:* seminar *Students:* mainly US
Costs: $4,900 & out-of-state tuition *incl* housing, some meals, intl airfare, fees, excursions *Nonrefundable fee*
Housing: *Arr by pgm:* apartments
Deadline: Jan 31
Other info: *US accredited sponsor:* yes *Began:* 2000 *Orient:* in US & abroad *Activities:* excursions, field trips, program travel, cultural events *URL:* http://gmorgan2.cob.vt.edu
Contact: George Morgan, VA Tech, 1016 Pamplin Hall (0221), Blacksburg, VA 24061 *Ph:* 540-231 7380 *Fax:* 540-231 3155 *E-mail:* gmorgan@vat.edu
Or Contact: Dilip Shome, VA Tech, 1016 Pamplin Hall (0221), Blacksburg VA 24061 *Ph:* 540-231 7380 *Fax:* 540-23331 3155 *E-mail:* dilip@vt.edu

---

1693
VIRGINIA POLYTECHNIC INSTITUTE & STATE UNIVERSITY
London Semester
Site: England: London *Host inst:* Foundation for Intl Educ
Dates: 4 wks or longer, May 20-Jun 17
Subjects: Political science/politics, Public policy
Eligibility: *Level:* sophs, jrs, srs *Requires:* 2.8 GPA *Age:* min 19, max 25, avg 20
Credit: *Undergrad:* 6 *Grad:* none *Doc:* transcript
Instruction: *In:* English *Format:* study tour *Students:* mainly US
Costs: $3,100 *incl* housing, intl airfare, insurance, fees, excursions, lectures *Nonrefundable fee*
Housing: *Arr by pgm:* residence halls, apartments
Deadline: Mar 1
Other info: *US accredited sponsor:* yes *Began:* 1999 *Orient:* abroad (1 day) *Activities:* field trips, program travel, cultural events *URL:* http://www.spia.vt.edu/lonsem
Contact: Virginia Tech, 108 Arch Annex, SPIA, Blacksburg VA 24061 *Ph:* 540-231 5517 *Fax:* 540-231 3367 *E-mail:* jayjon@vt.edu
Or Contact: Charles Taylor, Virginia Tech, Political Sci Dept, Blacksburg VA 24061 *Ph:* 540-231 5555 *Fax:* 540-231 6078 *E-mail:* clt@vt.edu

---

1694
WEBSTER UNIVERSITY
Graduate Program at Regent's College, London
Site: England: London *Host inst:* Webster Univ at Regent's Coll
Dates: 8 wks, summer
Subjects: Business/management, Computer sciences, Finance, International business, International relations, Marketing
Eligibility: *Level:* grads *Requires:* 2.5 GPA, bachelor's degree
Credit: *Undergrad:* avail *Grad:* 3-6 per term *Doc:* transcript, diploma
Instruction: *In:* English *Format:* music lesson, seminar *Students:* intl
Costs: $1,149 per 3-credit course *incl* tuition
Housing: *Sponsor assists:* apartments, hostels
Deadline: 6 mos before pgm
Other info: *US accredited sponsor:* yes *Began:* 1986 *Orient:* in US & abroad *Misc:* Registration fee applies for new degree-seeking students. *Financial aid:* scholarships *URL:* http://www.websteruniv.edu
Contact: Study Abroad Ctr, Webster Univ, 470 B Lockwood, St Louis MO 63119 *Ph:* 800-984 6857; 314-968 6988 *Fax:* 314-968 7119 *E-mail:* worldview@webster.edu

---

1695
WEBSTER UNIVERSITY and **REGENT'S COLLEGE**
Undergraduate Program in London
Site: England: London
Dates: 4 wks & 8 wks, Summer
Subjects: Business/management, Communications, Computer sciences, Economics, International relations, Liberal arts, Marketing, Media studies, Psychology
Eligibility: *Level:* sophs, jrs, srs *Requires:* 2.5 GPA
Credit: *Undergrad:* avail *Grad:* none *Doc:* transcript, diploma
Instruction: *In:* English *Format:* lecture, seminar *Students:* intl
Costs: $1,149 per 3-credit course *incl* tuition
Housing: *Sponsor assists:* residence halls, hostels
Deadline: 6 mos before pgm

Other info: *US accredited sponsor:* yes *Began:* 1986 *Orient:* in US & abroad *Activities:* excursions *Misc:* May contact former participants. *Financial aid:* scholarships *URL:* http://www.websteruniv.edu
Contact: Study Abroad Ctr, Webster Univ, 470 E Lockwood, St Louis MO 63119 *Ph:* 800-984 6988; 314-968 6988 *Fax:* 314-968 7119 *E-mail:* worldview@webster.edu

---

1696
WHITWORTH COLLEGE
British Culture Through Music or Theater
Site: England: London
Dates: 1 mo, Jan; offered in even-numbered yrs
Subjects: British studies, Civilization/culture, Drama/theater, Music
Eligibility: *Level:* sophs, jrs, srs
Credit: *Undergrad:* 3-4 *Grad:* none
Instruction: *In:* English *Format:* lecture *Students:* mainly US
Costs: About $3,500 *incl* housing, some meals, intl airfare, fees, excursions, books/materials
Housing: *Arr by pgm:* hotels
Deadline: Sep 15
Other info: *US accredited sponsor:* yes *Began:* 1986 *Activities:* excursions, cultural events *Misc:* Pgm offered in even-numbered yrs. May contact former participants. *URL:* http://www.whitworth.edu
Contact: Sue Jackson, Coord, Off-Campus Pgms, Ctr for Intl & Multicultural Educ, Whitworth Coll, Spokane WA 99251 *Ph:* 509-777 4596 *Fax:* 509-777 3723 *E-mail:* sjackson@whitworth.edu

---

1697
WIMBLEDON SCHOOL OF ART
Summer Courses
Site: England: London
Dates: 1 wk in Jul or Aug
Subjects: Costumes, Drawing, Fine arts, Homestay, Illustration, Painting, Photography, Sculpture, Theater design
Eligibility: *Level:* adults, teachers, professionals, precoll *Requires:* students under 16 must have legal guardian in UK *Age:* min 16, max 80
Credit: *Undergrad:* none *Grad:* none *Doc:* certificate
Instruction: *In:* English *Format:* art studio, practical training, workshop
Costs: UK 170-215 *Nonrefundable fee*
Housing: *Sponsor assists:* homestay
Deadline: Contact sponsor
Other info: *US accredited sponsor:* no *Orient:* abroad in London (5 days) *Activities:* excursions, field trips *URL:* http://www.wimbledon.ac.uk
Contact: Summer Course Administrator, Wimbledon Sch of Art, Merton Hall Rd, London SW19 3QA, UK *E-mail:* g.compton@wimbledon.ac.uk

---

NOTTINGHAM

1698
NOTTINGHAM TRENT UNIVERSITY
Internship Program
Site: England: Nottingham
Dates: 6-12 wks, yr-round
Subjects: Business/management, Communications, Education/teaching, Field study, Graphic arts/design, Health care/hospitals, Hotel management, Internships, Marketing, Media studies, Public administration, Public relations, Sports economics/management, Surveying, Tourism
Eligibility: *Level:* sophs, jrs, srs *Requires:* 2.8 GPA
Credit: *Undergrad:* none *Grad:* none *Doc:* transcript
Instruction: *In:* English *Format:* directed field study, independent study, internship, lecture, seminar, tutorial *Students:* mainly US
Costs: UK 2,400 per sem *incl* tuition, placement
Housing: *Sponsor assists:* residence halls, homestay
Deadline: 3 mos before pgm
Other info: *US accredited sponsor:* no *Began:* 1986 *Orient:* abroad *URL:* http://www.ntu.ac.uk
Contact: Yvonne Wroughton, Intl Off, Nottingham Trent Univ, Burton St, Nottingham NG1 4BU, UK *E-mail:* yvonne.wroughton@ntu.ac.uk

---

OUTER HEBRIDES

1699
BOSTON UNIVERSITY
Archaeological Field School-Scotland
Site: Scotland: Outer Hebrides *Host inst:* Flora MacDonald Project
Dates: 6 wks, Jun-Jul
Subjects: Archaeology
Eligibility: *Level:* sophs, jrs, srs, grads *Requires:* 3.0 GPA, in major, good acad standing
Credit: *Undergrad:* 8 *Grad:* 8 *Doc:* transcript
Instruction: *In:* English *Format:* directed field study, lecture, seminar *Students:* mainly US
Costs: $4,800 *incl* tuition, housing, all meals, excursions *Nonrefundable fee*
Housing: *Arr by pgm:* residence halls, rented house
Deadline: Mar 1; Apr 1 for scholarships
Other info: *US accredited sponsor:* yes *Began:* 1998 *Orient:* in US & abroad *Activities:* field trips, cultural events *Misc:* Full-time resident dir. 1-wk excursion to Glasgow. May contact former participants. *Financial aid:* scholarships *URL:* http://www.bu.edu/abroad/
Contact: Intl Pgms, Boston Univ, 232 Bay State Rd, Boston MA 02215 *Ph:* 617-353 9888 *Fax:* 617-353 5402 *E-mail:* abroad@bu.edu ▲

OXFORD

1700
ASSOCIATED COLLEGES OF THE SOUTH and RHODES COLLEGE
British Studies at Oxford
Site: England: Oxford *Host inst:* St John's Coll of Univ of Oxford
Dates: 6 wks, Jul-Aug
Subjects: Art history, British studies, English literature, Government, History, History of science, Music history, Political science/politics, Religion/theology
Eligibility: *Level:* fresh, sophs, jrs, srs, grads, adults *Requires:* 2.0 GPA *Age:* min 19, avg 21
Credit: *Undergrad:* 6-9 *Grad:* avail *Doc:* transcript, diploma
Instruction: *In:* English *Format:* lecture, seminar, study tour *Students:* mainly US
Costs: About $5,250 *incl* tuition, housing, all meals, fees, excursions *Nonrefundable fee*
Housing: *Arr by pgm:* residence halls
Deadline: Apply early; Jan 30 for scholarships
Other info: *US accredited sponsor:* yes *Began:* 1970 *Orient:* abroad *Activities:* excursions, field trips, cultural events *Misc:* Financial aid for consortium members only. May contact former participants. *Financial aid:* scholarships, work study *URL:* http://BSAO.Rhodes.edu
Contact: *See Index II for Members* Dr Michael Leslie or Mary Allie Baldwin, Rhodes Coll, 2000 North Pkwy, Memphis TN 38112-1690 *Ph:* 901-843 3715 *Fax:* 901-843 3717 *E-mail:* bsao@rhodes.edu

---

1701
DUKE UNIVERSITY
Duke in Oxford
Site: England: Oxford *Host inst:* New Coll of Univ of Oxford
Dates: Early Jul-mid-Aug
Subjects: British studies, English literature, History, Law, Political science/politics
Eligibility: *Level:* sophs, jrs, srs *Requires:* 3.0 GPA, good acad standing, transcript
Credit: *Undergrad:* 2 credits *Grad:* none *Doc:* transcript

Instruction: *In:* English *Format:* lecture, tutorial *Students:* mainly US
Costs: $6,075 for 2 courses *incl* tuition, housing, all meals, excursions
Housing: *Arr by pgm:* residence halls
Deadline: Feb 16
Other info: *US accredited sponsor:* yes *Began:* 1975 *Orient:* in US & abroad *Activities:* excursions, cultural events *URL:* http://www.aas.duke.edu/study_abroad/
Contact: Study Abroad, Duke Univ, 121 Allen Bldg, Box 90057, Durham NC 27708-0057 *Ph:* 919-684 2174 *Fax:* 919-684 3083 *E-mail:* abroad@asdean.duke.edu

---

1702
GEORGE WASHINGTON UNIVERSITY
International Human Rights Law
Site: England: Oxford *Host inst:* Univ of Oxford, New Coll
Dates: 4 wks, Jul-Aug
Subjects: Human rights, International law, Refugee studies, Women's studies
Eligibility: *Level:* grads, professionals *Requires:* good acad standing, demonstrated interest in human rights law *Age:* min 21
Credit: *Undergrad:* none *Grad:* 5 *Doc:* transcript
Instruction: *In:* English *Format:* lecture, seminar *Students:* US & intl
Costs: $5,350 *incl* tuition, housing, all meals, fees, books/materials *Nonrefundable fee*
Housing: *Arr by pgm:* residence halls
Deadline: Apr 15
Other info: *US accredited sponsor:* yes *Began:* 1994 *In coop with:* Univ of Oxford *Orient:* abroad (1 day) *Activities:* cultural events *Misc:* May contact former participants. *URL:* http://www.summer.gwu.edu
Contact: Summer, Special & Intl Pgms, George Washington Univ, 609 22nd St NW, Washington DC 20052 *Ph:* 202-994 6360 *Fax:* 202-994 9133 *E-mail:* sumprogs@gwu.edu

---

1703
GEORGETOWN UNIVERSITY
Comparative Strategic Management
Site: England: Oxford *Host inst:* Trinity Coll
Dates: Late-Jun-early Aug
Subjects: Business/management
Eligibility: *Level:* jrs *Requires:* 3.0 GPA, previous study in field
Credit: *Undergrad:* 6 *Grad:* none
Instruction: *In:* English *Format:* lecture, tutorial *Students:* mainly US
Costs: About $5,200 *incl* tuition, housing, some meals, fees, excursions
Housing: *Arr by pgm:* residence halls
Deadline: Feb 23
Other info: *US accredited sponsor:* yes *Activities:* field trips *Misc:* Study visits. *URL:* http://www.georgetown.edu/programs/oip/os
Contact: Dean Ann-Mary Kapusta, McDonough Sch of Bus, Georgetown Univ, Washington DC 20057-1008 *Ph:* 202-687 3851 *E-mail:* kapustaa@georgetown.edu
Or Contact: Rachel Rubin, Intl Pgms, Georgetown Univ, Washington DC 20057-1013 *Ph:* 202-687 9821 *Fax:* 202-687 5944 *E-mail:* rubinr@georgetown.edu

---

1704
GEORGETOWN UNIVERSITY
International Management Graduate Business Program in Oxford, England
Site: England: Oxford *Host inst:* Trinity Coll, Oxford Univ
Dates: Jun 27-Aug 8
Subjects: Business/management, International business
Eligibility: *Level:* grads
Credit: *Undergrad:* none *Grad:* 6 *Doc:* transcript
Instruction: *In:* English *Format:* directed field study, lecture, tutorial *Students:* mainly US
Costs: Contact sponsor
Housing: *Arr by pgm:* residence halls
Deadline: Feb 23
Other info: *US accredited sponsor:* yes *Activities:* excursions *Financial aid:* scholarships *URL:* http://www.georgetown.edu/ssce
Contact: Dean Ann-Mary Kapusta, McDonough Sch of Bus, Georgetown Univ, Washington DC 20057-1008 *Ph:* 202-687 3851 *E-mail:* kapustaa@georgetown.edu
Or Contact: Rachel Rubin, Intl Pgms, Georgetown Univ, Washington DC 20057-1013 *Ph:* 202-687 9821 *Fax:* 202-687 5944 *E-mail:* rubinr@georgetown.edu

---

1705
GEORGETOWN UNIVERSITY
Shakespeare Text and Performance
Site: England: Oxford *Host inst:* Oxford Univ, Lady Margaret Hall
Dates: 4 wks, early Jul-late Jul
Subjects: Drama/theater, Shakespeare studies
Eligibility: *Level:* fresh, sophs, jrs, srs, grads *Age:* min 18
Credit: *Undergrad:* 6 *Grad:* 6 *Doc:* transcript
Instruction: *In:* English *Format:* lecture, seminar, workshop *Students:* mainly US
Costs: About $3,550 *incl* tuition, housing, some meals, excursions, books/materials
Housing: *Arr by pgm:* residence halls
Deadline: Mid-Mar
Other info: *US accredited sponsor:* yes *Orient:* in US *Activities:* excursions, cultural events *Misc:* Pgm formerly offered at DeMontfort Univ in Leicester. Venue changed to provide opportunity to study at Oxford. May contact former participants. *URL:* http://www.georgetown.edu/programs/oip/os/sites/summer
Contact: Rachel Rubin, Intl Pgms, Georgetown Univ, PO Box 571013, Washington DC 20057-1013 *Ph:* 202-687 5620 *E-mail:* rubinr@georgetown.edu

---

1706
LEXIA INTERNATIONAL
LEXIA Summer in Oxford
Site: England: Oxford *Host inst:* Univ of Oxford
Dates: 8 wks, mid-Jun-mid-Aug
Subjects: Anthropology, Arts, Civilization/culture, Community service projects, Ecology/environmental studies, Economics, European studies, Fine arts, History, Homestay, Independent study, Internships, Literature, Political science/politics, Sociology
Eligibility: *Level:* fresh, sophs, jrs, srs, grads *Requires:* 2.5 GPA, 1 yr postsecondary educ completed *Age:* min 18, avg 21
Credit: *Undergrad:* 8-10 *Grad:* 8-10 *Doc:* transcript *Transfer credit through:* Western Washington Univ
Instruction: *In:* English *Format:* independent study, internship, lang study, lecture, seminar, volunteer/svc *Students:* mainly US
Costs: $5,650 *incl* tuition, housing, all meals, insurance, fees, excursions, ISIC, computer access *Nonrefundable fee*
Housing: *Arr by pgm:* residence halls with local students, homestay
Deadline: Apr 15; Apr 1 for scholarships
Other info: *US accredited sponsor:* no *Began:* 2000 *In coop with:* Western Washington Univ *Orient:* abroad (2 days, intensive lang study) *Activities:* excursions, field trips, program travel, cultural events, sports *Misc:* Student support svcs. May contact former participants. *Financial aid:* scholarships, work study *URL:* http://www.lexiaintl.org
Contact: LEXIA Intl, 25 S Main St, Hanover NH 03755 *Ph:* 800-775 3942; 603-643 9898 *Fax:* 603-643 9899 *E-mail:* info@lexiaintl.org
Or Contact: LEXIA Intl, West Coast, 378 Cambridge Ave, Palo Alto CA 94306 *Ph:* 650-327 9191 *Fax:* 650-327 9192

1707
NEW YORK UNIVERSITY, SCHOOL OF CONTINUING AND PROFESSIONAL STUDIES
Study Program at Oxford University
Site: England: Oxford *Host inst:* Oxford Univ at Christ Church Coll
Dates: 2 wks, Jul 28-Aug 11

Subjects: Elizabethan England, Victorian England
Eligibility: *Level:* fresh
Credit: *Undergrad:* avail *Grad:* none
Instruction: *In:* English *Format:* lecture *Students:* mainly US
Costs: $1,795 *incl* tuition, housing, all meals
Housing: *Arr by pgm:* residence halls
Deadline: Apr 1
Other info: *US accredited sponsor:* yes *Began:* 2000 *Orient:* in US (1 day) *Activities:* field trips *URL:* http://www.scps.nyu.edu
Contact: Vera Jelinek, NYU Sch of Continuing & Prof Studies, Intl Pgms, 48 Cooper Sq, Rm 101, New York NY 10003 *Ph:* 212-998 7133 *Fax:* 212-995 4134 *E-mail:* vera.jelinek@nyu.edu
Or Contact: Amber Devlin, NYU Sch of Continuing & Prof Studies, Intl Pgms, 48 Cooper Sq, Rm 101, New York NY 10003 *Ph:* 212-998 7133 *Fax:* 212-995 4134 *E-mail:* amber.devlin@nyu.edu

---

1708
NEW YORK UNIVERSITY, SCHOOL OF EDUCATION
English Education/Early Childhood and Elementary Education
Site: England: Oxford *Host inst:* Trinity Coll of Univ of Oxford
Dates: 8 wks, Jun 29-Aug 10
Subjects: Education/teaching, Elementary education, English
Eligibility: *Level:* grads *Requires:* 3.0 GPA, previous study in field
Credit: *Undergrad:* none *Grad:* avail *Doc:* transcript
Instruction: *In:* English *Format:* lecture, study tour *Students:* mainly US
Costs: $10,860 *incl* tuition, housing, some meals *Nonrefundable fee*
Housing: *Arr by pgm:* residence halls
Deadline: Apr 1
Other info: *US accredited sponsor:* yes *Began:* 1974 *Orient:* abroad *Activities:* field trips *Misc:* May contact former participants. *URL:* http://www.nyu.edu/summer
Contact: Harold Vine, Dir of English Educ Pgm, Teaching & Learning, New York Univ, 239 Greene St, Rm 635, New York NY 10003 *Ph:* 212-998 5237 *Fax:* 212-995 4198
Or Contact: Helen J Kelly, Dir of Special Pgms, New York Univ, 82 Washington Sq E, Rm 62, New York NY 10003 *Ph:* 212-998 5090 *Fax:* 212-995 4923 ▲

1709
NORTH CAROLINA STATE UNIVERSITY and **UNIVERSITY OF NORTH CAROLINA AT ASHEVILLE**
Summer at Oxford, England
Site: England: Oxford *Host inst:* Oxford Coll
Dates: 4 wks, Jun-Jul
Subjects: Art, British studies, Current events, History, Literature, Shakespeare studies
Eligibility: *Level:* fresh, sophs, jrs, srs *Requires:* 2.5 GPA
Credit: *Undergrad:* avail *Grad:* none *Doc:* transcript
Instruction: *In:* English *Format:* lecture, seminar, study tour *Students:* mainly US
Costs: $2,200 *incl* tuition, housing, some meals, fees, excursions
Housing: *Arr by pgm:* residence halls
Deadline: Feb
Other info: *US accredited sponsor:* yes *Began:* 1975 *Activities:* excursions, field trips, program travel, cultural events *URL:* http://www.ncsu.edu/study_abroad
Contact: Anne Haberkern, North Carolina State Univ, 2118 Pullen Hall, Box 7344, Raleigh NC 27695-7344 *Ph:* 919-515 2087 *Fax:* 919-515 6021 *E-mail:* study_abroad@ncsu.edu

---

1710
NORTHERN ILLINOIS UNIVERSITY
NIU at Oxford
Site: England: Oxford *Host inst:* Oriel Coll of Univ of Oxford
Dates: 6 wks, Jul-Aug
Subjects: Anthropology, Botany, British studies, English literature
Eligibility: *Level:* sophs, jrs, srs, grads *Requires:* 2.5 GPA, good acad standing *Age:* min 18, avg 22
Credit: *Undergrad:* 3-6 *Grad:* 3-6 *Doc:* transcript
Instruction: *In:* English *Format:* tutorial *Students:* mainly US
Costs: About $4,900 *incl* tuition, housing, some meals, insurance, fees, excursions
Housing: *Arr by pgm:* residence halls
Deadline: May 1 or until pgm filled
Other info: *US accredited sponsor:* yes *Began:* 1968 *Orient:* in US & abroad *Misc:* 32nd annual summer pgm offered by NIU & Oriel Coll taking advantage of the unique resources of the British setting. May contact former participants. *URL:* http://www.niu.edu/niuabroad/
Contact: Anne Seitzinger, Pgm Coord, Study Abroad, Williston 417, Northern Illinois Univ, DeKalb IL 60115 *Ph:* 815-753 0700 *Fax:* 815-753 0825 *E-mail:* niuabroad@niu.edu
Or Contact: Dr Gabriel Holbrook, Biological Scis, Northern Illinois Univ, DeKalb IL 60115 *Ph:* 815-753 3199 *E-mail:* gholbrook@niu.abroad

---

1711
OAKLAND UNIVERSITY and **UNIVERSITY OF DETROIT MERCY**
British Studies at Oxford, England
Site: England: Oxford *Host inst:* Corpus Christi Coll of Univ of Oxford
Dates: 3 or 6 wks, Jul 1-21; Jul 22-Aug 11
Subjects: Architecture, Art history, Business/management, Communications, Drama/theater, Education/teaching, English literature, Field study, History, Political science/politics
Eligibility: *Level:* fresh, sophs, jrs, srs, grads, adults *Requires:* 2.5 GPA *Age:* min 18
Credit: *Undergrad:* 3-8 *Grad:* 3-6
Instruction: *In:* English *Format:* directed field study, lecture, seminar *Students:* mainly US
Costs: $3,250 for 3 wks, $5,950 for 6 wks *incl* tuition, housing, all meals, fees, excursions, theater *Nonrefundable fee*
Housing: *Arr by pgm:* private rms in coll
Deadline: Apr 30 or until pgm filled
Other info: *US accredited sponsor:* yes *Began:* 1973 *Activities:* excursions, cultural events *Misc:* Optional wkend travel. Loans avail. May contact former participants. *URL:* http://www.oakland.edu/oxford
Contact: Prof Margaret Pigott, Ctr for Intl Pgms, Oakland Univ, Rochester MI 48309-4401 *Ph:* 248-370 4131, 248-652 3405 *Fax:* 248-650 9107 *E-mail:* pigott@oakland.edu
Or Contact: Prof Edward J Wolff, Study Abroad, Univ of Detroit Mercy, Box 19900, Detroit MI 48219-0900 *Ph:* 313-993 1082, 248-652 3405 *Fax:* 248-650 9107

1712
OXFORD STUDY ABROAD PROGRAMME
Oxford Study Abroad Program
Site: England: Oxford *Host inst:* New Coll, St Edmund Hall of Univ of Oxford, others
Dates: 4-12 wks, May 16-Sep 25
Subjects: Full curriculum, Shakespeare studies
Eligibility: *Level:* sophs, jrs, srs, grads, adults, teachers, professionals *Requires:* 3.0 GPA *Age:* min 17, avg 20
Credit: *Undergrad:* 1 per wk *Grad:* 1 per wk *Doc:* transcript *Transfer credit through:* Univ of the Pacific
Instruction: *In:* English *Format:* independent study, lab, lecture, study tour, tutorial *Students:* mainly US
Costs: $3,350 for 4 wks, $4,800 for 6 wks, $8,400 for 12 wks *incl* tuition, housing, all meals, fees, excursions
Housing: *Arr by pgm:* apartments with local students, residence halls with local students
Deadline: May 1 for May or Jun; Jun 15 for Jul, Aug, Sep
Other info: *US accredited sponsor:* no *Began:* 1994 *In coop with:* Univ of the Pacific *Orient:* abroad (3 days) *Activities:*

 See "How To Use This Book" for definitions of terms used above. ▲ = See program sponsor's ad(s) in this book.

excursions, field trips, program travel, cultural events, sports *Misc:* May contact former participants. *Financial aid:* scholarships, work study *URL:* http://www.osap.co.uk
Contact: Dr Holly Boren, Admin Dir, Oxford Study Abroad Pgm, Clarendon House, 52 Cornmarket St, Oxford OX1 3HJ, UK *E-mail:* osap@osap.co.uk

---

1713
SOUTHERN METHODIST UNIVERSITY
SMU in Oxford
Site: England: Oxford *Host inst:* Univ Coll of Univ of Oxford
Dates: Jul 1-Aug 5
Subjects: History, Literature, Political science/politics
Eligibility: *Level:* sophs, jrs, srs *Requires:* 2.5 GPA
Credit: *Undergrad:* 6 *Grad:* none *Doc:* transcript
Instruction: *In:* English *Format:* lecture, tutorial *Students:* mainly US
Costs: About $5,595 *incl* tuition, housing, most meals, fees, excursions, most meals *Nonrefundable fee*
Housing: *Arr by pgm:* residence halls
Deadline: Mar 1 or until pgm filled
Other info: *US accredited sponsor:* yes *Began:* 1978 *Activities:* excursions *Misc:* Guest lecturers & symposia. Scholarships for own students only. Loans avail. *Financial aid:* scholarships *URL:* http://www.smu.edu/studyabroad
Contact: Intl Pgms, Southern Methodist Univ, PO Box 0391, 3108 Fondren Dr, Dallas TX 75275-0591 *Ph:* 214-768 2338 *Fax:* 214-768 1061 *E-mail:* intlpro@mail.smu.edu
Or Contact: Dr Daniel Orlovsky, History, Southern Methodist Univ 0391, 3108 Fondren Dr, Dallas TX 75275 *Ph:* 214-768 2967 *E-mail:* dorlovsk@mail.smu.edu
Or Contact: Dr Michael Holahan, English, Southern Methodist Univ PO Box 0391, 3108 Fondren Dr, Dallas TX 75275 *Ph:* 214-768 2872 *E-mail:* mholahan@mail.smu.edu ▲

1714
UNIVERSITY OF ALABAMA
Alabama at Oxford
Site: England: Oxford
Dates: Jul 9-Aug 12
Subjects: English literature, History
Eligibility: *Level:* fresh, sophs, jrs, srs, grads *Age:* avg 20
Credit: *Undergrad:* avail *Grad:* none
Instruction: *In:* English *Format:* lecture *Students:* mainly US
Costs: About $3,950 *incl* tuition, housing, some meals, excursions
Housing: *Arr by pgm:* residence halls
Deadline: Mar 31
Other info: *US accredited sponsor:* yes *Began:* 1978 *Misc:* Optional travel. *URL:* http://www.ua.edu/international
Contact: Capstone Intl Pgm Ctr, Univ of Alabama, PO Box 870254, Tuscaloosa AL 35487-0254 *Ph:* 205-348 5256 *Fax:* 205-348 5298 *E-mail:* achannel@aalan.ua.edu

---

1715
UNIVERSITY OF MASSACHUSETTS AMHERST and **TRINITY COLLEGE, UNIVERSITY OF OXFORD**
Oxford Summer Seminar
Site: England: Oxford *Host inst:* Trinity Coll of Univ of Oxford
Dates: 6 wks, early Jul-mid-Aug
Subjects: Art, History, Law, Literature, Political science/politics
Eligibility: *Level:* fresh, sophs, jrs, srs, grads *Requires:* B avg in major
Credit: *Undergrad:* avail *Grad:* avail *Doc:* transcript
Instruction: *In:* English *Format:* tutorial *Students:* mainly US
Costs: $3,950-$4,150 *incl* tuition, housing, some meals, local transport
Housing: *Arr by pgm:* residence halls
Deadline: Mar 30
Other info: *US accredited sponsor:* yes *Began:* 1966 *Activities:* cultural events *Misc:* Theater trips incl. Optional travel to places of literary & historical interest. *Financial aid:* scholarships *URL:* http://www.umass.edu/oxford
Contact: Oxford Summer Seminar, English, Bartlett Hall, Univ of Massachusetts, Amherst MA 01003 *Ph:* 413-545 1914 *Fax:* 413-545 3880 *E-mail:* oxford@english.umass.edu

---

1716
UNIVERSITY OF MIAMI (FL)
Literature and History/Politics in Oxford, England
Site: England: Oxford *Host inst:* Univ of Oxford
Dates: 3-6 wks, early Jul-mid-Aug
Subjects: History, Literature, Political science/politics
Eligibility: *Level:* jrs, srs *Requires:* 3.5 GPA *Age:* min 18
Credit: *Undergrad:* 3 *Grad:* none *Doc:* transcript
Instruction: *In:* English *Format:* lecture *Students:* mainly US
Costs: $2,880 *incl* tuition, housing, all meals *Nonrefundable fee*
Housing: *Arr by pgm:* residence halls
Deadline: Apr 1
Other info: *US accredited sponsor:* yes *Began:* 1996 *Orient:* abroad (1 day) *Misc:* May contact former participants. *URL:* http://www.studyabroad.miami.edu
Contact: Intl Educ & Exch Pgms, Allen Hall 212, 5050 Brunson Dr, PO Box 248005, Univ of Miami, Coral Gables FL 33124-1610 *Ph:* 800-557 5421; 305-284 3434 *Fax:* 305-284 6629 *E-mail:* ieep@miami.edu

---

1717
UNIVERSITY OF MICHIGAN
Medieval or Environmental Studies at Oxford
Site: England: Oxford *Host inst:* St Peter's Coll of Univ of Oxford
Dates: 6 wks, early Jul-mid-Aug
Subjects: Ecology/environmental studies, Medieval studies
Eligibility: *Level:* jrs, srs, grads *Requires:* enrollment at accredited US or Canadian coll
Credit: *Undergrad:* 6-8 *Grad:* none
Instruction: *In:* English *Format:* directed field study, lecture, tutorial *Students:* mainly US
Costs: Contact Sponsor
Housing: *Arr by pgm:* residence halls
Deadline: Feb 16
Other info: *US accredited sponsor:* yes *Began:* 1989 *Activities:* excursions *Misc:* May contact former participants. *URL:* http://www.umich.edu/~iinet/oip/
Contact: Intl Pgms, Univ of Michigan, G513 Michigan Union, Ann Arbor MI 48109-1349 *Ph:* 734-764 4311 *Fax:* 734-764 3229 *E-mail:* oip@umich.edu

---

1718
UNIVERSITY OF SAN DIEGO, SCHOOL OF LAW
Oxford Institute on International and Comparative Law
Site: England: Oxford *Host inst:* Magdalen Coll of Univ of Oxford
Dates: About Jul 2-Aug 3
Subjects: Comparative law, European Union, International law
Eligibility: *Level:* grads, teachers, professionals *Requires:* law or bus students
Credit: *Undergrad:* none *Grad:* 6 *Doc:* certificate
Instruction: *In:* English *Format:* tutorial *Students:* mainly US
Costs: About $4,000, $4,500 with tutorial, *incl* tuition, housing, some meals, books/materials *Nonrefundable fee*
Housing: *Arr by pgm:* residence halls
Deadline: Mar 11
Other info: *US accredited sponsor:* yes *Began:* 1977 *Orient:* abroad *Misc:* Legal visits, some tourist visits arr at site. Correspondence re:pgm must be in English. Loans for US students only. *URL:* http://www.acusd.edu/lawabroad
Contact: Cindy King, Law Pgms Abroad, Univ of San Diego, 5998 Alcala Park, San Diego CA 92110-2492 *Ph:* 619-260 7460 *Fax:* 619-260 2230 *E-mail:* cking@acusd.edu

---

1719
UNIVERSITY OF TEXAS AT AUSTIN
Department of Geography Summer Program in England
Site: England: Oxford *Host inst:* Brasenose Coll of Univ of Oxford
Dates: 5 wks, mid-Jul-mid-Aug
Subjects: British studies, Civilization/culture, Geography
Eligibility: *Level:* fresh, sophs, jrs, srs
Credit: *Undergrad:* 6 *Grad:* none *Doc:* transcript
Instruction: *In:* English *Format:* lecture *Students:* mainly US
Costs: Contact sponsor
Housing: *Arr by pgm:* residence halls
Deadline: Early Dec for priority admission
Other info: *US accredited sponsor:* yes *Began:* 1990 *Orient:* in US *Activities:* field trips *Misc:* May contact former participants. *URL:* http://www.utexas.edu/student/abroad
Contact: Joy Williamson, Adviser, Study Abroad, Univ of Texas at Austin, Drawer A, Univ Station, Austin TX 78713-7206 *Ph:* 512-471 6490 *Fax:* 512-232 4363 *E-mail:* studyabroadinfo@mozart.io.utexas.edu

---

1720
WASHINGTON INTERNATIONAL STUDIES COUNCIL
Oxford Colleges Program (Summer)
Site: England: Oxford *Host inst:* New Coll & St Anne's Coll of Univ of Oxford
Dates: 4 or 6 wks, May 16-Sep 26
Subjects: Full curriculum
Eligibility: *Level:* adults *Requires:* 3.0 GPA, previous study in field *Age:* min 17, avg 20
Credit: *Undergrad:* 1 per wk *Grad:* 1 per wk *Doc:* transcript
Instruction: *In:* English *Format:* independent study, lab, lecture, study tour, tutorial *Students:* mainly US
Costs: $4,200 for 4 wks, $6,300 for 6 wks, $8,500 for 8 wks *incl* tuition, housing, fees, excursions
Housing: *Arr by pgm:* apartments with local students, residence halls with local students
Deadline: May 1 for May; Jun 1 for pgm beginning after Jun 10
Other info: *US accredited sponsor:* no *Began:* 1985 *Orient:* abroad (3 days) *Activities:* excursions, field trips, program travel, cultural events, sports *Misc:* Individual tutorial method. May contact former participants. *Financial aid:* scholarships, work study *URL:* http://www.studyabroad.com/wisc
Contact: Robert Schuettinger, Pres, WISC, 138 High St, Oxford OX1 4DN, UK *E-mail:* wiscox@earthdome.com

Or Contact: Stacy Swiger or Jessica O'Neill Ealick, Dir DC Off, WISC, 214 Massachusetts Ave NE, Ste 370, Washington DC 20002 *Ph:* 800-323 9472; 202-547 3275 *Fax:* 202-547 1470 *E-mail:* wisc@erols.com

---

READING

1721
UNIVERSITY STUDIES ABROAD CONSORTIUM
Modern Britain: British Literature and Theatre Studies
Site: England: Reading *Host inst:* Univ of Reading
Dates: 5 wks, Jul 2-Aug 3
Subjects: British studies, Civilization/culture, Contemporary issues, Economics, Education/teaching, History, Homestay, Literature, Political science/politics, Shakespeare studies, Theater arts
Eligibility: *Level:* grads *Requires:* 2.5 GPA, good acad standing *Age:* min 18, avg 22
Credit: *Undergrad:* 6 *Grad:* 6 *Doc:* transcript
Instruction: *In:* English *Format:* lecture, seminar *Students:* US & intl
Costs: $2,880 *incl* tuition, housing, all meals, insurance, fees, ISIC
Housing: *Arr by pgm:* residence halls with local students, homestay
Deadline: Apr 15
Other info: *US accredited sponsor:* yes *Began:* 1998 *Orient:* abroad *Activities:* field trips, cultural events, sports *Misc:* Beaches. Pgm organized flights. May contact former participants. *URL:* http://www.usac.unr.edu
Contact: *See Index II for Members* Carmelo Urza, Univ Studies Abroad Consortium, Univ of Nevada Library 323, Reno NV 89557-0093 *Ph:* 775-784 6569 *Fax:* 775-784 6010 *E-mail:* usac@unr.edu
▲

SAINT ANDREWS

1722
SUNY COLLEGE AT BROCKPORT
Scotland Geology Program
Site: Scotland: St Andrews *Host inst:* Univ of St Andrews
Dates: 2 wks, Jul
Subjects: Earth sciences, Field study, Geology
Eligibility: *Level:* jrs, srs *Requires:* 2.5 GPA, previous study in field *Age:* min 18
Credit: *Undergrad:* 3 *Grad:* none *Doc:* transcript
Instruction: *In:* English *Format:* directed field study, lecture, seminar *Students:* mainly US
Costs: $3,250 *incl* tuition, housing, some meals, intl airfare, fees, excursions *Nonrefundable fee*
Housing: *Arr by pgm:* residence halls
Deadline: May 1
Other info: *US accredited sponsor:* yes *Began:* 1999 *Activities:* excursions, field trips, program travel *Misc:* Faculty dir. May contact former participants. *URL:* http://www.brockport.edu/study_abroad

Contact: Dr John J Perry, Dir, Intl Educ, SUNY Coll at Brockport, 350 New Campus Dr, Brockport NY 14420-2914 *Ph:* 800-298 7869; 716-395 2119 *Fax:* 716-637 3218 *E-mail:* overseas@brockport.edu

SHEFFIELD

1723
ENGLISH LITERATURE SUMMER SCHOOL
The Writer and the Environment
Site: England: Sheffield
Dates: 2 wks, Jul 7-21
Subjects: English literature
Eligibility: *Level:* fresh, sophs, jrs, srs, grads, adults, teachers, professionals, precoll *Requires:* keen interest in English literature *Age:* min 16, avg 48
Credit: *Undergrad:* avail *Grad:* avail *Doc:* certificate
Instruction: *In:* English *Format:* seminar *Students:* intl
Costs: $1,450 *incl* tuition, housing, all meals, fees, excursions, books/materials
Housing: *Arr by pgm:* homestay
Deadline: 1 mo before pgm or until pgm filled
Other info: *US accredited sponsor:* no *Began:* 1976 *Activities:* field trips, program travel *Misc:* May contact former participants. *URL:* http://www.englishsummerschools.co.uk
Contact: Avril Meakin, English Literature Summer Sch, 10 Victoria Rd, Sheffield S10 2DL, UK *E-mail:* arthurmeakin@netscape.net

STIRLING

1724
BEAVER COLLEGE, CENTER FOR EDUCATION ABROAD
University of Stirling Summer Academic Program
Site: England: Stirling *Host inst:* Univ of Stirling
Dates: Jun 23-Aug 18
Subjects: Full curriculum
Eligibility: *Level:* sophs, jrs, srs, grads *Requires:* 3.0 GPA
Credit: *Undergrad:* 4, 6, or 8 *Grad:* none *Doc:* transcript
Instruction: *In:* English *Format:* lecture *Students:* mainly host country
Costs: $2,875 for 4 credits, $3,325 for 6 credits, $3,850 for 8 credits *incl* tuition, housing, insurance, ISIC card, transcript *Nonrefundable fee*
Housing: *Arr by pgm:* residence halls
Deadline: Mar 31
Other info: *US accredited sponsor:* yes *Orient:* avail *Misc:* May contact former participants. *URL:* http://www.beaver.edu/cea/
Contact: Ctr for Educ Abroad, Beaver Coll, 450 S Easton Rd, Glenside PA 19038 *Ph:* 888-232 8379; 215-572 2901 *Fax:* 215-572 2174 *E-mail:* cea@beaver.edu ▲

1725
ILLINOIS STATE UNIVERSITY
Stirling, Scotland Summer Program
Site: Scotland: Stirling *Host inst:* Univ of Stirling
Dates: 7 wks, Jun 26-Aug 18
Subjects: Adult education, Business/management, Ecology/environmental studies, Film studies, History, Literature, Media studies, Political science/politics, Scottish studies
Eligibility: *Level:* sophs, jrs, srs *Requires:* 3.0 GPA
Credit: *Undergrad:* 5-10 *Grad:* none *Doc:* transcript
Instruction: *In:* English *Format:* lecture, seminar, tutorial *Students:* mainly host country
Costs: $4,400 for 5 credit hours, $5,120 for 10 credit hours *incl* housing, all meals, intl airfare, insurance, fees, instructional costs
Housing: *Arr by pgm:* residence halls
Deadline: Feb 14
Other info: *US accredited sponsor:* yes *Orient:* abroad *Activities:* cultural events, sports *Misc:* Courses change annually. Contact sponsor for current course info. *URL:* http://www.its.ilstu.edu/intlstudies/
Contact: Intl Studies, Illinois State Univ, Campus Box 6120, Normal IL 61790-6120 *Ph:* 309-438 5365 *Fax:* 309-438 3987 *E-mail:* oisp@ilstu.edu

1726
NORTH AMERICAN INSTITUTE FOR STUDY ABROAD
Summer in Scotland
Site: Scotland: Stirling *Host inst:* Univ of Stirling
Dates: 6 wks, early Jul-mid-Aug
Subjects: Business/management, Ecology/environmental studies, English, Film studies, French language, Geology, History, Media studies, Political science/politics
Eligibility: *Level:* fresh, sophs, jrs, srs *Requires:* 2.80 GPA *Age:* min 18, avg 20
Credit: *Undergrad:* 6-8 *Grad:* none *Doc:* transcript
Instruction: *In:* English *Format:* lecture, seminar *Students:* mainly US
Costs: $2,990 for 4 credits, $3,590 for 6 credits, $3,990 for 8 credits *incl* tuition, housing, insurance, fees, ISIC
Housing: *Arr by pgm:* residence halls
Deadline: Apr 30; Nov 30 for scholarships
Other info: *US accredited sponsor:* no *Began:* 1998 *Orient:* abroad *Activities:* cultural events *Misc:* May contact former participants. *Financial aid:* scholarships *URL:* http://www.naisa.com
Contact: Dr Michael Currid, NAISA, 129 Mill St, Danville PA 17868 *Ph:* 570-275 5099 *Fax:* 570-275 1644 *E-mail:* naisa@naisa.com

1727
UNIVERSITY OF NORTH CAROLINA AT CHARLOTTE
Community Service and Enrichment in Scotland
Site: Scotland: Stirling
Dates: Jun 3-25
Subjects: Community service projects, Independent study
Eligibility: *Level:* fresh, sophs, jrs, srs, grads *Age:* avg 20
Credit: *Undergrad:* 3-6 *Grad:* none *Doc:* transcript
Instruction: *In:* English *Format:* independent study, seminar, volunteer/svc *Students:* mainly US
Costs: $2,400 *incl* tuition, housing, some meals, intl airfare, insurance *Nonrefundable fee*
Housing: *Arr by pgm:* hostels
Deadline: Feb 15
Other info: *US accredited sponsor:* yes *Began:* 1995 *Orient:* in US *Activities:* excursions, field trips, program travel, cultural events *Misc:* May contact former participants. *URL:* http://www.uncc.edu/oip/edabroad.htm
Contact: Joel Gallegos, Dir, Educ Abroad/Intl Pgms, UNC Charlotte, 9201 University City Blvd, Charlotte NC 28223-0001 *Ph:* 704-687 2464 *Fax:* 704-687 3168 *E-mail:* stennies@email.uncc.edu
Or Contact: Dr C D Fernald, Psychology, UNC Charlotte, 9201 University City Blvd, Charlotte NC 28223 *Ph:* 704-687 4741 *Fax:* 704-687 3096 *E-mail:* cdfernald@email.uncc.edu

1728
UNIVERSITY OF STIRLING
Summer Academic Program
Site: Scotland: Stirling *Host inst:* Univ of Stirling
Dates: 8 wks, Jun 28-Aug 21
Subjects: Adult education, Business/management, Civilization/culture, Ecology/environmental studies, English, Film studies, French language, History, Independent study, Media studies, Political science/politics
Eligibility: *Level:* fresh, sophs, jrs, srs, adults, teachers *Requires:* 3.0 GPA, previous study in field *Age:* min 18, avg 21
Credit: *Undergrad:* avail *Grad:* none *Doc:* transcript
Instruction: *In:* English *Format:* independent study, lecture, seminar, tutorial *Students:* mainly host country

Costs: $3,200 *incl* tuition, housing, some meals, books/materials *Nonrefundable fee*
Housing: *Arr by pgm:* apartments
Deadline: May 30
Other info: *US accredited sponsor:* no *Began:* 1994 *Orient:* avail yes *Activities:* excursions, field trips, cultural events *URL:* http://www.stir.ac.uk/departments/daice/sap/
Contact: Ms S McGiffen, Univ of Stirling, Stirling FK9 4LA, Scotland, UK *E-mail:* d.l.kelso@stir.ac.uk

---

STRATFORD-UPON-AVON

1729
AMERICAN INSTITUTE FOR FOREIGN STUDY (AIFS)
Shakespeare Summer Program in Stratford, England
Site: England: Stratford-upon-Avon *Host inst:* Richmond, The Amer Intl Univ in London
Dates: 3 or 6 wks, Jun 16-Aug 6
Subjects: Acting, Drama/theater, English, Shakespeare studies
Eligibility: *Level:* fresh, sophs, jrs, srs, grads, adults, precoll *Requires:* 2.0 GPA
Credit: *Undergrad:* 4 *Grad:* none *Doc:* transcript *Transfer credit through:* Richmond, The Amer Intl Univ in London
Instruction: *In:* English *Format:* directed field study, lecture, seminar *Students:* mainly US
Costs: $4,199 for 3 wks, $5,539 for 6 wks *incl* tuition, housing, some meals, intl airfare, excursions *Nonrefundable fee*
Housing: *Arr by pgm:* residence halls
Deadline: Mar 15
Other info: *US accredited sponsor:* no *Began:* 2000 *Orient:* abroad *Activities:* excursions, cultural events *Misc:* May contact former participants. *Financial aid:* scholarships *URL:* http://www.aifs.com
Contact: Dana Maggio, Coll Div, AIFS, River Plaza, 9 W Broad St, Stamford CT 06902 *Ph:* 800-727 2437 ext 6084 *E-mail:* college.info@aifs.com ▲

1730
FLORIDA INTERNATIONAL UNIVERSITY
Shakespeare at Stratford
Site: England: Stratford-upon-Avon
Dates: 2 wks, Jun 23-Jul 2
Subjects: Drama/theater, English literature, Shakespeare studies
Eligibility: *Level:* fresh, sophs, jrs, srs, grads, adults, teachers, professionals *Requires:* previous study in field
Credit: *Undergrad:* 6 *Grad:* 6 *Doc:* transcript
Instruction: *In:* English *Format:* directed field study, lecture, practical training, study tour *Students:* mainly US
Costs: $2,250 *incl* housing, all meals, intl airfare, excursions, railpass *Nonrefundable fee*
Housing: *Arr by pgm:* homestay
Deadline: May 15
Other info: *US accredited sponsor:* yes *Began:* 1997 *Orient:* in US (1 day) *Activities:* excursions, field trips, program travel, cultural events *Misc:* May contact former participants. *Financial aid:* scholarships *URL:* http://www.fiu.edu/~intered
Contact: Intl Studies, Florida Intl Univ, 11200 SW 8th St, DM 300B, Miami FL 33199 *Ph:* 305-348 1913, 305-348 1918 *Fax:* 305-348 1941 *E-mail:* intered@fiu.edu

---

TOTNES

1731
TOTNES SCHOOL OF GUITARMAKING
Guitarmaking (Guitars and Related Instruments)
Site: England: Totnes (Devon)
Dates: 12 wks, Jan 15-Apr 6, May 7-Jul 27, Sep 24-Dec 12
Subjects: Guitar, Homestay, Musical instrument making
Eligibility: *Level:* adults *Age:* min 16, avg 23
Credit: *Undergrad:* none *Grad:* none *Doc:* certificate
Instruction: *In:* English *Format:* workshop *Students:* intl
Costs: UK 3,200 *incl* tuition *Nonrefundable fee*
Housing: *Sponsor assists:* homestay
Deadline: None
Other info: *US accredited sponsor:* no *Began:* 1985 *Misc:* Students make instrument of their choice. Materials' costs vary with instrument. May contact former participants. *URL:* http://www.totnesschoolofguitarmaking.co.uk
Contact: Norman Reed or Philip Messer, Asst Tutor, Totnes Sch of Guitarmaking, Collins Rd, Totnes, Devon TQ9 5PJ, UK

YORK

1732
SUNY ROCKLAND COMMUNITY COLLEGE
Literature of England's Lake District
Site: England: York
Dates: 2 wks, Jun 25-Jul 9
Subjects: English, Literature, Poetry (beg/int)
Eligibility: *Level:* fresh, sophs, jrs, srs, adults, teachers, professionals *Requires:* 2.5 GPA *Age:* min 18
Credit: *Undergrad:* 3 *Grad:* none *Doc:* transcript
Instruction: *In:* English *Format:* study tour *Students:* mainly US
Costs: About $2,300 *incl* tuition, housing, intl airfare, fees, excursions
Housing: *Arr by pgm:* hotels
Deadline: April 1
Other info: *US accredited sponsor:* yes *Began:* 2001 *Orient:* abroad *Activities:* excursions, field trips *Misc:* May contact former participants. *Financial aid:* scholarships *URL:* http://www.studyabroad.com/suny/rockland
Contact: Judy Dudderar, SUNY Rockland, 145 College Rd, Suffern NY 10901 *Ph:* 845-574 4205 *Fax:* 845-574 4423

Middle East and North Africa

More Than One Country

1733
GEORGE MASON UNIVERSITY
Jordan/Palestine/Syria/Israel: Peace Process
Site: Israel, Jordan
Dates: 2 wks, Jan 2-17
Subjects: Economics, International studies, Peace studies, Political science/ politics
Eligibility: *Level:* sophs, jrs, srs, grads, adults, teachers, professionals *Requires:* 2.25 GPA, 3.0 for grads *Age:* min 18
Credit: *Undergrad:* 3 *Grad:* 3 *Doc:* transcript
Instruction: *In:* English *Format:* directed field study, lecture, seminar, study tour *Students:* mainly US
Costs: About $3,650 for VA residents, $4,150 for others *incl* tuition, housing, some meals, intl airfare, insurance, fees, excursions, ISIC *Nonrefundable fee*
Housing: *Arr by pgm*
Deadline: Oct 16
Other info: *US accredited sponsor:* yes *Began:* 1996 *Orient:* in US *Activities:* excursions, field trips, program travel, cultural events, sports *Misc:* Min 12 students for pgm. *URL:* http://www.gmu.edu/departments/cge
Contact: Ctr for Global Educ, George Mason Univ, Johnson Ctr, Rm 235, 4400 University Dr, Fairfax VA 22030-4444 *Ph:* 703-993 2155, 703-993 2156 *Fax:* 703-993 2153 *E-mail:* cge@gmu.edu

---

1734
INTERNS FOR PEACE
Interns for Peace
Site: Israel: Green Line; Palestine National Authority Area: Gaza *Host inst:* Nitzanei Shalom
Dates: Yr-round
Subjects: Arabic studies, Community service projects, Internships, Peace studies
Eligibility: *Level:* grads, adults, teachers, professionals *Requires:* coll educ, adv Hebrew or Arabic
Credit: *Undergrad:* none *Grad:* none
Instruction: *In:* Arabic, Hebrew *Format:* internship *Students:* mainly host country
Costs: Contact sponsor
Housing: *Arr by pgm:* apartments
Deadline: Rolling admissions
Other info: *US accredited sponsor:* no *Began:* 1977 *Orient:* abroad (30 days) *Misc:* May contact former participants.
Contact: Karen Wald Cohen, Interns for Peace, 475 Riverside Dr, New York NY 10115 *Ph:* 212-870 2226 *Fax:* 212-870 2119

1735
SUNY UNIVERSITY AT BUFFALO
Off the Beaten Path: A Summer Sojourn to Jordan & Syria
Site: Jordan: Amman; Syria: Damascus
Dates: 1 mo, Jul 5-Aug 5
Subjects: Arabic language, Arabic studies, Civilization/culture, Field study, Independent study, Middle Eastern studies, Political science/politics, Women's studies
Eligibility: *Level:* sophs, jrs, srs, grads, adults, teachers, professionals *Requires:* 2.67 GPA *Age:* min 18
Credit: *Undergrad:* 6 per month *Grad:* 6 per month
Instruction: *In:* English *Format:* directed field study, independent study, lecture, study tour *Students:* mainly US
Costs: $3,600 *incl* tuition, housing, all meals, fees, excursions
Housing: *Arr by pgm:* hotels
Deadline: Apr 1
Other info: *US accredited sponsor:* yes *Began:* 2000 *Orient:* in US & abroad (1 day) *Activities:* excursions, program travel, cultural events *URL:* http://www.buffalo.edu/studyabroad/
Contact: Dr Sandra J Flash, Dir of SA, SUNY Univ at Buffalo, 210 Talbert Hall, Box 601604, Buffalo NY 14260-1604 *Ph:* 716-645 3912 *Fax:* 716-645 6197 *E-mail:* studyabroad@buffalo.edu

---

1736
THUNDERBIRD, THE AMERICAN GRADUATE SCHOOL OF INTERNATIONAL MANAGEMENT
Winterim in the United Arab Emirates and Lebanon
Site: Lebanon; United Arab Emirates: Dubai
Dates: 3 wks
Subjects: Business/management, Economics, International studies, Middle Eastern studies, Political science/politics
Eligibility: *Level:* grads *Requires:* 3.0 GPA
Credit: *Undergrad:* none *Grad:* 3 *Doc:* transcript
Instruction: *In:* English *Format:* lecture *Students:* intl
Costs: $2,625 *incl* tuition, pgm fee
Housing: *Sponsor assists:* hotels
Deadline: Contact sponsor
Other info: *US accredited sponsor:* yes *Orient:* abroad *Activities:* field trips *Misc:* Pgm explores global & econ implications of oil. Field trips to oil-drilling operations, Jebel Ali free zone. *Financial aid:* scholarships *URL:* http://www.t-bird.edu
Contact: James Scott, Overseas Pgms, Thunderbird, 15249 N 59th Ave, Glendale AZ 85306 *Ph:* 602-978 7251 *Fax:* 602-547 1356 *E-mail:* scottj@t-bird.edu

Cyprus

MORE THAN ONE CITY

1737
COLLEGE CONSORTIUM FOR INTERNATIONAL STUDIES and **BROOKDALE COMMUNITY COLLEGE**
Summer Program in Cyprus
Site: Cyprus: Larnaca, Limassol, Nicosia *Host inst:* Intercoll of Cyprus
Dates: 7 wks, Jun 5-Jul 25
Subjects: Accounting, Archaeology, Business/management, Communications, Computer sciences, Finance, Greek language (beg/int/adv), Hotel management, International business, Internships, Liberal arts, Marketing, Psychology, Tourism
Eligibility: *Level:* fresh, sophs, jrs, srs, grads *Requires:* 2.5 GPA, 2 recommendation letters, transcript, essay, 15 credits prior to application *Age:* min 18
Credit: *Undergrad:* 7 *Grad:* none *Doc:* transcript
Instruction: *In:* English *Format:* internship, lecture, seminar, tutorial
Costs: $2,000 *incl* tuition, fees, excursions
Housing: *Arr by pgm:* residence halls, apartments
Deadline: Apr 15
Other info: *US accredited sponsor:* yes *Began:* 1990 *Orient:* in US & abroad *Activities:* excursions, field trips, cultural events *Misc:* Loans avail. May contact former participants. *Financial aid:* scholarships *URL:* http://www.ccisabroad.org
Contact: *See Index II for Members* CCIS, 2000 P St NW, Ste 503, Washington DC 20036 *Ph:* 800-453 6956; 202-223 0330 *Fax:* 202-223 0999 *E-mail:* info@ccisabroad.org
Or Contact: Emily Hagadorn, Mgr, Intl Ctr, Brookdale CC, 765 Newman Springs Rd, Lincroft NJ 07738-1597 *Ph:* 732-224 2174 *Fax:* 732-224 2980 *E-mail:* ehagadorn@brookdale.cc.nj.us ▲

Egypt

MORE THAN ONE CITY

1738
PENNSYLVANIA STATE UNIVERSITY
Archaeological Excavation in Egypt
Site: Egypt: Luxor, Mendes
Dates: 6 wks, Jun-Jul or Jul-Aug
Subjects: Archaeology, Field study
Eligibility: CIC students only *Level:* fresh, sophs, jrs, srs *Requires:* 2.5 GPA
Credit: *Undergrad:* 6 *Grad:* none
Instruction: *In:* English *Format:* directed field study, study tour *Students:* mainly US
Costs: Contact Sponsor
Housing: *Arr by pgm:* hotels, hostels
Deadline: Feb 15
Other info: *US accredited sponsor:* yes *Orient:* in US & abroad *Activities:* excursions, field trips *Misc:* May contact former participants. *Financial aid:* scholarships
Contact: Summer Abroad, Penn State Univ, 225 Penn State Conference Ctr, University Park PA 16802 *Ph:* 814-863 5170
Or Contact: Intl Pgm Adviser, Penn State Univ, 222 Boucke Bldg, University Park PA 16802 *Ph:* 814-865 7681 *Fax:* 814-865 3336

1739
PENNSYLVANIA STATE UNIVERSITY
Egypt
Site: Egypt: Luxor, Mendes
Dates: 4 wks, Jun-Jul
Subjects: Field study
Eligibility: *Level:* sophs, jrs, srs *Requires:* 2.5 GPA *Age:* min 18
Credit: *Undergrad:* 6 *Grad:* none *Doc:* transcript
Instruction: *In:* English *Format:* directed field study *Students:* mainly US
Costs: About $4,000 for PA residents, $5,700 for others *incl* tuition, housing, some meals, excursions, books/materials *Nonrefundable fee*
Housing: *Arr by pgm:* hotels, dig house
Deadline: Jan 15
Other info: *US accredited sponsor:* yes *Began:* 1999 *Orient:* in US & abroad *Activities:* field trips *Financial aid:* scholarships *URL:* http://www.outreach.psu.edu/pssea/
Contact: Summer Abroad, Penn State Univ, 225 Penn State Conference Ctr, University Park PA 16802-7005 *Ph:* 814-863 5170 *Fax:* 814-863 5190 *E-mail:* summerabroad@outreach.psu.edu

1740
SAN FRANCISCO STATE UNIVERSITY
RA Egypt Tour
Site: Egypt: Abu Simbel, Cairo, Luxor
Dates: Jan 1-21
Subjects: Classical studies, Egyptology
Eligibility: *Level:* adults *Requires:* previous study in field
Credit: *Undergrad:* avail *Grad:* none
Instruction: *In:* English *Format:* lecture, study tour *Students:* mainly US
Costs: $5,000 *incl* tuition, housing, some meals, intl airfare, excursions
Housing: *Arr by pgm:* hotels
Deadline: Nov 1
Other info: *US accredited sponsor:* yes *Began:* 1980 *Activities:* excursions, field trips, program travel
Contact: Marian Bernstein, Egyptologist, San Francisco State Univ, San Francisco CA 94103 *Ph:* 415-338 1500
Or Contact: Mary Pieratt, Extended Educ, San Francisco State Univ, 1600 Holloway Ave, Adm 153, San Francisco CA 94132 *Ph:* 415-338 1372 *Fax:* 415-338 7290 *E-mail:* travel@sfsu.edu

1741
SOUTHERN ILLINOIS UNIVERSITY AT CARBONDALE
Myth and Cosmos in Egypt
Site: Egypt: various sites
Dates: 2 wks, May 28-Jun 10
Subjects: Archaeology, Classical studies, Interdisciplinary studies, Philosophy
Eligibility: *Level:* fresh, sophs, jrs, srs, grads, teachers *Requires:* faculty approval
Credit: *Undergrad:* 1-3 *Grad:* 1-3 *Doc:* transcript
Instruction: *In:* English *Format:* lecture, seminar *Students:* mainly US
Costs: $3,650 *incl* tuition, housing, some meals, fees, excursions
Housing: *Arr by pgm:* hotels
Deadline: Apr 1
Other info: *US accredited sponsor:* yes *Began:* 1984 *Orient:* in US *Activities:* excursions *Misc:* Interdisciplinary seminar with primary focus on origins of philosophy. *URL:* http://www.siu.edu/departments/study_abroad/
Contact: Thomas A Saville, Study Abroad Pgms, Mailcode 6885, Southern Illinois Univ, Carbondale IL 62901-6885 *Ph:* 618-453 7670 *Fax:* 618-453 7647 *E-mail:* studyabr@siu.edu
Or Contact: Dr Robert Hahn, Philosophy, Southern Illinois Univ, Carbondale IL 62901 *Ph:* 618-536 6641

CAIRO

1742
AMERICAN UNIVERSITY IN CAIRO
Summer Intensive Arabic Language Program
Site: Egypt: Cairo
Dates: 7-8 wks, Jun 3-Jul 31
Subjects: Arabic language (beg/int/adv)
Eligibility: *Level:* fresh, sophs, jrs, srs, grads, adults, teachers, professionals *Age:* min 18, avg 24
Credit: *Undergrad:* none *Grad:* none *Doc:* transcript
Instruction: *In:* Arabic, English *Format:* lang study, study tour *Students:* intl
Costs: $5,356 *incl* tuition, housing, all meals, insurance, fees, books/materials, passport, visa *Nonrefundable fee*

Housing: *Arr by student:* residence halls, apartments
Deadline: Apr 1
Other info: *US accredited sponsor:* yes *Began:* 1965 *Orient:* abroad (intensive lang study) *Activities:* excursions, field trips, cultural events *Misc:* May contact former participants. *URL:* http://www.aucegypt.edu
Contact: Dean Davidson, Coord, Student Affairs, Amer Univ in Cairo, 420 Fifth Ave, 3rd Fl, New York NY 10018-2728 *Ph:* 212-730 8800 ext 224 *Fax:* 212-730 1600 *E-mail:* aucegypt@aucnyo.edu

---

1743
AMERICAN UNIVERSITY IN CAIRO
Summer Study Abroad Program
Site: Egypt: Cairo
Dates: 7 wks, Jun 8-Jul 31
Subjects: Anthropology, Arabic studies, Business administration, Chemistry, Communications, Economics, Egyptology, Journalism, Mathematics, Physics, Political science/politics
Eligibility: *Level:* sophs, jrs, srs, grads, teachers, professionals *Requires:* 2.5 GPA, good acad standing *Age:* min 18
Credit: *Undergrad:* 6 *Grad:* none *Doc:* transcript
Instruction: *In:* English *Format:* lecture *Students:* intl
Costs: $5,356 *incl* tuition, housing, all meals, insurance, fees, books/materials, passport/visa *Nonrefundable fee*
Housing: *Arr by student:* residence halls, apartments
Deadline: Apr 1
Other info: *US accredited sponsor:* yes *Began:* 1965 *Activities:* excursions, cultural events *Misc:* May contact former participants. *URL:* http://www.aucegypt.edu
Contact: Dean Davidson, Coord, Student Affairs, Amer Univ in Cairo, 420 Fifth Ave, 3rd Fl, New York NY 10018-2728 *Ph:* 212-730 8800 ext 224 *Fax:* 212-730 1600 *E-mail:* aucegypt@aucnyo.edu

---

1744
ANTIOCH COLLEGE
Middle East and North Africa-Studies in Egypt
Site: Egypt: Cairo *Host inst:* Inst for African & Intl Studies
Dates: May-Jul
Subjects: Arabic language, Arabic studies, Political science/politics, Religion/theology
Eligibility: *Level:* sophs, jrs, srs *Requires:* good acad standing
Credit: *Undergrad:* 16 per term *Grad:* none *Doc:* transcript
Instruction: *In:* Arabic, English *Format:* independent study, lang study, lecture, seminar *Students:* US & intl
Costs: Contact sponsor
Housing: *Arr by pgm:* pensions, hotels
Deadline: Mar 15
Other info: *US accredited sponsor:* yes *Began:* 2000 *In coop with:* Inst for African & Intl Affairs *Orient:* in US & abroad *URL:* http://www.antioch-college.edu/aea
Contact: Antioch Educ Abroad, 795 Livermore, Yellow Springs OH 45387 *Ph:* 800-874 7986; 937-769 1015 *Fax:* 937-769 1019

1745
CENTER FOR ARABIC STUDY ABROAD (CASA)
CASA III for Professors of Arabic as a Foreign Language
Site: Egypt: Cairo *Host inst:* Amer Univ in Cairo
Dates: Early Jun-early Aug
Subjects: Arabic language (adv), Foreign language teaching
Eligibility: *Level:* teachers *Requires:* US citizenship, specialization in humanities or Arabic as a foreign lang
Credit: *Undergrad:* none *Grad:* none
Instruction: *In:* Arabic *Format:* lang study, practical training *Students:* mainly US
Costs: $1,000 pgm fee; participants receive fellowship *incl* tuition, intl airfare, books/materials, maintenance allowance
Housing: *Arr by pgm:* apartments
Deadline: Dec 31
Other info: *US accredited sponsor:* yes *Began:* 1967 *In coop with:* US Dept of Educ *Orient:* abroad *Misc:* Optional excursions. *Financial aid:* scholarships *URL:* http://www.sais-jhu.edu/languages/casa
Contact: *See Index II for Members* Dr Mahmoud Al-Batal, ICIS, 428-B Candler Library, Emory Univ, Atlanta GA 20036-1983 *Ph:* 404-727 2536 *Fax:* 404-727 6724 *E-mail:* albata@emory.edu

---

1746
CENTER FOR ARABIC STUDY ABROAD (CASA)
Summer Institute
Site: Egypt: Cairo *Host inst:* Amer Univ in Cairo
Dates: Early Jun-early Aug
Subjects: Arabic language (adv)
Eligibility: *Level:* fresh, sophs, jrs, srs, grads *Requires:* US citizenship or permanent resident status, 2 yrs Arabic lang, passing score on exam in Arabic
Credit: *Undergrad:* avail *Grad:* avail
Instruction: *In:* Arabic *Format:* lang study *Students:* mainly US
Costs: $750 pgm fee; participants receive fellowship *incl* tuition, intl airfare, books/materials, maintenance allowance
Housing: *Arr by pgm:* residence halls, apartments
Deadline: Dec 31
Other info: *US accredited sponsor:* yes *Began:* 1967 *In coop with:* US Dept of Educ *Orient:* abroad *Misc:* Optional excursions. *Financial aid:* scholarships *URL:* http://www.sais-jhu.edu/languages/casa
Contact: *See Index II for Members* Dr Mahmoud Al-Batal, ICIS, 428-B Chandler Library, Emory Univ, Atlanta GA 30322 *Ph:* 404-727 2536 *Fax:* 404-727 6724 *E-mail:* albatal@emory.edu

---

1747
LEIDEN UNIVERSITY
Program in Archaeology/Egyptology
Site: Egypt: Cairo *Host inst:* Netherlands-Flemish Inst in Cairo
Dates: 2 mos, fall
Subjects: Archaeology, Art, Egyptology, Field study
Eligibility: *Level:* srs, grads *Requires:* 3.1 GPA *Age:* avg 25
Credit: *Undergrad:* avail *Grad:* avail *Doc:* certificate
Instruction: *In:* English *Format:* independent study, lecture, seminar, study tour *Students:* intl
Costs: $2,000 *incl* tuition
Housing: *Sponsor assists:* apartments
Deadline: Aug 1
Other info: *US accredited sponsor:* no *Began:* 1999 *Orient:* avail (1 day) *URL:* http://www.leidenuniv.nl/interuniv/nuic
Contact: Mrs T Mulder, Coord, Archaeology Pgm, NUIC, 1 Dr Mahmoud Azmist, PO Box 50, 111211 Zamalek Cairo, Egypt *E-mail:* nuic@rite.com

---

1748
SUNY COLLEGE AT CORTLAND
SUNY Cortland/American University Cairo (Summer Program)
Site: Egypt: Cairo *Host inst:* Amer Univ in Cairo
Dates: 6 wks, mid-Jun-early Aug
Subjects: Anthropology, Arabic language, Arabic studies, Egyptology, Islamic studies
Eligibility: *Level:* sophs, jrs, srs, adults, teachers *Requires:* 2.5 GPA, good acad standing, *Age:* min 19
Credit: *Undergrad:* avail *Grad:* none *Doc:* transcript
Instruction: *In:* Arabic, English *Format:* lang study, lecture, seminar *Students:* intl
Costs: $3,300 *incl* housing, all meals, insurance, fees, excursions, books/materials *Nonrefundable fee*
Housing: *Arr by pgm:* residence halls, apartments
Deadline: Mar 15
Other info: *US accredited sponsor:* yes *Began:* 2000 *Orient:* in US & abroad

Activities: excursions, cultural events, sports *Misc:* Advanced-level Arabic lang & lit are taught in Arabic. May contact former participants. *Financial aid:* scholarships *URL:* http://www.studyabroad.com/suny/cortand
Contact: Liz Kopp, Asst Dir, Intl Pgms, PO Box 2000, B-15 Old Main, SUNY Cortland, Cortland NY 13045 *Ph:* 607-753 2209 *Fax:* 607-753 5989 ▲

Israel

MORE THAN ONE CITY

1749
CENTRO CAMUNO DI STUDI PREISTORICI
Har Karkom, Holy Mountain in the Desert of Exodus
Site: Israel: Negev Desert
Dates: Mar-Apr, 3 wks in field, 3 mos min in lab
Subjects: Archaeology, Art, Biblical studies, Caving, Database management, Field study, Film studies, Photography, Rock art, Surveying
Eligibility: *Level:* grads, adults, teachers, professionals *Requires:* good physical health *Age:* min 18, avg 30
Credit: *Undergrad:* none *Grad:* none *Doc:* certificate
Instruction: *In:* English, French, Italian *Format:* directed field study, lab, practical training *Students:* intl
Costs: Contact sponsor
Housing: *Arr by pgm:* tent camp
Deadline: Jan
Other info: *US accredited sponsor:* no *Began:* 1980 *Orient:* abroad *Activities:* excursions *Misc:* Students must bring own tents. Archaeological excavation & survey fieldwork. *Financial aid:* scholarships, work study *URL:* http://www.rockart-ccsp.com
Contact: CCSP, 7 Via Marconi, Capo di Ponte, Valcamonica, Italy 25044 *E-mail:* ccsp@rockart-ccsp.com

---

1750
DUKE UNIVERSITY
Summer Program in Israel
Site: Israel: Jerusalem, Sepphoris
Dates: Late May-early Jul
Subjects: Archaeology, Christian studies, Civilization/culture, Jewish/judaic studies
Eligibility: *Level:* fresh, sophs, jrs, srs, grads *Requires:* good acad standing, transcript
Credit: *Undergrad:* 2 credits *Grad:* avail *Doc:* transcript
Instruction: *In:* English *Format:* directed field study, lecture, practical training *Students:* mainly US
Costs: $5,575 *incl* tuition, housing, all meals, excursions
Housing: *Arr by pgm:* (Mizpeh) guest facilities
Deadline: Feb 16
Other info: *US accredited sponsor:* yes *Began:* 1973 *Activities:* excursions *Misc:* Participation in dig at Sepphoris, the Galilee. *Financial aid:* scholarships *URL:* http://www.aas.duke.edu/study_abroad/
Contact: Study Abroad, Duke Univ, 121 Allen Bldg, Box 90057, Durham NC 27708-0057 *Ph:* 919-684 2174 *Fax:* 919-684 3083 *E-mail:* abroad@asdean.duke.edu

---

1751
LANGUAGE LIAISON
Hebrew Saturation
Site: Israel: Haifa, Jerusalem, Tel Aviv *Host inst:* Live in Learn
Dates: 1 wk or longer, yr-round
Subjects: Civilization/culture, Hebrew language (beg/int/adv), Homestay
Eligibility: *Level:* fresh, sophs, jrs, srs, grads, adults, teachers, professionals, precoll *Age:* min 10
Credit: *Undergrad:* none *Grad:* none *Doc:* transcript, certificate
Instruction: *In:* Hebrew *Format:* lang study, tutorial *Students:* intl
Costs: Contact sponsor
Housing: *Arr by pgm:* teacher's home
Deadline: 45 days before pgm
Other info: *US accredited sponsor:* no *Misc:* Scholarship research svc. *URL:* http://www.languageliaison.com
Contact: Nancy Forman, Dir, Lang Liaison, 4 Burnham Pkwy, Morristown NJ 07960 *Ph:* 800-284 4448 *Fax:* 973-898 1710 *E-mail:* learn@languageliaison.com

---

1752
MICHIGAN STATE UNIVERSITY
Archaeology and History of Religions
Site: Israel: Galilee, Jerusalem
Dates: 4 wks, Jun
Subjects: Anthropology, Field study, Religion/theology
Eligibility: *Level:* fresh, sophs, jrs, srs, grads *Requires:* 2.0 GPA, good physical condition *Age:* min 18
Credit: *Undergrad:* avail *Grad:* none *Doc:* transcript
Instruction: *In:* English *Format:* directed field study *Students:* mainly US
Costs: About $2,600 *incl* housing, all meals, insurance, fees, excursions, excavation equipment rental *Nonrefundable fee*
Housing: *Arr by pgm:* hostels
Deadline: Mar 2
Other info: *US accredited sponsor:* yes *Orient:* in US (1 day) *Activities:* excursions, field trips, program travel, cultural events *URL:* http://studyabroad.msu.edu
Contact: Cheryl Benner, Study Abroad, Michigan State Univ, 109 Intl Ctr, East Lansing MI 48824-1035 *Ph:* 517-353 8920 *Fax:* 517-432 2082 *E-mail:* bennerc@msu.edu ▲

1753
NATIONAL REGISTRATION CENTER FOR STUDY ABROAD (NRCSA)
Language Study in Israel
Site: Israel: Jerusalem, Tel Aviv *Host inst:* Home Lang Schs Intl
Dates: 1 wk or longer, yr-round
Subjects: Hebrew language, Homestay
Eligibility: *Level:* fresh, sophs, jrs, srs, grads, adults, teachers, professionals
Credit: *Undergrad:* none *Grad:* none *Doc:* certificate
Instruction: *In:* Hebrew *Format:* lang study, tutorial *Students:* intl
Costs: $1,135 per wk *incl* tuition, housing, all meals, insurance *Nonrefundable fee*
Housing: *Arr by pgm:* homestay
Deadline: 6 wks before pgm
Other info: *US accredited sponsor:* no *Misc:* Student lives in teacher's home. *URL:* http://www.nrcsa.com
Contact: Reuel Zielke, NRCSA, 823 N 2nd St, #206, Milwaukee WI 53203 *Ph:* 414-278 0631 *Fax:* 414-871 8884 *E-mail:* info@nrcsa.com

---

BEERSHEBA

1754
BEN-GURION UNIVERSITY OF THE NEGEV
Summer Institutes
Site: Israel: Beersheba
Dates: 6 wks, Jun-Jul
Subjects: Anthropology, Archaeology, Art, Creative writing, Ecology/environmental studies, Field study, Medicine, Sociology
Eligibility: *Level:* fresh, sophs, jrs, srs, grads, precoll *Age:* min 18, max 20
Credit: *Undergrad:* 6 *Grad:* none *Doc:* transcript
Instruction: *In:* English *Format:* art studio, directed field study, lecture, seminar, study tour, volunteer/svc *Students:* mainly host country
Costs: About $3,000 *incl* tuition, housing, insurance, fees, excursions
Housing: *Arr by pgm:* residence halls
Deadline: Apr 15; Apr 1 for scholarships
Other info: *US accredited sponsor:* no *Orient:* abroad (3 days) *Activities:* excursions, field trips, cultural events, sports *Misc:* May contact former participants. *Financial aid:* scholarships *URL:* http://www.bgu.ac.il/osp

Contact: Melissa Wright, Student Svcs, Ben-Gurion Univ, 342 Madison Ave, Ste 1224, New York NY 10173 *Ph:* 800-962 2248; 212-687 7721 *Fax:* 212-370 0686 *E-mail:* osp@aabgu.org

BEIT GAN

1755
UNIVERSITY OF TEXAS AT AUSTIN
Archaeological Expedition to Israel
Site: Israel: Beit Gan (lower Galilee)
Dates: Jun-Aug
Subjects: Archaeology
Eligibility: *Level:* sophs, jrs, srs, grads *Age:* min 18
Credit: *Undergrad:* 6 *Grad:* avail *Doc:* transcript
Instruction: *In:* English *Format:* directed field study, seminar *Students:* mainly US
Costs: Contact sponsor
Housing: *Arr by pgm*
Deadline: Contact sponsor
Other info: *US accredited sponsor:* yes *Began:* 1984 *Misc:* May contact former participants. *Financial aid:* scholarships *URL:* http://www.utexas.edu/student/abroad
Contact: Joy Williamson, Adviser, Study Abroad, Univ of Texas at Austin, Drawer A, Austin TX 78713 *Ph:* 512-471 6490 *Fax:* 512-232 4363 *E-mail:* studyabroadinfo@mozart.io.utexas.edu

CAESAREA

1756
UNIVERSITY OF KANSAS
Summer Institute: Caesarea Expedition
Site: Israel: Caesarea
Dates: 4 wks, May 30-Jun 25
Subjects: Archaeology, Classical studies, History
Eligibility: *Level:* fresh, sophs, jrs, srs *Age:* min 18
Credit: *Undergrad:* 3 *Grad:* none *Doc:* transcript
Instruction: *In:* English *Format:* directed field study, lecture *Students:* mainly US
Costs: $2,215 *incl* tuition, housing, some meals, insurance, fees *Nonrefundable fee*
Housing: *Arr by pgm:* residence halls
Deadline: Mar 1
Other info: *US accredited sponsor:* yes *Began:* 1999 *Orient:* in US & abroad *Misc:* May contact former participants. *URL:* http://www.ukans.edu/~osa
Contact: Susan MacNally, Coord of Summer Insts, Study Abroad, Univ of Kansas, 108 Lippincott, Lawrence KS 66045 *Ph:* 785-864 3742 *Fax:* 785-864 5040 *E-mail:* osa@ukans.edu ▲

HAIFA

1757
UNIVERSITY OF HAIFA
Summer Ulpan
Site: Israel: Haifa
Dates: 4 or 8 wks, Jul-Sep
Subjects: Full curriculum, Field study, Hebrew language, Internships
Eligibility: *Level:* fresh, sophs, jrs, srs *Age:* min 18, avg 20
Credit: *Undergrad:* avail *Grad:* none *Doc:* transcript
Instruction: *In:* Hebrew *Format:* directed field study, internship, lang study, lecture *Students:* intl
Costs: $1,070 for 4 wks, $1,840 for 8 wks *incl* tuition, housing, excursions, activities *Nonrefundable fee*
Housing: *Arr by pgm:* residence halls
Deadline: Contact sponsor
Other info: *US accredited sponsor:* no *Began:* 1996 *Orient:* abroad *Activities:* excursions, field trips, program travel, cultural events, sports *Misc:* May contact former participants. *Financial aid:* scholarships *URL:* http://www.haifa.ac.il
Contact: Stacey Sanders, Dir of Admissions, Univ of Haifa, 220 5th Ave, Ste 1301, New York NY 10001 *Ph:* 888-562 8813 *Fax:* 212-685 7883 *E-mail:* university-of-haifa@worldnet.att.net

JERUSALEM

1758
DICKINSON COLLEGE
Jerusalem Program
Site: Israel: Jerusalem
Dates: Late May-early Jul
Subjects: History, Religion/theology
Eligibility: *Level:* fresh, sophs, jrs
Credit: *Undergrad:* 4 *Grad:* none
Instruction: *In:* English *Format:* directed field study, seminar *Students:* mainly US
Costs: About $4,500 *incl* tuition, housing, all meals, intl airfare, local transport *Nonrefundable fee*
Housing: *Arr by pgm:* hospice
Deadline: Mar 1
Other info: *US accredited sponsor:* yes *Began:* 1997 *Orient:* in US *Activities:* program travel *URL:* http://www.dickinson.edu/departments/ocs/abroad.html
Contact: Global Educ, Dickinson Coll, PO Box 1773, Carlisle PA 17013-2896 *Ph:* 717-245 1341 *Fax:* 717-245 1688 *E-mail:* ocs@dickinson.edu

1759
FAIRFIELD UNIVERSITY
Intersession in Jerusalem
Site: Israel: Jerusalem
Dates: 10 days, Jan 2-14
Subjects: Religion/theology
Eligibility: *Level:* sophs, jrs, srs, grads, adults, teachers, professionals *Requires:* 3.0 GPA, essay, transcript *Age:* min 18, avg 20
Credit: *Undergrad:* 3 *Grad:* none *Doc:* transcript
Instruction: *In:* English *Format:* lecture, seminar, study tour *Students:* mainly US
Costs: Contact sponsor
Housing: *Arr by pgm:* pensions
Deadline: Nov 1
Other info: *US accredited sponsor:* yes *Began:* 1998 *Activities:* excursions, field trips *URL:* http://www.fairfield.edu/sce/studyabroad/jeru.htm
Contact: Christine Bowers, Study Abroad Coord, Fairfield Univ, Dolan House, Fairfield CT 06430 *Ph:* 888-254 1566; 203-254 4220 *Fax:* 203-254 4106 *E-mail:* cbbowers@fair1.fairfield.edu

1760
HEBREW UNIVERSITY OF JERUSALEM
Summer Courses
Site: Israel: Jerusalem
Dates: 3, 4 or 6 wks, beg Jul
Subjects: Arabic language, Archaeology, Architecture, Ethics, Film studies, Geography, International relations, Israeli studies, Jewish/judaic studies, Marine sciences, Middle Eastern studies, Political science/politics, Religion/theology, Sciences, Technology
Eligibility: *Level:* sophs, jrs, srs, grads, adults, teachers, professionals *Age:* avg 20
Credit: *Undergrad:* avail *Grad:* avail *Doc:* transcript
Instruction: *In:* English, Hebrew *Format:* lang study, lecture, seminar, study tour, tutorial *Students:* intl
Costs: About $2,800 *incl* tuition, housing, books/materials
Housing: *Arr by pgm:* residence halls
Deadline: May 15
Other info: *US accredited sponsor:* no *Began:* 1965 *Orient:* abroad *Activities:* excursions, field trips, program travel, cultural events, sports *Misc:* Financial aid avail. May contact former participants. *Financial aid:* scholarships *URL:* http://www.overseas.huji.ac.il

Contact: Acad Affairs, Rothberg Sch, Hebrew Univ of Jerusalem, 11 E 69th St, New York NY 10021 *Ph:* 800-404 8622; 212-472 2288 *E-mail:* hebrew@hebrewu.com

---

1761
JERUSALEM UNIVERSITY COLLEGE
Historical and Geographical Settings of the Bible
Site: Israel: Jerusalem
Dates: 3-wk courses, yr-round
Subjects: Biblical studies, Geography, History, Middle Eastern studies
Eligibility: *Level:* fresh, sophs, jrs, srs, grads, adults *Requires:* 2.0 GPA
Credit: *Undergrad:* avail *Grad:* avail *Doc:* certificate
Instruction: *In:* English *Format:* directed field study, lecture *Students:* US & intl
Costs: $1,865-$2,050 depending on housing *incl* tuition, housing, all meals, fees, excursions *Nonrefundable fee*
Housing: *Arr by pgm:* residence halls, hotels
Deadline: 3 mos before pgm
Other info: *US accredited sponsor:* yes *Began:* 1959 *Orient:* abroad *Activities:* excursions *URL:* http://www.juc.edu
Contact: *See Index II for Members* Jerusalem Univ Coll, 4249 E State St, Ste 203, Rockford IL 61108 *Ph:* 800-891 9408; 815-229 5900 *E-mail:* admissions@juc.edu

---

1762
MICHIGAN STATE UNIVERSITY
Jewish Studies
Site: Israel: Jerusalem *Host inst:* Hebrew Univ
Dates: 4 wks, Jun-Jul
Subjects: Civilization/culture, History, Jewish/judaic studies
Eligibility: *Level:* fresh, sophs, jrs, srs *Requires:* 2.5 GPA *Age:* min 18
Credit: *Undergrad:* avail *Grad:* none *Doc:* transcript
Instruction: *In:* English *Format:* lecture *Students:* intl
Costs: About $1,500 *incl* housing, insurance, fees, excursions *Nonrefundable fee*
Housing: *Arr by pgm:* residence halls with local students
Deadline: Mar 2
Other info: *US accredited sponsor:* yes *Began:* 1998 *Orient:* in US (1 day) *Activities:* excursions *URL:* http://studyabroad.msu.edu
Contact: Cheryl Benner, Study Abroad, Michigan State Univ, 109 Intl Ctr, East Lansing MI 48824-1035 *Ph:* 517-353 8920 *Fax:* 517-432 2082 *E-mail:* bennerc@msu.edu ▲

1763
RUTGERS UNIVERSITY
Summer Institute in Middle Eastern Studies
Site: Israel: Jerusalem
Dates: 6 wks, late-Jun-Jearly-Jul
Subjects: Middle Eastern studies
Eligibility: *Level:* sophs, jrs *Requires:* 2.5 GPA
Credit: *Undergrad:* avail *Grad:* none *Doc:* transcript
Instruction: *In:* English *Format:* lecture *Students:* mainly US
Costs: $1,986 for NJ residents, $2,326 for others *incl* tuition, housing, insurance, fees, excursions *Nonrefundable fee*
Housing: *Arr by pgm:* residence halls with local students
Deadline: Apr 15
Other info: *US accredited sponsor:* yes *URL:* http://www.rutgers.edu/Academics/Study_Abroad
Contact: Dir, Study Abroad, Rutgers Univ, 102 College Ave, New Brunswick NJ 08901 *Ph:* 732-932 7787 *Fax:* 732 932 8659

1764
UNIVERSITY OF DELAWARE
Winter Session in Israel
Site: Israel: Jerusalem
Dates: 1 mo, Jan
Subjects: Political science/politics, Sociology
Eligibility: *Level:* fresh, sophs, jrs, srs *Requires:* 2.0 GPA
Credit: *Undergrad:* 6 *Grad:* none *Doc:* transcript
Instruction: *In:* English *Format:* lecture, seminar, study tour *Students:* mainly US
Costs: Contact Sponsor
Housing: *Arr by pgm:* hotels, hostels, Kibbutz Guest House
Deadline: mid-Oct
Other info: *US accredited sponsor:* yes *Orient:* in US *Activities:* excursions, field trips, program travel, cultural events *Misc:* Contact sponsor to arrange honors credit. *Financial aid:* scholarships *URL:* http://www.udel.edu/studyabroad
Contact: Int Pgm & Special Sessions, Univ of Delaware, 4 Kent Way, Newark DE 19716 *Ph:* 888-831 4685; 302-831 2852 *Fax:* 302-831 6042 *E-mail:* studyabroad@udel.edu

---

NETANYA

1765
LANGUAGES ABROAD
Language and Cultural Immersion-Israel
Site: Israel: Netanya
Dates: 2 wks or longer, yr-round
Subjects: Civilization/culture, Hebrew language (beg/int/adv), Israeli studies
Eligibility: *Level:* adults *Age:* min 17, max 65, avg 25
Credit: *Undergrad:* none *Grad:* none *Doc:* certificate
Instruction: *In:* Hebrew *Format:* lang study *Students:* intl
Costs: $1,870 per mo *incl* tuition, some meals, fees, excursions, books/materials
Housing: *Arr by pgm:* residence halls, homestay
Deadline: None
Other info: *US accredited sponsor:* no *Began:* 1995 *Activities:* excursions, field trips, program travel, cultural events, sports *Misc:* May contact former participants. *URL:* http://www.languagesabroad.com
Contact: Ms Jesse Philippe, Langs Abroad, 317 Adelaide St W, Ste 900, Toronto, Ontario M5V 1P9, Canada *Ph:* 800-219 9924; 416-925 7117 *E-mail:* info@languagesabroad.com

---

TEL AVIV

1766
NEW YORK UNIVERSITY, TISCH SCHOOL OF THE ARTS
Documentary Workshop: Israel
Site: Israel: Tel Aviv *Host inst:* Tel Aviv Univ
Dates: 6 wks, about Jun 26-Aug 4
Subjects: Civilization/culture, Film studies, Journalism, Performing arts, Television/video
Eligibility: *Level:* fresh, sophs, jrs, srs, grads, adults, teachers, professionals *Requires:* previous study in field, prior filmmaking & video experience and/or training or permission of instructor *Age:* min 18
Credit: *Undergrad:* 8 *Grad:* none *Doc:* transcript
Instruction: *In:* English *Format:* lecture, practical training, seminar, workshop *Students:* mainly US
Costs: $5,949 *incl* tuition, housing, fees, excursions *Nonrefundable fee*
Housing: *Arr by pgm*
Deadline: About Apr 15
Other info: *US accredited sponsor:* yes *Began:* 2000 *In coop with:* Tel Aviv Univ *Orient:* in US & abroad *Activities:* excursions, field trips, cultural events *Misc:* Loans & scholarships for own students only. *URL:* http://www.nyu.edu/tisch/international/
Contact: Linda Kow, Assoc Dir, Tisch Intl Pgms, New York Univ, 721 Broadway, 12th Fl, New York NY 10003 *Ph:* 212-998 9175 *Fax:* 212-995 4578 *E-mail:* tisch.international@nyu.edu

---

1767
TEL AVIV UNIVERSITY, LOWY SCHOOL FOR OVERSEAS STUDIES
Summer Session/Summer Honors Study Tour
Site: Israel: Tel Aviv
Dates: 4-7 wks, Jun-Jul
Subjects: Hebrew language, History, Israeli studies, Jewish/judaic studies
Eligibility: *Level:* fresh, sophs, jrs, srs, grads, precoll *Requires:* 3.0 GPA, 3.25 GPA for honors
Credit: *Undergrad:* avail *Grad:* avail *Doc:* transcript
Instruction: *In:* English *Format:* study tour *Students:* mainly US
Costs: $2,000-$5,000 *incl* tuition, housing, all meals, intl airfare, insurance, fees, excursions, books/materials *Nonrefundable fee*
Housing: *Arr by pgm:* residence halls, hotels
Deadline: May 1
Other info: *US accredited sponsor:* no *Began:* 1968 *Orient:* abroad (1 day) *Activities:* excursions, field trips, program travel, cultural events, sports *Misc:* May contact former participants. *Financial aid:* scholarships *URL:* http://www.tau.ac.il/overseas
Contact: Hal Klopper, Dir, Acad Affairs, Tel Aviv Univ, 360 Lexington Ave, New York NY 10017 *Ph:* 800-665 9828 *Fax:* 212-687 4085 *E-mail:* tauoaa@aol.com

---

1768
TEMPLE UNIVERSITY SCHOOL OF LAW
Temple Law Summer Session in Israel
Site: Israel: Tel Aviv *Host inst:* Tel Aviv Univ
Dates: 6 wks, Jun-Jul
Subjects: Comparative law, Constitutional law, Law, Middle Eastern studies, Peace studies
Eligibility: *Level:* grads, grads *Requires:* 1 yr law sch, good acad standing
Credit: *Undergrad:* none *Grad:* 6 *Doc:* transcript, certificate
Instruction: *In:* English, English *Format:* lecture, lecture, seminar, seminar *Students:* US & US & intl & intl
Costs: About $6,401-$7,701 *incl* tuition, tuition, housing, housing, all meals, all meals, intl airfare, intl airfare, insurance, insurance, fees, fees, excursions, excursions, books/materials, books/materials, personal expenses *Nonrefundable fee*
Housing: *Arr by pgm, Arr by pgm:* apartments, apartments
Deadline: Apr 15
Other info: *US accredited sponsor:* yes *Began:* 1975 *Orient:* abroad (1 day) *Activities:* excursions, excursions, field trips, field trips, cultural events, cultural events *Misc:* May contact former participants. *Financial aid:* scholarships, scholarships *URL:* http://www.temple.edu/lawschool
Contact: Adelaide Ferguson, Asst Dean, Temple Law Sch, Intl Pgms, 1719 N Broad St, Room 710, Philadelphia PA 19122 *Ph:* 215-204 1448 *Fax:* 215-204 2282 *E-mail:* intl-law@vm.temple.edu

---

TEL BET SHEMESH

1769
INDIANA UNIVERSITY
Bet Shemesh Archaeological Dig
Site: Israel: Tel Bet Shemesh
Dates: 3 wks, mid-Jun-early Jul
Subjects: Archaeology, Biblical studies, Field study
Eligibility: Own students only. *Level:* fresh, sophs, jrs, srs, grads *Requires:* 3.0 GPA
Credit: *Undergrad:* 4 *Grad:* none *Doc:* transcript
Instruction: *In:* English *Format:* directed field study, lecture *Students:* mainly US
Costs: $2,100 or $2,600 *incl* tuition, housing, all meals, insurance, fees, excursions *Nonrefundable fee*
Housing: *Arr by pgm:* kibbutz
Deadline: Late Jan
Other info: *US accredited sponsor:* yes *Began:* 1996 *Orient:* in US & abroad *Activities:* field trips *Misc:* May contact former participants. *Financial aid:* scholarships *URL:* http://www.indiana.edu/~overseas
Contact: Overseas Study, Indiana Univ, Franklin Hall 303, Bloomington IN 47401 *Ph:* 812-855 9304 *Fax:* 812-855 6452 *E-mail:* overseas@indiana.edu

Jordan

AMMAN

1770
COUNCIL ON INTERNATIONAL EDUCATIONAL EXCHANGE (COUNCIL)
Jordan and Geopolitics
Site: Jordan: Amman *Host inst:* Univ of Jordan
Dates: 10 days, Jun
Subjects: Economics, Middle Eastern studies, Political science/politics, Religion/theology
Eligibility: *Level:* teachers, professionals
Credit: *Undergrad:* none *Grad:* none
Instruction: *In:* English *Format:* lecture *Students:* intl
Costs: $1,995 *incl* tuition, housing, some meals, insurance, fees, excursions *Nonrefundable fee*
Housing: *Arr by pgm:* hotels
Deadline: Mar 15
Other info: *US accredited sponsor:* no *Began:* 2001 *Misc:* May contact former participants. *URL:* http://www.ciee.org/ifds
Contact: Jennifer Ley, Dir, Faculty Pgms, Council, 633 3rd Ave, New York NY 10017 *Ph:* 212-822 2746 *Fax:* 212-822 2779 *E-mail:* jley@ciee.org ▲

1771
GEORGE MASON UNIVERSITY
Arabic Language at University of Jordan
Site: Jordan: Amman
Dates: 7 wks, Jul 2-Aug 24
Subjects: Arabic language
Eligibility: *Level:* fresh, sophs, jrs, srs *Requires:* 2.25 GPA *Age:* min 18
Credit: *Undergrad:* 6 *Grad:* none
Instruction: *In:* English *Format:* lecture, seminar *Students:* intl
Costs: Contact sponsor
Housing: *Sponsor assists:* apartments
Deadline: May 15
Other info: *US accredited sponsor:* yes *Orient:* in US (1 day) *Financial aid:* scholarships, work study *URL:* http://www.gmu.edu
Contact: Ctr for Global Educ, George Mason Univ, Johnson Ctr 235, 4400 University Dr, Fairfax VA 22030-4444 *Ph:* 703-993 2154 *Fax:* 703-993 2153 *E-mail:* cge@gmu.edu

---

1772
LANGUAGES ABROAD
Language and Culture-Amman
Site: Jordan: Amman
Dates: 2 wks or longer, yr-round
Subjects: Arabic language (beg/int/adv), Civilization/culture, Homestay
Eligibility: *Level:* adults *Age:* min 17, max 65, avg 25
Credit: *Undergrad:* none *Grad:* none *Doc:* certificate
Instruction: *In:* Arabic *Format:* lang study *Students:* mainly US
Costs: $2,950 for 4 wks *incl* tuition, housing, some meals, excursions, books/materials
Housing: *Arr by pgm:* residence halls, homestay
Deadline: None
Other info: *US accredited sponsor:* no *Began:* 1995 *Activities:* excursions, field trips, program travel, cultural events, sports *Misc:* May contact former participants. *URL:* http://www.languagesabroad.com
Contact: Ms Jesse Philippe, Langs Abroad, 317 Adelaide St W, Ste 900, Toronto, Ontario M5V 1P9, Canada *Ph:* 800-219 9924; 416-925 7117 *E-mail:* info@languagesabroad.com

---

IRBID

1773
UNIVERSITY OF ARKANSAS and **YARMOUK UNIVERSITY**
Bio-archaeological Field School in Jordan
Site: Jordan: Irbid
Dates: 8 wks, Jun 10-Aug 1
Subjects: Archaeology, Field study
Eligibility: *Level:* sophs, jrs, srs, grads, adults, teachers, professionals *Requires:* 3.0 GPA *Age:* min 18, avg 22
Credit: *Undergrad:* 6 *Grad:* 6 *Doc:* transcript
Instruction: *In:* English *Format:* directed field study *Students:* mainly US
Costs: $3,500 *incl* tuition, housing, intl airfare, insurance, fees, excursions, books/materials
Housing: *Arr by pgm:* residence halls
Deadline: Feb 1
Other info: *US accredited sponsor:* yes *Began:* 1995 *Orient:* in US & abroad *Activities:* excursions, field trips *Misc:* Work side by side with Jordanian students. Scholarships for own students only. May contact former participants.
Contact: Prof Jerry Rose, Anthropology, Univ of Arkansas, Old Main Rm 330, Fayetteville AR 72701 *Ph:* 501-575 2508 *Fax:* 501-575 2642 *E-mail:* jcrose@comp.uark.edu
Or Contact: Michelle Morris, Study Abroad, Fulbright Inst, 722 W Maple, Fayetteville AR 72701 *Ph:* 501-575 7582, 501-575 7582 *Fax:* 501-575 7402 *E-mail:* dslong@comp.uark.edu

Lebanon

BEIRUT

1774
AMERICAN UNIVERSITY OF BEIRUT
AUB Summer Program/Language and Culture
Site: Lebanon: Beirut
Dates: 5 wks, Jul 3-Aug 4
Subjects: Arabic language (beg)
Eligibility: *Level:* fresh, sophs, precoll *Age:* min 16, max 22, avg 18
Credit: *Undergrad:* none *Grad:* none *Doc:* certificate
Instruction: *In:* Arabic, English *Format:* lang study, seminar, study tour *Students:* intl & host country
Costs: $2,500 *incl* tuition, housing, some meals, fees, excursions, books/materials *Nonrefundable fee*
Housing: *Arr by pgm:* residence halls
Deadline: Apr 28
Other info: *US accredited sponsor:* yes *Began:* 1998 *Activities:* excursions, field trips, cultural events, sports *Misc:* May contact former participants. *URL:* http://www.aub.edu.lb
Contact: Miyada Musharbash, Amer Univ of Beirut, 850 3rd Ave, 18th Fl, New York NY 10022 *Ph:* 212-583 7372 *Fax:* 212-583 7351 *E-mail:* miyada@aub.edu

---

1775
AMERICAN UNIVERSITY OF BEIRUT
Summer Program/Visiting Students
Site: Lebanon: Beirut
Dates: 7 wks, Jul 1-Aug 25
Subjects: Arabic language, Banking, Behavioral sciences, Biology, Business administration, Chemistry, Economics, English, Geology, History, Mathematics, Physics, Political science/politics, Public administration, Social sciences
Eligibility: *Level:* fresh, sophs, jrs, srs *Requires:* 2.5 GPA, high sch diploma, transcript
Credit: *Undergrad:* 9 *Grad:* none *Doc:* transcript
Instruction: *In:* English *Format:* lang study, lecture *Students:* intl & host country
Costs: $3,350 for 9 credits *incl* tuition, housing, fees *Nonrefundable fee*
Housing: *Arr by pgm:* residence halls
Deadline: May 31
Other info: *US accredited sponsor:* yes *Misc:* May contact former participants. *URL:* http://www.aub.edu.lb
Contact: Julie Millstein, Asst to Pres, Amer Univ of Beirut, 850 3rd Ave, 18th Fl, New York NY 10022 *Ph:* 212-583 7678 *Fax:* 212-583 7650 *E-mail:* mills@aub.edu
Or Contact: Dr Salim Kanaan, Dir of Admissions, Amer Univ of Beirut, Beirut, Lebanon *E-mail:* admissions@aub.edu.lb

Morocco

MORE THAN ONE CITY

1776
UNIVERSITY OF DAYTON
Interdepartmental Summer Study Abroad (ISSAP)-Morocco
Site: Morocco: Casablanca, Fez, Ifrane, Rabat *Host inst:* Al Akhawayn Univ
Dates: 1 mo, May 24-Jun 23
Subjects: English, Liberal arts, Music, Philosophy
Eligibility: *Level:* fresh, sophs, jrs, srs, adults, teachers, professionals *Requires:* 2.0 GPA *Age:* min 18, avg 20
Credit: *Undergrad:* 7 *Grad:* avail *Doc:* transcript
Instruction: *In:* English *Format:* lecture *Students:* mainly US
Costs: $3,595 *incl* tuition, housing, some meals, fees, excursions
Housing: *Arr by pgm:* residence halls, pensions
Deadline: Mar 1; Jan 15 for scholarships
Other info: *US accredited sponsor:* yes *Began:* 1999 *In coop with:* Al-Akhawayn Univ *Orient:* in US & abroad (4 days) *Activities:* excursions, field trips, program travel, cultural events *Misc:* May contact former participants. *Financial aid:* scholarships
Contact: James Stiles, Univ of Dayton, 300 College Park, Dayton OH 45469-1481 *Ph:* 937-229 3728 *Fax:* 937-229 2766 *E-mail:* studyabroad@udayton.edu

---

1777
UNIVERSITY OF DELAWARE
Winter Session in Morocco
Site: Morocco: various sites
Dates: 1 mo, Jan
Subjects: Field study, Horticulture
Eligibility: *Level:* fresh, sophs, jrs, srs *Requires:* 2.0 GPA
Credit: *Undergrad:* 6 *Grad:* none *Doc:* transcript
Instruction: *In:* English *Format:* directed field study, lecture, seminar, study tour *Students:* mainly US
Costs: Contact sponsor
Housing: *Arr by pgm*
Deadline: Early Oct
Other info: *US accredited sponsor:* yes *Orient:* avail yes *Activities:* excursions, field trips, program travel, cultural events *Misc:* Contact sponsor to arrange honors credit. *Financial aid:* scholarships *URL:* http://www.udel.edu/studyabroad/
Contact: Intl Pgms, Univ of Delaware, 4 Kent Way, Newark DE 19716 *Ph:* 888-831 4685; 302-831 2852 *Fax:* 302-831 6042 *E-mail:* studyabroad@udel.edu

---

FEZ

1778
ARABIC LANGUAGE INSTITUTE IN FEZ (ALIF)
Modern Standard Arabic and Colloquial Moroccan Arabic
Site: Morocco: Fez
Dates: 6 wks or longer, yr-round
Subjects: Arabic language, Homestay, Independent study
Eligibility: *Level:* fresh, sophs, jrs, srs, grads, adults *Age:* avg 21
Credit: *Undergrad:* avail *Grad:* none *Doc:* transcript, certificate
Instruction: *In:* Arabic *Format:* independent study, lang study, lecture, study tour *Students:* intl
Costs: Contact sponsor
Housing: *Sponsor assists:* residence halls with local students, apartments, homestay, pensions, hotels, hostels
Deadline: 3 wks before pgm
Other info: *US accredited sponsor:* no *Began:* 1983 *In coop with:* Amer Lang Ctr

Orient: abroad (1 day) *Activities:* excursions, field trips, program travel, cultural events, sports *Misc:* May contact former participants. *Financial aid:* scholarships, work study *URL:* http://www.azure.net/alif
Contact: Martin Mayerchak, Asst to Dir, ALIF, BP 2136, Ville Nouvelle, Fez, Morocco *E-mail:* alif@fesnet.net.ma

---

1779
LANGUAGES ABROAD
Language and Culture-Fez
Site: Morocco: Fez
Dates: 2 wks or longer, yr-round
Subjects: Arabic language (beg/int/adv), Civilization/culture, Homestay, Moroccan studies
Eligibility: *Level:* adults *Age:* min 17, max 65, avg 25
Credit: *Undergrad:* none *Grad:* none *Doc:* certificate
Instruction: *In:* Arabic *Format:* lang study *Students:* intl
Costs: From $1,750 for 3 wks *incl* tuition, housing, some meals, insurance, excursions, books/materials
Housing: *Arr by pgm:* residence halls, homestay
Deadline: None
Other info: *US accredited sponsor:* no *Began:* 1995 *Activities:* excursions, field trips, program travel, cultural events, sports *Misc:* May contact former participants. *URL:* http://www.languagesabroad.com
Contact: Ms Jesse Philippe, Langs Abroad, 317 Adelaide St W, Ste 900, Toronto, Ontario M5V 1P9, Canada *Ph:* 800-219 9924; 416-925 7117 *E-mail:* info@languagesabroad.com

---

1780
NATIONAL REGISTRATION CENTER FOR STUDY ABROAD (NRCSA)
Arabic Language Study in Fez
Site: Morocco: Fez *Host inst:* ALIF
Dates: 3 wks, Jun 5-28, Jun 28-Jul 19 or Jul 19-Aug 9
Subjects: Arabic language (beg/int/adv), Homestay, Moroccan studies
Eligibility: *Level:* fresh, sophs, jrs, srs, grads, adults, teachers, professionals *Age:* min 18
Credit: *Undergrad:* none *Grad:* none *Doc:* certificate
Instruction: *In:* Arabic *Format:* lang study, lecture *Students:* intl
Costs: $595 for 3 wks *incl* tuition, housing, some meals, insurance *Nonrefundable fee*
Housing: *Arr by pgm:* residence halls, apartments, homestay, hotels
Deadline: 6 wks before pgm
Other info: *US accredited sponsor:* no *URL:* http://www.worldwide.edu
Contact: Reuel Zielke, NRCSA, 823 N 2nd St, #206, Milwaukee WI 53203 *Ph:* 414-278 0631 *Fax:* 414-278 8884 *E-mail:* info@nrcsa.com

---

IFRANE

1781
AL AKHAWAYN UNIVERSITY IN IFRANE
Arabic Language and Culture Program
Site: Morocco: Ifrane
Dates: 7 wks, early Jun-late Jul
Subjects: Arabic language (beg/int/adv), Arabic studies, Civilization/culture, Islamic studies, Moroccan studies
Eligibility: *Level:* fresh, sophs, jrs, srs, grads, adults, teachers, professionals *Requires:* 3.0 GPA
Credit: *Undergrad:* 8 *Grad:* 8 *Doc:* transcript *Transfer credit through:* SUNY Univ at Binghamton
Instruction: *In:* Arabic, English *Format:* lab, lang study, seminar *Students:* mainly US
Costs: $4,000 *incl* tuition, housing, all meals, insurance, fees, excursions, books/materials
Housing: *Arr by pgm:* residence halls
Deadline: Apr 1
Other info: *US accredited sponsor:* no *Began:* 1998 *Orient:* abroad *Activities:* excursions, field trips *Misc:* May contact former participants. *URL:* http://www.AlAkhawayn.ma
Contact: Al Akhawayn University in Ifrane, Dr Katharine C Krebs, Intl Pgms, NARC G-1, Binghamton Univ, Binghamton NY 13902-6000 *Ph:* 607-777 2336 *Fax:* 607-777 2889 *E-mail:* oip@binghamton.edu

---

1782
COLLEGE CONSORTIUM FOR INTERNATIONAL STUDIES and MONTANA STATE UNIVERSITY
Summer in Morocco Program
Site: Morocco: Ifrane *Host inst:* Al Akhawayn Univ
Dates: Late May-mid-Jul
Subjects: Arabic language, Arabic studies, Business administration, Civilization/culture, Engineering, Independent study, Social sciences
Eligibility: *Level:* sophs, jrs, srs, grads *Requires:* 2.5 GPA
Credit: *Undergrad:* 8 *Grad:* none *Doc:* transcript *Transfer credit through:* Montana State Univ
Instruction: *In:* English *Format:* independent study, lang study, lecture, seminar *Students:* mainly host country
Costs: $2,600 *incl* tuition, housing, airport transfer
Housing: *Arr by pgm:* residence halls with local students
Deadline: Apr 15
Other info: *US accredited sponsor:* yes *Began:* 2000 *Orient:* abroad (3 days) *Activities:* excursions, field trips, program travel, cultural events, sports *Financial aid:* scholarships *URL:* http://www.ccisabroad.org
Contact: *See Index II for Members* Kevin Hood, Study Abroad Adviser, Montana State Univ, 400 Culbertson Hall, Bozeman MT 59717 *Ph:* 406-994 4031 *Fax:* 406-994 1619 *E-mail:* khood@montana.edu
Or Contact: Julia Bruner, Study Abroad Coord, Montana State Univ, 400 Colbertson Hall, Bozeman MT 59717 *Ph:* 406-994 4031 *Fax:* 406-994 1619 *E-mail:* juliab@montana.edu ▲

1783
GEORGE WASHINGTON UNIVERSITY
Culture and Language in North Africa
Site: Morocco: Ifrane *Host inst:* Al Akahawayn Univ in Ifrane
Dates: 8 wks, May 28-Jul 20
Subjects: Arabic language, Humanities, International relations
Eligibility: *Level:* jrs, srs *Requires:* 2.75 GPA *Age:* min 18
Credit: *Undergrad:* 6 *Grad:* none *Doc:* transcript
Instruction: *In:* Arabic, English *Format:* lang study, lecture, seminar, study tour *Students:* US & intl
Costs: $4,230 *incl* tuition, housing, all meals, fees *Nonrefundable fee*
Housing: *Arr by pgm:* residence halls
Deadline: Contact Sponsor
Other info: *US accredited sponsor:* yes *Began:* 2000 *Orient:* abroad (1 day, intensive language study) *Activities:* excursions, field trips *Misc:* Summer pgms are updated in Dec. Contact sponsor for new info. *URL:* http://www.summer.gwu.edu
Contact: Summer, Special & Intl Programs, George Washinton Univ, 609 22nd St NW, Washington DC 20052 *Ph:* 202-994 6360 *Fax:* 202-994 9133 *E-mail:* sumprogs@gwu.edu

Tunisia

MORE THAN ONE CITY

1784
INTERNATIONAL BICYCLE FUND
Tunisia: Eden to Oasis
Site: Tunisia: various sites
Dates: 2 wks, Mar-Apr
Subjects: African studies, Agriculture, Civilization/culture, Development studies,

Ecology/environmental studies, Economics, Education/teaching, Field study, Geography, Geology, Health care/hospitals, History, Independent study, Political science/politics, Religion/theology
Eligibility: *Level:* adults
Credit: *Undergrad:* none *Grad:* none
Instruction: *In:* English *Format:* directed field study, independent study, seminar, study tour *Students:* mainly US
Costs: $1,190 *incl* tuition, housing, some meals, fees, excursions *Nonrefundable fee*
Housing: *Arr by pgm:* homestay, hotels, hostels
Deadline: Until pgm filled
Other info: *US accredited sponsor:* no *Began:* 1989 *Orient:* avail pre-departure packet *Misc:* May contact former participants. *URL:* http://www.ibike.org/bikeafrica
Contact: David Mozer, Dir, Intl Bicycle Fund, 4887 Columbia Dr S, Seattle WA 98108 *Ph:* 206-767 0848 *Fax:* 206-767 0848 *E-mail:* ibike@ibike.org

---

1785
INTERNATIONAL BICYCLE FUND
Tunisia: Historic North
Site: Tunisia: various sites
Dates: 13 days, Apr
Subjects: African studies, Agriculture, Civilization/culture, Development studies, Ecology/environmental studies, Economics, Education/teaching, Field study, Geography, Geology, Health care/hospitals, History, Independent study, Political science/politics, Religion/theology
Eligibility: *Level:* adults
Credit: *Undergrad:* none *Grad:* none
Instruction: *In:* English *Format:* directed field study, independent study, seminar, study tour *Students:* mainly US
Costs: $1,190 *incl* tuition, housing, some meals, fees, excursions *Nonrefundable fee*
Housing: *Arr by pgm:* homestay, hotels, hostels
Deadline: Unitl pgm filled
Other info: *US accredited sponsor:* no *Began:* 1989 *Orient:* avail pre-departure packet *Misc:* May contact former participants. *URL:* http://www.ibike.org/bikeafrica
Contact: David Mozer, Dir, Intl Bicycle Fund, 4887 Columbia Dr S, Seattle WA 98108 *Ph:* 206-767 0848 *Fax:* 206-767 0848 *E-mail:* ibike@ibike.org

---

MONASTIR

1786
COUNCIL ON INTERNATIONAL EDUCATIONAL EXCHANGE CONSORTIUM
Council Study Center, Tunisia
Site: Tunisia: Monastir *Host inst:* Natl Heritage Inst
Dates: 6 wks, late May-early Jul
Subjects: Archaeology, Art history, Field study, Studio arts
Eligibility: *Level:* fresh, sophs, jrs, srs, grads, adults, teachers, professionals *Requires:* 2.75 GPA, completion of 1 coll sem *Age:* min 18
Credit: *Undergrad:* 6 *Grad:* none
Instruction: *In:* English *Format:* directed field study, lecture *Students:* mainly US
Costs: $3,185 *incl* tuition, housing, some meals, insurance, excursions *Nonrefundable fee*
Housing: *Arr by pgm:* apartments
Deadline: Apr 1
Other info: *US accredited sponsor:* yes *Began:* 1996 *Orient:* abroad *Activities:* excursions, field trips, cultural events *Misc:* 2-wk archaeological dig required. Grade report. May contact former participants. *Financial aid:* scholarships *URL:* http://www.ciee.org/study
Contact: *See Index II for Members* Africa Pgm Adviser, Council-ISP, 633 3rd Ave 20th Fl, New York NY 10017-6706 *Ph:* 800-407 8839; 212-822 2600 *Fax:* 212-822 2779 *E-mail:* studyinfo@ciee.org

---

TUNIS

1787
LANGUAGES ABROAD
Language and Cultural Immersion Programs-Tunisia
Site: Tunisia: Tunis
Dates: 2 wks or longer, yr-round
Subjects: Civilization/culture, French language (beg/int/adv)
Eligibility: *Level:* adults *Age:* min 17, max 65, avg 25
Credit: *Undergrad:* none *Grad:* none *Doc:* certificate
Instruction: *In:* French *Format:* lang study *Students:* intl
Costs: From $2,950 for 4 wks *incl* tuition, housing, some meals, excursions, books/materials
Housing: *Arr by pgm:* apartments, homestay
Deadline: None
Other info: *US accredited sponsor:* no *Misc:* May contact former participants. *URL:* http://www.languagesabroad.com
Contact: Ms Jesse Philippe, Langs Abroad, 317 Adelaide St W, Ste 900, Toronto, Ontario M5V 1P9, Canada *Ph:* 800-219 9924; 416-925 7117 *E-mail:* info@languagesabroad.com

---

1788
UNIVERSITY OF KANSAS
Arabic Studies in Tunis, Tunisia
Site: Tunisia: Tunis *Host inst:* Bourguiba Inst of Univ Tunis
Dates: 1 mo, Jul 1-31
Subjects: Arabic language, Arabic studies, Independent study
Eligibility: *Level:* fresh, sophs, jrs, srs, grads, adults *Requires:* good acad standing *Age:* min 18
Credit: *Undergrad:* 6-8 *Grad:* none *Doc:* transcript
Instruction: *In:* Arabic *Format:* independent study, lecture, seminar, tutorial *Students:* intl
Costs: $1,660 *incl* tuition, housing, excursions, books/materials, medical evacuation svcs *Nonrefundable fee*
Housing: *Arr by pgm:* residence halls with local students
Deadline: Rolling admissions
Other info: *US accredited sponsor:* yes *Began:* 2000 *Orient:* in US (1 day) *URL:* http://www.ukans.edu/~osa
Contact: Susan MacNally, Asst Dir, Study Abroad, 108 Lippincott, Lawrence KS 66045 *Ph:* 785-864 3742 *Fax:* 785-864 5040 *E-mail:* osa@ukans.edu ▲

Turkey

MORE THAN ONE CITY

1789
COUNCIL ON INTERNATIONAL EDUCATIONAL EXCHANGE (COUNCIL)
International Faculty Development Seminars-Turkey
Site: Turkey: Ankara, Central Anatolia, Istanbul *Host inst:* Middle East Technical Univ
Dates: 12 days, Jun
Subjects: Economics, Education/teaching, Islamic studies, Political science/politics, Religion/theology
Eligibility: *Level:* teachers *Requires:* must be faculty at 2-yr or 4-yr inst
Credit: *Undergrad:* none *Grad:* none
Instruction: *In:* English *Format:* lecture, seminar *Students:* mainly US
Costs: $1,875 *incl* tuition, housing, some meals, insurance, fees, excursions, books/materials
Housing: *Arr by pgm:* hotels
Deadline: Mar 15
Other info: *US accredited sponsor:* no *Began:* 1996 *Orient:* abroad *Activities:*

excursions, field trips, cultural events *Misc:* Seminar title: Econ, Polity & Religion in Turkey. *URL:* http://www.ciee.org/ifds
Contact: Jennifer Ley, Dir, Intl Faculty Development Seminars, Council, 633 3rd Ave, New York NY 10017 *Ph:* 212-822 2747 *Fax:* 212-822 2779 *E-mail:* jley@ciee.org ▲

1790
GENCTUR TURIZM VE SEYAHAT ACENTASI
International Voluntary Work Camps
Site: Turkey: various sites *Host inst:* local municipalities or NGOs
Dates: 2 wks, May 1-Sep 30
Subjects: Community service projects
Eligibility: *Level:* adults *Age:* min 16, avg 22
Credit: *Undergrad:* none *Grad:* none
Instruction: *In:* English *Format:* volunteer/svc *Students:* intl
Costs: $50 *incl* housing, all meals, insurance
Housing: *Arr by pgm:* residence halls
Deadline: Aug 30
Other info: *US accredited sponsor:* no *Orient:* abroad (1 day) *URL:* http://www.genctur.com
Contact: Mr Zafer Yilmaz, GENCTUR, Istiklal Cad Zambak Sok 15/5, Istanbul 80080, Turkey *E-mail:* workcamps@genctur.com

---

1791
GEORGE MASON UNIVERSITY
Turkey: Dynamics of Political and Social Change
Site: Turkey: various sites
Dates: 4 wks, Jun 29-Aug 1
Subjects: Government, History, Political science/politics, Social policy
Eligibility: *Level:* fresh, sophs, jrs, srs *Requires:* 2.25 GPA *Age:* min 18
Credit: *Undergrad:* 6 *Grad:* none
Instruction: *In:* English *Format:* study tour *Students:* mainly US
Costs: About $3,800 for VA residents, $4,400 for others *incl* tuition, housing, some meals, insurance, fees, excursions, books/materials, ISIC *Nonrefundable fee*
Housing: *Arr by pgm:* hotels
Deadline: Apr 10
Other info: *US accredited sponsor:* yes *Began:* 1996 *Orient:* in US (1 day) *Misc:* May contact former participants. *Financial aid:* scholarships, work study *URL:* http://www.gmu.edu/departments/cge
Contact: Ctr for Global Educ, George Mason Univ, Johnson Ctr, Rm 235, 4400 University Dr, Fairfax VA 22030-4444 *Ph:* 703-993 2154 *Fax:* 703-993 2153 *E-mail:* cge@gmu.edu

---

ANKARA

1792
MIDDLE EAST TECHNICAL UNIVERSITY
METU International Summer School
Site: Turkey: Ankara *Host inst:* Middle East Technical University
Dates: 6 wks, Jun 28-Aug 7
Subjects: Architectural history, Art history, Central Asian studies, Economics, Engineering, Geology, History, Islamic studies, Middle Eastern studies, Political science/politics, Sociology, Turkish language, Turkish studies, Urban planning, Women's studies
Eligibility: *Level:* jrs, srs, grads *Requires:* 2.2 GPA, previous study in field, for specialized courses, good acad standing *Age:* min 19, max 36, avg 24
Credit: *Undergrad:* 6 *Grad:* 6 *Doc:* transcript
Instruction: *In:* English *Format:* lecture, study tour *Students:* mainly host country
Costs: $1,700 *incl* tuition, housing, fees, excursions, books/materials
Housing: *Arr by pgm:* residence halls with local students, homestay
Deadline: Apr 15 or until pgm filled
Other info: *US accredited sponsor:* no *Began:* 1994 *Orient:* abroad (intensive lang study) *Activities:* excursions, field trips *Misc:* Wkend trips to historical sites near Ankara, Central Anatolia & along Aegean. Participants assigned METU host students. *URL:* http://www.metu.edu.tr
Contact: Dr Shirley Epir, Dir, Intl Relations Off, Middle East Technical Univ, Inonu Blvd, Ankara 06531, Turkey *E-mail:* shirleyj@metu.edu.tr

---

ISTANBUL

1793
AMERICAN RESEARCH INSTITUTE IN TURKEY
Intensive Language Study in Turkey
Site: Turkey: Istanbul *Host inst:* Bosphorus Univ
Dates: 8 wks, Jul-Aug
Subjects: Turkish language (beg/int/adv)
Eligibility: US citizens only. *Level:* grads *Requires:* 3.0 GPA, must be grad student enrolled in degree pgm, proficiency test for adv applicants
Credit: *Undergrad:* none *Grad:* avail *Doc:* certificate
Instruction: *In:* Turkish *Format:* lang study *Students:* mainly US
Costs: Contact sponsor
Housing: *Sponsor assists:* residence halls with local students
Deadline: Feb 1
Other info: *US accredited sponsor:* yes *Began:* 1982 *Orient:* abroad (2 days, intensive lang study) *Activities:* field trips, cultural events *Misc:* ARIT is a fellowship pgm. May apply & pay for independently through Bosphorus Univ. May contact former participants. *Financial aid:* scholarships
Contact: *See Index II for Members* Iris Wright, Admin, Ctr for Study of Islamic Societies & Civilizations, Washington Univ, Campus Box 1230, One Brookings Dr, St Louis MO 63130-4899 *Ph:* 314-935 5166 *Fax:* 314-935 7462 *E-mail:* iwright@artsci.wustl.edu
Or Contact: Nancy Leinwand, Admin, Amer Research Inst in Turkey, Univ of Pennsylvania Museum, 33rd & Spruce Sts, Philadelphia PA 19104-6324 *Ph:* 215-898 3474 *Fax:* 215-898 0657 *E-mail:* leinwand@sas.upenn.edu

---

1794
DUKE UNIVERSITY
Duke in Turkey
Site: Turkey: Istanbul *Host inst:* Bogazici Univ
Dates: 9 wks, mid-Jun-mid-Aug
Subjects: Humanities, Philosophy, Social sciences
Eligibility: *Level:* fresh, sophs, jrs, srs *Requires:* good acad standing
Credit: *Undergrad:* avail *Grad:* none *Doc:* transcript
Instruction: *In:* English *Format:* lecture, seminar *Students:* mainly US
Costs: $5,225 *incl* tuition, housing, all meals, fees, excursions
Housing: *Sponsor assists:* residence halls
Deadline: Feb 16
Other info: *US accredited sponsor:* yes *Began:* 2001 *Orient:* abroad (2 days) *Activities:* excursions, field trips, program travel *Financial aid:* scholarships *URL:* http://www.aas.duke.edu/study_abroad
Contact: Study Abroad, Duke Univ, 121 Allen Bldg, Box 90057, Durham NC 27708-0057 *Ph:* 919-684 2174 *Fax:* 919-684 3083 *E-mail:* abroad@asdean.duke.edu

---

1795
LANGUAGES ABROAD
Language and Cultural Immersion-Istanbul
Site: Turkey: Istanbul
Dates: 2 wks or longer, yr-round
Subjects: Civilization/culture, Turkish language (beg/int/adv), Turkish studies
Eligibility: *Level:* adults *Age:* min 17, max 65, avg 25
Credit: *Undergrad:* none *Grad:* none *Doc:* certificate
Instruction: *In:* Turkish *Format:* lang study *Students:* intl
Costs: $3,000 per mo *incl* tuition, housing, some meals, excursions, books/materials

Housing: *Arr by pgm:* residence halls, homestay
Deadline: None
Other info: *US accredited sponsor:* no *Began:* 1995 *Activities:* excursions, field trips, program travel, cultural events, sports *Misc:* May contact former participants. *URL:* http://www.languagesabroad.com
Contact: Ms Jesse Philippe, Langs Abroad, 317 Adelaide St W, Ste 900, Toronto, Ontario M5V 1P9, Canada *Ph:* 800-219 9924; 416-925 7117 *E-mail:* info@languagesabroad.com

---

1796
SUNY UNIVERSITY AT BINGHAMTON
Summer Program at Bosphorus University
Site: Turkey: Istanbul *Host inst:* Bosphorus Univ
Dates: 7 wks, mid-Jun-early Aug
Subjects: Full curriculum, Economics, History, International relations, Literature, Political science/politics, Turkish language
Eligibility: *Level:* fresh, sophs, jrs, srs *Requires:* 3.0 GPA
Credit: *Undergrad:* 8 *Grad:* none *Doc:* transcript
Instruction: *In:* English *Format:* lang study, lecture, seminar *Students:* mainly host country
Costs: $4,500 for NY residents, $6,000 for others *incl* tuition, housing, all meals, intl airfare, insurance, fees, excursions, books/materials *Nonrefundable fee*
Housing: *Arr by pgm:* residence halls
Deadline: Mar 15
Other info: *US accredited sponsor:* yes *Began:* 1996 *Orient:* in US & abroad *Activities:* field trips *Misc:* May contact former participants. *URL:* http://www.binghamton.edu
Contact: Dr Katharine Krebs, Intl Pgms, NARC G-1 Binghamton Univ, Binghamton NY 13902-6000 *Ph:* 607-777 2336 *Fax:* 607-777 2889 *E-mail:* oip@binghamton.edu

United Arab Emirates

DUBAI

1797
AMERICAN INTERCONTINENTAL UNIVERSITY
Dubai Program
Site: United Arab Emirates: Dubai *Host inst:* Amer Univ in Dubai
Dates: 8-wk sessions, May-Jul, Jul-Sep
Subjects: Advertising, Arabic language (beg/int/adv), Business administration, Commercial art, Communications, Fashion design, Fine arts, Graphic arts/design, Intercultural studies, Interior design, Liberal arts, Marketing, Middle Eastern studies, Photography, Public relations
Eligibility: *Level:* fresh, sophs, jrs, srs, grads, adults *Requires:* good acad standing, approval by acad adviser & dean/dept head, coll transcript
Credit: *Undergrad:* 3-12 (5-20 qtr hrs) *Grad:* 3-9 (5-15 qtr hrs) *Doc:* transcript
Instruction: *In:* English *Format:* art studio, independent study, lang study, lecture, seminar *Students:* intl
Costs: About $2,706-$6,003 for undergrads, $5,487 for grads *incl* tuition, housing
Housing: *Arr by pgm:* apartments
Deadline: None; 6 mos before pgm recommended
Other info: *US accredited sponsor:* yes *Began:* 1995 *Orient:* in US & abroad *Activities:* excursions, field trips, program travel, cultural events, sports *Misc:* Classes meet Sun-Wed. May contact former participants. *Financial aid:* scholarships *URL:* http://studyabroad.aiuniv.edu
Contact: Study Abroad Pgms, Amer InterContinental Univ, 6600 Peachtree-Dunwoody Rd, 500 Embassy Row, Atlanta GA 30328 *Ph:* 800-255 6839; 404-965 5300 *Fax:* 404-965 8006 *E-mail:* studyabroad@aiuniv.edu ▲

Yemen

SANA'A

1798
LANGUAGE LIAISON
Arabic Language
Site: Yemen: Sana'a
Dates: 2 wks-1 yr, yr-round
Subjects: Arabic language
Eligibility: *Level:* fresh, sophs, jrs, srs, grads, adults, teachers, professionals, precoll *Age:* min 18
Credit: *Undergrad:* avail *Grad:* avail
Instruction: *In:* Arabic *Format:* lang study *Students:* intl
Costs: Contact sponsor
Housing: *Arr by pgm:* residence halls
Deadline: 60 days before pgm
Other info: *US accredited sponsor:* no *Began:* 1997 *Activities:* excursions, cultural events *URL:* http://www.languageliaison.com
Contact: Nancy Forman, Dir, Lang Liaison, 4 Burnham Pkwy, Morristown NJ 07960 *Ph:* 800-284 4448 *Fax:* 973-898 1710 *E-mail:* learn@languageliaison.com

---

1799
LANGUAGES ABROAD
Language and Cultural Immersion Programs
Site: Yemen: Sana'a
Dates: 2 wks or longer, yr-round
Subjects: Arabic language (beg/int/adv), Civilization/culture, Homestay
Eligibility: *Level:* adults *Age:* min 17, max 65, avg 25
Credit: *Undergrad:* none *Grad:* none *Doc:* certificate
Instruction: *In:* Arabic *Format:* lang study *Students:* intl
Costs: From $2,350 for 2 wks *incl* tuition, housing, some meals, excursions, books/materials
Housing: *Arr by pgm:* apartments, homestay
Deadline: None
Other info: *US accredited sponsor:* no *Misc:* May contact former participants. *URL:* http://www.languagesabroad.com
Contact: Ms Jesse Philippe, 317 Adeliade St W, Ste 900, Toronto, Ontario M5V 1P9, Canada *Ph:* 800-219 9924; 416-925 7117 *E-mail:* info@languagesabroad.com

Western Hemisphere

More Than One Country

1800
COUNCIL ON INTERNATIONAL EDUCATIONAL EXCHANGE (COUNCIL)
International Faculty Development Seminars-Argentina
Site: Argentina: Buenos Aires; Chile: Santiago *Host inst:* FLACSO
Dates: 9 days, Jun
Subjects: Contemporary issues, Economics, Political science/politics, Trade
Eligibility: *Level:* teachers, professionals *Requires:* must be faculty at 2-yr or 4-yr inst
Credit: *Undergrad:* none *Grad:* none
Instruction: *In:* English *Format:* lecture, seminar *Students:* mainly US
Costs: $1,995 *incl* tuition, housing, some meals, excursions, books/materials, receptions *Nonrefundable fee*
Housing: *Arr by pgm:* hotels
Deadline: Mar 15
Other info: *US accredited sponsor:* no *Began:* 1991 *Orient:* abroad *Activities:* excursions, field trips, program travel, cultural events *Misc:* Seminar title: Econ Reform, Regional Integration, & Democratization in Chile & Argentina. *URL:* http://www.ciee.org/ifds
Contact: Jennifer Ley, Dir, Council, 633 3rd Ave, New York NY 10017 *Ph:* 212-822 2747 *Fax:* 212-822 2779 *E-mail:* ifds@ciee.org ▲

1801
EASTERN MICHIGAN UNIVERSITY
Latin America Cultural History Tour
Site: Cuba, El Salvador, Guatemala, Mexico, Nicaragua
Dates: 6 wks, Jun 1-Jul 12
Subjects: History, Political science/politics
Eligibility: *Level:* fresh, sophs, jrs, srs *Requires:* 2.0 GPA, references *Age:* min 18
Credit: *Undergrad:* 6 *Grad:* none *Doc:* transcript
Instruction: *In:* English *Format:* lecture, seminar, study tour *Students:* mainly US
Costs: $2,995 *incl* tuition, housing, some meals, insurance, fees, excursions
Housing: *Arr by pgm:* residence halls, pensions, hotels
Deadline: Mar 1
Other info: *US accredited sponsor:* yes *Began:* 2001 *Orient:* abroad (2 days) *Activities:* excursions, field trips, program travel, cultural events *Misc:* May contact former participants.
Contact: Acad Pgms Abroad, Eastern Michigan Univ, 127 Boone Hall, Ypsilanti MI 48197 *Ph:* 800-777 3541; 734-487 2424 *Fax:* 734-487 4377 *E-mail:* programs.abroad@emich.edu

---

1802
FELLOWSHIP OF RECONCILIATION
Voluntarios Solidarios
Site: Argentina, Bolivia, Chile, Ecuador, Mexico, Panama, Paraguay, Puerto Rico
Dates: 3 mos or longer, yr-round
Subjects: Community service projects, Peace studies
Eligibility: *Level:* srs, grads, adults, teachers, professionals *Requires:* fluency in Spanish *Age:* min 21, avg 25
Credit: *Undergrad:* none *Grad:* none
Instruction: *In:* Spanish *Format:* volunteer/svc *Students:* mainly US
Costs: $200-$1,000 per mo depending on location *incl* housing, all meals *Nonrefundable fee*
Housing: *Sponsor assists:* apartments, homestay
Deadline: 2 mos before pgm
Other info: *US accredited sponsor:* no *Began:* 1994 *In coop with:* Latin Amer & Caribbean orgs *Activities:* excursions, program travel *Misc:* May contact former participants. *URL:* http://www.forusa.org
Contact: Luis Monterrosa, 2017 Mission St #305, Fellowship of Reconciliation, San Francisco CA 94110 *Ph:* 415-495 6334 *Fax:* 415-495 5628 *E-mail:* volfor@igc.org

---

1803
MICHIGAN STATE UNIVERSITY
Summer School in the Caribbean
Site: Barbados, Guyana, Trinidad & Tobago *Host inst:* Univ of the West Indies, Univ of Guyana at Turkeyan
Dates: 4 wks, Jun-Jul
Subjects: International relations, Political science/politics, Sociology
Eligibility: *Level:* fresh, sophs, jrs, srs *Requires:* 2.0 GPA, good acad standing *Age:* min 18
Credit: *Undergrad:* 8 *Grad:* none *Doc:* transcript
Instruction: *In:* English *Format:* lecture *Students:* mainly US
Costs: About $2,400 *incl* housing, some meals, insurance, excursions *Nonrefundable fee*
Housing: *Sponsor assists:* residence halls
Deadline: Mar 2
Other info: *US accredited sponsor:* yes *Began:* 1986 *Orient:* in US & abroad *Activities:* field trips *Misc:* Loans avail. May contact former participants. *Financial aid:* scholarships *URL:* http://studyabroad.msu.edu
Contact: Cheryl Benner, Study Abroad, Michigan State Univ, 109 Intl Ctr, East Lansing MI 48824-1035 *Ph:* 517-353 8920 *Fax:* 517-432 2082 *E-mail:* bennerc@msu.edu ▲

1804
NATIONAL REGISTRATION CENTER FOR STUDY ABROAD (NRCSA)
Learn Spanish in South America
Site: Argentina: Buenos Aires; Chile: Santiago *Host inst:* Home Lang Schs Intl
Dates: 1 wk, yr-round

Subjects: Homestay, Spanish language
Eligibility: *Level:* fresh, sophs, jrs, srs, grads, adults, teachers, professionals
Credit: *Undergrad:* avail *Grad:* avail *Doc:* certificate
Instruction: *In:* Spanish *Format:* lang study, tutorial *Students:* intl
Costs: $1,119 *incl* tuition, housing, all meals, insurance *Nonrefundable fee*
Housing: *Arr by pgm:* homestay
Deadline: 6 wks before pgm
Other info: *US accredited sponsor:* no *Misc:* Student lives in teacher's home. *URL:* http://www.nrcsa.com
Contact: June Domoe, NRCSA, 823 N 2nd St, #206, Milwaukee WI 53203 *Ph:* 414-278 0631 *Fax:* 414-271 8884 *E-mail:* info@nrcsa.com

---

1805
THUNDERBIRD, THE AMERICAN GRADUATE SCHOOL OF INTERNATIONAL MANAGEMENT
Winterim in Chile and Peru
Site: Chile: Santiago; Peru: Lima, Machu Picchu
Dates: 3 wks
Subjects: Business/management, Chilean studies, Civilization/culture, Economics, International business, Peruvian studies, Political science/politics, South American studies, Spanish language (adv)
Eligibility: *Level:* grads *Requires:* 3.0 GPA
Credit: *Undergrad:* none *Grad:* 3
Instruction: *In:* English, Spanish *Format:* lang study, lecture *Students:* intl
Costs: $2,625 *incl* tuition, pgm fee
Housing: *Sponsor assists:* hotels
Deadline: Contact sponsor
Other info: *US accredited sponsor:* yes *Orient:* abroad *Activities:* field trips *Misc:* Visits to companies, meetings with bus execs, govt officials. *URL:* http://www.t-bird.edu
Contact: James Scott, Overseas Pgms, Thunderbird, 15249 N 59th Ave, Glendale AZ 85306 *Ph:* 602-978 7251 *Fax:* 602-547 1356 *E-mail:* scottj@t-bird.edu

---

1806
THUNDERBIRD, THE AMERICAN GRADUATE SCHOOL OF INTERNATIONAL MANAGEMENT
Winterim in Cuba and Trinidad
Site: Cuba: Havana, Pinar del Rio; Trinidad: Varadero
Dates: 3 wks
Subjects: Business language, Civilization/culture, Economics, History, International business, International studies, Political science/politics, Spanish language
Eligibility: *Level:* grads *Requires:* 3.0 GPA
Credit: *Undergrad:* none *Grad:* 3
Instruction: *In:* English, Spanish *Format:* lang study, lecture *Students:* intl
Costs: $2,625 *incl* tuition, off-campus pgm fee
Housing: *Arr by pgm:* residence halls, hotels
Deadline: Contact sponsor
Other info: *US accredited sponsor:* yes *Orient:* abroad *Activities:* field trips *Misc:* Meet Cuban officials. May contact former participants. *URL:* http://www.t-bird.edu
Contact: James Scott, Overseas Pgms, Thunderbird, 15249 N 59th Ave, Glendale AZ 85306 *Ph:* 602-978 7251 *Fax:* 602-547 1356 *E-mail:* scottj@t-bird.edu

---

1807
TULANE UNIVERSITY, CENTER FOR LATIN AMERICAN STUDIES
Community Development Internship Program
Site: Cuba, Ecuador, Mexico
Dates: 3 wks for Cuba, 6 wks for others, yr-round
Subjects: Community service projects, Development studies, Internships
Eligibility: *Level:* fresh, sophs, jrs, srs, grads, adults, teachers, professionals *Requires:* 2.8 GPA, Spanish lang proficiency
Credit: *Undergrad:* avail *Grad:* avail *Doc:* transcript
Instruction: *In:* Spanish *Format:* internship, volunteer/svc *Students:* mainly US
Costs: $3,400 for 3 credits, $3,600 for 6 credits for 6 wks *incl* tuition, housing, some meals, insurance, excursions
Housing: *Arr by pgm:* homestay
Deadline: Contact sponsor
Other info: *US accredited sponsor:* yes *Began:* 1998 *Orient:* abroad *Activities:* excursions, cultural events *Misc:* Volunteers live with a family in rural Mexico & Ecuador, or semi-urban Cuba & work side by side with comm members. May contact former participants. *URL:* http://intern.tulane.edu
Contact: Dr Ana Lopez, Dir, Cuban Studies Inst, Tulane Univ, New Orleans LA 70118 *Ph:* 504-862 8629 *Fax:* 504-862 8678 *E-mail:* cuba@tulane.edu
Or Contact: Deborah Ramil, Cuban Studies Inst, Tulane Univ, Caroline Richardson Bldg, New Orleans LA 70118 *Ph:* 504-862 8629 *Fax:* 504-862 8678 *E-mail:* dramil@tulane.edu

---

1808
UNIVERSITY OF GEORGIA
Agriculture and Ecology in Tropical America
Site: Costa Rica (even-numbered yrs), Guatemala (odd-numbered yrs)
Dates: 18 days, late Jul-mid-Aug
Subjects: Agriculture, Agronomy, Animal production, Civilization/culture, Climatology, Deforestation, Ecology/environmental studies, History, Horticulture, Labor/labor relations, Latin American studies, Mayan studies, Soil/pasture management
Eligibility: *Level:* jrs, srs, grads, adults, teachers, professionals *Requires:* previous study in field, permission of dept, letter of reference, statement of interest
Credit: *Undergrad:* 3 *Grad:* 3 *Doc:* transcript
Instruction: *In:* English *Format:* lecture, study tour *Students:* mainly US
Costs: $2,000 *incl* tuition, housing, some meals, intl airfare, fees, excursions, local transport *Nonrefundable fee*
Housing: *Arr by pgm:* residence halls, hotels
Deadline: Mar 15
Other info: *US accredited sponsor:* yes *Began:* 1997 *Orient:* in US (1 day) or abroad (1 day) *Activities:* excursions, field trips, program travel, cultural events *Misc:* May contact former participants. *URL:* http://www.cropsoil.uga.edu/~tropag
Contact: Prof Mark Rieger, Univ of Georgia, 1111 Plant Scis, Athens GA 30602 *Ph:* 706-542 2471 *Fax:* 706-542 0624 *E-mail:* mrieger@uga.edu
Or Contact: Prof Wayne Parrott, Univ of Georgia, 3111 Plant Scis, Athens GA 30602 *Ph:* 706-542 0928 *E-mail:* wparrott@uga.edu

Anguilla

MORE THAN ONE CITY

1809
MICHIGAN STATE UNIVERSITY
Integrated Marine Resource Management and Coastal Tourism
Site: Anguilla: various sites
Dates: 4 wks, Jun-Jul
Subjects: Field study, Fishing/fisheries, Parks management, Recreation resources management, Wildlife
Eligibility: *Level:* jrs, srs, grads *Requires:* 2.5 GPA, previous study in field, DAN insurance, scuba certification, swimming competency *Age:* min 18
Credit: *Undergrad:* avail *Grad:* avail *Doc:* transcript
Instruction: *In:* English *Format:* directed field study *Students:* mainly US
Costs: About $2,600 *incl* housing, some meals, insurance, fees, excursions, tanks, air fills *Nonrefundable fee*
Housing: *Arr by pgm:* resort
Deadline: Mar 2
Other info: *US accredited sponsor:* yes *Began:* 1999 *Orient:* in US (2 days) *Activities:* excursions, program travel *URL:* http://studyabroad.msu.edu

Contact: Cheryl Benner, Study Abroad, Michigan State Univ, 109 Intl Ctr, East Lansing MI 48824-1035 *Ph:* 517-353 8920 *Fax:* 517-432 2082 *E-mail:* bennerc@msu.edu ▲

Argentina

MORE THAN ONE CITY

1810
AMERISPAN UNLIMITED
Spanish Study and Homestay in Argentina
Site: Argentina: Buenos Aires, Cordoba
Dates: 1 wk-1 yr, yr-round
Subjects: Business language, Civilization/culture, Homestay, Spanish language (beg/int/adv)
Eligibility: *Level:* fresh, sophs, jrs, srs, grads, adults, teachers, professionals, precoll *Age:* min 18
Credit: *Undergrad:* avail *Grad:* none *Doc:* transcript, certificate *Transfer credit through:* Univ of Southern Mississippi
Instruction: *In:* Spanish *Format:* lang study, lecture, tutorial *Students:* intl
Costs: $1,195 for 2 wks, $1,995 for 4 wks, $480 for each addtl wk *incl* tuition, housing, some meals, insurance, books/materials
Housing: *Arr by pgm:* homestay, hotels
Deadline: 4 wks before pgm
Other info: *US accredited sponsor:* no *Orient:* abroad *Activities:* excursions, cultural events, sports *Misc:* Transfer credit also avail through Seattle Central CC. May contact former participants. *Financial aid:* work study *URL:* http://www.amerispan.com/
Contact: AmeriSpan Unltd, PO Box 40007, Philadelphia PA 19106 *Ph:* 800-879 6640; 215-751 1100 *Fax:* 215-751 1986 *E-mail:* info@amerispan.com

---

1811
ILEE (INSTITUTO DE LENGUA ESPANOLA PARA EXTRANJEROS)
Spanish in Argentina at ILEE
Site: Argentina: Buenos Aires, Cordoba
Dates: 2 wks or longer, yr-round
Subjects: Argentine studies, Spanish language (beg/int/adv)
Eligibility: *Level:* fresh, sophs, jrs, srs, grads, adults, teachers, professionals, precoll *Age:* min 15, avg 28
Credit: *Undergrad:* avail *Grad:* none *Doc:* certificate, diploma *Transfer credit through:* Univ of Southern Mississippi
Instruction: *In:* Spanish *Format:* lang study *Students:* intl
Costs: Contact sponsor
Housing: *Arr by pgm:* homestay, hotels
Deadline: None
Other info: *US accredited sponsor:* no *Began:* 1988 *Orient:* in US & abroad *Activities:* excursions, field trips, program travel, cultural events, sports *Misc:* All teachers hold masters degrees in educ or literature. May contact former participants. *URL:* http://www.ilee.com.ar
Contact: Daniel Korman, Dir, ILEE, Av Callao 339, 3rd Fl, 1022 Buenos Aires, Argentina *E-mail:* info@ilee.com.ar

---

1812
ILEE (INSTITUTO DE LENGUA ESPANOLA PARA EXTRANJEROS)
Spanish Language School for Foreigners
Site: Argentian: Buenos Aires, Cordoba
Dates: Multiple pgm lengths, yr-round
Subjects: Literature, Political science/politics, Social sciences, Spanish language (beg/int/adv)
Eligibility: *Level:* adults *Age:* min 14, avg 25
Credit: *Undergrad:* avail *Grad:* none *Doc:* certificate, diploma *Transfer credit through:* University of Southern Mississippi
Instruction: *In:* Spanish *Format:* tutorial, workshop *Students:* intl
Costs: $1,600 per mo *incl* tuition, housing, some meals, books/materials *Nonrefundable fee*
Housing: *Arr by pgm:* homestay, hotels
Deadline: 1 mo before pgm
Other info: *US accredited sponsor:* no *Began:* 1987 *Orient:* abroad (1 day) *Activities:* excursions, cultural events, sports *Misc:* May contact former participants. *URL:* http://www.studyabroad.com/ilee
Contact: Daniel Korman, Dir, ILEE, Av Callao 339, 3rd Fl, 1022 Buenos Aires, Argentina *E-mail:* info@ilee.com.ar

---

1813
SAINT JOHN'S UNIVERSITY (NY)
Summer Program in Argentina
Site: Argentina: Buenos Aires, Corrientes *Host inst:* Instituto de Literatura Hispanoamericana of Univ of Buenos Aires, others
Dates: 1 mo, Jun-Jul
Subjects: Literature, Spanish language
Eligibility: *Level:* sophs, jrs, srs *Requires:* 2.75 GPA *Age:* min 18
Credit: *Undergrad:* avail *Grad:* none *Doc:* transcript
Instruction: *In:* Spanish *Format:* lang study, lecture *Students:* mainly US
Costs: $2,300-$2,500 *incl* housing, some meals, intl airfare, excursions *Nonrefundable fee*
Housing: *Sponsor assists:* residence halls, apartments
Deadline: Feb 1
Other info: *US accredited sponsor:* yes *Began:* 2000 *Orient:* in US *Activities:* excursions, field trips, program travel *Misc:* May contact former participants. *Financial aid:* scholarships
Contact: Study Abroad Pgms, St John's Univ, Bent Hall, Rm 388, 8000 Utopia Pkwy, Jamaia NY 11439 *Ph:* 718-990 6105 *Fax:* 718-990 2321 *E-mail:* intled@stjohns.edu

---

BUENOS AIRES

1814
ARGENTINE SPANISH LEARNING CENTER-CEDIC
Language and Argentine Literature-Contemporary Authors
Site: Argentina: Buenos Aires
Dates: 1 wk or longer, yr-round
Subjects: Adult education (int/adv), Argentine studies, Literature, Spanish language (int/adv)
Eligibility: *Level:* grads, adults, teachers, professionals *Requires:* knowledge of Spanish *Age:* min 17
Credit: *Undergrad:* avail *Grad:* none *Doc:* certificate
Instruction: *In:* Spanish *Format:* lang study, practical training, seminar *Students:* intl
Costs: Contact Sponsor
Housing: *Sponsor assists:* residence halls with local students, residence halls, apartments, homestay, hotels, hostels
Deadline: 2 wks before pgm
Other info: *US accredited sponsor:* yes *Began:* 1985 *Orient:* abroad *Activities:* excursions, cultural events, sports *Misc:* Customized pgms. Authors selected according to student's goals. May contact former participants. *URL:* http://www.cedic.com.ar
Contact: Martin Duh or Susana Bernardi, Argentine Spanish Learning Ctr-CEDIC, Reconquista 715, piso 11E, Buenos Aires, Argentina C1003 ABO *E-mail:* spanish@cedic.com.ar

---

1815
ARGENTINE SPANISH LEARNING CENTER-CEDIC
Spanish Course in Argentina
Site: Argentina: Buenos Aires
Dates: 1 wk or longer, year-round
Subjects: Argentine studies, Civilization/culture, Homestay, Spanish language
Eligibility: *Level:* adults *Age:* min 17
Credit: *Undergrad:* avail *Grad:* none *Doc:* certificate
Instruction: *In:* Spanish *Students:* intl
Costs: $105 per wk *incl* tuition
Housing: *Sponsor assists:* residence halls with local students, homestay, hotels, hostels

Deadline: Rolling admissions
Other info: *US accredited sponsor:* no *Orient:* abroad *Activities:* excursions, cultural events, sports *Misc:* Learning methods combined with audiovisual technology, conversation & grammar excercises. May contact former participants. *URL:* http://www.cedic.com.ar
Contact: Prof Martin Duh, Dir, or M A Susana Bernardi, Studies Dir, CEDIC-Argentine Spanish Learning Ctr, Reconquista 715, 11th Fl E, Buenos Aires, Argentina C1003 ABO *E-mail:* martinduh@act.net.ar

---

1816
ARGENTINE SPANISH LEARNING CENTER-CEDIC
Spanish for International Business-SIB
Site: Argentina: Buenos Aires
Dates: 1 wk or longer, yr-round
Subjects: Adult education (beg/int/adv), Business language, Spanish language (beg/int/adv)
Eligibility: *Level:* adults, professionals *Requires:* Spanih lang *Age:* min 18
Credit: *Undergrad:* avail *Grad:* none *Doc:* certificate
Instruction: *In:* Spanish *Format:* lang study, practical training *Students:* intl
Costs: Contact sponsor
Housing: *Sponsor assists:* apartments with local students, residence halls with local students, homestay, hotels, hostels
Deadline: 2 wks before pgm
Other info: *US accredited sponsor:* no *Began:* 1985 *Orient:* abroad *Activities:* excursions, program travel, cultural events, sports *Misc:* Flexible pgm designed according to client's work, schedule, lang needs & bus background. May contact former participants. *URL:* http://www.cedic.com.ar
Contact: Prof Martin Duh or Prof Susana Bernardi, CEDIC-Argentine Spanish Learning Ctr, Reconquista 715, piso 11 E, Buenos Aires, Argentina C1003 ABO *E-mail:* spanish@cedic.com.ar

---

1817
COOPERATING PROGRAMS IN THE AMERICAS and BUTLER UNIVERSITY, INSTITUTE FOR STUDY ABROAD and UNIVERSITY OF ILLINOIS AT URBANA-CHAMPAIGN
Argentine Language and Culture Program
Site: Argentina: Buenos Aires *Host inst:* Univ de Buenos Aires
Dates: 6 wks, early Jun-mid-Jul
Subjects: Argentine studies, Homestay, Latin American studies, Literature, Spanish language (adv)
Eligibility: *Level:* sophs, jrs, srs *Requires:* 3.0 GPA, 2 sems univ Spanish
Credit: *Undergrad:* 6 *Grad:* none *Doc:* transcript
Instruction: *In:* Spanish *Format:* lang study, lecture *Students:* mainly US
Costs: $3,400 *incl* tuition, housing, some meals, fees, excursions, ISIC
Housing: *Arr by pgm:* homestay
Deadline: Mar 15
Other info: *US accredited sponsor:* yes *Orient:* abroad (2 days) *Activities:* excursions, cultural events, sports *Misc:* May contact former participants. *Financial aid:* scholarships *URL:* http://www.isabutler.org
Contact: *See Index II for Members* COPA, Inst for Study Abroad, Butler Univ, 1100 W 42nd St, Ste 305, Indianapolis IN 46208 *Ph:* 888-344 9299; 317-940 9336 *Fax:* 317-940 9704 *E-mail:* copa@butler.edu

---

1818
GEORGIA INSTITUTE OF TECHNOLOGY
Business and Politics in Argentina
Site: Argentina: Buenos Aires *Host inst:* Salvador Univ
Dates: 6 wks, mid-May-early Jul
Subjects: Business/management, Economics, International relations, Political science/politics
Eligibility: *Level:* sophs, jrs, srs *Requires:* good academic standing
Credit: *Undergrad:* 6-9 *Grad:* none
Instruction: *In:* English *Format:* directed field study, lecture, seminar, study tour *Students:* US & host country
Costs: $3,100 GA residents, $3,350 others *incl* tuition, housing, some meals, fees, excursions, ground transportation
Housing: *Arr by pgm:* residence halls
Deadline: Contact sponsor
Other info: *US accredited sponsor:* yes *Began:* 1999 *Orient:* in US *Activities:* excursions, field trips, program travel, cultural events *Misc:* Courses fully integrated with students from Salvador Univ. May contact former participants.
Contact: Dr Kirk Bowman, Sam Nunn Sch of Intl Affairs, Georgia Inst of Technology, Atlanta GA 30332-0610 *Ph:* 404-894 6435 *Fax:* 404-894 1900

1819
LANGUAGE LIAISON
Spanish in Argentina
Site: Argentina: Buenos Aires
Dates: 2 wks-1 yr, yr-round
Subjects: Homestay, Spanish language
Eligibility: *Level:* fresh, sophs, jrs, srs, grads, adults, teachers, professionals, precoll *Age:* min 16
Credit: *Undergrad:* avail *Grad:* avail
Instruction: *In:* Spanish *Format:* lang study *Students:* intl
Costs: Contact sponsor
Housing: *Arr by pgm:* homestay
Deadline: 4 wks before pgm
Other info: *US accredited sponsor:* no *Began:* 1997 *Activities:* excursions, field trips, cultural events, sports *Misc:* Scholarship research svc. *URL:* http://www.languageliaison.com
Contact: Nancy Forman, Dir, Lang Liaison, 4 Burnham Pkwy, Morristown NJ 07960 *Ph:* 800-284 4448 *Fax:* 973-898 1710 *E-mail:* learn@languageliaison.com

---

1820
LANGUAGE LIAISON
Spanish Saturation-Buenos Aires
Site: Argentina: Buenos Aires *Host inst:* Live in Learn
Dates: 1 wk or longer, yr-round
Subjects: Civilization/culture, Homestay, Spanish language
Eligibility: *Level:* fresh, sophs, jrs, srs, grads, adults, teachers, professionals, precoll *Age:* min 10
Credit: *Undergrad:* none *Grad:* none
Instruction: *In:* Spanish *Format:* lang study *Students:* intl
Costs: Contact sponsor
Housing: *Arr by pgm:* teacher's home
Deadline: 45 days before pgm
Other info: *US accredited sponsor:* no *Misc:* Scholarship research svc. *URL:* http://www.languageliaison.com
Contact: Nancy Forman, Dir, Lang Liaison, 4 Burnham Pkwy, Morristown NJ 07960 *Ph:* 800-284 4448 *Fax:* 973-898 1710 *E-mail:* learn@languageliaison.com

---

1821
LEXIA INTERNATIONAL
LEXIA Summer in Buenos Aires
Site: Argentina: Buenos Aires *Host inst:* Univ de Buenos Aires
Dates: 8 wks, mid-Jun-mid-Aug
Subjects: Anthropology, Arts, Civilization/culture, Ecology/environmental studies, Economics, Fine arts, History, Homestay, Latin American studies, Literature, Political science/politics, Sociology, Spanish language (beg/int/adv)
Eligibility: *Level:* fresh, sophs, jrs, srs, grads, adults *Requires:* 2.5 GPA *Age:* min 18, avg 21
Credit: *Undergrad:* 8-10 *Grad:* 8-10 *Doc:* transcript *Transfer credit through:* Western Washington Univ
Instruction: *In:* English, Spanish *Format:* internship, lang study, lecture, seminar, volunteer/svc *Students:* mainly US
Costs: $4,950 *incl* tuition, housing, some meals, insurance, fees, excursions, ISIC, computer access *Nonrefundable fee*

Housing: *Arr by pgm:* residence halls with local students, homestay
Deadline: Apr 15; Apr 1 for scholarships
Other info: *US accredited sponsor:* no *Began:* 1995 *In coop with:* Western Washington Univ *Orient:* abroad *Activities:* excursions, field trips, program travel, cultural events, sports *Misc:* Student support svcs. May contact former participants. *Financial aid:* scholarships, work study *URL:* http://www.lexiaintl.org
Contact: LEXIA Intl, 25 S Main St, Hanover NH 03755 *Ph:* 800-775 3942; 603-643 9898 *Fax:* 603-643 9899 *E-mail:* info@lexiaintl.org
Or Contact: LEXIA Intl, West Coast, 378 Cambridge Ave, Palo Alto CA 94306-1544 *Ph:* 650-327 9191 *Fax:* 650-327 9192

1822
LINGUA SERVICE WORLDWIDE
Intensive Language and Culture in Argentina
Site: Argentina: Buenos Aires *Host inst:* ILEE
Dates: 1 wk-1 yr, yr-round
Subjects: Civilization/culture, Homestay, Spanish language (beg/int/adv)
Eligibility: *Level:* adults
Credit: *Undergrad:* avail *Grad:* avail *Doc:* transcript, certificate
Instruction: *In:* Spanish *Format:* lang study, lecture *Students:* intl
Costs: Contact sponsor
Housing: *Arr by pgm:* homestay, hotels
Deadline: 45 days before pgm
Other info: *US accredited sponsor:* no *Orient:* abroad *Activities:* excursions, field trips *Misc:* Special Survival Spanish in 10 Days course. May contact former participants. *URL:* http://www.linguaserviceworldwide.com
Contact: Dir, Lingua Svc Worldwide, 75 Prospect St, Ste 4, Huntington NY 11743 *Ph:* 800-394 5327; 631-424 0777 *Fax:* 631-271 3441 *E-mail:* itctravel@worldnet.att.net ▲

1823
LINGUA SERVICE WORLDWIDE
Total Immersion/Intensive Language and Culture-Buenos Aires
Site: Argentina: Buenos Aires *Host inst:* Home Lang Intl
Dates: 1 wk-1 yr, yr-round
Subjects: Civilization/culture, Homestay, Spanish language (beg/int/adv)
Eligibility: *Level:* adults *Age:* min 14
Credit: *Undergrad:* avail *Grad:* avail *Doc:* transcript, certificate
Instruction: *In:* Spanish *Format:* lang study *Students:* intl
Costs: Contact sponsor
Housing: *Arr by pgm:* apartments with local students, residence halls with local students, homestay, pensions, hotels, hostels
Deadline: 45 days before pgm
Other info: *US accredited sponsor:* no *Began:* 1993 *Activities:* excursions, cultural events *Misc:* May contact former participants. *URL:* http://www.linguaserviceworldwide.com
Contact: Dir, Lingua Svc Worldwide, 75 Prospect St, Ste 4, Huntington NY 11743 *Ph:* 800-394 5327; 631-424 0777 *Fax:* 631-271 3441 *E-mail:* itctravel@worldnet.att.net ▲

1824
LINGUATEC LANGUAGE CENTER
Learn Spanish in Argentina
Site: Argentina: Buenos Aires
Dates: 2 wks or longer, yr-round
Subjects: Homestay, Spanish language (beg/int/adv)
Eligibility: *Level:* adults, teachers, professionals, precoll *Age:* min 16, avg 28
Credit: *Undergrad:* avail *Grad:* none *Doc:* certificate
Instruction: *In:* Spanish *Format:* lang study *Students:* intl
Costs: $475 per wk *incl* tuition, housing, some meals, excursions *Nonrefundable fee*
Housing: *Arr by pgm:* homestay, hotels
Deadline: 1 wk before pgm
Other info: *US accredited sponsor:* no *Began:* 2000 *Orient:* abroad *Activities:* excursions *Misc:* May contact former participants. *URL:* http://www.linguatec.cl/argentina_index.htm
Contact: Mariano Decalzi, Dir, Linguatec Lang Ctr, Av Eduardo Madero 1020, Planta Baja 1106, Buenos Aires, Argentina *Ph:* 303-777 7783 *Fax:* 303-777 7246 *E-mail:* mariano@linguatec.com.ar

---

1825
NATIONAL REGISTRATION CENTER FOR STUDY ABROAD (NRCSA)
Spanish Study in Argentina
Site: Argentina: Buenos Aires *Host inst:* ILEE
Dates: 2 wks or longer, yr-round
Subjects: Homestay, Spanish language (beg/int/adv)
Eligibility: *Level:* fresh, sophs, jrs, srs, grads, adults, teachers, professionals *Age:* min 18
Credit: *Undergrad:* avail *Grad:* avail *Doc:* certificate
Instruction: *In:* Spanish *Format:* lang study, tutorial *Students:* intl
Costs: $1,616 for 4 wks *incl* tuition, housing, insurance
Housing: *Arr by pgm:* homestay
Deadline: Contact sponsor
Other info: *US accredited sponsor:* no *Orient:* abroad *Activities:* cultural events, sports *URL:* http://www.nrcsa.com
Contact: June Domoe, NRCSA, PO Box 1393, Milwaukee WI 53201 *Ph:* 414-224 3464 *Fax:* 414-224 3466 *E-mail:* info@nrcsa.com

---

1826
UNIVERSITY OF DELAWARE
Winter Session in Argentina
Site: Argentina: Buenos Aires *Host inst:* Univ of Palermo
Dates: 1 mo, Jan
Subjects: History, Homestay, Latin American studies, Literature, Spanish language
Eligibility: *Level:* fresh, sophs, jrs, srs, adults *Requires:* 2.0 GPA, 1 sem coll spanish or equiv
Credit: *Undergrad:* 6-7 *Grad:* none *Doc:* transcript
Instruction: *In:* English, Spanish *Format:* lang study, lecture, study tour *Students:* mainly US
Costs: Contact sponsor
Housing: *Arr by pgm:* homestay
Deadline: early Oct
Other info: *US accredited sponsor:* yes *Began:* 2001 *Orient:* in US & abroad *Activities:* excursions, field trips, program travel, cultural events *Misc:* Contact sponsor to arrange honors credit. *Financial aid:* scholarships *URL:* http://www.udel.edu/studyabroad
Contact: Lisa Chieffo, Study Abroad Coord, Univ of Delaware, Foreign Lang & Literatures, 326 Smith Hall, Newark DE 19716-1450 *Ph:* 302-831 6458 *Fax:* 302-831 0597 *E-mail:* lchieffo@udel.edu
Or Contact: Int Pgms & Special Sessions, Univ of Delaware, 4 Kent Way, Newark DE 19716-1450 *Ph:* 302-831 2852 *Fax:* 302-831 6042 *E-mail:* studyabroad@udel.edu

---

1827
UNIVERSITY OF MIAMI (FL)
Intensive Spanish in Buenos Aires
Site: Argentina: Buenos Aires *Host inst:* Univ del Salvador
Dates: 4 wks, late Jun-late Jul
Subjects: Homestay, Spanish language
Eligibility: *Level:* sophs, jrs, srs *Requires:* 2.75 GPA
Credit: *Undergrad:* avail *Grad:* none *Doc:* transcript
Instruction: *In:* Spanish *Format:* lang study *Students:* intl
Costs: $3,850 *incl* tuition, housing, some meals, excursions, books/materials *Nonrefundable fee*
Housing: *Arr by pgm:* residence halls, homestay
Deadline: Mar 30
Other info: *US accredited sponsor:* yes *Began:* 1997 *Orient:* abroad (1 day) *Misc:*

May contact former participants. *URL:* http://www.studyabroad.miami.edu
Contact: Intl Educ & Exch Pgms, Allen Hall 212, 5050 Brunson Dr, PO Box 248005, Univ of Miami, Coral Gables FL 33124-1610 *Ph:* 800-557 5421; 305-284 3434 *Fax:* 305-284 6629 *E-mail:* ieep@miami.edu

---

1828
UNIVERSITY OF SAN DIEGO, SCHOOL OF BUSINESS ADMINISTRATION
Graduate Business Study Abroad in Buenos Aires
Site: Argentina: Buenos Aires *Host inst:* Grad Bus Sch of Mgmt Development Inst of Argentina (IDEA)
Dates: 5 wks, mid-Jul-mid-Aug (3 wks distance learning, 2 wks in Buenos Aires)
Subjects: Business/management, Finance, Human resources, International business, International marketing, Latin American studies
Eligibility: *Level:* grads, professionals *Requires:* enrollment in or graduation from grad bus or related grad pgm, good acad standing
Credit: *Undergrad:* none *Grad:* 3 per course *Doc:* transcript
Instruction: *In:* English *Format:* lecture, seminar *Students:* US & intl
Costs: $1,450 for 1 course, $2,400 for 2 courses *incl* tuition *Nonrefundable fee*
Housing: *Sponsor assists:* apartments with local students, homestay, hotels
Deadline: None
Other info: *US accredited sponsor:* yes *Began:* 1999 *Orient:* abroad (1 day) *Activities:* excursions, field trips, program travel, cultural events *Misc:* Company visits. May contact former participants. *URL:* http://business.acusd.edu/ib/argen.html
Contact: Kate Vargas, Asst Dir, or Amanda Ryan, Admin Asst, Ahlers Ctr for Intl Bus, Univ of San Diego Sch of Bus Admin, 5998 Alcala Park, San Diego CA 92110-2492 *Ph:* 800-248 4873; 619-260 4896 *Fax:* 619-260 4891 *E-mail:* ib@acusd.edu

---

CORDOBA

1829
UNIVERSIDAD BLAS PASCAL
Argentum
Site: Argentina: Cordoba
Dates: 5 wks, Jun-Jul
Subjects: Civilization/culture, History, Homestay, Independent study, Latin American studies, Spanish language (beg/int/adv)
Eligibility: *Level:* fresh, sophs, jrs, srs, grads, adults, teachers, professionals, precoll *Requires:* 2.8 GPA, 1 sem coll Spanish or equiv *Age:* min 16, avg 22
Credit: *Undergrad:* 8 *Grad:* 8 *Doc:* transcript
Instruction: *In:* Spanish *Format:* independent study, lang study, lecture, seminar, tutorial *Students:* mainly US
Costs: $2,200 *incl* tuition, housing, all meals, excursions, cultural activities *Nonrefundable fee*
Housing: *Arr by pgm:* apartments, homestay
Deadline: Mar 15
Other info: *US accredited sponsor:* no *Began:* 1993 *Orient:* abroad *Activities:* excursions, field trips, cultural events, sports *Misc:* Intensive summer lang pgm. May contact former participants. *URL:* http://www.worldwide.edu/argentina/argentum
Contact: Prof Marta Rosso-O'Laughlin, Argentum, PO Box 99, Medford MA 02153-0099 *Ph:* 617-488 3552 *Fax:* 617-488 3552 *E-mail:* mrosso@aol.com
Or Contact: Prof Lucila Ravasi, Argentum, Univ Blas Pascal, Av Donato Alvarez 380, 5147 Arguello, Cordoba, Argentina *E-mail:* jravasi@ubp.edu.ar

---

MENDOZA

1830
UNIVERSITY OF HAWAII AT MANOA
Spanish Language and Hispanic Culture in Mendoza, Argentina
Site: Argentina: Mendoza *Host inst:* Univ Nacional de Cuyo
Dates: 5 wks, mid-May-late Jun
Subjects: Homestay, Spanish language (int/adv)
Eligibility: *Level:* sophs, jrs, srs *Requires:* 3.0 GPA, 1 yr coll Spanish
Credit: *Undergrad:* 6 *Grad:* none *Doc:* transcript
Instruction: *In:* Spanish *Format:* lang study, lecture *Students:* mainly US
Costs: $4,449 *incl* tuition, housing, some meals, intl airfare, insurance, fees, excursions, books/materials *Nonrefundable fee*
Housing: *Arr by pgm:* homestay
Deadline: Feb 17
Other info: *US accredited sponsor:* yes *Began:* 1992 *Orient:* in US & abroad *Activities:* excursions, field trips, cultural events *Misc:* UHM financial aid avail to eligible UHM students. *URL:* http://www2.hawaii.edu/study-abroad
Contact: Dir or Study Abroad Adviser, Study Abroad Ctr, Univ of Hawaii at Manoa, Moore Hall 115, 1890 East-West Rd, Honolulu HI 96822 *Ph:* 808-956 5143, 808-956 6958 *Fax:* 808-956 9319 *E-mail:* uhmsac@hawaii.edu

---

1831
WEBSTER UNIVERSITY
Spanish in Mendoza, Argentina
Site: Argentina: Mendoza *Host inst:* Espanola Lengua Extranjera, Univ Nacional de Cuyo
Dates: 5 wks, Jun-Jul
Subjects: Argentine studies, Civilization/culture, Literature, Spanish language, Written composition
Eligibility: *Level:* sophs, jrs, srs *Requires:* 2.5 GPA, beg Spanish
Credit: *Undergrad:* 6 *Grad:* none
Instruction: *In:* Spanish *Format:* lang study, lecture, study tour, workshop *Students:* mainly US
Costs: Contact sponsor
Housing: *Arr by pgm:* residence halls with local students, homestay
Deadline: Feb 1
Other info: *US accredited sponsor:* yes *Began:* 1997 *Orient:* in US & abroad *Activities:* excursions, field trips, program travel, cultural events, sports *URL:* http://www.websteruniv.edu
Contact: Dr Graciela Corvalan or Teresa Bruno, Webster Univ, 470 E Lockwood Ave, St Louis MO 63119 *Ph:* 800-984 6857; 314-968 6988 *Fax:* 314-968 7119 *E-mail:* corvalgv@websteruniv.edu

---

ROSARIO

1832
UNIVERSITY OF PITTSBURGH
Pitt in Argentina
Site: Argentina: Rosario
Dates: 6 wks, mid-May-Jun
Subjects: Argentine studies, Field study, Homestay, Spanish language (int/adv)
Eligibility: *Level:* sophs, jrs, srs *Requires:* 2.75 GPA, previous study in field, int/adv Spanish
Credit: *Undergrad:* 6-9 *Grad:* none *Doc:* transcript
Instruction: *In:* Spanish *Format:* independent study, lang study, lecture, seminar, study tour *Students:* mainly US
Costs: $3,125 for Univ of Pitt students, $3,425 for others *incl* tuition, housing, all meals, excursions *Nonrefundable fee*
Housing: *Arr by pgm:* homestay
Deadline: Feb 15
Other info: *US accredited sponsor:* yes *Began:* 1998 *In coop with:* Univ Nacl de Rosario *Orient:* in US & abroad *Activities:* excursions, field trips, cultural events *Misc:* Scholarships for own students only. Loans & grants avail. May contact former participants. *URL:* http://www.pitt.edu/~stdyabrd/
Contact: Jennifer Sill, Study Abroad Adviser, Univ of Pittsburgh, 802 William Pitt Union, Pittsburgh PA 15260 *Ph:* 412-648 2299 *Fax:* 412-383 7166 *E-mail:* jsill+@pitt.edu

---

Or Contact: Dr Mabel Morana, Hispanic Langs & Literature, Univ of Pittsburgh, Pittsburgh PA 15260 *Ph:* 412-624 5225 *Fax:* 412-624 8505 *E-mail:* mabel+@pitt.edu
Or Contact: Lola Ingles, Hispanic Langs & Literature, Univ of Pittsburgh, Pittsburgh PA 15260 *Ph:* 412-624 5225 *Fax:* 412-624 8505 *E-mail:* mdist6+@pitt.edu

Bahamas

SAN SALVADOR

1833
MICHIGAN STATE UNIVERSITY
Tropical Ecology and Management
Site: Bahamas: San Salvador
Dates: 2 wks, May
Subjects: Agriculture, Fishing/fisheries, Natural resources, Wildlife
Eligibility: *Level:* jrs, srs, grads *Requires:* 2.5 GPA, good acad standing, snorkeling equipment, swimming proficiency, zoology 355 *Age:* min 18
Credit: *Undergrad:* 6 *Grad:* 6 *Doc:* transcript
Instruction: *In:* English *Format:* lecture, seminar *Students:* mainly US
Costs: About $1,200 *incl* housing, most meals, insurance, excursions, boat rental *Nonrefundable fee*
Housing: *Arr by pgm:* Bahamian field station
Deadline: Mar 2
Other info: *US accredited sponsor:* yes *Orient:* in US *Activities:* excursions, field trips *Misc:* Loans avail. May contact former participants. *Financial aid:* scholarships *URL:* http://studyabroad.msu.edu
Contact: Cheryl Benner, Study Abroad, Michigan State Univ, 109 Intl Ctr, East Lansing MI 48824-1035 *Ph:* 517-353 8920 *Fax:* 517-432 2082 *E-mail:* bennerc@msu.edu ▲

1834
SUNY COLLEGE AT BROCKPORT
Bahamas Oceanography Practicum
Site: Bahamas: San Salvador
Dates: Late Dec-mid-Jan
Subjects: Ecology/environmental studies, Field study, Marine biology, Oceanography
Eligibility: *Level:* sophs, jrs, srs, grads *Requires:* background in biology, geology, or intro oceanography helpful
Credit: *Undergrad:* 3 *Grad:* avail *Doc:* transcript
Instruction: *In:* English *Format:* directed field study, lecture, practical training *Students:* US & host country
Costs: $2,700 *incl* tuition, housing, all meals, fees, excursions, books/materials, intl airfare from Florida
Housing: *Arr by pgm:* residence halls
Deadline: Sep 15
Other info: *US accredited sponsor:* yes *Began:* 1973 *Orient:* in US *Misc:* Faculty dir. *URL:* http://www.brockport.edu/study_abroad
Contact: Dr John Perry, Dir, Intl Educ, SUNY Coll at Brockport, 350 New Campus Dr, Brockport NY 14420 *Ph:* 800-298 7869 *Fax:* 716-637 3218 *E-mail:* overseas@brockport.edu

Barbados

MORE THAN ONE CITY

1835
COOPERATIVE CENTER FOR STUDY ABROAD
Barbados Program
Site: Barbados: various sites
Dates: 2 wks, Jun 7-25
Subjects: Criminal justice, Literature, Nursing, Political science/politics, Social work
Eligibility: *Level:* fresh, sophs, jrs, srs, grads, adults, teachers, professionals *Requires:* good acad standing, recommendation *Age:* min 18
Credit: *Undergrad:* 3 *Grad:* 3 *Doc:* transcript
Instruction: *In:* English *Format:* lecture, seminar, study tour, tutorial *Students:* mainly US
Costs: $2,495 *incl* housing, some meals, intl airfare, insurance, excursions, ISIC
Housing: *Arr by pgm:* residence halls
Deadline: Mar 1
Other info: *US accredited sponsor:* yes *Began:* 2001 *Orient:* in US & abroad *Activities:* excursions, field trips, cultural events *Misc:* May contact former participants. *Financial aid:* scholarships *URL:* http://www.nku.edu/ccsa
Contact: *See Index II for Members* Dr Michael A Klembara or Robin Byerly, Coop Ctr for Study Abroad, Northern Kentucky Univ, BEP 301, Highland Heights KY 41099 *Ph:* 800-319 6015; 859-572 6512 *Fax:* 859-572 6650 *E-mail:* ccsa@nku.edu

---

1836
VIRGINIA COMMONWEALTH UNIVERSITY
Barbados: People and Cultures of the Caribbean
Site: Barbados: various sites
Dates: 3 wks, Jul-Aug
Subjects: African-American studies, Anthropology, Archaeology, International studies, Sociology
Eligibility: *Level:* adults *Requires:* 2.0 GPA *Age:* min 18
Credit: *Undergrad:* 6 *Grad:* none *Doc:* transcript
Instruction: *In:* English *Format:* directed field study, independent study, lecture, study tour *Students:* mainly US
Costs: $3,700 *incl* tuition, housing, all meals, intl airfare *Nonrefundable fee*
Housing: *Arr by pgm:* residence halls
Deadline: Contact sponsor
Other info: *US accredited sponsor:* yes *Began:* 1997 *Activities:* program travel, cultural events *URL:* http://www.vcu.edu/cspweb/cspdocs/stdyabrd.html
Contact: Tina Murray, Asst Dir, Ctr for Intl Pgms, Virginia Commonwealth Univ, 916 W Franklin St, Box 843043, Richmond VA 23284-3043 *Ph:* 804-828 8471 *Fax:* 804-828 2552

Belize

MORE THAN ONE CITY

1837
AMERICAN UNIVERSITIES INTERNATIONAL PROGRAM (AUIP)
Belize: Marine Science Field Study
Site: Belize: South Water Caye, other sites
Dates: 4 wks, May 30-Jun 30
Subjects: Ecology/environmental studies, Field study, Marine biology, Oceanography
Eligibility: *Level:* sophs, jrs, srs, grads *Requires:* 2.0 GPA, biology background *Age:* min 18
Credit: *Undergrad:* avail *Grad:* none *Doc:* transcript *Transfer credit through:* Univ of Mississippi
Instruction: *In:* English *Format:* directed field study, lecture, study tour *Students:* mainly US
Costs: $4,495 *incl* tuition, housing, all meals, fees, excursions, ISIC, materials *Nonrefundable fee*
Housing: *Arr by pgm:* campsites/tents
Deadline: Apr 1
Other info: *US accredited sponsor:* no *Began:* 1999 *In coop with:* Univ of Mississippi *Orient:* in US & abroad *Activities:* excursions, field trips, program travel, cultural events *Misc:* May contact former participants. *URL:* http://www.auip.com
Contact: Linda Tomson or Tim Wakefield, AUIP, PMB 221,305 W Magnolia St, Ft Collins CO 80521 *Ph:* 970-495 0869 *Fax:* 970-484 6997 *E-mail:* info@auip.com ▲

1838
AMERICAN UNIVERSITIES INTERNATIONAL PROGRAM (AUIP)
Field Study: Neotropical Forest Amphibians, Reptiles & Birds
Site: Belize: various sites

Dates: 4 wks, Jul 3-30
Subjects: Field study, Herpetology, Ornithology
Eligibility: *Level:* sophs, jrs, srs, grads *Requires:* 2.0 GPA, some biology background
Credit: *Undergrad:* avail *Grad:* none *Doc:* transcript *Transfer credit through:* Univ of Mississippi
Instruction: *In:* English *Format:* directed field study, lecture, study tour *Students:* mainly US
Costs: $4,495 *incl* tuition, housing, all meals, insurance, excursions, ISIC, materials *Nonrefundable fee*
Housing: *Arr by pgm:* campgrounds, tents
Deadline: Apr 1
Other info: *US accredited sponsor:* no *Began:* 2001 *In coop with:* Univ of Mississippi *Orient:* avail in Mississippi & Belize (1 day) *Activities:* excursions, field trips, program travel, cultural events *Misc:* May contact former participants. *URL:* http://www.auip.com
Contact: Linda Tomson or Tim Wakefield, AUIP, PMB 221, 305 W Magnolia St, Ft Collins CO 80521 *Ph:* 888-921 2847; 970-495 0869 *Fax:* 970-484 6997 *E-mail:* info@auip.com ▲

1839
MONTCLAIR STATE UNIVERSITY
Montclair in Belize
Site: Belize: various sites
Dates: 1 wk, early Aug-mid-Aug
Subjects: Archaeology, Ecology/environmental studies, Field study
Eligibility: *Level:* fresh, sophs, jrs, srs, grads, adults, teachers, professionals *Requires:* good physical conditon *Age:* avg 25
Credit: *Undergrad:* none *Grad:* 3 *Doc:* transcript
Instruction: *In:* English *Format:* directed field study *Students:* mainly US
Costs: $1,800 *incl* housing, all meals, intl airfare, fees, excursions *Nonrefundable fee*
Housing: *Arr by pgm:* hotels
Deadline: May 1
Other info: *US accredited sponsor:* yes *Began:* 1999 *Orient:* in US (3 days) *Activities:* excursions, field trips *Misc:* May contact former participants.
Contact: Wendy Gilbert-Simon, Montclair State Univ, 22 Normal Ave, Upper Montclair NJ 07043 *Ph:* 973-655 4185 *Fax:* 973-655 7654 *E-mail:* simonw@mail.montclair.edu
Or Contact: Dr Jackie Willis, Montclair State Univ, 1 Normal Ave, Upper Montclair NJ 07043 *Ph:* 973-655 7753 *E-mail:* willisj@mail.montclair.edu

1840
SAN FRANCISCO STATE UNIVERSITY, WILDLANDS STUDIES PROGRAM
Ecosystems of Belize
Site: Belize: various sites
Dates: 4 wks, Jun 27-Jul 29; 6 wks, Jan 3-Feb 14 or Oct 1-Nov 12
Subjects: Biology, Civilization/culture, Ecology/environmental studies, Field study
Eligibility: *Level:* fresh, sophs, jrs, srs, adults, teachers, professionals *Requires:* application essay *Age:* min 18, avg 22
Credit: *Undergrad:* 6-9 per term *Grad:* none *Doc:* transcript
Instruction: *In:* English *Format:* directed field study *Students:* mainly US
Costs: $1,060 for Summer; $1,960 for Fall or Winter *incl* tuition
Housing: *Arr by pgm:* tents
Deadline: Rolling admissions
Other info: *US accredited sponsor:* yes *Began:* 1998 *Activities:* excursions, field trips, program travel, cultural events *Misc:* May contact former participants. *URL:* http://www.wildlandsstudies.com/ws
Contact: Crandall Bay, Dir, Wildlands Studies, 3 Mosswood Circle, Cazadero CA 95421 *Ph:* 707-632 5665 *Fax:* 707-632 5665 *E-mail:* wildlnds@sonic.net

1841
UNIVERSITY OF TEXAS AT AUSTIN
Maya Archaeology in Northwest Belize
Site: Belize: various sites
Dates: Mid-May-early Jun or mid-Jun-early Jul
Subjects: Archaeology, Mayan studies
Eligibility: *Level:* fresh, sophs, jrs, srs, grads
Credit: *Undergrad:* avail *Grad:* avail *Doc:* transcript
Instruction: *In:* English *Format:* directed field study *Students:* mainly US
Costs: Contact sponsor
Housing: *Arr by pgm*
Deadline: Mar 1
Other info: *US accredited sponsor:* yes *Activities:* excursions, field trips *Misc:* Survey to excavation at several Maya sites. Work directly with excavated Mayan artifacts. Max 25 students per session. *Financial aid:* scholarships
Contact: Joy Williamson, Adviser, Study Abroad, Univ of Texas at Austin, Univ Station, Drawer A, Austin TX 78713-7208 *Ph:* 512-471 6490 *Fax:* 512-232 4363 *E-mail:* studyabroadinfo@mozart.io.utexas.edu

SAN IGNACIO

1842
SOUTHWEST TEXAS STATE UNIVERSITY
Archaeological Field School in Belize
Site: Belize: San Ignacio
Dates: 4-1/2 wks, early Jul-mid-Aug
Subjects: Archaeology, Field study, Mayan studies, Research methods
Eligibility: *Level:* fresh, sophs, jrs, srs *Requires:* 2.0 GPA *Age:* avg 22
Credit: *Undergrad:* 6 *Grad:* none *Doc:* transcript
Instruction: *In:* English *Format:* directed field study, practical training *Students:* mainly US
Costs: Contact sponsor
Housing: *Arr by pgm:* hotels
Deadline: Contact sponsor
Other info: *US accredited sponsor:* yes *Activities:* excursions, field trips, program travel, cultural events *Misc:* May contact former participants. *Financial aid:* scholarships *URL:* http://www.ideal.swt.edu/extensions/study_abroad/
Contact: Prof James Garber, Chair, or Prof David M Glassman, Anthropology, Southwest Texas State Univ, San Marcos TX 78666 *Ph:* 512-245 8272 *Fax:* 512-245 8076 *E-mail:* dg02@academia.swt.edu

Bermuda

MORE THAN ONE CITY

1843
SAN FRANCISCO STATE UNIVERSITY, WILDLANDS STUDIES PROGRAM
Island Environment: The Bermuda Program
Site: Bermuda: various cities
Dates: 2 wks, Mar 17-Mar 30
Subjects: Biology, Ecology/environmental studies, Ethnography, Field study
Eligibility: *Level:* adults *Age:* min 18, avg 22
Credit: *Undergrad:* avail *Grad:* none *Doc:* transcript
Instruction: *In:* English *Format:* directed field study *Students:* mainly US
Costs: $465 *incl* tuition
Housing: *Arr by pgm:* Basecamps
Deadline: Rolling Admissions
Other info: *US accredited sponsor:* yes *Began:* 2000 *Orient:* abroad *Activities:* field trips *URL:* http://www.wildlandsstudies.com/ws
Contact: Crandall Bay, dir, or Marcene Bay, Asst, Wildlife Studies, San Francisco State Univ, 3 Mosswood Circle, Cazadero CA 95421 *Ph:* 707-632 5665 *Fax:* 707-632 5665

SAINT GEORGE'S

1844
BERMUDA BIOLOGICAL STATION FOR RESEARCH
Summer Courses in Marine Sciences
Site: Bermuda: St George's
Dates: 2-4 wk terms, May-Sep
Subjects: Field study, Marine sciences
Eligibility: *Level:* jrs, srs, grads *Requires:* consent of course instructor *Age:* min 18, avg 24
Credit: *Undergrad:* avail *Grad:* none
Instruction: *In:* English *Format:* directed field study, lab, lecture *Students:* intl
Costs: About $725 per wk *incl* tuition, housing, all meals, fees
Housing: *Arr by pgm:* residence halls
Deadline: Mar 1; late applications accepted
Other info: *US accredited sponsor:* no *Began:* 1973 *Orient:* in US *Misc:* May contact former participants. *Financial aid:* scholarships *URL:* http://www.bbsr.edu/
Contact: Educ Dept, Bermuda Biological Station for Research, Ferry Reach GE01, St George's, Bermuda *Ph:* 441-297 1880 *Fax:* 441-297 1919 *E-mail:* education@bbsr.edu

---

1845
BERMUDA BIOLOGICAL STATION FOR RESEARCH
Volunteer Internship Program
Site: Bermuda: St George's
Dates: 4 mos, summer
Subjects: Marine sciences
Eligibility: *Level:* jrs, srs, grads *Requires:* good sci background *Age:* min 18
Credit: *Undergrad:* none *Grad:* none
Instruction: *In:* English *Format:* practical training, volunteer/svc *Students:* intl
Costs: Contact sponsor
Housing: *Arr by pgm:* residence halls
Deadline: Feb 1
Other info: *US accredited sponsor:* no *Began:* 1970 *Financial aid:* work study *URL:* http://www.bbsr.edu/
Contact: Educ Dept, Bermuda Biological Station for Research, Ferry Reach GE01, St George's, Bermuda *Ph:* 441-297 1880 *Fax:* 441-297 1919 *E-mail:* education@bbsr.edu

Bolivia

MORE THAN ONE CITY

1846
OHIO UNIVERSITY
Global Studies in Plant Biology
Site: Bolivia: Copacabana, Coroico, La Paz, Sorata, Unduavi *Host inst:* Natl Herbarium, Inst of Ecology
Dates: 3 wks, late Nov-mid-Dec, late Jun-mid-Jul
Subjects: Ecology/environmental studies, Field study, Independent study
Eligibility: *Level:* jrs, srs *Requires:* 3.0 GPA, previous study in field
Credit: *Undergrad:* 3 qtr hrs *Grad:* none
Instruction: *In:* English *Format:* directed field study, independent study, lab *Students:* mainly US

Costs: Contact sponsor
Housing: *Arr by pgm:* pensions, hotels
Deadline: Oct 1
Other info: *US accredited sponsor:* yes *Began:* 2000 *Orient:* in US *Activities:* program travel *Misc:* May contact former participants. *Financial aid:* scholarships *URL:* http://oak.cats.ohiou.edu/~ballardh/globalstudies
Contact: Dr Harvey Ballard, Plant Biology, Ohio Univ, Porter Hall 406, Athens OH 45701 *Ph:* 740-593 1130 *E-mail:* ballardh@ohiou.edu
Or Contact: Dr Morgan Vis, Ohio Univ, Dept of Plant Biology, Porter Hall, Athens OH 45701 *Ph:* 740-593 1134 *Fax:* 740-593 1130 *E-mail:* vis-chia@ohiou.edu

---

COCHABAMBA

1847
AMIZADE
Bolivian Andes Volunteer Project
Site: Bolivia: Cochabamba
Dates: 1-4 wks, yr-round
Subjects: Community service projects
Eligibility: *Level:* adults *Age:* min 18
Credit: *Undergrad:* none *Grad:* none
Instruction: *In:* English *Format:* volunteer/svc *Students:* mainly US
Costs: $1,200-$1,500 for 2 wks *incl* tuition, housing, all meals, intl airfare, fees, excursions
Housing: *Arr by pgm:* residence halls
Deadline: Contact sponsor
Other info: *US accredited sponsor:* no *Began:* 1997 *Orient:* abroad (1 day) *Activities:* excursions, field trips, program travel, cultural events, sports *Misc:* May contact former participants. *URL:* http://amizade.org/Bolivia.htm
Contact: Mike Sandy, Ex Dir, Amizade Ltd, 367 S Graham St, Pittsburgh PA 15232 *Ph:* 888-973 4443 *Fax:* 412-648 1492 *E-mail:* volunteer@amizade.org

---

1848
LANGUAGES ABROAD
Language and Cultural Immersion-Bolivia
Site: Bolivia: Cochabamba
Dates: 2 wks or longer, yr-round
Subjects: Bolivian studies, Civilization/culture, Spanish language (beg/int/adv)
Eligibility: *Level:* adults *Age:* min 17, max 65, avg 25
Credit: *Undergrad:* none *Grad:* none *Doc:* certificate
Instruction: *In:* Spanish *Format:* lang study *Students:* intl
Costs: $1,125 per mo *incl* tuition, some meals, fees, books/materials
Housing: *Arr by pgm:* residence halls, homestay
Deadline: None
Other info: *US accredited sponsor:* no *Began:* 1995 *Activities:* excursions, field trips, program travel, cultural events, sports *Misc:* May contact former participants. *URL:* http://www.languagesabroad.com
Contact: Ms Jesse Philippe, Langs Abroad, 317 Adelaide St W, Ste 900, Toronto, Ontario M5V 1P9, Canada *Ph:* 800-219 9924; 416-925 7117 *E-mail:* info@languagesabroad.com

---

SUCRE

1849
AMERISPAN UNLIMITED
Spanish Study and Homestay in Sucre, Bolivia
Site: Bolivia: Sucre *Host inst:* Acad Latinamer, Casa de Lenguas
Dates: 1 wk-1 yr, yr-round
Subjects: Homestay, Spanish language (beg/int/adv)
Eligibility: *Level:* fresh, sophs, jrs, srs, grads, adults *Age:* min 16
Credit: *Undergrad:* avail *Grad:* none *Doc:* transcript, certificate *Transfer credit through:* Seattle Central CC
Instruction: *In:* Spanish *Format:* lang study, lecture *Students:* intl
Costs: $495 for 2 wks, $895 for 4 wks, $230 for each addtl wk *incl* tuition, housing, all meals, insurance, books/materials
Housing: *Arr by pgm:* homestay, hotels
Deadline: 4 wks before pgm
Other info: *US accredited sponsor:* no *Orient:* abroad *Activities:* excursions, field trips, cultural events *Misc:* Transfer credit also avail through Univ of Southern Mississippi. May contact former participants. *Financial aid:* work study *URL:* http://www.amerispan.com/
Contact: AmeriSpan Unltd, PO Box 40007, Philadelphia PA 19106 *Ph:* 800-879 6640; 215-751 1100 *Fax:* 215-751 1986 *E-mail:* info@amerispan.com

---

1850
NATIONAL REGISTRATION CENTER FOR STUDY ABROAD (NRCSA)
Spanish Study in Bolivia
Site: Bolivia: Sucre *Host inst:* Acad Latinoamericana
Dates: 2 wks or longer, yr-round
Subjects: Homestay, Spanish language (beg/int/adv)
Eligibility: *Level:* fresh, sophs, jrs, srs, grads, adults, teachers, professionals *Age:* min 17
Credit: *Undergrad:* avail *Grad:* avail *Doc:* certificate
Instruction: *In:* Spanish *Format:* lang study, tutorial *Students:* intl
Costs: $584 for 2 wks *incl* tuition, housing, some meals, insurance *Nonrefundable fee*
Housing: *Arr by pgm:* homestay
Deadline: 6 wks before pgm
Other info: *US accredited sponsor:* no *Activities:* field trips *URL:* http://www.nrcsa.com
Contact: June Domoe, NRCSA, 823 N 2nd St, #206, Milwaukee WI 53203 *Ph:* 414-278 0631 *Fax:* 414-271 8884 *E-mail:* iinfo@nrcsa.com

Brazil

MORE THAN ONE CITY

1851
COUNCIL ON INTERNATIONAL EDUCATIONAL EXCHANGE (COUNCIL)
International Faculty Development Seminars-Brazil
Site: Brazil: Rio de Janeiro, Sao Paulo *Host inst:* Univ of Sao Paulo
Dates: 9 days, Jun
Subjects: Brazilian studies, Civilization/culture, Contemporary issues, Economics, Political science/politics
Eligibility: *Level:* teachers, professionals *Requires:* must be full-time faculty at 2-yr or 4-yr insts
Credit: *Undergrad:* none *Grad:* none
Instruction: *In:* English *Format:* lecture, seminar *Students:* mainly US
Costs: $1,995 *incl* tuition, housing, some meals, fees, excursions, books/materials
Housing: *Arr by pgm:* hotels
Deadline: Mar 15
Other info: *US accredited sponsor:* no *Began:* 1993 *Orient:* abroad *Activities:* excursions, field trips, cultural events *Misc:* Seminar title: Brazil: Societal & Econ Perspectives. May contact former participants. *URL:* http://www.ciee.org/ifds
Contact: Jennifer Ley, Council, 633 3rd Ave, New York NY 10017 *Ph:* 212-822 2747 *Fax:* 212-822 2779 *E-mail:* ifds@ciee.org ▲

1852
KENTUCKY INSTITUTE FOR INTERNATIONAL STUDIES (KIIS)
Brazil
Site: Brazil: various sites
Dates: Late May-early Jul
Subjects: Brazilian studies, Civilization/culture
Eligibility: *Level:* fresh, sophs, jrs, srs, grads, adults *Requires:* 2.0 GPA
Credit: *Undergrad:* 3 *Grad:* 3 *Doc:* transcript
Instruction: *In:* English *Format:* lang

study, lecture, study tour *Students:* mainly US
Costs: About $3,330 *incl* housing, intl airfare, ISIC
Housing: *Arr by pgm:* hotels
Deadline: Feb 15 ($100 late fee); Mar 15 for scholarships
Other info: *US accredited sponsor:* yes *Began:* 2000 *Orient:* in US & abroad *Activities:* excursions, field trips, program travel, cultural events *URL:* http://www.kiis.org
Contact: *See Index II for Members* Dr J Milton Grimes, Exec Dir, KIIS, Murray State Univ, PO Box 9, Murray KY 42071 *Ph:* 270-762 3091 *Fax:* 270-762 3434 *E-mail:* kiismsu@murraystate.edu

---

1853
LANGUAGE LIAISON
Portuguese Language-Brazil
Site: Brazil: Maceio, Salvador da Bahia, Sao Paulo
Dates: 2 wks-1 yr, yr-round
Subjects: Brazilian studies, Homestay, Portuguese language (beg/int/adv)
Eligibility: *Level:* adults *Age:* min 16
Credit: *Undergrad:* avail *Grad:* avail *Doc:* transcript, certificate
Instruction: *In:* Portuguese *Format:* lang study *Students:* intl
Costs: Contact sponsor
Housing: *Arr by pgm:* homestay, hotels, guest house
Deadline: 30 days before pgm
Other info: *US accredited sponsor:* no *Activities:* excursions, cultural events, sports *Misc:* Scholarship research svc. *URL:* http://www.languageliaison.com
Contact: Nancy Forman, Dir, Lang Liaison, 4 Burnham Pkwy, Morristown NJ 07960 *Ph:* 800-284 4448 *Fax:* 973-898 1710 *E-mail:* learn@languageliaison.com

---

1854
LANGUAGES ABROAD
Language and Cultural Immersion-Brazil
Site: Brazil: Maceio, Rio de Janeiro
Dates: 2 wks or longer, yr-round
Subjects: Brazilian studies, Civilization/culture, Portuguese language (beg/int/adv)
Eligibility: *Level:* adults *Age:* min 17, max 65, avg 25
Credit: *Undergrad:* none *Grad:* none *Doc:* certificate
Instruction: *In:* Portuguese *Format:* lang study *Students:* intl
Costs: $1,400-$1,470 for 4 wks *incl* tuition, housing, some meals, books/materials
Housing: *Arr by pgm:* residence halls, homestay
Deadline: None
Other info: *US accredited sponsor:* no *Began:* 1995 *Activities:* excursions, field trips, program travel, cultural events, sports *Misc:* May contact former participants. *URL:* http://www.languagesabroad.com
Contact: Ms Jesse Philippe, Langs Abroad, 317 Adelaide St W, Ste 900, Toronto, Ontario M5V 1P9, Canada *Ph:* 800-219 9924; 416-925 7117 *E-mail:* info@languagesabroad.com

---

1855
LINGUA SERVICE WORLDWIDE
Total Immersion/Intensive Language and Culture in Brazil
Site: Brazil: Maceio, Salvador da Bahia *Host inst:* Dialogo, Fast Forward Idiomas
Dates: 1 wk-1 yr, yr-round
Subjects: Civilization/culture, Homestay, Portuguese language (beg/int/adv)
Eligibility: *Level:* fresh, sophs, jrs, srs, grads, adults, teachers, professionals, precoll *Age:* min 18
Credit: *Undergrad:* avail *Grad:* avail *Doc:* transcript, certificate *Transfer credit through:* Univ of Southern Mississippi
Instruction: *In:* Portuguese *Format:* lang study, lecture *Students:* intl
Costs: Contact sponsor
Housing: *Arr by pgm:* residence halls, apartments, homestay, pensions, hotels, hostels
Deadline: 45 days before pgm
Other info: *US accredited sponsor:* no *Activities:* excursions, cultural events *Misc:* Exec pgm. May contact former participants. *URL:* http://www.linguaserviceworldwide.com
Contact: Dir, Lingua Svc Worldwide, 75 Prospect St, Ste 4, Huntington NY 11743 *Ph:* 800-394 5327; 631-424 0777 *Fax:* 631-271 3441 *E-mail:* itctravel@worldnet.att.net ▲

1856
UNIVERSITY OF SOUTH FLORIDA
Eco-Brazil
Site: Brazil: Curitiba, various sites *Host inst:* Federal Univ of Parana (UFPR)
Dates: 3 wks, Jun
Subjects: Ecology/environmental studies, Field study
Eligibility: *Level:* fresh, sophs, jrs, srs, grads, teachers *Requires:* 2.5 GPA *Age:* min 18, avg 25
Credit: *Undergrad:* 6 *Grad:* 6 *Doc:* transcript, certificate
Instruction: *In:* English *Format:* directed field study, seminar, study tour, workshop *Students:* mainly US
Costs: About $1,800 *incl* tuition, housing, some meals, fees, excursions, books/materials, local transport
Housing: *Arr by pgm:* hotels
Deadline: Mar 30
Other info: *US accredited sponsor:* yes *Began:* 1998 *In coop with:* Univ Tuiuti do Parana *Orient:* in US & abroad *Activities:* excursions, field trips, program travel *Misc:* Emphasis on urban & rural ecology. Students will interact with native researchers. Pgm incl rainforest stay. May contact former participants. *Financial aid:* scholarships *URL:* http://www.usf.edu/~iac/
Contact: Julie Hale or James Pulos, USF Overseas Study Pgms, Univ of South Florida, 4202 E Fowler Ave, CPR 107, Tampa FL 33620-5550 *Ph:* 813-974 4043, 813-974 3933 *Fax:* 813-974 4613 *E-mail:* jpulos@iac.usf.edu
Or Contact: Dr Renu Khator, Pgm Dir, USF Environmental Sci & Policy, Univ of South Florida, 4202 E Fowler Ave, Tampa FL 33620-5550 *Ph:* 813-974 2978 *Fax:* 813-974 2184 *E-mail:* khator@luna.cas.usf.edu

---

BELO HORIZONTE

1857
UNIVERSITY OF TEXAS AT AUSTIN and **UNIVERSITY OF ILLINOIS AT URBANA-CHAMPAIGN**
Minas Gerais Exchange
Site: Brazil: Belo Horizonte *Host inst:* Univ Federal de Minas Gerais
Dates: 6 wks, Jun-Jul
Subjects: Civilization/culture, Portuguese language (beg/int/adv), Portuguese studies
Eligibility: *Level:* sophs, jrs, srs, grads *Requires:* 3.0 GPA
Credit: *Undergrad:* 6-9 *Grad:* avail *Doc:* transcript
Instruction: *In:* Portuguese *Format:* lang study, lecture *Students:* mainly US
Costs: $1,500 *incl* housing, some meals, excursions
Housing: *Arr by pgm:* homestay
Deadline: Mar 1
Other info: *US accredited sponsor:* yes *Began:* 1998 *Orient:* abroad *Misc:* Possible to continue into sem pgm at UFMG. May contact former participants. *URL:* http://www.utexas.edu/student/abroad
Contact: Joy Williamson, Adviser, Study Abroad, Univ of Texas at Austin, Drawer A, Austin TX 78713-7206 *Ph:* 512-471 6490 *Fax:* 512-232 4363 *E-mail:* studyabroadinfo@mozart.io.utexas.edu
Or Contact: Dr Joan Solaun, Univ of Illinois at Urbana-Champaign, 910 S Fifth St, Champaign IL 61820 *Ph:* 800-531 4404; 217-333 6168 *Fax:* 217-244 0249 *E-mail:* ipa@uiuc.edu

---

CURITIBA

1858
MICHIGAN STATE UNIVERSITY
Biodiversity, Ecosystem Protection and Management
Site: Brazil: Curitiba
Dates: 4 wks, May-Jun
Subjects: Development studies, Ecology/environmental studies, Forestry
Eligibility: *Level:* jrs, srs, grads *Requires:* 2.5 GPA, good acad standing, good physical condition *Age:* min 18
Credit: *Undergrad:* 6 *Grad:* 6 *Doc:* transcript
Instruction: *In:* English *Format:* lecture, seminar *Students:* mainly US
Costs: About $2,300 *incl* housing, some meals, insurance, excursions, support svcs
Housing: *Arr by pgm:* experiment station training ctr
Deadline: Mar 2
Other info: *US accredited sponsor:* yes *Began:* 1996 *Orient:* in US *Activities:* excursions *Misc:* Loans avail. *Financial aid:* scholarships *URL:* http://studyabroad.msu.edu
Contact: Cheryl Benner, Study Abroad, Michigan State Univ, 109 Intl Ctr, East Lansing MI 48824 *Ph:* 517-353 8920 *Fax:* 517-432 2082 *E-mail:* bennerc@msu.edu ▲

1859
UNIVERSITY OF SOUTH FLORIDA
USF in Brazil
Site: Brazil: Curitiba *Host inst:* Federal Univ of Parana (UFPR)
Dates: 3 wks, Jun
Subjects: Brazilian studies, Civilization/culture, Film studies, Independent study, Literature, Portuguese language
Eligibility: *Level:* adults, precoll *Requires:* 2.5 GPA, some Portuguese or Spanish helpful *Age:* min 18, avg 28
Credit: *Undergrad:* 8 *Grad:* 3-4 *Doc:* transcript, certificate
Instruction: *In:* English, Portuguese *Format:* independent study, lang study, study tour *Students:* mainly US
Costs: $1,700 *incl* tuition, housing, some meals, fees, excursions, local transport *Nonrefundable fee*
Housing: *Arr by pgm:* hotels
Deadline: Mar 30
Other info: *US accredited sponsor:* yes *Began:* 1997 *In coop with:* UFPR *Orient:* in US & abroad (2 days) *Activities:* excursions, field trips, program travel *Misc:* Scholarships for own students only. May contact former participants. *URL:* http://www.usf.edu/~iac/
Contact: Dr Edward Neugaard, Pgm Dir, Langs, Univ of South Florida, 4202 E Fowler Ave, CPR 107, Tampa FL 33620-5550 *Ph:* 813-974 3399 *Fax:* 813-974 4613 *E-mail:* neugaard@chuma1.cas.usf.edu
Or Contact: Julie Hale, Coord, Overseas Study Pgms, Univ of South Florida, 4202 E Fowler Ave, CPR 107, Tampa FL 33620-5550 *Ph:* 813-974 3933 *Fax:* 813-974 4613 *E-mail:* jhale@iac.usf.edu

---

FORTALEZA

1860
UNIVERSITY OF ARIZONA
Summer in Brazil
Site: Brazil: Fortaleza *Host inst:* Univ Federal do Ceara
Dates: 6 wks, Jun-Aug
Subjects: Homestay, Portuguese language (int/adv)
Eligibility: *Level:* sophs, jrs, srs, grads *Requires:* 2.5 GPA, 1 yr Portuguese
Credit: *Undergrad:* 6 *Grad:* 6 *Doc:* transcript
Instruction: *In:* Portuguese *Format:* lang study *Students:* mainly US
Costs: $2,800 *incl* tuition, housing, all meals, excursions, orient
Housing: *Arr by pgm:* residence halls, homestay
Deadline: May 1
Other info: *US accredited sponsor:* yes *Began:* 1993 *Orient:* in US & abroad *Misc:* May contact former participants. *Financial aid:* scholarships *URL:* http://w3.arizona.edu/~ciss/
Contact: Renee Griggs, Ctr for Global Student Pgms, Univ of Arizona, 939 N Tyndall Ave, Tucson AZ 85721 *Ph:* 520-626 7180 *Fax:* 520-626 9004 *E-mail:* griggsr@u.arizona.edu ▲

MACEIO

1861
EDUVACATIONS
Portuguese on the Brazilian Beach
Site: Brazil: Maceio
Dates: 1 wk or longer, yr-round
Subjects: Dance, Portuguese language (beg/int/adv), Sports
Eligibility: *Level:* adults *Age:* min 15
Credit: *Undergrad:* none *Grad:* none
Instruction: *In:* Portuguese *Format:* lang study *Students:* intl
Costs: Contact sponsor
Housing: *Sponsor assists:* apartments, homestay, guest houses
Deadline: Contact sponsor
Other info: *US accredited sponsor:* no *Activities:* excursions, field trips, cultural events, sports *Misc:* 5 students per class. *URL:* http://www.eduvacations.com
Contact: Mary Ann Puglisi, eduVacations, 1431 21st St NW, Ste 302, Washington DC 20036 *Ph:* 202-857 8384 *Fax:* 202-463 8091

1862
LANGUAGE STUDIES ABROAD, INC
Intensive Portuguese-Brazil
Site: Brazil: Maceio *Host inst:* LSA Maceio
Dates: 1 wk or longer, yr-round
Subjects: Homestay, Portuguese language (beg/int/adv)
Eligibility: *Level:* fresh, sophs, jrs, srs, grads, adults, teachers, professionals, precoll *Age:* min 8
Credit: *Undergrad:* avail *Grad:* avail
Instruction: *In:* Portuguese *Format:* lang study *Students:* intl
Costs: $988 for 4 wks *incl* tuition, housing, some meals, excursions, books/materials, airport transfer *Nonrefundable fee*
Housing: *Sponsor assists:* homestay, hotels
Deadline: 4 wks before pgm
Other info: *US accredited sponsor:* no *Began:* 1991 *Orient:* abroad *Activities:* excursions, sports *Misc:* May contact former participants. *URL:* http://www.languagestudiesabroad.com
Contact: Lang Studies Abroad, Inc, 103 Londonderry Ct, Reno NV 89511-2718 *Ph:* 800-424 5522; 775-849 9206 *Fax:* 775-849 9217 *E-mail:* info@languagestudiesabroad.com

---

RIO DE JANEIRO

1863
LINGUATEC LANGUAGE CENTER
Learn Portuguese in Brazil-Rio de Janeiro
Site: Brazil: Rio de Janeiro
Dates: 2 wks or longer, yr-round
Subjects: Homestay, Portuguese language (beg/int/adv)
Eligibility: *Level:* adults, precoll *Age:* min 16, avg 28
Credit: *Undergrad:* avail *Grad:* none *Doc:* certificate
Instruction: *In:* Portuguese *Format:* lang study *Students:* intl
Costs: $619 per wk *incl* tuition, housing, some meals, excursions *Nonrefundable fee*
Housing: *Arr by pgm:* homestay
Deadline: 1 wk before pgm
Other info: *US accredited sponsor:* no *Began:* 1988 *Activities:* excursions *Misc:* May contact former participants. *URL:* http://www.linguatec.cl
Contact: Ligia Pessoa, Linguatec Lang Ctr, Rua da Ajuda 35, Sobreloja 201, 20040-000 Rio de Janeiro RJ, Brazil *Ph:* 303-777 7783 *Fax:* 303-777 7246 *E-mail:* mligia@ancham.com.br

---

1864
NEW YORK UNIVERSITY, SCHOOL OF EDUCATION
Arts and Humanities: Art, Culture and Politics in Rio de Janeiro
Site: Brazil: Rio de Janeiro
Dates: Jul 2-20
Subjects: Humanities
Eligibility: *Level:* grads *Requires:* 3.0 GPA
Credit: *Undergrad:* none *Grad:* avail *Doc:* transcript
Instruction: *In:* English *Format:* lecture, seminar, tutorial *Students:* mainly US
Costs: $5,500
Housing: *Arr by pgm:* residence halls
Deadline: Mar 30
Other info: *US accredited sponsor:* yes *Orient:* abroad *Activities:* field trips, cultural events *Misc:* May contact former participants. *URL:* http://www.nyu.edu
Contact: Helen J Kelly, Dir, Special Pgms, NYU, 82 Washington Sq E, Rm 62, New York NY 10003 *Ph:* 212-998 5090 *Fax:* 212-995 4923 ▲

1865
NEW YORK UNIVERSITY, SCHOOL OF EDUCATION
International Studies in Human Rights
Site: Brazil: Rio de Janeiro
Dates: Jul 2-20
Subjects: Human rights, International education
Eligibility: *Level:* grads *Requires:* 3.0 GPA
Credit: *Undergrad:* none *Grad:* avail *Doc:* transcript
Instruction: *In:* English *Format:* lecture, seminar, tutorial *Students:* mainly US
Costs: $6,000 *incl* tuition, housing, excursions, books/materials *Nonrefundable fee*
Housing: *Arr by pgm:* residence halls
Deadline: Apr 1
Other info: *US accredited sponsor:* yes *Began:* 1999 *Orient:* in US & abroad *Activities:* field trips, cultural events *Misc:* May contact former participants. *URL:* http://www.nyu.edu/summer
Contact: Peter Lucas, New York Univ, 82 Washington Square E, Rm 72, New York NY 10003-6680 *Ph:* 212-998 5105 *E-mail:* peter.lucas@nyu.edu
Or Contact: Helen J Kelly, Dir, Special Pgms, New York Univ, 82 Washington Square E, Rm 62, New York NY 10003-6680 *Ph:* 212-998 5090 *Fax:* 212-995 4923 ▲

SALVADOR

1866
CASA DO BRASIL, CENTRO DE LINGUA, ARTE E CULTURA
Brazilian Portuguese Language Courses and Brazilian Culture
Site: Brazil: Salvador da Bahia
Dates: 2-3 wks, yr-round
Subjects: Business language, Folk dance, Folk music, Portuguese language (beg/int/adv)

Eligibility: *Level:* adults *Age:* min 18, max 70
Credit: *Undergrad:* none *Grad:* none
Instruction: *In:* Portuguese *Format:* lang study, lecture *Students:* intl
Costs: $630 for 2 wks *incl* tuition, excursions, books/materials *Nonrefundable fee*
Housing: *Sponsor assists:* homestay, hotels
Deadline: 2-3 wks before pgm
Other info: *US accredited sponsor:* no *Began:* 1988 *Orient:* abroad (intensive lang study) *Activities:* excursions, field trips, cultural events *Misc:* May contact former participants.
Contact: Dr Denise Scheyerl, Casa Do Brazil, Rua Milton de Oliviera 231, Barra, 40140-100 Salvador da Bahia, Brazil *E-mail:* casadobrasil@quasar.com.br

---

1867
LANGUAGES ABROAD
Language and Cultural Immersion Programs-Salvador
Site: Brazil: Salvador da Bahia
Dates: 2 wks or longer, yr-round
Subjects: Civilization/culture, Homestay, Portuguese language (beg/int/adv)
Eligibility: *Level:* adults *Age:* min 17, max 65, avg 25
Credit: *Undergrad:* none *Grad:* none *Doc:* certificate
Instruction: *In:* Portuguese *Format:* lang study *Students:* intl
Costs: About $2,250 for 4 wks *incl* tuition, housing, some meals, excursions, books/materials
Housing: *Arr by pgm:* apartments, homestay
Deadline: None
Other info: *US accredited sponsor:* no *Misc:* May contact former participants. *URL:* http://www.languagesabroad.com
Contact: Ms Jesse Philippe, Langs Abroad, 317 Adelaide St W, Ste 900, Toronto, Ontario M5V 1P9, Canada *Ph:* 800-219 9924; 416-925 7117 *E-mail:* info@languagesabroad.com

---

SANTAREM

1868
AMIZADE
Brazilian Amazon Volunteer Program
Site: Brazil: Santarem
Dates: 1-4 wks, yr-round
Subjects: Community service projects
Eligibility: *Level:* adults *Age:* min 18
Credit: *Undergrad:* none *Grad:* none
Instruction: *In:* English *Format:* volunteer/svc *Students:* mainly US
Costs: $1,000-$2,500 for 2 wks *incl* tuition, housing, all meals, intl airfare, fees, excursions
Housing: *Arr by pgm:* residence halls
Deadline: Contact sponsor
Other info: *US accredited sponsor:* no *Began:* 1994 *Orient:* abroad (1 day) *Activities:* excursions, field trips, program travel, cultural events, sports *Misc:* May contact former participants. *URL:* http://amizade.org/Brazil.htm
Contact: Mike Sandy, Ex Dir, Amizade Ltd, 367 S Graham St, Pittsburgh PA 15232 *Ph:* 888-973 4443 *Fax:* 412-648 1492 *E-mail:* volunteer@amizade.org

---

SAO PAULO

1869
COUNCIL ON INTERNATIONAL EDUCATIONAL EXCHANGE CONSORTIUM
Council Study Center in Sao Paulo, Brazil
Site: Brazil: Sao Paulo
Dates: 5 wks, mid-Jun-late Jul or mid-Jan-late Feb
Subjects: Brazilian studies, Civilization/culture, Homestay, Portuguese language
Eligibility: *Level:* fresh, sophs, jrs, srs, grads, adults, teachers, professionals *Requires:* 2.75 GPA, 2 yrs Portuguese or Spanish or 1 yr of each
Credit: *Undergrad:* 4 per sem *Grad:* none *Doc:* transcript
Instruction: *In:* Portuguese *Format:* lang study, lecture *Students:* mainly US
Costs: $2,625 *incl* tuition, housing, all meals, insurance, excursions, ISIC
Housing: *Arr by pgm:* homestay
Deadline: Apr 1 for Jun; Nov 1 for Jan
Other info: *US accredited sponsor:* yes *Orient:* abroad *Activities:* excursions, field trips *Misc:* May contact former participants. *Financial aid:* scholarships *URL:* http://www.ciee.org/study
Contact: *See Index II for Members* Latin Amer Pgm Adviser, Council-ISP, 633 3rd Ave, 20th Fl, New York NY 10017 *Ph:* 800-407 8839; 212-822 2758 *Fax:* 212-822 2779 *E-mail:* studyinfo@ciee.org

---

1870
LINGUATEC LANGUAGE CENTER
Learn Portuguese in Brazil-Sao Paulo
Site: Brazil: Sao Paulo
Dates: 2 wks or longer, yr-round
Subjects: Portuguese language (beg/int/adv)
Eligibility: *Level:* adults, precoll *Age:* min 16, avg 28
Credit: *Undergrad:* avail *Grad:* none *Doc:* certificate
Instruction: *In:* Portuguese *Format:* lang study *Students:* intl
Costs: $469 per wk *incl* tuition, excursions *Nonrefundable fee*
Housing: *Arr by student:* apartments, hotels
Deadline: 1 wk before pgm
Other info: *US accredited sponsor:* no *Began:* 1988 *Activities:* excursions *Misc:* May contact former participants. *URL:* http://www.linguatec.cl
Contact: ligia Pereira, Linguatec Lang Ctr, Ave Engenheiro Luiz Carlos, Berrini 1461, andar 8, 04571-011 Sao Paulo SP, Brazil *Ph:* 303-777 7783 *Fax:* 303-777 7246 *E-mail:* ligiap@linguatec.com.br

---

1871
RUTGERS UNIVERSITY
Rutgers Summer Internship in Brazil
Site: Brazil: Sao Paulo
Dates: 6 wks, early-Jun-early-Aug
Subjects: Brazilian studies
Eligibility: *Level:* sophs, jrs *Requires:* 2.5 GPA, previous study in field
Credit: *Undergrad:* avail *Grad:* none *Doc:* transcript
Instruction: *In:* Portuguese *Format:* internship, practical training *Students:* mainly US
Costs: $2,913 for NJ residents, $3,163 for others *incl* tuition, housing, some meals, intl airfare, insurance, fees, excursions *Nonrefundable fee*
Housing: *Arr by pgm:* hotels
Deadline: Apr 15
Other info: *US accredited sponsor:* yes *URL:* http://www.rutgers.edu/Academics/Study_Abroad
Contact: Dir, Study Abroad, Rutgers Univ, 102 College Ave, New Brunswick NJ 08901 *Ph:* 732-932 7787 *Fax:* 732-932 8659 *E-mail:* ru_abroad@email.rutgers.edu

---

1872
UNIVERSITY OF ILLINOIS AT URBANA-CHAMPAIGN
Brazil's Economy and Business Environment
Site: Brazil: Sao Paulo *Host inst:* Univ of Sao Paulo
Dates: 6 wks, May 20-Jul 1
Subjects: Business/management, Economics, Field study, Government, Homestay, Political science/politics, Portuguese language (beg)
Eligibility: *Level:* jrs, srs, grads *Requires:* previous study in field, B avg
Credit: *Undergrad:* 6 *Grad:* 6 *Doc:* transcript
Instruction: *In:* English *Format:* directed field study, lang study, lecture, seminar *Students:* mainly US
Costs: $3,300 *incl* tuition, housing, some meals, medical evacuation insurance *Nonrefundable fee*
Housing: *Arr by pgm:* homestay

See "How To Use This Book" for definitions of terms used above. ▲ = See program sponsor's ad(s) in this book.

Deadline: Mar 1
Other info: *US accredited sponsor:* yes *Began:* 1995 *Activities:* field trips, cultural events *Misc:* Company case study. Numerous company visits. Financial aid for own students only. May contact former participants. *URL:* http://www.uiuc.edu/providers/ips/sao
Contact: Illinois Pgms Abroad, Univ of Illinois, 115 Intl Studies Bldg, 910 S Fifth St, Champaign IL 61820 *Ph:* 217-333 6322 *Fax:* 217-244 0249 *E-mail:* ipa@uiuc.edu

---

VICTORIA

1873
UNIVERSITY OF KANSAS
Portuguese Language and Culture in Victoria, Brazil
Site: Brazil: Victoria *Host inst:* Federal Univ of Espirito Santo
Dates: 7 wks, mid-Jun-late Jul
Subjects: Brazilian studies, Civilization/culture, Homestay, Portuguese language
Eligibility: *Level:* sophs, jrs, srs, grads *Requires:* 3.0 GPA in Portuguese or Spanish and 2 sems coll Portuguese or 4 sems coll Spanish
Credit: *Undergrad:* 6 *Grad:* avail *Doc:* transcript
Instruction: *In:* Portuguese *Format:* lang study, lecture *Students:* mainly US
Costs: $2,180 *incl* tuition, excursions, books/materials
Housing: *Arr by pgm:* homestay, hotels on excursions
Deadline: Feb 15
Other info: *US accredited sponsor:* yes *Began:* 1995 *Activities:* excursions, field trips, program travel *Misc:* Excursions to Reserva Rio Doce, Bahia, Rio de Janeiro. May contact former participants. *URL:* http://www.ukans.edu/~osa
Contact: Renee Bergene, Coord, Study Abroad, Univ of Kansas, 108 Lippincott Hall, Lawrence KS 66045 *Ph:* 785-864 3742, 785-864 5040 *Fax:* 785-864 5040 *E-mail:* osa@ukans.edu ▲

Canada

MORE THAN ONE CITY

1874
INTERNATIONAL BICYCLE FUND
Rolling the Hoop Through Salish Country
Site: Canada: Tribal/reservation lands around Puget Sound; US
Dates: 13 days, Jul-Aug
Subjects: Art, Asian-American studies, Civilization/culture, Ecology/environmental studies, Economics, Ethnology, Field study, Geography, History, Homestay, Independent study, Native american studies, Political science/politics, Religion/theology
Eligibility: *Level:* adults
Credit: *Undergrad:* none *Grad:* none
Instruction: *In:* English *Format:* directed field study, independent study, seminar, study tour *Students:* intl
Costs: $1,290 *incl* tuition, housing, some meals, excursions *Nonrefundable fee*
Housing: *Arr by pgm:* homestay, hotels, hostels
Deadline: Until pgm filled
Other info: *US accredited sponsor:* no *Began:* 2000 *Orient:* avail *Activities:* excursions, field trips, program travel, cultural events *Misc:* May contact former participants. *URL:* http://www.ibike.org/ibike
Contact: David Mozer, Dir, Intl Bicycle Fund, 4887 Columbia Dr S, Seattle WA 98108 *Ph:* 206-767 0848 *Fax:* 206-767 0848 *E-mail:* ibike@ibike.org

---

1875
LINGUA SERVICE WORLDWIDE
Total Immersion/Intensive Language and Culture in Canada
Site: Canada: Montreal, Quebec City *Host inst:* Ctr Intl Linguistique Bouchereau, Greater Montreal Lang Schs
Dates: 1 wk-1 yr, yr-round
Subjects: Civilization/culture, French language (beg/int/adv), Homestay
Eligibility: *Level:* fresh, sophs, jrs, srs, grads, adults, teachers, professionals, precoll
Credit: *Undergrad:* avail *Grad:* avail *Doc:* transcript, certificate *Transfer credit through:* Univ of Southern Mississippi
Instruction: *In:* English *Format:* lang study *Students:* intl
Costs: Contact sponsor
Housing: *Arr by pgm:* apartments with local students, residence halls with local students, homestay, pensions, hotels, hostels
Deadline: 45 days before pgm
Other info: *US accredited sponsor:* no *Began:* 1993 *Activities:* excursions, cultural events *Misc:* May contact former participants. *URL:* http://www.linguaserviceworldwide.com
Contact: Dir, Lingua Svc Worldwide, 75 Prospect St, Ste 4, Huntington NY 11743 *Ph:* 800-394 5327; 631-424 0777 *Fax:* 631-271 3441 *E-mail:* itctravel@worldnet.att.net ▲

1876
MICHIGAN STATE UNIVERSITY
Natural Science in the Canadian Rockies
Site: Canada: various sites
Dates: 3 wks, Jul-Aug
Subjects: Field study, Natural sciences
Eligibility: *Level:* fresh, sophs, jrs, srs *Requires:* 2.0 GPA, camping equipment, essay, physical fitness *Age:* min 18
Credit: *Undergrad:* avail *Grad:* none *Doc:* transcript
Instruction: *In:* English *Format:* directed field study *Students:* mainly US
Costs: About $1,300 *incl* housing, insurance, excursions, camping fees *Nonrefundable fee*
Housing: *Arr by pgm:* campsites
Deadline: Mar 2
Other info: *US accredited sponsor:* yes *Orient:* in US (1 day) *Activities:* excursions, field trips, program travel, cultural events *Financial aid:* scholarships *URL:* http://studyabroad.msu.edu
Contact: Cheryl Benner, Study Abroad, Michigan State Univ, 109 Intl Ctr, East Lansing MI 48824-1035 *Ph:* 517-353 8920 *Fax:* 517-432 2082 *E-mail:* bennerc@msu.edu ▲

1877
UNIVERSITE LAVAL, ECOLE DES LANGUES VIVANTES
University Studies
Site: Canada: Quebec, Sainte-Foy
Dates: May-Jun
Subjects: Administration, Agronomy, Architecture, Dentistry, Education/teaching, Engineering, Forestry, Health sciences, Law, Literature, Mathematics, Music, Philosophy, Sciences, Visual arts
Eligibility: *Level:* fresh, sophs, jrs, srs, grads, adults, teachers, professionals *Requires:* good knowledge of French
Credit: *Undergrad:* avail *Grad:* avail
Instruction: *In:* French *Format:* art studio, directed field study, independent study, internship, lab, lang study, lecture, music lesson, practical training, seminar, student teaching, study tour, tutorial, volunteer/svc, workshop *Students:* mainly host country
Costs: Contact sponsor
Housing: *Sponsor assists*
Deadline: Feb 1
Other info: *US accredited sponsor:* no *Orient:* abroad *Activities:* cultural events, sports *Misc:* May contact former participants. *Financial aid:* scholarships, work study *URL:* http://www.ulaval.ca
Contact: Claire Sormany, Dir, Bureau d'Info, Pavillon Bonenfant, Local 2435, Quebec G1K 7P4, Canada *Ph:* 877-785 2825 *E-mail:* info@urd.ulaval.ca
Or Contact: Registrar, Univ Laval, Quebec G1K 7P4, Canada *Ph:* 877-785 2825 *E-mail:* reg@reg.ulaval.ca

---

1878
WILLING WORKERS ON ORGANIC FARMS (WWOOF) CANADA
Willing Workers on Organic Farms in Canada
Site: Canada: various sites
Dates: 1 wk-6 mos, early spring-late fall
Subjects: Community service projects, Farm management, Homestay
Eligibility: *Level:* adults *Requires:* a good attitude; one's best abilities *Age:* min 16
Credit: *Undergrad:* none *Grad:* none
Instruction: *In:* English *Format:* practical training, volunteer/svc *Students:* intl
Costs: $30 *incl* fees *Nonrefundable fee*
Housing: *Sponsor assists:* homestay
Deadline: None
Other info: *US accredited sponsor:* no *Began:* 1985 *Orient:* abroad (1 day) *Activities:* excursions, field trips, program travel, cultural events, sports *Misc:* Fees are for membership & descriptive booklet. *URL:* http://www.members.tripod.com/~wwoof
Contact: John Vanden Heuvel, Coord, Willing Workers on Organic Farms, RR2, S18, C9, Nelson BC V1L 5P5, Canada *Ph:* 250-354 4417 *Fax:* 250-354 4417 *E-mail:* wwoofcan@uniserve.com

---

CHICOUTIMI

1879
COLLEGE CONSORTIUM FOR INTERNATIONAL STUDIES and BROOKDALE COMMUNITY COLLEGE
Canada French and Snow Program
Site: Canada: Chicoutimi *Host inst:* Univ du Quebec a Chicoutimi
Dates: 3 wks, Jan 3-20
Subjects: Canadian studies, Field study, French language, Homestay
Eligibility: *Level:* fresh, sophs, jrs, srs, grads *Requires:* 2.5 GPA, transcript, essay, 2 references, 15 credits *Age:* min 18
Credit: *Undergrad:* 4 *Grad:* none *Doc:* transcript
Instruction: *In:* French *Format:* directed field study, lecture, seminar *Students:* mainly US
Costs: $1,770 *incl* tuition, housing, all meals, fees, excursions, books/materials, airport transfer, e-mail *Nonrefundable fee*
Housing: *Arr by pgm:* residence halls, homestay
Deadline: Nov 1
Other info: *US accredited sponsor:* yes *Began:* 2000 *Orient:* in US & abroad *Activities:* excursions, field trips, cultural events *Financial aid:* scholarships *URL:* http://www.ccisabroad.org
Contact: *See Index II for Members* CCIS, 2000 P St NW, Ste 503, Washington DC 20036 *Ph:* 800-453 6956; 202-223 0330 *Fax:* 202-223 0999 *E-mail:* info@ccisabroad.org
Or Contact: Emily Hagadorn, Mgr, Intl Ctr, Brookdale CC, 765 Newman Springs Rd, Lincroft NJ 07738-1597 *Ph:* 732-224 2174 *Fax:* 732-224 2980 *E-mail:* ehagadorn@brookdale.cc.nj.us ▲

1880
COLLEGE CONSORTIUM FOR INTERNATIONAL STUDIES and BROOKDALE COMMUNITY COLLEGE
Canada Summer Business French Program
Site: Canada: Chicoutimi *Host inst:* Univ du Quebec a Chicoutimi
Dates: 3 wks, Jul 2-21
Subjects: Field study, French language, Homestay, International business
Eligibility: *Level:* fresh, sophs, jrs, srs, grads *Requires:* 2.5 GPA, transcript, essay, 2 recommendations, 15 credits *Age:* min 18
Credit: *Undergrad:* 4 *Grad:* none *Doc:* transcript
Instruction: *In:* English, French *Format:* directed field study, lecture, seminar *Students:* US & intl
Costs: $1,681 *incl* tuition, housing, all meals, fees, excursions, books/materials, airport transfer, e-mail *Nonrefundable fee*
Housing: *Arr by pgm:* residence halls, homestay
Deadline: May 29
Other info: *US accredited sponsor:* yes *Began:* 2000 *Orient:* in US & abroad *Activities:* excursions, field trips, cultural events *Financial aid:* scholarships *URL:* http://www.ccisabroad.org
Contact: *See Index II for Members* CCIS, 2000 P St NW, Ste 503, Washington DC 20036 *Ph:* 800-453 6956; 202-223 0330 *Fax:* 202-223 0999 *E-mail:* info@ccisabroad.org
Or Contact: Emily Hagadorn, Mgr, Intl Ctr, Brookdale CC, 765 Newman Springs Rd, Lincroft NJ 07738 *Ph:* 732-224 2174 *Fax:* 732-224 2980 *E-mail:* ehagadorn@brookdale.cc.nj.us ▲

1881
COLLEGE CONSORTIUM FOR INTERNATIONAL STUDIES and BROOKDALE COMMUNITY COLLEGE
Canada Summer Language and Culture Program
Site: Canada: Chicoutimi *Host inst:* Univ du Quebec a Chicoutimi
Dates: 3 wks, Jul 2-21
Subjects: Canadian studies, Field study, French language, French studies, Homestay, Literature
Eligibility: *Level:* fresh, sophs, jrs, srs, grads *Requires:* 2.5 GPA, previous study in field, int French, transcript, 2 references, essay, 15 credits
Credit: *Undergrad:* 4 *Grad:* none *Doc:* transcript
Instruction: *In:* French *Format:* directed field study, lecture, seminar *Students:* US & intl
Costs: $1,700 *incl* tuition, housing, all meals, fees, excursions, books/materials, airport transfer *Nonrefundable fee*
Housing: *Arr by pgm:* residence halls, homestay
Deadline: May 29
Other info: *US accredited sponsor:* yes *Began:* 2000 *Orient:* in US & abroad *Activities:* excursions, field trips, cultural events *Misc:* E-mail access. *Financial aid:* scholarships
Contact: *See Index II for Members* CCIS, 2000 P St NW, Ste 503, Washington DC 20036 *Ph:* 800-453 6956; 202-223 0330 *Fax:* 202-223 0999 *E-mail:* info@ccisabroad.org
Or Contact: Emily Hagadorn, Mgr, Intl Ctr, Brookdale CC, 765 Newman Springs Rd, Lincroft NJ 07738-1597 *Ph:* 732-224 2174 *Fax:* 732-224 2980 *E-mail:* ehagadorn@brookdale.cc.nj.us ▲

1882
COLLEGE CONSORTIUM FOR INTERNATIONAL STUDIES and BROOKDALE COMMUNITY COLLEGE
Summer Program in Quebec
Site: Canada: Chicoutimi *Host inst:* Univ du Quebec a Chicoutimi
Dates: 3-5 wks, May or Jul
Subjects: Canadian studies, Civilization/culture, French language (beg/int/adv)
Eligibility: *Level:* fresh, sophs, jrs, srs, grads *Requires:* 2.5 GPA, 2 recommendation letters, transcript, essay, 15 credits prior to application *Age:* min 18
Credit: *Undergrad:* 4-7 *Grad:* none *Doc:* transcript
Instruction: *In:* French *Format:* lecture, seminar *Students:* US & intl
Costs: $1,700 for 3 wks, $2,000 for 5 wks *incl* tuition, housing, all meals, fees, excursions, e-mail, airport pickup
Housing: *Arr by pgm:* residence halls, homestay
Deadline: Apr 7 for May; May 29 for Jul
Other info: *US accredited sponsor:* yes *Orient:* in US & abroad *Activities:* excursions, field trips, cultural events *Misc:* Loans avail. May contact former participants. *Financial aid:* scholarships *URL:* http://www.ccisabroad.org
Contact: *See Index II for Members* CCIS, 2000 P St NW, Ste 503, Washington DC 20036 *Ph:* 800-453 6956; 202-223 0330 *Fax:* 202-223 0999 *E-mail:* info@ccisabroad.org

Or Contact: Emily Hagadorn, Mgr, Intl Ctr, Brookdale CC, 765 Newman Springs Rd, Lincroft NJ 07738-1597 *Ph:* 732-224 2174 *Fax:* 732-224 2980 *E-mail:* ehagadorn@brookdale.cc.nj.us ▲

1883
SUNY COLLEGE AT PLATTSBURGH
Chicoutimi, Quebec, in the Summer
Site: Canada: Chicoutimi *Host inst:* Univ du Quebec a Chicoutimi
Dates: 3 or 5 wks, May-Jun & Jul-Aug
Subjects: Civilization/culture, French language (int/adv), Homestay, Quebec studies
Eligibility: *Level:* adults *Requires:* 2.5 GPA *Age:* min 18
Credit: *Undergrad:* 5-7 *Grad:* none *Doc:* transcript
Instruction: *In:* French *Format:* lab, lang study, workshop *Students:* intl & host country
Costs: $1,600 for 3 wks, $2,200 for 5 wks for NY resident undergrads *incl* tuition, housing, all meals, insurance, fees, excursions, books/materials *Nonrefundable fee*
Housing: *Arr by pgm:* homestay
Deadline: Mar 15
Other info: *US accredited sponsor:* yes *Began:* 1983 *Orient:* abroad *Activities:* excursions, cultural events, sports *Misc:* Lang immersion, 12-17 students per class. Lang lab, conversation workshops, outdoor activity ctr. *Financial aid:* scholarships *URL:* http://www.plattsburgh.edu/studyabroad
Contact: Dodie Giltz, Asst Dir, Ctr for the Study of Canada, SUNY Coll at Plattsburgh, Plattsburgh NY 12901 *Ph:* 518-564 2086 *Fax:* 518-564 2112 *E-mail:* international@plattsburgh.edu

---

GOLD BRIDGE

1884
CHILCOTIN HOLIDAYS
One and Two Week Wilderness Guide Training Programs
Site: Canada: Gold Bridge
Dates: 1 & 2 wks, Apr 30-May 12, May 21-Jun 2, Jun 11-23, Jul 1-7, Jul 22-28, Aug 12-18
Subjects: Camping, Equestrian arts, Field study, Hiking/trekking, Homestay, Outdoor activities/education, Recreation resources management, Tourism
Eligibility: *Level:* adults, precoll *Age:* min 14, max 70, avg 24
Credit: *Undergrad:* none *Grad:* none *Doc:* certificate
Instruction: *In:* English *Format:* directed field study, internship, lecture, practical training, study tour *Students:* intl & host country
Costs: CN $1,200 per wk *incl* tuition, housing, all meals, excursions, books/materials *Nonrefundable fee*
Housing: *Arr by pgm:* homestay, tent cabins
Deadline: Rolling admissions
Other info: *US accredited sponsor:* no *Began:* 1991 *Orient:* abroad *Activities:* excursions, field trips, program travel, cultural events, sports *Misc:* May contact former participants. *URL:* http://www.chilcotinholidays.com
Contact: Brooke Bannerman or Sylvia Waterer, Chilcotin Holidays, Gun Creek Rd, Gold Bridge, BC Canada, VOK 1PO *E-mail:* adventures@chilcotinholidays.com

---

LAC-BEAUPORT

1885
EDUVACATIONS
Study in and Live in Your Teacher's Home-Canada
Site: Canada: Lac-Beauport
Dates: 1 wk or longer, yr-round
Subjects: French language (beg/int/adv), Homestay
Eligibility: *Level:* fresh, sophs, jrs, srs, grads, adults, teachers, professionals *Age:* min 18
Credit: *Undergrad:* none *Grad:* none *Doc:* certificate
Instruction: *In:* French *Format:* lang study *Students:* intl
Costs: Contact sponsor
Housing: *Arr by pgm:* homestay
Deadline: Contact sponsor
Other info: *US accredited sponsor:* no *Activities:* excursions, field trips, cultural events, sports *Misc:* May contact former participants. *URL:* http://www.eduvacations.com
Contact: Mary Ann Puglisi, eduVacations, 1431 21st St NW, Ste 302, Washington DC 20036 *Ph:* 202-857 8384 *Fax:* 202-463 8091

MONTREAL

1886
EDUVACATIONS
Intensive French in Montreal
Site: Canada: Montreal
Dates: 2 wks or longer, yr-round
Subjects: French language (beg/int/adv)
Eligibility: *Level:* adults
Credit: *Undergrad:* none *Grad:* none
Instruction: *In:* French *Format:* lang study, lecture *Students:* intl
Costs: Contact sponsor
Housing: *Arr by pgm:* residence halls, homestay, hostels
Deadline: Contact sponsor
Other info: *US accredited sponsor:* no *Activities:* excursions, field trips, cultural events, sports *Misc:* May contact former participants. *URL:* http://www.eduvacations.com
Contact: Mary Ann Puglisi, eduVacations, 1431 21st St NW, Ste 302, Washington DC 20036 *Ph:* 202-857 8384 *Fax:* 202-463 8091

1887
LANGUAGE LIAISON
French Language
Site: Canada: Montreal
Dates: 2 wks or longer, yr-round
Subjects: French language (beg/int/adv), Homestay
Eligibility: *Level:* fresh, sophs, jrs, srs, grads, adults, teachers, professionals, precoll *Age:* min 16
Credit: *Undergrad:* avail *Grad:* avail *Doc:* transcript, certificate
Instruction: *In:* French *Format:* lang study *Students:* intl
Costs: Contact sponsor
Housing: *Arr by pgm:* apartments, homestay
Deadline: 30 days before pgm
Other info: *US accredited sponsor:* no *Misc:* Scholarship research svc. *URL:* http://www.languageliaison.com
Contact: Nancy Forman, Dir, Lang Liaison, 4 Burnham Pkwy, Morristown NJ 07960 *Ph:* 800-284 4448 *Fax:* 973-898 1710 *E-mail:* learn@languageliaison.com

---

1888
LANGUAGE STUDIES ABROAD, INC
Intensive French
Site: Canada: Montreal *Host inst:* various LSA insts
Dates: 1 wk or longer, yr-round
Subjects: French language (beg/int/adv), Homestay
Eligibility: *Level:* fresh, sophs, jrs, srs, grads, adults, teachers, professionals, precoll *Age:* min 16
Credit: *Undergrad:* avail *Grad:* avail
Instruction: *In:* French *Format:* lang study *Students:* intl
Costs: $1,195 for 4 wks *incl* tuition, housing, some meals
Housing: *Sponsor assists:* apartments, homestay, hotels
Deadline: 4 wks before pgm
Other info: *US accredited sponsor:* no *Began:* 1962 *Orient:* abroad *Activities:* excursions *Misc:* May contact former participants. *URL:* http://www.languagestudiesabroad.com

Contact: Lang Studies Abroad, Inc, 103 Londonderry Ct, Reno NV 89511-2718 *Ph:* 800-424 5522; 775-849 9206 *Fax:* 775-849 9217 *E-mail:* info@languagestudiesabroad.com

---

1889
LANGUAGES ABROAD
Languages and Culture-Montreal
Site: Canada: Montreal
Dates: 2 wks or longer, yr-round
Subjects: Canadian studies, Civilization/culture, French language (beg/int/adv), Homestay
Eligibility: *Level:* adults *Age:* min 17, max 65, avg 25
Credit: *Undergrad:* none *Grad:* none *Doc:* certificate
Instruction: *In:* French *Format:* lang study *Students:* intl
Costs: $1,500 per mo *incl* tuition, housing, some meals, excursions, books/materials
Housing: *Arr by pgm:* residence halls, homestay
Deadline: None
Other info: *US accredited sponsor:* no *Began:* 1995 *Activities:* excursions, field trips, program travel, cultural events, sports *Misc:* May contact former participants. *URL:* http://www.languagesabroad.com
Contact: Ms Jesse Philippe, Langs Abroad, 317 Adelaide St W, Ste 900, Toronto, Ontario M5V 1P9, Canada *Ph:* 800-219 9924; 416-925 7117 *E-mail:* info@languagesabroad.com

---

1890
NATIONAL REGISTRATION CENTER FOR STUDY ABROAD (NRCSA)
Montreal Language School
Site: Canada: Montreal *Host inst:* LSC Montreal
Dates: 2-8 wks, yr-round
Subjects: French language (beg/int/adv), Homestay
Eligibility: *Level:* fresh, sophs, jrs, srs, adults, precoll *Age:* min 17
Credit: *Undergrad:* 3-6 *Grad:* 3-6 *Doc:* certificate
Instruction: *In:* French *Format:* lang study, lecture *Students:* intl
Costs: $862 for 2 wks, $1,352 for 4 wks *incl* tuition, housing, some meals, insurance
Housing: *Arr by pgm:* homestay, YMCA
Deadline: Contact sponsor
Other info: *US accredited sponsor:* no *Began:* 1962 *Orient:* abroad (intensive lang study) *Activities:* excursions *URL:* http://www.nrcsa.com
Contact: Reuel Zielke, NRCSA, 823 N 2nd St, #206, Milwaukee WI 53203 *Ph:* 414-278 0631 *Fax:* 414-271 8884 *E-mail:* info@nrcsa.com

---

1891
SUNY COLLEGE AT PLATTSBURGH
Montreal in the Summer
Site: Canada: Montreal *Host inst:* Univ de Montreal
Dates: 3 wks, late May-mid-Jun, early Jul-late Jul, late Jul-mid-Aug
Subjects: Business language, Civilization/culture, Composition, Foreign language teaching, French language (beg/int/adv), Quebec studies
Eligibility: *Level:* adults *Requires:* 2.5 GPA, placement exam *Age:* min 18
Credit: *Undergrad:* 3 *Grad:* none *Doc:* transcript
Instruction: *In:* French *Format:* lang study *Students:* intl & host country
Costs: About $1,136 *incl* tuition, insurance *Nonrefundable fee*
Housing: *Sponsor assists:* residence halls, homestay
Deadline: Mar 15
Other info: *US accredited sponsor:* yes *Began:* 1995 *Orient:* abroad (intensive lang study) *Activities:* cultural events, sports *Misc:* May contact former participants. *Financial aid:* scholarships *URL:* http://www.plattsburgh.edu/studyabroad
Contact: Dodie Giltz, Asst Dir, SUNY Coll at Plattsburgh, 133 Court St, Plattsburgh NY 12901 *Ph:* 518-564 2086 *Fax:* 518-564 2112 *E-mail:* international@plattburgh.edu

---

1892
UNIVERSITE DE MONTREAL, FACULTE DE L'EDUCATION PERMANENTE
Ecole de Francais: Intensive French Courses
Site: Canada: Montreal
Dates: 3-4 wks, May-Jun, Jun-Jul, Jul-Aug
Subjects: Business language, Foreign language teaching, French language (beg/int/adv), Quebec studies, Written composition
Eligibility: *Level:* adults *Age:* min 18
Credit: *Undergrad:* avail *Grad:* none *Doc:* transcript
Instruction: *In:* French *Format:* workshop *Students:* intl
Costs: CN $469 for 45 hrs, CN $569 for 60 hrs *incl* tuition, insurance, fees *Nonrefundable fee*
Housing: *Arr by student:* residence halls with local students, apartments, homestay
Deadline: 2 wks before pgm
Other info: *US accredited sponsor:* no *Began:* 1945 *In coop with:* ACTFL, AATF, Penn State Univ, SUNY, UAM, others *Activities:* excursions, field trips, cultural events, sports *URL:* http://www.fep.umontreal.ca/langues/index.html
Contact: Nicole Lavergne, Coord, Ecole de Francais, Faculte de l'Educ Permanente, Univ de Montreal, CP 6128, Succ Centre-Ville, Montreal, Quebec H3C 3J7, Canada *E-mail:* infolang@fep.umontreal.ca

---

1893
VIRGINIA COMMONWEALTH UNIVERSITY
Tout C'est Jazz: Intensive French and Jazz Festival
Site: Canada: Montreal *Host inst:* Lang Studies Canada
Dates: 1-2 mos, Jun-Jul
Subjects: French language, Homestay
Eligibility: *Level:* adults *Requires:* 2.0 GPA, 1 French course *Age:* min 18
Credit: *Undergrad:* avail *Grad:* none *Doc:* transcript
Instruction: *In:* English, French *Format:* lecture *Students:* mainly US
Costs: $1,600-$2,500 *incl* tuition, housing *Nonrefundable fee*
Housing: *Arr by pgm:* homestay
Deadline: Contact sponsor
Other info: *US accredited sponsor:* yes *Began:* 1996 *Activities:* cultural events *URL:* http://www.vcu.edu/cspweb/cspdocs/stdyabrd.html
Contact: Tina Murray, Asst Dir, Ctr for Intl Pgms, Virginia Commonwealth Univ, 916 W Franklin St, Box 843043, Richmond VA 23284-3043 *Ph:* 804-828 8471 *Fax:* 804-828 2552

QUEBEC CITY

1894
ARIZONA STATE UNIVERSITY
Quebec
Site: Canada: Quebec City
Dates: 4 wks, Jul 10-Aug 11
Subjects: Civilization/culture, French language, Homestay
Eligibility: *Level:* fresh, sophs, jrs, srs, grads, adults, teachers, professionals *Age:* min 18
Credit: *Undergrad:* 8 *Grad:* 8
Instruction: *In:* English, French *Format:* lang study, lecture, study tour *Students:* mainly US
Costs: $1,975 *incl* tuition, housing, some meals, excursions, ISIC *Nonrefundable fee*
Housing: *Arr by pgm:* residence halls, homestay
Deadline: Early Mar
Other info: *US accredited sponsor:* yes *Began:* 1999 *Orient:* in US *Activities:* excursions, field trips *Misc:* Loans avail. All students pay equiv of ASU resident

tuition. *Financial aid:* scholarships *URL:* http://www.asu.edu/ssc/StudyAbroad
Contact: Ara Pachmayer, Pgm Coord, Summer Sessions, Arizona State Univ, PO Box 873003, Tempe AZ 85287-3003 *Ph:* 480-965 0101 *Fax:* 480-965 3851 *E-mail:* study.programs@asu.edu

---

1895
COMMITTEE ON INSTITUTIONAL COOPERATION
CIC Summer Study Program in Quebec
Site: Canada: Quebec City *Host inst:* Univ Laval
Dates: 6 wks, late Jun-early Aug
Subjects: Civilization/culture, French language (int/adv), Homestay, Literature, Quebec studies
Eligibility: *Level:* fresh, sophs, jrs, srs, grads *Requires:* B avg, 1 yr coll French or equiv
Credit: *Undergrad:* 7-8 *Grad:* none *Doc:* transcript
Instruction: *In:* French *Format:* lang study, lecture *Students:* intl
Costs: $2,600 *incl* tuition, housing, all meals, fees, excursions, orient
Housing: *Arr by pgm:* residence halls, homestay
Deadline: Mar 15
Other info: *US accredited sponsor:* yes *Began:* 1980 *Orient:* abroad *URL:* http://www.uiowa.edu/~uiabroad
Contact: *See Index II for Members* Admin Coord, CIC, 120 Intl Ctr, Univ of Iowa, Iowa City IA 52242-1802 *Ph:* 319-335 0353 *Fax:* 319-335 2021 *E-mail:* cic-abroad@uiowa.edu

---

1896
GEORGE MASON UNIVERSITY
Intensive French Language
Site: Canada: Quebec City *Host inst:* Univ Laval
Dates: 1 mo, Jul 10-Aug 11
Subjects: French language (beg/int/adv)
Eligibility: *Level:* fresh, sophs, jrs, srs, grads, adults, teachers, professionals *Requires:* 2.25 GPA, previous study in field, 1 yr coll French *Age:* min 18
Credit: *Undergrad:* 6 *Grad:* none *Doc:* transcript
Instruction: *In:* French *Format:* lang study *Students:* intl
Costs: About $1,900 for VA residents, $2,500 for others *incl* tuition, housing, some meals, most meals, insurance, ISIC *Nonrefundable fee*
Housing: *Sponsor assists:* residence halls
Deadline: Apr 12
Other info: *US accredited sponsor:* yes *Began:* 1993 *Orient:* in US *Activities:* excursions, field trips, program travel, cultural events *Misc:* May contact former participants. *URL:* http://www.gmu.edu/departments/cge
Contact: Ctr for Global Educ, George Mason Univ, Johnson Ctr, Rm 235, 4400 University Dr, Fairfax VA 22030-4444 *Ph:* 703-993 2154 *Fax:* 703-993 2153 *E-mail:* cge@gmu.edu

---

1897
RAMAPO COLLEGE OF NEW JERSEY
Quebec City, Canada
Site: Canada: Quebec City
Dates: 4 wks, Jul-Aug
Subjects: French language, Literature
Eligibility: *Level:* fresh, sophs, jrs, srs, grads, adults, teachers, professionals *Requires:* 2.0 GPA *Age:* min 18, avg 22
Credit: *Undergrad:* 8 *Grad:* none *Doc:* transcript
Instruction: *In:* French *Format:* lang study, lecture, study tour *Students:* mainly US
Costs: $2,200 Ramapo students, $2,400 others *incl* tuition, housing, most meals, fees, excursions
Housing: *Arr by pgm:* residence halls
Deadline: May 1
Other info: *US accredited sponsor:* yes *Began:* 2000 *Orient:* in US (1 day) *Activities:* excursions, program travel, cultural events *Financial aid:* scholarships, work study
Contact: Ms Robyn Perricelli, Study Abroad, Ramapo Coll of New Jersey, 505 Ramapo Valley Rd, Mahwah NJ 07430 *Ph:* 201-684 7030 *Fax:* 201-684 7561 *E-mail:* rperrice@ramapo.edu

---

1898
SAINT JOSEPH'S UNIVERSITY (PA)
SJU at Laval
Site: Canada: Quebec City *Host inst:* Univ Laval
Dates: 5 wks, May 18-Jun 19 or Jul 6-Aug 7
Subjects: French language (beg/int/adv)
Eligibility: *Level:* fresh, sophs, jrs, srs, grads, adults *Age:* min 18
Credit: *Undergrad:* avail *Grad:* none
Instruction: *In:* French *Format:* lang study, lecture *Students:* mainly host country
Costs: $1,450 *incl* tuition, housing, fees
Housing: *Arr by pgm:* residence halls, homestay
Deadline: May 1
Other info: *US accredited sponsor:* yes *Began:* 1981 *Orient:* in US *Activities:* field trips *Misc:* May contact former participants.
Contact: Modern Lang, St Joseph's Univ, Philadelphia PA 19131-1395 *Ph:* 610-660 1848 *Fax:* 610-660 2160 *E-mail:* cip@sju.edu
Or Contact: Ctr for Intl Pgms, St Joseph's Univ, 5600 City Ave, Philadelphia PA 19131 *Ph:* 610-660 1835 *Fax:* 610-660 1697

1899
SUNY COLLEGE AT NEW PALTZ, LANGUAGE IMMERSION INSTITUTE
Learning Vacations to Quebec City
Site: Canada: Quebec City *Host inst:* Ctr Intl Linguistique Bouchereau
Dates: 2 wks or longer, yr-round
Subjects: Languages
Eligibility: *Level:* adults *Age:* min 18, avg 40
Credit: *Undergrad:* none *Grad:* none
Instruction: *In:* French *Format:* lang study, lecture *Students:* intl
Costs: $987 for 2 wks *incl* tuition, housing, some meals, fees, books/materials, airport transfers *Nonrefundable fee*
Housing: *Arr by pgm:* homestay
Deadline: 1 mo before pgm
Other info: *US accredited sponsor:* yes *Began:* 1976 *Activities:* excursions, field trips, cultural events, sports *Misc:* May contact former participants. *URL:* http://www.newpaltz.edu/lii
Contact: Dr Henry Urbanski, Dir, Lang Immersion Inst, SUNY New Paltz, 75 S Manheim Blvd, New Paltz NY 12561-2499 *Ph:* 914-257 3500 *Fax:* 914-257 3569 ▲

1900
SUNY COLLEGE AT PLATTSBURGH
Quebec City in the Summer
Site: Canada: Quebec City *Host inst:* Univ Laval
Dates: 5 wks, May-Jun & Jul-Aug
Subjects: French language (beg/int/adv), Homestay
Eligibility: *Level:* adults *Requires:* 2.5 GPA *Age:* min 18
Credit: *Undergrad:* 7 *Grad:* none *Doc:* transcript
Instruction: *In:* French *Format:* lang study *Students:* intl & host country
Costs: About $2,000 for NY resident undergrads *incl* tuition, housing, insurance, fees, books/materials
Housing: *Arr by pgm:* residence halls, homestay arr by student
Deadline: Mar 15
Other info: *US accredited sponsor:* yes *Began:* 1980 *Orient:* abroad *Activities:* excursions, field trips, cultural events, sports *Financial aid:* scholarships *URL:* http://www.plattsburgh.edu/studyabroad

Contact: Dodie Giltz, Asst Dir, Ctr for the Study of Canada, SUNY Coll at Plattsburgh, 133 Court St, Plattsburgh NY 12901 *Ph:* 518-564 2086 *Fax:* 518-564 2112 *E-mail:* international@plattsburgh.edu

SAINTE-FOY

1901
UNIVERSITE LAVAL, ECOLE DES LANGUES VIVANTES
French Courses for Non-Francophones (Summer Courses)
Site: Canada: Sainte-Foy
Dates: 5 wks, May-Jun or Jul-Aug
Subjects: French language, Homestay
Eligibility: *Level:* fresh, sophs, srs, adults, teachers, professionals *Age:* min 18, avg 22
Credit: *Undergrad:* avail *Grad:* none *Doc:* transcript
Instruction: *In:* French *Format:* lab, lecture, practical training, study tour, volunteer/svc *Students:* intl
Costs: CN $794 *incl* tuition, insurance
Housing: *Arr by pgm:* residence halls, homestay
Deadline: Apr 1 for 1st session, May 1 for 2nd session
Other info: *US accredited sponsor:* no *Activities:* excursions, cultural events, sports *URL:* http://www.ulaval.co
Contact: Marcel Tremblay, Ecole des Langues Vivantes, Univ Laval, Ste-Foy G1K 7P4, Quebec, Canada *Ph:* 418-353 2321 *Fax:* 418-656 7018 *E-mail:* elv@elv.ulaval.ca

STRATFORD

1902
BALL STATE UNIVERSITY
English Dramatic Literature: Field Study
Site: Canada: Stratford
Dates: 2 wks, late Jun or Jul
Subjects: Drama/theater, English, Field study, Shakespeare studies
Eligibility: *Level:* srs, grads, adults
Credit: *Undergrad:* 3 *Grad:* 3
Instruction: *In:* English *Format:* directed field study, lecture *Students:* mainly US
Costs: About $875 *incl* tuition, housing, insurance, fees, excursions, travel by van
Housing: *Arr by pgm:* residence halls
Deadline: May 10
Other info: *US accredited sponsor:* yes *Began:* 1976 *Activities:* excursions *URL:* http://www.bsu.edu/english
Contact: Prof William T Liston, English, Ball State Univ, Muncie IN 47306 *Ph:* 765-285 8473 *Fax:* 765-285 3765 *E-mail:* 00wtliston@bsu.edu

TORONTO

1903
OKLAHOMA STATE UNIVERSITY
Global Business-A US/Canadian Partnership
Site: Canada: Toronto
Dates: 3 wks, May 21-Jun 8
Subjects: International business
Eligibility: *Level:* sophs, jrs, srs, grads
Credit: *Undergrad:* avail *Grad:* avail *Doc:* transcript
Instruction: *In:* English *Format:* lecture, seminar, study tour *Students:* mainly US
Costs: $1,500 *incl* tuition, housing, intl airfare *Nonrefundable fee*
Housing: *Arr by pgm:* residence halls
Deadline: Apr 1
Other info: *US accredited sponsor:* yes *Began:* 1998 *Activities:* excursions, field trips, program travel, cultural events, sports *Financial aid:* scholarships
Contact: Dr Gregory C Mosier, Faculty Coord, Oklahoma State Univ, Coll of Bus Admin, Stillwater OK 74078 *Ph:* 405-744 5118 *Fax:* 405-744 6143 *E-mail:* gmosier@okstate.edu
Or Contact: Gaye Trivitt, Pgm Mgr, Bus Extension, Oklahoma State Univ, Coll of Bus Admin, Stillwater OK 74078 *Ph:* 405-744 5208 *Fax:* 405-744 6143 *E-mail:* glt@okstate.edu

TROIS-PISTOLES

1904
SUNY COLLEGE AT BUFFALO
French Immersion Program
Site: Canada: Trois-Pistoles *Host inst:* Trois-Pistoles French Immersion Sch, Univ of Western Ontario
Dates: 3-5 wks, Jul-Aug
Subjects: Civilization/culture, French language (beg/int/adv)
Eligibility: *Level:* fresh, sophs, jrs, srs, grads, adults, teachers *Requires:* 2.0 GPA *Age:* avg 28
Credit: *Undergrad:* 6-10 *Grad:* 6-10 *Doc:* transcript
Instruction: *In:* French *Format:* independent study, lang study, workshop *Students:* intl
Costs: $1,965 for NY residents, $2,475 for others for 3 wks, $2,168/$3,602 for 5 wks *incl* tuition, housing, all meals, insurance, fees, transport *Nonrefundable fee*
Housing: *Arr by pgm:* homestay
Deadline: Apr 1; rolling admissions
Other info: *US accredited sponsor:* yes *Began:* 1995 *Orient:* in US *Activities:* excursions, cultural events, sports *Misc:* May contact former participants. *URL:* http://www.buffalostate.edu/~intnated
Contact: Dr Lee Ann Grace, Dir, Intl Educ, SUNY Coll at Buffalo, 1300 Elmwood Ave, Buffalo NY 14222-1095 *Ph:* 716-878 4620 *Fax:* 716-878 3054 *E-mail:* intleduc@buffalostate.edu

VANCOUVER ISLAND

1905
SCHOOL FOR FIELD STUDIES
SFS BC: Conserving Marine Resources and Coastal Rainforests
Site: Canada: Vancouver Island
Dates: 4 wks, mid-Jun-mid-Jul or mid-Jul-mid Aug
Subjects: Agricultural economics, Anthropology, Biology, Botany, Conservation, Development studies, Ecology/environmental studies, Economics, Field study, Forestry, Marine biology, Natural resources, Water management, Wildlife
Eligibility: *Level:* fresh, sophs, jrs, srs, precoll *Age:* min 16, avg 20
Credit: *Undergrad:* avail *Grad:* none *Doc:* transcript *Transfer credit through:* Boston Univ
Instruction: *In:* English *Format:* directed field study, lecture, practical training *Students:* mainly US
Costs: $2,975 *incl* tuition, housing, all meals, excursions *Nonrefundable fee*
Housing: *Arr by pgm:* dormitory
Deadline: Rolling admissions
Other info: *US accredited sponsor:* no *Began:* 1996 *Orient:* abroad *Activities:* excursions, field trips, program travel, cultural events, sports *Misc:* Loans avail. May contact former participants. *Financial aid:* scholarships *URL:* http://www.fieldstudies.org
Contact: Admissions Off, Sch for Field Studies, 16 Broadway, Beverly MA 01915-4499 *Ph:* 800-989 4435; 978-927 7777 *Fax:* 978-927 5127 *E-mail:* admissions@fieldstudies.org

YUKON

1906
MICHIGAN STATE UNIVERSITY
Natural Resources and Tourism Management
Site: Canada: Yukon
Dates: 3 wks, Aug
Subjects: Agriculture, Field study, Fishing/fisheries, Independent study,

Natural resources, Parks management, Recreation, Tourism, Wildlife
Eligibility: *Level:* jrs, srs, grads *Requires:* 2.0 GPA, letter of interest *Age:* min 18
Credit: *Undergrad:* 4-6 *Grad:* none *Doc:* transcript
Instruction: *In:* English *Format:* directed field study, independent study *Students:* mainly US
Costs: About $ 2,100 *incl* housing, some meals, insurance, fees, excursions *Nonrefundable fee*
Housing: *Arr by pgm:* motor homes, campsites
Deadline: Mar 2
Other info: *US accredited sponsor:* yes *Began:* 2000 *Orient:* in US 1 day *Activities:* excursions, field trips, program travel, cultural events *Financial aid:* scholarships *URL:* http://www.studyabroad.msu.edu
Contact: Cheryl Benner, MSU Study Abroad, 109 Intl Ctr, East Lansing MI 448824-1035 *Ph:* 517-353 8920 *Fax:* 517-432 2082 *E-mail:* bennerc@msu.edu ▲

Cayman Islands

GRAND CAYMAN

1907
INDIANA UNIVERSITY
Tropical Biology in Grand Cayman
Site: Cayman Islands: Grand Cayman
Dates: 2 wks, mid-May
Subjects: Biology, Field study
Eligibility: Own students only. *Level:* jrs, srs *Requires:* 3.0 GPA, previous study in field
Credit: *Undergrad:* 3 *Grad:* none *Doc:* transcript
Instruction: *In:* English *Format:* directed field study *Students:* mainly US
Costs: $1,500 or $2,100 *incl* tuition, housing, all meals, insurance, fees, excursions *Nonrefundable fee*
Housing: *Arr by pgm:* hotels
Deadline: Late Jan
Other info: *US accredited sponsor:* yes *Began:* 1996 *Orient:* in US *Activities:* excursions, field trips *Misc:* May contact former participants. *Financial aid:* scholarships *URL:* http://www.indiana.edu/~overseas
Contact: Overseas Study, Indiana Univ, Franklin 303, Bloomington IN 47405 *Ph:* 812-855 9304 *Fax:* 812-855 6452 *E-mail:* overseas@indiana.edu

Chile

SANTIAGO

1908
AMERISPAN UNLIMITED
Spanish Study and Homestay in Chile
Site: Chile: Santiago *Host inst:* Linguatec Lang Ctr
Dates: 1 wk-1 yr, yr-round
Subjects: Business language, Civilization/culture, Homestay, Spanish language (beg/int/adv)
Eligibility: *Level:* srs, grads, adults, teachers, professionals, precoll *Age:* min 18
Credit: *Undergrad:* avail *Grad:* none *Doc:* transcript, certificate *Transfer credit through:* Seattle Central CC
Instruction: *In:* Spanish *Format:* lang study, lecture, tutorial *Students:* intl

Costs: $1,075 for 2 wks, $1,775 for 4 wks, $420 for each addtl wk *incl* tuition, housing, some meals, insurance, books/materials
Housing: *Arr by pgm:* homestay, hotels
Deadline: 4 wks before pgm
Other info: *US accredited sponsor:* no *Orient:* abroad *Activities:* excursions, cultural events *Misc:* Transfer credit also avail through Univ of Southern Mississippi. May contact former participants. *URL:* http://www.amerispan.com/
Contact: AmeriSpan Unltd, PO Box 40007, Philadelphia PA 19106 *Ph:* 800-879 6640; 215-751 1100 *Fax:* 215-751 1986 *E-mail:* info@amerispan.com

---

1909
LANGUAGE LIAISON
Spanish Saturation-Chile
Site: Chile: Santiago
Dates: 1 wk or longer, yr-round
Subjects: Civilization/culture, Spanish language (beg/int/adv)
Eligibility: *Level:* fresh, sophs, jrs, srs, grads, adults, teachers, professionals, precoll *Age:* min 10
Credit: *Undergrad:* avail *Grad:* avail *Doc:* transcript, certificate
Instruction: *In:* Spanish *Format:* lang study, tutorial *Students:* intl
Costs: Contact sponsor
Housing: *Arr by pgm*
Deadline: 45 days before pgm
Other info: *US accredited sponsor:* no *Misc:* Scholarship research svc. *URL:* http://www.languageliaison.com
Contact: Nancy Forman, Dir, Lang Liaison, 4 Burnham Pkwy, Morristown NJ 07960 *Ph:* 800-284 4448 *Fax:* 973-898 1710 *E-mail:* learn@languageliaison.com

---

1910
LANGUAGES ABROAD
Language and Cultural Immersion Programs-Santiago
Site: Chile: Santiago
Dates: 2 wks or longer, yr-round
Subjects: Civilization/culture, Homestay, Spanish language (beg/int/adv)
Eligibility: *Level:* adults *Age:* min 17, max 65, avg 25
Credit: *Undergrad:* none *Grad:* none *Doc:* certificate
Instruction: *In:* Spanish *Format:* lang study *Students:* intl
Costs: From $2,950 for 4 wks *incl* tuition, housing, some meals, excursions, books/materials
Housing: *Arr by pgm:* apartments, homestay
Deadline: None
Other info: *US accredited sponsor:* no *Misc:* May contact former participants. *URL:* http://www.languagesabroad.com
Contact: Ms Jesse Philippe, Langs Abroad, 317 Adelaide St W, Ste 900, Toronto, Ontario M5V 1P9, Canada *Ph:* 800-219 9924; 416-925 7117 *E-mail:* info@languagesabroad.com

---

1911
LINGUA SERVICE WORLDWIDE
Intensive Language and Culture in Chile
Site: Chile: Santiago *Host inst:* Home Lang Intl
Dates: 1 wk-1 yr, yr-round
Subjects: Civilization/culture, Homestay, Spanish language (beg/int/adv)
Eligibility: *Level:* adults
Credit: *Undergrad:* avail *Grad:* avail *Doc:* transcript, certificate
Instruction: *In:* Spanish *Format:* lang study, lecture *Students:* intl
Costs: Contact sponsor
Housing: *Arr by pgm:* homestay
Deadline: 45 days before pgm
Other info: *US accredited sponsor:* no *Activities:* excursions *Misc:* May contact former participants. *URL:* http://www.linguaserviceworldwide.com
Contact: Dir, Lingua Svc Worldwide, 75 Prospect St, Ste 4, Huntington NY 11743 *Ph:* 800-394 5327; 631-424 0777 *Fax:* 631-271 3441 *E-mail:* itctravel@worldnet.att.net ▲

1912
LINGUATEC LANGUAGE CENTER
Learn Spanish in Chile
Site: Chile: Santiago (Providencia)
Dates: 2 wks or longer, yr-round
Subjects: Homestay, Spanish language (beg/int/adv)
Eligibility: *Level:* adults, precoll *Age:* min 16, avg 28
Credit: *Undergrad:* avail *Grad:* none *Doc:* certificate
Instruction: *In:* Spanish *Format:* lang study *Students:* intl
Costs: $420 per wk *incl* tuition, housing, some meals, excursions *Nonrefundable fee*
Housing: *Arr by pgm:* apartments, homestay, hotels
Deadline: 1 wk before pgm
Other info: *US accredited sponsor:* no *Began:* 1990 *Activities:* excursions *Misc:* May contact former participants. *URL:* http://www.linguatec.cl
Contact: Bill Arnold, Asst Dir, Linguatec Lang Ctr, Los Leones 439, Providencia, Santiago, Chile *Ph:* 303-777 7783 *Fax:* 303-777 7246 *E-mail:* barnold@linguatec.cl

---

1913
NATIONAL REGISTRATION CENTER FOR STUDY ABROAD (NRCSA)
Linguatec
Site: Chile: Santiago *Host inst:* Linguatec Lang Ctr
Dates: 1 wk or longer, yr-round
Subjects: Homestay, Spanish language (beg/int/adv)
Eligibility: *Level:* fresh, sophs, jrs, srs, grads, adults *Age:* min 18
Credit: *Undergrad:* avail *Grad:* avail
Instruction: *In:* Spanish *Format:* lang study, tutorial *Students:* intl
Costs: $1,153 for 2 wks, $1,881 for 4 wks *incl* tuition, housing, some meals, insurance
Housing: *Arr by pgm:* homestay
Deadline: Contact sponsor
Other info: *US accredited sponsor:* no *Orient:* abroad (intensive lang study) *URL:* http://www.nrcsa.com
Contact: June Domoe, NRCSA, 823 N 2nd St, #206, Milwaukee WI 53203 *Ph:* 414-278 0631 *Fax:* 414-271 8884 *E-mail:* info@nrcsa.com

---

VALPARAISO

1914
ISA
Cursos de Lengua y Cultura: Summer Program in Valparaiso
Site: Chile: Valparaiso *Host inst:* Univ Catolica de Valparaiso
Dates: 5 wks, May 24-Jun 29 or Jun 26-Jul 29
Subjects: Civilization/culture, Homestay, Literature, Political science/politics, Spanish language
Eligibility: *Level:* fresh, sophs, jrs, srs, grads, adults, teachers, professionals, precoll *Requires:* 2.5 GPA, previous study in field, 2 sems coll Spanish, recommendation letter *Age:* min 17, avg 23
Credit: *Undergrad:* 6 sem hrs *Grad:* none *Doc:* transcript, certificate
Instruction: *In:* Spanish *Format:* internship, lang study, lecture, volunteer/svc *Students:* mainly US
Costs: $3,200 *incl* tuition, housing, all meals, insurance, fees, excursions, tutorial, resident dir *Nonrefundable fee*
Housing: *Arr by pgm:* homestay
Deadline: Apr 5
Other info: *US accredited sponsor:* no *Began:* 1997 *Orient:* abroad (1 day) *Activities:* excursions, field trips, program travel, cultural events, sports *Misc:* May contact former participants. *Financial aid:* scholarships *URL:* http://www.studiesabroad.com
Contact: Gustavo Artaza, Intl Studies Abroad, 901 W 24th, Austin TX 78705 *Ph:* 800-580 8826; 512-480 8522 *Fax:* 512-480 8866 *E-mail:* isa@studiesabroad.com ▲

Costa Rica

MORE THAN ONE CITY

1915
AMERISPAN UNLIMITED
Spanish Study and Homestay in Costa Rica
Site: Costa Rica: Flamingo Beach, Alajuela, Heredia, Manuel Antonio, Monteverde, San Joaquin de Flores, San Jose *Host inst:* various insts
Dates: 1 wk-1 yr, yr-round
Subjects: Civilization/culture, Current events, Folk dance, History, Homestay, Literature, Music, Spanish language (beg/int/adv)
Eligibility: *Level:* fresh, sophs, jrs, srs, grads, adults, teachers, professionals, precoll *Age:* min 16
Credit: *Undergrad:* avail *Grad:* avail *Doc:* certificate *Transfer credit through:* Univ of Southern Mississippi
Instruction: *In:* Spanish *Format:* lang study, lecture, practical training, study tour, tutorial, workshop *Students:* intl
Costs: $625-$1,000 for 2 wks, $1,095-$1,625 for 4 wks, $245-$525 each addtl *incl* tuition, housing, some meals, insurance, books/materials
Housing: *Arr by pgm:* homestay, hotels
Deadline: 4 wks before pgm
Other info: *US accredited sponsor:* no *Orient:* abroad *Activities:* excursions, field trips, cultural events *Misc:* Transfer credit also avail through Seattle Central CC. May contact former participants. *Financial aid:* work study *URL:* http://www.amerispan.com/
Contact: AmeriSpan Unltd, PO Box 40007, Philadelphia PA 19106 *Ph:* 800-879 6640; 215-751 1100 *Fax:* 215-751 1986 *E-mail:* info@amerispan.com

---

1916
CENTRO PANAMERICANO DE IDIOMAS
Spanish Language Immersion Program
Site: Costa Rica: Flamingo Beach, Heredia, Monteverde Cloud Forest
Dates: 1 wk or longer, yr-round
Subjects: Adult education, Biology, Career development, Costa Rican studies, Ecology/environmental studies, Foreign language teaching, Homestay, Latin American studies, Medicine, Social welfare/services, Social work, Spanish language (beg/int/adv), Sports, Sustainable development, Third World studies
Eligibility: *Level:* fresh, sophs, jrs, srs, grads, adults, teachers, professionals, precoll
Credit: *Undergrad:* 3-12 *Grad:* none *Transfer credit through:* Univ of Southern of Mississippi
Instruction: *In:* Spanish *Format:* lang study, practical training, seminar, study tour, volunteer/svc, workshop *Students:* US & intl
Costs: Contact sponsor
Housing: *Arr by pgm:* apartments, homestay, pensions, hotels
Deadline: Rolling admissions
Other info: *US accredited sponsor:* no *Began:* 1990 *Orient:* abroad *Activities:* excursions, field trips, cultural events *Misc:* May contact former participants. *URL:* http://www.cpi-edu.com
Contact: Carlos Najarro, Mgr, CPI, PO Box 151-3007, San Joaquin de Flores, Heredia, Costa Rica *Ph:* 888-682 0054 *E-mail:* anajarro@racsa.co.cr
Or Contact: Jerae Bjelland, Rep, Portland OR *Ph:* 888-682 0054 *E-mail:* cpi_costarica@hotmail.com

---

1917
COSI (COSTA RICA SPANISH INSTITUTE)
Spanish Lessons
Site: Costa Rica: Manuel Antonio, Quepos, San Jose
Dates: 1 wk or longer, yr-round
Subjects: Spanish language (beg/int/adv)
Eligibility: *Level:* fresh, sophs, jrs, srs, grads, adults, teachers, professionals, precoll
Credit: *Undergrad:* avail *Grad:* avail *Doc:* certificate *Transfer credit through:* Univ of Mississippi
Instruction: *In:* English, Spanish *Format:* independent study, internship, lang study, practical training, study tour, tutorial, volunteer/svc *Students:* intl
Costs: $315 per wk *incl* tuition, housing, some meals, books/materials *Nonrefundable fee*
Housing: *Arr by pgm:* apartments, homestay, hotels
Deadline: None
Other info: *US accredited sponsor:* no *Began:* 1994 *In coop with:* Univ of MS *Orient:* abroad *Activities:* excursions *Misc:* May contact former participants. *URL:* http://www.cosi.co.cr
Contact: Marvin Lopez, Dir, COSI, PO Box 1366-2050, San Pedro, San Jose, Costa Rica 1366-2050 *Ph:* 800-771 5184 *E-mail:* office@cosi.co.cr

---

1918
COUNCIL ON INTERNATIONAL EDUCATIONAL EXCHANGE (COUNCIL)
International Faculty Development Seminars-Costa Rica
Site: Costa Rica: Monteverde, San Jose *Host inst:* Monteverde Inst
Dates: 12 days, Jun
Subjects: Costa Rican studies, Women's studies
Eligibility: *Level:* teachers, professionals *Requires:* must be faculty at 2-yr or 4-yr inst
Credit: *Undergrad:* none *Grad:* none
Instruction: *In:* English *Format:* lecture, seminar *Students:* mainly US
Costs: $1,800 *incl* tuition, housing, some meals, excursions, books/materials, ITIC, receptions *Nonrefundable fee*
Housing: *Arr by pgm:* hotels
Deadline: Mar 15
Other info: *US accredited sponsor:* no *Began:* 1997 *Orient:* abroad *Activities:* excursions, field trips, program travel, cultural events *Misc:* Seminar title: Costa Rica: Perspectives on Women in a Central American Society. May contact former participants. *URL:* http://www.ciee.org/ifds
Contact: Jennifer Ley, Dir, Council, 633 3rd Ave, New York NY 10017 *Ph:* 212-822 2747 *Fax:* 212-822 2779 *E-mail:* ifds@ciee.org ▲

1919
DUKE UNIVERSITY and **ORGANIZATION FOR TROPICAL STUDIES**
Summer Program in Costa Rica
Site: Costa Rica: various sites
Dates: 4 wks, late May-late Jun
Subjects: Ecology/environmental studies
Eligibility: *Level:* sophs, jrs, srs *Requires:* previous study in field, ; Spanish preferred
Credit: *Undergrad:* 1 *Grad:* none *Doc:* transcript
Instruction: *In:* English *Format:* directed field study, lab, lecture, seminar *Students:* mainly US
Costs: $4,300 per term *incl* tuition, housing, all meals, fees, excursions, books/materials
Housing: *Arr by pgm:* residence halls
Deadline: Feb 16
Other info: *US accredited sponsor:* yes *Began:* 1999 *Orient:* abroad (1 day) *Activities:* field trips, program travel *Misc:* Tropical ecology course. May contact former participants. *URL:* http://www.aas.duke.edu/Study_Abroad/
Contact: Organization for Tropical Studies, Duke Univ, Box 90633, Durham NC 27708-0633 *Ph:* 919-684 5774 *Fax:* 919-684 5661 *E-mail:* nao@acpub.duke.edu

---

1920
INDIANA UNIVERSITY
Tropical Biology in Costa Rica
Site: Costa Rica: various sites
Dates: 2 wks, late Dec-mid-Jan
Subjects: Biology
Eligibility: Own students only. *Level:* jrs, srs *Requires:* 3.0 GPA, previous study in field, biology major or significant coursework in biology
Credit: *Undergrad:* 3 *Grad:* none *Doc:* transcript
Instruction: *In:* English *Format:* directed field study *Students:* mainly US
Costs: $1,400 or $1,900 *incl* tuition, housing, all meals, insurance, fees, excursions *Nonrefundable fee*
Housing: *Arr by pgm:* hotels, field stations
Deadline: Early Oct
Other info: *US accredited sponsor:* yes *Began:* 1990 *Orient:* in US *Activities:* excursions, field trips *Misc:* May contact former participants. *URL:* http://www.indiana.edu/~overseas
Contact: Overseas Study, Indiana Univ, Franklin 303, Bloomington IN 47405 *Ph:* 812-855 9304 *Fax:* 812-855 6452 *E-mail:* overseas@indiana.edu

---

1921
INTERCULTURA LANGUAGE CENTER
Intensive Spanish Language and Culture Program
Site: Costa Rica: Heredia, Samara Beach
Dates: 1 wk-6 mos, yr-round
Subjects: Business language (int/adv), Civilization/culture, Latin American studies (adv), Literature (int/adv), Media studies (int/adv), Medicine (int/adv), Spanish language (beg/int/adv), Spanish studies, Technical language (int/adv)
Eligibility: *Level:* fresh, sophs, jrs, srs, grads, adults, teachers, professionals, precoll *Age:* min 18
Credit: *Undergrad:* 3-12 *Grad:* 3-6 *Doc:* transcript, certificate *Transfer credit through:* Univ of Southern Mississippi
Instruction: *In:* Spanish *Format:* lang study, seminar, volunteer/svc *Students:* intl
Costs: $1,150 per mo *incl* tuition, housing, some meals, fees, Latin dance, cooking, films
Housing: *Arr by pgm:* apartments, homestay, pensions, hotels
Deadline: 2 wks before pgm; 4 wks before pgm in summer
Other info: *US accredited sponsor:* yes *Began:* 1993 *Orient:* abroad (1 day, intensive lang study) *Activities:* excursions, field trips, cultural events *Misc:* Cultural activities are an integral part of the pgm. May contact former participants. *Financial aid:* work study *URL:* http://www.spanish-intercultura.com
Contact: Laura Ellington, Founding Dir, or Melvin Montero, Co-Dir, Intercultura Lang Ctr, Apdo 1952-3000, Heredia, Costa Rica *E-mail:* info@spanish-intercultura.com
Or Contact: Intercultura Beach Campus--Isla Chora, Samara Beach, Peninsula de Nicoya, Costa Rica *E-mail:* intercul@racsa.co.cr

---

1922
LANGUAGE LIAISON
Spanish Language-Costa Rica
Site: Costa Rica: Quepos, San Jose, Santa Ana
Dates: 2 wks or longer, yr-round
Subjects: Civilization/culture, Homestay, Independent study, Spanish language (beg/int/adv)
Eligibility: *Level:* fresh, sophs, jrs, srs, grads, adults, teachers, professionals, precoll *Age:* min 15
Credit: *Undergrad:* avail *Grad:* avail *Doc:* transcript, certificate

See "How To Use This Book" for definitions of terms used above. ▲ = See program sponsor's ad(s) in this book.

Instruction: *In:* Spanish *Format:* independent study, lang study, lecture, study tour *Students:* intl
Costs: Contact sponsor
Housing: *Arr by pgm:* apartments, homestay, hotels, on-campus lodging
Deadline: 30 days before pgm
Other info: *US accredited sponsor:* no *Activities:* excursions, cultural events *Misc:* Scholarship research svc. *URL:* http://www.languageliaison.com
Contact: Nancy Forman, Dir, Lang Liaison, 4 Burnham Pkwy, Morristown NJ 07960 *Ph:* 800-284 4448 *Fax:* 973-898 1710 *E-mail:* learn@languageliaison.com

---

1923
LATIN AMERICAN LANGUAGE CENTER
Community Volunteer Program
Site: Costa Rica: Heredia, San Antonio de Belen *Host inst:* Ctr Linguistico Latinamericano de Costa Rica
Dates: 2 wks or longer, yr-round
Subjects: Community service projects, Costa Rican studies, Education/teaching, Health care/hospitals, Homestay, Public health, Social welfare/services, TEFL/TESL
Eligibility: *Level:* fresh, sophs, jrs, srs, grads, adults, teachers, professionals, precoll *Requires:* min 2 wks of Spanish at Ctr Linguistico *Age:* min 18
Credit: *Undergrad:* avail *Grad:* avail *Doc:* certificate
Instruction: *In:* Spanish *Format:* lang study, volunteer/svc *Students:* intl
Costs: $345 per wk *incl* tuition, housing, all meals, fees, books/materials, airport transfer, laundry *Nonrefundable fee*
Housing: *Arr by pgm:* homestay
Deadline: 3 days before pgm
Other info: *US accredited sponsor:* no *Began:* 1995 *Orient:* abroad (intensive lang study) *Activities:* excursions, field trips, cultural events *Misc:* May contact former participants. *URL:* http://www.madre.com/n/a/c/lalc.html
Contact: Susan Shores, Registrar, or Randall Shores, Assoc Registrar, Latin Amer Lang Ctr, PMB 123, 7485 Rush River Dr, Ste 710, Sacramento CA 95831-5260 *Ph:* 916-447 0938 *Fax:* 916-428 9542 *E-mail:* lalc@madre.com

---

1924
MICHIGAN STATE UNIVERSITY
Environmental Studies
Site: Costa Rica: various sites
Dates: 3 wks, Dec-Jan
Subjects: Ecology/environmental studies, Field study, Natural sciences
Eligibility: *Level:* fresh, sophs, jrs, srs *Requires:* 2.0 GPA, good acad standing, physical fitness *Age:* min 18
Credit: *Undergrad:* 6 *Grad:* none *Doc:* transcript
Instruction: *In:* English *Format:* directed field study, seminar *Students:* mainly US
Costs: About $1,300 *incl* housing, insurance, excursions *Nonrefundable fee*
Housing: *Arr by pgm:* biological field station
Deadline: Oct 20
Other info: *US accredited sponsor:* yes *Began:* 1975 *Orient:* in US & abroad *Activities:* field trips *Misc:* Loans avail. *Financial aid:* scholarships *URL:* http://studyabroad.msu.edu
Contact: Cheryl Benner, Study Abroad, Michigan State Univ, 109 Intl Ctr, East Lansing MI 48824-1035 *Ph:* 517-353 8920 *Fax:* 517-432 2082 *E-mail:* bennerc@msu.edu ▲

1925
MICHIGAN STATE UNIVERSITY
Tropical Field Studies in Geographical Informational Systems
Site: Costa Rica: various sites
Dates: 3 wks, May
Subjects: Geography, Zoology
Eligibility: *Level:* fresh, sophs, jrs, srs *Requires:* 3.0 GPA, essay *Age:* min 18
Credit: *Undergrad:* 6 *Grad:* none *Doc:* transcript
Instruction: *In:* English *Format:* directed field study, independent study *Students:* mainly US
Costs: About $1,700 *incl* housing, some meals, insurance, fees, excursions *Nonrefundable fee*
Housing: *Arr by pgm:* field station
Deadline: Mar 2
Other info: *US accredited sponsor:* yes *Began:* 2000 *Orient:* in US (1 day) *Activities:* excursions, field trips, program travel *Financial aid:* scholarships *URL:* http://studyabroad.msu.edu
Contact: Cheryl Benner, Study Abroad, Michigan State Univ, 109 Intl Ctr, East Lansing MI 448824-1035 *Ph:* 517-353 8920 *Fax:* 517-432 2082 *E-mail:* bennerc@msu.edu ▲

1926
NATIONAL REGISTRATION CENTER FOR STUDY ABROAD (NRCSA)
Study in Costa Rica
Site: Costa Rica: San Jose, Santa Ana *Host inst:* Conversa Linguistico, Forester Inst Intl, INTENSA
Dates: 2 wks or longer, yr-round
Subjects: Civilization/culture, Costa Rican studies, Homestay, Humanities, Spanish language (beg/int/adv), Spanish studies
Eligibility: *Level:* fresh, sophs, jrs, srs, grads, adults *Age:* min 18
Credit: *Undergrad:* avail *Grad:* avail *Doc:* certificate
Instruction: *In:* Spanish *Format:* lang study, lecture *Students:* intl
Costs: Contact sponsor
Housing: *Arr by pgm:* apartments, homestay
Deadline: 6 wks before pgm
Other info: *US accredited sponsor:* no *Activities:* excursions, field trips *URL:* http://www.nrcsa.com
Contact: Reuel Zielke, NRCSA, 823 N 2nd St, #206, Milwaukee WI 53203 *Ph:* 414-278 0631 *Fax:* 414-271 8884 *E-mail:* info@nrcsa.com

---

1927
NORTH CAROLINA STATE UNIVERSITY
Ethnographic Field School
Site: Costa Rica: various sites
Dates: 5 wks, May 6-Jun 10
Subjects: Anthropology, Ethnography, Field study, Homestay, Tourism
Eligibility: *Level:* sophs, jrs, srs, grads, adults, teachers *Requires:* previous study in field, 2 sems coll Spanish, 2 courses in anthropology
Credit: *Undergrad:* 6 per pgm *Grad:* avail *Doc:* transcript
Instruction: *In:* English *Format:* directed field study, seminar *Students:* mainly US
Costs: $2,600 *incl* tuition, housing, all meals, insurance, fees, excursions *Nonrefundable fee*
Housing: *Arr by pgm:* homestay
Deadline: Feb
Other info: *US accredited sponsor:* yes *Began:* 1996 *Orient:* in US & abroad *Activities:* excursions *Misc:* Anthropology of sustainable tourism. May contact former participants. *URL:* http://www.ncsu.edu/studyabroad
Contact: Anne Haberkern, North Carolina State Univ, 2118 Pullen Hall, Box 7344, Raleigh NC 27695-7344 *Ph:* 919-515 2087 *Fax:* 919-515 6021 *E-mail:* study-abroad@ncsu.edu

---

1928
PENNSYLVANIA STATE UNIVERSITY
Tropical Field Ecology
Site: Costa Rica: various sites
Dates: 2 wks, Dec 27-Jan 10
Subjects: Biology, Ecology/environmental studies, Field study
Eligibility: *Level:* fresh, sophs, jrs, srs, grads, adults, teachers, professionals *Requires:* 2.5 GPA, previous study in field
Credit: *Undergrad:* 3 *Grad:* none
Instruction: *In:* English *Format:* directed field study, lecture, practical training *Students:* mainly US
Costs: Contact sponsor
Housing: *Arr by pgm:* cottages
Deadline: Sep 1
Other info: *US accredited sponsor:* yes

Began: 1989 *Orient:* in US *Activities:* excursions *Misc:* May contact former participants. *Financial aid:* scholarships *URL:* http://www.cde.psu.edu/PSSEA/
Contact: Roberta Moore, Conferences & Insts, Penn State Univ, University Park PA 16802 *Ph:* 814-863 5100 *Fax:* 814-863 5190 *E-mail:* conferenceinfo1@cde.psu.edu
Or Contact: Kristi Wormhoudt, Asst Dir, Educ Abroad Pgms, Penn State Univ, 222 Boucke Bldg, University Park PA 16802 *Ph:* 814-865 7681 *Fax:* 814-865 3336

1929
SCHOOL FOR FIELD STUDIES
Alternative Strategies for Sustaining Tropical Ecosystems
Site: Costa Rica: Alajuela, Atenas
Dates: 1 mo, mid-Jun-mid-Jul or mid-Jul-mid-Aug
Subjects: Agriculture, Biology, Botany, Conservation, Ecology/environmental studies, Economics, Field study, Forestry, Horticulture, Latin American studies, Natural resources
Eligibility: *Level:* fresh, sophs, jrs, srs, precoll *Age:* min 16, avg 20
Credit: *Undergrad:* avail *Grad:* none *Doc:* transcript *Transfer credit through:* Boston Univ
Instruction: *In:* English *Format:* directed field study, lecture, practical training, volunteer/svc *Students:* mainly US
Costs: $3,150 *incl* tuition, housing, all meals, excursions *Nonrefundable fee*
Housing: *Arr by pgm:* dormitory
Deadline: Rolling admissions
Other info: *US accredited sponsor:* no *Began:* 1980 *Orient:* abroad *Activities:* excursions, field trips, program travel, cultural events, sports *Misc:* Loans avail, Spanish lessons. May contact former participants. *Financial aid:* scholarships *URL:* http://www.fieldstudies.org
Contact: Admissions Off, Sch for Field Studies, 16 Broadway, Beverly MA 01915-4499 *Ph:* 800-989 4435; 978-927 7777 *Fax:* 978-927 5127
E-mail: admissions@fieldstudies.org

1930
SUNY COLLEGE AT OSWEGO
Wintersession in Costa Rica
Site: Costa Rica: various sites
Dates: 3 wks, Dec 28-Jan 13
Subjects: Anthropology, Business/management, Chemistry, Literature, Spanish studies
Eligibility: *Level:* jrs, srs *Requires:* 2.50 GPA
Credit: *Undergrad:* 3 *Grad:* none *Doc:* transcript
Instruction: *In:* English *Format:* directed field study *Students:* mainly US
Costs: $3,400 *incl* tuition, housing, all meals, intl airfare, insurance, fees, books/materials
Housing: *Arr by pgm:* hotels
Deadline: Oct 1
Other info: *US accredited sponsor:* yes *Orient:* in US & abroad *Activities:* program travel *Misc:* May contact former participants. *URL:* http://www.oswego.edu/~intled
Contact: Intl Educ, SUNY Oswego, 102 Rich Hall, Oswego NY 13126 *Ph:* 888-467 9346; 315-341 2118 *Fax:* 315-341 2477
E-mail: intled@oswego.edu

1931
UNIVERSITY OF DELAWARE
Winter Session in Costa Rica/ Entomology
Site: Costa Rica: Corcovada & La Selva rainforests, Monteverde cloud forest, Santa Rosa dry forest
Dates: 1 mo, Jan
Subjects: Entomology
Eligibility: *Level:* fresh, sophs, jrs, srs *Requires:* 2.0 GPA
Credit: *Undergrad:* 3 *Grad:* none *Doc:* transcript
Instruction: *In:* English *Format:* lecture, seminar, study tour *Students:* mainly US
Costs: Contact sponsor
Housing: *Arr by pgm:* pensions
Deadline: Early Oct
Other info: *US accredited sponsor:* yes *Began:* 1999 *Activities:* excursions, field trips *Misc:* Contact sponser to arrange honors credit. Pgm offered even-numbered years. *Financial aid:* scholarships *URL:* http://www.udel.edu/studyabroad/
Contact: Intl Pgms & Special Sessions, Univ of Delaware, 5 Kent Way, Newark DE 19716-1450 *Ph:* 888-831 4685; 302-831 2852 *Fax:* 302-831 6042 *E-mail:* studyabroad@udel.edu

---

1932
UNIVERSITY OF DELAWARE
Winter Session in Costa Rica-Department of Philosophy
Site: Costa Rica: Peninsula de Osa
Dates: 1 mo, Jan
Subjects: Field study, Philosophy
Eligibility: *Level:* fresh, sophs, jrs, srs *Requires:* 2.0 GPA
Credit: *Undergrad:* 6 *Grad:* none *Doc:* transcript
Instruction: *In:* English *Format:* directed field study, lecture, seminar, study tour *Students:* mainly US
Costs: Contact sponsor
Housing: *Arr by pgm:* residence halls
Deadline: Early Oct
Other info: *US accredited sponsor:* yes *Orient:* avail *Activities:* excursions, field trips, program travel, cultural events *Misc:* Contact sponsor to arrange honors credit. *Financial aid:* scholarships *URL:* http://www.udel.edu/studyabroad/
Contact: Intl Pgms, Univ of Delaware, 4 Kent Way, Newark DE 19716 *Ph:* 888-831 4685; 302-831 2852 *Fax:* 302-831 6042
E-mail: studyabroad@udel.edu

1933
VIRGINIA POLYTECHNIC INSTITUTE & STATE UNIVERSITY
Tropical Ecology
Site: Costa Rica: various sites
Dates: 6 wks, May 21-Jun 28
Subjects: Ecology/environmental studies, Sociology
Eligibility: *Level:* sophs, jrs, srs, grads *Requires:* 2.5 GPA, ecology study recommended *Age:* min 18, avg 20
Credit: *Undergrad:* 6 *Grad:* 6
Instruction: *In:* English *Format:* study tour *Students:* mainly US
Costs: $3,500 *incl* tuition, housing, all meals, intl airfare, insurance *Nonrefundable fee*
Housing: *Arr by pgm:* residence halls, hotels
Deadline: Jan 25
Other info: *US accredited sponsor:* yes *Began:* 1999 *Activities:* field trips *Misc:* Course begins with Appalachian culture, ends with Costa Rican culture. May contact former participants. *URL:* http://www.genbio.vt.edu/buikema/costarica/
Contact: Arthur Buikema, Virginia Tech, Biology 0406, Blacksburg VA 24061 *Ph:* 540-231 5180 *Fax:* 540-231 9307 *E-mail:* buik@vt.edu

---

CARTAGO

1934
IYOK AMI
Iyok Ami
Site: Costa Rica: Cartago
Dates: 1 mo, yr-round
Subjects: Cartography, Conservation, Forestry, Hiking/trekking, Homestay, Horticulture, Natural resource management, Ornithology, Social anthropology, Water management
Eligibility: *Level:* fresh *Requires:* good physical health *Age:* avg 20
Credit: *Undergrad:* none *Grad:* none
Instruction: *In:* Spanish *Format:* lang study, volunteer/svc *Students:* intl
Costs: $500 for volunteers (work-study), $650 for students *incl* tuition, housing, all meals, laundry
Housing: *Arr by pgm:* homestay, hostels
Deadline: None
Other info: *US accredited sponsor:* no *Began:* 1999 *Orient:* abroad (intensive lang study) *Activities:* field trips *Misc:* May

contact former participants. *URL:* http://www.ecotourism.co.cr/IyokAmi
Contact: Mauren Vargas, Iyok Ami, Apdo 335-2100, Guadalupe, Costa Rica *E-mail:* ciprotur@sol.racsa.co.cr

---

GOLFITO

1935
UNIVERSITY OF KANSAS
Tropical Studies in Golfito, Costa Rica
Site: Costa Rica: Golfito
Dates: 6 wks, Jun 1-Jul 15
Subjects: Anthropology, Biology, Field study, Homestay
Eligibility: *Level:* fresh, sophs, jrs, srs *Requires:* 2.5 GPA, 2 or 4 sems Spanish depending on course
Credit: *Undergrad:* 6-7 *Grad:* none *Doc:* transcript
Instruction: *In:* English, Spanish *Format:* directed field study, lecture *Students:* mainly US
Costs: $2,500 *incl* tuition, housing, some meals, fees, excursions, med evacuation svcs
Housing: *Arr by pgm:* homestay
Deadline: Mar 15
Other info: *US accredited sponsor:* yes *Began:* 1998 *Activities:* excursions, field trips *URL:* http://www.ukans.edu/~osa
Contact: Amy Timkar, Pgm Coord, Study Abroad, Univ of Kansas, 108 Lippincott Hall, Lawrence KS 66045 *Ph:* 785-864 3742 *Fax:* 785-864 5040 *E-mail:* osa@ukans.edu ▲

HEREDIA

1936
LANGUAGE LINK
Spanish Study in Costa Rica
Site: Costa Rica: Heredia *Host inst:* Intercultura Lang Ctr
Dates: 1-16 wks, yr-round
Subjects: Civilization/culture, Latin American studies, Literature, Spanish language
Eligibility: *Level:* fresh, sophs, jrs, srs, grads, adults, teachers, professionals, precoll *Age:* min 17
Credit: *Undergrad:* 12 *Grad:* 6 *Doc:* transcript
Instruction: *In:* Spanish *Format:* lang study, tutorial, volunteer/svc *Students:* intl
Costs: $345 per wk *incl* tuition, housing, some meals, insurance, books/materials, airport transfer *Nonrefundable fee*
Housing: *Arr by pgm:* homestay
Deadline: None
Other info: *US accredited sponsor:* no *Began:* 1994 *In coop with:* Austin Peay State University *Orient:* abroad *Activities:* excursions, field trips, program travel, cultural events *Misc:* Optional 1-wk beach campus. May contact former participants. *URL:* http://www.langlink.com
Contact: Kay Rafool, Dir, Lang Link, PO Box 3006, Peoria IL 61612-3006 *Ph:* 800-552 2051; 309-692 2961 *Fax:* 309-692 2926 *E-mail:* info@langlink.com

---

1937
UNIVERSITY STUDIES ABROAD CONSORTIUM
Spanish and Latin American Studies
Site: Costa Rica: Heredia *Host inst:* Natl Univ of Costa Rica
Dates: May 27-Jun 30, Jun 25-Jul 28 and/or Jul 29-Aug 25
Subjects: Biology, Civilization/culture, Economics, History, Homestay, Literature, Political science/politics, Spanish language (beg/int/adv)
Eligibility: *Level:* fresh, sophs, jrs, srs, grads, adults, teachers, professionals *Requires:* 2.5 GPA *Age:* min 18, avg 21
Credit: *Undergrad:* 5 per session *Grad:* 5 per session *Doc:* transcript
Instruction: *In:* English, Spanish *Format:* lang study, lecture *Students:* US & intl
Costs: $1,980 Jun or Jul, $1,610 Aug, $3,190-$3,680 for 2 mos, $4,680 for all *incl* tuition, housing, insurance, fees, excursions, ISIC
Housing: *Arr by pgm:* homestay
Deadline: Apr 15
Other info: *US accredited sponsor:* yes *Began:* 1995 *Orient:* abroad (intensive lang study) *Activities:* excursions, field trips, program travel, cultural events *Misc:* Pgm organized flights. May contact former participants. *URL:* http://www.usac.unr.edu
Contact: *See Index II for Members*
Carmelo Urza, Univ Studies Abroad Consortium, Univ of Nevada Library 323, Reno NV 89557-0093 *Ph:* 775-784 6569 *Fax:* 775-784 6010 *E-mail:* usac@unr.edu
▲

1938
WORLDSTUDY
Spanish in Costa Rica
Site: Costa Rica: Heredia *Host inst:* Intercultura Lang Ctr
Dates: 4 wks or longer, May-Aug; 5 wks, Dec 16-Jan 21
Subjects: Business language, Literature, Spanish language (beg/int/adv), Technical language
Eligibility: *Level:* sophs, jrs, srs, grads, adults, teachers, professionals *Requires:* recommendation letter *Age:* min 18
Credit: *Undergrad:* none *Grad:* none *Doc:* certificate *Transfer credit through:* Univ of Southern Mississippi
Instruction: *In:* Spanish *Format:* lang study *Students:* intl
Costs: $1,670 for 4 wks, $330 for each addl wk *incl* tuition, housing, all meals, airport transfer, orient, ISIC *Nonrefundable fee*
Housing: *Arr by pgm:* homestay
Deadline: 1 mo before pgm
Other info: *US accredited sponsor:* no *Began:* 1994 *Orient:* abroad *Activities:* excursions, field trips, cultural events *Misc:* 4-6 students per teacher. Latin American dance, music & cooking lessons. May contact former participants. *Financial aid:* scholarships *URL:* http://ourworld.compuserve.com/homepages
Contact: Margarita Tonkinson, Exec Dir, WorldStudy, 9841 SW 73rd Ct, Miami FL 33156 *Ph:* 800-780 1095; 305-665 5004 *Fax:* 305-665 7085 *E-mail:* worldstudy@compuserve.com

---

LIMON

1939
RUTGERS UNIVERSITY
Rutgers Summer Study and Service in Costa Rica
Site: Costa Rica: Limon
Dates: Late May-early Jul
Subjects: Caribbean studies, Community service projects, Education/teaching
Eligibility: *Level:* fresh, sophs, jrs *Requires:* 2.5 GPA, recommendation letter
Credit: *Undergrad:* 6 *Grad:* none *Doc:* transcript
Instruction: *In:* English *Format:* seminar, student teaching, volunteer/svc *Students:* mainly US
Costs: $2,572 for NJ residents, $3,322 for others *incl* tuition, housing, insurance, fees
Housing: *Arr by pgm:* conference ctr
Deadline: Mar 1
Other info: *US accredited sponsor:* yes *Began:* 1994 *Orient:* in US *Activities:* excursions *URL:* http://studyabroad.rutgers.edu
Contact: Dir, Study Abroad, Rutgers Univ, 102 College Ave, New Brunswick NJ 08901 *Ph:* 732-932 7787 *Fax:* 732-932 8659 *E-mail:* ru_abroad@email.rutgers.edu
Or Contact: Melanie Andrich, Pgm Coord, Study Abroad, Rutgers Univ, 102 College Ave, New Brunswick NJ 08901 *Ph:* 732-932 7787 *Fax:* 732-932 8659 *E-mail:* mandrich@rci.rutgers.edu

---

MANUEL ANTONIO BEACH

1940
NATIONAL REGISTRATION CENTER FOR STUDY ABROAD (NRCSA)
Escuela de Idiomes d'Amore
Site: Costa Rica: Manuel Antonio Beach *Host inst:* Escuela de Idiomas d'Amore
Dates: 2 wks or longer, yr-round
Subjects: Homestay, Spanish language (beg/int/adv)
Eligibility: *Level:* fresh, sophs, jrs, srs, grads, adults, teachers, professionals
Credit: *Undergrad:* avail *Grad:* avail
Instruction: *In:* Spanish *Format:* lang study, lecture *Students:* intl
Costs: $1,048 for 2 wks *incl* tuition, housing, some meals, insurance *Nonrefundable fee*
Housing: *Arr by pgm:* homestay, hotels
Deadline: 6 wks before pgm
Other info: *US accredited sponsor:* no *Activities:* field trips *Misc:* May contact former participants. *URL:* http://www.nrcsa.com
Contact: June Domoe, NRCSA, 823 N 2nd St, #206, Milwaukee WI 53203 *Ph:* 414-278 0631 *Fax:* 414-271 8884 *E-mail:* info@nrcsa.com

---

MANUEL ANTONIO

1941
LANGUAGE STUDIES ABROAD, INC
General Spanish-Costa Rica
Site: Costa Rica: Manuel Antonio *Host inst:* LSA Manuel Antonio
Dates: 2 wks-6 mos, yr-round
Subjects: Homestay, Spanish language
Eligibility: *Level:* adults *Age:* min 18
Credit: *Undergrad:* avail *Grad:* none
Instruction: *In:* Spanish *Format:* lang study *Students:* intl
Costs: $1,590 for 4 wks *incl* tuition, housing, some meals, excursions
Housing: *Arr by pgm:* homestay, pensions, hotels, hostels
Deadline: 4 wks before pgm
Other info: *US accredited sponsor:* no *Began:* 1992 *Orient:* abroad *Activities:* excursions, sports *Misc:* May contact former participants. *URL:* http://www.languagestudiesabroad.com
Contact: Chris Cote or Dena Parkerson, Lang Studies Abroad, Inc, 103 Londonderry Ct, Reno NV 89511 *Ph:* 800-424 5522; 775-849 9206 *Fax:* 775-849 9217 *E-mail:* info@languagestudiesabroad.com

---

MONTEVERDE

1942
COUNCIL ON INTERNATIONAL EDUCATIONAL EXCHANGE CONSORTIUM
Council Study Center in Monteverde, Costa Rica
Site: Costa Rica: Monteverde *Host inst:* Monteverde Inst
Dates: Mid-Jun-mid-Aug
Subjects: Agronomy, Biology, Conservation, Ecology/environmental studies, Field study, Homestay, Independent study, Spanish language
Eligibility: *Level:* sophs, jrs, srs *Requires:* 2.75 GPA, 1 sem coll biology & 1 sem ecology or environmental studies

Credit: *Undergrad:* 10 *Grad:* none *Doc:* transcript
Instruction: *In:* English, Spanish *Format:* directed field study, independent study, lang study, lecture *Students:* mainly US
Costs: $4,300 *incl* tuition, housing, all meals, insurance, fees, excursions, ISIC
Housing: *Arr by pgm:* homestay, field station
Deadline: Apr 1
Other info: *US accredited sponsor:* yes *Began:* 1988 *Orient:* avail in San Jose *Activities:* excursions, field trips, program travel *Misc:* Full-time resident dir. May contact former participants. *Financial aid:* scholarships *URL:* http://www.ciee.org/study
Contact: *See Index II for Members* Latin Amer Pgm Adviser, Council-ISP, 633 3rd Ave 20th Fl, New York NY 10017 *Ph:* 800-408 839; 212-822 2600 *Fax:* 212-822 2779 *E-mail:* studyinfo@ciee.org

---

1943
GLOBAL SERVICE CORPS
Costa Rica Eco-Service Project
Site: Costa Rica: Monteverde Cloud Forest Preserve *Host inst:* Monteverde Conservation League, Monteverde Inst
Dates: 2 wks or longer, yr-round
Subjects: Civilization/culture, Development studies, Ecology/environmental studies
Eligibility: *Level:* fresh, sophs, jrs, srs, grads, adults, teachers, professionals *Requires:* good health, proper immunizations, travel insurance, int Spanish for long-term placements *Age:* min 20, avg 25
Credit: *Undergrad:* avail *Grad:* avail
Instruction: *In:* English *Format:* directed field study, independent study, internship, practical training, study tour, volunteer/svc *Students:* US & intl
Costs: $1,695 for 17 days, $495 for each addtl mo *incl* housing, all meals
Housing: *Arr by pgm:* residence halls, homestay, hotels
Deadline: 90 days before pgm
Other info: *US accredited sponsor:* no *Began:* 1993 *In coop with:* Earth Island Inst *Orient:* abroad & pre-trip material *Activities:* excursions, field trips, cultural events *URL:* http://www.globalservicecorps.org
Contact: Rick Lathrop, Exec Dir, or Costa Rica Project Coord, Global Svc Corps, 300 Broadway, Ste 28, San Francisco CA 94133 *Ph:* 415-788 3666 ext 128 *Fax:* 415-788 7324 *E-mail:* gsc@igc.apc.org

---

1944
MONTEVERDE STUDIOS OF THE ARTS
Monteverde Studios of the Arts
Site: Costa Rica: Monteverde
Dates: Jan 17-Aug 11
Subjects: Art, Ceramics/pottery, Crafts, Culinary arts, Drawing, Health/health education, Homestay, Jewelry/jewelry-making, Musical instrument making, Painting, Papermaking, Stained glass, Textiles, Woodworking, Yoga
Eligibility: *Level:* adults, precoll
Credit: *Undergrad:* none *Grad:* none
Instruction: *In:* Spanish *Format:* art studio *Students:* mainly US
Costs: $485-$560 per wk *incl* tuition, housing, some meals *Nonrefundable fee*
Housing: *Arr by pgm:* homestay, hotels
Deadline: None
Other info: *US accredited sponsor:* no *Began:* 1998 *Orient:* abroad *Misc:* May contact former participants. *URL:* http://www.mvstudios.com
Contact: Sybil Terres Gilmar, Monteverde Studios of the Arts, PO Box 766, Monteverde, Costa Rica *Ph:* 800-370 3331; 610-664 4045 *Fax:* 610-664 2437 *E-mail:* mstudios@pop.racsa.co.cr

---

SAN ANTONIO DE BELEN

1945
LATIN AMERICAN LANGUAGE CENTER
Spanish Language Immersion with Homestay
Site: Costa Rica: San Antonio de Belen *Host inst:* Ctr Linguistico Latinoamericano de Costa Rica
Dates: 1 wk or longer, yr-round
Subjects: Community service projects, Homestay, Spanish language (beg/int/adv)
Eligibility: *Level:* adults, precoll *Age:* min 14
Credit: *Undergrad:* avail *Grad:* avail *Doc:* certificate
Instruction: *In:* Spanish *Format:* lang study, practical training, volunteer/svc *Students:* US & intl
Costs: $345 per wk *incl* tuition, housing, all meals, fees, excursions, airport transfer, activities *Nonrefundable fee*
Housing: *Arr by pgm:* homestay, apartotel
Deadline: 30 days before pgm; $25 late registration fee
Other info: *US accredited sponsor:* no *Began:* 1982 *Orient:* abroad (intensive lang study) *Activities:* excursions, field trips, cultural events *Misc:* Students under 18 must be accompanied by an adult. May contact former participants. *URL:* http://www.madre.com/~lalc/lalc.html
Contact: Susan Shores, Registrar, or Randall Shores, Assoc Registrar, Latin Amer Lang Ctr, PMB 123, 7485 Rush River Dr, Ste 710, Sacramento CA 95831-5260 *Ph:* 916-447 0938 *Fax:* 916-428 9542 *E-mail:* lalc@madre.com

---

SAN CARLOS

1946
KENTUCKY INSTITUTE FOR INTERNATIONAL STUDIES (KIIS)
Costa Rica
Site: Costa Rica: San Carlos
Dates: Jun 16-Jul 6
Subjects: Costa Rican studies, Education/teaching
Eligibility: *Level:* teachers *Requires:* 2.0 GPA, previous study in field *Age:* min 18
Credit: *Undergrad:* 3 *Grad:* 3 *Doc:* transcript *Transfer credit through:* Murray State Univ
Instruction: *In:* English *Format:* directed field study, lecture, study tour *Students:* mainly US
Costs: About $1,980 *incl* tuition, housing, some meals, intl airfare, excursions, ISIC *Nonrefundable fee*
Housing: *Arr by pgm:* residence halls
Deadline: Feb 15 ($100 late fee); Mar 15 for scholarships
Other info: *US accredited sponsor:* yes *Began:* 2000 *In coop with:* Inst Tecnologico de Costa Rica *Orient:* in US & abroad *Activities:* excursions, field trips *Misc:* Topic: The Schs of Costa Rica: A Comparative Perspective. May contact former participants. *Financial aid:* scholarships *URL:* http://www.kiis.org
Contact: *See Index II for Members* Dr J Milton Grimes, Exec Dir, KIIS, Murray State Univ, PO Box 9, Murray KY 42071 *Ph:* 270-762 3091 *Fax:* 270-762 3434 *E-mail:* kiismsu@murraystate.edu

---

SAN JOSE

1947
ASESORIA GERENCIAL, S A
International Career Enhancement Program
Site: Costa Rica: San Jose
Dates: 4, 8 or 12 wks, Jun-Aug
Subjects: Field study, History, Homestay, Independent study, Internships, Spanish language (beg/int/adv)
Eligibility: *Level:* jrs, srs, grads, adults, teachers, professionals *Requires:* 3.0 GPA, previous study in field *Age:* min 20, avg 24
Credit: *Undergrad:* none *Grad:* none *Doc:* certificate
Instruction: *In:* English, Spanish *Format:* directed field study, independent study,

internship, lang study, lecture, practical training, seminar, tutorial, volunteer/svc *Students:* mainly US
Costs: $2,500 for 8 wks, $3,700 for 12 wks *incl* tuition, housing, all meals, fees, excursions *Nonrefundable fee*
Housing: *Arr by pgm:* homestay
Deadline: 6 wks before pgm
Other info: *US accredited sponsor:* no *Began:* 1985 *Orient:* abroad (2 days) *Activities:* excursions, field trips, cultural events *Misc:* Internship option avail for 8- & 12-wk pgms only. May contact former participants. *URL:* http://www.studyabroad.com/asesoria
Contact: Marielos Calvo or Maria Hernandez, Pgm Dirs, Asesoria Gerencial SA, Apdo 1379, San Jose 1100, Costa Rica *E-mail:* agsamac@sol.racsa.co.cr

---

1948
CENTRO CULTURAL COSTARRICENSE-NORTEAMERICANO
Spanish for Foreigners
Site: Costa Rica: San Jose
Dates: mulitple pgm lengths yr-round
Subjects: Homestay, Spanish language (beg/int/adv)
Eligibility: *Level:* fresh, sophs, jrs, srs, grads, adults
Credit: *Undergrad:* none *Grad:* avail *Doc:* transcript, certificate
Instruction: *In:* Spanish *Format:* lang study, lecture, student teaching, tutorial *Students:* intl
Costs: $1,500 per mo *incl* tuition, housing, all meals, intl airfare, fees, books/materials
Housing: *Arr by pgm:* homestay, hotels
Deadline: 1 mo before pgm
Other info: *US accredited sponsor:* no *Orient:* abroad (1 day, intensive lang study) *Activities:* excursions, field trips, program travel, cultural events *Misc:* 1-on-1 tutorials avail. May contact former participants. *URL:* http://www.cccncr.com
Contact: Alonso Murillo, Ctr Cultural, PO Box 1489-1000, San Jose, Costa Rica *Ph:* 506-207 7521 *Fax:* 506-224 1480 *E-mail:* acccnort@sol.racsa.co.cr

---

1949
CENTRO LINGUISTICO CONVERSA
Intensive Spanish in San Jose
Site: Costa Rica: San Jose
Dates: 2-12 wks, yr-round
Subjects: Languages, Literature, Spanish language (beg/int/adv)
Eligibility: *Level:* adults *Age:* min 7, avg 25
Credit: *Undergrad:* avail *Grad:* none *Doc:* transcript *Transfer credit through:* Miami-Dade CC
Instruction: *In:* Spanish *Format:* lang study *Students:* mainly US
Costs: $1,500 per mo for Intensive, $1,800 per mo Super Intensive *incl* tuition, housing, most meals, books/materials *Nonrefundable fee*
Housing: *Arr by pgm:* homestay
Deadline: None
Other info: *US accredited sponsor:* no *In coop with:* Miami-Dade CC, Truman State Univ *Orient:* abroad *Activities:* excursions, field trips *Misc:* May contact former participants. *URL:* http://www.conversa.net
Contact: David Kaufman, Dir, Ctr Linguistico Conversa, Apdo 17, 1007 Centro Colon, Costa Rica *Ph:* 800-367 7726 *E-mail:* conversa@sol.racsa.co.cr
Or Contact: Dr Sherman Thomas, USA Conversa Rep, 30601 Lower Valley Rd, Bear Valley Springs CA 93561 *Ph:* 800-354 5036; 661-821 1607 *Fax:* 661-821 0379 *E-mail:* thomashouse@thegrid.net

---

1950
COLLEGE CONSORTIUM FOR INTERNATIONAL STUDIES and **MIAMI-DADE COMMUNITY COLLEGE** and **TRUMAN STATE UNIVERSITY**
Intensive Spanish in Costa Rica
Site: Costa Rica: San Jose *Host inst:* Ctr Linguistico Conversa
Dates: 1 mo or longer, yr-round
Subjects: Spanish language
Eligibility: *Level:* fresh, sophs, jrs, srs, grads, adults, teachers, professionals *Requires:* 2.5 GPA *Age:* min 18
Credit: *Undergrad:* 6 per mo *Grad:* none *Doc:* transcript
Instruction: *In:* English, Spanish *Format:* lang study *Students:* mainly US
Costs: $1,464 per mo *incl* tuition, housing, some meals, books/materials *Nonrefundable fee*
Housing: *Arr by pgm:* apartments, homestay
Deadline: Rolling admissions
Other info: *US accredited sponsor:* yes *Began:* 1973 *Orient:* abroad (1 day) *URL:* http://www.ccisabroad.org
Contact: *See Index II for Members* CCIS, 2000 P St NW, Ste 503, Washington DC 20036 *Ph:* 800-453 6956; 202-223 0330 *Fax:* 202-223 0999 *E-mail:* info@ccisabroad.org
Or Contact: Reinaldo Changsut, Study Abroad, Miami-Dade CC, 11011 SW 104th St, Miami FL 33176-3393 *Ph:* 305-237 2535 *Fax:* 305-237 2949 *E-mail:* rchangsu@mdcc.edu ▲

1951
COLLEGE CONSORTIUM FOR INTERNATIONAL STUDIES and **MIAMI-DADE COMMUNITY COLLEGE** and **TRUMAN STATE UNIVERSITY**
Veritas Summer Program in San Jose, Costa Rica
Site: Costa Rica: San Jose *Host inst:* Univ Veritas
Dates: 5-7 wks, early Jul-late Aug
Subjects: Ecology/environmental studies, Homestay, Literature, Spanish language
Eligibility: *Level:* fresh, sophs, jrs, srs, grads, adults, teachers, professionals *Requires:* 2.5 GPA *Age:* min 18
Credit: *Undergrad:* 11-12 *Grad:* none
Instruction: *In:* English, Spanish *Format:* lang study, lecture *Students:* mainly US
Costs: About $2,500 for 5 wks *incl* tuition, housing, some meals, excursions, books/materials
Housing: *Arr by pgm:* homestay
Deadline: Jun 1
Other info: *US accredited sponsor:* yes *Began:* 1996 *Orient:* abroad (1 day) *Activities:* excursions, field trips *URL:* http://www.ccisabroad.org
Contact: *See Index II for Members* CCIS, 2000 P St NW, Ste 503, Washington DC 20036 *Ph:* 800-453 6956; 202-223 0330 *Fax:* 202-223 0999 *E-mail:* info@ccisabroad.org
Or Contact: Dr Robert Vitale or Reinaldo Changsut, Study Abroad, Miami-Dade CC, 11011 SW 104th St, Miami FL 33176-3393 *Ph:* 305-237 2533, 305-237 2535 *Fax:* 305-237 2949 *E-mail:* rchangsu@mdcc.edu ▲

1952
COMPTON COMMUNITY COLLEGE
Summer Study Abroad
Site: Costa Rica: San Jose *Host inst:* Inst Universal de Idiomas
Dates: 4 wks, Jun 30-Jul 28
Subjects: Civilization/culture, Homestay, Spanish language (beg/int/adv), Spanish studies
Eligibility: *Level:* fresh, sophs, jrs, srs, grads, adults *Age:* min 17
Credit: *Undergrad:* 2-9 *Grad:* none *Doc:* certificate
Instruction: *In:* Spanish *Format:* independent study, lang study, lecture, study tour *Students:* mainly US
Costs: $1,790 *incl* tuition, housing, some meals, intl airfare, fees, excursions, books/materials, transport at San Jose airport *Nonrefundable fee*
Housing: *Arr by pgm:* homestay
Deadline: May 18 or until pgm filled
Other info: *US accredited sponsor:* yes *Began:* 1974 *Orient:* in US & abroad *Activities:* excursions *Misc:* May contact former participants. *URL:* http://www.compton.cc.ca.us

Contact: Study Abroad Coord, Compton CC, 1111 E Artesia Blvd, Compton CA 90221-5393 *Ph:* 310-900 1600 ext2545 *Fax:* 310-900 1697

1953
CSA, CENTER FOR STUDY ABROAD
INTENSA-Spanish Language Studies
Site: Costa Rica: San Jose *Host inst:* INTENSA
Dates: 1 wk or longer, yr-round
Subjects: Homestay, Spanish language
Eligibility: *Level:* adults *Age:* min 17
Credit: *Undergrad:* avail *Grad:* avail *Doc:* transcript, certificate
Instruction: *In:* Spanish *Format:* lang study *Students:* intl
Costs: $600 per wk *incl* tuition, housing, all meals, insurance, fees, books/materials *Nonrefundable fee*
Housing: *Sponsor assists:* homestay, hotels
Deadline: None
Other info: *US accredited sponsor:* no *Orient:* abroad *Activities:* excursions, field trips, program travel, cultural events, sports *URL:* http://www.studyabroad.com/csa
Contact: Alima Khan, Assoc Dir, CSA, Ctr for Study Abroad, 2802 E Madison St, MS #160, Seattle WA 98112 *Ph:* 206-726 1498 *Fax:* 206-583 8192 *E-mail:* virtuecsa@aol.com

---

1954
CULTURAL EXPERIENCES ABROAD (CEA)
Study Spanish Language, Ecology and Latin American Studies
Site: Costa Rica: San Jose *Host inst:* Veritas Univ
Dates: 4 wks, Jun-Aug
Subjects: Costa Rican studies, Ecology/environmental studies, Homestay, Independent study, International relations, Latin American studies, Literature, Marine biology, Spanish language (beg/int/adv)
Eligibility: *Level:* fresh, sophs, jrs, srs, grads, precoll *Requires:* 2.7 GPA, previous Spanish lang study recommended *Age:* min 17, avg 20
Credit: *Undergrad:* 4-5 per term *Grad:* avail *Doc:* transcript, certificate
Instruction: *In:* English, Spanish *Format:* independent study, lang study, lecture, study tour, tutorial, volunteer/svc *Students:* intl
Costs: $2,495-$2,695 per 4-wk session *incl* tuition, housing, most meals, insurance, fees, excursions, orient, airport transfers *Nonrefundable fee*
Housing: *Arr by pgm:* homestay
Deadline: Rolling admissions
Other info: *US accredited sponsor:* no *Orient:* abroad *Activities:* excursions, field trips, program travel, cultural events, sports *Misc:* E-mail. On-site dir. May contact former participants. *Financial aid:* scholarships *URL:* http://www.travelabroad.com
Contact: CEA Study Abroad, 1400 E Southern Ave, Ste B-108 AZ 85282-8011 *Ph:* 480-557 7900 *Fax:* 480-557 7926 *E-mail:* costarica@travelabroad.com

---

1955
FAIRFIELD UNIVERSITY
International Environmental Management and Policy
Site: Costa Rica: San Jose
Dates: 3 wks, about Dec 27-Jan 16
Subjects: Ecology/environmental studies, Environmental law
Eligibility: *Level:* sophs, jrs, srs, grads, adults, teachers, professionals *Requires:* 2.5 GPA, recommendation letters *Age:* min 18, avg 20
Credit: *Undergrad:* 3 *Grad:* none *Doc:* transcript
Instruction: *In:* English *Format:* directed field study, lecture, study tour *Students:* mainly US
Costs: About $2,600 *incl* tuition, housing, some meals, intl airfare, excursions
Housing: *Arr by pgm:* homestay
Deadline: Oct 1 or until pgm filled
Other info: *US accredited sponsor:* yes *Began:* 1998 *In coop with:* Costa Rican Lang Acad *Orient:* avail avail *Activities:* field trips, cultural events *Misc:* May contact former participants. *URL:* http://www.fairfield.edu/sce/studyabroad
Contact: Christine Bowers, Study Abroad Coord, Fairfield Univ, Dolan House, Fairfield CT 06430 *Ph:* 888-254 1566; 203-254 4220 *Fax:* 203-254 4106 *E-mail:* cbbowers@fair1.fairfield.edu

---

1956
FLORIDA STATE UNIVERSITY
FSU/Costa Rica Summer Program
Site: Costa Rica: San Jose *Host inst:* Univ de Costa Rica
Dates: 6 wks, Jun 22-Aug 3
Subjects: Business/management, History, Political science/politics, Spanish language
Eligibility: *Level:* sophs, jrs, srs *Requires:* 2.5 GPA, 2 terms coll Spanish
Credit: *Undergrad:* 10 *Grad:* none
Instruction: *In:* English, Spanish *Format:* lang study, lecture *Students:* mainly US
Costs: $3,295 *incl* housing, some meals, intl airfare, insurance, fees, excursions, ISIC
Housing: *Arr by pgm:* homestay
Deadline: Jan 19
Other info: *US accredited sponsor:* yes *Began:* 1980 *Orient:* abroad *Activities:* excursions *URL:* http://www.international.fsu.edu
Contact: Bonnie Snyder, Costa Rica Pgm, Florida State Univ, 5500 UCA, Tallahassee FL 32306-2420 *Ph:* 800-374 8581; 850-644 3272 *Fax:* 850-644 8817 *E-mail:* intprog@www.fsu.edu

---

1957
FORESTER INSTITUTO INTERNACIONAL
Spanish Language Courses
Site: Costa Rica: San Jose
Dates: 1 wk or longer, yr-round
Subjects: Homestay, Spanish language (beg/int/adv)
Eligibility: *Level:* adults, teachers, professionals, precoll *Age:* min 14
Credit: *Undergrad:* avail *Grad:* avail *Doc:* certificate *Transfer credit through:* Univ of Connecticut
Instruction: *In:* Spanish *Format:* lang study, lecture *Students:* intl
Costs: $140 per wk *incl* tuition, books/materials
Housing: *Arr by pgm:* homestay
Deadline: None
Other info: *US accredited sponsor:* no *Began:* 1979 *Orient:* abroad *Activities:* excursions, field trips, cultural events *Misc:* May contact former participants. *URL:* http://www.fores.com
Contact: Horacio Loprete, Forester Inst Intl, Los Yoses, del Automercado, 75m Sur, San Jose, Costa Rica *E-mail:* forester@sol.racsa.co.cr

---

1958
GEORGIA INSTITUTE OF TECHNOLOGY
Costa Rica Study Abroad
Site: Costa Rica: San Jose *Host inst:* Univ de Costa Rica
Dates: May 27-Jul 7
Subjects: Ecology/environmental studies, Field study, Homestay, Political science/politics
Eligibility: *Level:* fresh, sophs, jrs, srs, grads *Requires:* 2.5 GPA *Age:* min 18
Credit: *Undergrad:* 6 *Grad:* 6 *Doc:* transcript
Instruction: *In:* English *Format:* directed field study, lecture, seminar *Students:* mainly US
Costs: $3,095 for GA resident, $3,345 for others *incl* tuition, housing, some meals, fees, excursions
Housing: *Sponsor assists:* homestay
Deadline: Feb 1
Other info: *US accredited sponsor:* yes *Began:* 2000 *Orient:* abroad (1 day) *Activities:* excursions, field trips, program travel, cultural events, sports *Misc:* Next pgm offered summer 2002. May contact former participants.

Contact: Kirk Bowman, Georgia Inst of Technology, Intl Affairs 0610, 781 Marietta St NW, Atlanta GA 30332-0610 *Ph:* 404-894 6435 *Fax:* 404-894 1900 *E-mail:* kirk.bowman@inta.gatech.edu

---

1959
IPEE SPANISH LANGUAGE SCHOOL
Intensive Spanish Language Course
Site: Costa Rica: San Jose
Dates: 1 wk-3 mos, yr-round
Subjects: Homestay, Spanish language (beg/int/adv)
Eligibility: *Level:* fresh, sophs, jrs, srs, grads, adults, teachers, professionals, precoll *Age:* min 15
Credit: *Undergrad:* avail *Grad:* avail *Doc:* transcript, certificate
Instruction: *In:* Spanish *Format:* lang study *Students:* intl
Costs: Contact sponsor
Housing: *Arr by pgm:* apartments, homestay, hotels
Deadline: Contact sponsor
Other info: *US accredited sponsor:* no *Began:* 1994 *Orient:* abroad (1 day, intensive lang study) *Activities:* excursions, field trips, cultural events *Misc:* May contact former participants. *Financial aid:* scholarships *URL:* http://www.ipee.com
Contact: Robert Levy, Dir, IPEE Spanish Lang Sch, 1112 Estatewood Dr, Brandon FL 33510 *Ph:* 813-643 0416 *Fax:* 813-643 0416 *E-mail:* ipee@gate.net

---

1960
IPEE SPANISH LANGUAGE SCHOOL
IPEE-Spanish Language School
Site: Costa Rica: San Jose
Dates: 1 wk-3 mos, yr-round
Subjects: Business language, Foreign language teaching, Spanish language (beg/int/adv)
Eligibility: *Level:* fresh, sophs, jrs, srs, grads, adults, teachers, professionals, precoll *Age:* min 15
Credit: *Undergrad:* depending on length *Grad:* avail *Doc:* transcript, certificate
Instruction: *In:* Spanish *Format:* lang study *Students:* US & intl
Costs: $374 for 1 wk, $679 for 2 wks, $1,002 for 3 wks, $1,229 per mo *incl* tuition, housing, some meals, excursions, books/materials, laundry, airport transfer *Nonrefundable fee*
Housing: *Arr by pgm*
Deadline: 2 wks before pgm
Other info: *US accredited sponsor:* no *Activities:* excursions, field trips, cultural events *Misc:* May contact former participants. *URL:* http://www.ipee.com

Contact: Robert Levy, Dir, IPEE Spanish Lang Sch, 1112 Estatewood Dr, Brandon FL 33510 *Ph:* 813-643 0416 *Fax:* 813-643 0416 *E-mail:* ipee@gate.net

---

1961
IPEE SPANISH LANGUAGE SCHOOL
Language Acquisition and Culture for Professionals
Site: Costa Rica: San Jose
Dates: 1-4 wks, Jun-Jul
Subjects: Civilization/culture, Homestay, Spanish language
Eligibility: *Level:* jrs, srs, grads, adults, teachers *Age:* min 20
Credit: *Undergrad:* 3 *Grad:* 3 *Doc:* transcript *Transfer credit through:* Kansas State Univ
Instruction: *In:* English, Spanish *Format:* lecture, study tour, workshop *Students:* US & intl
Costs: $2,500 per mo *incl* tuition, housing, some meals, books/materials *Nonrefundable fee*
Housing: *Arr by pgm:* homestay
Deadline: 2 wks before pgm
Other info: *US accredited sponsor:* no *In coop with:* Kansas State Univ *Orient:* abroad *Activities:* excursions, field trips, program travel, cultural events *Misc:* May contact former participants. *URL:* http://www.ipee.com
Contact: Robert Levy, Dir, IPEE Spanish Lang Sch, 1112 Estatewood Dr, Brandon FL 33647 *Ph:* 813-643 0416 *Fax:* 813-643 0416 *E-mail:* ipee@gate.net

---

1962
IPEE SPANISH LANGUAGE SCHOOL
Latin American Literature
Site: Costa Rica: San Jose
Dates: 4 wks, yr-round
Subjects: Homestay, Latin American studies, Literature
Eligibility: *Level:* fresh, sophs, jrs, srs, grads, adults, teachers, professionals, precoll *Requires:* int Spanish *Age:* min 15, avg 21
Credit: *Undergrad:* avail *Grad:* avail *Doc:* transcript, certificate *Transfer credit through:* Kansas State Univ
Instruction: *In:* Spanish *Format:* lecture *Students:* US & intl
Costs: $1,229 *incl* tuition, housing, some meals, books/materials *Nonrefundable fee*
Housing: *Arr by pgm:* homestay
Deadline: 2 wks before pgm
Other info: *US accredited sponsor:* no *In coop with:* Kansas State Univ *Orient:* abroad *Activities:* excursions, field trips, program travel, cultural events *Misc:* May contact former participants. *URL:* http://www.ipee.com

Contact: Robert Levy, Dir, IPEE Spanish Lang Sch, 1112 Estatewood Dr, Brandon FL 33510 *Ph:* 813-643 0416 *Fax:* 813-643 0416 *E-mail:* ipee@gate.net

---

1963
IPEE SPANISH LANGUAGE SCHOOL
Spanish Medical Terminology
Site: Costa Rica: San Jose
Dates: 2 wks, yr-round
Subjects: Homestay, Spanish language (adv), Technical language
Eligibility: *Level:* fresh, sophs, jrs, srs, grads, adults, teachers, professionals, precoll *Requires:* int Spanish lang *Age:* min 15, avg 25
Credit: *Undergrad:* avail *Grad:* avail *Doc:* transcript, certificate
Instruction: *In:* Spanish *Format:* lang study, lecture, practical training *Students:* intl
Costs: $165 per wk *incl* tuition, books/materials *Nonrefundable fee*
Housing: *Arr by pgm:* homestay
Deadline: 2 wks before pgm
Other info: *US accredited sponsor:* no *Began:* 1997 *Orient:* abroad (1 day) *Activities:* cultural events *Misc:* This pgm is an add-on. Students must be enrolled in a standard long course. May contact former participants. *Financial aid:* scholarships *URL:* http://www.ipee.com
Contact: Robert Levy, Dir, IPEE Spanish Lang Sch, 1112 Estatewood Dr, Brandon FL 33510 *Ph:* 813-643 0416 *Fax:* 813-643 0416 *E-mail:* ipee@gate.net

---

1964
ISA
Spanish Language: Summer Program in San Jose
Site: Costa Rica: San Jose *Host inst:* Univ Veritas
Dates: 5 wks, May 27-Jun 30 or Jul 8-Aug 11
Subjects: Homestay, Spanish language (beg/int/adv)
Eligibility: *Level:* fresh, sophs, jrs, srs, grads, adults *Requires:* 2.5 GPA, recommendation letters
Credit: *Undergrad:* 5-6 sem hrs *Grad:* none *Doc:* transcript, diploma
Instruction: *In:* Spanish *Format:* lang study *Students:* mainly host country
Costs: $2,450-$2,750 per mo *incl* tuition, housing, all meals, insurance, fees, excursions, tutoring, resident dir
Housing: *Arr by pgm:* homestay
Deadline: Apr 5
Other info: *US accredited sponsor:* no *Began:* 1998 *Orient:* in US & abroad (1 day) *Activities:* excursions, field trips, program travel, cultural events *Misc:* May contact former participants. *Financial aid:*

scholarships *URL:* http://www.studiesabroad.com
Contact: Gustavo Artaza, Intl Studies Abroad, 901 W 24th St, Austin TX 78705 *Ph:* 800-580 8826; 512-480 8522 *Fax:* 512-480 8866 *E-mail:* isa@studiesbroad.com ▲

1965
LANGUAGE LINK and **ILISA**
Immersion Spanish in Costa Rica
Site: Costa Rica: San Jose
Dates: 2-16 wks, yr-round
Subjects: Homestay, Spanish language
Eligibility: *Level:* fresh, sophs, jrs, srs, grads, adults, teachers, professionals, precoll *Age:* min 8, avg 30
Credit: *Undergrad:* 12 *Grad:* 6 *Doc:* transcript
Instruction: *In:* Spanish *Format:* lang study, tutorial *Students:* intl
Costs: $435 per wk *incl* tuition, housing, some meals, insurance, fees, books/materials, airport transfer *Nonrefundable fee*
Housing: *Arr by pgm:* homestay
Deadline: None
Other info: *US accredited sponsor:* no *Began:* 1990 *In coop with:* Austin Peay State Univ *Orient:* abroad (intensive lang study) *Activities:* excursions, field trips, program travel, cultural events *Misc:* Special pgm for families incl nanny svc. May contact former participants. *URL:* http://www.langlink.com
Contact: Kay Rafool, Dir, Lang Link, PO Box 3006, Peoria IL 61612 *Ph:* 800-552 2051; 309-692 2961 *Fax:* 309-692 2926 *E-mail:* info@langlink.com

---

1966
LANGUAGE STUDIES ABROAD, INC
Learn Spanish in Costa Rica
Site: Costa Rica: San Jose *Host inst:* LSA San Jose
Dates: 2 wks or longer, yr-round
Subjects: Civilization/culture, Homestay, Independent study, Spanish language (beg/int/adv)
Eligibility: *Level:* fresh, sophs, jrs, srs, grads, adults, teachers, professionals, precoll *Age:* min 13
Credit: *Undergrad:* avail *Grad:* avail *Doc:* certificate
Instruction: *In:* Spanish *Format:* independent study, lang study, lecture, study tour *Students:* US & intl
Costs: $1,080 for 4 wks *incl* tuition, housing, some meals *Nonrefundable fee*
Housing: *Arr by pgm:* homestay
Deadline: 4 wks before pgm
Other info: *US accredited sponsor:* no *Began:* 1979 *Orient:* abroad *Activities:* excursions, cultural events *Misc:* May contact former participants. *URL:* http://www.languagestudiesabroad.com
Contact: Lang Studies Abroad, Inc, 103 Londonderry Ct, Reno NV 89511-2718 *Ph:* 800-424 5522; 775-849 9206 *Fax:* 775-849 9217 *E-mail:* info@languagestudiesabroad.com

---

1967
LANGUAGES ABROAD
Language and Cultural Immersion Programs-San Jose
Site: Costa Rica: San Jose
Dates: 2 wks or longer, yr-round
Subjects: Civilization/culture, Homestay, Spanish language (beg/int/adv)
Eligibility: *Level:* adults *Age:* min 17, max 65, avg 25
Credit: *Undergrad:* none *Grad:* none *Doc:* certificate
Instruction: *In:* Spanish *Format:* lang study *Students:* intl
Costs: About $2,250 for 4 wks *incl* tuition, housing, some meals, excursions, books/materials
Housing: *Arr by pgm:* apartments, homestay
Deadline: None
Other info: *US accredited sponsor:* no *Misc:* May contact former participants. *URL:* http://www.languagesabroad.com
Contact: Ms Jesse Philippe, Langs Abroad, 317 Adelaide St W, Ste 900, Toronto, Ontario M5V 1P9, Canada *Ph:* 800-219 9924; 416-925 7117 *E-mail:* info@languagesabroad.com

---

1968
LEHIGH UNIVERSITY
Lehigh in Costa Rica
Site: Costa Rica: San Jose *Host inst:* Org for Tropical Studies
Dates: 3 wks, Dec 28-Jan 15
Subjects: Conservation, Deforestation, Ecology/environmental studies, Sustainable development
Eligibility: *Level:* fresh, sophs, jrs, srs *Requires:* 2.0 GPA
Credit: *Undergrad:* 3 *Grad:* none
Instruction: *In:* English *Format:* study tour *Students:* mainly US
Costs: $3,300 *incl* tuition, housing, some meals, intl airfare, fees *Nonrefundable fee*
Housing: *Arr by pgm:* residence halls, hotels
Deadline: May 1
Other info: *US accredited sponsor:* yes *Began:* 1998 *Orient:* in US & abroad *Misc:* May contact former participants. *URL:* http://www.Lehigh.edu/~incis/incis.html
Contact: Dr Sandi Smith, Dir, Study Abroad, Lehigh Univ, 5 E Packer Ave, Whitaker Lab 354, Bethlehem PA 18015 *Ph:* 610-758 3351 *Fax:* 610-758 5156 *E-mail:* incis@lehigh.edu

---

1969
LINGUA SERVICE WORLDWIDE
Total Immersion/Intensive Language and Culture in Costa Rica
Site: Costa Rica: San Jose *Host inst:* Forester Inst Intl
Dates: 2 wks or longer, yr-round
Subjects: Civilization/culture, Homestay, Spanish language (beg/int/adv)
Eligibility: *Level:* fresh, sophs, jrs, srs, grads, adults, teachers, professionals, precoll *Age:* min 15
Credit: *Undergrad:* avail *Grad:* avail *Doc:* transcript, certificate *Transfer credit through:* Univ of Southern Mississippi
Instruction: *In:* Spanish *Format:* lang study, lecture *Students:* intl
Costs: Contact sponsor
Housing: *Arr by pgm:* residence halls, apartments, homestay, pensions, hotels, hostels
Deadline: 45 days before pgm
Other info: *US accredited sponsor:* no *Activities:* excursions, cultural events *Misc:* May contact former participants. *URL:* http://www.linguaserviceworldwide.com
Contact: Dir, Lingua Svc Worldwide, 75 Prospect St, Ste 4, Huntington NY 11743 *Ph:* 800-394 5327; 631-424 0777 *Fax:* 631-271 3441 *E-mail:* itctravel@worldnet.att.net ▲

1970
MONTCLAIR STATE UNIVERSITY
Costa Rica Rainforest and Whitewater Adventure
Site: Costa Rica: San Jose *Host inst:* La Selva Biological Research Station
Dates: 1 wk, early Aug-mid-Aug
Subjects: Biology, Independent study
Eligibility: *Level:* fresh, sophs, jrs, srs, grads, adults, teachers, professionals, precoll *Requires:* good physical condition, ability to swim
Credit: *Undergrad:* 1 *Grad:* none *Doc:* transcript
Instruction: *In:* English *Format:* directed field study, independent study, study tour *Students:* mainly US
Costs: About $1,600 *incl* housing, some meals, intl airfare, excursions
Housing: *Arr by pgm:* hotels, hostels
Deadline: Jun 1
Other info: *US accredited sponsor:* yes *Began:* 1998 *Orient:* in US (1 day) *Misc:* 3 days at biological research station in rainforest, 3 days of whitewater rafting. May contact former participants.
Contact: Wendy Gilbert-Simon, Global Educ Ctr, Montclair State Univ, 22 Normal Ave, Upper Montclair NJ 07043 *Ph:* 973-655 4185 *Fax:* 973-655 7654 *E-mail:* gilbertsimon@saturn.montclair.edu

Or Contact: Dr Martin Greenwald, Montclair State Univ, Upper Montclair NJ 07043 *Ph:* 973-655 4142 *E-mail:* greenwaldm@saturn.montclair.edu

---

1971
NORTHERN ILLINOIS UNIVERSITY
Intensive Latin American Culture Program for Spanish Teachers
Site: Costa Rica: San Jose
Dates: Jul 6-Aug 11
Subjects: Costa Rican studies, Education/teaching, Spanish language (int)
Eligibility: *Level:* adults, teachers, professionals *Requires:* 2.75 GPA, previous study in field *Age:* min 18, avg 25
Credit: *Undergrad:* none *Grad:* 3-6 *Doc:* transcript
Instruction: *In:* Spanish *Format:* directed field study, lang study *Students:* mainly US
Costs: $2,475 *incl* tuition, housing, all meals, insurance, excursions
Housing: *Arr by pgm:* homestay
Deadline: May 1 or until pgm filled
Other info: *US accredited sponsor:* yes *Began:* 2000 *In coop with:* Asesoria Gerencial SA of Costa Rica *Orient:* in US & abroad *Misc:* High sch Spanish teachers & comm coll instructors develop lang skills & achieve a total Spanish environment. May contact former participants. *URL:* http://www.niu.edu/niuabroad/
Contact: Anne Seitzinger, Pgm Coord, Study Abroad, Williston 417, Northern Illinois Univ, DeKalb IL 60115 *Ph:* 815-753 0700 *Fax:* 815-753 0825 *E-mail:* niuabroad@niu.edu
Or Contact: Prof Michael Morris, Foreign Langs & Literatures, Northern Illinois Univ, DeKalb IL 60115 *Ph:* 815-753 0700 *Fax:* 815-753 0825 *E-mail:* niuabroad@niu.edu

---

1972
NORTHERN ILLINOIS UNIVERSITY
International Career Development and Spanish Language Program in Costa Rica
Site: Costa Rica: San Jose
Dates: 8 wks, Jun 1-Jul 28
Subjects: Costa Rican studies, Development studies, Ecology/environmental studies, Geology, Health/health education, Homestay, Human resources, Intercultural studies, International business, Internships, Nutrition, Political science/politics, Public administration, Spanish language (int)
Eligibility: *Level:* sophs, jrs, srs, grads, professionals *Requires:* 2.75 GPA, 2 yrs coll Spanish *Age:* min 19, avg 25
Credit: *Undergrad:* 9 *Grad:* none *Doc:* transcript
Instruction: *In:* Spanish *Format:* independent study, internship, lang study, lecture *Students:* mainly US
Costs: $2,600 *incl* tuition, housing, all meals, insurance, excursions
Housing: *Arr by pgm:* homestay
Deadline: Apr 1
Other info: *US accredited sponsor:* yes *Began:* 1984 *Orient:* abroad *Misc:* May contact former participants. *URL:* http://www.niu.edu/niuabroad/
Contact: Anne Seitzinger, Pgm Coord, Study Abroad, Northern Illinois Univ, Williston Hall 417, DeKalb IL 60115 *Ph:* 815-753 0700 *Fax:* 815-753 0825 *E-mail:* niuabroad@niu.edu

---

1973
NORTHERN ILLINOIS UNIVERSITY
Spanish Language and Literature in Costa Rica
Site: Costa Rica: San Jose
Dates: May 25-Jul 20
Subjects: Costa Rican studies, Spanish language (int)
Eligibility: *Level:* sophs, jrs, srs *Requires:* 2.75 GPA, previous study in field *Age:* min 18, avg 20
Credit: *Undergrad:* 3-6 *Grad:* none *Doc:* transcript
Instruction: *In:* Spanish *Format:* lang study *Students:* mainly US
Costs: $2,725 *incl* tuition, housing, all meals, insurance, excursions
Housing: *Arr by pgm:* homestay
Deadline: Apr 1 or until pgm filled
Other info: *US accredited sponsor:* yes *Began:* 2000 *In coop with:* Asesoria Gerencial *Orient:* in US & abroad *Misc:* May contact former participants. *URL:* http://www.niu.edu/niuabroad/
Contact: Anne Seitzinger, Pgm Coord, Study Abroad, Williston 417, Northern Illinois Univ, DeKalb IL 60115 *Ph:* 815-753 0700 *Fax:* 815-753 0825 *E-mail:* niuabroad@niu.edu

---

1974
RAMAPO COLLEGE OF NEW JERSEY
Costa Rica-Intensa
Site: Costa Rica: San Jose *Host inst:* INTENSA
Dates: 4 wks, Jun
Subjects: Civilization/culture, Costa Rican studies, Homestay, Literature, Spanish language (beg/int/adv)
Eligibility: *Level:* adults *Requires:* 2.0 GPA *Age:* min 18
Credit: *Undergrad:* 8 *Grad:* none
Instruction: *In:* Spanish *Format:* lang study, lecture *Students:* intl
Costs: $2,400 for Ramapo students, $2,600 for others *incl* tuition, housing, most meals, intl airfare, fees, excursions, books/materials, orient
Housing: *Arr by pgm:* homestay
Deadline: May 1
Other info: *US accredited sponsor:* yes *Began:* 1992 *Activities:* excursions, field trips, cultural events *Misc:* May contact former participants. *URL:* http://www.ramapo.edu/Academics/Abroad/
Contact: Robyn Perricelli, Study Abroad, Ramapo Coll of New Jersey, 505 Ramapo Valley Rd, Mahwah NJ 07430 *Ph:* 201-684 7463 *Fax:* 201-684 7651 *E-mail:* rperrice@ramapo.edu

---

1975
RAMAPO COLLEGE OF NEW JERSEY
Summer Study Abroad-Costa Rica
Site: Costa Rica: San Jose, various biological research stations, natl parks, nature reserves *Host inst:* Organization for Tropical Studies
Dates: 3 wks, late May-early Jun
Subjects: Ecology/environmental studies, Field study
Eligibility: *Level:* fresh, sophs, jrs, srs, adults *Requires:* 2.0 GPA, good physical health
Credit: *Undergrad:* 4 *Grad:* none *Doc:* transcript
Instruction: *In:* English *Format:* directed field study *Students:* mainly US
Costs: $2,400 for Ramapo students, $2,600 for others *incl* tuition, housing, all meals, intl airfare, fees, excursions, ground transport
Housing: *Arr by pgm:* residence halls, hotels
Deadline: Apr 22
Other info: *US accredited sponsor:* yes *Began:* 1990 *Orient:* abroad *Activities:* excursions, field trips *Misc:* Visits to La Selva, Palo Verde, Monteverde, volcanos & Manuel Antonio. White river rafting on Pacuare River. *URL:* http://www.ramapo.edu/Academics/Abroad/
Contact: Ms Robyn Perricelli, Coord, Study Abroad, Ramapo Coll of New Jersey, 505 Ramapo Valley Rd, Mahwah NJ 07430-1680 *Ph:* 201-684 7030 *Fax:* 201-684 7651 *E-mail:* studabrd@ramapo.edu
Or Contact: Dr Richard Lowell, Pgm Dir, Ramapo Coll of New Jersey, 505 Ramapo Valley Rd, Mahwah NJ 07430-1680 *Ph:* 201-684 7741 *Fax:* 201-684 7651

1976
SUNY COLLEGE AT NEW PALTZ, LANGUAGE IMMERSION INSTITUTE
Learning Vacations in Costa Rica
Site: Costa Rica: San Jose *Host inst:* Forester Inst Intl
Dates: 2 wks or longer, yr-round
Subjects: Homestay, Spanish language (beg/int/adv)
Eligibility: *Level:* grads, adults, teachers, professionals *Age:* min 18, avg 35

Credit: *Undergrad:* avail *Grad:* none *Doc:* certificate
Instruction: *In:* Spanish *Format:* lang study, lecture *Students:* intl
Costs: About $1,035 for 2 wks *incl* tuition, housing, fees, books/materials
Housing: *Arr by pgm:* homestay
Deadline: 4 wks before pgm
Other info: *US accredited sponsor:* yes *Began:* 1981 *Activities:* excursions, cultural events *Misc:* May contact former participants. *URL:* http://www.newpaltz.edu/lii
Contact: Dr Henry Urbanski, Dir, Lang Immersion Inst, SUNY New Paltz, 75 S Manheim Blvd, New Paltz NY 12561-2499 *Ph:* 845-257 3500 *Fax:* 845-257 3569 *E-mail:* lii@newpaltz.edu ▲

1977
SYRACUSE UNIVERSITY
Costa Rican: A Land of Contrasts
Site: Costa Rica: San Jose
Dates: 5 wks, May 28-Jun 26
Subjects: Field study, Geography, Independent study, Latin American studies
Eligibility: *Level:* fresh, sophs, jrs, srs, grads, adults *Requires:* 2.5 GPA *Age:* min 18
Credit: *Undergrad:* 6 *Grad:* 6 *Doc:* transcript
Instruction: *In:* English *Format:* directed field study, independent study, lecture, seminar *Students:* mainly US
Costs: $6,000 *incl* tuition, housing, some meals, fees, excursions
Housing: *Arr by pgm:* hotels
Deadline: Mar 15
Other info: *US accredited sponsor:* yes *Began:* 2001 *Orient:* abroad *Activities:* excursions *Misc:* May contact former participants. *Financial aid:* scholarships *URL:* http://sumweb.syr.edu/dipa/summer
Contact: Daisy Fried, Assoc Dir, Syracuse Univ, 119 Euclid Ave, Syracuse NY 13244 *Ph:* 800-251 9674; 315-443 9419 *Fax:* 315-443 4593 *E-mail:* dsfried@summon3.syr.edu ▲

1978
UNIVERSIDAD DE COSTA RICA and **MODERN LANGUAGE STUDIES ABROAD**
Summer Study at the Universidad de Costa Rica
Site: Costa Rica: San Jose *Host inst:* Univ de Costa Rica
Dates: 4 wks, May 19-Jun 18 or Jun 25-Jul 25
Subjects: Full curriculum, Art, Civilization/culture, International business, Internships, Literature, Philosophy, Spanish language (beg/int/adv)
Eligibility: *Level:* fresh, sophs, jrs, srs, grads, adults, teachers, professionals *Age:* min 17
Credit: *Undergrad:* 6 *Grad:* 6 *Doc:* transcript, certificate, diploma
Instruction: *In:* Spanish *Format:* internship, lab, lang study, lecture *Students:* intl
Costs: $1,995 *incl* tuition, housing, some meals, intl airfare, excursions, books/materials
Housing: *Arr by pgm:* homestay
Deadline: Apr 15
Other info: *US accredited sponsor:* no *Began:* 1989 *Orient:* abroad (intensive lang study) *Activities:* excursions, field trips, program travel, cultural events, sports *Misc:* May contact former participants. *URL:* http://www.mlsa.com
Contact: Modern Lang Studies Abroad, Univ of Costa Rica, PO Box 548, Frankfort IL 60423 *Ph:* 815-464 1800 *Fax:* 815-464 9458 *E-mail:* mlsa@sprintmail.com

---

1979
UNIVERSITY OF CONNECTICUT
Forester Institute Spanish Language Study
Site: Costa Rica: San Jose *Host inst:* Forester Inst Intl
Dates: 3 wks-4 mos, fall, spring or summer
Subjects: Homestay, Spanish language (beg/int/adv)
Eligibility: *Level:* fresh, sophs, jrs, srs, grads, adults, teachers, professionals *Requires:* 2.5 GPA
Credit: *Undergrad:* avail *Grad:* none *Doc:* transcript
Instruction: *In:* Spanish *Format:* lang study, lecture *Students:* intl
Costs: $910-$1,420 *incl* tuition, housing, some meals
Housing: *Arr by pgm:* homestay
Deadline: 8 wks before pgm
Other info: *US accredited sponsor:* yes *Began:* 1992 *Orient:* abroad (intensive lang study) *Misc:* May contact former participants. *URL:* http://www.studyabroad.uconn.edu
Contact: Study Abroad Pgms, Univ of Connecticut, U-207 Intl Affairs, Storrs CT 06269-1207 *Ph:* 860-486 5022 *Fax:* 860-486 2976 *E-mail:* sabadm03@uconnum.uconn.edu

---

1980
UNIVERSITY OF DELAWARE
Winter Session in Costa Rica-Department of Foreign Languages
Site: Costa Rica: San Jose *Host inst:* Univ de Costa Rica
Dates: 1 mo, Jan
Subjects: Civilization/culture, Homestay, Latin American studies, Spanish language
Eligibility: *Level:* fresh, sophs, jrs, srs *Requires:* 2.0 GPA, 2 sems coll Spanish or 4 yrs high school
Credit: *Undergrad:* 6-7 *Grad:* none *Doc:* transcript
Instruction: *In:* English, Spanish *Format:* lang study, lecture, seminar *Students:* mainly US
Costs: Contact sponsor
Housing: *Arr by pgm:* homestay
Deadline: Early Oct
Other info: *US accredited sponsor:* yes *Orient:* avail yes *Activities:* excursions, field trips, program travel, cultural events *Misc:* Contact sponsor to arrange honors credit. *Financial aid:* scholarships *URL:* http://www.udel.edu/studyabroad/
Contact: Lisa Chieffo, Univ of Delaware, Foreign Langs & Literature, 326 Smith Hall, Newark DE 19716 *Ph:* 302-831 6458 *Fax:* 302-831 0597 *E-mail:* lchieffo@udel.edu
Or Contact: Int Pgms & Special Sessions, Univ of Delaware, 4 Kent Way, Newark DE 19716 *Ph:* 888-831 4685; 302-831 6458 *Fax:* 302-831 6042 *E-mail:* studyabroad@udel.edu

---

1981
UNIVERSITY OF GEORGIA
Costa Rica Study Abroad
Site: Costa Rica: San Jose
Dates: 10 wks, May 26-Aug 4
Subjects: Ecology/environmental studies, Gender studies, Literature, Spanish language (int/adv), Women's studies
Eligibility: *Level:* jrs, srs *Requires:* Spanish 1001, 1002, 2001 or equiv
Credit: *Undergrad:* 6-12 *Grad:* none
Instruction: *In:* English *Format:* independent study, lang study, lecture *Students:* mainly US
Costs: About $6,500 *incl* tuition, housing, some meals, intl airfare, insurance, fees, excursions
Housing: *Arr by pgm:* homestay
Deadline: Feb with $250 deposit
Other info: *US accredited sponsor:* yes *Began:* 2000 *In coop with:* AIFS *Orient:* in US *Activities:* excursions *Misc:* Pgm designed for jrs & srs in Women's Studies or Spanish. *URL:* http://www.uga.edu/wsp/
Contact: Dr Patricia Del Rey, UGA Women's Studies, 1200 S Lumpkin St, Athens GA 30602-3647 *Ph:* 706-542 2846 *Fax:* 706-542 0049 *E-mail:* pdelrey@coe.uga.edu
Or Contact: Dr Roberta Fernandez, Romance Langs, Gilbert Hall, Athens GA 30602 *Ph:* 706-542 1865 *Fax:* 706-542 0049 *E-mail:* robertaf@arches.uga.edu

---

1982
UNIVERSITY OF NORTH CAROLINA AT CHARLOTTE
Spanish Language and Culture in Costa Rica
Site: Costa Rica: San Jose *Host inst:* Forester Inst Intl
Dates: 4 wks, Jun
Subjects: Civilization/culture, Homestay, Spanish language (beg/int/adv)
Eligibility: *Level:* fresh, sophs, jrs, srs, grads, adults
Credit: *Undergrad:* 6 *Grad:* none *Doc:* transcript
Instruction: *In:* Spanish *Format:* lang study, lecture *Students:* mainly US
Costs: About $2,300 *incl* tuition, housing, some meals, insurance, fees, excursions *Nonrefundable fee*
Housing: *Arr by pgm:* homestay
Deadline: Mar 5
Other info: *US accredited sponsor:* yes *Began:* 1989 *Orient:* in US & abroad *Activities:* excursions *Misc:* May contact former participants. *URL:* http://www.uncc.edu/oip/edabroad.htm
Contact: Educ Abroad/Intl Pgms, UNC Charlotte, 9201 University City Blvd, Charlotte NC 28223 *Ph:* 704-687 2464 *Fax:* 704-687 3168 *E-mail:* stennies@email.uncc.edu
Or Contact: Mary Frances Castro, 1998 Costa Rica Pgm Dir, Foreign Langs, UNC Charlotte, 9201 University City Blvd, Charlotte NC 28223 *Ph:* 704-687 4332 *Fax:* 704-687 3496

1983
UNIVERSITY OF SOUTH FLORIDA
USF in Costa Rica
Site: Costa Rica: San Jose *Host inst:* ILISA
Dates: 4 wks or longer, yr-round; 4-5 wks intensive immersion pgm
Subjects: Ecology/environmental studies, Homestay, Spanish language (beg/int/adv), Written composition
Eligibility: *Level:* adults *Requires:* good acad standing, beg Spanish recommended *Age:* min 18
Credit: *Undergrad:* 6 *Grad:* none *Doc:* transcript, certificate
Instruction: *In:* Spanish *Format:* lang study *Students:* intl
Costs: $1,450 *incl* housing, some meals, fees, excursions *Nonrefundable fee*
Housing: *Arr by pgm:* homestay
Deadline: 6 wks before pgm
Other info: *US accredited sponsor:* yes *Began:* 1985 *Orient:* in US & abroad (1 day, 1/2 day) *Activities:* excursions *Misc:* May contact former participants. *URL:* http://www.usf.edu/~iac/
Contact: James Pulos, Coord, Overseas Study Pgms, Univ of South Florida, 4202 E Fowler Ave, CPR 107, Tampa FL 33620-0550 *Ph:* 813-974 4043 *Fax:* 813-974 4613 *E-mail:* jpulos@iac.usf.edu
Or Contact: Dr Warren Hampton, Pgm Dir, USF in Costa Rica, Univ of South Florida, 4202 E Fowler Ave, CPR 107, Tampa FL 33620-5550 *Ph:* 813-974 6747 *Fax:* 813-974 4613

SAN PEDRO

1984
INSTITUTE FOR CENTRAL AMERICAN DEVELOPMENT STUDIES (ICADS)
ICADS Intensive Spanish Program
Site: Costa Rica: San Pedro
Dates: 1 mo, yr-round
Subjects: Community service projects, Homestay, Latin American studies, Spanish language (beg/int/adv)
Eligibility: *Level:* adults *Age:* min 17, max 70, avg 30
Credit: *Undergrad:* avail *Grad:* avail *Doc:* certificate
Instruction: *In:* Spanish *Format:* lang study, lecture, volunteer/svc *Students:* intl
Costs: $1,500 *incl* tuition, housing, some meals, fees, excursions, books/materials, laundry, volunteer placements
Housing: *Arr by pgm:* homestay
Deadline: 1 mo before pgm; 2 mos before pgm in summer
Other info: *US accredited sponsor:* no *Began:* 1987 *Orient:* abroad *Activities:* excursions, field trips *Misc:* Volunteer placements. May contact former participants. *URL:* http://www.icadscr.com
Contact: ICADS, Dept 826, PO Box 025216, Miami FL 33102-5216 *E-mail:* icads@netbox.com

---

1985
INSTITUTE FOR CENTRAL AMERICAN DEVELOPMENT STUDIES (ICADS)
Internship-only Program
Site: Costa Rica: San Pedro
Dates: 10 wks, Jun-Aug
Subjects: Community service projects, Conservation, Education/teaching, Field study, Health care/hospitals, Homestay, Human rights, Internships, Public health, Spanish language, Wildlife, Women's studies
Eligibility: *Level:* jrs, srs, grads, adults, teachers, professionals, precoll *Requires:* 1 yr Spanish
Credit: *Undergrad:* none *Grad:* none
Instruction: *In:* Spanish *Format:* directed field study, internship, lang study, lecture, student teaching, study tour, volunteer/svc *Students:* mainly US
Costs: $3,500 *incl* tuition, housing, some meals, fees, excursions, books/materials *Nonrefundable fee*
Housing: *Arr by pgm:* homestay
Deadline: Rolling admissions
Other info: *US accredited sponsor:* no *Orient:* abroad (2 days) *Activities:* excursions, field trips, program travel, cultural events *Misc:* Evaluation letter. May contact former participants. *Financial aid:* scholarships *URL:* http://www.icadscr.com
Contact: Dr Sandra Kinghorn, ICADS, Dept 826, Box 025216, Miami FL 33102-5216 *E-mail:* icads@netbox.com

---

SAN RAMON

1986
GEORGE MASON UNIVERSITY
Costa Rica: Spanish Language and Culture
Site: Costa Rica: San Ramon *Host inst:* Univ of Costa Rica
Dates: 2 wks, Jan 1-15
Subjects: Spanish language
Eligibility: *Level:* fresh, sophs, jrs, srs, adults, teachers, professionals, precoll *Requires:* 2.25 GPA *Age:* min 18
Credit: *Undergrad:* 3 *Grad:* none *Doc:* transcript
Instruction: *In:* Spanish *Format:* lang study *Students:* mainly US
Costs: About $2,927 for VA residents, $3,527 for others *incl* tuition, housing, all meals, intl airfare, insurance, fees, excursions, ISIC *Nonrefundable fee*
Housing: *Arr by pgm:* homestay
Deadline: Oct 16
Other info: *US accredited sponsor:* yes *Began:* 1996 *Orient:* in US (1 day) *Misc:* May contact former participants. *Financial aid:* scholarships, work study *URL:* http://www.gmu.edu/departments/cge
Contact: Ctr for Global Educ, George Mason Univ, Johnson Ctr, Rm 235, 4400 University Dr, Fairfax VA 22030-4444 *Ph:* 703-993 2154 *Fax:* 703-993 2153 *E-mail:* cge@gmu.edu

---

1987
UNIVERSITY OF NEW ORLEANS
UNO-Costa Rica
Site: Costa Rica: San Ramon *Host inst:* Univ de Costa Rica, Sede de Occidente
Dates: 5 wks, late May-late Jun
Subjects: Anthropology, Archaeology, Biology, English, Geography, Geology, History, Homestay, Literature, Political science/politics, Spanish language
Eligibility: *Level:* fresh, sophs, jrs, srs, teachers *Requires:* 2.0 GPA *Age:* min 17, max 50
Credit: *Undergrad:* 6 *Grad:* none *Doc:* transcript
Instruction: *In:* English, Spanish *Format:* lang study, lecture, study tour *Students:* mainly US

Costs: $1,995 *incl* tuition, housing, some meals, insurance, fees, excursions
Housing: *Arr by pgm:* homestay
Deadline: Apr 1
Other info: *US accredited sponsor:* yes *Began:* 1993 *Orient:* in US & abroad *Activities:* excursions, field trips, cultural events, sports *Misc:* May contact former participants. *URL:* http://www.uno.edu/~inst/Welcome.html
Contact: Marie Kaposchyn, Univ of New Orleans, PO Box 569, New Orleans LA 70148 *Ph:* 504-280 7455 *Fax:* 504-280 7317 *E-mail:* mkaposch@uno.edu

---

SANTA ANA

1988
CENTRO LINGUISTICO CONVERSA
Learn Spanish in Santa Ana, Costa Rica
Site: Costa Rica: Santa Ana
Dates: 4-wk courses, yr-round; students may enroll for 2 wks or more
Subjects: Literature, Spanish language (beg/int/adv)
Eligibility: *Level:* fresh, sophs, jrs, srs, grads, adults, teachers, professionals, precoll *Age:* avg 25
Credit: *Undergrad:* avail *Grad:* none *Doc:* transcript *Transfer credit through:* Miami-Dade CC
Instruction: *In:* Spanish *Format:* lang study *Students:* mainly US
Costs: $2,200 for 80 hrs, $2,500 for 110 hrs *incl* tuition, housing, all meals, books/materials, transport *Nonrefundable fee*
Housing: *Arr by pgm:* homestay, lodge (at addtl cost)
Deadline: None
Other info: *US accredited sponsor:* no *Began:* 1980 *In coop with:* Miami-Dade Community College & Truman State University (CCIS members) *Orient:* abroad *Activities:* sports *Misc:* Sports facilities. 6-acre campus. May contact former participants. *URL:* http://www.conversa.net
Contact: David Kaufman, Ctr Linguistico Conversa, Apdo 17, 1007 Centro Colon, San Jose, Costa Rica *Ph:* 800-367 7726 *E-mail:* conversa@sol.racsa.co.cr
Or Contact: Dr Sherman Thomas, US Rep, Conversa, Bear Valley Springs, 30601 Lower Valley Rd, Tehachapi CA 93561 *Ph:* 800-354 5036; 661-821 1607 *Fax:* 661-821 0379 *E-mail:* thomashouse@thegrid.net

---

1989
COLLEGE CONSORTIUM FOR INTERNATIONAL STUDIES and **MIAMI-DADE COMMUNITY COLLEGE** and **TRUMAN STATE UNIVERSITY**
Intensive Spanish in Costa Rica
Site: Costa Rica: Santa Ana *Host inst:* Ctr Linguistico Conversa
Dates: 1 mo, yr-round
Subjects: Homestay, Spanish language (beg/int/adv)
Eligibility: *Level:* fresh, sophs, jrs, srs, adults, teachers, professionals *Requires:* 2.5 GPA *Age:* min 18
Credit: *Undergrad:* 6-8 *Grad:* none *Doc:* transcript
Instruction: *In:* Spanish *Format:* lang study, lecture *Students:* intl
Costs: $2,770 *incl* housing, some meals, fees, excursions *Nonrefundable fee*

Housing: *Arr by pgm:* homestay, campus lodge at extra cost
Deadline: Rolling admissions
Other info: *US accredited sponsor:* yes *Began:* 1993 *Orient:* abroad *Activities:* excursions, field trips, cultural events *Financial aid:* scholarships *URL:* http://www.ccisabroad.org
Contact: *See Index II for Members* CCIS, 2000 P St NW, Ste 503, Washington DC 20036 *Ph:* 800-453 6956; 202-223 0330 *Fax:* 202-223 0999 *E-mail:* info@ccisabroad.org
Or Contact: Reinaldo Changsut, Study Abroad Adviser, Miami-Dade CC, 11011 SW 104th St, Miami FL 33176-3393 *Ph:* 305-237 2535 *Fax:* 305-237 2949 *E-mail:* rchangsu@mdcc.edu ▲

1990
UNIVERSITY OF WISCONSIN-STEVENS POINT
Tropical Ecology Interim
Site: Costa Rica: San Jose
Dates: Dec 28-Jan 17
Subjects: Biology, Field study, Natural history, Natural resources
Eligibility: *Level:* fresh, sophs, jrs, srs, grads, adults
Credit: *Undergrad:* 3 *Grad:* avail *Doc:* transcript
Instruction: *In:* English *Format:* lecture, study tour *Students:* mainly US
Costs: About $2,795 *incl* housing, some meals, intl airfare, excursions, local transport *Nonrefundable fee*
Housing: *Arr by pgm:* hotels, research stations
Deadline: Oct 1 or until pgm filled
Other info: *US accredited sponsor:* yes *Began:* 1985 *Orient:* in US *Activities:* excursions *Misc:* Parks incl Palo Verde, Santa Rosa, Monteverde & Corcovado. *Financial aid:* scholarships *URL:* http://www.uwsp.edu/studyabroad
Contact: Intl Pgms, Univ of Wisconsin-Stevens Point, Stevens Point WI 54481 *Ph:* 715-346 2717 *Fax:* 715-346 3591 *E-mail:* intlprog@uwsp.edu

Cuba

MORE THAN ONE CITY

1991
COUNCIL ON INTERNATIONAL EDUCATIONAL EXCHANGE (COUNCIL)
Contemporary Cuban Society
Site: Cuba: Havana, Santiago de Cuba
Host inst: Ctr Felix Varela
Dates: Dec-Jan or Jun-Jul
Subjects: Civilization/culture, Contemporary issues, Cuban studies, Latin American studies
Eligibility: *Level:* sophs, jrs, srs, grads *Requires:* 2.75 GPA, min 1-2 sems Spanish
Credit: *Undergrad:* 3 *Grad:* none *Doc:* transcript
Instruction: *In:* English, Spanish *Format:* directed field study, lecture, seminar, study tour *Students:* mainly US
Costs: $2,500 *incl* tuition, housing, all meals, insurance, excursions, cultural events *Nonrefundable fee*
Housing: *Arr by pgm:* pensions
Deadline: Nov 1 for Dec; Apr 1 for Jun
Other info: *US accredited sponsor:* no *Began:* 2000 *Orient:* abroad (1 day) *Activities:* excursions, field trips, program travel, cultural events *Misc:* Full-time resident dir. May contact former participants. *Financial aid:* scholarships *URL:* http://www.ciee.org/study
Contact: Pgm Adviser, Latin Amer, Intl Study Pgm, Council, 633 3rd Ave, New York NY 10017 *Ph:* 800-407 8839; 212-822 2600 *E-mail:* studyinfo@ciee.org ▲

1992
COUNCIL ON INTERNATIONAL EDUCATIONAL EXCHANGE (COUNCIL)
International Faculty Development Seminars-Cuba
Site: Cuba: Havana, Santiago de Cuba
Host inst: Ctr Felix Varela
Dates: 11 days, Jan or Jun
Subjects: Contemporary issues, Current events
Eligibility: *Level:* teachers, professionals *Requires:* must be faculty at 2-yr or 4-yr inst
Credit: *Undergrad:* none *Grad:* none
Instruction: *In:* English *Format:* seminar *Students:* mainly US
Costs: $1,995 *incl* tuition, housing, some meals, excursions, books/materials *Nonrefundable fee*
Housing: *Arr by pgm:* hotels
Deadline: Oct 15 for Jan; Mar 15 for Jun
Other info: *US accredited sponsor:* no *Began:* 2000 *Orient:* abroad *Activities:* excursions, field trips, program travel, cultural events *Misc:* Seminar title: Contemporary Cuba. May contact former participants.
Contact: Jennifer Ley, Dir, Faculty Pgms, Council, 633 3rd Ave, New York NY 10017 *Ph:* 212-822 2746 *Fax:* 212-822 2779 *E-mail:* jley@ciee.org ▲

1993
GEORGE MASON UNIVERSITY
History and Culture of Cuba
Site: Cuba: Havana, Matanzas, Santiago, Trinidad
Dates: 2 wks, beg Dec 2
Subjects: Civilization/culture, Cuban studies, History, Spanish language
Eligibility: *Level:* fresh, sophs, jrs, srs, grads, adults, teachers, professionals *Requires:* 2.25 GPA *Age:* min 18
Credit: *Undergrad:* 3 *Grad:* none *Doc:* transcript
Instruction: *In:* English *Format:* lecture *Students:* mainly US
Costs: $2,884 for GMU students, $3,484 for others *incl* tuition, housing, some meals, intl airfare, insurance, fees, excursions *Nonrefundable fee*
Housing: *Arr by pgm:* hotels
Deadline: Oct 15
Other info: *US accredited sponsor:* yes *Began:* 1998 *Orient:* in US (1 day) *Activities:* excursions, program travel, cultural events *Misc:* May contact former participants. *Financial aid:* scholarships, work study
Contact: Ctr for Global Educ, George Mason Univ, Johnson Ctr 235, 4400 University Dr, Fairfax VA 20111 *Ph:* 703-993 2154 *Fax:* 703-993 2153 *E-mail:* cge@gmu.edu

---

1994
INTERNATIONAL BICYCLE FUND
Cuba People-to-People Tour
Site: Cuba: various sites
Dates: 13 days, Nov-May
Subjects: Agriculture, Civilization/culture, Cuban studies, Development studies, Ecology/environmental studies, Economics, Education/teaching, Field study, Geography, Geology, Health care/hospitals, History, Independent study, Political science/politics, Religion/theology
Eligibility: *Level:* adults
Credit: *Undergrad:* none *Grad:* none
Instruction: *In:* English *Format:* directed field study, independent study, seminar, study tour *Students:* mainly US
Costs: $990 *incl* tuition, housing, some meals, fees, excursions *Nonrefundable fee*
Housing: *Arr by pgm:* homestay, hotels, hostels
Deadline: Until pgm filled
Other info: *US accredited sponsor:* no *Began:* 1997 *Orient:* avail (pre-departure packet) *Misc:* May contact former participants. *URL:* http://www.ibike.org/bikecuba
Contact: David Mozer, Dir, Intl Bicycle Fund, 4887 Columbia Dr S, Seattle WA 98108 *Ph:* 206-767 0848 *Fax:* 206-767 0848 *E-mail:* ibike@ibike.org

---

 See "How To Use This Book" for definitions of terms used above. ▲ = See program sponsor's ad(s) in this book.

HAVANA

1995
CENTER FOR CROSS-CULTURAL STUDY and WILLAMETTE UNIVERSITY
Summer Language & Culture Program in Cuba
Site: Cuba: Havana *Host inst:* Univ of Havana
Dates: 3 or 6 wks, Jun 7-29, Jun 28-Jul 20 or Jun 7-Jul 20
Subjects: Contemporary issues, Cuban studies, Homestay, Spanish language (int)
Eligibility: *Level:* fresh, sophs, jrs, srs, grads *Requires:* 2.5 GPA, must be a degree-seeking coll student *Age:* min 18, avg 21
Credit: *Undergrad:* 4-8 *Grad:* none *Doc:* transcript, certificate
Instruction: *In:* English, Spanish *Format:* lecture, study tour *Students:* mainly US
Costs: $2,825 for 3 wks, $4,990 for 6 wks *incl* tuition, housing, some meals, insurance, excursions, books/materials, Cancun-Havana airfare, orient, e-mail
Housing: *Arr by pgm:* residence halls, homestay, hotels
Deadline: Mar 15
Other info: *US accredited sponsor:* yes *Began:* 1996 *Orient:* avail in Cancun, Mexico & Havana, Cuba *Activities:* excursions, field trips, program travel, cultural events *Misc:* Orient & overnight stay in Cancun, Mexico. Excursions. May contact former participants. *URL:* http://www.studyincuba.org
Contact: *See Index II for Members* Dr Judith Ortiz, Dir, US, Ctr for Cross-Cultural Study, 446 Main St, Amherst MA 01002-2314 *Ph:* 800-377 2621; 413-256 0011 *Fax:* 413-256 1968 *E-mail:* iie@cccs.com ▲

1996
CENTER FOR CROSS-CULTURAL STUDY
Winter Language & Culture Program in Cuba
Site: Cuba: Havana *Host inst:* Univ of Havana
Dates: 3 wks, Dec 29-Jan 20
Subjects: Civilization/culture, Contemporary issues, Cuban studies, Homestay, Spanish language
Eligibility: *Level:* fresh, sophs, jrs, srs, grads *Requires:* 2.5 GPA, Int lang students must have 1 yr Spanish or equiv *Age:* min 18, avg 21
Credit: *Undergrad:* 4 *Grad:* none *Doc:* transcript, certificate
Instruction: *In:* English, Spanish *Format:* lecture *Students:* mainly US
Costs: $2,825 *incl* tuition, housing, some meals, insurance, excursions, books/materials, local airfare, email *Nonrefundable fee*
Housing: *Arr by pgm:* residence halls, homestay, hotels
Deadline: Oct 5
Other info: *US accredited sponsor:* yes *Began:* 1996 *Orient:* in US & abroad (2 days) *Activities:* excursions, field trips, program travel, cultural events *Misc:* Excursions. May contact former participants. *URL:* http://www.studyincuba.org
Contact: *See Index II for Members* Dr Judith M Ortiz, CC-CS, 446 Main St, Amherst, MA 01002-2314 *Ph:* 800-377 2621; 413-256 0011 *Fax:* 413-256 1968 ▲

1997
DUKE UNIVERSITY
Duke in Cuba
Site: Cuba: Havana *Host inst:* Casa de las Americas
Dates: 6 wks, late May-early Jul
Subjects: Civilization/culture, History, Literature
Eligibility: *Level:* fresh, sophs, jrs, srs *Requires:* 2 yrs coll Spanish, good acad standing, transcript
Credit: *Undergrad:* 2 credits *Grad:* none *Doc:* transcript
Instruction: *In:* English, Spanish *Format:* lecture, seminar, study tour *Students:* mainly US
Costs: $5,325 *incl* tuition, housing, all meals, excursions
Housing: *Arr by pgm:* apartments
Deadline: Feb 16
Other info: *US accredited sponsor:* yes *Began:* 1998 *Orient:* in US & abroad *Activities:* excursions *Misc:* May contact former participants. *URL:* http://www.aas.duke.edu/study_abroad/
Contact: Amanda Toler Kelso, Asst Dir, Study Abroad, Duke Univ, 121 Allen Bldg, Box 90057, Durham NC 27708-0057 *Ph:* 919-684 2174 *Fax:* 919-684 3083 *E-mail:* abroad@asdean.duke.edu

---

1998
GEORGE WASHINGTON UNIVERSITY
International Business and Tourism Studies in Cuba
Site: Cuba: Havana
Dates: 3 wks, summer
Subjects: Field study, International marketing, Tourism
Eligibility: *Level:* jrs, srs, grads *Age:* min 21
Credit: *Undergrad:* none *Grad:* 6 *Doc:* transcript
Instruction: *In:* English *Format:* directed field study, lecture, study tour *Students:* intl
Costs: $3,209 for 1 course, $4,664 for 2 courses *incl* tuition, housing, some meals, intl airfare, fees, excursions *Nonrefundable fee*
Housing: *Arr by pgm*
Deadline: Contact sponsor
Other info: *US accredited sponsor:* yes *Began:* 1997 *Orient:* in US & abroad (2 days) *Activities:* excursions, field trips, program travel, cultural events *Misc:* New summer pgm announced in December. Contact sponsor for updated info. *URL:* http://www.gwu.edu/~specprog
Contact: George Washington Univ, Summer, Special & Intl Pgms, George Washington Univ, 609 22nd St NW, Washington DC 20052 *Ph:* 202-994 6360 *Fax:* 202-994 9133 *E-mail:* sumprogs@gwu.edu

---

1999
GLOBAL EXCHANGE
Cuba Language School
Site: Cuba: Havana *Host inst:* Univ of Havana
Dates: 2 wks-1 mo, yr-round
Subjects: Development studies, Languages (beg/int/adv), Peace studies, Social change, Third World studies
Eligibility: *Level:* fresh, sophs, jrs, srs, grads, adults, teachers, professionals, precoll
Credit: *Undergrad:* avail *Grad:* avail *Doc:* certificate
Instruction: *In:* English, Spanish *Format:* lang study, study tour *Students:* mainly US
Costs: Contact sponsor
Housing: *Arr by pgm:* guest house
Deadline: Contact sponsor
Other info: *US accredited sponsor:* no *Activities:* program travel, cultural events *Misc:* May contact former participants.
Contact: Global Exch, Reality Tours, 2017 Mission, #303, San Francisco CA 94110 *Ph:* 800-497 1994; 415-255 7296 *Fax:* 415-255 7498 *E-mail:* info@globalexchange.org

---

2000
LEXIA INTERNATIONAL
LEXIA Summer in Havana
Site: Cuba: Havana *Host inst:* Univ of Havana
Dates: 8 wks, mid-Jun-mid-Aug
Subjects: Anthropology, Arts, Civilization/culture, Community service projects, Ecology/environmental studies, Economics, Fine arts, History, Homestay, Internships, Latin American studies, Literature, Political science/politics, Sociology, Spanish language (beg/int/adv)
Eligibility: *Level:* fresh, sophs, jrs, srs, grads *Requires:* 2.5 GPA, 1 yr postsecondary educ completed *Age:* min 18, avg 21
Credit: *Undergrad:* 8-10 *Grad:* 8-10 *Doc:* transcript *Transfer credit through:* Western Washington Univ
Instruction: *In:* English, Spanish *Format:* internship, lang study, lecture, seminar, volunteer/svc *Students:* mainly US
Costs: $4,650 *incl* tuition, housing, all meals, insurance, fees, excursions, ISIC *Nonrefundable fee*
Housing: *Arr by pgm:* residence halls with local students, homestay
Deadline: Apr 15; Apr 1 for scholarships
Other info: *US accredited sponsor:* no *Began:* 2000 *In coop with:* Western Washington Univ *Orient:* abroad (2 days, intensive lang study) *Activities:* excursions, field trips, program travel, cultural events, sports *Misc:* Student support svcs. May contact former participants. *Financial aid:* scholarships, work study *URL:* http://www.lexiaintl.org
Contact: LEXIA Intl, 25 S Main St, Hanover NH 03755 *Ph:* 800-775 3942; 603-643 9898 *Fax:* 603-643 9899 *E-mail:* info@lexiaintl.org
Or Contact: LEXIA Intl, West Coast, 378 Cambridge Ave, Palo Alto CA 94306 *Ph:* 650-327 9191 *Fax:* 650-327 9192

2001
SUNY COLLEGE AT NEW PALTZ
Summer Study in Havana, Cuba
Site: Cuba: Havana
Dates: 2 wks, Jun 23-Jul 7
Subjects: Cuban studies, Literature, Political science/politics, Spanish language
Eligibility: *Level:* fresh, sophs, jrs, srs, grads *Requires:* good acad standing *Age:* min 18
Credit: *Undergrad:* 3 *Grad:* 3 *Doc:* transcript
Instruction: *In:* Spanish *Format:* lecture *Students:* intl
Costs: $2,295 for NY residents, $2,921 for others *incl* tuition, housing, some meals, intl airfare, insurance, fees, excursions *Nonrefundable fee*
Housing: *Arr by pgm:* hotels
Deadline: Mar 1
Other info: *US accredited sponsor:* yes *Began:* 2000 *Orient:* abroad *Activities:* field trips *Financial aid:* scholarships *URL:* http://www.newpaltz.edu/oie/
Contact: Ctr for Intl Pgm, SUNY New Paltz, 75 S Manheim Blvd, New Paltz NY 12561 *Ph:* 845-257 3125 *Fax:* 845-257 3129 *E-mail:* international@newpaltz.edu ▲

2002
SUNY ROCKLAND COMMUNITY COLLEGE
Cuba Today
Site: Cuba: Havana
Dates: 2 wks, Jun 15-Jun 29
Subjects: Civilization/culture, Cuban studies, Music, Performing arts, Visual arts
Eligibility: *Level:* fresh, sophs, jrs, srs, adults *Requires:* 2.5 GPA *Age:* min 18
Credit: *Undergrad:* 3 *Grad:* none *Doc:* transcript
Instruction: *In:* English *Format:* study tour *Students:* mainly US
Costs: Contact Sponsor
Housing: *Arr by pgm:* hotels
Deadline: Apr 1
Other info: *US accredited sponsor:* yes *Began:* 2001 *Orient:* abroad *Activities:* field trips, cultural events *Misc:* May contact former participants. *Financial aid:* scholarships *URL:* http://www.studyabroad.com/suny/rockland

Contact: Jody Dudderar, Dir, SUNY Rockland, 145 College Rd, Suffern NY 10901 *Ph:* 845-574 4205 *Fax:* 845-574 4423 *E-mail:* Study-Abroad@sunyrockland.edu

---

2003
SUNY UNIVERSITY AT BUFFALO
Beyond the Embargo: Culture & Politics in Cuba
Site: Cuba: Havana *Host inst:* Univ of Havana
Dates: 4 wks, May 25-Jun 26
Subjects: Architecture, Area studies, Art history, Caribbean studies, Civilization/culture, Comparative literature, Field study, Latin American studies, Political science/politics, Social sciences, Spanish language, Spanish studies, Urban planning
Eligibility: *Level:* sophs, jrs, srs, grads *Requires:* 3.0 GPA *Age:* min 18
Credit: *Undergrad:* 6 *Grad:* 6 *Doc:* transcript
Instruction: *In:* English, Spanish *Format:* directed field study, lang study, lecture *Students:* mainly US
Costs: $3,200 *incl* tuition, housing, most meals, excursions, local transport, orient *Nonrefundable fee*
Housing: *Arr by pgm:* ctr for visiting students
Deadline: Mar 15; rolling admissions
Other info: *US accredited sponsor:* yes *Began:* 1997 *Orient:* in US & abroad (1-1/2 day) *Activities:* field trips *Financial aid:* scholarships *URL:* http://www.buffalo.edu/studyabroad/
Contact: Dr Sandra J Flash, Dir, Study Abroad Pgms, Intl Educ, SUNY Univ at Buffalo, 210 Talbert Hall, Box 601604, Buffalo NY 14260-1604 *Ph:* 716-645 3912 *Fax:* 716-645 6197 *E-mail:* studyabroad@acsu.buffalo.edu

---

2004
TULANE UNIVERSITY, CENTER FOR LATIN AMERICAN STUDIES
Summer in Cuba
Site: Cuba: Havana
Dates: 3 wks, Jun 2-Jun 23
Subjects: African studies, Civilization/culture, Cuban studies, Ecology/environmental studies, Historical preservation/restoration, History, Public health, Social change, Spanish language (beg/int/adv)
Eligibility: Must be enrolled in degree-seeking pgm. *Level:* fresh, sophs, jrs, grads *Requires:* 2.5 GPA
Credit: *Undergrad:* 3-6 *Grad:* 3-6 *Doc:* transcript
Instruction: *In:* English, Spanish *Format:* lang study, lecture, seminar *Students:* mainly US
Costs: $3,115 for 1 course, $4,115 for 2 courses *incl* tuition, housing, some meals, insurance, excursions
Housing: *Arr by pgm:* residence halls, hotels
Deadline: Apr 10
Other info: *US accredited sponsor:* yes *Began:* 1997 *Orient:* abroad *Activities:* excursions *Misc:* May contact former participants. *URL:* http://cuba.tulane.edu
Contact: Dr Ana López, Dir, Cuban Studies Inst, Tulane Univ, Caroline Richardson Bldg, New Orleans LA 70118 *Ph:* 504-862 8629 *Fax:* 504-862 8678 *E-mail:* cuba@tulane.edu
Or Contact: Deborah Ramil, Cuban Studies Inst, Caroline Richardson Bldg, New Orleans LA 70118 *Ph:* 504-862 8629, 504-862 8629 *Fax:* 504-862 8678 *E-mail:* dramil@tulane.edu

---

2005
UNIVERSITY OF ILLINOIS AT URBANA-CHAMPAIGN
Summer Study in Havana, Cuba
Site: Cuba: Havana *Host inst:* Ctr de Estudios Martianos
Dates: 3 wks, May 30-Jun 20
Subjects: Latin American studies, Literature, Spanish language
Eligibility: *Level:* sophs, jrs, srs, grads *Requires:* 3.0 GPA, previous study in field, 2 yrs Spanish lang study
Credit: *Undergrad:* 3 *Grad:* none *Doc:* transcript
Instruction: *In:* Spanish *Format:* directed field study, lecture *Students:* mainly US
Costs: $3,000 *incl* tuition, housing, some meals, excursions, medical evacuation insurance *Nonrefundable fee*
Housing: *Arr by pgm:* residence halls
Deadline: Mar 1
Other info: *US accredited sponsor:* yes *Began:* 1999 *Activities:* excursions *Misc:* Scholarships & loans for own students only. May contact former participants. *URL:* http://www.uiuc.edu/providers/ips/sao
Contact: Illinois Pgm Abroad, Univ of Illinois, 115 Intl Studies Bldg, 910 S Fifth St, Champaign IL 61820 *Ph:* 800-531 4404; 217-333 6168 *Fax:* 217-244 0249 *E-mail:* ipa@uiuc.edu

---

2006
UNIVERSITY OF PITTSBURGH
Pitt in Cuba
Site: Cuba: Havana *Host inst:* Univ de la Habana
Dates: 6 wks, mid-May-Jun
Subjects: Anthropology, Caribbean studies, Cuban studies, History, Independent study, Latin American studies, Spanish language
Eligibility: *Level:* sophs, jrs, srs *Requires:* 2.75 GPA, previous study in field, 2 yrs coll Spanish, previous coursework in Latin Amer/Caribbean studies *Age:* avg 20
Credit: *Undergrad:* 6-9 *Grad:* none *Doc:* transcript
Instruction: *In:* Spanish *Format:* independent study, lang study, lecture, seminar, study tour *Students:* mainly US
Costs: $2,895 for Univ of Pitt students, $3,195 for others *incl* tuition, housing, excursions, 2 wkend field trips *Nonrefundable fee*
Housing: *Arr by pgm:* hotels
Deadline: Feb 15
Other info: *US accredited sponsor:* yes *Began:* 2000 *Orient:* in US & abroad *Activities:* excursions, field trips, cultural events *Misc:* Scholarships for own students only. Grants & loans avail. Courses taught by Cuban faculty. May contact former participants. *Financial aid:* scholarships *URL:* http://www.pitt.edu/~stdyabrd
Contact: Jennifer Sill, Study Abroad, Univ of Pittsburgh, 802 William Pitt Union, Pittsburgh PA 15260 *Ph:* 412-648 2299 *Fax:* 412-383 7166 *E-mail:* jsill+@pitt.edu
Or Contact: Dr Jose Moreno, Sociology, Univ of Pittsburgh, Pittsburgh PA 15260 *Ph:* 412-648 7561 *Fax:* 412-648 2799 *E-mail:* moreno+@pitt.edu

---

SANTIAGO

2007
GEORGE MASON UNIVERSITY
Afro-Cuban Dance in Cuba
Site: Cuba: Santiago
Dates: 2 wks, Dec 28-Jan 12
Subjects: Cuban studies, Folk dance
Eligibility: *Level:* fresh, sophs, jrs, srs, grads, adults, teachers, professionals *Requires:* 2.25 GPA, previous study in field *Age:* min 18
Credit: *Undergrad:* 3 *Grad:* 3 *Doc:* transcript
Instruction: *In:* English *Format:* workshop *Students:* mainly US
Costs: $2,790 for GMU students, $3,390 for others *incl* tuition, housing, some meals, intl airfare, insurance, fees, excursions *Nonrefundable fee*
Housing: *Arr by pgm:* hotels
Deadline: Oct 15
Other info: *US accredited sponsor:* yes *Began:* 1999 *Orient:* in US (1 day) *Activities:* excursions, program travel, cultural events *Misc:* May contact former participants. *Financial aid:* scholarships, work study
Contact: Ctr for Global Educ, George Mason Univ, Johnson Ctr 235, 4400 University Dr, Fairfax VA 20111 *Ph:* 703-993 2154 *Fax:* 703-993 2153 *E-mail:* cge@gmu.edu

Dominica

ROSEAU

2008
INSTITUTE FOR TROPICAL MARINE ECOLOGY
Marine Resource Conservation
Site: Dominica: Roseau
Dates: 6 wks, Jun 10-Jul 23
Subjects: Conservation, Ecology/environmental studies, Marine biology, Marine sciences, Natural resource management
Eligibility: *Level:* sophs, jrs, srs, grads *Requires:* previous study in field *Age:* min 18, avg 20
Credit: *Undergrad:* avail *Grad:* none *Doc:* transcript, certificate *Transfer credit through:* Eastern Michigan Univ
Instruction: *In:* English *Format:* lab, lecture, practical training, seminar *Students:* mainly US
Costs: Contact sponsor
Housing: *Arr by pgm:* residence halls
Deadline: Jun 1
Other info: *US accredited sponsor:* no *Began:* 1999 *In coop with:* Eastern Michigan Univ *Orient:* abroad (4 days) *Activities:* excursions, field trips, program travel *Misc:* May contact former participants. *Financial aid:* scholarships *URL:* http://www.itme.org
Contact: Dr Sasha C C Steiner, ITME, PO Box 944, Roseau, Dominica *E-mail:* admin@itme.org

Dominican Republic

MORE THAN ONE CITY

2009
NATIONAL REGISTRATION CENTER FOR STUDY ABROAD (NRCSA)
Spanish in the Caribbean
Site: Dominican Republic: Santo Domingo, Sousa *Host inst:* Inst Intercultural del Caribe
Dates: 2 wks or longer, yr-round
Subjects: Homestay, Spanish language
Eligibility: *Level:* fresh, sophs, jrs, srs, grads, adults, teachers, professionals
Credit: *Undergrad:* avail *Grad:* avail
Instruction: *In:* Spanish *Format:* lang study, lecture, tutorial *Students:* mainly US
Costs: $1,476 per mo *incl* tuition, housing, some meals, insurance *Nonrefundable fee*
Housing: *Arr by pgm:* residence halls, homestay
Deadline: 6 wks before pgm
Other info: *US accredited sponsor:* no *Misc:* May contact former participants. *URL:* http://www.nrcsa.com
Contact: June Domoe, NRCSA, 823 N 2nd St, 206, Milwaukee WI 53203 *Ph:* 414-278 0631 *Fax:* 414-271 8884 *E-mail:* info@nrcsa.com

---

SANTIAGO DE LOS CABALLEROS

2010
COUNCIL ON INTERNATIONAL EDUCATIONAL EXCHANGE CONSORTIUM
Council Study Center in Santiago, Dominican Republic
Site: Dominican Republic: Santiago de los Caballeros *Host inst:* Pontificia Univ Catolica Madre y Maestra
Dates: Early Jun-late Jul
Subjects: Health care/hospitals, Homestay, Public health, Spanish language
Eligibility: *Level:* sophs, jrs, srs, professionals *Requires:* 2.75 GPA, 4 sems coll Spanish
Credit: *Undergrad:* 9 *Grad:* none
Instruction: *In:* Spanish *Format:* lang study, seminar, volunteer/svc *Students:* mainly US
Costs: $3,185 *incl* tuition, housing, all meals, insurance, fees, excursions, ISIC, pre-departure advising
Housing: *Arr by pgm:* homestay, rural clinic
Deadline: Apr 1
Other info: *US accredited sponsor:* yes *Orient:* avail in Puerto Plata & Santiago *Activities:* excursions, field trips, program travel *Misc:* Full-time resident dir. Comm svc. Pre-departure advising. May contact former participants. *Financial aid:* scholarships *URL:* http://www.ciee.org/study
Contact: *See Index II for Members* Latin Amer Pgm Adviser, Council-ISP, 633 3rd Ave 20th Fl, New York NY 10017-5706 *Ph:* 800-407 8839; 212-822 2600 *Fax:* 212-822 2779 *E-mail:* studyinfo@ciee.org

---

SANTO DOMINGO

2011
AMERISPAN UNLIMITED
Spanish Study and Homestay in Santo Domingo
Site: Dominican Republic: Santo Domingo *Host inst:* Inst de Lengua y Cultura
Dates: 1 wk-1 yr, yr-round
Subjects: Civilization/culture, Homestay, Spanish language (beg/int/adv)
Eligibility: *Level:* fresh, sophs, jrs, srs, grads, adults, teachers, professionals *Age:* min 21
Credit: *Undergrad:* avail *Grad:* none *Doc:* transcript, certificate *Transfer credit through:* Seattle Central CC
Instruction: *In:* Spanish *Format:* lang study, lecture, study tour, tutorial *Students:* intl
Costs: $730 for 2 wks, $1,410 for 4 wks, $340 for each addtl wk *incl* tuition, housing, all meals, insurance
Housing: *Arr by pgm:* homestay, hotels
Deadline: 4 wks before pgm
Other info: *US accredited sponsor:* no *Orient:* abroad *Activities:* excursions, field trips, cultural events *Misc:* May contact former participants. *URL:* http://www.amerispan.com/
Contact: AmeriSpan Unltd, PO Box 40007, Philadelphia PA 19106 *Ph:* 800-879 6640; 215-751 1100 *Fax:* 215-751 1986 *E-mail:* info@amerispan.com

---

2012
COMMITTEE ON INSTITUTIONAL COOPERATION
Latin American Health, Nutrition and Environmental Issues
Site: Dominican Republic: Santo Domingo *Host inst:* Entrena SA
Dates: 8 wks, mid-Jun-mid-Aug
Subjects: Caribbean studies, Field study, Health/health education, Homestay, Independent study, Medicine, Nutrition, Sociology, Spanish language (int)
Eligibility: *Level:* sophs, jrs, srs, adults, teachers, professionals *Requires:* 2.5 GPA, previous study in field, or previous experience, 2 sems Spanish or equiv *Age:* min 18
Credit: *Undergrad:* 8 *Grad:* none *Doc:* transcript
Instruction: *In:* English, Spanish *Format:* directed field study, independent study, lang study, lecture, seminar *Students:* mainly US
Costs: About $3,400 *incl* tuition, housing, most meals, fees, excursions, orient
Housing: *Arr by pgm:* homestay
Deadline: Mar 15
Other info: *US accredited sponsor:* yes *Began:* 1994 *Orient:* abroad *Activities:* field trips, cultural events *Misc:* May contact former participants. *URL:* http://www.uiowa.edu/~uiabroad
Contact: *See Index II for Members* Hannah Covert, Admin Coord, CIC Study Abroad, 120 Intl Ctr, Univ of Iowa, Iowa City IA 52242-1802 *Ph:* 319-335 0353 *Fax:* 319-335 2021 *E-mail:* cic-abroad@uiowa.edu

---

2013
EDUVACATIONS
Learn Spanish in the Caribbean
Site: Dominican Republic: Santo Domingo
Dates: 2 wks or longer, yr-round
Subjects: Civilization/culture, Culinary

arts, Dance, Spanish language (beg/int/adv)
Eligibility: *Level:* adults *Age:* min 16
Credit: *Undergrad:* none *Grad:* none
Instruction: *In:* Spanish *Format:* lang study *Students:* intl
Costs: Contact sponsor
Housing: *Arr by pgm:* apartments, homestay, hotels
Deadline: Contact sponsor
Other info: *US accredited sponsor:* no *Activities:* excursions, field trips, cultural events, sports *Misc:* 20 hrs/wk Spanish instruction. Max 8 students per class. *URL:* http://www.eduvacations.com
Contact: Mary Ann Puglisi, eduVacations, 1431 21st St NW, Ste 302, Washington DC 20036 *Ph:* 202-857 8384 *Fax:* 202-463 8091

2014
HISPANIOLA ACADEMIA CARIBE DE LENGUAS
Spanish Abroad
Site: Dominican Republic: Santo Domingo
Dates: 2-24 wks, yr-round
Subjects: Caribbean studies (beg/int/adv), Spanish language (beg/int/adv)
Eligibility: *Level:* adults, teachers, professionals *Age:* min 16, avg 27
Credit: *Undergrad:* none *Grad:* none *Doc:* certificate, diploma
Instruction: *In:* Spanish *Format:* lang study *Students:* intl
Costs: $670-$1,140 for 2 wks *incl* tuition, housing, some meals, fees, books/materials
Housing: *Arr by pgm:* apartments, homestay, pensions, hotels
Deadline: 1 mo before pgm; 2 mos for scholarships
Other info: *US accredited sponsor:* no *Began:* 1995 *Orient:* abroad (1 day) *Activities:* excursions, field trips, cultural events *Misc:* May contact former participants. *Financial aid:* scholarships *URL:* http://www.hispaniola.org
Contact: Luca Pellegrini, Dir, Hispaniola Acad Caribe de Lenguas, c/ Mercedes 155, Edf San Pedro, Zona Colonial, Santo Domingo, Dominican Republic *E-mail:* luca@hispaniola.org

---

2015
LANGUAGES ABROAD
Language and Cultural Immersion Programs-Santo Domingo
Site: Dominican Republic: Santo Domingo
Dates: 2 wks or longer, yr-round
Subjects: Civilization/culture, Homestay, Spanish language (beg/int/adv)
Eligibility: *Level:* adults *Age:* min 17, max 65, avg 25
Credit: *Undergrad:* none *Grad:* none *Doc:* certificate
Instruction: *In:* Spanish *Format:* lang study *Students:* intl
Costs: From $2,250 for 4 wks *incl* tuition, housing, some meals, excursions, books/materials
Housing: *Arr by pgm:* apartments, homestay
Deadline: None
Other info: *US accredited sponsor:* no *Misc:* May contact former participants. *URL:* http://www.languagesabroad.com
Contact: Ms Jesse Philippe, Langs Abroad, 317 Adelaide St W, Ste 900, Toronto, Ontario M5V 1P9, Canada *Ph:* 800-219 9924; 416-925 7117 *E-mail:* info@languagesabroad.com

---

2016
SUNY COLLEGE AT NEW PALTZ, LANGUAGE IMMERSION INSTITUTE
Learning Vacations in the Caribbean
Site: Dominican Republic: Santo Domingo *Host inst:* Hispaniola Academia Caribe de Lenguas
Dates: 2 wks or longer, yr-round
Subjects: Languages
Eligibility: *Level:* adults *Age:* min 18, avg 40
Credit: *Undergrad:* none *Grad:* none
Instruction: *In:* Spanish *Format:* lang study, lecture *Students:* intl
Costs: $880 for 2 wks *incl* tuition, housing, some meals, fees, books/materials *Nonrefundable fee*
Housing: *Arr by pgm:* homestay
Deadline: 1 mo before pgm
Other info: *US accredited sponsor:* yes *Activities:* excursions, cultural events, sports *Misc:* May contact former participants. *URL:* http://www.newpaltz.edu/lii
Contact: Dr Henry Urbanski, Dir, Lang Immersion Inst, SUNY New Paltz, 75 S Manheim Blvd, New Paltz NY 12561-2499 *Ph:* 914-257 3500 *Fax:* 914-257 3569 ▲

2017
SUNY UNIVERSITY AT ALBANY
Language and Cultural Studies in the Dominican Republic
Site: Dominican Republic: Santo Domingo *Host inst:* Univ PUCMM
Dates: 7 wks, Jun-Aug
Subjects: African-American studies, Caribbean studies, Civilization/culture, Dominican studies, Latin American studies, Spanish language (beg/int/adv)
Eligibility: *Level:* fresh, sophs, jrs, srs *Requires:* fluent Spanish for direct enrollment
Credit: *Undergrad:* 6 *Grad:* none *Doc:* transcript
Instruction: *In:* English *Format:* lang study, lecture, volunteer/svc *Students:* mainly US
Costs: $2,215 for NY residents *incl* tuition, housing, all meals, fees, excursions, student support svcs *Nonrefundable fee*
Housing: *Arr by pgm:* homestay
Deadline: Apr 15; late applications considered
Other info: *US accredited sponsor:* yes *Began:* 1996 *Orient:* in US & abroad *Activities:* field trips *Misc:* Addtl charge for direct enrollment. May contact former participants. *URL:* http://www.albany.edu/intled
Contact: Joan N Savitt, Intl Pgm, SUNY Univ at Albany, LI 66, Albany NY 12222 *Ph:* 518-422 3525 *Fax:* 518-442 3338 *E-mail:* intled@uamail.albany.edu

---

2018
UNIVERSITY OF MICHIGAN
Summer Program in Santo Domingo, Dominican Republic
Site: Dominican Republic: Santo Domingo *Host inst:* Entrena SA
Dates: 9 wks, mid-Jun-mid-Aug
Subjects: Caribbean studies, Civilization/culture, History, Homestay, Spanish language (int/adv)
Eligibility: *Level:* sophs, jrs, srs *Requires:* 2.5 GPA, 2 sems coll Spanish
Credit: *Undergrad:* 6-8 *Grad:* none
Instruction: *In:* English, Spanish *Format:* lang study, lecture *Students:* mainly US
Costs: Contact sponsor
Housing: *Arr by pgm:* homestay
Deadline: Feb 16
Other info: *US accredited sponsor:* yes *Began:* 1997 *Orient:* abroad *Activities:* excursions, field trips *URL:* http://www.umich.edu/~iinet/oip/
Contact: Intl Pgms, Univ of Michigan, G513 Michigan Union, Ann Arbor MI 48109-1349 *Ph:* 734-764 4311 *Fax:* 734-764 3229 *E-mail:* oip@umich.edu

Ecuador

MORE THAN ONE CITY

2019
AMERISPAN UNLIMITED
Spanish Study and Homestay in Ecuador
Site: Ecuador: Cuenca, Quito *Host inst:* Acad de Espanol Quito, Acad Latinoamer de Espanol, Estudio Intl Sampere
Dates: 1 wk-1 yr, yr-round
Subjects: Business language, Civilization/culture, Homestay, Spanish language (beg/int/adv)
Eligibility: *Level:* fresh, sophs, jrs, srs, grads, adults *Age:* min 16
Credit: *Undergrad:* avail *Grad:* avail *Doc:* transcript, certificate *Transfer credit through:* Univ of Southern Mississippi
Instruction: *In:* Spanish *Format:* lang study, study tour, tutorial *Students:* intl

Costs: $495-$895 for 2 wks, $990-$1,595 for 4 wks, $215-$405 each addtl wk *incl* tuition, housing, all meals, insurance, books/materials
Housing: *Arr by pgm:* homestay, hotels
Deadline: 4 wks before pgm
Other info: *US accredited sponsor:* no *Orient:* abroad *Activities:* excursions, field trips, cultural events *Misc:* Transfer credit also avail through Seattle Central CC. May contact former participants. *Financial aid:* work study *URL:* http://www.amerispan.com/
Contact: AmeriSpan Unltd, PO Box 40007, Philadelphia PA 19106 *Ph:* 800-879 6640; 215-751 1100 *Fax:* 215-751 1986 *E-mail:* info@amerispan.com

---

2020
ARIZONA STATE UNIVERSITY
Andes and the Amazon
Site: Ecuador: various sites
Dates: 3 wks, Jun 7-30
Subjects: Civilization/culture, Folk arts, Folk dance, Folk music, History, Literature, Quechua/Quichua language (beg), Religion/theology
Eligibility: *Level:* fresh, sophs, jrs, srs, grads, adults, teachers, professionals *Age:* min 18
Credit: *Undergrad:* 7 *Grad:* none
Instruction: *In:* English *Format:* lang study, lecture, study tour, volunteer/svc *Students:* mainly US
Costs: $1,995 *incl* tuition, housing, all meals, fees, ground transport, ISIC
Housing: *Arr by pgm:* camping, health spa
Deadline: Early Mar
Other info: *US accredited sponsor:* yes *Began:* 1999 *Activities:* excursions, field trips, program travel *Misc:* Loans avail. All students pay equiv of ASU resident tuition. *Financial aid:* scholarships *URL:* http://www.asu.edu/ssc/StudyAbroad
Contact: Ara Pachmayer, Pgm Coord, Summer Sessions, Arizona State Univ, PO Box 873003, Tempe AZ 85287-3003 *Ph:* 480-965 0101 *Fax:* 480-965 3851 *E-mail:* study.programs@asu.edu

---

2021
GEORGE MASON UNIVERSITY
Ecology of the Galapagos Islands and Ecuador's Culture
Site: Ecuador: Galapagos Islands, Quito
Dates: 3 wks, Dec 28-Jan 17
Subjects: Biology
Eligibility: *Level:* fresh, sophs, jrs, srs, grads, adults, teachers, professionals *Requires:* 2.25 GPA *Age:* min 18
Credit: *Undergrad:* 6 *Grad:* 6 *Doc:* transcript
Instruction: *In:* English *Format:* lecture, study tour *Students:* intl
Costs: About $4,500 for VA residents, $5,100 for others *incl* tuition, most meals, intl airfare, insurance, excursions, ISIC *Nonrefundable fee*
Housing: *Arr by pgm:* pensions, cruise boat
Deadline: Oct 16
Other info: *US accredited sponsor:* yes *Began:* 1996 *Orient:* in US *Activities:* excursions, field trips, program travel *Misc:* May contact former participants. *URL:* http://www.gmu.edu/departments/cge
Contact: Ctr for Global Educ, George Mason Univ, Fairfax VA 22030-4444 *Ph:* 703-993 2154 *Fax:* 703-993 2153 *E-mail:* cge@gmu.edu
Or Contact: Ms Tanith Fowler, Pgm Officer, Ctr for Global Educ, George Mason Univ, Fairfax VA 22030-4444 *Ph:* 703-993 2167 *Fax:* 703-993 2153 *E-mail:* tfowler2@gmu.edu

---

2022
LANGUAGE LIAISON
Spanish Saturation-Ecuador
Site: Ecuador: Cuenca, Quito
Dates: 2 wks or longer, yr-round
Subjects: Homestay, Spanish language
Eligibility: *Level:* adults
Credit: *Undergrad:* avail *Grad:* avail *Doc:* certificate
Instruction: *In:* Spanish *Format:* lang study, tutorial *Students:* intl
Costs: Contact sponsor
Housing: *Arr by pgm:* homestay, hotels, hostels
Deadline: 30 days before pgm
Other info: *US accredited sponsor:* no *Misc:* Scholarship research svc. *URL:* http://www.languageliaison.com
Contact: Nancy Forman, Dir, Lang Liaison, 4 Burnham Pkwy, Morristown NJ 07960 *Ph:* 800-284 4448 *Fax:* 973-898 1710 *E-mail:* learn@languageliaison.com

---

2023
LINGUA SERVICE WORLDWIDE
Total Immersion/Intensive Language and Culture in Quito
Site: Ecuador: Cuenca, Quito *Host inst:* Acad de Espanol Quito, Estudio Intl Sampere
Dates: 2-10 wks, yr-round
Subjects: Homestay, Spanish language (beg/int/adv)
Eligibility: *Level:* fresh, sophs, jrs, srs, grads, adults, teachers, professionals, precoll *Age:* min 14
Credit: *Undergrad:* none *Grad:* none *Doc:* certificate *Transfer credit through:* Univ of Southern Mississippi
Instruction: *In:* Spanish *Format:* lang study, tutorial *Students:* intl
Costs: Contact sponsor
Housing: *Arr by pgm:* apartments, homestay, hotels
Deadline: Rolling admissions
Other info: *US accredited sponsor:* no *Began:* 1982 *Activities:* excursions, cultural events, sports *Misc:* Individual instruction. May contact former participants. *URL:* http://www.linguaserviceworldwide.com
Contact: Dir, Lingua Svc Worldwide, 75 Prospect St, Ste 4, Huntington NY 11743 *Ph:* 800-394 5327; 631-424 0777 *Fax:* 631-271 3441 *E-mail:* itctravel@worldnet.att.net ▲

2024
UNIVERSITY OF CONNECTICUT
Culture & Ecology of Ecuadorian Tropical Rainforest
Site: Ecuador: various sites
Dates: 3 wks, Jun 4-25
Subjects: Anthropology, Civilization/culture, Ecology/environmental studies, Field study
Eligibility: *Level:* fresh, sophs, jrs, srs, grads, precoll *Requires:* 2.5 GPA, good physical condition for field work *Age:* min 18
Credit: *Undergrad:* 3 *Grad:* none *Doc:* transcript
Instruction: *In:* English *Format:* directed field study, lecture, seminar, study tour *Students:* mainly US
Costs: $3,395 *incl* tuition, housing, all meals, intl airfare, fees *Nonrefundable fee*
Housing: *Arr by pgm:* hotels, lodge at rainforest reserve
Deadline: Mar 1
Other info: *US accredited sponsor:* yes *Began:* 1999 *Orient:* in US & abroad *Activities:* excursions, field trips, program travel, cultural events *Misc:* Rigorous hiking, trips to local villages, animal habitats, rehab ctrs. May contact former participants. *URL:* http://www.studyabroad.uconn.edu
Contact: Sally Innis Klite, Study Abroad Prg, Univ of Connecticut, U-207 943 Bolton Rd, Storrs CT 06269-1207 *Ph:* 860-486 5022 *Fax:* 806-486 2976 *E-mail:* sabadmo3@uconnum.uconn.edu
Or Contact: Dr Pamela Erickson, Univ of Connecticut *E-mail:* pamelaerickson@uconn.edu

---

CUENCA

2025
ESTUDIO INTERNACIONAL SAMPERE
Curso Intensivo de Lengua y Cultura
Site: Ecuador: Cuenca
Dates: 2-16 wks, yr-round
Subjects: Civilization/culture, Ecuadorian studies, Spanish language

See "How To Use This Book" for definitions of terms used above. ▲ = See program sponsor's ad(s) in this book.

Eligibility: *Level:* adults *Requires:* previous study in field, beg Spanish *Age:* min 18, max 65
Credit: *Undergrad:* none *Grad:* none *Doc:* transcript, certificate
Instruction: *In:* Spanish *Format:* lang study *Students:* intl
Costs: $985 per mo *incl* tuition, housing, all meals, fees, excursions, books/materials, Quito-Cuenca air transfers
Housing: *Arr by pgm:* apartments, homestay
Deadline: 2 wks before pgm
Other info: *US accredited sponsor:* no *Began:* 1995 *Orient:* abroad *Activities:* excursions, field trips, program travel, cultural events, sports *Misc:* May contact former participants. *URL:* http://www.sampere.com
Contact: Juan Manuel Sampere, EIS, Lagasca 16, E-28001 Madrid, Spain *E-mail:* madrid@eisampere.es

---

2026
LANGUAGE STUDIES ABROAD, INC
Intensive Spanish-Ecuador
Site: Ecuador: Cuenca *Host inst:* LSA Cuenca
Dates: 1 wk or longer, yr-round
Subjects: Homestay, Spanish language
Eligibility: *Level:* fresh, sophs, jrs, srs, grads, adults, teachers, professionals, precoll *Age:* min 18
Credit: *Undergrad:* avail *Grad:* avail
Instruction: *In:* Spanish *Format:* lang study *Students:* intl
Costs: $990 for 4 wks *incl* tuition, housing, all meals, insurance, excursions, books/materials, airfare from Quito to Cuenca *Nonrefundable fee*
Housing: *Sponsor assists:* apartments, homestay, hotels
Deadline: 4 wks before pgm
Other info: *US accredited sponsor:* no *Began:* 1995 *Orient:* abroad *Misc:* May contact former participants. *URL:* http://www.languagestudiesabroad.com
Contact: Lang Studies Abroad, Inc, 103 Londonderry Ct, Reno NV 89511-2718 *Ph:* 800-424 5522; 775-849 9206 *Fax:* 775-849 9217 *E-mail:* info@languagestudiesabroad.com

---

2027
NATIONAL REGISTRATION CENTER FOR STUDY ABROAD (NRCSA)
Spanish in Cuenca
Site: Ecuador: Cuenca *Host inst:* EIS Cuenca
Dates: 2 or 4 wks, yr-round
Subjects: Homestay, Spanish language (beg/int/adv)
Eligibility: *Level:* fresh, sophs, jrs, srs, grads, adults, teachers, professionals *Age:* min 18
Credit: *Undergrad:* avail *Grad:* avail *Doc:* certificate
Instruction: *In:* Spanish *Format:* lang study, lecture, tutorial *Students:* intl
Costs: $598 for 2 wks, $1,032 for 4 wks *incl* tuition, housing, all meals, insurance *Nonrefundable fee*
Housing: *Arr by pgm:* homestay
Deadline: 6 wks before pgm
Other info: *US accredited sponsor:* no *Misc:* May contact former participants. *URL:* http://www.nrcsa.com
Contact: June Domoe, NRCSA, 823 N 2nd St, #206, Milwaukee WI 53203 *Ph:* 414-278 0631 *Fax:* 414-271 8884 *E-mail:* info@nrcsa.com

---

GUAYAQUIL

2028
COLLEGE CONSORTIUM FOR INTERNATIONAL STUDIES and **COLLEGE OF STATEN ISLAND, CITY UNIVERSITY OF NEW YORK** and **BROOKDALE COMMUNITY COLLEGE**
Summer Program in Guayaquil
Site: Ecuador: Guayaquil *Host inst:* Univ Catolica de Santiago de Guayaquil
Dates: Jul 2-27
Subjects: Ecuadorian studies, Homestay, Spanish language (beg/int/adv)
Eligibility: *Level:* fresh, sophs, jrs, srs, grads, adults *Requires:* 2.5 GPA, recommendation letter, essay, transcript *Age:* min 18
Credit: *Undergrad:* 6-8 *Grad:* none *Doc:* transcript
Instruction: *In:* Spanish *Format:* lang study *Students:* mainly US
Costs: $1,860 *incl* tuition, housing, some meals, fees, excursions *Nonrefundable fee*
Housing: *Arr by pgm:* homestay
Deadline: May 15
Other info: *US accredited sponsor:* yes *Began:* 1989 *Orient:* in US & abroad *Activities:* excursions *Misc:* May contact former participants. *URL:* http://www.ccisabroad.org
Contact: *See Index II for Members* CCIS, 2000 P St NW, Ste 503, Washington DC 20036 *Ph:* 800-453 6956; 202-223 0330 *Fax:* 202-223 0999 *E-mail:* info@ccisabroad.org
Or Contact: Emily Hagadorn, Mgr, Intl Ctr, Brookdale CC, 765 Newman Springs Rd, Lincroft NJ 07738 *Ph:* 732-224 2577 *Fax:* 732-224 2980 *E-mail:* ehagadorn@brookdale.cc.nj.us
Or Contact: Coord, Ecuador Pgms, Ctr for Intl Svc, Coll of Staten Island/CUNY, Bldg 2A, Rm 206, 2800 Victory Blvd, Staten Island NY 10314 *Ph:* 718-982 2100 *Fax:* 718-982 -2108 *E-mail:* studyab@postbox.csi.cuny.edu ▲

2029
FLORIDA ATLANTIC UNIVERSITY
Study Abroad in Guayaquil, Ecuador
Site: Ecuador: Guayaquil *Host inst:* Blue Hill Coll
Dates: 5 wks, May-late Jun or early Jul-early Aug
Subjects: Accounting, Anthropology, Business/management, Civilization/culture, Ecology/environmental studies, Economics, Finance, Geography, Geology, International business, Latin American studies, Spanish language (beg/int/adv), Spanish studies
Eligibility: *Level:* fresh, sophs, jrs, srs *Requires:* 2.5 GPA *Age:* min 18
Credit: *Undergrad:* 7 *Grad:* none *Doc:* transcript
Instruction: *In:* English, Spanish *Format:* internship, lang study, lecture *Students:* mainly host country
Costs: $2,600 *incl* tuition, housing, all meals, fees, excursions, books/materials *Nonrefundable fee*
Housing: *Arr by pgm:* apartments, homestay
Deadline: May 15; Apr 15 for scholarships
Other info: *US accredited sponsor:* yes *Began:* 1994 *Orient:* in US (1 day) *Activities:* excursions *Misc:* Single rm avail for addtl fee. May contact former participants. *Financial aid:* scholarships *URL:* http://www.fau.edu/ecuador
Contact: Intl Pgms, Florida Atlantic Univ, 777 Glades Rd, GCS 259, Boca Raton FL 33431-0991 *Ph:* 800-935 5734; 561-297 2580, 561-297 3282 *Fax:* 561-297 2850 *E-mail:* goabroad@fau.edu

---

2030
MICHIGAN STATE UNIVERSITY
Primary Health Care
Site: Ecuador: Guayaquil
Dates: 4 wks, Jul-Aug
Subjects: Health care/hospitals
Eligibility: *Level:* grads *Requires:* 2.0 GPA, good acad standing, interview *Age:* min 18
Credit: *Undergrad:* 6 *Grad:* 6 *Doc:* transcript
Instruction: *In:* English *Format:* lecture, seminar *Students:* mainly US
Costs: About $2,000 *incl* housing, some meals, insurance, excursions *Nonrefundable fee*
Housing: *Arr by pgm:* hotels
Deadline: Mar 2
Other info: *US accredited sponsor:* yes *Began:* 1996 *Orient:* in US *Activities:* excursions, field trips *Misc:* Loans avail. *Financial aid:* scholarships *URL:* http://studyabroad.msu.edu
Contact: Cheryl Benner, Study Abroad, Michigan State Univ, 109 Intl Ctr, East Lansing MI 48824 *Ph:* 517-353 8920 *Fax:* 517-432 2082 *E-mail:* bennerc@msu.edu ▲

2031
SUNY COLLEGE AT NEW PALTZ
Summer Studies in Guayaquil, Ecuador
Site: Ecuador: Guayaquil *Host inst:* Espiritu Santo Univ
Dates: 4 wks, Jun 20-Jul 18, Jul 19-Aug 17
Subjects: Area studies, Community service projects, Internships, Spanish language (beg/int/adv)
Eligibility: *Level:* fresh, sophs, jrs, srs *Requires:* 2.5 GPA *Age:* min 18
Credit: *Undergrad:* 6 *Grad:* none *Doc:* transcript
Instruction: *In:* Spanish *Format:* internship, lang study, seminar, volunteer/svc *Students:* mainly host country
Costs: $2,357 per session *incl* tuition, housing, all meals, insurance, fees, excursions, books/materials, internship placement
Housing: *Arr by pgm:* homestay
Deadline: Mar 1
Other info: *US accredited sponsor:* yes *Began:* 1995 *Orient:* abroad (intensive lang study) *Activities:* excursions, cultural events *Misc:* Loans avail. Student's area of interest matched with local bus, sch, social svc or organization for internships. May contact former participants. *Financial aid:* scholarships *URL:* http://www.newpaltz.edu/oie/
Contact: Ctr for Intl Pgms, SUNY New Paltz, 75 S Manheim Blvd, Ste 9, New Paltz NY 12561 *Ph:* 845-257 3125 *Fax:* 845-257 3129
E-mail: international@newpaltz.edu ▲

QUITO

2032
ACADEMIA DE ESPANOL QUITO
Activa Spanish Program
Site: Ecuador: Quito
Dates: 1 wk or longer, yr-round
Subjects: Homestay, Spanish language (beg/int/adv)
Eligibility: *Level:* adults, teachers, professionals *Age:* min 17, avg 30
Credit: *Undergrad:* avail *Grad:* avail *Doc:* transcript *Transfer credit through:* Univ of Southern Mississippi
Instruction: *In:* Spanish *Format:* lang study *Students:* intl
Costs: $469 per wk *incl* tuition, housing, all meals, fees, excursions, books/materials, airport transfer *Nonrefundable fee*
Housing: *Arr by pgm:* homestay
Deadline: None
Other info: *US accredited sponsor:* no *Began:* 1982 *Activities:* excursions, field trips, cultural events *Misc:* Dance lessons, daily excursions. May contact former participants. *URL:* http://www.academiaquito.com.ec
Contact: Edgar J Alvarez, Dir, Acad de Espanol Quito, 130 Marchena St & 10 de Agosto Ave, Quito, Ecuador *E-mail:* edalvare@ecnet.ec
Or Contact: Dra Syla Mendoza, Acad Dir, Acad de Espanol Quito, 130 Marchena St & 10 de Agosto Ave, Quito, Ecuador
E-mail: edalvare@pi.pro.ec

2033
ACADEMIA DE ESPANOL QUITO
Anaconda Spanish Program
Site: Ecuador: Quito
Dates: 1 wk, yr-round
Subjects: Spanish language (int/adv)
Eligibility: *Level:* adults, teachers, professionals *Requires:* previous study in field, previous Spanish lang study *Age:* min 17, avg 30
Credit: *Undergrad:* none *Grad:* none *Doc:* transcript
Instruction: *In:* Spanish *Format:* lang study *Students:* intl
Costs: $580 *incl* tuition, housing, all meals, fees, excursions, books/materials, airport transfer *Nonrefundable fee*
Housing: *Arr by pgm:* hotels
Deadline: None
Other info: *US accredited sponsor:* no *Began:* 1982 *Activities:* excursions, field trips, cultural events *Misc:* Daily excursions with native guides. May contact former participants. *URL:* http://www.academiaquito.com.ec
Contact: Edgar J Alvarez, Dir, Acad de Espanol Quito, 130 Marchena St & 10 de Agosto Ave, Quito, Ecuador *E-mail:* edalvare@ecnet.ec
Or Contact: Dra Syla Mendoza, Acad Dir, Acad de Espanol Quito, 130 Marchena St & 10 de Agosto Ave, Quito, Ecuador
E-mail: edalvare@pi.pro.ec

2034
ACADEMIA DE ESPANOL QUITO
Intensiva Spanish Program
Site: Ecuador: Quito
Dates: 1 wk or longer, yr-round
Subjects: Homestay, Spanish language (beg/int/adv)
Eligibility: *Level:* adults, teachers, professionals *Age:* min 17, avg 30
Credit: *Undergrad:* avail *Grad:* avail *Doc:* transcript *Transfer credit through:* Nicholls State Univ
Instruction: *In:* Spanish *Format:* lang study *Students:* intl
Costs: $429 per wk *incl* tuition, housing, all meals, fees, books/materials, airport transfer *Nonrefundable fee*
Housing: *Arr by pgm:* homestay
Deadline: None
Other info: *US accredited sponsor:* no *Began:* 1982 *Activities:* excursions, field trips, cultural events *Misc:* Dance lessons. May contact former participants. *URL:* http://www.academiaquito.com.ec
Contact: Edgar J Alvarez, Dir, Acad de Espanol Quito, 130 Marchena St & 10 de Agosto Ave, Quito, Ecuador *E-mail:* edalvare@ecnet.ec
Or Contact: Dra Syla Mendoza, Acad Dir, Acad de Espanol Quito, 130 Marchena St & 10 de Agosto Ave, Quito, Ecuador
E-mail: edalvare@pi.pro.ec

2035
ALMA COLLEGE
Alma College Program of Studies in Ecuador
Site: Ecuador: Quito *Host inst:* Acad Latinoamericana
Dates: 1-4 mos, yr-round
Subjects: Art, Business/management, Civilization/culture, Ecuadorian studies, History, Homestay, Internships, Literature, Spanish language
Eligibility: *Level:* sophs, jrs, srs, grads, adults, teachers, professionals *Requires:* 2.5 GPA, 3.0 for internships *Age:* min 18, avg 20
Credit: *Undergrad:* avail *Grad:* none *Doc:* transcript
Instruction: *In:* Spanish *Format:* internship, lang study, lecture, seminar *Students:* intl
Costs: Contact sponsor
Housing: *Arr by pgm:* homestay
Deadline: 2 mos before pgm; Oct 15 & Mar 15 for scholarships
Other info: *US accredited sponsor:* yes *Began:* 1999 *Orient:* abroad (1 day) *Activities:* excursions, cultural events, sports *Misc:* Direct enrollment possible. May contact former participants. *Financial aid:* scholarships *URL:* http://www.alma.edu/academics/international
Contact: Chris Musick, Dir, Intl Educ, Alma Coll, 614 W Superior, Alma MI 48801 *Ph:* 800-321 2562; 517-463 7055 *Fax:* 517-463 7126 *E-mail:* intl_studies@alma.edu

2036
COLLEGE CONSORTIUM FOR INTERNATIONAL STUDIES and **COLLEGE OF STATEN ISLAND, CITY UNIVERSITY OF NEW YORK** and **BROOKDALE COMMUNITY COLLEGE**
Program in Quito
Site: Ecuador: Quito *Host inst:* Univ San Francisco de Quito
Dates: 9 wks, late May-late Jul
Subjects: Andean studies, Anthropology, Art, Civilization/culture, Drama/theater, Ecology/environmental studies, History, Latin American studies, Literature, Sociology, Spanish language (int/adv)
Eligibility: *Level:* fresh, sophs, jrs, srs,

grads, adults *Requires:* 2.5 GPA, 2 recommendation letters, essay, transcript, int/adv coll Spanish *Age:* min 18
Credit: *Undergrad:* 6-8 *Grad:* none *Doc:* transcript
Instruction: *In:* English, Spanish *Format:* lang study, lecture, study tour *Students:* mainly US
Costs: $3,065 *incl* tuition, housing, some meals, fees, excursions *Nonrefundable fee*
Housing: *Arr by pgm:* homestay
Deadline: Apr 15
Other info: *US accredited sponsor:* yes *Began:* 1989 *Orient:* abroad *Activities:* excursions *Misc:* Loans avail. May contact former participants. *URL:* http://www.ccisabroad.org
Contact: *See Index II for Members* CCIS, 2000 P St NW, Ste 503, Washington DC 20036 *Ph:* 800-453 6956; 202-223 0330 *Fax:* 202-223 0999 *E-mail:* info@ccisabroad.org
Or Contact: Emily Hagadorn, Mgr, Intl Studies, Brookdale CC, 765 Newman Springs Rd, Lincroft NJ 07738 *Ph:* 732-224 2577 *Fax:* 732-224 2980 *E-mail:* ehagadorn@brookdale.cc.nj.us
Or Contact: Coord, Ecuador Pgms, Ctr for Intl Svc, Coll of Staten Island/CUNY, Bldg 2A, Rm 206, 2800 Victory Blvd, Staten Island NY 10314 *Ph:* 718-982 2100 *Fax:* 718-982 2108 *E-mail:* studyab@postbox.csi.cuny.edu ▲

2037
GEORGETOWN UNIVERSITY
Quito MAT Program
Site: Ecuador: Quito *Host inst:* Univ de las Americas
Dates: 6 wks for 3 summers, early Jun-late-Jul
Subjects: Education/teaching (adv), Foreign language teaching (adv), Spanish language (adv)
Eligibility: *Level:* grads, teachers *Requires:* 3.2 GPA, previous study in field, adv Spanish
Credit: *Undergrad:* none *Grad:* 9 per summer *Doc:* transcript, degree
Instruction: *In:* Spanish *Format:* lang study, lecture, seminar *Students:* mainly US
Costs: About $3,850 per term *incl* tuition, housing, some meals, insurance, fees, excursions, books/materials *Nonrefundable fee*
Housing: *Arr by pgm:* homestay
Deadline: Mid-Mar
Other info: *US accredited sponsor:* yes *Began:* 1970 *Orient:* in US *Activities:* excursions *Misc:* Master of Arts in teaching Spanish earned after completing 3 summers & thesis. May contact former participants. *URL:* http://www.georgetown.edu/programs/oip/os/sites/summer
Contact: Dr Hector Campos or Rachel Rubin, Intl Pgms, Georgetown Univ, Box 571013, Washington DC 20057-1013 *Ph:* 202-687 5620 *Fax:* 202-687 5944 *E-mail:* rubinr@georgetown.edu

---

2038
GEORGETOWN UNIVERSITY
Summer Session in Quito
Site: Ecuador: Quito *Host inst:* Univ de las Americas
Dates: 6-7 wks, late May or early Jun-late Jul
Subjects: Civilization/culture, Homestay, Linguistics, Literature, Spanish language (beg/int/adv)
Eligibility: *Level:* fresh, sophs, jrs, srs, grads, teachers, precoll *Requires:* 3.2 GPA, previous study in field, high beg proficiency in Spanish *Age:* min 18
Credit: *Undergrad:* 6-8 *Grad:* 6-8 *Doc:* transcript
Instruction: *In:* Spanish *Format:* lang study, lecture, seminar, volunteer/svc *Students:* intl
Costs: About $3,550, $3,850 for accelerated pgm *incl* tuition, housing, some meals, insurance, fees, excursions, books/materials *Nonrefundable fee*
Housing: *Arr by pgm:* homestay
Deadline: Mid-Mar
Other info: *US accredited sponsor:* yes *Began:* 1970 *Orient:* in US *Misc:* Placement exam given on site. Competency exam given at the end of pgm. May contact former participants. *URL:* http://www.georgetown.edu/programs/oip/os/sites/summer
Contact: Hector Campos or Rachel Rubin, Intl Pgms, Georgetown Univ, Box 571013, Washington DC 20057-1013 *Ph:* 202-687 5620 *E-mail:* rubinr@georgetown.edu

---

2039
KENTUCKY INSTITUTE FOR INTERNATIONAL STUDIES (KIIS)
Program in Ecuador
Site: Ecuador: Quito
Dates: Jun-Jul
Subjects: Biology, Ecology/environmental studies, Geoscience
Eligibility: *Level:* fresh, sophs, jrs, srs, grads, adults, teachers, professionals *Requires:* 2.0 GPA, faculty recommendations, good acad standing *Age:* min 18
Credit: *Undergrad:* 3-6 *Grad:* none *Doc:* transcript *Transfer credit through:* Murray State Univ
Instruction: *In:* English *Format:* independent study, lecture, seminar, study tour *Students:* mainly US
Costs: $3,500 for students at member schs, $3,800 for others *incl* tuition, housing, all meals, intl airfare, fees, excursions, ISIC *Nonrefundable fee*
Housing: *Arr by pgm:* guest houses
Deadline: Feb 15 ($100 late fee)
Other info: *US accredited sponsor:* yes *Began:* 1995 *Orient:* in US & abroad *Activities:* excursions, cultural events *Misc:* Excursion to Galapagos Islands. May contact former participants. *Financial aid:* scholarships *URL:* http://www.kiis.org
Contact: *See Index II for Members* Dr J Milton Grimes, Exec Dir, KIIS, Murray State Univ, PO Box 9, Murray KY 42071-0009 *Ph:* 270-762 3091 *Fax:* 270-762 3434 *E-mail:* kiismsu@murraystate.edu

---

2040
LANGUAGE LINK and **ACADEMIA DE ESPANOL QUITO**
One-on-One Spanish Instruction in Ecuador
Site: Ecuador: Quito
Dates: 1-16 wks, yr-round
Subjects: Spanish language
Eligibility: *Level:* fresh, sophs, jrs, srs, grads, adults, teachers, professionals, precoll *Age:* avg 28
Credit: *Undergrad:* 12 *Grad:* 6 *Doc:* transcript
Instruction: *In:* Spanish *Format:* lang study, tutorial *Students:* intl
Costs: $294 per wk *incl* tuition, housing, some meals, insurance, books/materials, airport transfer *Nonrefundable fee*
Housing: *Arr by pgm:* homestay
Deadline: None
Other info: *US accredited sponsor:* no *Began:* 1985 *In coop with:* Austin Peay State Univ *Orient:* abroad *Activities:* excursions, field trips, cultural events, sports *Misc:* Amazon pgm & Pacific Beach pgm. May contact former participants. *URL:* http://www.langlink.com
Contact: Kay G Rafool, Dir, Lang Link, PO Box 3006, Peoria IL 61612-3006 *Ph:* 800-552 2051; 309-692 2961 *Fax:* 309-692 2926 *E-mail:* info@langlink.com

---

2041
LANGUAGES ABROAD
Language and Cultural Immersion Programs-Quito
Site: Ecuador: Quito
Dates: 2 wks or longer, yr-round
Subjects: Civilization/culture, Homestay, Spanish language (beg/int/adv)
Eligibility: *Level:* adults *Age:* min 17, max 65, avg 25
Credit: *Undergrad:* none *Grad:* none *Doc:* certificate
Instruction: *In:* Spanish *Format:* lang study *Students:* intl
Costs: $2,250 for 4 wks *incl* tuition, housing, some meals, excursions, books/materials

Housing: *Arr by pgm:* apartments, homestay
Deadline: None
Other info: *US accredited sponsor:* no *Misc:* May contact former participants. *URL:* http://www.languagesabroad.com
Contact: Ms Jesse Philippe, Langs Abroad, 317 Adelaide St W, Ste 900, Toronto, Ontario M5V 1P9, Canada *Ph:* 800-219 9924; 416-925 7117 *E-mail:* info@languagesabroad.com

---

2042
NATIONAL REGISTRATION CENTER FOR STUDY ABROAD (NRCSA)
Study in Ecuador
Site: Ecuador: Quito *Host inst:* Acad de Espanol Quito, Acad Latinoamer de Espanol
Dates: 2-3 wks or longer, yr-round
Subjects: Civilization/culture, Homestay, Latin American studies, Spanish language (beg/int/adv), Spanish studies
Eligibility: *Level:* fresh, sophs, jrs, srs, grads, adults *Age:* min 18
Credit: *Undergrad:* avail *Grad:* avail
Instruction: *In:* Spanish *Format:* lang study, lecture *Students:* intl
Costs: Contact sponsor
Housing: *Arr by pgm:* homestay
Deadline: None
Other info: *US accredited sponsor:* no *Misc:* Optional excursions. *URL:* http://www.nrcsa.com
Contact: June Domoe, NRCSA, 823 N 2nd St, #206, Milwaukee WI 53203 *Ph:* 414-278 0631 *Fax:* 414-271 8884 *E-mail:* info@nrcsa.com

---

2043
QUITO SPANISH INSTITUTE
Spanish in the Middle of the World
Site: Ecuador: Quito *Host inst:* Intl Benedict Schs of Langs
Dates: 1 wk or longer, yr-round
Subjects: Ecuadorian studies, Geography, History, Homestay, Spanish language (beg/int/adv)
Eligibility: *Level:* fresh, sophs, jrs, srs, grads, adults, precoll
Credit: *Undergrad:* avail *Grad:* none *Doc:* certificate, diploma
Instruction: *In:* Spanish *Format:* lang study *Students:* US & intl
Costs: $5 per hr *incl* books/materials, activities
Housing: *Sponsor assists:* homestay, hostels
Deadline: None
Other info: *US accredited sponsor:* no *Began:* 1990 *In coop with:* Benedict Schs *Orient:* abroad *Activities:* field trips, cultural events, sports *Financial aid:* work study *URL:* http://www.quitospanish.com
Contact: Maria Clara de Wohlermann, SI Spanish Inst, Edmundo Chiriboga N47 133, Jorge Paez (La Concepcion), Quito, Ecuador *E-mail:* info@quitospanish.com
Or Contact: Teresa Bershaw, Benedict Schs, Edmundo Chiriboga N47 133, Jorge Paez (La Concepcion), Quito, Ecuador *E-mail:* benedict@accessinter.net

---

2044
SYRACUSE UNIVERSITY
Exploring Ecuador: From the Andes to the Amazon
Site: Ecuador: Quito
Dates: 6 wks, Jun 8-Jul 22
Subjects: Anthropology, Field study, Homestay, Independent study, Spanish studies
Eligibility: *Level:* fresh, sophs, jrs, srs, grads, adults *Requires:* 2.5 GPA *Age:* min 18
Credit: *Undergrad:* 6 *Grad:* 6 *Doc:* transcript
Instruction: *In:* English *Format:* directed field study, independent study, lecture, seminar *Students:* mainly US
Costs: $6,000 *incl* tuition, housing, some meals, fees, excursions *Nonrefundable fee*
Housing: *Arr by pgm:* homestay
Deadline: Mar 15
Other info: *US accredited sponsor:* yes *Began:* 2001 *Orient:* abroad *Activities:* excursions, field trips *Misc:* May contact former participants. *Financial aid:* scholarships *URL:* http://sumweb.syr.edu/dipa/summer
Contact: Daisy Fried, Assoc Dir, Intl Pgms Abroad, Syracuse Univ, 119 Euclid Ave, Syracuse NY 13244 *Ph:* 800-251 9674; 315-443 9419 *Fax:* 315-443 9419 *E-mail:* dsfried@summer3.syr.edu ▲

Guadeloupe

SAINTE-ANNE

2045
EDUVACATIONS
Learn French in the Caribbean
Site: Guadeloupe: Sainte-Anne
Dates: 2 wks or longer, yr-round
Subjects: Caribbean studies, Civilization/culture, French language (beg/int/adv), Music, Outdoor activities/education, Scuba diving
Eligibility: *Level:* adults, precoll *Age:* min 16
Credit: *Undergrad:* none *Grad:* none
Instruction: *In:* French *Format:* directed field study, lang study *Students:* intl
Costs: Contact sponsor
Housing: *Sponsor assists:* apartments, homestay, hotels
Deadline: None
Other info: *US accredited sponsor:* no *Activities:* excursions, field trips, cultural events, sports *Misc:* Excursions to rain forest. May contact former participants. *URL:* http://www.eduvacations.com
Contact: Mary Ann Puglisi, eduVacations, 1431 21st St NW, Ste 302, Washington DC 20036 *Ph:* 202-857 8384 *Fax:* 202-463 8091

Guatemala

MORE THAN ONE CITY

2046
AMERISPAN UNLIMITED
Spanish Study and Homestay in Guatemala
Site: Guatemala: Antigua, Quetzaltenango *Host inst:* various insts
Dates: 1 wk-1 yr, yr-round
Subjects: Civilization/culture, Current events, Homestay, Latin American studies, Spanish language (beg/int/adv)
Eligibility: *Level:* fresh, sophs, jrs, srs, grads, adults *Age:* min 16
Credit: *Undergrad:* avail *Grad:* avail *Doc:* certificate *Transfer credit through:* Univ of Southern Mississippi
Instruction: *In:* Spanish *Format:* lang study, study tour, tutorial, volunteer/svc *Students:* intl
Costs: $385 for 2 wks, $750 for 4 wks, $175 for each addtl wk *incl* tuition, housing, all meals, insurance, books/materials
Housing: *Sponsor assists:* homestay, hotels
Deadline: 4 wks before pgm
Other info: *US accredited sponsor:* no *Orient:* abroad *Activities:* excursions, field trips, cultural events, sports *Misc:* Transfer credit also avail through Seattle Central CC. May contact former participants. *Financial aid:* work study *URL:* http://www.amerispan.com/
Contact: AmeriSpan Unltd, PO Box 40007, Philadelphia PA 19106 *Ph:* 800-879 6640; 215-751 1100 *Fax:* 215-751 1986 *E-mail:* info@amerispan.com

---

2047
HIGHER EDUCATION CONSORTIUM FOR URBAN AFFAIRS
Environment, Economy and Community in Guatemala
Site: Guatemala: Guatemala City, Lake Atitlan region
Dates: 1 mo, Jan 3-29
Subjects: Anthropology, Development studies, Ecology/environmental studies, Economics, Humanities, International studies, Justice, Latin American studies, Peace studies, Political science/politics, Rural studies, Social policy, Social welfare/services, Sociology, Women's studies

Eligibility: *Level:* sophs, jrs, srs *Requires:* 1 yr coll Spanish or equiv
Credit: *Undergrad:* 4 *Grad:* none *Doc:* transcript *Transfer credit through:* Hamline Univ
Instruction: *In:* English, Spanish *Format:* directed field study, lecture, seminar *Students:* mainly US
Costs: $2,275 *incl* tuition, housing, some meals, intl airfare, excursions *Nonrefundable fee*
Housing: *Arr by pgm:* homestay, hotels
Deadline: Oct 4
Other info: *US accredited sponsor:* yes *Began:* 1999 *Orient:* in US & abroad *Activities:* excursions, field trips, program travel *Misc:* 1 wk homestay in rural Guatemala. May contact former participants. *URL:* http://www.hecua.org
Contact: *See Index II for Members* Rebecca Rassier, Dir, Campus Relations & Student Svcs, HECUA, Mail #36 at Hamline Univ, 1536 Hewitt Ave, St Paul MN 55104-1284 *Ph:* 800-554 1089; 651-646 8831 *Fax:* 651-659 9421 *E-mail:* info@hecua.org

---

2048
LANGUAGE LIAISON
Spanish Saturation-Guatemala
Site: Guatemala: Antigua, Quetzaltenango
Dates: 2 wks or longer, yr-round
Subjects: Civilization/culture, Homestay, Spanish language, Spanish studies
Eligibility: *Level:* adults, precoll
Credit: *Undergrad:* avail *Grad:* avail *Doc:* certificate
Instruction: *In:* Spanish *Format:* lang study, tutorial *Students:* intl
Costs: Contact sponsor
Housing: *Arr by pgm:* apartments, homestay, pensions
Deadline: 45 days before pgm
Other info: *US accredited sponsor:* no *Misc:* Scholarship research svc. *URL:* http://www.languageliaison.com
Contact: Nancy Forman, Dir, Lang Liaison, 4 Burnham Pkwy, Morristown NJ 07960 *Ph:* 800-284 4448 *Fax:* 973-898 1710 *E-mail:* learn@languageliaison.com

---

2049
LINGUA SERVICE WORLDWIDE
Intensive Language and Culture in Guatemala
Site: Guatemala: Antigua, Quetzaltenango *Host inst:* UTATLAN, others
Dates: 1 wk-1 yr, yr-round
Subjects: Culinary arts, Embroidery, History, Homestay, Literature, Painting, Quiche language, Spanish language (beg/int/adv), Sports
Eligibility: *Level:* adults
Credit: *Undergrad:* avail *Grad:* avail *Doc:* transcript, certificate
Instruction: *In:* Spanish *Format:* lang study, lecture *Students:* intl
Costs: Contact sponsor
Housing: *Arr by pgm:* homestay, hotels
Deadline: 45 days before pgm
Other info: *US accredited sponsor:* no *Orient:* abroad *Activities:* excursions, field trips, cultural events, sports *Misc:* May contact former participants. *URL:* http://www.linguaserviceworldwide.com
Contact: Dir, Lingua Svc Worldwide, 75 Prospect St, Ste 4, Huntington NY 11743 *Ph:* 800-394 5327; 631-424 0777 *Fax:* 631-271 3441 *E-mail:* itctravel@worldnet.att.net ▲

ANTIGUA

2050
ACADEMIA DE ESPANOL PROBIGUA
Spanish Immersion Program
Site: Guatemala: Antigua
Dates: 1 wk or longer, yr-round
Subjects: Spanish language (beg/int/adv)
Eligibility: *Level:* adults *Age:* avg 25
Credit: *Undergrad:* none *Grad:* none *Doc:* certificate
Instruction: *In:* Spanish *Format:* lang study *Students:* intl
Costs: $135 per wk *incl* tuition, housing, all meals, books/materials
Housing: *Arr by pgm:* homestay, hotels
Deadline: None
Other info: *US accredited sponsor:* no *Began:* 1994 *Activities:* excursions, field trips, cultural events *Misc:* PROBIGUA provides the beg, int or adv student of Spanish with an intensive, total immersion experience. *URL:* http://probigua.conexion.com
Contact: Rigoberto Zamora Charuc, Probigua, 6a Ave Norte 41B, Antigua, Guatemala 03001 *E-mail:* probigua@conexion.com.gt

---

2051
ACADEMIA DE ESPANOL SAN JOSE EL VIEJO
San Jose El Viejo Spanish Language Study
Site: Guatemala: Antigua
Dates: 1 wk-6 mos, Jan 4-Dec 27
Subjects: Spanish language (beg/int/adv)
Eligibility: *Level:* fresh, sophs, jrs, srs, grads, adults, teachers, professionals, precoll
Credit: *Undergrad:* avail *Grad:* avail *Doc:* transcript, certificate
Instruction: *In:* Spanish *Format:* lang study *Students:* intl
Costs: $185 per week *incl* tuition, housing, some meals, books/materials
Housing: *Sponsor assists:* apartments, homestay, pensions, hotels
Deadline: 4 days before pgm
Other info: *US accredited sponsor:* no *Orient:* abroad *Activities:* excursions, field trips, cultural events *Misc:* May contact former participants. *URL:* http://www.guate.net/spanish/
Contact: Joan Ashton, Spanish Sch San Jose El Viejo, PO Box 1218, 50 Beowawie Rd, Crystal Bay NV 89402-1218 *Ph:* 800-562 6274; 775-831 5678 *Fax:* 775-832 5678 *E-mail:* joanash@aol.com
Or Contact: Jorge L Guzman, San Jose El Viejo, 5 Ave Sur 34, Antigua, Guatemala *E-mail:* spanish@guate.net

---

2052
ART WORKSHOPS IN GUATEMALA
Art Workshops in Guatemala
Site: Guatemala: Antigua
Dates: 10 days, Jan, Feb, Mar, Apr, Oct or Nov
Subjects: Book arts, Civilization/culture, Creative writing, Fiber art, Mayan studies, Photography, Visual arts, Weaving
Eligibility: *Level:* adults, teachers, professionals *Age:* min 18
Credit: *Undergrad:* none *Grad:* none
Instruction: *In:* English, Spanish *Format:* study tour, workshop *Students:* mainly US
Costs: Contact sponsor
Housing: *Arr by pgm:* hotels, bed & breakfasts
Deadline: Contact sponsor
Other info: *US accredited sponsor:* no *Began:* 1995 *Orient:* abroad *Activities:* excursions, field trips, program travel *Misc:* May contact former participants. *URL:* http://www.artguat.org
Contact: Lisa Fourre, Dir, Art Workshops in Guatemala, 4758 Lyndale Ave S, Minneapolis MN 55409-2304 *Ph:* 612-825 0747, 502-832 6403 *Fax:* 612-825 6637 *E-mail:* info@artguat.org

---

2053
LANGUAGES ABROAD
Language and Cultural Immersion Programs-Guatemala
Site: Guatemala: Antigua
Dates: 2 wks or longer, yr-round
Subjects: Civilization/culture, Homestay, Spanish language (beg/int/adv)
Eligibility: *Level:* adults *Age:* min 17, max 65, avg 25
Credit: *Undergrad:* none *Grad:* none *Doc:* certificate
Instruction: *In:* Spanish *Format:* lang study *Students:* intl
Costs: From $2,250 for 4 wks *incl* tuition, housing, some meals, excursions, books/materials
Housing: *Arr by pgm:* apartments, homestay
Deadline: None
Other info: *US accredited sponsor:* no

Misc: May contact former participants. *URL:* http://www.languagesabroad.com
Contact: Ms Jesse Philippe, Langs Abroad, 317 Adelaide St W, Ste 900, Toronto, Ontario M5V 1P9, Canada *Ph:* 800-219 9924; 416-925 7117 *E-mail:* info@languagesabroad.com

---

2054
PROYECTO LINGUISTICO FRANCISCO MARROQUIN
One-on-One Spanish Study
Site: Guatemala: Antigua
Dates: 2-16 wks, yr-round
Subjects: Homestay, Mayan languages (beg/int/adv), Spanish language (beg/int/adv)
Eligibility: *Level:* adults *Age:* min 14, avg 28
Credit: *Undergrad:* 12 hrs per sem *Grad:* 6 hrs per sem *Doc:* transcript
Instruction: *In:* Spanish, Mayan *Format:* lang study, tutorial *Students:* intl
Costs: $200 per wk *incl* tuition, housing, all meals *Nonrefundable fee*
Housing: *Arr by pgm:* homestay
Deadline: None
Other info: *US accredited sponsor:* yes *Began:* 1972 *In coop with:* Austin Peay State Univ *Orient:* abroad *Activities:* excursions, cultural events *Misc:* May contact former participants. *URL:* http://www.plfm-antigua.org
Contact: Kay G Rafool, Dir, Lang Link/PLFM, PO Box 3006, Peoria IL 61612-3006 *Ph:* 800-552 2051; 309-692 2961 *Fax:* 309-692 2926 *E-mail:* info@langlink.com

---

QUETZALTENANGO

2055
CASA XELAJU
Casa de Espanol Xelaju
Site: Guatemala: Quetzaltenango
Dates: 2-12 wks, yr-round
Subjects: Civilization/culture, Culinary arts, Ecology/environmental studies, Folk dance, Government, History, Languages, Latin American studies, Social sciences, Spanish language (beg/int/adv), Weaving, Women's studies
Eligibility: *Level:* fresh, sophs, jrs, srs, grads, teachers, professionals *Requires:* 3.0 GPA, for grads, 2.5 GPA for undergrads *Age:* min 17, avg 30
Credit: *Undergrad:* 3-12 *Grad:* 3-12 *Doc:* transcript *Transfer credit through:* Univ of Southern Mississippi
Instruction: *In:* Spanish *Format:* tutorial *Students:* intl
Costs: Contact sponsor
Housing: *Sponsor assists:* apartments, homestay
Deadline: 2 wks before pgm
Other info: *US accredited sponsor:* no *Began:* 1987 *Orient:* abroad *Activities:* excursions, field trips, program travel, cultural events *Misc:* Daily activities. Extra charge for univ credit. Rain forest expeditions. May contact former participants. *URL:* http://www.casaxelaju.com
Contact: Julio Batres, Dir, Casa Xelaju, 3034 47th Ave S, Minneapolis MN 55406 *Ph:* 888-729 9253; 612-729 9253 *Fax:* 612-729 9264 *E-mail:* info@casaxelaju.com
Or Contact: Dir, Casa Xelaju, Casa de Espanol Xelaju, Callejon 15, Diagonal 13-02, Zona 1, Quetzaltenango, Guatemala *E-mail:* office@casaxelaju.com

---

2056
CASA XELAJU
Xela Tours
Site: Guatemala: Quetzaltenango
Dates: 3 wks, summer
Subjects: Archaeology, Civilization/culture, Human rights, Latin American studies, Mayan studies, Spanish language, Women's studies
Eligibility: *Level:* srs, grads, adults, teachers, professionals *Requires:* 3.0 GPA, previous Spanish lang study *Age:* min 20, max 70, avg 30
Credit: *Undergrad:* avail *Grad:* 3 *Doc:* transcript *Transfer credit through:* Univ of Southern Mississippi
Instruction: *In:* Spanish *Format:* study tour *Students:* mainly US
Costs: $1,500 *incl* housing, all meals, insurance, fees, excursions, in-country transport *Nonrefundable fee*
Housing: *Arr by pgm:* homestay, pensions, hotels
Deadline: 4 wks before pgm
Other info: *US accredited sponsor:* no *Began:* 1996 *Orient:* abroad (1 day, intensive lang study) *Activities:* excursions, field trips, program travel, cultural events *Misc:* May contact former participants. *URL:* http://www.casaxelaju.com
Contact: Julio Batres, Dir, Casa Xelaju, 2034 47th Ave S, Minneapolis MN 55406 *Ph:* 888-796 2272; 612-729 9253 *Fax:* 612-729 9264 *E-mail:* info@casaxelaju.com
Or Contact: Dir, Casa Xelaju, Callejon 15, Diagonal 13-02, Zona 1, Quetzaltenango, Guatemala *E-mail:* office@casaxelaju.com

---

2057
CENTRO DE ESTUDIOS DE ESPANOL POP WUJ
Centro de Estudios de Espanol Pop Wuj
Site: Guatemala: Quetzaltenango
Dates: Contact sponsor
Subjects: Civilization/culture, History, Latin American studies, Mayan studies, Quiche language, Spanish language
Eligibility: *Level:* fresh, sophs, jrs, srs, grads, adults, teachers, professionals, precoll *Age:* avg 24
Credit: *Undergrad:* none *Grad:* none *Doc:* certificate
Instruction: *In:* Spanish *Format:* lang study, lecture *Students:* intl
Costs: $140 per wk Jun, Jul, Aug, Jan, $125 per wk for other mos *incl* tuition, housing, all meals *Nonrefundable fee*
Housing: *Arr by pgm:* homestay
Deadline: Contact sponsor
Other info: *US accredited sponsor:* no *Began:* 1991 *In coop with:* Williams Coll (MA), Greenbrier E HS (WV) *Orient:* abroad *Activities:* excursions, field trips, cultural events *Misc:* One-on-one lang instruction. May contact former participants. *URL:* http://www.popwuj.org
Contact: Coord, Ctr Pop Wuj, Apdo Postal 68, Quetzaltenango, Guatemala *E-mail:* popwujxel@pronet.net.gt
Or Contact: Rebecca Walters or Numa Marlborough, Registration, Ctr de Estudios Pop Wuj, PO Box 11127, Santa Rosa CA 95406 *Ph:* 707-869 1116 *Fax:* 707-869 1116 *E-mail:* popwuj@juno.com

---

2058
ESCUELA DE ESPANOL JUAN SISAY
Spanish Language School-Total Immersion
Site: Guatemala: Quetzaltenango
Dates: 1 wk-1 yr, yr-round
Subjects: Spanish language (beg/int/adv)
Eligibility: *Level:* adults *Age:* min 12, max 70, avg 28
Credit: *Undergrad:* none *Grad:* none *Doc:* certificate
Instruction: *In:* Spanish *Format:* lang study *Students:* intl
Costs: $125 per wk, $140 per wk *incl* tuition, housing, all meals, fees
Housing: *Arr by pgm:* homestay
Deadline: None
Other info: *US accredited sponsor:* no *Began:* 1991 *Activities:* excursions, field trips, program travel, cultural events, sports
Contact: Jean Dodge Totzke, Escuela Juan Sisay, 3465 Cedar Valley Ct, Smyrna GA 30080 *Ph:* 770-436 6283 *E-mail:* juansisay@aol.com

---

2059
INSTITUTO CENTRAL AMERICA (ICA)
Spanish Language and Guatemalan Culture Program
Site: Guatemala: Quetzaltenango
Dates: 1 wk or longer, yr-round
Subjects: Spanish language (beg/int/adv)
Eligibility: *Level:* grads, adults, teachers, professionals, precoll
Credit: *Undergrad:* none *Grad:* none

Instruction: *In:* Spanish *Format:* lang study, lecture, tutorial *Students:* intl
Costs: $120 per wk Sep-May, $130 per wk Jun-Aug *incl* tuition, housing, all meals, excursions, books/materials, activities *Nonrefundable fee*
Housing: *Arr by pgm:* homestay
Deadline: 1 mo before pgm recommended
Other info: *US accredited sponsor:* no *Activities:* excursions, field trips *Misc:* Strictly one-on-one courses. May contact former participants. *URL:* http://www.spanishschoolica.com
Contact: Dale & Bonnie Barth, 83969 570 Ave, Stanton NE 68779 *Ph:* 402-439 2943 *Fax:* 402-439 2943 *E-mail:* dbbarth@stanton.net

---

2060
JAMES MADISON UNIVERSITY
Summer Program in Guatemala
Site: Guatemala: Quetzaltenango
Dates: 4 wks, May 10-Jun 6
Subjects: Ecology/environmental studies, Information science/systems
Eligibility: *Level:* fresh, sophs, jrs, srs *Requires:* 2.8 GPA, previous study in field *Age:* min 18, avg 20
Credit: *Undergrad:* 3 *Grad:* none *Doc:* transcript
Instruction: *In:* English *Format:* directed field study, lecture *Students:* mainly US
Costs: $2,670 for VA residents, $3,230 for others *incl* tuition, housing, some meals, fees, excursions, books/materials
Housing: *Arr by pgm:* residence halls, hotels
Deadline: Feb 1
Other info: *US accredited sponsor:* yes *Began:* 1999 *Orient:* in US & abroad *Activities:* excursions, field trips, program travel, cultural events *Misc:* May contact former participants. *URL:* http://www.jmu.edu/international/
Contact: Dr Bruce Clemens, James Madison Univ, Harrisonburg VA 22807 *Ph:* 540-568 8770 *Fax:* 540-568 8080 *E-mail:* clemenbw@jmu.edu

---

2061
LA HERMANDAD EDUCATIVA
La Hermandad Educativa
Site: Guatemala: Quetzaltenango
Dates: 1 wk or longer, yr-round
Subjects: Mam language, Spanish language
Eligibility: *Level:* adults, precoll
Credit: *Undergrad:* avail *Grad:* none *Doc:* certificate
Instruction: *In:* Spanish, Mayan *Format:* lang study *Students:* intl
Costs: $130 per wk Sep-May, $150 per wk Jun-Aug *incl* tuition, housing, all meals *Nonrefundable fee*
Housing: *Arr by pgm:* homestay
Deadline: Rolling admissions
Other info: *US accredited sponsor:* no *Orient:* abroad (1/2 day) *Activities:* excursions, field trips, program travel, cultural events *Misc:* May contact former participants. *URL:* http://www.hermandad.com
Contact: Dane Johnson or Jeannie Kapple, La Hermandad Educativa, PO Box 452, Manson, Manson WA 98831 *Ph:* 800-963 9889 *E-mail:* johsond@televar.com

---

2062
NATIONAL REGISTRATION CENTER FOR STUDY ABROAD (NRCSA)
Language Study in Guatemala
Site: Guatemala: Quetzaltenango *Host inst:* SAB Lang Ctr
Dates: 1-8 wks, yr-round
Subjects: Humanities, Spanish language (beg/int/adv)
Eligibility: *Level:* fresh, sophs, jrs, srs, teachers, precoll *Requires:* good acad standing, 1 yr Spanish *Age:* min 18, avg 25
Credit: *Undergrad:* avail *Grad:* avail
Instruction: *In:* Spanish *Format:* lang study, lecture, seminar, tutorial *Students:* intl
Costs: $742 for 4 wks, $1,238 for 8 wks *incl* tuition, housing, all meals, fees, books/materials
Housing: *Arr by pgm:* homestay
Deadline: 6 wks before pgm
Other info: *US accredited sponsor:* no *Began:* 1980 *Orient:* abroad (1 wk) *Activities:* field trips, cultural events *Misc:* May contact former participants. *URL:* http://www.nrcsa.com/
Contact: Reuel Zielke, NRCSA, 823 N 2nd St, Milwaukee WI 53203 *Ph:* 414-278 0631 *Fax:* 414-271 8884 *E-mail:* info@nrcsa.com

---

SAN ANDRES

2063
NATIONAL REGISTRATION CENTER FOR STUDY ABROAD (NRCSA)
Eco-Escuela
Site: Guatemala: San Andres *Host inst:* Eco-Escuela
Dates: 8 wks, yr-round
Subjects: Community service projects, Homestay, Spanish language (beg/int/adv)
Eligibility: *Level:* fresh, sophs, jrs, srs, grads, adults, teachers, professionals *Age:* min 18
Credit: *Undergrad:* avail *Grad:* avail *Doc:* certificate
Instruction: *In:* Spanish *Format:* lang study, tutorial, volunteer/svc *Students:* intl
Costs: $1,712 *incl* tuition, housing, all meals, insurance *Nonrefundable fee*
Housing: *Arr by pgm:* homestay
Deadline: 6 wks before pgm
Other info: *US accredited sponsor:* no *URL:* http://www.nrcsa.com
Contact: June Domoe, NRCSA, 823 N 2nd St, #206, Milwaukee WI 53203 *Ph:* 414-278 0631 *Fax:* 414-271 8884 *E-mail:* info@nrcsa.com

---

SAN JOSE

2064
NATIONAL REGISTRATION CENTER FOR STUDY ABROAD (NRCSA)
Spanish in the Rainforest
Site: Guatemala: San Jose *Host inst:* Bio-Itza
Dates: 2 or 4 wks, yr-round
Subjects: Homestay, Spanish language (beg/int/adv)
Eligibility: *Level:* fresh, sophs, jrs, srs, grads, adults, teachers, professionals *Age:* min 18
Credit: *Undergrad:* avail *Grad:* avail *Doc:* certificate
Instruction: *In:* Spanish *Format:* tutorial, volunteer/svc *Students:* intl
Costs: $448 for 2 wks, $856 for 4 wks *incl* tuition, housing, all meals, insurance *Nonrefundable fee*
Housing: *Arr by pgm:* homestay
Deadline: 6 wks before pgm
Other info: *US accredited sponsor:* no *Misc:* May contact former participants. *URL:* http://www.nrcsa.com
Contact: June Domoe, NRCSA, 823 N 2nd St, #206, Milwaukee WI 53203 *Ph:* 414-278 0631 *Fax:* 414-271 8884 *E-mail:* info@nrcsa.com

Haiti

MORE THAN ONE CITY

2065
FLORIDA INTERNATIONAL UNIVERSITY
Haitian Summer Institute
Site: Haiti: various sites
Dates: 1 wk, Jul 18-26
Subjects: Civilization/culture, Creole studies
Eligibility: *Level:* fresh, sophs, jrs, srs, grads, adults, teachers, professionals *Requires:* 3 wks of FIU course (in Miami)
Credit: *Undergrad:* avail *Grad:* avail *Doc:* transcript
Instruction: *In:* English *Format:* lang study, study tour *Students:* mainly US
Costs: $1,200-$1,500 *incl* housing, some meals, intl airfare, railpass
Housing: *Arr by pgm:* hotels
Deadline: May 15
Other info: *US accredited sponsor:* yes *Began:* 1999 *Orient:* in US (1 day) *Activities:* excursions, field trips, program

travel, cultural events *Misc:* May contact former participants. *URL:* http://www.fiu.edu/~intered
Contact: Intl Studies, Florida Intl Univ, 11200 SW 8th St, DM 300B, Miami FL 33199 *Ph:* 305-348 1913, 305-348 1918 *Fax:* 305-348 1941 *E-mail:* intered@fiu.edu

Honduras

COPAN

2066
AMERISPAN UNLIMITED
Spanish Study and Homestay in Honduras
Site: Honduras: Copan *Host inst:* Ctr Intl de Idiomas, Ixbalanque Escuela de Espanol
Dates: 1 wk-1 yr, yr-round
Subjects: Homestay, Spanish language (beg/int/adv)
Eligibility: *Level:* fresh, sophs, jrs, srs, grads, adults, teachers, professionals, precoll *Age:* min 16
Credit: *Undergrad:* avail *Grad:* avail *Doc:* transcript, certificate *Transfer credit through:* Seattle Central CC
Instruction: *In:* Spanish *Format:* lang study, tutorial *Students:* intl
Costs: $425 for 2 wks, $825 for 4 wks, $200 for each addtl wk *incl* tuition, housing, all meals, insurance, books/materials
Housing: *Arr by pgm:* homestay, hotels
Deadline: 4 wks before pgm
Other info: *US accredited sponsor:* no *Activities:* excursions, field trips, cultural events *Misc:* 1 mile from Mayan ruins of Copan. May contact former participants. *URL:* http://www.amerispan.com/
Contact: AmeriSpan Unltd, PO Box 40007, Philadelphia PA 19106 *Ph:* 800-879 6640; 215-751 1100 *Fax:* 215-751 1986 *E-mail:* info@amerispan.com

---

2067
LANGUAGES ABROAD
Language and Culture-Copan
Site: Honduras: Copan
Dates: 2 wks or longer, yr-round
Subjects: Civilization/culture, Homestay, Spanish language (beg/int/adv)
Eligibility: *Level:* adults *Age:* min 17, max 65, avg 25
Credit: *Undergrad:* none *Grad:* none *Doc:* certificate
Instruction: *In:* Spanish *Format:* lang study *Students:* intl
Costs: Contact sponsor
Housing: *Arr by pgm:* residence halls, homestay
Deadline: None
Other info: *US accredited sponsor:* no *Began:* 1995 *Activities:* excursions, field trips, program travel, cultural events, sports *Misc:* May contact former participants. *URL:* http://www.languagesabroad.com
Contact: Ms Jesse Philippe, Langs Abroad, 317 Adelaide St W, Ste 900, Toronto, Ontario M5V 1P9, Canada *Ph:* 800-219 9924; 416-925 7117 *E-mail:* info@languagesabroad.com

---

LA CEIBA

2068
NATIONAL REGISTRATION CENTER FOR STUDY ABROAD (NRCSA)
Spanish Study in Honduras
Site: Honduras: La Ceiba *Host inst:* Central Amer Spanish Sch
Dates: 2 wks or longer, yr-round
Subjects: Community service projects, Homestay, Spanish language
Eligibility: *Level:* fresh, sophs, jrs, srs, grads, adults, teachers, professionals *Age:* min 18
Credit: *Undergrad:* avail *Grad:* avail *Doc:* certificate
Instruction: *In:* Spanish *Format:* internship, lang study, tutorial, volunteer/svc *Students:* intl
Costs: $936 for 4 wks *incl* tuition, housing, all meals, insurance
Nonrefundable fee
Housing: *Arr by pgm:* homestay
Deadline: 6 wks before pgm
Other info: *US accredited sponsor:* no *Misc:* May contact former participants. *URL:* http://www.nrcsa.com
Contact: June Domoe, NRCSA, 823 N 2nd St, #206, Milwaukee WI 53203 *Ph:* 414-278 0631 *Fax:* 414-271 8884 *E-mail:* info@nrcsa.com

---

SAN PEDRO

2069
JAMES MADISON UNIVERSITY
Summer in Honduras
Site: Honduras: San Pedro
Dates: May
Subjects: Field study, Health administration/planning, Health sciences, Homestay, Independent study, Nutrition, Spanish language
Eligibility: *Level:* jrs, srs, grads *Requires:* 2.8 GPA, previous study in health scis *Age:* min 18, max 26, avg 20
Credit: *Undergrad:* 3 *Grad:* 3 *Doc:* transcript
Instruction: *In:* English, Spanish *Format:* directed field study, independent study, lab, lang study, lecture, practical training *Students:* mainly US
Costs: $1,200 for VA residents, $1,750 for others *incl* tuition, housing, some meals, fees, excursions, books/materials
Nonrefundable fee
Housing: *Arr by pgm:* homestay, hotels
Deadline: Feb 1
Other info: *US accredited sponsor:* yes *Began:* 1995 *Orient:* in US & abroad (1 wk, intensive lang study) *Activities:* excursions, cultural events *Misc:* May contact former participants. *URL:* http://www.jmu.edu/international/
Contact: Dr Marcia Hall, James Madison Univ, Moody 117, Harrisonburg VA 22807 *Ph:* 540-568 3951 *Fax:* 540-568 3336 *E-mail:* ballml@jmu.edu
Or Contact: Intl Pgms, James Madison Univ, Harrisonburg VA 22807 *Ph:* 540-568 6419 *Fax:* 540-568 8080 *E-mail:* international@jmu.edu

Jamaica

MORE THAN ONE CITY

2070
UNIVERSITY OF SOUTHERN MISSISSIPPI
Caribbean Studies Program
Site: Jamaica: Kingston, Ocho Rios *Host inst:* Univ of the West Indies
Dates: 3 wks, May 13-May 30
Subjects: Anthropology, Caribbean studies, Criminal justice, Development studies, Field study, Geography, History, Literature, Music, Nursing, Social work, Sociology, Women's studies
Eligibility: *Level:* fresh, sophs, jrs, srs, grads *Requires:* 2.0 GPA, Clear academic standing, applicants for bus course must have completed 54 sem hours with a min GPA of 2.0 for undergrads
Credit: *Undergrad:* 4 *Grad:* 4 *Doc:* transcript
Instruction: *In:* English *Format:* directed field study, lecture *Students:* mainly US
Costs: $2,199 for undergrads, $2,499 for grads *incl* tuition, housing, intl airfare, fees, excursions, ground transport
Nonrefundable fee
Housing: *Arr by pgm:* hotels, condominium resort
Deadline: Apr 29
Other info: *US accredited sponsor:* yes *Began:* 1986 *Orient:* in US & abroad *Activities:* excursions, field trips, program travel, cultural events *Misc:* May contact former participants. *Financial aid:* scholarships *URL:* http://www.usm.edu
Contact: Dr Tim W Hudson, Intl & Continuing Educ, Univ of Southern Mississippi, Box 10047, Hattiesburg MS 39406-0047 *Ph:* 601-266 4344 *Fax:* 601-266 5699 *E-mail:* melissa.ravencraft@usm.edu

Or Contact: Dr Mark Miller, Dir, Caribbean Studies Pgm, Univ of Southern Mississippi, Box 10047, Hattiesburg MS 39406-0047 *Ph:* 601-266 4729 *Fax:* 602-266 5699

LUCEA

2071
SOUTHWESTERN UNIVERSITY
Jamaica Service Learning
Site: Jamaica: Lucea
Dates: 3 wks, May 15-Jun 5
Subjects: Community service projects, Education/teaching, Social sciences
Eligibility: Own students preferred. *Level:* fresh, sophs, jrs, srs *Requires:* 2.5 GPA, previous svc experience *Age:* min 18, avg 21
Credit: *Undergrad:* 3 *Grad:* none *Doc:* transcript
Instruction: *In:* English *Format:* volunteer/svc *Students:* mainly US
Costs: $1,500 *incl* tuition, housing, intl airfare, insurance, fees, excursions *Nonrefundable fee*
Housing: *Arr by pgm:* homestay
Deadline: Mar 1
Other info: *US accredited sponsor:* yes *Began:* 1997 *Orient:* in US & abroad (5 days) *Activities:* excursions, field trips, cultural events *Misc:* May contact former participants. *Financial aid:* scholarships *URL:* http://www.southwestern.edu/academic/
Contact: Sue Mennicke, Dir, Study Abroad, Southwestern Univ, PO Box 770, Georgetown TX 78627 *Ph:* 512-863 1857 *Fax:* 512-863 1535 *E-mail:* mennicks@southwestern.edu

PRIORY

2072
ROGER WILLIAMS UNIVERSITY
Tropical Ecology
Site: Jamaica: Priory (northern coast)
Dates: Dec 27-Jan 10
Subjects: Ecology/environmental studies, Field study
Eligibility: *Level:* sophs, jrs, srs, grads *Requires:* some coll biology preferred
Credit: *Undergrad:* 3 *Grad:* none
Instruction: *In:* English *Format:* directed field study, lecture *Students:* mainly US
Costs: $1,900 *incl* tuition, housing, all meals, intl airfare, fees, excursions
Housing: *Arr by pgm:* apartments
Deadline: Sep 30
Other info: *US accredited sponsor:* yes *Began:* 1979 *Orient:* in US *Activities:* field trips
Contact: Dr Harold F Pomeroy, Roger Williams Univ, Bristol RI 02809 *Ph:* 401-254 3170 *Fax:* 401-254 3310 *E-mail:* hfp@alpha.rwu.edu

Martinique

FORT-DE-FRANCE

2073
LONGWOOD COLLEGE (VA)
Summer Study Abroad Program in Fort-de-France
Site: Martinique: Fort-de-France *Host inst:* Univ of Fort-de-France
Dates: 4 wks, May 13-Jun 12
Subjects: Civilization/culture, Creole studies, French language (int/adv), Homestay
Eligibility: *Level:* sophs, jrs, srs *Requires:* 2.5 GPA, previous study in field, 2 sems coll French *Age:* min 19
Credit: *Undergrad:* 6 *Grad:* none *Doc:* transcript, certificate
Instruction: *In:* French *Format:* lang study, study tour *Students:* mainly US
Costs: $2,600 *incl* tuition, housing, all meals, fees, excursions
Housing: *Arr by pgm:* homestay
Deadline: Mar 15
Other info: *US accredited sponsor:* yes *Began:* 1990 *In coop with:* CIRECCA *Orient:* in US (intensive lang study) *Activities:* excursions, program travel, cultural events *Misc:* Scholarships for Longwood Coll students only. May contact former participants. *URL:* http://www.lwc.edu
Contact: Dr Linda Goff, Intl Affairs, Longwood Coll, 201 High St, Farmville VA 23909-1899 *Ph:* 804-395 2172 *Fax:* 804-395 2141 *E-mail:* lgoff@longwood.lwc.edu

2074
UNIVERSITY OF DELAWARE
Winter Session in Martinique
Site: Martinique: Fort-de-France *Host inst:* Univ Antilles-Guyanne
Dates: 1 mo, Jan
Subjects: Caribbean studies, French language (int), Homestay, Literature
Eligibility: *Level:* fresh, sophs, jrs, srs, adults *Requires:* 2.0 GPA
Credit: *Undergrad:* 6-7 *Grad:* none *Doc:* transcript
Instruction: *In:* English, French *Format:* lang study, lecture, study tour *Students:* mainly US
Costs: Contact sponsor
Housing: *Arr by pgm:* homestay
Deadline: Early Oct
Other info: *US accredited sponsor:* yes *Began:* 1993 *Orient:* avail yes *Activities:* excursions, field trips, program travel, cultural events *Misc:* Contact sponsor to arrange honors credit. *Financial aid:* scholarships *URL:* http://www.udel.edu/studyabroad/
Contact: Lisa Chieffo, Study Abroad Coord, Foreign Langs & Literatures, Univ of Delaware, 326 Smith Hall, Newark DE 19716 *Ph:* 302-831 6458 *Fax:* 302-831 0597 *E-mail:* lchieffo@udel.edu
Or Contact: Intl Pgms & Special Sessions, Univ of Delaware, 4 Kent Way, Newark DE 19716 *Ph:* 888-831 4685; 302-831 2852 *Fax:* 302-831 6042 *E-mail:* studyabroad@udel.edu

Mexico

MORE THAN ONE CITY

2075
AMERISPAN UNLIMITED
Spanish Study and Homestay in Mexico
Site: Mexico: Buena Vista, Cancun, Cuernavaca, Guanajuato, Merida, Morelia, Oaxaca, San Miguel de Allende *Host inst:* various insts
Dates: 1 wk-1 yr, yr-round
Subjects: Arts, Crafts, Current events, History, Homestay, Literature, Mexican studies, Spanish language (beg/int/adv)
Eligibility: *Level:* fresh, sophs, jrs, srs, grads, adults *Age:* min 16
Credit: *Undergrad:* avail *Grad:* avail *Doc:* transcript, certificate *Transfer credit through:* Univ of Southern Mississippi
Instruction: *In:* Spanish *Format:* lang study, lecture, practical training, study tour, tutorial, workshop *Students:* intl
Costs: $550-$850 for 2 wks, $950-$1,450 for 4 wks, $225-$345 each addtl wk *incl* tuition, housing, all meals, insurance, books/materials
Housing: *Arr by pgm:* homestay, hotels
Deadline: 4 wks before pgm
Other info: *US accredited sponsor:* no *Orient:* abroad *Activities:* excursions, field trips, cultural events, sports *Misc:* Transfer credit also avail through Seattle Central CC. May contact former participants. *Financial aid:* work study *URL:* http://www.amerispan.com/
Contact: AmeriSpan Unltd, PO Box 40007, Philadelphia PA 19106 *Ph:* 800-879 6640; 215-751 1100 *Fax:* 215-751 1986 *E-mail:* info@amerispan.com

2076
LANGUAGE LIAISON
Spanish in Mexico
Site: Mexico: Cancun, Cuernavaca *Host inst:* Live in Learn
Dates: 1 wk-1 yr, yr-round
Subjects: Homestay, Spanish language
Eligibility: *Level:* adults
Credit: *Undergrad:* none *Grad:* none

Instruction: *In:* Spanish *Format:* lang study *Students:* intl
Costs: Contact sponsor
Housing: *Arr by pgm:* teacher's home
Deadline: 45 days before pgm
Other info: *US accredited sponsor:* no *Began:* 1997 *Activities:* excursions, cultural events, sports *Misc:* Scholarship research svc. *URL:* http://www.languageliaison.com
Contact: Nancy Forman, Dir, Lang Liaison, 4 Burnham Pkwy, Morristown NJ 07960 *Ph:* 800-284 4448 *Fax:* 973-898 1710 *E-mail:* learn@languageliaison.com

---

2077
LANGUAGE LIAISON
Spanish Language-Mexico
Site: Mexico: Cancun, Cuernavaca, Guadalajara, Nayarit, Oaxaca, Puerta Vallarta, San Miguel de Allende
Dates: 2 wks or longer, yr-round
Subjects: Art history, Economics, Folk dance, Folk music, History, Homestay, Humanities, Latin American studies, Literature, Mexican studies, Social welfare/services, Spanish language (beg/int/adv)
Eligibility: *Level:* fresh, sophs, jrs, srs, grads, adults, teachers, professionals, precoll *Age:* min 14
Credit: *Undergrad:* avail *Grad:* avail *Doc:* transcript, certificate
Instruction: *In:* Spanish *Format:* lang study *Students:* intl
Costs: Contact sponsor
Housing: *Arr by pgm:* apartments, homestay, hotels
Deadline: 30 days before pgm
Other info: *US accredited sponsor:* no *Activities:* excursions, field trips, cultural events *Misc:* Scholarship research svc. *URL:* http://www.languageliaison.com
Contact: Nancy Forman, Dir, Lang Liaison, 4 Burnham Pkwy, Morristown NJ 07960 *Ph:* 800-284 4448 *Fax:* 973-898 1710 *E-mail:* learn@languageliaison.com

---

2078
LANGUAGE STUDIES ABROAD, INC
Intensive Spanish-Mexico
Site: Mexico: Cuernavaca, Merida, Morelia, Puebla, San Miguel de Allende *Host inst:* various LSA insts
Dates: 1 wk or longer Merida & San Miguel de Allende/2 wks or longer Cuernavaca, yr-round
Subjects: Homestay, Mexican studies, Spanish language (beg/int/adv)
Eligibility: *Level:* fresh, sophs, jrs, srs, grads, adults, teachers, professionals, precoll *Age:* min 16
Credit: *Undergrad:* avail *Grad:* avail
Instruction: *In:* Spanish *Format:* lang study, tutorial *Students:* intl
Costs: From $1,265 for 4 wks *incl* tuition
Housing: *Arr by pgm:* apartments, homestay, hotels
Deadline: 4 wks before pgm; 8 wks before pgm for scholarships
Other info: *US accredited sponsor:* no *Orient:* abroad *Activities:* excursions, field trips, cultural events *Misc:* Scholarships for San Miguel de Allende pgm only. May contact former participants. *URL:* http://www.languagestudiesabroad.com
Contact: Lang Studies Abroad, Inc, 103 Londonderry Ct, Reno NV 89511-2718 *Ph:* 800-424 5522; 775-849 9206 *Fax:* 775-849 9217 *E-mail:* info@languagestudiesabroad.com

---

2079
LANGUAGES ABROAD
Language and Cultural Immersion-Mexico
Site: Mexico: various sites
Dates: 2 wks or longer, yr-round
Subjects: Civilization/culture, Mexican studies, Spanish language (beg/int/adv)
Eligibility: *Level:* adults *Age:* min 17, max 65, avg 25
Credit: *Undergrad:* none *Grad:* none *Doc:* certificate
Instruction: *In:* Spanish *Format:* lang study *Students:* intl
Costs: From $670 for 2 wks *incl* tuition, some meals, excursions, books/materials
Housing: *Arr by pgm:* residence halls, homestay
Deadline: None
Other info: *US accredited sponsor:* no *Began:* 1995 *Activities:* excursions, field trips, program travel, cultural events, sports *Misc:* May contact former participants. *URL:* http://www.languagesabroad.com
Contact: Ms Jesse Philippe, Langs Abroad, 317 Adelaide St W, Ste 900, Toronto, Ontario M5V 1P9, Canada *Ph:* 800-219 9924; 416-925 7117 *E-mail:* info@languagesabroad.com

---

2080
LINGUA SERVICE WORLDWIDE
Total Immersion/Intensive Language and Culture in Mexico
Site: Mexico: Cozumel, Cuernavaca, Merida, Oaxaca *Host inst:* Ctr Idiomas del Sureste, Experiencia, Inst Cultural Oaxaca, Univ Intl
Dates: 1 wk-1 yr, yr-round
Subjects: Civilization/culture, Homestay, Spanish language (beg/int/adv)
Eligibility: *Level:* fresh, sophs, jrs, srs, grads, adults, teachers, professionals, precoll *Age:* min 15, avg 30
Credit: *Undergrad:* avail *Grad:* avail *Doc:* transcript, certificate *Transfer credit through:* Univ of Southern Mississippi
Instruction: *In:* Spanish *Format:* art studio, lang study, lecture *Students:* intl
Costs: Contact sponsor
Housing: *Arr by pgm:* apartments, homestay, pensions, hotels, furnished rooms
Deadline: 45 days before pgm
Other info: *US accredited sponsor:* no *Activities:* excursions, cultural events *Misc:* May contact former participants. *URL:* http://www.linguaserviceworldwide.com
Contact: Dir, Lingua Svc Worldwide, 75 Prospect St, Ste 4, Huntington NY 11743 *Ph:* 800-394 5327; 631-424 0777 *Fax:* 631-271 3441 *E-mail:* itctravel@worldnet.att.net ▲

2081
MICHIGAN STATE UNIVERSITY
Documentary Film Making
Site: Mexico: Acapulco, Cocotitlan, Oaxaca, Puebla, Taxco
Dates: 2 wks, Dec-Jan
Subjects: English, Film studies
Eligibility: *Level:* sophs, jrs, srs, grads *Requires:* 2.0 GPA, good acad standing, interview *Age:* min 18
Credit: *Undergrad:* 4 *Grad:* avail *Doc:* transcript
Instruction: *In:* English *Format:* directed field study, seminar *Students:* mainly US
Costs: About $950 *incl* housing, insurance, excursions *Nonrefundable fee*
Housing: *Arr by pgm:* hotels
Deadline: Oct 20
Other info: *US accredited sponsor:* yes *Began:* 1992 *Orient:* in US & abroad *Activities:* excursions *Misc:* Loans avail. *Financial aid:* scholarships *URL:* http://studyabroad.msu.edu
Contact: Cheryl Benner, Study Abroad, Michigan State Univ, 109 Intl Ctr, East Lansing MI 48824-1035 *Ph:* 517-353 8920 *Fax:* 517-432 2082 *E-mail:* bennerc@msu.edu ▲

2082
NATIONAL REGISTRATION CENTER FOR STUDY ABROAD (NRCSA)
Study in Mexico
Site: Mexico: Cuernavaca, Guadalajara, Merida, Mexico City, Morelia, Oaxaca, San Cristobal, Queretaro, other sites *Host inst:* Cemanahuac, CMI, Concepto, Ctr Bilingue, Escuela de Espanol, OLE, others
Dates: 1 wk or longer, yr-round
Subjects: Civilization/culture, Culinary arts, History, Homestay, Humanities, Latin American studies, Literature, Mayan studies, Mexican studies, Spanish language (beg/int/adv), Spanish studies
Eligibility: *Level:* adults *Age:* min 18, avg 25
Credit: *Undergrad:* avail *Grad:* avail *Doc:* certificate
Instruction: *In:* Spanish *Format:* lang

study, lecture, seminar, tutorial *Students:* intl
Costs: Contact sponsor
Housing: *Arr by pgm:* apartments, homestay, pensions, hotels
Deadline: 6 wks before pgm
Other info: *US accredited sponsor:* no *Activities:* cultural events *Misc:* Addtl host insts: Ctr de Idiomas, Univ of Guadalajara, Vancouver Lang Ctr. Optional excursions. *URL:* http://www.nrcsa.com
Contact: June Domoe, NRCSA, 823 N 2nd St, #206, Milwaukee WI 53203 *Ph:* 414-278 0631 *Fax:* 414-271 8884 *E-mail:* info@nrcsa.com

---

2083
SOUTHWEST TEXAS STATE UNIVERSITY
SWT in Mexico
Site: Mexico: Yucatan, various sites
Dates: Mid-May-early Jun
Subjects: Anthropology, Field study, Independent study, Spanish language (int/adv)
Eligibility: *Level:* sophs, jrs, srs, grads, adults, teachers, professionals *Requires:* 2.0 GPA, intro Spanish for Spanish courses *Age:* min 18
Credit: *Undergrad:* 6 *Grad:* 6 *Doc:* transcript
Instruction: *In:* English, Spanish *Format:* directed field study, independent study, lang study, lecture, seminar, study tour, tutorial, volunteer/svc *Students:* mainly US
Costs: $1,600 *incl* tuition, housing, intl airfare, fees, excursions, ground transport
Housing: *Arr by pgm:* hotels
Deadline: Contact sponsor
Other info: *US accredited sponsor:* yes *Began:* 1996 *Activities:* excursions, field trips, program travel, cultural events *Misc:* May contact former participants. *Financial aid:* scholarships *URL:* http://www.ideal.swt.edu/extension/study_abroad/
Contact: Dr Jon McGee, Anthropology, Southwest Texas State Univ, 601 University Dr, San Marcos TX 78666 *Ph:* 512-245 8272 *Fax:* 512-245 8072 *E-mail:* rm08@swt.edu
Or Contact: Isis de la O Gomez, Extension Studies Coord, Southwest Texas State Univ, 601 University Dr, San Marcos TX 78666 *Ph:* 512-245 2322 *Fax:* 512-245 8934 *E-mail:* ig02@swt.edu

---

2084
SUNY UNIVERSITY AT BUFFALO
Ancient Art and Cities of Yucatan
Site: Mexico: Yucatan, various sites
Dates: 2 wks, Jan 2-15
Subjects: Anthropology, Archaeology, Field study, Yucatan studies
Eligibility: *Level:* fresh, sophs, jrs, srs *Requires:* 2.67 GPA *Age:* min 18
Credit: *Undergrad:* 3 *Grad:* none *Doc:* transcript
Instruction: *In:* English *Format:* directed field study, study tour *Students:* mainly US
Costs: $2,170 *incl* housing, most meals, fees, excursions *Nonrefundable fee*
Housing: *Arr by pgm:* hotels
Deadline: Nov 1; rolling admissions
Other info: *US accredited sponsor:* yes *Began:* 1999 *Orient:* abroad (1 day) *Activities:* field trips, program travel *Misc:* US pgm dir on-site. May contact former participants. *URL:* http://www.buffalo.edu/studyabroad/
Contact: Dr Sandra J Flash, Dir, Study Abroad Pgms, SUNY Univ at Buffalo, 210 Talbert Hall, Box 601604, Buffalo NY 14260-1604 *Ph:* 716-645 3912 *Fax:* 716-645 6197 *E-mail:* studyabroad@acsu.buffalo.edu

---

2085
THUNDERBIRD, THE AMERICAN GRADUATE SCHOOL OF INTERNATIONAL MANAGEMENT
Winterim in Mexico
Site: Mexico: Mexico City, Puebla
Dates: 3 wks, Jan 8-26
Subjects: Business language, Spanish language (adv)
Eligibility: *Level:* grads *Requires:* 3.0 GPA, faculty permission, knowledge of Spanish
Credit: *Undergrad:* none *Grad:* 3
Instruction: *In:* Spanish *Format:* lang study, lecture *Students:* intl
Costs: $2,250, $375 off-campus fee *incl* tuition
Housing: *Sponsor assists:* hotels
Deadline: Contact sponsor
Other info: *US accredited sponsor:* yes *Orient:* abroad *Activities:* field trips *URL:* http://www.t-bird.edu
Contact: James Scott, Overseas Pgms, Thunderbird, 15249 N 59th Ave, Glendale AZ 85306 *Ph:* 602-978 7251 *Fax:* 602-547 1356 *E-mail:* scottj@t-bird.edu

---

2086
UNIVERSIDAD LA SALLE
Special Programs for Foreigners
Site: Mexico: Cancun, Cuernavaca, Mexico City, Morelia, Pachuca
Dates: 1-16 wks, yr-round
Subjects: Art, Business/management, History, Homestay, Mexican studies, Spanish language (beg/int/adv)
Eligibility: *Level:* fresh, sophs, jrs, srs, grads, adults, teachers, professionals *Age:* min 18
Credit: *Undergrad:* avail *Grad:* avail *Doc:* transcript
Instruction: *In:* English, Spanish *Format:* lang study, lecture, seminar, study tour *Students:* intl
Costs: $40-$100 per day *incl* tuition, housing, all meals, fees, excursions, books/materials *Nonrefundable fee*
Housing: *Arr by pgm:* homestay
Deadline: 3 mos before pgm
Other info: *US accredited sponsor:* no *Began:* 1994 *Orient:* abroad *Activities:* field trips *Misc:* Tailored to objectives. *URL:* http://www.ulsa.edu.mx
Contact: Joan Landeros, Dir, or Zulema Rashid, Coord Special Pgms, Ctr for Intl Educ, Univ la Salle, Benjamin Franklin 47, Col Condesa, 06140 Mexico DF, Mexico *E-mail:* zra@aixulsa.ulsa.mx

---

2087
UNIVERSIDAD NACIONAL AUTONOMA DE MEXICO
Intensive Spanish Language and Latin American Culture
Site: Mexico: Mexico City, Taxco *Host inst:* Ctr de Ensenanza para Extranjeros of UNAM
Dates: 6 wks, yr-round
Subjects: Art history, Civilization/culture, History, Homestay, Latin American studies, Literature, Mexican studies, Spanish language (beg/int/adv)
Eligibility: *Level:* adults *Requires:* high sch diploma & completion of Level III Spanish for culture courses *Age:* min 18
Credit: *Undergrad:* avail *Grad:* avail *Doc:* transcript
Instruction: *In:* Spanish *Format:* lang study, lecture *Students:* intl
Costs: From $300-$375 depending on location & pgm *incl* tuition *Nonrefundable fee*
Housing: *Sponsor assists:* apartments, homestay
Deadline: Contact sponsor
Other info: *US accredited sponsor:* no *Orient:* abroad *Activities:* field trips, cultural events, sports *URL:* http://www.cepe.unam.mx
Contact: Marta Basave, Head, Info Dept, CEPE, Apdo Postal 70-391, CU, Delegacion Coyoacan, 04510 Mexico DF, Mexico *E-mail:* marta@servidor.unam.mx
Or Contact: Gustavo Pena, Dir, CEPE Taxco, Apdo Postal 70, 40200 Taxco, Gro, Mexico *E-mail:* guspe@servidor.unam.mx

---

2088
UNIVERSITY OF ALABAMA
Alabama in Yucatan
Site: Mexico: Yucatan, various sites
Dates: 2 wks, May 18-Jun 1
Subjects: Anthropology, Economics, History, Sociology
Eligibility: *Level:* fresh, sophs, jrs, srs,

grads, adults, teachers, precoll *Requires:* 2.0 GPA *Age:* min 17, avg 22
Credit: *Undergrad:* 3 *Grad:* 3
Instruction: *In:* English *Format:* study tour *Students:* mainly US
Costs: $3,000 *incl* housing, intl airfare, excursions
Housing: *Arr by pgm:* hotels
Deadline: Mar 15; Apr 15 for scholarships
Other info: *US accredited sponsor:* yes *Began:* 1974 *Orient:* in US (1 day) *Activities:* excursions, field trips, program travel, cultural events *Financial aid:* scholarships *URL:* http://www.ua.edu/international
Contact: Dr J Selwyn Hollingsworth, Sociology/Anthropology, Univ of Alabama, Box 870210, 12 Ten Hoor Hall, Tuscaloosa AL 35487-0250 *Ph:* 205-348 1947 *Fax:* 205-348 5298 *E-mail:* sholling@tenhoor.as.ua.edu
Or Contact: Angie Channell, Pgm Coord, Intl Pgms, Univ of Alabama, Box 870254, 135 BB Comer Hall, Tuscaloosa AL 35487-0250 *Ph:* 205-348 5256 *Fax:* 205-348 5298 *E-mail:* achannel@aalan.ua.edu

---

2089
UNIVERSITY OF NEBRASKA-LINCOLN
Intensive Language Program in Mexico
Site: Mexico: Monterrey or Queretaro *Host inst:* ITESM
Dates: 6 wks, about Jun 12-Jul 24
Subjects: Business language, Business/management, Homestay, Mexican studies, Spanish language (beg/int/adv)
Eligibility: *Level:* fresh, sophs, jrs, srs, teachers *Requires:* 2.5 GPA
Credit: *Undergrad:* 6 *Grad:* none *Doc:* transcript
Instruction: *In:* English, Spanish *Format:* lang study *Students:* mainly US
Costs: $1,750 for NE residents, $2,645 for others *incl* tuition, intl airfare, insurance, fees *Nonrefundable fee*
Housing: *Arr by pgm:* residence halls, homestay
Deadline: Feb 15
Other info: *US accredited sponsor:* yes *Began:* 1987 *Orient:* in US *Activities:* field trips *Misc:* Doing Business in Mexico course offered at Queretaro campus. *URL:* http://www.iaffairs.unl.edu
Contact: Christa Joy, Study Abroad Coord, Intl Affairs, Univ of Nebraska-Lincoln, 420 University Terrace, Lincoln NE 68588-0286 *Ph:* 402-472 5358 *Fax:* 402-472 5383 *E-mail:* iaffairs@unl.edu

---

ACAPULCO

2090
LINGUA SERVICE WORLDWIDE
Intensive Language and Culture in Acapulco
Site: Mexico: Acapulco *Host inst:* Home Lang Intl
Dates: 1 wk-1 yr, yr-round
Subjects: Civilization/culture, Homestay, Spanish language (beg/int/adv)
Eligibility: *Level:* adults
Credit: *Undergrad:* avail *Grad:* avail *Doc:* transcript, certificate
Instruction: *In:* Spanish *Format:* lang study, lecture *Students:* intl
Costs: Contact sponsor
Housing: *Arr by pgm:* homestay
Deadline: 45 days before pgm
Other info: *US accredited sponsor:* no *Activities:* excursions, field trips *Misc:* May contact former participants. *URL:* http://www.linguaserviceworldwide.com
Contact: Dir, Lingua Svc Worldwide, 75 Prospect St, Ste 4, Huntington NY 11743 *Ph:* 800-394 5327; 631-424 0777 *Fax:* 631-271 3441 *E-mail:* itctravel@worldnet.att.net ▲

CANCUN

2091
LANGUAGE LINK and **INTERNATIONAL LANGUAGE CENTER EL BOSQUE DEL CARIBE**
Learn Spanish on the Beach!
Site: Mexico: Cancun *Host inst:* El Bosque del Caribe
Dates: 1-16 wks, yr-round
Subjects: Spanish language
Eligibility: *Level:* fresh, sophs, jrs, srs, grads, adults, teachers, professionals, precoll *Age:* min 18, avg 28
Credit: *Undergrad:* 12 *Grad:* 6 *Doc:* certificate
Instruction: *In:* Spanish *Format:* lang study, tutorial *Students:* intl
Costs: $430 per wk *incl* tuition, housing, all meals, insurance, fees, airport pickup *Nonrefundable fee*
Housing: *Arr by pgm:* apartments, homestay, hotels
Other info: *US accredited sponsor:* no *Began:* 1996 *In coop with:* Austin Peay State Univ *Orient:* abroad *Activities:* excursions, field trips, cultural events *Misc:* May contact former participants. *URL:* http://www.langlink.com
Contact: Kay Rafool, Dir, Lang Link, PO Box 3006, Peoria IL 61612 *Ph:* 800-552 2051; 309-692 2961 *Fax:* 309-692 2926 *E-mail:* info@langlink.com

---

COLIMA

2092
UNIVERSITY OF NORTHERN IOWA
UNISSIST in Mexico
Site: Mexico: Colima
Dates: 7-8 wks, late Jun-early Aug
Subjects: Civilization/culture, Composition, Homestay, Literature, Spanish language (adv)
Eligibility: *Level:* grads, teachers *Requires:* previous study in field, Previous Spanish study *Age:* avg 35
Credit: *Undergrad:* none *Grad:* 9 *Doc:* transcript, diploma, degree
Instruction: *In:* English *Format:* lang study, lecture, seminar *Students:* mainly US
Costs: $2,700 *incl* tuition, housing, all meals, excursions *Nonrefundable fee*
Housing: *Arr by pgm:* homestay
Deadline: Jan 1
Other info: *US accredited sponsor:* yes *Began:* 1996 *Orient:* abroad (1 day) *Activities:* excursions, cultural events *Misc:* may attend for no credit or earn MA by attending several summers. *URL:* http://www.uni.edu/modlangs/institutes-abroad
Contact: Dr. Nile Vernon, Coord, Dept of Modern Lang, Univ of Northern Iowa, Cedar Falls IA 50614-0504 *Ph:* 319-273 6102 *Fax:* 319-273 2848 *E-mail:* nile.vernon@uni.edu
Or Contact: Mark Welty, Inst Abroad Clerk, Dept of Modern Lang, Univ of Northern Iowa, Cedar Falls IA 50614-0504 *Ph:* 319-273 2200 *Fax:* 319-273 2848 *E-mail:* modlangs@uni.edu

---

CUERNAVACA

2093
CALE (CENTRO DE ARTES Y LENGUAS)
Study Intensive Spanish
Site: Mexico: Cuernavaca
Dates: 1 wk or longer, yr-round
Subjects: Homestay, Spanish language (beg/int/adv)
Eligibility: *Level:* adults *Age:* min 14
Credit: *Undergrad:* none *Grad:* none *Doc:* certificate
Instruction: *In:* Spanish *Format:* lang study, tutorial *Students:* intl
Costs: About $1,200 per mo *incl* tuition, housing, all meals, fees, excursions, books/materials *Nonrefundable fee*
Housing: *Arr by pgm:* residence halls, apartments, homestay, pensions, hotels, hostels
Deadline: Rolling admissions
Other info: *US accredited sponsor:* no *Began:* 1969 *Orient:* abroad *Activities:* excursions, field trips, program travel, cultural events, sports *Misc:* May contact

former participants. *Financial aid:* scholarships, work study *URL:* http://www.gl.com.mx/cale
Contact: CALE, Calle Nueva Tabachin #22-A Bis, Colonia Tlaltenango, Apdo 1777, Cuernavaca, Morelos, Mexico *E-mail:* scale@infosel.net.mx

---

2094
CETLALIC (CENTRO TLAHUICA DE LENGUAS E INTERCAMBIO CULTURAL, AC)
Alternative Spanish Language School
Site: Mexico: Cuernavaca
Dates: 1 wk or longer, yr-round
Subjects: Art, Civilization/culture, Ecology/environmental studies, Economics, Education/teaching, Gender studies, Health/health education, History, Latin American studies, Literature, Political science/politics, Religion/theology, Spanish language (beg/int/adv), Women's studies
Eligibility: *Level:* fresh, sophs, jrs, srs, grads, adults *Age:* avg 25
Credit: *Undergrad:* avail *Grad:* none *Doc:* certificate
Instruction: *In:* Spanish *Format:* lang study, study tour, volunteer/svc, workshop *Students:* intl
Costs: $340-$375 per wk *incl* tuition, housing, all meals, excursions, books/ materials
Housing: *Arr by pgm:* apartments, homestay, hotels
Deadline: None
Other info: *US accredited sponsor:* no *Began:* 1987 *Activities:* excursions, field trips, program travel, cultural events *Misc:* Partial scholarships only. Contact sponsor for alternative housing arr. *Financial aid:* scholarships, work study *URL:* http://www.giga.com/~cetlalic
Contact: Jorge Torres Viveros, PO Box 1-201, Cuernavaca, Morelos 62000, Mexico *E-mail:* cetlalic@mail.giga.com
Or Contact: Brian Eklund, 2273 W 31st St, Los Angeles CA 90018 *Ph:* 323-735 6156 *Fax:* 323-731 3400 *E-mail:* brianeklund@msn.com

---

2095
CUAUHNAHUAC
Intensive Spanish Program
Site: Mexico: Cuernavaca
Dates: 1 wk or longer, yr-round; 1 mo recommended
Subjects: Homestay, Mexican studies, Spanish language (beg/int/adv)
Eligibility: *Level:* fresh, sophs, jrs, srs, grads, adults
Credit: *Undergrad:* avail *Grad:* avail *Doc:* certificate
Instruction: *In:* Spanish *Format:* lang study, lecture *Students:* intl
Costs: $1,220 per mo *incl* tuition, housing, all meals, fees *Nonrefundable fee*
Housing: *Arr by pgm:* apartments, homestay, pensions, hotels, furnished rms
Deadline: None
Other info: *US accredited sponsor:* no *Began:* 1972 *Orient:* abroad *Activities:* excursions, cultural events *Misc:* Conversation intercambios with Mexican students. May contact former participants. *URL:* http://www.cuauhnahuac.edu.mx/
Contact: Cuauhnahuac, AP #5-26, Cuernavaca, Morelos, Mexico 62051 *E-mail:* inform@cuauhnahuac.edu.mx
Or Contact: Marcia Snell, 519 Park Ave, Kenilworth IL 60043 *Ph:* 800-245 9335; 847-256 7570, 847-251 4587 *Fax:* 847-256 9475 *E-mail:* mexmarcia@hotline.com ▲

2096
IDEAL LATINOAMERICA LANGUAGE SCHOOL
Total Immersion Spanish Language and Culture Program
Site: Mexico: Cuernavaca
Dates: 1 wk or longer, yr-round
Subjects: Business language, Foreign language teaching, Homestay, Mexican studies, Spanish language (beg/int/adv), Technical language, Traditional medicine
Eligibility: *Level:* adults *Age:* min 15, max 90, avg 30
Credit: *Undergrad:* none *Grad:* none *Doc:* certificate, diploma
Instruction: *In:* Spanish *Format:* lang study *Students:* intl
Costs: $270 per wk *incl* tuition, housing, all meals *Nonrefundable fee*
Housing: *Arr by pgm:* apartments, homestay
Deadline: Contact sponsor
Other info: *US accredited sponsor:* no *Began:* 1996 *Activities:* excursions, field trips, cultural events *Misc:* May contact former participants. *URL:* http://www.IDEAL-L.com
Contact: Lisa Hansel, Registrar, or Hugo R Brito, Admin, IDEAL, Privada Narciso Mendosa 107, Colonia Pradera, Cuernavaca, Morelos, CP 62170, Mexico *E-mail:* ideal@ideal-l.com

---

2097
INDIANA UNIVERSITY
Summer Study in Mexico
Site: Mexico: Cuernavaca *Host inst:* Inst Tech (ITESM)
Dates: 6 wks, early Jun-late Jul
Subjects: Homestay, Spanish language
Eligibility: Own students only. *Level:* fresh, sophs, jrs, srs *Requires:* 1 yr coll Spanish
Credit: *Undergrad:* 6 *Grad:* none *Doc:* transcript
Instruction: *In:* Spanish *Format:* lang study *Students:* mainly US
Costs: $2,400 or $3,500 *incl* tuition, housing, all meals, insurance, fees, excursions *Nonrefundable fee*
Housing: *Arr by pgm:* homestay
Deadline: Mid-Feb
Other info: *US accredited sponsor:* yes *Began:* 1998 *Orient:* abroad *Activities:* excursions *Misc:* May contact former participants. *Financial aid:* scholarships *URL:* http://www.indiana.edu/~overseas
Contact: Overseas Study, Indiana Univ, Franklin Hall 303, Bloomington IN 47405 *Ph:* 812-855 9304 *Fax:* 812-855 6452 *E-mail:* overseas@indiana.edu

---

2098
LANGUAGE LINK and **SPANISH LANGUAGE INSTITUTE (SLI)**
Immersion Spanish In Cuernavaca
Site: Mexico: Cuernavaca
Dates: 1-16 wks, yr-round
Subjects: Civilization/culture, Mexican studies, Spanish language
Eligibility: *Level:* fresh, sophs, jrs, srs, grads, adults, teachers, professionals, precoll *Age:* min 13, avg 28
Credit: *Undergrad:* 12 *Grad:* 6 *Doc:* transcript
Instruction: *In:* Spanish *Format:* lang study, tutorial *Students:* intl
Costs: $255 per wk with shared rm, $304 with private rm *incl* tuition, housing, all meals, insurance *Nonrefundable fee*
Housing: *Arr by pgm:* homestay
Deadline: None
Other info: *US accredited sponsor:* no *Began:* 1990 *In coop with:* Austin Peay State Univ *Orient:* abroad *Activities:* excursions, field trips, cultural events *Misc:* Special summer teen pgm. Professional exec pgm. May contact former participants. *URL:* http://www.langlink.com
Contact: Kay Rafool, Dir, Lang Link, PO Box 3006, Peoria IL 61612-3006 *Ph:* 800-552 2051; 309-692 2961 *Fax:* 309-692 2926 *E-mail:* info@langlink.com

---

2099
NORTH CAROLINA STATE UNIVERSITY
Study and Travel in Mexico
Site: Mexico: Cuernavaca *Host inst:* Ctr for Bilingual & Multicultural Studies
Dates: May-Jun
Subjects: Art, History, Homestay, Mexican studies, Spanish language (beg/int/adv), Written composition
Eligibility: *Level:* fresh, sophs, jrs, srs *Requires:* 1 sem coll Spanish
Credit: *Undergrad:* 6 *Grad:* none *Doc:* transcript
Instruction: *In:* Spanish *Format:* lang

study, lecture, practical training, seminar, study tour *Students:* mainly US
Costs: $2,600 *incl* tuition, housing, all meals, intl airfare, insurance, excursions, airport taxes
Housing: *Arr by pgm:* homestay
Deadline: Feb
Other info: *US accredited sponsor:* yes *Orient:* abroad *Activities:* excursions, field trips, program travel, cultural events *URL:* http://www.ncsu.edu/studyabroad
Contact: Anne Haberkern, North Carolina State Univ, 2118 Pullen Hall, Box 7344, Raleigh NC 27695-7344 *Ph:* 919-515 2087 *Fax:* 919-515 6021 *E-mail:* study_abroad@ncsu.edu

---

2100
SANTA BARBARA CITY COLLEGE
Intensive Spanish Language Program
Site: Mexico: Cuernavaca *Host inst:* Ctr Bilingue
Dates: 4 wks, Jun-Jul
Subjects: Spanish language (beg/int/adv)
Eligibility: *Level:* fresh, sophs, adults, teachers *Age:* min 18
Credit: *Undergrad:* avail *Grad:* none *Doc:* transcript
Instruction: *In:* Spanish *Students:* mainly US
Costs: $1,800 *incl* housing, some meals, insurance, excursions
Housing: *Arr by pgm:* homestay
Deadline: Mar
Other info: *US accredited sponsor:* yes *Began:* 1973 *Orient:* in US & abroad (2 days) *Activities:* excursions, field trips, cultural events *Financial aid:* scholarships *URL:* http://www.sbcc.cc.ca.us/academic/StudyAbroad/
Contact: Naomi Sullwold, Santa Barbara City Coll, 721 Cliff Dr, Santa Barbara CA 93109 *Ph:* 805-965 0581 ext 2494 *Fax:* 805-963 7222 *E-mail:* sullwold@sbcc.net
Or Contact: Carola Smith, Dir, Study Abroad, Santa Barbara City Coll, 721 Cliff Dr, Santa Barbara CA 93109 *Ph:* 805-965 0581 ext 2243 *Fax:* 805-963 7222 *E-mail:* smithc@sbcc.net

---

2101
SUNY COLLEGE AT BROCKPORT
Intensive Spanish in Mexico
Site: Mexico: Cuernavaca *Host inst:* Univ Intl-The Ctr for Bilingual Multicultural Studies
Dates: Jul- early Aug
Subjects: Homestay, Internships, Spanish language (beg/int)
Eligibility: *Level:* sophs, jrs, srs, grads *Requires:* 2.5 GPA
Credit: *Undergrad:* 6 *Grad:* avail
Instruction: *In:* English, Spanish *Format:* internship, lang study, lecture, tutorial *Students:* intl
Costs: About $2,900 *incl* tuition, housing, all meals, intl airfare, insurance, fees, excursions, books/materials
Housing: *Arr by pgm:* homestay
Deadline: May 1
Other info: *US accredited sponsor:* yes *Began:* 1971 *Orient:* abroad *Activities:* excursions, field trips *Misc:* Resident dir. *URL:* http://www.brockport.edu/study_abroad
Contact: Dr John Perry, Dir, Intl Educ, 350 New Campus Dr, SUNY Coll at Brockport, Brockport NY 14420 *Ph:* 800-298 7869 *Fax:* 716-637 3218 *E-mail:* overseas@brockport.edu

---

2102
SUNY COLLEGE AT CORTLAND
Cortland International Programs at Cuernavaca
Site: Mexico: Cuernavaca *Host inst:* Univ Intl-The Ctr for Bilingual Multicultural Studies
Dates: 3 wks, Jan
Subjects: Civilization/culture, Homestay, Mexican studies, Spanish language (beg/int/adv)
Eligibility: *Level:* fresh, sophs, jrs, srs *Requires:* 2.5 GPA
Credit: *Undergrad:* 3 *Grad:* none *Doc:* transcript
Instruction: *In:* Spanish *Format:* lang study, lecture *Students:* mainly US
Costs: $2,000 *incl* housing, all meals, intl airfare, insurance, fees, excursions, books/materials, land transport
Housing: *Arr by pgm:* homestay
Deadline: Oct 1
Other info: *US accredited sponsor:* yes *Began:* 1987 *Orient:* in US & abroad *Activities:* excursions *Misc:* Independent study avail for adv students. May contact former participants. *URL:* http://www.studyabroad.com/suny/cortland
Contact: Liz Kopp, Intl Pgms, SUNY Coll at Cortland, PO Box 2000, Cortland NY 13045 *Ph:* 607-753 2209 *Fax:* 607-753 5989 *E-mail:* koppl@cortland.edu ▲

2103
SUNY COLLEGE AT NEW PALTZ, LANGUAGE IMMERSION INSTITUTE
Learning Vacations in Mexico
Site: Mexico: Cuernavaca *Host inst:* Cemanahuac Educ Comm
Dates: 2 wks or longer, yr-round
Subjects: Homestay, Spanish language
Eligibility: *Level:* adults *Age:* min 18, avg 40
Credit: *Undergrad:* avail *Grad:* none
Instruction: *In:* Spanish *Format:* lang study *Students:* mainly US
Costs: About $878 for 2 wks *incl* tuition, housing, fees
Housing: *Arr by pgm:* homestay, hotels
Deadline: 2 mos before pgm
Other info: *US accredited sponsor:* yes *Activities:* excursions, field trips *Misc:* May contact former participants. *URL:* http://www.newpaltz.edu/lii
Contact: Lang Immersion Inst, SUNY New Paltz, 75 S Manheim Blvd, New Paltz NY 12561-2499 *Ph:* 914-257 3500 *Fax:* 914-257 3569 *E-mail:* lii@newpaltz.edu ▲

2104
UNIVERSITY OF SOUTHERN MISSISSIPPI
Spanish in Mexico
Site: Mexico: Cuernavaca *Host inst:* Cemanahuac Educ Comm
Dates: 4 wks, May 15-Jun 19
Subjects: Civilization/culture, Geography, History, Mexican studies, Spanish language (beg/int/adv)
Eligibility: *Level:* sophs, jrs, srs, grads *Requires:* 2.0 GPA, good acad standing, enrollment in accredited US univ, previous study in Spanish
Credit: *Undergrad:* 6 *Grad:* 6 *Doc:* transcript
Instruction: *In:* Spanish *Format:* lang study *Students:* mainly US
Costs: $2,699 for undergrads, $2,999 for grads *incl* tuition, housing, all meals, intl airfare, fees, excursions *Nonrefundable fee*
Housing: *Arr by pgm:* homestay
Deadline: Apr 2
Other info: *US accredited sponsor:* yes *Began:* 1989 *Orient:* in US & abroad *Activities:* excursions, field trips, program travel *Misc:* Classes limited to 5 students. *Financial aid:* scholarships *URL:* http://www.usm.edu
Contact: Dr Tim W Hudson, Intl & Continuing Educ, Univ of Southern Mississippi, Box 10047, Hattiesburg MS 39406 *Ph:* 601-266 4344 *Fax:* 601-266 5699 *E-mail:* melissa.ravencraft@usm.edu
Or Contact: Dir, Mexican Studies Pgm, Foreign Langs & Literatures, Univ of Southern Mississippi, Box 5038, Hattiesburg MS 39406-5038 *Ph:* 601-266 4964 *Fax:* 601-266 5699

2105
XAVIER UNIVERSITY
Xavier University Summer Program in Mexico
Site: Mexico: Cuernavaca *Host inst:* Cemanahuac Educ Comm
Dates: 3 or 6 wks, May 20-Jun 10 or May 20- Jun 30
Subjects: Field study, Latin American studies, Spanish language (beg/int/adv)
Eligibility: *Level:* fresh, sophs, jrs, srs, grads, adults, teachers, professionals *Requires:* 2.5 GPA *Age:* min 18
Credit: *Undergrad:* 2-3 per term *Grad:* 2-3 per term *Doc:* transcript

Instruction: *In:* English, Spanish *Format:* lang study, lecture, seminar *Students:* mainly US
Costs: $1,550 for 3 wks, $2,495 for 6 wks *incl* tuition, housing, some meals, excursions *Nonrefundable fee*
Housing: *Arr by pgm:* homestay
Deadline: Mar 25
Other info: *US accredited sponsor:* no *Began:* 1991 *Orient:* in US *Activities:* excursions, field trips, cultural events, sports *Misc:* May contact former participants. *URL:* http://www.xu.edu
Contact: Margaret McDiarmid, Xavier Univ, 3800 Victory Pkwy, Cincinnati OH 45207-5184 *Ph:* 800-344 4698; 513-745 3406 *Fax:* 513-745 1955 *E-mail:* mcdiarmi@xu.edu
Or Contact: Dr Irene B. Hodgson, Xavier Univ 3800 Victory Parkway, Cincinnati OH *Ph:* 800-344 4698; 513-745 3541 *Fax:* 513-745 1955 *E-mail:* hodgson@xu.edu

ENSENADA

2106
BAJA CALIFORNIA LANGUAGE COLLEGE
Baja California-Spanish in Ensenada
Site: Mexico: Ensenada
Dates: 1-20 weeks, yr-round
Subjects: Anthropology, Education/teaching, Health care/hospitals, Homestay, Human resources, International business, Law enforcement, Spanish language
Eligibility: *Level:* adults *Age:* avg 36
Credit: *Undergrad:* avail *Grad:* none *Doc:* transcript, certificate
Instruction: *In:* Spanish *Format:* lang study *Students:* intl
Costs: $240 per wk *incl* tuition, some meals, fees, excursions, books/materials *Nonrefundable fee*
Housing: *Arr by pgm:* homestay, hotels
Deadline: 2 wks before pgm
Other info: *US accredited sponsor:* no *Began:* 1996 *Orient:* abroad (1 day) *Activities:* excursions, field trips, cultural events *Misc:* Classes offered at all levels of Spanish proficiency. Discounts for longer stays. May contact former participants. *URL:* http://www.bajacal.com
Contact: Keith Rolle, Pres, Rolle Enterprise Intl, Inc, PO Box 7556, San Diego CA 92167 *Ph:* 877-444 2252; 619-758 9711 *E-mail:* college@bajacal.com
Or Contact: Yolanda Camacho, Dir, Baja California Lang Coll, Barcelona y Belgrado 191, Fracc Chapultepec, Ensenada BC, Mexico *E-mail:* bajaalumno@aol.com

2107
UNIVERSITY OF CALIFORNIA, SAN DIEGO EXTENSION
Spanish Immersion Program: Ensenada, Mexico
Site: Mexico: Ensenada *Host inst:* Center of Langs & Latin Amer Studies
Dates: 3 days-1 wk, yr-round
Subjects: Spanish language (beg/int/adv)
Eligibility: *Level:* fresh, sophs, jrs, srs, grads, adults, teachers, professionals, precoll *Age:* min 18
Credit: *Undergrad:* none *Grad:* none *Doc:* transcript, certificate
Instruction: *In:* Spanish *Format:* lang study, lecture *Students:* mainly US
Costs: $200 per wkend, $380 per wk *incl* tuition, housing, all meals, books/materials
Housing: *Sponsor assists:* homestay, hotels
Deadline: 2 wks before pgm
Other info: *US accredited sponsor:* yes *Began:* 1996 *Orient:* abroad *Activities:* excursions *Misc:* Ages 13-17 can attend with a parent or legal guardian. May contact former participants. *URL:* http://www.extension.ucsd.edu/laip
Contact: Tanya Knebel, Pgm Rep, UCSD Extension, Liberal Arts & Intl Pgms 0176Z, 9500 Gilman Dr, La Jolla CA 92093-0176 *Ph:* 858-822 2747 *Fax:* 858-534 7385 *E-mail:* travelstudy@ucsd.edu

2108
UNIVERSITY OF CALIFORNIA, SAN DIEGO EXTENSION
Travel Photography Workshop in Ensenada, Mexico
Site: Mexico: Ensenada
Dates: 2 days, yr-round
Subjects: Photography
Eligibility: *Level:* fresh, sophs, jrs, srs, grads, adults, teachers, professionals, precoll *Age:* min 18
Credit: *Undergrad:* none *Grad:* none *Doc:* transcript
Instruction: *In:* English *Format:* directed field study, lecture *Students:* mainly US
Costs: $295 *incl* tuition, housing, fees, excursions *Nonrefundable fee*
Housing: *Sponsor assists:* homestay
Deadline: Contact sponsor
Other info: *US accredited sponsor:* yes *Began:* 1996 *Orient:* in US *Activities:* excursions *Misc:* Incls pre- & post-workshop meetings. *URL:* http://www.extensions.ucsd.edu/laip
Contact: Julie Halter, Pgm Rep, UCSD Extension, Liberal Arts & Intl Pgms 0176Z, 9500 Gilman Dr, La Jolla CA 92093-0176 *Ph:* 858-534 9891 *Fax:* 858-534 7385 *E-mail:* jhalter@ucsd.edu

GUADALAJARA

2109
BEAVER COLLEGE, CENTER FOR EDUCATION ABROAD
Summer in Mexico
Site: Mexico: Guadalajara *Host inst:* Univ Panamericana
Dates: Jun 6-Jul 21
Subjects: Anthropology, Art history, Civilization/culture, Economics, Mexican studies, Political science/politics, Spanish language
Eligibility: *Level:* sophs, jrs, srs *Requires:* 3.0 GPA
Credit: *Undergrad:* 6 *Grad:* none *Doc:* transcript
Instruction: *In:* Spanish *Format:* lang study, lecture, seminar *Students:* mainly host country
Costs: $2,595 *incl* tuition, housing, all meals, insurance, excursions, ISIC, orient, transcript *Nonrefundable fee*
Housing: *Arr by pgm:* homestay
Deadline: Mar 31
Other info: *US accredited sponsor:* yes *Began:* 1993 *Orient:* abroad (4 days) *Activities:* excursions *Misc:* May contact former participants. *URL:* http://www.arcadia.edu/cea/
Contact: Ctr for Educ Abroad, Beaver Coll, 450 S Easton Rd, Glenside PA 19038 *Ph:* 888-232 8379 *E-mail:* cea@beaver.edu ▲

2110
CENTRAL WASHINGTON UNIVERSITY
CWU Program in Guadalajara, Mexico
Site: Mexico: Guadalajara *Host inst:* Univ Autonoma de Guadalajara
Dates: 4 wks, yr-round
Subjects: Full curriculum, Homestay, Literature, Spanish language
Eligibility: *Level:* fresh, sophs, jrs, srs, grads, adults, teachers *Requires:* 2.5 GPA *Age:* min 18, avg 20
Credit: *Undergrad:* avail *Grad:* none *Doc:* transcript
Instruction: *In:* Spanish *Format:* lang study *Students:* intl
Costs: $500 *incl* tuition, fees, excursions
Housing: *Arr by pgm:* homestay
Deadline: 45 days before pgm
Other info: *US accredited sponsor:* yes *Began:* 1997 *In coop with:* CCIS *Orient:* in US & abroad (1 day) *Activities:* excursions, cultural events *Misc:* General curriculum for adv students only. *URL:* http://www.cwu.edu/~intlprog/mexicohome.html
Contact: Heather Barclay, Central Washington Univ, 400 E 8th Ave, Ellensburg WA 98926-7408 *Ph:* 809-963 3616 *Fax:* 809-963 1558 *E-mail:* goabroad@cwu.edu

 See "How To Use This Book" for definitions of terms used above. ▲ = See program sponsor's ad(s) in this book.

2111
COUNCIL ON INTERNATIONAL EDUCATIONAL EXCHANGE (COUNCIL)
International Faculty Development Seminars-Guadalajara
Site: Mexico: Guadalajara *Host inst:* Univ de Guadalajara
Dates: 10 days, Jun
Subjects: Contemporary issues, Economics, Political science/politics, Trade
Eligibility: *Level:* teachers *Requires:* must be faculty at 2-yr or 4-yr inst
Credit: *Undergrad:* none *Grad:* none
Instruction: *In:* English *Format:* lecture, seminar *Students:* mainly US
Costs: $1,800 *incl* tuition, housing, some meals, insurance, fees, excursions, books/materials
Housing: *Arr by pgm:* hotels
Deadline: Mar 15
Other info: *US accredited sponsor:* no *Began:* 1998 *Orient:* abroad *Activities:* excursions, field trips, cultural events *Misc:* Seminar title: Mexico's Transition to a Free Market Econ. May contact former participants. *URL:* http://www.ciee.org/ifds
Contact: Jennifer Ley, Dir, Intl Faculty Development Seminars, Council, 633 3rd Ave, New York NY 10017 *Ph:* 212-822 2747 *Fax:* 212-822 2779 *E-mail:* jley@ciee.org ▲

2112
COUNCIL ON INTERNATIONAL EDUCATIONAL EXCHANGE CONSORTIUM
University of Guadalajara
Site: Mexico: Guadalajara *Host inst:* Univ de Guadalajara
Dates: 2, 5 or 10 wks, Jun-Aug
Subjects: Civilization/culture, Homestay, Mexican studies, Spanish language (beg/int/adv)
Eligibility: *Level:* sophs, jrs, srs, grads, adults *Requires:* 2.5 GPA, for undergrads
Credit: *Undergrad:* avail *Grad:* none *Doc:* transcript
Instruction: *In:* English, Spanish *Format:* lang study, lecture, seminar, tutorial *Students:* intl
Costs: $600 for 2 wks, $1,150 for 5 wks, $1,750 for 10 wks *incl* tuition, some meals, insurance, ISIC
Housing: *Arr by pgm:* residence halls, homestay
Deadline: 2 wks before pgm
Other info: *US accredited sponsor:* yes *Began:* 1996 *Orient:* abroad (1 day) *Activities:* excursions, cultural events *Misc:* Pre-departure advising. Guitar lessons avail. May contact former participants. *URL:* http://www.ciee.org/study
Contact: *See Index II for Members* Pgm Adviser, Council-ISP, 633 3rd Ave 20th Fl, New York NY 10017-6706 *Ph:* 800-407 8839; 212-822 2600, 212-822 2762 *Fax:* 212-822 2779 *E-mail:* studyinfo@ciee.org

---

2113
CULTURAL EXPERIENCES ABROAD (CEA)
Spanish Language and Latin American Studies in Guadalajara
Site: Mexico: Guadalajara *Host inst:* Univ of Guadalajara
Dates: 5 wks, Jun-Jul or Jul-Aug
Subjects: Art history, Business/management, Economics, History, Homestay, Independent study, International business, Latin American

studies, Literature, Mexican studies, Political science/politics, Spanish language (beg/int/adv)
Eligibility: *Level:* fresh, sophs, jrs, srs, grads, precoll *Requires:* 2.5 GPA, previous Spanish lang study recommended *Age:* min 17, avg 20
Credit: *Undergrad:* avail *Grad:* avail *Doc:* transcript, certificate
Instruction: *In:* English, Spanish *Format:* independent study, lang study, lecture, study tour, tutorial, volunteer/svc *Students:* intl
Costs: $2,495 *incl* tuition, housing, all meals, insurance, fees, excursions, books/materials, orient, airport transfers *Nonrefundable fee*
Housing: *Arr by pgm:* homestay
Deadline: Rolling admissions
Other info: *US accredited sponsor:* no *Orient:* abroad *Activities:* excursions, field trips, cultural events, sports *Misc:* Support svcs. E-mail. May contact former participants. *URL:* http://www.travelabroad.com
Contact: CEA Study Abroad, 1400 E Southern Ave St, B-108 AZ 85282-8011 *Ph:* 480-557 7900 *Fax:* 480-557 7926 *E-mail:* mexico@travelabroad.com

---

2114
MONTCLAIR STATE UNIVERSITY
Montclair in Mexico
Site: Mexico: Guadalajara *Host inst:* UNIVA
Dates: 4 wks, late Jun-late Jul
Subjects: Homestay, Latin American studies, Spanish language (beg/int)
Eligibility: *Level:* fresh, sophs, jrs, srs, grads *Age:* avg 20
Credit: *Undergrad:* 6 *Grad:* none *Doc:* transcript
Instruction: *In:* English, Spanish *Format:* lang study, lecture, seminar, study tour *Students:* mainly US
Costs: About $2,000 *incl* housing, some meals, intl airfare, fees, excursions
Housing: *Arr by pgm:* homestay, hotels
Deadline: Apr 1
Other info: *US accredited sponsor:* yes *Began:* 2000 *In coop with:* UNIVA *Orient:* in US (1 Day) *Activities:* excursions, field trips, program travel, cultural events *Misc:* May contact former participants.
Contact: Wendy Gilbert-Simon, Montclair State Univ, 22 Normal Ave, Upper Montclair NJ 07043 *Ph:* 973-655 4185 *Fax:* 973-655 7654 *E-mail:* simonw@mail.montclair.edu
Or Contact: Dr John Hwang, Montclair State Univ, 1 Normal Ave, Upper Montclair NJ 07043 *Ph:* 973-655 7508 *E-mail:* hwangj@mail.montclair.edu

---

2115
NATIONAL REGISTRATION CENTER FOR STUDY ABROAD (NRCSA)
Spanish in Guadalajara
Site: Mexico: Guadalajara *Host inst:* Spanish Lang Sch
Dates: 2 wks or longer, yr-round
Subjects: Homestay, Spanish language (beg/int/adv)
Eligibility: *Level:* fresh, sophs, jrs, srs, grads, adults, teachers, professionals *Age:* min 18
Credit: *Undergrad:* avail *Grad:* avail *Doc:* certificate
Instruction: *In:* Spanish *Format:* lang study, lecture, tutorial *Students:* intl
Costs: $527 for 2 wks *incl* tuition, housing, all meals, insurance *Nonrefundable fee*
Housing: *Arr by pgm:* apartments, homestay, hotels
Deadline: 6 wks before pgm
Other info: *US accredited sponsor:* no *Misc:* May contact former participants. *URL:* http://www.nrcsa.com
Contact: June Domoe, NRCSA, 823 N 2nd St, # 206, Milwaukee WI 53203 *Ph:* 414-278 0631 *Fax:* 414-271 8884 *E-mail:* info@nrcsa.com

---

2116
SPANISH EDUCATION FOR WOMEN
Three Weeks in Guadalajara
Site: Mexico: Guadalajara
Dates: 3 wks, Jul
Subjects: Art, Civilization/culture, Creative writing, Mexican studies, Political science/politics, Spanish language (beg/int/adv)
Eligibility: Women only. *Level:* grads, adults, teachers, professionals *Requires:* previous study in field, some Spanish *Age:* min 25, avg 45
Credit: *Undergrad:* none *Grad:* none *Doc:* certificate
Instruction: *In:* Spanish *Format:* lang study, tutorial, workshop *Students:* mainly US
Costs: About $1,400 *incl* tuition, housing, all meals, fees, excursions, books/materials, airport transfer
Housing: *Arr by pgm:* homestay
Deadline: Contact sponsor
Other info: *US accredited sponsor:* no *Began:* 1986 *Orient:* abroad (1 day) *Activities:* field trips, cultural events *Misc:* May contact former participants. *URL:* http://www.seww@erols.com
Contact: Debbie Polhemus or Denise Curry, Spanish Educ for Women, PO Box 29338, Washington DC 20017 *Ph:* 202-529 0620 *Fax:* 202-529 0620 *E-mail:* seww@erols.com

---

2117
THUNDERBIRD, THE AMERICAN GRADUATE SCHOOL OF INTERNATIONAL MANAGEMENT
Thunderbird Guadalajara, Mexico Program
Site: Mexico: Guadalajara
Dates: Summer
Subjects: Business/management, Finance, International business, International studies, Latin American studies, Mexican studies, Spanish language (int/adv), Trade
Eligibility: *Level:* grads *Requires:* 3.0 GPA, previous lang study recommended
Credit: *Undergrad:* none *Grad:* 9-12
Instruction: *In:* English *Format:* lang study, lecture *Students:* intl
Costs: Contact sponsor
Housing: *Sponsor assists:* apartments, hotels
Deadline: Contact sponsor
Other info: *US accredited sponsor:* yes *Orient:* abroad *Activities:* field trips *Misc:* May contact former participants. *Financial aid:* scholarships *URL:* http://www.t-bird.edu
Contact: Dr Earl Gibbons, Assoc VP, Overseas Pgms, Thunderbird, 15249 N 59th Ave, Glendale AZ 85306 *Ph:* 602-978 7367 *Fax:* 602-978 7419 *E-mail:* gibbonse@t-bird.edu
Or Contact: Diane Hayton, Coord, Overseas Pgms, Thunderbird, 15249 N 59th Ave, Glendale AZ 85306 *Ph:* 602-978 7367 *Fax:* 602-978 7419 *E-mail:* haytond@t-bird.edu

---

2118
UNIVERSITY OF ARIZONA
Guadalajara Summer School
Site: Mexico: Guadalajara *Host inst:* Col Guadalajara
Dates: 3, 5 or 6 wks, Jul 3-Aug 17
Subjects: Anthropology, Bilingualism, Field study, Film studies, Homestay, Independent study, Literature, Mexican studies, Political science/politics, Spanish language (beg/int/adv)
Eligibility: *Level:* fresh, sophs, jrs, srs, grads, adults, teachers, professionals, precoll *Age:* min 17
Credit: *Undergrad:* 3-8 *Grad:* 3-6 *Doc:* transcript
Instruction: *In:* English, Spanish *Format:* directed field study, independent study, lang study, lecture *Students:* mainly US
Costs: $500-$2,000 *incl* tuition, housing, all meals, fees *Nonrefundable fee*
Housing: *Sponsor assists:* homestay
Deadline: Contact sponsor
Other info: *US accredited sponsor:* yes *Began:* 1952 *Activities:* excursions *Misc:* Folklorico dance class *Financial aid:* scholarships *URL:* http://w3.arizona.edu/~ciss/

Contact: Dr Macario Saldate IV, Dir, Guadalajara Summer Sch, Univ of Arizona, PO Box 40966, Tucson AZ 85717 *Ph:* 520-621 5137 *Fax:* 520-621 8141 *E-mail:* gss@u.arizona.edu ▲

2119
UNIVERSITY OF CALIFORNIA, SAN DIEGO EXTENSION
Spanish Immersion Program: Guadalajara, Mexico
Site: Mexico: Guadalajara *Host inst:* Univ of Guadalajara
Dates: 2 or 5 wks, yr-round
Subjects: Civilization/culture (adv), History (adv), Latin American studies (adv), Literature (adv), Mexican studies (adv), Political science/politics (adv), Spanish language (beg/int/adv)
Eligibility: *Level:* fresh, sophs, jrs, srs, grads, adults, teachers, precoll *Age:* min 18
Credit: *Undergrad:* none *Grad:* none *Doc:* transcript, certificate
Instruction: *In:* Spanish *Format:* lang study, lecture, seminar *Students:* mainly US
Costs: $699 for 2 wks, $1,383 for 5 wks *incl* tuition, housing, all meals, insurance *Nonrefundable fee*
Housing: *Sponsor assists:* residence halls, homestay, hotels
Deadline: 4-6 wks before pgm
Other info: *US accredited sponsor:* yes *Began:* 1948 *Orient:* abroad *Activities:* excursions, field trips, cultural events *Misc:* May contact former participants. *URL:* http://www.extension.ucsd.edu/laip
Contact: Tanya Knebel, Pgm Rep, UCSD Extension, Liberal Arts & Intl Pgms 0176Z, 9500 Gilman Dr, La Jolla CA 92093-0176 *Ph:* 858-822 2747 *Fax:* 858-534 7385 *E-mail:* travelstudy@ucsd.edu

---

2120
UNIVERSITY OF COLORADO AT BOULDER
Study Spanish in Guadalajara
Site: Mexico: Guadalajara *Host inst:* Univ de Guadalajara
Dates: 5 or 10 wks, Jun-Aug
Subjects: Area studies, Homestay, Humanities, Social sciences, Spanish language (beg/int/adv)
Eligibility: *Level:* sophs, jrs, srs, adults, teachers, professionals *Requires:* 2.5 GPA, no more than 3 sems coll Spanish *Age:* avg 23
Credit: *Undergrad:* avail *Grad:* none *Doc:* transcript
Instruction: *In:* Spanish *Format:* lang study, lecture *Students:* intl
Costs: $1,358-$2,260 for CO residents, $2,358-$3,260 for others *incl* tuition, housing, all meals, insurance, fees
Housing: *Arr by pgm:* homestay
Deadline: Mar 1
Other info: *US accredited sponsor:* yes *Began:* 1984 *Orient:* in US *Activities:* excursions, field trips, cultural events *Misc:* May contact former participants. *URL:* http://www.colorado.edu/OIE/StudyAbroad
Contact: Intl Educ, Univ of Colorado, Campus Box 123, Boulder CO 80309-0123 *Ph:* 303-492 7741 *Fax:* 303-492 5185 *E-mail:* studyabr@colorado.edu

---

2121
UNIVERSITY OF KANSAS
Summer Language and Culture Institute in Guadalajara
Site: Mexico: Guadalajara *Host inst:* Univ del Valle de Atemajae (UNIVA)
Dates: 8 wks, Jun 2-Jul 28
Subjects: Civilization/culture, Homestay, Literature, Mexican studies, Spanish language
Eligibility: *Level:* fresh, sophs, jrs, srs, grads *Requires:* 2 sems coll Spanish
Credit: *Undergrad:* 7 *Grad:* avail *Doc:* transcript
Instruction: *In:* Spanish *Format:* lang study, lecture *Students:* mainly US
Costs: $1,235 *incl* tuition, housing, some meals, fees
Housing: *Arr by pgm:* homestay
Deadline: Rolling admissions; Feb 15
Other info: *US accredited sponsor:* yes *Began:* 1963 *Activities:* excursions, cultural events, sports *Misc:* Optional excursion to Mexico City, colonial towns. May contact former participants. *URL:* http://www.ukans.edu/~osa
Contact: Renee Bergene, Coord, Study Abroad, Univ of Kansas, 108 Lippincott Hall, Lawrence KS 66045 *Ph:* 785-864 3742 *Fax:* 785-864 5040 *E-mail:* osa@ukans.edu ▲

GUANAJUATO

2122
COMMITTEE ON INSTITUTIONAL COOPERATION
CIC Summer Study Program in Mexico
Site: Mexico: Guanajuato *Host inst:* Univ de Guanajuato
Dates: 8 wks, Jun-Aug
Subjects: Art, Civilization/culture, History, Homestay, Latin American studies, Literature, Mexican studies, Spanish language (adv)
Eligibility: *Level:* fresh, sophs, jrs, srs, grads *Requires:* 3.0 GPA, 5 sems coll Spanish or equiv
Credit: *Undergrad:* 6-9 *Grad:* avail *Doc:* transcript
Instruction: *In:* Spanish *Format:* lang study, lecture *Students:* mainly US
Costs: About $2,700 *incl* tuition, housing, all meals, fees, excursions
Housing: *Arr by pgm:* homestay
Deadline: Mar 1
Other info: *US accredited sponsor:* yes *Began:* 1967 *Orient:* abroad *Activities:* excursions, field trips, cultural events *Misc:* May contact former participants. *URL:* http://www.uiowa.edu/~uiabroad
Contact: *See Index II for Members* Hannah Covert, Admin Coord, CIC Study Abroad, 120 Intl Ctr, Univ of Iowa, Iowa City IA 52242-1802 *Ph:* 319-335 0353 *Fax:* 319-335 2021 *E-mail:* cic-abroad@uiowa.edu

---

2123
ISA
Cursos de Lengua Espanola: Summer Program in Guanajuato
Site: Mexico: Guanajuato *Host inst:* Univ de Guanajuato
Dates: 5 wks, May 20-Jun 24, Jul 8-Aug 12
Subjects: Homestay, Literature, Spanish language (beg/int/adv)
Eligibility: *Level:* fresh, sophs, jrs, srs, grads, adults, teachers *Requires:* 2.5 GPA, recommendation letter *Age:* min 18, avg 21
Credit: *Undergrad:* 6-8 sem hrs *Grad:* none *Doc:* transcript, certificate
Instruction: *In:* Spanish *Format:* lang study, lecture *Students:* intl
Costs: $2,150 *incl* tuition, housing, all meals, insurance, fees, excursions, ground transport, tutoring
Housing: *Arr by pgm:* homestay
Deadline: Apr 5; Mar 10 for scholarships
Other info: *US accredited sponsor:* no *Began:* 1989 *Orient:* in US & abroad *Activities:* excursions *Misc:* Resident dir incl in costs. May contact former participants. *Financial aid:* scholarships *URL:* http://www.studiesabroad.com
Contact: Gustavo Artaza, Exec Dir, ISA, 901 W 24th St, Austin TX 78705 *Ph:* 800-580 8826; 512-480 8522 *Fax:* 512-480 8866 *E-mail:* isa@studiesabroad.com ▲

2124
SOUTHWEST TEXAS STATE UNIVERSITY
SWT in Guanajuato
Site: Mexico: Guanajuato
Dates: 3 wks, Jul
Subjects: Field study, Geography
Eligibility: Students with no geography background need faculty approval *Level:* grads, professionals *Age:* min 18, avg 39
Credit: *Undergrad:* none *Grad:* avail *Doc:* transcript
Instruction: *In:* English *Format:* directed field study, lecture, study tour *Students:* mainly US
Costs: $1,175 *incl* tuition, housing, some meals, fees, excursions, books/materials
Housing: *Arr by pgm:* hotels
Deadline: Contact sponsor
Other info: *US accredited sponsor:* yes *Began:* 2000 *Orient:* in US *Activities:* excursions, field trips *Misc:* May contact former participants. *Financial aid:* scholarships *URL:* http://www.ideal.swt.edu/extension/study-abroad/
Contact: Dr David Stea, Southwest Texas State Univ, 601 Univ Dr, San Marcos TX 78666 *Ph:* 512-245 7975 *Fax:* 512-245 8353 *E-mail:* ds34@swt.edu
Or Contact: Isis Gomez Extension Studies Coord, Southwest Texas State Univ, 601 Univ Dr, San Marcos TX 78666 *Ph:* 512-245 2322 *Fax:* 512-245 8934 *E-mail:* ig02@swt.edu

---

2125
STETSON UNIVERSITY
Guanajuato Summer
Site: Mexico: Guanajuato *Host inst:* Univ de Guanajuato
Dates: Jun 10-Jul 9
Subjects: Architectural history, Crafts, Folk arts, Folk dance, History, Homestay, Interdisciplinary studies, Literature, Mexican studies, Spanish language, Written composition
Eligibility: *Level:* sophs, jrs *Requires:* 2.5 GPA, previous study in field
Credit: *Undergrad:* 6 *Grad:* none *Doc:* transcript
Instruction: *In:* English, Spanish *Format:* lang study *Students:* intl
Costs: $2,400 *incl* tuition, housing, all meals, excursions, laundry *Nonrefundable fee*
Housing: *Arr by pgm:* homestay
Deadline: Mar 1
Other info: *US accredited sponsor:* yes *Began:* 1999 *Orient:* abroad (1 day) *Activities:* excursions, field trips, program travel, cultural events *Misc:* Resident director. May contact former participants. *URL:* http://www.ugto.mx/Universidad.html
Contact: Alma Montes Hernandez, Resident Dir, Ctr de Idiomas, Univ de Guanajuato, Guanajuato, GTO 36000, Mexico *Ph:* 904-822 8165 *Fax:* 904-822 8167 *E-mail:* montesa@quijote.ugto.mx

---

2126
STUDY ABROAD/A LIFE EXPERIENCE
Spanish Language
Site: Mexico: Guanajuato
Dates: 1-6 wks, May 19-Jun 30 or Jul 7-Aug 18
Subjects: Civilization/culture, History, Homestay, Literature, Spanish language (beg/int/adv), Spanish studies
Eligibility: *Level:* fresh, sophs, jrs, srs, adults, teachers, professionals, precoll *Requires:* 2.5 GPA *Age:* min 18, avg 22
Credit: *Undergrad:* 6-8 *Grad:* none *Doc:* transcript, diploma
Instruction: *In:* English, Spanish *Format:* lang study, lecture, study tour, tutorial *Students:* mainly US
Costs: Contact sponsor
Housing: *Arr by pgm:* homestay

Deadline: Contact sponsor
Other info: *US accredited sponsor:* no *Began:* 1996 *Orient:* abroad *Activities:* excursions, field trips, program travel *Misc:* May contact former participants. *URL:* http://www.foreignstudies.net
Contact: Clayton Murphy, Dir, Study Abroad/A Life Experience, 4573 Albatross Dr, Seabrook TX 77586 *Ph:* 888-722 5346; 281-291 7344 *Fax:* 281-291 7355

2127
UNIVERSITY OF ARIZONA
Verano Mexico: Education Program in Mexico
Site: Mexico: Guanajuato *Host inst:* Inst Falcon
Dates: 4 wks, Jul 6-Aug 5
Subjects: Bilingualism, Education/teaching, Field study, Homestay, Spanish language (beg/int/adv), Special education
Eligibility: *Level:* srs, grads, teachers *Requires:* 3.0 GPA, bachelor's degree or approval of instructor
Credit: *Undergrad:* 6 *Grad:* 6 *Doc:* transcript
Instruction: *In:* English, Spanish *Format:* directed field study, lang study *Students:* mainly US
Costs: $1,200 *incl* tuition, excursions
Housing: *Arr by pgm:* apartments, homestay, hotels
Deadline: May 20
Other info: *US accredited sponsor:* yes *Orient:* in US *Activities:* field trips, program travel *Financial aid:* scholarships *URL:* http://w3.arizona.edu/~ciss/
Contact: Todd Fletcher, Special Educ & Rehabilitation, Univ of Arizona, Tucson AZ 85721 *Ph:* 520-621 0939 *Fax:* 520-626 9004 *E-mail:* cpatrick@u.arizona.edu
Or Contact: Ctr for Global Student Pgms, Univ of Arizona, 939 N Tyndall Ave, Tucson AZ 85721 *Ph:* 520-626 9211 *Fax:* 520-626 9004 ▲

LEON

2128
MICHIGAN STATE UNIVERSITY
Veterinary Medicine
Site: Mexico: Leon
Dates: 7 wks, Jul-Aug
Subjects: Field study, Homestay, Independent study, Spanish language, Veterinary science
Eligibility: *Level:* fresh, sophs, jrs, srs *Requires:* 2.5 GPA, previous study in field, pre-vet studies *Age:* min 18
Credit: *Undergrad:* 7 *Grad:* avail *Doc:* transcript
Instruction: *In:* English, Spanish *Format:* directed field study, independent study, lang study, lecture *Students:* mainly US
Costs: About $1,700 *incl* housing, all meals, insurance, support svcs
Housing: *Arr by pgm:* homestay
Deadline: Mar 2
Other info: *US accredited sponsor:* yes *Began:* 1999 *Orient:* in US & abroad *Misc:* May contact former participants. *Financial aid:* scholarships *URL:* http://studyabroad.msu.edu
Contact: Cheryl Benner, Study Abroad, Michigan State Univ, 109 Intl Ctr, East Lansing MI 48824 *Ph:* 517-353 8920 *Fax:* 517-432 2082 *E-mail:* bennerc@msu.edu ▲

MERIDA

2129
INSTITUTO BENJAMIN FRANKLIN DE YUCATAN
Spanish in Yucatan
Site: Mexico: Merida
Dates: 1 wk or longer, yr-round
Subjects: Homestay, Latin American studies, Spanish language (beg/int/adv)
Eligibility: *Level:* adults *Age:* min 17, avg 21
Credit: *Undergrad:* avail *Grad:* avail *Doc:* transcript, certificate
Instruction: *In:* Spanish *Format:* lang study, lecture, tutorial *Students:* intl
Costs: $150 per wk *incl* books/materials *Nonrefundable fee*
Housing: *Arr by pgm:* homestay, hotels
Deadline: 2 wks before pgm
Other info: *US accredited sponsor:* no *Began:* 1958 *In coop with:* US State Dept *Activities:* excursions, field trips, program travel, cultural events *Misc:* Conversation pgm, library, video rm, colonial bldg. May contact former participants. *URL:* http://www.benjaminfranklin.com.mx
Contact: Guillermo Vales, Dir, Inst Benjamin Franklin, Calle 57, #474-A-A x 54, Merida, Yucatan, Mexico *E-mail:* franklin@finred.com.mx

---

2130
MICHIGAN STATE UNIVERSITY
Intensive First and Second Year Spanish
Site: Mexico: Merida
Dates: 9 wks, May-Jul
Subjects: Homestay, Spanish language (beg/int)
Eligibility: *Level:* fresh, sophs, jrs, srs *Requires:* 2.0 GPA *Age:* min 18
Credit: *Undergrad:* avail *Grad:* none *Doc:* transcript
Instruction: *In:* English *Format:* lang study *Students:* mainly US
Costs: About $1,200 *incl* housing, all meals, insurance, fees, excursions *Nonrefundable fee*
Housing: *Arr by pgm:* homestay
Deadline: Mar 2
Other info: *US accredited sponsor:* yes *Began:* 1999 *Orient:* in US (1 day) *Activities:* field trips *URL:* http://studyabroad.msu.edu
Contact: Cheryl Benner, Study Abroad, Michigan State Univ, 109 Intl Ctr, East Lansing MI 48824-1035 *Ph:* 517-353 8920 *Fax:* 517-432 2082 *E-mail:* bennerc@msu.edu ▲

2131
MICHIGAN STATE UNIVERSITY
Land Use, the Environment and Social Capital
Site: Mexico: Merida
Dates: 3 wks, Dec-Jan
Subjects: Agriculture, Field study, Geography, Natural resources, Social sciences
Eligibility: *Level:* fresh, sophs, jrs, srs *Requires:* 2.0 GPA *Age:* min 18
Credit: *Undergrad:* avail *Grad:* none *Doc:* transcript
Instruction: *In:* English *Format:* directed field study, lecture *Students:* mainly US
Costs: About $1,300 *incl* housing, all meals, insurance, fees, excursions *Nonrefundable fee*
Housing: *Arr by pgm:* homestay
Deadline: Oct 20
Other info: *US accredited sponsor:* yes *Began:* 1999 *Orient:* in US (1 day) *Activities:* excursions, field trips *URL:* http://studyabroad.msu.edu
Contact: Cheryl Benner, Study Abroad, Michigan State Univ, 109 Intl Ctr, East Lansing MI 48824-1035 *Ph:* 517-353 8920 *Fax:* 517-432 2082 *E-mail:* bennerc@msu.edu ▲

2132
NATIONAL REGISTRATION CENTER FOR STUDY ABROAD (NRCSA)
CIS-Merida
Site: Mexico: Merida *Host inst:* Ctr de Idiomas
Dates: 2 wks or longer, yr-round
Subjects: Homestay, Spanish language (beg/int/adv)
Eligibility: *Level:* fresh, sophs, jrs, srs, grads, adults, teachers, professionals *Age:* min 18
Credit: *Undergrad:* avail *Grad:* avail *Doc:* certificate
Instruction: *In:* Spanish *Format:* lang study, lecture *Students:* mainly US
Costs: $738 for 2 wks *incl* tuition, housing, all meals, insurance *Nonrefundable fee*
Housing: *Arr by pgm:* homestay
Deadline: 6 wks before pgm
Other info: *US accredited sponsor:* no *Misc:* May contact former participants. *URL:* http://www.nrcsa.com

Contact: June Domoe, NRCSA, 823 N 2nd St, #206, Milwaukee WI 53203 *Ph:* 414-278 0631 *Fax:* 414-271 8884 *E-mail:* info@nrcsa.com

---

2133
UNIVERSITY OF DELAWARE
Winter Session in Mexico
Site: Mexico: Merida *Host inst:* Merida Inst of Technology
Dates: 1 mo, Jan
Subjects: Art history, Homestay, Independent study, Latin American studies, Political science/politics, Spanish language (int)
Eligibility: *Level:* fresh, sophs, jrs, srs, adults *Requires:* 2.0 GPA
Credit: *Undergrad:* 6-7 *Grad:* none
Instruction: *In:* English, Spanish *Format:* independent study, lang study, lecture, study tour *Students:* mainly US
Costs: Contact sponsor
Housing: *Arr by pgm:* homestay
Deadline: Early Oct
Other info: *US accredited sponsor:* yes *Began:* 1992 *Orient:* avail yes *Activities:* excursions, field trips, program travel, cultural events *Misc:* Contact sponsor to arrange honors credit. May contact former participants. *Financial aid:* scholarships *URL:* http://www.udel.edu/studyabroad/
Contact: Lisa Chieffo, Study Abroad Coord, Foreign Langs & Literatures, Univ of Delaware, 326 Smith Hall, Newark DE 19716 *Ph:* 302-831 6458 *Fax:* 302-831 0597 *E-mail:* lchieffo@udel.edu
Or Contact: Intl Pgms & Special Sessions, Univ of Delaware, 4 Kent Way, Newark DE 19716 *Ph:* 888-831 4685; 302-831 2852 *Fax:* 302-831 6042 *E-mail:* studyabroad@udel.edu

---

2134
UNIVERSITY OF SAINT THOMAS
UST Summer Program in Merida
Site: Mexico: Merida
Dates: 6 wks, May 31-Jul 4
Subjects: Civilization/culture, Field study, Independent study, Literature, Mexican studies, Sociology, Spanish language (int/adv)
Eligibility: *Level:* fresh, sophs, jrs, srs, grads, adults, teachers, professionals, precoll *Requires:* previous study in field, 2 sems coll Spanish *Age:* avg 20
Credit: *Undergrad:* 6 *Grad:* none *Doc:* transcript
Instruction: *In:* Spanish *Format:* directed field study, independent study, lang study, lecture, seminar, study tour, tutorial *Students:* US & intl
Costs: $3,199 *incl* tuition, housing, all meals, intl airfare, fees, excursions
Housing: *Arr by pgm:* villa
Deadline: May 1
Other info: *US accredited sponsor:* yes *Began:* 1975 *Orient:* in US & abroad (2 wks, intensive lang study) *Activities:* excursions, field trips, program travel, cultural events *Misc:* Scholarships & work-study avail for UST students only. Costs do not incl rm & board during 2-wk training at UST. May contact former participants. *Financial aid:* scholarships, work study
Contact: Prof E Zambosco-Thomas, Dir, Spanish, Univ of St Thomas, 3800 Montrose Blvd, Houston TX 77006 *Ph:* 713-525 3123 *Fax:* 713-525 2125 *E-mail:* ezt@basil.stthom.edu
Or Contact: Fr Jack Hanna, Spanish, Univ of St Thomas, 3800 Montrose Blvd, Houston TX 77006 *Ph:* 713-864 6348, 713-868 2909 *Fax:* 713-864 5750

MEXICO CITY

2135
ALMA COLLEGE
Summer Program of Studies in Mexico
Site: Mexico: Mexico City *Host inst:* Univ Iberoamericana
Dates: 6 wks, Jun-mid-Jul, 4-6 wks, mid-Jun-early Aug for intensive lang study
Subjects: Latin American studies, Mexican studies, Spanish language (beg/int/adv)
Eligibility: *Level:* sophs, jrs, srs *Requires:* 2.5 GPA, faculty recommendations
Credit: *Undergrad:* 3-9 *Grad:* none *Doc:* transcript
Instruction: *In:* English, Spanish *Format:* lang study, lecture *Students:* mainly US
Costs: $3,199 for 6 wks Latin Amer study, $2,949-$3,408 for 4-6 wks Spanish *incl* tuition, housing, all meals, insurance, fees, excursions, e-mail
Housing: *Arr by pgm:* homestay
Deadline: 2 mos before pgm
Other info: *US accredited sponsor:* yes *Began:* 1983 *Orient:* abroad *Activities:* excursions, cultural events *Misc:* Direct study in univ possible. Fitness, internet facilities. *URL:* http://www.alma.edu/academics/international
Contact: Chris Musick, Intl Educ, Alma Coll, 614 W Superior St, Alma MI 48801-1599 *Ph:* 800-321 2562; 517-463 7055 *Fax:* 517-463 7126 *E-mail:* intl_studies@alma.edu

---

2136
ENDICOTT COLLEGE
Endicott College, Mexico City
Site: Mexico: Mexico City *Host inst:* Endicott Coll Mexico City campus
Dates: 4 wks, Jul and/or Aug
Subjects: Civilization/culture, Independent study, Internships, Latin American studies, Spanish language
Eligibility: *Level:* fresh, sophs, jrs, srs, adults *Requires:* 2.0 GPA *Age:* min 18
Credit: *Undergrad:* 6 *Grad:* none *Doc:* transcript
Instruction: *In:* English, Spanish *Format:* lang study, seminar *Students:* intl
Costs: $1,400 *incl* tuition, housing, some meals, fees, ISIC *Nonrefundable fee*
Housing: *Arr by pgm:* homestay
Deadline: Apr 15
Other info: *US accredited sponsor:* yes *Began:* 1998 *Orient:* abroad (2 days) *Activities:* excursions, field trips, cultural events *URL:* http://www.cis-spain.com/
Contact: Dr James L Citron, Dean, Intl Studies & Pgms, Endicott Coll, 376 Hale St, Beverly MA 01915 *Ph:* 978-232 2271 *Fax:* 978-232 3100 *E-mail:* jcitron@endicott.edu
Or Contact: Dra Vivian Antaki, Dean, Endicott Coll Mexico, Aristoteles No 80, 11560 Mexico DF, Mexico *E-mail:* vantaki@endicott.edu ▲

2137
SUNY COLLEGE AT OSWEGO
Mexico City
Site: Mexico: Mexico City *Host inst:* Univ Iberoamericana
Dates: 6 wks, late May-mid-Jul
Subjects: Anthropology, Arts, Crafts, Dance, Folklore, Homestay, International relations, Latin American studies, Literature, Mexican studies, Music, Spanish language (beg/int/adv)
Eligibility: *Level:* adults, precoll *Requires:* good acad standing
Credit: *Undergrad:* 6 *Grad:* none *Doc:* transcript
Instruction: *In:* Spanish *Format:* lang study, lecture *Students:* mainly US
Costs: $3,100 *incl* tuition, housing, some meals, intl airfare, excursions, cultural events *Nonrefundable fee*
Housing: *Arr by pgm:* homestay
Deadline: Apr 1
Other info: *US accredited sponsor:* yes *Began:* 1985 *Orient:* in US *Activities:* field trips, cultural events *Misc:* May contact former participants. *URL:* http://www.oswego.edu/~intled
Contact: Susan Ansara, Dir, Intl Educ, SUNY Coll at Oswego, 102 Rich Hall, Oswego NY 13126 *Ph:* 888-467 9346; 315-341 2118 *Fax:* 315-341 2477 *E-mail:* intled@oswego.edu

---

2138
UNIVERSIDAD LA SALLE
Year-Round Spanish Acquisition and Perfection Program
Site: Mexico: Mexico City
Dates: 3 wks, yr-round

Subjects: Latin American studies, Literature, Spanish language (beg/int/adv)
Eligibility: *Level:* fresh, sophs, jrs, srs, grads, adults, teachers, professionals, precoll *Age:* min 18
Credit: *Undergrad:* avail *Grad:* avail *Doc:* transcript
Instruction: *In:* Spanish *Format:* lang study, lecture, practical training, tutorial *Students:* intl
Costs: $170 for semi-intensive classes, $310 for intensive *incl* tuition, books/materials
Housing: *Sponsor assists*
Deadline: 3 days before pgm
Other info: *US accredited sponsor:* no *Began:* 1992 *Orient:* abroad *Misc:* Intensive & semi-intensive pgms avail. Span. for specific purposes. Cultural, acad courses avail. *URL:* http://www.ulsa.edu.mx
Contact: Leonor Lemus, Coord, Spanish Pgms & Housing, CIEL, Univ La Salle, Benjamin Franklin 47, Col Condesa, 06140 Mexico DF, Mexico *E-mail:* lla@aixulsa.ulsa.mx

---

2139
UNIVERSITY OF MIAMI (FL)
Spanish and Area Studies at Ibero-Americana, Mexico
Site: Mexico: Mexico City *Host inst:* Univ Ibero-Americana
Dates: 6 wks, Jun-Jul
Subjects: Civilization/culture, Homestay, Mexican studies, Spanish language
Eligibility: *Level:* sophs, jrs, srs *Requires:* 2.75 GPA, 1 yr Spanish *Age:* min 18
Credit: *Undergrad:* 6 *Grad:* none *Doc:* transcript
Instruction: *In:* English, Spanish *Format:* lang study, lecture *Students:* mainly US
Costs: $3,950 *incl* tuition, housing, all meals, excursions *Nonrefundable fee*
Housing: *Arr by pgm:* homestay
Deadline: Mar 30
Other info: *US accredited sponsor:* yes *Began:* 2000 *Orient:* abroad (1 day) *Misc:* May contact former participants. *URL:* http://www.studyabroad.miami.edu
Contact: Chris Tingue, Allen Hall 212, 5050 Brunson Dr, PO Box 248005, Univ of Miami, Coral Gables FL 33124-1610 *Ph:* 800-557 54521; 305-284 3434 *Fax:* 305-284 6629 *E-mail:* ieep@miami.edu

---

2140
UNIVERSITY OF SOUTHERN MISSISSIPPI
Mexico Studies Program
Site: Mexico: Mexico City
Dates: 2 wks, May 14-31
Subjects: Civilization/culture, International business, Psychology
Eligibility: *Level:* fresh, sophs, jrs, srs, grads *Requires:* 2.0 GPA, previous study in field *Age:* min 18, avg 24
Credit: *Undergrad:* 4 *Grad:* 4 *Doc:* transcript
Instruction: *In:* English *Format:* directed field study, lang study *Students:* mainly US
Costs: $2,599 for undergrads, about $2,899 for grads *incl* tuition, housing, intl airfare *Nonrefundable fee*
Housing: *Arr by pgm:* homestay
Deadline: Apr 1

Other info: *US accredited sponsor:* yes *Began:* 1995 *Activities:* field trips, cultural events *Financial aid:* scholarships *URL:* http://www.usm.edu
Contact: Dr Tim W Hudson, Intl & Continuing Educ, Univ of Southern Mississippi, Box 10047, Hattiesburg MS 39406-0047 *Ph:* 601-266 4344 *Fax:* 601-266 5699 *E-mail:* melissa.ravencraft@usm.edu
Or Contact: Dr Tony Henthorne, Dir, Univ of Southern Mississippi, Box 5059, Hattiesburg MS 39406-5059 *Ph:* 601-266 4635 *Fax:* 601-266 5699

MONTERREY

2141
OKLAHOMA STATE UNIVERSITY
Global Business-A US/Latin American Partnership
Site: Mexico: Monterrey
Dates: Jan 30-Mar 29
Subjects: International business
Eligibility: *Level:* sophs, jrs, srs, grads
Credit: *Undergrad:* avail *Grad:* avail *Doc:* transcript
Instruction: *In:* English *Format:* lecture, study tour *Students:* mainly US
Costs: $1,500 *incl* tuition, housing, intl airfare *Nonrefundable fee*
Housing: *Arr by pgm:* hotels
Deadline: Jan 14
Other info: *US accredited sponsor:* yes *Began:* 1995 *Activities:* excursions, field trips, program travel, cultural events *Financial aid:* scholarships
Contact: Dr Andrew Urich, Faculty Coord, Oklahoma State Univ, Coll of Bus Admin, Stillwater OK 74078 *Ph:* 405-744 8619 *Fax:* 405-744 6143 *E-mail:* aurich@okstate.edu
Or Contact: Gaye Trivitt, Pgm Mgr, Bus Extension, Oklahoma State Univ, Coll of Bus Admin, Stillwater OK 74078 *Ph:* 405-744 5208 *Fax:* 405-744 6143 *E-mail:* glt@okstate.edu

2142
SOUTHWEST TEXAS STATE UNIVERSITY
SWT in Monterrey
Site: Mexico: Monterrey *Host inst:* ITESM
Dates: 4 wks, Jul
Subjects: Business language, Business/management, Spanish studies
Eligibility: *Level:* jrs, srs *Requires:* 2.5 GPA, previous study in field, Int Spanish *Age:* min 18, avg 22
Credit: *Undergrad:* 6 *Grad:* none *Doc:* transcript
Instruction: *In:* Spanish *Format:* lang study, lecture, tutorial *Students:* mainly US
Costs: $2,270 *incl* tuition, housing, intl airfare, fees, excursions
Housing: *Arr by pgm:* residence halls
Deadline: Contact sponsor
Other info: *US accredited sponsor:* yes *Began:* 2000 *Orient:* in US & abroad (1 day) *Activities:* excursions, cultural events, sports *Misc:* May contact former participants. *Financial aid:* scholarships *URL:* http://www.ideal.swt.edu/extension/study-abroad/
Contact: Dr Lucy Harney, Southwest Texas State Univ, 601 Univ Dr, San Marcos TX 78666 *Ph:* 512-245 2360 *Fax:* 512-245 8298 *E-mail:* lharneyswt@aol.com
Or Contact: Isis Gomez Extension Studies Coord, Southwest Texas State Univ, 601 Univ Dr, San Marcos TX 78666 *Ph:* 512-245 2322 *Fax:* 512-245 8934 *E-mail:* ig02@swt.edu

2143
UNIVERSITY OF PITTSBURGH
Pitt/Monterrey Exchange Program
Site: Mexico: Monterrey *Host inst:* Monterrey Tech
Dates: 6 wks, early Jun-mid-Jul
Subjects: Engineering, Mexican studies, Spanish language (beg/int/adv)
Eligibility: Own students only. *Level:* fresh, sophs, jrs, srs *Requires:* 2.75 GPA *Age:* avg 20
Credit: *Undergrad:* 6 *Grad:* none *Doc:* transcript
Instruction: *In:* English, Spanish *Format:* lang study, lecture *Students:* intl
Costs: About $1,700 *incl* tuition, housing, all meals, fees *Nonrefundable fee*
Housing: *Arr by pgm:* residence halls with local students, homestay
Deadline: Mar 15
Other info: *US accredited sponsor:* yes *Orient:* in US & abroad *Activities:* excursions, field trips, cultural events *Misc:* May contact former participants. *Financial aid:* scholarships *URL:* http://www.pitt.edu/~stdyabrd/
Contact: Erin Sunday, Study Abroad, Univ of Pittsburgh, B-80G Benedum Hall, Pittsburgh PA 15261 *Ph:* 412-624 5942 *Fax:* 412-624 2728 *E-mail:* abroad@engrng.pitt.edu

2144
UNIVERSITY OF SAN DIEGO, SCHOOL OF BUSINESS ADMINISTRATION
Graduate Business Study Abroad in Monterrey
Site: Mexico: Monterrey *Host inst:* EGADE, ITESM Campus Monterrey
Dates: Jan 3-24 (2 wks distance learning, Jan 13-20 in Monterrey)
Subjects: Homestay, International business, Latin American studies, Mexican studies
Eligibility: *Level:* grads, professionals *Requires:* enrollment in or graduation from grad bus or related grad pgm, good acad standing
Credit: *Undergrad:* none *Grad:* 3 per course *Doc:* transcript
Instruction: *In:* English *Format:* lecture, seminar *Students:* intl
Costs: $1,450 for one course, $2,400 for 2 courses *incl* tuition, housing, some meals *Nonrefundable fee*
Housing: *Arr by pgm:* apartments with local students, homestay, hotels
Deadline: None
Other info: *US accredited sponsor:* yes *Began:* 1996 *Orient:* abroad (1 day) *Activities:* excursions, field trips, program travel, cultural events *Misc:* Company visits. May contact former participants. *URL:* http://business.acusd.edu/ib/mexico.html
Contact: Kira Mende, Coord, or Amanda Ryan, Admin Asst, Ahlers Ctr for Intl Bus, Univ of San Diego Sch of Bus Admin, 5998 Alcala Park, San Diego CA 92110-2492 *Ph:* 800-248 4873; 619-260 4896 *Fax:* 619-260 4891 *E-mail:* ib@acusd.edu

MORELIA

2145
CENTRAL WASHINGTON UNIVERSITY
CWU Program in Morelia, Mexico
Site: Mexico: Morelia *Host inst:* Ctr Mexicano Intl, Univ Latina
Dates: 4 or 10 wks, Sep 6-Nov 5, Jan 8-Mar 9, Mar 26-May 25, Jun 19-Jul 14, Jul 14-Aug 11 or Jun 19-Aug 11
Subjects: Bilingualism, Business/management, Education/teaching, History, Homestay, Literature, Mexican studies, Political science/politics, Spanish language (beg/int/adv)
Eligibility: *Level:* fresh, sophs, jrs, srs, grads, adults, teachers, professionals *Requires:* 2.5 GPA *Age:* min 18, avg 20
Credit: *Undergrad:* 12 per term *Grad:* 12 per term *Doc:* transcript
Instruction: *In:* Spanish *Format:* lang study, lecture, seminar *Students:* US & host country
Costs: $3,133 for 10 wks *incl* tuition, housing, all meals, fees, excursions, books/materials *Nonrefundable fee*
Housing: *Arr by pgm:* apartments, homestay
Deadline: 45 days before pgm
Other info: *US accredited sponsor:* yes *Began:* 1978 *In coop with:* CCIS *Orient:* in US & abroad (1 day) *Activities:* excursions, cultural events *URL:* http://www.cwu.edu/~intlprog/mexicohome.html

Contact: Heather Barclay, Central Washington Univ, 400 E 8th Ave, Ellensburg WA 98926-7408 *Ph:* 809-963 3616 *Fax:* 809-9631558 *E-mail:* goabroad@cwu.edu

---

2146
COLLEGE OF WILLIAM & MARY
Hispanic Studies in Mexico
Site: Mexico: Morelia *Host inst:* CMI
Dates: 1 mo, about Jun 3-Jul 1
Subjects: Civilization/culture, Mexican studies, Spanish language
Eligibility: *Level:* fresh, sophs, jrs, srs, grads, teachers *Requires:* 2.8 GPA, previous study in field, 2 yrs Spanish or equiv
Credit: *Undergrad:* 7 *Grad:* none *Doc:* transcript
Instruction: *In:* Spanish *Format:* lecture *Students:* intl
Costs: $3,000 *incl* tuition, housing, intl airfare, excursions
Housing: *Arr by pgm:* homestay
Deadline: Feb 15
Other info: *US accredited sponsor:* yes *Began:* 1998 *Orient:* avail *Activities:* excursions *URL:* http://www.wm.edu/academics/reves/programs_abroad/
Contact: Guru Ghosh, Coll of William & Mary, PO Box 8795, Williamsburg VA 23187-8795 *Ph:* 757-221 3595 *Fax:* 757-221 3597 *E-mail:* gxghos@wm.edu

---

2147
KENTUCKY INSTITUTE FOR INTERNATIONAL STUDIES (KIIS)
Program Mexico
Site: Mexico: Morelia
Dates: 5 wks, late May-Jun
Subjects: Civilization/culture, Homestay, Humanities, Spanish language (beg/int/adv)
Eligibility: *Level:* fresh, sophs, jrs, srs, grads, adults, teachers, professionals *Requires:* 2.0 GPA, faculty recommendations, good acad standing *Age:* min 18
Credit: *Undergrad:* 3-6 *Grad:* none *Doc:* transcript *Transfer credit through:* Murray State Univ
Instruction: *In:* English, Spanish *Format:* lang study, lecture, seminar, study tour *Students:* mainly US
Costs: About $1,990 for students at member schs, $2,290 for others *incl* tuition, housing, all meals, intl airfare, fees, excursions, ISIC *Nonrefundable fee*
Housing: *Arr by pgm:* homestay
Deadline: Feb 15 ($100 late fee)
Other info: *US accredited sponsor:* yes *Began:* 1992 *Orient:* in US & abroad *Activities:* excursions, cultural events *Financial aid:* scholarships *URL:* http://www.kiis.org
Contact: *See Index II for Members* Dr J Milton Grimes, Exec Dir, KIIS, Murray State Univ, PO Box 9, Murray KY 42071-0009 *Ph:* 270-762 3091 *Fax:* 270-762 3434 *E-mail:* kiismsu@murraystate.edu

---

2148
WESTERN WASHINGTON UNIVERSITY and CENTRO MEXICANO INTERNACIONAL (CMI)
Summer Program in Morelia
Site: Mexico: Morelia
Dates: 4 or 8 wks, Jun 18-Aug 10
Subjects: Anthropology, Art, Dance, Education/teaching, Mexican studies, Music, Spanish language (beg/int/adv), TEFL/TESL
Eligibility: *Level:* fresh, sophs, jrs, srs, grads, adults *Requires:* 2.5 GPA
Credit: *Undergrad:* 10-18 qtr hrs *Grad:* none *Doc:* transcript
Instruction: *In:* English, Spanish *Format:* art studio, lang study, lecture, seminar *Students:* mainly US
Costs: About $2,009 for 4 wks, $3,583 per qtr *incl* tuition, housing, all meals, insurance, fees, excursions, books/materials *Nonrefundable fee*
Housing: *Arr by pgm:* homestay, other arrangements
Deadline: Apr 15
Other info: *US accredited sponsor:* yes *Began:* 1977 *Orient:* in US & abroad *Activities:* excursions *Misc:* Optional travel, dance, guitar, crafts. Limited grants, loans & scholarships. Financial aid for WWU students only. *Financial aid:* scholarships *URL:* http://www.wwu.edu/~ipewwu
Contact: Evelyn Rupaal, Coord Dir, Intl Pgms & Exchs, Western Washington Univ, Bellingham WA 98225-9046 *Ph:* 800-426 1349; 360-650 3298 *Fax:* 360-650 6572 *E-mail:* ipewwu@cc.wwu.edu
Or Contact: CMI AC, 14542 Brookhollow Ste 279, San Antonio TX 78232 *Ph:* 800-835 8863 *E-mail:* cmi@spanish-language.com

---

OAXACA

2149
CITY COLLEGE OF SAN FRANCISCO
Learn Spanish in Oaxaca, Mexico
Site: Mexico: Oaxaca *Host inst:* Inst Cultural Oaxaca
Dates: 3-4 wks, Jun 23-Jul 17
Subjects: Crafts, Culinary arts, Homestay, Literature, Spanish language (beg/int/adv)
Eligibility: *Level:* fresh, sophs, jrs, srs, adults *Age:* min 18
Credit: *Undergrad:* avail *Grad:* none *Doc:* transcript
Instruction: *In:* Spanish *Format:* lang study, lecture, workshop *Students:* mainly US
Costs: $1,882 *incl* tuition, housing, most meals, intl airfare, ISIC
Housing: *Arr by pgm:* homestay
Deadline: Apr 2
Other info: *US accredited sponsor:* yes *Began:* 1994 *Orient:* in US & abroad *Activities:* cultural events *Misc:* Optional wkend excursions. Loans & grants for eligible students. *Financial aid:* scholarships *URL:* http://www.ccsf.org/studyabroad
Contact: Jill Heffron, Study Abroad Coord, City Coll of San Francisco, 50 Phelan Ave, Box C212, San Francisco CA 94112 *Ph:* 415-239 3778 *Fax:* 415-239 3804 *E-mail:* jheffron@ccsf.org

---

2150
HORIZONS TO GO
Horizons in Mexico: Oaxaca During Three-Kings Day
Site: Mexico: Oaxaca
Dates: 1 wk, Jan 5-12
Subjects: Art, Ceramics/pottery, Civilization/culture, Crafts, Mexican studies, Textiles, Weaving, Woodcarving
Eligibility: *Level:* adults *Age:* min 19, max 85, avg 45
Credit: *Undergrad:* none *Grad:* none
Instruction: *In:* English *Format:* study tour, workshop *Students:* mainly US
Costs: $1,325 *incl* housing, all meals, fees, excursions, books/materials
Housing: *Arr by pgm:* hotels
Deadline: Contact sponsor
Other info: *US accredited sponsor:* no *Began:* 1983 *Activities:* excursions, field trips, cultural events *Misc:* Workshops with local artisans in various mediums. May contact former participants. *URL:* http://www.horizons-art.org
Contact: Jane Sinauer, Horizons To Go, PO Box 2206, Amherst MA 01004 *Ph:* 413-549 2900 *Fax:* 413-549 5995 *E-mail:* horizons@horizons-art.org

---

2151
INSTITUTO CULTURAL OAXACA
Spanish Language and Culture Program in Oaxaca
Site: Mexico: Oaxaca
Dates: 1 wk or longer, yr-round
Subjects: Archaeology, Ceramics/pottery, Culinary arts, Folk dance, History, Homestay, Literature, Mexican studies, Spanish language (beg/int/adv), Weaving
Eligibility: *Level:* adults *Age:* min 16, avg 35
Credit: *Undergrad:* avail *Grad:* none *Doc:* certificate
Instruction: *In:* Spanish *Format:* art studio, lang study, lecture, practical

training, study tour, workshop *Students:* US & intl
Costs: $450 per 4-wk session *incl* tuition, fees *Nonrefundable fee*
Housing: *Arr by pgm:* apartments, homestay, pensions, hotels
Deadline: 1 mo before pgm; 2-3 mos before pgm for Jun or Jul
Other info: *US accredited sponsor:* no *Began:* 1984 *Orient:* abroad *Activities:* excursions, cultural events *Misc:* Art workshops avail. May contact former participants. *URL:* http://www.instculturaloax.com.mx
Contact: Lic Lucero Topete, Inst Cultural Oaxaca, Apdo 340, Oaxaca 68000, Oaxaca, Mexico *E-mail:* inscuoax@antequera.com ▲

2152
LANGUAGE LINK and **BECARI LANGUAGE SCHOOL**
Spanish Immersion in Oaxaca, Mexico
Site: Mexico: Oaxaca City
Dates: 1-16 wks, yr-round
Subjects: Spanish language
Eligibility: *Level:* fresh, sophs, jrs, srs, grads, adults, teachers, professionals, precoll *Age:* min 18, avg 30
Credit: *Undergrad:* 12 *Grad:* 6 *Doc:* transcript
Instruction: *In:* Spanish *Format:* lang study, tutorial *Students:* intl
Costs: $225 per wk *incl* tuition, housing, some meals, insurance, fees, airport pickup *Nonrefundable fee*
Housing: *Arr by pgm:* homestay
Deadline: Contact sponsor
Other info: *US accredited sponsor:* no *Began:* 1994 *In coop with:* Austin Peay State Univ *Orient:* abroad *Activities:* excursions, field trips, cultural events *Misc:* May contact former participants. *URL:* http://www.langlink.com
Contact: Kay Rafool, Dir, Lang Link, PO Box 3006, Peoria IL 61612 *Ph:* 800-552 2051; 309-692 2961 *Fax:* 309-692 2926 *E-mail:* info@langlink.com

---

2153
SOUTHWESTERN UNIVERSITY
Intensive Spanish Language and Culture Program
Site: Mexico: Oaxaca
Dates: Contact sponsor
Subjects: Latin American studies (int), Spanish language (adv), Written composition
Eligibility: *Level:* fresh, sophs, jrs, srs *Requires:* 2.5 GPA, 1 or 2 yrs coll Spanish
Credit: *Undergrad:* 6 *Grad:* none *Doc:* transcript
Instruction: *In:* Spanish *Format:* lang study, seminar *Students:* mainly US
Costs: $2,650 *incl* tuition, housing, all meals, intl airfare, insurance, fees, excursions
Housing: *Arr by pgm:* homestay
Deadline: Contact sponsor
Other info: *US accredited sponsor:* yes *Began:* 1992 *Orient:* in US & abroad (spring sem sessions in US, 1 day abroad) *Activities:* excursions, field trips *Misc:* May contact former participants. *URL:* http://www.southwestern.edu/academic/
Contact: Sue Mennicke, Dir, Study Abroad, Southwestern Univ, Georgetown TX 78626 *Ph:* 512-863 1857 *Fax:* 512-863 1535 *E-mail:* mennicks@southwestern.edu

---

2154
UNIVERSITY OF GEORGIA
Study of Mexican Culture through Crafts, Textiles and Dress
Site: Mexico: Oaxaca
Dates: 9 days, mid-late May
Subjects: Civilization/culture, Crafts, Mexican studies
Eligibility: *Level:* fresh, sophs, jrs, srs, grads
Credit: *Undergrad:* 3 per term *Grad:* 3 per term
Instruction: *In:* English *Format:* lecture, study tour *Students:* mainly US
Costs: $1,500 for pgm *incl* housing, all meals, fees, excursions *Nonrefundable fee*
Housing: *Arr by pgm:* hotels
Deadline: Mid-Nov
Other info: *US accredited sponsor:* yes *Began:* 1999 *Orient:* in US *Misc:* May contact former participants. *URL:* http://www.uga.edu/oie
Contact: Dr Karen K Leonas, 317 Dawson Hall, Univ of Georgia, Athens GA 30602 *Ph:* 706-542 4898 *Fax:* 706-542 4890 *E-mail:* kleonas@fcs.uga.edu

---

2155
UNIVERSITY OF ROCHESTER
Spanish in Mexico
Site: Mexico: Oaxaca *Host inst:* El Instituto Cultural
Dates: 1 mo, Jun 2-Jul 2
Subjects: Civilization/culture (beg/int/adv), History, Homestay, Literature, Spanish language, Spanish studies
Eligibility: *Level:* fresh, sophs, jrs, srs *Requires:* 1 yr coll spanish *Age:* min 18, max 22, avg 20
Credit: *Undergrad:* 6 *Grad:* none *Doc:* transcript
Instruction: *In:* Spanish *Format:* lang study *Students:* mainly US
Costs: $2,300 per term *incl* tuition, housing, some meals, intl airfare, excursions
Housing: *Arr by pgm:* homestay
Deadline: Mar 15
Other info: *US accredited sponsor:* yes *Began:* 1992 *Orient:* in US & abroad (3 days) *Activities:* excursions, field trips, program travel, cultural events, sports *Misc:* May contact former participants.
Contact: Anne Lutkins, Modern Langs & Cultures, Univ of Rochester, Lattimore 403, Rochester NY 14627-0082 *Ph:* 716-275 2235

2156
UNIVERSITY OF WISCONSIN-MADISON
Academic Summer Program in Oaxaca
Site: Mexico: Oaxaca *Host inst:* Inst Cultural Oaxaca
Dates: 8 wks, late May-late Jul
Subjects: Civilization/culture, Homestay, Internships, Literature, Spanish language (int)
Eligibility: *Level:* sophs, jrs, srs *Requires:* 2.5 GPA, 4 sems Spanish with B avg
Credit: *Undergrad:* avail *Grad:* none *Doc:* transcript
Instruction: *In:* Spanish *Format:* internship, lang study, lecture *Students:* mainly US
Costs: $4,000 for WI residents, $4,250 for others *incl* tuition, housing, some meals, intl airfare, excursions, books/materials *Nonrefundable fee*
Housing: *Arr by pgm:* homestay
Deadline: 1st Fri in Mar
Other info: *US accredited sponsor:* yes *Began:* 1990 *Orient:* in US & abroad *Activities:* excursions *Misc:* Loans for qualifying degree-seeking undergrads. May contact former participants. *Financial aid:* scholarships *URL:* http://www.wisc.edu/studyabroad
Contact: Intl Studies & Pgms, Univ of Wisconsin-Madison, 261 Bascom Hall, 500 Lincoln Dr, Madison WI 53706 *Ph:* 608-265 6329 *Fax:* 608-262 6998 *E-mail:* peeradvisor@bascom.wisc.edu

---

PLAYA DEL CARMEN

2157
SOLEXICO
Intensive Spanish Programs
Site: Mexico: Playa del Carmen
Dates: 1 wk or longer, yr-round
Subjects: Spanish language (beg/int/adv)
Eligibility: *Level:* fresh, sophs, jrs, srs, grads, adults, teachers, professionals, precoll *Age:* min 15, avg 27
Credit: *Undergrad:* avail *Grad:* avail *Doc:* certificate
Instruction: *In:* Spanish *Format:* lang study *Students:* intl
Costs: About $178 per wk *incl* tuition, housing, all meals, excursions, books/materials *Nonrefundable fee*
Housing: *Arr by pgm:* apartments, homestay, pensions, hotels, hostels

Deadline: Rolling admissions
Other info: *US accredited sponsor:* no *Began:* 1998 *Orient:* abroad *Activities:* excursions, cultural events, sports *Misc:* Max of 5 students per class. May contact former participants. *URL:* http://www.solexico.com
Contact: Gerardo Diego, Dir, Solexico, Ave 35 y Calle 6, Playa del Carmen, Quintano Roo, Mexico 77710 *E-mail:* gerardo@solexico.com
Or Contact: Juan Carlos Delgado, Solexico, Ave 35 s/n y Calle 6, Playa del Carmen, Quintano Roo, Mexico *E-mail:* juan@solexico.com

---

PUEBLA

2158
BENTLEY COLLEGE
Summer Program in Puebla, Mexico
Site: Mexico: Puebla *Host inst:* Univ de las Americas
Dates: 4 wks, late May-early Jul
Subjects: Homestay, Mexican studies, Spanish language (beg/int/adv)
Eligibility: *Level:* fresh, sophs, jrs, srs *Requires:* 2.7 GPA, faculty reference
Credit: *Undergrad:* 6 *Grad:* none *Doc:* transcript
Instruction: *In:* Spanish *Format:* lang study, lecture *Students:* intl
Costs: $2,500 *incl* tuition, housing, fees, excursions, ISIC *Nonrefundable fee*
Housing: *Arr by pgm:* residence halls, homestay
Deadline: Mar 1
Other info: *US accredited sponsor:* yes *Began:* 1993 *Orient:* in US & abroad *Activities:* excursions, field trips, cultural events *Misc:* May contact former participants. *URL:* http://ecampus.bentley.edu/dept/sa
Contact: Jill A Perry Redin, Dir, Study Abroad, Intl Ctr, Bentley Coll, 175 Forest St, Waltham MA 02452-4705 *Ph:* 781-891 3474 *Fax:* 781-891 2819 *E-mail:* study_abroad@bentley.edu

---

2159
MIAMI UNIVERSITY (OH)
Intensive Spanish
Site: Mexico: Puebla *Host inst:* Univ de las Americas
Dates: 6 wks, beg late May
Subjects: Art, Civilization/culture, History, Homestay, Political science/politics, Spanish language (int/adv), Spanish studies
Eligibility: *Level:* sophs, jrs, srs, grads *Requires:* 2 yrs coll Spanish, placement test administered by UDLA
Credit: *Undergrad:* 8 *Grad:* 6
Instruction: *In:* Spanish *Format:* lang study, lecture *Students:* mainly US
Costs: $1,942 grads, $1,896 OH resident undergrads, $2,877 other undergrads *incl* tuition, some meals, excursions
Housing: *Arr by pgm:* residence halls, homestay
Deadline: Feb 15
Other info: *US accredited sponsor:* yes *Began:* 1988 *Orient:* in US & abroad *Activities:* excursions *URL:* http://MiaVX1.MUOhio.Edu/~spocwis/

Contact: Prof Reed Anderson, Acting Chair, Spanish & Portuguese, Miami Univ, Oxford OH 45056 *Ph:* 513-529 4500 *Fax:* 513-529 1807 *E-mail:* adamskr@muohio.edu

---

2160
PENNSYLVANIA STATE UNIVERSITY
Summer Abroad Spanish Language, Art and Mexican Culture
Site: Mexico: Puebla *Host inst:* Casa del Cultura
Dates: 2 mos, May-Jul
Subjects: Civilization/culture, Homestay, Linguistics, Mexican studies, Spanish language (beg/int), Studio arts
Eligibility: *Level:* fresh, sophs, jrs, srs *Requires:* 2.5 GPA, previous study in field, Spanish lang study, reference letter, transcript, goal statement *Age:* min 18, avg 20
Credit: *Undergrad:* 9 *Grad:* none *Doc:* transcript
Instruction: *In:* English, Spanish *Format:* art studio, lang study, lecture, study tour *Students:* mainly US
Costs: About $4,130 for PA residents, $6,794 for others *incl* tuition, housing, some meals, excursions *Nonrefundable fee*
Housing: *Arr by pgm:* apartments, homestay
Deadline: Feb 1
Other info: *US accredited sponsor:* yes *Orient:* in US (1 day) *Misc:* May contact former participants. *Financial aid:* scholarships *URL:* http://www.outreach.psu.edu/PSSEA/
Contact: Summer Abroad, Penn State Univ, 225 Penn State Conference Ctr, University Park PA 16802 *Ph:* 814-863 5170 *Fax:* 814-863 5190 *E-mail:* SummerAbroad@outreach.psu.edu

---

2161
UNIVERSITY OF ARKANSAS
Spanish Language and Culture in Puebla
Site: Mexico: Puebla *Host inst:* Benemevita Univ Autonoma de Puebla (BUAP)
Dates: 5 wks, Jul 1-Aug 4
Subjects: Latin American studies, Spanish language (int/adv)
Eligibility: *Level:* fresh, sophs, jrs, srs, teachers *Requires:* 2.7 GPA, previous study in field, 2 sems coll Spanish, recommendation from home univ *Age:* avg 21
Credit: *Undergrad:* 6 *Grad:* none *Doc:* transcript
Instruction: *In:* English, Spanish *Format:* lecture, seminar *Students:* mainly US
Costs: $2,800 *incl* tuition, housing, some meals, insurance, fees, excursions
Housing: *Arr by pgm:* homestay
Deadline: Apr 1
Other info: *US accredited sponsor:* yes *Began:* 1998 *Orient:* in US & abroad (1 day) *Activities:* excursions, field trips, cultural events *Misc:* May contact former participants.
Contact: Michelle Morris, Study Abroad Adviser, Fulbright Inst, 722 W Maple, Fayetteville AR 72701 *Ph:* 501-575 7582 *Fax:* 501-575 7402 *E-mail:* studyabr@cavern.uark.edu
Or Contact: Steven Bell, Kimpel Hall 425, Univ of Arkansas, Fayetteville AR 72701 *Ph:* 501-575 2951 *E-mail:* studyabr@cavern.uark.edu

---

2162
WICHITA STATE UNIVERSITY
Summer Program in Puebla
Site: Mexico: Puebla
Dates: Jun 18-Jul 27
Subjects: Civilization/culture (adv), Internships, Literature (adv), Mexican studies (adv), Spanish language (int/adv)
Eligibility: *Level:* sophs, jrs, srs, grads *Requires:* some knowledge of Spanish
Credit: *Undergrad:* 6-8 *Grad:* 6-8
Instruction: *In:* Spanish *Format:* lang study, lecture *Students:* mainly US
Costs: About $1,795 *incl* tuition, housing, all meals, insurance, fees, excursions
Housing: *Arr by pgm:* homestay, hotels
Deadline: Apr 15
Other info: *US accredited sponsor:* yes *Began:* 1965 *Orient:* abroad *Activities:* excursions, program travel *URL:* http://www.twsu.edu
Contact: Dr John Koppenhaver, Summer Pgm in Puebla, Modern & Classical Langs, Wichita State Univ, Wichita KS 67260-0122 *Ph:* 316-978 3232 *Fax:* 316-978 3777 *E-mail:* koppenha@twsuvm.uc.twsu.edu
Or Contact: Robert Phillips, Summer Pgm in Puebla, Modern & Classical Langs, Wichita State Univ, Wichita KS 67260-0011 *Ph:* 316-978 3180, 316-978 3180 *E-mail:* phillips@twsuvm.uc.twsu.edu

---

PUERTO SAN CARLOS

2163
SCHOOL FOR FIELD STUDIES
SFS Mexico: Marine Mammal Conservation & Coastal Ecosystem Studies
Site: Mexico: Puerto San Carlos (Magdalena Bay, Baja)
Dates: 30 days, mid-Jun-mid-Jul or mid-Jul-mid-Aug
Subjects: Conservation, Development studies, Ecology/environmental studies, Economics, Field study, Fishing/fisheries, Latin American studies, Marine biology, Marine sciences, Natural resource management, Water management
Eligibility: *Level:* fresh, sophs, jrs, srs, precoll *Age:* min 16, avg 20
Credit: *Undergrad:* avail *Grad:* none *Doc:* transcript *Transfer credit through:* Boston Univ
Instruction: *In:* English *Format:* directed field study, lecture *Students:* mainly US
Costs: $2,975 *incl* tuition, housing, all meals, excursions *Nonrefundable fee*
Housing: *Arr by pgm:* rustic cabins
Deadline: Rolling admissions
Other info: *US accredited sponsor:* no *Began:* 1996 *Orient:* abroad *Activities:* excursions, field trips, program travel, cultural events, sports *Misc:* Loans avail, Spanish lessons. May contact former participants. *Financial aid:* scholarships *URL:* http://www.fieldstudies.org
Contact: Admissions Off, Sch for Field Studies, 16 Broadway, Beverly MA 01915 *Ph:* 800-989 4435; 978-927 7777 *Fax:* 978-927 5127 *E-mail:* admissions@fieldstudies.org

---

QUERETARO

2164
EASTERN MICHIGAN UNIVERSITY
Spanish Language Program
Site: Mexico: Queretaro *Host inst:* Univ de Queretaro
Dates: Jul 7-Aug 25
Subjects: Spanish language (int/adv)
Eligibility: *Level:* fresh, sophs, jrs, srs, grads, adults *Requires:* good acad standing, references *Age:* min 18
Credit: *Undergrad:* 6-9 *Grad:* 6-9 *Doc:* transcript
Instruction: *In:* Spanish *Format:* lang study, lecture, study tour *Students:* mainly US
Costs: $3,095 *incl* tuition, housing, some meals, most meals, insurance, fees, excursions, transport in Mexico
Housing: *Arr by pgm:* homestay
Deadline: Mar 1
Other info: *US accredited sponsor:* yes *Began:* 1977 *Orient:* avail by mail *Activities:* excursions *Misc:* May contact former participants. *URL:* http://www.emich.edu/abroad
Contact: Acad Pgms Abroad, Eastern Michigan Univ, 127 Boone Hall, Ypsilanti MI 48197 *Ph:* 800-777 3541; 734-487 2424 *Fax:* 734-487 4377 *E-mail:* programs.abroad@emich.edu

---

2165
ILLINOIS STATE UNIVERSITY
Summer Study in Mexico
Site: Mexico: Queretaro *Host inst:* ITESM Queretaro

Dates: 6 wks, Jun 7-Jul 19
Subjects: Civilization/culture, Homestay, International business, Mexican studies
Eligibility: *Level:* jrs, srs *Requires:* 2.5 GPA, previous study in field, bus major/minors preferred
Credit: *Undergrad:* 6 *Grad:* none
Instruction: *In:* English *Format:* lecture, seminar *Students:* mainly US
Costs: $3,862 *incl* tuition, housing, all meals, intl airfare, insurance, fees, excursions, books/materials, ISIC *Nonrefundable fee*
Housing: *Arr by pgm:* homestay
Deadline: Mar 1
Other info: *US accredited sponsor:* yes *Orient:* avail avail *Activities:* excursions, field trips, cultural events *URL:* http://www.its.ilstu.edu/intlstudies/
Contact: Nancy Baldoni, Illinois State Univ, Campus Box 5500, Normal IL 61790-5500 *Ph:* 309-438 8385
Or Contact: Intl Studies & Pgms, Illinois State Univ, Campus Box 6120, Normal IL 61790-6120 *Ph:* 309-438 5365 *Fax:* 309-438 3987 *E-mail:* oisp@ilstu.edu

---

2166
INTERAMERICAN UNIVERSITY STUDIES INSTITUTE and UNIVERSITY OF OREGON
Summer Spanish
Site: Mexico: Queretaro *Host inst:* Interamerican Univ Studies Inst
Dates: 6 wks, Jun 18-Jul 29 or Jul 30-Sep 9
Subjects: Mexican studies, Spanish language
Eligibility: *Level:* sophs, jrs, srs, grads, adults *Requires:* 2.75 GPA, previous study in field, 1 yr coll Spanish *Age:* min 18
Credit: *Undergrad:* 12 *Grad:* 12 *Doc:* certificate *Transfer credit through:* Univ of Oregon
Instruction: *In:* Spanish *Format:* lang study, lecture, seminar *Students:* mainly US
Costs: $2,324 *incl* tuition, housing, all meals, fees, excursions *Nonrefundable fee*
Housing: *Arr by pgm:* homestay
Deadline: Mar 1
Other info: *US accredited sponsor:* yes *Began:* 1994 *Orient:* in US *Activities:* excursions, field trips, program travel *Misc:* May contact former participants. *URL:* http://www.iusi.org
Contact: Jennifer Jewett, Pgm Coord, IUSI, PO Box 10958, Eugene OR 97440 *Ph:* 800-345 4874; 541-686 5947 *Fax:* 541-686 5947 *E-mail:* office@iusi.org

---

2167
ITESM CAMPUS QUERETARO
ITESM Campus Queretaro
Site: Mexico: Queretaro
Dates: 6 wks, Jun-Jul
Subjects: Business/management, Civilization/culture, Literature, Mexican studies, Spanish language (beg/int/adv)
Eligibility: *Level:* fresh, sophs, jrs, srs, grads, adults, teachers, professionals *Age:* min 18, avg 22
Credit: *Undergrad:* avail *Grad:* avail *Doc:* transcript
Instruction: *In:* English, Spanish *Format:* lang study, lecture *Students:* mainly host country
Costs: About $2,500 *incl* tuition, housing, all meals, insurance, fees, excursions, books/materials *Nonrefundable fee*
Housing: *Sponsor assists:* homestay
Deadline: May 17
Other info: *US accredited sponsor:* yes *Began:* 1996 *Orient:* abroad *Activities:* excursions, field trips, program travel, cultural events, sports *Misc:* Campus is not 100wheelchair accessible. May contact former participants. *Financial aid:* work study *URL:* http://www.qro.itesm.mx/departamentos/prog_interna
Contact: Jorge Lujan, ITESM Campus Queretaro, Epigmenio Gonzalez 500, San Pablo, 76130 Queretaro, Mexico

---

2168
UNIVERSITY OF CINCINNATI
UC-ITESM Queretaro Summer Program
Site: Mexico: Queretaro *Host inst:* ITESM-Queretaro
Dates: 6 wks, Jun 8-Jul 23
Subjects: Civilization/culture, Homestay, Independent study, Mexican studies, Spanish language
Eligibility: *Level:* sophs, jrs, srs, grads *Requires:* 1 yr coll spanish *Age:* min 18
Credit: *Undergrad:* 13 qtr hrs *Grad:* none *Doc:* transcript
Instruction: *In:* Spanish *Format:* independent study, lang study, lecture, study tour *Students:* mainly US
Costs: $3,666 for OH residents *incl* tuition, housing, some meals, intl airfare, insurance, fees, excursions, books/materials
Housing: *Arr by pgm:* homestay
Deadline: Apr 1
Other info: *US accredited sponsor:* yes *Began:* 1992 *Orient:* in US & abroad *Activities:* excursions, field trips, program travel, cultural events *Misc:* scholarships for U of C students only May contact former participants. *Financial aid:* scholarships
Contact: Dr Arthur Neisberg, Educ Abroad Coord, Univ of Cincinnati, PO Box 210640, Cincinnati OH 45221-0640 *Ph:* 513-556 1363 *Fax:* 513-556 2990 *E-mail:* arthur.neisberg@uc.edu

---

SAN CRISTOBAL DE LAS CASAS

2169
NATIONAL REGISTRATION CENTER FOR STUDY ABROAD (NRCSA)
Spanish in Chiapas
Site: Mexico: San Cristobal de las Casas *Host inst:* Ctr Bilingue
Dates: 2 wks or longer, yr-round
Subjects: Homestay, Spanish language (beg/int/adv)
Eligibility: *Level:* fresh, sophs, jrs, srs, grads, adults, teachers, professionals *Age:* min 18
Credit: *Undergrad:* avail *Grad:* avail *Doc:* certificate
Instruction: *In:* Spanish *Format:* lang study, lecture, tutorial *Students:* mainly US
Costs: $475 for 2 wks *incl* tuition, housing, all meals, insurance *Nonrefundable fee*
Housing: *Arr by pgm:* homestay
Deadline: 6 wks before pgm
Other info: *US accredited sponsor:* no *Misc:* May contact former participants. *URL:* http://www.nrcsa.com
Contact: June Domoe, NRCSA, 823 N 2nd St, #206, Milwaukee WI 53203 *Ph:* 414-278 0631 *Fax:* 414-271 8884 *E-mail:* info@nrcsa.com

---

SAN MIGUEL DE ALLENDE

2170
ACADEMIA HISPANO AMERICANA
Intensive Spanish and Related Subjects
Site: Mexico: San Miguel de Allende
Dates: 4 wks, yr-round; shorter/longer courses avail
Subjects: Banking, Elementary education, Homestay, Internships, Law, Medicine, Mexican studies, Spanish language (beg/int/adv), Special education, TEFL/TESL
Eligibility: *Level:* adults, precoll *Age:* min 15
Credit: *Undergrad:* avail *Grad:* none *Doc:* transcript, certificate, diploma *Transfer credit through:* Univ of Southern Mississippi
Instruction: *In:* Spanish *Format:* internship, lang study, lecture *Students:* intl
Costs: $1,772 *incl* tuition, housing, all meals, books/materials
Housing: *Arr by pgm:* homestay
Deadline: Until pgm filled
Other info: *US accredited sponsor:* no *Began:* 1960 *Activities:* cultural events *Financial aid:* scholarships *URL:* http://www.mexonline.com/academ1.htm

Contact: Gary de Mirjyn, Acad Hispano Americana, Mesones 4, San Miguel de Allende, Guanajuato 37700, Mexico *E-mail:* academia@unisono.net.mx
Or Contact: Glenda Mikeska, Lang Studies Intl, 5006 Highland Ct, Austin TX 78731 *Ph:* 512-458 8008 *Fax:* 512-453 2441 *E-mail:* gmikeska@spanishstudy.com

---

2171
ACADEMIA HISPANO AMERICANA
Uno Con Uno
Site: Mexico: San Miguel de Allende
Dates: 1 wk or longer, yr-round
Subjects: Homestay, Spanish language (beg/int/adv)
Eligibility: *Level:* adults, precoll *Age:* min 13, avg 25
Credit: *Undergrad:* none *Grad:* none *Doc:* transcript, certificate, diploma *Transfer credit through:* Univ of Southern Mississippi
Instruction: *In:* Spanish *Format:* lang study, lecture *Students:* intl
Costs: $456 per wk *incl* tuition, housing, all meals, books/materials
Housing: *Arr by pgm:* homestay
Deadline: 1 mo before pgm
Other info: *US accredited sponsor:* no *Began:* 1975 *Orient:* in US *Misc:* Optional excursions. *URL:* http://www.mexonline.com/academ1.htm
Contact: Gary de Mirjyn, Acad Hispano Americana, Mesones 4, San Miguel de Allende, Guanajuato 37700, Mexico *E-mail:* academia@unisono.net.mx
Or Contact: Glenda Mikeska, Lang Studies Intl, 5006 Highland Ct, Austin TX 78731 *Ph:* 512-458 8008 *Fax:* 512-453 2441 *E-mail:* gmikeska@spanishstudy.com

---

2172
INSTITUTO HABLA HISPANA
Communicative Spanish Courses
Site: Mexico: San Miguel de Allende
Dates: 4 wks, beg Jan 8, Feb 6, Mar 5, Apr 2, May 7, Jun 4, Jul 22, Jul 30, Aug 27, Oct 1, Oct 23, Nov 26
Subjects: Homestay, Spanish language (beg/int/adv)
Eligibility: *Level:* adults *Requires:* previous lang study for int & adv levels *Age:* min 14
Credit: *Undergrad:* none *Grad:* none *Doc:* certificate
Instruction: *In:* Spanish *Format:* lang study, practical training, seminar, study tour, workshop *Students:* intl
Costs: $380 *incl* tuition, books/materials *Nonrefundable fee*
Housing: *Sponsor assists:* homestay, hotels
Deadline: Contact sponsor
Other info: *US accredited sponsor:* no *Began:* 1990 *Activities:* excursions, cultural events *Misc:* 20 hrs/wk intensive Spanish in classroom of max 10 students. 10 hrs/wk seminars, working groups, guided walking tours. May contact former participants. *URL:* http://www.mexicospanish.com
Contact: Angelica Rodriguez, Dir, Inst Habla Hispana, Calzada de la Luz #25, Apdo 689, CP 37700 San Miguel de Allende, Guanajuato, Mexico *Fax:* 313-557 0805 *E-mail:* info@mexicospanish.com
Or Contact: Kima Cargill, US Agent, Inst Habla Hispana, 814 E 45th, Austin TX 78751 *Ph:* 512-452 2405 *E-mail:* kcargill@mac.com

---

TAXCO

2173
ILLINOIS STATE UNIVERSITY
Summer Program in Mexico
Site: Mexico: Taxco *Host inst:* Univ Nacional Autonoma de Mexico
Dates: 7 wks, Jun-Aug
Subjects: Civilization/culture, Field study, Homestay, Latin American studies, Literature, Mexican studies, Spanish language
Eligibility: *Level:* sophs, jrs, srs, grads *Requires:* 2.5 GPA, previous study in field, 1 yr coll Spanish
Credit: *Undergrad:* 6 *Grad:* 6 *Doc:* transcript
Instruction: *In:* English, Spanish *Format:* directed field study, lang study, lecture *Students:* mainly US
Costs: $3,350 *incl* housing, all meals, intl airfare, excursions, books/materials, overseas tuition *Nonrefundable fee*
Housing: *Arr by pgm:* homestay
Deadline: Feb 14
Other info: *US accredited sponsor:* yes *Began:* 1990 *Orient:* abroad *URL:* http://www.its.ilstu.edu/intlstudies/
Contact: Dr James J Alstrum, 4300 Foreign Langs, Illinois State Univ, Normal IL 61790-4300 *Ph:* 309-438 7620, 309-438 3604 *E-mail:* oisp@ilstu.edu
Or Contact: Intl Studies, Illinois State Univ, Campus Box 6120, Normal IL 61761-6901 *Ph:* 309-438 5365 *Fax:* 309-438 3987 *E-mail:* oisp@ilstu.edu

---

2174
UNIVERSITY OF MARYLAND and **UNIVERSITY OF MARYLAND BALTIMORE COUNTY** and **TOWSON UNIVERSITY**
Maryland in Taxco, Mexico
Site: Mexico: Taxco *Host inst:* Univ Nacional Autonoma de Mexico
Dates: 6 wks, Jun 18-Aug 5
Subjects: Literature, Mexican studies, Spanish language
Eligibility: *Level:* fresh, sophs, jrs, srs, adults, teachers *Requires:* 2.5 GPA, previous study in field, 1 sem coll Spanish with B avg
Credit: *Undergrad:* 6 *Grad:* none *Doc:* certificate
Instruction: *In:* Spanish *Format:* seminar *Students:* intl
Costs: $1,325 *incl* tuition, excursions, Mexico City-Taxco transport *Nonrefundable fee*
Housing: *Arr by pgm:* homestay
Deadline: Apr 1
Other info: *US accredited sponsor:* yes *Began:* 1995 *Orient:* in US *Activities:* excursions, field trips *Misc:* May contact former participants. *URL:* http://www.inform.umd.edu/INTL/studyabroad
Contact: Dr Richard Weaver, Intl Studies Coord, Study Abroad, Univ of Maryland, 3125 Mitchell Bldg, College Park MD 20742 *Ph:* 301-314 7746 *Fax:* 301-314 9347 *E-mail:* studyabr@deans.umd.edu

---

2175
UNIVERSITY OF NORTH CAROLINA AT CHAPEL HILL
UNC-CH Summer Language Program in Mexico
Site: Mexico: Taxco *Host inst:* Univ Nacional Autonoma de Mexico
Dates: 6 wks, Jun 17-Aug 4
Subjects: Homestay, Latin American studies, Spanish language (beg/int/adv)
Eligibility: *Level:* adults *Requires:* 2.5 GPA
Credit: *Undergrad:* 6-9 *Grad:* none *Doc:* transcript, certificate
Instruction: *In:* English, Spanish *Format:* lang study, seminar *Students:* intl
Costs: $1,624 *incl* tuition, housing, all meals, insurance, fees *Nonrefundable fee*
Housing: *Arr by pgm:* homestay
Deadline: Early Feb
Other info: *US accredited sponsor:* yes *Began:* 1988 *Orient:* in US & abroad in Mexico City *Activities:* excursions *Misc:* On-site resident dir. May contact former participants. *Financial aid:* scholarships *URL:* http://www.unc.edu/depts/abroad
Contact: Study Abroad, UNC-Chapel Hill, 12 Caldwell Hall, CB-3130, Cameron Ave, Chapel Hill NC 27599-3130 *Ph:* 919-962 7001 *Fax:* 919-962 2262 *E-mail:* abroad@unc.edu

---

XALAPA

2176
SOUTHERN METHODIST UNIVERSITY
Xalapa Language Study Program
Site: Mexico: Xalapa *Host inst:* Univ Veracruzana

See "How To Use This Book" for definitions of terms used above. ▲ = See program sponsor's ad(s) in this book.

Dates: 6 wks, Jun 17-Jul 28
Subjects: Civilization/culture, Homestay, Spanish language (int/adv)
Eligibility: *Level:* sophs, jrs, srs, grads *Requires:* 2.5 GPA, 2 sems coll Spanish
Credit: *Undergrad:* 6 *Grad:* none *Doc:* transcript
Instruction: *In:* Spanish *Format:* lang study *Students:* intl
Costs: $3,800 *incl* tuition, housing, all meals, excursions *Nonrefundable fee*
Housing: *Arr by pgm:* homestay
Deadline: Contact sponsor
Other info: *US accredited sponsor:* yes *Began:* 1993 *Activities:* excursions, cultural events *Misc:* Scholarships for own students only. May contact former participants. *Financial aid:* scholarships *URL:* http://www.smu.edu/studyabroad
Contact: Intl Pgms, Southern Methodist Univ, PO Box 0391, 3108 Fondren Dr, Dallas TX 75275-0391 *Ph:* 214-768 2338 *Fax:* 214-768 1051 *E-mail:* intlpro@mail.smu.edu
Or Contact: Veronica Leon, Spanish, Southern Methodist Univ, Dallas TX 75275 *Ph:* 214-768 1410 *E-mail:* vleon@mail.smu.edu ▲

2177
UNIVERSIDAD VERACRUZANA
Summer Program
Site: Mexico: Xalapa
Dates: 6 wks, mid-Jun-Jul
Subjects: Anthropology, Business/management, Civilization/culture, History, Homestay, Latin American studies, Literature, Mexican studies, Spanish language (beg/int/adv), Women's studies
Eligibility: *Level:* fresh, sophs, jrs, srs, grads, adults, teachers, professionals *Requires:* good acad standing
Credit: *Undergrad:* avail *Grad:* avail *Doc:* transcript
Instruction: *In:* Spanish *Format:* lang study, lecture, seminar, workshop *Students:* mainly US
Costs: $2,193 *incl* tuition, housing, all meals, fees, excursions *Nonrefundable fee*
Housing: *Arr by pgm:* homestay
Deadline: 1 mo before pgm
Other info: *US accredited sponsor:* no *Began:* 1957 *Orient:* abroad (1 day) *Activities:* excursions, field trips, cultural events, sports *URL:* http://www.skynet.eee-uv.mx
Contact: Edith Hernandez or Elida Sanchez, Escuela para Estudiantes Extranjeros, Univ Veracruzana, Zamora 25 Ctr Xalapa, Veracruz 91000, Mexico *E-mail:* eeeuv@dino.coacade.uv.mx

---

2178
UNIVERSITY OF MISSOURI-KANSAS CITY
Summer Study in Mexico
Site: Mexico: Xalapa *Host inst:* Univ Veracruzana
Dates: 6 wks, Jun 5-Jul 27
Subjects: Art, Civilization/culture, Contemporary issues, History, Homestay, Literature, Mexican studies, Spanish language (beg/int/adv), Women's studies
Eligibility: *Level:* sophs, jrs, srs, grads *Requires:* 2.70 GPA, previous study in field, Spanish lang study
Credit: *Undergrad:* 9 *Grad:* 9 *Doc:* transcript
Instruction: *In:* English, Spanish *Format:* lang study, lecture, study tour, tutorial *Students:* intl
Costs: $3,200 *incl* tuition, housing, all meals, intl airfare, insurance, fees, excursions *Nonrefundable fee*
Housing: *Arr by pgm:* homestay
Deadline: Late Apr
Other info: *US accredited sponsor:* yes *Began:* 1985 *Orient:* abroad *Activities:* excursions, field trips, cultural events, sports *Misc:* Scholarships for own students only. May contact former participants. *URL:* http://www.umkc.edu/international
Contact: Foreign Langs, Univ of Missouri-Kansas City, 5100 Rockhill Rd, Kansas City MO 64110-2499 *Ph:* 816-235 1311 *Fax:* 816-235 1312 *E-mail:* international@umkc.edu
Or Contact: Coord, Ctr for Intl Affairs, Univ of Missouri-Kansas City, 5100 Rockhill Rd, Kansas City MO 64110 *Ph:* 816-235 5759 *Fax:* 816-235 5610 *E-mail:* international@umkc.edu

Nicaragua

MORE THAN ONE CITY

2179
VIRGINIA POLYTECHNIC INSTITUTE & STATE UNIVERSITY
Labor and Labor Movements in Nicaragua (Sociology)
Site: Nicaragua: various sites *Host inst:* Witness for Peace
Dates: Aug
Subjects: Sociology
Eligibility: Space is limited, early application is recommended *Level:* adults *Requires:* approval by the NGO Witness for Peace *Age:* min 17, avg 21
Credit: *Undergrad:* 3 *Grad:* 3
Instruction: *In:* English *Format:* study tour *Students:* mainly US
Costs: About $850 *incl* housing, all meals, excursions, translation *Nonrefundable fcc*
Housing: *Arr by pgm:* homestay, pensions
Deadline: Apr 30
Other info: *US accredited sponsor:* yes *Began:* 2000 *Orient:* avail *Activities:* program travel *URL:* http://fbox.vt.edu:10021/international/studyabroad/index.html
Contact: Dr Dale Wimberley, Virginia Tech, Dept of Sociology, Blacksburg VA 24061 *Ph:* 540-231 8960 *Fax:* 540-231 3860 *E-mail:* dale.wimberley@vt.edu

---

LAGUNA DE APOYO

2180
VIRGINIA POLYTECHNIC INSTITUTE & STATE UNIVERSITY
Global Issues in Natural Resources
Site: Nicaragua: Laguna de Apoyo *Host inst:* Univ of Central Amer
Dates: 3 wks, May 15-Jun 7
Subjects: Ecology/environmental studies, Forestry, Natural resources
Eligibility: *Level:* jrs, srs, grads, adults, teachers, professionals *Age:* min 20, avg 35
Credit: *Undergrad:* 3 *Grad:* 3 *Doc:* certificate
Instruction: *In:* English *Format:* directed field study, lecture, practical training, study tour, workshop *Students:* US & intl
Costs: $1,700 *incl* housing, all meals, excursions *Nonrefundable fee*
Housing: *Arr by pgm:* pensions
Deadline: Feb 1; Apr or May for scholarships
Other info: *US accredited sponsor:* yes *Began:* 2000 *In coop with:* USAID *Orient:* in US & abroad *Activities:* excursions, field trips, program travel *Misc:* Must complete a journal while in course. May contact former participants. *Financial aid:* scholarships, work study *URL:* http://www.cyber.vt.edu/wd3784mic/
Contact: Dr A L Hammett, Virginia Tech, 210 Cheatham Hall, Mailcode 0323, Blacksburg VA 24061 *Ph:* 540-231 2716 *Fax:* 540-231 8176 *E-mail:* himal@vt.edu
Or Contact: Dr Jeff McCrary, Univ of Central Amer, Managua, Nicaragua *E-mail:* jmcrary@lbw.com.nl

Panama

BOCAS DEL TORO

2181
UNIVERSITY OF COLORADO AT BOULDER
Field Methods in Primate Ecology
Site: Panama: Bocas del Toro *Host inst:* Inst for Tropical Ecology & Conservation
Dates: 3 wks, Dec 22-Jan 15, May 10-31
Subjects: Anthropology, Biology, Ecology/environmental studies, Field study
Eligibility: *Level:* jrs, srs, grads *Requires:* 2.75 GPA, previous study in field, anthropology or biology *Age:* min 18, avg 21

Credit: *Undergrad:* 6 *Grad:* 6 *Doc:* transcript
Instruction: *In:* English *Format:* directed field study, seminar *Students:* mainly US
Costs: $3,060 for CO residents, $4,060 for others *incl* tuition, housing, all meals, insurance, fees, excursions *Nonrefundable fee*
Housing: *Arr by pgm:* rustic cabins at field station
Deadline: Mar 1
Other info: *US accredited sponsor:* yes *Began:* 1999 *Orient:* in US & abroad 1 day *Activities:* excursions *Misc:* scholarships avail for CU-Boulder students only. May contact former participants. *Financial aid:* scholarships *URL:* http://www.colorado.edu/OIE/StudyAbroad
Contact: Intl Educ, Univ of Colorado, Campus Box 123, Boulder CO 80309-0123 *Ph:* 303-492 7741 *Fax:* 303-492 5185 *E-mail:* studyabr@colorado.edu

---

PANAMA CITY

2182
AMERISPAN UNLIMITED
Spanish Study and Homestay in Panama
Site: Panama: Panama City *Host inst:* Inst de Lenguas y Relaciones Intl
Dates: 1 wk-1 yr, yr-round
Subjects: Business language, Civilization/culture, Homestay, Spanish language (beg/int/adv)
Eligibility: *Level:* fresh, sophs, jrs, srs, grads, adults, teachers, professionals, precoll *Age:* min 16
Credit: *Undergrad:* avail *Grad:* none *Doc:* transcript, certificate *Transfer credit through:* Seattle Central CC
Instruction: *In:* Spanish *Format:* lang study, lecture, tutorial *Students:* intl
Costs: $765 for 2 wks, $1,075 for 4 wks, $270 for each addtl wk *incl* tuition, housing, some meals, insurance, books/materials
Housing: *Arr by pgm:* homestay, hotels
Deadline: 4 wks before pgm
Other info: *US accredited sponsor:* no *Activities:* excursions, field trips, cultural events *Misc:* May contact former participants. *Financial aid:* work study *URL:* http://www.amerispan.com/
Contact: AmeriSpan Unltd, PO Box 40007, Philadelphia PA 19106 *Ph:* 800-879 6640; 215-751 1100 *Fax:* 215-751 1986 *E-mail:* info@amerispan.com

---

2183
FLORIDA STATE UNIVERSITY
Panama Summer Program
Site: Panama: Panama City
Dates: 6 wks, Jun 21-Aug 4 or 13 wks, May 2-Aug 10
Subjects: Civilization/culture, Ecology/environmental studies, History, Latin American studies, Liberal arts, Primatology
Eligibility: *Level:* fresh, sophs, jrs, srs, grads, precoll *Requires:* 2.5 GPA
Credit: *Undergrad:* 10 *Grad:* avail
Instruction: *In:* English *Format:* lecture *Students:* mainly US
Costs: $3,195 for 6 wks, $4,335 for 13 wks *incl* tuition, housing, intl airfare, insurance
Housing: *Arr by pgm:* apartments
Deadline: Jan 19
Other info: *US accredited sponsor:* yes *Began:* 1957 *Orient:* in US & abroad (2 days) *Activities:* excursions, field trips, program travel, cultural events *Misc:* May contact former participants. *URL:* http://www.international.fsu.edu
Contact: Elizabeth Trelenberg or Bonnie Snyder, Intl Pgms, Florida State Univ, 5500 UCA, Tallahassee FL 32306-2420 *Ph:* 800-374 8581; 850-644 3272 *Fax:* 850-644 8817 *E-mail:* intprog@www.fsu.edu

---

2184
LANGUAGES ABROAD
Language and Culture-Panama
Site: Panama: Panama City
Dates: 2 wks or longer, yr-round
Subjects: Civilization/culture, Homestay, Spanish language
Eligibility: *Level:* adults *Age:* min 17, max 65, avg 25
Credit: *Undergrad:* none *Grad:* none *Doc:* certificate
Instruction: *In:* Spanish *Format:* lang study *Students:* intl
Costs: $1,195 per mo *incl* tuition, some meals, fees, excursions, books/materials
Housing: *Arr by pgm:* residence halls, homestay
Deadline: None
Other info: *US accredited sponsor:* no *Began:* 1995 *Activities:* excursions, field trips, program travel, cultural events, sports *Misc:* May contact former participants. *URL:* http://www.languagesabroad.com
Contact: Ms Jesse Philippe, Langs Abroad, 317 Adelaide St W, Ste 900, Toronto, Ontario M5V 1P9, Canada *Ph:* 800-219 9924; 416-925 7117 *E-mail:* info@languagesabroad.com

Paraguay

ASUNCION

2185
NATIONAL REGISTRATION CENTER FOR STUDY ABROAD (NRCSA)
Instituto Privado de Ensenanza de Espanol
Site: Paraguay: Asuncion
Dates: 1 wk, yr-round
Subjects: Guarani language, Homestay, Spanish language (beg/int/adv)
Eligibility: *Level:* fresh, sophs, jrs, srs, grads, adults *Age:* min 18
Credit: *Undergrad:* avail *Grad:* avail
Instruction: *In:* Spanish, Guarani *Format:* lang study, tutorial *Students:* intl
Costs: $435 *incl* tuition, housing, all meals, insurance
Housing: *Arr by pgm:* homestay
Deadline: Contact sponsor
Other info: *US accredited sponsor:* no *Orient:* abroad (intensive lang study) *Activities:* cultural events *URL:* http://www.nrcsa.com
Contact: June Domoe, NRCSA, 823 N 2nd St, #206, Milwaukee WI 53203 *Ph:* 414-278 0631 *Fax:* 414-271 8884 *E-mail:* info@nrcsa.com

Peru

MORE THAN ONE CITY

2186
GEORGE MASON UNIVERSITY
Peru and Amazon Extension
Site: Peru: Amazon Jungle, Cusco, Lima, Machu Picchu
Dates: Mar 2-14
Subjects: Civilization/culture, History, Peruvian studies
Eligibility: *Level:* fresh, sophs, jrs, srs, grads, adults, teachers, professionals, precoll *Requires:* 2.25 GPA *Age:* min 18
Credit: *Undergrad:* avail *Grad:* avail *Doc:* transcript
Instruction: *In:* English *Format:* study tour *Students:* mainly US
Costs: About $1,600 for VA residents, $2,300 for others *incl* tuition, housing, some meals, intl airfare, insurance, fees, excursions *Nonrefundable fee*
Housing: *Arr by pgm:* hotels
Deadline: Late Jan
Other info: *US accredited sponsor:* yes *Began:* 1996 *Orient:* in US (1 day) *Financial aid:* scholarships, work study *URL:* http://www.gmu.edu/departments/cge

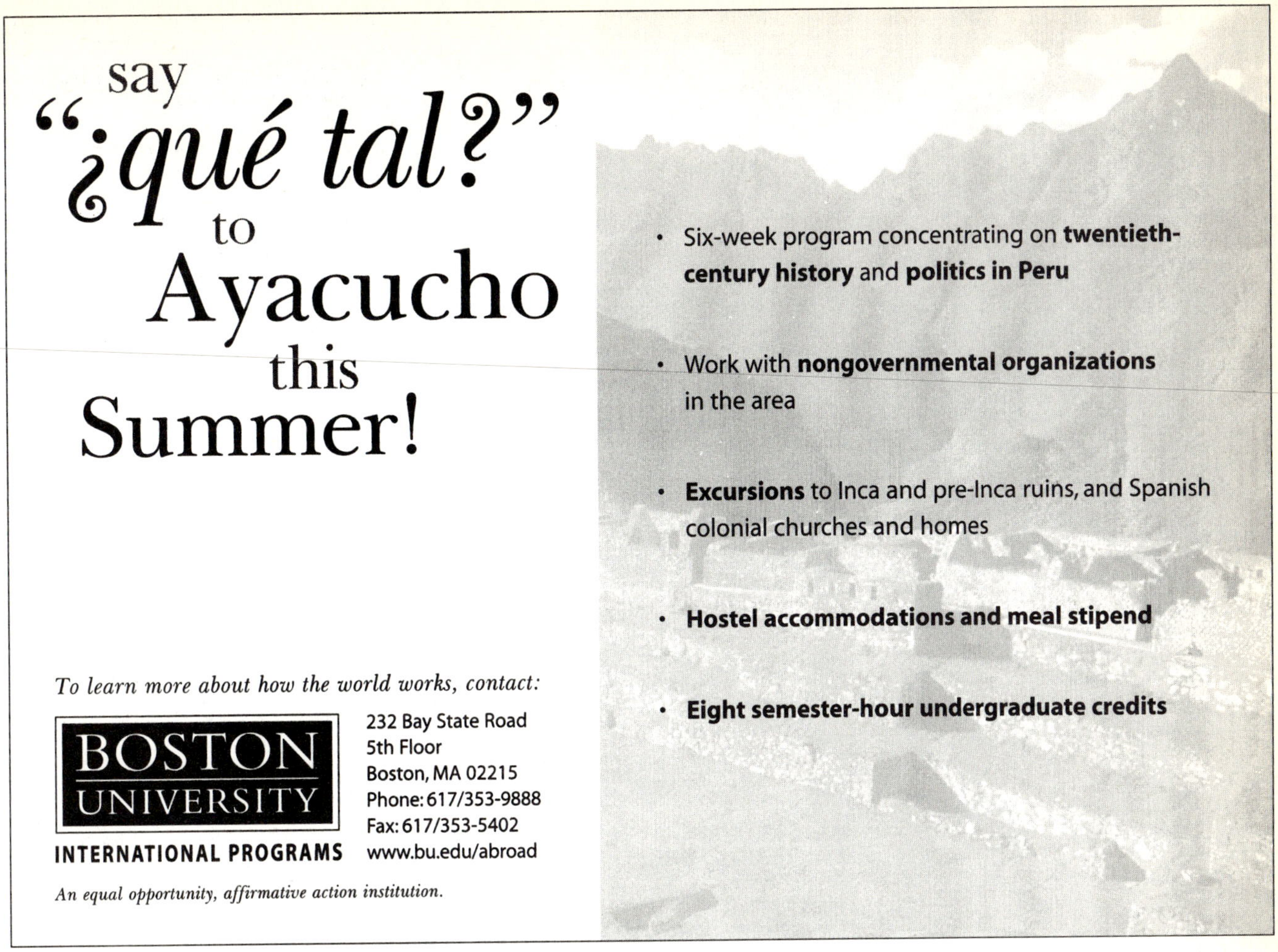

Contact: Ctr for Global Educ, George Mason Univ, Johnson Ctr, Rm 235, 4400 University Dr, Fairfax VA 22030-4444 *Ph:* 703-993 2154 *Fax:* 703-993 2153 *E-mail:* cge@gmu.edu

---

2187
VIRGINIA COMMONWEALTH UNIVERSITY
Peru: Art Studio and Intensive Spanish
Site: Peru: Cuzco, Lima
Dates: 3 wks, May 31-Jun 24
Subjects: Spanish language, Studio arts
Eligibility: *Level:* adults *Requires:* 2.0 GPA *Age:* min 18
Credit: *Undergrad:* 3-6 *Grad:* 3-6 *Doc:* transcript
Instruction: *In:* English *Students:* mainly US
Costs: $3,800 *incl* tuition, housing, some meals, intl airfare, fees, excursions, in-country transport *Nonrefundable fee*
Housing: *Arr by pgm:* residence halls, hostels
Deadline: None
Other info: *US accredited sponsor:* yes *Began:* 1997 *Orient:* in US & abroad (1 day, intensive lang study) *Activities:* excursions, field trips, program travel, cultural events, sports
Contact: Tina Murray, CIP, Virginia Commonwealth Univ, PO Box 843043, Richmond VA 23284 *Ph:* 804-828 8471 *Fax:* 804-828 2552 *E-mail:* csmurray@vcu.edu
Or Contact: Javier Tapia, Painting Dept, Virginia Commonwealth Univ, PO Box 842519, Richmond VA 23284 *Ph:* 804-828 3729 *Fax:* 804-828 2552

AYACUCHO

2188
BOSTON UNIVERSITY
Summer Program in Peru
Site: Peru: Ayacucho
Dates: 6 wks, Jun-Jul
Subjects: History, International relations, Latin American studies, Political science/ politics
Eligibility: *Level:* jrs, srs *Requires:* 3.0 GPA, in major
Credit: *Undergrad:* 8 *Grad:* none *Doc:* transcript
Instruction: *In:* Spanish *Format:* lecture, seminar *Students:* mainly US
Costs: $4,550 *incl* tuition, housing, all meals, insurance, excursions *Nonrefundable fee*
Housing: *Arr by pgm:* hotels
Deadline: Mar 1; Apr 1 for scholarships
Other info: *US accredited sponsor:* yes *Began:* 1999 *Orient:* in US & abroad *Activities:* excursions, field trips *Misc:* Full-time resident dir. May contact former participants. *Financial aid:* scholarships *URL:* http://www.bu.edu/abroad/
Contact: Intl Pgms, Boston Univ, 232 Bay State Rd, Boston MA 02215 *Ph:* 617-353 9888 *Fax:* 617-353 5402 *E-mail:* abroad@bu.edu ▲

CUZCO

2189
AMERISPAN UNLIMITED
Spanish Study and Homestay in Peru
Site: Peru: Cuzco

Dates: 1 wk-1 yr, yr-round
Subjects: Dance, Homestay, Music, Spanish language, Weaving
Eligibility: *Level:* fresh, sophs, jrs, srs, grads, adults *Age:* min 16
Credit: *Undergrad:* avail *Grad:* none *Doc:* transcript, certificate *Transfer credit through:* Seattle Central CC
Instruction: *In:* Spanish *Format:* lang study, tutorial, workshop *Students:* intl
Costs: $450 for 2 wks, $860 for 4 wks, $200-$240 for each addtl wk *incl* tuition, housing, all meals, insurance, books/ materials
Housing: *Arr by pgm:* homestay, hostels
Deadline: 4 wks before pgm
Other info: *US accredited sponsor:* no *Orient:* abroad *Activities:* excursions, field trips, cultural events *Misc:* Transfer credit also avail through Univ of Southern Mississippi. May contact former participants. *Financial aid:* work study *URL:* http://www.amerispan.com/
Contact: AmeriSpan Unltd, PO Box 40007, Philadelphia PA 19106 *Ph:* 800-879 6640; 215-751 1100 *Fax:* 215-751 1986 *E-mail:* info@amerispan.com

---

2190
LANGUAGE LINK and **AMAUTA**
One-on-One Spanish in Peru
Site: Peru: Cuzco
Dates: 1-16 wks, yr-round
Subjects: Spanish language
Eligibility: *Level:* fresh, sophs, jrs, srs, grads, adults, teachers, professionals, precoll *Age:* min 18, avg 28
Credit: *Undergrad:* 12 *Grad:* 6 *Doc:* transcript
Instruction: *In:* Spanish *Format:* lang study, tutorial *Students:* intl
Costs: $275 per wk *incl* tuition, housing, all meals, insurance, fees, excursions, books/materials, airport transfer *Nonrefundable fee*
Housing: *Arr by pgm:* residence halls, homestay, hotels
Deadline: None
Other info: *US accredited sponsor:* no *Began:* 1994 *In coop with:* Austin Peay State Univ *Orient:* abroad *Activities:* excursions, field trips *Misc:* Trip to Machu Picchu, Inca Trail & Sacred Valley. Optional location Urubamba. Rainforest pgm. May contact former participants. *URL:* http://www.langlink.com
Contact: Kay Rafool, Dir, Lang Link, PO Box 3006, Peoria IL 61612 *Ph:* 800-552 2051; 309-692 2961 *Fax:* 309-692 2926 *E-mail:* info@langlink.com

---

2191
LANGUAGES ABROAD
Language and Cultural Immersion Programs-Cuzco
Site: Peru: Cuzco
Dates: 2 wks or longer, yr-round
Subjects: Civilization/culture, Homestay, Spanish language (beg/int/adv)
Eligibility: *Level:* adults *Age:* min 17, max 65, avg 25
Credit: *Undergrad:* none *Grad:* none *Doc:* certificate
Instruction: *In:* Spanish *Format:* lang study *Students:* intl
Costs: From $2,250 for 4 wks *incl* tuition, housing, some meals, excursions, books/ materials
Housing: *Arr by pgm:* apartments, homestay
Deadline: None
Other info: *US accredited sponsor:* no *Misc:* May contact former participants. *URL:* http://www.languagesabroad.com
Contact: Ms Jesse Philippe, Langs Abroad, 317 Adelaide St W, Ste 900, Toronto, Ontario M5V 1P9, Canada *Ph:* 800-219 9924; 416-925 7117 *E-mail:* info@languagesabroad.com

---

2192
NATIONAL REGISTRATION CENTER FOR STUDY ABROAD (NRCSA)
Spanish Study in Peru
Site: Peru: Cuzco *Host inst:* AMAUTA
Dates: 2 wks or longer, yr-round
Subjects: Community service projects, Homestay, Spanish language (beg/int/adv)
Eligibility: *Level:* fresh, sophs, jrs, srs, grads, adults, teachers, professionals *Age:* min 18
Credit: *Undergrad:* avail *Grad:* avail *Doc:* certificate
Instruction: *In:* Spanish *Format:* tutorial, volunteer/svc *Students:* intl
Costs: $1,246 for 4 wks *incl* tuition, housing, all meals, insurance, excursions *Nonrefundable fee*
Housing: *Arr by pgm:* homestay
Deadline: 6 wks before pgm
Other info: *US accredited sponsor:* no *Began:* 1995 *Activities:* excursions *URL:* http://www.nrcsa.com
Contact: June Domoe, NRCSA, 823 N 2nd St, #206, Milwaukee WI 53203 *Ph:* 414-278 0631 *Fax:* 414-271 8884 *E-mail:* info@nrcsa.com

---

LIMA

2193
CROSS-CULTURAL SOLUTIONS
Peru Program
Site: Peru: Lima
Dates: 3 wks, yr-round
Subjects: Community service projects
Eligibility: *Level:* adults, precoll *Age:* min 18
Credit: *Undergrad:* none *Grad:* none *Doc:* certificate
Instruction: *In:* Spanish *Format:* volunteer/svc *Students:* intl
Costs: $1,950 *incl* housing, all meals, excursions *Nonrefundable fee*
Housing: *Arr by pgm*
Deadline: Rolling admissions
Other info: *US accredited sponsor:* no *Orient:* abroad (3 days) *Activities:* excursions *Misc:* May contact former participants. *URL:* http://www.crossculturalsolutions.org
Contact: Volunteer Coord, Cross-Cultural Solutions, 47 Potter Ave, New Rochelle NY 10801 *Ph:* 800-280 4777; 914-632 0022 *Fax:* 914-632 8494

2194
GEORGE MASON UNIVERSITY
Peru in the 90's: The Challenge of Development and Democracy
Site: Peru: Lima *Host inst:* Pontificia Univ Catolica del Peru
Dates: 2 wks, May 17-31
Subjects: Government, Peruvian studies, Sociology
Eligibility: *Level:* fresh, sophs, jrs, srs, grads, adults, teachers, professionals *Requires:* 2.25 GPA *Age:* min 18
Credit: *Undergrad:* 3 *Grad:* 3 *Doc:* transcript
Instruction: *In:* English *Format:* study tour *Students:* mainly US
Costs: About $2,400 for VA residents, $2,900 for others *incl* tuition, housing, some meals, insurance, fees, excursions, ISIC *Nonrefundable fee*
Housing: *Arr by pgm:* residence halls with local students
Deadline: Apr 10
Other info: *US accredited sponsor:* yes *Began:* 1996 *Orient:* in US (1 day) *Misc:* May contact former participants. *Financial aid:* scholarships, work study *URL:* http://www.gmu.edu/departments/cge
Contact: Ctr for Global Educ, George Mason Univ, Johnson Ctr, Rm 235, 4400 University Dr, Fairfax VA 22030-4444 *Ph:* 703-993 2154 *Fax:* 703-993 2153 *E-mail:* cge@gmu.edu

---

2195
LANGUAGE LIAISON
Spanish Saturation-Peru
Site: Peru: Lima region *Host inst:* Live in Learn
Dates: 1 wk or longer, yr-round
Subjects: Homestay, Spanish language (beg/int/adv)
Eligibility: *Level:* adults, precoll

Credit: *Undergrad:* none *Grad:* none *Doc:* certificate
Instruction: *In:* Spanish *Format:* lang study, tutorial *Students:* intl
Costs: Contact sponsor
Housing: *Arr by pgm:* teacher's home
Deadline: 45 days before pgm
Other info: *US accredited sponsor:* no *Misc:* Scholarship research svc. *URL:* http://www.languageliaison.com
Contact: Nancy Forman, Dir, Lang Liaison, 4 Burnham Pkwy, Morristown NJ 07960 *Ph:* 800-284 4448 *Fax:* 973-898 1710 *E-mail:* learn@languageliaison.com

---

2196
LINGUA SERVICE WORLDWIDE
Intensive Language and Culture in Peru
Site: Peru: Lima *Host inst:* Home Lang Intl
Dates: 1 wk-1 yr, yr-round
Subjects: Civilization/culture, Homestay, Spanish language (beg/int/adv)
Eligibility: *Level:* adults
Credit: *Undergrad:* avail *Grad:* avail *Doc:* transcript, certificate
Instruction: *In:* Spanish *Format:* lang study, lecture *Students:* intl
Costs: Contact sponsor
Housing: *Arr by pgm:* homestay
Deadline: 45 days before pgm
Other info: *US accredited sponsor:* no *Activities:* excursions, field trips *Misc:* May contact former participants. *URL:* http://www.linguaserviceworldwide.com
Contact: Dir, Lingua Svc Worldwide, 75 Prospect St, Ste 4, Huntington NY 11743 *Ph:* 800-394 5327; 631-424 0777 *Fax:* 631-271 3441 *E-mail:* itctravel@worldnet.att.net ▲

2197
NORTH CAROLINA STATE UNIVERSITY
Peru Summer Program
Site: Peru: Lima
Dates: 6 wks, Jun
Subjects: Homestay, Latin American studies, Literature, Spanish language
Eligibility: *Level:* sophs, jrs, srs, adults, teachers *Requires:* 2.0 GPA, 3 sems coll level Spanish *Age:* min 18
Credit: *Undergrad:* 6 *Grad:* none *Doc:* transcript
Instruction: *In:* Spanish *Format:* lang study, lecture, seminar *Students:* mainly US
Costs: $3,475 *incl* tuition, housing, all meals, intl airfare, insurance, fees, excursions, books/materials *Nonrefundable fee*
Housing: *Arr by pgm:* homestay, hotels
Deadline: Feb 20
Other info: *US accredited sponsor:* yes *Began:* 2000 *Orient:* abroad (2 days) *Activities:* excursions, program travel, cultural events *Misc:* incl 2 wk travel in Cuzco & visits to Macchu Picchu & other sites. May contact former participants. *URL:* http://www.ncsu.edu/studyabroad
Contact: Anne Haberkern, North Carolina State Univ, 2118 Pullen Hall, Box 7344, Raleigh NC 27695-7344 *Ph:* 919-515 2087 *Fax:* 919-515 6021 *E-mail:* study_abroad@ncsu.edu

---

2198
UNIVERSIDAD PERUANA DE CIENCIAS APLICADAS
UPC-Peru Intensive Spanish Program
Site: Peru: Lima *Host inst:* UPC
Dates: 3 wks, Feb and/or Aug
Subjects: Civilization/culture, Homestay, Latin American studies, Peruvian studies, Spanish language (beg/int/adv)
Eligibility: *Level:* fresh, sophs, jrs, srs, grads, teachers, professionals *Requires:* good acad standing, 1 yr Spanish, intl health insurance *Age:* min 18, max 25, avg 21
Credit: *Undergrad:* 3 *Grad:* none *Doc:* transcript, certificate
Instruction: *In:* Spanish *Format:* lang study, lecture, seminar, study tour, tutorial *Students:* intl
Costs: $1,500 *incl* tuition, housing, all meals, fees, excursions, books/materials, support svcs, lang lab
Housing: *Arr by pgm:* homestay
Deadline: Jan 1; Jul 1
Other info: *US accredited sponsor:* no *Began:* 1996 *Orient:* abroad (3 wks, intensive lang study) *Activities:* excursions, field trips, cultural events *Misc:* Multimedia computer & lang lab. Avg class size 5-10. Personal tutorial provided as needed. May contact former participants. *URL:* http://www.upc.edu.pe
Contact: Claudio Draghi, Coord, Intl Relations, Ave Prolongacion, Primavera 2390, Monterrico, Surco/Lima 33, Peru *E-mail:* studyabroad@upc.edu.pe

Puerto Rico

MORE THAN ONE CITY

2199
SCHOOL OF THE MUSEUM OF FINE ARTS, BOSTON
Painting in the Rainforest
Site: Puerto Rico: the Rainforest
Dates: Aug 4-Aug 12
Subjects: Studio arts (beg/int/adv)
Eligibility: *Level:* fresh, sophs, jrs, srs, grads, adults, teachers, professionals *Age:* min 18
Credit: *Undergrad:* avail *Grad:* none *Doc:* transcript
Instruction: *In:* English *Format:* art studio *Students:* mainly US
Costs: $1,520 *incl* tuition, housing, all meals, excursions, facilities
Housing: *Arr by pgm:* hotels
Deadline: Apr 6 or until pgm filled
Other info: *US accredited sponsor:* yes *Began:* 2000 *Activities:* excursions, program travel *URL:* http://www.smfa.edu
Contact: Nathaniel Bradley, SMFA Continuing Educ, 230 The Fenway, Boston MA 02115 *Ph:* 617-267 1219 *Fax:* 617-369 3679 *E-mail:* coned@smfa.edu

---

MAYAGUEZ

2200
SUNY COLLEGE AT OSWEGO
Puerto Rico Winter Study Opportunity
Site: Puerto Rico: Mayaguez *Host inst:* Univ of Puerto Rico, Mayaguez
Dates: 3 wks, Jan
Subjects: Anthropology, Business/management, Marketing
Eligibility: *Level:* adults *Requires:* 2.5 GPA, previous study in field
Credit: *Undergrad:* 3 *Grad:* 3 *Doc:* transcript
Instruction: *In:* English *Format:* lang study, lecture *Students:* mainly US
Costs: $2,500 for undergrads, $2,700 for grads *incl* tuition, housing, all meals, intl airfare, excursions *Nonrefundable fee*
Housing: *Arr by pgm:* residence halls
Deadline: Oct 1
Other info: *US accredited sponsor:* yes *Began:* 1991 *Orient:* in US *Activities:* excursions, field trips, cultural events *Misc:* May contact former participants. *URL:* http://www.oswego.edu/~intled
Contact: Susan Ansara, Dir, Intl Educ, SUNY Coll at Oswego, 102 Rich Hall, Oswego NY 13126 *Ph:* 888-467 9346; 315-341 2118 *Fax:* 315-341 2477 *E-mail:* intled@oswego.edu

---

SAN JUAN

2201
AMERISPAN UNLIMITED
Spanish Study and Homestay in Puerto Rico
Site: Puerto Rico: San Juan *Host inst:* Euskalduna Inst Intl
Dates: 1 wk-1 yr, yr-round
Subjects: Civilization/culture, Current events, History, Homestay, Literature, Spanish language (beg/int/adv)
Eligibility: *Level:* grads, adults *Age:* min 16
Credit: *Undergrad:* avail *Grad:* none *Doc:* certificate *Transfer credit through:* Univ of Southern Mississippi

Instruction: *In:* Spanish *Format:* lang study *Students:* intl
Costs: $840 for 2 wks, $1,595 for 4 wks, $390 for each addtl wk *incl* tuition, housing, insurance
Housing: *Sponsor assists:* homestay, pensions, hotels
Deadline: 4 wks before pgm
Other info: *US accredited sponsor:* no *Orient:* abroad *Activities:* excursions, field trips, cultural events *Misc:* Transfer credit also avail through Seattle Central CC. May contact former participants. *Financial aid:* work study *URL:* http://www.amerispan.com/
Contact: AmeriSpan Unltd, PO Box 40007, Philadelphia PA 19106 *Ph:* 800-879 6640; 215-751 1100 *Fax:* 215-751 1986 *E-mail:* info@amerispan.com

---

2202
LANGUAGE LIAISON
Spanish Saturation in Puerto Rico
Site: Puerto Rico: San Juan
Dates: Varying pgm lengths, yr-round
Subjects: Civilization/culture, Homestay, Spanish language, Spanish studies
Eligibility: *Level:* adults *Age:* min 18
Credit: *Undergrad:* avail *Grad:* avail
Instruction: *In:* Spanish *Format:* lang study *Students:* intl
Costs: Contact sponsor
Housing: *Sponsor assists:* homestay, hotels
Deadline: 45 days before pgm
Other info: *US accredited sponsor:* no *Orient:* abroad *Activities:* excursions, field trips, cultural events, sports *Misc:* Scholarship research svc. *URL:* http://www.languageliaison.com
Contact: Nancy Forman, Dir, Lang Liaison, 4 Burnham Pkwy, Morristown NJ 07960 *Ph:* 800-284 4448 *Fax:* 973-898 1710 *E-mail:* learn@languageliaison.com

---

2203
LANGUAGES ABROAD
Language and Cultural Immersion-San Juan
Site: Puerto Rico: San Juan
Dates: 2 wks or longer, yr-round
Subjects: Civilization/culture, Spanish language (beg/int/adv)
Eligibility: *Level:* adults *Age:* min 17, max 65, avg 25
Credit: *Undergrad:* none *Grad:* none *Doc:* certificate
Instruction: *In:* Spanish *Format:* lang study *Students:* intl
Costs: $1,835 per mo *incl* tuition, housing, some meals, excursions, books/materials
Housing: *Arr by pgm:* residence halls, homestay
Deadline: None
Other info: *US accredited sponsor:* no *Began:* 1995 *Activities:* excursions, field trips, program travel, cultural events, sports *Misc:* May contact former participants. *URL:* http://www.languagesabroad.com
Contact: Ms Jesse Philippe, Langs Abroad, 317 Adelaide St W, Ste 900, Toronto, Ontario M5V 1P9, Canada *Ph:* 800-219 9924; 416-925 7117 *E-mail:* info@languagesabroad.com

---

2204
NATIONAL REGISTRATION CENTER FOR STUDY ABROAD (NRCSA)
Spanish Study in Puerto Rico
Site: Puerto Rico: San Juan *Host inst:* Inst Euskalduna
Dates: 2 wks or longer, yr-round
Subjects: Homestay, Spanish language (beg/int/adv)
Eligibility: *Level:* fresh, sophs, jrs, srs, grads, adults, teachers, professionals *Age:* min 18
Credit: *Undergrad:* avail *Grad:* avail *Doc:* certificate
Instruction: *In:* Spanish *Format:* lang study *Students:* mainly US
Costs: $998 for 2 wks *incl* tuition, housing, some meals, insurance *Nonrefundable fee*
Housing: *Arr by pgm:* homestay, guest house
Deadline: 6 wks before pgm
Other info: *US accredited sponsor:* no *Activities:* field trips *URL:* http://www.nrcsa.com
Contact: June Domoe, NRCSA, 823 N 2nd St, #206, Milwaukee WI 53203 *Ph:* 414-278 0631 *Fax:* 414-271 8884 *E-mail:* info@nrcsa.com

St Lucia

CASTRIES

2205
SUNY ROCKLAND COMMUNITY COLLEGE
St Lucia & the US: Comparative Issues & Trends in Education
Site: St Lucia: Castries
Dates: 2 wks, Jan 6-Jan 20
Subjects: Civilization/culture, Education/teaching, Social sciences, Sociology
Eligibility: *Level:* fresh, sophs, jrs, srs, adults, teachers, professionals *Requires:* 2.5 GPA *Age:* min 18
Credit: *Undergrad:* 3 *Grad:* none *Doc:* transcript
Instruction: *In:* English *Format:* directed field study, lecture, seminar, tutorial *Students:* mainly US
Costs: About $1,500 *incl* tuition, housing, some meals, intl airfare
Housing: *Arr by pgm:* pensions
Deadline: Nov 1
Other info: *US accredited sponsor:* yes *Began:* 2001 *Orient:* abroad *Activities:* excursions, field trips *Misc:* May contact former participants. *Financial aid:* scholarships *URL:* http://www.studyabroad.com/suny/rockland
Contact: Jody Dudderar, Dir, SUNY Rockland CC, 145 College Rd, Suffern NY 10901 *Ph:* 845-574 4205 *Fax:* 845-574 4423 *E-mail:* studyabroad@sunyrockland.edu

Trinidad and Tobago

MORE THAN ONE CITY

2206
UNIVERSITY OF SOUTH FLORIDA
Caribbean Popular Culture: USF in Trinidad & Tobago
Site: Trinidad & Tobago
Dates: 6 wks, May-Jun
Subjects: Caribbean studies, Civilization/culture, Research methods
Eligibility: *Level:* sophs, jrs, srs, grads, teachers, professionals *Requires:* 2.5 GPA, previous study in field, intro anthropology course, good physical health *Age:* min 20, max 25
Credit: *Undergrad:* 6 *Grad:* 6 *Doc:* transcript
Instruction: *In:* English *Format:* directed field study, lecture *Students:* mainly US
Costs: $2,700 *incl* tuition, housing, some meals, intl airfare, fees, excursions *Nonrefundable fee*
Housing: *Arr by pgm:* homestay, hotels
Deadline: Feb 15
Other info: *US accredited sponsor:* yes *Began:* 1996 *Orient:* in US & abroad (1 day) *Activities:* excursions, field trips, cultural events *URL:* http://www.usf.edu/~iac/
Contact: Dr Christine Ho, Pgm Dir, Anthropology, Univ of South Florida, 4202 E Fowler Ave, SOC 107, Tampa FL 33620 *Ph:* 813-974 0807 *Fax:* 813-974 2668 *E-mail:* ho@luna.cas.usf.edu
Or Contact: James Pulos, Coord, USF Overseas Study Pgms, Univ of South Florida, 4202 E Fowler Ave, CPR 107, Tampa FL 33620 *Ph:* 813-974 4043 *Fax:* 813-974 4613 *E-mail:* jpulos@iac.usf.edu

---

SAINT AUGUSTINE

2207
UNIVERSITY OF MIAMI (FL)
Caribbean Studies at UWI, Trinidad
Site: Trinidad: St Augustine *Host inst:* Univ of West Indies
Dates: 8 wks, late May-late Jul
Subjects: Business/management, Caribbean studies, Economics, History,

International relations, Literature, Political science/politics, Sociology
Eligibility: *Level:* jrs, srs *Requires:* 3.0 GPA *Age:* min 18
Credit: *Undergrad:* 6-9 *Grad:* none *Doc:* transcript
Instruction: *In:* English *Format:* lecture, seminar *Students:* mainly host country
Costs: $5,200 *incl* tuition, housing *Nonrefundable fee*
Housing: *Arr by pgm:* residence halls
Deadline: Apr 1
Other info: *US accredited sponsor:* yes *Began:* 2000 *Misc:* May contact former participants. *URL:* http://www.studyabroad.miami.edu
Contact: Intl Educ & Exch Pgms, Allen Hall 212, 5050 Brunson Dr, PO Box 248005, Univ of Miami, Coral Gables FL 33124-1610 *Ph:* 800-557 5421; 305-284 3424 *Fax:* 305-284 6629 *E-mail:* ieep@miami.edu

Turks and Caicos Islands

SOUTH CAICOS ISLAND

2208
SCHOOL FOR FIELD STUDIES
SFS Caribbean: Marine Parks Management
Site: Turks & Caicos Islands: South Caicos Island
Dates: 1 mo, mid-Jun-mid-Jul or mid-Jul-mid-Aug
Subjects: Anthropology, Caribbean studies, Conservation, Ecology/environmental studies, Economics, Field study, Fishing/fisheries, Marine biology, Natural resources
Eligibility: *Level:* fresh, sophs, jrs, srs, precoll *Age:* min 16, avg 20
Credit: *Undergrad:* avail *Grad:* none *Doc:* transcript *Transfer credit through:* Boston Univ
Instruction: *In:* English *Format:* directed field study, lecture, practical training *Students:* mainly US
Costs: $3,275 *incl* tuition, housing, all meals, excursions *Nonrefundable fee*
Housing: *Arr by pgm:* campsites, rustic cabins
Deadline: Rolling admissions
Other info: *US accredited sponsor:* no *Began:* 1980 *Orient:* abroad *Activities:* excursions, field trips, program travel, cultural events, sports *Misc:* Scuba & snorkeling. Loans avail. May contact former participants. *Financial aid:* scholarships *URL:* http://www.fieldstudies.org
Contact: Admissions Off, Sch for Field Studies, 16 Broadway, Beverly MA 01915-4499 *Ph:* 800-989 4435; 978-927 7777 *Fax:* 978-927 5127 *E-mail:* admissions@fieldstudies

Uruguay

MONTEVIDEO

2209
AMERISPAN UNLIMITED
Spanish Study and Homestay in Uruguay
Site: Uruguay: Montevideo *Host inst:* Inst de Lenguas Extranjeras
Dates: 2 wks-1 yr, yr-round
Subjects: Civilization/culture, Current events, History, Homestay, Latin American studies, Literature, Spanish language (beg/int/adv)
Eligibility: *Level:* srs, grads, adults, teachers, professionals, precoll *Age:* min 18
Credit: *Undergrad:* avail *Grad:* none *Doc:* transcript, certificate *Transfer credit through:* Seattle Central CC
Instruction: *In:* Spanish *Format:* lang study, lecture, study tour, tutorial *Students:* intl
Costs: $1,050 for 2 wks, $2,050 for 4 wks, $500 for each addtl wk *incl* tuition, housing, some meals, insurance
Housing: *Arr by pgm:* apartments, homestay, hotels
Deadline: 4 wks before pgm
Other info: *US accredited sponsor:* no *Orient:* abroad *Activities:* excursions, field trips, cultural events *Misc:* May contact former participants. *URL:* http://www.amerispan.com/
Contact: AmeriSpan Unltd, PO Box 40007, Philadelphia PA 19106 *Ph:* 800-879 6640; 215-751 1100 *Fax:* 215-751 1986 *E-mail:* info@amerispan.com

---

2210
LANGUAGES ABROAD
Language and Cultural Immersion Programs-Montevideo
Site: Uruguay: Montevideo
Dates: 2 wks or longer, yr-round
Subjects: Civilization/culture, Homestay, Spanish language (beg/int/adv)
Eligibility: *Level:* adults *Age:* min 17, max 65, avg 25
Credit: *Undergrad:* none *Grad:* none *Doc:* certificate
Instruction: *In:* Spanish *Format:* lang study *Students:* intl
Costs: About $2,950 for 4 wks *incl* tuition, housing, some meals, excursions, books/materials
Housing: *Arr by pgm:* apartments, homestay
Deadline: None
Other info: *US accredited sponsor:* no *Misc:* May contact former participants. *URL:* http://www.languagesabroad.com
Contact: Ms Jesse Philippe, Langs Abroad, 317 Adelaide St W, Ste 900, Toronto, Ontario M5V 1P9, Canada *Ph:* 800-219 9924; 416-925 7117 *E-mail:* info@languagesabroad.com

---

2211
NATIONAL REGISTRATION CENTER FOR STUDY ABROAD (NRCSA)
Instituto de Lenguas Extranjeras
Site: Uruguay: Montevideo *Host inst:* Inst de Lenguas Extranjeras
Dates: 2 wks or longer, yr-round
Subjects: Homestay, Spanish language (int/adv)
Eligibility: *Level:* fresh, sophs, jrs, srs, grads, adults *Age:* min 18
Credit: *Undergrad:* avail *Grad:* avail *Doc:* certificate
Instruction: *In:* Spanish *Format:* lang study, tutorial *Students:* intl
Costs: $1,155 for 2 wks, $490 for each addtl wk *incl* tuition, housing, some meals, insurance
Housing: *Arr by pgm:* apartments, homestay
Deadline: Contact sponsor
Other info: *US accredited sponsor:* no *Orient:* abroad (intensive lang study) *Activities:* field trips *URL:* http://www.nrcsa.com
Contact: June Domoe, NRCSA, 823 N 2nd St, #206, Milwaukee WI 53203 *Ph:* 414-278 0631 *Fax:* 414-271 8884 *E-mail:* info@nrcsa.com

Venezuela

MORE THAN ONE CITY

2212
AMERISPAN UNLIMITED
Spanish Study and Homestay in Venezuela
Site: Venezuela: Caracas, Merida *Host inst:* Ctr Venezolano de Espanol, Inst Latinoamer de Idiomas
Dates: 1 wk-1 yr, yr-round
Subjects: Homestay, Spanish language (beg/int/adv)
Eligibility: *Level:* fresh, sophs, jrs, srs, grads, adults *Age:* min 18
Credit: *Undergrad:* avail *Grad:* none *Doc:* transcript, certificate *Transfer credit through:* Univ of Southern Mississippi
Instruction: *In:* Spanish *Format:* lang study, lecture, study tour, tutorial *Students:* intl
Costs: $560 for 2 wks, $1,090 for 4 wks, $260 for each addtl wk *incl* tuition, housing, some meals, insurance, books/materials
Housing: *Arr by pgm:* homestay, hotels
Deadline: 4 wks before pgm
Other info: *US accredited sponsor:* no

Orient: abroad *Activities:* excursions, field trips, cultural events *Misc:* Transfer credit also avail through Seattle Central CC. May contact former participants. *Financial aid:* work study *URL:* http://www.amerispan.com/
Contact: AmeriSpan Unltd, PO Box 40007, Philadelphia PA 19106 *Ph:* 800-879 6640; 215-751 1100 *Fax:* 215-751 1986 *E-mail:* info@amerispan.com

---

2213
CULTURELINK INTERNATIONAL PROGRAMS
Internships in Venezuela
Site: Venezuela: all cities
Dates: 4 wks or longer, yr-round
Subjects: Field study, Independent study, Internships
Eligibility: *Level:* fresh, sophs, jrs, srs, grads, adults, teachers, professionals, precoll *Requires:* 2.5 GPA, previous Spanish lang study *Age:* min 18, avg 22
Credit: *Undergrad:* avail *Grad:* avail *Doc:* transcript, certificate *Transfer credit through:* Univ of Utah
Instruction: *In:* Spanish *Format:* directed field study, independent study, internship *Students:* intl
Costs: $2,000 per sem *incl* tuition, fees
Housing: *Sponsor assists:* homestay
Deadline: 1 mo before departure
Other info: *US accredited sponsor:* no *Began:* 1995 *Orient:* abroad (1 day) *Misc:* May contact former participants. *URL:* http://www.culturelinkinc.com
Contact: Beatriz Guzman, Culturelink, 585 NW 129th Way, Pembroke Pines FL 33028 *Ph:* 954-432 2355, *Fax:* 954-433 5787 *E-mail:* culture@interpoint.net

---

2214
LANGUAGE LIAISON
Spanish in Venezuela
Site: Venezuela: Caracas, Merida
Dates: 2 wks-1 yr, yr-round
Subjects: Homestay, Spanish language
Eligibility: *Level:* fresh, sophs, jrs, srs, grads, adults, teachers, professionals, precoll *Age:* min 16
Credit: *Undergrad:* avail *Grad:* avail
Instruction: *In:* Spanish *Format:* lang study *Students:* intl
Costs: Contact sponsor
Housing: *Arr by pgm:* homestay, hotels
Deadline: 30 days before pgm
Other info: *US accredited sponsor:* no *Began:* 1997 *Activities:* excursions, cultural events, sports *Misc:* Scholarship research svc. *URL:* http://www.languageliaison.com
Contact: Nancy Forman, Dir, Lang Liaison, 4 Burnham Pkwy, Morristown NJ 07960 *Ph:* 800-284 4448 *Fax:* 973-898 1710 *E-mail:* learn@languageliaison.com

---

2215
LANGUAGES ABROAD
Language and Cultural Immersion-Venezuela
Site: Venezuela: Caracas, Merida
Dates: 2 wks or longer, yr-round
Subjects: Civilization/culture, Spanish language (beg/int/adv), Venezuelan studies
Eligibility: *Level:* adults *Age:* min 17, max 65, avg 25
Credit: *Undergrad:* none *Grad:* none *Doc:* certificate
Instruction: *In:* Spanish *Format:* lang study *Students:* intl
Costs: $1,200 per mo *incl* tuition, housing, some meals, excursions, books/materials
Housing: *Arr by pgm:* residence halls, homestay
Deadline: None
Other info: *US accredited sponsor:* no *Began:* 1995 *Activities:* excursions, field trips, program travel, cultural events, sports *Misc:* May contact former participants. *URL:* http://www.languagesabroad.com
Contact: Ms Jesse Philippe, Langs Abroad, 317 Adelaide St W, Ste 900, Toronto, Ontario M5V 1P9, Canada *Ph:* 800-219 9924; 416-925 7117 *E-mail:* info@languagesabroad.com

---

CARACAS

2216
CENTRO VENEZOLANO DE ESPANOL
Learn Spanish Facil in Venezuela
Site: Venezuela: Caracas
Dates: 2-32 wks, yr-round
Subjects: Homestay, Latin American studies, Spanish language (beg/int/adv)
Eligibility: *Level:* fresh, sophs, jrs, srs, grads, adults, teachers, professionals *Age:* min 16, avg 23
Credit: *Undergrad:* avail *Grad:* none *Doc:* certificate
Instruction: *In:* English, Spanish *Format:* lang study, study tour *Students:* intl
Costs: $1,100 per mo *incl* tuition, housing, some meals, fees, excursions, books/materials *Nonrefundable fee*
Housing: *Arr by pgm:* homestay, hotels
Deadline: 4 wks before pgm
Other info: *US accredited sponsor:* no *Began:* 1990 *Orient:* abroad *Activities:* excursions, program travel, cultural events, sports *Misc:* Visits to 8 sites per mo. May contact former participants. *URL:* http://www.ceves.org.ve
Contact: Cristina Nino, Acad Dir, or Torre Phelps, Ctr Venezolano de Espanol,, PO Box 54583, Caracas, Venezuela 1050 *Ph:* 800-835 1341 *E-mail:* ceves@ceves.org.ve

---

2217
LANGUAGE LIAISON
Spanish Saturation-Venezuela
Site: Venezuela: Caracas *Host inst:* Live in Learn
Dates: 1 wk or longer, yr-round
Subjects: Civilization/culture, Homestay, Spanish language (beg/int/adv)
Eligibility: *Level:* fresh, sophs, jrs, srs, grads, adults, teachers, professionals, precoll *Age:* min 10
Credit: *Undergrad:* none *Grad:* none *Doc:* transcript, certificate
Instruction: *In:* Spanish *Format:* lang study *Students:* intl
Costs: Contact sponsor
Housing: *Arr by pgm:* teacher's home
Deadline: 45 days before pgm
Other info: *US accredited sponsor:* no *Misc:* Scholarship research svc. *URL:* http://www.languageliaison.com
Contact: Nancy Forman, Dir, Lang Liaison, 4 Burnham Pkwy, Morristown NJ 07960 *Ph:* 800-284 4448 *Fax:* 973-898 1710 *E-mail:* learn@languageliaison.com

---

MARACAIBO

2218
CENTRO VENEZOLANO AMERICANO DEL ZULIA (CEVAZ)
Study in Venezuela
Site: Venezuela: Maracaibo
Dates: Jan-1st wk in Dec
Subjects: Homestay
Eligibility: *Level:* fresh, sophs, jrs, srs, grads, adults *Age:* min 9, max 50, avg 20
Credit: *Undergrad:* none *Grad:* none *Doc:* certificate, diploma
Instruction: *In:* English *Format:* lang study *Students:* mainly host country
Costs: $80 per mo *incl* tuition
Housing: *Sponsor assists:* residence halls, homestay
Deadline: Rolling Admissions
Other info: *US accredited sponsor:* no *Began:* 1973 *Orient:* abroad *Activities:* cultural events *Financial aid:* work study *URL:* http://www.cevaz.org.
Contact: Ilse Chemaly or Ann Kuggler, Cevaz, Calle 63, #3E-60, Maracaibo, Venezuela 4001 *E-mail:* cevazdi@cantv.net

---

MERIDA

2219
NATIONAL REGISTRATION CENTER FOR STUDY ABROAD (NRCSA)
VENUSA
Site: Venezuela: Merida *Host inst:* VENUSA CPSA
Dates: 1 wk or longer, yr-round
Subjects: Homestay, Spanish language, Venezuelan studies
Eligibility: *Level:* fresh, sophs, jrs, srs, grads, adults, teachers, precoll *Age:* min 18
Credit: *Undergrad:* avail *Grad:* avail *Doc:* certificate
Instruction: *In:* Spanish *Format:* tutorial *Students:* intl
Costs: $446 per wk, $741 for 2 wks *incl* tuition, housing, all meals, insurance
Housing: *Arr by pgm:* homestay
Deadline: 6 wks before pgm
Other info: *US accredited sponsor:* no *Activities:* excursions *URL:* http://www.nrcsa.com
Contact: June Domoe, NRCSA, 823 N 2nd St, #206, Milwaukee MI 53203 *Ph:* 414-278 0631 *Fax:* 414-271 8884 *E-mail:* info@nrcsa.com

---

2220
SUNY COLLEGE AT CORTLAND
Cortland at Merida Summer Sessions
Site: Venezuela: Merida *Host inst:* VENUSA CPSA
Dates: Mid-May-late Jun and/or late Jun-early Aug
Subjects: Anthropology, Communications, Ecology/environmental studies, History, Homestay, Intercultural studies, International business, Internships, Latin American studies, Sociology, Spanish language, TEFL/TESL
Eligibility: *Level:* fresh, sophs, jrs, srs *Requires:* 2.5 GPA, good acad standing; 1 sem Spanish preferred *Age:* min 18
Credit: *Undergrad:* 6-8 per session *Grad:* none *Doc:* transcript
Instruction: *In:* English, Spanish *Format:* internship, lang study, lecture, seminar, tutorial *Students:* US & intl
Costs: $3,800 per session *incl* tuition, housing, all meals, intl airfare, insurance, fees, books/materials, passport, transfers
Housing: *Arr by pgm:* homestay
Deadline: Apr 1
Other info: *US accredited sponsor:* yes *Began:* 1994 *In coop with:* VENUSA CPSA *Orient:* in US & abroad *Activities:* field trips, cultural events *Misc:* Loans avail. May contact former participants. *URL:* http://www.studyabroad.com/suny/cortland
Contact: Liz Kopp, Intl Pgms, SUNY Coll at Cortland, Cortland NY 13045 *Ph:* 607-753 2209 *Fax:* 607-753 5989 *E-mail:* studyabroad@cortland.edu ▲

2221
SUNY COLLEGE AT CORTLAND
Global Internships for Professionals
Site: Venezuela: Merida *Host inst:* VENUSA CPSA
Dates: 10 wks, late May-early Aug
Subjects: Business/management, Internships, Social welfare/services
Eligibility: *Level:* jrs, srs, adults *Requires:* 2.5 GPA, previous study in field, adv Spanish
Credit: *Undergrad:* avail *Grad:* none *Doc:* transcript
Instruction: *In:* Spanish *Format:* internship, lang study *Students:* mainly US
Costs: $3,300 *incl* tuition, housing, some meals, intl airfare, insurance, fees, books/materials, orient, passport *Nonrefundable fee*
Housing: *Arr by pgm:* homestay
Deadline: Feb 1
Other info: *US accredited sponsor:* yes *Began:* 1999 *Orient:* in US & abroad (intensive lang study) *Activities:* excursions, field trips, cultural events *Misc:* May contact former participants. *URL:* http://www.studyabroad.com/suny/cortland
Contact: Liz Kopp, Asst Dir, Intl Pgms, SUNY Coll at Cortland, PO Box 2000, Cortland NY 13045 *Ph:* 607-753 2209 *Fax:* 607-753 5989 *E-mail:* koppl@cortland.edu ▲

2222
UNIVERSITY OF ALABAMA
Alabama in Venezuela
Site: Venezuela: Merida *Host inst:* Fundalinga Inst, Univ de los Andes
Dates: 3 wks, Jun 26-Jul 16
Subjects: Education/teaching, Field study, Homestay
Eligibility: *Level:* grads, teachers, professionals *Requires:* 3.0 GPA *Age:* min 18, avg 25
Credit: *Undergrad:* none *Grad:* 6 *Doc:* transcript
Instruction: *In:* English *Format:* directed field study, lecture, practical training, student teaching, volunteer/svc *Students:* mainly US
Costs: $2,600 *incl* tuition, housing, all meals, intl airfare, fees, excursions, travel insurance
Housing: *Arr by pgm:* homestay
Deadline: Mar 1
Other info: *US accredited sponsor:* yes *Began:* 2000 *In coop with:* Culturelink *Orient:* in US & abroad *Activities:* excursions *Misc:* may be open to undergrads in 2001 *Financial aid:* scholarships *URL:* http://www.ua.edu/international
Contact: Ms. Angie Channell, CIPS - Univ of Alabama, 135 BB comer Hall/Box 870254, Tuscaloosa AB 35487-0254 *Ph:* 205-348 5256 *Fax:* 205-348 5298 *E-mail:* achannel@aalan.ua.edu

---

2223
UNIVERSITY OF MINNESOTA
Study Abroad in Venezuela
Site: Venezuela: Merida *Host inst:* VENUSA CPSA
Dates: 6 wks, May 19-Jun 30 and/or Jun 30-Aug 11
Subjects: Area studies, Botany, Economics, Geography, Homestay, Latin American studies, Literature, Political science/politics, Spanish language, TEFL/TESL
Eligibility: *Level:* fresh, sophs, jrs, srs, grads, adults, teachers, professionals *Requires:* 2.5 GPA
Credit: *Undergrad:* 8-9 *Grad:* none *Doc:* transcript
Instruction: *In:* English, Spanish *Format:* directed field study, lang study, lecture, volunteer/svc *Students:* mainly US
Costs: About $3,350 for Univ of MN Students, $3600 others *incl* tuition, housing, some meals, insurance, fees, excursions *Nonrefundable fee*
Housing: *Arr by pgm:* homestay
Deadline: Mar 15 for session I; Apr 25 for session II
Other info: *US accredited sponsor:* yes *Began:* 1994 *Orient:* in US & abroad *Activities:* excursions *Misc:* Scholarships for own students only. *URL:* http://www.UMabroad.umn.edu
Contact: Study Abroad in Venezuela, Global Campus, Univ of Minnesota, 230 Heller Hall, 271 19th Ave S, 271 19th Ave S, Minneapolis MN 55455-0138 *Ph:* 612-626 9000 *Fax:* 612-626 8009 *E-mail:* UMabroad@tc.umn.edu
Or Contact: Study Abroad in Venezuela, VENUSA CPSA, Inst of Intl Studies, 6342 Forest Hill Blvd, Ste 287, West Palm Beach FL 33415 *Ph:* 561-357 8802 *Fax:* 407-753 3758 *E-mail:* venusa@flinet.com

Virgin Islands

MORE THAN ONE CITY

2224
MICHIGAN STATE UNIVERSITY
Natural Science
Site: Virgin Islands: St Croix, St John
Dates: 3 wks, Dec-Jan
Subjects: Biology, Ecology/environmental studies
Eligibility: *Level:* fresh, sophs, jrs, srs *Requires:* 2.0 GPA, good physical condition *Age:* min 18

Credit: *Undergrad:* 6 *Grad:* none *Doc:* transcript
Instruction: *In:* English *Format:* directed field study *Students:* mainly US
Costs: About $1,500 *incl* housing, some meals, insurance, excursions
Nonrefundable fee
Housing: *Arr by pgm:* campsites
Deadline: Oct 20
Other info: *US accredited sponsor:* yes *Orient:* in US *Activities:* excursions, field trips, program travel *Misc:* Students must have own camping equipment & snorkeling supplies. May contact former participants. *Financial aid:* scholarships *URL:* http://studyabroad.msu.edu
Contact: Cheryl Benner, Study Abroad, Michigan State Univ, 109 Intl Ctr, East Lansing MI 48824 *Ph:* 517-353 8920 *Fax:* 517-432 2082 *E-mail:* bennerc@msu.edu ▲

SAINT THOMAS

2225
SUNY COLLEGE AT NEW PALTZ
Summer Study in the Virgin Islands-Saint Thomas
Site: Virgin Islands: St Thomas *Host inst:* Univ of the Virgin Islands-St Thomas
Dates: 6 wks, Jun 30-Jul 31
Subjects: Full curriculum
Eligibility: *Level:* fresh, sophs, jrs, srs, precoll *Requires:* good acad standing, *Age:* min 17
Credit: *Undergrad:* 6 *Grad:* none *Doc:* transcript
Instruction: *In:* English *Format:* lecture, seminar *Students:* intl
Costs: $2,957 for NY residents, $4,211 for others *incl* tuition, housing, all meals, intl airfare, insurance, fees, excursions
Nonrefundable fee
Housing: *Arr by pgm:* residence halls
Deadline: Mar 1
Other info: *US accredited sponsor:* yes *Orient:* abroad *Financial aid:* scholarships *URL:* http://www.newpaltz.edu/oie/
Contact: Ctr for Intl Pgms, SUNY New Paltz, 75 S Manheim Blvd, New Paltz NY 12561 *Ph:* 845-257 3125 *Fax:* 845-257 3129 *E-mail:* international@newpaltz.edu ▲

Index I: Sponsoring Institutions

Programs are indexed alphabetically by sponsoring institution. References are to sequential book entry numbers, not to the page on which the sponsor's entry appears.

If provided by the sponsor at the time of information-gathering, the URL (Uniform Resource Locator) indicating the program sponsor's home page address on the World Wide Web appears after the name of the sponsoring institution. Please keep in mind that this information was current at the time IIE conducted its research for this book. At publication, some addresses may have changed in this evolving area of media technology.

Study-abroad programs with up to three sponsors are indexed by the name of one, two or three sponsor organizations. Other programs are sponsored by larger groups of colleges and universities, or consortia. **Index I: Sponsoring Institutions** identifies these programs by the name of the consortium only. **Index II: Consortia** lists the member colleges and universities of each consortium that sponsors a program.

A

B

C

D

E

F

G

H

I

J

K

L

M

N

O

P

Q

R

S

T

U

V

W

X, Y, Z

Index II: Consortia

Many programs are sponsored by consortia of colleges and universities. This index lists the member institutions of all consortia that sponsor programs in this book. For the book's purposes, a consortium is a group of more than three colleges and universities that jointly offer a study abroad program.

If provided by the consortium at the time of information-gathering, the URL (Uniform Resource Locator) indicating the consortium's home page address on the World Wide Web appears after the contact address. Please keep in mind that this information was current at the time IIE conducted its research for this book. At publication, some addresses may have changed in this evolving area of media technology.

Students enrolled at a member institution of the consortia listed below should typically apply for admission through their home campus. Others should apply to the administering school or consortium office.

Accent Paris Consortium

Accent, 870 Market St, Ste 1026, San Francisco CA 94102; 800-869 9291, 415-835 3744; Fax: 415-835 3749 http://www.accentintl.com
Program(s) 0699

California State Polytechnic Univ-Pomona, 3801 West Temple Ave, Pomona CA 91768; Samira Matta, 909-869 6841
Cerritos Coll, 11110 Alondra Blvd, Norwalk CA 90650; Roland Bellugue, 310-860 2451 ext 2827
Coast CC District, 1370 Adams Ave, Costa Mesa CA 92626; Christine Russell, 714-432 4704
Los Angeles Pierce Coll, 6201 Winnetka Ave, Woodlands Hills CA 91371; Scarlett Gani, 818-719 6402
Napa Valley Coll, 2277 Napa-Vallejo Hwy, Napa CA 94558; Anne-Marie McEligot, 707-253 3795
Palomar Coll, 1140 West Mission Rd, San Marcos CA 92069; Elisabeth Clark, 619-744 1150 ext 2390
Santa Barbara City Coll, 712 Cliff Dr, Santa Barbara CA 93109; Carola Smith, 805-965 0581

Adventist Colleges Abroad

Odette Ferreira, Dir, 12501 Old Columbia Pike, Silver Spring MD 20904-6600; 301-680 6444; Fax: 301-680 6463 http://www.nadadventist.org/aca
Program(s) 0502, 0649, 1026, 1354

Andrews Univ, Coll of Arts & Scis, Berrien Springs MI 49104
Antillean Adventist Univ, Apdo 118, Mayaguez PR 00681
Atlantic Union Coll, South Lancaster MA 01561
Canadian Union Coll, PO Box 430, College Heights, Alta TOC 0Z0, Canada
Col Adventista de Sagunto, Carretera de Petres s/n, Apdo 52, 46500 Sagunto (Valencia), Spain
Columbia Union Coll, 7600 Flower Ave, Takoma Park MD 20912
Home Study Intl, PO Box 4437, Silver Spring MD 20904-6600
Inst Adventista de Ensino, CP 12630, CEP 04798-970, Sao Paulo, SP, Brazil
Inst Adventiste du Saleve, BP 74, 74165 Collonges-sous-Saleve, Cedex, France
Ist Avventista Villa Aurora, via del Pergolina 12, 50139 Florence, Italy
La Sierra Univ, Riverside CA 92515
Oakwood Coll, Huntsville AL 35896
Pacific Union Coll, Angwin CA 94508
Seminar Schloss Bogenhofen, A-4963 St Peter am Hart, bei Braunau am Inn, Austria
Southern Coll of SDA, Collegedale TN 37315
Southwestern Adventist Univ, Keene TX 76059
Union Coll, 3800 S 48th St, Lincoln NE 68506
Walla Walla Coll, College Place WA 99324

American Research Institute in Turkey

Iris Wright, Admin, Ctr for Study of Islamic Socys & Civilizations, Washington Univ, Campus Box 1230, One Brookings Dr, St Louis MO 63130-4899
Program(s) 1793

Archaeological Inst of America, Boston MA 02215
Brown Univ, Providence RI 02912
Bryn Mawr Coll, Bryn Mawr PA 19010
Columbia Univ, New York NY 10027
Cornell Univ, Ithaca NY 14853
Duke Univ, Durham NC 27706
Dumbarton Oaks, Washington DC 20007
Georgetown Univ, Washington DC 20007
Harvard Univ, Cambridge MA 02138
Indiana Univ, Bloomington IN 47405
Loyola Univ, New Orleans LA 70118
Metropolitan Museum of Art, New York NY 10028
New York Univ, New York NY 10003
Ohio State Univ, Columbus OH 43210
Portland State Univ, Portland OR 97207
Princeton Univ, Princeton NJ 08540
Texas A&M Univ, Commerce TX 75429
Tulane Univ, New Orleans LA 70118
Univ of Arizona, Tucson AZ 85721
Univ of California San Diego, La Jolla CA 92093
Univ of California, Berkeley CA 94720
Univ of California, Los Angeles CA 90024
Univ of Chicago, Chicago IL 60637
Univ of Cincinnati, Cincinnati OH 45221
Univ of Illinois, Champaign IL 61820
Univ of Michigan, Ann Arbor MI 48109
Univ of North Carolina, Chapel Hill NC 27514
Univ of Pennsylvania, Philadelphia PA 19104
Univ of Texas, Austin TX 78712
Univ of Toronto, Toronto ON MS5 1A1, Canada
Univ of Utah, Salt Lake City UT 84112
Univ of Washington, Seattle WA 98105
Univ of Wisconsin, Madison WI 53706
Washington Univ, St Louis MO 63130

Associated Colleges of the South (ACS)

Michael Leslie, Rhodes Coll, 2000 North Parkway, Memphis TN 38112-1690; 901-843 3715; E-mail: bsao@rhodes.edu
Program(s) 1700

Birmingham-Southern Coll, Birmingham AL 35254
Centenary Coll of Louisiana, Shreveport LA 71134
Centre Coll, Danville KY 40422
Davidson Coll, Davidson NC 28036
Furman Univ, Greenville SC 29613
Hendrix Coll, Conway AR 72032
Millsaps Coll, Jackson MS 39210
Morehouse Coll, Atlanta GA 30314
Rhodes Coll, Memphis TN 38112
Rollins Coll, Winter Park FL 32789
Southwestern Univ, Georgetown TX 78626
Trinity Univ, San Antonio TX 78212
Univ of Richmond, Richmond VA 23173

Center for Arabic Study Abroad (CASA)

Dr Gerald E Lampe, Dir, SAIS, Johns Hopkins Univ, 1619 Massachusetts Ave NW, Washington DC 20036-1983; 202-663 5750
http://www.sais-jhu.edu/languages/casa
Program(s) 1745, 1746

Center for Cross-Cultural Study

Dr Judith Ortiz, US Dir, Dept Y, 446 Main St, Amherst MA 01002; 800-377 2621, 413-256 0011; Fax: 413-256 1968
Program(s) 1397, 1398, 1995, 1996

College Consortium for International Studies (CCIS)

2000 P St NW, Ste 503, Washington DC 20036; 800-453 6956, 202-223 0330; Fax: 202-223 0999
http://www.ccisabroad.org
Program(s) 0151, 0338, 0405, 0519, 0579, 0600, 0628, 0842, 0956, 1034, 1035, 1118, 1204, 1399, 1477, 1573, 1594, 1595, 1737, 1782, 1879, 1880, 1881, 1882, 1950, 1951, 1989, 2028, 2036

Univ of Southern Maine
Univ of Texas at Arlington
Univ of Texas at Dallas
Univ of Texas at Tyler
Univ of Texas Southwestern Medical Ctr
Univ of the Virgin Islands
Univ of Wisconsin-Platteville
Valencia CC
Virginia Union Univ
Westfield State Coll
Wiley Coll
William Paterson Univ of New Jersey
Worcester State Coll
Youngstown State Univ

College Consortium for Study Abroad

Prof Seymour J Fader, Pgm Dir, CCSA, PO Box 562, Paramus NJ 07653-0562; 201-261 8753; Fax: 201-261 6389
Program(s) 1484

Clark State CC, Springfield OH 45501
Elgin CC, Elgin IL 60123
Fisher Coll, Boston MA 02116
Gadsden State CC, Gadsden AL 35902
Saint Paul's Coll, Lawrenceville VA 23868
Southside Virginia CC, Alberta VA 23821
Tennessee State Univ, Nashville TN 37209

Committee on Institutional Cooperation

Janis Perkins, Admin Dir, CIC-Study Abroad Pgms, 120 Intl Ctr, Univ of Iowa, Iowa City IA 52242-1802; 319-335 0353; Fax: 319-335-2021 http://www.uiowa.edu/~uiabroad
Program(s) 1895, 2012, 2122

Indiana Univ, Bloomington IN 47405
Michigan State Univ, East Lansing MI 48824
Northwestern Univ, Evanston IL 60201
Ohio State Univ, Columbus OH 43210
Pennsylvania State Univ, University Park PA 16802
Purdue Univ, West Lafayette IN 47907
Univ of Chicago, Chicago IL 60637
Univ of Illinois, Chicago IL 60607
Univ of Illinois, Urbana IL 61801
Univ of Iowa, Iowa City IA 52242
Univ of Michigan, Ann Arbor MI 48109
Univ of Minnesota, Minneapolis MN 55455
Univ of Wisconsin, Madison WI 53706
Univ of Wisconsin, Milwaukee WI 53201

Committee on Institutional Cooperation/AESOP London Internships

Study Abroad, Univ of Illinois, 115 Intl Studies Bldg, 910 S Fifth, Champaign IL 61820; 217-333 6322; Fax: 217-244 0249; E-mail: sao@uiuc.edu http://www.server.ips.uiuc.edu/ips/sao/index.html
Program(s) 1596

Indiana Univ, Bloomington IN 47405
Michigan State Univ, East Lansing MI 48824
Northwestern Univ, Evanston IL 60201
Ohio State Univ, Columbus OH 43210
Pennsylvania State Univ, University Park PA 16802
Purdue Univ, West Lafayette IN 47907
Univ of Chicago, Chicago IL 60637
Univ of Illinois, Chicago IL 60607
Univ of Illinois, Urbana IL 61801
Univ of Iowa, Iowa City IA 52242
Univ of Michigan, Ann Arbor MI 48109
Univ of Minnesota, Minneapolis MN 55455
Univ of Wisconsin, Madison WI 53706

Consortium for the Teaching of Indonesian and Malay (COTIM)

Ms Marie Kruger, Pgm Asst, Ctr for Southeast Asian Studies, 1155 Observatory Dr, Ingraham Hall, Rm 207, University of Wisconsin-Madison, Madison WI 53706; Fax: 608-263 3735; E-mail: mkruger@student.wisc.edu http://www.wisc.edu/ctrseasia/cotim.html
Program(s) 0237

Arizona State Univ
Cornell Univ
Northern Illinois Univ
Ohio Univ
Univ of British Columbia
Univ of California-Berkeley
Univ of California-Los Angeles
Univ of Hawaii
Univ of Michigan
Univ of Washington
Univ of Wisconsin-Madison
Yale Univ

Cooperating Programs in the Americas

Inst for Study Abroad, Butler Univ, 1100 W 42nd St, Ste 305, Indianapolis IN 46208; 888-344 9299; Fax: 317-940 9704 http://www.isabutler.org
Program(s) 1817

Butler Univ, Indianapolis IN 46208
Intl Student Exch Pgm (ISEP), Washington DC
Univ of Illinois, Champaign IL 61820
Univ of North Carolina, Chapel Hill NC 27514
Univ of Texas, Austin TX 78712

Cooperative Center for Study Abroad

Dr M Klembara, Northern Kentucky Univ, BEP 301, Highland Heights KY 41099; 800-319 6015, 859-572 6512; Fax: 859-572 6650; E-mail: ccsa@nku.edu http://www.nku.edu/ccsa
Program(s) 0087, 0108, 0134, 0205, 0916, 0917, 1486, 1597, 1598, 1835

Abilene Christian Univ, Mabee Bus Bldg 264, ACU Box 29354, Abilene TX 79699; Dr John E Timmerman, 915-674 2815
Austin Peay State Univ, Browning 105, Clarksville TN 37044; Dr Ivan Joe Filippo, Acad Affairs, 931-221 6236
Bellarmine Coll, 2001 Newburg Rd, Louisville KY 40205; Prof Gabriele Bosley, Intl Pgms, 502-452 8476
Belmont Univ, 1900 Belmont Blvd, Nashville TN 37212; Dr Margaret Monteverde, Literature & Lang, 615-460 6197
Eastern Kentucky Univ, Case Annex 467, Richmond KY 40475; Dr Bonnie C Plummer, 859-622 1364
Huntingdon Coll, 1500 E Fairview Ave, Montgomery AL 36106; Maxine Goldner, 334-833 4433
Kentucky State Univ, Whitney M Young Jr Coll of Leadership Studies, 128A Carver Hall, Frankfort KY 40601; Dr Edwin Conner, 502-227 6732
Middle Tennessee State Univ, 202 Cope Admin Bldg, Murfreesboro TN 37132; Dr Tech Wubneh, Dir, Intl Pgms & Svcs, 615-898 2238
Mississippi State Univ, PO Drawer EH, Mississippi State MS 39762; Dr Jack H White, Univ Honors Pgm, 662-325 2522
Morehead State Univ, RH 243 UPO 715, Morehead KY 40351; Dr Janet Gross, Nursing, 606-783 5173
Murray State Univ, 7C Faculty Hall, Murray KY 42071; Dr Ronald Cella, English, 270-762 4532
Northern Kentucky Univ, BEP 301, Highland Heights KY 41099; Dr Michael A Klembara, Exec Dir, 859-572 6512
Saint Francis Coll, Loretto PA 15940; Dr Kirk Weixel, English, 814-472 3194
Spring Hill Coll, 4000 Dauphin St, Mobile AL 36608; Dr David Sauer, English, 334-380 4644
Thomas More Coll, Crestview Hills KY 41017; Dr Raymond Hebert, Dean Emeritus of the Coll, 859-344 3375
Univ of Kentucky, B108B William T Young Library, Lexington KY 40506; Ms Constance Baird, Dir, Distance Learning, 859-257 3377
Univ of Louisville, Brodschi Hall, Louisville KY 40292; Ms Andrea Stephan, Intl Ctr, 502-852 6602
Univ of Mississippi, University MS 38677; Ms Susan Oliphant, Study Abroad Coord, 662-915 1508
Univ of Tennessee at Chattanooga, 233 University Ctr, Chattanooga TN 37403; Dr Hugh Prevost, Intl Educ, 423-755 4735
Univ of Tennessee at Martin, 322K Humanities Bldg, Martin TN 38238; Mr Stan Sieber, History, 901-587 7467
Walsh Univ, Farrell Hall 212, 2020 Easton St NW, North Canton OH 44720; Dr Mark Rogers, 330-490 7154
Western Kentucky Univ, One Big Red Way, Bowling Green KY 42101; Dr John Peterson, Dir, Intl Ctr, 270-745 5468
Western Oregon Univ, 107 West House, Monmouth OR 97361; Ms Martha Sargent, Bus Div, 503-838 8350

Council on International Educational Exchange Consortium

Council, 205 E 42nd St, New York NY 10017; 212-822 2600; Fax: 212-822 2699 http://www.ciee.org/study
Program(s) 0187, 0214, 0320, 0662, 0706, 0773, 1264, 1400, 1786, 1869, 1942, 2010, 2112

Adelphi Univ, Garden City NY 11530
Albion Coll, Albion MI 49224
Alma Coll, Alma MI 48801
Aquinas Coll, Grand Rapids MI 49506
Assoc Colls of the Midwest, Chicago IL 60606
Auburn Univ, Auburn AL 36849-5159
Augustana Coll, Sioux Falls SD 57197

Bates Coll, Lewiston ME 04240
Bellarmine Coll, Louisville KY 40250-0671
Beloit Coll, Beloit WI 53511
Boston Coll, Chestnut Hill MA 02215
Bradley Univ, Peoria IL 61625
Brandeis Univ, Waltham MA 02254
Brown Univ, Providence RI 02912
Bucknell Univ, Lewisburg PA 17837
Butler Univ, Indianapolis IN 46208
California State Univ at Long Beach, Long Beach CA 90840-1004
California State Univ System, Long Beach CA 90802
Central Coll, Pella IA 50219
Central Michigan Univ, Mt Pleasant MI 48859
Claremont McKenna Coll, Claremont CA 91711
Clark Atlanta Univ, Atlanta GA 30314
Clark Univ, Worcester MA 01610-1477
Coll of Lake Co, Grayslake IL 60030-1198
Coll of Notre Dame, Baltimore MD 21210
Coll of Saint Catherine, St Paul MN 55105
Coll of Wooster, Wooster OH 44691
Colorado State Univ, Ft Collins CO 80523
Columbia Univ, New York NY 10027
Cornell Univ, Ithaca NY 14853
Curtin Univ, Perth, Western Australia 6001
Dartmouth Coll, Hanover NH 03755
DePauw Univ, Greencastle IL 46135
Doane Coll, Crete NE 68333
Dominican Coll of San Rafael, San Rafael CA 94901
Drake Univ, Des Moines IA 50311
Drexel Univ, Philadelphia PA 19104
Emory Univ, Atlanta GA 30322
Endicott Coll, Beverly MA 01915
Fairfield Univ, Fairfield CT 06430-7524
Florida Atlantic Univ, Boca Raton FL 33431-0991
Florida Intl Univ, Miami FL 33199
George Washington Univ, Washington DC 20052
Georgetown Univ, Washington DC 20057
Georgia State Univ, Atlanta GA 30303
Goshen Coll, Goshen IN 46526
Grand Valley State Univ, Allendale MI 49401-9403
Great Lakes Colls Assn, Ann Arbor MI 48103
Greensboro Coll, Greensboro NC 27401-1875
Grinnell Coll, Grinnell IA 50112
Guilford Coll, Greensboro NC 27410
Gustavus Adolphus Coll, St Peter MN 56082
Hamline Univ, St Paul MN 55104
Harvard Univ, Cambridge MA 02138
Hobart & William Smith Colls, Geneva NY 14456
Hood Coll, Frederick MD 21701
Hope Coll, Holland MI 49423
Howard Univ, Washington DC 20059
Idaho State Univ, Pocatello ID 83209
Illinois State Univ, Normal IL 61761
Indiana Univ, Bloomington IN 47405
Intl Christian Univ, Japan
James Madison Univ, Harrisonburg VA 22807
Johns Hopkins Univ, Baltimore MD 21218
Kalamazoo Coll, Kalamazoo MI 49006-3295
Kenyon Coll, Gambier OH 43022
Lehigh Univ, Bethlehem PA 18015-3198
Lewis & Clark Coll, Portland OR 97219
Long Island Univ, Greenvale NY 11548
Loyola Marymount Univ, Los Angeles CA 90045
Lynchburg Coll, Lynchburg VA 24501
Macalester Coll, St Paul MN 55105
Michigan State Univ, East Lansing MI 48824
Michigan Tech Univ, Houghton MI 49931-1295
Mills Coll, Oakland CA 94613
Monterey Inst of Intl Studies, Monterey CA 93940
Morehouse Coll, Atlanta GA 30314
Mount Saint Mary's Coll, Emmitsburg MD 21727
Mount San Antonio Coll, Walnut CA 91789
Murdoch Univ, Perth, Western Australia 6150
Nebraska Wesleyan Univ, Lincoln NE 68504-2796
North Carolina State Univ, Raleigh NC 27411
Northeastern Univ, Boston MA 02115
Northern Illinois Univ, DeKalb IL 60115
Oberlin Coll, Oberlin OH 44074
Occidental Coll, Los Angeles CA 90041
Ohio State Univ, Columbus OH 43210
Ohio Univ, Athens OH 45701
Oklahoma City Univ, Oklahoma City OK 73106
Oklahoma State Univ, Stillwater OK 74078
Old Dominion Univ, Norfolk VA 23529
Ottawa Univ, Ottawa KS 66067-3399
Pace Univ, New York NY 10038
Pennsylvania State Univ, University Park PA 16802
Pitzer Coll, Claremont CA 91711
Plymouth State Coll, Plymouth NH 03264
Pomona Coll, Claremont CA 91711
Portland State Univ, Portland OR 97207
Princeton Univ, Princeton NJ 08544
Purdue Univ, West Lafayette IN 47906-6207
Rhodes Coll, Memphis TN 38112
Rice Univ, Houston TX 77251
Rutgers Univ, New Brunswick NJ 08903
Saint John's Univ, Jamaica NY 11439
Saint Norbert Coll, DePere WI 54115
Saint Olaf Coll, Northfield MN 55057
Santa Clara Univ, Santa Clara CA 95053
Sarah Lawrence Coll, Bronxville NY 10708-5999
Scripps Coll, Claremont CA 91711
Seattle Univ, Seattle WA 98122-4460
Simmons Coll, Boston MA 02115
Southern Illinois Univ, Carbondale IL 62901
Southern Methodist Univ, Dallas TX 75275
Spelman Coll, Atlanta GA 30314
Stanford Univ, Stanford CA 94305-3089
SUNY Univ at Buffalo, Buffalo NY 14260
Sweet Briar Coll, Sweet Briar VA 24595
Syracuse Univ, Syracuse NY 13244
Temple Univ, Philadelphia PA 19122
Texas A&M Univ, College Station TX 77843
Texas Christian Univ, Fort Worth TX 76129
Texas Tech Univ, Lubbock TX 79409-5004
Thunderbird, Amer Grad Sch of Intl Mgmt, Glendale AZ 85306
Towson Univ, Towson MD 21204
Trinity Coll, Hartford CT 06106
Trinity Univ, San Antonio TX 78112-7200
Tufts Univ, Medford MA 02155
Tulane Univ, New Orleans LA 70118
Univ del Salvador, Buenos Aires, Argentina
Univ Estacio de Sa, Rio de Janeiro, Brazil
Univ of Alabama at Birmingham, Birmingham AL 35294
Univ of Arizona, Tucson AZ 85721
Univ of California System, Santa Barbara CA 93106
Univ of Chicago, Chicago IL 60637
Univ of Colorado, Boulder CO 80309
Univ of Connecticut, Storrs CT 06269-1207
Univ of Evansville, Evansville IN 47722
Univ of Florida, Gainesville FL 32611
Univ of Hartford, West Hartford CT 06117-1599
Univ of Idaho, Moscow ID 83844
Univ of Illinois, Urbana-Champaign IL 61820
Univ of Iowa, Iowa City IA 52242
Univ of Kansas, Lawrence KS 66045
Univ of Kentucky, Lexington KY 40506
Univ of Limburg, Ctr for European Studies, Maastricht, Netherlands
Univ of Maine, Orono ME 04469
Univ of Maryland, College Park MD 20742
Univ of Massachusetts Amherst, Amherst MA 01003
Univ of Michigan, Ann Arbor MI 48109
Univ of Minnesota, Minneapolis MN 55455
Univ of Mississippi, Oxford MS 38677
Univ of Nebraska, Lincoln NE 68588
Univ of New Hampshire, Durham NH 03824
Univ of New Mexico, Albuquerque NM 87131-1056
Univ of North Carolina, Chapel Hill NC 27514
Univ of North Carolina, Charlotte NC 28223
Univ of Oklahoma, Norman OK 73019
Univ of Oregon, Eugene OR 97403
Univ of Pennsylvania, Philadelphia PA 19104
Univ of Pittsburgh, Pittsburgh PA 15260
Univ of Puerto Rico, San Juan PR 00936
Univ of Rhode Island, Kingston RI 02881
Univ of Rochester, Rochester NY 14627
Univ of Saint Thomas, Houston TX 77006-4696
Univ of Saint Thomas, St Paul MN 55105
Univ of South Carolina, Spartanburg SC 29303
Univ of Southern California, Los Angeles CA 90089
Univ of Tennessee, Knoxville TN 37996
Univ of Texas, Austin TX 78712-7206
Univ of Texas, San Antonio TX 78249
Univ of the Pacific, Stockton CA 95211
Univ of Toledo, Toledo OH 43606
Univ of Utah, Salt Lake City UT 84112
Univ of Virginia, Charlottesville VA 22903
Univ of Washington, Seattle WA 98195
Univ of Wisconsin, Madison WI 53706
Univ of Wisconsin, Milwaukee WI 53201
Univ of Wyoming, Laramie WY 82701
Univ System of Georgia, Atlanta GA 30303
Ursinus Coll, Collegeville PA 19426-1000
Utah State Univ, Logan UT 84322
Vanderbilt Univ, Nashville TN 37240
Villanova Univ, Villanova PA 19085
Washington & Jefferson Coll, Washington PA 15301
Washington Coll, Chestertown MD 21620-1197
Washington State Univ, Pullman WA 99163
Washington Univ, St Louis MO 63130
Wesleyan Univ, Middletown CT 06457
Western Michigan Univ, Kalamazoo MI 49008
Western Washington Univ, Bellingham WA 98225
William Woods Univ, Fulton MO 65251
Wittenberg Univ, Springfield OH 45501
Wofford Coll, Spartanburg SC 29301

DIS, Denmark's International Study Program

Vestergade 7, DK-1456 Copenhagen K, Denmark; 800-247 3477, 45-331 10144; Fax: 45-339 32624
http://www.disp.dk
Program(s) 0564, 0565, 0912, 0913, 1601

Alfred Univ, Saxon Dr, Herrick Library, Alfred NY 14802-1205; Pamela A Lakin, Study Abroad
Alverno Coll, 3400 S 43rd St, Milwaukee WI 53234-3922; Dimitri Lazo, Study Abroad
American Univ, 4400 Massachusetts Ave NW, Washington DC 20016-8083; Elizabeth Bell Townsend, World Capital Pgms
Auburn Univ, 201 Hargis Hall, Auburn Univ AL 36849-5159; Nick Conrad, Study Abroad/Exch
Ball State Univ, Muncie IN 47306; Yukie Kurosawa, Study Abroad Pgms
Bates Coll, Andrews Rd, Lewiston ME 04240-6028; Stephen W Sawyer, Study Abroad
Bowdoin Coll, 4800 College Station, Brunswick ME 04011; Stephen Hall, Off-Campus Study
Bradley Univ, Peoria IL 61625-0002; Elmo Roach, Intl Pgms
Brown Univ, Rhode Island Hall, Box 1973, Providence RI 02912; Linda Brault, Intl Pgms
California Polytechnic State Univ, San Luis Obispo CA 93407; Monica Schecter, Intl Educ & Pgms

Wesleyan Univ, 307 Fisk Hall, 262 High St, Middletown CT 06459; Jane Edwards, Intl Studies
Western Illinois Univ, 5 Horrabin Hall, 1 Univ Circle, Macomb IL 61455; Gloria Barr, Travel & Study Abroad Pgms
Whittier Coll, Whittier CA 90608; Michael J McBride, Study Abroad
Williams Coll, Williamstown MA 01267; Laura McKeon, Intl Educ Pgms
Wittenberg Univ, PO Box 720, Springfield OH 45501; JoAnn Bennett, Intl Educ
Wofford Coll, 429 N Church St, Spartanburg SC 29303-3663; Annemarie Wiseman, Pgms Abroad

European Studies Association (ESA)

Dr Thomas Blair, Dir, 424 Dorado Terrace, San Francisco CA 94112-1753; 415-334 4222; Fax: 415-334 4222; E-mail: tblair@ccsf.org
http://www.jps.net/tblair
Program(s) 0715

California State Univ-Hayward, Hayward CA 94542; Dr Yolanda Patterson, 510-885 3211
San Diego State Univ, CES, San Diego CA 92182-1920; Ginny Foster, Travel/Study Pgm, 619-594 5154
San Francisco State Univ, CEL, San Francisco CA 94132; Mary Pieratt, Travel/Study Pgm, 415-338 1533

Higher Education Consortium for Urban Affairs (HECUA)

Hamline Univ, Mail #36, 1536 Hewitt Ave, St Paul MN 55104-1284; 800-554 1089, 651-646 8831; Fax: 651-659 9421; E-mail: info@hecua.org
http://www.hecua.org
Program(s) 0165, 2047

Augsburg Coll, Minneapolis MN 55454
Augustana Coll, Sioux Falls SD 57197
Carleton Coll, Northfield MN 55057
Coll of Saint Benedict, St Joseph MN 56374
Coll of Saint Catherine, St Paul MN 55105
Concordia Univ, St Paul MN 55104
Gustavus Adolphus Coll, St Peter MN 56082
Hamline Univ, St Paul MN 55104
Macalester Coll, St Paul MN 55105
Saint John's Univ, Collegeville MN 56321
Saint Mary's Univ, Winona MN 55987
Saint Olaf Coll, Northfield MN 55057
Univ of Minnesota, Minneapolis MN 55455
Univ of Saint Thomas, St Paul MN 55105
Viterbo Coll, La Crosse WI 54601

IES, Institute for the International Education of Students

Admissions, 223 W Ohio St, Chicago IL 60610-4196; 312-944 1750; Fax: 312-944 1448
http://www.IESabroad.org
Program(s) 0172, 0191, 0266, 0722, 0941, 1100, 1324, 1367, 1613

Allegheny Coll, Meadville PA 16335
Amherst Coll, Amherst MA 01002
Austin Coll, Sherman TX 75090-4440
Bates Coll, Lewiston ME 04240
Boston Coll, Chestnut Hill MA 02167-3934
Boston Univ, Boston MA 02215
Bowdoin Coll, Brunswick ME 04011
Brandeis Univ, Waltham MA 02254-9110
Brown Univ, Providence RI 02912-1973
Bucknell Univ, Lewisburg PA 17837
Carleton Coll, Northfield MN 55057
Carnegie Mellon Univ, Pittsburgh PA 15213
City Coll of New York, New York NY 10031
Claremont McKenna Coll, Claremont CA 91711
Clark Atlanta Univ, Atlanta GA 30314
Colby Coll, Waterville ME 04901
Coll of the Holy Cross, Worcester MA 01610-2395
Coll of William & Mary, Williamsburg VA 23185
Coll of Wooster, Wooster OH 44691
Colorado State Univ, Ft Collins CO 80524
Connecticut Coll, New London CT 06320
Cornell Univ, Ithaca NY 14853
Denison Univ, Granville OH 43023
DePauw Univ, Greencastle IN 46135
Dickinson Coll, Carlisle PA 17013-2896
Dominican Univ, River Forest IL 60305
Drake Univ, Des Moines IA 50311
Emory Univ, Atlanta GA 30322
Franklin & Marshall Coll, Lancaster PA 17604-3003
George Washington Univ, Washington DC 20052
Grinnell Coll, Grinnell IA 50112-0810
Gustavus Adolphus Coll, St Peter MN 56082
Hampden-Sydney Coll, Hampden-Sydney VA 23943
Hampton Univ, Hampton VA 23668
Harvard Univ, Cambridge MA 02138
Haverford Coll, Haverford PA 19041-1392
Hope Coll, Holland MI 49422-9000
Illinois Wesleyan Univ, Bloomington IL 61701
Indiana Univ, Bloomington IN 47405-2801
Intl Christian Univ, Tokyo, Japan
Ithaca Coll, Ithaca NY 14850
Kenyon Coll, Gambier OH 43022-9623
Knox Coll, Galesburg IL 61401-4999
Lafayette Coll, Easton PA 18042-1798
Lehigh Univ, Bethlehem PA 18015
Luther Coll, Decorah IA 52101-1045
Macalester Coll, St Paul MN 55105
Manhattan Coll, Riverdale NY 10471
Marietta Coll, Marietta OH 45750
Massachusetts Inst of Technology, Cambridge MA 02139
Millikin Univ, Decatur IL 62522-2084
Millsaps Coll, Jackson MS 39210-0001
Morehouse Coll, Atlanta GA 30314
Mount Holyoke Coll, S Hadley MA 01075
North Carolina State Univ, Raleigh NC 27695-7344
Northwestern Univ, Evanston IL 60208-4195
Oberlin Coll, Oberlin OH 44074
Occidental Coll, Los Angeles CA 90041
Ohio State Univ, Columbus OH 43210-1358
Pacific Lutheran Univ, Tacoma WA 98447
Pennsylvania State Univ, University Park PA 16802
Pomona Coll, Claremont CA 91711
Princeton Univ, Princeton NJ 08544
Purdue Univ, West Lafayette IN 47906
Rhodes Coll, Memphis TN 38112-1690
Rice Univ, Houston TX 77251
Santa Clara Univ, Santa Clara CA 95053
Scripps Coll, Claremont CA 91711
Simmons Coll, Boston MA 02115
Skidmore Coll, Saratoga Springs NY 12866-1632
Southwestern Univ, Georgetown TX 78626
Spelman Coll, Atlanta GA 30314
Susquehanna Univ, Selinsgrove PA 17870-9989
Texas Christian Univ, Ft Worth TX 76129
Trinity Coll, Hartford CT 06106-3100
Trinity Univ, San Antonio TX 78212-7200
Tufts Univ, Medford MA 02155
Univ of California-Davis, Davis CA 95616
Univ of Califonia-San Diego, La Jolla CA 92093
Univ of Colorado, Boulder CO 80309-0123
Univ of Denver, Denver CO 80208
Univ of Georgia, Athens GA 30602-3108
Univ of Illinois, Champaign IL 61820
Univ of Illinois-Chicago, Chicago IL 60607-2919
Univ of Iowa, Iowa City IA 52242
Univ of Minnesota, Minneapolis MN 55455
Univ of Missouri-Columbia, Columbia MO 65211
Univ of New Hampshire, Durham NH 03824
Univ of North Florida, Jacksonville FL 32224
Univ of Notre Dame, Notre Dame IN 46556
Univ of Pennsylvania, Philadelphia PA 19104-6275
Univ of Pittsburgh, Pittsburgh PA 15260-0001
Univ of Portland, Portland OR 97203
Univ of Puget Sound, Tacoma WA 98416
Univ of Redlands, Redlands CA 92373-0999
Univ of Rochester, Rochester NY 14627-0408
Univ of Saint Thomas, St Paul MN 55105
Univ of San Diego, San Diego CA 92110
Univ of San Francisco, San Francisco CA 94117-1080
Univ of Southern California, Los Angeles CA 90089-1261
Univ of Texas at Austin, Austin TX 78713-7206
Univ of the Pacific, Stockton CA 95211
Univ of the South, Sewanee TN 37375-4013
Univ of Tulsa, Tulsa OK 74104-3189
Univ of Vermont, Burlington VT 05405-0384
Univ of Virginia, Charlottesville VA 22903
Vassar Coll, Poughkeepsie NY 12601
Virginia Military Inst, Lexington VA 24450
Wabash Coll, Crawfordsville IN 47933
Wagner Coll, Staten Island NY 10301
Wake Forest Univ, Winston-Salem NC 27109
Washington & Lee Univ, Lexington VA 24450
Washington State Univ, Pullman WA 99163-5110
Wellesley Coll, Wellesley MA 02181-8201
Wesleyan Coll, Macon GA 31210-4462
Westminster Coll, Fulton MO 65251-1299
Wheaton Coll, Norton MA 02766
Whitman Coll, Walla Walla WA 99362
Willamette Univ, Salem OR 97301
William Jewell Coll, Liberty MO 64068
Williams Coll, Williamstown MA 01267
Wittenberg Univ, Springfield OH 45501
Wofford Coll, Spartanburg SC 29301
Xavier Univ, Cincinnati OH 45207-5184
Xavier Univ, New Orleans LA 70125

IH Espana

c/o Trafalgar 14 entlo, 08010 Barcelona, Spain
Program(s) 1233, 1275, 1276, 1277, 1278, 1279, 1280, 1281, 1307, 1325, 1326, 1327, 1328, 1329, 1330, 1378, 1379, 1380, 1381, 1382, 1383, 1403, 1404, 1405, 1406, 1407, 1408, 1409, 1410

CLIC International House Sevilla
International House Barcelona
International House Madrid
Lacunza International House San Sebastian

Inter-University Program for Chinese Language Studies

Inst of East Asian Studies, 2223 Fulton St #2318, Berkeley CA 94720-2318; 510-642 3873; Fax: 510-643 7062
http://www.ieas.berkeley.edu/iup
Program(s) 0193

Columbia Univ, New York NY
Cornell Univ, Ithaca NY
Harvard Univ, Cambridge MA
Indiana Univ, Bloomington, IN
Princeton Univ, Princeton NJ
Stanford Univ, Stanford CA
Univ of California, Berkeley CA
Univ of California, Los Angeles CA
Univ of Chicago, Chicago IL
Univ of Michigan, Ann Arbor MI
Univ of Pennsylvania, Philadelphia PA
Univ of Washington, Seattle WA
Univ of Wisconsin, Madison WI
Yale Univ, New Haven CT

International Campus Consortium

Dr Earl Gibbons, Assoc VP, Overseas Pgms, Thunderbird, AGSIM, 15249 N 59th Ave, Glendale AZ 85306; 602-978 7367; Fax: 602-978 7419
http://www.t-bird.edu
Program(s) 0071, 0109, 0173, 0226, 0267, 0457, 0624

Arizona State Univ, Tempe AZ 85287
Claremont Grad Sch, Claremont CA 91711
Fordham Univ, New York NY 10023
ITESM, Monterrey NL 64849, Mexico
James Madison Univ, Harrisonburg VA 22807
San Diego State Univ, San Diego CA 92182
Syracuse Univ, Syracuse NY 13244
Texas A&M Univ, College Station TX 77843
Univ of Calgary, Calgary AB T2N 1N4, Canada
Univ of Colorado, Boulder CO 80309-0123
Univ of Houston, Houston TX 77204
Univ of Notre Dame, Notre Dame IN 46556
Univ of Utah, Salt Lake City UT 84112
Vanderbilt Univ, Nashville TN 37240

Iowa Regents' Institutions

http://www.uni.edu/modlangs/institutes-abroad
Program(s) 1431

Univ of Iowa, Iowa City IA 52242
Univ of Northern Iowa, Cedar Falls IA 50614

Japan Center for Michigan Universities

John Hazewinkel, 108 Intl Ctr, Michigan State Univ, East Lansing MI 48824-1035; 517-355 4654; Fax: 517-353 8727
http://www.isp.msu.edu/JCMU
Program(s) 0250

Central Michigan Univ, 348 Moore Hall, Mt Pleasant MI 48858; Dianne DeSalvo, 517-774 4308
Eastern Michigan Univ, 307 Goodison Hall, Ypsilanti MI 48197; Geoffrey Voght, World Coll, 734-487 0178
Ferris State Univ, 303 Bishop Hall, Big Rapids MI 49307; Paul Landen, Intl Affairs, 616-592 2405
Grand Valley State Univ, 104 STU, Allendale MI 49401; Rebecca Chomos, Intl Studies, 616-895 3898
Lake Superior State Univ, Sault Ste Marie MI 49783; James W T Moody, Arts & Letters, 906-635 2120
Michigan State Univ, 108 Intl Ctr, East Lansing MI 48824-1035; John Hazewinkel, JCMU, 517-355 4654
Michigan Technological Univ, Houghton MI 49931; James Cross, Dir, Intl Pgms, 906-487 3055
Northern Michigan Univ, Marquette MI 49855; John Weting, Dir, Intl Affairs, 906-227 2510
Oakland Univ, Rochester MI 48063; Bonnie Abiko, Art & Art History, 810-370 3382
Saginaw Valley State Univ, 2250 Pierce Rd, University Center MI 48710; Woody Pelton, 517-790 4473
Univ of Michigan-Ann Arbor, Ann Arbor MI 48109; Jordan Pollack, Intl Pgms, 734-764 4311
Univ of Michigan-Dearborn, Dearborn MI 48128; Richard Roehl, Arts & Letters, 313-593 5490
Univ of Michigan-Flint, Flint MI 48502-2186; Roy Hanashiro, History, 313-762 3366
Wayne State Univ, 4137 Faculty Admin Bldg, Detroit MI 48202; Jack Kay, 313-577 2310
Western Michigan Univ, B-200 Ellsworth Hall, Kalamazoo MI 48008-5177; Margaret Riley, Intl Affairs, 616-387 5890

Jerusalem University College

4249 E State St, Ste 203, Rockford IL 61108; 815-229 5900; Fax: 815-229 5901
http://www.juc.edu
Program(s) 1761

Anderson Univ Sch of Theology, Anderson OH
Asbury Coll, Wilmore KY
Asbury Theological Seminary, Wilmore KY
Ashland Coll, Ashland OR
Ashland Theological Seminary, Ashland OH
Azusa Pacific Univ, Azusa CA
Baptist Bible Coll, Clarks Summit PA
Baptist Sch of Theology, Clarks Summit PA
Bethel Coll, Mishawaka IN
Bethel Coll, St Paul MN
Bethel Theological Seminary, St Paul MN
Bible Coll of New Zealand, Auckland, New Zealand
Biblical Theological Seminary, Hatfield PA
Calvary Bible Coll, Kansas City MO
Calvin Coll, Grand Rapids MI
Calvin Theological Seminary, Grand Rapids MI
Canadian Bible Coll, Regina, Saskatchewan, Canada
Canadian Theological Seminary, Regina, Saskatchewan, Canada
Capital Baptist Seminary, Korea
Cedarville Coll, Cedarville OH
Central Coll, McPherson KS
Christian Heritage Coll, El Cajon CA
Chungshin Univ, Korea
Cincinnati Bible Coll, Cincinnati OH
Cincinnati Theological Seminary, Cincinnati OH
Columbia Intl Univ, Columbia SC
Concordia Lutheran, Edmonton AB, Canada
Concordia Seminary, St Louis MO
Concordia Univ Coll, Edmonton AB, Canada
Cornerstone Coll & Grand Rapids Baptist Coll & Seminary, Grand Rapids MI
Covenant Coll, Lookout Mountain GA
Covenant Theological Seminary, St Louis MO
Dallas Theological Seminary, Dallas TX
Denver Seminary, Denver CO
Evangel Coll, Springfield MO
Evangelical Sch of Theology, Myerstown PA
Fuller Theological Seminary, Pasadena CA
Geneva Coll, Beaver Falls PA
George Fox Univ, Portland OR
Gordon Coll, Wenham MA
Gordon-Conwell Theological Seminary, South Hamilton MA
Grace Coll, Winona Lake IN
Grace Theological Seminary, Winona Lake IN
Grace Univ, Omaha NE
Grand Canyon Univ, Phoenix AZ
Grand Rapids Baptist Seminary, Grand Rapids MI
Hoseo Univ, Korea
Houghton Coll, Houghton NY
Huntington Coll, Huntington IN
Indiana Wesleyan Univ, Marion IN
Intl Coll & Grad Sch, Honolulu HI
John Brown Univ, Siloam Springs AR
John Wesley Coll, High Point NC
Judson Coll, Elgin IL
King Coll, Briston TN
King's Univ Coll, Edmonton, Canada
Kobe Lutheran Theological Seminary, Kobe, Japan
Lancaster Bible Coll, Lancaster PA
LeTourneau Univ, Longview TX
Messiah Coll, Grantham PA
Mid-Continent Coll, Mayfield KY
Minnesota Bible Coll, Rochester MN
Multnomah Bible College and Biblical Seminary, Portland OR
Nairobi Evangelical Grad Sch, Nairobi, Kenya
North Amer Baptist Seminary, Sioux Falls SD
North Park Coll, Chicago IL
North Park Theological Seminary, Chicago IL
Northern Baptist Theological Seminary, Lombard IL
Northwest Christian Coll, Eugene OR
Northwest Coll, Kirkland WA
Northwest Nazarene Coll, Nampa ID
Northwestern Coll, St Paul MN
Nyack Coll, Nyack NY
Oak Hills Christian Coll, Bemidji MN
Oklahoma Baptist Univ, Shawnee OK
Olivet Nazarene Univ, Kankakee IL
Oral Roberts Univ, Tulsa OK
Patten Coll, Oakland CA
Philadelphia Coll of Bible, Langhorne PA
Point Loma Nazarene Coll, San Diego CA
Prairie Bible Coll & Grad Sch, Three Hills AB, Canada
Presbyterian Coll & Theological Seminary, Seoul, Korea
Providence Coll, Otterburne, Manitoba, Canada
Providence Theological Seminary, Otterburne, Ontario, Canada
Puget Sound Christian Coll, Edmonds WA
Redeemer Coll, Hamilton, Ontario, Canada
Reformed Theological Coll, Australia
Reformed Theological Seminary, Seoul, Korea
Regent Univ Sch of Divinity, Virginia Beach VA
Roberts Wesleyan Coll, Rochester NY
Seoul Theological Univ, Seoul, Korea
Simpson Coll, Redding CA
Southern Baptist Theological Seminary, Louisville KY
Southern California Coll, Costa Mesa CA
Southwestern Assemblies of God Coll, Waxahachie TX
Southwestern Baptist Theological Seminary, Louisville KY
Spring Arbor Coll, Spring Arbor MI

Sung Kyul Christian Univ, Anyang, Korea
Taeshin Christian Univ, Korea
Taylor Univ, Upland IN
Tokyo Christian Univ, Chiba-ken, Japan
Trinity Evangelical Divinity Sch, Deerfield IL
Trinity Intl Univ, Deerfield IL
Trinity Western Univ, Langley BC, Canada
Tyndale Bible Coll, Willowdale, Ontario, Canada
Tyndale Theological Seminary, Willowdale, Ontario, Canada
Union Univ, Jackson TN
Western Evangelical Seminary, Portland OR
Westminster Theological Seminary, Philadelphia PA
Westmont Coll, Santa Barbara CA
Wheaton Coll, Wheaton IL
Whitworth Coll, Spokane WA

Kentucky Institute for International Studies (KIIS)

Dr J Milton Grimes, Exec Dir, Murray State Univ, PO Box 9, Murray KY 42071-0009; 270-762 3091; Fax: 270-762 3434
http://www.kiis.org
Program(s) 0211, 0241, 0458, 0503, 0504, 0521, 0727, 0856, 0984, 1235, 1236, 1852, 1946, 2039, 2147

Antioch Coll, Yellow Springs OH 45387; Dr Andrzej Bloch, Educ Abroad, 937-767 6366
Ball State Univ, Muncie IN 47306; Mr Larry Laffrey, Intl Pgms, 765-285 5422
Bellarmine Coll, Louisville KY 40205; Ms Gabriele Bosley, Foreign Langs, 502-452 8476
Berea Coll, Berea KY 40404; Ms Suzanne Kifer, Intl Ctr, 606-985 3924
Eastern Kentucky Univ, Richmond KY 40475; Dr Jed Deppman, Humanities & Foreign Langs, 606-622 1179
Georgetown Coll, Georgetown KY 40324; Dr Sigrid Suesse, Foreign Langs, 502-863 8168
Middle Tennessee State Univ, Murfreesboro TN 37132; Dr Richard Pace, Sociology & Anthropology, 615-904 8058
Midway Coll, Midway KY 40347-1120; Ms Lesia Holder, Acad Affairs, 606-846 5792
Morehead State Univ, Morehead KY 40351; Ms Mary Jo Netherton, UPO 1215, 606-783 2779
Murray State Univ, Murray KY 42071; Dr J Milton Grimes, Foreign Langs, 270-762 3091
Northern Kentucky Univ, Highland Heights KY 41099; Dr Michael Klembara, Intl Pgms, 606-572 6512
Transylvania Univ, Lexington KY 40508; Ms Kathy Simon, Special Pgms, 606-233 8124
Union Coll, Barbourville KY 40906; Dr Christine Marley, Foreign Langs, 606-546 1675
Univ of Kentucky, Lexington KY 40506; Dr David Bettez, Intl Affairs, 606-257 4067, ext 229
Univ of Louisville, Louisville KY 40292; Ms Andrea Stephan, Intl Ctr, 502-852 6602
Western Kentucky Univ, Bowling Green KY 42101; Ms Kimberly Erwin, Intl Pgms, 270-745 6146

Midwest Consortium for Study Abroad (MCSA)

AHA Intl, 741 SW Lincoln St, Portland OR 97201-3178; 800-654 2051, 503-295 7730; Fax: 503-295 5969
http://www.aha-intl.org
Program(s) 1394

Alma Coll, Alma MI 48801-1599; Intl Educ, 517-463 7247
Ball State Univ, Muncie IN 47306-0175; Ctr for Intl Pgms, 765-285 5422
Central Michigan Univ, Mt Pleasant MI 48859; Intl Educ, 517-774 4308
Concordia Coll, Ann Arbor MI 48105; Overseas Study, 313-995 7390
Indiana State Univ, Terre Haute IN 47809; Intl Affairs, 812-237 3427
Madonna Univ, Livonia MI 48150-1173; Ctr for Intl Studies, 734-432 5636
Northern Michigan Univ, Marquette MI 49855; Intl Affairs, 906-227 2510
Oakland Univ, Rochester MI 48309-4401; Ctr for Intl Pgms, 810-370 2154
Saginaw Valley State Univ, Univ Ctr MI 48710; Intl Pgms, 517-790 4473
Wheeling Jesuit Univ, Wheeling WV 26003; Political Sci, 304-243 2201
Wilmington Coll, Wilmington OH 45177; Intl Educ, 937-382 6661 ext 246

Northwest Council on Study Abroad (NCSA)

AHA Intl, 741 SW Lincoln St, Portland OR 97201-3178; 800-654 2051, 503-295 7730; Fax: 503-295 5969
http://www.aha-intl.org
Program(s) 0614, 1142, 1351

Central Washington Univ, Ellensburg WA 98926-7408; Intl Pgms, 509-963 3615
Oregon State Univ, Corvallis OR 97331; Intl Educ, 541-737 3006
Portland State Univ, Portland OR 97207; Intl Educ Svcs, 503-725 4011
Southern Oregon Univ, Ashland OR 97520; Intl Pgms, 541-552 6336
Univ of Alaska Anchorage, Anchorage AK 99508; Enrollment Svcs, 907-786 1558
Univ of Alaska Fairbanks, Fairbanks AK 99775; Intl Pgms, 907-474 5327
Univ of Alaska Southeast, Novatney Bldg, Rm 204, Juneau AK 99801; 907-465 6455
Univ of Oregon, Eugene OR 97403; Intl Educ, 541-346 3207
Univ of Washington, Seattle WA 98195; Intl Pgms, 206-543 9272
Washington State Univ, Pullman WA 99164-5110; Intl Pgms, 509-335 4508
Western Oregon Univ, Monmouth OR 97361; Intl Educ & Svcs, 503-838 8095
Western Washington Univ, Bellingham WA 98225-9046; Intl Pgms, 360-650 3299

Summer Academy

Keynes Coll, Univ of Kent, Kent CT2 7NP, UK
http://www.ukc.ac.uk/sa
Program(s) 0477

Univ of Bristol, Bristol, UK
Univ of Durham, Durham, UK
Univ of East Anglia, Norwich, Norfolk, UK
Univ of Exeter, Exeter, Devon, UK
Univ of Kent, Canterbury, UK
Univ of Manchester, Inst of Sci & Technology (UMIST), Manchester, UK
Univ of Reading, Reading, UK
Univ of Sheffield, Sheffield, UK
Univ of Stirling, Stirling, UK
Univ of Strathclyde, Glasgow, UK
Univ of Wales, Aberystwyth, Aberystwyth, Dyfed, Wales
Univ of Wales, Bangor, Bangor, Wales
Univ of Wales, Swansea, Swansea, Wales
Univ of York, York, UK

Texas Christian University Business in Budapest Consortium

Kristi Dill, Asst Dean, Texas Christian Univ, PO Box 29850, Fort Worth TX 76129; 817-257 7527; Fax: 817-257 6049
http://www.neeley.tcu.edu
Program(s) 0373

Groupe ESC Dijon, France
Tec de Monterrey-Chihuahua, Chihuahua, Mexico
Texas Christian Univ, Fort Worth TX 76129
Univ de Las Americas, Puebla, Mexico

University of Southern Mississippi British Studies Consortium

Frances Sudduth or Dr Tim Hudson, Univ of Southern Mississippi, Southern Station Box 10047, Hattiesburg MS 39406; 601-266 4344; Fax: 601-266 5699
http://www.usm.edu
Program(s) 1686

Henderson State Univ, Arkadelphia AR 71999-0001
Hinds CC, Raymond MS 39154-0999
Midwestern State Univ, Wichita Falls TX 76308
Mississippi Coll, Clinton MS 39058
Northeast Louisiana Univ, Monroe LA 71209
Southeastern Louisiana Univ, Hammond LA 70402
Texas A&M Univ, Commerce TX 75429
Univ of Memphis, Memphis TN 38152
Univ of South Alabama, Mobile AL 36688
Univ of Southern Mississippi, Hattiesburg MS 39406

University Studies Abroad Consortium

Dr Carmelo Urza, Univ of Nevada, Reno, Univ Library 323, Reno NV 89557-0093; 775-784 6569; Fax: 775-784 6010
http://www.usac.unr.edu
Program(s) 0201, 0323, 0569, 0597, 0852, 1146, 1384, 1721, 1937

Boise State Univ, Boise ID 83725
California State Univ, Chico CA 95929
California State Univ, Fresno CA 93740
California State University, Dominguez Hills, Carson CA 90747
California State University, Stanislaus, Turlock CA 95380

Waseda Oregon Office

Index III: Fields of Study

Programs are indexed by field of study, and by country within field. Most fields of study are as given in the *Classification of Instructional Programs of the National Center for Education Statistics.* However, IIE has adapted the classification to accommodate the especially rich study-abroad opportunities in languages, civilization, culture, and other subjects specific to international study, adding a number of additional fields to the basic set.

A

C

D

E

F

I

M

N

O

P

T

Index IV: Special Options

Most programs in this book are intended for undergraduate students beyond the first year. However, a substantial number of programs offer graduate credit, or will accept freshmen or precollege students, or provide special opportunities for teachers, adults and professionals. This index can help to identify study opportunities for the many study-abroad candidates who are not upper-level undergraduates.

Users of this book can also use this index to find programs that offer study options other than the typical academic lecture, seminar or tutorial. Indexed below are such options as art studios, directed field study, independent study, internships, practical training, student teaching, study tours and voluntary service.

Adult courses

Art studios

Directed field study

Freshmen courses

Graduate courses

Independent study

Internships

Music lessons

Practical training

Precollege programs

Professionals courses

Student teaching

Study tours

Teacher courses

Volunteer/service

Workshops

Index V: Cost Ranges

Use this index for approximate guidance only. Programs are indexed on the lowest cost option they offer as a package fee, which is virtually always for the shortest period of study offered.

Each range indicates specifically whether international travel is included in the cost or not. However, readers must consult individual program entries to determine what else is included in the program fee. Tuition, housing, food, fees, insurance, books and materials, and international and local transportation are the basic categories of expenses incurred in studying abroad. Program fees may include all or only some of these costs.

Remember that IIE conducts the research for this book approximately one year before actual program dates. Program sponsors have the option of providing current actual charges or projected fees for the year covered by this book. Entries indicate which year's charges are provided.

Programs sponsored by foreign organizations often provide their costs in foreign currency. Because of exchange fluctuations, it is not useful to provide dollar equivalents for prices stated in foreign currencies. Use exchange rates current at the time of application to calculate approximate costs.

All applicants are well-advised to contact the program sponsor directly for the most up-to-date information on program charges before making a decision. Although program sponsors typically seek to stabilize prices, many factors can influence the cost of an international program. Contact the program sponsor for final information.

Under $1,000 Not Incl Intl Travel

$1,000 to $2,500 Incl Intl Travel

$1,000 to $2,500 Not Incl Intl Travel

$2,500 to $5,000 Incl Intl Travel

$2,500 to $5,000 Not Incl Intl Travel

$5,000 to $10,000 Incl Intl Travel

$5,000 to $10,000 Not Incl Intl Travel

$10,000 to $15,000 Incl Intl Travel

$10,000 to $15,000 Not Incl Intl Travel

$15,000 and Over Incl Intl Travel

$15,000 and Over Not Incl Intl Travel

Costs in Foreign Currency

Contact Sponsor

Index VI: Duration

Short-Term Study Abroad provides information on programs of varying length that take place in the summer—and on short-term programs in the fall, winter and spring. (IIE's companion volume, *Academic Year Abroad,* describes programs that last one or more academic terms.)

Use this index to identify programs that offer study opportunities for the period of time you have available. Remember that short-term study can be scheduled during interim sessions, academic holidays or semester breaks during the academic year as well as in the summer. Adult students, professionals and others not bound by the traditional US academic calendar will find opportunities year-round, including many courses that can be taken for varying lengths of time at any season.

Summer

Under 2 Wks

2 to 4 Wks

4 to 6 Wks

6 to 8 Wks

8 to 12 Wks